AMERICAN HANDBOOK OF PSYCHIATRY

Volume Two

AMERICAN HANDBOOK OF PSYCHIATRY

Silvano Arieti, EDITOR-IN-CHIEF

Volume One
The Foundations of Psychiatry
EDITED BY SILVANO ARIETI

Volume Two
Child and Adolescent Psychiatry, Sociocultural and Community Psychiatry
EDITED BY GERALD CAPLAN

Volume Three
Adult Clinical Psychiatry
EDITED BY SILVANO ARIETI AND EUGENE B. BRODY

Volume Four
Organic Disorders and Psychosomatic Medicine
EDITED BY MORTON F. REISER

Volume Five
Treatment
EDITED BY DANIEL X. FREEDMAN AND JARL E. DYRUD

Volume Six
New Psychiatric Frontiers
EDITED BY DAVID A. HAMBURG AND H. KEITH H. BRODIE

AMERICAN HANDBOOK OF PSYCHIATRY

SECOND EDITION

Silvano Arieti · Editor-in-Chief

VOLUME TWO

Child and Adolescent Psychiatry, Sociocultural and Community Psychiatry

GERALD CAPLAN · *Editor*

BASIC BOOKS, INC., PUBLISHERS · NEW YORK

Second Edition
© 1974 by Basic Books, Inc.
Library of Congress Catalog Card Number: 72–89185
SBN: 465–00148–3
Manufactured in the United States of America
76 77 78   10 9 8 7 6 5 4 3 2

CONTRIBUTORS

Nathan W. Ackerman, M.D.
Deceased. Formerly Director of the Professional Program of the Nathan W. Ackerman Family Institute, New York; Formerly Clinical Professor of Psychiatry at the College of Physicians and Surgeons, Columbia University, New York.

James R. Allen, M.D.
Associate Professor of Psychiatry and Behavioral Sciences, College of Medicine, and Associate Professor of Human Ecology, College of Health, University of Oklahoma Health Sciences Center, Oklahoma City.

Suzanne Taets van Amerongen, M.D.
Director of Training of the Boston University Department of Child Psychiatry; Associate Professor of Child Psychiatry, Boston University.

E. James Anthony, M.D.
Blanche F. Ittleson Professor of Child Psychiatry, and Director, Eliot Division of Child Psychiatry, Washington University School of Medicine, St. Louis.

Edgar Auerswald, M.D.
Chief, Maui Mental Health Center, Wailuku, Maui, Hawaii; Associate Professor of Clinical Psychiatry, School of Medicine, University of Hawaii.

Marjorie L. Behrens
Research Associate, Nathan W. Ackerman Family Institute, New York.

Irving N. Berlin, M.D.
Professor of Psychiatry and Pediatrics, Head of the Division of Child Psychiatry, and Co-Director, Social and Community Psychiatry Programs, University of Washington School of Medicine, Seattle.

Harry R. Brickman, M.D.
Deputy Director for Mental Health, Los Angeles County Department of Health Services; Clinical Professor of Psychiatry, University of California at Los Angeles Medical School.

Eugene B. Brody, M.D.
Chairman and Professor, Department of Psychiatry, and Director, Institute of Psychiatry and Human Development, University of Maryland School of Medicine.

Bertram S. Brown, M.D.
Director, National Institute of Mental Health.

Hilde Bruch, M.D.
Professor of Psychiatry, Baylor College of Medicine, Texas Medical Center, Houston.

Gerald Caplan, M.D.
Professor of Psychiatry and Director, Laboratory of Community Psychiatry, Harvard Medical School, Boston.

John C. Cassel, M.D., M.P.H.
Professor and Chairman, Department of Epidemiology, School of Public Health, University of North Carolina, Chapel Hill.

Morris E. Chafetz, M.D.
Director, National Institute on Alcohol Abuse and Alcoholism, Department of Health, Education, and Welfare, Rockville, Maryland.

Jacob Christ, M.D.
Clinical Associate Professor, Department of Psychiatry, Woodruff Medical Center of Emory University, Atlanta; Visiting Lecturer, Medical University of South Carolina, Charleston.

Raquel E. Cohen, M.D.
Associate Professor of Psychiatry and Associate Director, Laboratory of Community Psychiatry, Harvard Medical School, Boston.

Shirley Cooper, M.S.W.
Chief Psychiatric Social Worker and Executive Director, Children's Service, Mt. Zion Hospital and Medical Center, Department of Psychiatry.

Robert E. Davidson, M.D.
Medical Director of Preschool Program and Medical Director of Central Intake, Emma

Pendleton Bradley Hospital, Providence, Rhode Island.

Harold W. Demone, Jr., Ph.D.

Executive Director, United Community Services of Metropolitan Boston; Associate Clinical Professor of Social Welfare in the Department of Psychiatry, Laboratory of Community Psychiatry, Harvard Medical School, Boston.

George A. DeVos, Ph.D.

Professor of Anthropology, University of California at Berkeley.

Jackson Dillon, M.D.

Project Director, Greater Lynn Community Memorial Health Center, Union Hospital; Lecturer on Psychiatry, Laboratory of Community Psychiatry, Harvard Medical School, Boston.

Barbara Snell Dohrenwend, Ph.D.

Professor of Psychology, City College, City University of New York.

Bruce P. Dohrenwend, Ph.D.

Professor of Social Science, Department of Psychiatry, College of Physicians and Surgeons, Columbia University, New York.

Matthew P. Dumont, M.D.

Assistant Commissioner for Drug Rehabilitation, Massachusetts Department of Mental Health; Lecturer on Psychiatry, Laboratory of Community Psychiatry, Harvard Medical School, Boston.

Leon Eisenberg, M.D.

Professor of Psychiatry, Harvard Medical School; Chief of Psychiatry, Massachusetts General Hospital, Boston.

Dana L. Farnsworth, M.D.

Professor of Hygiene, Emeritus, Harvard University; Consultant on Psychiatry, Harvard School of Public Health, Boston.

George E. Gardner, M.D., Ph.D.

Professor of Psychiatry, Emeritus, Harvard Medical School; Director, Emeritus, Judge Baker Guidance Center, Boston.

Alan Gartner, Ph.D.

Professor of Education, Queens College, New York; Co-Director, New Human Services Institute, New York; Publisher, Social Policy magazine.

Albert J. Glass, M.D.

Professor of Psychiatry and Behavioral Sciences, University of Oklahoma Health Sciences Center, Oklahoma City.

William Goldfarb, M.D., Ph.D.

Director, Henry Ittleson Center for Child Research, a Division of the Jewish Board of Guardians, Riverdale, New York; Clinical Professor of Psychiatry, Columbia University.

Ernest M. Gruenberg, M.D., Dr. P.H.

Professor of Psychiatry, College of Physicians and Surgeons, Columbia University; Director, Psychiatric Epidemiology Research Unit, Hudson River State Hospital, Poughkeepsie, New York.

Beatrix A. Hamburg, M.D.

Assistant Professor and Director, Child Psychiatry Clinic, Department of Psychiatry, Stanford University School of Medicine.

Norris Hansell, M.D.

Superintendent, Adolf Meyer Center, Decatur, Illinois; Professor of Psychiatry, Northwestern University, Chicago.

Portia Bell Hume, M.D.

Clinical Professor in Psychiatry, Emeritus, School of Medicine, University of California at San Francisco; Lecturer, School of Public Health, University of California at Berkeley.

James D. Isbister

Deputy Director, National Institute of Mental Health.

Gerald F. Jacobson, M.D.

Executive Director, Los Angeles Psychiatric Service; Executive Director, Benjamin Rush Centers for Problems of Living, Los Angeles.

John J. Laffey, Ph.D.

Associate Professor of Psychology and Director, The Learning Center, Rhode Island College, Providence; Consultant in Psychology, Emma Pendleton Bradley Hospital, Providence.

Maurice W. Laufer, M.D.

Director and Physician-in-Chief, Emma Pendleton Bradley Hospital, Providence; Clinical Professor of Psychiatry and Chairman, Committee of Child Psychiatry, Brown University, Providence.

Alexander H. Leighton, M.D.

Professor of Social Psychiatry and Head, Department of Behavioral Sciences, Harvard School of Public Health, Boston.

Alan I. Levenson, M.D.

Professor and Head, Department of Psychiatry, College of Medicine, University of Arizona.

Reginald S. Lourie, M.D.

Professor of Child Health and Human Development, Department of Psychiatry and Behavioral

Science, George Washington University, Washington, D.C.; Director, Department of Psychiatry, Children's Hospital National Medical Center, Washington, D.C.

Alan A. McLean, M.D.

Medical Director, Eastern Region, International Business Machines; Clinical Associate Professor of Psychiatry, Cornell University Medical College.

Irwin M. Marcus, M.D.

Clinical Professor of Psychiatry, Louisiana State University Medical School, New Orleans; Chairman of the Child Psychoanalysis Program and Past President of the New Orleans Psychoanalytic Institute.

James F. Masterson, M.D.

Clinical Professor of Psychiatry, Cornell University Medical College; Head, Adolescent Program, New York Hospital Payne Whitney Clinic.

Salvador Minuchin, M.D.

Director, Philadelphia Child Guidance Clinic; Professor of Child Psychiatry and Pediatrics, University of Pennsylvania.

Peter B. Neubauer, M.D.

Director, Child Development Center, a Division of the Jewish Board of Guardians; Professor of Clinical Psychiatry, Downstate Medical Center, State University of New York.

Harris B. Peck, M.D.

Professor of Psychiatry, Albert Einstein College of Medicine; Acting Director of Social and Community Psychiatry, Albert Einstein College of Medicine, New York.

Chester M. Pierce, M.D.

Professor of Education and Psychiatry in the Faculty of Medicine and at the Graduate School of Education, Harvard University; Visiting Psychiatrist, Massachusetts General Hospital, Boston.

Raymond Prince, M.D.

Research Director, Mental Hygiene Institute, Montreal; Associate Professor, Department of Psychiatry, McGill University.

Eveoleen N. Rexford, M.D.

Divisional Professor of Child Psychiatry, Formerly Director, Department of Child Psychiatry, Boston University School of Medicine;

Instructor at the Boston Psychoanalytic Society and Institute.

Rebecca E. Rieger, Ph.D.

Chief Psychologist, Hillcrest Children's Center, Washington, D.C.; Chief Psychologist, Children's Hospital National Medical Center.

Frank Riessman, Ph.D.

Professor of Education, Queens College, New York; Co-Director, New Human Services Institute, New York; Editor, Social Policy magazine.

Donald B. Rinsley, M.D.

Director, Children's Section, Topeka State Hospital; Member of the Executive and Training Faculty in Child Psychiatry, Menninger Foundation; Associate Clinical Professor of Psychiatry, University of Kansas School of Medicine.

Alexander S. Rogawski, M.D.

Professor and Director, Division of Social and Community Psychiatry, School of Medicine, University of Southern California; Chief Mental Health Consultant, Department of Public Social Service, County of Los Angeles.

John L. Schimel, M.D.

Associate Director, William Alanson White Institute of Psychiatry, Psychoanalysis, and Psychology, New York; Associate Clinical Professor of Psychiatry, New York University Medical Center.

Edwin S. Shneidman, Ph.D.

Professor of Medical Psychology and Director, Laboratory for the Study of Life-Threatening Behavior, University of California at Los Angeles.

Albert J. Solnit, M.D.

Sterling Professor of Pediatrics and Psychiatry, School of Medicine, Yale University; Director, Child Study Center, Yale University, New Haven.

Bessie M. Sperry, Ph.D.

Chief Psychologist, Judge Baker Guidance Center, Boston.

Zena A. Stein, M.D.

Director, New York State Department of Mental Hygiene, Epidemiology of Mental Retardation Research Unit; Professor of Public Health, Division of Epidemiology, Columbia University.

Mervyn Susser, M.D.

Professor and Head, Division of Epidemiology, School of Public Health, Columbia University.

James M. Toolan, M.D.

Assistant Professor, University of Vermont College of Medicine; Medical Director, United Counseling Service of Bennington County, Bennington, Vermont; Psychiatric Consultant to Bennington College and to Marlboro College.

Paul H. Wender, M.D.

Professor of Child Psychiatry, University of Utah Medical School, Salt Lake City.

Sidney L. Werkman, M.D.

Professor of Psychiatry and Director of Medical School Teaching in Psychiatry, University of Colorado School of Medicine.

Eric D. Wittkower, M.D.

Professor of Psychiatry, Emeritus, McGill University, Montreal; Honorary Consulting Psychiatrist, Royal Victoria Hospital, Montreal General Hospital, Queen Elizabeth Hospital, and the Reddy Memorial Hospital, Montreal.

Stanley F. Yolles, M.D.

Chairman, Department of Psychiatry, School of Medicine, Health Sciences Center, State University of New York at Stony Brook.

Israel Zwerling, M.D., Ph.D.

Director, Bronx State Hospital; Professor of Psychiatry, Albert Einstein College of Medicine, New York. (Currently Professor and Chairman, Department of Mental Health Sciences, Hahnemann Medical College, Philadelphia.)

CONTENTS

Volume Two

PART THREE: *Sociocultural Psychiatry*

PART FOUR: *Community Psychiatry*

PART ONE

Child Psychiatry

CHAPTER 1

PSYCHIATRIC AND PSYCHOLOGICAL EXAMINATION OF CHILDREN*

Reginald S. Lourie and Rebecca E. Rieger

THE DIAGNOSTIC PROCESS in child psychiatry has gradually evolved over the last 150 years into a usually trustworthy pattern of study in trained hands. It began as a descriptive approach and made its greatest gains during the past sixty years, with the development of dynamic concepts of human behavior and the perfection of a variety of pertinent psychological instruments. More modern diagnostic efforts began around the turn of the century, with interested and concerned pediatricians moving into the dis-

turbed child's home and living with the family for a period. A modification of this was what Leo Kanner called "noodle soup psychiatry," in which the diagnostician was invited to have dinner with the patient and his family. The most significant statements of the most current status of the psychiatric and psychological diagnostic examination of the young are in the Group for the Advancement of Psychiatry's "The Diagnostic Process in Child Psychiatry,"[17] Anna Freud's "Normality and Pathology in Childhood: Assessment of Development,"[33] and James Simmons' "Psychiatric Examination of Children."[107]

The present form of diagnostic examination

* Chapters on mental retardation will be found in Volume IV: *Organic Conditions and Psychosomatic Medicine.*

of children had its beginnings in the retroactive studies initiated by Sigmund Freud in psychoanalysis and Adolf Meyer in psychobiology. Its greatest impetus came from the development of the child guidance movement and the fields of child psychoanalysis, clinical psychology, and pediatric psychiatry. Important contributions about constitutional factors came from the pioneers in developmental neurology, such as Bronson Crothers and Samuel Orton, from such pediatricians as Donald Winnicott, and from the fields of mental retardation and cerebral palsy. Psychology contributed not only intelligence testing, projective techniques, and basic information about learning but also their use as sources of clinical information. Psychiatric social work added the important component of family dynamics and environmental influences on the child, leading to the more recent inclusion of information from anthropology and sociology about cultural and societal forces. Add to these the specialist in educational diagnosis and the speech pathologist, and one sees not only how the classical clinical team concept became an accepted approach to the diagnostic process but also how the team has expanded.

It is also obvious that there needs to be a coordinator of the team, an integrator of the information about the individual child and the influences from his family, school, and community. The more or less expanded team functions chiefly in the outpatient clinic, treatment center, community mental health program, and hospital, but it is also found in such settings as school systems, juvenile courts, family agencies, and more recently in comprehensive child health programs. The private practitioner may combine the roles of various team members or work with collaborators from other disciplines who are also in private practice. Similar combining of roles takes place in many clinics. The role in diagnosis for the rapidly growing category of nonprofessional mental health workers is an expanding one. These valuable additions to the clinical team, if properly trained and supervised, have provided an extension of the clinical team in the inner city and rural areas for communication with otherwise hard to reach community resources, including neighborhood and regional action programs.

(Goals

Almost everybody is a diagnostician. Almost everybody has an opinion as to what is wrong with a disturbed child. The goal of the psychiatric and psychological examinations, however, is to obtain as complete and valid a picture as possible of the child's current status. This includes evaluating the areas of weakness and strength in the child, his family and living situation, his environment, and his community as a basis for defining not only what has gone wrong and how the patient became the way he is but also what can be done about it correctively.

In dealing with the child himself, one begins with how he is put together constitutionally. In addition to information about developmental milestones and medical history, a current physical examination should be part of every diagnostic study. The pertinent information about contributing constitutional factors may come from the prenatal period. For example, a hyperactive child may have been a "whirling dervish" even in utero. Individual differences beginning in the newborn period are important to annotate, such as hyper- or hyposensitivities to touch and sound, excessive passivity, high or low impulse levels, imbalances, poor coordination and integration, poor control patterns, and tolerance for anxiety. Here Lois Murphy's vulnerability inventory[78] has been quite valuable.

The constitutional "givens" of the child should be matched with their interaction in and with the environmental matrix. What have been the facilitators, the inhibitors, the distorters, and perpetuators of any constitutional hazards to normal development? This information comes both from history and direct observation.

There should be an evaluation of how the child has developed in a range of expectable (ego) functions. These include his patterns of coping and adapting (defenses), cognitive abilities, memory, relationship patterns, reality testing, self-image, autonomous functions, space orientation, language, and synthetic functions. The latter should particularly be examined in terms of the response of patterns of organization and integration in the presence of stress. Especially important is knowing whether there is disorganization of thinking and acting in the presence of anxiety or pressure. This body of information is also obtainable from both history and direct observation and testing.

Another area of information gathering about an emotionally disturbed or malfunctioning child is in terms of how he has moved along the lines of development in a range of maturational patterns. These include patterns of relationships and socializations both within and outside his family. How have dependency and basic trust developed? How has the individual dealt with survival problems, with separation problems, with negativism, with aggression, with sexual interests, with work, with impulse control and body control (including sphincters)? What kind of conscience (and other superego components) does the child have, what concepts of property rights (including "owning" people), and what response to rules? Are there identity distortions? Are there habit and/or fear patterns that indicate earlier fixations and immaturities? These questions too can be answered by both history and direct examination.

([Technical Aspects of Psychiatric and Psychological Examination of the Child

The basic components of a diagnostic study for children are the history, the psychiatric examination, and psychological testing. The clinical team of psychiatric social worker, clinical psychologist, and child psychiatrist traditionally divided these facets, but there has been considerable blurring of disciplinary lines and overlapping of functions as professionals who developed more than one area of competence

progressed in the child mental health field and trained others in their fields. Thus, in every step of an evaluation, clinical observations are being made, beginning with history taking. The psychiatric social worker, the public health mental health nurse, the psychologist, and the child psychiatrist use their formal examinations, including contributions about constitutional factors, to obtain history information and define dynamic processes. It is no longer valid to treat the psychological study simply as a form of laboratory testing, as was true in many settings in the past. Sometimes, where indicated, more than one member of the team will see children and parents together for a combined history and clinical examination in a family diagnostic type of study.[52]

The History

Usually there is a scrutiny of preliminary information about a patient (in the clinic most often in an intake conference) as a basis for deciding the most appropriate patterns of examination by psychologist and psychiatrist.

Where indicated, additional information may need to be obtained first from the members of the extended team, or the pediatrician, neurologist, geneticist, biochemist, teacher, special educator, speech therapist, police, and/or probation officer.

History taking in child psychiatry needs to include information from the prime child-care agents, who may be parents or outsiders. These outsiders may be relatives such as a grandmother, or a babysitter, nurse, or governess. This is especially important when the mother works full time or is otherwise relatively unavailable. In addition, there should be information about the parents' health, developmental problems, and value systems, as well as their interests and relationships and/or problems with their own families. It is useful to have information on intercurrent events that influenced critical stages in personality. The patient's systems and the parent's understanding and handling of them are important, but should not preclude obtaining a comprehensive picture including the social and cultural influences on the family. Finally, the history taking should end with helping the parents prepare the child for the diagnostic visits. One way this can be done is to explain that there are people who know how to help children get over troubles or to make plans, such as about school.

The Psychiatric Examination

The setting for the examination and battery of tests will be determined by the age of the child, his symptom complex, and the questions to be answered. The preschool child will need different toys and tests than the school-age child. The pubertal child may need to be seen in a playroom or, depending on maturity, to be treated more like the adolescent in an office interviewing setting. An especially fearful child or one with marked separation problems may need to be seen with a parent present, so that history taking cannot then be simultaneous. Sometimes the examinations must take place in other than clinic or office settings. Thus, children are seen in day-care centers, nursery and other schools, detention centers, welfare programs, or child-care institutions. A portable kit with appropriate toys and/or testing materials is useful for such purposes. It can be particularly appropriate for examination of hospitalized children. Some have used the World Game for this purpose.[54]

For the psychiatric examination of preschool and school-age children, a playroom is ideal. It is also quite possible to carry out such studies with toys in a closet, desk drawer, or in a box. As is well established, toys serve a triple purpose. First is the need for interesting, even enticing, a child patient who usually sees no reason of his own for a visit to the examiner. Second is the child's use of playthings as a means of working out developmental problems. Third is the child's use of play as a means of expressing himself, both as a nonverbal language and as a medium and expeditor of fantasy. In observation of and participation in their play there is also the opportunity to take note of children's body language as still another form of nonverbal communication.

It is particularly important for the examiner to become expert in "reading" children's nonverbal language, because by four or five years of age children have usually learned to use words to cover up how they really feel. Dr. Charles West, who founded the Hospital for Sick Children (Great Ormond Street) in London in 1854, wrote in his lectures to medical students,[19] "Your old means of investigating disease will here to a degree fail you, and you will feel almost as if you had to learn your alphabet again. [It is] as if you were to hear around you everywhere the sounds of a foreign tongue, and to observe manners and customs such as you had never seen before." He then added, "If you are not fond of little children you cannot learn it, for they soon make up their minds as to who loves them, and when ill, they will express their real feelings, whether by words or signs, to no one else."

The variety of toys is planned to explore the child's developmental and interpersonal concerns and his method of dealing with them. For exploring relationship interests and patterns, there should be human figures, puppets, and an unstructured dollhouse where possible, with the usual furniture, including kitchen, toilet, and bedroom items. Toy animals should be available for those children who are too sensitized to deal directly with their feelings about people. Some children may need to avoid anything resembling the living (dolls, stuffed animals) and can only respond to relationship play with families of inanimate objects, such as blocks or cars.

Movement toys, such as cars, trucks, and airplanes, help to define a child's motor and control problems. Soldiers, blown-up clowns, and guns and rubber-tipped darts help to show the child's interests and solutions to aggressive patterns. A few games, appropriate for different ages (and not time consuming), can show competetive interests and attitudes toward rules. For younger children, a pull toy is useful. Communication toys are useful, such as one or two toy telephones, a typewriter, and a few books for children with difficulties in communication. Blocks are good to provide demonstration of constructive and destructive interests, motor and spatial orientation. In their use for house building, they can give clues to body image.[31] Drawing materials are helpful for this purpose as well as providing an avenue for constructive interests, fantasy, self-image, and such scorable tests as the Goodenough Draw-A-Person test and the house, tree, and person drawings (see discussion of psychological approaches). For adolescents it is useful to have such materials readily at hand for doodling or drawing as a basis for face saving (hopefully), temporary retreat, or regrouping of defenses. Other construction materials, such as clay, fingerpaints, and Play-Doh, are helpful not only in expressing feelings and ideas but in showing interest in messiness or orderliness. A traveling toy kit for a playroom interview on a spontaneous basis, such as on hospital ward rounds, consists of pipe cleaners, tongue blades, blank paper, and paper clips. Pipe cleaners can make people, animals, and houses. Tongue blades can become people, animals, autos, planes, trains, and so on. Paper for drawing, making cutouts, or folding to make planes and helicopters is useful. Origami is a helpful skill.

The psychiatric examination begins in the waiting room. There is considerable value in structured waiting-room observations. A method to accomplish this has been developed, utilizing a checklist, which can be filled in by a receptionist, secretary, or mental health aide.[64] Not infrequently parent-child interaction goes on in the waiting room and ceases when the examiner appears. The mothers and children who are very close or far apart, the fearful mother or child, the permissive mother whose child climbs all over her with hands under her clothes, the hyperactive child whose parent sits helplessly, unnoticingly, or mildly reproves him from across the room when he hits another, throws things around, or pulls the paper out of the secretary's typewriter are providing usable information often otherwise unavailable.

The examiner's role in the psychiatric examination is to establish a working relationship with the patient in which the child is free to share feelings, thoughts, actions, and fantasies. With a warm, friendly, interested approach, most children will respond favorably, particu-

larly since they want to be liked. The examiner's manner should be calculated to establish confidence and a feeling that he is there to help the child. To minimize the child's mistrust, the parent or substitute should be helped as part of the intake process to prepare for the examination by explaining that the examiner is there to find ways to help children get over troubles and to make the best kind of plans for school, for example, and not because he is "crazy." This is not always effective, however, because the child may have been threatened that, for example, if he did not stop wetting his bed, he would be taken to a place where they would make him stop. The child is then wondering all through the visit when and how he will be made to stop. Or the child has been tricked into stopping at the clinic or office on the way to the movies or to see Santa Claus. The examiner's neutrality and interest in the child must be established, especially when the patient has been sent for evaluation by the juvenile court, school authorities, or lawyers or judges in a custody suit.

After the usual introductions, it is useful with verbal children for the examiner to explain what will happen, stating, for example, "We have a room with all kinds of toys and we invite boys and girls to visit with us there to play and talk. Do you know what happens when we are finished? [Without waiting for an answer] Then you go home [or back to school and so on]. Let me show you where it is." The child and often the parent are relieved when a complete gestalt is presented in some such way about a feared unknown experience. Comfort or discomfort with separation is seen at this point. Some children need the visual (more than verbal) permission of the parent before making a move.

On the way to the playroom a number of mental notes can be made about gait and other large muscle movements. A hand briefly on the child's shoulder (not with adolescents) will show the individual who melts into the examiner's side or pulls away, uncomfortable with closeness or with a stranger. Some children will wait to have their hand taken to be led to the playroom or will insist on the parent's accompanying them. Some will run on ahead, acting all knowing, or having to explore every door or touch every picture on the way. Some show their negativism, fear, or need to control the situation by stubbornly refusing to go. The resulting parental cajoling, bribing, anger, or helplessness can be the reenactment of a familiar script or tableau as a demonstration for the examiner. With the fearful or willful preschooler, a pull-toy may be brought out or a ball bounced to woo the child or change the subject. When a child brings a favorite toy or book with him, he can be invited to bring it along.

Once in the playroom (or other examining setting) it is important to note the patient's first interest. The child with relationship problems often will go first to the dolls or dollhouse. A boy may only look at it carefully, then back away and perhaps say "Only girls play with that," thus suggesting an underlying interest. The hyperactive child who goes first to the movement toys and plays patterns of controlling movement tells of an interest in solving his difficulty with control. The aggressive child may pick up the guns. The child with communication problems may go first to a telephone or a typewriter. The child concerned with fears of bodily hurt will spot a doll or a toy soldier with a part missing, sometimes even when these are not obvious, and may ask how it happened. The child concerned with problems of order or impulse control may say "This is a messy place" and proceed to line up the toys. On the other hand, the child with any of these problems who studiously avoids the toys or play related to his underlying problems, even when later introduced by the examiner, is also telling something about his motivation and defenses.

The anxious child may flit from toy to toy, touching or testing, and moving on. The child concerned with dependency may pick up something he knows quite well, such as a gun or ball, and ask "What's this?" or "Can I take this home?" to test the examiner's interest in helping, giving, or responding to him. The inhibited, shy, or overly passive child may stand immobilized in the middle of the playroom and wait for help in getting involved. The too uninhibited child who is the tyrant or "bad

one" in the family or the bully may immediately turn a gun on the examiner or throw something at him to test from the start who is in control. The all-knowing child who is the family autocrat may declare that he knows all about the games, has all these toys, and much better ones. The exhibitionistic child will demonstrate something he knows or a dance step he has learned. The rivalrous or competitive child will ask to start a game in which scores are kept, sometimes setting his own rules or changing them if he is losing.

With the younger (preschool) child one may need to structure the play for most of the examination. Describing the examining situation is important with children available to verbal approaches. The first step is to explain the ground rules, such as saying "This is a place where you can play with anything you want and do anything you want here, but we have one rule." If one asks the child to guess what this rule is, interesting and often telling answers result. Then the usual playroom rule is shared with the child, such as "You can't hurt yourself, and you can't hurt me." This is not only reassuring but also gives the examiner considerable leeway in deciding what will be harmful to the patient.

Then it is useful to repeat the examiner's function as one to help children get over troubles or make plans: "The best way he knows to help is to get to know the child and his views by having a visit with him and by not having to rely on what others have said." This also provides an opening for a question, such as "Tell me what troubles [problems] 'they' say you have." Then confidentiality should be stressed in such terms as "Whatever we talk about here is just for us here." Some prefer to add "You can say anything about it to anyone. We won't."

For those examiners who prefer to take notes during the visit, it is good to clarify the basis for this with the child and even ask his permission. This can be done in terms such as "I like to write down some of the things we talk about. My memory isn't always so good and I would rather not forget. Is that all right with you? I don't have to if you would rather not." Seldom, if ever, will a child refuse permission. However, the mistrustful or suspicious child may later ask what is being written or surreptitiously peek at the notes. It is useful to note at which point this occurs during the examination. Reading the last sentence aloud, letting the child look at the notes, or simply saying that only what has been happening is being noted is usually enough to stop the questions. With adolescents note taking is adjusted to the individual situation and attitude. More often than otherwise, notes are not taken, particularly with hostile, reluctant, rebellious, or paranoid teenagers. With any age group it is well to put aside pencil and paper when discussing particularly sensitive areas, such as sexual interests, details of a stealing episode, and runaway plans. On the other hand, it is important to make an obvious note of suicidal thoughts and attempts.

In order for the examination to provide information that will achieve the goals and objectives outlined above, both the psychological and psychiatric studies should be a combination of structured and unstructured approaches. The psychological is obviously the more formally structured. In contrast to treatment interviews, diagnostic examinations are calculated to obtain as much information about a child as possible in the time available.

For those who have the luxury of an extended diagnostic period with a number of visits, usually less structure is necessary for the psychiatric examination. However, the pressures for service have made it more appropriate to obtain the necessary information in a single visit if possible. There are exceptional situations in which additional visits are necessary. Usually, sufficient data can be made available in the single hour, particularly if the psychological examination can be counted on to complement the needed clinical data for a useful evaluation. The one-shot psychiatric examination, which is part of a consultation or the private office visit, thus has the hazard of providing only a single time segment of behavior, which can give less than a comprehensive picture of the child.

The less structured part of the examination provides opportunity for tuning in on the child's nonverbal communication. One watches for the points at which he changes play patterns, such as what was happening in play at the moment when one activity is given up. Was it in relation to the reaction of the examiner as a participant, as an observer, or as a questioner of what is happening? Particularly if a question was raised, watch for the next bit of activity because it may be a playing out of the real answer, in spite of what verbal answer was given. Watch for the reactions to frustration or failure, whether it is giving up, persistence, projecting blame elsewhere, wanting his mother, or becoming disorganized, awkward, demanding, aggressive, destructive, dependent, unavailable, overactive, messy, and so on. Watch for the body language. What is the point at which a brain-damaged child begins to drool? Can the child calm himself down when he becomes overstimulated? At what point does the enuretic or encopretic child begin to wet or soil himself or ask for the toilet? What is happening at the point at which the child puts his hands to his genitals to protect or reassure himself about them? Glances, grimaces, looking over the shoulder at the examiner, eyes beginning to tear, blushes, and fearfulness are examples of forms of communication, as in the old song "Every Little Movement Has a Meaning All Its Own." With a large majority of verbal children it is quite possible to have a productive diagnostic interview sitting at a desk, with emphasis on verbal communication while the child is playing or otherwise occupied. It has been commonly said that child psychiatrists stop seeing children when at age fifty they can not get down on the floor so easily. Lippman, however, described and demonstrated how one can be less physically active and still effective as a diagnostician (and therapist) with children and, as always, with adolescents.[69]

The verbal approach, following the preparatory comments to set the stage as described above, should begin with some evidence of the examiner's personal interest in the child. One time-honored way of starting this is to say "I know very little about you. I am not even sure about your age. Can I guess?" Then the guess is at least a year older than the child really is, which is almost always flattering. If the child indicates that he is often thought of as being older or younger, this can be followed by an inquiry as to whether that is good or bad.

Explorations into specific areas of a child's functioning should begin with a neutral area, much as in a physical examination, where the sore throat or abdomen are examined last, if one wants a cooperative patient. The exception is where the complaints about him, his troublesome symptom, the habits he wants to get rid of, the basis for his failure, the parent, the sibling, the bully giving him trouble, the unjust accusations of the police, the unfair teacher, and so on are on the surface, and the child himself may introduce it. Sometimes a parent will, as the last word as the child leaves with the examiner.

A cardinal principle in the verbal approach to school-age and pubertal children is to avoid direct questions as much as possible. Particularly the word "why" is the most abused word in the examiner's lexicon and should be avoided whenever possible. Children have usually become expert at parrying questions, especially to "why," or giving the answer that they feel is the "right" or expected one. Besides, mostly they want to please. The exceptions are the passive child who cannot resist pressure for a reply to questions about even the most sensitive areas and the resistant sullen, suspicious, or withdrawn child who retreats into silence. Even with the latter group, there are nonverbal responses, particularly when key areas are touched on. For example, if they are drawing or doodling suddenly the spaces must be filled in, or the lines become fragmented or wild or tighter. Examples of the use of positive statements, the "tell me" approach, instead of questions will be given in the discussion of specific areas to be investigated. It should also be kept in mind that one should not stop with the factual information about a specific area. The thinking or fantasies behind it should also be looked into. The examiner should also realize that the objective of the examination is to get a rounded picture of the child's personality development and the factors underlying it. Therefore, the frequent tendency to spend most of the in-

quiry on the presenting symptoms should be avoided. Thus, in spite of the child's and examiner's often necessary pressure to get the details of a rape, suicidal attempt, stealing episode, runaway, or acid trip, the questions to be ultimately answered are "How did it get there?" and "What can be done about it?"

Where possible, the sequence of areas explored should lead naturally into each other. If one begins by looking into the school situation as a neutral subject (where the major complaints do not center around school), this can be structured to lead into attitudes toward aggression, friends, and fantasies. An example of one way this can be done is with the following sequence:

"Everybody goes to school. Tell me about your school. I don't even know which grade you are in."

"Tell me how many other schools you were in and which was the best one."

"Tell me about the best [easiest] thing in school."

"Tell me about the worst [hardest] thing." Specifically, learning problems should be looked at further.

"You know how in every school that there are bad children and ones who get into trouble. Tell me about the ones who fight and what you do if they fight you." Where there is complete denial of anything bad or aggressive in the child's experience, one can add: "Tell me what you heard that the bad ones do in other schools and outside of school. Tell me about the ones who tease and call names and the best thing to do about it." If stealing has been a problem, this is an easy place to introduce it.

"Tell me about children who steal in your school [neighborhood] and why they steal." The child can then, on a face-saving basis, tell about at least conscious awareness of motives.

"You know how some children like to help each other and like to play together. Tell me if you like to be with friends or to be alone."

"Tell me what kind of fun you have with friends." With the girls who prefer sports, horses, and boy's games and boys who like girl's games this should be further explored as to sex identity preferences.

"Tell me what you like to do when you are alone. Lots of boys and girls like to pretend when they are alone or play or make-believe." With adolescents, talk about daydreaming. "Tell me what you like to pretend." Particularly with those children who avoid fantasy (and usefully with all children) one can add: "I'll bet I know one thing you like when you're alone—television. Tell me which are your favorite programs." This can be varied to include movies, comics and books. "Tell me one thing that happened in that program [movie, book], the first thing you think of. I don't mean the whole story, just one thing that happened."

The use of the child's favorite media as a projective approach can lead to further insights about dynamics, since each child seeing a program is looking at it in terms of his own experience, motives, and interests and usually is reported in a version that includes the individual's own preoccupations and concerns. The incident reported should be followed up. Questions are more appropriate for this, such as "I wonder what made him do that?" or "How come that happened?" One may add "How did it end?" "Why?" For children who attend Sunday school or church, the Bible can be used as a similar projective technique, such as "Tell me one thing that happened in the Bible." One can hear some startling versions of incidents in the Good Book and the motivations behind them. And the Bible is a remarkably complete record of human experience.

In exploring the patient's family and relationships, one can get a picture of where the child sees himself and the others in terms of closeness or being left out by asking him to draw a picture of his family. "Tell me which one is the biggest nuisance [or who makes the most trouble, or is bad, if the child does not know what a nuisance is]." Attitudes about parents are better assessed by impersonalizing. "Tell me what a mother has to do to be a good mother. Any mother, not yours." "You must know what bad mothers do; you see them on television and in movies." "Tell me what old witches do." The witch is the age-old symbol for the bad mother. Similarly for good and bad fathers. One can usefully explore sleeping arrangements or have the child draw the interior of the house for this purpose.

In some situations it is helpful to check on early memories, especially screen memories. One way to accomplish this is to say, "Some children can remember way back when they were little. Tell me how far back you can remember. What is the first thing you can recall, not what somebody told you?"

Patterns of closeness, alienation, trust, and self-image relationships to others can be explored by the use of selected Duss fables.[23,29,32,83] One of the most useful of these is the desert island story. It can be introduced by saying "Let's pretend again for a few minutes. Let's say you had to go far away to live on a desert island [or on a piece of land in the middle of the ocean with no one living there]. But you could take one person from the whole world. Tell me whom you would take." Some children will need additional reassurance that this is only daydreaming or fantasy. The usual school-age child will take a friend. The deprived, untrusting child will take God, Jesus, an angel. The child reaching out hungrily for any port in a storm will want the examiner, never having seen him before. The rivalrous, hurt, or neglected child may go alone or take a sibling or a pet animal. The fearful child may take Superman, Batman, or Hercules. The immature child or the oedipal child will want one or the other parent. The answer should be interpreted in terms of the normal expectations about relationships at any given age.

Another form of projective approach to check on a child's self-image as to competence, dependency, separation, and close relationships is the game of providing an ending for a structured story. One of the most frequently used Duss fables for this purpose is the baby bird story. "Let's pretend that there was a baby bird living in a nest with a mother bird and father bird. The baby bird could fly just a little bit. Then along came a big wind which blew the mother bird out one way and blew the father bird out the opposite way. Let's make up a story about what happened to the baby bird. Remember it could fly just a little bit." The answers forthcoming give clues to the child's own fears about hurt and survival, to hopelessness with separation and abandonment, to trust that someone will care for it, to feelings of readiness to be on one's own and coping with outside dangers, to magical solutions, to optimism versus pessimism, to getting rid of one or the other parent, and so on. Here, too, it may be necessary to say "Tell me how it ended for the mother and the father."

When exploring fears, it is well to establish that the examiner is comfortable talking about fears, that he knows that all children have had them, and that the patient is expected to be like all other children. This area can be opened with a statement such as "You [and I] know how children are afraid of things when they are little, like before they go to kindergarten or the first grade. They are afraid of the dark and animals and storms and ghosts and witches and robbers and kidnappers, and monsters. Tell me what you were afraid of when you were little." Later one can add, "Sometimes these fears don't stop when you go to school." Then it should be followed up by finding out who takes care of the fears, and what is done about them. Similarly one approaches dreams. "You [and I] know how everyone has dreams, good ones and bad ones. Tell me something that happened in a dream. Only one thing, not a whole dream." This can be followed up by exploring how the dreams are cared for. Especially with nightmares: Does the child then have to get into bed with someone, and who is it?

Sexual areas can be explored in the same way, that is, first establishing the normality of such interests and then expecting that this child has been like others. This type of structuring in terms of normality often is most reassuring and relieving to a youngster who had never dared to talk about this part of his makeup. "You [and I] know how when children are little, even before they go to school, they like to play with their wee wees or whatever they call them. Tell me how old you were when you first found out about it. Some children find out at home, some outside, some from friends, some from brothers or sisters or big boys and girls, and some find out by themselves. Tell me how you found out." The leads opened up can be followed, such as fears of self-hurt or hurt by others as a basis for giving up sex activities. With the overstimulated or sexually active child one may need to talk in the child's vernacular about "getting pussy."

With teenagers this area can be explored in terms of "making out," "going all the way," "making first, second, third bases, or a home run," and so on. One must use judgment in opening up the question of sexual fantasies with adolescents, keeping in mind the risk of creating a crisis in a borderline psychotic individual or one close to a homosexual panic. In general, it is surprising to some how much of this type of information is available in a diagnostic interview, in contrast to treatment interviews. One often has an opportunity at this time to find out about a girl's concept of menstruation, her preparation, difficulties, and understanding of it. With young adolescent boys, asking factually about wet dreams can be helpful. With younger children, it may be appropriate to look into their concept of how babies are born as well as sex differences and how one finds out about these.

Health and medical background as seen by the child should be looked into, including reaction to hospitalizations, operations, accidents, and so on. In the child with psychosomatic manifestations, finding out what helped and his own views of what's wrong in contrast to those of others can be useful. "Drawing the pain" is a technique developed at the Children's Hospital, Washington, D.C. The child with headaches or abdominal pain is asked to draw a picture or an outline of a head or an abdomen of the size and shape of the pain. The child with an organically based pain will look at the examiner as though there is something wrong with him. However, the child with a psychological basis for the pain usually seems to know just what is meant. Often the resulting drawing will be inconsistent with anatomical nerve distribution, for example, a sharply outlined small square or a pinpoint or a circle the size of a dime. One girl with headaches, who had been raped by her father, drew the area of the pain in the shape of a penis. One girl drew the shape of her chronic back pain as a bell. On being asked what the shape reminded her of, she replied "It's a bell, but the clapper is missing." Adolescents, especially those with poor self-concept or in an identity crisis, can be asked: "If this were a physical examination and you were examining yourself, what would you find wrong or think could be better?"

If the symptoms or complaints that brought the child for study have not yet been discussed, they should be covered before ending the interview. Important to bring out is not only the child's picture of the situation but also what he has been told about the basis for the problem, incident, or manifestation and what the child really believes.

An additional area to explore is a child's present interest for the future, as well as what he used to want to be. The psychiatric examination should be ended where possible on an optimistic forward-looking note. One way of doing this is to return to the open-ended fantasy such as these two time-honored approaches to underlying fantasies: (1) "Let us pretend again for a little bit before we have to stop. Suppose you were walking down the street and found $100. Tell me what you would do with it if it is all yours." (2) "Let us pretend that there is someone magic, maybe with the powers of God, and they gave you three wishes. Tell me what you would wish for."

Structured play as part of the psychiatric examination is preferred by some examiners to the purely verbal approaches. It is also an important adjunct with the less verbal child, with the shy, reticent child, and with the otherwise unavailable child, such as those with autism or other psychiatric features. It is useful, too, as a means of validating or clarifying an ambiguous verbal response or one that is suspect of being the response the child thinks the examiner wants or that the child feels is the "right" one. It is also the approach of choice with the preverbal child.

The use of structured play was highlighted by David Levy in his research studies on sibling rivalry[67,68] and maternal overprotection. It was further refined by Conn[18] and Hambidge.[44] It can be facilitated by having the range of toys available in the world game as developed by Margaret Lowenfeld.[74]

The principle involved is setting up a play situation that creates an opportunity for the child to bring his own reactions and solutions to an area of functioning to be evaluated. This offers the possibility of re-creating and reenacting traumatic situations encountered in the patient's life about which details have been repressed. One can also set up details of school, home, neighborhood, aggression, property rights, habits, special symptoms, and so on. It is possible too, to play out open-ended projective approaches, such as the Duss fables.

The use of puppets and role playing in expressing feelings go back in history to long before psychology and psychiatry were developed.[9] One variation in the use of puppets in diagnostic settings is for the examiner to adopt a puppet character, which explores the areas to be investigated and acts as commentator as the child plays.

With the preverbal child, the psychiatric and psychological examinations are attempting to explore the same areas of constitutional personality and mental makeup as with the older child and with the same goals outlined earlier. Mother-child interactions should be closely observed, both in and out of the examining room. With the very young child who has separation fears, it is better for the examiner as a stranger not to look directly at the child for the first few minutes, concentrating on the mother until the youngster decides from the mother's responses that the examiner is safe. Otherwise, one has a crying, fearful, uncooperative subject from the start. When the mother is in the playroom as necessary, it is well to include her in the child's play at the examiner's direction or else she becomes the observer or examiner of the examiner, a less than comfortable examining climate.

It may be necessary with many young children to "prime the pump" as a means of initiating play. This may take the form of rolling a ball back and forth, building with blocks and knocking them down, rolling cars and having them bump into one another, and so on. In addition to the child's own specific play interests, structured play situations should include relationship situations, a child getting hurt, getting punished (spanked), toileting, bathing, aggressive play (hitting), sleeping, fears, dreaming, and so on. The desert island story and baby bird story can be played out. Mothers and fathers can go out together, fight, or go to sleep together. At a family meal, one of the family can eat poisoned food or have a stomachache. A sleeping child can wake up, perhaps on a far off place (desert island), and be afraid or have a bad dream. What is the fear or the bad dream?

The clinical psychiatric examination of infants has not yet been developed into an organized art and science. However, it is in the process of being defined, and portions of the process are more or less refined. The problems and principles involved have been outlined by Cytryn.[21] A great deal has been written about mother-infant transactions and their observations as well as about infants in institutions for research purposes.[89] Individual differences in babies and their meaning in terms of vulnerability to developmental distortions have been defined by Heide,[50] Murphy,[77] Thomas, Chess, Birch, Hertzig, and Korn.[113] Psychosomatic responses have been studied by Lourie[72] and Richmond.[98] Psychological patterns have been defined by Wolff[123] and autonomic responses by Lipton, Steinschneider, and Richmond.[70] Nutritional[28] and developmental neurological pathology[26] are increasingly available.

As this type of information becomes accessible, the reluctance to think of particularly vulnerable infants having emotional problems is gradually disappearing. Also, as the searchlights increasingly highlight the first few years of life at the time when the roots of personality and adjustment problems are laid down,[73] a more defined basis for infant psychiatric evaluation becomes necessary and will be available.

In the psychiatric examination of adolescents, a few additional technical points can be added to those already mentioned. Though the diagnostician is usually better advised not to use teenage slang or "hip" language, it is often helpful to let the individual know of the examiner's familiarity with such colloquial communication patterns. Some teenagers are afraid to talk about themselves because they might find that they are "crazy," particularly as they are afraid of the nature and intensity of their wishes, fantasies, impulses, and so on. In other words, many adolescents come to the diagnostic interview on a basis that handicaps communication. Such individuals require patient approaches, sometimes repeat visits and an opportunity to test out the examiner's integrity before trust can develop.

There are many ways in which the psychiatrist can be fooled by the adolescent. The florid quality of symptoms may convince the psychiatrist that he is dealing with a schizophrenic patient, whereas he may only be seeing a transient episode of short duration from which his patient returns to adequate functioning without residual deficit. Episodes of great aggressiveness, running away, or seemingly total disorganization can be short-lived and have no ominous implications. On the other hand, one sees seemingly inexplicable suicides and psychotic episodes for which only the most minor antecedents can be discovered. There has been a trend to underestimate the seriousness of adolescent psychological conflict and to hope that the developmental process will take care of it. Careful assessment will forestall the great waste of therapeutic time that can occur when a patient is overtreated or treated inappropriately. For example, the impulse-ridden, delinquent teenager may be taken into intensive outpatient psychotherapy under the false notion that he can utilize this treatment situation effectively. Obviously, he cannot, and the result is that the therapist becomes the rider of a runaway horse.

Toward whom is the problem directed? Planning is greatly facilitated by narrowing down the areas of major conflict into manageable proportions. This helps both diagnostician and adolescent to see what their work will be. Is the conflict between mother and child or father and child? Is the problem one of displacement from parental figure to a schoolteacher? Since school failure or a drop in grades is often the signal for psychiatric consultation by the parents of teenagers, it is exceedingly important to understand the true significance of such phenomena. For example, failing in courses may be secondary to preoccupation with sexuality or jealousy and have little to do with the actual school situation. It may reflect a conflict between teacher and youngster. It may also reflect a lag in the conceptual and abstractive development of the youngster. Each would require a different kind of therapeutic intervention.

The Psychological Tests

The point at which the psychological examination enters the psychiatric diagnostic process is a function of the preferences of the team members, or of practical scheduling problems, or most importantly, of the questions that are asked about the child. In some private psychiatric practice, the psychologist-clinician is asked to make a preliminary survey of the child's difficulties, to secure the pertinent history (either directly or through a social work colleague), and to advise the psychiatrist where the principal locus of the problem appears to lie, that is, in an inhospitable or inappropriate environment, in the child's constitutional (including neurological) deficits, in the child's emotional and social development, or in some combination of these factors. A preliminary review by the psychologist is particularly useful when the child's principal presenting problem is focused on the school—the underachiever, who is presumed to be emotionally disturbed, the slow learner, who is presumed to be constitutionally handicapped, the hyperactive disruptive child, who is viewed as handicapped or hostile according to the forbearance of the teacher—since in many such cases the psychologist may clarify the primary or secondary nature of the omnipresent emotional problem. In some instances, the psychiatrist may then see an approach to the problem that obviates the need for direct psychiatric intervention, for example, the psychologist's communication to the school with suggestions for remedial teaching and/or better classroom handling. More usually, the psychological examination is seen by the psychiatrist as a complementary concomitant to the psychiatric examination and the developmental history.

The psychological examination within the psychiatric diagnostic study has as its primary goal the exploration of aspects of the child's functioning not easily accessible to the psychiatric interview nor established decisively by the developmental history.* In addition, the psychological examination may investigate areas covered by the psychiatrist from a different vantage point, with the possibility of corroborating, extending, or questioning the latter's interview findings, thus leading to the need for reconciliation of the disparate interpretations from the data and the emergence of a fuller picture of the child and his difficulties.

The formal psychological examination[20] is primarily mediated through the use of psychological tests, though it often encompasses an interview and always includes clinical observations of the child's elicited and spontaneous behavior in the test setting. The psychological test may be defined as a systematic procedure for comparing the behavior (performance, characteristics, responses) of an individual to a criterion, the criterion usually being the age-appropriate behavior of the population on which the test was standardized. In contrast to most other interview techniques (for the psychological examination is itself a type of standardized interview), a psychological test is characterized by reproducibility, standard administration, systematic recording and scoring, and explicit criteria for interpretation and evaluation. (The structured psychiatric interview, used primarily with adults for research purposes, has many qualities that approximate a formal psychological test.)

Psychological tests used by the clinician may be classified according to the structure of the test and the purpose or domain of the test: There is a class of tests described as structured, objective, or psychometric. These tests typically focus on the subject's response as a product, a discrete, scorable answer to a definite question or to the request for an act demonstrating skill in nonverbal tasks. At the other end of a continuum are unstructured, projec-

---

* The psychological examination will vary in its goals and emphases depending on the referral source (for example, pediatrician, neurologist, schoolteacher, or parent) and the nature of the presenting problems and questions to be answered.[43,59,65]

tive, or open-ended tests, which typically focus on the subject's individual mode of responding, the coping process he engages in when confronted with conditions of relative ambiguity. Stated another way, with the class of structured tests both the subject and the examiner have a clear idea of the nature of the expected answer (even if the subject does not know the "correct" answer). A child asked "Who discovered America?" will respond with the name of a person (or "God"). Asked "How many legs does a dog have?" he will respond with a number. Asked to copy a design, he will attempt to make his product look similar to the model. Asked to arrange picture cards to tell a sensible story, he will move them around to form a sequence corresponding to his story. In the case of the unstructured, or projective, tests, the subject is not privy to the examiner's frame of reference for judging the response, and in fact the subject is given to understand that there are no right or wrong answers, and is invited to respond in his own way, which leads to a revelation of his personal associations, mode of response, and style, with only incidental information about his level of knowledge or ability. Asked to tell what a Rorschach inkblot resembles, the subject has as his only clear cue that a verbal response is expected, but no guidance as to the nature of the expected answer (the subject matter category, the level of organizational complexity, the dominant determinant reform or color, the portion of the blot to be interpreted, and so on). Asked to tell a story to a Children's Apperception Test (CAT) picture, the child is ignorant of the examiner's intention to see his responses to animal pictures as analogues of his responses to humans and, more particularly, as reflections of his perceptions of himself and his interpersonal world. Although structured and unstructured tests differ along the dimension of the explicitness of the examiner's response expectations, they also exist along a continuum of more or less structure and more or less opportunity for revelation of personal style. As an example, the Bender Motor Gestalt Test, which requires the subject to copy nine designs, may be seen as a highly structured test with explicit directions to make the product closely resemble the stimulus, that is, to reproduce the form with accuracy; unspecified are such aspects as the size of the copied designs, their arrangement on the page, and the quality of the lines. The Bender has both psychometric and projective aspects, both of which contribute to the examiner's understanding of the subject. In similar fashion, the relatively structured Wechsler Intelligence Scale for Children (WISC) has questions that permit the observation of personal style, while the test is formally scored on the basis of a limited range of acceptable answers for each task. For example, to the question "What should you do if you saw a train approaching a broken track?" with the expectation of an answer reflecting the child's awareness that one needs to warn the train and/or summon help, following are some of the answers that seem to reveal more about the child's self-concept than about his level of intellectual functioning. A thirteen-year-old underachiever answered: "I wouldn't do anything; what's the use, after all, the engineer would look out and see a little kid trying to signal, and would ignore him." An aggressive eleven-year-old boy said: "Nothing, I'd just stand back and watch the action." An anxious ten-year-old girl replied: "I'd move back as fast as I could; you could get hurt, you know."

The relatively unstructured Rorschach, though permitting open-ended response possibilities, does consist of a standardized set of ten cards, each having discriminable objective attributes of size, shape, shading, and color, as well as complex gestalt stimulus properties which tend to elicit certain responses far more often than others (the "populars," which represent the subject's ability and/or willingness to give a socially expected response). The Rorschach responses are scored on several variables, including the level of form perception, that is, whether the subject's match of a verbalized image to the stimulus is among those that can be or have been consensually validated. There are then psychometric aspects to performance on an unstructured test, related to reality testing and the acceptance of group norms.

A second classification of tests in terms of

their purpose or domain would include tests of cognitive functioning, such as intelligence tests, tests of perceptual-motor functioning, tests of language function, those revealing personality structure and interpersonal perceptions, those reflecting vocational interests or vocational aptitudes, achievement tests in specific subject matter or skills, and tests empirically developed to reflect the presence of impaired neurological functioning.

When we turn from the classification of individual tests to the psychological examination, we can consider some of the factors that influence our choice of the tests we use with an individual patient. One basic assumption underlies the psychological examination, namely, that the behavior we observe, elicit, and record in the testing situation, in relation to the tests, the examiner, the environment, or to a combination of all these factors, is in some sense representative behavior, from which we may generalize to the subject's real life. This assumption, relating to the validity of the tests and the examination process, can only be tested against the success of the resultant prediction, postdiction, or contribution to understanding of the subject's behavior. Within the testing situation, we need to get a representative sample of the subject's behavior, that is, we need to observe the subject's responses across enough stimuli, under varying conditions of difficulty, so that we can be confident that the behavior is somehow typical of the subject and not a momentary aberration. Further, this broad sampling permits us to specify the contingencies that elicit various behaviors. For example, we may observe that a child handles questions on the structured tests very confidently, but shows uncertainty and agitation when faced with the projective tests. Or, we may see that a child is very slow and seemingly inhibited in handling verbal tasks, yet comes to life with the nonverbal tasks. It is therefore generally desirable to rely on batteries of tests rather than on single tests, since the broader sampling permits a wider range of observations, a comparison between intratest and intertest variability, the testing of tentative hypotheses across situations (permitting a statement concerning internal consis-

tency, which is one criterion of validity), and sequential observations, including responses to fatigue, variability in concentration, and motivation.

In planning the test battery, it is important to include tests sensitive to the child's overt problem areas as stated in the presenting complaints or uncovered during the course of the playroom interview and/or developmental history. If, for example, a child is described as absent minded and forgetful, it would be desirable to include tasks tapping recent and remote memory and his ability to concentrate, as well as tests that might reveal the role of fantasy in his lapses of attention; if a child comes with a history of slow speech development and learning problems, it is important to include verbal tasks of sufficient range and difficulty to assess the current problem and its contribution to the learning difficulties, as well as other tests related to school performance (such as an intelligence test and the Bender Gestalt).

A cardinal principle in test selection is to choose a test or battery of tests appropriate to the subject. Thus, we would not use a test of adult intelligence with an eight-year-old, nor a test requiring vision with a blind subject, nor a test involving full command of English with a Spanish-speaking subject. It is assumed that a test is valid only when applied to subjects similar to those in the standardization sample. When we test members of minority groups[24] with instruments standardized on the dominant cultural group, where their test performance is judged against the majority norms, we violate one of the assumptions in test administration. While it may be possible to compare their performance with the standardization norms, and to assess their ability to adjust and/or compete where the majority standards hold sway, it is hazardous to extrapolate further.*

* There is, particularly in the communication of IQ scores to school authorities, the constant danger of setting up conditions to foster self-fulfilling prophecies in the case of poor inner-city black and other minority children. The IQ scores for the majority of such children are below the national norms. School authorities accept the idea that IQ scores are predictive of school performance, which is generally true for the

Where there is a sufficient background of experience with minority group children, such that there exist formal or informal norms for their performance, it is possible to report their performance in relation to their own peers. In addition, such tests as the intelligence tests can be legitimately used as clinical instruments, exploring the child's strategies for coping with a variety of problem situations, some within his grasp and some frustrating, leading to insight into his cognitive processes, attitudes toward school-related tasks, ability and/or willingness to concentrate, and feelings about authority figures who make demands on him. Then the child's relative standing in his peer group and the clinical observations of his functioning can be reported with attention to his individual needs and recommendations for remediation.

The psychological examination is often spoken of as objective, scientific, and partaking of the validity of a laboratory procedure, because its tools are standardized tests— reproducible, scorable, and using explicit criteria for interpretation. Though there is some truth in this assertion for many of the more structured tests, particularly tests of cognitive function, it is far less true of the projective tests, which are really specialized, standardized interview techniques with certain rules of procedure, standard stimuli, scoring criteria, and general rules of interpretation, in fact, multiple systems of scoring and interpretation.

The face-to-face testing situation with an examiner and an individual patient shares many characteristics of other two-person interactions, and in assessing the formal test findings, it is important to recognize and take into account various factors that may influence the test results. Under the heading of examiner variables, it is important to consider the examiner's philosophy of testing, which includes his perception of his role, whether he views himself as a diagnostician who relates to

the patient neutrally and divorces the diagnostic interview from the helping process or whether he relates to the patient with more positive affect and believes that any contact with a professional should have therapeutic implications. In both cases, it is possible to follow standard testing procedures, but the atmosphere and stimulus to rapport are quite different. In the same connection, examiners differ in their view of whether the patient should be examined under minimal stress conditions,[10] to elicit his best functioning, or under greater stress conditions, to investigate his breakdowns in functioning. The testing situation is, of course, inherently stressful for many children and adults who perceive it as a threat to their privacy and to their defenses against feelings of inadequacy. A case can be made for testing under conditions facilitating the greatest cooperation and effort on the patient's part. His failures and difficulties are usually reported at length in the presenting complaints and developmental history. What often remains unreported, unless the interviewer of the parents is very skilled and knowledgeable, is the area of strengths and assets. A sympathetic examiner, supplying reassuring structure and appreciation of the child's efforts, can begin to sort out the basic capacities from the inefficiencies associated with internal and/or external stress. In addition, the accepting, interested adult may lessen the child's need for a defensive armor, so that more of his covert problems may be open to exploration.

Another set of examiner variables includes his own personality makeup, race, social class and professional identification, and self-awareness regarding prejudices, stereotyped expectations, and power needs in relation to a patient. These variables may exert a subtle influence on the test results either through their effect on the examination itself, mainly in terms of the rapport and level of encouragement of the patient's optimum efforts, or in the evaluation of the test results, and possibly in both. Though there is clearly a serious problem in the validity of test results where the examiner is openly antagonistic, contemptuous, condescending, or admiring of the pa-

majority population, but in the case of areas where there are large numbers of underprivileged minority children, the schools are discouraged by the implied prediction of their poor learning ability, and school personnel lower their expectations, lose their enthusiasm, and lessen their investment in these children, thus helping to fulfill the prophecy.

tient, or where the examiner and the patient cannot communicate adequately because of a significantly different cultural frame of reference or language barrier, the greater danger lies in the less blatant, more covert examiner attitudes and practices.

On the patient's part, there are also variables influencing his performance in both obvious and covert ways. The issue of trust is perhaps paramount: In the very young child, it will come in immediately and directly in the child's refusal or willingness to leave his parent and participate in the test situation. In the latency child, it is more likely to take the form of reticence or willingness to verbalize freely or to engage in any projective task. In the adolescent, the issue of trust may be expressed in a direct confrontation with the examiner regarding the implied invasion of privacy, the examiner's perceived role as the agent for the complaining parents, and against the examiner's identification with the establishment. In all cases, the basic issue is the patient's concern and fantasies as to the purpose of the examination. From the child's viewpoint, his degree of cooperation with the examiner will be very different if he feels the examiner is a benevolent adult, interested in his side of any reported troubles and understanding of his worries, as against his perception of a demanding, punitive, authority figure who has the power to recommend significant changes in his way of life. Though the child's responses may reflect his habitual pattern of reaction to perceived threat, and therefore provide valid data for observation, his responses to a particular examiner may not be representative of his responses to stress situations generally and may be more a function of his fears and expectations regarding school authorities, probation officers, or doctors. His approach to the examination may limit the amount of information available to the examiner, or obscure his assets and conflict-free areas of functioning, or give a distorted picture of his functioning in other situations.

It is the examiner-clinician's role to be aware of the interpersonal, situational, and intrapersonal factors affecting the psychological evaluation and to assess the validity and rep-

resentativeness of the findings.[93] The process[94] is analytic, inferential, synthetic, and evaluative, and the report communicated to his mental health colleagues is neither a laboratory summary nor a direct reading of the raw test data but ideally an integrated clinical judgment. Overall, the criteria for evaluating the child's test performance relate to his coping ability: How adaptive or maladaptive is his behavior, that is, does it seem to further the goals of the organism, to reduce discomfort, achieve individuation, maintain dependency, achieve mastery, and so on? How efficiently does the child achieve his goals, that is, with what degree of effort and at what cost to other competing needs? How appropriate are his solutions to his chronological age, that is, what is his level of maturity in relation to the expected stages of development (cognitive, psychosexual, social)? How well can he communicate with significant others to elicit environmental support, to give necessary feedback, or to relieve stress, and so on?

The movement in psychological assessment is away from diagnostic classification[75] with its inherent emphasis on pathology and with its potential for hampering a flexible approach to remediation (for example, the despair of mental health professional with an autistic child, the distrust and despair toward a sociopath, the frequent loss of interest in the emotional problems of a retarded child). In fact, the clinical psychologist as diagnostician has recently come in for increasingly heavy criticism from several sources: from minority groups who see the tests as invalid instruments inimical to the needs of their children;[121] from schoolteachers and special education teachers who feel the tests do not speak directly to methods of remediation and therefore offer them little useful information; from behaviorally oriented psychologists,[118] who feel the findings are too inferential and the tests invalid because their rationale is frequently unsupported by research and there is insufficient spelling out of the contingencies under which behavior is elicited and maintained, and therefore insufficient information for effecting change.

In the light of all the above, following is a

discussion of psychological test instruments and their principal uses. The instruments cited are those used in individual diagnosis with children and adolescents, omitting group intelligence and achievement tests, which are typically administered in a school setting. This list of tests is selective and consists of those common in clinical child psychology practice[100] rather than highly specialized instruments reserved for intensive neurological diagnosis or research.

Let us first consider the area of cognitive development and functioning,[51] which is usually assigned to the psychologist for formal investigation in the psychiatric diagnostic process. The principal tools in this investigation are the individual intelligence tests,[90] which have a comparatively long history, beginning with the first attempt to predict a child's capacity to profit from school experience. The test devised by Binet in 1905 was different from previous laboratory tests of single functions in that it assumed that the capacity to learn in a school setting was a complex function including adequate language development, problem-solving ability, computational skills, social judgment, and command of other complex tasks. Here the concept of intelligence is broad and related to the capacity to learn from experience, where experience is assumed to be daily life experiences, not directly linked to school learning. The usual distinction between intelligence and achievement tests is misleading in that it implies that the intelligence test is not an achievement test. In fact, it is a generalized achievement test with emphasis on a wider sampling of behavior and of acquired concepts than the usual standardized achievement test, which focuses on specific subject matter or skills.

The intelligence tests most commonly in use report their results as a summary IQ, which reflects the relative standing of a subject in comparison to his own age group.* It is a deviation IQ, based on the assumption of a statistically normal distribution of intelligence within each age group, and expresses the degree to which a subject resembles the average or deviates from it in either direction. Underlying the use of a summary score is a concept of general mental ability reflecting the finding of high correlations among the mental tests making up the intelligence scales. But the many tasks also provide an opportunity for the observation of individual patterns of ability.

There are two basic assumptions underlying the interpretation of intelligence test results: (1) the subject taking the test has been exposed to the relevant experiences reflected in the test questions; (2) one can best predict future learning capacity on the basis of the evidence of past learning. Differences in the level of achievement on the intelligence test are therefore interpreted as evidence of the organism's capacity to learn, where environmental opportunities have been similar to those of the standardization population. The leading individual intelligence tests have been standardized on white subjects from a range of socioeconomic groups and geographical areas but with the predominant socioeconomic level within the middle class and white collar workers in urban settings. The assumption of comparability of experience is challenged when these same tests are given to children of different racial-cultural backgrounds, socioeconomic level, and social status in the society.

Opposition to the use of intelligence tests with nonwhite, minority group children is particularly intense where the test results are interpreted as bearing on the genetic superiority of one group over another. There is little argument that genetic and other biological factors operate in the realm of mental ability, but there has been a lively controversy for many years on the relative importance of nature and nurture, and the controversy has boiled up anew with the publication of a review by Jensen[53] purporting to support the greater role of heredity in explaining white-black differences in IQ results.[102]

---

* The IQ no longer retains its meaning of "intelligence quotient," that is, a ratio between the mental age (the chronological age at which the average child does as well as the subject does) and the child's actual chronological age, where level of performance higher than chronological age (the precocious child)

yielded an IQ over 100 and level of performance below chronological age yielded an IQ below 100, with the majority of subjects having IQs between 90 and 110. The IQ was originally meant to represent the child's rate of mental development.

For the clinician, the study of the individual child in the context of his own racial-cultural peer group is more defensible and diagnostically more significant for highlighting individual differences in ability and coping style. Thus, intelligence test results of minority group children are best reported in terms of their more restricted but relevant norms, with appropriate comments regarding the qualitative aspects of their performance. Where a minority group child is in a situation of direct confrontation with the majority norms, or where it is anticipated that he will be, it can be useful to indicate his standing in the larger group, together with the implications for his success or need for compensatory work. The concept of intelligence as reflected in the intelligence tests is held to include nonverbal problem-solving ability and the area of social competence and judgment. Though the tests were designed to evaluate cognitive functioning, the level of functioning at any one time is a function of basic capacity (genetic-biological, modified by environmental-experiential influences); attitudinal, emotional, and motivational factors[124] (habitual and pertaining to the immediate situation); environmental factors (the setting and the examiner); and the subject's way of meeting intellectual challenge (including test-taking experience, expectations, and behavior). The individual intelligence tests are moderately successful in predicting school performance, with implications for future work possibilities, for groups of subjects, but have less success in predicting the school performance of individuals whose rate of growth may vary from the norm and whose environment may undergo marked alterations. Significant changes in a child's health, life experiences, emotional development, or environmental expectations may greatly affect his functional intelligence in either a positive or a negative direction, though for most children in stable living conditions the IQ, reflecting their relative standing among their peers, tends to remain relatively constant (that is, within five to ten IQ points).

The predictive value of intelligence tests declines sharply as we go down the age scale. The best prediction comes from sampling of behavior comparable to the later requirements of the criterion, that is, in predicting school performance, language development and concept formation are most relevant. Infant scales[3] survey the repertoire of responses and behaviors of the infant and toddler, but language development is in its preliminary stages and cannot be assessed reliably. It is possible to observe whether the child is showing developments normal for its age, what pediatricians call developmental milestones, but few of the observations will be predictive of later performance. The only two areas correlating somewhat with school-age performance are early vocalization and fine motor control. Moderately and severely retarded children usually show lags in development while still in infancy, but the mildly retarded child may show sensorimotor development and relationship patterns within normal limits until the stage of language and concept development, when the deficit first becomes apparent. The rise in predictive capacity of tests for two- and three-year-old children, though still modest, in some sense reflects not only the increasing appearance of speech and language development but the inherently more reliable test subject, reattention and alertness. Early childhood is a period of a very rapid rate of maturation and change and the acquisition of new responses to environmental stimuli. Until the repertoire of behaviors is reasonably well stabilized, attempts to conduct a formal examination are necessarily unreliable.

The most recently standardized infant scale is the Bayley Scale of Mental and Motor Development[4] for children two to thirty months. The standardization sample included minority group children (about 25 per cent of the total sample of 1,200 to 1,400 babies). The Bayley scale took items from the Gesell, Cattell, and Griffith (an English scale) scales, through standardization determined the best items, and added some new features to form the best standardized infant scale now in use. The Cattell Infant Intelligence Scale [5] is a downward extension of the Stanford-Binet (see below), for testing ages two to thirty months; the Gesell Developmental Schedules,[37] for ages four weeks to six years, is a schedule of behaviors in the areas of motor, adaptive, language, and personal-social behavior, similar to a careful pediatric examination.

In the age range from eighteen months to five years, the preschool period, the intelligence tests have greater predictive power than the infant scales, but the young child's short attention span, distractibility, insistence on immediate gratification and discharge of tension make for considerable unreliability in single session samples of behavior. It is in this age range that the examiner's patience, skill, and flexibility are put to the greatest test.[63] The preschool tests have many performance tasks that have a play quality, helping to engage the child's attention and cooperation. With some overlap with infant scales, the most commonly used scales for the preschool child are the Stanford-Binet Intelligence Scale,[112] for the child who does not perform below a two-year level on any function measured by the scale (the Binet is discussed further under the school-age tests), the Merrill-Palmer Scale of Mental Tests[110] (ages two to five), and the Minnesota Preschool Scale (ages one and one-half to six).[38] For the developmental assessment of infants and preschool children, who for behavioral or physical reasons are unable to participate in the testing, it is possible to interview the mother or other responsible adult with the Vineland Social Maturity Scale.[27] The Vineland, developed to evaluate the social competence of mental retardates in conjunction with an intelligence test, has a substantial correlation with IQ and can yield developmental information in areas of socialization, self-help, self-direction, communication, locomotion, and occupation. The largely nonverbal Merrill-Palmer can be helpful in surveying the abilities of children with delayed speech or language problems, but the absence of verbal items makes it hazardous to predict to later school adjustment.

Bridging the preschool-school range is the relatively new Wechsler Preschool and Primary Scale of Intelligence (WPPSI)[117] for children from four to six and one-half years of age, a downward extension of the WISC. For children of elementary school age, and up to middle adolescence, the two most commonly

used instruments are the Stanford-Binet, form L-M, and the WISC.[115] The Stanford-Binet can be used from early childhood through the entire age range, including adult life. There is a set of Wechsler scales covering the range from age four to six and one-half (WPPSI), five to fifteen (WISC), and sixteen through adult life (Wechsler Adult Intelligence Scale [WAIS]),[116] all of which are descendants of the Wechsler-Bellevue Intelligence Scale, dating from 1939. There exists a vast literature on the Binet and Wechsler Scales[71] as intelligence tests and as diagnostic instruments, and this survey will touch only briefly on their characteristics and uses.

The Binet scale is organized by age levels, from age two to superior adult 3, and at each level the subject is presented with tasks appropriate to that level, so that the test given to the three-year-old is different from the test given to the eight-year-old, not only in the level of difficulty but in the very nature of the tasks. Below age six, the tasks are fairly evenly divided between verbal and nonverbal, but above age six the test is heavily weighted on the verbal side. The range of abilities surveyed is very wide, including language development and usage, reasoning, concept formation, computational skills, rote and meaningful memory, planfulness, verbal abstraction, understanding of absurdities, visual-motor development, and problem-solving. Though the test is not organized to focus on evidence of differential abilities within the scale, it is possible to analyze patterns of successes and failures to reveal consistent areas of handicap or deficiency. Qualitatively, the Binet test is particularly useful in the evaluation of very bright children and adolescents because it has so high a ceiling (into the superior adult range) and because it presents the intelligent subject with many different novel and challenging tasks, thereby sustaining interest and motivation. Its low floor (at the two-year level) permits an adequate sampling of behavior and abilities in young children and retardates, with economy of time, which is important in the testing of subjects with short attention spans. The Binet provides varied opportunities for clinical observations of cognitive style as well as cognitive efficiency. The inclusion of the absurdities tasks and interpretation of proverbs within the under sixteen age range provides the examiner with samples of verbal behavior useful in the identification of a developing thought disorder.*

The Wechsler scales consist of verbal and performance subtests, leading to separate verbal and performance IQs as well as a full-scale IQ, each computed on the basis of the subject's relative standing in his age group. In contrast to the Binet grouping of items in age levels with mixed content tasks, the Wechsler scales are point scales which expose each subject to the same range of subtest tasks; within each subtest, items are arranged in order of difficulty, and the raw scores attained on the subtests are converted into scaled scores, that is, normalized standard scores, with a mean of ten and standard deviation of three. There are five or six verbal and five performance subtests, affording opportunities to observe varied classes of behaviors, some general problem-solving behavior across modalities, and a more explicit analysis of abilities in different areas from those possible with the Binet. Correlation between the WISC full-scale IQs and the Binet are high, [20, p. 197] but the WISC verbal scale IQs are even more highly correlated with the predominantly verbal Binet. Yet, IQs of bright young children run consistently higher on the Binet. Average or bright children above six with visual-motor handicaps, might fare better on the largely verbal Binet, because there would be little opportunity to reveal the deficit, whereas the timed performance tasks on the WISC would highlight the problem. Between the ages of four and six and one-half, the WPPSI is an interesting and varied test, but mainly for bright, highly motivated children; for the slower and/or duller child, it takes too long to administer, leading frequently to loss of attention and frustration, and it tends to underestimate the IQs of the bright children in comparison to the well-

established Binet.[101] Thus, its purpose to extend the WISC downward, where the WISC has proven weakest (in the five to seven year period), has been only partially achieved.

As a group, the Wechsler scales permit analysis of the patterning of subtest scores, from which one may derive diagnostic hypotheses beyond the issue of overall mental ability, but the "profile analysis" must be used cautiously in individual diagnosis, where careful qualitative examination of responses may reveal supporting evidence, or may lead to a rejection of the hypothesis. As one example, the finding that the verbal IQ is significantly greater than the performance IQ may, on closer examination, be a function of (1) the fact that all the performance tasks are timed, whereas only the arithmetic subtest is timed on the WISC, resulting in a lower performance IQ in the case of a depressed subject; or (2) the inadequate visual-motor ability of a mildly neurologically handicapped subject of average verbal ability, whose qualitative performance on the nonverbal tasks as well as timing are relatively poor; and (3) the relative verbal-language acceleration in development of a bright young subject, whose physical motoric maturation is proceeding at a more average pace.

A performance test concerned with a special aspect of intelligence, namely, foresight and planning ability, is the Porteus Maze Test,[87] which has been used extensively since 1922, usually in conjunction with standard intelligence scales (in fact, mazes have been included in the performance scale of the WISC as an optional task). It can be analyzed quantitatively, in terms of level of achievement, and also qualitatively, in terms of details of performance in the areas of impulsivity and persistence.[88] (It was among the tests used to study the effects of prefrontal lobotomy, and reflected the loss of future-oriented behavior in the lobotomized patient.)

For the examination of physically handicapped children, it is possible to give the verbal or performance Wechsler scales, depending on the area of handicap. The Columbia Mental Maturity Scale[12] is a brief nonverbal test consisting of large cards with three or

---

* My first experience with the Binet as a clinical instrument was with adult psychotic patients at St. Elizabeth's Hospital in Washington, D.C., where it proved to be very sensitive to schizophrenic modes of thinking, particularly in the aforementioned tasks.

more items, requiring the child only to point to the item that does not belong with the others, yielding two derived age-based scores: the Age Deviation Score and the Maturity Index. In its 1971 edition, it is standardized on a new sample of children purported to be representative of socioeconomic level and ethnic group membership as determined in the 1970 census, and suitable for ages three and one-half to nine years. Spanish directions are included in the manual for Spanish-speaking subjects. It gives information on abstract reasoning, an important component of intelligence. As was noted earlier, the Vineland Social Maturity Scale is suitable where subjects cannot themselves cooperate for physical or emotional reasons and an informant is available.

A truly developmental approach to cognitive maturation is offered by Jean Piaget[85] and his followers,[30] which traces the orderly sequence of changes in the nature of thought processes as the child grows from infancy to maturity in adolescence.[35] An increasing number of psychologists are becoming interested in assessing a child's cognitive processes in terms of his stage of intellectual development in the Piaget sense, rather than in comparison to other children in his peer group.[106] It would then be possible to have a scale of the developmental maturity of the thought processes.[114] One endeavor to construct a standardized test using Piaget's concepts of development was that of Laurandeau and Pinard,[62] who investigated the mode of precausal thinking, one of the early stages of cognitive development, which they found generally decreasing with the increase in chronological age.

There is a burgeoning field of writers on the applications of Piaget's[36] developmental theories to the process of education,[84] establishing direct links between the child's stage of functioning and efforts at education and remediation.[109]

A host of tests were designed to explore the child's level of perceptual-motor maturation, integration, and intactness of functioning. They offer developmental norms and often include scoring criteria for pathological deviations, or there are pertinent research findings permitting assessment of neurological central processing functions and dysfunctions.[16] They are particularly useful in studying children with learning disabilities because they deal with less complex, more basic response capacities of the child than are generally tapped in the intelligence tests, and frequently have associated remediation suggestions and programs. For most children, these tests generate relatively little anxiety and represent conflict-free areas of functioning. The exceptions are of course the children with moderate to severe perceptual-motor problems, who are aware of their inadequacies and may find such tests very trying. However, the clinician is then in a position to observe how the child deals with his anxieties and frustrations in tasks similar to classroom requirements in learning to read and write. The tests, as a group, can give information as to the child's readiness for classroom learning, can indicate children who constitute high risks and need special handling before or on entering the formal educational channels, and can tag some children as needing careful neurological study because of pathologically deviant performance. Though these tests are relatively culture free, that is, less directly reflective of differences in socioeconomic level and cultural group than the intelligence tests, there are indications that rate of maturation and other normative criteria may differ between groups, and deviations from majority group norms should be treated cautiously in diagnosing pathology in minority group children.[120]

Following are pencil and paper perceptual-motor tests that involve copying of designs, where both the visual-perceptual and motor-expressive aspects are necessary for successful performance: The Developmental Test of Visual-Motor Integration by Beery and Buktenica[5] can be used with children as young as two years of age and goes up to age fifteen. The Haworth Primary Visual Motor Test[49] can also be used with young children.

The Bender Visual-Motor Gestalt Test (1938) has become a standard part of most test batteries for children from five years of age (with no upper age limit on its use). With the appearance of the Koppitz scoring system for ages five to eleven,[60] and with the widely used Pascal-Suttell system,[82] which is applicable in adolescence and adulthood, its usefulness as a developmental test and as a diagnostic instrument for neurological dysfunction in the visual-processing sphere has been enhanced. The Background Interference Procedure[13] was designed to increase the sensitivity of the Bender to neurological dysfunction.[14,56] The Bender is a useful diagnostic tool beyond the issues of neurological maturation and dysfunction since it permits observations on the management of motility—the strength of drive, the capacity to control, the style of control, that is, the defensive patterns—and in this area of motility patterns are many diagnostic clues in cases of hyperactivity, behavior disorders generally, compulsivity, and childhood psychosis. Within the Wechsler intelligence scales, the WISC Coding subtest and WAIS Digit Symbol are speed tests that demand adequate visual perception of simple geometrical figures and rapid motor reproduction, with norms for ages five and above. They also afford an opportunity to observe attention and concentration since the subject is required to move along rows of symbols, shift constantly from one to another, and monitor his own performance without any help from the examiner. The fact that there is no inherent structure to engage the subject's attention, nor inherent interest in the material, makes this type of task useful in extrapolating behavioral expectations to other situations, such as the classroom, where the child is put to work on his own to master dull repetitive material. Among the pencil and paper tests, the Graham-Kendall Memory for Designs[40] introduces an immediate memory factor since the subject draws each of fifteen geometric designs after looking at it for five seconds, then the stimulus card is removed. The test was empirically developed as a test of neurological dysfunction, and errors resembling those most frequent in an independently diagnosed population of brain-damaged subjects are most heavily penalized with a higher score. There

are some manifestly brain-injured subjects whose performance on the Bender, though slow and uncertain, is not clearly pathological, but whose Memory for Designs performance reveals gross errors in perception of the gestalt, with loss of symmetry and fragmentation of the gestalt most prominent.

The Frostig Development Test of Visual Perception[34] surveys different areas for children four to seven, such as spatial relationships, position in space, form constancy, figure-ground relationships, and eye-hand coordination. Also an associated remedial program is offered to develop proficiency in visual perceptual abilities. The Frostig test and remedial program are specifically aimed at identifying and helping the child with potential learning difficulties.

Another group of tests, also involving visual perception and motoric execution, is constructional in nature, the assembling of a gestalt out of discrete pieces. The Wechsler Object Assembly has the subject put together a concrete object (a manikin, horse, auto, hand), where the subject will usually have guessed the nature of the object early on, and the task then requires the integration of the parts into a perceived whole. The Wechsler Block Design, on the other hand, has the subject reproduce a nonrepresentational design from the examiner's model or a drawing, using discrete blocks. This entails perceptual analysis first, into the component parts, then organization and synthesis. In both the object assembly and block design tasks, the motor element is minimized in that the subject has only to move the pieces around, which requires much less manual dexterity and fine motor control than the drawing tasks. The mosaic test[74] is a much less structured task, in which the subject is invited to construct something using multicolored, multishaped flat plastic chips. The completed product is judged on a variety of dimensions,[97] with the overall criterion the successful construction of a recognizable gestalt, representational or nonrepresentational, using the forms and colors to form patterns showing inner coherence and organization, appropriate to the child's age and developmental level. The task calls on internalized imagery and self-organization, as well as awareness of the adequacy of the overt production and is particularly difficult for brain-injured subjects.

Another test in the area of visual perception, the Draw-A-Person (or any of its variants, for example, House-Tree-Person and Harris-Goodenough) calls on the internalized body image of the subject and therefore has a memory factor, a perceptual factor, and a motor factor. The test originated in 1926 with Florence Goodenough's Draw-A-Man test as a measure of intellectual maturation, gained considerable prominence as a projective technique for adolescents and adults with the Machover description of the drawings as projections of personality (1948), and was expanded into the Buck House-Tree-Person test (1948); it has been brought back into the area of intellectual maturation with the Harris (1963) adaptation of the original Goodenough test.[45] More recently, Koppitz[61] published a scoring method for children's human figure drawings with explicit developmental considerations, drawing attention to the elements expected at each age level as well as other normative information. The figure drawings are a source of information about the child's self-concept and concern about body functioning, often expressed through omissions, exaggerations, and distortions of parts of the body, and sometimes displaced from the locus of anxiety.[22] It is particularly important to judge personality dynamics in the context of the developmental expectations, or else there can be a confounding of intellectual-maturational and personality conflict features.[25] The human figure drawings are often very useful in the diagnosis of neurological dysfunction, with special attention to such elements as consistent unilateral disproportions (asymmetry) and 90-degree rotations of the figures.[81] It is often true that children with emotional difficulties, with or without neurological dysfunction, will produce human figure drawings that score below chronological age expectations, and it is therefore unwise to use the drawings as a primary source of information about intellectual maturation.

The Lincoln-Oseretsky Motor Development Scale,[108] for children six to fourteen, is primarily a motor test, with associated perceptual elements. It is a revision and restandardization by Sloan of a test of motor proficiency originally published in Russia in 1923. It consists of thirty-six items, about one-third of which involve gross motor behavior, and the remainder, hand and arm movements that demand speed, coordination, rhythm, and dexterity. It provides age norms, yields developmental and maturational information, and has proved useful in the diagnosis of neurological dysfunction.

The foregoing tests all involve some motor expressive components. On the other hand, the Columbia Mental Maturity Scale (revised 1971) requires the subject only to point to the pattern that is different, making it almost purely a test of visual discrimination. It is useful as a nonlanguage screening test of intelligence, but it demands comprehension of the concept of "different." Raven's Progressive Matrices[95] also largely eliminates the motor element and requires the subject to indicate which one of four possible choices is appropriate to complete a series of items. It has complex visual-discrimination elements and is also used as a test of nonverbal intelligence.

The Illinois Test of Psycholinguistic Abilities (ITPA)[58] was described by its authors as a diagnostic test of communication abilities for children two to ten years of age designed to delineate specific abilities and disabilities in children's communications with a view to remediation. It is called a diagnostic test of specific cognitive abilities, as well as a molar test of intelligence.[57] The twelve ITPA subtests are intended to pinpoint problems in two channels of language input and output (auditory-vocal and visual-motor), three processes of communication (receptive, expressive, and a central mediating organizing process between the receptive and expressive), and two levels of language organization (the representational and the automatic). It shares with the foregoing tests of central processing in the perceptual-motor area immediate relevance to learning problems, with associated remedial implications, and the ITPA has become a respected test in the repertoire of the school psychologist. Its applicability to the preschool child makes it particularly valuable in helping the clinician to analyze early language disturbances, such as delayed speech, and permits early intervention where appropriate. Taken together with the verbal material on the intelligence scales, the language usage observed on the projective tests, and the spontaneous language interchange with the examiner in the test situation, the child's varied communications patterns can be surveyed and described in rich detail.

Of all the psychologists' test instruments, the projectives are the most well known and the most frequently requested in a diagnostic study.[47,91] This is so despite the fact that the psychiatrist has interview techniques for children at his disposal that overlap with the domain of the unstructured and semistructured tests (see the discussion above on playroom observations, the World Test, Duss fables, and so on.) Among the projective techniques, the Rorschach is most in demand by the psychiatrist-client and is rarely omitted from a clinician's test battery. The Rorschach is considered a multidimensional test of personality, but it is at its base, according to Rorschach,[99] "a diagnostic test based on perception." Rorschach believed that through the ten symmetrical inkblots, with their variations in form, shading, and color and ambiguity of associative value, he could elicit an individual's unique way of perceiving, interpreting, and responding. He further believed that the person's way of responding bore a lawful relationship to that person's view of the world, his reality orientation, defensive structure, and diagnostic group. It is important to stress that underlying is the assumption that the person is capable of performing the basic perceptual task—finding in his mind a matching engram, a memory image to correspond to the ambiguous visual stimulus before him. In fact, the individual must repeat this process of searching the stimulus and his associations for an appropriate fit at least ten times. With some neurologically damaged subjects the task is too difficult, and they fall back on perseveration, primitive naming of stimulus proper-

ties, and repeated expressions of impotence.[86] In such cases, the individuality of the subject is obscured by the pathological interference with spontaneity and normal variability, much as a patient with Parkinson's syndrome, seen at a distance, will resemble other Parkinson victims rather than reveal a unique gait and expressive movement. The Rorschach may indeed reflect the neurologically damaged organism's problems with lack of structure, but will scarcely do justice to the multidimensional personality of the subject. For the same reason, when the task is developmentally beyond a young child,[42] the results are meager regarding personality structure.

The Rorschach has definable overt properties and response tendencies (from normative studies),[1,2] and yet provides an open-ended opportunity for response (except for some group administration versions that require the subject to choose a response from a fixed number of alternatives). As a test based on perception and association, predictions regarding the subject's behavior are inferential, and there can be no direct translation from the verbal behavior elicited by the test stimuli to actual behavior in life situations.[68] What can be defined are response tendencies of the organism, but the probabilities governing their emergence would depend on environmental contingencies and the internal state of the organism at some particular moment in time. The information regarding personality structure would be useful in clarifying the subject's expectations and needs from the environment, his probable competence in unstructured situations, and his repertoire of responses in comparison with others of his peer group, but would not help specific, short-term prediction without other kinds of information, such as evidences of past performance under similar conditions.

As an example, a sixteen-year-old boy, hospitalized for wild acting-out episodes, including the taking of hallucinogenic drugs, multiple and varied sexual experiences, and gradual withdrawal of interest from school and other adolescent peer activities, presented the picture of adequate if slightly shaky reality testing on the WAIS and a floridly anxious, bizarre, confused picture on the Rorschach. On the hospital unit, where a conscientious psychiatrist-administrator surrounded him with firm but appropriate behavioral expectations and limits, his behavior was controlled and steady, but he complained a lot and his room was chaotically messy. Could one predict from the Rorschach to the hospital behavior? Not without assessing the degree of structure in the hospital setting and the firm parental role taken by the administrator, and certainly not from the Rorschach alone, since a predictive clinical judgment should rest on an adequate sampling of the patient's behavior, which in this case would include his performance on the more structured, emotionally less stimulating intelligence test.

Within the class of projective tests, the Rorschach is one of the least structured. There is a group of semistructured tests requiring the subject to make up a story,[46] largely involving pictures of human beings interacting in different combinations and situations. These tests retain open-ended response possibilities, but their effective range is greatly restricted. The oldest and most famous is Murray's Thematic Apperception Test (TAT),[79] supplemented by Bellak's Children's Apperception Test (CAT)[7] involving animal figures, and a later CAT (1965) using human figures.[8] There is also the Michigan Picture Test[48] and Schneidman's Make-A-Picture Story.[104] These tests are called "content" tests, in contrast to the Rorschach, which is a test of personality structure, and the content they are eliciting is largely interpersonal: the protagonist in relation to a single significant figure; in relation to a group; in relation to parental figures, peers, sexual love objects; and by himself in relation to situations suggesting a coercive environment, a state of depression, loneliness, fearful fantasy, suicidal concerns, and so forth. There are multiple ways of analyzing these content tests, beginning with Murray's thematic approach to the subject's need and the environmental press, but in most approaches there is interest in representing the subject's view of his world, his drives, his emotional reactions to the different figures, his conception of the parental role, his overt and covert presentation of the protagonist's role, his mode of resolving conflict and dealing with anxiety, his level of immersion in fantasy and the quality thereof, and his ability to organize and present his ideas, with implications for diagnosis. However, the content tests are particularly useful as part of a test battery for clarification of interpersonal perceptions rather than as a primary contribution to diagnostic classification. With adolescents, the TAT is the best instrument; with elementary school children, probably the Michigan Picture Test is most useful (particularly selected cards, including the first, which is the only card showing a whole family together); for younger school and preschool children, the CAT in either version is useful. The Make-A-Picture Story test can be given to children and adolescents and offers an attractive theatrical quality, since the subject can choose his own dramatis personae and backgrounds for his stories.

Sentence completion tests are attempts to survey a subject's interpersonal attitudes, self-concept, and relations to such institutions as school and job and are suitable for older children and adolescents for whom reading is not difficult, since they are usually self-administering.

Though any of the semistructured content tests permit interpretation along psychoanalytic lines, only the Blacky test[11] was expressly designed to evaluate psychoanalytic concepts and to analyze the subject in terms of his psychosexual development. The protagonist of twelve cartoon drawings is a dog named "Blacky," whose adventures are supposed to relate to the psychoanalytic stages of development, oral, anal, and genital, with subthemes around oral eroticism and oral sadism, anal sadism, guilt over masturbation, castration anxiety, oedipal rivalry, and penis envy. Thus, the Blacky pictures provide a specific structure within which personality dynamics are studied in a developmental context. It is appropriate for children six to twelve years of age.

A new approach to assessment comes from the behaviorists, some of whom hold that operant technology is consistent with an approach to the study of individual differences:

"An effective diagnostic procedure would be one in which the eventual therapeutic methods can be directly related to the information obtained from a continuing assessment of the patient's current behaviors and their controlling stimuli."[55] A major point is that knowledge of a subject's responsiveness to reinforcing contingencies could lead to successful prediction of behavior. In an experiment reported by Moore and Goldiamond,[76] form discrimination was taught to preschool children using a behavioral fading technique. Such behavioral approaches might lead to the observation that a differential rate of learning under specified conditions might be seen as an assessment technique for separating out children with various types and degrees of learning problems.[80]

Let us now reconsider the psychologist's contribution to the total diagnostic process with children, in terms of the areas where his contributions are of primary importance, or secondary but significant, to flesh out or test hypotheses derived from other sources. Within the division of labor between the psychiatrist and psychologist in their formal examinations, (and before other specialists are brought in, such as neurologists, educators, speech and hearing experts), the psychologist has primary responsibility for formal investigation of what Hartmann and Rapaport[92] discussed under the autonomous ego functions, those inborn biological apparatuses that form the core of ego development—memory, perception, and motility—as well as others such as affect expression and stimulus barrier. In addition, the psychologist is particularly charged with investigating the direct derivatives, such as cognitive development, synthetic functions and their vicissitudes under stress, concept formation and language development, and the relationship of these functions to the central processing efficiency of the nervous system. Still of interest but not crucial for the psychologist are patterns of adapting and coping in the interpersonal sphere, the role of fantasy, self-concept, and reality orientation with respect to meeting environmental pressures and demands (for example, school, home). In terms of developmental lines, the psychiatrist

can usually investigate psychosocial and psychosexual development adequately without psychological test inputs, but in the larger framework of psychobiological growth and development, including the maturation of the perceptual-motor apparatus, cognition, and the management of motility patterns, the psychologist's input is immediately relevant and important. A detailed exposition of how each of these goals is to be met through the psychological examination is outside the scope of this chapter, but following is a brief survey of the psychologist's approach.

Perception and the association of perception with motor patterns (perceptual-motor functioning) can be investigated through tasks within the intelligence tests, through the tests of visual perception and visual-motor processing, such as the Beery-Buktenica Developmental Test of Visual-Motor Integration, the Bender Visual-Motor Gestalt Test, or the Frostig Developmental Test of Visual Perception, and through the ambiguous stimulus properties of the Rorschach. Motility patterns can be studied through any of the performance tasks on the Wechsler scales, through many items on the Merrill-Palmer and Binet tests for younger children, through the Lincoln-Oseretsky Motor Development Scale, and through the motor expressive aspects of the Bender. Affect expression can be examined in relation to the Rorschach and the content tests and often is a part of the human figure drawings. Stimulus barrier is studied across all the tests in a battery, in terms of the inherent neutrality versus stimulus attributes of the different tasks, but can be looked at in a focused way in the differential nature and sequence of Rorschach responses to the varied and known stimulus properties of each of the ten cards. Overall cognitive development and the related areas of concept formation and language development are in the domain of the intelligence tests, including the Piaget approach to cognitive maturation, but can also be studied with the ITPA, particularly where the issue is one of efficiency of communication. The synthetic functions need to be looked at in the context of the entire psychological examination, in terms of the subject's baseline level (his habitual patterns in the area of higher cortical functioning where the synthetic functions are mediated) and in terms of breakdowns in functioning (when they occur in the temporal sequence of the test; where they occur in relation to the neutrality or emotional charge inherent in the particular task; how and to what degree the inefficiency is expressed behaviorally, for example, in delayed responses, in confused sequence, in manifest disorganization; and how discrete or pervasive does the breakdown become, that is, can the subject recover when a new task is presented or does the incipient or manifest disorganization immobilize his usual coping resources). Within the test battery, the Rorschach, with its combination of anxiety-inducing ambiguity (that is, stress), variability in stimulation attributes (the color, chiefly), and sequence of stressful and relatively unstressful cards (cards 1 and 5 are relatively neutral stimuli, whereas cards 2 and 9 are frequently experienced as stressful), proves to be a useful microcosm for the study of the synthetic function. A full TAT analysis could also contribute significantly.

In general, specific questions within the diagnostic process regarding interpersonal behavioral patterns, self-concept, and fantasy can be answered from analysis of the projective tests, including the human figure drawings.

In the exploration of structural or constitutional or organic versus functional or emotional factors in children's difficulties in coping,[111] the psychologist is not so much called on to rule in the emotional, which is usually present as a primary or secondary factor, but rather to rule in the organic factors, if they can be identified. In any sense, we can never rule out a factor that may be resistant to our examination, but we can speak to the probability of its contribution to the genesis or persistence of the presenting problem. Certain test findings have the consistency of syndromes, and as such can be readily identified. For example, a combination of adequate or better verbal-language development, relatively poor perceptual-motor development, excessive stimulability with a tendency to cogni-

tive disorganization, poor self-concept, and observed behavioral hyperactivity in the test session leads to the diagnosis of minimal chronic brain dysfunction (or whatever current term is more acceptable to a behavioral approach). In most instances, the psychologist's suggested diagnosis of neurological dysfunction rests on the integration of several lines of inquiry: Are the inefficiencies and errors in performance related to basic processes such as attention, retention, motor control, perceptual discrimination, perceptual flexibility versus perseveration, and excessive concreteness versus appropriate levels of abstraction? Is there greater difficulty with tasks requiring self-organization and perceptual flexibility than with structured, specific answer tasks? Are the breakdowns pervasive or limited to emotionally charged material? Are the elicited verbalizations appropriate in content, mood, and intensity, aside from their level of cognitive maturation? Does the self-concept fairly approximate the level of deficit? Is there a depressive response to the self-concept of damage? What are the compensatory and/or defense operations in relation to the deficit, and how adaptive are they? There are very few pathognomonic signs, which taken in isolation are valid indicators of neurological dysfunction, and the usual clinical test battery is not geared to explore neuropsychological connections in any detail. For that, such batteries as the Reitan-Halstead[96] are recommended and should be administered by an experienced neuropsychologist.

(Summary

The analysis and interpretations of the findings from these examinations can seem like putting together a complex jigsaw puzzle, unless there is an organizational pattern in which they are structured. This pattern starts with the information about what kind of basic constitutional makeup the child has as gleaned from his history and the physical, psychological, and psychiatric examinations. This is then matched with the parental and family makeup and situation and any special problems and conditions that would influence the manner in which the child has dealt with expectable stages of personality development and ego functions. Stock is then taken of the resolution or lack of it for each of these stages and functions. Any unresolved areas and developmental defects and lags are annotated. These then are examined in terms of their interaction with the child's living situation and both daily and out of the ordinary events in it. Particularly the reactions to anxiety-producing situations are looked at, whether they are created by the child's own fixations at earlier levels along unresolved developmental lines or by inappropriate or distorting handling or life experience which perpetuates or exaggerates them. Then the child's symptoms and other manifestations internalized and externalized are correlated with these reactions and examined as his attempts to defend against the anxieties, to find better answers to the unsolved problem areas, to maintain homeostasis and/or to perpetuate and reenact the conditions and situations that led to the unsolved problem area. One takes stock of the cumulative poor answers as the unresolved answers to earlier stages make for additional poor or incomplete answers to later stages. The end result should be a picture of the child's current functioning with as logical as possible an ordering of the factors and forces that created and continue to influence it.

This process is carried out by picking up clues from any part of the examination and looking for validation of these leads. The data one uses involve soft facts for the most part, and care should be taken not to be misled by unvalidated clues. Interweaving the material from psychological and psychiatric clinical and testing examinations enlarges the opportunity for such validation.

Unused clues are not discarded but are stored. Later information or observation may not only provide their validation but also may change the emphasis in the diagnostic formulation. It is always interesting to look back at the diagnostic study after a treatment program has filled in the fine print to go with the headlines written in the diagnostic formula-

tion. One usually finds that the diagnostic study never can provide a complete picture.

The recommendations are logical outgrowths of the factors and forces underlying, perpetuating, and/or exaggerating the child's symptoms, his family's current status, and the conditions and resources in his community. Therefore, the survey of assets and weaknesses in the child, family, school, and community, matched with dynamic and genetic factors, should be made with an eye on the possible resources for remedial approaches, the ideal and the practical and possible. This should include a picture of the availability and readiness of the child and family for change. It should be kept in mind that one does not give up on the possibility of change in the child even if the family is unavailable or resistant. It has been reassuring to learn how much tolerance children can learn to have for the difficulties parents can present.

Diagnostic labels may need to be carried out on two levels. The ideal type of diagnostic formulation identifies the etiology, psychodynamics, and predominant symptom and/or character patterns. At times, however, from a practical point of view, another component should be added to indicate what treatment plan is needed. This can help a school, court, treatment institution, or insurance company understand the legitimate nature of the problem and the child's needs for a therapeutic program they can support.

The diagnostic study is never complete until it is shared with the family and/or other responsible individuals. The principles of interpretation of findings so that they can be heard, understood, and carried out should be always kept in mind. These principles include the translation of findings into understandable words, presenting the present problems in developmental terms to assist in seeing how the difficulties arose, relieving guilt (such as inappropriate handling or mistakes having been made not on the basis of hate but in the interests of helping the child), and describing what can be done about relief or help with the problems. The latter should include practical suggestions about trying changes in handling, appropriate medications where indicated, and contacts to be made. The family, school, referring physician, court, and so on should not be left with only promises of help in the future. They should not be left helplessly waiting while a treatment plan is being worked out. They should be given things to try or do.

The mental health professional often can feel helpless when social pathology or distortions in the system are heavily implicated in some cases. The questions one must ask are how has this child and this family responded to these conditions and what can be mobilized to help and modify these responses. At the same time, the needed changes in the system should be shared with community planners, community change agents, and community advocate programs.

(Bibliography

1. AMES, L. B., LEARNED, J., METRAUX, R. W., and WALKER, R. N. *Child Rorschach Responses*. New York: Hoeber, 1952.

2. ——, METRAUX, R. W., and WALKER, R. N. *Adolescent Rorschach Responses*. Rev ed. New York: Brunner/Mazel, 1971.

3. BAYLEY, N. "Consistency and Variability in the Growth of Intelligence from Birth to Eighteen." *Journal of Genetic Psychology*, 75 (1949), 165.

4. ——. *The Bayley Scales of Mental and Motor Development*. New York: Psychological Corporation, 1969.

5. BEERY, K. E., and BUKTENICA, N. A. *Developmental Test of Visual-Motor Integration*. Chicago: Follett Educational Corporation, 1967.

6. BEISER, H. R. "Psychiatric Diagnostic Interviews with Children." *Journal of the American Academy of Child Psychiatry*, 1 (1962), 656.

7. BELLAK, L., and BELLAK, S. S. *Children's Apperception Test*. Larchmont, N.Y.: C.P.S., 1949.

8. ——, and BELLAK, S. S. *Children's Apperception Test (Human Figures)*. Larchmont, N.Y.: C.P.S., 1965.

9. BENDER, L., and WOLTMAN, A. G. "The Use of Puppet Shows as a Psychotherapeutic Method for Behavior Problems in Chil-

dren." *American Journal of Orthopsychiatry*, 6 (1936), 341–354.

10. BERSOFF, D. N. " 'Current Functioning' Myth: An Overlooked Fallacy in Psychological Assessment." *Journal of Consulting and Clinical Psychology*, 37, no. 3 (1971), 391–393.

11. BLUM, G. S. *The Blacky Pictures: A Technique for the Exploration of Personality Dynamics*. New York: Psychological Corporation, 1950.

12. BURGOMEISTER, B., BLUM, L. H., and LORGE, I. *Columbia Mental Maturity Scale* (1953). New York: Harcourt, Brace, Jovanovich, 1971.

13. CANTER, A. *The Background Interference for the Bender-Gestalt Test: Preliminary Manual of Scoring and Interpretation*. Iowa City: University of Iowa Press, 1966.

14. ——. "A Background Interference Procedure To Increase Sensitivity of the Bender-Gestalt Test to Organic Brain Damage." *Journal of Consulting Psychology*, 30 (1966), 91–97.

15. CATTELL, P. *The Measurement of Intelligence of Infants and Young Children*. New York: Psychological Corporation, 1947.

16. CHALFANT, J. C., and SCHEFFELIN, M. A. *Central Processing Dysfunction in Children: A Review of Research*. NINDS Monograph, no. 9. Bethesda, Md.: U.S. Department of Health, Education and Welfare, 1969.

17. COMMITTEE ON CHILD PSYCHIATRY, GROUP FOR ADVANCEMENT OF PSYCHIATRY. *The Diagnostic Process in Child Psychiatry*. New York, 1957.

18. CONN, J. H. "Play Interview Therapy of Castration Fears." *American Journal of Orthopsychiatry*, 25 (1955), 747–754.

19. CREAK, M. "Child Health and Child Psychiatry: Neighbors or Colleagues." *Lancet*, 1 (1959), 481–485.

20. CRONBACH, L. J. *Essentials of Psychological Testing*. 3d ed. New York: Harper & Row, 1970.

21. CYTRYN, L. "Methodological Issues in Psychiatric Evaluation of Infants." *Journal of the American Academy of Child Psychiatry*, 7 (1968), 510–521.

22. ——, CYTRYN, E., and RIEGER, R. E. "Psychological Implications of Cryptorchism." In *Annual Progress in Child Psychiatry and Child Development*. New

York: Brunner/Mazel, 1968. Pp. 396–418.

23. DESPERT, J. L. "Psychosomatic Study of Fifty Stuttering Children." *American Journal of Orthopsychiatry*, 16 (1946), 100–173.

24. DEUTSCH, M., FISHMAN, J., KOGAN, L., NORTH, R., and WHITMAN, M. "Guidelines for Testing Minority Group Children." *Journal of Social Issues*, 20 (1964), 129–145.

25. DI LEO, J. H. *Young Children and Their Drawings.* New York: Brunner/Mazel, 1970.

26. DODGE, P. R. "Neurologic History and Examination." In T. W. Farmer, ed., *Pediatric Neurology.* New York: Harper & Row, 1964. Pp. 1–64.

27. DOLL, E. A. *The Vineland Social Maturity Scale.* Publication of the Training School Department of Research, series 1936, no. 3. Vineland, N.J., 1936.

28. DUBOS, R., "Biological Freudianism." *Pediatrics*, 38 (1966), 789–796.

29. DUSS, L. "La Methode des Fables en Psychanalyse Infantile." *Psyche-Paris*, 2 (1947), 534–552.

30. ELKIND, D., and FLAVELL, J. H., eds. *Studies in Cognitive Development. Essays in Honor of Jean Piaget.* New York: Oxford University Press, 1969.

31. ERIKSON, E. H. "Sex Differences in the Play Configurations of Pre-Adolescents." *American Journal of Orthopsychiatry*, 21 (1951), 667–692.

32. FINE, R. "Use of the Despert Fables (Revised Form) in Diagnostic Work with Children." *Rorschach Research Exchange and The Journal of Projective Technique*, 12 (1948), 106–118.

33. FREUD, A. *Normality and Pathology in Childhood: Assessment of Development.* New York: International Universities Press, 1965.

34. FROSTIG, M. *The Marianne Frostig Developmental Test of Visual Perception.* Palo Alto, Cal.: Consulting Psychologists, 1964.

35. FURTH, H. G. *Piaget and Knowledge.* Englewood Cliffs, N.J.: Prentice-Hall, 1969.

36. ———. *Piaget for Teachers.* Englewood Cliffs, N.J.: Prentice-Hall, 1970.

37. GESELL, A., et al. *Gesell Development Schedules.* New York: Psychological Corporation, 1949.

38. GOODENOUGH, F. L., and VAN WAGENEN, M. J. *Minnesota Preschool Scales.* Minneapolis, Minn.: Educational Test Bureau, 1940.

39. GOODMAN, J., and SOURS, J. *The Child Mental Status Examination.* New York: Basic Books, 1967.

40. GRAHAM, F. K., and KENDALL, B. S. *Memory for Designs Test.* Missoula, Mont.: Psychological Test Specialists, 1960.

41. GROUP FOR THE ADVANCEMENT OF PSYCHIATRY. *Psychopathological Disorders in Childhood: Theoretical Consideration and a Proposed Classification.* Report no. 62. New York, 1966.

42. HALPERN, F. *A Clinical Approach to Children's Rorschachs.* New York: Grune & Stratton, 1953.

43. ———. "Diagnostic Methods in Childhood Disorders." In *Handbook of Clinical Psychology.* New York: McGraw-Hill, 1965. Pp. 621–638.

44. HAMBIDGE, G., JR. "Structured Play Therapy." *American Journal of Orthopsychiatry*, 25 (1955), 601–617.

45. HARRIS, D. B. *Children's Drawings as Measures of Intellectual Maturity.* Harcourt, Brace and World, 1963.

46. HARRISON, R. "Thematic Apperceptive Methods." In *Handbook of Clinical Psychology.* New York: McGraw-Hill, 1965. Pp. 562–620.

47. HARROWER, M. *Appraising Personality: An Introduction to the Projective Techniques.* New York: Simon & Schuster, 1964.

48. HARTWELL, S. W., HUTT, M. L., ANDREW, G., and WALTON, R. E. "The Michigan Picture Test: Diagnostic and Therapeutic Possibilities of a New Projective Test for Children." *American Journal of Orthopsychiatry*, 21 (1951), 124–137.

49. HAWORTH, M. R. *The Primary Visual Motor Test: With Test Manual and Scoring Instructions.* New York: Grune & Stratton, 1970.

50. HEIDER, G. M. "Vulnerability in Infants and Young Children: A Pilot Study." *Genetic Psychology Monographs*, 73 (1966), 1–216.

51. HORROCKS, J. E. *Assessment of Behavior.* Columbus, Ohio: Merrill, 1964.

52. JACKSON, D., and SATIR, V. "A Review of Psychiatric Developments in Family Diagnosis and Family Therapy." In N. W. Ackerman, ed., *Exploring the Base for*

Family Therapy. New York: Family Service Association of America, 1961. Pp. 29–51.

53. JENSEN, A. "How Much Can We Boost IQ and Scholastic Achievement?" *Harvard Educational Review,* 39 (1969), 1–123.

54. KAMP, L. N. J., and KESSLER, E. S. "The World Test: Developmental Aspects of a Play Technique." *Journal of Child Psychology and Psychiatry,* 11 (1970), 81–108.

55. KANFER, F. H., and SASLOW, G. "Behavioral Analysis." *Archives of General Psychiatry,* 12 (1965), 533.

56. KENNY, T. J. "Background Interference Procedure: A Means of Assessing Neurologic Dysfunction in School-Age Children." *Journal of Consulting and Clinical Psychology,* 37, no. 1 (1971), 44–46.

57. KIRK, S. A., McCARTHY, J. J., and KIRK, W. D. *Examiner's Manual, Illinois Test of Psycholinguistic Abilities.* Rev. ed. Urbana, Ill.: University of Illinois Press, 1968.

58. ———, McCARTHY, J. J., and KIRK, W. D. *Illinois Test of Psycholinguistic Abilities.* Rev. ed. Urbana, Ill.: University of Illinois Press, 1968.

59. KLOPFER, W. G. "The Role of Diagnostic Evaluation in Clinical Psychology." In B. Lubin and E. E. Levitt, eds., *The Clinical Psychologist.* Chicago: Aldine, 1967. Pp. 152–154.

60. KOPPITZ, E. M. *The Bender Gestalt Test for Young Children.* New York: Grune & Stratton, 1964.

61. ———. *Psychological Evaluation of Children's Human Figure Drawings.* New York: Grune & Stratton, 1968.

62. LAURANDEAU, M., and PINARD, A. *Causal Thinking in the Child.* New York: International Universities Press, 1962.

63. LAYMAN, E. M. "Psychological Testing of Infants and Preschool Children." *Clinical Proceedings of the Children's Hospital* (Washington, D.C.), 11, no. 6 (1955), 126–136.

64. ———, and LOURIE, R. S. "Waiting Room Observations as a Technique of Analysis of Communication Behavior in Children and Their Parents." In P. Hoch and J. Rubin, eds., *Psychopathology of Communication.* New York: Grune & Stratton, 1957. Pp. 227–249.

65. LEVINE, M. "Psychological Testing of Children." In *Review of Child Development*

Research. Vol. 2. New York: Russell Sage Foundation, 1966. Pp. 257–310.

66. LEVY, D. M. "Hostility Patterns in Sibling Rivalry Experiments." *American Journal of Orthopsychiatry,* 6 (1936), 183–257.

67. ———. "Projective Techniques in Clinical Practice." *American Journal of Orthopsychiatry,* 19 (1949), 140–144.

68. LEVY, L. H. *Psychological Interpretation.* New York: Holt, 1963.

69. LIPPMAN, H. S. *Treatment of the Child in Emotional Conflict.* 2d ed. New York: McGraw-Hill, 1962.

70. LIPTON, E. L., STEINSCHNEIDER, A., and RICHMOND, J. B. "The Autonomic Nervous System in Early Life." *New England Journal of Medicine,* 273, nos. 3 & 4 (1965), 147–153, 201–208.

71. LITTELL, W. M. "The Wechsler Intelligence Scale for Children: Review of a Decade of Research." *Psychological Bulletin,* 57 (1960), 132–156.

72. LOURIE, R. S. "Experience with Therapy of Severe Psychosomatic Problems in Infants." In P. Hoch and J. Zubin, eds., *Psychopathology of Childhood.* New York: Grune & Stratton, 1955. Pp. 254–264.

73. ———. "The First Three Years of Life: An Overview of a New Frontier of Psychiatry." *American Journal of Psychiatry,* 127, no. 11 (1971), 1457–1463.

74. LOWENFELD, M. *The Lowenfeld Mosaic Test.* London: Newman Neame, 1954.

75. McREYNOLDS, P., ed. *Advances in Psychological Assessment.* Vol. 1. Palo Alto, Cal.: Science & Behavior Books, 1968.

76. MOORE, R., and GOLDIAMOND, I. "Errorless Estimate of Visual Discrimination Using Fading Process." *Journal of Experimental Analysis of Behavior,* 7(3) (1964), 269–272.

77. MURPHY, L. B. "Assessment of Infants and Young Children." In C. A. Chandler, R. S. Lourie, A. D. Peters and L. L. Dittmann, eds., *Early Child Care: The New Perspectives.* New York: Atherton, 1968. Pp. 107–139.

78. ———. "The Vulnerability Inventory." In C. A. Chandler, R. S. Lourie, A. D. Peters, and L. L. Dittmann, eds., *Early Child Care: The New Perspectives.* New York: Atherton, 1968. Pp. 364–372.

79. MURRAY, H. A., et al. *Thematic Apperception Test Manual.* Cambridge, Mass.: Harvard University Press, 1943.

80. OZER, M. N. "The Use of Operant Conditioning in the Evaluation of Children with Learning Problems." *Clinical Proceedings of Children's Hospital* (Washington, D.C.), 22, no. 8 (1966), 235–245.

81. PAINE, R. "Minimal Chronic Brain Syndromes." *Clinical Proceedings of Children's Hospital* (Washington, D.C.), 22, no. 1 (1966), 21–40.

82. PASCAL, G. R., and SUTTELL, B. J. *The Bender-Gestalt Test.* New York: Grune & Stratton, 1951.

83. PEIXOTTO, H. E. "Use of the Despert Fables with Disturbed Children." *Journal of Clinical Psychology,* 16 (1960), 173–179.

84. PIAGET, J. *Science of Education and the Psychology of the Child.* New York: Orion Press, 1970.

85. ———, and INHELDER, B. *The Psychology of the Child.* New York: Basic Books, 1969.

86. PIOTROWSKI, Z. A. "The Rorschach Inkblot Method." In *Handbook of Clinical Psychology.* New York: McGraw-Hill, 1965. Pp. 522–561.

87. PORTEUS, S. C. *The Porteus Maze Test and Intelligence.* Palo Alto, Cal.: Pacific Books, 1950.

88. ———. *The Maze Test and Clinical Psychology.* Palo Alto, Cal.: Pacific Books, 1959.

89. PROVENCE, S., and LIPTON, R. C. *Infants in Institutions.* New York: International Universities Press, 1962.

90. RABIN, A. I. "Diagnostic Use of Intelligence Tests." *Handbook of Clinical Psychology.* New York: McGraw-Hill, 1965. Pp. 477–497.

91. ———, and HAWORTH, M. R., eds. *Projective Techniques with Children.* New York: Grune & Stratton, 1960.

92. RAPAPORT, D. "The Autonomy of the Ego." In R. P. Knight, ed., *Psychoanalytic Psychiatry and Psychology.* New York: International Universities Press, 1954. Pp. 248–258.

93. ———. "The Theoretical Implications of Diagnostic Testing Procedures." In R. P. Knight, ed., *Psychoanalytic Psychiatry and Psychology.* New York: International Universities Press, 1954. Pp. 173–195.

94. ———, GILL, M. M., and SCHAFER, R. *Diagnostic Psychological Testing.* Rev. Ed. ed. by R. R. Holt. New York: International Universities Press, 1968.

95. RAVEN, J. C. *Progressive Matrices.* New York: Psychological Corporation, 1956.

96. REED, J. C. "Brain Damage and Learning Disabilities: Psychological Diagnosis and Remediation." In L. Tarnapol, ed., *Learning Disorders in Children: Diagnosis, Medication, and Education.* Boston: Little, Brown, 1971.

97. REIMAN, M. G. "The Mosaic Test: Its Applicability and Validity." *American Journal of Orthopsychiatry,* 20 (1950), 600–615.

98. RICHMOND, J. B. "Toward Developmental Psychosomatic Medicine." *Psychosomatic Medicine,* 25 (1963), 567–573.

99. RORSCHACH, H. *Psychodiagnostics.* 4th ed. New York: Grune & Stratton, 1949.

100. ROSS, A. O. *The Practice of Clinical Child Psychology.* New York: Grune & Stratton, 1959. Pp. 34–56.

101. RUSCHIVAL, M., LENA, G., and WAY, J. "The WPPSI and the Stanford-Binet: A Validity and Reliability Study Using Gifted Preschool Children." *Journal of Consulting and Clinical Psychology,* 37, no. 1 (1971), 163.

102. SCARR-SALAPATEK, S. "Unknowns in the IQ Equation." *Science,* 174, no. 4015 (December 1971), 1223–1228.

103. SCHAFER, R. "Interpersonal Dynamics in the Test Situation." *Psychoanalytic Interpretation in Rorschach Testing.* New York: Grune & Stratton, 1954. Pp. 6–73.

104. SCHNEIDMAN, E. S. "Manual for the Make-A-Picture-Story Method." *Journal of Projective Techniques,* monogr. no. 2 (1952).

105. SHORE, M. F. "Psychological Testing." In R. H. Woody and J. D. Woody, eds., *Clinical Assessment in Counseling and Psychotherapy.* New York: Appleton-Century-Crofts, 1972.

106. SIGEL, I. E. "The Attainment of Concepts." In *Review of Child Development Research.* Vol. 1. New York: Russell Sage Foundation, 1964. Pp. 209–248.

107. SIMMONS, J. E. *Psychiatric Examination of Children.* Philadelphia: Lea & Febiga, 1969.

108. SLOAN, W. "The Lincoln-Oseretsky Motor Development Scale." *Genetic Psychology Monograph,* 51 (1955), 183–252.

109. STEPHENS, W. B., PIAGET, J., and INHELDER, B. "Application of Theory and Diagnostic Techniques to the Area of Mental Retardation." *Education and Training of Mentally Retarded,* 1 (1966), 75–87.

110. STUTSMAN, R. *Mental Measurement of Pre-school Children with a Guide for the Administration of the Merrill-Palmer Scale of Mental Tests.* Yonkers-on-Hudson, N.Y.: World, 1931.

111. TAYLOR, E. M. *Psychological Appraisal of Children with Cerebral Defects.* Cambridge, Mass.: Harvard University Press, 1959.

112. TERMAN, L. M., and MERRILL, M. A. *Stanford-Binet Intelligence Scale.* Form L-M. Geneva, Ill.: Houghton Mifflin, 1960.

113. THOMAS, A., CHESS, S., BIRCH, H. G., HERTZIG, M., and KORN, S. *Behavioral Individuality in Early Childhood.* New York: New York University Press, 1963.

114. TUDDENHAM, R. D. "Psychometrizing Piaget's Methode Clinique." In I. Athey and D. Rubadeau, eds., *Educational Implication's of Piaget's Theory.* Waltham, Mass.: Ginn/Blaisdell, 1970. Pp. 317–324.

115. WECHSLER, D. *Wechsler Intelligence Scale for Children.* New York: Psychological Corporation, 1949.

116. ———. *Wechsler Adult Intelligence Scale Manual.* New York: Psychological Corporation, 1955.

117. ———. *Wechsler Preschool and Primary Scale of Intelligence.* New York: Psychological Corporation, 1967.

118. WEISS, R. L. "Operant Conditioning Techniques in Psychological Assessment." In *Advances in Psychological Assessment.* Palo Alto, Cal.: Science and Behavior Books, 1968. Pp. 169–190.

119. WERKMAN, S. L. "The Psychiatric Diagnostic Interview with Children." *American Journal of Orthopsychiatry,* 35 (1965), 764.

120. WETZEL, K. H., WELCHER, D. W., and MELLITIS, E. D. "The Possibility of Overdiagnosing Brain Dysfunction from a Single Administration of the Bender Gestalt Test." *Johns Hopkins Medical Journal,* 129 no. 6 (1971).

121. WILLIAMS, R. L. "Danger: Testing and Dehumanizing Black Children." *Clinical Child Psychology Newsletter,* 9, no. 1 (1970), 5–6.

122. WITMER, H. L., ed. *Psychiatric Diagnostic Interviews with Children.* New York: Commonwealth Fund, 1946.

123. WOLFF, P. H. "The Causes, Controls, and Organization of Behavior in the Neonate." *Psychological Issues,* 5, no. 1 (1966), monogr. no. 17.

124. ZIGLER, E., and BUTTERFIELD, E. C. Motivational Factors and IQ Changes in Culturally Deprived Children Attending Nursery School. Unpublished manuscript, 1967.

CHAPTER 2

FAMILY DIAGNOSIS AND CLINICAL PROCESS*

Nathan W. Ackerman and Marjorie L. Behrens

OUR APPROACH to the concept of family diagnosis evolves from the nature of the clinical encounter. To diagnose means to distinguish by knowing. In this special context, the clinician acquires a "knowing" through his involvement in a series of exploratory family interviews. It is through this participatory experience of face to face confrontation that the therapist empathically "feels into" and "sees into" a troubled family. The method involves continuous observation and interpretation of relevant events. The encounter stimulates in the therapist a progression of clinical hunches, deriving from and enriched by his knowledge of psychodynamic and psychosocial processes and by his past personal and professional experience. These hunches are continually put to the test of the prevailing interpersonal realities. Across time, the therapist develops fragments of theory concerning family diagnosis which must be tested, amended, and verified in an ongoing process of consensual validation. This, in effect, is our "manner of inquiry"† into the problem of family diagnosis, a stage by stage development of diagnostic insight derived from the experience of therapeutic involvement. What is learned is a function of how we learn it.

Thus, family diagnosis and family therapy are parallel, interdependent activities. Insofar as the family is an ever-changing phenomenon, the diagnosis changes as the family changes. Diagnosis serves as a guide to action. It provides a strategy for therapeutic intervention.

Within the limits of present-day knowledge, does the task of family diagnosis make sense? Is it realistic? Is it feasible? Whatever one thinks and however one does it, whether well

I received this chapter from Nathan Ackerman a few weeks before his untimely death. Its vivid style and content help us realize the magnitude of our loss. —G.C.

* Grateful acknowledgment is offered to Dr. Walter Sencer and Judith Lieb for thoughtful criticism of this chapter.

† What is called truth constantly changes. Since no fact is immune to new information, what remains much longer is a viewpoint of "manner of inquiry."[8]

or badly, it is a fact of everyday clinical practice. The issue is not shall we but rather *how* shall we diagnose. Clinicians inevitably draw judgment on the families they treat. They describe, compare, and contrast them; they draw meaningful distinctions among them. In a tentative way, therapists hypothesize certain correlations between family transactions and the adaptation of individual members. They cannot help but do so. The functions of observing, conceptualizing, and interpreting such correlations are inherent in the therapeutic encounter. The issue is, therefore, family diagnosis toward what ends, by what means, with what criteria, by whom, and with what measure of reliability.

In taking this posture on the problem of family diagnosis, we are fully cognizant of the existing climate of opinion. The disenchantment with the medical model of psychiatric illness is widespread. The bias against labeling people and families is sharp. In many quarters, psychiatric classification is viewed as passé, useless in therapy, or even harmful. Nonetheless, the challenge is there to be met. The answer to bad diagnosis or the abuse of diagnosis is better diagnosis—not to toss out this responsibility altogether.

The turbulence of contemporary behavior theory, the disillusionment with traditional standards of diagnosis, these are precisely the products of new knowledge. What is called for now is a fresh start, a new, more effective paradigm for the responsibility of clinically oriented family diagnosis. Such a model needs to take into account the ecological perspective, the changing theory of behavior, of therapeutic process, of mental illness and its causation. Within this framework we must underscore the contagious and communicable nature of pathogenic emotion in family group process. We are impelled, also, to adopt a broader interpretation of psychiatric disorder as a family phenomenon, a cluster of multiple disturbances among the members of the family group, interdependent, interacting, and emerging in series across time. Individual diagnosis, whether child or adult, achieves a fuller meaning within the matrix of the family as a behavior system.

To sum up the argument thus far, family diagnosis begins with a clinical hunch, an intuitive, informal fragment of theory; it then moves gradually toward a more formal, explicit, systematic diagnostic judgment, a shift by progressive stages from a subjective toward a more objective formulation. The use of multiple observers facilitates this process.

The Family Group

In the family-group procedure, we are evaluating a group different from other groups, a culturally patterned biosocial unit embracing two or more generations, both sexes, a constellation of persons sharing emotion, identity, a way of life, and a related quality of struggle and growth. We are judging persons within the family, the family within the community. We are assessing a path of movement, what the family is, was, and where it is going. The family is a living entity, an open system of behavior, characterized by a life cycle uniquely its own. It grows up; it grows outward. It undergoes periods of slow change and rapid change. It experiences a sequence of crises. To maintain its functions, it must weather each crisis in turn. The family moves forward, or else it loses its vital force (gets "sick") and "dies". Following each upset, it must mobilize its homeodynamic powers to restore equilibrium and yet preserve its potential for movement and growth.

We evaluate what goes on inside and outside the family, inside and between the minds of individual members. We examine the structure and functions of the family, how the family fulfills its multiple responsibilities or fails to do so, and how this molds the experience, development, and emotional health of its members.

The family is a unit of living, yet its parts are divided and differentiated. It has male and female, old and young, big and small, strong and weak, smart and stupid, appealing and unappealing members. Within its larger representations of unity, there are shifting alignments and splits. A conflict of identity, values, and strivings brings a rift, a split in the family group which mobilizes one faction against another. These factions do battle with one another for a position of dominance in determining what the family does for, with, and against its members; what they do, in turn, for, with, and against the family. Such splits within the group may be horizontal, vertical or diagonal. They may be male against female, mother and son against father and daughter, mother and children against father, the younger against the older generation. Fragmentation and alienation of family relationships may proceed to the extreme where finally it becomes each member for himself. Such trends divide the family, throw its functions off balance, favoring some, disabling and warping others.

It is the character of a living system that it has a boundary, and across this boundary there is an incessant exchange from outside in and from inside out. How we define the family, its boundary, whom we include and whom we exclude, depends on what we are trying to do. We expand or contract the "rubber fence" (L. Wynne) of family in accordance with our special interests and purposes. If we adopt too narrow a focus, we get more precise data but are in danger of omitting important processes. If we use too broad a focus, we clutter our understanding with an overabundance of unmanageable data. Of necessity, our focus is selective; it concentrates on those components of family experience that are relevant and specific for the emotional destiny of the members. Within this framework, diagnosis has a special meaning related to the clinical goal, a program of intervention that seeks to exert a favorable influence on the critical balance of forces as between those that predispose to breakdown and those that enhance health.

⟨ The Functions of a Family Therapist

As indicated, diagnosis and therapy depend on the clinician's use of self as family therapist. Therapeutic family interviewing is a personal art; yet each artist is called on to optimize existing knowledge of the dynamics of family and individual behavior. The role of the family therapist is that of a participant observer. He engages a family group in a face-to-face interview, searching for the forces, both open and hidden, that affect the well-being of the family and its members. The encounter is a free-wheeling, open-ended adventure, limited only by the potentials of the fit between family and therapist. With a particular family, one clinician may make it; another may fail. A special kind of human chemistry is involved. It is the idiosyncratic quality of the match of family and therapist that determines the potentials both of therapy and of diagnostic understanding.

With the involvement of the therapist, the family group is instantly "repeopled." The therapist becomes part of what he is observing. He is drawn into the whirlpool of the family struggle. He moves in but must also know when and how to move out. He must be continuously aware of the risk of being sucked into the family system and thus lose his capacity for autonomous, flexible, and appropriate intervention. Stage by stage, the therapist evolves the priorities and sequences of his actions. The selection and timing of his interventions are of the essence. Through his active participation, the therapist shakes up the existing alignments and splits of the family.

In face-to-face confrontation, the therapist makes instant observations of appearance, mood, and behavior of the members and their integration into family roles. He pays attention to their demeanor, manner of entry, and seating arrangements. Who joins with whom? Who is against whom? Who speaks? Who is silent? Who is open, who closed? Who looks cheerful, who seems sad? Who moves quickly into the fray? Who slides into retreat?

The mood is all important. What part of the group is alive and spirited; what part is depressed and dying? Which of the members are hopeful, expectant, or on the other hand, resigned and despairing? What are the expressions of hurt, fright, and anger? Of confusion, mistrust, and hostility? Do the members reach out to one another and to the therapist? Are they receptive? Do they turn coercive? Do

they sink into apathy and cease to ask for anything?

A first concern of the therapist is to establish
rapport, a feeling of trust and empathy (a
touching quality of contact and communication), and to rekindle the hope of something
better. The therapist reaches out to meet the
family members on their own ground, to join
them emotionally where they live. He feels his
way toward the idiosyncratic mood and language of the family, how they talk, what they
talk about, what they do not talk about. The
therapist, through his openness and candor,
catalyzes the interchange of conflict-loaded
material. When the members engage in a silent pact to evade such confrontation, the therapist seeks ways to penetrate their complic-
itous denials. He draws judgments as to how
far these family secrets are valid, or false, how
far they are on the side of health, or on the
side of sickness. To whatever extent they are
judged to be pathogenic pseudosecrets, the
therapist supports the family in exposing and
sharing the hidden content. In a white family
with three daughters and one son, it was necessary to crack open the pseudosecret: One
daughter lives with a black man, and the only
son is homosexual. Every member knows yet
pretends not to know, a conspiracy of silence.

The therapist zeroes in on the most destructive levels of conflict, on those relationships
that generate the most intense anxiety. To stir
movement, he engages in a tactic characterized by "tickling" the defenses. He catches the
family by surprise, pointedly confronting them
with contradictions between their self-justify-
ing rationalizations and the truer emotions. He
exposes the discrepancies between verbal ut-
terances and what is felt below the level of
words in facial expression, gesture, and bodily
posture. He challenges empty verbalisms,
clichés, and pat formulae for the problems of
living. Maximizing the stream of empathic
emotional interchange, he invites increasingly
candid disclosures. Stage by stage, he reaches
out for a deeper, more meaningful emotional
interchange.

He assays the main patterns of conflict and
coping, the patterns of complementarity, the
interplay of family defense and individual de-

fense. He traces the sources of anxiety that
freeze the reaching out of members, the asking for closeness one with the other and with
the therapist.

He cuts through the vicious cycle of blame
and punishment, which is nothing less than an
unconscious collusion to prevent change.
When one part of the family armors itself to
assault and scapegoat another, the therapist
intervenes to neutralize and soften the assault.
By counteracting scapegoating as a pathogenic defense, he retransposes the conflict to
its place of origin within the group. By identifying a cluster of interrelated roles—persecu-
tor, victim, and peacemaker or healer—he is
enabled to support and strengthen the forces
of healing within the family.

The emotions and images evoked in the
therapist by the crisscross currents of feeling
moving among the family members and toward himself serve, in effect, as a diagnostic
yardstick for what is being experienced below
the surface. Sequence by sequence, and in a
selective way, the therapist puts his clinical
hunches and insights to the test. The face-to-
face interview provides a continuous opportunity for consensual validation of hypotheses.
What one member conceals, another reveals.
What one expresses in a twisted, prejudicial
way is counterbalanced by another. The social
structuring of the interview promotes a sustained process of working through of partly
shared, partly clashing, images and emotions.
The therapist acts as a balance wheel, check-
ing experience against the prevailing interpersonal realities.

The core of the exploratory process involves
colliding images, the family's image of itself,
the conflicting images of the warring factions,
the community's image, and the therapist's
own image of the family. Throughout the entire process, the therapist is engaged in a
subtly shifting encounter, joining or jousting
with one or another family factions. What is
involved is a kaleidoscope of forces epitomiz-
ing a shifting balance of continuity within
change, change within continuity. The quest
for relevant insights moves from the family as
a whole, to the warring subgroups, to the cluster of interlocking disturbances, and finally, to

the pathogenic effect on the labeled patient. In so doing, the therapist assays the relative severity of disturbance and the family's capacity for change and growth. Step by step, he optimizes the opportunity for teasing out the essential character of the family.

This is our picture of an exploratory family interview; the how of the encounter determines the what; the information we gather depends on how we get it.

[A Clinical Illustration*

This family consists of the two parents in their thirties and five children. The mother is Italian Catholic; the father is half-Jewish. This is a working-class family. The first issue is survival. The mother is depressed and shabby looking. She has made repeated attempts at suicide. Her face is marred with acne; she has a facial tic. The father is a good-looking man; neat and trim, fearful and yet overbearing.

This couple has been separated for a month, but is again joined. The father has terminated an affair with another woman, whom the mother contemptuously calls "the pig."

During the interview, the mother seats herself next to the therapist. The father leans away; he "plays it cool". The presenting mood is one of explosive rage between husband and wife, barely controlled. The eldest son, twelve years, has a masked, frightened look; the eldest daughter, ten years, seems depressed. The younger children are restless and noisy.

The therapist comments on the mood and facial expression of the older children. He asks the son how he feels about having his two parents together again. The boy likes it, but feels helpless as to how to keep them together. The father is distracted by the noise making of the younger children. He tosses them a menacing look, as if he would kill them. The therapist gives explicit recognition to the father's mean look. The father admits he hits them if they do not behave. They must keep their place.

*For other examples see *Treating the Troubled Family*.[3]

The therapist points out that the father has been unable to keep the mother in her place. He now confronts the father and mother with their spatial separation in the interviewing room. The wife agrees she does not want to be close to her husband; she feels safer that way. At this point, the therapist removes himself from his chair between husband and wife and challenges the parents to talk with one another. They choose to argue about the children. The mother wants the children present at the interview; the father wants them out. The children are frightened and stay out of the parental war. The mother uses the children as allies against the father. He, in turn, scapegoats them. The therapist now excuses the children.

Once the mother and father are alone with the therapist, the mother speaks up in a pained, martyred manner. The husband always treats her as a "kook," the sick one. He is severely critical of her. She feels deprived and fed up. She screams that he cares more about that other woman than he does about her. The husband denies this. The wife angrily asserts that she has tried to be a good wife and mother but never got any approval. The therapist asks the husband what he wants from his wife. His answer: She must take care of the children, the home, and feed and sleep with him. He accuses her of being sloppy, disorganized, and neglecting the children. He blames this on his wife's family. Her mother was a drinker and lived a promiscuous life, like a whore. "It made me sick," says the wife. She sobs agitatedly about her mother's abuse of her and her husband's infidelity.

She tells of a telephone call from her father alleging that her husband had made a sexual advance to her sister. He denies this and rebuts with a countercharge that the wife's father had made a sexual advance to her. This she affirms; she bows her head, crying now in a softer way. She discusses her suicide attempts but agrees with the therapist that despite her anguish, she very much wants to live.

This leads to an exploration of their sexual life. At first, the wife brags; no matter what, she can keep her husband happy in bed. She then contradicts herself; she does not even feel loved in bed. In fact, she is nowhere satisfied. She reverts to screaming at her husband that as a man he never makes it; he's gutless. Alone with him, she would not dare expose him because he would beat her. In the meantime, he screws around with "this other woman." In a flash of fury, "Yes, you can feel powerful on the outside, but at home with me, you're nothing!"

The only time she is happy is when her belly is filled with a baby. At her husband's insistence, she had her tubes tied. She reacted with a sense of loss and depression. Her husband wanted her to have an operation because he felt her vagina was too big. She, in turn, felt his penis was too small.

Diagnostic Comment

This is a family with recurrent crises. The marriage relationship is immature and unstable. Each partner is still tied to family of origin. Each parentifies the other. The prime need is for security and service. The pattern is one of mutual dependency in which neither partner satisfies the other. Of the two partners, the husband is stronger and more adequate. The wife suffers a cyclic mood disturbance. She is infantile, demanding, insatiable, rebellious, and vindictive. When depressed and agitated, she insults and emasculates her husband, and sabotages her domestic functions. Incest guilt makes her feel low, dirty, and unworthy. The husband responds by turning dictatorial and violent. Having failed in his original role of savior for his wife, he overreacts with an exaggerated assertion of male supremacy that barely cloaks his underlying panic regarding a total loss of power. The mother allies with the children against the father, who turns tyrant and scapegoats the children. In crisis, all family functions collapse.

⟦ A Conceptual Framework for Family Diagnosis

The work of building a theory of the psychosocial dynamics of the family and a corresponding concept of family diagnosis is barely begun. At this moment, we are betwixt and between; we are in a kind of no man's land, striving to discover an appropriate conceptual framework. At best, we have evolved a set of partial hypotheses, relatively unintegrated, a far cry still from a unified theory. The biopsychoanalytic model of family and individual personality is inadequate and biased, as is the medical model of mental illness. The science of psychodynamics and psychopathology shows progress but has its own built-in limitations. Signs of diminishing returns begin to appear in the framework of individual psychology. Now come two further developments, the psychosocial model and the systems theory model. Both are in the formative stages.

The psychosocial model, therapeutically oriented, places a main emphasis on the internal dynamics of the family while leaving room for conceptualization of events at the interface of family and community. Recognizing that the external environment cannot be viewed as a constant, the psychosocial approach must nonetheless specialize on the inner life of the family. It seeks the psychotherapeutic contribution to a theory of the family.

Systems theory is an ecologically oriented model; as such, it holds a rich potential for illuminating the issues of conceptualization. Yet, in the opinion of its founder, von Bertalanffy, it is neither exhaustive nor final. At present, the effort to implement systems theory reveals certain limitations and risks.[9] The abstract quality of systems theory opens a large gap between the theory model and a concrete case. Discrepancies emerge between the model and reality. There is often a lack of fit between theory and empirical events. Systems theory lacks a methodology. As von Bertalanffy puts it: "New horizons have been opened up but the relations to empirical facts remain tenuous."

Systems theory aspires to universality. But, the more a theory approximates a mathematical model, the less easy it is to apply to a human situation. To quote Einstein: "Insofar as the laws of mathematics refer to reality, they are not certain; insofar as they are certain, they do not refer to reality." Therapeutic experience suggests that an upper-range theory must be reduced to a lower order of generalization before we can make practical use of it in analysis of a clinical problem. A middle-range theory provides a closer connection with the time- and space-bound vicissitudes of the human struggle with conflict.

(Criteria for Family Diagnosis

Family diagnosis here signifies a means of identifying the psychosocial configuration of the family entity, a basis of classification and differential diagnosis of family types according to potentials of health and growth, and finally, a method of correlating the dynamics of family and individual behavior.

For twenty-five years we have worked and reworked the criteria for family diagnosis in order to make them more simple, practical, and authentic, and at the same time render a live image of the character of the family. For the examination of family, we propose the following criteria.

The Most Destructive Foci of Conflict

The most destructive foci of conflict are the contagion of anxiety; the alignments and splits within the group and related coping patterns; and the interplay of family and individual coping.

The first step in diagnosis is to mark out the most destructive levels of conflict, the contagious flow of anxiety, and the family relationships within which conflict and anxiety are trapped. The coping patterns are reflected in the organization of alignments and splits and in the interaction of these competing factions. One part of the family clashes with another about what the family is and ought to be, how the family serves or fails to serve the needs of its members, and what the members do, ought to do, or fail to do with the family. Family conflict revolves around issues of security, need satisfaction, love expectation, struggle for control or support of a needed self-image.

Family coping has as its purpose the protection of the integrity, continuity, and growth of the family. *The levels of coping* may be identified as follows:

1. A shared search for specific and suitable solutions to conflict, leading to a changed configuration of family relationships.
2. A strengthening of family unity, integrity, and functional competence through an enhancement of the bonds of love and loyalty, and with this a consolidation of sound family values.
3. "Repeopling" of the family, that is, removing a person from or adding a person to the functioning family unit.
4. Mobilization of external support for family integrity through social service, psychotherapy, religious guidance, and so on.
5. A spiritual rebirth, an enhancement of family closeness and health, after recovery from a family crisis such as the death of a family member.
6. Reintegration of family role relationships through: (a) tightening of the family organization, rigidification of authority, sharper division of labor, constriction and compartmentalization of roles; (b) a loosening of the family organization, dilution of the family bond, distancing, alienation, role segregation, thinning of the boundary between family and community, and displacement of family functions from inside to outside; and (c) reorganization of the complementarity of the family roles by a reversal of sex-linked parental roles and/or reversal of parent-child roles.
7. Reduction of conflict and danger through avoidance, denial, and isolation.
8. Reduction of conflict and danger through compromise, compensation, and escape, that is, sexual escapades, delinquency, alcohol, drugs, and the like.
9. Realignment of family relationships through splitting of the group, scapegoating, and compensatory healing.

The Typical Family Role Relationships and Patterns of Complementarity

As the second step, we identify the typical family role relationships and complementary patterns. In the reciprocal adaptations of husband-wife, father-mother, parent-child, parent-grandparent, we examine the question of complementarity in terms of five items: (1) self-esteem; (2) need satisfaction; (3) a shared search for solutions to conflict; (4) buttressing of needed defenses against anxiety; and (5) support of growth and creative development.

At what specific levels is complementarity preserved; at what other levels is it sacrificed? We draw a further judgment: In the emotional involvement of triangular relationships, such as mother-father-child, do the needs and anxieties of a family pair impose an emotional sacrifice on the third member, or do the needs and anxieties of one member of the threesome invade and impair the emotional complementarity of the other two?

We classify role complementarity in three broad categories: (1) lacking; (2) partial; and (3) complete. A lack of complementarity exists when there is a critical reduction at all levels. Complementarity is partial when it exists on some levels and is absent on others. For example, a satisfactory quality of complementarity may prevail in terms of need satisfaction and support of defenses against anxiety, but it may be lacking at other levels—in the support of self-esteem, in the quest for solutions to conflict, in nourishment of growth and development. Partial complementarity may contribute to the control of anxiety by offsetting possible breakdown in one of the partners, while limiting growth of the relationship and of each partner as an individual. We characterize this as a form of negative complementarity. Complementarity is high or relatively complete where there is reciprocal emotional satisfaction on all five items.

The diagnosis of the marital partnership is a part of family diagnosis. To be considered are the capacity for love, mutual adaptation, adaptation to external change, and adaptation for growth.

We are concerned with evaluating the role complementarity of the marital partnership, the levels of conflict, benign and destructive, and the patterns of coping. Worthy of emphasis here are two special features: (1) the use of the marital partnership to compensate anxiety and support one or both partners against the threat of breakdown; the use of external relationships to mitigate marital failure and provide compensatory gratification, and (2) the quality of integration of each partner into the marital role and the fit of marital and parental roles.

The performance of the parental pair can be similarly judged by:

1. The complementarity of parental roles, the mutuality of adaptation, adaptation to external change and adaptation for growth.
2. The levels of conflict, benign or destructive.
3. The integration of each partner into the parental role.
4. The effects of parental behavior on the child and the effects of the child's behavior on the parents.

Fulfillment, Harmonization, and Balancing of Family Functions

We may assess the family's capacity to fulfill, harmonize and balance its multiple functions according to the following items: (1) survival and security; (2) affection; (3) the balance between dependency and autonomous development; (4) social and sexual training; and (5) growth and creative development.

What priorities are assigned to these functions? How are they integrated and balanced? Which are selectively safeguarded? Which others are neglected or distorted? Which are sacrificed so as to protect which others?

Identity, Stability, Value Striving, and Growth

We come now to the question of family identity. Family identity is what the family stands for. It pertains to a dominant identity, a representation of shared goals, values, and strivings. Family identity is never fixed; it represents a fluid, continuously evolving image of the family as a living, growing entity. It is crystallized out of an ongoing clash of multiple competing and cooperating partial identity representations. It is molded by the manner in which each subgroup, whether a family pair, triad, or an individual member, strives to reconcile personal identity and values with shifting representations of family identity across time. This highlights the value struggle within the family and between the family and community. Family identity answers the question: Who are we as a family at a given time and place and in a defined life situation?

Family identity and stability must be considered together. Stability epitomizes the family's capacity to protect the continuity and integrity of the family's identity under the pressure of changing life conditions. It assures the intactness of family adaptation in the face of new experience. This is the conservative phase of stability. The other aspect must provide for the capacity to adapt flexibly to new experience, to learn and achieve further development. It represents the potentials of change and growth. Effective adaptation or homeodynamic equilibrium requires a favorable balance between the protection of sameness and continuity and the need to accommodate to change. It requires the preservation of the old coupled with receptivity to the new, a mixture of conservatism and readiness to live dangerously.

Evaluation of the Family's Capacity for Change and Growth: Discrepancy between Actual Performance of Family and a Theoretical Model of a Healthy Family

In determining the performance of a family one can assess:

1. Fulfillment of strivings and values.
2. The stability, maturity, and realism of the family.
3. The presence or absence of regressive and disintegrative trends.
4. The quality and degree of successful adaptation.

Our concern here is to evaluate how far the family gets stuck at different points in the growth curve, how far the family falls short of what it might be in the family's view of itself, in the community's view of family, and finally, in terms of a professional standard of a healthy family unit. We try then to conceptualize the relations of family performance to the alignments and splits within the group and the effect on the emotional development and health of individual members. In this way we strive for a clearer picture of the balance of forces within the family, those that predispose to breakdown and illness and those that protect health and growth.

⟮ Guide for Family Diagnosis

For the gathering and organization of comparable data on a range of family types, we offer a guide for family diagnosis, which should be implemented in a flexible and appropriate manner for each family.

1. *Identifying data*
   a. Age and sex of family members and of other persons, in or outside the home, who are significant participants
   b. Living arrangements
   c. Number of years married
   d. Occupations and incomes
   e. Education
   f. Religious, ethnic, and cultural factors
   g. Special features: previous marriages, separations, pregnancies, illnesses, deaths, and so on
2. *The problem: presenting complaints*
   a. Disturbance of "labeled" member; disturbances of other members
   b. Family conflicts; stress factors; crisis in relationships; impairment of family functions
   c. Family attitudes toward problem and toward intervention
   d. Previous intervention

3. *Conflict and coping*
   a. Conflicts: explicit, implicit, benign, destructive
   b. Mechanisms of control and coping
   c. Interplay of family and individual defense and coping
4. *Internal organization*
   a. Typical family role relationships (husband-wife, parent-child, and so on)
   b. Alignments and splits
   c. Complementarity: lacking, partial, complete, or "negative complementarity"
   d. Adaptation of individual members
5. *Family functions: integration, harmonization, balance*
6. *External adaptation*
   a. Kin network
   b. School, work
   c. Social network
   d. Religious, ethnic, cultural factors
7. *Historial development of family group*
8. *Identity and stability: standards, values, and strivings*
9. *Family's capacity for change and growth: discrepancy between actual performance of family and a theoretical model of a healthy family*

❨ Case Illustration of the Guide for Family Diagnosis*

Identifying Data

A white, Jewish, conservative family consisting of Mr. O, forty-two; Mrs. O, forty-one; Helen, eighteen; Judy, sixteen. Mr. O works as a printing salesman, earning $17,000 yearly. Judy is in junior high school. Helen quit college after one semester and is now working as a secretary. Mrs. O held a job as stenographer for four years; she quit when trouble with Helen began.

* This summary of family diagnosis was written by Peggy Papp, staff member of The Family Institute.

Referral

Family referred by psychiatrist; Helen was the "labeled" patient.

Problem

When Helen was sixteen, the family received an anonymous letter saying she was dating a black boy. She became pregnant, and the parents helped to arrange an abortion. This fall Helen became pregnant again, this time by a white boy she met in a bar. She wanted to get married. He did not. When she contacted the black boy, he proposed marriage and she accepted. Later, she restored contact with her parents, left her husband, and with the parents' help had a second abortion and divorced her husband.

Family as a Group

This family is laden with contradictions. Helen enters, looking every inch the streetwalker. Her own description of herself, "I'm no plain Jane," is the understatement of the year. She is pretty, blond, overweight, heavily made up, wearing false eyelashes, a bright orange dress, and dangling jewelry. In contrast, her father sits next to her looking like Herbert Marshall, gentle, controlled, conservative. He is the kindly philosopher trying to light the road of life of the family with a Norman Vincent Peale approach.

Judy and her mother resemble each other; they are not so attractive nor so flamboyant as Helen. There is something just slightly blowsy in their dress and grooming. The mother is overweight, has tinted red hair, and is wearing a red suit and black blouse. Judy just misses the poor taste of her mother, mainly through dint of her youthful figure and teenage garb.

The father, in his characteristically controlled manner, relates the above harrowing experiences; he finishes by stating that things are better now, that he has faith in Helen's courage and strength of character, that he knows she is going to come through "true-blue." He concedes there has always been difficulty between Helen and her mother, but they are both wonderful people. He knows they will work things out between them, and everyone is going to be happy. During all this, the mother is crying, Helen looks depressed, and Judy sits nervously twisting her hair and cracking her knuckles, the picture of guilt.

During one session, while the father was saying how well things were going, the mother was literally choking in the corner. She could not get her breath, blaming it on asthma, though she had never had asthma before.

Helen's appearance sharply contradicts her manner. If one were to hear her without seeing her one would visualize a shy, withdrawn, frail, colorless girl. She speaks barely above a whisper with a slight speech impediment. It took a long time before she was able to say anything beside "I guess so." Once she found her voice, however, her statements were terse, and pregnant with hostility and bitterness. "Why try to express myself, Mother always has the last word." "She wins every battle. If I talk back to her, I take away her role as mother. She'd feel unwanted."

She summed up her relationship with the black boy in one sentence. "I could never be myself at home. With Joe I was myself." She gave Joe the same kind of treatment he gave her. She was bossy, domineering, and always had the last word.

Though the family describes the mother as being loud and domineering at home, unable to tolerate anyone's opinion but her own, in the interviews she is submissive, silent, appears frightened, constantly cries and timidly defends herself against Helen's accusations. She emerges as a fragile monster who through the years has dominated the family with a combination of sergeant commands and unnerving tears.

The two sisters themselves are an interesting study in contrasts. Helen, the beauty, the sexpot, has always had difficulty dating. Her greatest fear is that she will be an old maid. Judy, the plainer one, is the belle of the ball. She has a steady boyfriend and is barraged with phone calls. Despite Judy's popularity, she is jealous of Helen's beauty. Helen is jeal-ous of Judy's outgoing personality and her relationship with her parents. Judy is aware she is favored by both parents and that she constantly overshadows Helen because of her natural vivacity. She feels responsible for Helen's unhappiness. Despite her guilt over hogging the spotlight, however, she also enjoys it and is most reluctant to share it. When Helen began expressing herself in the interviews, Judy suddenly became uncomfortable, accusing Helen of sounding like a "queen" and "highflown." Though Judy constantly talks back to her mother she finds it intolerable when Helen does. She feels she has to protect her mother from Helen's intense hostility.

Recently Judy was distressed, as Helen had become despondent over having no dates and threatened to commit suicide. Judy felt it was due to her popularity.

Family Mood

The underlying mood of this family is one of apprehension and guilt. They are suffering from shell shock from the many bombs Helen has exploded during the past two years. They live in constant fear of another explosion. They are currently engaged in trying to patch up the blanket of pretense and denial under which they have lived and go on as though nothing had happened. Sex, death, hostility, jealousy are taboo subjects in this family. There has always been an aura of mystery surrounding sex in the home. The parents never close their bedroom door, and the girls wonder when they have intercourse. When Helen, as a child, asked her mother about babies, Mrs. O was embarrassed to talk about it as grandmother was there. She said she would tell her later. Helen never asked again.

Helen feels she must cover up her depressed moods on a weekend to keep the family from becoming upset. She pretends to be in good spirits; the parents pretend to believe her, though they never go out for fear of leaving her alone. They deny suicide has ever entered their minds regarding Helen or anyone else. Yet Judy remembers her mother threatening to drive the car off the bridge and kill both herself and Judy when she received the anonymous letter about Helen. The mother has no recollection of this incident.

This denial has a demolishing effect on Helen. Her experiences over the past two years are being ignored and wiped out by the family. She herself feels wiped out. "Mother pretends I was never married to Joe. I'll never forget it as long as I live. So I don't know how to relate to people from here on. I don't know what she expects of me."

Internal Organization

MARITAL RELATIONSHIP

The parents have formed a united front in covering up any dissatisfaction they may feel in the marriage. They have insisted that they have "average sexual relationships" and "seldom quarrel." The father is extremely protective of the mother, frequently jumping to her defense. However, his description of her as a "good woman, well-meaning, hard-working, and conscientious" is a damning one. His hostility has emerged little by little as the interviews progressed until he recently blurted out "Yes I always obeyed her. Who'd want to tangle with her? She is a very tough customer." Through the years, whenever he showed the slightest resistance to her plans, she burst into tears, and he was forced to back down. He takes his revenge by "turning her off." He does not mind her loud voice as he simply does not hear it. Mrs. O denied she had any awareness of his "shutting her out." Yet Judy recalled her mother as having said only yesterday, "He never hears a thing I say. It's like talking to a wall." Mr. O also retaliates by teasing, saying to the girls, "watch your mother bite at this one." She always bites and ends up agitated and crying.

Their only open conflict has been over the disciplining of the girls. Mr. O has felt the girls should have stricter rules and regulations. However, he wanted the mother to enforce them. He has been squeamish in dealing with the girls. He admits he does not understand women and he likes to "avoid scenes."

The parents met at a dance in an old ladies' home when Mrs. O was sixteen and Mr. O eighteen. Then followed what appeared to be a conservative courtship. They dated for two years. Mr. O broke off the relationship when his father lost the store and he had to help support the family. Two years later he resumed the courtship. They dated for another two years before marrying.

PARENT-CHILD RELATIONSHIP

Both parents have always had a communication problem with Helen. She was a quiet child, and they never knew what she was thinking or feeling. Mrs. O has been able to cope with Judy because she fights back openly, and they can clear the air. Helen never opposes her mother openly. When Mrs. O criticizes her for eating too much ice cream, she just quietly has another dish.

Despite the father's distance from the girls there is a measure of warmth, affection, and humor expressed between them in the interviews. He seems to be more free and easy with Judy than with Helen. Helen finally turned to him in desperation about a year ago. She confided her hatred of her mother in what seemed to be a plea for his interference with the mother's intrusiveness. He made one feeble effort. He sided with Helen against the mother's waiting at the door every morning to give her the critical once over.

Both girls feel he should have actively intervened to give them more protection from the mother's family. Helen's fear of being an old maid seems to be related to her fear of being unable to break her symbiotic tie with the mother. Her fantasy is that she will be going to work, coming home to her parents every night, just as she is now, when she is fifty. Actually, she is more concerned with her own rejection of boys than she is with their rejection of her. She doubts her ability to love anyone for very long. She quickly grew tired of Jerry, her first steady boyfriend at fifteen, and lost interest in Joe after she married him. She felt her mother did not approve of Jerry, though the mother denies this. Helen feels helplessly dominated and overwhelmed by her mother who constantly nags and criticizes her. The father summed up their relationship succinctly when he stated "they devastate each other."

FAMILIES OF ORIGIN

This family is a carbon copy of the mother's original family even to the number, sex, and spacing of the children—two girls three years apart. Mrs. O's older sister was the bane of her family as Helen is the bane of this one. Though the older sister was never involved in delinquent behavior such as Helen's, Mrs. O describes her as "a slouch, irresponsible, and fat." It is this irresponsible quality she identifies with Helen. When it came time for work, her sister always disappeared just as Helen does. Mrs. O would always do her sister's work to keep her mother from being agitated. "My older sister ate my mother up inside"—precisely what Mrs. O feels Helen is doing to her. Mrs. O considered it her responsibility to save her mother from her older sister, the role in which Judy is cast in the present family. Mrs. O's relationship with her mother was the same as Judy's is with her. They were able to fight openly and clear the air.

Mrs. O continues in an extremely close and dependent relationship with her original family, whom Judy, Helen, and Mr. O dislike intensely and describe as being "terribly loud and overbearing." They have secretly resented the weekly visits they have been subjected to over the years but until now have not expressed this resentment for fear of "devastating Mrs. O." Mrs. O would not dare interrupt them for fear of "devastating mother." She is deathly afraid of her mother's "hysterics."

Helen in particular has felt overwhelmed and depressed by the enforced visits. According to her, the grandparents speak of nothing but scholastic achievement and rave about her eighteen-year-old male cousin who is going to Yale. When Helen and this cousin were leaving for college last year, their grandparents gave them a sending off party. But only the cousin's name was on the cake. No one in Helen's family took issue with the grandmother, although they were all aware of the glaring omission.

The maternal grandmother is much closer to the older sister's children (two boys and a girl) than to Helen and Judy. Mrs. O pretends this does not bother her; it does. Her sister's family lived with the grandparents for five years after the sister's husband died.

None of the relatives was informed of Helen's relationship with Joe or the two abortions. The parents were forced into revealing her marriage only after she disappeared. The maternal grandparents were enraged that they were not informed earlier, feeling they could have prevented the whole thing.

The father is the middle child in a family of three boys. His father was a salesman who owned a clothing store at one time, which he lost during the depression. Mr. O quit school to work to support the family. Very little of significance can be gleaned about his family relationships because of his positive thinking approach to life. He insists he had a happy childhood and a good relationship with both parents and siblings. At present he has a warm, affectionate but not overly involved relationship with his parents. The family sees them about once a month. Helen and Judy are fond of them.

External Organization

SOCIAL FUNCTIONING, VALUES, AND STRIVINGS

The values of this family are conventional, constricted, and tightly bound up with the older generation. The father has inherited the salesman's approach to life from his own father. The mother is still trying to fulfill the standards and expectations of her parents through the performance of her children. Helen wanted to get a secretarial job after high school, but allowed her mother to maneuver her into college. She stayed one semester, hated the experience and failed every subject. She is currently performing well at a secretarial job.

Family Diagnosis

This family illustrates in graphic terms the transmission of pathology from one generation to another. The family is isolated, feeds on itself, and reinforces a regressive, destructive, symbiotic pattern. Mrs. O duplicates in her own family the mother-daughter-sister triangle she experienced in her original family. Mrs. O unconsciously identified Helen with her older sister, molding her through her anticipatory attitudes into her sister's image. Helen's statement, "I could never be myself at home," indicates the influence of the sister's ghost. She proved to her mother just how much of a "slouch" she could be since this was what was expected of her. This is indicated in Helen's retort regarding Joe. "Since you disapproved of Jerry I thought I'd bring you someone who was really good enough for me." Her pregnancies were a desperate attempt to establish her identity as a person and free herself from the symbiotic tie with her mother. One cannot underestimate their shock value either. They served as a temporary means of smashing her parents' denial. From the feeling in the interviews, Helen's unspoken bitter communication seems to be "Stop pretending; sex exists; it's here in my belly. Hostility exists; I hate you. Jealousy exists; you prefer my sister. Death exists; I feel suicidal. I exist; I'm not your sister."

The part the father has played in Helen's acting out is not clear except by virtue of his absence as a person who might have intervened to dilute the relationship between Helen and her mother. Being afraid and bewildered by these strange creatures, women, he withdrew from the fray, giving Helen little support.

Although Judy seems to be functioning well socially and scholastically, she shows signs of nervousness and anxiety. Her job as mediator between Helen and her mother is proving too big a burden for her.

(Conclusions

In this essay we have outlined a perspective on the relations of the concept of family diagnosis to clinical process. In our view, family diagnosis and family therapy are twin processes, each dependent on the other. We have described here our version of a clinician's encounter with a troubled family. The functions of observing, conceptualizing, and interpreting relevant emotional events are inherent in the nature of this encounter. The testing of clinical hunches, step by step, against the existing interpersonal realities leads to hypotheses concerning the relations of family transaction and individual adaptation. We have presented here a conceptual framework for family diagnosis, a guide that enables us to compare and contrast family types, and have illustrated these themes with clinical examples.

(Bibliography

1. ACKERMAN, N. W. *The Psychodynamics of Family Life.* New York: Basic Books, 1958.

2. ———. "Family Psychotherapy: Theory and Practice." *American Journal of Psychotherapy,* 20, no. 3 (1966).

3. ———. *Treating the Troubled Family.* New York: Basic Books, 1966.

4. ———. "The Role of the Family in the Emergence of Child Disorders." In E. Miller, ed., *Foundations of Child Psychiatry.* New York: Pergamon Press, 1968.

5. ———, and BEHRENS, M. L. "A Study of Family Diagnosis." *American Journal of Orthopsychiatry,* 26, no. 1 (January 1956).

6. ———, PAPP, P., and PROSKY, P. "Childhood Disorders and Interlocking Pathology in Family Relationships." In *International Yearbook for Child Psychiatry.* Vol. 1. *The Child in His Family.* New York: Wiley, 1970.

7. ———, and SOBEL, R. "Family Diagnosis: An Approach to the Pre-School Child," *American Journal of Orthopsychiatry,* 20, no. 4 (October 1950).

8. COLES, R. "Profile of Erik H. Erikson. *The New Yorker,* November 14, 1970.

9. STEIN, I. L. Systems Theory and Casework. Unpublished monograph.

CHAPTER 3

DISORDERS OF
EARLY CHILDHOOD

Peter B. Neubauer

❰ Problems in the Establishment of Diagnosis

CHILD PSYCHIATRY is a comparatively new discipline. It is still struggling against the effort to apply to children the experiences and diagnostic categories that have been established for adult patients. At the same time, over the last decades, and in this field more than in any other in psychiatry, extraordinary progress has been made: A large number of discoveries have made child psychiatry a discipline in which research, and the development of new clinical techniques, have been increasingly gaining in significance. Moreover, the now general recognition of the existence of early childhood pathology, along with the difficulties encountered in the establishment of corrective measures later in life, have made services for the very young child a national priority.

During World War II, when large sections of the population were being drawn into military service, the nation became alerted to the great numbers of people who, for various health reasons, were unable to fulfill the requirements for induction; many were simply incapable of standing the stresses of army life and combat. This discovery contributed to a marked increase in mental health services. Similarly, the emerging national awareness of the fact that large portions of the population live at less than minimal standards has also brought with it recognition of the great numbers of children who are living under conditions of deprivation, with consequent serious impact on their development. Legislation was introduced to cope with this problem, and for the first time programs were devised for services to children during the first years of life.

This thrust toward social action on behalf of sections of the population that had hitherto not been reached by traditional mental health services challenged the child psychiatrists and members of allied professions to extend their knowledge in many new directions. New disorders were described stemming from a confluence of economic, nutritional, maturational, and environmental dysfunction; new techniques of treatment had to be devised; and new forms of delivery of services became essential. This has made it even more important for a sound clinical base to be established, resting of necessity on the appropriate diagnostic assessment of young children.

The younger the child, the more often do we find that our existing diagnostic categories are not appropriate for the complex clinical picture. The more differentiated the mental and psychic apparatus, the greater the degree of independence that it has achieved from maturational and environmental influences, the more precisely are we able to define psychic and mental dysfunction. Conversely, any nutritional imbalance, or any biological disorder in early life, has an immediate impact on psychic and mental development. Similarly, environmental influences on the child's emotional life will show direct effects in physiological functioning as well as having an impact on further development.

Thus, it is not surprising that the history of the establishment of early disorders reveals that some investigators, depending on their preferences, will stress either the neurophysiological or the biological components as the primary source of the disorder, whereas others will be far more impressed by the influence on the child of the specific environment, ascribing to it pathogenic powers as a way of explaining the most serious emotional disorders. Most clinicians and researchers have accepted the proposition that innate constitutional forces are in continuous interplay with the environment, and that very often the outcome is decided by both factors. But, as the search goes on for the primary etiological factor, a clearer distinction between causation and outcome has been found to be needed. That is to say, the prognosis in itself cannot make a sufficient explanatory contribution to the etiology.

⟨ The Developmental Factor

Infant observation, profile assessments, and research in early development have given us increasing information about ego formation and its relationship to drive expressions and to the variety of maturational factors that are operative and enter in sequence into the process of psychic organization. The role played by ego equipment and by the emerging ego function is capable of being seen from the beginning in its interplay with the object.

Early interest focused on the evolution of the infantile neurosis—the drama and fate of the particular oedipal conflict, as well as the crystallizations resulting from the subsequent emergence of the superego. Interest also became directed toward preoedipal contributions, derived from earlier fixation points, and the effects these had on shaping the infantile neurosis, as well as character formation. These questions were explored mainly in terms of the conflict between instinctual drives and ego and superego forces, along with the resolutions arrived at in relation to that conflict. At the same time, S. Freud[23,24] was always interested in constitutional contributions, those that were derived both from the varying strengths of inborn drives and from the innate endowment and proclivities of the ego, insofar as these might influence the course of later conflicts and also their resolution. Hartmann's[32] concept of autonomous ego factors that exerted their own independent impact on developmental processes added to this a further dimension, in terms of the intertwining of these ego factors with the structures that were formed out of conflict.

During recent years, interest has increasingly turned toward the intricate details of the preoedipal organization of development, and in particular toward the processes of early ego formation. Two major contributions have been Erikson's[19] mapping out of the epigenetic sequence of phase development and of developing ego modalities and Margaret Mahler's[42] delineation of the processes of self-object differentiation through the vicissitudes of separation-individuation.

There has also been an efflorescence of infant studies, investigating the processes of the earliest evolution of psychic life, and particularly of incipient ego formation. Such studies too have focused on the effects of the infant's innate equipment (for example, activity type, tension-discharge patterns, or the particular infant's specific kind of perceptual sensitivity and discrimination) on the early evolution of ego organization. They have pointed to the highly complex way in which innate and maturing equipmental factors will relate to one another, as well as to the differing experiences offered by the environment. We are referring, of course, especially to the work in this field done by Kris,[38] Escalona,[20] Wolff,[76] and Spitz.[66] Crucial to this area of study is the monumental work done by Piaget in investigating the sequences of learning and of cognitive development, starting from earliest infancy.

The developmental point of view, that is, the observation of the processes of unfolding and of the interrelationship between maturation and the repeated interchange with, hopefully, a relatively consistent environment, permits us to see how the primitive regulatory mechanisms are increasingly differentiated, ordered, and systematized.

As we have attempted to identify more clearly the apparent sequence of stages—the organization and reorganization of libidinal phases and the concomitant maturational and ego components—we have come to enlarge our view of the role of conflict in development. We are now able to observe the many individual variations, reflecting innate predispositions, and with them the quantitative and qualitative imbalances of the drives as well as of ego equipment and ego functions. While still taking note of the object's influence, we also recognize the infant's own selectivity as to what he will react to and how, by which he is in effect codetermining what is to become his significant environment. Early perceptual preferences, differences in levels of threshold and motor energy, and variations in drive endowment all make possible an early impression of the child's strength and vulnerabilities in his interactions with his specific environment.

Such studies lead into two directions: (1) They provide us with a greater awareness of the many factors that have to be taken into account, as we attempt to follow the organizing and structuring development processes; (2) such data make it less easy to reduce later psychic conflicts to some simple psychic mechanism of infancy, such as introjection, incorporation, projection.

The great degree of individual variability that is operative from infancy on has begun to help us to more fully understand the relationship of symptoms and character disorders within the context of individual consultations.

Anna Freud[22] pointed to the psychosomatic matrix in terms of which the child's endowments and reactions can be understood. Annemarie Weil[72] spoke of a basic core, which attempts to explain those particular clusterings of factors that are specific for any individual child; these can be assessed very early, their importance lying in the fact that they tend to be stable and to have a determining influence on future development. The child's pathology is thus capable of being viewed within the context of these constellations.

Within this broad view of the interplay between internal conflicts and structural variations we are able to include individual variations in the developmental process itself. In addition to either the precocious or delayed mode of development, we have been able to see children in whom there is not only an overlapping of phases but situations where early conflicts and structures continue to exist alongside later ones or become interwoven with them. While the progressive thrust continues, phase specificity does not take place; in other words, phallic primacy is not achieved. This, of course, affects the formation of the infantile neurosis, as well as the treatment of these children during prelatency.

Our awareness of multiple inter- and intrastructural interactions, and of the individual variability in this regard, has increased our ability to detect maturational and developmental deviations; faulty ego and equipment; atypical ego variations, resulting from either constitutional or congenital defects; deficient or inappropriate stimulation, or a combination of the two.

Any assessment of childhood disorders is, of necessity, in many ways bound to our notion of the normal developmental process. At present, our diagnostic categories are continuously in need of refinement, and very few of us are as yet satisfied with the usefulness or appropriateness of our present definitions. We need to study more intensively the sequences of developmental progression.

If we accept Anna Freud's proposition that one can use the primary task of childhood, namely, developmental progression, as a yardstick in order to decide on the health or pathology of a child, we thereby adopt a new way of arriving at an assessment of childhood disorders. Freud very early proposed the normal occurrence of the infantile neurosis, a proposition that implied that in our picture of normal development we must expect to include many problems, conflicts, symptoms, and even neurotic constellations. For as long as the child's development continues, various symptoms, rituals, compulsive manifestations, phobic phenomena, and so forth will be found to be part of those stresses that we can observe in young children and that are transitory in nature. Any decision, therefore, as to whether they are to be regarded as within the range of normal expectations must rest on a determination of whether they are likely to last longer, without being resolved by succeeding stages and thus interfering with further development. Furthermore, even the developmental process itself may be pathological, and today we have a number of categories that address themselves to this condition.

⟨ Individual Variations in Development

An outline of normal development, or of developmental deviations would be incomplete without a consideration of individual variations in development such as takes cognizance of the variety of modalities of development as well as the variety of environments in which development takes place. These developmental variations have their source in factors of time and structure formation. Is development proceeding according to the expected timetable, or does it show signs of cautiousness or slowness? Furthermore, is the rate of development even in all areas of psychic development, or are certain faculties emerging with different speed?

Uneven development and maturation are very often observed, and within certain limits they belong among the individual variations. The structural aspect, which addresses itself to the formation of psychic function, is based on our assumption of stages of development. Instead, we very often see overlapping of stages, in which earlier psychic organization is carried into the next succeeding stage without there being any signs of fixation, or in which, at a later stage, psychic functioning from earlier stages continues to exist alongside the stage-appropriate function.

Another way of looking at individual variation is based on a broader concept, which includes the developmental aspects mentioned previously but also takes into account a variety of personality characteristics. This concept has to do with the temperament of the child.[14] Seven variables are regarded as being characteristic components in the definition of temperament, and the question of normality or abnormality in an individual case is tested against the constellation of these factors. Though we have thus made progress in our ability to define the individual condition, we have not proceeded with similar distinction toward a solution of how to assess the environment in which the child develops and to which he has to adapt. Family diagnoses and family dynamics have been in the foreground of our interest for a long time, but attempts to assess those variables that have a specific influence on the child at various stages have not yet brought about a profiling of the environment. Hopefully, in the future, this will be part of our overall assessment of the child.

In addition, we have become quite aware of the developmental differences between boys and girls, and thus we now know that a single outline of development, designed to cover both, may distort our capacity for assessing a child appropriately. New discoveries as to the role of gender in development seem very promising.

❲ Infantile Neurosis

The concept of infantile neurosis has played a major historical role in the establishment of childhood disorders. It was arrived at, during the earliest period of psychoanalysis, by way of reconstruction of the childhood of those adults who were coming into treatment. Freud therefore put forward the proposition that every adult neurosis can be traced to an infantile neurosis. This proposition implies, first, that no adult neurosis occurred later in life without first having existed in early childhood and, second, that the infantile neurosis is part of normal development. This gave significant weight to the understanding of early pathology and to a recognition of the need to investigate the development of children during the first years of life.

We define neurosis in terms of those conflicts that arise during the oedipal stage of development. This means (1) that superego, ego, and id derivatives are involved in the conflict; (2) that the child is unable to arrive at a resolution of the conflict; and (3) that specific symptoms emerge as part of the compromise formation between the internal and external struggle. In order for a neurosis to be formed, the conflict has to arise out of an anticipation of punishment and guilt at a level of social evolution. The symptom picture that can be observed varies greatly; at times, the variability can be greater among children than among adults. Later psychic structuring and patterning of psychic life has the effect of stabilizing these symptoms and thereby reducing their variability. The younger the child, the more often do we find changes in symptomatology. Old symptoms may disappear and new ones emerge, as new compromise solutions are established. Various forms of phobic manifestations, obsessive compulsive phenomena, habit and conduct disorders may reach the neurotic level. The diagnosis of this disorder therefore rests on our ability to determine what characteristics we will assign to the neurosis.

The proposition that every adult neurosis is based on an infantile one does not imply that every infantile neurosis has to lead to an adult neurosis. The possibility of a spontaneous cure or of a change in this disorder during childhood to a regressive state of earlier pathology also has to be considered. Thus, during prelatency, diagnosis of an infantile neurosis does not imply a prognostic view that it will inevitably lead to an adult disorder, and this raises the question of whether and when treatment is indicated.

When Freud formulated this clinical picture in the cases of Little Hans and the Wolfman, he made a significant contribution to our understanding of early childhood pathology. Today we are able to add to his original clinical formulation a clearer view of those developmental disorders that precede the infantile neurosis and that both influence its emergence and color the clinical picture of the neurotic pathology that is found between the ages of four and six. We now assume that, when an infantile neurosis occurs, pathology at earlier levels of development is a necessary precondition for its evolvement. Just as Freud traced the adult to the infantile neurosis, so we now trace the infantile neurosis to earlier pathological conditions. This widened view indicates the importance of earlier diagnostic evaluations. Such an evaluation will affect the decision as to the choice of treatment and reveals the need to outline treatment interventions that are able to assist the child during the earlier years of life.

❲ Infantile Autism

During 1943 Kanner[35] proposed the diagnosis of infantile autism for a group of children, as differentiated from the overall classification of childhood schizophrenia. This step was significant in that it initiated the classification of children with psychoses into subgroupings and thus opened up a new search for etiologies and differential treatment procedures. At the same time, a review of the literature will reveal the many questions that are still unsettled in our understanding of this and similar disorders. One can utilize Kanner's initial category in order to highlight the state in which we find ourselves at present, in terms of the manifold views that authors hold when they are examining psychotic disorders of early childhood.

On a descriptive level, Kanner's outline was clear enough. He spoke about the affective disorder (most often the absence of affect); the ensuing difficulties in speech development and in the thinking processes; the hypersensitivity to various sensory modalities, or the absence of responses to normal sensory stimuli together with the obsessive need for the preservation of sameness; the attachment to inanimate objects; and the inability to use the mother for orienting and for organizing psychic structuring. Kanner related this condition to an inborn defect; but soon others were using this term in order to refer to less severe disorders. With the broadening of the knowledge of symptomatology, researchers have included such disorders as schizophrenia and many others that are simply labelled "atypical." Instead of maintaining the specific and somewhat circumscribed conditions of early infantile autism, we have extended them to other autistic mechanisms and thereby confused the diagnostic process.

Similarly, we now find a wide variety of opinions as to the etiology of this disorder. Kanner assumed an inborn defect, but he did add to it the possibility of parental refrigeration, that is, an environmental factor that contributes to the clinical picture. Some writers consider autism to be the result of a diffuse encephalopathy or of some form of brain damage encountered during pregnancy. Others have suggested that one may be able to differentiate two forms of infantile autism: one based on a constitutional disorder; the other the result of severe environmental interference with the child's development. If one follows Kanner's original proposition, one has to be clear that the term "autism" does not refer there to a schizoid symptom, connoting withdrawal or detachment, but rather to a syndrome that permits the differentiation of infantile psychosis from infantile autism. Without recognition of these differences, one may lose the significance of this diagnosis. Insistence on maintaining this differential diagnosis will help to distinguish between those disorders based on interpersonal difficulties and those that stem from a different core, in this somatopsychological makeup of the child. It is clear that the outcome of a disorder will always depend on the interplay of the child's personality structure with the environment in which it is involved and that the prognostic possibilities also depend on the environment in which the child's problems are expressed. Yet this interplay of factors should not obscure the clarification that has been attained with regard to the primary etiology, nor should it minimize the role played by environmental conditions in determining the outcome.

A study of the epidemiology of infantile autism,[68] carried out by assessing an entire state population under twelve, has shown how rare this condition actually is. Schizophrenia and infantile autism together gave a prevalence of 3.1 per 10,000 children. The 280 patients fell into three groups: infantile autism (25 per cent), psychosis of childhood (57 per cent), and psychosis complicated by organicity (18 per cent). Infantile autism was thus very rare, with a prevalence of 0.7 per 10,000 children. This is particularly so if the meaning of this diagnostic category is maintained, rather than being changed by regarding infantile autism as a symptom rather than as a disease entity.

❲ Developmental Deviations

Great progress has been made over the last decades in the classification of children's disorders through an understanding of those changes that are owing to deviations in the developmental process itself. The importance of being able to differentiate these disorders from ego disorders or from those that are based on conflicts, accompanied by symptom formations, lies in the fact that the prognostic implications as well as the choice of treatment will be affected by it.

When we address ourselves to the developmental process, we generally refer to its essential aspects, the time factor as well as psychic structure formation. Deviations can occur that involve either of these components or a combination of the two. For quite some time now it has been recognized that some children show a cautious or slow development, whereas others show unevenness as to the speed of development; that is to say, at different periods of development there may be a different rate of development, as the result either of acceleration or of the slowing down of progression.

The developmental factor may be connected with the maturational sequences, in which central nervous system maturation, along with its neuromuscular expressions, may follow various rates, within or outside the normal range. The pediatrician has long studied the physical growth patterns of children and established certain variations in that regard within and outside the norm. We know that puberty may exercise a significant influence, thus indicating the role that hormonal changes can play in maturation and, with it, in psychic development.

One can today outline quite early a timetable for development and thus what should be the individual rate of development during the first years of life. Psychic structuring is generally assumed to proceed according to phases or stages of development. Along with this concept goes the assumption that, with the establishment of new hierarchies in psychic organization, there is a discontinuation of earlier psychic structure. It has been recognized that we can often find an overlapping of phases within the normal range; but one can also find children in whom there is a total absence of phase distinction, so that early and later stages appear together for a long period of time. Furthermore, one can outline those developmental variations in which earlier developmental organization exists side by side with later ones.

Moreover, one can see variations expressed in the progression-regression balance of a child. There are those children who show a wide swing in both the forward movement of development and regressive trends, whereas other children show a very narrow range of developmental mobility, in which the maintenance of function is closely held to and the psychic structure shows signs of rigidity. Thus, one could refer to this as the "elasticity factor" in development.

⟪ Ego Deviation

In addition to developmental variations, some writers have outlined ego deviations that have to do with unevenness in areas of psychic function. Thus, one can observe children with very low or very high thresholds in the sensory modalities, so that their reactions to sound, light, or touch are outside the norm. Such children may respond to normal stimuli with abnormal sensitivity, fright reactions, and anxieties or with gestures of avoidance of the stimulus. There are others in whom normal contact with the child has not reached a high enough degree of intensity to stimulate the child sufficiently into an appropriate interaction with his environment. If one extends this latter ego deviation, one then approaches categories that are close to infantile autism or other psychotic disorders. We are not referring here to a range of response, from the more normal to the more pathological, such as would encompass all forms of disorders and would indicate that, the same set of factors being always operative, the diagnosis is to be determined by the degree of intensity of the pathology. What we are maintaining is rather the notion of a clear differentiation of diseases, based on etiology as well as on a clustering of symptoms, in spite of the fact that we are able to find similarities in clinical symptomatology.

Many decades ago, children were being categorized by reference to their *activity patterns*. In a group of children studied from infancy on or even during their uterine life, hypermotility was found to be characteristic of the children's functioning, along with a tendency for that characteristic to maintain itself throughout childhood. Some of these have been referred to as congenital activity patterns, with modality of function that could be recognized early and that later on led to a great range of difficulties in social interaction and social behavior. Such forms of hyperactivity must be differentiated from those that are based on a recognizable organic pathology, in which the motility disorder emerges as a symptom of cerebral pathology. Follow-up studies[25] of these children show that the majority show a modification of this abnormal deviation during adolescence, whereas those in whom it is the organic component that is significant continue to maintain impulse disorders and other discharge phenomena in the motor area for a more protracted period of time.

Similarly, one can outline developmental deviations in the area of the affective life of the children. Pleasure-displeasure responses, the early smile, and the degree of stranger reaction indicate variations in the affective modality of psychic life. The threshold component discussed earlier in connection with sensory stimuli seems here to be significant as well in the affective area. There are affect-placid children and there are those with a wide range of affective responses. At times, it is difficult to be certain whether one is dealing primarily with a developmental deviation in the emotional area or whether this is in itself a response to deviations in the area of sensory modalities (it could even be a mixture of both). Such deviations will have a strong effect on the degree of interrelationship with the mother, with its varied forms of object interaction. Whereas some children maintain a strong interplay cathexis with the mother, others seem to have a wider scanning or interplay with the environment and are thus less bound to the mother as the sole source of gratification.

At the extreme, we find the case of an individual whose variations are described by Mahler[41] as the "symbiotic child." The deviations of the "symbiotic child" are rooted in the separation-individuation process. There are children in whom the smile appears either very early or quite late and children in whom the intensity of pleasure or displeasure is quite great, so that the stranger reaction can lead to panic and clinging. In these children, the necessary separation from the mother, during their toddler phase, cannot be negotiated, in that the child shows extreme fear of the loss of the object. These deviations will have an effect on imitation and identification with the object, so that anticipation of events and sequences will not lead to providing regularity and continuity in psychic function. These clusterings of symptoms in connection with the mother can of course be reinforced by the mother's attitude; in severe cases, they may even be the effect of her pathology. We are addressing ourselves here to variations that seem to stem primarily from the child's innate equipment and psychic apparatus, though they manifest themselves in the interplay with the environment in its specific forms. Annemarie Weil[71] suggested which groups of children fall within these categories of deviational development.

The Atypical Child

This category refers to those disorders that can be observed in infancy as affecting some specific ego function. These children show a variety of symptoms in the areas of the development of thinking, language development, motility controls, reality testing, social judgment, and defensive psychic organization. They are similar to children who have been affected by various forms of psychosis in childhood; but once again it is important to differentiate these groups and to establish specific categories for them.

The absence of a psychotic process, and the prognosis of these conditions, as well as the early beginning, permit such a differentiation. At times, what we see is a clustering that points to a deviation in maturation; one example of this is late language development. When it does finally take place, the child's thinking indicates an undue influence on the part of primary-process qualities. There seem to be difficulties in differentiating those stimuli that have arisen in the internal psychic life from those that come from the outside, and thus reality testing is very often affected. What the child sees as real, and what he wishes or feels, emerge only very slowly. Fears reach a severe level of intensity, to the extent that one part of the clinical picture is early phobic manifestations, with avoidance of situations and undue clinging to the mother. At times, one can observe in the child an inability to move from the concrete to the more abstract, and thus to reliable concept formation. One gets the impression that it may be the integrative or synthesizing function of the ego that has been primarily impaired.

Similarly, psychic control over impulses and motility may be involved. What is observed as restlessness may be the sign of a continuous high level of anxiety. At times, infants with this disorder can be comforted only in the arms of the caretaker; at other times, they show very strong resistance to any tactile closeness, as if the influence of the mother had already gone beyond the limits of their tolerance. Bowel control may be delayed, and one may find an erratic symptomatology. Among those functions that have suffered may be the process of differentiating internal and external life, developing logical sequences and concepts, establishment of the sense of time and sex differentiation. Frequently, these atypical children show hypersensitivity in certain areas, for example, to sound or to light; they may respond with panic to silence, to the sounds of the vacuum cleaner, or to the flushing of the toilet. They may be finicky in their food selection, and show an early development of food fads. Enumeration of these clinical manifestations may remind us how closely they resemble those symptom formations that we associate with schizophrenia in childhood. Yet these symptoms, as part of atypical development, may at times be quite mild; they may go hand in hand with many strengths in the child, and they may not impair progression in development, at least with regard to stage sequences, nor be connected with strong regressive phenomena or fixations. Basically, it is insufficiency or inability in areas of ego function that is characteristic. The child may slowly evolve

his own corrective measures, which, as other aspects of the psychic equipment become strengthened, may in turn lead to the development of appropriate compensatory measures.

⟦ Personality Disorders

The category of personality disorders has great significance for that part of childhood when psychic organization and function have been sufficiently established. Still, it would be a mistake not to use it and to make its diagnosis, since it is possible very early to determine significant character and personality traits that are already deviant from the normal. Today we assume that these personality disorders stem from the specific makeup of the child, the child's preferred employment of defense mechanisms, and the transmission of conflicts from parent to child.

Within this disorder there are many subcategories. At times, it is possible to determine those clearly (for instance, the obsessive-compulsive personality type or the overdependent or overly independent child); but most often we find the various disorders commingled, with the result that hysterical and anxiety reactions, together with some compulsive features, occur concomitantly. We can find, at about the age of three, a specific core constellation, which is determined by both the healthy and the abnormal psychic functioning of the child, in which symptoms, character traits and specific ego functions together determine the direction of further development. Stability of function is a prerequisite for the ascription of personality disorders, since in this category we assume that the disorder has become part of the defense system and the adaptive process. Since we are indeed able to discover these conditions quite early, it is important to make such an assessment and to initiate the appropriate treatment. We have learned about the existence of a continual change of symptom pictures in young children, that is, that while the personality disorder can be described, the symptom pictures within it can shift.

At times, these personality malfunctions interfere with further development, so that the stage of oedipal organization or of latency cannot take place in appropriate sequence. At other times, these disorders are modified by later stages; or the child does engage in further psychic organization, but brings to it the earlier deviations.

The successful assessment of large numbers of children shows how frequently one is able to make these diagnoses. In the past, the diagnosis was formulated in relation to those manifestations that were a direct outcome of conflicts in oral, anal, phallic, or oedipal constellations. One therefore used the diagnosis of oral-anal-phallic character disorders. Outlines and descriptions were made early of incorporative greediness or oral aggressivity; compulsiveness in connection with either cleanliness-orderliness or its opposite as the result of anal conflicts.

(Primary Behavior Disorders

In addition, we have a diagnosis of primary behavior disorders in which the internalization of the process has not yet been established. Psychic organization from the higher oedipal conflict has yet not added to those psychic functions that deal with guilt and social consciousness.

Originally, the category of primary behavior disorder was divided into two parts: (1) habit disorders and (2) conduct disorders. The category of habit disorders refers to those difficulties related primarily to body function, such as thumb sucking, nail biting, sleep disorders, and excessive masturbation, whereas that of conduct disorders refers to the behavior of the child in relation to his environment, for example, the biting child, the aggressive child, and the overdependent child. These forms of behavior have been regarded as being the consequence of the child's experience and, in particular, inappropriate care by the parents. Since these symptoms tended to be part of the child's functioning for a long period of time (at times, over a number of

years) they had to be separated from the category of reactive disorders.

(Reactive Disorders

Under the category of reactive disorders, we observe that the child is showing a strong and abnormal response to a specific event, but we assume that that response is transient in nature. The transitory aspect of the disorder can be related to the fact that the environmental condition may change to normal, or that the child may be able, after a comparatively short period of time, to find a more normal adaptive response. Reactive responses may be expressed in a number of different ways: We may find a depression in early childhood, in which the affect is dulled, there is a deceleration of the function of the child, the thriving developmental pull is retarded, or the somatic vegetative function of the child is slowed down. It may be important to recognize the possibility of a state of depression in young children and not to neglect its significance, since very often the quiet state of the child to which one would otherwise refer may actually conceal an underlying depression.

The reactive response of some children may constitute a regression to earlier modes of function, for instance, at a time when a sibling is born; other children may respond to that same situation with aggressivity, irritability, or increased dependency. It is clear that, in all areas of psychic function, we may find symptom formation to be dependent on the age of the child, as well as on his psychic development up to that time.

Thus we have learned to pay particular attention to those events in the life of the young child that may have a strong, or even decisive, influence on further development. This may be, for example, the death or absence of a parent, particularly the mother, that is, the loss of the caretaking person. It may be connected with particular handicapping illnesses on the part of the child himself. The emotional condition of the mother—her own illness, which may handicap her in her functioning with the child; her depression or other forms of mental illnesses—may also have a crucial effect on the early years of the child. There are a host of circumstances that have direct relevance to the child's early development; in dealing with these, early intervention on a primary or secondary level will be essential, and the resources and mechanisms for it should be part of the community facilities.

Reactive disorders are very often discussed today under the headings of *crisis conditions* and *interventions*. One assumes here that the cause of the interference in parent-child relationship has occurred suddenly and that therefore there are no advance preparations available for the care of the child. Yet such by no means uncommon events as the death of a parent or acute hospitalization may create a serious upheaval in the child's life, particularly among children in those families for whom the prevailing economic and social conditions do not permit easy solutions or substitute measures.

There are a good many studies dealing with these conditions, ranging from Spitz's anaclitic depression[63] and hospitalism[62] to interferences during the first few years of life as the result of various depriving conditions. The experienced observer will be able to discover and study these various forms of interference with normal development, one good example being the findings that have been made in connection with the separation of the young child from the mother.

([Principles of Treatment

It may be advisable to discuss the modes of psychiatric intervention under one single heading, instead of in relation to each psychiatric disorder. This will avoid needless repetition, and it will also make for an understanding of the therapeutic approach, which may be similar in relation to a number of different symptom formations. Moreover, there is often a similar treatment for disorders that share basic dynamic constellations.

1. The younger the child, the more the treatment approach will be based on the need for supporting the environment that has direct responsibility for the care of the child. Thus, one will help the mother to provide the appropriate conditions for modifying or correcting the child's disorder. If the mother proves to be unable to use such assistance, or is unavailable, one would then have to consider that other caretakers need to be brought in in order to provide such function. It is clear, therefore, that our ability to help will greatly depend on the parent's ability to cooperate and to participate in the intervention that is required for the child.

2. It is necessary, when we outline the treatment program, for us to assess the parents' capacity for collaborating with the program, in addition to making an assessment of the pathology of the child.

In addition to relying on the participation of parents in our efforts to carry out an appropriate treatment program, we have become more aware that we have to involve community participation. In our present social climate, the outlining of needs for services by the community, the feasibility of the programs, and the mobilization of resources for these programs have all become essential factors when one is planning services designed to reach large groups of those children who are at present outside of the orbit of appropriate care. Again, this becomes particularly significant with regard to services for children during their first years of life. Collaboration with well-baby clinics, outpatient departments of hospitals, community clinics, prenursery and nursery facilities, day-care centers and so forth is an essential condition for success in these efforts. It is necessary if we are to detect those children who are in need of such services and to build in a clinical arm for those children whose pathology warrants specialized programming.

3. To the degree that the child has reached a more stable psychic organization and that the child's difficulties have become internalized, that is, have influenced defensive patterning and have resulted in symptom formations based on intrapsychic conflict, one is able to address oneself directly to the child's psychic life.

4. It is in the American tradition of child guidance that the individual therapeutic approach to the child is coordinated with the guidance or treatment of the parents and is carried out in collaboration with the essential persons in the child's life. Often enough, a number of different combinations are made in which a teacher or a nurse provides appropriate developmental stimulation for the child, oriented toward the correction of ego function, while individual therapy may at the same time attempt to alter the internal psychic conditions. These combinations may vary in accordance with the therapeutic needs of the child and with the availability of the resources needed to fulfill such a program. We have only begun to make available adequate professional assistance for the correction of early psychiatric disorders; there is a great need to rapidly increase the training of people from various professions for effective participation in treatment programs for the very young child. There is also a need for adequate caretaking programs for children, as is now established in the Department of Welfare, for those children who do not have available a family condition that can be guaranteed to provide for the minimal care of the child. If these programs are appropriate, they may be of great help; but they cannot take the place of the special skill that is necessary to help those children who already show signs of special psychiatric conditions.

One essential prerequisite for carrying out these functions in early childhood is a knowledge of child development. One must be able to provide assistance to the developmental progression of the child by buttressing the thriving components, and to do this effectively one has to be acquainted with the milestones in developmental progression. The ability of the child during the first year of life to achieve an attachment to the mother, along with the emergence of the smile or the stranger reaction, becomes one of the significant criteria by which one observes and measures development.

5. One could outline treatment procedures in accordance with the degree to which the child's disorder either is based on innate or congenital conditions or is the result of reaction to environmental influences. There is convincing evidence that, even if one has to deal with constitutional disorders or with diagnostic categories whose etiologies are unknown, one nevertheless does not have to, for that reason, feel helpless with regard to the possibilities for treatment; one can rely on the child's responsiveness to his environmental conditions, which may make the margin of difference for his further development. Even in the event of the most serious early pathology, one has the right to expect that some maturation, and with it some form of development, will take place. Without a full assessment of this capacity of the child, therefore, a capacity that will reveal itself only over a period of time, it would be inappropriate to adopt a nihilistic treatment approach.

We have already described above the serious disabilities of the child with infantile autism (see page 55); the general lack of responsiveness; the turn toward inanimate objects for stimulation; and the insistence on sameness and repetitiveness. Experience with these children is likely to make the establishment of any treatment program seem extraordinarily difficult: Since the etiology of the illness is unknown, we are unable, it would appear, to construct an appropriate treatment program. Yet, one can recommend that, precisely in recognition of these behavioral problems, one can utilize these very functions to provide stimulation at the level of the present psychic organization. The manipulation of inanimate objects by an adult, for example, may slowly gain in significance; over a period of time, a shift may occur in the child from activities engaged in solely with the inanimate world to include as well the person who will then have the opportunity to bring the social influences to bear on the child. A caretaker who is specially skilled in these functions can be introduced into the child's environment from infancy on.

It is important that the child not be stimulated in directions that are, in fact, beyond his capacities and that stimuli not be introduced in such a way as to create displeasure and discomfort, for that will surely counteract their usefulness. The reason why the normal environment is very often inappropriate for these children is that it exposes them to a world that does not fit their actual condition and that will therefore increase, instead of diminish, the gaps between psychic organization and environmental conditions. It is very often impossible to create such a special environment in the home, since it would have too great an effect on the living milieu of all the family members involved.

This principle of therapy is applicable not only to infantile autism but also to the symbiotic condition, as well as to deficiency syndromes, maturational unevennesses, and developmental deviations, except that, when the child's condition is less serious, one is very often able to provide the appropriate therapeutic milieu within the home. Special treatment techniques have been developed and applied to children who are suffering from developmental fixations and who therefore require a special form of intervention by a trained person, who will spend many hours with him in order to provide the appropriate stimulation. Dr. Alpert's[1] corrective object relations program provided just such a technique, based on the following treatment processes:

1. A special form of object relationship occurs. While the child permits the therapist to provide need satisfaction, he also recovers the wish for the mother, the hitherto distant and unavailable adult. In this relationship with the therapist, the child reexperiences the loss, the frustration, and the disappointments. It is the task of the special teacher to satisfy the child's need and, at the same time, to make possible not only the testing of the availability of the original primary object but also the emergence of longing for her. During this period, the special teacher has to be readily available, when and as she is needed.

2. Separation and differentiation processes become involved in the relationship to the therapist, as well as to the environment. In this step, orientation toward the outside world, both spatially and in terms of relations to both adults and peers, becomes one part of the practicing activities of the child. The teacher supports this activity by verbal reinforcement of the child's search and by the very fact of the dependability of the therapeutic relationship. The child is then able to progress from the initial one-to-one relationship to an increasingly expanding environment, and to experience for the first time certain steps in the separation-individuation process.

3. A change appears in the fantasy-reality balance. The child moves from the more autistic, self-contained fantasy world to one that not only includes the teacher but one in which the child expresses his fantasy, verbally or through direct action toward and with her. This step can now include reality testing, during the course of which the fantasies expressed by the child can be explored in terms of the capacity of the environment to fulfill them. At times, this reality testing will lead to an eruption of the child's frustration, resistance, and anger. As in normal development, such angry turning against the teacher may further the developmental progression of turning to other persons in the environment.

4. The capacity to form relationships with peers emerges on the strength of these hitherto unexperienced progressive developments. In these new relationships, too, the child expresses all the primitive mechanisms that we know from our work with younger children. There is imitation, incorporative identification, and the trying on of other children's functions, as evidence of newly found identity. Slowly, a more complex orchestration of relationships can be observed, which then leads to a more realistic interaction with other children and adults.

Dr. Alpert's form of therapeutic intervention is based on two factors. One factor carefully follows the child's own modalities of behavior when a one-to-one relationship is being established. No technique is imposed on the child, nor is any specific area selected for improvement. In the past, enrichment treatment was often either based on the problem of nutritional supplies or addressed itself to the cognitive or motor control areas. If Dr. Alpert's suggested therapy is followed carefully, we find that all these areas—the affective, the cognitive, and that of body skill functions—are included within the context of the social experience.

The second factor involves the fact that the therapist must be aware of the detailed steps of the developmental process. Since so much in this method is conditional on the effective return to a point of fixation, and then from there to the exercise of those developmental steps that had never before been taken by the child, it is essential that the appropriateness of the developmental experience be understood. Otherwise, various aspects of the child's behavior, which may be quite appropriate when they are seen as fulfilling the necessary task of developmental progression, may be regarded as pathological simply because they appear to be age-inappropriate. Moreover, those aspects of the child's activity that follow a line of developmental organization must be differentiated from those that are pathological in nature, being based on conflicts and experiences that may add to the child's differentiation syndrome. Nor can one assume, whatever the degree of developmental inhibition, that the possibilities of other emotional pathology are excluded.

This detailed description of a technique has been presented in order to highlight the fact that therapeutic intervention, to be effective, must be based on a clear knowledge of the developmental processes, as well as on carefully outlined technical maneuvers, and thus on trained personnel. The treatment of the atypical child with ego deviations and of those children in whom the developmental sequences deviate from the norm, will be based primarily on a clear profiling of the child's overall function and development. With these guarantees, detection of the specific area of disorder, whether it be motility, language development, thought process problems affecting judgment, or reality testing, can lead to the appropriate therapeutic maneuver.

Development of a treatment plan for developmental disorders requires that one observe the child's growth for a long period of time, in order to determine the specific forms of developmental deviation. At different periods, different modalities of intervention may have to be employed; retesting and reassessing will help to determine the degree of progress the child may be expected to make or the degree of the fixation and unevenness from which he is suffering. It is clear that such programs will have to draw on the skills of specialists in language correction or training, or of those who deal with perceptual problems in the visual area (problems that very often contribute to dyslexia), or of hearing specialists. Often enough children who suffer from these conditions have also developed conflicts at various levels of psychic organization, with preneurotic or neurotic symptoms and other personality disorders based on inappropriate conflict solutions. Therefore, one has to keep in mind the necessity for individual psychotherapy.

The criteria for effective therapy are by now well established: (1) The child must have developed the capacity to form a specific relationship with the therapist, and there must also be adequate capacity for verbal expression and for self-observation; (2) A certain degree of individuation and differentiation must have occurred; (3) A degree of internalization of conflicts is necessary.

Frequently, the child needs preparatory help by a teacher, a nurse, or some other specially trained person, in order to arrive at the evolvement of the conditions mentioned. It is clear that one can establish indications for the psychoanalysis of prelatency children. Neurotic conflicts, sometimes the infantile neurosis, which has already reached an intensity beyond the norm and is intervening with further development; obsessive-compulsive character disorders; the early appearance of sexual confusion; perversions; and a host of other symptoms have all been proven to yield to psychoanalytic treatment.

In the largest number of cases, it is only the intensive and careful exploration of the child's inner life—his fantasies, along with his defensive organization and its relationship to his external reality—that makes possible a clear diagnostic assessment of the child's condition.

(Bibliography

1. ALPERT, A. "Treatment of an Autistic Child: Introduction and Theoretical Discussion." *Journal of the American Academy of Child Psychiatry*, 3 (1964), 591–616.

2. ————. "Institutes on Programs for Children Without Families." *Journal of the American Academy of Child Psychiatry*, 4 (1965), 163.

3. ————, and KROWN, S. "Treatment of a Child with Severe Ego Restriction in a Therapeutic Nursery." *Psychoanalytic Study of the Child*, 8 (1953), 333–354.

4. ANTHONY, E. J. "An Experimental Approach to the Psychopathology of Childhood: Encopresis." *British Journal of Medical Psychology*, 30 (1957), 146.

5. BENDER, L. "Childhood Schizophrenia." *American Journal Orthopsychiatry*, 27 (1947), 68.

6. BOWLBY, J. *Maternal Care and Mental Health*. Geneva: World Health Organization, 1952.

7. ————. "The Nature of the Child's Tie to His Mother." *International Journal of Psycho-Analysis*, 39 (1958), 350.

8. CALDWELL, B. M. "The Effects of Infant Care." In M. Hoffman, ed., *Review of Child Development Research*. Vol. 1. New York: Russell Sage Foundation, 1964. Pp. 9–87.

9. ————, and RICHMOND, J. B. "Social Class Level and Stimulation Potential of the Home." In *Exceptional Infant*. Vol. 1. *The Normal Infant*. Seattle, Wash.: Special Child Publications, 1967. Pp. 453–466.

10. CAPLAN, G. *Principles of Preventive Psychiatry*. New York: Basic Books, 1964.

11. ————, ed. *Prevention of Mental Disorders in Children*. New York: Basic Books, 1961.

12. CAPLAN, R. B., and CAPLAN, G. *Psychiatry and the Community in Nineteenth-Century America*. New York: Basic Books, 1969.

13. CHESS, S., THOMAS, A., BIRCH, H. G., and HERTZIG, M. "A Longitudinal Study of Primary Reaction Patterns in Children." *Comprehensive Psychiatry*, 1 (1960), 103.

14. ————, THOMAS, A., RUTTER, M., and BIRCH, H. G. "Interaction of Temperament and Environment in the Production of Behavioral Disturbances in Children." *American Journal of Psychiatry*, 20 (1963), 142.

15. COMMITTEE ON CHILD PSYCHIATRY, GROUP FOR THE ADVANCEMENT OF PSYCHIATRY. *Psychopathological Disorders in Childhood: Theoretical Considerations and a Proposed Classification*. Report no. 62. New York, 1966.

16. EISENBERG, L., and KANNER, L. "Early Infantile Autism, 1943–1955." *American Journal of Orthopsychiatry*, 26 (1956), 556.

17. ERIKSON, E. H. "Ego Development and Historical Change." *Psychoanalytic Study of the Child*, 2 (1946), 359–396.

18. ————. "The Problem of Ego Identity." *Journal of the American Psychoanalytic Association*, 4 (1956), 56–121.

19. ————. "Identity and the Life Cycle." *Psychological Issues*, monogr. no. 1 (1959).

20. ESCALONA, S., and HEIDER, G. M. *Prediction and Outcome: A Study in Child Development*. New York: Basic Books, 1959.

21. FREUD, A. *The Ego and the Mechanisms of Defence*. New York: International Universities Press, 1946.

22. ————. *Normality and Pathology: Assessment of Development*. New York: International Universities Press, 1965.

23. FREUD, S. "Disposition to Obsessional Neurosis." In *Standard Edition*. Vol. 12. London: Hogarth, 1958. Pp. 317–326.

24. ————. "Types of Onset of Neuroses." In *Standard Edition*. Vol. 12. London: Hogarth, 1958. Pp. 231–238.

25. FRIES, M. E., and WOOLF, P. J. "The Influence of Constitutional Complex on Developmental Phases." In *Separation-Individuation*. New York: International Universities Press, 1971. Pp. 274–296.

26. ————, and WOOLF, P. J. "Some Hypotheses on the Role of the Congenital Activity Type in Personality Development." *Psychoanalytic Study of the Child*. 8 (1953), 48–63.

27. FURMAN, E. "An Ego Disturbance in a Young Child." *Psychoanalytic Study of the Child* 11 (1956), 312–336.

28. GELEERD, E. R. The Borderline States in Childhood and Adolescence. Paper presented to the New York Psychoanalytic Institute, 1958.

29. GLAZER, K., and EISENBERG, L. "Maternal Deprivation." *Pediatrics*, 18 (1956), 626.

30. GREENACRE, P. "Early Physical Determinants in the Development of the Sense of Iden-

tity." *Journal of the American Psycho-analytic Association*, 6 (1958), 612–627.

31. HARLEY, M. "Analysis of a Severely Disturbed Three-and-a-Half-Year-Old Boy." *Psychoanalytic Study of the Child*, 6 (1951), 206–234.

32. HARTMANN, H. "Problems of Infantile Neurosis: A Discussion." *Psychoanalytic Study of the Child*, 9 (1954), 16.

33. ———. "Technical Implications of Ego Psychology." In *Ego Psychology: The Problem of Adaptation*. New York: International Universities Press, 1958. Pp. 142–154.

34. JAHODA, M. *Current Concepts of Positive Mental Health*. New York: Basic Books, 1960.

35. KANNER, L. "Early Infantile Autism." *American Journal of Orthopsychiatry*, 19 (1949), 416.

36. ———, and EISENBERG, L. "Notes on the Follow-Up Studies of Autistic Children." In P. Hoch et al., eds., *Psychopathology of Childhood*. New York: Grune & Stratton, 1955. Pp. 227–239.

37. KAPLAN, D. M. "A Concept of Acute Situational Disorders." *Social Work*, 7 (1962), 15.

38. KRIS, E. "Development and Problems of Child Psychology." *Psychoanalytic Study of the Child*, 5 (1950), 18–46.

39. LEVY, D. M. "Primary Affect Hunger." *American Journal of Psychiatry*, 94 (1937), 643.

40. LUSTMAN, S. "Defense, Symptom, and Character." *Psychoanalytic Study of the Child*, 17 (1962), 216–244.

41. MAHLER, M. "Autism and Symbiosis: Two Extreme Disturbances of Identity." *International Journal of Psycho-Analysis*, 39 (1958), 77.

42. ———. *On Human Symbiosis and the Vicissitudes of Individuation: Infantile Psychosis*. Vol. 1. New York: International Universities Press, 1968.

43. NEUBAUER, P. B. "Psychoanalytic Contributions to the Nosology of Childhood Psychic Disorders." *Journal of the American Psychoanalytic Association*, 11 (1963), 595.

44. ———. "The Deviant Infant: Perceptual Misinformation." *Exceptional Infant*. Vol. 1. *The Normal Infant*. Seattle, Wash.: Special Child Publications, 1967. Pp. 415–426.

45. PAVENSTEDT, E. "History of a Child with Atypical Development, and Some Vicissitudes of His Treatment." In G. Caplan, ed., *Emotional Problems of Early Childhood*. New York: Basic Books, 1955. Pp. 379–405.

46. ———. "A Comparison of the Child-Rearing Environment of Upper-Lower and Very Low-Lower Class Families." *American Journal of Orthopsychiatry*, 35 (1965), 89–98.

47. PIAGET, J. *Structuralism*. New York: Basic Books, 1970.

48. POLLAK, O. "A Family Diagnosis Model." *Social Service Review*, 34 (1960), 19–28.

49. PROVENCE, S. "Some Determinants of Relevance of Stimuli in an Infant's Development." *Exceptional Infant*. Vol. 1. *The Normal Infant*. Seattle, Wash.: Special Child Publications, 1967. Pp. 443–452.

50. PRUGH, D. G. "Toward an Understanding of Psychosomatic Concepts in Relation to Illness in Children." In A. Solnit and S. Provence, eds., *Modern Perspectives in Child Development*. New York: International Universities Press, 1963. Pp. 246–367.

51. RANK, B. "Intensive Study and Treatment of Preschool Children Who Show Marked Personality Deviations, or 'Atypical Development,' and Their Parents." In G. Caplan, ed., *Emotional Problems of Early Childhood*. New York: Basic Books, 1955. Pp. 491–501.

52. RAPAPORT, D. "Cognitive Structures." In *Collected Papers*. New York: Basic Books, 1967. Pp. 631–664.

53. RITVO, S., and PROVENCE, S. "Form Perception and Imitation in Some Autistic Children: Diagnostic Findings and Their Contextual Interpretation." *Psychoanalytic Study of the Child*, 8 (1953), 155–161.

54. ———, and SOLNIT, A. J. "The Relationships of Early Identifications to Superego Formation." *International Journal of Psycho-Analysis*, 41 (1960), 295–300.

55. ROBERTSON, J. *Young Children in Hospitals*. New York: Basic Books, 1958.

56. ROCHLIN, G. "Loss and Restitution." *Psychoanalytic Study of the Child*, 8 (1953), 288–309.

57. SANDLER, J., and JOFFE, W. G. "Notes on Childhood Depression." *International Journal of Psycho-Analysis*, 46 (1965), 88.

58. SAYEGH, Y., and DENNIS, W. "The Effect of Supplementary Experiences upon the Be-

havioral Development of Infants in Institutions." *Child Development*, 36 (1965), 81.

59. SCHAFER, R. "Generative Empathy in the Treatment Situation." *Psychoanalytic Quarterly*, 28 (1959), 347–373.

60. SEARS, R. R., MACCOBY, E. E., and LEVIN, H. *Patterns of Child Rearing*. Evanston, Ill.: Row, Peterson, 1957.

61. SETTLAGE, C. F. "Psychologic Development." In W. E. Nelson, ed., *Textbook of Pediatrics*. 8th ed. Philadelphia: Saunders, 1964. Pp. 61–69.

62. SPITZ, R. "Hospitalism." *Psychoanalytic Study of the Child*, 1 (1945), 53.

63. ———. "Anaclitic Depression." *Psychoanalytic Study of the Child*, 2 (1946), 313.

64. ———. "Hospitalism, An Inquiry into the Genesis of Psychiatric Conditions in Early Childhood: A Follow-Up Report." *Psychoanalytic Study of the Child*, 2 (1946), 113.

65. ———. *No and Yes: On the Genesis of Human Communication*. New York: International Universities Press, 1957.

66. ———. *A Genetic Field Theory of Ego Formation*. New York: International Universities Press, 1959.

67. THOMAS, A., BIRCH, H. G., CHESS, S., and ROBBINS, L. "Individuality in Responses of Children to Similar Environmental Situations." *American Journal of Psychiatry*, 117 (1961), 798.

68. TREFFERT, D. A. "Epidemiology of Infantile Autism." *Archives of General Psychiatry*, 22 (1970), 431–438.

69. VAN OPHUIJSEN, J. H. W. "Primary Conduct Disturbances: Their Diagnosis and Treatment." In N. D. C. Lewis and B. L. Pacella, eds., *Modern Trends in Child Psychiatry*. New York: International Universities Press, 1945. Pp. 35–42.

70. WAELDER, R. "The Principles of Multiple Function." *Psychoanalytic Quarterly*, 5:1 (1936), 45–62.

71. WEIL, A. "Certain Severe Disturbances of Ego Development in Childhood." *Psychoanalytic Study of the Child*, 8 (1953), 271–287.

72. ———. "The Basic Core." *Psychoanalytic Study of the Child*, 25 (1970), 442–460.

73. WINNICOTT, D. W. "Psychoses and Child Care." *British Journal of Medical Psychology*, 26 (1953), 68.

74. ———. "The Capacity To Be Alone." *International Journal of Psycho-Analysis*, 39 (1958), 416–420.

75. ———. "Transitional Objects and Transitional Phenomena." In *Collected Papers*. New York: Basic Books, 1958. Pp. 229–242.

76. WOLFF, P. H. "Observations on Newborn Infants." *Psychosomatic Medicine*, 21 (1959), 110–118.

77. WORLD HEALTH ORGANIZATION. *Deprivation of Maternal Care: A Reassessment of Its Effects*. Public Health Papers, no. 14. Geneva: World Health Organization, 1962.

78. YARROW, L. J. "Separation from Parents During Early Childhood." In *Review of Child Development Research*. Vol. 1. New York: Russell Sage Foundation, 1964. Pp. 89–136.

CHAPTER 4

PSYCHOLOGICAL DISORDERS OF THE GRADE SCHOOL YEARS

Eveoleen N. Rexford and
Suzanne Taets van Amerongen

SINCE THE LAST EDITION of the *American Handbook of Psychiatry* was published, the confluence of a number of trends has brought changes in the course and evolution of child psychiatric activities that we did not clearly foresee a decade ago. The effective treatment of neurotic children has led to the demand that we similarly treat children with other disturbances and that we care for many, rather than a modest number of, boys and girls. The mental health outreach into poverty areas brought the role of cultural deprivation and racial discrimination into our work with inner-city children and involved us with a larger number of children showing developmental arrests and deviations. When education became imperative in a technological society, our clinics received more referrals of children with serious learning disorders and perceptual handicaps. A growing emphasis in theoretical discussions on the role of interpersonal relations in mental health and illness of children placed a focus on the importance of object relations and object loss in a child's growth and development. Medical advances made it possible for children with serious congenital handicaps to survive and to present later problems in personality organization, learning, and behavior. The increasing societal pressures to which all of us are vulnerable have put a premium on the issues of self-esteem, flexibility, and adaptation to change. All these trends contributed to the changing character of the caseloads in our clinics and in our consultation work, namely, a larger number of children with developmental deviations, minimal brain damage, and personality disorders.[71] They drew attention inevitably to the status of our nosology and pressed us to refine our classifications so that our work could be based more securely on a psychological understanding of the child and his milieu.[42]

As the community mental health movement gained momentum during the 1960's, demands for children's services led to the creation of a blueprint, a comprehensive range of services for children from birth to adulthood, from all socioeconomic and racial groups, with varying modalities to carry out prevention and treatment efforts for all types of emotional disturbances.[55] Though few programs have as yet been funded and staffed sufficiently well to replicate such an ambitious model, most child psychiatric facilities have moved toward the blueprint, providing a greater variety of services for a wider range of children. Programs of education for paraprofessional and indigenous workers and inservice training of personnel for specialized but limited skills proliferate to try to solve the pressing personnel problems.

These institutional changes highlighted the shortcomings of all nosological schemata of the emotional and personality disorders of children. In discussions of the Joint Commission on the Mental Health of Children, the criticisms varied with the orientation and responsibilities of the speakers, but the need for feasible schemata for all child mental health activities was generally accepted.

In his chapter on "Common Neuroses of Childhood" in the first edition of Volume I of the *American Handbook of Psychiatry*, Cramer referred to the difficulties in constructing a classification of children's emotional problems and concluded, "it is probably not possible clearly to delineate one."[16, p. 803] However, because of all the changes and trends outlined above, we in the profession have been forced to give our attention to nosological schemata and to make determined efforts to devise more satisfactory classifications.

We remember vividly an experience over fifteen years ago when we were involved in consultations about diagnostic studies in a state youth service facility. Three fifteen-year-old youths were committed for the identical crime, namely, stealing an automobile. Our diagnostic studies revealed that one boy was floridly schizophrenic, another a young person whose life pattern of impulsive, disruptive, and antisocial behavior had begun before his school years and had continued uninterruptedly, and the third boy was caught up in an intense neurotic guilt reaction related to his unhappiness over his relationship with a recently widowed mother. Each of these boys obviously required a different plan if more than custodial aims were to be met by his commitment to the youth services.

Child-care agencies, community mental health programs, and child psychiatric facilities alike need to incorporate within their operations some systematic sorting out process that offers guidance, however imperfect and incomplete, in setting up management plans and provides some useful prognostications about children and adolescents. The evolution of family diagnosis and therapy and the model of treating the family may create even more confusion if little attention is paid to the specific elements of the child's disturbance and to his special needs.

The problems of constructing a satisfactory classification of children's emotional disorders are great, the reason undoubtedly that all attempts thus far have met with serious criticisms. The very nature of childhood and of the many factors that can influence a child's growth and development positively or negatively create a large number of variables, with interrelationships extremely difficult to formulate.[58] Nonetheless, during the years since the first edition of the *American Handbook of Psychiatry* was published, we have witnessed significant progress in grasping the intricacies of the classification process and in bringing to diagnostic thinking concepts of considerable value for assessment and management planning.[20,21,32,50,65]

The 1966 Group for the Advancement of Psychiatry (GAP) report on psychopathological disorders in childhood[15] represents the most ambitious and effective attempt thus far to provide a nosology bringing together psychosomatic, developmental, and psychosocial propositions in positing major categories of childhood disturbances. The report was the culmination of work begun by members of previous committees on child psychiatry, and in it the 1966 committee succeeded in preparing a synthesis of conceptualizations and clinical experiences more nearly adequate to our evaluative needs than any previously constructed. The committee took as its point of departure the nature of twentieth-century scientific thinking, which "strives to be multidimensional, relativistic and dynamic in character, relying on probabilities rather than certainties."[15, p. 176] They formulated:

a conceptual framework that would encompass the characteristics of personality formation and development in childhood in sufficiently comprehensive fashion to permit professional people from differing schools of thought to agree at least upon a point of departure to a classification of disturbances and deviations. The influence of hereditary factors, the impact of familial and other environmental influences, the significance of developmental capacities and vulnerabilities, the fluidity and plasticity of the young child's personality characteristics, and other considerations obviously had to be taken into account. In addition, the tendency of the clinician to see and classify pathology rather than health was recognized. Accordingly, the conceptual scheme evolved must permit in some measure an understanding and classification of healthy as well as unhealthy reactions and behaviors. Above all such a conceptual framework must be clinically relevant if it is to be at all helpful in undergirding a classification constructed for everyday clinical usage.

In searching for a theoretical framework that would meet the various tests it must survive, the Committee felt that three basic propositions were vital: (a) the psychosomatic concept, involving the unity of mind and body and the inter-relatedness between psychological and somatic processes; (b) the developmental dimension, so central to the study of the child; and (c) the psychosocial aspects of the child's existence in the family and society.[15, p. 178]

The following major categories are proposed:

1. Healthy responses
2. Reactive disorders
3. Developmental deviations
4. Psychoneurotic disorders
5. Personality disorders
6. Psychotic disorders
7. Psychophysiologic disorders
8. Brain syndromes
9. Mental retardation
10. Other disorders.[15, p. 217]

Each major category is broken down into subcategories, and a symptom list encourages further specificity in assigning a diagnostic formulation to an individual child.

Specific aspects or isolated items of this schema may be criticized; perhaps its most important weakness lies in conceptualizations of disorders in which social and cultural factors play a predominant role.[44,69] In a paper for the Clinical Committee of the Joint Committee, the chairman of the GAP Child Psychiatry Committee, Dane Prugh,[54] tried to deal more fully with the psychosocial dimension. Whatever flaws the report presents, it is an effort at once practical and creative in a field to which many experienced clinicians have contributed without producing an end result as effective as this classification schema.

The GAP report reflects the influence of important bodies of clinical work and theoretical considerations which encourage a more sophisticated level of diagnostic thinking and more precise treatment planning. It is difficult to estimate the influence of Anna Freud's concepts of developmental lines,[26,27,28] the end product of the research of her child psychoanalytic group at Hampstead, England. The group proposed a complex diagnostic profile[43,46] through which a child's development could be traced, indicating the evolution of energies, defenses, traits, relations to others, modes of behavior, and adaptation over a period of years. The process clearly rests on a very detailed clinical history taking, and a mastery of the underlying principles requires intense study and developmental sophistication. Despite the fact that the profile is attuned to the collection of data through the psychoanalytic method, the concepts of the developmental lines are being applied to historical and cross-sectional data accumulated through other techniques.

A. Freud's 1970 preliminary classification of the symptomatology of childhood[29] demonstrated a continuing thrust of the Hampstead clinical research into the areas of assessment of children not treated by the psychoanalytic method. Her concluding comment contains the thesis of this chapter, namely, "it is reasonable to expect that any step forward in the refinement of diagnostic assessment will, in the long run, lead to improvements in matching disorders and therapy in the children's field."[29, p. 40]

Erikson's concepts of psychosocial maturation according to epigenetic principles[18] continue to provide guidance to the diagnostic thinking of many child clinicians who decry the inner directedness of psychoanalytic schemata but find the usual symptomatic rubrics too slight for the assessment task to be done. However, Dane Prugh illustrated how far-reaching Erikson's psychosocial schema actually is:

In Erikson's "house of many mansions" we can thus fit various types of learning theory including operant conditioning; Piaget's and other concepts regarding intellectual development; cybernetic theory; small group and family theory; sociocultural theories; field theory; systems theory and communication theory, not to mention the more classical theory of psychosexual development derived from Sigmund Freud and Anna Freud's recent elaboration of "developmental lines."[54, pp. 153–154]

Certain themes relevant to understanding childhood emotional disturbances appear and reappear in the literature. Though neither the supporting work nor the concepts first appeared during the last decade or so, they have nonetheless lately received emphasis and elaboration so that they strongly influence diagnostic and therapeutic thinking.[11]

One of these themes is the focus on constitutional and/or congenital deficits which limit and distort the child's developmental capacities from birth on and strongly influence the responses and behaviors of caretakers. Studies of the congenitally blind child (Fraiberg),[23,74] many papers concerning the minimal brain damage syndrome,[17] and studies of children with other serious physical handicaps reflect the growing appreciation of the influence of such conditions on personality organization and parental response to the child, and provide cues for more effective management when such children are brought to the child psychiatrist.

A second theme that strongly influences diagnostic thinking and hence treatment planning is that of object relations and object loss.[14,51,67] We are indebted to the Kleinian group of English analysts for studies and formulations that centered our attention on the crucial roles of the child's objects and their images in his inner life. Fairbairn's writing on object relations and their key place in personality development and organization and Bowlby's work on early maternal deprivation promoted the search for ways of understanding human relatedness and its vicissitudes. The other side of object relations, the loss of the object, again is not new to our theorizing about personality development and child psychopathology; however, the emphasis given to it by Rochlin[59,60] underlined the ubiquitous character of loss, the constant fear of it, and the crucial power of these to shape character and future experiences.

The issue of object relations and object loss[49] appears to be one of the most cogent and useful considerations in viewing the natural history of a child's emotional disturbance and in setting up what needs to be done to free the progressive developmental forces for the child's growth and maturation. The child's actual experiences of loss, when they occurred, the support available to him, and the manner in which he could cope with the loss are definitive in determining the degree of his vulnerability to future stress and the quality of the resources he can muster to master a real or fantasied recapitulation. New developmental challenges or life's vicissitudes have a way of probing the weaknesses in trust and self-esteem that previous experience of loss can engender; the more global defenses available to counter massive anxiety and rage at an early age may need to be remobilized when later traumata or extreme stress break through the current adaptive equilibrium. In addition, each developmental step carries with it the abdication of prior gratification and the giving up of previous modes of behavior; along with the gains of mastery and a new level of adaptation go the losses of parts of the past. Loss as well as gain is an inevitable component of change and adaptation.

Mahler[38,39] intensively studied the nature and significance of the period of separation-individuation during infancy, and her concepts have value for identifying basic difficulties and for tracing the vicissitudes of effective or faulty adaptations to the developmental task of self-other differentiation.

Still another theme frequently used for its diagnostic and explanatory value is that of the need of the infant and young child for an optimal degree, kind, and variety of stimulation and interaction with his caretakers. There are many controversies about whether certain inner-city children have too much or too little stimulation. The issue probably is more wisely phrased in terms of the child's relationship to the one stimulating him, his preferred sensory modalities, and the timing, intensity, or nature of the stimulation.[58]

The concept of adaptation plays a larger role in diagnostic thinking about childhood emotional disorders since the developmental point of view and the teachings of psychoanalytic ego psychology became more widely used by clinicians. This issue was dealt with at some length in the report of the Clinical Committee for the Joint Commission:

Concepts of health and illness or of function and dysfunction in children differ somewhat from those applicable to adults, depending upon the child's capacities at a particular stage of development, the current nature of the family transactional operations, and other factors. Nevertheless, the concept of adaptation to the environment (or of effective coping, mastery or psychosocial functioning) is central in relation to both children and adults. In the modern unitary theory of health and illness, health and disease are considered phases of life. Health represents the phase of positive adaptation by the human organism, and in the child, the phase of growth and development. In this phase, the child is able to master his environment and himself, within stage-appropriate limits, to learn effectively, and is reasonably free from pain, disability or limitations in social capacities. Illness or dysfunction represents the phase of failure in adaptation or of breakdown in the attempts of the organism to maintain an adaptive equilibrium or the dynamic steady state (at any one moment in the forward development of the particular child).[54, p. 148]

These themes and concepts have played their part in the growing tendency to use the developmental point of view in clinical assessment and management planning. The developmental approach to the evaluation of children's emotional difficulties and to the planning for their amelioration offers the clinician many advantages.[25] He is oriented to a point of view that postulates a series of developmental stages during the course of which the child's constitutional givens interact with his experiences to the end of mastering psychobiological tasks and adapting to the demands of growth and maturation in ways acceptable to his society.[19] The clinician looks, therefore, for information about the child's makeup and his health; he looks for data bearing on the effectiveness and the fit of the way the child was raised by his parents or their surrogates. He wants to know how the child met traumatic situations and adapted to such normal but often taxing events as the birth of a sibling, change of domicile, and leaving home to enter school. He assesses whether the child experienced the support of his milieu as predominantly positive and helpful or whether he lacked trust and confidence. The clinician tries to discover what the child's coping modes are and under what circumstances he is able to use them; he wants to know of the people and the structures in the child's life that promote or could promote his growth and maturation. Within such a context, he studies the child's symptoms, their history and course, and he is alerted to evidence of earlier, even if transient, childhood disturbances which left vulnerabilities in the child's capacities for object relating, tolerating frustration, mastering anxieties, and reality testing. The clinician looks for data bearing on the points of great inner stress and tries to follow the vicissitudes of the child's handling of sexual and aggressive impulses.

The growth process hence becomes the central focus, and the child's symptomatology is viewed as a manifestation of disruptions in it.[37]

❬ Groupings of Children's Emotional Disturbances

It is in line with such reasoning that we describe below groupings of children's emotional disturbances and present suggestions for therapeutic management. It is obvious that in the space of this brief review we cannot list and discuss all the disorders considered in the GAP report, the American Psychiatric Association diagnostic classification 2, or other nosological outlines in use. The following are groupings of children we find coming frequently to our attention in today's more comprehensive programs and/or presenting evaluation problems often interfering with their effective management.

Physiologically Based Disturbances

The first grouping we wish to discuss is that of children with a major disturbance in the early years owing to constitutional defect, congenital handicaps, or serious ailment during infancy. Our knowledge of the influence of these disabilities on cognitive development and personality organization is still fragmentary, but clinical research studies and experiences with individual children are filling in some of the gaps. It is clear that such conditions alter and distort the course of the child's progression, but it seems also that the extent of the developmental deviation depends a great deal on the feedback from the baby's surroundings, whether positive or negative, and to what degree. Children with a major sensory defect, such as congenital blindness or deafness, show marked but differing developmental deviations. Selma Fraiberg[22,24] has illustrated how certain blind babies escape the arrest in growth pattern, the passivity, lack of motoric achievement, and limited relatedness to people characteristic of many blind infants;

they were encouraged by mothers (and fathers) who could help them relate to others and find a different but an effective route toward personality organization. From such parents and babies Fraiberg's group learned how to teach other parents to provide the positive feedbacks that enabled their infants to progress. Such infant studies open up a whole new area of intervention in infants with a variety of serious physical conditions hindering the usual growth process.

Those disturbances of growth and development secondary to central nervous system deficits appear to be occurring more frequently. The physical disabilities of cerebral palsy are often accompanied by distortions, irregularities, or failures in different development lines, the most common of which is mental retardation.

The syndrome called most often minimal brain damage is highly controversial, but children displaying the symptoms of hyperkinesis,[64,72] distractability, impulsivity, and difficulties in learning are generally considered to suffer from cerebral cortical damage of a diffuse nature. It is these children who respond well in a high proportion of instances to the amphetamines. They show diffuse abnormalities in the electroencephalogram and in electromyography. Their difficulties in learning to read and write and in developing abstract concepts are associated with difficulties in perceptual motor functions, spatial orientation, and cerebral integration or organizational capacities.[17] Specific neurological lesions are rarely found, and the diagnosis must usually be made on history and the above symptomatology. Recent studies indicate that though the hyperkinesis often abates during adolescence, the defects in learning capacities, social adaptation, frustration tolerance, and other basic ego functions persist.[72]

The evaluation of the developmental status and level of functioning of a child with a major sensory or central nervous system handicap or other major physical impairment requires a synthesis of information from neurologists, educators, pediatricians, and other specialists with the history given by the parents and the assessment of child and family by the child psychiatrist at the time of referral. However, a careful psychological evaluation may be minimized in the study of the many dimensions to be assessed in a child with severe epilepsy, cerebral palsy, serious birth defects, club feet, or cleft palate. Nonetheless, there are certain key psychological issues that require attention and must be the focus of management planning from the standpoint of personality growth and development. The first is the profound effect of such disabilities and defects on the self-esteem of the child. The vulnerability of his sense of self and self-worth may lead to an exaggeration of the significance of a defect, for instance, a convulsive disorder or a cleft palate, so that the child's self-image is that of one generally and severely defective or hopelessly inadequate. Such a self-image will interfere with the thrust of progressive development and may make all efforts at education of the child very disappointing. The second point is the role of the child's guilt, which may be overlooked in the perception of the family's complicated ways of dealing with its own ubiquitous feelings of guilt. The child must deal with the hostility he feels because of his condition; increased aggressive impulses may be mobilized by the physical care of his handicap, for instance, immobilization in a plastic cast, painful operative procedures, hospitalizations, medications, and restriction of activity. If the child internalizes his hostility, he suffers from a heavy load of guilt which interferes with his relationships with people and with his achieving and predisposes him for masochistic destructive character formation. If he has to project his feeling of hostility, a greater or lesser degree of paranoid thinking and behavior will color his reactions and interactions. The latter occurs frequently in juvenile diabetics.

The management of these handicapped children depends on a skillful synthesis of the evaluations of their total potential for growth and the coordination of efforts of several specialists from different disciplines to promote the child's development. Psychoeducation, psychotherapy, drug treatment, and parental counseling may be needed concomitantly, intermittently, or sequentially for longer or shorter periods. These various treatments may be indicated particularly at such times when maturational and developmental milestones tend to create additional stress situations for these children (for example, during the early school years, on entering puberty, and in the course of adolescence).

Developmental Irregularities or Failures

The grouping of developmental irregularities or failures is a far more significant sector of childhood emotional disorders than we have realized and one about which we have somewhat more understanding today than we had a decade ago. The work of the Hampstead Clinic, studies of psychotic children, the experiences of our colleagues in psychoeducation, and clinical contacts with culturally deprived children have demonstrated to us that in certain children, specific ego functions have not developed or developed more slowly or faster than others, or developed only partially, leading to a wide range of symptoms. The model of childhood neurosis on which the concepts of child psychotherapy were built does not apply directly to these children, and there is no doubt but that many of our failures in management have come because we have assumed that we were treating neurotic children whose achievements had been lost or undone through regression. The distinction is an important one to make, since quite different therapeutic approaches may be needed to ameliorate a developmental failure from those useful for a child in a neurotic regressive state. It is, however, a differentiation that may be confusing and difficult to make. Our need for more careful and systematic clinical research is obvious.[47]

A child's failure to reach the expected level of growth may show up anywhere within the structure of his personality. It may concern the milestones of his first year, it may involve a lagging in drive development or in a wide variety of ego functions, it may appear in superego formation. Anna Freud wrote,[29, p. 35]

Developmental irregularities and failures confront the clinician with many problems, foremost among them the need to differentiate between the causes for them. Retardation of milestones in the first year of life raises the suspicion of organic damage. Delay in drive development may either be due to constitutional factors or may be determined environmentally by inadequate response from the parental objects. Ego retardation is frequently due to poor endowment, but, as the study of many underprivileged children has revealed, equally often the consequence of lack of proper environmental stimulation. Arrested superego development may be part of general ego retardation and share its causation or it may be due to the lack of adequate objects in the child's environment or to separation from them; or to internal failure to form relations to other objects; or to the qualities of the parental personalities with whom the child identifies. Traumatic experience may at any time endanger progress in any direction or, at worst, bring forward development to a standstill.

A. Freud agrees to the difficulties in distinguishing between these types of damages to development and those that represent the undoing of developmental achievements after they have been acquired and which are due to regressions and inhibitions based on conflict.[29, p. 35]

The most reliable hallmarks of neurosis are anxiety, guilt and conflict while in contrast to these, the various types of developmental arrest may remain internally undisputed, especially in those cases where the arrest affects more than one sector of the personality. But this diagnostic indicator too cannot be trusted in all instances.

The management of developmental irregularities and failures is best effected by variants of educational methods directed at the promotion of the functions that have been arrested or distorted.[8] Psychoeducational programs, behavioral modification techniques,[73] and group therapy with a heavy emphasis on ego training are among the most effective modes presently employed. Whatever modality is chosen, the issue of relatedness to the teacher, clinician, or therapist is of primary importance. We learned years ago in the pioneer work with psychotic young children that ego growth, ego synthesis, and integration can be promoted only in the setting of an object relation; this lesson holds for children whose de-

velopmental failures are based on less overwhelming traumatic experiences or failures to thrive.[1]

Psychoneuroses of Childhood

The psychoneuroses of childhood, the most familiar category of the diagnoses associated with psychoanalytic concepts and dynamic psychiatry, are among the more controversial today.[33] Of course, the model was derived from the psychoanalysis of adults; as more sophistication in determining developmental stages and particularly the development of various ego functions emerged, it was observed that these stages of development and functions of the ego did not always mature in unison; hence a more frequent difficulty in using the adult diagnoses arose. It became apparent that full-blown psychoneurotic syndromes did not appear as often in childhood as in later life and that this finding was to be expected.

The obsessive-compulsive neurosis in children resembles more closely the adult picture, and there is little disagreement about these cases.[63]

The picture of a hysterical psychoneurosis in a child appears more severe than its adult counterpart, and on examination, the child usually presents an hysterical character with many pregenital features, especially of an oral nature. The more transient reversible neurotic behaviors no longer are commonly seen in child psychiatric clinics, since pediatricians, school counselors, or social workers are more likely to deal with them than psychiatrists.

The very nature of childhood complicates the process of diagnosis and nowhere more clearly than in the category of the psychoneuroses. The very same factors, however, contribute to a fluidity and a potential for change that can alter the psychopathological state and the developmental stasis in a fashion that would be astonishing in an adult. Our management measures and prognostications need to reflect the range of possibilities for change that development and life events can bring about.

The disorders in the oedipal period present

some of the most clear-cut examples of psychoneuroses seen in children. The struggles of the young child to maintain his psychic equilibrium in the face of conflicting wishes to win the favor of one parent while vanquishing the other, both of whom he needs and cherishes, precede the thrust of active exploration of the outside world which entering first grade provides. His conflicts in this triangular situation in which both sexual and aggressive impulses are invested are unconscious, and the pursuant anxiety leads to a number of defensive operations and symptoms that characterize the neurotic picture. Little Hans[30] is the classical example in the psychoanalytic literature of a neurotic youngster of this age; his phobias, his behavior toward his parents, and his shifting explanations of his difficulties illustrate his preoccupations with his parents and the resulting picture when the boy could not handle his conflicting needs, wishes, and fears.

Psychoneuroses are based on unconscious conflicts over the handling of sexual and aggressive impulses, which though removed from awareness through the mechanism of repression in combination with a number of other defenses, such as denial and displacement, remain active and unresolved. Though conflicts may begin and remain to some degree active during the preschool years, the life situation triggering a neurotic formation is the child's sharp conflict in the triangular position with his parents. His sexual and aggressive wishes toward them become unbearable, and he develops symptoms of anxiety, regression, phobias, physical complaints, and so on. If the child cannot resolve his conflicts and renounce his wishes as the developmental progression provides him with more flexible and effective defenses, his conflicts about and with his parents become internalized and tend to assume a chronic character. Modifications can occur with development; environmental change and manipulation can influence the symptomatology, but the more usual natural history demonstrates a self-perpetuating or repetitive nature. The neurotic difficulties usually manifest themselves in an interference with an important object relationship, the child's own feelings and wishes become incongruent with the expectations of parent or sibling and later with the child's own inner standards of acceptability. The resulting ambivalences toward parent or sibling figures are readily transferred in school or play to teachers and playmates who are invested with strong emotions and fantasies displaced from the actual situation and original cast of characters. In other children the ambivalences hold them fast to the family and prevent the child's moving toward new objects.

Much energy can be spent on futile discussions of whether a child's conflicts existed before the oedipal period or rather arose only at that time. Problems during early childhood can provide fertile soil for intensified conflict, symptom formation, and defense evoked by the oedipal struggles.

Neurotic children usually relate well to a clinician; there is a history of developmental achievements and of positive attitudes toward neighbors, friends, or teachers which contrast with the dismal history that may accompany more disturbed children. This contrast leads some mental health professionals to minimize the needs of the neurotic child for specific treatment because "he isn't as sick as the others, and they need it more" (for instance, the disorganized, borderline, or psychotic child) and because they expect that "he will grow out of" his disability.

There is a related belief that poor and minority group children do not suffer from psychoneuroses and that only middle- or upper-class boys and girls do so. Though it is probably true that the proportions vary in the two populations it is likely that there are many more instances of psychoneuroses in the inner-city population than are correctly diagnosed in busy mental health facilities.

The clinical judgment that neurotic children are less sick and so deserve less attention leaves out of consideration several significant factors: (1) the constricting and warping influence of unresolved neurotic conflicts on personality and character formation; (2) the necessity for appropriate treatment if more than transient symptom relief is to be attained;

and (3) the potential of these children for optimal self-realization and contributions to our society if their capacities can be freed for growth and progression.

Two eventualities are observed repeatedly in families studied in clinics, and each illustrates the burden of unresolved childhood neuroses extending into adult life and distorting adult functioning, namely, chronic underachievement in work, in love, and in play and an often painful interference with parental functioning.[48]

As mentioned earlier, the older divisions of the neuroses of childhood and youth into the hysterias and the obsessive-compulsive neuroses have recently met with dissatisfaction. The latter condition is one most observers describe in a similar fashion:[13] The anxieties produced by unconscious conflict and involving particularly aggressive impulses and wishes are defended against and defused by a preoccupation with stereotyped acts or rituals also serving the purpose of binding anxieties. The nuclear conflict from which the child regresses is that engendered by the triangular situation with the wishes toward the parent of the opposite sex poised against those of an aggressive nature toward the parent of the same sex. The neurotic child does not know why he pursues these thoughts or acts, but failure to think such aggressive thoughts brings on such anxiety that it is difficult indeed to persuade him to refrain from them long enough to discover their links to charged affects and memories. Obsessional children are often highly intellectual, deeply interested in acquiring facts, valuing knowledge, and isolating from their awareness feelings or the memories of fantasies and emotions. They rely heavily on denying their aggressive thoughts and impulses, persuading themselves of holding precisely the opposite sentiments: These reaction formations protect them from a guilty awareness of their hostile and cruel impulses. Their internalized standards are very strict and can lead to a progressive restriction as the child struggles to defuse the dangerous impulses and take distance from them. A strong belief in magic pervades the obsessional

child's attitude toward the world, and words are especially invested with power, being equated with acts. As we learn more of such a child, we are likely to find that his relations with people at one point were less ambivalent and less polarized between love and hate, and we can find evidence that the triangular relationship with his parents was a highly stressful one for him. The nature of the obsessional's preoccupations and of his object relations suggests a regression to anal-retentive modes with the sadistic coloring often characteristic of fantasies and impulses of this developmental level.

Current doubts about an entity of hysterical psychoneurosis are illustrated by the omission of this diagnosis in the GAP report.[15,61] There is a rubric of hysterical personality disorder, but the section on the psychoneuroses lists in addition to the obsessional neurosis the following: psychoneurosis anxiety type, phobic type, conversion type, dissociative type, and depressive type. The likelihood is that many clinicians would place the children that the GAP report describes in these subcategories into the group of hysterical psychoneurosis.[34,41] These children are apt to be lively, warm, perhaps seductive, and rather charmingly immature. They cling in a coy manner to important objects and give the impression of accomplishing less than they are capable of. Their ways of relating and behaving are often highly eroticized, and therapy with them may become stalemated on this issue. Often they come to our attention because of a physical complaint "for which no organic cause has been found," and their attitude toward a serious dysfunction is one of apparent indifference unless or until therapeutic work with them begins to disturb their defensive facade.

The immature and dependent stance of these children coupled with considerable oral preoccupation leads the unwary to assume the child's psychopathology is centered at an earlier level than that of the oedipal struggles. Their easy regression and preference for this mode of combatting anxiety can be problems in therapy as well as diagnosis. Careful history taking reveals that the child has mastered relatively well the various developmental tasks, but at the time of referral is functioning less maturely than that history would lead one to expect. Phobias of a fleeting or more lasting nature, nightmares, temper tantrums, and impulsiveness are reported. Particularly common is underachieving in school.[2]

In some children, overt anxiety is such a prominent symptom that anxiety hysteria or anxiety neurosis is the diagnostic label applied. The impression one receives is that the defenses of repression, denial, and regression were not sufficient to contain the anxiety engendered by the conflicts over sexual and aggressive impulses. Though phobias are the example par excellence of the neuroses of early childhood, grade school children may demonstrate this symptom as the predominant compromise formation.[9,53,57] Similarly, though depressive moods may appear in any hysterical neurosis, some children respond to their guilt and anxiety with sufficient depression so that the sadness, expressions of unworthiness, and self-abnegation take precedence over the other symptoms.[3,70]

The treatment of choice for most psychoneuroses of childhood is psychoanalytic psychotherapy.[10] Aimed at helping the child overcome the blocks to his progressive development, the psychotherapy utilizes an object relation with a reliable and interested adult to strengthen the child's more mature defensive and adaptive ego functions and to diminish the hold of pathological modes of dealing with conflict and anxiety. Fantasy material and transference elements often appear and may be used in psychotherapy. When developmental stasis threatens several important lines of development and the child's problems though clearly neurotic are of long-standing, psychoanalysis should be considered, since it permits a systematic exploration and working through of the neurotic conflicts. A consultation with a child analyst, followed perhaps by his diagnostic exploration, can clarify issues of diagnosis, choice of management, and prognosis for the family and referring agent. Each child psychiatric facility regularly sees children for whom psychoanalysis is indicated: Where

child analysts are available, their services for diagnosis and psychoanalytic treatment should be utilized as one element in the range of comprehensive child services.

Psychoeducational techniques, group activities, and/or drug therapy may be needed to supplement psychotherapy. To use these approaches as replacements for one-to-one psychotherapy does not give the child an optimal opportunity to master developmental and situational conflicts and to promote his personality growth.

The Personality Disorders

A large number of grade school children referred to child psychiatrists, clinics, and mental health centers today make up a fourth major grouping, the character and chronic behavioral disturbances or as the GAP report terms them, the personality disorders. The GAP classification lists the following subcategories: compulsive personality; hysterical personality; anxious personality; the overly dependent, oppositional, overly inhibited, overly independent personalities; the isolated and the mistrustful personalities; the tension-discharge disorders, the sociosyntonic personality disorders, sexual deviation; and other personality disorders.[35,56] The descriptions of these subcategories point to the usefulness of the continuum concept in discussing this major grouping:

At one end are relatively well organized personalities with, for example, constructively compulsive traits or somewhat over dependent characteristics representing mild to moderate exaggeration of healthy personality trends. . . . At the other end are markedly impulsive, sometimes poorly organized personalities that dramatically come into conflict with society over their sexual or social patterns of behavior.[15, p. 238]

Each classifier and many clinicians have tended to divide up this group using terms to suit their own preferences and experiences. However, whether their disturbances are called character disorders, behavioral disturbances, or personality disorders, these children tend to resemble one another in the relative rigidity and chronicity of their pathological trends.[31,40] The extent of the pathological handicaps will of course vary with the location of the condition on the diagnostic continuum, and within any one subcategory, children will differ in their susceptibility to change and limitation of functioning.

In contrast to the children suffering from neurotic disorders, children with serious personality or character disorders do not experience an inner sense of conflict, always present in the former group. The battle is between them and the outside world, that is, their parents, the teacher, the police, or courts but not within themselves. They are markedly unable to tolerate delay or frustration, and their capacity to bear ambivalance, anxiety, and depression is conspicuously low; in serious cases it is almost absent. It is not surprising, therefore, that their attempts at coping are geared mainly to adapting their environment to their needs rather than adapting to it. Their relationships to people are shallow and mainly based on need fulfillment. Their orientation is self- rather than other-directed. Their superego is not patterned after an identification with a respected and loved parent figure, but appears mainly the product of early childhood projections and views of adults as cruel, ruthless, intransigent, and exceptionally powerful.

We find, on closer scrutiny of these children, serious defects in reality testing, distortions in their self-image of almost delusional fixity, and a paucity of adaptive and defensive ego mechanisms perhaps best characterized by the phrase "few strings on his bow."[62]

In their histories we repeatedly encounter serious disturbances in the quality of the early mother-child relationships, such as emotional neglect owing to depression and withdrawal on the part of one or both parents, unpredictability and inconsistency on the part of the child's mother, an identification of the child by the parent with a hated, disturbed, or delinquent relative, wife, or husband. These are factors that seriously affect a child's relationship to his early love objects and from them, people in general.[4]

Bowlby's first work with delinquents led him to study the early history of these boys: He found a conspicuous number of instances of separation from and loss of the mother during the first three years of life.[5] Such an experience of maternal loss was particularly common in those children whom he called "affectionless characters," that is, those boys with no apparent relatedness to others and a very limited capacity to make a relationship when one was available to them.[6,7] The refinements of Bowlby's formulations,[75] which further research has elucidated, brought out (1) that the loss of the mother may have been symbolic and not actual, due to a mother's postpartum depression, a chaotic family situation, or her serious physical illness; and (2) that the provision, planned or fortuitous, of a mother surrogate during the early months and years of a child's life could counter the destructive effects of physical or psychological absence of the biological mother.

Some of these patients have been moved from one foster home to another, deserted at birth by their parents and adopted by no one. Some lost their parents because of the latter's severe psychopathology, which rendered the child intolerable to them when he began to assert his independence. A series of losses not infrequently punctuates the child's life, and his capacity to care about others is seriously incapacitated.[36]

These children suffer from low self-esteem, which they try to counter by negation. They have to prove their power, vulnerability, and cunning repeatedly to themselves and to deny their rage and frustration by rationalization, denial, and projection.[45]

The concept of the continuum of severity of personality disorders is useful to alert us to the possibility that a child's emotional disorder may change over a period of observation. Though we are more apt to be impressed by the children who move from the less to the more serious end of the emotional disturbance continuum, we need to keep in mind that precisely because our patients are children, change toward less restrictive and more hopeful states is possible and does occur. Developmental thrusts and unexpected life situations can influence pathological trends so that significant positive change takes place even in a child with relatively fixed and widespread pathological trends. Certainly until puberty and adolescent reorganization have wrought their changes, we cannot view even severe character disorders as rarely susceptible to change. During the grade school years, the coming together of such a youngster with an adult who cares for him can effect a significant change in his object relating, his behavior, and his general ego growth. These possibilities should be kept in mind in planning therapeutic management for all the boys and girls who fall within this broad rubric of personality disorders.

For many grade school children with personality disorders on the nearer to the neurotic end of the continuum, psychotherapy may be very effective. A consistent caring object who will become a stable element in the child's life, to whom he can return when new crises, losses, or developmental demands again restrict or cut him off from rewarding relationships and activities, can help the child modulate his fixed attitudes and reach out for new objects and achievements. These children can become attached to the setting so that they expect help from "that place" even if the therapist is no longer there. A long-term investment of the facility, even though there will be many periods of silence from the child, is indicated; it is not likely that one round of treatment will be sufficient to keep him moving forward unless he is fortunate indeed in his life situation. This is particularly the case with children displaying schizoid, paranoid, or obsessional character traits.

Time-limited psychotherapy with a focus on loss and separation offers a great deal to these children. They are more apt to be referred when their equilibrium is upset by significant losses, a father leaving, the death of an older brother, a depression of the mother. The re-experiencing of recent and more remote losses in the setting of a therapeutic relationship, which the child knows is specifically limited in time, can promote a degree of mastery of loss and a forward thrust that is surprising if one

has not witnessed the changes possible. Follow up and contacts with the family after the termination of the treatment are wise.

Group therapy is a felicitous approach for most children in this large category. Because of early deprivations and ambivalences toward adults, they are prone to reach out to their peers and gain important nutriment for growth through group identifications, support, and new activities. Individual and group therapy can go on simultaneously or one follow the other. In the interests of using professional time and the family's time wisely, the decision about which modality or what sequence should be made following the diagnostic process.

Psychoeducational techniques in psychiatric day-care programs are becoming popular and may well hold promise as they stimulate the child to learn and to achieve with his peers and in an understanding milieu.

Drug therapy for overactive, overanxious, depressed, or paranoid children is a modality that should be used alone or in combination with other treatment approaches on the basis of a diagnostic rationale. Careful medical supervision and evaluation of drug effects are important.

For certain very deprived and character-disordered children, the encouragement and support of their relationship with an adult important to them are the key to promoting their development. A scoutmaster, agency worker, probation officer, or "big brother" may with professional guidance use his tie to the child to achieve far more than a new therapist or a specific new modality could. Agency resources for camping, recreational programs in settlement houses, and medical care can make up useful facets of a total push program to which the child's response can be gratifying to all.

Children with antisocial character disorders may be more amenable to a variety of treatment modalities if these are carried out within the context of a court or youth service connection. Limits put on these children and their families are apt to be necessary if any psychiatric or mental health approach is to be helpful; the personnel of such agencies can often supply important relationships and opportunities so that more of a total push on the child's behalf is feasible.

❴ Conclusions

We have presented the thesis that events of the past decade have propelled us to plan for and work with a much wider variety of children as well as a much larger number of children than was true in the past. We have pointed out the crucial role of nosological classifications and the diagnostic process in selecting the most likely modes of therapeutic management for a specific child at that point in time. Our conviction that we need more systematic and sophisticated clinical and epidemiological research to guide our efforts in planning for and caring for hundreds of thousands of disturbed children in this country has, we hope, been made vividly evident. We have encouraged our colleagues to use the GAP report classification, or others if they prefer these, but to press on with planning our comprehensive services for children on a more rational and scientific basis. We have discussed four major groupings of children and offered certain management suggestions.

The number of children with serious emotional disturbances in this country faces us with an urgent problem in child care. We identify daily in our clinics and offices many examples of severe emotional and intellectual dysfunctioning. But these are children; they have the forces of development on their side. They are susceptible to positive as well as negative changes in their life situations. We have much to hope for and much to do if we use our knowledge, refine our techniques, and unearth more precise ways of fitting our management measures to the assets and needs of the children for whom we are responsible.

❴ Bibliography

1. ACK, M. "Julie: The Treatment of a Case of Developmental Retardation." *Psychoanaly-*
tic Study of the Child, 21 (1966), 127–149.
2. ANTHONY, J. "Panel Report: Learning Difficulties in Childhood." *Journal of the American Psychoanalytic Association,* 9 (1961), 124–134.
3. ASCH, S. S ."Depression: Three Clinical Variations." *Psychoanalytic Study of the Child,* 21 (1966), 150–171.
4. BERES, D. "Ego Disturbances Associated with Early Deprivation." *Journal of the American Academy of Child Psychiatry,* 4 (1965), 188–200.
5. BOWLBY, J. *Maternal Care and Mental Health.* Monogr. series, no. 2. Geneva: World Health Organization, 1951.
6. ———. "The Nature of the Child's Tie to His Mother." *International Journal of Psycho-Analysis,* 39 (1958), 350.
7. ———. "Grief and Mourning in Infancy and Early Childhood." *Psychoanalytic Study of the Child,* 5 (1960), 9.
8. BRAZELTON, T. B., YOUNG, G. G., and BULLOWA, M. "Inception and Resolution of Early Developmental Pathology: A Case History." *Journal of the American Academy of Child Psychiatry,* 10 (1971), 124–135.
9. BRODIE, S., and FEENEY. "A Ten-Year Follow-Up Study of Sixty-Six School Phobic Children." *Journal of the American Orthopsychiatric Association,* 34 (1964), 675–684.
10. BRODY, S. "Aims and Methods in Child Psychotherapy." *Journal of the American Academy of Child Psychiatry,* 3 (1964), 385–412.
11. ———. "Some Infantile Sources of Childhood Disturbances." *Journal of the American Academy of Child Psychiatry,* 6 (1967), 615–643.
12. CHESS, S., THOMAS, A., and BIRCH, H. G. "Behavior Problems Revisited: Findings of an Anterospective Study." *Journal of the American Academy of Child Psychiatry,* 6 (1967), 321–331.
13. CHETHIK, M. "The Therapy of an Obsessive-Compulsive Boy: Some Treatment Considerations." *Journal of the American Academy of Child Psychiatry,* 8 (1969), 465–484.
14. ———. "The Impact of Object Loss on a Six-Year-Old." *Journal of the American Academy of Child Psychiatry,* 9 (1970), 624–643.
15. COMMITTEE ON CHILD PSYCHIATRY. GROUP FOR THE ADVANCEMENT OF PSYCHIATRY.

Psychopathological Disorders in Childhood: Theoretical Considerations and a Proposed Classification. Report no. 62. New York, 1966.

16. CRAMER, J. "Common Neurosis of Childhood." In S. Arieti, ed., *American Handbook of Psychiatry*. Vol. 1. New York: Basic Books, 1959. Pp. 797–815.

17. DORIS, J., SOLNIT, A., and PROVENCE, S. "The Evaluation of the Intellect of the Brain-Damaged Child." In *Modern Perspectives in Child Development*. New York: International Universities Press, 1963. P. 162.

18. ERIKSON, E. H. "Growth and Crises of the Healthy Personality." In *Identity and the Life Cycle. Psychological Issues*, monogr. series, no. 1. New York: International Universities Press.

19. ESCALONA, S., and HEIDER, G. *Prediction and Outcome: A Study in Child Development*. New York: Basic Books, 1959.

20. FISH, B., and SHAPIRO, T. "A Typology of Children's Psychiatric Disorders: I. Its Application to a Controlled Evaluation of Treatment." *Journal of the American Academy of Child Psychiatry*, 4 (1965), 32–52.

21. ———, and SHAPIRO, T. "A Descriptive Typology of Children's Psychiatric Disorders: II. A Behavioral Classification." In R. Jenkins and J. Cole, eds., *Diagnostic Classification in Child Psychiatry*. Psychiatric Report No. 18, Washington, D.C.: American Psychiatric Association, 1964.

22. FRAIBERG, S. "Parallel and Divergent Patterns in Blind and Sighted Infants." *Psychoanalytic Study of the Child*, 23 (1968), 264–300.

23. ———, and FREEDMAN, D. A. "Studies in the Ego Development of the Congenitally Blind Child." *Psychoanalytic Study of the Child*, 9 (1964), 113–169.

24. ———, SIEGEL, B. L., and GIBSON, R. "The Role of Sound in the Search Behavior of a Blind Infant." *Psychoanalytic Study of the Child*, 21 (1966), 327–357.

25. FRANK, L. "Human Development: An Emerging Scientific Discipline." In A. Solnit and S. Provence, eds., *Modern Perspectives in Child Development*. New York: International Universities Press, 1963. Pp. 10–36.

26. FREUD, A. "Assessment of Childhood Disturbances." *Psychoanalytic Study of the Child*, 17 (1962), 149–158.

27. ———. "The Concept of Developmental Lines." *Psychoanalytic Study of the Child*, 18 (1963), 245–265.

28. ———. *Normality and Pathology: Assessment of Development*. New York: International Universities Press, 1965.

29. ———. "The Symptomatology of Childhood: A Preliminary Attempt at Classification." *Psychoanalytic Study of the Child*, 25 (1970), 19–44.

30. FREUD, S. "Analysis of a Phobia in a Five-Year-Old Boy (1909)." In *Standard Edition*. Vol. 10. London: Hogarth Press, 1955.

31. FRIJLING-SCHREUDER, E. C. M. "Borderline States in Children." *Psychoanalytic Study of the Child*, 24 (1969), 307–327.

32. JENKINS, R., and COLE, J., eds. *Diagnostic Classification in Child Psychiatry*. Psychiatric report, no. 18. Washington, D.C.: American Psychiatric Association, 1964.

33. KAPLAN, E. B. "Panel Report: Classical Forms of Neurosis in Infancy and Early Childhood." *Journal of the American Psychoanalytic Association*, 10 (1962), 571–578.

34. KAUFMAN, I. "Conversion Hysteria in Latency." *Journal of the American Academy of Child Psychiatry*, 1 (1962), 385–396.

35. ———, HEIMS, L., and REISER, D. "Re-evaluation of the Psychodynamics of Firesetting." *Journal of the American Orthopsychiatric Association*, 31 (1961), 123–136.

36. KHAN, M., and MASUD, R. "The Concept of Cumulative Trauma." *Psychoanalytic Study of the Child*, 18 (1963), 286–306.

37. KORNER, A. F., and OPSVIG, P. "Developmental Considerations in Diagnosis and Treatment: A Case Illustration." *Journal of the American Academy of Child Psychiatry*, 5 (1966), 594–616.

38. MAHLER, M. S. "On Sadness and Grief in Infancy and Childhood: Loss and Restoration of the Symbiotic Love Object." *Psychoanalytic Study of the Child*, 16 (1961), 332–351.

39. ———. *Separation-Individuation*. New York: International Universities Press, 1970.

40. MAKKAY, E. S., and SCHWAAB, E. H. "Some Problems in the Differential Diagnosis of Antisocial Character Disorders in Early Latency." *Journal of the American Academy of Child Psychiatry*, 1 (1962), 414–430.

41. MALMQUIST, C. P. "School Phobia: A Problem in Family Neurosis." *Journal of the*

Academy of Child Psychiatry, 4 (1965), 293–319.

42. McDonald, M. "The Psychiatric Evaluation of Children." *Journal of the American Academy of Child Psychiatry*, 4 (1965), 569–612.

43. Meers, D. R. "A Diagnostic Profile of Psychopathology in a Latency Child." Foreword by R. S. Lurie. *Psychoanalytic Study of the Child*, 21 (1966), 483–526.

44. ———. "Contributions of a Ghetto Culture to Symptom Formation: Psychoanalytic Studies of Ego Anomalies in Childhood." *Psychoanalytic Study of the Child*, 25 (1970), 209–230.

45. Minuchin, S. "The Study and Treatment of Families That Produce Multiple Acting-Out Boys." *Journal of the American Orthopsychiatric Association*, 34 (1964), 125–133.

46. Nagera, H. "The Developmental Profile: Notes on Some Practical Considerations Regarding Its Use." *Psychoanalytic Study of the Child*, 18 (1963), 511–540.

47. ———. "On Arrest in Development, Fixation, and Regression." *Psychoanalytic Study of the Child*, 19 (1964), 222–239.

48. ———. *Early Childhood Disturbances: The Infantile Neurosis and the Adulthood Disturbances*. New York: International Universities Press, 1966.

49. ———. "Children's Reactions to the Death of Important Objects: A Developmental Approach." *Psychoanalytic Study of the Child*, 25 (1970), 360–400.

50. Neubauer, P. B. "Panel Report: Psychoanalytic Contributions to the Nosology of Childhood Psychic Disorders." *Journal of the American Psychoanalytic Association*, 21 (1963), 595–604.

51. Norton, A. H. "Management of Catastrophic Reactions in Children." *Journal of the American Academy of Child Psychiatry*, 4 (1965), 701–710.

52. Noshpitz, J., ed. *Report of Committee on Clinical Issues*. Washington, D.C.: Joint Commission on Mental Health of Children, May 1969. Pp. 148–149.

53. Poznanski, E., and Zrull, J. P. "Childhood Depression: Clinical Characteristics of Overtly Depressed Children." *Archives of General Psychiatry*, 23 (1970), 8–15.

54. Prugh, D. "Psychosocial Disorders in Childhood and Adolescence: Theoretical Considerations and an Attempt at Classification." In J. Nospitz, ed., *Report of the Committee on Clinical Issues*. Washington, D.C.: Joint Commission on Mental Health of Children, May 1969. Pp. 153–154.

55. ———, ed. *Planning Child Psychiatric Services. Report on Conference on Planning Children's Services in Community Mental Health Center Programs*. American Psychiatric Association, 1963.

56. Rexford, E. N., ed. "Symposium on a Developmental Approach to Problems of Acting Out." *Journal of the American Academy of Child Psychiatry*, 2 (1963), 1–175.

57. Rie, H. E. "Depression in Childhood: A Survey of Some Pertinent Contributions." *Journal of the American Academy of Child Psychiatry*, 5 (1966), 653–685.

58. Ritvo, S., McCollum, A., Omwake, E., Provence, S., and Solnit, A. "Some Relations of Constitution, Environment and Personality as Observed in a Longitudinal Study of Child Development." In A. Solnit and S. Provence, eds., *Modern Perspectives in Child Development*. New York: International Universities Press, 1963. Pp. 107–143.

59. Rochlin, G. "The Dread of Abandonment: A Contribution to the Etiology of the Loss Complex and to Depression." *Psychoanalytic Study of the Child*, 16 (1961), 451–470.

60. ———. *Grief and Its Discontents*. Boston: Little, Brown, 1965.

61. Rock, N. L. "Conversion Reactions in Childhood: A Clinical Study on Childhood Neuroses." *Journal of the American Academy of Child Psychiatry*, 10 (1971), 65–93.

62. Rosenberg, R. M., and Mueller, B. C. "Preschool Antisocial Children. Psychodynamic Considerations and Implications for Treatment." *Journal of the American Academy of Child Psychiatry*, 7 (1968), 421–441.

63. Sandler, J., and Joffe, W. G. "Notes on Obsessional Manifestations in Children." *Psychoanalytic Study of the Child*, 20 (1965), 425–440.

64. Schrager, J., Lindy, J., Harrison, S., McDernott, J., and Wilson, P. "The Hyperkinetic Child: An Overview of the Issues." *Journal of the American Academy of Child Psychiatry*, 5 (1966), 526–533.

65. Settlage, C. F. "Psychoanalytic Theory in Relation to the Nosology of Childhood

Psychic Disorders." *Journal of the American Psychoanalytic Association*, 12 (1964), 776–801.

66. SHAMBAUGH, B. "A Study of Loss Reactions in a Seven-Year-Old." *Psychoanalytic Study of the Child*, 16 (1961), 510–522.

67. SOLNIT, A. "Object Loss in Infancy." *Psychoanalytic Study of the Child*, 25 (1970), 257.

68. SPERLING, M. "School Phobias: Classification, Dynamics and Treatment." *Psychoanalytic Study of the Child*, 22 (1967), 375–401.

69. SPURLOCK, J. "Panel Report: Social Deprivation in Childhood and Character Formation." *Journal of the American Psychoanalytic Association*, 18 (1970), 622–630.

70. SYMONDS, M. "The Depressions in Childhood and Adolescence." *American Journal of Psychoanalysis*, 28 (1968), 189–195.

71. VAN AMERONGEN, S. T., HILTNER, R., and HUNTINGTON, D. *Children and Clinics.* New York: The American Association of Psychiatric Services for Children, 1968. P. 3.

72. WEISS, G., MINDE, K., WERRY, J. S., DOUGLAS, V., and NEMETH, E. "Studies on the Hyperactive Child." *Archives of General Psychiatry*, 24, no. 5 (1971), 409.

73. WERRY, J. S., and WOOLERSHEIM, J. P. "Behavior Therapy with Children: A Broad Overview." *Journal of the American Academy of Child Psychiatry*, 6 (1967), 346–370.

74. WILLS, D. M. "Vulnerable Periods in the Early Development of Blind Children." *Psychoanalytic Study of the Child*, 25 (1970), 461–482.

75. WORLD HEALTH ORGANIZATION. *Deprivation of Maternal Care: A Reassessment of Its Effects.* Public Health Papers, no. 14. Geneva, 1962.

CHAPTER 5

DISTINGUISHING AND CLASSIFYING THE INDIVIDUAL SCHIZOPHRENIC CHILD

William Goldfarb

CHILDHOOD SCHIZOPHRENIA covers a wide range of the most extreme forms of behavior disorder in children in the period between birth and pubescence. In psychiatric discussion, it is sometimes known by other names as well, for example, "childhood psychosis." All these names refer to a very wide variety of disorders, so that it is usually uncertain what specific range of deviations is covered in the use of these terms. However, most workers with particular interest in this broad range of childhood deviancy have doubts about the usefulness of applying in mechanical and uncritical fashion to the condition of childhood schizophrenia the principles and facts that pertain to the symptoms, processes, and etiology of adult schizophrenia.

Whatever may be the relationship between childhood and adult reactions, it is still wise to study and illuminate schizophrenic reactions in childhood apart from those noted in adulthood. Our most urgent requirements are sensitivity to individual variations among schizophrenic children in their patterns of adaptation and life course and precise subclassification in order to accomplish more homogeneous subclusters of schizophrenic children.

Even though it is often not clear just which specific aspects of the broad category of childhood schizophrenia may be under consideration in a given study or report, there is general agreement regarding the broad diagnosis of childhood schizophrenia. There is an increasingly clearer understanding of its relationship to other childhood disorders, based on sharper delineations of the contributing factors and the phenomenological expressions. Thus, therapeutic skill has grown and key issues have emerged more precisely.

It is accordingly the purpose of this chapter to present a summary of the historical diagnostic and etiological issues connected with the study of childhood schizophrenia in a manner that might be of practical use in developing an approach to the management and observation of those children who are found in this category of behavioral disorder. This brief presentation will be utilized to cast light on some important questions which urgently need to be answered at this time. What is the link between childhood schizophrenia and adult schizophrenia? How homogeneous are children diagnosed as schizophrenic? For clarifying the study of the growth and development of schizophrenic children, how can schizophrenic children be subclassified so as to achieve homogenous subclusters of children?

Detailed reviews of childhood schizophrenia[9,29,42,64] and annotated bibliographies[43,95] are available, and these will not be replicated. Rather, an effort will be made to draw out of the vast, oftimes confusing, literature essential conviction and information that can be applied in a simple and direct fashion in the treatment and study of childhood schizophrenia. In this distillation of thought and practice, we have been influenced by pragmatic experience in the treatment and investigation of psychotic conditions in childhood.

A review of the history of the construct embodied in the phrase "the schizophrenic syndrome of childhood" will serve to expose some major contemporary issues in the study and treatment of the behavioral impairments to which it refers. In the historical review we will first consider the relationship of childhood schizophrenia to adult schizophrenia. A historical perspective will serve to emphasize the key significance of maturation and its disturbance in the manifestations of childhood schizophrenia. Then the presentation of criteria for diagnosis will stress the very broad range of children who are filtered out by present diagnostic methods. Similarly, the discus-

sion of etiology that follows will evaluate the merits of multicausal versus unicausal hypotheses as a basis for elaborating programs of treatment and research. Based on an awareness of the diversity of children termed schizophrenic and the complex kind of interplay between social, intrapsychic, and biological factors, a practical basis for subclassification will be suggested. The transactional point of view of the deviations of schizophrenic children is used in deciding how to subclassify the children in meaningful and homogeneous subclusters. It is also the basis for an individualized approach to their care and corrective treatment.

([Historical Sources of the Construct "Childhood Schizophrenia"

Currently, there is a strong disposition in the field of psychiatry to link childhood and adult schizophrenia. The similarity in names has reinforced this trend; but this is hardly a relevant or logical basis for such association, since similar-names could have been supplied to different conditions. A historical perspective is more useful for casting light on the impetus to connect the two classes of disorder, although historic association in the evolution of thought regarding the two psychiatric entities is also not evidence in itself that they represent a single class of disorder manifested at different times in life.

Contemporary concepts of childhood psychosis generally followed in the wake of developments in the delineation of adult psychosis. Even the names assigned the very severe behavioral disturbances in childhood were borrowed from those assigned to adult disturbances. For example, diagnostic labels, such as "dementia infantilis"[53] and "dementia praecocissima"[23] followed Kraepelin's definition of dementia praecox in adolescence and adult years. In the same way, the diagnostic phrase "childhood schizophrenia" followed Bleuler's definitions of the adolescent and adult schizophrenia.

In their fundamental contributions to adult psychiatry, both Kraepelin[61] and Bleuler[15] referred to on occasional, albeit infrequent, onset of the psychiatric disorders in childhood years. Kraepelin, for example, reported that 3.5 percent of his patients with dementia praecox had been under ten years of age at time of onset; Bleuler[15] similarly reported that 5 percent of his schizophrenic patients had been under ten years of age at onset. It is difficult to interpret what bearing these data have on the question of the link between adult and childhood schizophrenias. Both writers had little experience with young children, and they did not offer descriptions of predisposing traits and circumstances in childhood. Nor is it clear what modifications they made in applying criteria for adult diagnosis to children. Kraepelin's descriptions of simple, hebephrenic, paranoid, and catatonic reactions in dementia praecox are still considered pertinent in the categorization of adult schizophrenic reactions. However, generally speaking, these four syndromes have not been regarded as applicable to childhood reactions. Bleuler's precise definition of the symptoms of schizophrenia were more applicable to children. During the 1930's and 1940's child psychiatrists[3,17,24,80] became intrigued by the likelihood that typical schizophrenic reactions could appear long before adolescence. On the other hand, they recognized that symptomatic expression of psychosis in childhood was influenced by the child's cognitive immaturity. Potter,[80] for example, explained the infrequency and simplicity of the delusional reactions in psychotic children by their limitations in language and their concreteness of thought. Even Bleuler's symptoms had to be modified if they were to be used in the categorization of aberrant behaviors in children.

Progress in the definition and understanding of the psychoses of childhood thus began with the elaboration of symptomatic criteria uniquely suited to the forms and boundaries of childhood expression. Even more crucially, a great impetus to the evolution of understanding and diagnosis of childhood psychoses was the recognition that the definable entities of childhood psychosis all represented patterns of disorganization or impairment in behavioral maturation. Thus, psychiatrists were impelled first to search for early onset histories of schizophrenia. They soon discovered, however, that the criteria used in the diagnosis of schizophrenic reactions in adolescent or later years had to be modified to include forms of behavior that are uniquely evident in early childhood. In this extrapolation, they made the rather large assumption of equivalence in psychopathological and dynamic significance of the different forms of deviant expression in childhood and later years. Finally, they discarded their efforts to find childhood equivalents of adult schizophrenic symptoms. Instead they tended to stress maturational deficit as the primary signs of psychosis. When they took this necessary diagnostic step it became evident that the presumed link between childhood schizophrenia and adult schizophrenia was tenuous indeed. It became clear that though historically there had been expressed a historic relationship between the two classes of impairment which had led to an equivalence in names, it did not follow that there was an equivalence in psychological significance and certainly not in etiology.

This historic trend toward differentiation of the two conditions should become evident if one compares Bleuler's criteria for the diagnosis of adult schizophrenia with more recent criteria for diagnosis of childhood psychosis. Bleuler[15] described primary and secondary symptoms of schizophrenia. Primary symptoms included (1) autism, that is, the unusual predominance of inner fantasy life over reality, (2) fragmentation and lack of continuity of association, (3) affective disharmony and disturbance, and (4) extreme emotional ambivalence. Secondary symptoms included (1) hallucinations, (2) delusions, (3) illusions, and (4) motor aberrations, such as catatonia.

In one of the earlier applications of Bleuler's criteria in the diagnosis of childhood schizophrenia, Potter[80] proposed the following criteria: (1) a generalized retraction of interests from the environment; (2) unrealistic thinking, feeling, acting; (3) disturbances of thought, for example, blocking, condensation, symbolization, perseveration, incoherence, and diminution; (4) defect in emotional rapport; (5) diminution, rigidity, and distortion of affect; (6) behavioral alteration, exaggerated increase or decrease in motility, or bizarre, perseverative, stereotyped behavior. The absence of Bleuler's secondary symptoms, such as hallucinations and delusions, in Potter's criteria for diagnosis of childhood schizophrenia is noteworthy, inasmuch as Potter felt this reflected the immaturity of the children. Potter's criteria are, perhaps, more related to Bleuler's primary symptoms, although even these adult and child criteria do not precisely replicate each other. Potter's symptoms of childhood schizophrenia represent an early recognition that, quite unlike the approach to adult schizophrenia, diagnosis of childhood schizophrenia is based on the observation of developmental deviation in crucial, purposeful functions.

Bradley and Bowen[18] reflected the developing empiricism and the recognition that adult criteria were not suitable for diagnosis of childhood schizophrenia. They asked themselves what traits do in fact characterize schizophrenic children. They described observable, objective symptoms in a group of children under therapeutic observation, including four children with actual schizophrenic psychosis and ten children with evidences of schizoid personalities. (Implicitly, none of the children replicated precisely all the attributes of Bleuler's adult schizophrenia and certainly not of Kraepelin's dementia praecox.) Eight characteristics differentiated these 14 children from 124 other children admitted to residential treatment. In order of frequency these traits were (1) seclusiveness, (2) instability when seclusiveness was disturbed, (3) daydreaming, (4) bizarre behavior, (5) diminution in number of personal interests, (6) regressive nature of personal interests, (7) sensitivity to comment and criticism, (8) physical inactivity. Bradley was impressed, however, with the primary symptomatic significance of seclusiveness, bizarre behavior, and regression. These three primary or key symptoms have little obvious link to Bleuler's primary symptoms of adult schizophrenia,

which still represent the current key criteria of adolescent and adult schizophrenia. Bradley recommended that the diagnosis of childhood schizophrenia be founded chiefly on aberrations in the child's psychological growth.

Beginning in the 1950's, the emphasis on dysmaturation as the key to diagnosis of childhood schizophrenia was represented in the work of two major observers in the field, Lauretta Bender[3] and Leo Kanner.[56]

Although convinced from the beginning that childhood schizophrenia was related etiologically to adult schizophrenia and that both were genetically determined, Bender's many important descriptions of childhood schizophrenia have emphasized the central significance of disturbances in growth. The symptoms she recommended for diagnosis had little obvious link to the adult manifestations of schizophrenia. Indeed at one point, she noted that childhood schizophrenia could assume forms that subsumed every variety of childhood disorder.[8] Thus she described a pseudodefective type, a pseudoneurotic type, a psychosomatic type, a pseudopsychopathic type, a type with frank psychotic expression, and a latent type. Suffice it to say that she proposed that the central core of schizophrenia, which is expressed in many forms, is "a total psychological disorder in the regulation of maturation of all the basic behavior functions seen clinically in childhood. Thus it is a maturation lag with embryonic features as characterized by primitive (embryonic) plasticity in all patterned behavior in the autonomic or vegetative, perceptual, motor, intellectual, emotional and social areas." It is difficult to appreciate sufficiently the historic significance of Bender's exquisite clinical descriptions which anticipated virtually all later descriptive and phenomenological investigation of schizophrenic children and which focused the attention of all subsequent observers on disturbances in biological and psychological maturation as a key to diagnosis. Again, however, we should like to stress that, although convinced herself of the unity of childhood and adult schizophrenia, Bender's criteria for diagnosis of childhood schizophrenia had no prima facie connection with Bleuler's primary and secondary symptoms of adult schizophrenia.

The second major observer was Kanner[56] who, during 1942, published his classical report on early infantile autism. This report is still the best description of the autistic syndrome. Kanner's criteria for the diagnosis of infantile autism were as follows:

1. Aloneness, extreme in degree and evident in earliest infancy. The babies do not respond with normal anticipatory gestures as the adults reach to pick them up and do not adapt to the bodies of those who hold them.

2. Impaired communication. Speech and language are not used for the purposes of communication. Often the children are entirely mute or, if speech is present, it is echolalic and does not convey meaning. Pronomial reversals and literalness are frequent; and affirmation is expressed by repetition rather than the use of the word "yes."

3. Obsessive insistence on the maintenance of sameness, with great anxiety in new and unfamiliar situations, and with repetitive ritualistic preoccupation.

4. Fascination for objects, in contrast to disinterest in people.

Kanner and his closest colleague, Eisenberg,[58] differentiated infantile autism from schizophrenia on the basis of onset history, course, and familial background. Thus, they held that, in contrast to schizophrenia, autism starts extremely early in infancy and the relatives of autistic children presumably do not show abnormally high incidence of schizophrenia. They also differentiated autism from mental deficiency, since the autistic child presumably shows segmental areas of normal or even superior intellectual capacity. Eisenberg[28] recommended that the expression "infantile autism" be restricted in use to children with psychotic onset during the first year of life and schizophrenia to children with psychotic onset at eight years or older. Bender[7] included autistic aberrations in her concept of multiple manifestations of a total psychological and maturational failure termed "schizophrenia." Others[86,87] supported Kanner's separation of the early autistic reaction from childhood schizophrenia. In contrast to Kanner and Rutter, some workers[10,74] observed an unusually large ratio of schizophrenic parents in the families of children with early psychotic onset. Certainly Rimland's[86] recommendations for differentiating the autistic children from schizophrenic children on the basis of signs in the former such as physical beauty, normal electroencephalograms, excellence in motor capacity, uniformly high intelligence and education of the parents, and the "idiot savant" character of intellectual organization are not supported by systematic clinical or experimental observation; indeed, these characteristics are often missing in children with early onset. It is safe to assume that apart from age of onset, the sharp differentiation of infantile autism from other psychotic reactions in early childhood is still uncertain.

As in Bender's work, Kanner emphasized developmental impairment in a broad array of psychological functions. His diagnostic criteria also had little apparent relationship to the criteria of adult psychosis. All important observers after Bender and Kanner have similarly called attention to the primary importance of maturational disorder in childhood as a key to the understanding and diagnosis of schizophrenic children.

Of special interest among these observers are those who, while recognizing predisposing factors, emphasized psychodynamic forces impeding the psychological growth of psychotic children. Of particular significance is the work of Mahler. In a series of papers[66–72] Mahler and her colleagues developed a psychodynamic approach derived from classical psychoanalysis. Mahler proposed that normal children move through three states of self-differentiation. (1) During the autistic phase between birth and three months, the normal infant is presumably aware of inner stimuli only and does not perceive objects outside his body. (2) During the symbiotic phase of development, beginning at about three months, the child is incipiently aware of an external object capable of satisfying his needs but does not sharply differentiate his mother from his image of self. (3) Then at twelve to eighteen months, during the separation-individuation phase, the baby begins more sharply to differentiate himself from the nonself. Mahler postulated that children suffering from the autistic psychosis have not developed beyond the normal autistic phase. In the symbiotic psychosis, Mahler postulated that the children have not been able to accommodate to the challenge of separation and individuation. In a state of panic, these children may regress to the autistic state, in which a clear personal identity is totally lacking.

Other workers, too, have represented a psychodynamic bias. Earlier than most, Despert[24] took a psychotherapeutic position and described the difficulties of schizophrenic children in attaining normal emotional relatedness to reality. For many years, Szurek (Boatman and Szurek[16]) related his therapeutic management of schizophrenic children to a psychodynamic hypothesis. He proposed that the disorders of schizophrenia result from emotional conflict and their miscarried resolution. He thus attempted to alleviate the disorders by intensive psychotherapy of the children and their parents. Rank[83] and Putnam[81] also emphasized psychodynamic and developmental features of the disorder.

Apart from their contributions to the issue of etiology, which we shall be considering later in this report, Despert, Mahler, Szurek, Rank, Putnam, and many others like them represent a group of psychiatric observers who have been impelled by therapeutic, rehabilitative objectives. With this orientation, they have been primarily concerned with the psychic growth of individual children over time. This is a developmental approach to childhood psychosis, in which schizophrenic children are appraised in terms of ontogenetic history and in the context of normal child development.

To recapitulate, psychiatrists first looked for expressions of adult psychosis in childhood. They then found that criteria for diagnosis of adult psychosis needed extensive modification before they could be applied to children. Soon, also, psychiatrists began to develop criteria that were uniquely suited to the delineation of extreme behavioral aberrations in childhood and that were quite unlike those employed for adult diagnosis. Theoretical or factual links between the criteria used in childhood and those employed in adulthood have not been well elaborated. These links thus remain ambiguous.

What hard facts, however, bear on the question? Certainly, virtually by definition, few individuals who manifest first signs of schizophrenia in adolescence or adult life will have shown manifestations of childhood schizophrenia during their early childhood. Follow-up studies of schizophrenic children do show more suggestive overlap between diagnosed schizophrenia of children and schizophrenia of adolescent or later years. The most frequently reported study, that of Bender and Grugett,[10] stated that 87 percent of a group of children who had been diagnosed schizophrenic during childhood were diagnosed as schizophrenic during adolescence or adult life. The very high incidence of adult schizophrenia when schizophrenic children reach adulthood has been confirmed in virtually all follow-up studies.*

In Bennett and Klein's[11] follow up of fourteen schizophrenic children thirty years after the diagnosis of childhood schizophrenia, nine were in hospitals and only one was maintaining himself outside. (Two were dead, and two could not be located.) Of particular interest was their observation that the nine hospitalized cases could not be differentiated from other chronically deteriorated adult schizophrenic patients in the same hospitals. How accurate is this observation, which at best is a qualitative one? It is undoubtedly difficult to distinguish the markedly deteriorated adult patient from the very regressed schizophrenic child who has not succeeded in maturing in adaptive function as he has grown older. Most follow-up studies are after all retrospective. There is obvious advantage in observing the schizophrenic child in a prospective fashion as

---

* See references 1, 11, 19, 20, 25, 27, 50, 84, and 87.

he matures; for then it frequently becomes evident that the highly impaired or primitive schizophrenic child changes very little as he grows older and that his personality in adult years is quite like that in his childhood. Since he has not deteriorated in his adult years, he has not "become" an adult schizophrenic. He is still in a sense a childhood schizophrenic in personality organization; and his early personality is merely residing in an older body.

A genetic study, such as that of Kallmann and Roth[55] would seem to support the notion that childhood schizophrenia and adult schizophrenia are both processes related to the same gene-specific deficiency state. However, this study focused on children who had grown normally before onset of the psychotic disorder. Thus the average age of onset was 8.8 years. In this sense, the study has little bearing on the processes involved in the very early childhood psychoses.

In addition to differences in their diagnostic criteria, childhood schizophrenia and adult schizophrenia each subsume a wide diversity of disorders. Among schizophrenic children, the range in personality and adaptive capacity is so great that the diagnosis of childhood schizophrenia ordinarily has virtually no bearing on the treatment plans formulated for each individual child. Some of the children are largely devoid of adaptive skills, including intelligence, language, and social capacity. Others are extremely bright and verbal but laden with complex psychological defenses. In view of the heterogeneity of schizophrenic children and the broad diversity of adult schizophrenic reactions as well, it would seem wise to explore the problems of childhood schizophrenia apart from any links to adult schizophrenia. In addition, empirical experience in the follow up of schizophrenic children has demonstrated that while a large proportion are ultimately classified as schizophrenic in late adolescence or adulthood, others are reasonably classified in other categories of adult pathology, for example, mental deficiency, organic brain syndrome, and a variety of other classes of disorder. A primary need is the longitudinal observation of schizophrenic children for detailed study of variations in life course to be noted among individual schizophrenic children. Since all of the schizophrenic children to be studied as individuals are, nevertheless, members of the same gross diagnostic class, a standard set of diagnostic criteria is required to select such children for purposes of treatment and study.

◖ Diagnosis of Childhood Schizophrenia

As a general background for discussion of the diagnosis of childhood schizophrenia, Eisenberg's[28] approach to a wider classification of childhood psychoses recommends itself. As in adulthood, psychoses of childhood refer to deep functional impairments relative to normal children of equal age including gross disorders in personality, regressive defenses, bizarre and socially unacceptable behavior, and markedly deficient testing of reality. In this larger group of psychoses, Eisenberg first differentiated disorders caused by or associated with impairment of brain tissue and with demonstrable pathology of brain tissue from psychotic disorders in which structural changes in the brain have not as yet been demonstrated.

The psychoses with unequivocally demonstrable brain tissue pathology include the toxic psychoses (for example, atropine poisoning), metabolic psychoses (for example, pellagra), degenerative psychoses (for example, Schilder's disease), and infectious psychoses (for example, paresis), disrhythmic psychoses (for example, psychomotor seizures), traumatic psychoses, and neoplastic psychoses. These are often easily diagnosed and warrant immediate and appropriate treatment.

The remaining psychoses are those in which demonstrable and unequivocal brain tissue changes have not as yet been demonstrated. This group of functional disorders has never been adequately subdivided. It includes children previously described under a wide assortment of labels including infantile autism,[56] childhood schizophrenia,[3] atypical child syndrome,[83] childhood psychosis,[16] psychosis on top of mental deficit,[61,97] and rare reactions termed "folie à deux."[28] As previously reported, Eisenberg himself recommended restricting the infantile autistic reactions to disorders with onset during the first year and schizophrenia to disorders with onset after eight years of age. The latter disorders presumably satisfy the criteria for diagnosis of schizophrenia in adulthood. Eisenberg also implied that the categories of infantile autism and schizophrenia encompass the bulk of the functional psychotic disorders. In view of the obvious overlapping among the children included in each of the above subgroups, there would seem to be wisdom in disregarding the many descriptive labels, in continuing to deal with the functional disorders as a large heterogeneous group termed "schizophrenic syndromes of childhood," and in seeking bases for subdividing the larger group along a series of empirically determined dimensions. Onset history, for example, is an example of a useful kind of parameter for such subclassification. Other dimensions for such subdivision will be recommended.

It is necessary first to have a set of diagnostic criteria for the diagnosis of the broad category of childhood schizophrenia that most workers could agree on. During 1961, after extensive discussion, a group of British workers[22] agreed on the following criteria:

1. Gross and sustained impairment of emotional relationships with people. This includes the more usual aloofness and the empty clinging (so-called symbiosis); also abnormal behavior towards other people as persons, such as using them impersonally. Difficulty in mixing and playing with other children is often outstanding and long lasting.

2. Apparent unawareness of his own personal identity to a degree inappropriate to his age. This may be seen in abnormal behavior towards himself, such as posturing or exploration and scrutiny of parts of his body. Repeated self-directed aggression, sometimes resulting in actual damage, may be another aspect of his lack of integration (see also point 5) as

is also the confusion of personal pronouns (see point 7).

3. Pathological preoccupation with particular objects or certain characteristics of them without regard to their accepted function.

4. Sustained resistance to change in the environment and a striving to maintain or restore sameness. In some instances behavior appears to aim at producing a state of perceptual monotony.

5. Abnormal perceptual experience (in the absence of discernible organic abnormality) is implied by excessive, diminished, or unpredictable response to sensory stimuli—for example, visual and auditory avoidance (see also points 2 and 4), insensitivity to pain and temperature.

6. Acute, excessive and seemingly illogical anxiety is a frequent phenomenon. This tends to be precipitated by change, whether in material environment or in routine, as well as by temporary interruption of a symbiotic attachment to persons or things (compare points 3 and 4, and also 1 and 2). (Apparently commonplace phenomena or objects seem to become invested with terrifying qualities. On the other hand, an appropriate sense of fear in the face of real danger may be lacking.)

7. Speech may have been lost or never acquired, or may have failed to develop beyond a level appropriate to an earlier stage. There may be confusion of personal pronouns (see point 2), echolalia, or other mannerisms of use and diction. Though words or phrases may be uttered, they may convey no sense of ordinary communication.

8. Distortion in motility patterns—for example, (a) excess as in hyperkinesis, (b) immobility as in catatonia, (c) bizarre postures, or ritualistic mannerisms, such as rocking and spinning (themselves or objects.)

9. A background of serious retardation in which islets of normal, near normal, or exceptional function or skill may appear.

Since the criteria were reported by the British working group in 1961, they have been widely applied to diagnosis of schizophrenic children. In one treatment center,* a review of the symptoms of all children discharged over a ten-year period with the diagnosis of childhood schizophrenia demonstrated that all the symptoms of the children were encompassed in the nine signs listed above. All these children evidenced at least five of the nine signs. In addition, all the children manifested impairment in human relationships, defects in personal identity, excessive anxiety provoked by change, and disturbance in speech and communication. As further support for the practical utility of the nine signs, a review of a large number of reports, which included descriptions of symptoms of childhood schizophrenia,[42] showed that all the symptoms described by the many authors were encompassed by the nine points.

It can be stated unequivocally that the children who are filtered out by these clear though broad criteria are highly heterogeneous in behavioral attributes and capacities, in psychosocial and social class characteristics of the family, and in neurological manifestations. Beyond the mere diagnosis of childhood schizophrenia, there is an obvious need to subdivide the children into homogeneous subclasses. In this regard, the dominant disposition of psychiatric observers is still to propose systems of subclassification in which adult schizophrenia remains a central referent. In other words, these observers tend to ask only if childhood psychosis is or is not an extension of adult schizophrenia; and, by implication, they have no reason to subclassify. Thus some workers would tend to term the reactions of all the children "schizophrenic" (for example, Bender[9]). Others distinguish infantile autism from schizophrena.[28,56,86,87] The latter restrict infantile autism to children with onset of their behavioral disorders in infancy, that is, birth to approximately two years. Eisenberg[28] and Rutter[87] restricted the diagnosis of schizophrenia even further to children with onset of their symptoms after eight years of

age. Presumably, these children are examples of schizophrenic reaction that does not differ from the schizophrenic reactions of later years. Children with histories of onset between two and eight years are considered most often to be cases of primary organic psychosis other than autism or schizophrenia.

Perhaps the most explicit and most precise differentiation of early childhood psychosis and schizophrenia is that of Rutter.[88] Beyond the obvious differences in age of onset, Rutter believed childhood psychosis and schizophrenia to be independent, non-overlapping conditions. Thus, he pointed out that unlike schizophrenia, which rarely appears before pubescence, childhood psychosis is frequently associated with mental subnormality and cerebral dysfunction and is only rarely associated with the secondary symptoms of adult schizophrenia, such as hallucinations, delusions, and paranoid ideation. In addition, familial history of adult schizophrenia is presumably rare in childhood psychosis.[58,87,88] However, even these findings of difference have not been established in a totally unequivocal fashion. Most systematic studies have confirmed the frequent association of early childhood psychosis with mental subnormality, and by implication, the weaker association between low intelligence and adult schizophrenia. However, a significant proportion of children with early childhood psychosis have very superior intelligence. Sizable changes in IQ over a three-year period have been noted in a high percentage of psychotic children in residential treatment with a consequent tendency to augment the number with high IQs, though the children with lowest IQs tend not to change.[44] Similarly, although a very high proportion gives signs of cerebral dysfunction, a sizable (albeit smaller) proportion does not present these neurological signs. To complicate matters, it would now appear that a large percentage of patients with onset of schizophrenia in adolescence also give evidence of cerebral dysfunction.[13] In Pollin's very important studies of adult twins discordant for schizophrenia, the schizophrenic twin was more likely to manifest soft evidence of neurological dysfunctions.[77] It is true, too, that

* Henry Ittleson Center for Child Research

children with very early onset of psychosis rarely present symptoms such as hallucinations, delusions, and elaborate paranoid reactions. (However, we have been more impressed than Rutter by the frequent paranoid expressions, perhaps restricted to the brighter, more verbal children.) Finally, some workers[10,74] have diagnosed schizophrenia in the parents, especially the mothers, with much greater frequency than noted by Kanner[57] and Rutter.[87]

Other data differentiating autistic from schizophrenic children have been described by a number of authors.[57] For example, the superior educational and vocational status of parents of autistic children has been noted. Yet more recent studies have demonstrated families of children with early infantile psychosis come from all social classes.[40,73] Recently, with increased referral of children by poverty agencies, the ratio of cases of early infantile psychosis among low social class families in therapeutic installations has been increased. Obviously, the artifact of sampling will influence the distribution of families in regard to social class position.

Among diagnosed schizophrenic children, there are wide variations in personality organization, symptomatology, clinical course, patterns and level of intellectual organization, and contributing circumstances. They range from near total absence of affective and social response, language, and cognitive capacity to high levels of ideational response and affectivity. In some, affective meagerness and social withdrawal are the dominant behavior. In others, the children show complex protective mechanisms, including phobic, obsessional, paranoid and depressive reactions, and at times, delusional responses. Some grow up quite unchanged in clinical manifestation. Others improve dramatically and attain normal levels of educational and social response. The contributions to the child's symptoms of factors, such as familial or neurological deviance, vary from child to child. While Rutter[87] has stressed the failures in language in the children he has studied, as shown, for example, in superiority of performance capacity over verbal capacity as measured in standard tests, such intellectual patterning and segmental failure in verbal response have not been confirmed in other samplings of schizophrenic children (for example, see Goldfarb and Goldfarb[44]).

Differences among observers of schizophrenic children undoubtedly reflect the heterogeneity of the children and the artifact of sampling. No single description of a necessarily limited sample of children suffering from early childhood psychosis can be generalized to the entire population of psychotic children. Therefore, there is no simple answer to the question of whether schizophrenia is one condition encompassing the bulk of childhood as well as adult psychoses or, on the other hand, whether the adult and childhood psychoses are totally disparate and non-overlapping.

Fortunately, the absence of unequivocal evidence as to the presence or absence of association between childhood schizophrenia and adult schizophrenia is not a serious hindrance to the creative evolution of treatment methods and of programs of investigation. After all, the diagnosis of a treatment plan for an individual schizophrenic child should not be linked crucially to the fact that he has been classified as schizophrenic. Rather, the treatment plan should be determined by a careful evaluation of each child's unique pattern of ego organization, his specific adaptive strengths and weaknesses, and the life experiences to which he has been exposed. In research, too, the most meaningful information will reflect the highly individual interplay between constitutional and environmental factors.

⟮ Subclassification of Schizophrenic Children

The primary necessity is to have more information regarding the life course of individual schizophrenic children and to gather such knowledge through the use of precise baselines for description and appraisal of change. By grouping the children on the basis of common patterns of change in the appropriate factors, the clusters of children that emerge provide homogeneous groupings which otherwise remain hidden behind nonspecific categories such as schizophrenia and autism.

As will be stressed, a more profitable basis for subclassification of schizophrenic children, therefore, is one that takes into account the broad range in individual adaptive capacity of the children and in factors, both internal and external, that influence their psychological growth. In such subclassification, also, the association between the psychotic child's individual growth, the adaptive capacities of the child, his neurological integrity, and the level of psychosocial functioning of his family should be noted.

For deciding which adaptive attributes might be included in systematic subclassification, investigations of purposeful functions in schizophrenic children are already helpful. The levels of behavior that have been reported include sensation, perception, conceptualization, and psychomotor response. The functions represented are involved in the child's efforts to orient himself and contact reality, to make meaningful generalizations about reality, to test these generalizations, and to manipulate them in the service of adaptation and survival.

Frequently in clinical study of schizophrenic children, the possibility of sensory loss or marked elevation in sensory thresholds has had to be considered. Pseudodeafness, for example, has been noted frequently. In contrast, observations of hypersensitive reactions have stimulated the hypothesis of diminished sensory thresholds. Actual studies of sensory thresholds,[36] however, have demonstrated normal thresholds for vision (A-O charts at twenty feet), for hearing (pure tone audiometry), and for touch (Von Frey Test). Though they have demonstrated normal auditory thresholds to pure tone stimulation, schizophrenic children showed more elevated thresholds for speech than for pure tones.[52] While further studies are needed, this discrepancy would support the conclusion that the phenomenon of not hearing may reflect altered attention to and awareness of human speech rather than impaired sensory acuity.

In contrast to the evidence that the schizophrenic child's apparatus for receiving sensory impression is intact, all investigations have demonstrated inferiority, relative to normal children, in perceptual discrimination.[12,32–34,36] Numerous studies have also confirmed deficits in abstract and conceptual behavior.[31,36, 75,90] Included in these studies of conceptual failure are the many investigations that have demonstrated the strong trend to low intellectual response[78] and impairments in communication.[36] Psychomotor behavior is found to be equally impaired.[36]

Inferences regarding the defects in perceptual discrimination, in the ordering of perceptual information for the attainment of meaning, and in the execution of adaptive acts refer to studies using summary statistics based on groups of children. However, there is a very broad range of capacity in all the purposeful functions among individual schizophrenic children, which often remains unnoticed in the group summary statistics. For example, the children range from extreme intellectual deficiency, so severe that mental testing is not feasible, to very superior intellectual functioning (see for example, Goldfarb and Goldfarb.[44]) Some of the children are totally devoid of language and are extremely restricted in educability and capacity for self-care. Others are superior in intellectual and educational competence.

In addition, the children differ greatly among themselves in course of development. A large proportion of the children do remain chronically impaired. Others attain fairly normal levels of capacity for schooling and community living. In most follow-up studies, the ratio of children who attain such moderately normal levels range from a quarter to a third of the children.[5,19,50,58] Recent studies of changes in specific adaptive functions show comparable variations. Individual curves of growth in reading in response to schooling while in residential treatment vary from a reflection of complete uneducability to a reflection of advanced educational response.[49] Similarly, in recent studies of change in the Wechsler Full IQ of schizophrenic children while in a therapeutic residence, some of the children showed no change and others showed dramatic changes that seem to be linked to comparable shifts in clinical status.[44]

In anticipation of a proposal for subclassifying schizophrenic children, it should be noted at this point that the general level of adaptive capacity of schizophrenic children at the start of therapeutic observation is associated with their later and ultimate progress. Clinical follow-up studies, for example, have confirmed that children who have very low intelligence quotients and who are devoid of verbal speech at five to six years of age show uniformly poor clinical progress.[50,58,87] Systematic observation of longitudinal change in specific perceptual, conceptual, and psychomotor functions confirm the fact that children with lowest intellectual functioning (Wechsler Full IQs below 45) remain quite unchanged, whereas children of greater initial capacity show significant improvements.[44]

Although schizophrenic children manifest failures at all levels of behavior, including receptor, integrative, and executive levels, a number of observers have emphasized particularly the deficiencies in perceptual-afferent response. Clinical and experimental observation has confirmed abnormality in the hierarchy of receptor organization[35,51,89] and in intersensory integration.[14] Thus, schizophrenic children often avoid focused visual and auditory attention to objects in their environment; touching, tasting, and smelling are substituted. The apparent auditory and visual imperception may well be a later and defensive reaction to the discomfort of initial hyperacusis. Such primary failure in the afferent organization of behavior apparently precludes discriminative response, separation of figure from ground, anticipatory response, and monitored learning more generally. It may be presumed that the failure to achieve a pattern of auditory commitment, for example, is a factor in the impaired speech of schizophrenic children or that the schizophrenic child's deficits in discrimination of difference in shape and directional orientation[51] are exaggerated by visual inattention.

While stressing the deficiencies of schizophrenic children in the reception and organization of sensory input, it must be repeated that failures have been noted in all aspects of adaptive functioning, that is, in central organization or conceptualization of perceptual information and in the motor and executive levels of behavior. In addition, a serious consequence of the failures in adaptive response is a drastic absence of sharp inner awareness of the self in action as differentiated from the nonself.[38] Beyond this, schizophrenic children suffer intense anxiety as an outcome of their inability to achieve feelings of familiarity, permanence, and predictability.

How can a theory of etiology help in subclassifying the children? The precise cause of the above noted adaptive failures in childhood schizophrenia has not been established. Three kinds of etiological hypothesis have been formulated. One variety of hypothesis emphasizes primary and intrinsic deficiencies in the schizophrenic child. Another variety of hypothesis proposes that the psychosocial environment is the primary causal agent leading to the development of the schizophrenic syndrome. The third view of etiology proposes that all schizophrenic reactions reflect the influence of both intrinsic and extrinsic factors. The latter position is favored in the present report for its value in diagnosis, subclassification, formulating individual treatment plans, and designing research. This point of view assumes that primary atypism and deviant psychosocial influence are dimensional in character, that is, they vary in observable degree among individual schizophrenic children. The symptoms and character attributes embodied in the schizophrenic reaction reflect the interaction of the child's potentialities for adaptive response and the expectations and reinforcements of his outer world.

There are two general bodies of evidence in support of a primary atypism.[13] One body of evidence supports the etiological significance of inheritance and refers chiefly to familial concordance for psychosis. The other body of evidence refers to dysfunction and trauma of the central nervous system.

Bender and her coworkers argued most cogently that childhood schizophrenia and adult schizophrenia are both caused by the same genotype.[10] Her evidence is twofold, that is, the observation that the large majority of schizophrenic children who had been under her care ultimately developed symptoms of adult schizophrenia and the further observation that an unusual proportion of the children's mothers (43 percent) and fathers (40 percent) were mentally ill. Other studies of prevalence of schizophrenia in the families of schizophrenic children have tended to support the high incidence of parental schizophrenia, but to a lesser degree. Most significantly, there are wide statistical variations in the studies reported. In one sample of parents of early school-age schizophrenic children at the Ittleson Center, 28 percent of the mothers and 13 percent of the fathers were classified as schizophrenic.[74] In Kallmann and Roth's study[55] of fifty-two twins and fifty singletons, the parental schizophrenia rate was 9 percent. On the other hand, Kanner[56] noted that only one of one hundred parents showed major mental illness. Nor is it possible to explain the range of frequencies by the fact that Bender had fewer cases of infantile autism in her sample than Kanner, since Bender's sampling undoubtedly included a large percentage of cases of infantile autism by Kanner's criteria. Certainly, although the Kanner and Ittleson frequencies are quite different, a large percentage of the Ittleson Center population[74] were cases of very early infantile psychosis.

Methodologically, there can be no doubt that Kallmann and Roth's study of twin concordance in preadolescent schizophrenia was the most mature methodologically for studying the hereditary factor and freest of ordinary contaminants. In their study, dizygotic and monozygotic twins differed in concordance rates for preadolescent schizophrenia (17.1 percent and 70.6 percent) and for adult schizophrenia (14.7 percent and 85.8 percent). In this study, as in Kallmann's study of twin concordance rates for adult schizophrenia,[54] the differences between one-egg and two-egg twins were significant. The reporters concluded that preadolescent schizophrenia was determined by the same gene-specific deficiency state as adult schizophrenia. However, it must be emphasized again that the mean

age of onset of Kallmann's group, about 8.8 years, was much older than that of children with early psychosis. In addition, Kallmann and Roth excluded mentally deficient children, who represent the bulk of children in most studies of children with early childhood psychosis. The Kallmann and Roth results obviously are not applicable to children ordinarily included in investigations of early childhood schizophrenia.

Beyond these restrictions on the Kallmann and Roth findings for explaining childhood schizophrenia, more recent twin concordance studies (e.g. Kringlen[63]) in adult schizophrenia have tended to show smaller differences in concordance rates between one-egg and two-egg twins. In addition, as Birch and Hertzig[13] have argued, concordance rates in twins may reflect the greater risk of reproductive complications in the development of twins than in the development of singletons and also greater risk in the development of monozygotic twins than in dizygotic twins. This is of key importance since, as will be seen, the evidence of damage to the central nervous system in many children suffering from early childhood schizophrenia is very strong. The part played by a genetic factor in childhood schizophrenia still needs to be studied. Such study will have to include careful control of nervous and psychosocial factors.

Evidence for central nervous system impairment in a proportion of diagnosed schizophrenic children, however, is quite convincingly derived from many sources. Many studies have demonstrated a higher incidence of prenatal and perinatal complications.* Developmental deviations supporting the inference of dysfunction in the central nervous system have been noted by many observers.[6,21,30] In addition to deviations in neurological history, a proportion of schizophrenic children tend to give observable, though soft, evidence of neurological dysfunction in physical examination, including deviations in gait, posture, balance, motor coordination, muscle tone, and integration of multiple simultaneous stimuli.† In one

---

* See references 36, 60, 76, 93, 94, 96, and 99.
† See references 4, 36, 62, 79, 82, and 91.

clinical sample,[36] neurological examination diagnosed neurological dysfunction in 65 percent of a group of schizophrenic children. Severe restrictions in level and pattern of perceptual, perceptuomotor, and cognitive response as measured in formal tests have been interpreted as evidence of neurological dysfunction.[14,36,78,87] Perhaps of more direct significance, encephalographic studies have shown more frequent electroencephalogram abnormalities in schizophrenic children than in normals,[59,98] and high incidence of convulsions has been reported.[7,21]

In summary, therefore, prenatal and perinatal history, developmental trends, neurological histories, neurological examination, and systematic and controlled studies of neurological functions all offer strong evidence of a primary atypism in a high proportion of schizophrenic children. Historically, the disorders in integration of the central nervous system generally occur in the reproductive phase of development in early infancy. They express themselves early in infancy in disorders of sensorimotor integration and later in childhood in more complex cognitive and social failure.

The second general class of theories regarding the etiology of childhood schizophrenia refers to theories of environmental and psychosocial causation. The elucidation of psychogenic and environmental factors has come in large measure from the therapeutic case study and is represented in the descriptions of observers with strong and primary motivation to heal. The therapeutic and case approaches to investigation are highly vulnerable to such errors as insufficient clinical documentation, vagueness of definition, and bias. Nevertheless, they are still our most valid tools for observing individual children in living situations and in process of growth, and for grasping the private, very subjective meanings and experiences of schizophrenic children. The high incidence of mental illness in the parents of schizophrenic children has been noted. While this can be interpreted as evidence for a specific genotype, it is also likely that schizophrenic parents represent an environmental challenge to the children as well. In support of

this thesis, a systematic study of the psychosocial functioning of the families of schizophrenic children revealed that the families with one or two schizophrenic parents were less adequate in psychosocial functioning than those in which neither parent was schizophrenic.[74] Finally, direct observations of family functioning and patterns of communication have tended to support the hypothesis that the families and parents of schizophrenic children deviate from normal.*

However, it has always been clear that not all the schizophrenic children show evidence of neurological dysfunctioning and not all the parents and families are functionally aberrant. A significant proportion of the children also offer fairly clear evidence of dysfunction of the central nervous system and, in addition, have families that are unequivocally and extremely aberrant. A multicausal theory of etiology inclusive enough to explain all the known evidence would seem to be the most effective way of rationalizing the manifestations of childhood schizophrenia.

A multicausal theory of etiology facilitates a transactional approach to the comprehension of schizophrenic children as individuals. In this approach the disordered adaptation of each schizophrenic child is presumed to reflect the interplay of intrinsic deficits in the child and of deviation in psychosocial organization of the family. It is also presumed that each of these classes of aberration varies dimensionally from none to marked and that the relative contributions of each class of disorder to the functional impairments of the child vary from child to child. In some children, primary atypism of the child is the dominant causal factor; in others, the deviant family climate is the dominant causal factor. The former would be illustrated in the very seriously brain-damaged child in a normal family, and the latter would be illustrated in the neurologically and somatically intact child in a highly deviant family. Often too, one may note a neurologically impaired child who has been reared in a functionally deviant family. In a recent qualitative, psychiatric appraisal of

---

* See references 2, 36, 37, 47, 65, 74, 85, and 92.

neurological and familial contributions to the ego aberrations of forty schizophrenic children under intensive therapeutic care and very detailed observation (for purposes of longitudinal study), the children were distributed as in Table 5–1. By clinical judgment, tend not to show significant improvement in IQ during three years of residential treatment. In contrast, children at higher, measurable levels of intellectual response often do show significant improvement in WISC IQ. While absence of language by the age of five to six

TABLE 5–1.

Psychosocial factors dominant; no evidence of neurological dysfunction	30.0%
Evidence of neurological dysfunction	70.0%
Neurological dysfunction dominant; no evidence of psychosocial factors	27.5%
Psychosocial factors more dominant than neurological dysfunction	20.0%
Both psychosocial factors and neurological dysfunction signficant	22.5%

therefore, while the majority of the schizophrenic children appraised showed evidence of cerebral dysfunction, psychosocial and familial influences contributed in a primary or crucial way to the adaptive failures of the children in almost 73 percent of the cases. We are proposing that subclassification include an assay of neurological and psychosocial influences.

In conclusion, we are now prepared to recommend a system of subclassification. It has demonstrated its usefulness for attaining meaningful subgroupings of schizophrenic children. In other words, the subgroupings differ from each other in average adaptive capacity and etiological influence. In addition we have already been able to demonstrate that the subgroupings show significant differences in growth patterns.[44]

Level of Intellectual Functioning

Tests of intelligence are viewed as tests of overall adaptive functioning and the IQ is seen as a measure of clinical status and functional capacity.[36] The value of the IQ as a predictor of clinical improvement has been demonstrated by a number of follow-up studies.[26,50,87] Children who cannot speak and have the most extremely inferior IQs (for example, below fifty) show no significant clinical progress. In a recent study,[44] children with intellectual functioning so inferior at admission as to be unmeasurable in the WISC

years has also been regarded as an important indication of bad prognosis,[26,50,87] Rutter has demonstrated, however, that such language failure is of key predictive significance if linked to low intellectual functioning.

Age of Onset and Age of Admission to Treatment

Age of onset has been emphasized by many observers as a factor of major import in defining the diagnosis and life course of schizophrenic children.[24,27,87] Quality of onset is in itself related to age of onset. Presumptively insidious onset, for example, is more likely to be associated with very early onset, and acute onset implies later onset. In experience with schizophrenic children of early elementary school age in treatment at the Ittleson Center, virtually all the children demonstrated developmental aberrations and symptoms from the earliest months of life, including the small percentage (about 13 percent) who also showed clear historic evidence of acute reactions. On the other hand, age of admission may be defined in an objective and reliable fashion. A gross relationship between the constructs age of onset and age of admission to treatment may be presumed. It does emerge that age of admission to treatment does differentiate among schizophrenic children in terms of level of integrative and adaptive response and life course, even where the range of admission age is fairly narrow. This has been noted, for example, in a comparison of early school-age schizophrenic children admitted to residential treatment at eight years of age or older and those admitted below eight years of age.[44] The children admitted at eight years or older showed higher levels of IQ than those admitted to treatment at younger ages. While both groups improved significantly in WISC Full IQ over three years of residential treatment, the younger children improved to a greater degree in IQ. Even so, the children admitted at the older ages maintained their cognitive superiority at each year of treatment over those children admitted at ages below eight years.

Sex

All investigations of childhood schizophrenia have confirmed the greater proportion of boys than of girls in those who are diagnosed as schizophrenic. The boy to girl ratio varies among subclusters of schizophrenic children grouped by a variety of other independent variables. For example, the proportion of boys is considerably higher among schizophrenic children with evidence of neurological dysfunction than among those without evidence of neurological dysfunction, where the proportion of boys and girls are about equal.[44,74] If we take into account the overlapping between sex and other variables and the evidence that differences between boys and girls in longitudinal change reflect, at least in part, the influence of these overlapping variables and of sampling as well, there is still great validity in including gender in a system of subclassification inasmuch as the boys and girls seem to differ as groups. At the Ittleson Center, where attention has been paid to the issue of sex, group differences between schizophrenic boys and girls have been observed in psychodynamics, intelligence, level of ego organization, educability, and the influence of cerebral and psychosocial factors.

Level of Neurological Integration

Employing the judgment of qualified psychiatric neurologists and using neurological history and examination, it has been feasible to subdivide schizophrenic children with and without evidence of cerebral dysfunction. The neurological examination, of course, seeks hard evidence of neurological impairment, such as alteration in normal reflexes, abnormal reflexes, asymmetrical failures in sensory and motor response, and EEG abnormalities. However, in recent years, more emphasis has been placed on refined observation of impairments in gait, posture, balance, motor coordination and control, muscle tone, and the integration of multiple or multimodal stimuli. When the schizophrenic children are grossly subdivided into those who give these evidences of cerebral impairment (organic) and those who do not (nonorganic), a number of empirical findings distinguish the two subclusters. For example, the nonorganic children are superior to the organic children in most adaptive functions, including perceptual, conceptual, and psychomotor response.[36] The nonorganic and organic children also differ in regard to family patterns of interaction,[36,37] psychiatric status of the parents,[74] and in maternal communication.[48] Direct observations of families have tended to confirm that families of nonorganic children are virtually always deviant in psychosocial functioning, while organic children have families which are more heterogeneous in regard to adequacy of functioning and which include average as well as deviant families. A higher proportion of the mothers of nonorganic children than of organic children are schizophrenic. The mothers of nonorganic children have poorer speech[47] and are less clear in their communication.[48] Finally the two groups of children differ in course of development,[50] in response to day and residential treatment,[45] and in changes in specific ego functions.[44] The organic children include the most impaired and most unchanging children. On the other hand, while the organic children respond equally well to day and residential treatment, nonorganic children appear to show more progress in residential care, that is, the most comprehensive form of environmental treatment.[45] Neurological appraisal is a cardinal step in the differentiation of intrinsic and extrinsic influences.

Social Class Position

Schizophrenic children come from families at every level of social class position. Increasingly, too, it has become evident that the social class position of their families is associated with differences among the schizophrenic children. For example, in a recent longitudinal investigation, the schizophrenic children at high, middle, and low social class position differed in mean IQ at admission to treatment and in amount of change in IQ between admission and third year of treatment.[44] Thus, mean WISC Full IQs at admission and after three years of treatment were as shown in Table 5–2.

Then I discussed the diagnosis of childhood schizophrenia to arrive at a common basis for the classification of schizophrenic children. I emphasized the empirical finding that in spite of careful diagnosis, schizophrenic children were highly diversified in many important abilities and attributes, interpersonal and family experience, social class, and neurological integrity. Paralleling this diversity, a multiplicity of factors would appear to be linked to the adaptive disorders of schizophrenic children. In some children, intrinsic factors were linked to the schizophrenic child's manifestations. Thus, a high percentage of the children gave strong evidence of deficits in neurological and cerebral integrity. In some children, deviations

TABLE 5–2.

SOCIAL CLASS	HOLLINGSHEAD-REDLICH INDEX	MEAN WISC ADMISSION	FULL IQ THIRD YEAR
High	I, II	61.6	68.2
Middle	III	77.2	82.5
Low	IV, V	79.2	89.2

⟨ Conclusions

The reader has been asked to accompany me through a complex discussion of the ambiguities and inconsistencies in the construct of childhood schizophrenia. This discussion first stressed that the emergence of the category of childhood disorders termed "childhood schizophrenia" followed the prior evolution of the category of adult disorders termed "adult schizophrenia" and the confusing consequences of this historic association were noted. Though there was some apparent overlap between the two classes of disorder, they were not completely identical in symptoms and life course. I concluded that it was still wise to study and treat childhood schizophrenia as a set of conditions apart from adult schizophrenia. In addition, the most relevant focus in the study of schizophrenic children was presumed to be on the disturbances in maturation of purposeful functions and on factors influencing these disorders in psychological growth.

in family organization and functioning seemed to be associated with the schizophrenic child's behavior. In the latter connection, paralysis in parental functioning and unclear maternal communication have been noted.

In view of the heterogeneity of schizophrenic children and the apparent multiplicity of causative influences, there is little doubt that specific and precise therapeutic design to meet the needs of the individual schizophrenic child requires careful assay of his unique psychodynamic dispositions, functional capacities, and developmental experiences. In research and observation, too, it has seemed most profitable to seek a point of view that does not reject the seeming contradiction in observational data but rather rationalizes them. These inconsistencies are more apparent than real since such inconsistencies are inferred only if one begins with the assumption that schizophrenic children are homogeneous and that there is a single cause of childhood schizophrenia. Disparate findings begin to show a pattern if one assumes that schizophrenic children are highly diverse and that the causes are multiple. I have concluded that the key to the discovery of this pattern is the intensive developmental study of individual schizophrenic children. I have also proposed that the many levels of capacity, motivation, and experience need to be seen in dynamic interplay with one another as the child grows. For example, there is little value in merely labeling the social class position of the families of schizophrenic children as high (a currently favored conviction) or low. There is more profit, however, in defining the developmental implications of low or high social class experience for a specific schizophrenic child.

Finally, we have concluded that just as study of the growth of individual schizophrenic children is essential to dispel current ambiguities, it is equally essential to characterize these children individually by certain pertinent dimensions. The purpose of such characterization of individual children is to achieve homogeneous subclusters of schizophrenic children that permit generalization from the data. The present discussion has offered one system for subdividing schizophrenic children in which the dimensions employed reflect empirical experience as well as theoretic considerations.

⟨ Bibliography

1. ANNELL, A. L. "The Prognosis of Psychotic Syndromes in Children." *Acta Psychiatrica Scandinavica*, 39 (1963), 235–297.

2. BEHRENS, M., and GOLDFARB, W. "A Study of Patterns of Interaction of Families of Schizophrenic Children in Residential Treatment." *American Journal of Orthopsychiatry*, 28 (1958), 300–312.

3. BENDER, L. "Childhood Schizophrenia." *Nervous Child*, 1 (1941–1942), 138–140.

4. ———. "Childhood Schizophrenia: Clinical Study of One Hundred Schizophrenic Children." *American Journal of Orthopsychiatry*, 17 (1947), 40–56.

5. ———. "Childhood Schizophrenia." *Psychiatric Quarterly*, 27 (1953), 663–681.

6. ———. "Schizophrenia in Childhood: Its Recognition, Description, and Treatment." *American Journal of Orthopsychiatry*, 26 (1956), 499–506.

7. ———. "Autism in Children with Mental Deficiency." *American Journal of Mental Deficiency*, 63, no. 7 (1959), 81–86.

8. ———. "Treatment in Early Schizophrenia." *Progress in Psychotherapy*, 5 (1960), 177–184.

9. ———. "The Nature of Childhood Psychosis." In J. G. Howells, ed., *Modern Perspectives in International Child Psychiatry*. Edinburgh: Oliver & Boyd, 1969. Pp. 649–684.

10. ———, and GRUGETT, A. "A Study of Certain Epidemiological Factors in a Group of Children with Childhood Schizophrenia." *American Journal of Orthopsychiatry*, 26 (1956), 131–145.

11. BENNETT, S., and KLEIN, H. R. "Childhood Schizophrenia: 30 Years Later." *American Journal of Psychiatry*, 122 (1966), 1121–1124.

12. BERKOWITZ, P. H. "Some Psychological Aspects of Mental Illness in Children." *Genetic Psychology Monographs*, 63 (1961), 103–148.

13. BIRCH, H. G. and HERTZIG, M. E. "Etiology of Schizophrenia: An Overview of the Relation of Development to Atypical Behavior." In J. Romano, ed., *The Origins of Schizophrenia: Proceedings*. Amsterdam: Excerpta Medica Foundation, 1967. Pp. 92–111.

14. ———, and WALKER, H. A. "Perceptual and Perceptual-Motor Dissociation." *Archives of General Psychiatry*, 14, no. 2 (1966), 113–118.

15. BLEULER, E. *Dementia Praecox or the Group of Schizophrenias*. Trans. by Joseph Zinkin. New York: International Universities Press, 1952.

16. BOATMAN, M. J., and SZUREK, S. A. "A Clinical Study of Childhood Schizophrenia." In D. D. Jackson, ed., *The Etiology of Schizophrenia*. New York: Basic Books, 1960. Pp. 389–440.

17. BRADLEY, C. *Schizophrenia in Childhood*. New York: Macmillan, 1941.

18. ———, and BOWEN, M. "Behavior Characteristics of Schizophrenic Children." *Psychiatric Quarterly*, 15 (1941), 296–315.

19. BROWN, J. L. "Follow-Up of Children with Atypical Development (Infantile Psychosis)." *American Journal of Orthopsychiatry*, 33, no. 5 (1963), 855–861.

20. COLBERT, E. G., and KOEGLER, R. R. "The Childhood Schizophrenia in Adolescence." *Psychiatric Quarterly,* 35 (1961), 693–701.

21. CREAK, M. "Childhood Psychosis: A Review of 100 Cases." *British Journal of Psychiatry,* 109 (1963), 84–89.

22. ———, et al. "Schizophrenia Syndrome in Childhood: Report of a Working Party." *British Medical Journal,* 2 (1961), 889–890.

23. DESANCTES, S. "La Neuropsychiatria Infantile." *Infanzia Abnormale,* 18 (1925), 633–661.

24. DESPERT, J. L. "Schizophrenia in Childhood." *Psychiatric Quarterly,* 12 (1938), 366–371.

25. EATON, L., and MENOLASCINO, M. D. "Psychotic Reactions of Childhood: A Follow-Up Study." *American Journal Orthopsychiatry,* 37 (1967), 521–529.

26. EISENBERG, L. "The Autistic Child in Adolescence." *American Journal of Psychiatry,* 112 (1956), 607–613.

27. ———. "The Course of Childhood Schizophrenia." *Archives of Neurology and Psychiatry,* 78 (1957), 69–83.

28. ———. "Psychotic Disorders in Childhood." In R. E. Cook, ed., *Biological Basis of Pediatric Practice.* New York: McGraw-Hill, 1966.

29. EKSTEIN, R., BRYANT, K., and FRIEDMAN, S. W. "Childhood Schizophrenia and Allied Conditions." In L. Bellak and P. K. Benedict, eds., *Schizophrenia: A Review of the Syndrome.* New York: Logo Press, 1958. Pp. 555–593.

30. FISH, B. "Longitudinal Observations on Biological Deviation in the Schizophrenic Infant." *American Journal of Psychiatry,* 116, no. 1 (1959), 25–31.

31. FRIEDMAN, G. "Conceptual Thinking in Schizophrenic Children." *Genetic Psychology Monograph,* 63 (1961), 149–196.

32. FULLER, G. B. "A Further Study on Rotation: Cross Validation." *Journal of Clinical Psychology,* 19, no. 1 (1963), 127–128.

33. ———. "The Objective Measurement of Perception in Determining Personality Disorganization among Children." *Journal of Clinical Psychology,* 2, no. 3 (1965), 305–307.

34. ———, and CHAGNON, G. "Factors Influencing Rotation in the Bender Gestalt Performance of Children." *Journal of Projective Techniques,* 26 (1962), 36–46.

35. GOLDFARB, W. "Receptor Preferences in Schizophrenic Children." *Archives of Neurology and Psychiatry,* 76 (1956), 643–652.

36. ———. *Childhood Schizophrenia.* Cambridge, Mass.: Harvard University Press, 1961.

37. ———. "Families of Schizophrenic Children." In L. C. Kolb et al., eds., *Mental Retardation.* Baltimore, Md.: Williams & Wilkins, 1962. Pp. 256–269.

38. ———. "Self-awareness in Schizophrenic Children." *Archives of General Psychiatry,* 118 (1962), 902–915.

39. ———. "An Investigation of Childhood Schizophrenia: A Retrospective View." *Archives of General Psychiatry,* 11, no. 6 (1964), 620–634.

40. ———. "Factors in the Development of Schizophrenic Children: An Approach to Subclassification." In J. Romano, ed., *The Origins of Schizophrenia: Proceedings.* Amsterdam: Excerpta Medica Foundation, 1967. Pp. 70–92.

41. ———. "The Subclassification of Psychotic Children: Application to a Study of Longitudinal Change." In D. Rosenthal and S. Kety, eds., *The Transmission of Schizophrenia.* London: Pergamon Press, 1968. Pp. 333–334.

42. ———. "Childhood Psychosis." In P. H. Mussen, ed., *Manual of Child Psychology.* Vol. 2. New York: Wiley, 1970. Pp. 765–830.

43. ———, and DORSEN, M. *An Annotated Bibliography of Childhood Schizophrenia and Related Disorders.* New York: Basic Books, 1956.

44. ———, and GOLDFARB, N. *Schizophrenic Children in Residential Treatment: A Longitudinal Study of Growth and Change.* In preparation.

45. ———, GOLDFARB, N., and POLLACK, R. "A Three Year Comparison of Day and Residential Treatments of Schizophrenic Children." *Archives of General Psychiatry,* 14 (1966), 119–128.

46. ———, GOLDFARB, N., and POLLACK, R. "Changes in IQ of Schizophrenic Children During Residential Treatment." *Archives of General Psychiatry,* 21 (1969), 673–690.

47. ———, GOLDFARB, N., and SCHOLL, H. H. "The Speech of Mothers of Schizophrenic Children." *American Journal of Psychiatry*, 122 (1966), 1220–1227.

48. ———, LEVY, D. M., and MEYERS, D. I. "The Verbal Encounter between the Schizophrenic Child and His Mother." In G. S. Goldman and D. Shapiro, eds., *Developments in Psychoanalysis at Columbia University*. New York: Hafner, 1966.

49. ———, and POLLACK, R. C. "The Childhood Schizophrenic's Response to Schooling in a Residential Treatment Center." In P. H. Hoch and J. Zubin, eds., *The Evaluation of Psychiatric Treatment*. New York: Grune & Stratton, 1964. Pp. 221–246.

50. ———, SCHIMEL, P. L., MEYERS, D. I., POLLACK, R. C., ZEICHNER, G., GOLDFARB, N., and FISHKIN, H. "A Follow-Up Investigation of Schizophrenic Children Treated in Residence." *Psychosocial Process*, 1, no. 1 (1970).

51. HERMELIN, B. Response Behavior of Autistic Children and Subnormal Controls. Paper presented to the Seventeenth International Congress of Psychology, August 1963.

52. HOBERMAN, S. B., and GOLDFARB, W. "Speech Reception Thresholds in Schizophrenic Children." *Journal of Speech and Hearing Research*, 6 (1963), 101–106.

53. HULSE, W. C. "Dementia Infantilis." *Journal of Nervous and Mental Disease*, 319 (1954), 471–477.

54. KALLMAN, F. J. "Heredity-Genetic Theory: Analysis of 691 Twin Index Families." *American Journal of Psychiatry*, 103 (1946), 309–332.

55. ———, and ROTH, B. "Genetic Aspects of Preadolescent Schizophrenia." *American Journal of Psychiatry*, 112 (1956), 599–606.

56. KANNER, L. "Autistic Disturbances of Affective Contact." *Nervous Child*, 2 (1942), 217–250.

57. ———. "Problems of Nosology and Psychodynamics of Early Infant Autism." *American Journal of Orthopsychiatry*, 19 (1949), 416–426.

58. ———, and EISENBERG, L. "Notes on the Follow-Up Studies of Autistic Children." In P. H. Hoch and J. Zubin, eds., *Psychopathology of Childhood*. New York: Grune & Stratton, 1955. Pp. 227–239.

59. KENNARD, M. A. "The Characteristics of Thought Disturbance as Related to Electroencephalographic Findings in Children and Adolescents." *American Journal of Psychiatry*, 115 (1959), 911–921.

60. KNOBLOCH, H., and PASAMANICK, B. Etiologic Factors in Early Infantile Autism and Childhood Schizophrenia. Paper presented to the Tenth International Congress of Pediatrics, Lisbon, September 1962.

61. KRAEPELIN, E. *Dementia Praecox*. Trans. by M. R. Barclay. Edinburgh: Livingstone, 1919.

62. KRAMER, Y., RABKIN, R., and SPITZER, R. L. "Whirling as a Clinical Test in Childhood Schizophrenia." *Journal of Pediatrics*, 52, no. 3 (1958), 295–303.

63. KRINGLEN, E. "Schizophrenia in Twins: An Epidemiological Study." *Psychiatry*, 29, no. 2 (1966).

64. LAUFER, M. W., and GAIR, D. S. "Childhood Schizophrenia." In L. Bellack and L. Loeb, eds., *The Schizophrenic Syndrome*. New York: Grune & Stratton, 1969. Pp. 378–461.

65. LENNARD, H. L., BEAULIEU, M. R., and EMBREY, M. G. "Interaction in Families with a Schizophrenic Child." *Archives of General Psychiatry*, 12, no. 2 (1965), 166–183.

66. MAHLER, M. S. "Remarks on Psychoanalysis with Psychotic Children." *Quarterly Journal of Child Behavior*, 1 (1949), 18–21.

67. ———. "On Child Psychosis and Schizophrenia: Autistic and Symbiotic Infantile Psychoses." *Psychoanalytic Study of the Child*, 7 (1952), 286–305.

68. ———. "Perceptual De-differentiation and Psychotic Object Relationships." *International Journal of Psycho-Analyses*, 41, pts. 4–5 (1960), 548–553.

69. ———. "On Sadness and Grief in Infancy: Loss and Restoration of the Symbiotic Love Object." *Psychoanalytic Study of the Child*, 16 (1961), 332–351.

70. ———, and FURER, M. "Observations on Research Regarding the 'Symbiotic Syndrome' of Infantile Psychosis." *Psychoanalytic Quarterly*, 29 (1960), 317–327.

71. ———, FURER, M., and SETTLAGE, C. F. "Severe Emotional Disturbances in Childhood: Psychosis." In S. Arieti, ed., *American Handbook of Psychiatry*. Vol. 1. New York: Basic Books, 1959. Pp. 816–839.

72. ———, and GOSLINER, B. J. "On Symbiotic

Child Psychosis: Genetic, Dynamic and Restitutive Aspects." *Psychoanalytic Study of the Child*, 10 (1955), 195–214.

73. McDermott, J. F., et al. "Social Class and Mental Illness in Children: The Question of Childhood Psychosis." *American Journal of Orthopsychiatry*, 37, no. 3 (1967), 548–557.

74. Meyers, D. I., and Goldfarb, W. "Psychiatric Appraisal of Parents and Siblings of Schizophrenic Children." *American Journal of Psychiatry*, 118 (1962), 902–915.

75. Norman, E. "Reality Relationships of Schizophrenic Children." *British Journal of Medical Psychology*, 27 (1954), 126–141.

76. Osterkamp, A., and Sands, D. J. "Early Feeding and Birth Difficulties in Childhood Schizophrenia: A Brief Study." *Journal of Genetic Psychology*, 101 (1962), 363–366.

77. Polin, W., Stabenau, J. R., Mosher, L., and Tupin, J. "Life History Differences in Identical Twins, Discordant for Schizophrenia." *American Journal of Orthopsychiatry*, 36 (1966), 492–501.

78. Pollack, M. "Mental Subnormality and Childhood Schizophrenia." In P. H. Hoch and J. Zubin, eds., *Psychopathology of Mental Development*. New York: Grune & Stratton, 1967.

79. ———, and Krieger, H. P. "Oculomotor and Postural Patterns in Schizophrenic Children." *Archives of Neurology and Psychiatry*, 79 (1958), 720–726.

80. Potter, H. W. "Schizophrenia in Children." *American Journal of Psychiatry*, 12, no. 6 (1933), 1253–1270.

81. Putnam, M. C. "Some Observations on Psychosis in Early Childhood." In G. Caplan, ed., *Emotional Problems of Early Childhood*. New York: Basic Books, 1955. Pp. 519–523.

82. Rachman, S., and Berger, M. "Whirling and Postural Control in Schizophrenic Children." *Journal of Child Psychology and Psychiatry*, 4 (1963), 137–155.

83. Rank, B. "Adaptation of the Psychoanalytic Technique for the Treatment of Young Children with Atypical Development." *American Journal of Orthopsychiatry*, 19 (1949), 130–139.

84. Reiser, D. E., and Brown, J. L. "Patterns of Later Development in Children with Infantile Psychosis." *Journal of the American Academy of Child Psychiatry*, 3, no. 4 (1964), 650–667.

85. Rice, G., Kepecs, J. G., and Yohalom, I. "Differences in Communicative Impact between Mothers of Psychotic and Nonpsychotic Children." *American Journal of Orthopsychiatry*, 36 (1966), 529–543.

86. Rimland, B. *Infantile Autism: The Syndrome and Its Implications for a Neutral Theory of Behavior*. New York: Appleton-Century-Crofts, 1964.

87. Rutter, M. "The Influence of Organic and Emotional Factors on the Origins, Nature and Outcome of Childhood Psychosis." *Developmental Medicine and Child Neurology*, 7 (1965), 518–528.

88. ———. "Prognosis: Psychotic Children in Adolescence and Early Adult Life." In J. Wing, ed., *Childhood Autism: Clinical, Educational and Social Aspects*. London: Pergamon Press, 1966.

89. Schopler, F. "Early Infantile Autism and Receptor Processes." *Archives of General Psychiatry*, 13, no. 5 (1965), 327–335.

90. Schulman, I. "Concept Formation in the Schizophrenic Child: A Study of Ego Development." *Journal of Clinical Psychology*, 9 (1953), 11–15.

91. Silver, A., and Gabriel, H. P. "The Association of Schizophrenia in Childhood with Primitive Postural Responses and Decreased Muscle Tone." *Developmental Medicine and Child Neurology*, 6, no. 5 (1964), 495.

92. Singer, M., and Wynne, L. C. "Differentiating Characteristics of the Parents of Childhood Schizophrenics." *American Journal of Psychiatry*, 120, no. 3 (1963), 234–243.

93. Taft, L. T., and Goldfarb, W. "Prenatal and Perinatal Factors in Childhood Schizophrenia." *Developmental Medicine and Child Neurology*, 6, no. 1 (1964), 32–43.

94. Terris, M., Lapouse, R., and Monk, M. A. "The Relations of Prematurity and Previous Fetal Loss to Childhood Schizophrenia." *American Journal of Psychiatry*, 121 (1964), 476–481.

95. Tilton, J. R., DeMyer, M. K., and Loew, L. H. *Annotated Bibliography on Childhood Schizophrenia*. New York: Grune & Stratton, 1966.

96. Vorster, D. "An Investigation into the Part Played by Organic Factors in Childhood

Schizophrenia." *Journal of Mental Science*, 106 (1960), 494–522.

97. WEYGANDT, W. "Idiotic and Imbezillitat." In G. Aschaffenberg, ed., *Handbook de Psychiatrie*. Vol. 2. Wein: Spezieller Teil, 1915.

98. WHITE, P. T., DeMYER, W., and DeMYER, M. "EEG Abnormalities in Early Childhood Schizophrenia: A Double Blind Study of Psychiatrically Disturbed and Normal Children during Promozene Sedation." *American Journal of Psychiatry*, 120 (1964), 950–958.

99. ZITRIN, A., FERBER, P., and COHEN, D. "Pre- and Paranatal Factors in Mental Disorders in Children." *Journal of Nervous and Mental Disease*, 139 (1964), 357–361.

CHAPTER 6

DEPRESSION
AND MOURNING

Albert J. Solnit

DEPRESSION IN CHILDHOOD has been a controversial subject in clinical and theoretical circles because there is a lack of agreement about the relationship between the intent and significance of utilizing the same terms and psychological concepts for children as for adults. This controversy has historic roots centered on the changing meaning that children have for adults, especially during the past 300 or 400 years. During this period, children have gradually been recognized as representing the adults' claim on the future—immortality—rather than as chattel to be exploited for the present. Thus, there have been many obstacles to the recognition that children are not homunculi, having their developmentally appropriate emotional and mental reactions which are different than but forerunners to adult reactions.

In the consideration of depression and mourning in childhood, the major question is not whether these reactions and processes are the same as for adults. They are not. The major question is whether it is productive, recognizing the dynamic maturational and developmental continuum that is encompassed, to use the same terms and to establish connections between these childhood and adult conditions.

Emotional responses are universal in children and adults, though the understanding of their tone, content, and meaning often require interpretation. Certainly, emotional expressions and processes are motivated as well as reactive. In an important sense, emotional responses[27] and expressions are adaptive or coping devices, but they also can become associated with or characteristic of deviant or inhibited development and behavior. Depression should be viewed as related to deviant as well as to normative development in children as well as in adults. Depressive reactions may constitute first steps toward restitution, as well as an indicator of success or failure in coping with loss, or a symptom and sign of illness. Thus, depression cannot be understood unless it is related both to the dynamic human psychological context in which it arises and to the developmental tasks confronting the individual who is depressed.

In this chapter the terms "depression," "depressive reactions," and "mourning" will be used, with the assumption that it is productive to use the same terms in childhood as in adulthood, though their meaning is not identical. Developmental considerations and qualifications will enable us to avoid the major disadvantages of utilizing the same terms for children as for adults.

⟨ Developmental Perspectives

When a child is sad, feels hopeless or inadequate, his capacity, before adolescence, to tolerate and cope with these reactions as a mood or emotional state (affect) is limited. It is questionable whether the affect of sadness, depression, and feelings of helplessness can be experienced and communicated before certain levels of ego and superego development are achieved. For these reasons, depression in childhood is usually observed as behavior to ward off or react against the impact of feelings of sadness and a sense of loss, hopelessness, or inferiority.

Paradoxically, in children under the age of two years, as demonstrated by Spitz,[45-47] Provence and Lipton,[38] and others[7,8,13,33,39] the child initially may show the reaction to loss by facial expressions and lack of motor activity. The facial expressions in these abandoned infants, and also those who have been significantly maternally deprived, have been described by scientific observers as forlorn, sad, apathetic, blank, unresponsive, and nonsmiling. Later, psychophysiological equivalents such as diarrhea, anorexia, vomiting, and skin disorders may be noted.[43-45,47] As the child becomes a toddler, motor activity away from what is intolerable, namely, feeling sad or unloved and helpless, and toward relief, namely, a replacement or distraction, is increasingly characteristic.

In adults, the emotions and moods that are characteristic of depression can be tolerated to a much greater extent. In normative depressive reactions, the adult is able to tolerate the mood and to reflect about what can be done,

if anything, about it. If there is no immediate action that is appropriate, the adult will use thinking and memory, adaptive trial actions, to understand, tolerate, and get beyond the depression to other aspects of experience and life.

Assuming that the perception of emotional states (affects) and their communication are an ego function, depression as experienced by adults would require the following preconditions:

1. The availability of memory and thinking as a sense of the past and their continuity with the present and future.
2. The capacity to inhibit or store up motor discharge when psychic tension or discomfort is increasing.
3. The capacity for the closeness and tenderness that is characteristic of the oedipal period and the resolution of the oedipal conflict in which there are haunting sad feelings of loss and failure to achieve a romantic intimacy with the primary love object.

Many observers[18,19,26,34,42] indicated that such a structure and intensity of sadness, depression, and painful nostalgia (helpless to win out in terms of oedipal strivings) is not available and not experienced until adolescence.

Before the prepubertal and adolescent periods of awareness, the conditions of sadness (loss), loneliness (aloneness), and helplessness are warded off by motor discharge or by obsessional preoccupations because memory, capacity for postponement, and anticipation are not adequately developed to promote the feeling and expression of depression. In fact, when a younger child is depressed and because of traction or paralysis cannot move adequately, the failure of defense against depression is often manifest as withdrawal, apathy, and regression.

In a young child the capacity is lacking to use memory as a dependable, comforting mental activity that will enable the child to have the loved person with them psychologically, as well as to project ahead and anticipate that the lost love object can or will return in the near future. The young child also lacks the capacity for generalizing to an expectation that a substitute can be found or provided for the dead or lost love object. This is also a function of the inability to differentiate and individuate in the young child. Consequently, the young child, not fully understanding loss and not being able to cope with feelings of helplessness, attempts to erase or deny the loss, to pretend that the loved person will return, or to attempt to latch on immediately and relatively indiscriminately to another adult as a concrete replacement.

When the panic or discomfort associated with feelings of loss, hopelessness, helplessness, and inferiority is experienced, the young child appropriately attempts to lessen the shattering, painful feelings by acting concretely. He moves to discharge tension and to get away from the internal overwhelming sadness or helpless feeling by externalizing his concerns and fears. Instead of feeling sad, he is afraid there will not be enough food and tends to overeat. Instead of feeling helpless, he more actively becomes busy to reassure himself that he can do what he had done before the impact of his depressed reactions. Instead of feeling hopeless and inadequate, he tries to find out in concrete ways that life, food, warmth, love, and gratifications will continue.

A five-year-old boy's father was killed suddenly in an automobile accident. When the boy, who had been very close to his father, was told, he blinked, moved away from his mother, came back, and asked fearfully, "Will we have enough to eat?" Although depression in childhood is not limited to the loss of a love object, this experience is most commonly used as an example of a condition that evokes the reactions associated with depressive and mourning reactions characteristic of childhood.

It should be clear that sadness and other depressive reactions are also an essential part of the emotional repertoire that well-functioning adults are assumed to have a capacity for if their development has been full and balanced. As Hartmann[28] stated, "A healthy person must have the capacity to suffer and be depressed." Later, Hartmann[29] added that "what appears as 'pathological' in a cross-section of development may, viewed in the longitudinal dimension of development, represent the best possible solution of a given infantile conflict." There can be no human life without loss and disappointment. At the same time, no human being can adequately relate to other human beings in an affectionate and enduring manner unless he can identify and empathize with his friends, relatives, coworkers, and fellow citizens, including those times when people are depressed. Thus, we expect that a child who is developing well, who is healthy and able to achieve object constancy,[34] will be able to increase his capacity to feel and cope with sadness, loneliness, hopelessness, and inadequacy when it is appropriate and when it becomes the basis for understanding others as well as accepting oneself in a more realistic and understanding way.

⟮ Theoretical and Clinical Perspectives

Greenacre[26] stated

Depression, as a symptom, is as ubiquitous as life itself, and, in a mild degree, appears "naturally" as a reaction to loss which no life escapes. Its occurrence under these conditions is so regularly present as to be accepted as an accompaniment or sequel to loss which need hardly be questioned. It is, however, a positive, forceful affective state, though in a negative direction as in contrast to apathy or indifference which it may superficially simulate, and it implies inherently some degree of identification of the subject with the object loss. It is certainly the intensity, the excessive duration and the domination of the organism by the affect rather than its occurrence, which is pathological.

In childhood, the intensity of feeling depressed is not tolerable as an emotional state, and therefore the depressed child acts to relieve himself and to ward off the threatening, overwhelmingly painful feeling. There is also evidence[43,44] in instances of permanent loss, that until the child has become prepubertal (approximately nine to eleven years of age), he cannot conceptualize the permanence and inevitability of the process of dying and of death. Loss is experienced according to the developmental capacity, cognitively and emotionally. In fact, it may be heuristically productive to view the permanent loss of a primary maternal person in the first two or three years of a child's life as productive of a psychosomatic depressive state. As Anna Freud[20] indicated, "It is an old finding that the satisfaction of early body needs opens up the way to object attachment and following this to the individual's general capacity for object relationships." Conversely, the loss of this primary love object, who has served as a vital source of stimulation and regulation, as an activator and auxiliary ego, will evoke depression that has its physiological as well as psychological expression.

In this connection, Edward Bibring[5] stated,

Basic depression represents a state of the ego whose main characteristics are a decrease of self-esteem, a more or less intensive and extensive inhibition of functions, and a more or less intensely felt particular emotion; in other words, depression represents an affective state, which indicates a state of the ego in terms of helplessness and inhibition of functions.

Bibring further linked anxiety and depression as basic feeling states characterized by helplessness, when he said,

It may be helpful to compare depression with the feeling of anxiety, particularly since the latter has been brought in close connection with the feeling of helplessness [by Freud[21,22]]. Both are frequent—probably equally frequent—ego reactions, scaling from the mildest to the most intensive pathological structures. Since they cannot be reduced any further, it may be justified to call them basic ego reactions. From the point of view elaborated here, anxiety and depression represent diametrically opposed basic ego responses. Anxiety as reaction to (external or internal) danger indicates the ego's desire to survive. The ego, challenged by the danger, mobilizes the signal of anxiety and prepares for fight or flight. In depression the opposite takes place; the ego is paralyzed because it finds itself incapable to meet the "danger." In extreme situations the wish to live is replaced by the wish to die.

However, anxiety and depression are not mutually exclusive. A person may be anxious and depressed, a mixed state often noted in children with an underlying failure of self-esteem. In such child patients the anxiety state may cover an underlying and threatening depression with a paradoxical increase in manifest motor activity.

Direct observations of children, especially those in intensive psychotherapy or psychoanalytic treatment, have confirmed the utility and theory-building productivity of Bibring's formulations. In the context of intensive therapy, as reported by Furman,[24,25] Kliman,[31] McDonald,[32] and others,[3] many of these characteristics of sadness, depression, and mourning can be discerned. This suggests that the ego-strengthening effects of the treatment and the therapist enable the child to forego the defensive, warding-off reactions to the depressive condition, the very reactions that ordinarily indicate an underlying depression in children. This would clarify the apparent controversy in the literature about children's capacity to experience depression and to mourn when there is a permanent loss of a primary love object.

An elemental manifestation of depression is that seen in anaclitic depressions. Spitz[46] characterized this state as follows: "Apprehension, sadness, weepiness. Lack of contact, rejection of environment, withdrawal. Retardation of development, retardation of reaction to stimuli, slowness of movement, dejection, stupor. Loss of appetite, refusal to eat, loss of weight. Insomnia." He added to this by saying: "To this symptomatology should be added the physiognomic expression in these cases, which is difficult to describe. This expression would in an adult be described as depression."

The following case illustrates many of the clinical and theoretical issues that are involved. An eight-and-one-half-year-old boy had been in psychoanalytic treatment for almost two years when his father died suddenly of a subarachnoid hemorrhage. Just prior to his father's death Eddie had been expressing a great deal of aggressive rivalrous feelings toward his older sister and brother and had begun to realize that much of this feeling was displaced from his father onto his siblings. Eddie was referred for treatment because his stubborn, provocative behavior had begun to interfere with his social relationships at school, to be associated with a negative attitude toward his school work, and to lead into physically daring and risk-taking acts.

In the two interviews just prior to his father's death, Eddie was preoccupied with his envy of his analyst's children and expressed his resentment about the analyst's involvement with his wife and children. Negative oedipal longings were clearly expressed in the transference and could be verbalized and interpreted in preparation for working through his defensive and regressive reactions and tendencies.

Because of his father's sudden death the analyst was the first person to inform Eddie about his father's death. Eddie's first reaction was that of sadness and helplessness conveyed by his facial expression and the posture of his body. Then he asked anxiously and slowly, "Will we have to move? How can we pay for the house? Can you help my mother? She doesn't have enough money to buy food for us." He then spoke apprehensively about money for the treatment and wondered if I would have to stop seeing him. The sadness and apprehension about insufficient supplies and helplessness were replaced after one week by wild, provocative behavior.

Interpretations were not very helpful, and as the analyst conveyed his acceptance of Eddie's sadness and fearfulness, the little boy began to communicate through behavior and verbalization his fear of dying, of joining his father. He played out his fear of being caged or unable to move. He dramatized dangerous behavior, pretending he would jump from the tallest building. During the second week after his father's death he began tearfully to review his father's recent life and work, to express his fear of losing control of himself and his apprehension that his mother would become sick and go away.

During the third week he began to give evidence of sporadic overeating, followed by a poor appetite for a short period. His fear of not having enough food was played out, and as he became more clear about this unrealistic apprehension he wondered how they could get along without his daddy. There were then several play episodes in which he utilized regressive reviews of himself as a baby to review his feelings about his father and to express resentful feeling that his father could not leave him if he was supposed to grow up.

In the transference, over the next six to nine months, Eddie also "recovered" his father by playing out and talking about the fantasy that his mother and the analyst would marry and Eddie would become the analyst's son. About six months after his father's death, Eddie responded with sadness and reflective memories about his mother and father when his longing for his father was interpreted in the context of the fantasy transference play that his mother and the analyst would marry.

Of course, there was a great deal of the mourning process that reflected regressive, developmentally appropriate reviews and revisions of his relationship to and longing for his father. For example, his fearful identification with his dead father was prominent in his transient phobic reactions to sleep and to small rooms at the same time as he was engaged in eating binges.

Eddie's analysis was completed two and a half years after his father's death. Toward the end of the analysis the mourning process appeared to be well along. However, there was still a good deal of guilt about the father's death that turned up as a reluctance to do well at school. When it was suggested that Eddie was fearful of the consequences of doing well at school he initially ridiculed such an idea. Thereupon, through the analysis of a dream that was evoked in part by this interpretation, he completed part of the mourning process that had not been worked through.

In this dream Eddie is alone with his mother who is dying. He is frantic and cries out. This awakened Eddie and brought his mother running into his room. The analysis of the dream revealed Eddie's longing for his father to protect him from a threatening closeness to his mother, especially from a feminine identification with his mother. This led to an important reconstruction in which Eddie recovered repressed memories of his father expressing concern that he would not live long enough to see his youngest child well launched into adulthood. Eddie also recovered his angry reactive feelings that his father would cheat him as compared to his two older siblings. This unacceptable anger and the magic connection of, if I live (succeed), father will die (reject me) were key factors in Eddie's reluctance to succeed academically.

Another factor was involved in this reconstruction that enabled Eddie to complete a great deal of his mourning reaction. The analysis, by agreement, was in its final phase. Eddie was fearful that ending the treatment would finish off his analyst, himself, or both. Not doing well at school represented the fear of the future and the effort to make time stand still, perhaps even to turn it back so his father would be there to help him. It represented a regressive effort to make anger safe and limit closeness to the mother.

The mourning process is periodically reawakened in children as they take on new developmental tasks in which the tie to the dead parent is an important bridge from the past to the future. It is a bridge that is so basic that it must be repeatedly traversed, especially in regard to those crucial identifications and progressive individuations that promote or can interfere with the process of identity formation as it continues on throughout the life cycle.

In her 1960 discussion of John Bowlby's paper, "Grief and Mourning in Infancy," Anna Freud[18] stated,

The process of mourning (Trauerarbeit) taken in its analytic sense means to us the individual's efforts to accept a fact in the external world (the loss of the cathected object) and to effect corresponding changes in the inner world (withdrawal of libido from the lost object, identification with the lost object). At least the former half of this task presupposes certain capacities of the mental apparatus such as reality testing, the acceptance of the reality principle, partial control of id tendencies by the ego, etc., i.e. capacities which are still undeveloped in the infant according to all other evidence. We have hesitated therefore to apply the term mourning in its technical sense to the bereavement reactions of the infant. Before the mental apparatus has matured and before, on the libidinal side, the stage of object constancy has been reached, the child's reactions to loss seem to us to be governed by the more primitive and direct dictates of the pleasure-pain principle.

Later she stated, "Any assessment of the eventual pathological consequences of a separation trauma is inseparable, in our belief, from the assessment of the level of libido development at the time of its occurrence." A. Freud concluded this passage with the concept that if the child has attained the level of so-called object constancy, "the image of the cathected person can be maintained internally for longer periods, irrespective of the real object's presence or absence in the external world, and much internal effort will be needed before the libido is withdrawn."

In this same series of discussions about Bowlby's paper, Spitz[47] pointed out, "I agree with him [Bowlby] that loss of the mother figure—or, as I prefer to call it for the age below one year, loss of love object—is responded to by the infant with grief."

Though mourning is a special or specific instance of depression, in childhood the consideration of this phenomenon raises to theoretical and clinical visibility the developmental issues and the future research that is necessary to clarify how children react to loss and how they express sadness, grief, and depression. These insights, in turn, will enable us to develop interventions that will assist the depressed child immediately as well as interventions that are designed to protect the child's future development from delayed distortions and obstacles resulting from the trauma and disabling identifications associated with an inadequate or stunted mourning process.

(Familial and Epidemiological Factors

There is a high incidence of parental depression associated with depressive reactions in childhood, a function of the child's identification with parental attitudes and expectations.[10,14,16,35,39] Also, there appears to be significant correlation between parental death and depressions that may have been initiated in childhood but manifested during adulthood.

In examining the treatment records of 100 children treated psychoanalytically at the Hampstead Child Therapy Clinic, Sandler and Joffe[42] reported that a number of children of all ages showed a depressive reaction in response to a wide range of environmental or internally psychological precipitating factors. They did not report on the incidence because they found a tendency toward depression mixed with defensive reaction in most of the children in analysis with great variation of intensity and duration.

Many clinicians associate the child who is depressed with a severe object loss in his childhood.[7,9,12,36,37,40,41] Others associate depression during childhood with a failure of self-esteem or unresolved dependency conflicts.[35,39,18,49] Depressions in childhood, as with adults, are overdetermined in that a wide variety of inner conflicts and environmental pressures may be associated with depressive reactions. It is also clear that depressive reactions and depressions can be more easily discernible if the child is in an intensive psychotherapeutic alliance in which the psychotherapist serves as an auxiliary ego for the young child.

tion, the evidence that a child is depressed usually emerges gradually during an effective treatment. In fact, most children are referred for treatment because of a school learning problem, impulsive behavior, or other problems. In the course of the treatment, the underlying depression becomes uncovered, and with the support and interpretive assistance of the therapist the child is able to feel and cope with the depressive reactions. The interpretation of the defenses against these sad feelings and sense of loss and helplessness will gradually enable the child to reexperience his depressive reactions and work them through.

There are depressive attitudes and feelings that are reactive to a child's handicaps, physical and intellectual. Often this tendency or trait persists in a recurrent fashion. The principles of treatment and prevention are, of course, the same in these situations.

Although the use of phenothiazines can be considered in providing relief for agitated states in association with clinical depressions, drugs are usually not necessary or helpful unless the child is suffering from a psychotic condition. In neurotic or reactive depressive conditions the child's own defensiveness wards off the feelings of depression. The aim of the treatment in these instances is to help the child through play, verbalization, and interpretations to experience the depressed state gradually in order to gain insight, overcome the trauma, and resolve the conflicts related to the depression.

⟮ Treatment and Prevention

Prevention is mainly based on protecting the child's affectionate bonds with his primary love objects and on providing him with opportunities to gain approval and to be active in following his own interests. The latter enables the child to develop a realistic and resilient self-esteem.

In the treatment of depressed children and adolescents there often is a good deal of resistance to treatment because the child fears exposure to the threatening depression. However, as has been cited earlier in this presenta-

⟮ Bibliography

1. ARTHUS, B., and KEMME, M. "Bereavement in Childhood." *Journal of Child Psychology and Psychiatry*, 5 (1964), 37–49.
2. AXELRAD, S., and MAURY, L. "Identification as a Mechanism of Adaptation." In G. B. Wilbur and W. Muensterberger, eds., *Psychoanalysis and Culture*. New York: International Universities Press, 1965. Pp. 168–184.
3. BARNES, J. J. "Reactions to the Death of a Mother." *Psychoanalytic Study of the Child*, 19 (1964), 334–357.

4. BENDER, L., and SCHILDER, P. "Suicidal Preoccupations and Attempts in Children." *American Journal of Orthopsychiatry*, 7 (1937), 225–234.

5. BIBRING, E. "The Mechanism of Depression." *Psychoanalytic Contributions to the Study of Affective Disorders.* New York: International Universities Press, 1953.

6. BIRTSCHNELL, J. "The Possible Consequences of Early Parent Death." *British Journal of Medical Psychology*, 42 (1969), 1–12.

7. BOWLBY, J. *Maternal Care and Mental Health.* 2d. ed. Geneva: World Health Organization, 1952.

8. ———. "Grief and Mourning in Infancy and Early Childhood." *Psychoanalytic Study of the Child*, 15 (1960), 9–52.

9. ———. "Separation Anxiety." *International Journal of Psycho-Analysis*, 41 (1960), 89–113.

10. ———. "Childhood Mourning and Its Implications for Psychiatry." *American Journal of Psychiatry*, 118 (1961), 481–498.

11. ———. "Processes of Mourning." *International Journal of Psycho-Analysis*, 42 (1961), 317–340.

12. ———. "Pathological Mourning and Childhood Mourning." *Journal of the American Psychoanalytic Association*, 11 (1963), 500–541.

13. ———. *Attachment and Loss.* Vol. 1. *Attachment.* New York: Basic Books, 1969.

14. BROWN, F. "Depression and Child Bereavement." *Journal of Mental Science*, 107 (1961), 754–777.

15. BURKS, H. L., and HARRISON, S. I. "Aggressive Behavior as a Means of Avoiding Depression." *American Journal of Orthopsychiatry*, 32 (1962), 416–422.

16. CAPLAN, J. G., and DOUGLAS, V. I. "Incidence of Parental Loss in Children with Depressed Mood." *Journal of Child Psychology and Psychiatry*, 10 (1969), 225–232.

17. DAVIDSON, J. "Infantile Depression in a 'Normal' Child." *Journal of the American Academy of Child Psychiatry*, 7 (1968), 522–535.

18. FREUD, A. "Discussion of Dr. Bowlby's Paper." *Psychoanalytic Study of the Child*, 15 (1960), 53–62.

19. ———. *Normality and Pathology in Childhood: Assessments of Development.* New York: International Universities Press, 1965.

20. ———. "The Infantile Neurosis: Genetic and Dynamic Considerations." *Psychoanalytic Study of the Child*, 26 (1971).

21. FREUD, S. "Mourning and Melancholia" (1917). *Standard Edition.* Vol. 14. London: Hogarth Press, 1957. Pp. 237–258.

22. ———. "Inhibitions, Symptoms and Anxiety" (1926). *Standard Edition.* Vol. 20. London: Hogarth Press, 1959. Pp. 87–175.

23. FROMMER, E. A. "Depressive Illness in Childhood, Recent Developments in Affective Disorders: A Symposium." *British Journal of Psychiatry*, 2 (1968), 117–136.

24. FURMAN, R. "Death of a Six-Year-Old's Mother During His Analysis." *Psychoanalytic Study of the Child*, 19 (1964), 377–397.

25. ———. "Death and the Young Child." *Psychoanalytic Study of the Child*, 19 (1964), 321–333.

26. GREENACRE, P. "Introduction." *Psychoanalytic Contributions to the Study of Affective Disorders.* New York: International Universities Press, 1953.

27. HAMBURG, D. A. "Evolution of Emotional Responses: Evidence from Recent Research on Nonhuman Primates." In Jules H. Masserman, ed., *Science and Psychoanalysis.* Vol. 12. New York: Grune & Stratton, 1968. Pp. 39–52.

28. HARTMANN, H. "Psychoanalysis and the Concept of Health." In *Essays on "Ego Psychology."* New York: International Universities Press, 1939. London: Hogarth, 1964.

29. ———. "Problems of Infantile Neurosis." In *Essays on "Ego Psychology."* New York: International Universities Press, 1939. London: Hogarth, 1964.

30. JACOBSON, E. "Adolescent Moods and the Remodeling of Psychic Structures in Adolescence." *Psychoanalytic Study of the Child*, 16 (1961), 164–183.

31. KLIMAN, G. *Bibliography of Scientific Works.* White Plains, N.Y.: Foundation for Research in Preventive Psychiatry, 1969 & 1970.

32. McDONALD, M. "A Study of the Reactions of Nursery School Children to the Death of a Child's Mother." *Psychoanalytic Study of the Child*, 19 (1964), 358–376.

33. MAHLER, J. S. "On Sadness and Grief in Infancy and Childhood: Loss and Restora-

tion of the Symbiotic Love Object." *Psychoanalytic Study of the Child*, 16 (1961), 332–351.

34. ———. *On Human Symbiosis and the Vicissitudes of Individuation*. New York: International Universities Press, 1968.

35. MALMQUIST, C. "Depressions in Childhood and Adolescence: Parts I and II." *New England Journal of Medicine*, 284 (1971), 887–893, 995–961.

36. NEUBAUER, P. B. "The One-Parent Child and His Oedipal Development." *Psychoanalytic Study of the Child*, 15 (1960), 286–309.

37. PAZNANSKI, E., and ZRULL, J. P. "Childhood Depression: Clinical Characteristics of Overtly Depressed Children." *Archives of General Psychiatry*, 23 (1970), 8–15.

38. PROVENCE, S., and LIPTON, R. *Infants in Institutions*. New York: International Universities Press, 1967.

39. RIE, H. E. "Depression in Childhood: A Survey of Some Pertinent Contributions." *Journal of the American Academy of Child Psychiatry*, 5 (1966), 653–686.

40. ROCHLIN, G. "The Loss Complex." *Journal of the American Psychoanalytic Association*, 7 (1959), 299–316.

41. ———. "The Dread of Abandonment: A Contribution to the Etiology of the Loss Complex and to Depression." *Psychoanalytic Study of the Child*, 16 (1961), 451–470.

42. SANDLER, J., and JOFFE, W. G. "Notes on Childhood Depression." *International Journal of Psycho-Analysis*, 46 (1965), 88–96.

43. SOLNIT, A. J. "The Dying Child." *Developmental Medicine and Child Neurology*, 7 (1965), 693–704.

44. ———. "A Study of Object Loss in Infancy." *Psychoanalytic Study of the Child*, 25 (1970), 257–271.

45. SPITZ, R. "Hospitalism: An Inquiry into the Genesis of Psychiatric Conditions in Early Childhood." *Psychoanalytic Study of the Child*, 1 (1945), 53–74.

46. ———. "Anaclitic Depression." *Psychoanalytic Study of the Child*, 2 (1946).

47. ———. *A First Year of Life*. New York: International Universities Press, 1968.

48. TOOLAN, J. M. "Depression in Children and Adolescents." *American Journal of Orthopsychiatry*, 32 (1962), 404–415.

49. WINNICOTT, D. W. "The Depressive Position in Normal Emotional Development." In *Collected Papers of D. W. Winnicott*. London: Tavistock, 1958.

50. WOLFENSTEIN, M. "How Is Mourning Possible?" *Psychoanalytic Study of the Child*, 21 (1966), 93–123.

CHAPTER 7

SCHOOL PROBLEMS— LEARNING DISABILITIES AND SCHOOL PHOBIA

George E. Gardner and Bessie M. Sperry

THE SCHOOL is an important segment of the life of the child, taking, in many ways, the position of work in the life of the adult. Psychologically, it requires some ability for the child to separate without undue anxiety from his family and to relate to the teacher and his school peers as an enlargement of his social experience. He must tolerate a new and possibly less protective authority figure and test his own abilities in comparison with age mates. If he approaches this situation with sensory or neurological handicaps, anxiety about competition in this situation as well as the effect of the actual disabilities will be experienced.

Some school learning disabilities are known to be due to various and different etiological factors that affect brain functioning. These causative agents may be genetic, infectious, endocrinological, metabolic, or traumatic in nature; all result in organic brain dysfunction, maximal or minimal. In addition to these, deficiencies or abnormalities related to the sensory modalities are also known to impair and modify learning achievement. Impairments of this nature will be dealt with in another section of the present volume. In this chapter we shall be dealing primarily with the school difficulties of children in which an organic factor does not appear to be primary.

❨ Learning Disabilities

In children not handicapped by sensory or perceptual deficits there are two major possibilities to be considered as contributing to the child's inability to learn in school. One of these is that he comes to school with cognitive deficits from an impoverished environment that has failed to develop his capacity for perceiving spatial relationships, time, number, classification of objects, and vocabulary in a way that will make his school experience a process continuous with his previous learning. Poorer performance of intelligence tests and a higher rate of dropping out of school have been consistently shown in children from lower socioeconomic levels. Preschool education has been shown to have a favorable effect on first-grade IQ scores.[11] Reports of studies of structured preschool experiences for children with their mothers being involved shows that from preschool programs conducted in a variety of centers there is a favorable effect on cognition as measured by conventional intelligence tests.[18,20] The impact of such studies has been seen in the Headstart Program for preschool education and the television program "Sesame Street." The parent-child centers advocated by Hunt[21] rest on his theoretical analysis of the effects of poverty on cognitive development.[20]

Children from a low socioeconomic status emerge in the literature as being less well prepared also in the socialization processes needed for successful school attendance.[5] Numerous sociopsychological studies have found the lower-class child more likely to be hyperactive, to have more difficulty in delaying gratification, and to be more hostile toward authority than his middle-class agemate. Negro children have also been found to share many of the characteristics attributed to the lower class,[2] with special disadvantages due to the caste system.

The problem of Negro children's ability to score as well as white children on school-oriented intelligence tests lends itself to biological interpretations partly because a degree of dark skin color is an easily ascertainable piece of research data, though it may not, in fact, define a unitary heredity. The American child with dark skin frequently comes to school from a highly disadvantaged urban or rural situation with a family history whose known origins are in the period of enslavement in the United States. His self-image and achievement motivation are affected by his

history as well as by the prejudice toward him and the adult members of his group in American society.

The growing theoretical position in psychological theory is that biological endowment and the environment interact from the beginning, that attempts to measure abilities determined by biology as separate from the effects of the environment surrounding their development are unsound.[1,35]

The problem of school integration posed by the 1954 Supreme Court decision, that public schools in the United States must achieve an effective integration of black and white students, has probably affected the reemergence of the nature-nurture controversy at a time when scientifically it should have become a logically irrelevant issue. Fortunately, the problems of the integrated urban schools have also stimulated important contributions from such psychologists as Martin Deutsch, who is concerned with compensatory measures to stimulate more complex aspects of cognitive development in children whose early environments provided less cognitive stimulation than the preschool environments of more advantaged children.

The lower-class children and their parents are also more frequently vulnerable to mental illness than are their middle-class counterparts[19] and are more often subjected to precarious living conditions and traumatic events. If one were to think in terms of statistical findings with regard to class membership, one might conclude that being a member of the middle class should make children relatively immune to school learning problems. Unfortunately this is not true. Though cultural deprivation is mainly characteristic of the lower socioeconomic groups, emotional disturbances are present in children of all social classes and commonly affect school learning. Of the children with emotional disturbances who came to an urban child guidance clinic (Judge Baker Guidance Center) during the past year about 50 percent came with disturbances in school learning as a major presenting complaint.

As in many other childhood disturbances, the number of boys referred for learning disabilities far exceeds the number of girls who are referred for similar disabilities. Various theories have been used to account for this, dealing essentially with three factors: (1) presumed slower neurological maturation in males; (2) greater achievement pressures in this society on males, and hence a greater vulnerability to conflict around achievement; and (3) the fact that elementary school teachers are predominantly female, and therefore may be seen as attempting to feminize the boy in the learning situation. Definitive evidence for the saliency of these factors in creating the sex differential in the incidence of learning problems is not known to us, but it seems quite probable that each may contribute something of explanatory significance.

The types of learning problems most intensively studied as individual cases by mental health clinicians are those in which family relationships and individual emotional reactions have combined to produce in children of normal intelligence neurotic reactions around various aspects of the learning processes. These reactions have been commonly viewed as psychological inhibitions about knowing and about growing up.[28]

The refusal to learn in school is seen as a defense against anxiety; the child is defending himself against a deeper and more important fear than that involved in school failure itself. Liss[30,31] pointed out that failures in the management of sadomasochistic feelings made it difficult for the child to manage the alternation of receptivity and activity that are necessary for effective learning; Mahler-Shoenberger[32] pointed out that the assumption of stupidity made it possible for parent and child to enjoy certain libidinal pleasures that would otherwise be forbidden. Sperry, Staver, and Mann[37] reported cases in which the child's mobilization of aggressive activity in the service of learning appeared in fantasy to be the equivalent of destroying his interpersonal world. The psychoanalytic literature[33,34,38] involves primarily theoretical formulations in which the child's fears of his impulse life have become unconsciously involved with symbolic aspects of the learning situation: the forms of letters and numbers, the operations involved

in their manipulation, and the acquisition or display of knowledge through them. At an intrapsychic level these conflicts appear to be mediated by pictorial imagery replete with interpersonal and body referents.[17]

By a complex process of denial of anxiety in other life situations and a displacement of its residues into school learning, many children are able to maintain a restricted way of life without acute anxiety. School learning is dealt with by avoidance through a flight into fantasy or excessive motor behavior that prevents attending to the precision learning tasks with which children are confronted in school. Their school failure functions as a moderate punishment to the child and as a reproach to his parents without involving the cataclysmic effects that the repressed fantasy would have should it be activated. The neurotic balance achieved by such a relationship to learning is often a difficult one to shift for both child and parents.

An intensive study of twenty-six elementary school boys with neurotic learning problems was carried out at the Judge Baker Guidance Center in Boston during the 1960's. The group studied were boys who previously had been tutored, both at school and at home, with little effect on school performance. They came from intact homes and social-class membership included all but the lowest social class. Representation from the middle- and lower-middle classes was most frequent. These children and their parents were seen in weekly treatment sessions as well as being studied by psychological tests and research interviews. The following family problems were found to be frequent:

1. The presence of a family secret involving either present or past activities thought by the family to be disgraceful, for example, alcoholism, illegitimacy, financial misdealings, brutality with the family group.

2. A defensive pattern involving the family communication; a policy of nonmention or minimal mention spreading beyond the particulars of the situation being concealed and, less frequently, a cruel

overexposure of the child to painful information without adequate opportunity to integrate it by reasonable discussion.

3. Sibling-like rivalry on the part of the parent or parents (most frequently the father) toward the son's possible achievements.

4. Parental derogation of the child's ability to learn or to assume independent and responsible roles. (Though this may be in part a secondary effect of the children's school failures, the parental attitudes seemed in the case material to be more pervasive than current school achievement deficits and related at least in part to painful parental experiences in which they felt defeated or less favored than their own siblings.)

In addition to these parental attitudes, the children had in fact been exposed to traumatic circumstances within the family group or to illness or injury to themselves in excess of what is expectable within the preschool years. Although one criterion of selection for this study was family intactness, threats to life by illness in a family member, temporary separations, and threats of separation were common. A later study[4] confirmed the earlier clinical hypotheses of more frequent trauma in children with neurotic learning disabilities as compared with a matched control group of good achievers. Earlier, Liss[27,29] reported a high incidence of respiratory disorders in learning-problem children seen by him.

In this population two types of learning problems were discriminated:

1. The acquisition problem was seen in children whose prevailing mode of relating to school learning was characterized by an inability to acquire basic school skills in reading, spelling, and arithmetic. They were usually inattentive in school, and when they tried to relate to the learning their performances were characterized by anxious blocking. Though they appeared willing to comply, they frequently were unable to understand the teachers' directions, engaged in excessive preparatory activity before task engagement, and tried to get the teachers' help and confirma-

tion of the correctness of each step taken. Their comprehension of meaning from material presented by symbols was poor, and a frightened rigidity was characteristic of their approaches to the technical aspects of reading.

2. Children with the production problem showed fairly intact skills on individually administered achievement tests in spite of minimal productivity in school. They were often considered willfully uncooperative by their teachers, and sometimes were in fact defiant and derogatory of both the teacher and the tasks assigned. Though this was their prevailing mode of behavior and some of them believed that they could produce when they wished to do so, experiments in meeting the demanding conditions for productivity revealed their anxiety and limited ability to produce work even under highly specialized conditions.

These groupings are somewhat overlapping, and from time to time individual children manifested some aspects of each problem. Clinically both groups were seen as dealing with depressive affects stemming both from traumatic life experiences and their devalued role in the family.

Children with the confusion and blocking characteristic of the acquisition problem showed a pattern of interpersonal relationships oriented to the role of the victim. Many were beaten or teased by a sibling without adequate countermeasures, and they were reluctant to ask parents or teachers directly for things they wanted but used their helplessness as an appeal for attention. Their social roles were primarily as appeasers; their affects were mildly depressive with occasional outbursts of irritability.

Boys with the production problem type of difficulty were as a group more provocative and seemed more openly angry rather than depressed. From time to time they were subject, however, to acute depressive episodes. From the clinical material it appeared that they used a defensive, unstable identification with the aggressor as a defense against depression.

Identity conflicts characterized both groups. Although neither group evidenced marked feminine tendencies, discomfort with the masculine role and what they viewed as the necessary hostility to maintain it was common. Enuresis had been a problem for about one-third of the boys. Few in either group had comfortable relationships with peers, and most tended to function as marginal members of the peer group without close friendships. The discrimination between assertive activity and hostility was poorly made in the life styles of the boys as well as in the school learning situation.

In the learning situation both groups appeared to be lacking in goal direction with regard to the primary school tasks. They were occupied with the acting out of more personal conflicts. Teachers acquired a highly personal significance of a transference type, and school learning operations had affective connotations displaced from interpersonal conflicts.

All young children normally have fears when they confront the learning situation. These fears are partly inculcated by parents in an effort to protect him from real dangers in his environment and are partly the product of his own imaginative organization of his observations. He has not learned to distinguish possibilities of danger from probabilities, nor does he have causality with regard to illness and injury completely separated from personal systems of causality in which his own aggressive feelings may play an important role. Children who have or are experiencing within the family traumatic events, communication patterns that fail to make life sequences understandable, and covert or open derogation of their own coping and learning abilities are vulnerable to the displacement of anxiety onto the precision learning required in school.

The successful treatment of an entrenched pattern of marginal learning in school with a dependent, devalued role in the family may require prolonged psychological intervention and some remedial education. Milder learning disorders that are reactive to immediate life crises are sometimes responsive to shorter interventions. The assessment of the sources of anxiety in the child's life and of his own and his family's coping maneuvers is important in planning intervention.

In psychotherapeutic treatment,[36] bridges between intrapsychic conflicts and actual difficulties in learning operations are frequently necessary in order to facilitate symptom change. Therapeutic activity is also necessary around avoided areas in the child's life. Since defenses that cluster around avoidance and denial of unpleasant reality are most commonly used by children with neurotic learning disorders, a passive therapeutic attitude may prolong treatment unduly or foster mutual discouragement of the participants. On the other hand, since many children with this disorder also tend to assume the passive victim position in interpersonal relationships, a careful nurturing of the child's initiative interspersed with judicious therapist activity is necessary. If conflicts are not dealt with in relation to the confusion in learning operations, the child may improve socially, while the learning symptom retains a negative autonomy little altered by the general considerations and affects discussed in therapy.

In less severe difficulties supportive tutoring that takes into account the fears of the child and furnishes an external support for the ego in confronting tasks onto which these fears have been displaced may be sufficient to neutralize the learning problem. In fact, tutoring of this kind may be a profitable adjunct to psychotherapy in the most severe cases of neurotic learning disability.

We have dealt in this part of our presentation with the neurotic learning problems in childhood occurring as a primary symptom. Learning problems are well known to occur frequently as a secondary complaint with psychosomatic disorders, acting out problems, and delinquency and borderline schizophrenic problems. Clinical observations confirm the existence of problems around separation and sadomasochism to be also important in the learning problems of these patients, but a more systematic review of these will not be attempted in this chapter.

We have outlined two sources of difficulty in school learning: inadequate cognitive stimulation and anxiety displaced by intrapsychic defense mechanisms to schoolwork. The investigations of these difficulties have not been parallel in methods or in choices of populations. The difficulties of cognitive development have been concerned with the lower-class child as the target population; the therapeutically oriented investigations have a middle-class to lower-middle-class bias in population sampling since this is the group that seeks this type of intervention. The lower-class child does sometimes get clinical diagnosis and treatment for severe learning disorders; the assessment of such cases makes it clear that suffering from one kind of deficit does not exclude difficulties with an emotional source. Some middle-class children in the clinic population have also shown deficits in cognitive organization that resemble developmental immaturities. There are at this point no systematic data relating these two major sources of difficulty in the development of effective school learning, but the presumption from existing data would be that the lower-class child is more vulnerable from two sources: The cognitive apparatus receives less positive stimulation from the environment during the early years, and he is subjected more frequently to a chronically traumatic milieu.

(School Phobia

A not infrequently encountered neurosis in middle childhood and preadolescence is the school phobia. In its classical form its symptomatology is triadic in that the child exhibits (1) severe anxiety, (2) dread and apprehension, and (3) psychosomatic complaints associated almost exclusively with the necessity to attend school. When the child is permitted to stay home during weekends and vacation periods when school is not in session the symptoms usually disappear in a matter of a few hours, only to reappear when school attendance is anticipated or forced.

The most helpful instructional method to emphasize and clarify the cogent items relating to this neurosis (symptoms, reaction of parents, cause, psychodynamic motivation, meanings, treatment emphases, and progno-

sis) is to cite a classical clinical case and then refer to the research impressions and research results of those workers who have dealt with statistically important numbers of cases of this syndrome. We shall follow this format in the present communication and cite the case of seven-year-old Alice.[16]

Alice was in the second grade when she was referred to the Judge Baker. She lives with her father and mother and an older brother Frank, aged ten, who is in the fifth grade. She lives in a good neighborhood, and her home is a comfortable one. Her brother has never had any difficulty in school or any fears of attending it.

Mother stated that she was bringing Alice to the Clinic because of her intense fear of going to school and her intense fear of being separated from Mother at any time. Mother said Alice does very well in school when she goes, but she has not been in school during the first three months of this school year and missed considerable time from school at the end of last year. Alice has remained out of school on the advice of the family pediatrician, who, along with the school nurse, recently recommended the Judge Baker. Mother said that she first noticed Alice's concern two or three years ago (at four and one-half years), when she went into town for an evening and left Alice with the paternal grandmother. That evening Alice complained of pain in the abdomen, vomited after eating her supper, and seemed in a "panic" because her mother and father had not returned. When Mother returned home she called the pediatrician, who decided to wait till morning before referring Alice to the hospital with a question of appendicitis. Alice went directly to sleep and the next morning seemed entirely well.

At this point Mother abruptly switched to the current situation and stated that school this year was to begin on Tuesday, and that the Sunday before, Mother found Alice in bed crying. This continued until the following day, and Mother reassured Alice that she did not have to go to school if she really felt she could not. Mother stated that although Alice says she wants to go, enjoys school, and reads avidly, she seems literally terrified. In an attempt to handle the situation this year, Father stayed home from work the first day of school; but even so, Alice was not able to go. Mother said that last year, when Alice was in the first grade, she had taken her to school and remained with her until she seemed to be absorbed in the work. Then Mother would leave.

f

Now Alice will not believe Mother when she says she would not leave her like that now.

In the first grade Alice was fearful but did not have too much trouble until six months ago, when she told Mother she had decided not to go to school any more. Previously she had been complaining for several weeks that she did not like school. In May the teacher began telling Mother to come to school and get Alice because she was nauseated and vomiting. When this continued she finally had to be taken out of school. Prior to this, Mother said, she would send Alice to school but the child kept coming back, claiming to have forgotten something—"she did not know what." Mother said that Alice hates to admit that she does not want to go to school and that she is afraid. She hates anyone to see her crying and they usually find her alone in her room crying. But even then she will deny that she is afraid.

About Alice's early years, Mother feels that Alice was always inclined to be shy, even as a baby. Mother said that Father was in the Service when Alice was born. During Alice's first year he came home nearly every weekend, and after that was home permanently. Father took over Alice's care on weekends—and to a greater extent after he was discharged from the Service. At that time Father had his own business and frequently took Alice to the office with him. Mother remarked a little sadly that Alice never bothered with her then. She was, and still is, Father's favorite and seems at times to actually dislike her mother. In association with this, Mother said that Alice has never been corrected in the same way that Frank has and that there has never been any necessity to scold or discipline her. Mother remarked that Frank, in contrast to Alice, does not get very good grades in school but is not particularly troubled about this. He is very easygoing and has many friends and outside interests. Alice, on the other hand, always brought home perfect papers from school, and on one occasion when she had made one error on a paper she had first refused to show it to her parents. Mother laughingly commented that she could perhaps understand Alice's fear better if they had been harsh with her, but she said that if they ever even scold her mildly, she looks as if she is going to cry, and Mother just does not have the heart to say anything to her.

Mother said very frankly that she feels at a loss to know how to help Alice. The worker's feeling was that Mother has considerable warmth and sympathy for the child. Mother has talked on many occasions with the pediatrician, who, she says, blames her for leaving Alice in school last year and "sneaking out." Mother has tried to talk to Alice about what she fears will happen if she is separated from Mother, but Alice is unable to tell her anything. Mother stated, as one would expect, that Alice never volunteers to recite in class and is very fearful on being made to stand up and sing alone in front of the class. It is only very recently that Alice will go into the candy store and ask the clerk for candy herself, even when Mother is with her, although she is very fond of candy.

Mother brought up the fact that she thinks she may have some idea as to what Alice is afraid of even though Alice cannot tell her. Recently the mother of a child in the neighborhood had to be hospitalized for a chronic illness. For several days Alice acted out in play the story of a family in which the mother and father both died. Last year Father was in the hospital. The day before he was to go to the hospital Alice began vomiting; Mother assumed that she had a virus infection since this was going around at the time and Frank had it.

Mother said that Alice seems to be very bright and alert and wants to learn. She apparently reads quite well for her age, and Mother tries to keep her supplied with books. Mother had asked either for a home teacher or that she at least be given some help in guiding Alice in her reading at home. The principal refused both requests on the basis that if Alice is permitted to stay at home, she will then make no effort to get over her fears and go back to school.

Similar illustrative classical cases are cited by Coolidge et al.,[6,8,9] Kessler,[23] and Waldfogel, Coolidge, and Hahn.[39] We shall comment on the features that recur again and again in such cases.

Sex Ratio

School phobia is one of the very few behavioral disabilities in childhood that occurs somewhat more frequently in girls than in boys. A compilation of 124 cases in six studies by Kessler[23] indicated that of the 124 cases, 68 were girls and 56 were boys, meaning that for every six girl patients referred for clinic treatment, there are five boys referred with the same disability. One's general impression is that the sex difference is greater than this, and most writers in any general discussion of the condition will refer to the patient as "she" or "her." The figures, however, do not substantiate the impression. This sex preference in school phobia becomes all the more interesting and unusual when one considers childhood emotional disorders in general. Bentzen,[3] for example, in reviewing numerous studies of sex ratios in childhood learning and behavior problems, emphasized the agreement in the results of investigators that there is a marked preponderance of boy patients in at least seven diagnostic categories (reading disorders, learning difficulties, school behavior problems, stuttering, autism, childhood schizophrenia, and juvenile delinquency) and suggested that boys from the very beginning are more vulnerable to stress than girls, probably due to the fact that the maturation rates of boys are slower. Many of the ratios cited by Bentzen ran as high as four boys to one girl, or even eight boys to one girl. Bentzen, however, did not include reviews of the studies on school phobia and anorexia nervosa, the two not infrequently encountered neuroses where girls tend to outnumber boys slightly as patients. And investigators dealing with these latter two conditions rarely attempt to explain or account for this fact of altered sex ratio in their case series.

Age at Onset

There is a general agreement among research workers that a school phobia can and does appear at any age in the child's school career. It occurs at the kindergarten age level, but its onset may be noted for the first time in the preadolescent or adolescent in the junior or senior high school grades. However, there seems to be a clustering of cases at two very particular age-grade levels: (1) at the seven- to nine-year third-grade level, and (2) at the twelve- to fourteen-year eighth- to tenth-grade level.[8,9,12,39,41]

Intelligence or Learning

The child with school phobia rarely states that she is afraid to go to school because the work is too hard or because she cannot do the work, and the reports of teachers' and parents' impressions almost universally allege that these children are good to excellent learners in those periods before and after their illness when they have been able to attend school for any appreciable length of time. However, in one of their follow-up studies, Coolidge, Brodie, and Feeney[7] stated:

Many clinicians have noted that school-phobic children, particularly younger children, are of superior intelligence and perform at an advanced level in school when they are able to attend. We were impressed by the frequency of such remarks in the school reports written by kindergarten teachers or teachers in the first two grades. School IQ tests were available on thirty-six subjects and yielded a median Otis IQ of 113 with a range of 84 to 135. Thus the median IQ, while well above average on national norms, falls slightly below the median for the suburban area from which most of the sample was drawn. The clinical impression of the original research group, that these children are intellectually alert, eager, and prepared to excel, was not borne out by their subsequent intellectual development.

It is probably correct to conjecture that a large series of cases tested on standardized reliable tests of intelligence would show that the distribution of IQ figures would approach a normal bell-shaped curve slightly skewed to the right with the median at or somewhat above the 113 found by these authors. Such a skew to the right at the kindergarten and first two grades age levels probably can be attributable to the excess in any such series of girls with the expected earlier maturation that they have attained when compared with boys of the same age.

A second impression that has taken on the respectability of a clinical fact is the repeated statement that school-phobic children are almost invariably excellent achievers in school learning. This impression has led to the balanced and antithetical clinical statements that "The school-phobic child is always an excellent achiever; the learning disability child is never school phobic." Both of these allegations are myths. For in respect to the learning achievements of the forty-nine children in the Coolidge group study[7] the authors stated:

With respect to actual school achievement, IQ scores were compared with school grades and teachers' reports. The children's IQ-Achievement was then rated on a five-point scale, ranging from being significantly below to significantly above expectation. Forty-three percent of the children were performing below, while only twelve percent were performing above expectation. Although we recognize that IQ scores alone are a dubious criterion for predicting academic success, it does appear that the weight of the evidence points to a large number of learning problems among these children, predominantly of the production type.

And they add, "It was of interest to us that proportionately more boys than girls were showing [accompanying] problems in learning."

Associated Physical Complaints

In from 50 percent to 75 percent of school-phobic children, in addition to their voicing of feelings of anxiety and dread in relation to school attendance they will complain of pains in various parts of the body or of a feeling of a general sickness. Such complaints typically are abdominal pain, nausea, vomiting, and, less common, pain in the extremities. It has been pointed out by some authors that the primary associated physical complaint pattern (abdominal pain, nausea in the morning, vomiting) in these patients is quite similar to the "morning sickness" of pregnant women. Be that as it may, Gardner[16] stated:

Inasmuch as these physical complaints usually emerge at the point in time when the child is supposed to go to school, either in the sense of daily attendance (in the morning) or at the close of the summer vacation when school attendance is imminent, they give rise to the suspicion in the minds of many people that these physical complaints are entirely faked and that the child is, in essence, a malingerer. Such, however, proves not to be the case on intensive investigation, because the physical disabilities that emerge usually have specific reference to some of the underlying unconscious conflicts and are not at all seized upon "just in order to stay out of school."

Etiology or Psychodynamic Meanings

There is a general consensus as to the cause, or better, meaning, of the symptomatology ex-

hibited by the school-phobic child. In its interpretive dissection by the therapist it is noted that the child is not afraid primarily of going to school or afraid of the schoolwork or of the teacher but rather that she is afraid of leaving her mother. Inevitably the child selects and names any number of things, objects or people that she states are the loci of her dread and anxiety, but these are projections on selected external factors and are seen to be such after the mother carefully investigates each and every one of them in her anxious concern, bafflement, and lack of understanding of the child's sudden terror of school attendance.[16]

The consensus that we mentioned above is best outlined by Coolidge et al.,[6] as these authors deal with the patterns of aggression existing in the overt behaviors of the phobic child and her mother:

The central concern in the child is the fear of abandonment by the parents. The child fears that some danger from the outside world will befall the parents, particularly the mother, and that thus abandoned, he will either die of lack of care or because of lack of protection be a victim of violence from the outside world.

To see that this annihilative result is not carried out, the child stays at home, as close to the mother as possible. The Coolidge team continue as follows:

This underlying fear is considerably intensified at the outbreak of the symptoms, bringing with it an increase in the dammed-up aggressive fantasies which stem from murderous wishes toward the parents. These are experienced as too dangerous, and the child defends herself by regressing to increased dependence on the mother while displacing [projecting?] the anger associated with her hostile wishes to the outside world, notably the school.

However, most authors emphasize, too, the possible evoking (and demonstrable furtherance) of the child's neurotic dread by the mother herself. The child and mother have set up (or continue) a seeming symbiotic relationship, one with the other, and this relationship is a sadomasochistic expression that has needed neurotic gains for both mother and child. An extreme overprotective and antiseptic attitude on the part of the mothers of these patients was stressed by Waldfogel et al.[39] and Estes, Haylett, and Johnson,[14] and they attributed the cause of the child's condition to the mother's own neurotic needs responses. In addition, Waldfogel et al.[39] included the fathers of these children as being partners with the mother in the creation of the child's psychopathology in that they too were not infrequently noted to be overprotective and to act competitively with the mother, acting thereby more as anxious mothers than as fathers.

Eisenberg[13] stressed the fact that it is the mother's own anxiety that is transmitted to the child. This transmission is not through words but by means of cues or gesture language that involve facial expression, attitudes, and moods. The mother fears the cold, impersonal attitude of the school and its teachers and fears that the other children attending it are bad or hurtful. The school-phobic child has picked up these fears from the cues of the mother and responds in the same vein in an attempt to please the mother.

Finally, Cramer[10] attributed the causation of this childhood condition not specifically to the responses of the mother or the father but indicated rather that the neurotic expression in the child is due to the total family climate. The etiological importance of the family situation is stressed by him as follows:

The unconscious involvement of the total family in reciprocal systems of neurotic adaptation frequently provides a climate, before the child has to go to school, in which the tolerance of his defenses forestalls the breakthrough of symptoms. His [later] attempts to deal similarly with exacerbations of anxiety in the school environment cannot be so easily tolerated.

Presumably, with the additional stress involved in school attendance the child's previous defenses against family-engendered and family-member-associated anxiety break down and the neurosis emerges.

Jane Kessler,[23] on the basis of her clinical studies of school-phobic children, outlined serious doubts as to the repeated allegations that the child's mother is the cause of this condition in the child and cited the need for further research to establish its truth. Kessler stated:

The literature on school phobia abounds with statements to the effect that it never exists in isolation but is always intimately associated with a complementary neurosis in the mother, leaving the impression that the other is the cause. This explanation must be regarded as a partial one for several reasons. First, the same dynamic conflicts have been observed in mothers of children with different kinds of problems (e.g., psychosomatic problems and psychoses), so it is questionable that there is a specific cause-and-effect relationship between the mother's problem and the child's. Secondly, school phobia does not especially run in families. Why is only one child so affected? Third, investigations of parental psychopathology have not involved the use of control groups, so one cannot know how many mothers with the same conflicts are raising children who are free of phobias. . . . However, whatever the origin of the child's school phobia, there is no doubt that the mother's reaction will affect its duration and intensity. . . . Reading the clinical case material, one wonders what was primary and what secondary—that is, how much of the mother's anxiety was engendered by the child's obvious distress, and to what extent her anxiety created his distress. Even when the separation anxiety starts with the mother, the psychopathology will, after a time, be internalized, becoming an integral part of the child's personality structure. The child learns the psychology of the mother and makes it his own. In most of these cases, one sees only a continuous cycle with no clear-cut starting point.

To add to the heuristic value of her discussion, Professor Kessler[23] suggested: "It would be worthwhile to investigate patterns of maternal behavior in respect to children's fears. All children are reluctant to go to school at some time or other, but no effort has been made to see what parents normally do about it. Careful study might define more sharply the unique features of the 'phobogenic' mother."

Kessler's alluding to the separation anxiety of these children leads one to comment on the general diagnostic classification by numerous researchers of these children with school phobia as residing under the rubric of separation anxiety.[22] Though this may not be specifically stated by the score or so of investigators who over recent years have worked intensively with this childhood clinical condition, it is certainly implied as their preferred clinical diagnosis. To this Anna Freud[15] outlined a serious objection that should give us pause. She stated:

In clinical diagnoses one hears it, [i.e., separation anxiety] applied indiscriminately to the states in separated infants as well as to the states of mind causing school phobias (i.e., the inability to leave home) or homesickness (a form of mourning) in latency children. Here also, to employ the same name for two sets of disorders with similar manifest appearances tends to obscure the essential metapsychological differences which are characteristic of them. To separate, for whatever reason, a young infant from his mother during the period of biological unity between them represents an unwarranted interference with major inherent needs. It is reacted to as such by the infant with legitimate distress which can be relieved only by the return of the mother or, in the longer run, by establishing a mother substitute mother-tie. There is no correspondence here, except in behavior, with the states of mind of the homesick or the school-phobic child. In these latter cases the distress experienced at separation from the mother, parents, or home is due to an excessive ambivalence toward them. The conflict between love and hate of the parents can be tolerated by the child only in their reassuring presence. In their absence, the hostile side of the ambivalence assumes frightening proportions, and the ambivalently loved figures of the parents are clung to so as to save them from the child's own death wishes, aggressive fantasies, etc. In contrast to the separation distress of the infant, which is relieved by reunion with the parent, in ambivalent conflicts reunion with the parents acts merely as a palliative; here only analytic insights into conflict of feelings will cure the symptom.

In this passage, with the clear enunciation of the differing unmet physiological needs of the infant and the existence of the ambivalence conflicts of the school-age child in respect to separation or abandonment, Anna Freud warned us of a needed differentiation of each of these specific clinical conditions.

What seems to be lacking in all of these observations and reports on the possible genesis of the school phobia that involves in its causation both the parents (usually the mother) and the child (usually the daughter), is a genesis referable to the problems for solution faced by the child at this particular stage and age in its development. In the light of usually agreed on milestones in the personality development with which the usual school-phobic child is still struggling are the problems attendant on, and associated with, an unresolved (or imperfectly resolved) oedipal conflict. It is in the unfinished business of this stage in development that most of the children are caught.

These patients seem to be still battling with the conflicts engendered by the rejection of the parent of the opposite sex and the (for whatever reason) continuing negative and aggressive impulses toward the parent of the same sex. The response of renunciation of oedipal impulses has not yet been acceptable to the child, and she or he still harbors, but resists, the feelings of defeat and loss of prestige within the family group. And the parents by their reactions continue to contribute to the child's delay in the satisfying and satisfactory resolution of the conflict. Put in another context, the child's phobic reaction seems to be a continuing and delayed grief reaction, a delay in the modification of the love and hate of a lost love object. Out of this continuing conflict arises the manifest ambivalence and the demanded closeness to the parent (mother) to ensure that unconscious death wishes will not be carried out through the magic power of the wish or the thought. In the florid disabling stage of this condition, the child would seem to need a psychotherapeutic process aimed sympathetically at the child's attainment of insight relating to his or her unconscious conflicts.

Prognosis

It can be stated with reasonable certitude that the prognosis for the child suffering from school phobia is excellent. In a large percentage of cases the condition lasts a few weeks, a few months, or recurs in a few episodes spread over one or two months' time.

It should be remembered that there are scores of children who manifest, for a time, some of the well-known symptoms of school phobia but go undetected, or certainly undiagnosed as such, because of the shortness of the duration of the attack or because the condition does not develop to a florid state of disability. The child is not referred for clinic treatment nor, indeed, is she or he referred for help to the school psychologist or school counselor by the teacher. (In such cases it is reasonable that both the parents and the teacher feel that the child's reluctance to go to school because of being afraid is nothing but malingering.)

It is just these items of self-limitation and the absence of an accurate diagnosis of the condition that make certain aspects of research difficult or render research studies unreliable. For example, if a clinical condition is for the most part self-limiting and may in appreciable numbers terminate itself, all claims to the efficacy of one treatment approach as compared to a different treatment approach are questionable. For the recovery could have been spontaneous, no treatment at all being necessary. Also, if appreciable numbers of school-phobic children are not considered to be suffering from the condition, that is, are undiagnosed, any research results relative to the incidence are open to question. Corroboration of this unreliability of incidence figures was one of the interesting items that came to light in the classical intervention study of Waldfogel, Tessman, and Hahn.[40] When this research team actually went into the selected schoolrooms to observe the children, to talk with the teachers and with parents, during a two-year period, thirty-six cases of mild to severe school phobia were noted whereas the alleged incidence previous to that time was said to be five or six cases per year. If one were permitted to generalize on the basis of these figures of incidence, one might assert that probably less than one case of school phobia in three is detected and so diagnosed.

Even though the prognosis, as above stated, is excellent and the recovery rate high, as shown by the results of a ten-year follow-up study of sixty-six cases by Coolidge et al.,[7] this same investigator in two other studies[8,9]

called attention to the fact that though the recovery rate is high in school children aged seven, eight, and nine, the recovery rate in the preadolescent or adolescent child is by no means as high. In fact, these two research teams[8,9] emphasized the fact that the adolescent school phobia can be a manifestation of a severe character disturbance or become a way of life rather than indicating a neurotic crisis, as seems to be so evident in children in the lower grades of the elementary school.

Intervention and Treatment

The effectiveness of the treatment of the child suffering from school phobia depends on the presence of at least three propitious conditions: (1) early detection, (2) prompt intervention, and (3) the cooperation of the child, his family members (mother and father), and the school in a broad-gauged treatment program.

The remarkable results of early detection and intervention are clearly demonstrated in the study of Waldfogel et al.[40] These investigators became observers somewhat after the manner of teachers' aides in selected classrooms with the hope of detecting the first signs of a developing school-phobic condition in the various pupils. The teachers of these classrooms were welcomed and utilized as important members of the research team and were made thoroughly acquainted with the signs and symptoms of the condition.*

During the two-year period of the study, thirty-six children were thought by the investigators to be exhibiting the prodromal signs of school phobia. The parents of the child were interviewed immediately, and in twenty-five cases they cooperated in the treatment

---

* In any such intervention programs contemplated one must bear in mind that not infrequently the child patient sometimes, and the mother more often, blames the teacher for the existing fear of going to school. Teachers have suffered because of this palpably unjust accusation. To gain their very necessary cooperation, either in intervention studies or, indeed, in treatment programs for the patient, it is well for the members of the research team, or the therapists, to realize it is important to eliminate one's adherence to this traditionally held notion that the teacher is to be discovered to be the psychogenic agent causing the condition.

program. Sixteen of the twenty-five cases were treated through counseling in the school setting (in the schoolroom itself or an adjacent office), four were referred to a child guidance clinic, and five were cases of spontaneous recovery. In a follow-up study twenty-two of the twenty-five treated cases showed no signs of a return of the phobia, whereas three of the eleven untreated children were still school phobic. The results of this study seem to indicate clearly that whatever treatment method used—individual psychothcrapy, group therapy, family therapy, psychoanalysis,[24] or behavior therapy[25]—early intervention in its utilization offers the best chance for early recovery and minimal loss of important school attendance. (And all investigators agreed that at the earliest possible moment the child should face the phobic situation, that is, return to school.)

Additional general suggestions in regard to treatment approaches are made by Gardner[16]:

Here again one can begin by stating first what single devices or actions do not seem to be efficacious or effective in treatment. In the first place, it seems to be of little help to change the child to another teacher or to another school. Nor is it surprising that this is so, in the light of the true meaning of the condition. As you can see, it is not primarily school-centered. Again, from time to time, the plan has been used of having the mother always accompany the child to school or, very frequently, of having the mother sit in the classroom with the child. This usually works, but it cannot be used indefinitely because of its impracticability, both from the point of view of the mother, who must attend to other duties in the home, and from the point of view of the teacher and other pupils, both of whom do not relish the indefinite presence in the schoolroom of a mother of one of the pupils. Usually, too, when the mother withdraws or for the first time does not stay, the child's symptoms return with all their former acuteness. Allowing the child to stay home and be taught by a home teacher, though temporarily solving the difficulty, also cannot be resorted to forever. In addition, with regard to such treatment as the only treatment, although it may result in a long protracted self-recovery, the child taught at home during this long period is losing much in respect to social development and social adjustment that accrues to association with

other children through day-by-day attendance at school.

Finally, it should be emphasized again that the cooperation of the school administrator, and particularly of the child's teacher, must be sought and maintained throughout the treatment procedure. Many problems in the overall management of the child with school phobia involve one or both of these school personnel; it is not mere speculation to assume that a large number of those children who recover spontaneously do so through the day after day individual help and guidance extended to them by an insightful and sympathetic classroom teacher.

(Bibliography

1. ANASTASI, A. *Differential Psychology.* 3d ed. New York: Macmillan, 1958.
2. AUSUBEL, D., and AUSUBEL, P. *Ego Development Among Segregated Negro Children: Education in Depressed Areas.* New York: Teachers College Press, Teachers College, Columbia University Press, 1963.
3. BENTZEN, F. "Sex Ratios in Learning and Behavior Problems." *American Journal of Orthopsychiatry,* 33 (1963), 92–98.
4. BRODIE, R. D., and WINTERBOTTOM, M. R. "Failure in Elementary School Boys as a Function of Traumata, Secrecy, and Derogation." *Child Development,* 38 (1967), 701–711.
5. CHILMAN, C. S. *Growing Up Poor.* Welfare Administration Publication, U.S. Department of Health, Education and Welfare. Washington, D.C.: U.S. Government Printing Office, 1966.
6. COOLIDGE, J. C., et al. "Patterns of Aggression in School Phobia." *Psychoanalytic Study of the Child,* 17 (1962).
7. ——, BRODIE, R. D., and FEENEY, B. "A Ten Year Follow-Up Study of Sixty-Six School Phobic Children." *American Journal of Orthopsychiatry,* 34 (1964).
8. ——, HAHN, P. B., and PECK, A. L. "School Phobia: Neurotic Crisis or Way of Life?" *American Journal of Orthopsychiatry,* 27 (1957), 296–306.
9. ——, WILLER, M. L., TESSMAN, E., and WALDFOGEL, S. "School Phobia in Adolescence: A Manifestation of Severe Charac-

ter Disturbance." *American Journal of Orthopsychiatry*, 30 (1960), 599–607.

10. CRAMER, J. B. "Common Neuroses of Childhood." In S. Arieti, ed., *American Handbook of Psychiatry*. Vol. 1. New York: Basic Books, 1959. Pp. 797–815.

11. DEUTSCH, M., and BROWN, B. "Social Influences in Negro-White Intelligence Differences." *Journal of Social Issues*, 20 (1964), 24–35.

12. EISENBERG, L. "School Phobia: Diagnosis, Genesis, and Clinical Management." *Pediatric Clinics of North America*, 5 (1948).

13. ———. "School Phobia: A Study of Communication of Anxiety," *American Journal of Psychiatry*, 114 (1958), 712–718.

14. ESTES, H. R., HAYLETT, C. H., and JOHNSON, E. M. "Separation Anxiety." *American Journal of Psychotherapy*, 10 (1956), 682–695.

15. FREUD, A. *Normality and Psychopathology in Childhood*. New York: International Universities Press, 1965.

16. GARDNER, G. E. "The Child with School Phobia." *Post Graduate Medicine*, 34 (1963).

17. ———, and SPERRY, B. M. "Basic Word Ambivalence and the Learning Disabilities in Childhood and Adolescence." *American Journal of Orthopsychiatry*, 18 (1964), 377–392.

18. GORDON, E. "Review of Programs of Compensatory Education." *American Journal of Orthopsychiatry*, 35 (1965), 640–651.

19. HOLLINGSHEAD, A. B., and REDLICH, F. C. *Social Class and Mental Illness: A Community Study*. New York: Wiley, 1958.

20. HUNT, J. M. *The Challenge of Incompetence and Poverty*. Urbana: University of Illinois Press, 1969.

21. ———. "Parent-Child Centers: Their Basis in Behavioral and Educational Science." *American Journal of Orthopsychiatry*, 41 (1971), 13–39.

22. JOHNSON, A. M. "School Phobia: Discussion." *American Journal of Orthopsychiatry*, 27 (1957), 307–309.

23. KESSLER, J. W. *Psychopathology of Childhood*. Englewood Cliffs, N.J.: Prentice-Hall, 1966.

24. KLEIN, E. "Reluctance To Go to School." *Psychoanalytic Study of the Child*, 1 (1945), 263–279.

25. LAZARUS, A. A., DAVISON, G. C., and POLEFKA, D. A. "Classical and Operant Factors in the Treatment of a School Phobia." *Journal of Abnormal Psychology*, 70 (1965), 225–230.

26. LEVENSTEIN, P. "Cognitive Growth in Pre-Schoolers: Verbal Interaction with Mothers." *American Journal of Orthopsychiatry*, 40 (1970), 426–432.

27. LISS, E. "Emotional and Biological Factors Involved in Learning Processes." *American Journal of Orthopsychiatry*, 7 (1937).

28. ———. "Learning Difficulties." *American Journal of Orthopsychiatry*, 11 (1941).

29. ———. "Physiology of Learning." *American Journal of Orthopsychiatry*, 13 (1943), 275.

30. ———. "The Psychiatric Implications of the Failing Student." *American Journal of Orthopsychiatry*, 19 (1949), 501.

31. ———. "Motivations in Learning." *Psychoanalytic Study of the Child*, 10 (1955).

32. MAHLER-SHOENBERGER, M. "Pseudo-Imbecility: A Magic Cap of Invincibility." *Psychoanalytic Quarterly*, 11 (1942).

33. PEARSON, G. H. "A Survey of Learning Difficulties in Children." *Psychoanalytic Study of the Child*, 7 (1952).

34. ———. *Psychoanalysis and the Education of the Child*. New York: Norton, 1954.

35. PETTIGREW, T. "Negro-American Intelligence." In J. Roberts, ed., *School Children of the Urban Slum*. Ontario: Collier Macmillan, 1964.

36. ROSEN, V. "Strephosymbolia: An Intrasystemic Disturbance in the Synthetic Function of the Ego." *Psychoanalytic Study of the Child*, 10 (1955).

37. SPERRY, B., STAVER, N., and MANN, H. "Destructive Fantasies in Certain Learning Difficulties." *American Journal of Orthopsychiatry*, 22 (1952), 356–365.

38. STRACHEY, J. "Some Unconscious Factors in Reading." *International Journal of Psychoanalysis*, 11 (1930).

39. WALDFOGEL, S., COOLIDGE, J. C., and HAHN, P. B. "The Development, Meaning and Management of School Phobia." *American Journal of Orthopsychiatry*, 27 (1957), 754–780.

40. ———, TESSMAN, E., and HAHN, P. "A Program for Early Intervention in School Phobia." *American Journal of Orthopsychiatry*, 29 (1959), 324–333.

41. WEISS, M., and CAIN, B. "The Residential Treatment of Children and Adolescents with School Phobia." *American Journal of Orthopsychiatry*, 34 (1964), 103–112.

CHAPTER 8

MINIMAL BRAIN DYSFUNCTION IN CHILDREN

Paul H. Wender and Leon Eisenberg

FEW CLINICAL problems incite such dispu-
tation as the concept of minimal brain
dysfunction (MBD). There are those
who deny its existence and others who see the
syndrome in the majority of troublesome children. The confusion stems from an interaction
of the following factors: the differing viewpoints of the professionals who encounter its
manifestations; the variability of its manifestations in different settings; the variability in the
syndrome itself; and the variable meanings inferred from the diagnosis by professionals and
parents when it is encountered.[10]

Children so labeled are seen by neurologists, psychiatrists, pediatricians, psychologists, and schoolteachers. To some neurologists a diagnosis of brain damage cannot be
made unless the classical neurological signs
associated with nervous system lesions (that
is, sensory defects, reflex changes, motor ab-

normalities, and so on) can be positively identified. The limitation of this viewpoint is evident from the fact that the classical neurological signs are the result of injury to only
certain fractions of the brain substance; most
of its bulk is silent in this respect, though it is
very noisy in relation to complex behavior.
There may be a marked discrepancy between
neurological impairment, on the one hand,
and behavior disturbance, on the other, following brain pathology. A child whose motor
function is severely crippled by cerebral palsy
may nonetheless display superior intelligence.
Conversely, a child with severe intellectual
impairment on the basis of brain disorder (as
in Heller's disease) may have normal reflexes
and gross motor behavior.[28] Conceptually, it
is essential at the outset to differentiate the
child with evidence of identifiable other neurological disease from the category of children

considered here. The term "minimal" in minimal brain dysfunction is meant to indicate that the syndrome does not fit an otherwise recognized pattern and is associated with soft signs and presumptive evidence of brain disorder in the regulation of complex behavior.

The psychiatrist often fails to make the diagnosis, but for quite different reasons. The problems he is accustomed to dealing with are so often psychogenic or sociogenic that he may fail to consider that a behavior disorder may be secondary to brain dysfunction. His set is reinforced by the fact that disturbed family relations often accompany the syndrome. The difficult child may engender difficult behavior in his parents; organic lesions in a child do not preclude the simultaneous existence of psychogenic problems in his family.

The problem for the pediatrician is again different. The variability and unpredictability of development make the distinction between a transient behavioral aberration and one that is enduring difficult to discern except over time. If he has reassured a parent that the child will grow out of his problem and the problem persists, he may find it hard to extricate himself from his earlier commitment. Under such circumstances, he will continue to provide ineffectual reassurance while morbidity continues.

The psychologist is likely to base his diagnostic judgment on test results. The correlation between minimal brain dysfunction and defective cognitive and perceptual performance is significant but not one to one.[5] That is, a normal child may show quite uneven developmental attainments, whereas one with this syndrome may score in the average range. Except at the extremes, psychological test performance and neurological status may fail to correspond. The psychologist is in the difficult dilemma of making an inference about brain function from the test results. If he turns to the neurologist for confirmation, he may find the neurologist in turn relying upon him. This is no indictment of either profession but a simple consequence of the lack of pathognomonic criteria.

The educator observes the child in the classroom. He infers the diagnosis from overt behavior without necessarily having the skill to discriminate between the causal factors underlying common behavioral patterns. Moreover, he sees the child in a group setting, whereas the other specialists observe him alone in examining rooms.

This last feature brings us to a second major characteristic of the brain dysfunction syndrome: the variability of its manifestations in different settings. The symptoms are most evident in an environment that provides a maximum of stimulation. The child who is a "whirling dervish" in a classroom or on a playground may be able to sit quietly and pleasantly in a small room with a friendly examiner who can command his attention. Thus, professionals may engage in fruitless arguments about the description of the child because they fail to understand the significance of the settings in which each observes him.

Finally, the very broadness of the category minimal brain dysfunction should prepare us for the fact that children so affected differ markedly from one another, presumably in relationship to the presence or absence of an anatomical lesion, size of the lesion, site of the lesion, number of lesions, the age of acquisition, the total amount of brain tissue involved, and perhaps even the cause of the lesions.[10] Since present techniques do not enable us to determine the state of tissue function except indirectly, we do not have the anatomical information to correlate structure and function. Without the ability to do this, we use a common label for children suffering from what we can assume to be quite different anatomical or physiological defects. And yet there is sufficient commonality to the behavioral syndromes and sufficient responsiveness to similar treatment regimes to warrant the continued clinical use of the diagnostic term.

Finally, the connotations of the term can lead to unanticipated consequences. To some parents (and some professionals) it connotes irreversibility and poor prognosis. But biochemical or even structural defects need not have such consequences in a growing organism if the extent is limited and if rehabilitation is provided. Indeed, clinical experience suggests that the outcome can be quite favorable if gross disability is not present.

For the present, it would be useful if the diagnosis of minimal brain dysfunction is always followed by a brief list of its major clinical manifestations as well as by a statement of cause, if cause can be established. When the behavioral syndrome is seen in a child whose basic disorder fits a better-defined category (postencephalitic syndrome, cerebral palsy, and so on), that diagnosis should take precedence over this behavioral term.

(Characteristics of the Minimal Brain Dysfunction Syndrome

There is disagreement as to the boundaries of the MBD syndrome. We will discuss those signs and symptoms found in classical instances.

Motor Behavior

The major abnormalities of motor function are high activity level and impaired coordination (dyspraxia). When these symptoms are present, the history is surprisingly stereotyped. As an infant, the child is reported to have been active, colicky, and a poor sleeper. As soon as he entered the toddler stage, he was into everything, constantly touching and/or mouthing and having to be watched at all times for his own protection as well as that of his household. As an older child he is described as having been driven like a motor, constantly fidgeting, unable to keep still at the dinner table and even (*mirabile dictu*) in front of the television set. At school, his teacher reports that he is unable to sit still, gets up and walks around, whistles, drums, and annoys her as well as his fellows. As he enters adolescence, gross hyperactivity is apt to disappear, but other characteristics of the syndrome may not. Hyperactivity is not a necessary sign for the diagnosis of the MBD syndrome. There are children with other characteristics of the syndrome who are normally active or even hypoactive.

The second abnormality seen in perhaps three-quarters of MBD children is incoordination. The distribution of MBD children may be bimodal in this regard. Some are reported as having passed developmental landmarks at an early age and of always having been agile. More common is the clumsy, inept child. The child is frequently reported as always having had two left feet, constantly tripping over himself or any object in his path. Fine motor coordination problems may have been reflected in the slowness in learning to button buttons, tie shoelaces, color, cut with scissors, or write with legibility. Balance difficulties impair riding a two-wheel bicycle or roller skating. Many will have difficulty in throwing, catching, or hitting a ball. This difficulty is "diagnosed" by the child's peers, who select him last when choosing up sides for baseball.

Attentional Difficulties

The most striking abnormality of the MBD child is his short attention span and poor ability to concentrate. His parents report that he has never remained with one activity for a reasonable period of time. At school age, his teacher comments that "he has a short attention span. He is distractible. You can't get him to pay attention for long. He doesn't listen." These difficulties, like all the others, occur on a continuum. Some MBD children are able to persist in a few activities that they like. In others, attentional problems may be masked by perseverative behavior. This may be labeled "compulsive."

As with hyperactivity, distractibility and inattentiveness tend to diminish with age, but the problems may remain in a muted form.

Cognitive Difficulties

Cognitive disabilities are variable. There are three groups of children: those with perceptual-cognitive problems and no behavioral difficulties; those with behavioral difficulties and no perceptual-cognitive problems; and last, and most common, children with difficulties in both spheres.

Among the difficulties are problems with orientation in space (manifested by right-left confusion, by reversals in reading and writing, and poor performance on the Bender Gestalt Test); difficulties in auditory discrimination (confusing similar sounds); difficulties in auditory synthesis (so that phonemes cannot be combined to sound out a word); difficulties in transferring information from one sensory modality to another (e.g., recognizing equivalence between a printed Morse code and its sounding out) and from a static to a temporal sequence (e.g., recognizing equivalence between flashing lights and a printed pattern).[15]

Learning Difficulties

The area in which the MBD child's difficulties combine to produce maximum dysfunction is in school performance. Capacity, motivation, previous preparation, and adequacy of teaching contribute to how well a child performs. There are many reasons for inadequate school performance besides MBD. But a substantial fraction of MBD children (perhaps one-half) manifest learning difficulties. Among children with normal intelligence, normal environment and preparation, and reasonable school experience MBD would appear to be a frequent source of academic difficulty. The most common difficulty is in learning to read, though problems in writing and in arithmetic may be present as well. This group of children overlaps the ill-defined syndrome of dyslexia.[12]

Attentional and perceptual-cognitive difficulties impede academic progress. When untreated, the MBD child falls further and further behind academically.[49] Since his IQ is apt to be normal, he will be labeled an underachiever. Falling cumulatively further behind, the MBD child is probably at greater risk to drop out than his peers. One study[21] of nonselected adolescent underachievers found that two-thirds of the nonretarded underachievers were MBD children grown up.

Difficulty in Impulse Control

A common characteristic of the MBD child is poor impulse control as manifested by low frustration tolerance, inability to delay gratification, impaired sphincter control in the young (enuresis, encopresis), and antisocial behavior in the older child (destructiveness, stealing, lying, firesetting, sexual acting out). Impaired impulse control is also manifested in poor planning and judgment. The ability to think ahead develops with age; the MBD child is behind in accomplishment for his age.

The overlap between MBD and acting-out behavior is important. That MBD children contribute to social deviance in adolescence is suggested by retrospective cross-sectional studies of delinquents.[23] These findings suggest that effective treatment of the younger MBD child might be useful in minimizing adolescent problems.

Interpersonal Relations

The MBD child is apt to be extroverted, resistant to social demands, controlling, and independent. In extreme instances, he is stubborn, negativistic, and impervious to ordinary disciplinary measures. "He always wants things his own way. Punishment doesn't faze him. You can't reach him." In relation to his peers, "he is bossy. He wants to play the game his way or not at all. He's too aggressive."

Emotional Abnormalities

The child with minimal brain dysfunction exhibits increased lability, altered reactivity, increased aggressiveness, and dysphoria. His response to pain is often diminished: He seems indifferent to the bumps, falls, and scrapes that are the common lot of childhood. On the other hand, he overreacts to frustration and excitement. Temper tantrums are frequent.

Although these children are often described as angry, the behavior is usually irritability and lack of consideration. The child is often described as having a low boiling point and a short fuse.

The major dysphoric characteristics are anhedonia, depression, low self-esteem, and anxiety. Anhedonia (reduced ability to experience pleasure) is evident from such parental comments as "He never gets a real kick out of anything. It seems impossible to satisfy him. He wants something for a long time, and then when he gets it he's tired with it right away." Insatiability is often interpreted as the result of spoiling; in the MBD child, such parental behavior may be a response to the child's non-gratifiability. MBD children are sometimes said to have a masked depression or to have depressive equivalents. The behavior that suggests this interpretation includes concern about injury or death for parents or selves, low self-esteem, and lack of zest and initiative. Self-evaluation may be hidden by bravado or assumed indifference, but parents and teachers will report that the child has described himself as stupid, worthless, or bad.[34]

Familial Problems

Problems between the child and his parents, between the child and his siblings, and between parents themselves occur with sufficient frequency to be listed among the key characteristics of the syndrome. Although these problems are frequently interpreted as though they reflected familial pathology, it is probably more accurate to view them as a reaction to the child's difference. Most parents of MBD children feel guilty. Everyone "knows" that a child's behavior is the product of his upbringing, particularly his mothering. If the parents do not reach this conclusion independently, they are often helped to do so by mental health professionals. The guilt may produce depression or be projected onto the spouse. The difficulty in socializing the child is a major source of arguments between parents: Each views the other's attempts as ineffectual. Since neither succeeds, the possibilities for mutual recrimination are endless. The MBD child demands more attention than his peers; they in turn react with jealousy and amplify the problem. The possibilities for disruptive family alliances, triangles, and the like are numerous.

Neurological Concomitants

There is an increased prevalence of minor, or soft, neurological signs in children with minimal brain dysfunction (as high as 50–60 percent in some series). The neurological findings labeled "soft" are so called because of their variability and lack of correlation with anatomical lesions. They include difficulties in fine motor coordination, visual-motor coordination and balance, choreiform movements, clumsiness, and poor speech.

The prevalence of abnormal EEGs among MBD children varies greatly, as a function of the population surveyed and the criteria employed. There is considerable overlap with the EEG records of other psychiatrically disturbed children. Except when epilepsy is suspected, the EEG is not particularly helpful. The one specific abnormality that has been reported but not yet replicated is that described by Laufer et al.[31] These investigators demonstrated decreased photometrazol thresholds in hyperkinetic children.

It should be emphasized that many children with minimal brain dysfunction have no detectable neurological abnormalities. Neurological findings may support the diagnosis, but the absence of neurological abnormalities does not rule out the diagnosis.

Physical Stigmata

A number of workers have reported an increased prevalence of minor anatomic abnormalities in MBD children.[48] In general, the stigmata are similar to those seen in schizophrenic children and overlap those seen in mongolism: anomalies of the epicanthus and ears, high arched palates, short incurving fifth finger, single palmar crease, abnormally long and webbed third toe, strabismus, and, perhaps, unusually large, small, or abnormally shaped skulls.

Psychological Test Performance

There are no pathognomonic psychological test findings; but the absence of abnormalities does not rule out the presence of the syndrome. As with the neurological examination, the psychological report may suggest the diagnosis but is not definitive. Children with minimal brain dysfunction display a varying degree of perceptual and cognitive dysfunction. Many of the abnormalities are not revealed on the standard psychological test batteries but may be revealed by educational testing techniques. Variability of WISC subtest scores is often regarded as criterional; no evidence clearly supports this view. Abnormalities on the Bender Gestalt test (particularly reversals) are common. Difficulties in sorting tests, tests of figure-ground discrimination, and tests requiring cross-modal transfer of information are frequent. The difficulty is, as Conners[5] concluded, that evaluations of children with documented cerebral lesions have failed to show a single pattern of dysfunction on intelligence tests; the same may be expected to be true of children without documented lesions.

Clinical Subsyndromes and Changing Manifestations with Age

Minimal brain dysfunction is generally associated with the picture of the hyperactive child: the driven, impulsive, distractable hellion. Many of the same psychological deficiencies seen in the hyperactive child are seen in children who are assigned to other diagnostic categories. We include these children within the boundaries of the syndrome. That is, we employ a Bleulerian rather than a Kraeplinian model. Minimal brain dysfunction would seem to be involved in the following subsyndromes: (1) the classic hyperactive syndrome; (2) the neurotic; (3) the psychopathic; and (4) the special learning disorder. In each of these variants, one or another aspect of the syndrome's varying manifestations are salient. In the "neurotic" it may be the rigidity and the "fixed" fear pattern; in the psychopathic, it is the recalcitrance to social expectations and impulsivity; in the special learning disorder, it is the inattentiveness and/or perceptual-cognitive problems.

Together with the variable clustering of attributes, the changing behavioral manifestations of the syndrome with age tends to mask its diagnosis. The reasons for age changes include physiological alterations with maturation; learned consequences of continuing deviant behavior (a child is more hostile toward school after repeated failure); and most important, changing social expectations of the norms. In schematic form, the career of the MBD child might be summarized as follows: As an infant he is irritable, overalert, colicky, and difficult to soothe. As a toddler, he is always on the go, threatening imminently to injure himself or family possessions. As he enters kindergarten and elementary school, his attentional and social problems become salient. His distractability, low frustration tolerance, aggressiveness, and domineeringness win him the favor of neither his teacher nor his peers. Academic problems, though often present, tend to be ignored at first; by the time he reaches the third grade he is discovered to have a learning problem. Concomitant with the increased academic demands, the child's school behavior turns from inattentiveness to directed hostility. Associated with increased academic and peer problems, acting-out problems now appear. When antisocial behavior is present, it frequently claims the limelight, obscuring the existence and contributions of academic and learning problems. During preadolescence and early adolescence antisocial behavior constitutes the reason for referral. The academic problems persist but are accepted; the school generally attempts to promote a delinquent out of its confines. The postadolescent development of the MBD child is not fully known; the available information will be reviewed in the section on prognosis. It should be emphasized that the developmental changes discussed should not be construed as a fatalistic timetable of developmental difficulty; fortunately many children, either because of therapeutic intervention or maturation, return to a normal developmental sequence.

(Diagnosis

The major tools for diagnosing the minimally brain dysfunctioned child are the history and current naturalistic observations of the child's behavior. The history can most rapidly be obtained by employing a structured format. Open-ended questions, successively becoming more specific, should be directed at the areas described under "characteristics." Multiple informants are useful. Teacher observations are of particularly great importance. The teacher, to a greater degree than the parents, has the opportunity of comparing the child with thirty or more of his peers in his daily activities. Discrepancy between home and teacher reports should not be discounted as documenting poor interrater reliability; it may provide useful information. If the child is reported to be normal at home and a dervish at school, one should determine whether the parents have aberrant norms of child behavior, whether the parents have devised effective techniques of control, or whether the disturbed school behavior is the product of learning difficulties or school management. Similarly, a history of good adjustment at school and disturbed behavior at home suggests that the home situation be explored more fully.

The clinical interview with the child has a limited role in diagnosis. It is common for teachers to report that the child will do well briefly in a one-to-one situation; the psychiatrist thus may be misled. The psychiatrist obtains the most unrepresentative sample of the child's behavior. (For example, Zrull et al.[54] found that when mothers', teachers', and social workers' reports and psychiatrists' playroom evaluations were all intercorrelated, the evaluations that correlated least well with the others were those of the psychiatrists). The differential diagnostic consideration for which the psychiatrist's evaluation is most important is in determining whether the child is psychotic. Although parents and teachers are quick to spot the unruly, they frequently fail to notice the bizarre; the differential diagnosis between MBD and borderline schizophrenia has major therapeutic implications.

The physical and neurological examinations are contributory rather than diagnostic. It is important to screen for sensory defects. This is particularly important in lower-class populations in whom hearing or visual defects may have long remained undetected. A neurological exam may suggest the diagnosis; approximately one-half of MBD children have soft neurological signs. The presence or absence of these signs does not have any implications for pharmacological management, but the boy who is reported to be poorly coordinated can frequently be helped by specific programs in physical education. When this results in improved sports performance, it may bolster the child's deflated self-esteem. The electroencephalogram is relevant neither diagnostically nor in planning management, except when historical information leads one to believe that a seizure disorder is present. There is no evidence indicating that epilepsy is more common in children with minimal brain dysfunction than in children without the syndrome.

While projective testing is of little, if any, value, diagnostic educational testing may be of the greatest practical importance. Those MBD children who have specific perceptual-cognitive difficulties may require remedial special education; those who do not have such difficulties are nonetheless frequently behind grade level and will continue to remain academic misfits unless they receive correct academic placement.

With the disturbed child diagnosis is not a sterile exercise but a determinant of action. A good general principle for any physician to remember is that since he cannot diagnose with perfect accuracy, he must decide whether to overdiagnose or underdiagnose. If a disorder is moderately serious and the treatment very safe, he should overdiagnose (e.g., if one suspects a strep throat and has no laboratory facilities, it is safer to treat with a nonallergenic antibiotic than risk the possibility of rheumatic fever). If the disorder is not very serious or if the treatment is dangerous, one should diagnose with much greater caution. In the case of the MBD child, recognition of the classical hyperkinetic case imposes no diagnostic difficulty. The problem is in the borderline areas. There will be many children in whom the diagnosis is suspected but cannot be ascertained. A therapeutic trial of medication is easy, safe, and permits a rapid evaluation of a child's drug responsiveness.

❨ Prevalence of the MBD Syndrome

There are two separate questions. (1) What is the prevalence of minimal brain dysfunction among children? (2) What is the prevalence of the syndrome among diagnosed disturbed children? Despite imprecision in diagnosis, a number of surveys of school-age children have produced prevalence figures that are in surprising agreement. Prechtl and Stemmer[38] surveyed the prevalence in the Netherlands of the choreiform syndrome, which they defined as the presence of minimal choreiform movements together with behavioral problems. They found the syndrome present in 20 percent of elementary school boys and severe in 5 percent of them; its prevalence in girls was 10 percent with less than 1 percent having severe problems. Of children with this syndrome, 90 percent were reported as having appreciable reading difficulties. Stewart et al.[47] reported the hyperactivity syndrome to be present in approximately 4 percent of a St. Louis grade school population between the ages of five and eleven. Huessey[26] found hyperkinesis in 10 percent of Vermont second grade children; he reported that 80 percent of the children whom teachers felt had serious behavioral difficulties fell into this category. Despite the different diagnostic criteria employed and the different areas surveyed, the reported figures fall into the same range: 5 to 10 percent. The prevalence of the disorder may be linked to social class, being more frequent among disadvantaged children. The syndrome, as reported in clinic populations, shows clear sex linkage: the male-to-female ratios ranging from three- or four-to-one[36] to nine-to-one.[53] Some of the manifestations of minimal brain dysfunction may be different in girls. (It is our impression that hyperactivity itself may be less prominent with undirectedness and resistance to socialization being more salient.)

The prevalence of the disorder in clinical populations is difficult to ascertain; until recently, the syndrome could not be coded except as chronic brain syndrome. Current American Psychiatric Association nomenclature permits the additional category of hyperkinetic reaction of childhood. Employing a broad definition of minimal brain dysfunction, one finds that half of the children referred to outpatient clinics can be encompassed within this category. The situation is analogous to that with schizophrenia. The clinics and practitioners who use a dementia praecox model report very few schizophrenics in ordinary outpatient populations, whereas clinicians employing a Bleulerian model[18] may report as many as one-half of their outpatients in this category. This issue clearly requires further study.

❨ Etiology

It is probable that the MBD syndrome is a final common expression of distinct and separate causal factors. It may be produced by extrinsic brain insults, genetic transmission, intrauterine random variation in biological development, fetal maldevelopment, or psychosocial experience.

The earliest description of MBD behavior in children[2] was in those who developed behavioral abnormalities following von Economo's encephalitis. Subsequently, similar behavioral abnormalities were associated with other forms of infection, poisoning, and trauma. These causal associations led to the first diagnostic labels for the syndrome: "postencephalitic behavior disorder," "organic drivenness," "minimal brain injury." Studies by Knobloch and Pasamanick[29] demonstrated an association between prematurity, prenatal difficulties, and paranatal complications and a variety of psychological, behavioral, and neurological abnormalities in children (including cerebral palsy, epilepsy, mental deficiency, behavior disorders, and reading disabilities). The highest association between reproductive pathology and behavior abnormality was found for the group of children who were hyperactive, confused, and disorganized, a group obviously resembling and/or overlapping the MBD syndrome.[41]

It is these early studies that have willed the term "minimal brain damage" to child psychiatry. It is an unfortunate inheritance for both logical and empirical reasons. Logically, it is incorrect because one cannot argue that since some brain-injured children have the MBD syndrome, all children with MBD are brain injured. Empirically it is misleading because in a large fraction of children with MBD, one can neither obtain a history suggestive of neurological damage nor find signs of neurological impairment.

A second cause for minimal brain dysfunction is very probably genetic. Clinicians have long noted the familial clustering of the disorder, with an apparent increased prevalence among siblings and parents. Two studies documented the familial clustering of dyslexia.[17, 20] These studies reported MBD behavioral abnormalities associated with the dyslexia and an increased prevalence of MBD behavior among the nondyslexic siblings. (In clinical experience, one sibling of a MBD child may have learning difficulties but no behavioral problems, a second may have behavioral problems but no learning difficulties, while a third may be clumsy but have no behavioral or learning difficulties.) Such observations are compatible not only with genetic transmission but with familial transmission of behavioral patterns. The only sound way to disentangle the effects of nature and nurture is to study the siblings of MBD children who have been reared separately. Safer[42] was able to locate fourteen MBD children whose siblings or half-siblings had been reared in foster homes. This study disclosed that approximately 50 percent of the full siblings versus 14 percent of the half-siblings were characterized by short attention span, repeated behavior problems and a diagnosis (by an independent rater) of hyperactivity. This study must be viewed with caution because of the small sample size. Nongenetic, nontraumatic, prenatal variation may play a role in the development of behavioral pathology. This is suggested by the study of premature infants and monozygotic twins. In these groups increased MBD pathology is repeatedly seen in the lower birth-weight infants.[29,37]

A fourth possible cause of MBD pathology is fetal maldevelopment. Several investigators have noticed an association between MBD behavior pathology and anatomical stigmata.[48] There are no data indicating whether such anatomical abnormalities are familial. The pathology of mongolism (trisomy versus translocation) suggests the question of whether the minimal brain dysfunction disorder is associated with maternal pathology or genetic abnormalities. One must further inquire if there is an association between MBD and maternal exposure to toxins or infection during pregnancy.

Finally, there is reason to believe that minimal brain dysfunction behavior may be produced by psychosocial experience. For example, prolonged institutionalization[19] during early childhood may produce a child who not only has difficulties in forming relationships but who also has certain temperamental and cognitive abnormalities, including hyperactivity, inability to concentrate, and difficulties in abstraction. Some clinicians distinguish between organic and psychogenic subgroups of hyperactivity. The disorder can occur in the absence of organic signs, but there is no firm basis for supposing that these children manifest a different pattern nor that the syndrome has appeared in them solely as a response to stress. Psychosocial experience may interact with physiological predisposition to aggravate or minimize the manifestations of the syndrome.

❨ Mechanism

The pathophysiology of the minimal brain dysfunction syndrome is unknown, but Wender[51] proposed a model linking the observed behavior to a hypothesized physiological dysfunction. Briefly, it asserts that the primary psychological characteristics of the syndrome are directly produced by the physiological dysfunction. The primary characteristics generate, in the course of life experience, the psychological signs and symptoms seen in the clinical syndrome. There are three postulated primary abnormalities: (1) a difficulty in attention characterized by a high and poorly modulated level of activation; (2) a decreased ability to experience both pleasure and pain, manifested behaviorally by decreased sensitivity to reinforcement; and (3) extroversion.

The second hypothesis about mechanism is that some forms of the disorder are produced by a dysfunction in monoamine metabolism. The reasons adduced are clinical and experimental. To begin with, von Economo's encephalitis, which produced Parkinsonism in adults, also produced minimal brain dysfunction in children. The inference is that the virus had a predilection for monoaminergic neurones (since postencephalitic Parkinsonism is known to be associated with dopeaminergic lesions). A second naturalistic datum suggesting that decreased function of monoaminergic neurones lies at the basis of the syndrome is the dramatic response of MBD children to amphetamines and tricyclic antidepressants. It has been hypothesized[44] that these drugs act by increasing the functional amounts of monoamines, most probably norepinephrine, which function as central nervous system neurotransmitters. They act, in effect, as stimulators or amplifiers of the monoaminergic systems. Animal experiments suggest that norepinephrine is probably the neurohumor critically involved in mediating the effects of reinforcement; decreases in norepinephrine result in decreased responding to both positive and negative reward. Decreased norepinephrine is also thought, in the human, to be accompanied by depression. Decreased functioning of the noradrenergic system would be expected to produce an unhappy and socially unresponsive child. Similarly, although the mechanisms are not so well worked out, norepinephrine seems to be involved in arousal. It is unclear whether the inattentiveness seen in MBD children is a manifestation of overarousal or of underarousal (as suggested by Satterfield et al.[43]). Though amphetamine is clearly arousing in adults, there is some suggestion that noradrenergic neurones may be involved in diminishing attention and arousal.[32]

The testable consequences of this theory are that at least one group of MBD children should be characterized by decreased synthesis, release, or sensitivity to norepinephrine. If the decreased synthesis is peripheral as well as central, it might be reflected in decreased excretion of monoamine metabolites in the urine. This hypothesis has been tested, but it was not supported.[52] If the syndrome results from decreased sensitivity to normally produced norepinephrine, such children should manifest less autonomic responsiveness to exogenous norepinephrine. This test has not yet been conducted, but it too presumes that peripheral metabolism parallels central.

The monoamine theory, although plausible, suffers from lack of direct empirical verifiability; at present, we lack methods for direct measurement of the activity of central neurones in humans.

⁌ Prognosis

Pediatricians and child psychiatrists have tended to believe that the hyperactive child outgrows his difficulties with age. This belief was supported by the diminution of certain MBD signs with age: enuresis, fine motor difficulties, classroom disruptiveness, and immature behavior. Several studies disputed this assumption. The first group of studies were follow-up studies. The most direct were those of Menkes et al.[33] and Weiss et al.[49] Menkes et al. studied the outcome of fourteen children who had been evaluated and labeled as MBD while outpatients at Johns Hopkins twenty-five years previously. The population consisted of children with probable organic brain injury and serious rather than mild brain dysfunction. At the time of reexamination, four of the original fourteen were institutionalized psychotics; only eight were self-supporting, and of these four had been institutionalized for some time. Weiss et al. followed their own sample for a mean of five years (to the age of thirteen). Their sample was composed of nonretarded, nonpsychotic hyperactive children who had shown no evidence of serious brain dysfunction. On follow up it was found that hyperactivity had diminished, but that disorders of attention remained and that a significant proportion of the children continued to show immature behavior, low self-esteem, and poor school performance. Compared to their peers, the children were more aggressive and inclined to antisocial behavior. A one- to nine-year follow up of postencephalitic children who had been institutionalized[2] found that approximately two-thirds showed chronic and serious behavioral difficulties.

Another follow-up study of children who may have suffered from a severe form of the minimal brain dysfunction syndrome is that of Morris et al.[35] who reported a follow up after more than twenty-one years, of ninety children who had been admitted to a psychiatric hospital for severe acting out in the presence of normal intelligence and in the absence of psychosis or overt brain damage. The sample is described as disobedient and markedly restless and would seem to constitute a severely disturbed antisocial group of MBD children. Of sixty-eight children followed until age eighteen or older, twelve had become psychotic, ten were diagnosed as borderline, seven had acquired a criminal record, and only fourteen were described as doing well. Robins[40] reported a thirty- to forty-year follow up of children seen in psychiatric outpatient clinics. The population consisted largely of children with acting-out problems; retrospectively, many of these children might be considered to have had minimal brain dysfunction. Robins's data documented the fact that acting out children are at greater risk not only for sociopathy but for psychosis as well. All these studies except that of Weiss et al. were skewed toward the more severely disturbed MBD child. There are no available follow-up studies describing the postadolescent fate of moderately to mildly impaired MBD children.

The other group of studies that shed some light on the prognosis of the MBD child were retrospective studies. A number of these studies revealed an increased prevalence of histories reminiscent of minimal brain dysfunction among adult psychiatric patients with a variety of diagnoses.[23] Healy and Bronner found that delinquents (as compared to sibling controls) demonstrated significantly more cross and fussy babyhood, enuresis, hyperactivity, restlessness, and impulsiveness. Studying a far less disturbed population, a group of adolescent underachievers, Hammar[21] reported that approximately one-half of these children (and two-thirds of the nonretarded subsample) constituted MBD children grown up. A number of studies of psychiatric inpatients revealed an increased prevalence of signs and/or histories of MBD problems in earlier life. Hertzig and Birch[25] reported soft neurological signs in 30 percent of a heterogeneous group of hospitalized adolescents as compared to a 5 percent prevalence of such signs in a control population. Hartocollis[22] examined the childhood characteristics of adult psychiatric inpatients whose psychological tests had suggested possible organic impairment. Of inpatients meeting these characteristics he found historical signs strongly suggestive of minimal brain dysfunction (clumsiness, hyperactivity, temper tantrums, aggressiveness, lability, reading difficulty, and the like). Of particular interest was the variety of adult diagnostic groupings into which these patients fell: Personality types were mainly infantile but included impulsive, schizoid, phobic, and hysteric; diagnoses included schizophrenia, depression, and infantile personality.

Another relevant study linking minimal brain dysfunction problems in childhood and psychiatric disorders of adulthood is that of Quitkin and Klein.[39] Examining adult inpatients under the age of twenty-five, they found that 30 percent had definite histories of soft neurological signs and/or hyperkinesis, impulsivity, clumsiness, and other problems suggestive of minimal brain dysfunction. These adult inpatients fell into two major diagnostic groupings: the impulsive-destructive and the awkward-withdrawn. The former included mainly emotionally unstable character disorders, while the awkward-withdrawn subgroup was constituted of process schizophrenics and schizoid and passive dependent characters.

A final source of information came from interviewing adults, including the parents of

MBD children, who described themselves as MBD children grown up. Anderson and Plymate[1] reported that even in the more benign instances the MBD child is prone to continuing attention problems, social imperceptiveness, and interpersonal difficulties.

Two points deserve particular emphasis. (1) The increased prevalence of neurological signs in psychiatrically disturbed populations does not document that neurological impairment causes psychiatric illness. It is entirely possible that both the neurological signs and the psychological problems are common manifestations of an underlying disease process (as is seen in Huntington's chorea). (2) The increased prevalence of MBD histories among psychiatric patients does not imply that most, or even many, minimally brain dysfunctioned children become psychiatrically disturbed adults. As may be easily shown,[50] these figures imply that only a small fraction of MBD children subsequently develop the psychiatric syndrome studied. Nonetheless, these studies have several important implications. (1) The usual complacency regarding prognosis may not be justified; it appears that MBD children are at greater than average risk for subsequent psychiatric disorder. (2) The studies implied that not only do the psychological abnormalities associated with minimal brain dysfunction persist, but these abnormalities may change their form. What we need to know is what types of MBD children develop in which ways. In particular the fate of the most common and least seriously afflicted, the hyperactive inattentive child who is amiable and has minor learning difficulties, is unknown.

❰ Management

The care of the child with minimal brain dysfunction will obviously vary from case to case in relation to the predominant manifestations, the family setting, and community resources. Since cause is unknown and theories of pathophysiology are speculative, treatment is necessarily symptomatic. The four major therapeutic modalities are medication, family counseling, remedial education, and psychotherapy for the child.

The responsiveness of the symptoms of hyperkinesis and distractability to stimulant drug treatment is so remarkable as to have been suggested as a diagnostic test. In a number of well-controlled studies,[15] it was established that two-thirds to four-fifths of children will show a favorable response if a stimulant drug is used properly.[46] Contrariwise, sedative drugs often exacerbate the behavior disturbance.[11] Methylphenidate in dosage level from 10 to 100 milligrams per day and dextroamphetamine from 5 to 50 milligrams per day are the drugs of choice. Side effects may be fewer with methylphenidate.

The drug should be begun at the lowest dose and the child's response observed. If little or no response is recorded, the dose should be doubled at two- to three-day intervals until a beneficial result is obtained, troublesome side effects intervene, or the maximum safe dose has been reached. All too often, treatment is abandoned after only minimal doses have been tried; some children may show little response until the maximum dose and then improve strikingly. Anorexia and insomnia are the most common side effects. Both symptoms may disappear even if dosage is maintained over a seven- to ten-day period. If they continue to be troublesome, the dose may have to be diminished and a compromise sought between effectiveness and unwanted side effects. One drug may succeed where another has failed. Since the symptoms tend to diminish with age, periodic discontinuation of medication is necessary in order to determine whether it is still necessary. We routinely suspend the drug during summer vacations except in severely troubled children. We then recommend a trial in school without medication in order to determine whether it must be restarted. Clinicians have maintained children on stimulant drugs for as long as five years with no evidence of tolerance or habituation. The drug can be discontinued from one day to the next with no need to taper off.

For children who fail to respond to stimulants, phenothiazines (thioridazine) may prove useful, although there is reason for concern that learning may be adversely affected by the sedative effect of these drugs.[24,45] More recently, there have been reports of good results from the use of tricyclic antidepressants.[27] Preliminary trials have suggested that magnesium pemoline may be an effective stimulant drug.[6]

Family counseling is an essential ingredient of care. The parents are distraught and upset by behavior they cannot understand and for which they may blame themselves or have been blamed by others. It is essential that the physician attempt to clarify the nature of the syndrome, its cause, and its prognosis and provide guidelines for appropriate management. The child's overresponsiveness to stimulation indicates the usefulness of environmental restriction (parties, trips to department stores, and the like had best be postponed). The missing brake in the control of behavior by the child points to the need for the parents to intervene early when behavior begins to get out of control. They will need help in working with the teacher on such educational programs as are appropriate to the particular case. At the same time, attention must be paid to family problems that, though independent of the syndrome of brain dysfunction, nonetheless interact with it because of the greater vulnerability of the child to psychological stress. Psychiatric care for marital discord, parental disagreement about child care, anger toward the patient, or any of the manifestations of family psychopathology will be essential if the program of management is to succeed.

There is no single educational prescription for this category of children but rather a need for an individual assessment of each in order to set out a sensible course of action. To the attentional defects that are so common there may be added in a particular case specific perceptual and cognitive defects that will further complicate learning. If the child cannot be helped to overcome his learning disability, the experience of school failure may lead to a train of psychological consequences which will further complicate the organic behavior disorder. What needs emphasis is the importance of a thorough psychoeducational work-up of each patient to provide the basis for a program of educational rehabilitation. In the absence of educational remediation for the child with a major learning disorder, medical efforts will be futile. In this sense, education is the single most important modality of treatment.

Psychotherapy is of limited value in treating the common symptoms in contrast to their good response to medication. On the other hand, psychotherapy may be essential if family pathology coexists with the minimal brain damage. Drug therapy may enable the child to make use of psychotherapy in instances in which he is unresponsive. A useful rule of thumb is to gauge the response to drug treatment alone. If the target symptoms improve, but other problems remain sharply evident, psychotherapeutic intervention is not only indicated but can be more sharply focused.

(Public Health Policy Questions

In 1970, a grossly inaccurate newspaper account, alleging that large numbers of elementary school children in a mid-Western city were being placed on stimulant drugs at the behest of teachers and without parental consent, touched off a storm of public protest, which culminated in congressional hearings and the appointment of a Department of Health, Education, and Welfare advisory panel. The two questions, on which lay and medical debates centered, were the following. (1) Are stimulant drugs mind-control agents to suppress rebellion against excessively rigid teachers and schools? (2) Does their use in children lead to drug abuse when these children become adolescents?

As to the first question, there is no reliable information about what stimulant drugs would do if administered to normal children. There are obvious ethical reasons why we cannot give stimulants to normal children to satisfy academic curiosity even on so important an issue. Since the phenomenon is age related, studies with adult volunteers do not help. But let us be clear: Overactivity and distractability can occur under at least three sets of circumstances in which drug use would be grossly inappropriate and medically reprehensible. The first is the child who exhibits intense anxiety in the midst of grossly disorganized family life. It is the physician's task in the diagnostic evaluation to explore this possibility; if it is identified, the therapeutic task is to restore family equilibrium before entertaining the use of medication. The second is the fidgetiness and inability to concentrate that can be produced by hypoglycemia in a child who is malnourished and regularly has no breakfast. Food is the appropriate pharmacological treatment for such problems. The third differential point to be considered in diagnosis is the character of the classroom; if it is overcrowded, if the teacher is incompetent (or simply overwhelmed), or if the classroom is above a busy fire station, what is needed is attention to the classroom setting and not to the chaotic activity that will characterize the majority of the children in such a classroom. Those who point out the danger of the indiscriminate use of stimulant drugs do so with justification. Any potent agent can be abused. But exclusive preoccupation with the possibility of misuse can lead to the abandonment of the hyperkinetic child along with the drug. Furthermore, it is a myth that stimulants make hyperkinetic children into conforming robots. Restlessness, distractability, and impulsivity are constraints on freedom, not freedom; the child is not free to behave but is driven. Is a child whose attention is commanded by every passing sight and sound, meaningful and meaningless alike, to be considered independent? Is a child who is not learning to read, when most of his classmates are, in any sense expressing creativity? Stimulant drugs reduce fidgeting not purposeful motor activity; they lessen distractability so that the child can concentrate, but what he chooses to monitor is his decision; they diminish impulsivity so that his behavior is more reflective. There can be no argument that they should not be given except after a thorough diagnostic evaluation, under careful medical supervision and with informed parental consent.

What of the potential for adolescent drug abuse? One of the remarkable aspects of stimulant drug use with children in contrast to adolescents is its consistent failure to produce euphoria. If the child notes a change in feeling tone, he is apt to report sadness or drowsiness rather than feeling high. Most children have to be reminded to take their medicine; few ask for it. Those who feel positive about it do so because they are grateful for no longer being called stupid or bad. The point to be emphasized is that it is the high produced by these agents in the adolescent that leads to repeated usage. Since children do not become euphoric, there is no motivating force for drug abuse.

Taking a drug over a prolonged period of time under medical prescription and management is a very different matter from either being encouraged to experiment with drugs or watching one's parents employ cocktails, downers, and uppers at their own initiative in order to get through a stressful life. There are no data that suggest that epileptic children on anticonvulsants, diabetic children on insulin, children with rheumatic carditis on prophylactic sulfonamides, or asthmatics on steroids are at any higher risk than the rest of the adolescent population for drug abuse. We anticipate that such youngsters may be less likely, rather than more likely, to become drug abusers because of having learned to take medicine for the proper business of suppressing illness.

Theoretical arguments are no substitute for empirical data. What are the facts? The only available data stem from a preliminary study by our clinic. Dr. Maurice Laufer of Providence, one of the pioneers in stimulant drug therapy, was good enough to give our staff permission to contact the parents of 110 children whom he had treated with dextroamphetamine for hyperkinetic impulse disorder some ten to fifteen years earlier. A letter was sent to each family, explaining the purpose of the study and asking them to cooperate. Eighty agreed to do so; of these, sixty-three completed the lengthy questionnaire sent to them. We hope to locate the missing respondents. Although a 60 percent response rate to a mailing is surprisingly good, and although the respondents did not differ in any significant way from the missing cases by history, the attrition in the sample limits the confidence to be placed in the data. To summarize the information we do have, the patients had now attained a mean age of twenty. As children, 40 percent had received medication for less than six months; only 30 percent, for more than three years. Of the sixty-three, only three were known by their parents to have tried marijuana, none as frequent users. Not a single one of these former patients was reported to have experimented with other drugs, although four were described as drinking to excess. In the absence of a control sample, one can only compare these data to general experience: A contemporary college-aged population might include half who were experienced with marijuana and some 10 percent who had tried lysergic acid, mescaline, or psilocybin.

Despite the lack of evidence that hyperkinetic children treated with stimulant drugs become adolescent drug abusers, even the remote possibility of such an outcome justifies the call for more follow-up studies than are now at hand. Stimulant drugs are grossly abused in American society. The only medical conditions in which they have been demonstrated to be effective are the hyperkinetic syndrome and narcolepsy. Their temporary effects in obesity and depression are far outweighed by the risk they pose for habituation. Yet physicians continue to prescribe them almost indiscriminantly; they are manufactured in entirely excessive amounts; they circulate through an extensive black market. They constitute a major public health hazard. Whatever faith we place in legal controls, an approach not conspicuously successful in containing the heroin pandemic, there is no excuse for poor medical practice and unethical pharmaceutical promotion. Recent efforts by medical societies to exhort their members to limit drug use to legitimate indications represent a much to be applauded, if somewhat belated, step in the right direction. It would indeed be regrettable if the patients for whom stimulants have been shown to be strikingly effective were to be denied access to them by draconian legislation resulting from the failure of other measures of control. The hyperkinetic syndrome is no mere matter of a developmental phase to be endured until it is outgrown. The data from the longitudinal studies reviewed earlier provide evidence for persisting educational handicap and enduring behavior disorder. Stimulant drugs, though only one element in a program of treatment, can be key factors in enabling the child to benefit from remedial education and parent counseling. Continuing pediatric supervision is essential to success in rehabilitating what we are beginning to see as a chronic disorder and about which we have much yet to learn.

In January 1971, the Office of Child Development of the U.S. Department of Health, Education, and Welfare convened the "Conference on the Use of Stimulant Drugs in the Treatment of Behaviorally Disturbed Young School Children." We can think of no better way to conclude this chapter than by quoting the last three paragraphs of the conference report:

Clinical pharmacologists have repeatedly found that drugs may act differently in children than in adults. To use medicines of all kinds effectively in children, more specialists must be trained in drug investigation—pharmacologists who can develop basic knowledge about the action of drugs in the developing organism. There is the obvious need for better and more precisely target drugs for the whole range of severe childhood behavior disorders. This requires intense research and training efforts. Such efforts provide the means for developing, testing and delivering better treatment programs. There is a similar need for research in the techniques of special education and also a need to make these techniques available to children who can benefit. It would appear to be a sound Federal investment to conduct such research and training.

In summary, there is a place for stimulant medications in the treatment of the hyperkinetic behavioral disturbance, but these medications are not the only form of effective treatment. We recommend a code of ethical practices in the promotion of medicines, and candor, meticulous care and restraint on the part of the media, professionals and the public. Expanded programs of continuing education for those concerned with the health care of the young, and also sustained research into their problems, are urgently needed.

Our society is facing a crisis in its competence and willingness to develop and deliver authentic knowledge about complex problems. Without such knowledge, the public cannot be protected against half-truths and sensationalism, nor can the public advance its concern for the health of children.

❲ Bibliography

1. ANDERSON, C., and PLYMATE, H. B. "Management of the Brain-damaged Adolescent." *American Journal of Orthopsychiatry*, 32 (1960), 492–500.

2. BOND, E. D., and SMITH, L. H. "Post-encephalitic Behavior Disorders." *American Journal of Psychiatry*, 92 (1935), 17–33.

3. CAMPBELL, S. B., DOUGLAS, V. I., and MORGENSTERN, G. "Cognitive Styles in Hyperactive Children and the Effect of Methylphenidate." *Journal of Child Psychology and Psychiatry*, 12 (1971), 55–67.

4. COMLY, H. H. "Cerebral Stimulants for Children with Learning Disorders." *Journal of Learning Disabilities*, 4 (1971), 484–490.

5. CONNERS, C. K. "The Syndrome of Minimal Brain Dysfunction: Psychological Aspects." *Pediatric Clinics of North America*, 14 (1967), 749–766.

6. ———. "Psychological Effects of Stimulant Drugs in Children with Minimal Brain Damage." *Pediatrics*, 49 (1972), 702–708.

7. ———, et al. "Effect of Dextroamphetamine in Children." *Archives of General Psychiatry*, 17 (1967), 478–485.

8. CONRAD, W. G., et al. "Effects of Amphetamine Therapy and Prescriptive Tutoring on the Behavior and Achievement of Lower Class Hyperactive Children." *Journal of Learning Disabilities*, 4 (1971), 509–517.

9. DENHOFF, E., et al. "Effects of Dextroamphetamine on Hyperkinetic Children." *Journal of Learning Disabilities*, 4 (1971), 491–498.

10. EISENBERG, L. "Behavioral Manifestations of Cerebral Damage in Childhood." In H. G. Birch, ed., *Brain Damage in Children*. Baltimore, Md.: Williams & Wilkins, 1964. Pp. 61–73.

11. ———. "The Management of the Hyperkinetic Child." *Developmental Medicine and Child Neurology*, 5 (1966), 593–598.

12. ———. "Neuropsychiatric Aspects of Reading Disability." *Pediatrics*, 37 (1966), 352–365.

13. ———. "Principles of Drug Therapy in Child Psychiatry." *American Journal of Orthopsychiatry*, 41 (1971), 371–379.

14. ———. The Clinical Use of Stimulant Drugs in Children. Paper presented to the American Academy of Pediatrics, Chicago, 1971.

15. ———, and CONNERS, C. K. "Psychopharmacology in Childhood." In N. Talbot, J. Kagan, and L. Eisenberg, eds., *Behavioral Science in Pediatric Medicine*. Philadelphia: Saunders, 1971. Pp. 397–423.

16. FINNERTY, D., et al. "The Use of D-Amphetamine with Hyperkinetic Children." *Psychopharmacologia*, 21 (1971), 302–308.

17. FRISK, M., et al. "The Problem of Dyslexia in Teenage." *Acta Paediatrica Scandinavica*, 56 (1967), 333–343.

18. GAW, E. "How Common Is Schizophrenia?" *Bulletin of the Menninger Clinic*, 17 (1953), 20–28.

19. GOLDFARB, W. "Emotional and Intellectual Consequences of Psychologic Deprivation in Infancy." In P. H. Hoch and J. Zubin, eds., *Psychopathology of Childhood*. New York: Grune & Stratton, 1955. Pp. 105–119.

20. HALLGREN, B. "Specific Dyslexia (Congenital Word Blindness)." *Acta Psychiatrica Scandinavica*, suppl. 65 (1950).

21. HAMMAR, S. L. "School Underachievement in the Adolescent: A Review of 73 Cases." *Pediatrics*, 40 (1967), 373–381.

22. HARTOCOLLIS, P. "Minimal Brain Dysfunction in Young Adult Patients." *Bulletin of the Menninger Clinic*, 32 (1968), 102–114.

23. HEALY, W., and BRONNER, A. F. *New Light on Delinquency and Its Treatment*. New Haven: Yale University Press, 1936.

24. HELPER, M., et al. "Effects of Chlorpromazine on Learning and Related Processes in Emotionally Disturbed Children." *Journal of Consulting Psychology*, 27 (1966), 1–9.

25. HERTZIG, M. E., and BIRCH, H. "Neurologic Organization in Psychiatrically Disturbed Adolescents." *Archives of General Psychiatry*, 19 (1968), 528–537.

26. HUESSY, H. R. "Study of the Prevalence and Therapy of the Hyperkinetic Syndrome in Public School Children in Rural Vermont." *Acta Paedopsychiatrica*, 34 (1967), 130–135.

27. ———, and WRIGHT, A. L. "The Use of Imipramine in Children's Behavior Disorders." *Acta Paedopsychiatrica*, 37 (1970), 194.

28. KANNER, L. *Child Psychiatry*. 3d ed. Springfield, Ill.: Charles C Thomas, 1957.

29. KNOBLOCH, H., and PASAMANICK, B. "Prospective Studies on the Epidemiology of Reproductive Casualty." *Merrill-Palmer Quarterly of Behavior and Development*, 12 (1966), 27–43.

30. KORNETSKY, C. "Psychoactive Drugs in the Immature Organism." *Psychopharmacologia*, 17 (1970), 105–136.

31. LAUFER, M. W., et al. "Hyperkinetic Impulse Disorder in Children's Behavior Problems." *Psychosomatic Medicine*, 19 (1957), 38–49.

32. MANDELL, A. J., and SPOONER, C. E. "Psychochemical Research Studies in Man." *Science*, 162 (1968), 1442–1453.

33. MENKES, M., et al. "A Twenty-five-Year Follow-Up Study on the Hyperkinetic Child with Minimal Brain Dysfunction." *Pediatrics*, 39 (1967), 393–399.

34. MINDE, K., et al. A Five-Year Follow-Up Study of 91 Hyperactive School Children. Paper presented to the American Academy of Child Psychiatry, Boston, October 1971.

35. MORRIS, H. H., Jr., et al. "Aggressive Behavior Disorders of Childhood: A Follow-Up Study." *American Journal of Psychiatry*, 112 (1956), 991–997.

36. PAINE, R. S. "Minimal Chronic Brain Syndromes in Children." *Developmental Medicine and Child Neurology*, 4 (1962), 21–27.

37. POLLIN, E., et al. "Life History Differences in Identical Twins Discordant for Schizophrenia." *American Journal of Orthopsychiatry*, 36 (1966), 492–509.

38. PRECHTL, H. F. R., and STEMMER, C. J. "The Choreiform Syndrome in Children." *Developmental Medicine and Child Neurology*, 4 (1962), 119–127.

39. QUITKIN, F., and KLEIN, D. F. "Two Behavioral Syndromes in Young Adults Related to Possible Minimal Brain Dysfunction." *Journal of Psychiatric Research*, 7 (1969), 131–142.

40. ROBINS, L. *Deviant Children Grown Up*. Baltimore, Md.: Williams & Wilkins, 1966.

41. ROGERS, M. E., et al. "Prenatal and Paranatal Factors in the Development of Childhood Behavior Disorders." *Acta Psychiatrica et Neurologica Scandinavica*, suppl. 102 (1955).

42. SAFER, D. J. "The Familial Incidence of Minimal Brain Dysfunction." Unpublished manuscript, 1971.

43. SATERFIELD, J. H., et al. Physiological Studies of the Hyperkinetic Child. Paper presented to the American Psychiatric Association, May 1971.

44. SCHILDKRAUT, J. J., and KETY, S. S. "Pharmacological Studies Suggest a Relationship Between Brain Biogenic Amines and Affective State." *Science*, 156 (1967), 3771.

45. SPRAGUE, R., et al. "Methylphenidate and Thioridazine: Learning, Reaction Time, Activity and Classroom Behavior in Disturbed Children." *American Journal of Orthopsychiatry*, 40 (1970), 615–628.

46. STEINBERG, G. G., et al. "Dextroamphetamine-Responsive Behavior Disorders in School Children." *American Journal of Psychiatry*, 128 (1971), 174–179.

47. STEWART, M., et al. "The Hyperactive Child Syndrome." *American Journal of Orthopsychiatry*, 36 (1966), 861–867.

48. WALDROP, M. F., et al. "Minor Physical Anomalies and Behavior in Preschool Children." *Child Development*, 39 (1968), 391–400.

49. WEISS, G., et al. "Studies on the Hyperactive Child: VIII. Five-Year Follow-Up." *Archives of General Psychiatry*, 24 (1971), 409–414.

50. WENDER, P. H. "On Necessary and Sufficient Conditions in Psychiatric Explanation." *Archives of General Psychiatry*, 16 (1967), 41–47.

51. ———. *Minimal Brain Dysfunction in Children*. New York: Wiley, 1971.

52. ———, et al. "Urinary Monamine Metabolites in Children with Minimal Brain Dysfunction." *American Journal of Psychiatry*, 127 (1971), 1411–1415.

53. WERRY, J. S. "Studies on the Hyperactive Child: An Empirical Analysis of the Minimal Brain Dysfunction Syndrome." *Archives of General Psychiatry*, 19 (1968), 9–16.

54. ZRULL, J. P., et al. "An Evaluation of Methodology Used in the Study of Psychoactive Drugs for Children." *Journal of the American Academy of Child Psychiatry*, 5 (1966), 284–291.

CHAPTER 9

CHILD THERAPY TECHNIQUES

E. James Anthony

THE EMERGENCE OF THE CHILD as a treatable patient was accomplished over a protracted period of time and through a succession of stages. First came the recognition of the child as a child; in his illuminating biography of the child through the ages, Aries[7] pointed out that the social identity subsumed under the term "child" was of comparatively recent origin and that for many centuries of Western culture children were regarded as incomplete adults. It was not until the early seventeenth century that childhood was accorded a special status in its own right. The recognition of the child as emotionally disturbed, as opposed to brain damaged or mentally defective, came much later and can be considered partly a twentieth-century phenomenon. However, it was not until Freud's[20] 1909 detailed clinical description of a phobia in a five-year-old boy that the intangibles of neurosis were separated from willfulness and naughtiness. With characteristic boldness, he declared that problems of this kind in childhood were "quite extraordinarily frequent" but were generally "shouted down in the nursery."

With equal audacity he suggested that children suffering from such conditions were treatable in the same sense that adults were treatable, and he then proceeded to the first successful treatment of a neurotic child.

This recognition of psychological disturbance in the child and its treatability obtained further elaboration over the next few decades as the scope of diagnosis and treatment was widened. The concept of the child as an individual gave place to that of the child as a whole within a total environment. This at once added several new dimensions to the picture, taking into account the interactions of mind and body, the conscious and unconscious determinants of his behavior, the influences emanating from his family, as well as the effects of class, culture, and environment. With each additional facet the responsibility for the disturbance was increasingly shared with the parents, the family, the neighborhood, and even society, which led to some diffuseness of the therapeutic aim. At the same time, this expansive movement was counteracted by another that set limits to treatability. The potential for this came to be assessed predominantly in terms of suitability for psychotherapy, and it soon transpired that therapist and patient, more often than not, came from the same exclusive neighborhood and shared the same cultural advantages, such as verbal fluency, testable intelligence, and the capacity for abstract thinking.

The portrait of the child as a patient, however, had still to be completed since the important dimension of time had been omitted from previous accounts. He was now seen as developing through a sequence of stages, each of which might influence the nature and outcome of his disturbance. His status, in the general life cycle of the individual, was now assured; from being the incomplete man, he had become the father to the man, and his treatment assumed preventive significance.

In all this development the child had ceased to be a passive victim of circumstance and was considered not only an active agent in the setting up of his own disturbance but an instigator of disturbance in others in his immediate environment. As a patient, he was susceptible to as wide as spectrum of disturbances as those affecting adults, matching most of their diagnoses and adding several peculiar to himself. To the variety of diagnoses, a variety of treatments have been added, indicating a new need for careful and more specific prescription and treatment planning.

In its most recent evolution the overemphasis on pathology has been corrected by the further consideration of psychological assets, such as natural endowment, constitutional resilience, and the capacity to cope with anxiety, frustration, novelty, and other stresses. The assessment of the child as a patient now needed to include an inventory of his potentials as a person and as a patient.

❲ Pioneers of Child Therapy Techniques

The emergence of the child as a patient had its correlates in the emergence of the child therapist and his techniques. The first systematic piece of child therapy was carried out by a father on his son under the supervision of Freud,[20] and although the treatment could be regarded as highly successful both at termination and subsequent follow up, this particular treatment model has not stimulated too many imitators. In fact, fathers have proved notoriously difficult to involve in the therapy of a child. In the follow-up evaluation, some seventeen years after the treatment, the above mentioned child patient met all the requirements for a cure. He was perfectly well and free from troubles and inhibitions, and his emotional life had successfully undergone the severest of ordeals, the divorce of his parents and the consequent separation from his much loved sister. There had been no detrimental consequences as a result of opening up his unconscious mind, and the uncovered events, together with the therapy, had both been "overtaken by amnesia." He had also traversed the pitfalls of puberty without damage. At this point in history it was not sufficient to demonstrate that child therapy did good; it was also necessary to show that it did no harm, and Freud's case was a double success from this point of view.

Child Therapy and the Delinquent

The treatment of the phobic child proved a stimulus to the field. The next step was taken by Healy,[26] who synthesized the relevant and burgeoning knowledge in this area and fashioned it into a therapeutic instrument that provided the basis for the child guidance approach of study and treatment by an interdisciplinary team. In Healy's clinic, the child, together with his family, was confronted by a group of experts who carefully assessed both internal and external realities in terms of past and present experiences. For the first time in clinical history the child was invited to tell his own story in his own way and in his own time, a truly radical departure from being peremptorily dosed and discharged. Although the child's problems were considered within the framework of a dynamic, developmental psychopathology, its antisocial nature demanded extensive manipulations of the environment, meaning active social work. Within the analytic context, the concept of environment itself underwent change and came to be viewed as "fluid, intimate—composed of living, changing, reacting personalities."[37] Shifts in the external environment, however dynamically conceived, were not sufficient in themselves to alter the delinquent tendency, and, as its etiology was traced to the earliest deprivations and disadvantages, the need to establish a working therapeutic alliance with the delinquent patient was seen to be fundamental. A special kind of therapist, with an inordinate capacity for tolerating antisocial behavior, undertook the job of rendering the patient treatable by establishing a relationship and subsequently neuroticizing the problem. Unlike the phobic child treated by Freud, this type of patient required preparatory treatment before he was able to tolerate an uncovering or probing therapy.

The Development of Child Analysis

Psychoanalysis as a specific technique made comparatively little contribution to child therapy until the development of child analysis during the second and third decades of this century. This was associated with the discovery of play as a major mode of communication and expression for the child in treatment. As early as 1924, Abraham[1] remarked that the future of psychoanalysis itself lay in the play analysis of children, and that he looked to it for future theoretical developments. The work of the child analysts Melanie Klein[32] and Anna Freud,[16] during the subsequent period, testified to the truth of this prediction. Klein developed a new metapsychology on the basis of her child analytic work, and further, her experience convinced her that children were analyzable to the same extent as adults and that one could even go "deeper" with them. Children, she felt, developed a transference neurosis similiar to that in the adult patient and were technically treatable from the second year onward. Anna Freud had many reservations in the beginning regarding the child's potential for analysis, and, at an earlier phase, limited its application to children of

latency age whose parents had themselves undergone analysis. In place of the direct symbolic interpretation of Klein she substituted a more cautious analysis of resistance, and whereas Klein made use of play as free association, Anna Freud tended to regard it as one of several important ways of learning about the child from the child. At this earlier time she was impressed by the limitations of the child as an analytic patient. The differences from the adult counterpart seemed to her then striking: The child did not come for treatment but was brought; it was not he who complained but his parents; he was unable to lie on a couch, free associate, analyze his dreams, work through his resistances, or develop a transference neurosis. All this meant that he was not analyzable in the classical meaning of the term but only in an applied sense. In recent years, Anna Freud has veered around to Klein's position. She regards many more children as analyzable and recognizes the development of transference neurosis in some children, Whereas she began her work in analytically oriented psychotherapy, she is now training her students in child analysis.

Nondirective Psychotherapy

According to Carl Rogers[45] there is a powerful creative force within every individual that strives continually for self-realization, independence, maturity, and self-determination, and, if given an opportunity to act, it can work out a constructive adjustment to even the most difficult realities confronting the person. It is the therapist's role to release this curative element by providing the growing ground for its development. He may accomplish this simply by giving tacit permission to the individual to be accepted by himself and others. Once self-confidence has been established, the rest can be left to the growth impulse, the operation of which will make mature behavior preferable to immature behavior. The patient assumes direction and responsibility for his own treatment since the cure resides within him. Axline[8] adapted the Rogerian technique to child therapy, applying the same principles both to individual and group situations. There is an inspirational quality about this approach that, together with its somewhat reverential attitude toward the child, its positivistic philosophy, its insistent high-mindedness, and its simplistic theoretical structure, has turned away the average secular therapist. The idea that spontaneous expression of itself is the key to therapeutic change takes little account of the complex system of defenses set up in the disturbed individual as well as the variety of reaction patterns brought into play by different life experiences and constitutions. It is, therefore, not surprising that Axline disdained the diagnostic evaluation and believed that "regardless of symptomatic behavior, the individual is met by the therapist *where* he is."

A number of similiar therapies have also stemmed from the work of Otto Rank[43] and Alfred Adler,[2] all having in common an emphasis on the living relationship and a primary focus of the patient. The so-called client-centered therapy also views the relationship as a significant growth experience but treats the therapist and child as separate individuals, the role of the therapist being to reflect, clarify, and demonstrate an empathic understanding of his client's predicament.

Allen,[3] deriving his therapeutic stance from Rank, put special stress on the here and now. The relationship is "an immediate experience," and therapeutic reality exists in the present not in the "past present." The therapist himself is "a living symbol of the present world" and must maintain his own realness and not retreat through transference into the dark recesses of the past. The therapeutic setting is in essence an encounter with a world of pressing realities. The past holds a measure of safety, and it is in the present that the anxieties and insecurities lie. The therapist is not there to change the patient but to help the patient to change himself. His skill and training have no therapeutic value unless they are used by the patient. It is what the child does spontaneously on his own and in his own way, without prompting or coercion, that helps to induce the change. Immediacy, spontaneity, creativity, and uniqueness make up the prime components of this unusual encounter. Psycho-

therapy in this sense is not a rite or a ritual but a realization. The encounter movement in its present form has turned even further away from intellectual understanding and has made spontaneous affective experience the critical dynamic factor in treatment.

Release Therapy

Classical catharsis was given a new lease on life when Levy[33] formulated his technique of release therapy, which he felt was appropriate for uncomplicated problems in family relationships of recent onset and of short duration in children under the age of ten years, where a definite symptom picture had been precipitated by some disturbing specific event, such as birth, divorce, death, or frightening experience. Levy described three types of situations in which the technique appeared to work effectively: (1) where there is a simple release of inhibited aggressive or infantile regressive behavior by means of acting out such behaviors in a permissive setting; (2) where there is a release of feeling in a standardized provocative situation in which, for example, two sibling dolls compete for a mother, or a nude doll demonstrates sex differences, or two parent dolls are brought together in a primal scene; and (3) where there is a release of feelings in a specific play situation set up to resemble the recent traumatic experience in the life of the patient. In this third situation, the therapist acts "like a friendly property man" who selects the props, sets the stage, and depicts the plot, occasionally acting as prompter. The acting-out principle assumed to function in this situation could be compared to a dilation process designed to stretch a somewhat constricted personality. The result can at times be tempestuous, and Levy warned that a cardinal rule of the situation should be that the therapist be spared. He is likely to get involved when transference is activated, and when this happens, of course, the treatment proceeds beyond the limits of release therapy. This particular technique can be best regarded as crisis intervention and therefore limited to particular situations. Levy's suggestion that it might be used as a prelude to insight therapy or as an interlude in a resistant psychotherapy would not be accepted by analytically oriented psychotherapists today. Such shock procedures create many more problems than they solve and can interfere seriously with the careful and systematic work of psychotherapy. As Allen[3] pointed out, "The mere release or getting out of feeling has little value therapeutically. It is the incorporation of that feeling into himself and the ability to be responsible for its use and direction that constitutes growth."

Suppressive Therapy

At the opposite pole from release therapy is suppressive therapy, proposed by Escalona[14] for children showing extreme weakness in ego functioning and at times a disintegrative dependency that inteferes profoundly with ego development. In such cases, the children have failed to repress the psychic experiences that normally should be unconscious; their spontaneous verbalization of conscious content resembles the dreams of other children, and their play during the initial interviews is like the play of neurotic children who have been in therapy for some time. Thus the therapy is directed at discouraging the expression and acting out of fantasies, and at providing many opportunities for realistic activities together with the strengthening of reality testing. Whether suppressive therapy could work in practice is still a moot point since the procedure has not been systematically studied in a large enough number of children. It does suggest, however, the possibility that expressive types of psychotherapy in some cases may tend to operate in antitherapeutic ways to the detriment of the child's condition.

Projection Therapy

Projection therapy is merely an example of the way in which therapists, somewhat grandiosely, attach labels to some particular medium by which communication with the child is channeled. Play therapy, in which the child is given a free choice in the use of small toys and freedom in the way in which they are to

be used, is a particular example of such a tendency. Differences exist in the extent to which the therapist participates or makes interpretations. The assumption is that the child will endeavor to play out his problems if given this opportunity. There is still much difference of opinion as to whether play is a medium of therapy or therapeutic in itself. All the great dynamic therapists were directly or indirectly alive to the endless theoretical issues latent in the play of children. For Freud[21] the interest lay in its creativity, and he compared the child at play to an imaginative writer creating a world of his own or rearranging his world to please himself. He was aware of the essential seriousness of play for the child. Jung[29] was equally aware of its seriousness for the adult and described how even into old age he was often able to deal successfully with his anxieties by resorting to play. For Erikson,[12] the play situation was a human laboratory in which the child experimented with reality by creating model situations in which he relived the past, redeemed his present failures, and anticipated the future. Ever since Freud,[18] child therapists have been aware that the child will play compulsively and repetitively in order to master inner and outer traumatic anxieties, especially if he is able to reverse the roles and become the master and not the victim of the experience. All these elements of creative problem-solving, catharsis, repetition compulsion, tension reduction, wish fulfillment, vacation from reality, and passivity into activity have been built up into a comprehensive psychoanalytic theory of play that, in turn, could be appropriately applied to the therapeutic situation. The possibilities for the child in this miniature world are so varied that it is not surprising that he visits it so frequently in the service of self-therapy. In his make believe he can animate a lifeless object, invent an imaginary companion, identify with a fearsome character, vent his hostility without reprisal, exercise his primitive magic, test out limits, and investigate solutions to his conflicts. Under the eye of the therapist the therapeutic elements of play can be further enhanced through more systematic deployment. Play can help, for example, to bolster the therapeutic alliance and afford the therapist easier access to the inner problems of his patient. Even with minimal intervention or interpretation, the playing child may improve in a way comparable to the relief that certain dreams afford the dreaming adult even before he has understood their meaning.

The play equipment itself has been overemphasized by some therapists and underrated by others. For Lowenfeld,[36] it consists of no more than the culinary implements and raw food material in the kitchen. "It is what the cook does with these implements and food elements that determines the dish." Lowenfeld provided her patients with an entire world in which the child could reconstruct his inner vision of life together with the rules and regulations that govern it. In a rough sense, the outer world is isomorphic with the internal one. Lowenfeld is not so concerned as other therapists in connecting the two but in making contact with the mind behind the construction and understanding it better. Klein[32] was of the opinion that the play material should be essentially nebulous and malleable and therefore easily convertible to the child's projected needs. Bender[9] insisted that one could do play therapy with children near the equator using sand, stones, and palm trees, and in the arctic regions, snow and ice, since it was important for the material to be meaningful to the lives of the children. Many play therapists maintain a separate box of play equipment for each child patient that remains at his service throughout his treatment. The contents of a box is often a motley collection of things that allows for the expression of family feeling, aggression, regression, rivalry, and restitution.

In the older child, games can substitute for play and can be used ingeniously by the therapist to portray the essentials of both interpersonal and intrapsychic conflicts. Loomis,[35] Gardner,[22] and others have described how the game of checkers, played since the days of the Pharaohs, can be used as a modality in therapeutic work with children, helping to externalize a large number of problems. The game ingredients, described by Redl,[44] can be adapted with advantage to the progress of treatment. Winning or losing, playing fair or cheating, laying traps for your opponent, sacrificing in order to gain, manipulating the ground rules, giving up under pressure, playing chaotically or compulsively, breaking up the game, and losing interest or becoming tired may all reflect the current intrapsychic state of the child and his interpersonal situation with the therapist. Some have gone so far as to call this "checkers therapy," but it is really no more than a sometimes useful maneuver when the verbal interchange has come to a standstill.

Conditioning Therapy

The classic study in this field is Watson and Rayner's[48] conditioning of a fear response to a white rat in a little boy called Albert, and this was followed a little later by Jones's[28] methods of eliminating fear, using such procedures as disuse, verbal appeal, negative adaptation, repression, distraction, direct conditioning, and social imitation. Only the methods of direct conditioning (or deconditioning) and social imitation proved very successful. Behavior therapy is based on the assumption that the symptom is the illness and not merely the external manifestation of some underlying disturbance. On the basis of learning theory, behavior can be reinforced or inhibited at the discretion of the therapist, and some behaviors may be replaced by others considered less disturbing to the environment. The changes are not only produced rapidly but are observable, and from this point of view behavior therapy is more likely to impress the unsophisticated patient or parent than treatments conducive to an alteration of inner state without external evidence of that state.

❨ The Basic Ingredients of Child Therapy

Theory and Child Therapy

Therapists vary considerably in their need of theory or technique. There are some who need a minimum of both and rely on the impact of their personalities (often charismatic in these cases) on the patient. The child improves because he is impressed by the therapist, wishes to please him, and wants to be like him. Other therapists are top-heavy with theory or so dedicated to the exclusive use of particular techniques that much of the flexibility and spontaneity are eliminated from the treatment, with a consequent deadening of the process. An adequate therapist gradually learns to weld theory, technique, and experience into his therapeutic style, making it both personal to himself and generalizable to the theory and practice of other practitioners.

Psychoanalytic theory has the advantage of emerging from psychoanalytic practice and at the same time influencing the nature of that practice. The tripartite structure of the psyche, according to psychoanalysis, helps to illuminate the process of therapy in every stage of its development. The id impulses are constantly striving to make themselves conscious and achieve fulfillment, either completely or derivatively. The ego struggles as actively by means of a complex system of defenses to keep such impulses from consciousness. In analytic treatment, this aspect of the ego's function comes under analysis. Since the purpose of analytic treatment is to enable repressed instincts to enter awareness in ideational form, the ego automatically sets up defenses against the analysis and eventually the analyst. This resistance to the analyst's work eventually becomes part of the transference resistances. The ego defends itself not only against the instincts but also against the affects associated with the instincts, and it develops a wide variety of measures to master the concomitant feelings. These ego defenses vary with the stage of development, and the child analyst may therefore find himself dealing predominantly with different defense mechanisms, not only in different patients at different developmental stages but also in the same patient at different phases of the treatment. In later childhood some of the resistances become incorporated into the character and are therefore extremely laborious to analyze because of the apparent absence of intrasystemic conflict. In the treatment process of child

analysis, the technique often begins with the analysis of the patient's defense against affects and then proceeds to the investigation of the transference resistances. In the early days of psychoanalysis the following reasons were given as to why the child was not analyzable in the usual sense of analysis: A child generally did not come voluntarily to treatment; he was generally not able to relax on a couch; he was not able to free associate; he was unable to develop a transference neurosis; he was unable to work through certain resistances; he was unable to undertake dream work; and his ego and superego were too immature to deal with anything but a minimum of id material. In the last few decades the situation has changed remarkably, mainly because of the influence of Melanie Klein, who had insisted from the beginning that the analysis of the child was in every way comparable to the analysis of the adult. Anna Freud has since come to an almost similar conclusion, although by a different path. Klein[32] felt that a free flow of play was equivalent to the free flow of a patient's thoughts and that the content of play can therefore be treated as associations. Anna Freud[15] was unable to accept this equation, but, for her part, thought that the analysis of affects as they undergo transformation in treatment may offer opportunities similar to free associations and have, moreover, the advantage of not requiring the child's voluntary cooperation. Freud is currently in agreement with Klein that transference neurosis can develop in the child and is susceptible of analysis. As in the case of adult psychoanalysis, transference has gradually come to occupy a major role in child analysis.

The Rankian approach is somewhat different. Transference, like resistance, is accepted as a stage in the growth process of the self becoming autonomous. The analyst tries to accept what is happening without letting his own feelings interfere with the young patient's struggle to find himself. It is up to the child to do what he can for himself with the steady support of the analyst, the latter tolerating all the vicissitude of the transference. The Rankian emphasis on time may play an integral part in the treatment, and its most crucial development may lie in dealing with the series of endings and separations that analysis, like life, imposes on the situation. The termination, willed and accepted by the patient, is an active beginning as well as ending. In all this the therapeutic process becomes strangely coterminous with the life process.[47]

In child analysis, therefore, the unconscious conflicts underpinning a neurosis are interpreted systematically; the transference manifestations may develop and may mature to a full transference neurosis; the Oedipus complex is reached, worked through, and resolved in keeping with the psychosexual level of the child, and treatment is carried out three to five times a week for as long as four to five years.

By comparison, analytic psychotherapy with the child is directed at the alleviation of a specific neurotic symptom or the reduction of some related anxiety by means of interpreting the specific underlying conflict. The therapist attempts to stabilize the reasonably intact personality of his patient and to prevent any aggravation of pathology. He attempts to function as a real rather than as a transference object, to deal with current reality, to respond actively with verifications, suggestions, and reassurance, to encourage the expression of thoughts and feelings, to leave useful defenses alone, and to deal with dynamic rather than genetic issues. In so doing, according to Brody,[10] he cannot but develop a "parental aura." He usually sees the patient not more than once or twice a week over a period of one to three years. Brody felt that the psychoanalytic framework is the only practical one for effective child psychotherapy because, as she said, "if psychotherapy is to be rational, one theory of personality development and of symptom formation must obtain for all methods." McClure[38] outlined the basic principles of play therapy somewhat differently. In her scheme, the therapist must attempt to make contact with the child's unconscious, split the ambivalence, participate in the guilt released, probe no deeper into the unconscious than is necessary for therapy, and foster a reconstruction of the personality on its own lines, true to its own basic reaction type. She grouped patients according to their reaction types (hysterical, obsessional, and labile) and modified her therapeutic activity accordingly. With the hysteric the therapist attempts to act as a stabilizing force and then to find, in the historical emotional environment of the child, the obstruction that first disorientated the child's reactions. With the obsessional the therapist attempts to harness the creativity of the child, especially in terms of his fantasies of punishment, and with this will come the first contact with the child's feelings. With the labile reaction type much of the treatment can be carried out at a positive, extroverted reality level, attempting to give the child some insight into the restraint of his primitive impulses. McClure pointed out that verbal interpretation can be helpful but should not be systematic or intellectual. In general, she stated that the therapist should adopt a warmer approach toward obsessional than toward other types of children.

Within the Therapeutic Environment

Milner[40] likened the therapeutic environment to a framed picture, the frame standing for the boundary between the comparative unreality and illusion within the frame and the everyday reality outside it. The frames (or walls) are there to specify that the situation is unusual and that what takes place can occur nowhere else in the outside world. The frame may be complete or incomplete, or the system may be closed or open. In the case of younger children many therapists prefer to work with an open system that allows regular contact with the parents so that information they give may be used in the service of therapy. However, such openness may lead to problems of confidentiality even in very young children, who may rapidly assume a conspiracy of adults attempting conjointly to domesticate them. The parents, in fact, represent a technical problem for all ages of children, and the general rule is to involve them less in the system in direct relation to the age of the child.

The therapist creates the therapeutic environment in which he is best able to work, but to some extent his therapeutic posture is determined by his theoretical leanings. If he is a classical child analyst, for example, he takes his stand at a point "equidistant from the id, the ego, and the superego."[15] If he is a Rankian, he must "maintain his own realness," provide a "steady background," and help the patient gradually to be himself, gain a sounder evaluation of his own differences, and become free to make creative and responsible use of these differences in the continuing realities of his life.[3] Allen[3] had enough confidence in this approach to state, somewhat categorically, that "we have gone far beyond the idea of therapy as the application of techniques and the giving of insight." If he is a Rogerian, the therapist is basically nondirective, but within the relationship he is warm and friendly, establishes a good rapport as soon as possible, accepts the child exactly as he is, establishes a feeling of permissiveness so that the child feels free to express his feelings completely, reflects these feelings back to the child in such a way that he gains insight into his behavior, maintains a deep respect for the child's ability to solve his own problems if given an opportunity to do so, encourages the responsibility to make choices and to institute change, and establishes only those limitations necessary to anchor the therapy to the world of reality and to make the child aware of his share in the relationship. The child always leads the way, and the therapist follows unhurriedly. These are the basic principles outlined by Axline[8] by means of which she structured the therapeutic alliance.

All therapists are aware or should be aware that during the other twenty-three hours of the day the child is exposed to a variety of pro- and antitherapeutic forces operating in his general environment. Unless the therapist makes himself aware of these factors he may find to his surprise that his patients make sudden and inexplicable therapeutic changes for the better or worse that leave him surprised and perplexed. He may understand fully what is going on in therapy but not what is going on outside therapy. The facilitating environment[49] may have special significance for certain needy and dependent children without too much autonomous capacity of their own.

Erikson[12] structured the world of the playing child into three areas: a sphere directly related to the small manipulatable toys with which he plays; a sphere relating to his body; and a sphere relating to the larger world. The therapeutic environment can be differentiated in the same way: a microsphere where the child can project his internal feelings and conflicts; the autosphere to which he retreats or regresses in a need of comfort and satisfaction; a macrosphere which contains the rest of the environment; and the transference sphere containing and surrounding the therapist. The child's movements within this system can be plotted and interpreted in relation to the significant figure of the therapist.

Winnicott's[49] full conception of the therapeutic environment was in dynamic terms. Every part of it—the resisting walls, the openings into the outer world, the little things that could be broken and put together again—were all understood in dynamic terms, as if the environment was structured rather like the mental apparatus.

The therapeutic environment congenial to relationship therapy has been fully described by Moustakas.[41] It has been compared to the atmosphere of a Japanese tea ceremony: harmonious, reverential, pure, and tranquil, exuding a constant sense of peace. All this sounds remote from the often scarifying, disturbing child analytic situation in which murderous and incestuous wishes and fears may pervade the environment. As Klein remarked, the psychoanalytic treatment of children is not a gentle matter, since the impulses involved are far from gentle. It would not be feasible to conduct a child analysis in the atmosphere of a Japanese tea ceremony.

The therapeutic relationship that develops within the therapeutic environment begins first with the breakdown of strangeness, the establishment of confidence and trust in the therapist, the resolution of the initial suspicions and misgivings and fears, and finally the growth of a therapeutic alliance in which the observing and healthy portion of the patient's ego joins forces with the therapist in the battle against the patient's neurosis. The relationship undergoes many changes during the course of therapy; sometimes it is used for symbiotic ends, for regressive needs, for the working out of transference, for support, for understanding reality, for transitional purposes and for learning how to become therapeutic with regard to oneself. The communications that punctuate this relationship are frequently nonverbal, empathic understandings that need no overt expression, sometimes comments, sometimes questions, sometimes direct confrontations, and every now and then, when the timing is appropriate, an interpretation given with tact and clarity in brief and concrete terms.[5]

As the child moves from one sphere to another in relation to the therapist, from one mode of expression to another in terms of his fantasies, dreams, play, games, and dramatic performances, he also passes through cycles of affect that follow one another in logical sequence: Aggressiveness, giving place to guilt, and then to fear of retaliation, and then to the desire to make reparation, eventuates in loving feelings and a movement toward the therapist. Erotic feelings may be followed by fears of seduction and penetration, giving place to anger and attack and distancing from the therapist.[5]

Newcomers to the field of child therapy are often puzzled by the vague and nebulous content of the sessions and the capacity for the child to be productive in the therapeutic situation without need to communicate. Even after long experience the child therapist must be prepared to deal with less certitude than the adult therapist. A gifted commentator, outside the field,[11] had this to say about the contact with children: "Children need not talk, even when they can. Much goes in but little comes out. We may ask but win few direct answers. We can at best only interpret. . . . I believe those who can win nearest to childhood and be wholly at peace, at liberty, and at ease in its company would be the first to acknowledge

that they can never get nearer than very near, never actually there."[11]

(Preliminary Considerations in Child Therapy

Assessment of Therapeutic Potential

An important part of the diagnostic process is the assessment of therapeutic potential, which is a global consideration depending in part on factors in the child, in his family, in the community around him, and in the clinician or clinical team that is preparing to treat him.

The important factors in the child have to do with the extent of the disturbance, its duration, the amount of secondary gain deriving from the symptoms, and the proportion of reactive to internal elements in the disorder. A second area has to do with the personal characteristics of the patient, such as his stage of development, his capacity for relating to others, his ability to conceptualize and communicate, his tolerance of anxiety and frustration, his repertoire of defensive and coping mechanisms, his potential for transference, his "psychological mindedness," and his proneness to regression. The third area is related to the personality as a whole in both its healthy and unhealthy parts, considered separately with regard to drives, conscience, and ego, especially in its conflict-free functions. The final area is concerned with the degree of physical and central nervous system impairment.

In more detail, the evaluation attempts to assess the cooperation and motivation of the parents, their familiarity with psychological treatment, their experience of treatment with other children in the family, their sophistication with respect to inner and unconscious factors or causality, and their general belief in the malleability of the human psyche. In the developmental context, significant factors include the quality of the primary mother-infant relationship, the presence or absence of pregenital fixations, the intensity of the symbiotic tie to the mother, the presence or absence of

Oedipal configurations, and the amount of trauma, such as separation, hospitalization, illness, death, or divorce, in the early part of the life cycle.

Psychological elements within the child include his level of intelligence, the availability of his affects, his introspectiveness, his recognition of problems and willingness to consider them, and his motivation to come "in order to get on better."

The characteristics of the family as a unit, whether stable, cohesive, divisive, close, or distant, and its relationship, in turn, to the community, whether isolated or involved, may also exert a determining influence on the child's level of therapeutic responsiveness. To the extent that he also shares in a general family pathology that is in a relative state of equilibrium, this can also impede the progress of change. The child's role in the psychic economy of the parental relationship is sometimes so crucial that a shift in his balance is likely to prove disruptive to the marital tie. The extended family of near and distant relatives may also play a part in supplementing, implementing, or undermining the therapeutic management, particularly when they become part of the practical arrangements and are required to transport, babysit, or pay the fees. The arrangements in general have to be carefully considered in the overall assessment and should not add a burdensome load of their own to the treatment undertaking.

The factors in the community that may affect therapy, either positively or negatively, include the school and its investment in the child, the child's pediatrician and his attitude toward psychological treatment, and religious and social organizations in close touch with the family.

The result of the assessment should generally throw conclusive light on the treatability of the child, but this is sometimes still in doubt after all the factors have been carefully considered. It is then good practice to undertake a trial period of therapy before any child is labeled "untreatable." There are many children who are unreachable and untreatable when the classical techniques are rigidly applied but who respond very well following a period of preparation or modification of method. These and other related matters have been fully considered in a recent report.[25]

Assessment of the Degree and Level of Disturbance

Although it is customary for the growth and relationship school of child therapy to eschew the process of diagnosis and to endeavor to meet the child where he is, the more usual practice for those working with the medical model is to make a careful diagnosis and construct a diagnostic profile or working model of the child's therapeutic strengths and weaknesses prior to any consideration of treatment. The diagnostic classification that has most to recommend it for ordinary clinical purposes[24] has the additional advantage of some research evaluation. Its most striking feature is the inclusion of a diagnostic category of health (rarely considered when a child is referred to a clinic) as well as the further useful category of developmental deviation.

A special psychoanalytically oriented profile has also been devised by Anna Freud[17] and her colleagues, which is based on both external factors, such as the referral symptoms, the family background and history, other possibly significant environmental influences, and internal factors dealing with the structure of his personality, the dynamic interplay within the structure, the economic factors relating to the relative strength of id and ego forces, the psychogenetic assumptions, and the adaptation of the child to the realities of his circumstances. In the overall consideration the total personality of the child is scrutinized in terms of his frustration tolerance, his sublimation potential, his handling of anxiety, and the proportion of aggressive to regressive tendencies.

Differential Treatment Planning

This important interlude is fully considered in a Group for the Advancement of Psychiatry report.[25] There is sometimes an awkward gap between diagnosis and treatment, which may be extended indefinitely by a lengthy waiting list procedure. The logical sequence of events that take place in the interim period following evaluation is often unclear not only to the clinician himself but also to the family. Most clinics today have progressed beyond the point where a patient is rejected as being unsuitable for treatment. Clinics are increasingly able to provide a range of treatments to match a range of diagnoses, so that individual, group, family, psychoeducational, drug, and behavior therapies are prescribed after very careful consideration of the diagnostic circumstances. For purposes of treatment planning, diagnostic classification in the narrow sense of the child's liabilities is insufficient and at times even misleading and needs to be complemented by a differential assessment of his assets. The planning may result in a number of treatment recommendations in which one or more may be combined, and although the clinician may favor a particular approach, he may well alter his recommendation after full discussion with the family. The consumer's point of view is therefore represented in the final plan. Communicating the findings and recommendations of the clinician to the child and his family is a small art in itself, and strong resistances may arise when suggestions are made in an atmosphere of reproach instigating guilt and shame. Resistance may also arise from a lack of clarity or a failure to empathize with special anxieties and concerns at the receiving end.

❡ The Course of Treatment

An overall view of treatment generally tends to categorize it into a beginning, middle, and terminal phase, which Freud[19] once compared to a game of chess in which the opening gambit and end game could be taught and learned to some extent. The long phase between the two was so complex in its development that the student had to learn to play it by ear with the help of certain general principles and a variety of technical procedures.

Anthony[5] made an attempt to trace the evolution of the therapeutic process in individual psychotherapy and child analysis. In his paradigm he envisaged four stages in treatment:

1. There was a varying period of initial contact during which familiarization to the therapeutic environment and to an unknown person occurs. The duration of this stage bears a close relationship to the level of anxiety that the patient brings in with him and to his habitual sensitivity to strangers and strange situations. It is essentially an encounter between real people, with transference factors playing a minimal part.

2. The next stage, termed Phase I, functions essentially as an open system modeled on the early parent-child union with its anaclitic-diatrophic form of relatedness. Communication is dominated by primitive ego functioning on the part of both therapist and patient, with heavy reliance on empathy, intuition, imitation, and identification. The patient's thinking is largely of the primary-process variety and is apt to be colored by ideas of magic and omnipotence. The focal conflict has to do with dependency and the ambivalent feelings engendered by it. In keeping with this issue, the drives are predominantly pregenital in origin, with attacking and sadistic elements especially prominent. The symbiotic transference tends to be floating and sporadic, and the countertransference is parental in orientation, involving areas of care, contact, and control. The major therapeutic influences at work involve suggestion, persuasion, and catharsis, and consequently the therapist's personality plays a crucial role in directing the course of treatment. The therapeutic task for this first phase comprises the resolution of the ambivalent dependency, the crystallization of identifications into a more genuine object relationship and a corresponding individuation of the patient as a whole.

3. As a result of these developments, the course of treatment undergoes an often dramatic transformation, which is characteristic of Phase II. During this state the therapeutic system can be described as closed, and the working therapeutic model would include representations of both mother and father within

a triangular frame of reference. Communication is typically verbal and explicit, and the thinking operations of both patient and therapist involve logical secondary processes, with the observing ego of the patient demonstrating a capacity for doing a certain amount of analytic work itself in the form of self-analysis and working through, indicating that the therapist, as therapist, has been to some extent internalized. Because libidinal drives are more to the forefront, there seems to be a general softening of the treatment milieu. It is during the course of this stage that transference neurosis develops and is resolved with the methodical use of interpretation and defense analysis. The countertransference experiences show erotic and genital components, depending on the sex of the patient and the positive or negative direction of the therapist's Oedipal complex.

Anthony was of the impression that for the majority of cases seen in a children's psychiatric clinic, the Phase I period of therapy only is sufficient, since the resolution of the ambivalent dependence could lead to lasting changes within the personality through the medium of identification. In certain cases, however, where the neurosis is classical, circumscribed, internalized, and structuralized, a shift to Phase II becomes necessary. When this fails to occur, the fault may be attributable to unforeseen diagnostic complications in the patient, to the excessive use of gratification in the treatment environment, or to certain subtle countertransference resistances in the therapist himself.

4. With the passing of the transference, a termination stage can usually be demarcated during which the therapist once again emerges predominantly as a real person who is more knowable than the previously nebulous transference figure. This person-to-person encounter is associated with a general mellowing of the therapist's affective response toward the patient, and the major therapeutic work to be conducted in this phase focuses on the separation anxiety stimulated by the prospect of termination.

In the relationship field, Moustakas[41] also described stages in treatment under the aegis of a therapist who believes deeply in his patient as a person and in his potentialities for growth. At the beginning, the child is required to become aware of his real feelings, fear, anger, immaturity, and destructiveness. As the relationship with the therapist is clarified and strengthened, the child's deeper feelings of hostility also become gradually sharpened, and anger is expressed more directly and more relevantly to the person or situation concerned. At the next stage, he is no longer so completely negative, and ambivalent feelings, both negative and positive, predominate. In the final stage, positive feelings emerge, and the child begins to see himself and relations with people more as they really are. In the anxious child, as opposed to the angry child, anxiety is at first all pervasive and general and then begins to crystallize around some particular person. At this point, he feels very inadequate, and this persists until the next phase when the doubts about himself are gradually replaced by confidence and courage, though for a while the child oscillates between these two sets of feelings. Finally, he becomes clear about positive and negative fears toward particular people and can relate them to actual situations, and when this happens they slowly diminish in intensity.

In children who have not undergone a primary mothering experience, to use Winnicott's[49] term, and in children heavily traumatized in the first period of life and who have developed what used to be called primary behavior disorders, there is often a singular lack of motivation and anxiety on which to base the treatment. A long period of preparation for treatment may finally result in the emergence of a treatable child, but the task of preparation is not easy, and the chink in the armor may be hard to find. Work with the parents may make all the difference between success and failure in treatment.

The classical treatments have not only been modified for certain previously untreatable disorders, but they have also been shortened to fit the needs of acute or critical circumstances. Release or abreactive therapy for the traumatic neuroses has already been mentioned. Green and Rothenberg[23] suggested certain guidelines in the first aid treatment for children. In order to prevent emotional damage to the child, they advised that the parents be informed of the possible risk to the child involved in the situation and educated in the role of secondary prevention by receiving an understanding of the child's language of behavior in nontechnical terms. The parents are given some concrete and practical advice, such as the need to maintain self-control in the child's presence, the importance of listening to the child without teasing, ridiculing, or beating him for his symptoms, of allowing him to recount his complaints as often as he wishes, of not telling him to go away and forget his problems, of investigating the situation as much as possible before taking action and not pushing the child into any frightening or disturbing situation to which he feels unequal. Listening, encouraging, reassuring, abreacting, and interpreting are the foundations of these short-term therapies. With younger children, treatment can often be abbreviated by working with the parents to affect those environmental forces playing on the child. The reason why brief interventions are so effective in the emotional predicament of crisis is that at these times the defenses are labile and the cathexes fluid. Caplan (quoted by Klein and Lindemann[31]) likened the critical intervention to the giving of a gentle push to a man standing on one leg, thereby hoping to restore him to his precrisis balance; the results are also gained with much less effort than might generally be required. However, although the push may be gentle and brief, the inner reverberations set up by it may continue long beyond the actual encounter. Stierlin[46] argued that certain developmental crises may be propitious occasions in which you may alter life situations so that the decision as to when to treat may be a crucial therapeutic decision. The therapist's responsiveness and sensitivity carry even greater importance in brief than in long-term therapy. Malan[39] pointed to some of the advantages of the time limited situation. The brevity of contact makes it easier to tolerate the tensions and negative feelings engendered by the relationship. The therapist tries to deal with termination at the onset of therapy, activating the capacity to mourn. The end of treatment, therefore, becomes the main focus of the therapeutic process.

Behavior therapies of various kinds are becoming increasingly used in child guidance clinics. Phobias have been desensitized; disturbing symptoms have been eradicated by punishment and nonsymptomatic behavior reinforced by rewards; social adjustment has been improved by means of treatment based on social learning theory. The results obtained are often so striking that it is not surprising that more and more clinics are climbing on to this particular bandwagon. More recent evaluations, however, especially long-term ones, are less enthusiastic, and there have been several suggestions in recent years that insight and behavior therapy are not mutually exclusive or incompatible and might advantageously be used in conjunction.

❰ The Role of the Therapist

Child therapy is an arduous business, and few child therapists remain active practitioners beyond the fourth decade; thereafter, they either tend to switch to adult patients or become supervisors. The wear and tear of person and property can be considerable and discouraging and, to paraphrase Winnicott,[49] there are at least twenty-one good reasons why the average good enough therapist sometimes hates his child patient. He may hate him because he is unwilling to come, reluctant to stay, and eager to go; he may hate him because he is obstinately silent, garrulously irrelevant or monotonously confined to cliches, such as "I don't know." He may hate him for being physically aggressive, destructive, or dirty and messy; for inquisitively investigating all his private drawers and papers; for demanding food and rejecting interpretations; for making the therapist doubt his theory, his technique, his ability to understand even himself. There is no other situation that engenders so much countertransference for the therapist except perhaps the treatment of psychosis.

Apart from feelings generated by the patient, the therapist may also react to the child's parents, by identifying either with them against the child or with the child against the parents. In both instances the responses ricochet on the therapist.

The facilitating factors that the child therapist brings with him to the treatment situation are his empathy, deriving from his own mother-child relationship, his capacity to tolerate immaturities, his ability to regress therapeutically along with his patient, a general familiarity and at homeness in childhood, and a childlike quality that is often recognized immediately by the child patient and responded to with a sense of kinship. A touch of anality makes the general messiness of child therapy not so distasteful to the child therapist.

The psychological distance between the child therapist and his child patient is therefore much less than that between the average adult and child, and further bridging measures include a learned capacity to talk to the child without condescension. Anthony[4] commented on the usefulness of Piaget's[42] technique of clinical interrogation in communicating therapeutically with children, and Gardner introduced a special technique of storytelling which is tape-recorded during the treatment session. The therapist also tells a story following a few principles of story analysis, similiar to dream analysis. In the story analysis, the symbolic significance of each figure is clarified, and the moral of the story becomes a dynamic interpretation.

The therapist therefore plays a large number of roles in child therapy, and he wears so many hats that he is likely at times to become confused or feel confused. He can be a real figure, a transitional figure, a transference figure, a parent surrogate, a trustworthy friend, an untiring playmate, a model of good consistent adult behavior, a seductive agent in the expression of bad, aggressive, and erotic thoughts, a prohibitor and limit setter, a frightening "head shrinker," and above all, someone who has an uncanny sense of what it feels like to be small and helpless and who knows, in Erikson's terms, "the humiliation of being a child."[13]

(Evaluation of Child Therapy

Psychotherapy outcome studies are logically necessary within the framework of scientific treatment. It makes not too much sense to stress the exactitudes of diagnosis and the details of treatment planning if there is a lack of confidence in the treatment that follows and a lack of knowledge of its efficacy. Outcome studies are so difficult to carry out in a way that would please both the practitioners and the research pundits that each year finds a decrease in the number of investigations undertaken. The old crude methods of evaluation have given place to the setting up of laboratory analogues, computer simulation, and psychophysiological measures, but nearly all the studies to date suffer from the same deficiencies—narrow and superficial scope with little clinical depth, follow ups undertaken too soon, therapy variables contaminated by interpersonal affects, and no real control of observer bias.

Anthony[6] reviewed the outcome studies in child therapy and came up with the usual admixture of findings, similar to the results in adult therapy. The variables are so many and so complex that it is almost impossible to find comparison and control groups.

There have been more than eighty studies of the effects of various psychotherapeutic techniques in which some form of control procedure or comparison has been made. Of these, about seventeen have had to do with child psychotherapy. Heinicke and Goldman[27] carried out a review of these studies, in all of which some type of eclectic psychotherapy was used and at least three criteria of outcome status were employed during the follow-up study. A pooling of these studies revealed that in approximately 80 percent of the cases, psychotherapy was found to be either completely or partially successful at follow up.

Although such results were extremely favorable, the question is whether these children would have changed as much without therapy. Favorable environmental influences or normal maturational processes could have led to the disappearance of the difficulties. Therefore it was clearly not suffcient to pronounce in favor of psychotherapy without comparing the degree and quality of change in children equivalent in all respects except that they do not receive psychotherapy.

A number of factors may have been responsible for the lack of significant differences between the two groups.[30] The children were examined five to six years after treatment, and some of them had only a very brief course of therapy. The longer the follow up, the more likely the specific effects of treatment are to be overshadowed by life experiences, so that the differences between treated and untreated are likely to decrease with the passage of time. Again, the children followed up and tested were only a small proportion of the initial sample and therefore may not have been representative. However, an average of 18 percent of parents gave improvement in the child as one of the reasons for defection, and therefore the defectors may have had a larger proportion of remissions before they were due for treatment. It is thus doubtful whether defectors can be regarded as a suitable control group.

In summing up, it is clear that psychotherapy research has been carried out on greatly varied samples, and the techniques of treatment and assessments employed have been so diverse that some of the studies have very little in common. The evidence would suggest that all the various methods of psychotherapy with children are effective to a degree and that different techniques lead to changes of a different kind.[30]

⟮ Bibliography

1. ABRAHAM, K. Quoted in M. Klein, *The Psycho-Analysis of Children*. London: Hogarth Press, 1932.
2. ADLER, A. *Individual Psychology*. New York: Harper & Row, 1956.
3. ALLEN, F. H. *Psychotherapy with Children*. New York: Norton, 1942.
4. ANTHONY, E. J. "Communicating Therapeutically with the Child." *Journal of the American Academy of Child Psychiatry*, 3 (1964), 106–125.
5. ———. "Varieties and Vicissitudes of the Therapeutic Situation in the Treatment of Children." *Psychotherapy and Psychosomatics*, 13 (1965), 15–28.
6. ———. "The Behavior Disorders of Childhood." In P. Mussen, ed., *Carmichael's Manual of Child Psychology*. Vol. 2. New York: Wiley, 1970. Pp. 667–764.
7. ARIES, P. *Centuries of Childhood: A Social History of Family Life*. New York: Knopf, 1962.
8. AXLINE, V. *Play Therapy*. Boston: Houghton Mifflin, 1947.
9. BENDER, L., and SCHILDER, P. "Form as a Principle in the Play of Children." *Journal of Genetic Psychology*, 49 (1936), 254–261.
10. BRODY, S. "Aims and Methods in Child Psychotherapy." *Journal of the American Academy of Child Psychiatry*, 3 (1964), 385–412.
11. DE LA MARE, W. *Early One Morning in the Spring*. New York: Macmillan, 1935.
12. ERIKSON, E. H. "Studies in the Interpretation of Play." *Genetic Psychology Monographs*, 22 (1940), 557–671.
13. ———. *Identity: Youth and Crisis*. New York: Norton, 1968.
14. ESCALONA, S. K. "Some Considerations Regarding Psychotherapy with Psychotic Children." *Bulletin of the Menninger Clinic*, 12 (1948), 126–134.
15. FREUD, A. *The Ego and the Mechanisms of Defense*. New York: International Universities Press, 1946.
16. ———. *The Psychoanalytical Treatment of Children*. London: Imago, 1946.
17. ———. "Assessment of Childhood Disturbances." *Psychoanalytic Study of the Child*, 17 (1962), 149–158.
18. FREUD, S. *Beyond the Pleasure Principle*. London: Hogarth Press, 1922.
19. ———. "Analysis Terminable and Interminable." In *Collected Papers*. Vol. 5. London: Hogarth, 1953. Pp. 316–357.
20. ———. "A Phobia in a Five-Year-Old Boy" (1909). In *Collected Papers*. Vol. 3. London: Hogarth, 1953.
21. ———. "The Relation of the Poet to Daydreaming." In *Collected Papers*. Vol. 4. London: Hogarth, 1953. Pp. 173–183.
22. GARDNER, R. *Therapeutic Communications*

with Children. New York: Science House, 1971.

23. GREEN, S., and ROTHENBERG, A. *A Manual of First Aid for Mental Health in Childhood and Adolescence.* New York: Julian Press, 1953.

24. GROUP FOR THE ADVANCEMENT OF PSYCHIATRY. *Psychopathological Disorders in Childhood.* Report no. 62. New York, 1968.

25. ———. *From Diagnosis to Treatment (Differential Treatment Planning).* In press.

26. HEALY, W., BRONNER, A., and BOWERS, A. *The Structure and Meaning of Psychoanalysis.* New York: Knopf, 1930.

27. HEINICKE, C., and GOLDMAN, A. "Research on Psychotherapy with Children." *American Journal of Orthopsychiatry,* 30 (1960), 483.

28. JONES, M. C. "Elimination of Children's Fears." *Journal of Experimental Psychology,* 7 (1924), 382–390.

29. JUNG, C. *Memories, Dreams, Reflections.* New York: Pantheon Books, 1963.

30. KELLNER, R. "The Evidence in Favor of Psychotherapy." *British Journal of Medical Psychology,* 40 (1967), 341.

31. KLEIN, D., and LINDEMANN, E. "Preventive Intervention in Individual and Family Crisis Situations." In G. Caplan, ed., *Prevention of Mental Disorders in Children.* New York: Basic Books, 1961. Pp. 283–306.

32. KLEIN, M. *The Psycho-Analysis of Children.* London: Hogarth, 1932.

33. LEVY, D. "Projective Techniques in Clinical Practice." *American Journal of Orthopsychiatry,* 19 (1949), 140–144.

34. LIPPMAN, H. *Treatment of the Child in Emotional Conflict.* New York: McGraw-Hill, 1956.

35. LOOMIS, E. "The Use of Checkers in Handling Certain Resistances in Child Therapy." *Journal of the American Psychoanalytic Association,* 5 (1957), 130–135.

36. LOWENFELD, M. *Play in Childhood.* London: Gollanez, 1935.

37. LOWERY, L. G. "Trends in Therapy." *American Journal of Orthopsychiatry,* 9 (1939), 669–706.

38. McCLURE, A. "Reaction Types in Maladjusted Children." *British Journal of Medical Psychology,* 20 (1945), 389–392.

39. MALAN, D. *A Study of Brief Psychotherapy.* London: Tavistock, 1963.

40. MILNER, M. *On Not Being Able To Paint.* New York: International Universities Press, 1967.

41. MOUSTAKAS, C. *Psychotherapy with Children.* New York: Harper & Row, 1959.

42. PIAGET, J. *Language and Thought of the Child.* New York: Harcourt, Brace, 1930.

43. RANK, O. *Will Therapy and Truth and Reality.* New York: Knopf, 1945.

44. REDL, F. "Implications for Our Current Models of Personality." In B. Schaffner, ed., *Group Processes.* New York: Josiah Macy Jr. Foundation, 1959. Pp. 83–131.

45. ROGERS, C. *Client-Centered Therapy.* Boston: Houghton Mifflin, 1951.

46. STIERLIN, H. "Short-term vs. Long-term Psychotherapy in the Light of a General Thing of Human Relationships." *British Journal of Medical Psychology,* 41 (1968), 357.

47. TAFT, J. *The Dynamics of Therapy in a Controlled Relationship.* New York: Dover, 1962.

48. WATSON, J. B., and RAYNER, R. "Conditioned Emotional Reactions." *Journal of Experimental Psychology,* 3 (1920), 1–14.

49. WINNICOTT, D. W. *Collected Papers.* London: Tavistock, 1958.

CHAPTER 10

TREATMENT OF PARENTS

Shirley Cooper

⟨ Introduction

The Changing Family

Work with parents in behalf of the psychotherapy of children is influenced by changes within our culture and the consequent pressures these place on the family. Within a short period historically, the American family has been forced to redefine its role and function to a degree almost unknown in history.

Along the path of its development, the American family shed in-laws, grandparents, cousins, aunts and retainers: It handed over production to the factory and the office, religion to the churches, the administration of justice to the courts, formal education to the schools, medical attention to the hospitals, and it has even begun to hand over some of the basic life decisions to the psychotherapist. It has been stripped down to the bare frame of being marriage centered and child fulfilled.[13,p.552]

No longer is the family a productive unit economically, gathered together in one place close to its kin, providing continuity and stability. Fathers no longer unquestionably rule the roost, and more and more women perform dual roles as homemakers and breadwinners.* For stability we have substituted mobility; for authority the possibility of greater mutuality. Confronted with rapid and constant change, parents are plagued by intense anxiety about their children. Older bonds of tradition, religious and moral cohesion, economic necessity, and occupational certainty no longer support today's family. Opportunities for varied models provided by the extended family are less available to children, while parents must purchase help formerly offered by family members. Simultaneously, we have learned that what occurs within the family is of central importance to the health and psychological well-being of its members.

Children have moved from a position without rights to one with many claims. Such change creates its own tensions. Benign neglect in child rearing has become unacceptable in middle-class families. The parent who observes a child doing nothing often experiences a vague sense of guilt and rushes to

---

* In 1965 4 million mothers with children under the age of six were employed full time.

occupy him. This can diminish the child's opportunities for privacy and lead to the parent's compensating reactions of overcare. The boundaries of safety become confused for the child, while his demands may become tyrannical. The parent risks succumbing to living in the shadow of his child, feeling cheated and uneasy, unable to define the limits of his own giving and his child's demanding.

The role of women is also shifting. Until recently women were a particularly handy group for scapegoating. Seen as powerful, tender, magically strong, they are at the same time capricious, vain, a bit foolish, scheming, and irrational.[12] Women have been made to feel they must be completely selfless and devoted to their children. It is as though the child remains always the infant needing his parent's attention exclusively. The more emancipated role of women provides opportunities for greater mutuality in marriage as well as opportunities for self-fulfillment apart from child-rearing. We are only now coming to recognize that women who feel unfulfilled are unlikely to provide good mothering.

The Role of the Expert

Unable to rely upon past tradition as a guide, troubled and confused parents invited the experts to move into the vacuum. The experts rarely demurred. Instead, they offered advice that was at times conflicting, slimly supported by evidence, and partially contaminated by cultural bias. Usually the advice was given predominantly from the standpoint of the child and his development. "How to's" and "not to's" were offered in plenty as experts became ever more interested and skillful in observing the child. Threaded throughout the diverse and often conflicting views of the experts one finds an attitude that the child is an artless innocent, always potentially the victim, while the adult is always "the guilty fumbler, bumbler, meddler and destroyer."[13, p. 564] *The Rights of Infants*,[18] a challenging publication of the 1940s, contributed understanding of the needs of the very young. Nevertheless, it seemed permeated by attitudes about good and evil. Infancy was good, precious, and

needed immediate "in-tune" response; otherwise the fragile infant was in mortal danger. For example, "breast feeding is the very essence of 'mothering' and the most important means of immunizing a baby against anxiety;"[18, p. 53] "any curbing of the child's natural ways at an early age may very well endanger the smooth functioning of delicate mechanisms that make it possible for the human body to live and breathe and have its being;"[18, p. 72] "babies of mothers who are emotionally detached or absorbed in social, professional or artistic pursuits suffer retardation in speech or locomotion."[18, p. 98]

Popular literature, further distorting professional insights, exhorted parents to adhere to demand schedules, to consider themselves as both responsible for and blameworthy about all that went awry in child development. It was not until the 1950s* that a more reciprocal view of parent-child interaction was presented. We moved from Ribble and in-tune mothering in 1943 to Winnicott, who offered the concept of good enough mothering in 1956.[20]

Winnicott and others recognized that it was impossible to talk about adequate or inadequate mothering in the light of highly complicated parent-child interactions. Nor was it possible to prescribe the amount and kind of parenting for all children: "the child's needs vary according to his state of development, his individuality, and his previous experiences. These variations do not allow us to talk about a specific amount of care as being adequate or inadequate for all children. What is adequate for one child may not be nearly adequate for another. An experience that imposes a task which one child masters successfully and that strengthens him may be traumatic for another."[17]

Anna Freud[8, p. 4] noted the temptation to apply psychoanalytic insights about adults to the upbringing of children.

The therapeutic analysis of adult neurotics left no doubt about the detrimental influence of many environmental attitudes and actions such as dishonesty in sexual matters, unrealistically high moral standards, over-strictness or over-indul-

---

* See references 4, 7, 14, 15, 17, 19, and 20.

gence, frustrations, punishments or seductive behavior. It seemed a feasible task to remove some of these threats from the next generation of children by enlightening parents and altering the conditions of upbringing and to devise thereby "a psychoanalytic education" serving the prevention of neurosis.

This hope has never been fulfilled. Freud noted that some of the advice was contradictory and generated unwanted, unpredicted side effects. For example, the advice to parents to reduce a child's fear of them partially provoked the child's increasing fears of his own conscience, and "produced the deepest of all anxieties, i.e. the fear of human beings who feel unprotected against the pressure of their drives."[8, p. 9]

The study of individual differences in neonates since the 1940s countered the view that all pathology originates with the parents. There are children who for reasons not yet completely understood seem incapable of accepting comfort, and others who seem so quixotic even in the earliest stages as to make reading their signals almost impossible, as well as chance events that create their own momentum of trauma, dissonance between maturational spurts and developmental readiness, and the impact of wider cultural influences on the child and his parents. Moreover, recent work with different socioeconomic and ethnic populations supports the view that there is considerable variety in styles of parenting, each providing benefits and potential hazards. Most recently, understanding about parents has been enriched by the recognition that parenthood is itself a developmental process, influenced significantly by the marital configuration. Until now grossly neglected, the psychology of parenthood is coming into its own. Related to its central socializing function, parenthood in its own right is beginning to stir scientific interest. Observations suggest that the child may initiate and stimulate reactions in the parent drawn from his own history, these reactions in turn further influencing the child and parent.

The child's absolute need lays claim on a mother whose need for her child is relative. This unequal partnership between mother and child (influenced importantly by the father's differentiated participation with each) is a complicated affair. If the mother's need is absolute, the possibility for growth and individuation for child and mother is seriously impaired. In such instances one is likely to see the mother behaving toward the child as she experienced or fantasized her parents' behavior toward herself. A three-generational condensation forces the mother to vacillate between being the child herself as well as her own parent in dealing with her child.

Mrs. Jones illustrates this well. In her treatment hour, she reports observing her thirteen-year-old son Frank being picked up by the school bus. No one welcomed him or made a place for him to sit. Suffering for her son, Mrs. Jones vigorously berated the other youngsters for the lack of consideration. Frank, embarrassed, experienced his mother's outburst not as protection but as interference. Later in the same hour, Mrs. Jones reports hearing sounds from her son's bedroom. Without knocking she entered his room to observe him struggle into his pajamas. Clearly she had caught Frank in the act of masturbating. In her account she speaks of this with guilt apparently related to Frank's masturbation as well as her intrusion. Almost without pause, she shows her therapist a letter from her mother who had recently visited. The letter berates Mrs. Jones for seeing and hearing too much about her children. Mrs. Jones experiences her mother's letter not only as critical intrusion but also as demonstrable evidence that her mother has never permitted her to gain the status of an adult. Mrs. Jones seems to experience herself as child, parent, and grandparent simultaneously. She is the guilty victim as well as the judging intruder.

Though we have become increasingly sophisticated in our understanding of relevant components in the interactional spiral of child-rearing and parenthood, the picture is neither complete nor thoroughly synthesized. Fatherhood remains an uncharted psychological territory. And in spite of heightened sophistication, the temptation to require saintliness of parents continues.

❴ Direct Work with Parents

Goals

Work with parents involves three basic aims: (1) to develop an alliance that will support the child's growth in treatment; (2) to secure necessary information about the child and his experiences; and (3) to help bring about changes in the environment to further the child's growth and development. At minimum, the parent will need to help by getting the child to his interviews regularly, paying fees, and providing information about the child's daily life and important events. When a parent is allied with the goals of treatment for his child and is not now contributing to the child's problems, parental participation may be limited to these contributions. On the other hand, the work with parents may set as its goal the modification of a parent's personality in significant ways. This may involve intensive treatment for the parent. Between these extremes work with parents may have other goals. Some parents will benefit by advice and suggestions in the handling of a child. These may include environmental suggestions as well as proposals for parental handling of particular child behavior. Other times the work will involve helping the parent loosen his neurotic tie to the child by offering a new object (the therapist) toward whom he can direct some of his energy. On occasion, the parent will be required to alter specific pathological interactions which may yield thorough identification with the therapist. At other times the parent who is incapable of changing significantly may be asked to temporarily yield the major role of parenting to surrogates.

To put it another way: An early effort must be made to sort out where the interventions and therapeutic strategies can best take place in order to (1) create optimum conditions for protecting the child's treatment; (2) release forces to help the child develop; (3) reduce or alter contributing parental pathological interactions; and/or (4) significantly alter personality difficulties within the parent that impinge on the child's development.

Parents change and their needs differ from time to time. No initial diagnosis and disposition, no matter how skillful, is immutable. A parent with whom we have established a good working tie, who arranges for his child's regular attendance, provides useful and relevant information, and pays his bills, may suddenly become a bit distant and develop car trouble or babysitting difficulties that disrupt the child's treatment. In these ways he may be announcing that his child's change, so very much wanted at an earlier time when symptoms were rampant, is now a threat. The parent may find himself in internal conflict, deeply though unconsciously ambivalent about his wish to permit the child's progress. The therapist must now intervene to chart a new course of action if the child's opportunity for continued growth is to be safeguarded.

Conversely, a parent driven by guilt in the initial phase of the work may experience considerable relief as he discovers that his therapist does not judge him and hold him responsible for his child's difficulty. Confusion and uncertainty may be replaced by tenderness, affection, and firmness. The altered parent-child interaction may dictate a change in the direction of reduced interviews. At other times, shifts in emphasis occur within the same framework, requiring no change in frequency but a highly flexible approach and style.

Mrs. Thomas, the sole support of her family, considers returning to work. Her child has been subject to a variety of separations that are central to his pathology. The mother, seen by the child's therapist weekly, discusses her concerns about preparing her child for her going to work. In several interviews, the mother ruminates about how to correctly prepare her child, discarding one suggestion after the other. It is not until several hours later that the therapist catches on to the idea that this obsessive concern with the proper way of preparing the child is in fact a reflection of the mother's own ambivalence about going to work. The mother has been using the child's difficulties, when in fact these are her own worries. Until now, work with Mrs. Thomas centered on the child's behavior and the ways in which the mother could be helped to deal more appropriately with him. At this point the focus must shift to the mother's own concerns, with the recognition that preparing the child is in fact a piece of resistance.

The ability to alter prior ways of working consonant with the changing needs of parent and child deepens support for the child's treatment, while simultaneously helping the adult function with greater choice over life decisions. The purposes for which we involve a parent in collaborative work do not automatically dictate the treatment method, its frequency, or its timing. Some parents will profit most from regular individual sessions, others from intermittent meetings; some make gains through groups, while others may benefit most from family therapy. If a parent's difficulty is of such an order that it is crippling the child's growth at this developmental stage and in the near future, collateral work is in order. However, a parental neurosis is not necessarily expressed through a child even when the child may at one time have lent himself to this expression. Neither does the parent's neurosis inevitably have relevance to the child's development. Whatever the goals of work with the parent, this treatment requires all the diagnostic and treatment skill necessary to any psychotherapeutic endeavor.

The Request for Help

Rarely does the child himself initiate the request for help. The parent is often directed to seek help from an institution such as school or court, institutions that represent authority. His own reactions to authority are quickly mobilized. How he defends in such situations will partially dictate whether he can engage as an ally in the treatment partnership.

Asking for help is stressful for almost every family except the rare few who feel no home is complete without a psychological advisor. Almost all parents experience bewilderment, inadequacy, helplessness, shame, anxiety, guilt, and anger during the normal process of child rearing. When a parent acknowledges

that he is no longer able to cope with the care of his child, these feelings become sharply aggravated, shaking his self-esteem. In a sense, the child's behavior serves as the parent's report card. Parents ask themselves the questions put poignantly by Deborah's parents in *I Never Promised You a Rose Garden*: "How did we share in this thing? What awful wrongs did we do?" "Do I know," he answered. "If I knew would I have done them? It seemed like a good life. Now they say it wasn't." Deborah's mother wonders: "Sometimes it even seemed that with Deborah's illness coming to a head, the whole thrust and purpose of their lives was forced under scrutiny."[10, p. 28]

Parents worry about being judged by and exposed to people to whom they must turn for help. Usually the request for help comes after other painfully unsuccessful efforts have been made. On occasion, their request for help with a child may disguise a request for help for themselves.

As with all patients, the parent's experience dictates how he will approach the helping process. It is important to elicit the parent's theories about the meaning of help. From what do these theories derive? Do they come from prior experience, propaganda, extensions of how the referral agent is understood, or from his own intrapsychic and interpersonal problems? It matters a very great deal how the parent perceives the cause of his child's problem, and whether he seeks to fix blame or recognizes complex contributing factors. These attitudes can be observed as the parent reports his experience with the referral agent, his view of the child's problems, the efforts he has made to cope with these, and his expectations of the therapist. Is he fearful that an important relationship with the child will be split up? Does he hope the therapist will side with him against the child? Is he asking the therapist to assume all parental responsibility, wishing the therapist to take over for him? Is the parent ambivalent, yet passively expecting immediate and miraculous change? Does he competitively invite the therapist to fail to assuage his sense that the child, not he, is totally responsible? Is he overly ready to accept all responsibility? Is he hostile and threatened, again aware of some complicity in the child's pathology, resistant to the change that the therapist by his presence represents? As with all patients, attitudes about dependency and authority are mobilized by the very act of seeking help. Unrecognized, these can create difficulties in the treatment of child and parent.

Moreover, the parent is not simply dealing with attitudes toward taking help; he is here about another, his child. The very feelings that color his relationship to the child may affect his attitudes toward the therapist. If he is angered or humiliated, made vulnerable to exposure by his child's behavior, these feelings may be displaced on the therapist. Unless the child is already grown, able to finance his own treatment, and no longer so dependent on parental approval, the parent can decide whether the child will be treated or not. Yet too often the work with the parent develops as a wrestling with the enemy to exorcise the noxious power of parent over child. It is difficult indeed to make an ally of an enemy. The parent who comes as captive and is not helped to become participant endangers the treatment of both child and parent.

There are hazards the therapist may bring to his work. He may overidentify with the child and seek to rescue him to prove that he can provide better parenting. Or he may side with the parent to behave suppressively with his child patient. The overzealous therapist may require commitments parents are unwilling to make and which are unnecessary for the work with the child. After all, the ideal patient is one who is clearly motivated, does not injure therapeutic narcissism by rejecting therapeutic offerings, wants change for himself rather than for someone else, and invests heavily in this process. This is rarely true of anyone; it is perhaps even less true for the parent. Unless these hazards are recognized, they can impede the treatment of child and parent.

In the first sessions an emotional climate is established out of which parent and therapist engage in serious work to determine how to best help the child. There are no magical ways to overcome resistance with parents any more than with any other patient. The tact, skill, and benign but committed neutrality central to the treatment of all patients is paradigmatic for work with parents. Good treatment is never simply a discussion; it is an experience. From the experience of these early hours the parent forms his decision about whether to choose treatment for his child and how he will participate in it. The importance of utilizing the first hours to decrease resistance, to enhance motivation, and to set in motion a partnership aimed at problem-solving cannot be overstressed.

On Exchanging Information

A child cannot be treated without knowledge of his environment. Anthony[1, p. 28] observed that though the child's world may encompass "not much more than a half dozen houses, a handful of people, a school, a church, and a playground . . . we need to know it well and be familiar with every corner of it, if we aim to talk to him smoothly and easily." Much can be supplied by the child; more is usually needed from the parent. The child cannot always draw an accurate representation of his environment. It may be altered and distorted by his defenses. Though this holds for all patients, the child's immaturity makes it mandatory that we understand his world both as he conveys it and as it exists more objectively.

For example, Sara, age seven, is an active, bright, and precocious child. Bossy with peers and resistant to following directions, she is underachieving at school. Mrs. Johnson, the mother, concerned that her placement of Sara with the grandparents after her divorce is responsible for the child's difficulties, rapidly accepts the teacher's suggestion for psychiatric help. Placed at age four, Sara remained with her grandparents for almost two years while her mother moved to a new city, found employment, and recovered from her depression. The grandmother's death precipitated Sara's return to her mother, who remarried shortly before Sara came home. Sara is very fond of her stepfather.

Sara's initial hours are filled with activity. Masterfully and cheerfully, she orders her therapist to help with the many games and projects she devises. Shortly before Sara arrives for this particular hour, the mother informs the therapist that Mr. Johnson's job required that he be away from home for two or three weeks. Sara starts the hour typically by ordering the therapist to get her the family of dolls. Then, in atypical desultory fashion, she sets up housekeeping under the desk, shielding her play from the therapist. The therapist's efforts to discover what is going on are met with stubborn silence, angry comments to be quiet, assaults on the mother doll who is called stupid, and an alternating cuddling and pummeling of the girl doll. The therapist's comment that it is sometimes hard to feel alone leads to a play disruption. The dolls are swooped up, followed by angry comments about the poor quality of the toys and a period of aimless rummaging in the toy cabinet. Sara discovers the jacks, setting several of them twirling just outside the interview room. Firmly closing the door on them, Sara announces almost tearfully that they are lost, will have to take care of themselves, or "maybe they are dead."

Without the information provided by the mother that her husband was away temporarily, this atypical play would be incomprehensible; even more, the therapist's ability later in the hour to help Sara express her concern that when people leave she fears they will die would be sharply diminished.

Gathering data about the child is an important part of the work between parent and therapist, yet such facts may at times be gotten at the expense of the working alliance. The ability to shift with the parents' interests and needs and to hear out what they consider most critical cannot be deflected by the therapist's need for information. The child and his family are not only the victims of their problems but the participants in their creation who will now participate in their solution. Evaluation and diagnosis cannot simply be a fact-gathering process. Rather it must be the beginning of an active working toward a commitment to change. To be sure, important milestones and traumas, developmental progressions and regressions, skills, interfamilial

and peer relationships, medical history, current experiences, and so on must be understood in order to institute remedial help. But parents are not computer storers of developmental statistics who spew forth at the push of a button. Unless memory is jogged by tactful inquiry, it may not be possible to distinguish between resistance, uncertainty, or repression of information. For example, to ask whether a child was planned may provide clues about the child's conception; it may offer slim information about the child's reception. The latter may be better understood by such inquiry as: Did you want a boy or girl? How did you choose the child's name? Who helped with that? What baby equipment did you have? Did you have help when you came home with the baby? Where was his crib placed? In addition, the gathering of history cannot be a one-time event. As with all patients, parents will correct and elaborate historical and other information as situations arise that trigger memory and as their trust in the therapist develops.

In short, the gathering of information is a skillful process that enlists the active participation of the parent, takes cognizance of human defensive operations, and proceeds at a pace and in the style that will make it a graphic sample of what help is about.

No diagnostic evaluation is complete without reporting to the parent judgments made by the therapist about the child and the proposed treatment design. Again, this is not simply a rendering of one-sided judgments; it is as with all aspects of treatment a process actively involving all the participants. Parents often base their expectations of treatment on past experiences. A parent who has taken his child to a physician expects him to report his findings, including those involving tests, and to get advice about remedial procedures. If the diagnostic process has been well done, the parents' expectation for finite statements and judgments will have yielded some such statements, but they will still need to hear what is known and understood and what must still be left for future discovery. When diagnostic findings are offered in perfunctory ways, parents are left with great uncertainty about the nature and degree of their child's problems and the uncomfortable feeling that their questions are intrusions. It is in just such soil that suspicion and rivalry flourish. The permission to inquire, to exchange useful information, and to clarify confusion enlists cooperation and alliance, a process that can be promoted during the post-diagnostic sessions, to be continued throughout the work.

As indicated, bringing a child for treatment often reflects on one's parenting. Worries about what goes on during the treatment hours may not only reflect concern about what the child may be revealing but touch off concerns about turning one's child over to someone else. Helping parents to know what goes on in the treatment room, to give them some understanding of the very paraphernalia used in work with children, can sometimes resolve or mitigate some of these concerns. As the parent senses the therapist's willingness to share his knowledge about the child, his own participation is enlisted. There is a great difference between maintaining the confidentiality of patients and reporting so little or in such constrained ways as to give the impression that vast secrets are being guarded. Sometimes confidentiality is invoked when the therapist is himself unsure about what and how to present information usefully.

The mother of a congenitally impaired youngster applies on behalf of her son, aged twelve. Among other factors, the mother's guilt about producing a "damaged" child is central to her overprotectiveness. In addition to the expected curiosity about what is going on during the early hours in her son's treatment, the mother is worried about the therapist's appraisal of her. She informs the therapist about her curiosity, directly and indirectly. The therapist, concerned for guarding the child's confidential experience with him, responds to these messages by a short lecture announcing that he cannot tell the mother specifically what the child does and says, but that he will hold himself responsible for reporting on the child's general progress in treatment. He has done his duty. He has acknowledged the mother's rights by agreeing to keep her informed of the child's progress. The therapist is puzzled and irritated when the

mother continues to question her son about what goes on during the sessions. The therapist, hewing close to the letter of psychological law, has obscured his vision about its spirit. The mother's guilt cannot so easily recede nor can her symbiotic tie diminish because she has been told that she can know some things and not others. There is no reason to withhold from her the fact that the boy is beginning to work on his worries about being curious, which contribute to his learning problems. The mother's help can be enlisted by advising her to encourage the boy's curiosity and demonstrating to the mother that curiosity is valued, both hers and her child's. Moreover, failing to address himself to the mother's guilt, to her worry that her child perceives her as bad, a reflection in part of her own self-image, the therapist leaves her to find alternative routes for her concern, routes further away from him and thus not so easily available to handle.

Dispositional Issues

Dispositional judgments with parents in a child's case rest on many factors, among which are the age of the child, the purpose for which one engages the parent or parents, the timing of assignments, the frequency of meetings with each of the "members" in the case, the mode of treatment (individual, conjoint, family, group, or combinations of these) and whether one or several therapists will work on the case.

Whether a family is treated by one therapist or collaboratively by several clinicians is dictated both by conviction and style. Advocates for the thesis that all cases must be separated are matched by equally strong advocates for the view that cases are best handled by one therapist alone. Each has its own set of advantages and problems. Collaborative work built on the model of the team has its difficulties. Many therapists report difficulty in finding time to meet. Jealousies and rivalry often develop between collaborators. Dissonance in viewpoints about goals develops. Unless collaborating colleagues are relatively evenly matched, each respecting the other's skills, one member of the collaborating team is likely to assume leadership over the others. In some settings where social workers only treat parents while other disciplines treat the child, interdisciplinary rivalries may develop. How to use the data provided by a collaborator in one's own case may pose thorny problems. It is not a rare occurrence that the case begins to falter at precisely such moments when one or another of the collaborating team finds himself unsure about how to use the information secured from a colleague. If the parent is being treated in his own right, the information about the child's life that the child therapist requires may not be forthcoming. Here, too, the collaboration may falter. The parent's therapist may see it as an imposition to interrupt his work with his adult patient to get information about the child. The simple practice of having the child therapist see the parent for such information is often overlooked.

On the other hand, a case carried by one therapist has its own potential hazards. Remaining equidistant from each patient is not always an easy task. As indicated, the child therapist is often drawn toward his smaller child patient. Covert rivalries with the parent, who is often a factor in the child's pathology, occur. While the family's being treated by one therapist may save time, since collaboration if practiced carefully requires time, it is with some cases clearly contraindicated. More typically, adolescents struggling to achieve independence from their parents may be unable to trust their therapists if they know the parent is also being seen. However, age alone may not be the only factor in dictating the separation of a case. Therapeutic style may weigh as heavily as any other variable.

No matter what the style or the level of skill of treatment, there are cases that do not succeed. There are parents who must for reasons of their own unyielding pathology have a sick child. There are parents who dare not yield their child to another. The child and parent may collude to maintain this tie, allowing no helper to intrude on such unity. The parent who needs his child for his own completeness may never be able to develop an alliance with a therapist, who represents a threat to his balance.

Special problems occur with those who seek to turn over the parenting role entirely to the therapist. Treatment cannot substitute for daily care. Concrete services to help the parent feel less burdened may be necessary. However, when the parent can no longer assume any parental responsibility, the treatment of choice may be placement of the child away from home, either briefly until the parent regains the strength to do his job or for a longer time to permit the child to develop in an atmopshere of greater safety and care. When the aims of the treatment are significantly opposed to those the parent holds for his child, the child may by the very act of continuing treatment be placed in the completely untenable position of trying to be loyal to two opposing pulls. Unless the child is willing to renounce the parental object, as is sometimes the case with adolescents whose development permits such options, the child will not be able to choose. In such instances we do the child no favor by continuing his treatment.

Ongoing Work

How we expect to help the parent function more effectively with his child will dictate the treatment plan. As suggested where parents are in harmony with the treatment goals for the child and do not contribute to the child's pathology, some regular plan for sharing information may be all that is necessary.

Where other issues are at stake, an understanding of the parent's needs, strivings, and problems must be taken into account to work effectively and flexibly. For example, giving advice is predicated not alone on what the child requires but on whether the parent can use the advice. This is in turn dependent on whether the advice is consonant with the parent's hope for his child, his style of parenting, his capacity to try new ways of functioning or on sufficient identification with the therapist so that the parent will trust and try a new way.

For example, a seven-year-old, deeply disturbed youngster is brought to treatment because of inability to function in a normal school setting. His sudden verbal outbursts and strange hand gestures are frightening to peers. In the beginning it becomes clear that the mother, pressed by outside institutions, wished that the child would become less noticeably bizarre yet she maintained an intense investment in some of his pathology. Although the hand gestures had bothered her, she rationalized and denied some of her concern. After a period of treatment, the gestures disappear and the youngster begins to cut out the first letters of his name, taking these with him everywhere, to school, and to his treatment sessions. The therapist clearly understands from the child that these letters represent a progressive step forward in development. The strange hand gestures have yielded away from his own body to an external representation, which he makes "to help keep me safe."

The mother, disturbed and puzzled by this new behavior, begins to institute repressive disciplinary tactics. Unconsciously she is trying to hold onto her child's difficulty in its most primitive form. The tricky business of attempting to help a mother at such a moment, when unconscious fears operate and when the reality is for her both noxious and incomprehensible, becomes a central factor in the work with her. The therapist must help the mother permit the emergence of new transitional behavior before more acceptable behavior can be evolved.

The interest and concern demonstrated by the therapist for this woman's barren life has helped to build a trusting relationship, decisive now in helping this mother support the treatment. The mother's identification with the therapist makes it possible for her to act on the advice not to repress the child's new progressive efforts.

Work with families invariably involves divergencies in therapeutic goals held by different family members. At times these may be in sharp conflict, disrupting the treatment completely. More often there will be out of phase periods, when the child's advances may for a time confront the parent with unwanted insults or doubts. What helps to sustain the parent through these periods is his general confidence in the therapeutic endeavor.

Other goals focus on specific pathological interactions without aiming to alter the parent's basic character structure. Family therapy may be particularly useful in these instances, since the therapist can observe such interactions as they occur and intervene to modify them.*

Another level of parental work involves marital counseling where marital conflicts intrude on the child's development. It is in such instances that conjoint interviewing techniques that require the careful equidistant stance of the therapist are often most useful.

The parents of a six-year-old child are seen separately and together during the diagnostic process. The father thinks the child will outgrow his difficulties, whereas the mother maintains that the father's laissez-faire attitude reflects his wish to turn over all parenting responsibilities to her. Beneath this complaint is the mother's view that her husband is indifferent to her, considering her only as a useful and necessary homemaker. The mother's application for treatment for her son in part involves the hope that the therapist will support her in her complaints and accusations. The father, sensing this, defends himself by greater withdrawal, but does acknowledge that his son seems troubled. Clearly this six-year-old son represents the battleground upon which marital struggles are being fought. Unless the existing relationships within this family can be altered, the child's anxiety, based in part on his confused and constantly shifting sense of loyalty to each of his parents, cannot be modified.

Whatever the goals, we must directly engage the parent with the aim of helping him as an adult to function more effectively as a parent. Whenever a parent is seen in behalf of his child, there is the danger that the child enters as a ghost into the interview room. The

* See Chapter 2.

therapist may be tempted to become the advocate for the ghost child. The effort to reach one human being through the needs of another almost invariably ensures that the person in the room will see himself as less valued and less important to the therapist than the ghost hovering between them. To illustrate: Mrs. Ferrari, age forty-six, deserted by her husband fourteen years ago, had raised her sixteen-year-old daughter, Maria, alone and by dint of much hard work and sacrifice. For the last three years Maria had refused to attend school. Mrs. Ferrari went from one doctor to another seeking the necessary medical recommendation for home teachers. Now with the doctors' refusal, and upon the school's insistence, Mrs. Ferrari and Maria arrived at the psychiatric clinic. Both were accepted for treatment and each assigned a therapist. It soon became evident that the mother's terror of losing Maria, the only pleasure in her life, was a major factor in the girl's school avoidance. During her treatment hours, Mrs. Ferrari spoke of her daughter's virtues, her confusion about Maria's symptoms, and her detailed and lengthy accounts of the many efforts she had made to give Maria all the things a young girl should have. The therapist found few places to intervene to help change the course of events. However, during one session, although Mrs. Ferrari began as usual, gradually more and more irritation with Maria began to show. She was annoyed with Maria's tentative steps into the world of dating and her insistence on getting a new dress for a dance. Recognizing that Mrs. Ferrari was at last talking pointedly to the problems at hand, the therapist reported, "Gently I spoke to Mrs. Ferrari of adolescence and tried to educate and prepare her for Maria's need to make some separation from her."

This comment was unfortunate, for what the therapist was trying to do was understandable. Certainly Maria and her mother were doomed to a life of symbiosis if neither could let the other go. However, Mrs. Ferrari was clearly describing her desperate fear of loneliness and desertion, and unless the therapist could help the mother with such feelings, her freeing Maria would be impossible. No amount of education about Maria's evolving adolescence could serve to break these unhealthy ties. By reaching for the ghost child through the mother, without stopping to attend to the mother herself, the therapist lost both. Mrs. Ferrari felt misunderstood and threatened. Her next move was out of the clinic with Maria close behind.

In all instances, short of work with the parent in his own right, which does not differ from work with any adult, work with parents can be viewed as collateral to the work with the child, with the aim of helping each to live one with the other in more self-respecting and satisfying ways.

Work with Fathers

Fathers are truly the forgotten men in treatment. If the psychology of parenthood has been grossly neglected, fatherhood remains even less well understood. Earlier endowed, at least in the idealized version, with the greatest clarity, the father's position is now one of considerable ambiguity. The compelling biological position of the mother, coupled with its cultural imperatives of child-rearing does not hold for the father. While fathers are expected to function as protectors and providers,[3-5] they no longer keep a stern but distant watch over the child's discipline and work habits. Although not invariably, the father is now far more engaged in the daily care of his children, sharing in their rearing with his wife.[16] The father's greater intimacy can offer wider opportunities for satisfaction and pride in his child's development. If, instead, he feels displaced by his children, he may turn away from the family in search of gratifications other than those inherent in fatherhood. This in turn can leave the mother and child without important sources of support while the child and mother deepen their dependence on one another.

For example: Mr. Thornton, Tom's father, was uncertain that his son needed treatment. He felt that the mother exaggerated five-and-a-half-year-old Tom's aggressive behavior, which deeply worried his wife. The mother was also troubled by Tom's rubbing up against her and masturbating in front of her, yet she seemed incapable of stopping him. In a joint meeting with both parents, the mother complains that Mr. Thornton spends too little time with Tom. She appeals to the therapist: "Don't boys need their fathers?" The father listens uncomfortably to these and other complaints, then asserts that the mother seems unable to recognize when Tom is overly demanding, exhausting herself during the nighttime rituals instead of putting a stop to Tom's endless requests before he finally goes to sleep. With mounting anger he announces that Tom always turns to her for help. For example, Tom will always ask his mother to help him tie his shoelaces though his father often offers assistance. Mr. Thornton states that when this happens his wife seems unaware that he has offered help, and he feels "elbowed out during these scenes."

Clearly both parents contribute to Tom's difficulty. The mother's ambivalent wish for her son and husband to become close leads her to demand more of her husband for Tom while at other times she elbows him out of the relationship. The father, who feels left out by son and wife, cannot offer a firm hand in parenting, thus leaving Tom to retain an overcloseness with his mother, which should now be receding. This engenders Mr. Thornton's anger with his wife and his son, which further reduces his ability to act as father and husband. Mr. Thornton's assistance will be needed in helping Tom develop; even more his participation can alter the balance in this basically good marriage so that he and his wife can return to a more satisfactory and adult relationship.

In his own right, a father's overbalanced need for pride in his offspring may turn into driving or perfectionistic ambition creating the potential for pathology in the child and other members of the family.

Fathers rarely initiate a request for help. This is logically so, since they are typically less involved in the child's care than the mother, and perhaps also because men even more so than women are imbued with the view that to ask for help is an admission of weakness, to experience tenderness is less than manly. It is more common to hear fathers assert that their child's troubles will pass with time, that too much is being made of the trouble. Yet many fathers have much to contribute to an understanding of the child. Out of their own needs, they may become strong allies in therapy when they feel their wives' overinterest in the children leaves them unattended and uncertain of their place in their families.

Experience suggests that when mothers proclaim with certainty that their husbands are too busy or unable to participate because of other commitments this may not always be the case. It is wise to attempt to meet directly with the father to determine how he views the child's problem and his part in its solution. When both parents disagree sharply about whether help is needed, additional strains are added to the family and to the treatment. Unless these are resolved, the child will be pulled in opposing ways.

If we are persuaded that fathers are important for the health and well-being of their family and are themselves altered by its health or disturbance, we are bound to reach out for the fathers' help.

Work with Poor or Minority Families

Wealth does not invariably immunize against pathology nor does poverty inevitably breed it. Yet as the old adage would have it, if you are going to be unhappy, you might as well also be rich. The maladaptive effects of poverty or oppression, and often these go together, are difficult to withstand. It is, however, important to distinguish between stable, low-income families and families who have experienced intense and chronic social and economic deprivation, which often leads to family disorganization. Families almost exclusively involved in a struggle to survive and subsist rarely have energy to spare for participation in remedial work for their children. However, even within this latter group there is a wide range of disorganization and pathology, which heightens and recedes at different times. Generally, however, the poor have a greater tendency to view themselves as alienated from the rest of society. A sense of distrust for professional authority is not uncommon. The professional himself, usually drawn from social strata other than the poor, is often uneasy when treating people not of his own group. Hence psychological barriers are maintained from both directions, and the mutual process of exploring and understanding can be more difficult. One consequence of such barriers has been the tendency to stereotype poor and ethnic families and to see them as far more homogeneous in their parenting practices than recent inquiry suggests.

The recent rise of ethnic interest, a by-product of more active struggles by minority people for equality, has begun to provide important insights about differences within these groups, the effects of oppression on personality formation and child-rearing practices. We are only now beginning to accumulate some experience with poor and minority families. As a consequence, our knowledge about effective treatment strategies with these groups, where and in what ways the more traditional styles of treatment require modification, is not fully developed.

Chilman observed that "many of the very poor suffer from a chronic, deep depression, linked to a hopeless anxiety springing out of a lifetime of frustration, failure and rejection. Often this depression is dealt with in an impulsive, dramatic expressive style, rather than in the more compulsive, intellectualized, instrumentalist style generally employed by the middle class in dealing with their hopeful, goal-oriented anxiety."[6, p. 223]

In a study of a small group of severe multiproblem families, Bandler[2] delineated five basic pathogenic characteristics: (1) a sense of psychological, educational, social, and cultural deprivation; (2) the constant and intense sense of danger from inner impulses and from violent and unexpected behaviors from the outer world; (3) the excesses derived from extremes of disorganized stimuli; (4) the absence of patterned, predictable behavior which contributes to a sense of uncertainty and inconsistency; and (5) the lethargy and hopelessness that become organized into pervasive passivity.

Despite such overwhelming difficulties,

Bandler observed that mothers in such families were often capable, with help, of developing sufficient parental altruism to offer their children love, competence, and a sense of value derived from their own enjoyment of the children when these mothers were "no longer faced with near starvation"[2, p. 228] themselves.

Certainly parents cannot give to their children what they do not themselves possess. Parents who were themselves impoverished will need considerable help and support before they can make themselves available to their children. In such instances, clearly programmatic help in sharing the burdens of parenting may be needed to supplement direct work with the family. One may need to help the family by reducing the pathogenic pressures from the environment in order to enable the parents to function more effectively. In such instances, interventions traditionally associated with casework and social work, including direct services with concrete assistance, may be required. These may include assistance with income, jobs, housing, child care, and transportation to the agencies providing help to the child and his parent. However, such help cannot be forthcoming from social work alone. The problems of poverty, racism, health, education, welfare, and work will not be solved by professional groups. They confront our society as a whole. However, when such problems create personality distortion and human suffering, we cannot wait until society acts. Nevertheless, we must recognize that there are some children and parents who are so impaired that psychological and social work rehabilitation with today's tools is no longer possible. While such cases are more likely to be found among the poor, it is important to exercise special caution to ensure that our decisions and dispositions spring from understanding rather than bias.

❲ Conclusion

The family, a changing institution, retains its importance as the most significant shaping influence on its members and more particularly its children. Parenthood in its own right offers opportunities for the further evolution of adult personality. Work with parents in behalf of children requires careful assessment and differentiated treatment and disposition strategies. Efforts to assist the child without engaging the parent through involvement with his [the parent's] needs and psychology are likely to fail.

([Bibliography

1. ANTHONY, E. J. "Communicating Therapeutically with the Child." *Journal of the American Academy of Child Psychiatry*, 33 (1964), 106–125.
2. BANDLER, L. "Family Functioning: A Psycho-Social Perspective." In E. Pavenstedt, ed., *The Drifters: Children of Disorganized Lower Class Families*. Boston: Little, Brown, 1967. Pp. 225–253.
3. BENEDEK, T. "Adaptation to Reality in Early Infancy." *Psychoanalytic Quarterly*, 7 (1938), 200–215.
4. ———. "Fatherhood and Providing." In E. J. Anthony and T. Benedek, eds., *Parenthood: Its Psychology and Psychopathology*. Boston: Little, Brown, 1970. Pp. 167–183.
5. ———. "Parenthood as a Developmental Phase." *Journal of the American Psychoanalytic Association*, 7 (1959), 389–417.
6. CHILMAN, C. S. "Poor Families and Their Patterns of Child Care: Some Implications for Service Programs." In C. A. Chandler, R. S. Lourie, A. D. Peters, and L. L. Dittmann, eds., *Early Child Care*. New York: Atherton, 1968. Pp. 217–236.
7. COLEMAN, R. W., KRIS, E., and PROVENCE, S. "The Study of Variation of Early Parental Attitudes." *Psychoanalytic Study of the Child*, International Universities Press, vol. 8 (1953), 20–47.
8. FREUD, A. *Normality and Pathology in Childhood*. New York: International Universities Press, 1965.
9. FRIEDMAN, S. W. "The Diagnostic Process as Part of the Treatment and Process." *Reiss Davis Bulletin*, 3, no. 2 (1966).
10. GREEN, H. *I Never Promised You a Rose Garden*. New York: New American Library, 1964.
11. KORNER, A. F. "The Parent Takes the Blame." *Social Casework*, 42, no. 7 (1961), 339–341.
12. LEDERER, W. *The Fear of Women*. New York: Grune & Stratton, 1968.
13. LERNER, M. *America as a Civilization*. New York: Simon & Schuster, 1957.
14. MAHLER, M. S. "Notes on the Development of Basic Moods: The Depressive Affect." In R. M. Lowenstein, L. M. Newman, M. Schur, and A. J. Solnit, eds., *Psychoanalysis: A General Psychology*. New York: International Universities Press, 1966. Pp. 152–168.
15. MURPHY, L. B. *Personality in Young Children*. 2 vols. New York: Basic Books, 1956.
16. MUSSEN, P., and BEYTAGH, L. A. M. "Industrialization, Child-Rearing Practices, and Children's Personality." In S. Chess and A. Thomas, eds., *Annual Progress in Child Psychiatry and Child Development*. New York: Brunner/Mazel, 1970. Pp. 195–217.
17. PROVENCE, S. "The First Year of Life: The Infant." In C. A. Chandler, R. S. Lourie, A. D. Peters, and L. L. Dittman, eds., *Early Child Care*. New York: Atherton, 1968. Pp. 27–38.
18. RIBBLE, M. *The Rights of Infants*. New York: Columbia University Press, 1943.
19. SPITZ, R. A. "The Psychogenic Diseases in Infancy." *Psychoanalytic Study of the Child*, (1951), 255–275.
20. WINNICOTT, D. W. "On Transference." *International Journal of Psycho-Analysis*, 37 (1956), 386–388.

CHAPTER 11

STRUCTURAL
FAMILY THERAPY

Salvador Minuchin

THE BODY OF THEORY and the interventive techniques labeled "family therapy" are concerned, fundamentally, with changing dysfunctional aspects of a family system. The goal of therapy is a more adequate family organization, one that will maximize the growth potential of each member of that family.

A family is a natural social system that has evolved ways of organizing and transacting that are economical and effective for that particular group. It comes into therapy when some stress overloads the system's adaptive and coping mechanisms, thus handicapping the optimal functioning of its members.

The family's diagnosis of the problem is usually that one of their members is behaving in ways that are stressful for the family. They want the therapist to change the member who is having or causing difficulties. The family therapist, however, focuses on the whole group. One of the members may be expressing the family stress in ways that are clearly visi-

ble, but the problem is not confined to the identified patient. The whole family is responding to a stressful situation.

The source of family stress may be internal or external. It may spring from internal problems around a transitional stage in the family's development, such as the emergence of a child into adolescence, the inclusion of a new family member, or the separation of a member. It may spring from idiosyncratic problems, such as a child's retardation or physical handicap. Or family stress may spring from one member's stressful contact with the extrafamilial world, for example, a child's having problems in school or a father at his job. It may come from total family contact with the extrafamilial world. The family may be pressured by poverty, discrimination, separation from natural systems of support, and so on.

In any case, when the family comes into therapy, the therapist will enter the family, buttress or change the system in whatever ways seem necessary, and then leave the family to continue its own enhanced growth-encouraging, supportive, and reparative functions. Therapy is a transitional process, which can be schematized as [family] + [therapist] → [family + therapist] → [family + therapist's ghost] − [therapist].

◖ Concepts of Family Therapy

The Prospective Approach

Family therapy is prospective; its orientation is to the present and future. This is one of the aspects that distinguishes it from dynamic theory, which is retrospective. In dynamic theory the patient's present transactions are seen as a projection of the past, and growth is defined as casting loose from this past. Understanding the past is seen as necessary for changing the present. In family therapy, the tool of therapy is not the exploration and understanding of the past but the manipulation of the present. The past history of the family was instrumental in the creation of the family's present organization and functioning; it is, therefore, manifest in the present and available to change-producing interventions. Manipulation of the present is the tool for changing the present and the future.

The Scope of the Therapist

The family is a socializing, educational, and reparative unit. In family therapy, therefore, the family itself is seen as performing many of the functions that in individual dynamic theory are the functions of the therapist.

The family therapist does not join the family to educate or socialize. His function is to be the enabler of the family's own functioning, so that it can perform these tasks. Many of his transactions will have educational input, and this may sometimes be essential for family functioning. But his main input will be in terms of the family's structure and organization.

The scope of the therapist is also affected by reliance on the systemic properties of the family. In dynamic theory, change is seen as having to occur in the interaction between the therapist and the patient. As in the traditional healing by the laying on of hands, the therapist must be present for change to occur. By contrast, in family therapy, the family is recognized as a self-perpetuating system. The processes that the therapist has initiated within the family may be perpetuated in his absence. In other words, when family change has been effected, the system properties of the family will preserve that change; the input of the therapist will affect family members even in his absence.

This quality of therapy makes new ways of using time in therapy possible. For example, the therapist can spend the initial phases of therapy in intensive work with the family. At the point at which dysfunctional sets begin to change, he can recess the family and reconvene later to see if it is continuing the new organization. He can then continue therapy or recess again, with the understanding that he is available for problems that may arise. Like a general practitioner, the therapist brings the family to a level of health and then stands ready to be called in if necessary. The advantages of brief and prolonged therapy are thus combined.

Orientation toward Sets

Family sets are patterned sequences of interaction among family members. Family pathology can be conceived of as the development of dysfunctional sets. These are nonproblem-solving reactions of family members as the result of stress, reactions that repeat in the family without modification when there is conflict. Changes that could restore a functional equilibrium—a realignment of family members, adaptations of rules, and so on—become blocked. For example, the father experiences stress at work. He comes home and attacks the mother. She counterattacks, and symmetrical or escalating nonstress-resolving interactions develop, continue without change, and finish when one member of the dyad abandons the field. Each member suffers from the sense of nonresolution. A similar situation can involve a triad. The mother and father attack each other, then both become concerned with controlling a misbehaving child. Or the father, under stress, attacks the mother, and the mother seeks a coalition with the son against the father. The father counters by seeking coalition with the son against the mother.

Dysfunctional sets can also involve the entire family group. For example, a child emerges into adolescence. His participation and status in the extrafamilial world increase. Problems around control and autonomy develop within the family. The relationship between the adolescent and the mother resists the changes necessary for adaptation. The mother attacks the adolescent, the father enters the conflict on the adolescent's side, and younger children enter the conflict, attacking the adolescent. When all family members participate in dysfunctional sequences, a variety of groupings and coalitions can occur. The situation generalizes. All family members become involved in the conflict, but the family organization does not change. The dysfunctional sets will, therefore, repeat in the next stressful situation.

Sets may also be functional. For example, a man experiencing stress at work comes home and attacks his wife. She withdraws and a few moments later returns to support him. Or there may be a fight, but it finishes with closure in spite of escalation and increased level of attacks. The field is not abandoned with a sense of the lack of resolution.

Functional sets can change. Realignment, changes in rules, and other conflict-resolution sequences are possible. They tend to resolve or diminish stress for family members. Dysfunctional sets do not change; they repeat when stress occurs, and they tend to maintain stress. Or if stress in one subsystem is alleviated, this is at the expense of another subsystem in which stress is maintained or increased (see the example of the T family, below).

Dysfunctional sets can assume a salience in family life that obfuscates functional sets that are supportive and encourage growth. The therapist scans family structure to pinpoint salient sets. He will explore functional sets and search for steps to buttress them. He will emphasize family strengths, mobilizing supportive mechanisms to enhance what is functional. Change-producing interventions will be directed toward the dysfunctional sets.

Points of Entry

The common mode of describing an interaction is like stopping a motion picture. We say "Father provoked mother," excluding the factors that the mother provoked the father to provoke her and that the sequence has impact on the father, mother, and other family members.

The family therapist sees individuals as subsystems of larger systems; these individuals initiate processes that have impact on the system, and they react to system processes. The therapist deals with the sequences of interpersonal interaction. This broadens possible points of entry. He can work with individuals as subsystems of the family. He can work with dyadic family subsystems, that is, helping parents strengthen interactions as adults, so as to strengthen the boundary between adults and children in the family. He can work at the interface of the family system and societal systems. In other words, he can direct interventions to any promising point in a sequence. When working with a child's problem, the family therapist can enter to utilize any useful part of that child's ecosystem.

Implications for Therapy

Theoretically, child psychiatry encompasses an understanding of the importance of the child's ecosystem; but for therapeutic purposes, the child may be conceptualized as an intrapsychic entity preserved unchanged through the vicissitudes of an average environment. This retrospective approach minimizes exploration and manipulation of the present life context.*

* The Group for the Advancement of Psychiatry report[10] contains innumerable examples of this point of view.

The boundaries imposed by the artificial dichotomy between internal and external processes and influences limit the child therapist. If a child is referred to treatment because of a school phobia, the 1966 Group for the Advancement of Psychiatry report said "the child has unconsciously displaced the content of his original conflict onto . . . a situation in the external environment that has symbolic significance for him. . . . Thus the child avoids those . . . situations that revive or intensify his displaced conflict. . . ."[10, p. 232] The focus of this diagnosis does not take into account the environment of the child or the target of the phobia. But looking at the child with school phobia in his current life contexts broadens possible points of entry. The problem and/or an area available to therapeutic intervention might be found in the school, the home, or at the interface between school and home.

In exploring the school context for possible points of entry, the therapist would look at the child's perception of himself as a learner and his performance as a student. He would explore the child's position in the peer group and his self-perception as a member of this peer group, his relationship with the teacher and the ways he perceives the teacher as similar to or different from other significant adults, the teacher's view of the child and how correct and differentiated that view is, and how the child and the teacher work together.[21]

Both home and school have, in a broad sense, an educational style and expectations of the child. The child can be seen as operating at the interface of two socializing institutions. Are the two syntonic, or do they interact with him in conflicting ways?[28]

Exploring the family context, the therapist would look for the possibility that dysfunctional sets in the family are rewarding the child's phobia. The needs of the mother, creating dysfunctional sets in the mother-child dyad, might be keeping the child at home. Or there might be a conflict between the parents in which the child's symptoms are useful; if so, dysfunctional sets in the triad might be reinforcing his not going to school. Or the school phobia could be supporting the child in a position of strength in his sibling group. Or the siblings might be supporting his symptoms as part of a scapegoating process.[1,34]

Given this expanded focus of observation, the family therapist can look at the multiple forces impinging on the child in his current contexts and select areas for intervention that his analysis and goals have highlighted as promising.

These concepts could only be a product of twentieth-century philosophy and technology. The old idea of the individual acting on his environment becomes the concept of the individual interacting in his environment. As Bateson[5, p. 6] writes:

Consider a man felling a tree with an axe. Each stroke of the axe is modified or corrected, according to the shape of the cut face of the tree left by the previous stroke. This self-corrective . . . process is brought about by a total system, tree-eyes-brain-muscles-axe-stroke-tree; and it is this total system that has the characteristics of immanent mind.

In nineteenth-century thought, actions were expressed simply: "The boy chopped the tree down." But twentieth-century cybernetic thought recognizes that a human being is controlled, in Bateson's words,[5, p. 5] "by information from the system and must adapt his own actions to its time characteristics and to the effects of his own past action. Thus in no system . . . can any part have unilateral control over the whole." The individual influences his context and is influenced by it in constantly recurring sequences of interactions.

The broadening of focus implied by this approach affects every aspect of therapy, including its diagnostic categories. A diagnosis is no longer a nonevolving label pasted on a contextless intrapsychic entity. It is an evolving, broader description of relevant sequences. Furthermore, it includes implications for therapeutic interventions. The diagnosis of encopresis implies only that the child should be cleaned up. The diagnosis of a child's responding to unresolved conflict in the family's spouse subsystem, or the diagnosis of sequences of enmeshed interactions between mother and child that isolate the husband-father, contain the germ of possible therapeutic interventions.

Another implication of this broadened theory is the recognition of diagnosis as something achieved by therapeutic strategy. In a systems-oriented framework, the entrance of the therapist into the family group is recognized as a massive intervention in itself. He becomes part of a new system—the therapeutic unit [family + therapist]—and he acts and reacts as a subsystem of that system.

His diagnosis is an evolving analysis.[24] For example, a family comes into therapy with a teenage girl because she is shy and withdrawn and has difficulties in her social life. The therapist notices that when the family enters the therapy room, the girl moves quickly to sit next to her mother and pushes the two chairs close. The therapist asks what the problem is, and the mother responds. When the daughter tries to add something, the mother continues talking about her as though she had not spoken. There is a great deal of noise and confusion in the family, with the girl's siblings talking while the mother talks. The mother's knowledge of her daughter's life is intimate, going far beyond material usually shared by adolescent girls. Four minutes after the beginning of the session, the therapist makes his first intervention, asking the mother and father to change chairs. This intervention tests the flexibility of the family, suggests to the family an interpretation of pathology in the mother-child dyad, and brings the father into the picture, in general providing a reframing of the problem with a larger focus.

The idea that the child responds to stresses that affect the family, which is accepted by both child and family psychiatry, is the basic tenet of family therapy.* It has largely been a clinical supposition, based on observation, but recent family research gives it experimental grounding.

For example, in one psychophysiological research project,[26] parents are subjected to a stress interview while their children observe

them through a one-way mirror. Blood samples are taken from all family members at fifteen-minute intervals for later analysis of the free fatty acid level changes at different times in the interview.† The children can see and hear their parents, but they are physically unable to take part in the conflict situation. Nevertheless, their free fatty acid levels rise as they observe their parents under stress. The cumulative impact of current psychological stress is powerful enough to cause physiological changes, even in children who are not directly involved.

This experiment also shows the utilization of a child in dysfunctional sets. In the T family interview, for instance, the parents were engaged in their usual spiral of nonresolving conflicts, with the wife blaming her husband and her husband apologizing but indicating no intention of changing. During this period the parents' free fatty acid levels increased significantly. The identified patient, a nine-year-old diabetic boy who was having trouble in school, was observing their bickering. His free fatty acid level rose almost twice as much as those of his parents.‡

When this boy was brought into the therapy room, each parent tried to entice him into a coalition against the other parent. The spouse conflicts were submerged in the sequences of triangulating the child. In the half hour of this situation the parents' free fatty acid levels returned to their basal levels. The child's increased and remained high.

The stress associated with chronic nonresolved spouse conflicts was lessened for the parents by the possibility of triangulating the child. The stress associated with this type of position in the family system is shown by the child's large rise in free fatty acid, poignantly demonstrating the price paid by what Ackerman calls the "family healer."[1] The family healer's instability is necessary to lessen the

---

* See references 1–3, 7, 13–17, 23, 29, 32, and 38.

† Free fatty acid level is a biochemical variable that rises within five to fifteen minutes in response to stress. It is used in this study as a physiological indicator of emotional arousal.

‡ In a nonstressful control period his free fatty acid level remained close to his basal level.

stress in another subsystem. The triadic dysfunctional set operates at his expense.

Techniques of Family Therapy

Family therapy is not a technique to be defined by the number of people in a therapy room during a session. It is an interactional theory, which encompasses any number of techniques.

Bell[6] is generally considered the therapist who first treated families as a group. He originated a distinct procedure for treating disturbed children, seeing first the parents and then the parents and child, emphasizing the refocusing of the problem from the child's behavior to parental conflict.

As the concept of family therapy began to gain currency in the 1960s, interventions directed toward every conceivable unit were tried.* There have been experiments with different locations.[9,27] Different time units have been used.[1,20] Different cotherapists have been utilized.[18,24,29] Various mechanical devices have been used; and total-family diagnostic tools have been developed.[37]

When a child is brought into therapy by his family, he has already been diagnosed by the school, his pediatrician, the court, the police, or his peers. This diagnosis reinforces the family's labeling of the child as a problem.

The family therapist's initial objective is to transform this individual label into a diagnosis that includes the family. For example, if the child is caught in enmeshed interactions between his parents, either trapped in the position of a go-between, as in the previous example, or used as the battleground, the diagnosis will reflect this dysfunctional set. The therapeutic goal will be to achieve a family organization in which the spouse dyad can function without triangulating the child.

In order to work toward this goal, the therapist will look at the sets of spouse interaction, pinpointing the ones that seem to have to utilize the child's symptoms. These will be the targets of his change-producing interventions.

Therapeutic Tactics

Therapeutic tactics will in general fall into two categories: coupling and change production. Coupling can be defined as everything the therapist does to enhance his therapeutic leverage within the therapeutic unit. Change production is the strategems directed toward changing dysfunctional sets.

Coupling†

When two different systems adjust themselves in terms of direction and become one system, this is coupling. The union in space of a lunar module and the command ship is an example. The therapist, one system, joins the family system, and the two become one therapeutic system. The therapist facilitates his entrance into the family by accepting the family organization. Coupling operations are obviously vital to therapy. If the family drops out or the therapist loses the leadership of the therapeutic unit, nothing can be accomplished. There are three types of coupling interventions.

1. Maintenance involves supporting the family structures. A family system is governed by rules that regulate the behavior of its members. The therapist joining the family feels the pressure to behave according to these rules. He may accept them in the beginning as a way of gaining entrance to the system. For example, if the mother is the central pathway by which family communication is routed, the therapist also talks to her and allows her to mediate his communications to the family. The therapist must be aware of the family's threshold of stress. When family members need support, he will provide it. When change-

* See references 7, 8, 12, 13, 19, 29, 30, 31, 33, and 35.

† I am indebted to Braulio Montalvo for labeling this operation. An elaboration can be found in his film, "Analysis of a C. Whitaker Consultation Interview," which is available from the Philadelphia Child Guidance Clinic.

producing strategems are pushing the family toward its threshold, he will use maintenance techniques to move back to a point where the family is more comfortable. Other examples of maintenance operations are supporting areas of family strength, rewarding or affiliating with a family member, supporting an individual member who feels threatened by therapy, and explaining a problem.

2. Tracking* is a method of adopting the content of family communications. As a phonograph follows a record's grooves, producing sound, the therapist takes over the family content and uses it in a therapeutic maneuver. For example, a family may be complaining about the father's authoritarian stance. The father says, "I want to be a leader, but I want to be a democratic leader. I want to be the president of this family." The therapist says, "okay, if you want to be a democratic leader, let's hold an election." In tracking, the therapist does not challenge the family. It is a method that has its roots in hypnotic suggestion, in which the patient is never confronted. If the patient refuses a suggestion, the hypnotist accepts his refusal but manipulates the situation so that the refusal is a form of obeying the hypnotist's command. As in the technique of jujitsu, one uses the opponent's own movement to propel him. With a family, the therapist utilizes the family's movement to propel it. But he maintains the framework that he is propelling it in the direction it wants to go in. He seems to enter the family as a supporter of family rules. But he makes the family rules work in the direction of his goals for it.

3. Mimesis is a coupling technique aimed at the family's style and affect, as reflected in the members' activity and mood. The therapist may use the tempo of family communications. If the family is restricted, his communications may be sparse. He may adopt the family's affective style. In a jovial, expansive family he may use expansive body movements. He pays attention to their language and begins to use some of their terms. If they discuss a bar mitzvah, he may use a Yiddish word. If a Puerto

Rican family is urging a daughter to find a husband, he may suggest that she turn St. Anthony's statue upside down. Mimetic operations are mostly nonexplicit and quite spontaneous. Experienced therapists perform them without realizing it. In one family, a father who was derrogating himself took his coat off. Immediately, the therapist took his own coat off. But he did not recognize this as an intervention until an observer pointed it out in a postsession discussion.

Change Production

Unlike coupling, change production involves some form of challenge to the family's natural style, in order to change dysfunctional* sets. It is helpful in conveying this to picture the family as a jazz group. Music is produced by improvisation, but the tempo, the order the instruments will solo in, and sometimes the key are firmly predetermined. The many improvisations open to the individual player are chosen according to his mood and the possibilities of his instrument. There are areas of great flexibility within a strictly patterned organization, but they are governed by the sets.

Change-producing interventions will be directed toward the sets, or the system "memory," which dictates the repetition of accustomed interactional patterns. Coupling operations will continue throughout, but they are not to be confused with the change-producing operations that will be directed toward pathogenic sets. Therapy is often unnecessarily long because therapists waste their effort on areas in which flexibility is already possible, instead of identifying and concentrating on pathogenic sets.

The following example may help present some of the clinical consequences of family therapy theory. The presenting problem was a serious case of anorexia nervosa in a ten-year-old girl. The priority of intervention was, obviously, the abandonment of the symptoms in the child. Once this had been accomplished,[25] we embarked on a nine-month course of family therapy, vital to the continued change of the family patterns, which had generated and supported the anorexia nervosa.

---

* I am indebted to Mariano Barragan for labeling this operation and for the example.

The following data are presented in terms of an analytic schema, rather than in process recording form. When one thinks of therapy as a process involving a system's needs, interventions oriented toward a goal, and outcome, this organization of data becomes cogent. It is not sequential. Much of the material in the diagnostic formulation, for instance, was explored only after the anorexia symptoms had been abandoned. But it is a logical course of phases that the family therapist must think through.

The schema divides therapy into four phases:

1. Determination of family structure, areas of strength, and dysfunctional sets. Assignment of priorities for intervention (diagnosis).
2. Determination of objectives, or goals for change. This will be closely related to the diagnostic assessment, but will evolve through therapy.
3. Assessment of therapeutic options and selection of strategies. Given a diagnostic assessment that includes objectives, there are many possible strategies. The therapist must assess the potential impact of each option in terms of its power, its type, and its cost. In terms of power, does it mainly affect the individual, another subsystem such as the spouses, the entire family, two interlocked systems such as family and classroom, and so on? In terms of its type, is it change production or prevention? What will it cost in therapeutic time and input, psychological pain and financial burden to the family? Strategem selection takes into account the family's assessment of its needs, the therapist's assessment of priority, the pathways open within the limitations imposed by the family's style and the therapist's style and capability.
4. Evaluation. Periodic evaluation of the results of strategems leads to the reassessment of priorities, new evaluation of therapeutic alternatives, the selection of further strategems, and further evaluation of implementation.

Case Example

The Smith family is composed of the father, a successful architect in his mid-forties, the mother, and four daughters, Helen, fourteen and one-half, Barbara, twelve, Sally, ten, and Jane, eight. The family was referred to family therapy by its pediatrician.* Sally had been hospitalized, diagnosed as suffering from anorexia nervosa, after losing fifteen pounds during two and a half months. On her arrival in the hospital she had weighed forty-two pounds; after a week in the hospital, she weighed forty pounds. The family assessed itself as a "normal American family." Its goal was that Sally eat.

Diagnostic Formulation

The priority of therapy was obvious—the abandonment of the anorexia symptomatology. In priority, the therapist's assessment coincided with the family's. But because he saw the anorexia syndrome as a response to family organization, rather than as an individual's illness, his diagnostic formulation of needs was much broader than the family's perceived needs. Both the immediate and long-term objectives depended on a broader diagnostic formulation.

The therapist's assessment of the family was that they were operating in a tight, enmeshed system.[29] Dyadic transactions rarely occurred. They became triadic or group transactions. These interactions were characterized by a rigid sequence that promoted a sense of vagueness and confusion in all family members. A parent criticized one of the girls. The other parent or a sibling joined in to protect the child. Another family member joined the critic or the criticized. The original issue would be diffused, to start again through a similar sequence, to be similarly unresolved. There was a helpful, protective quality to the enmeshed interactions. The avoidance of ag-

* Robert Kaye was in charge of the pediatric aspects of this case and was a member of the family therapy team.

gression or even disagreement was striking. The family described all interactions as harmonious.

In the therapist's assessment, there were many unnegotiated husband-wife conflicts. Such conflicts were submerged and never allowed to become explicit. They were expressed in a family organization in which the mother joined the daughters in a coalition of females that left the husband-father trapped in a position of helpless isolation. He was perceived by the women as an absolute despot. In reality, his power within his family was negligible. The mother parented the daughters; the husband-father was disengaged and peripheral. Only in the area of parenting were spouse disagreements expressed. The father felt the mother was too lenient with the girls.

Another expression of disagreement that might have been related to the selection of the anorexia symptom was the mother's constant attempts to improve the father's table manners. This was a disagreement that had run throughout the twenty years of the marriage and was now discussed with bantering by all the family members, particularly at mealtime.

The boundaries of the spouse subsystem were very weak. The peripheral husband-father had strong ties to extrafamilial systems, particularly his business and his own family of rearing. The mother was firmly bound in the female subsystem, which was an enmeshed, high resonance system. Small movements by members of this system brought countermovement from the other members. The mother was the main point of contact between this system and others. The father communicated with the girls through the mother. Therefore, the mother controlled the nature of their communication, screening out nurturant elements of the interactions but letting controlling elements pass, thus strengthening the coalition of the girls with her against their father. Her relationship with the girls was overcontrolling, intrusive, and overnurturing. The close communication, appropriate with younger children, had led to difficulties beginning a number of years before when the older daughter, emerging into adolescence, had begun to make demands for age-appropriate increased

autonomy. At this point, the relationship of mother and oldest daughter was fraught with demands for autonomy, countered by the mother's demands for obedience. Barbara was allied with her older sister in this conflict.

This family malfunctioning was affecting all the family members. The symptomatology of anorexia nervosa overshadowed the symptomatology of the parents and the "well" siblings, but clinical scrutiny of the total group showed each member responding to the family stress in idiosyncratic ways. The anorexia nervosa syndrome was deeply imbedded in the family's pathogenic sets.

The Smiths, like other pathologically enmeshed families, were highly resistant to change. When a situation that required family change occurred, they typically insisted on retaining their accustomed methods of interaction. Consequently, situations of chronic imbalance were maintained for long periods.

When significant members of a pathologically enmeshed family system feel that the family can neither withstand change nor adapt to it, the system demands that particular family members change in a way that will maintain the malfunctioning homeostasis. A symptom bearer is selected (and self-selected) as a conflict-avoidance circuit. Whenever the rather low perceived danger point of family stress is approached, the symptom bearer will be activated for use in conflict-detouring sequences. The family system reinforces the development of symptomatology and rewards its continuance because the symptomatology is necessary to the conflict-detouring sequences that maintain the status quo of the family system.

In the Smith family, Sally was functioning as the chief conflict-detouring pathway. Her most important use and source of reinforcement was in the spouse subsystem, but the symptomatology was, of course, multideterminate.

SPOUSE SUBSYSTEM

The never negotiated conflicts between the parents were perceived as a particular danger area. All the children were involved in keeping these submerged; but when one arose, it was most often Sally who crossed the generational boundary to diffuse the parental conflict. Her function was to allow her parents to detour their conflict via concern for her.

Furthermore, the symptom defined one safe area in which spouse conflicts could surface. The father thought the mother should make Sally eat. The mother, though very worried, thought that Sally should not be forced to eat.

The coalition of the mother and daughter against the father was explicitly manifested in the mother's protecting Sally against the father's assertion that she should eat. At the same time, the selection of the symptom was an implicit coalition with the father, whose fight with the mother had also been allowed to surface in the area of eating.

SIBLING SUBSYSTEM

Sally was the least powerful member of the rather undifferentiated group. She was isolated and excluded. The sibling subgroup, of course, conformed to the family style. Whenever conflict arose, there was immediate bunching in coalitions. Sally was always excluded from these coalitions, and was often their target. Since open disagreement was to be avoided, her isolation took the form of tomboy interests. The girls said Sally did not want to play with them because she preferred boys' games, and Sally agreed.

The anorexia nervosa kept the structure of the sibling subgroup intact, but it improved Sally's position. She was still isolated, but the coalitions against her became coalitions of concern and protectiveness.

INDIVIDUAL SUBSYSTEM

The anorexia syndrome was a means of self-assertion. By not eating, Sally was asserting herself in a way that was permissible within the value system of the family. She was disagreeing, but not openly. The family's priority of avoidance of conflict was maintained because her not eating was not an explicit confrontation or rule breaking.

The symptom, then, was being reinforced by the spouses as a conflict-avoidance circuit, by one spouse in coalition against the other, by

Sally's experience of "legal" self-assertion, and by Sally's being able to protect her family and even ally herself, on an implicit level, with her father. The siblings also reinforced the symptom as part of a protective and scapegoating system.

OBJECTIVES POSED BY DIAGNOSTIC FORMULATION

The objectives posed by diagnostic formulation were:

1. The disappearance of the anorexia nervosa symptomatology.
2. A change in the spouse subsystem. Supportive, complementary transactions between the spouses must increase. A strongly bounded subsystem of mother and father, parenting their children in a mutually supportive relationship, must appear. The mother must be disengaged from parenting to give her more space for spouse subsystem operations and for clear supportive parenting operations. The father must be more engaged in parenting, able to contact his daughters directly without going through the mother; the mother's function as contact must disappear.
3. A change in the sibling subsystem. The enmeshed functioning of the subsystem must decrease. The boundaries must be weakened so that the girls can interact with their parents and with the extrafamilial world without choosing a representative of their needs. There must be clear differentiation, with clear age-appropriate increased autonomy for the adolescents and a change in Sally's powerless, scapegoated position.
4. The possibility of effective dyads and triads in the total family system. The degree of flexibility must increase, and enmeshment must decrease. Flexible alliances and coalitions, capable of shifting, must be possible.
5. Clear communication among all family members. This must be fostered, so that the real nature of transactions can be recognized.

It will be obvious that these objectives are mutually interdependent. All changes are predicated on generic change in the family's enmeshed style and the degree of flexibility possible. Furthermore, the goals are interlocked within the system just as the pathology is. The older daughters cannot become adolescents until the mother becomes a wife. The mother cannot be a wife until her husband pulls her away from her daughters. The daughters will not let their mother go until the mother has some support from the father as a husband in the areas of spouse support and tenderness. As long as contact between the father and daughters has to go via sequences that include the mother, the father cannot get his wife into his own orbit. While the mother and father are divided, the girls will have to struggle with the mother's intrusive overnurturance and overcontrol. As long as the girls remain part of an undifferentiated, highly enmeshed sibling subgroup, they will struggle through the use of the anorectic sibling, further reinforcing the symptomatology.

Assessment of Therapeutic Options and Stratagem Selection

It is clear from the diagnostic formulation that only an approach to the whole family system will respond to family needs. If an option directed toward only part of the family system, such as individual therapy, were selected, this would still be an intervention affecting the total family (whether or not the therapist recognized and utilized this impact). Working with the child on an outpatient basis brings the therapist into the family system. He uses the therapeutic relationship to block the child's participation in the family interactions as a conflict-avoidance circuit; and he attempts to use the changes in the child as a modifier of family transactions. Furthermore, in working with the parents as part of the treatment of the child, the therapist has another handle in changing family organization. When the child is hospitalized, the forced separation of the child from the family joins the factors that can help mobilize family conflicts

that will have to be dealt with in the absence of the anorectic child.

But therapeutic interventions directed toward an anorectic child without explicit attempts at changing the family organization of which she is a subsystem would be expensive. Even if they were successful, they would be costly in terms of psychological pain for the identified patient, the pain of duration of the anorexia symptomatology, financial burden on the family, and lack of preventive qualities for siblings and parents. The family therapist is particularly aware of the parents and three siblings, each of whom is currently showing responses to family stress and might become the new scapegoat if the presenting problem were dealt with without change in the family system.

Accordingly, the option chosen for the Smith family was family therapy. Sally had already been hospitalized prior to referral. The therapist's preference was to work with the child in her family, shortening the period of hospitalization insofar as this was consistent with medical needs. The pediatrician and family therapist collaborated in a strategy of iatrogenic family crisis, designed to break the symptomatology so that Sally could return home quickly.*

Change-producing strategies are always predicated on the therapist's opening up repetitive vicious pathogenic sets as he joins the family system. Though he does not have absolute freedom to manipulate the system in the ways he wants, he does have several options within the mode of family therapy. He can, for instance, elect to defuse the stress that brought the family into therapy, returning the family to a sort of status quo ante and continuing long-term therapy to change the pathogenic sets. But in working with a rigidly dysfunctional family system such as the Smiths', this approach would only reinforce the dysfunctional organization. A return to the status

---

* A pediatrician may be reluctant to allow an anorectic child to return home to the family, fearing the medical consequences. The family therapist may find himself in the position of having to educate both the family and the pediatrician, so that the pediatrician does not unwittingly reinforce the family's labeling of their symptom bearer.

quo ante would not be even an interim solution.

When working with pathologically enmeshed families with psychosomatically ill children, it is preferable to work in the development of crisis, organizing the family transactions in such a way that the family is forced to deal with the stresses it has been submerging. The therapist monitors the resulting crises, creating experiential situations in which the family members can and must learn to deal with one another in new and different ways. In a family that insists on defining itself as perfectly normal, except for one member's medical problem, a medically induced crisis opens up the significance of family sets which have created and supported the symptom. The symptom area offers the obvious route to this crisis. During the first session with the Smith family, the signs of pathological enmeshment were obvious.

Since the first step in iatrogenic crisis is to observe the family's reaction to and handling of conflict, the therapist searched for an area in which a conflict could be framed. But the family was extremely resistant to attempts to elicit conflict. Only after an hour and a half of probing was an area of difficulty brought out —the mother's constant attempts to nag her husband into improving his table manners. This provided a cue for asking the family to order lunch.* The session stopped while sandwiches were brought in and a lunch table was set up in the therapy room.

The technique of having lunch with an anorectic family is valuable for several reasons. For one thing, it makes things happen in the session with the therapist. When a conflict around eating can be enacted in the session, talking about anorexia nervosa would be a waste of time. Furthermore, organizing a family crisis around the anorexia symptom makes it available to direct intervention. Interventions on an individual level directed at the anorexia symptomatology, such as exploration of the anorectic's ideation about food and the like, might only serve to reinforce and further crystallize the symptom. But when a family crisis is organized around the syndrome, it is the interpersonal negotiation of parents and child around the eating that gains salience, rather than the symptom itself. Not eating becomes "ground" instead of "figure" because of the dramatic emergence of interactional factors, which then become available for change-producing interventions.

During the session with the Smith family, the crisis was produced by directing the parents to demand that Sally eat. They were unable to state their demand clearly or to get her to eat. The results highlighted their powerlessness, the anorectic's power over her family, and the family members' lack of negotiation skills within their web of enmeshed protectiveness and caused an experimential, here-and-now crisis in which the therapist could intervene.†

Evaluation of Implementation

The strategy of increasing stress between parents and daughter around the anorexia syndrome yielded immediate results. Sally started eating during the session, continued to eat during two more days in the hospital, and kept eating after her return home. In a month her weight had returned to normal.

Once the dramatic presenting symptom had disappeared, the needs of other family members came more sharply into focus, forcing a reassessment of therapeutic goals. Since the core of the problem was the inability of the spouses to negotiate together, the next therapeutic priority became change in the spouse subsystem.

Sessions with the spouse subsystem were interspersed with total family sessions. Once the facade of mutual agreement had been broken, the spouse sessions dealt with the wife's sense of being unacceptable to her husband, her sense of being in competition with her mother-in-law, her complaints of her husband's not supporting her in parenting and not respecting her as an adult. The husband brought issues of being isolated in the family, being needed to intervene with his daughters only

---

* Initial sessions with anorexia cases start at eleven A.M.

† A film of this session is available from the Philadelphia Child Guidance Clinic.

when the wife failed, and feeling that his wife was not interested in him as a sexual partner. Therapeutic interventions in these subsystem sessions were addressed to facilitating the negotiation and resolution of disagreements and encouraging the experience of mutually supportive and pleasurable nonparenting interactions.

Meanwhile, total family sessions continued. Various strategems were utilized in the intrafamilial sphere. During total family sessions, communication style was challenged. When a conflict between two members developed, the therapist made them continue until they achieved a resolution or until a third member could join in explicit form, either asking to be included or being invited by the original dyad. Members of the family changed chairs so that the two or three people involved in a discussion sat next to each other; the others moved out of the circle and observed.

This technique was particularly useful in differentiating the siblings. For example, as the eldest girl's conflicts with the mother became prominent, the father was requested to intervene. The three brought their chairs to the center of the room while the other girls moved out. With the mother strongly supported by her husband, negotiations ensued that gave Helen much more autonomy, explicitly related to her status as the eldest. The therapist increased this differentiation by treating her as an adult. He also assigned a task[11] to the mother. She was to watch for actions Helen performed that deserved her approval and reward them. This was directed to a double audience. Helen heard the task assignment and increased the type of actions that her mother could reward. Helen began to emerge as a teenager.

The individuation and disengagement of Helen from the sibling subsystem left Barbara the playmate of Jane; Sally was excluded. Now the three girls occupied the center of the room, with the mother and father helping them from outside the circle. Jane and Barbara were directed to play with Sally. The three played a board game together, and the game became enmeshed and chaotic. Therefore, the girls were assigned the task of playing board games at home. The parents bought the games, helped select them, and saw that the rules were followed.

Barbara, the brightest and most psychologically minded of the family, began to ally with the therapist, sitting near him and commenting on family functioning. She began to have more school friends, spending more time with them in an age-appropriate process of contacting the extrafamilial. Sally and Jane became closer.

In one session, Jane complained that Sally played roughly and threatened her with frightening fury. Now Jane and Sally took the center, with Helen asked to act as the mediator, helping Jane to understand Sally's explanation. Her role as eldest sister was buttressed by participation in a play that differentiated her two youngest siblings.

In all these sessions, the clear demarcation of the parties in a negotiation and the resolution of clearly stated conflicts were emphasized. This use of space to create explicit proximity and distance, delimit subgroups (actors and observers), intensify affect, potentialize the enactments of fantasies or roles, and so on is useful in rigid, deeply enmeshed, undifferentiated families. It enables the therapist to function like the director of a play, setting the stage, creating a scenario, assigning a task, and requiring the family members to function within the new sets that he has imposed.

Therapy with this family terminated successfully after nine months.

(Conclusion

The Smith family case demonstrates that a child presenting a symptom is presenting a symptom of family stress. If one broadens the focus, the forces within the family that maintain the symptom will appear and can be dealt with.

It will be obvious that the case example concentrates on the change-producing interventions done with this family. Change-producing strategems can best be conveyed by describing family members and the therapist as though they were cybernated robots. The inaccuracies of this approach in describing human beings and describing therapy with human beings are too obvious to need elaboration. But coupling operations are so idiosyncratic to a therapist's style, a family's style, and the way the two interact that a description of them would simply be case recording. Change-producing interventions can be described in more generic fashion.

In conclusion, an orientation that takes the child's ecosystem into account will combine the possibility of maximally potent interventions with preventive operations. This approach involves the least possible psychological pain for the people involved, and therefore becomes the most humanitarian as well as the most effective way of approaching a problem.

(Bibliography

1. ACKERMAN, N. W. "Prejudicial Scapegoating and Neutralizing Forces in the Family Group, with Special Reference to the Role of Family Healer." *International Journal of Social Psychiatry*, spec. ed. no. 2 (1961), 90–96.

2. ——. *Treating the Troubled Family*. New York: Basic Books, 1966.

3. ——. ed. *Family Therapy in Transition*. Boston: Little, Brown, 1970.

4. BARCAI, A. From the Individual to the Family and a Step Beyond. Paper presented to the American Orthopsychiatric Association, Washington, D.C., 1967.

5. BATESON, G. "The Cybernetics of Self: A Theory of Alcoholism." *Psychiatry*, 34 (1971), 1–18.

6. BELL, J. E. *Family Group Therapy*. Public Health Monograph, no. 64. Washington, D.C.: U.S. Government Printing Office, 1961.

7. BOSZORMENYI-NAGY, I., and FRAMO, J. L., eds. *Intensive Family Therapy*. New York: Harper & Row, 1965.

8. BOWEN, M. Presentation of a Family Experience. Paper presented to the Conference on Systemic Research in Family Interaction, Philadelphia, 1967.

9. FRIEDMAN, A. S., et al. *Family Treatment of Schizophrenics in the Home*. New York: Springer, 1965.

10. GROUP FOR THE ADVANCEMENT OF PSYCHIATRY. *Psychopathological Disorders in Childhood: Theoretical Considerations and a Proposed Classification*. Report no. 62. New York, 1966.

11. HALEY, J. *Strategies of Psychotherapy*. New York: Grune & Stratton, 1963.

12. ——, and GLICK, I. D. *Family Therapy and Research: An Annotated Bibliography of Articles and Books 1950–1970*. New York: Grune & Stratton, 1971.

13. ——, and HOFFMAN, L. *Techniques of Family Therapy*. New York: Basic Books, 1967.

14. HOFFMAN, L. "Deviation Amplifying Processes in Natural Groups." In J. Haley, ed., *Changing Families*. New York: Grune & Stratton, 1971. Pp. 285–310.

15. ——, and LONG, L. "A Systems Dilemma." *Family Process*, 8 (1969), 211–234.

16. JACKSON, D. D., ed. *Communication, Family and Marriage*. Palo Alto: Science and Behavior Books, 1968.

17. ——, ed. *Therapy, Communication and Change*. Palo Alto: Science and Behavior Books, 1968.

18. LANDES, J. and WINTER, W. D. "A New Strategy for Treating Disintegrating Families." *Family Process*, 5 (1966), 1–20.

19. LAQUEUR, H. P., et al. "Multiple Family Therapy: Further Developments." *International Journal of Social Psychiatry*, spec. ed. no. 2 (1961), 70–80.

20. MACGREGOR, R., et al. *Multiple Impact Therapy with Families*. New York: McGraw-Hill, 1964.

21. MINUCHIN, P., et al. *The Psychological Impact of School Experience*. New York: Basic Books, 1969.

22. MINUCHIN, S. "Conflict-Resolution Family Therapy." *Psychiatry*, 28 (1965), 278–286.

23. ——. "Family Therapy: Technique or Theory?" In J. H. Masserman, ed., *Science and Psychoanalysis*. Vol. 14. New York: Grune & Stratton, 1969.

24. ——. "The Use of an Ecological Framework in Child Psychiatry." In E. J. Anthony and C. Koupernik, eds., *The Child in His Family*. New York: Wiley, 1970.

25. ——. Anorexia Nervosa: Interactions around the Family Table. In preparation.

26. ——, and BAKER, L. Childhood Psycho-

somatic Illness and the Family. In preparation.

27. ———, and BARCAI, A. "Therapeutically Induced Family Crisis." In J. H. Masserman, ed., *Science and Psychoanalysis*. Vol. 14. New York: Grune & Stratton, 1969.

28. ———, et al. "A Project to Teach Learning Skills to Disturbed Delinquent Children." *American Journal of Orthopsychiatry*, 37 (1967), 558–567.

29. ———, MONTALVO, B., et al. *Families of the Slums: An Exploration of Their Structure and Treatment*. New York: Basic Books, 1967.

30. SATIR, V. *Conjoint Family Therapy*. Palo Alto: Science and Behavior Books, 1964.

31. SPECK, R. V. "Psychotherapy and the Social Network of a Schizophrenic Family." *Family Process*, 6 (1967), 208–214.

32. SPIEGEL, J., and BELL, N. "The Family of the Psychiatric Patient." In S. Arieti, ed., *American Handbook of Psychiatry*. Vol. 1. New York: Basic Books, 1959. Pp. 114–149.

33. TABER, R. H. "A Systems Approach to the Delivery of Mental Health Services in Black Ghettos." *American Journal of Orthopsychiatry*, 40 (1970), 702–709.

34. VOGEL, E. S., and BELL, N. W. "The Emotionally Disturbed Child as the Family Scapegoat." *Psychoanalysis and Psychoanalytic Review*, 47 (1960), 21–42.

35. WATZLAWICK, P., et al. *Pragmatics of Human Communication: A Study of Interactional Patterns, Pathologies, and Paradoxes*. New York: Norton, 1967.

36. WHITAKER, C. A. "Psychotherapy with Couples." *American Journal of Psychotherapy*, 12 (1958), 18–23.

37. WINTER, W. D., and FERREIRA, A. J., eds. *Research in Family Interaction: Readings and Commentary*. Palo Alto: Science and Behavior Books, 1969.

38. ZUK, G. H., and BOSZORMENYI-NAGY, I., eds. *Family Therapy and Disturbed Families*. Palo Alto: Science and Behavior Books, 1967.

CHAPTER 12

RESIDENTIAL TREATMENT
FOR CHILDREN
AND ITS DERIVATIVES

Maurice W. Laufer, John J. Laffey,
and Robert E. Davidson

A CONFERENCE on inpatient psychiatric treatment for children was held under the auspices of the American Psychiatric Association and the American Academy of Child Psychiatry in 1956, with the assistance of the National Institute for Mental Health (NIMH). The inpatient treatment of emotionally disturbed children was as yet a new field of development. The conference was held to share concepts and methods and develop a basis for minimal standards. Yet, and in many ways fortunately, diversity still reigns.

The first inpatient psychiatric services for emotionally disturbed children appeared in the 1920s. The rather basic care function of these institutions was rooted in the Poor Law of 1601 in England, whereby public responsibility for the poor—including many children with physical, cognitive, and emotional handicaps—was established. In the 1800s, there emerged also a view of children as separate and distinct from adults. Amendments to the Poor Law in England in 1868 and 1889 provided for the removal of children from their parents in cases of neglect. At that time, specific hospitals geared to the special needs of children were first established, and children identified as mental retardates were admitted to institutions for custodial care. Then, private voluntary children's aid societies emerged, focused upon the dependent, neglected child. Even so, by 1900, children were generally not to be found in specialized programs and facilities. They were, rather, in the custodial care environments of almshouses, orphanages, state hospitals, jails, training schools, and group homes. Significant subsequent developments included the evolution of social work to professional status; the contributions of psychoanalysis and psychobiology, indicating the importance of early child development and the environmental influences of child-rearing practices; the preparation of the public for a more positive attitude toward the mentally ill and their need for specialized services by the mental hygiene movement; and the establishment (in 1912) of the Children's Bureau as an arm of the federal government, and (in 1931) of "the first inpatient psychiatric services for children in the United States . . . to care for children with post-encephalitic behavior disorders following the encephalitis lethargica epidemic at the close of World War I."[8]

Another stimulus for the growth or conversion of treatment institutions for the emotionally disturbed was added by the passage of the Social Security Act of 1935 with its aid to dependent children provisions. Many children so classed were enabled to remain with their mothers. Institutions formerly geared to group living programs now received increasing referrals of disturbed children, enforcing a change from staffs with many volunteers and laymen to more and more professionals. Overall, there was a progression from custodial care, to modifying behavior by utilizing the environment, to intervening attempts at internal change by forms of psychotherapy. This led to the addition and various uses of social case workers with a psychiatric orientation, social group workers, educational experts, occupational therapists, clinical psychologists, psychiatric nurses, and psychiatrists, as institutions altered their programs from providing continuing care to that of providing psychiatric treatment and return home. As a result of the addition of such personnel and of programs utilizing them during the 1940s, "it was demonstrated that treatment in a residential setting was possible for children who could not be satisfactorily treated on an out-patient basis."[8]

By the 1950s, residential treatment offered various combinations of approaches and de-pended greatly on the setting in which the service was offered. There certainly was no standard method, approach, or staffing. The inpatient treatment of emotionally disturbed children has evolved from a wide variety of philosophical viewpoints encompassing different views of children in relation to the adult role, concerns for special needs of children as they develop in a variety of environments from total dependency to relative autonomy in the face of ever-changing demands by rapidly changing environments, and a remarkably rapid growth of a technology of behavioral science with its many diverse theories.

Other factors influencing the manifold diversity of developments have been differing philosophies as to the role of parents (varying from all-important, much to be condemned and shunned etiological factors, to bewildered victims who both need and can provide help, plus all kinds of versions and mixtures in between). The kinds of children being treated play a large role, as do the expectations of institution and community for either symptomatic improvement or total internal psychological change. Freedom to limit intake and freedom to determine duration of treatment are two among a host of important variables.

Introduction of family therapy, group methods, halfway houses, specialized foster homes, group homes, behavior therapy, and day hospitals all have added to a mix of infinite variety.

(Residential Institutions for Children

The Setting

In 1964, the National Association for Mental Health published a *Directory of Facilities for Mentally Ill Children in the United States.*[86] For criteria of selection they included residential and educational facilities that by "stated policy, function and intake criteria planfully accept mentally ill children and render continued service in facilities which are distinct and separate from adults." In the term "children" they included infancy to eighteen years of age. Many authors limit "children" to age twelve years. No doubt many facilities were omitted, for many reasons. This publication listed 116 such facilities, with sixteen of the fifty states having no such facility. It was considered that fourteen more facilities might have been included had more information been available.

Only four years later, the NIMH biometry branch cited 149 residential treatment centers.[104] It was admitted that only limited information on children served in such facilities was available. This fact permitted only an estimate of the number of children served, which was placed at 55,400 in 1966.

There is a great variety of facilities, listed under a bewildering variety of names, many of which do not even connote treatment. Reid and Hagan[101] considered that such "specialized institutions . . . have one thing in common—the development of a total approach to therapy." They go on to describe twelve organizations as "a base from which to evaluate and better understand clinical studies and reports from residential treatment centers."

There are four general categories of inpatient treatment facilities for children: (1) the shelter or placement unit; (2) the residential treatment center; (3) the inpatient psychiatric service; and (4) the state hospital unit.

1. The shelter or placement unit is usually under private auspices and finds financial support under contract with a government unit. Generally, shelters provide custody, care, and management of children in residence, are inadequately staffed, and more often offer psychiatric evaluation and separation from the community and family than continuance of care for emotional aspects. Such facilities tend to draw from children unmanageable in the community and involved in court and child welfare services.

2. The residential treatment center is most often under private auspices with financial support through public agencies. There may be psychiatrists, social workers, educators, or psychologists as administrative directors, with psychiatric and medical directors often in the structure. In addition to custody, care, and management are a therapeutic, structured milieu, routine medical care, individual and group psychotherapies, special school, and an adequate staff-child ratio. The staff is usually multidisciplined and highly specialized. In contrast to the usual social pathology found in the children in shelters, one finds a large number of emotionally disturbed children, who may have parents who cannot cope with the child. Most of the children in these settings[104] are ten to seventeen years of age; with 1 percent under five years of age and 5 percent in the five-to-nine-year age group. Seventy-three percent of the ten- to seventeen-year-olds are diagnosed as having psychosis, personality disorder, or transient situational disorder. The five- to nine-year-old group are usually diagnosed chronic brain syndrome, personality disorder, or schizophrenia.

An attempt to bring some order out of diversity is provided in our draft of an operational definition for residential treatment centers. A residential treatment center is an institution or a unit of an institution existing specifically for the round-the-clock, long-term treatment of emotionally disturbed children who have sufficient intellectual potential for responding to active treatment and for whom outpatient treatment is not indicated but for whom inpatient treatment is the treatment of choice at the time. It does not provide custodial care. Children will not be admitted because of central nervous system disorders or other organic difficulties as such. However, the existence of such difficulties will be no bar to admission if they contribute to or complicate emotional disturbance, provided proper medical facilities are available. The staff must have control over intake and discharge, based upon diagnostic and therapeutic study.

The institution must provide a total therapeutically planned group living and learning situation and a milieu within which individual psychotherapeutic approaches are integrated. The living arrangements, physical and personal, should provide a psychologically safe milieu for dynamic maneuvering and experimentation without fear of trauma or retaliation. It should offer support for growth as well as for internal reexamination, with individual psychotherapeutic interviews available in proportion to the needs of each individual child. Schooling may be provided within or outside the institution. Adequate recreational facilities (including gross sports and major muscle activity and hobbies, arts, and crafts) must be available within it.

The institution will usually provide the combined contributions of the disciplines of psychiatry, psychology, education, social casework, and social group work, which must be integrated in a responsible and dynamic interplay with the group living aspects and the personnel who provide these, though there will be no standard pattern for the form of combination or role of each of these. All, however, must have special therapeutic training and orientation for work with children and for work together as a team along with the childcare workers, teachers, nurses, pediatricians, and all who deal with the children. It is hoped that all such institutions would also provide centers for clinical training and for research.

A specific variant, which has been offered as a means of carrying out the task of residential treatment in a more economical, focused and shorter-term manner is the modality known as "Project Re-Ed," modeled somewhat on the French *educateur*. In this, specially trained teachers, in essence, provide all the needed teaching, group living, and change in emotional status of their charges, with appropriate consultation from other disciplines. Enthusiastic claims for the results and devastating attacks on the concept have both appeared. It is too soon for any definitive evaluation, but it may be expected that with time it will become clear that this can be an excellent approach for many, leaving a residual for which only the classical methods of residential treatment will suffice.

3. The inpatient psychiatric service of the general hospital is under private, public, or university auspices. Such facilities are administered and directed by psychiatrists. Many provide the range of services of the residential treatment center and can provide more totally for the medical needs of the children. Generally, they serve the child for shorter periods of time than the usual residential treatment center. Psychiatrists are more involved in the day to day treatment of the children, with a characteristic emphasis on intrapsychic change and the opportunity for more individual psychotherapy than in the residential centers. It is estimated that in 1966 there were three to four times as many children in this type of facility (20,000) than in a residential treatment center (8,000) and that there are nearly five times as many such units as residential centers.[104] In 1966, 14 percent of the children in these units were under five years of age and 52 percent were older adolescents. Under five the predominant diagnosis is chronic brain syndrome. In the five-to-nine-year age group, convulsive disorder and mental deficiency are the most common diagnoses. Schizophrenia, psychoneurosis, and personality disorder account for more than 50 percent of the ten- to fourteen-year-olds and schizophrenia, neurosis, and transient situational disorders account for more than 60 percent of the fifteen- to seventeen-year-olds.

4. The state hospital unit is under the auspices of a state health or hospital system and utilizes psychiatrists as administrators and directors. Like the residential treatment centers, these institutions provide for the total needs of the children but generally have insufficient professional staff to adequately carry out longterm treatment and rehabilitation. They serve about the same number of children as the inpatient psychiatric units in general hospitals, have a greater prevalence of children over ten, and more than half have the more severe chronic diagnoses of schizophrenia and chronic brain syndrome.[104] Many children with a poor prognosis, who have failed to benefit sufficiently in other inpatient settings, may be found in these state units.

Reports since that quoted for 1966 have shown a steady rise in the actual numbers and percentages of adolescents admitted to both state and nongovernmental mental hospitals. This is especially true of the latter, with their smaller capacity. Increasingly, the private hospitals are reporting that a majority of their census consists of adolescents.

As the percentage of adolescents increases, the mental hospital tends to take on more and more of the coloration of the residential center (as described and defined here), including the all-important educational aspects and group approaches. Discussions of hospital treatment for adolescents almost always raise the issue of whether it is preferable to have a separate adolescent unit or have them intermingled with the older patients. Articles and arguments on each side abound and neatly cancel each other out. This being so, it must be concluded that the results depend upon the particular staff and that with which it is comfortable. The same would seem to apply to isolation or mixing of the sexes.[58]

An increasingly vexing issue is the problem of how to deal with adolescent drug users. Many settings are limiting the numbers of such youngsters that they will take. One respected private hospital, which had been quite successful in dealing with alcoholics, finally decided to ban entirely the admission of teenage drug addicts.[88] In essence, it was felt that severe character disorder and a lack of motivation for treatment, along with easy continuing availability of drugs in the community, were what caused this program to fail.

Such observations may have significance for treatment of other patterns of adolescent dysfunctional behavior related to character disorders. It is our opinion that success in treatment in such cases requires the availability of, and initial placement in, a locked ward, with graded and earned increases in "openness" and a readiness to return the adolescent to the locked ward and start all over again, as often as necessary.[58,102]

The Child

Criteria for placement of a child in an inpatient treatment facility vary from institution to institution. Generally, the children selected for inpatient treatment are those who cannot be treated on an outpatient basis because of severity of symptoms or breadth of symptoms. Selection is not on the basis of diagnosis or because outpatient treatment is not available. Relevant are the severity of the child's dis-

order, the family's disturbance, the severity of maladaptive child behavior, and the danger to the child, to other persons, and to property posed by the child's behavior. Institutions may specialize to the point of providing admission for children with specific types of behavior. Age, intelligence, the presence of an intact family, geographic proximity to the child's home, the willingness of the family to participate in casework, the length of inpatient treatment considered to be necessary, and the presence or absence of special sensory and physical disabilities are further factors considered as influencing admission. Individual institutions, such as state hospitals, may have little or no choice (a child may be court committed, for example), or they may feel that they need to offer their services as equally as possible to all comers. Institutions functioning with greater freedom of choice of patient may create a total environment geared to the special needs of a certain behaviorally disturbed group. For example, a highly controlled and structured environment may be created for the aggressive, acting-out child, or the treatment program may be geared to behavior modification principles and applied only to autistic-like children, or it may be permissive and encouraging to the shy, anxious, withdrawn child.

Contraindications also vary from institution to institution. It has been a rule of thumb that a child under six should not be taken from his family for such a placement. Children under six in placement are relatively few and tend to have serious disorders, such as psychosis, brain syndrome, or retardation. The problem of eventual reentry into the community of a burdensome child, unwanted by his family, may influence admission. Parental opposition to placement or unwillingness to voluntarily give up custody, or lack of motivation for family casework or therapy may be considered as cause for rejection of a child for admission.

Particularly in private residential units, the ability to finance the treatment is a major consideration.

The structure of the setting is more often a matter of chance than design, as it is still true that the majority of residential treatment centers represent the outcome of new uses of old buildings. A recent article by Clemens[30] relates the happy results of being able to plan from the outset as to how a center could be built to meet the needs of the children, and its bibliography gives some further thoughts on the matter.

A frequent question is whether it is best to have a single congregate building with other supporting structures, or to have a cottage system. Experience suggests that the results are more dependent on staff than on structure, there having been outstanding successes and failures with each plan. Regardless of design, children must feel that the staff care more for them than for the building.

Treatment

Classically present in child inpatient treatment have been individual psychotherapy, milieu treatment, group therapy, parents in therapy, and the use of medications.[76] Family therapy may be employed. It is not currently utilized to the same extent as the above modalities, but is increasingly so. A new approach, assuming increasing prominence, is that of behavior therapy.

Intrinsic to the treatment of a child in residence are the concepts of separation of the child from his environment as not only necessary but as therapeutically useful (and only to the extent that it is); involvement in a milieu, not only promoting desirable development and behaviors but also acting as an agent to change and improve attachment behaviors; and reintegration of the child into his community, not only as necessary to physical termination but as a therapeutic series of actions of an ongoing, not just a terminal, nature. In addition to the specific therapies, these treatment concepts gain support in residential units by employment of controlled and manipulatable groupings of children and parent surrogates, by control over the degree of offered life structure, by variations in the life tasks expectations in terms of frequency, duration, and sequencing, and by control over the quality and quantity of exposure to the outside world.

Inpatient units specifically offer (1) planned and controlled living, with flexibility for greater responsibility and independence and protection against destructive impulses; (2) an emphasis on health via achievement and work; (3) group living and individualization; (4) identification figures of a positive nature; (5) a medium for treatment and change through child-staff and child-child interaction; (6) a community in which a child feels himself as integral; and (7) integration of a collective effort.[2]

The treatment goals for the child are to build a stronger ego, to enable him to sublimate and modify drives in a socially acceptable manner, and to help him develop more mature defenses, a realistic superego, and new and more useful identifications.[1]

Length of treatment varies widely from institution to institution and from child to child. The depth of the illness, the requirements of ego growth, and the nature of the treatment process are determinants of length of treatment. Some consider that one- or two-year treatment programs are vulnerable to the child's use of compliance, and surface change may be accepted as expressive of deeper change. Some consider that the child needs inpatient placement until he reaches adulthood. Factors leading to a rationale for such long-term treatment are the severity of the child's illness, the nature and complexity of psychic growth, the length of time required for establishment of a relationship to the ego defective child, the time required for new positive experiences to ward off pernicious effects of earlier traumatic experiences, and the concept of the child setting the treatment pace.[1]

Although it is convenient to state all this in terms of the child, such an orientation leaves out a most important factor, the adult grouping to which the child belongs and to which, hopefully, he will return. In most cases, this represents an existing family. To most workers in the field, an absolute essential is that there be involvement of the total family from the time of consideration of admission, through the actual admission-separation process, throughout the period of residential treatment, with its increasing home and community visiting, and the postdischarge reintegration. This involvement may be developed by individual casework with the parents, but there is an increasing tendency to make use of total family sessions for this purpose. As noted elsewhere, the availability of transitional measures, such as halfway houses and day hospitals, enhances this technique tremendously and may speed the process of reintegration.

Where there is no intact family, or where the child's best interests require continuing separation, experience suggests that work with the sponsoring agency (if the treating agency does not have a network of its own services) can be crucial and must continue all through the contact with the child.

The kind of thinking previously offered has been based upon psychodynamic premises. It must be recognized that acceptance of behavior therapy concepts and mode of operation may shorten the stay and lead to different goals.

Discharge is considered clinically indicated when the child has sufficient adaptive capabilities for usual life stress. Postdischarge adequacies and the child's institutional performance are relatable only when the situation to which the child returns is taken into account.[41] Slow integration into the community, such as can be accomplished by discharge to a group home or halfway house or day hospital, is useful in gauging the child's readiness for full community life.

Education

One of the major tasks of a growing child is to learn. In this culture, learning is generally done in school.

Most children coming to residential treatment have problems both learning and behaving in a standard learning situation. One of the most important and difficult tasks in a residential treatment center is that of bringing about improvement in these areas. An all too common tragedy is for a child of normal intelligence to leave at the age of twelve, capable only of second-grade work, despite the best endeavors. This is one of the areas most in need of improvement, generally. Perhaps this is one area where behavioral approaches will be of value.

The Professionals in Residential Units

Perhaps in no other place in mental health facilities will one find such a wide range of professionals as in residential units. Impinging on the daily routines of the children are the child-care personnel, the special educators (subspecialized in some instances), pediatric and psychiatric nursing personnel, the physician (pediatric and psychiatric), the occupational therapist, the recreational specialists, the special skill technician (for example, speech, language, visual-perceptual-motor), social group and case worker, and individual psychotherapist (variously, child-care worker, nurse, social worker, psychologist, psychiatrist). In addition, one finds a widely varied group of consultants, diagnosticians, and treatment personnel as special resources from the fields of child development, child care, education, and medicine.

Although not conceptually a professional in terms of the treatment of children, the supporting staff of the institution (cooks, maintenance and janitorial personnel, seamstresses, and so on) often spontaneously or by design form important relationships with children and thus become a part of the total treatment program and staff.

There are increasing experiments in using indigenous personnel from a community as treatment agents in settings such as community mental health centers. One special role that commends itself for residential treatment centers is in the two-way communication between parents-community and staff-institution.

Though not professionals, no reference to staff would be complete without consideration of volunteers. They have demonstrated their value in many capacities. Included are the roles of visitors to children who have none; introducing children into community activities; providing special skills not possessed by regular staff; supplementing the work of staff, for instance, as teacher aides. Above all, they bring the warmth and feeling of the community to these children in a most impressive and personal way and make children and staff feel: "We are not alone."

Outcome

Highly refined data on outcome are lacking, and there are but few follow-up studies available. The concept of success in residential treatment is a difficult one. Current intake criteria lack precision, so as to limit major comparisons between settings. There is the question of defining how much intrapsychic or environmental change there must be for success. It has been said that progress is best seen in terms of total case modifiability, the components of which include individual modifiability and family involvement in individual circumstances.[79] Maximal success has been said to occur with neurotic, nonacting-out children.[112] Treatment variables and subsequent adjustment following discharge have shown no relationship to each other; however, the presenting symptoms and chief complaints at admission have been found to be the best predictors of postdischarge adjustment.[34]

The Bellefaire follow-up study[5] found the greatest growth in terms of school and relationships with adults, peers, and general living tasks to be evidenced in those admitted before the age of thirteen. Also it found that this growth in and of itself was not useful in predicting postdischarge adaptability and adaptation. The postdischarge environment was found to be a major consideration in determining success or failure.

In nearly every worker's experience there has been little doubt of benefit of inpatient psychiatric treatment for some children. The presence of an intact family that desires a reintegration with the child appears to greatly increase the chances of postdischarge success. Availability of such resources as day hospitals, group homes, and outpatient treatment services, in addition to allowing for a smoother reintegration into a full community life, also allow for more accurate predictions as the child proceeds to become reinvolved in his community in a gradual and stepwise fashion.

(Day Hospitals

Although by the mid-1950s the need for some such program as day hospital for children had been seen, as of 1956 no experience had yet been reported in a day hospital program at public psychiatric hospitals for children.[116] Increasingly in the last decade day hospital treatment has been stressed as a vital component in the continuum of services for emotionally disturbed children,[9,33,77] but the professional literature concerned with children had yielded relatively few relevant papers up to 1969.[24]

The Setting

A day hospital for children is a therapeutic milieu in which psychotherapeutic, educational, sometimes behavioral, recreational, social work, and other services (for example, nursing, pediatrics, communication skills, and perceptual training) are integrated under the direction of clinically trained staff, on a day basis, with the child returning home for the night.

The distinction between the terms "day hospital" and "therapeutic day school" may at times be difficult to draw. For example, some day schools operate more in the manner typical of a day hospital.[37,39,40] One of the distinctions cited by Dingman[36,37] is that the day hospital's major programming control is in the hands of clinicians, whereas the day school, though it may have similar facilities and services, operates with the guidance and consultations of clinical staff rather than under its direct supervision.

The term "day care" has often been used to refer to day hospital programs.[51,65,91] It has been suggested that the term "day care" might best be restricted to programs intended primarily for children who are not in need of treatment for emotional disturbance but rather in need of day-to-day nurturant care in the absence of parents.[37] With the increasing emphasis on publicly supported day-care centers for young children of working mothers, this distinction may well need to be asserted. This is not to ignore the fact that many youngsters may benefit from a therapeutic milieu under the auspices of day-care programs,[57] but points to a difference in intent, population, and scope of services.

In its emphasis on the integration of a variety of approaches within one program, the day hospital comes to resemble the residential treatment center, with the obvious distinction that the child returns to his family daily and generally spends the entire weekend with his family. The fact of continual daily return to the family means that the parents continue to have major responsibility for fulfilling the nurturing needs of the child, as contrasted with the assumption of virtually total responsibility for the child's needs by the residential treatment center.[77] The child maintains his status as a family member physically present in the home, and parents continue to fulfill the parental role, so that in this sense the family unity is preserved intact.

In addition to helping maintain the degree of family cohesion already present, there are other advantages of a day hospital as opposed to residential treatment. Fenichel[39] indicated some of the disadvantages often attending residential treatment.

1. Residential treatment centers are usually distant from the child's home, making work with parents more difficult.
2. The family may reorganize in the child's absence so as to exclude the child's reentry.
3. The child may become institutionalized and thus have further difficulties in reintegrating into community life.
4. Removal of the child from his home causes the child to lose whatever positive aspects of family life exist, which harms both child and parents.

To this list may be added the stigmatizing of the child as bad or different, which may serve to mask underlying family problems, and the increased guilt and feelings of failure that many parents experience when the child leaves the home. In addition, the residential placement may allow the child to maintain

fantasies (often difficult to work through) of the family home, quite discrepant from what it actually was.

Clearly, removal of the child from his family is a drastic step, but one that in some instances is necessary. All too often, when guidance clinic services do not meet the needs of a particular child and family, and community educational facilities cannot cope with the child, there is no adequate alternative available except to seek a residential facility. It is this gap, between inpatient and outpatient services, that a day hospital can often fill. In a 1969 survey of needs for children's residential facilities in San Diego County, California, day treatment facilities were listed as most needed for children up to age twelve. Moreover, while the need for residential facilities for adolescents was stressed overall, it was felt most economical to invest in a day treatment facility because it offered services needed for the largest percentage of children in all age groups.[105]

The Child

The day hospital may be the treatment of choice and a useful alternative to full-time hospitalization and to outpatient treatment, both for children[24] and adolescents.[47] With adolescents it has been employed as a flexible service offering rehabilitation of former inpatients, follow-up service for discharged patients, and a testing ground for those long hospitalized.[65,91] While providing treatment it can also serve a diagnostic function and help to determine the extent to which a structured day for the child and relief for the parents along with casework will prove sufficient to avoid the need for complete removal of the child from the home. Availability of day hospital programs offers the promise of earlier discharge of children from residential treatment centers. Actually, as a rough rule of thumb, we have surmised that one-third of child referrals for residential treatment can have their needs better met by day hospital; and one-third, as well by day hospital as by residential treatment; and for the final one-third, residential treatment represents by far the treatment of choice.

Studies have indicated that up to two-thirds of adult patients treated in partial hospitalization settings would have required full-time hospitalization had day hospital facilities not been available.[10] Controlled studies in which patients were randomly assigned to inpatient or day hospital programs have shown that approximately two-thirds of those assigned to day hospitals were able to make use of treatment in that modality.[55,120] Devlin[35] reported on the results of randomly assigning to a day program, children who had met the criteria for residential treatment at the Ittelson Center. Tentative conclusions, based on those children either withdrawn from the program or transferred to the residential program, were that parental factors were the most significant determinants of suitability for either modality, although all children were deemed to have made some gains. Commenting on day hospitals in general, Astrachan et al.[10] stated that rather than any specific patient characteristic, it is the family's willingness to participate in the treatment program that influences the suitability of day hospital treatment. On the subject of criteria for the differential use of treatment settings, Atkins[11] reported that day treatment programs also served seriously disturbed children with results apparently comparable to those of residential treatment programs, a fact that made the search for differential criteria even more complicated. Schizophrenic children have been treated on a day basis at the League School for more than a decade.[39,40] On the basis of seven years experience in day treatment, La Vietes et al.[70] included among criteria for admission to the program the willingness and ability of parents to participate in the program plus a certain amount of basic stability in the home. Psychotic children have been treated directly, on a day basis,[56] and more recently indirectly, through the training of parents to work in the home with the child, with an operant conditioning approach.[107,108] Lovaas, et al. have recently reported a follow-up study, utilizing operant techniques with autistic children in a variety of programs, including day settings.[72]

It would seem, then, that no diagnostic classification of itself indicates the specific treatment modality of choice. The severity of the disorder as such is also not an absolute indicator, although one might think that a child or adolescent who demonstrates extremely poor impulse control and/or poor judgment and has clearly endangered himself or others may need the controls that only a residential setting can provide. This has not been substantiated in the literature with regard to day hospitalization. Frequent reference has been made to the need for the child to be removed from the family as an indication for residential treatment. In general, it appears that some degree of parental stability, including parental willingness to support the treatment program of the child, and sufficient parental resources to participate in their own treatment program (be this casework, group therapy, family therapy, or the like) are essential to the success of a day hospital approach. Greater precision with regard to criteria on the part of the child or the parents remains to be delineated. Despite this uncertainty, the need for the day treatment center to maintain control over its intake policy has been stressed.[36,116]

Treatment Program

The basic elements in most day hospital programs are specialized education, competence-producing recreational activities, group socializing experiences, provision for individual psychotherapy where indicated, and intensive work with parents.[24,87,47] The integration of these elements is generally through a multidisciplinary team approach.[51]

Education must be tailored to the special needs of the child, while the content of specific educational activities and their emphasis within the total program will vary.[39,42,56,69] Day treatment center clinical and educational services have been successfully coordinated with classroom experience in a metropolitan school system.[42] The integration of educational experiences with other therapeutic experiences has been stressed, while maintaining the view that in a day hospital, treatment, rather than modified education, is the primary function.[24]

Psychotherapy is most likely to be offered on an individual basis for the preadolescent in day hospitals and therapeutic day schools.[32,42, 48,63] Adolescents may be treated individually as well, but typically much emphasis is placed on group interaction, including frequent, often daily, patient-staff discussion groups.[47,91] A basic tool recommended for staff to employ in helping children make use of the therapeutic milieu is the "life space interview."[24]

Day treatment programs for psychotic children must be highly modified to cope with the severe limitations of functioning generally present. In a study of the effects of structure on the development of autistic children, results suggested that autistic children responded best to relatively high structure.[109]

The importance of helping the parents of psychotic children in day treatment centers to care for their disordered child in the home, with a more collaborative, rather than analytic approach to the parents, has increasingly been stressed.[38,56,70] In recent years, autistic children, for the most part inaccessible to psychodynamic therapies, have been involved in specially modified day treatment approaches, often with the application of principles of operant conditioning. The most recent findings indicated that the key to maintenance of gains in behavior modification programs for autistic children lies in assisting the parents to assume the training role in the home.[72,107,108]

In terms of staffing patterns, experience derived from residential treatment centers in general offers a reliable estimate of types of positions and staff ratios needed.[62] Programming of activities and staffing patterns will depend on the age of the children being treated and the types of disorder. Day treatment programs for children span the age range from preschool through adolescence and include children with emotionally based learning problems, those with personality disorders, and those termed psychotic or autistic. D'Amato[33] presented models of types of programs, the staffing of a program complex for fifty children, and corresponding space requirements.

Some clinicians who advocate day hospitalization as the principal treatment resource for a broad range of severely disturbed adolescents and adults[103] cite the disadvantages of the day hospital being physically and organizationally an appendage of a parent institution, and stress the need for institutional autonomy in order to maximize utilization of the day hospital as a treatment modality. Astrachan et al.[10] discussed the problems arising in a given day hospital when it attempts to attain a variety of goals. They pointed out that all secondary tasks will interfere with performance of the primary task and urged that task primacy and priorities be designated to ensure the survival of the organization. As an example, a day hospital that functions primarily to prevent inpatient hospitalization would be seen as being compromised in this task to the extent that it attempted to provide ongoing follow-up services to former inpatients.

At this point, day treatment programs for children appear to be (1) offshoots of residential treatment or inpatient facilities[51,77] or (2) attempts at either adding educational programming to outpatient clinical services or bringing these clinical services to existing educational settings.[43,44,48]

Where day hospital facilities are developed on the same grounds as residential or inpatient facilities, the question arises whether to integrate or keep separate day hospital and residential patients. Beneficial effects of integrating adolescent day and residential patients have been reported.[91] Arguments in favor of integrating day hospital with residential children, and in favor of separating the two programs, have been presented by Marshall and Stewart.[77] While their institution adopted a compromise resolution (schooling is the major area integrated), they pointed out that although theoretically able to differentiate goals and time factors in the two programs, in practice staff did have difficulty in modifying their patterns of treatment, based as they were on the preexisting residential treatment program.

Outcome

Outcome studies of the results of day treatment for children are sparse and generally lacking in precision. As Wilder et al.[120] reported, research on day hospitalization "has not kept pace with its expanded use." Guy and Gross[54] found in the literature "the almost unanimous opinion that day hospitals are an effective alternative to hospitalization," and cited the success reported with almost every variety of psychiatric disturbance in adults and children. They discussed proposals aimed at reducing confusion in the identification of patient populations, definitions of treatment, treatment effects, and assessment procedures.

An outcome study of a day treatment unit school with a psychoeducational program for primarily nonpsychotic children has been reported by Gold and Reisman.[44] Utilizing information from case records of fifty children treated over a four-year period and comparing this with follow-up data, including parent and teacher ratings, results indicated an approximately two-thirds improvement rate, regardless of the provision of psychotherapy. More favorable outcomes were found for children identified and treated at younger (five to eight) ages. Of the thirty-seven children who enrolled in public school following treatment, twenty-six still required some special class placement. La Vietes et al.[70] reported on thirty-eight children who completed a three-year day treatment program, indicating that 76 percent had "good results," while of the four children who required residential treatment, "the factor chiefly responsible was the parental one." Halpern[56] found that about one-fourth of autistic patients moved directly from the day treatment unit into a residential facility. As pointed out by Gold and Reisman[44] "reported results of day school programs dealing with primarily non-psychotic youngsters are not as readily available" as are those with psychotic or autistic youngsters. As for the latter, although there is an increased emphasis on quantifiable data, the newness of the programs and the relatively small number of children in them limit statements as to long-term treatment effectiveness.[72,108,109]

The cost of day treatment is generally estimated at somewhat less than half that of full residential treatment. Obviously, since the type of program, kinds of children served, and staffing patterns all may vary, there are differences in costs from one program to another. One difficulty that is being overcome in many instances is that of obtaining third-party payment, without which most comprehensive day treatment programs would be beyond the resources of the average family.

There are no exact figures available on the number of day hospitals or therapeutic day schools currently operating. As of April 1970, the National Association of Private Psychiatric Hospitals listed twenty-one private hospitals that offered day treatment programs for children and/or adolescents;[87] in the following year at least two more such programs were known to have been initiated.

In one reported instance, over a two-year period, the number of inpatient children decreased by approximately 16 percent, while the number in day treatment nearly tripled.[33] If day treatment fulfills its promise as an alternative to residential treatment for a significant number of children, it seems likely that similar trends will become prevalent. It is with such an expectation in mind, coupled with the belief that day treatment is a needed and useful treatment of choice in many instances, that those involved in mental health planning for children[9,95,113] continue to emphasize the role of day treatment in the spectrum of services.

⟪ Group Homes

The concept of the group home has been receiving increasing attention from those concerned with providing services to children. Although definitions vary, since they have been derived for the most part pragmatically, the general structure of the concept and the definite need for such homes, especially for adolescents, are clear enough in the literature.[92] A group home occupies a place in the continuum of services between institutional care and foster home, with some measure of each. Although at times there have been difficulties in the literature in distinguishing between group and foster homes, several authors, especially Herstein[59] have emphasized that the group home is a residential setting that provides professionally guided help for disturbed adolescents while retaining the small-group autonomy of the foster family for the growth benefits the latter provides. Both Herstein[59] and Gula[53] stressed the need for agency control and supervision of care and treatment (with provisions for casework and/or social group work supervision and psychiatric consultation). The child-care staff are viewed as counselors or houseparents rather than as foster parents, and each group home is limited in size, numbers, and composition of members. The nuclear child-care staff may be either a couple or a group of adults, but neither the staffing patterns nor the degree of openness or closedness to the community is crucial to the definition of a group home.[50]

Group homes are believed to meet the living and treatment needs of many adolescents who (1) may be able to move from residential treatment to community living but have no suitable family or (2) have had multiple unsuccessful foster home placements and cannot meet the demands for intimacy and conformity to family life.[92]

Admission criteria to group homes generally refer to the inability of the adolescent to cope with family or foster home life (or unavailability or unsuitability of the latter). The adolescent's behavioral or emotional problems must not be of such severity as to prevent functioning in the community, including school and peer activities, given the support and treatment that may be available. While some degree of psychiatric disorder may be present, the degree and kind of acting-out behavior must not be of such nature or severity as to be disruptive of the home itself or of its relationship to the community.[59]

In addition to discussions of the composition and supervision of the child-caring staff of group homes, the overall direction and integration of services has been described.[45] Relationship of the home to its neighborhood, and of preparation to enter the neighborhood, have been discussed.[117]

In view of the diversity of staffing patterns, it is difficult to discuss costs with any generality. Compared to residential treatment in a similar locale, group home costs may be approximately one-third to one-fourth per resident.

The usefulness of small-group homes for adolescents (the need among younger children has not been so much emphasized) may be seen both in terms of ongoing aftercare (following residential treatment) and as a means of providing stability in the lives of those who might otherwise develop more delinquent or other symptomatic behavior. For the adolescent boy or girl who has some emotional disturbance, who is unable to adjust to the foster home or family setting that is available but unsuitable, or who needs an ongoing, supportive living situation that can provide security and consistency, with overall professional direction, supervision, and consultation, the group home may be a placement of choice.[110]

As mental health planning focuses more deservedly on the needs of adolescents, the concept of the group home may be expected to flourish.

◖ Retrospect and Forecast

Ongoing social changes and concepts have helped to bring about a shift from institutions designed to provide congregate living for orphans or dependent and neglected children, to residential treatment centers, designed to help children and parents reconstruct inner distortions and pathological interaction. The child-care origin of most of these institutions helped to determine a social work orientation, while the hospital origin of others led toward a medical orientation. Various settings have sprung up, reflecting the concepts of psychiatry, casework, group work, education, and the like.

Regardless of this past, it is noteworthy that

the best among such settings came to emphasize an integrated approach, utilizing and requiring the contribution of each discipline in an integrated manner. Very often this was exemplified in the treatment team of which the particular child was the unseen but much felt center, in which all who were involved with child or parent or agency met, conferred, planned, and with increasing maturity and independence set and pursued their goals. Not only did this require a heavy concentration of staff per child, but the spoken or unspoken contract of the treatment center was apt to be: "We will cure the child; we will cure the family; and we will cure the society which has afflicted them both, so that we may guarantee an everlasting successful life after leaving our doors." The consequence is somewhat like analysis interminable. The combination of high staff ratio, heavy cost, and prolonged treatment has placed the classical form of residential treatment in jeopardy.

Owing to the resultant economic pressures from third-party payors; the spirit of the times, which emphasizes a colleague rather than an autocratic approach and stresses flexibility; the felt and asserted need for a comprehensive, integrated network of services readily and locally available, involving community change agents as much as possible; the appearance, often forceful pushing, of behavior therapy and its delimited set of goals—we see today a great ferment.

It is likely that there will be a variety of experiments and hybrid forms of treatment. Goals will be more flexible, realistic, and differentiated. Community involvement, extending into the operation of these facilities, will most likely increase, and many more facilities will become part of a community network rather than stand alone. The next decade will probably record 1972 as the end of that phase of residential treatment and its offshoots which began with the Social Security Act of 1935.

❲ Bibliography

1. ADESSA, S., and LAATSCH, A. "Extended Residential Treatment: Eighth-year Anxiety." *Social Work*, 10, no. 4 (1965), 16–24.

2. ADLER, J. "General Concepts in Residential Treatment of Disturbed Children." *Child Welfare*, 47, no. 9 (1968), 524.

3. AICHORN, A. *Wayward Youth*. New York: Viking Press, 1915.

4. ALLERHAND, M. E., WEBER, R. E., et al. "The Bellefaire Follow-Up Study: Research Objectives and Method." *Child Welfare*, 40, no. 7 (1961).

5. ————, WEBER, R. E., et al. *Adaptation and Adaptability: The Bellefaire Follow-up Study*. New York: Child Welfare League of America, 1966.

6. ALT, H. "The Role of the Psychiatric Social Worker in the Residential Treatment of Children." *Social Casework*, 32, no. 9 (1951).

7. ————. *Residential Treatment for the Disturbed Child: Basic Principles in Planning and Design of Programs and Facilities*. New York: International Universities Press, 1961.

8. AMERICAN PSYCHIATRIC ASSOCIATION. *Psychiatric Inpatient Treatment of Children*. Baltimore, Md.: Lord Baltimore Press, 1957.

9. ————. *Planning Psychiatric Services for Children in the Community Mental Health Program*. Washington, D.C.: The Association, 1964.

10. ASTRACHAN, B. M., et al. "Systems Approach to Day Hospitalization." *Archives of General Psychiatry*, 22 (1970), 550–559.

11. ATKINS, T. "Summary." In *Criteria for the Differential Use of Treatment Settings for Children with Emotional Disorders*. New York: Child Welfare League of America, 1962.

12. BERWALD, J. F. "Cottage Parents in a Treatment Institution." *Child Welfare*, 39, no. 10 (1960).

13. BETTELHEIM, B. "Closed Institutions for Children." *Bulletin of the Menninger Clinic*, 12 (1948).

14. ————. *Love Is Not Enough*. Glencoe, Ill.: The Free Press, 1950.

15. ————. *Truants from Life*. Glencoe, Ill.: The Free Press, 1955.

16. ————, and SYLVESTER, E. "A Therapeutic Milieu." *American Journal of Orthopsychiatry*, 18 (1948), 191.

17. BOWLBY, J. "Separation Anxiety: A Critical

Review of the Literature." *Journal of Child Psychology and Psychiatry*, 1 (1961), 251–269.

18. BRADLEY, C. "A Pioneer Hospital for Children's Behavior Disorders." *Modern Hospital*, 50 (1938).

19. ———. "Education in a Children's Psychiatric Hospital." *Nervous Child*, 73 (1944).

20. ———. "Indications for Residential Treatment of Children with Severe Neuropsychiatric Problems." *American Journal of Orthopsychiatry*, 19, no. 3 (1949).

21. BROWN, I. H. D. "The Development of Family-Group Homes in Manchester." *Child Care*, 15, nos. 2 and 3 (1961), 45–50, 89–92.

22. BURMEISTER, E. *The Professional Houseparent*. New York: Columbia University Press, 1960.

23. CAMERON, K., et al. "Symposium on the Inpatient Treatment of Psychotic Adolescents." *British Journal of Medical Psychology*, 23 (1950), 107.

24. CHAZIN, R. M. "Day Treatment of Emotionally Disturbed Children." *Child Welfare*, 48 (1969), 212–218.

25. CHILD WELFARE LEAGUE OF AMERICA. *Group Home Programs: A Study of Some Programs Operated by League Member Agencies*. New York, 1962.

26. ———. *Standards for Services of Child Welfare Institutions*. New York, 1963.

27. ———. *Group Homes in Perspective*. New York, 1964.

28. CHILDREN'S BUREAU. *Research Relating to Emotionally Disturbed Children*. Washington, D.C.: U.S. Government Printing Office, 1968.

29. CHRIST, A. E., and WAGNER, N. N. "Iatrogenic Factors in Residential Treatment: The Psychiatric Team's Contribution to Continued Psychopathology." *American Journal of Orthopsychiatry*, 35, no. 2 (1965), 253–254.

30. CLEMENS, D. W. "Functional Design in Building a Residential Treatment Facility." *Child Welfare*, 50 (1971), 513–518.

31. COLVIN, R. W. "The Education of Emotionally Disturbed Children in a Residential Treatment Center." *American Journal of Orthopsychiatry*, 31, no. 3 (1961), 591–597.

32. COMMUNITY CHEST OF SAN FRANCISCO. *Residential Treatment for Emotionally Disturbed Children*. San Francisco, 1954.

33. D'AMATO, G. *Residential Treatment for Child Mental Health*. Springfield, Ill.: Charles C Thomas, 1969.

34. DAVIDS, A., RYAN, R., and SALVATORE, P. D. "Effectiveness of Residential Treatment for Psychotic and Other Disturbed Children." *American Journal of Orthopsychiatry*, 38, no. 3 (1968), 469–475.

35. DEVLIN, M. "Criteria for a Day Treatment Type of Setting." In *Criteria for the Differential Use of Treatment Settings for Children with Emotional Disorders*. New York: Child Welfare League of America, 1962.

36. DINGMAN, P. R. "Day Hospitals for Children." In *Day Care of Psychiatric Patients*. Springfield, Ill.: Charles C Thomas, 1964.

37. ———. "Day Programs for Children: A Note on Terminology." *Mental Hygiene*, 53, no. 4 (1969), 646–647.

38. DOERNBERG, N., et al. *A Home Training Program for Young Mentally Ill Children*. Brooklyn, N.Y.: League School for Emotionally Disturbed Children, 1969.

39. FENICHEL, C., et al. "Day School for Schizophrenic Children." *American Journal of Orthopsychiatry*, 30, no. 1 (1960).

40. FREEDMAN, A. "Day Hospital for Severely Disturbed Children." *American Journal of Orthopsychiatry*, 115 (1959), 893–898.

41. FRENCH, E. L. "Therapeutic Education: Theory and Practice in a Residential Treatment Center for Emotionally Disturbed Adolescents." In J. Hellmuth, ed., *Educational Therapy*. Vol. 1. Seattle, Wash.: Special Child Publications of the Seattle Sequin School, 1966. Pp. 425–437.

42. GODWIN, M. P., et al. "The Role of the Educational Program in a Psychotherapeutic Day Care Center for Children and Teenagers." *American Journal of Orthopsychiatry*, 36, no. 2 (1966), 345–346.

43. GOLD, J. "Child Guidance Day Treatment and the School: A Clinic's Use of Its Psychoeducational Facility for New Programming in the Public Schools." *American Journal of Orthopsychiatry*, 37, no. 2 (1967), 276–277.

44. ———, and REISMAN, J. "An Outcome Study of a Day Treatment Unit School in a Community Mental Health Center." *Bulletin Rochester Mental Health Center*, 3, no. 1 (1971), 71–78. (Also in *American Journal of Orthopsychiatry*, 40, no. 2 [1970].)

45. GOLDSTEIN, H. "The Role of a Director in a Group Home." *Child Welfare*, 45 (1966), 501–508.

46. GORDON, G., and SIEGEL, L. "The Evolution of a Program of Individual Psychotherapy for Children with Aggressive Acting-out Disorders in a New Residential Treatment Unit." *American Journal of Orthopsychiatry*, 27, no. 1 (1957).

47. GRADOLPH, P. C., and SIEGEL, B. "Adolescent Day Treatment Project." *American Journal of Orthopsychiatry*, 37 (1967), 273–274.

48. GRAFFAGNINO, P. N., et al. "Psychotherapy in Latency-Age Children in an Inner City Therapeutic School." *American Journal of Psychiatry*, 127, no. 5 (1970), 626–634.

49. GREEN, R. K., and CLARK, W. P. "Therapeutic Recreation for Aggressive Children in Residential Treatment." *Child Welfare*, 44, no. 10 (1965), 578–582.

50. GREENBERG, A. "Agency-Owned and -Operated Group Foster Homes for Adolescents." *Child Welfare*, 42, no. 4 (1963), 173–179.

51. GRITZKA, K., et al. "An Interdisciplinary Approach in Day Treatment of Emotionally Disturbed Children." *Child Welfare*, 49 (1970), 468–472.

52. GULA, M. *Child-Caring Institutions*. Washington, D.C.: U.S. Government Printing Office, 1958.

53. ——. "Group Homes–New and Differentiated Tools in Child Welfare, Delinquency and Mental Health." *Child Welfare*, 43 (1964), 393–398.

54. GUY, W., and GROSS, G. "Problems in Evaluation of Day Hospitals." *Community Mental Health Journal*, 3 (1967), 111–118.

55. ——, et al. "A Controlled Evaluation of Day Hospital Effectiveness." *Archives of General Psychiatry*, 20 (1969), 329–338.

56. HALPERN, W. I. "The Schooling of Autistic Children: Preliminary Findings." *American Journal of Orthopsychiatry*, 40 (1970), 665–671.

57. HANSAN, J. E., and PEMBERTON, K. "Day Care: A Therapeutic Milieu." *Child Welfare*, 44 (1965), 149–155.

58. HARTMANN, E., et al. *Adolescents in a Mental Hospital*. New York: Grune & Stratton, 1968.

59. HERSTEIN, N. "What Is a Group Home?" *Child Welfare*, 43 (1964), 403–414.

60. HOBBS, N. "Helping Disturbed Children: Ecological and Psychological Strategies." *American Psychologist*, 21 (1966), 1105–1115.

61. HYLTON, L. *Residential Treatment Cost Study*. New York: Child Welfare League of America, 1962.

62. ——. *The Residential Treatment Center: Children, Programs, and Costs*. New York: Child Welfare League of America, 1964.

63. JACKSON, J. "Child Psychotherapy in a Day School for Maladjusted Children." *Journal of Child Psychotherapy*, 2, no. 4 (1970), 54.

64. JOINT COMMISSION ON MENTAL HEALTH OF CHILDREN. *Crisis in Mental Health: Challenge for the 1970's*. New York: Harper & Row, 1969, 1970.

65. JONES, C. H. *Mental Hospitals*, 12 (1961), 4–6.

66. JONES, M. *The Therapeutic Community*. New York: Basic Books, 1953.

67. KESTER, B. C. "Indications for Residential Treatment of Children." *Child Welfare*, 44, no. 6 (1966).

68. KONOPKA, G. "The Role of the Group in Residential Treatment." *American Journal of Orthopsychiatry*, 25, no. 4 (1955).

69. LA VIETES, R. "The Teacher's Role in the Education of the Emotionally Disturbed Child." *American Journal of Orthopsychiatry*, 32 (1962), 854–862.

70. ——, et al. "Day Treatment Center and School: Seven Years' Experience." *American Journal of Orthopsychiatry*, 35, no. 1 (1965), 160–169.

71. LEWIS, W. W. "Project Re-Ed: Education Intervention in Discordant Child Rearing Systems." In *Emergent Approaches to Mental Health Problems*. New York: Appleton-Century-Crofts, 1967.

72. LOVAAS, et al. "Some Generalization and Follow-Up Measures on Autistic Children in Behavior Therapy." *Journal of Applied Behavior Analysis*, in press.

73. MAIER, H. W. *Group Work as Part of Residential Treatment*. New York: National Association of Social Workers, 1965.

74. ——, et al. "The Role of Residential Treatment for Children." *American Journal of Orthopsychiatry*, 25 (1955), 699.

75. MARSDEN, G., et al. *Selection of Children for Residential Treatment: A Study of the Process*. Ann Arbor: Children's Psychiatric Hospital, University of Michigan Medical Center, 1967.

76. ———, et al. "Residential Treatment of Children: A Survey of Institutional Characteristics." *Journal of Child Psychiatry*, 9, no. 2 (1970).

77. MARSHALL, K., and STEWART, M. F. "Day Treatment as a Complementary Adjunct to Residential Treatment." *Child Welfare*, 48, no. 1 (1969), 40–44.

78. MATSUSHIMA, J. "Group Work with Emotionally Disturbed Children in Residential Treatment." *Social Work*, 7, no. 2 (1962).

79. ———. "Some Aspects of Defining 'Success' in Residential Treatment." *Child Welfare*, 44, no. 5 (1965), 272–277.

80. MAYER, M. F. In "Symposium (1954), The Role of Residential Treatment for Children." *American Journal of Orthopsychiatry*, 25 (1955), 667–668.

81. ———. *A Guide for Child-Care Workers*. New York: Child Welfare League of America, 1958.

82. ———. "The Use of Vocational Guidance as a Part of Residential Treatment." *Journal of Jewish Communal Service*, 40, no. 2 (1963), 212–221.

83. ———. "A Research Attempt in a Residential Treatment Center: An Administrative Case History." In M. Norris and B. Wallace, eds., *The Known and Unknown in Child Welfare Research*. New York: Child Welfare League of America and National Association of Social Workers, 1965.

84. ———, and WOLFENSTEIN, C. M. "Diagnostic Criteria for Intramural and Extramural Schooling of Disturbed Children in a Residential Treatment Center." *American Journal of Orthopsychiatry*, 24, no. 2 (1954).

85. MORA, G., et al. "A Residential Treatment Center Moves Toward the Community Mental Health Model." *Child Welfare*, 48 (1969), 585–590, 628–629.

86. NATIONAL ASSOCIATION FOR MENTAL HEALTH. *Directory of Facilities for Mentally Ill Children in the United States*. New York: National Association for Mental Health, 1967.

87. NATIONAL ASSOCIATION OF PRIVATE PSYCHIATRIC HOSPITALS. Personal Communication, April 2, 1970.

88. NEUMANN, C. P. and TAMERIN, J. S. "The Treatment of Adult Alcoholics and Teen-Age Drug Addicts in One Hospital." *Quarterly Journal of Studies on Alcohol*, 32, no. 1 (1971), 82–93.

89. PAPENFORT, D., et al. *Population of Children's Residential Institutions in the United States*. Chicago: University of Chicago Press, 1968.

90. PASAMANICK, B. "Liaison Committee to the Joint Commission on Mental Health of Children: Position Statement of the American Orthopsychiatry Association on the Work of the Joint Commission on Mental Health of Children." *American Journal of Orthopsychiatry*, 38 (1968), 402–409.

91. PFAUTZ, H. W. "The Functions of Day-Care for Disturbed Adolescents." *Mental Hygiene*, 46, no. 2 (1962), 222–229.

92. PIPPERT, E., et al. Report of the Group Home Committee. Riverside, R.I.: Emma Pendleton Bradley Hospital, 1970.

93. POLSKY, H. W., and CLASTER, D. S. *The Dynamics of Residential Treatment: A Social System Analysis*. Chapel Hill, N.C.: University of North Carolina Press, 1968.

94. RABINOVITCH, R. D., et al. "Primary Functions of Occupational and Recreational Therapy in the Psychiatric Treatment of Children." *American Journal of Occupational Therapy*, 5 (1951).

95. RAFFERTY, F. T. "Child Psychiatry Service for a Total Population." *Journal of Child Psychiatry*, 6, no. 2 (1967), 295–308.

96. REBENOW, I. "Agency Operated Group Homes." *Child Welfare*, 43 (1964), 415–422.

97. REDL, F. "New Ways of Ego Support in Residential Treatment of Disturbed Children." *Bulletin of the Menninger Clinic*, 13 (1949).

98. ———. "The Concept of a 'Therapeutic Milieu.'" *American Journal of Orthopsychiatry*, 24, no. 4 (1959).

99. ———. *When We Deal with Children*. New York: The Free Press, 1966.

100. ———, and WINEMAN, D. *The Aggressive Child*. Glencoe, Ill.: The Free Press, 1957.

101. REID, J. H., and HAGAN, H. R. *Residential Treatment of Emotionally Disturbed Children*. New York: Child Welfare League of America, 1952.

102. RINSLEY, D. B. "The Adolescent in Residential Treatment—Some Critical Reflections." *Adolescence*, 2, no. 5 (1967), 83.

103. ROCHE REPORT. "Frontiers of Clinical Psychiatry." *Roche Report*, 7, no. 18 (November 1970), 5–11.

104. ROSEN, B. M., et al. "Utilization of Psychiatric Facilities by Children: Current Status, Trends, Implications." *Mental Health*

Statistics, Series 13, no. 1. Public Health Service publication, no. 1868. Washington, D.C.: National Institution of Mental Health, 1968.

105. SATTLER, J. M., and LEPPLA, B. W. "A Survey of the Need for Children's Mental Health Facilities." *Mental Hygiene*, 53, no. 4 (1969), 643–645.

106. SCHER, B. "Specialized Group Care for Adolescents." *Child Welfare*, 37 (1958), 12–17.

107. SCHOPLER, E. Developmental Therapy for Autistic Children: Individual and Social Implications. Paper presented to the National Society for Autistic Children, June 1971.

108. ——, and REICHLER, R. J. "Parents as Cotherapists in the Treatment of Psychotic Children." *Journal of Autism and Childhood Schizophrenia*, 1, no. 1 (1971), 87–102.

109. ——, et al. "Effect of Treatment Structure on Development in Autistic Children." *Archives of General Psychiatry*, 24 (1971), 415–421.

110. SCHWARTZ, M. and KAPLAN, I. "Small Group Homes: Placement of Choice for Adolescents." *Child Welfare*, 40, no. 9 (1961), 9–13.

111. SHODELL, M. "Day Center for Severely Disturbed Children." *Journal of Rehabilitation*, July–August 1967, pp. 22–25.

112. SILVER, H. "The Residential Treatment of Emotionally Disturbed Children: An Evaluation of 15 Years' Experience." *Journal of Jewish Communal Service*, 38, no. 2 (1961).

113. SONIS, M. "Implications for the Child Guidance Clinic of Current Trends in Mental Health Planning." *American Journal of Orthopsychiatry*, 38, no. 3 (1968), 515–526.

114. SPECHT, R., and GLASSER, B. "A Review of the Literature on Social Work with Hospitalized Adolescents and Their Families." *Social Service Review*, 37, no. 3 (1963), 295–306.

115. TRIESCHMAN, A. E. *The Other 23 Hours: Child-Care Work with Emotionally Disturbed Children in a Therapeutic Milieu.* Chicago: Aldine, 1969.

116. VAUGHAN, W. T., Jr., and DAVIS, F. E. "Day Hospital Programming in a Psychiatric Hospital for Children." *American Journal of Orthopsychiatry*, 33, no. 3 (1963), 542–544.

117. WALSH, R. R. "Small Group Care Facilities: Their Neighborhoods and Their Neighbors." *Child Welfare*, 43 (1964), 279–286.

118. WEINSTEIN, L. "Project Re-Ed Schools for Emotionally Disturbed Children: Effectiveness as Viewed by Referring Agencies, Parents, and Teachers." *Exceptional Children*, 35 (1969), 703–711.

119. WEISS, V., and WEISS, S. *Follow-Up Study of Children Released from Residential Treatment Centers.* New Orleans, La.: Jewish Children's Home Service, 1969.

120. WILDER, J. F., et al. "A Two Year Follow-Up Evaluation of Acute Psychiatric Patients Treated in a Day Hospital." *American Journal of Psychiatry*, 122 (1966), 1095–1101.

CHAPTER 13

WORKING WITH SCHOOLS

Raquel E. Cohen

M ENTAL HEALTH professionals are participating in school programs where their knowledge of the psychological needs of children and their skills of working within organizational structures are becoming integrated into systematic methods of dealing with the problems inherent in educating students.[11,21] A wide range of possibilities exists for becoming involved in schools and these possibilities will be influenced by the focus of the mental health professional's activity, the organization and auspices from which he comes, and his approach, procedures, and goals. The professional can focus on: (1) individual emotionally disturbed children; (2) a population of children that present severe emotional disturbance; or (3) both the population of emotionally disturbed children and the climate in which they function, which would include the teachers' approach and the administrative design of a program for the child.

Although in the past most mental health consultation has focused on these problems, it is becoming evident that as the mental health professionals take an interest in broader areas of intervention, they are increasingly concerned about other groups of children, such as the mentally retarded and children who have serious learning difficulties.[32] As this concern and intervention enlarges to incorporate these children, it becomes evident that the mental health professional, who is using a conceptual framework of open social systems, will further enlarge his focus to reach out to children in the classroom who may be acutely disturbed for a brief period of time and for a variety of reasons as well as to children who are chronically mildly disturbed.[17,19,31] Again it is difficult to establish a definite boundary between this population and the normal population in the classrooms of schools. In reality then, if a mental health professional wants to work within a school system, he will have to pay attention to the total population in that school but may want to place emphasis on certain groups of children at different times of his intervention.

The opportunity to do this may be facilitated by the stance the mental health professional may develop for himself. For example, a private therapist will work with his patient along with some of the teachers and administrators who work with this child, while a mental health professional working in a mental health center, whose mission is to look at the problems of a population within a "catchment area," might want to work with the totality of the school system.

The focus of intervention will vary depending on what the issues are with respect to individual children, so that the mental health professional may find himself working with (1) special classes; (2) special educational services (retardation, programs for dyslexics); or (3) teachers and principals within the total school. This means, then, that the professional must be aware of the necessity to coordinate his activities with pupil personnel services within the school at different administrative levels so as to prevent duplication of services. He should ally himself with individuals within these services in such a way as to integrate his activities with theirs. This means he should direct his efforts in order to create a framework of comprehensive and collaborative actions around the child's problems.

The mental health professional will find that these special services activities and his own may be vaguely defined and will tend to develop overlapping responsibilities. This can result in poor communication, lack of trust, excessive manipulation, and conflicting goals and priorities unless attention is paid to the necessary steps to avoid this. Although professionals working in schools and mental health clinics are concerned about the welfare of individual children, hierarchical aspects of a school's structure can make it difficult for them to ally their efforts with the educators.

When mental health services are well organized within a school, they tend to be integrated into the ongoing activities of the educational system. The professionals who staff these services have easy access to information from the teacher or the principal and are sanctioned to enter the children's homes and obtain relevant material from community agencies. This means, then, that the mental health professional working within the special education system can be integrated further into the rest of the system as his efforts and activities are seen as useful and as he participates in a meaningful way with areas of concern of administrators and teachers.

❲ Establishing a Collaborative Coprofessional Practice in the School

Let us assume that, for a multitude of reasons or motivations—as the therapist of an individual child with specific emotional problems who is having difficulties adapting to school or as a regular consultant invited by the school— a mental health professional decides to participate in a school program. He will wonder what principles can be adapted from the traditional one-to-one treatment model and how to order and modify these principles so that he can use them in the development of collaborative approaches within the school system. As a coprofessional collaborator he will want to know how he can relate most effectively to the school personnel and help them plan programs for the emotionally disturbed child, regardless of whether this condition is due to a poor school program, to temperament, or to outside social or familial conditions.[5,12,14,16,23,26] With whom will he work, and how can he intervene in an existing school program? These issues, and many more, are continually raised by experiences that are being accumulated, as an increasing number of mental health professionals join with the schools to look at the abundance of children experiencing different ranges and levels of emotional disturbance.

Areas of Inquiry

There are many questions that a mental health professional should ask himself when entering a school. The four major lines of inquiry pertain to (1) the academic climate, (2) the emotional climate permeating the educational tasks, (3) the existing programs and personnel within the educational system, and (4) the populations at risk within the school.

ACADEMIC CLIMATE

Is this school characterized by an open or relatively closed culture?[22] What are the educators' attitudes about emotionally disturbed youngsters, in terms of the process of adjustment to the school environment? How do the school's pedagogical approaches relate to the psychosocial tasks of students in the school?

EMOTIONAL CLIMATE

What is the level of sensitivity to children with special needs? What type of emotional climate exists? That is, do the teachers listen to the children? Do they accept the differences between children without placing value judgments on these differences? Are there programs planned for the special and individual needs of children? Do activities have, as their ultimate goal, the integration of all children, including the emotionally disturbed child, into the mainstream of school life? Are there teachers selected and trained specifically for dealing with emotionally disturbed children?

EXISTING PROGRAMS AND PERSONNEL

Considering the special programs in existence, what type of infrastructural program communication does the school have? Do special programs have a highly compartmentalized, fragmented character (as is so often the case) that impedes dialogue between people who are functioning in different areas and levels of the school's hierarchy? How complex are the special services offered, and what are the quality and quantity of their specialists and the administrators and teachers who interact with the children? What characterizes the personnel for special services, in terms of numbers, training, and interest?

POPULATIONS AT RISK

What is the range of psychopathology in the area of emotional disturbance and retardation represented by children in the school? For what age child are existing programs designed? Do special programs reflect the appropriate range of age and need, and, if necessary, do they function for children with mild, moderate, and severe psychopathology?

How to Begin Working in the Schools

Let us now consider the classical aspects of entering a school system and developing relationships within it.[8]

ENTERING THE SYSTEM

Caplan[3,4] gave us a well-documented and extensive description of the fundamentals of entering a school system. His work can help the mental health professional to conceptualize principles, attitudes, and goals, which can guide him as he moves through different levels of a school's hierarchy. It also suggests ways of establishing rapport between mental health professional and educator.

At his initial entry into a school a mental health professional should make personal contact with the top authority figure of the school. This will help him to understand the overall climate of the school and to get sanction for his future work. He should be continually aware that although he is dealing specifically within the classroom with one teacher, the influences on this teacher reflect the surrounding administrative and peer network. The more direct information the mental health professional has about this network, the more feasible his suggestions can be. Depending on hearsay will give him a distorted view of the organizational and social patterns he has to work with. He needs to learn as much as possible about the way the school goes about accomplishing its goals, about the values and traditions of the educators there, and about the climate of trust and respect at every level of the school.

Although few mental health professionals have the time or inclination to study organizational school charts and predefined roles, having this larger picture is as important as being aware of personal idiosyncrasies and abilities of specific individuals in a school or school system. Within what tends most often to be a conservative, traditional organizational structure, the mental health professional sets out to find some shared values to facilitate open communication with educators. Most schools are interested in the help that mental health professionals can offer to alleviate problems occasioned by the disruptive behavior of emotionally disturbed children. But it is the mental health professional who must offer his initiative, creativity, and expertise in a positive and affirmative manner if he is to help the educators solve their problems. At this particular historical moment, explicitly energetic, active approaches are imperative: Our past professional neglect of the schools has fostered many negative, ambivalent, and consequently detrimental stereotypes about school mental health workers.

Learning the Language of the Educators

Once the mental health professional has an overall sense of the organization of the school system, he has to learn the style of communication that school personnel share. The communication used by the mental health professional must respect both the educational-technical language (developed by educators to describe their own activities and socioaffective climate) and the language of local cultural and historical traditions. Though it will take time to acquire intimate knowledge of the details and characteristics of the local language, the mental health professional needs to be constantly aware of it, using every available opportunity to ascertain that he is getting the right message, which relates not only to verbal messages but also to nonverbal behavior. An inability to understand some of the symbolic shorthand of the school communication methods puts him at a disadvantage, which he can acknowledge; on occasion he should be prepared to ask for more explanation in a situation that seems obscure to him.

Building Relationships and Developing Trust

Mental health professionals must realize that when working in schools, it is essential to build mutually respecting relationships with the teachers before the teacher can hear and, in turn, modify attitudes and ways of dealing with the children. Often a child's problems require a group of educators and staff personnel to work together as a team. If the mental health professional is not accepted and re-

spected, the potential for his contribution on this team is minimal. Educators must be convinced that the mental health professional is in general sympathy with the educational goals of the school. He will probably have to neutralize the threatening stereotype that educators have about mental health workers; he will also have to prove that he will not slight the personal status of teachers and special services personnel. There is a high degree of dread in the schools that professionals, coming in from outside, will make use of information they obtain there to humiliate and vilify people already working in the schools. The mental health professional must sincerely make school personnel feel that, although in his field he has expert knowledge that can be directly helpful to them, he lacks knowledge in those areas where the educators are experts. He should acknowledge very explicitly that he knows the chief responsibility for educating children is theirs. He can also point out that, being trained to understand problem situations from different points of view, he is willing and able to make his knowledge and training available to them and to collaborate with them in overcoming problems created by the mentally or emotionally handicapped child within the classroom setting.

Policy, tradition, lack of manpower or of funds can create predicaments for teachers and special services personnel. The mental health professional who is concentrating on the well-being of a specific vulnerable child will find himself extremely unhappy at conditions in the school that impose added stress; he may have difficulty balancing his awareness of the realistic issues confronting the educators with his own affective reactions to specific situations, which he labels sociopathologic. This is one of the crucial conflicts that mental health professionals have to resolve before they can be helpful within a system already overburdened with impediments to good programming for handicapped children. To be a truly effective collaborator with educators who, by law, have to work with children who have severe learning problems takes a great deal of time. The multiplicity of issues that affect a child's experience must be continuously kept in mind. Often the very high expectations that most mental health professionals have of the ideal milieu for handicapped children can impede effective collaboration with educators who, for so many reasons beyond their control (such as lack of adequate space, a governmental local body cutting the school budget, or a restrictive teachers' union policy), may not be producing the optimum environment.

DEVELOPING COLLABORATIVE RULES FOR WORKING IN SCHOOLS

Together mental health professionals and school personnel should work out their ground rules for collaboration. When a mental health professional first comes to a school, he should define his particular interest, approach, and mode of working. He should be as clear as possible about the type of child he is most interested in discussing, thereby indicating to educators just what they may expect from collaboration with him. Ground rules then demonstrate what goals and aims they share and circumscribe the procedures they will mutually undertake, as for instance how often they will meet, where these meetings will take place, and how the mental health professional will set treatment programs into motion after conferences. In other words, everyone needs to be very clear about just what a mental health professional can and cannot do within the structure of the school.

TESTING THE METTLE OF THE MENTAL HEALTH PROFESSIONAL

When he is first asked to participate in programming for emotionally disturbed children, a mental health professional should expect the initial cases to be test cases. School personnel generally use these opportunities to scrutinize a mental health professional's ability and to assess his willingness and capacity to collaborate and communicate within their structure. If the mental health professional realizes that a case is being used as a means of establishing relationships with school personnel he will not neglect these first challenges in a school and will address his efforts both to the child and to the needs of the educators. Details of individ-

ual cases need to be discussed in general terms, with full respect for the rights of the child for confidential and competent diagnosis and treatment. Educators are rarely interested in specific dynamics, and generally they lack the framework in which to understand theoretical psychiatric material, which should be kept to a minimum, with elimination of psychiatric jargon.

Techniques Available to the Mental Health Professional

As more experience is being accumulated by mental health professionals working in the schools, it is evident that there has been an evolution of roles and techniques. Although there are differences in the amount of interest demonstrated by mental health workers in entering schools and that of educators in accepting their efforts, a resulting interaction can no longer be subsumed under the umbrella of classical consultation; new techniques are being developed that could be classified by the degree of responsibility and activism. Within the circumscribed area of dealing with the ranges of severely to mildly emotionally disturbed children, the following techniques are often used: education in mental health principles, consultation, collaboration, coordination, and liaison.[6,7,25,28]

EDUCATION IN MENTAL HEALTH PRINCIPLES

It is essential for the mental health professional to realize that of all professional adults in a school the teacher has the most constant contact with students and hence the greatest potential for effectiveness.[4] Many teachers come to the classroom without having had much experience with children whose egos are disorganized and weak. Mental health professionals need to share their knowledge of ego development, particularly as it relates to a child's concept of self and sense of being meaningful to others. Teachers must understand the child's approaches and the levels on which he communicates his feelings and attitudes and how these relate to the maintenance need of ego integrity. Some teachers need to know which classroom activities promote opportunities for increasing ego organization. Principles of child psychology, special education, and group dynamics can be integrated into the curriculum. A teacher may have to be helped to develop specific skills for communicating with an individual child so that the child is not confused by distortions and so that the teacher can carry out effective educational projects.[24] The hope is that, by educating a teacher in the principles of mental health, he may increase his repertoire of approaches.[1,13]

CONSULTATION

In the process of socializing the child, educating him, and coping with his tension, consultation between mental health professional and educator can be of help.[20] Interaction and communication between mental health professionals and educators come about when they [the educators] are having difficulty with some current work problems and decide that this may be within the province of the mental health professional's expertise. We should emphasize again that the same care of the multi-level process and sequential steps necessary in entering a system and establishing relationships should be reproduced in a relatively simpler setting when establishing consultation relationships with individuals.[4,30]

A teacher in special classes is often confronted with activity and behavior that are beyond the pedagogical sphere, and with which he cannot deal appropriately.[15] He needs to build up a repertoire of techniques for working with emotionally disturbed children. This is core material for him to discuss with mental health personnel. Consultation helps a teacher to increase his knowledge and diminish his feelings of helplessness and his lack of understanding.

Even though a teacher can become more and more experienced in handling difficult situations, there may be certain categories of classroom problems that will continue to create an unusual set of circumstances that he may not feel competent to handle and for which he would like continuous consultation. It appears that the need for consultation, and the value it has, increases according to the competence of the consultee. This is because

as the consultee becomes more aware of the mental health dimensions involved in working with emotionally disturbed children, he is more likely to benefit and profit from discussion with an expert.

Different categories of consultation between mental health professionals and administrators, special services staff, and teachers have been defined by many descriptive terms according to different authors.[2,31] Distinctions were made by Caplan[4] primarily on the basis of whether the focus of concern is on an individual case or on an administrative problem having to do with a special program or policy. He also distinguished between those cases where the consultant's primary job is to give his own specialized opinion and recommendation and those where he should attempt to help the consultee by letting him find a way of solving his own problem.

COLLABORATION

Collaboration refers to the process whereby the mental health professional actively helps a teacher and takes part of the responsibility for dealing with problems in the classroom or with specific emotionally disturbed children. It enables the mental health specialist not only to discuss and advise but also to participate in implementing a program.[18] He shares the responsibility of resolving problem situations; he and the teacher work together in ways appropriate to their respective, professional training and roles. The mental health specialist may sit in the classroom and participate in some activities. He may be part of a group session, including the child and his family, in an administrator's office. He may see the family and the child in his own clinic and then come to school to discuss the care of the child in the classroom. In collaborative situations, both teacher and mental health professional continually have direct contact with the child and his family; both contribute to the actual therapeutic program.[10]

In collaborating, the mental health professional accepts direct responsibility for codetermining what action will be taken, depending on the need of the child. In this type of working relationship between professionals, the differences between the value systems and goals of the mental health professional and the teacher tend to emerge very clearly. Many of the mental health professional's activities are of a very specialized nature and have no direct applicability to the classroom situation. However, his activities must be undertaken in conjunction with what is going on in the classroom; he should understand that he is most likely to enhance the therapeutic program if he keeps the specific teacher and school system clearly in mind. If, in addition to giving advice and guidance, the mental health professional is sharing responsibilities for a case, and if his expectations for change are not being met, hostility may develop between himself and the educators. It is important that the mental health professional's sense of a case's evolution be realistic, and if he finds that his frustration and anxiety make it hard for him to act as a collaborative ally, he himself should ask for consultation.

COORDINATION

We ascribe to coordination those efforts that mental health professionals make when they endeavor to link together departments or individuals who participate in the care of a given child.[29] For example, there are many occasions when children need special programs that clash with a school's policy and tradition. Individual arrangements may have to be worked out. In such cases, mental health professionals can recommend types of settings in which a particular child might function better. Frequently, children benefit from having a different teacher or a different peer group with whom to relate. On these occasions mental health consultants work with administrators whose job it is to form the groups and design the programs within the school.

A school is sometimes unable to understand the functions of different professionals in its own hierarchy as being relevant to the totality of care for a single child. A coordinator can help design a program that meets different needs of a child even though it may seem diversified or superfluous to school administrators. In such cases an aide or a nurse, for example, who does not ordinarily interact

educationally with an emotionally disturbed child, may be important in collecting all the information and executing the therapeutic program. There will be opportunities for group meetings, discussions between individuals, the sharing of responsibility by departments in a school that may not have worked together in the past. This affords the mental health professional the opportunity to practice both educational and consultative techniques.

LIAISON

The principle underlying the concept of liaison is that coordinated approaches enhance the development of comprehensive programs and provide follow through within the health, welfare, and education areas.[4,27] Liaison techniques have special relevance for low socioeconomic groups whose needs are varied and usually not met by the compartmentalized, fragmented, and discontinuous network of services existing in most communities. The mental health professional should try to stimulate and occasionally himself establish connections between the services, educational approaches, and activities of the school and outside community agencies. He should try to reach as many outside areas of activity as possible: mental health clinics, hospitals, welfare agencies, recreational centers, community legal services, police stations, and the courts. This is a new territory for mental health professionals working with emotionally or mentally handicapped children, but it is evident that many children who are involved with any of these outside agencies are in need of an integrated advocacy approach. Community liaison work is viewed ambivalently by some mental health professionals, who would rather like to ascribe this very large responsibility to school personnel. But the potential of the school as a mental health or human services center for a deprived child has just begun to be recognized, and school personnel will have to conceptualize their jobs in broader terms than they have in the past. Mental health professionals should see the school as the focus for efforts that not only reinforce the child's own capacities but also influence the total milieu in which he is living. And if mental health professionals can help inform school personnel about services available in the community, they can also promote the involvement of school people and parent groups in community planning, particularly when such planning concerns itself with mental health needs. The hope is that a school's active participation in community affairs will come to be respected and requested, contributing, as it can, a valuable dimension to the many programs needed for good child care.

⟨ Perspectives for the Future

Although the issues and problems brought about by the disruptive behavior of intellectually and emotionally disturbed children within the school system are not considered significant areas of concern for many school professionals relative to their major problem of educating the majority of students, it is emerging as a fighting cry for a large group of parents in the core urban communities who are becoming sophisticated in the needs of their children. The leadership is emerging from parents who are becoming cognizant of new mental health programs while participating as aides or ethnic indigenous paraprofessionals in community mental health centers. Through the work in the mental health or antipoverty programs they are recognizing the situation in the schools as an acute one and are going to be demanding more cooperative programs between professionals concerned with these problems. They are also beginning to use the component offered by the legal aid groups and learning to use the judicial channels as a way of obtaining better services for children with emotional disturbance or mental retardation problems. It is foreseeable that in the future the mental health professional will be placed in the stressful position of having to become an intermediary systems-bridge person, trying to help the overloaded, understaffed, underbudgeted school systems, which are dealing with problems that necessitate expensive and sophisticated manpower, versus the frustrated, long-suffering emergent em-

powered parents. This will necessitate a continued reevaluation and innovative efforts of mental health professionals who are working in one of the most potentially therapeutic systems to influence the mental health of children in our community. Hopefully the mental health professional will rise to this challenge.

⟨ Bibliography

1. BERLIN, I. N. "Mental Health Consultation in Schools as a Means of Communicating Mental Health Principles." *Journal of the American Academy of Child Psychiatry,* 1:4 (October 1962), 671–680.

2. BINDMAN, A. J. "Mental Health Consultation: Theory and Practice." *Journal of Consulting Psychology,* 23 (1959), 473–482.

3. CAPLAN, G. "Mental Health Consultation in Schools." In *The Elements of a Community Mental Health Program.* Proceedings of a Round Table at the 1955 Annual Conference. New York: Milbank Memorial Fund, 1956. Pp. 77–86.

4. ———. *The Theory and Practice of Mental Health Consultation.* New York: Basic Books, 1970.

5. CHESS, S. "Temperament and Learning Ability of School Children." In S. Chess and A. Thomas, eds., *Annual Progress in Child Psychiatry and Child Development.* New York: Brunner/Mazel, 1969. Pp. 125–136.

6. COHEN, R. E. "Anatomy of a Local Mental Health Program: A Case History." *American Journal of Orthopsychiatry,* 42:3 (April 1972), 490–498.

7. ———. "The Collaborative Coprofessional: Developing a New Mental Health Role." *Hospital and Community Psychiatry,* 24:4 (April 1973), 242–246.

8. ———. "The Gradual Growth of a Mental Health Center." *Hospital and Community Psychiatry,* 19:4 (April 1968), 103–106.

9. ———. "Consultation to an Open School." *Contemporary Education,* 44:2 (November 1972), 80–83.

10. ———. "Principles of Preventive Mental Health Programs for Ethnic Minority Populations: The Acculturation of Puerto Ricans to the United States." *American Journal of Psychiatry,* 128:12 (June 1972), 1529–1533.

11. ———. "Team Consultation in a School

System." *College Student Journal*, 6:1 (February–March 1972), 100–105.

12. COLES, R. *Children of Crisis*. New York: Dell, 1964.

13. DONAHUE, G. T., and NICHTERN, S. *Teaching the Troubled Child*. New York: The Free Press, 1965.

14. EISENBERG, L. "Racism, the Family, and Society: A Crisis in Values." In S. Chess and A. Thomas, eds., *Annual Progress in Child Psychiatry and Child Development*. New York: Bruner/Mazel, 1969. Pp. 252–264.

15. ELLIS, D. B., and MILLER, L. W. "Teachers' Attitudes and Child Behavior Problems." *Journal of Educational Psychology*, 27 (1936), 501–511.

16. FREUD, A. *Normality and Pathology in Childhood*. New York: International Universities Press, 1965.

17. GLIDEWELL, J. C., MENSH, I. N., and GILDEA, M. C.-L. "Behavior Symptoms in Children and Degree of Sickness." *American Journal of Psychiatry*, 114 (1957), 47–53.

18. GROUP FOR THE ADVANCEMENT OF PSYCHIATRY. *The Psychiatrist in Mental Health Education: Suggestions on Collaboration with Teachers*. Report no. 35. New York, 1956.

19. ———. *Psychopathological Disorders in Childhood: Theoretical Considerations and a Proposed Classification*. Report no. 62. New York, 1966.

20. HASOL, L., and COOPER, S. "Mental Health Consultation in a Preventive Context." In H. Grunebaum, ed., *Practice of Community Mental Health*. Boston: Little, Brown, 1970. Pp. 711–726.

21. HETZHECKER, W., and FORMAN, M. A. *Community Child Psychiatry: Evolution and Direction*. Philadelphia: Temple University, 1969.

22. HIRSCHOWITZ, R. G. "Psychiatric Consultation in the Schools: Sociocultural Perspec-

tives." *Mental Hygiene*, 50 (1966), 218–225.

23. JENSEN, S. E. "Children with School Adjustment Problems." *Canada's Mental Health*, 17 (1969), 33–34.

24. LAYCOCK, S. R. "Teachers' Reactions to Maladjustments of School Children." *British Journal of Educational Psychology*, 4 (1934), 11–19.

25. MACHT, L. B. "Education and Mental Health: New Directions for Interaction." *Elementary School Guidance and Counseling*, 47 (1969), 855.

26. MENSH, I. N., KANTOR, M. B., DOMKE, H. R., GILDEA, M. C.-L., and GLIDEWELL, J. C. "Children's Behavior Symptoms and Their Relationships to School Adjustment, Sex, Social Class." *Journal of Social Issues*, 15 (1959), 8–15.

27. NATIONAL HEALTH COUNCIL. *Health Education in Our Schools Today: The Need for Agency Action*. New York, 1965.

28. NEWMAN, R. G. *Psychological Consultation in the Schools*. New York: Basic Books, 1967.

29. RICHMOND, J. B., and COVERT, C. "Mental Health and Education Conference: A Report." *Archives of General Psychiatry*, 17 (1967), 513–520.

30. STRINGER, L. "Consultation: Some Expectations, Principles and Skills." In P. Cook, ed., *Community Psychology and Community Mental Health*. San Francisco: Holden Day, 1970. Pp. 95–102.

31. WHITE HOUSE CONFERENCE ON CHILDREN. "Educational Technology: Constructive or Destructive." In *Report of Forum 9*. Washington, D.C.: U.S. Government Printing Office, 1970. Pp. 1–16.

32. ZAX, M., COWEN, E. L., IZZO, L. D., and TROST, M. A. "Identifying Emotional Disturbance in the School Setting." *American Journal of Orthopsychiatry*, 34 (1964), 447–454.

PART TWO

Adolescent Psychiatry

CHAPTER 14

PSYCHIATRIC DISORDERS

OF ADOLESCENCE

Sidney L. Werkman

ADOLESCENCE is a period dominated by the concept of development and its deviations and directly related to earlier childhood in the intense metamorphosis of behavioral manifestations. Although a number of relatively static psychiatric disorders emerge during the adult period of life, adolescence is the time during which physical and psychological elements surge ahead together to result in many changing combinations of normal and healthy characterological results, as well as a variety of psychological distortions.

As the normal sequence of development must be known accurately in order for the clinician to comprehend and be useful to adolescents, this chapter will refer often to developmental issues. However, it will concentrate, primarily, on deviations from usual growth patterns that result in behavioral distortions and psychiatric disorders that are characteristic of the age period.

Several factors relating to development must be kept in mind constantly in studying and treating adolescents. Most adolescent psychological problems are the direct results of exaggerations, fixations, or inhibitions in expected growth sequences. These sequences must be dissected separately and somewhat artificially in order to be understood effectively.[5,10,12,13,15,23] Three different sets of coordinates must be kept in mind in order to understand the problems of adolescence: (1) developmental and chronological age and their related deviations; (2) the historically based social, psychological, and cultural advances and problems of adolescence; (3) the psychiatric disorders that characteristically arise at this time. We will define adolescence as a tripartite sequence, beginning at approximately twelve years of age and concluding at approximately twenty-one years of age, or when the growing person becomes settled on a career and achieves relative autonomy and individuation and independence from his family. The following discussion of the relation of developmental-chronological age to various disorders is summarized in the following list.

1. *Early adolescence (12–14 years)*
   a. Continuation of childhood problems (enuresis, inhibitions)
   b. Learning problems (defects in ability to abstract; problems in larger social network of junior high school)
   c. Obesity
   d. Acne
   e. Menstrual irregularities
   f. Anorexia nervosa
2. *Middle adolescence (15–17 years)*
   a. Rebellion and turmoil
   b. Running away
   c. Learning problems (inundation with primary-process thought)
   d. Sexual acting out
   e. Fighting
3. *Late adolescence (18–21+ years)*
   a. Schizophrenia
   b. Acute confusional states
   c. Career choice uncertainties
   d. Suicide
   e. Depression

⟮ Age-Linked Concerns

In early adolescence, approximately ages twelve through fourteen, psychological and structural changes in the body are of major concern. The adolescent becomes preoccupied with the effective development of primary and secondary sexual characteristics. Important milestones for the young adolescent are increase in body hair, genital, breast, and body conformity changes, and the onset of menstruation and seminal emission. Linear growth and changes in general body status are major sources of concern and anxiety. The myriad deviations in these developmental characteristics may result in a variety of symptomatic problems involved with growth. As the young adolescent needs to begin making a transition to a larger social network, it is exceedingly important that variations in body development be understood and dealt with in a healthy manner so that they do not become niduses for significant psychopathological problems.

In middle adolescence, approximately ages fifteen through seventeen, much somatic growth has been accomplished, and the adolescent, both because of greater ability and changes in his social situation, is ejected into a much larger society. During this time, the teenager must work out his relationship to his parents in a new way, develop external identification figures, and begin an exploration of questions of values and career.

Not unexpectedly, it is during this period that the most characteristic adolescent turmoil occurs. This turmoil is reflected in generally rebellious attitudes toward parents, an exceedingly self-centered quality, and turning away from traditional career and learning experiences. Because of the central importance of sexuality to the adolescent, many of his rebellious impulses are reflected in sexual disturbances.[22]

During later adolescence, approximately ages eighteen through twenty-one or more, the primary challenges are those of developing a sense of identity and a relationship to the larger society. During this period the adolescent may well founder on issues of career choice, sexual autonomy and expression, and the beginnings of true intimacy and shared cooperative love and work responsibility. Though defects in these developmental challenges often are not recognized until some years later in marital difficulties and serious defects in child-rearing practices, their seeds are found during this age period. Thus, adolescence constitutes a long period of development whose deviations and problems reach far into the adult years. It is valuable for the clinician to identify the adolescent bases of adult psychiatric disorders, for it is in understanding and reworking adolescent themes that therapy is accomplished even with people of considerably mature years.

While struggling with physical and social pressures, the adolescent must deal with a number of internal challenges and decisions. Biologically, he must come to terms with his own body and learn to regulate individually the great rhythmic patterns of food, sleep, sexuality, motor activity, and the need for sensation. Together with physical growth deviations, such psychosomatic problems as acne, obesity or unusual thinness, sleep disturbances, menstrual irregularities, and preoccupation with sexuality in the form of masturbation, inhibition of sexuality, or frantic heterosexual activity, as well as anger, aggression, and fighting, are seen.

Parental relationships must change. The adolescent must work through a healthy independence from parental domination, be able to accept his parents as they are, and work toward obtaining a nonincestuous love object.[14]

Socially, the adolescent must work toward the development of a system of values and responsibilities, a tolerance for frustration, and the ability to achieve reasonable impulse control and direct himself toward an adult economic status as typified in a career.

Finally, the adolescent must work toward developing a sense of identity, a sense of "persistent sameness within oneself and a persistent sharing of some kind of essential character with others."[10]

On a characterological level, the period of healthy adolescent development results in the solidification of a group of processes crucially important for understanding the technical problems and psychotherapeutic strategies of the period. Because of growth and hormonal changes, the adolescent is stronger, larger, more sexually mature, and capable of infinitely more effective, as well as destructive, cognitive, and aggressive acts than previously. All these factors, primarily expressed as a potential for competence, action, and overt motor skill, must be channeled, modified, and transformed in order for adolescence to be traversed in a psychologically effective fashion.

Because of this grouping of discontinuous forces, adolescence can result in most unusual problems. The intensity of impulses must be transformed and controlled in the direction of resistance to regression, while there must be an allowance for flexibility for the adolescent to experiment with and express impulses appropriately. The adolescent must have the good fortune to be offered appropriate role models in order that he may learn how to function effectively even during periods of great stress. He must direct himself toward a career, the crystallization of values, and a way of expressing sexuality that will be psychologically satisfying to himself and still acceptable by his general society.

Because of the large number of often competing pressures, adolescence is a period in which many lapses from psychological normality occur. Unless the diagnostician and psychotherapist are able to recognize grossly the difference between inevitable discontinuities in psychological integration, such as self-centeredness, moodiness, and rapid changes in identifications, as opposed to the deeply ingrained character problems centering around severe narcissistic regression or totally unresolved oedipal issues, they will make many errors in planning and carrying out treatment.

❲ Specific Psychiatric Disorders

Adolescent disorders can be divided empirically into two groups. The first group comprises those problems linked to the developmental stages described above. The second group consists of deeply ingrained intrapsychic difficulties and those of unknown etiology, such as schizophrenia, psychotic depressions, and some suicidal states. As we describe syndromes in some detail, it is important to keep in mind the various dimensions and coordinates described above, for they comprise a kind of interwoven foundation, each set of factors depending on the others for the understanding of the final development of categories of psychiatric disorders in adolescence (see outline which follows).

1. *Disorders of regulation*
   a. Sleep
   b. Eating
   c. Work
   d. Sexuality
   e. Aggression

f. Defenses (asceticism, intellectualization, intense concentration on athletics or hobbies)

2. *Transient behavior, mood, and thought disorders*
   a. Short periods of regression
   b. Moodiness, anger, intransigence
   c. Distorted sexuality
   d. Egocentricity, grandiosity
   e. Exaggerated ideological commitments

3. *Characterological problems*
   a. Rebelliousness
   b. Acting out and frank delinquency
   c. Sexuality, homosexuality, promiscuity
   d. Identity diffusion
   e. Depressive, obsessive-compulsive, hysterical character

4. *Neuroses*
   a. Hysterical and conversion reactions
   b. Obsessive-compulsive reactions
   c. Anxiety reactions
   d. Depressive reactions
   e. Phobic reactions

5. *Schizophrenias*
   a. Borderline (schizoid) personality
   b. Severe obsessional and panphobic reactions
   c. Simple and hebephrenic reactions
   d. Acute catatonic reactions

6. *Psychotic disorders of affect*
   a. Psychotic depression and suicidal pressure
   b. Manic-depressive reactions

7. *Psychosomatic (psychophysiological) disorders*
   a. "Growing pains"
   b. Orthopedic handicaps
   c. Skin disorders
   d. Rheumatoid arthritis
   e. Diabetes
   f. Peptic ulcer and ulcerative colitis
   g. Anorexia nervosa

8. *Historically and culturally linked symptom expressions*
   a. Drug use and abuse
   b. Innovation and rebellion in life style
   c. The communitarian movement and earlier separation from the nuclear family

Disorders of Regulation of Drives, Needs, and Motivation

It is tempting for the clinician to lump all adolescent problems together and see them as examples of the various configurations of rebellion against parents and society, the anxiety and guilt that constitute signals of unacceptable impulse, and the defenses that are erected to protect against the experience of anxiety. Such a classification, by its very global inclusiveness, ignores many facets of syndromes and disorders, even transient and historically based ones, that can be valuable in diagnosis, the prescription for treatment, and the treatment process itself. A description of specific disorders follows, but one must recognize the danger of being overly precise in a developmental period that is primarily characterized by alteration, movement, and transformation.

SLEEP

As a means of evading reality, regressing, and returning to infantile means of gaining satisfaction, sleep or spending a great deal of time in bed are important psychopathological problems. Unusual sleep patterns may also be a signal of the presence of overwhelming regressive fantasy activity and a preoccupation with masturbation. The inability to be roused from bed in the morning or staying up extremely late at night are examples both of attempts to stretch experience and of problems in internal regulation. Serious insomnia is a relatively new development of adolescence and in some ways mirrors the pavor nocturnus and sleep disturbances of very early childhood.[16]

EATING

Difficulties in this area are represented by fasting, the development of unusual and faddish diets, or frank obesity. The ascetic wish to deny all impulse gratification out of guilt, identification with great leaders, or a sense of grandiosity may be seen beneath many of the dietary quirks of adolescent patients. Such denial of eating may also betray severe depression. Obesity, a prominent adolescent symptom, usually represents a problem in perceptual inaccuracy, an aspect of regression or of difficulty in external control between the adolescent and his environment.[6,28] Like the other symptoms discussed here, it represents a regression to an infantile form of gaining gratification, a way that circumvents anxiety, and the need to deal persistently with contemporary reality.

WORK

One sees intense spurts of concentrated activity in school work, recreation, and creative activity. It is during adolescence that the astonishing poetic spurts are seen,[25] often as poorly disguised derivatives of drive activity. Excessive studying and an anxiety-ridden attention to learning, to the exclusion of other interests, are frequently seen in adolescence. A kind of work addiction may become a defense that hides the serious pain experienced by the adolescent. Conversely, many adolescents have great difficulty in marshaling their energies and spend endless hours in daydreaming, dawdling, and wandering. Together with work inhibition, one usually sees a regressive, compulsive masturbatory activity in the adolescent and a concomitant withdrawal from social activity. In such cases, the major issue is not that of sexuality but rather a pulling back from pressing personal problems.

SEXUALITY AND AGGRESSION

Orgies of denial, or direct expression of these impulses, are seen in episodic fashion during adolescence. The entire range of homosexual, heterosexual, and group sexual and aggressive activities are played out. Though sadistic or masochistic fantasies and acts, as well as directly sexual ones, are concomitants of most of the problems of regulation, they often are seen nakedly as expressions of direct impulse gratification and total difficulty in deferring or transforming impulses.

INHIBITING DEFENSES

Asceticism, overintellectualization, and intense concentration on work or hobbies or on athletics and body development are frequently seen.[11] There is a tendency for the disturbed adolescent to concentrate on a single defense to the exclusion of other mechanisms that might be more adaptive and to become a kind of caricature of a whole personality. He often lacks flexibility, reality-testing capacity, or perceptiveness in social situations. Though the healthy adult may choose from a variety of adaptation mechanisms to relate himself to society, the intensely egocentric adolescent finds himself at best playing a succession of often jarring, incongruous, incomplete, and painful roles.

All the disorders of regulation represent either a legacy of inadequately internalized impulse control mechanisms from earlier childhood, unsolved characterological problems, or frank regression. A further complicating problem for the adolescent is his built-in need for sensation, the wish to stay up all night, to feel intense pain or cold, to extend his body as far as possible either in gorging or denying food. Joseph Conrad described this phenomenon magnificently in *Youth*:[7]

I remember my youth and the feeling that will never come back any more—the feeling that I could last forever, outlast the sea, the earth, and all men; the deceitful feeling that lures us on to joys, to perils, to love, to vain effort—to death; the triumphant conviction of strength, the heat of life in the handful of dust, the glow in the heart that with every year grows dim, grows cold, grows small, and expires, too soon, too soon,—before life itself.

Thus, although it is urgent that he begin effective self-regulation of basic needs and drives, the adolescent is caught in a period of the most intense internal pressure to express these very primitive kinds of desires, sensations, and wishes. If he is not helped in the process of developing self-regulation, he will forever remain an impulse-ridden character.

Transient Disorders of Mood, Thought and Behavior

Short periods of regressive messiness and obstinacy, moodiness, anger, acting out, withdrawal, arrogance, or grandiosity are the rule during adolescence. This large range of disturbing affects and behaviors is by far the most bothersome aspect of adolescence to therapists and families. In part, such disorders represent a normal phase of development and must be tolerated. In part, they express the need of the adolescent to individuate and his groping attempts to do so. Such disorders also may be the result of a desperate kind of role playing or an identification with an intensely cathected friend or leader. Finally, they may be early symptoms of serious disturbances in thinking or personality disorganization. However, it is their very transience, changeableness, and variety of expression that label them as short-term problems, often of no ominous pathological significance.

Such disorders illustrate symbolically the discontinuity of development between growth and stability, rebellion and dependence, impulse and defense, and, at bottom, the struggle between love and hate. In this discontinuity and struggle, the adolescent, both consciously and unconsciously, reaches blindly for ways of gaining some stability and feeling of psychological comfort. It is in that reaching, which so often misses the mark, that we see the quick formation and disappearance of the symptoms described above.[20]

Characterological Problems

Characterological disorders are the ultimate crystallizations of difficulties described under the category of transient disorders. If developmental stages are not traversed adequately or unfortunate identification figures become available during adolescence, serious, permanent character deformations may result. Inhibition in social activities and inability to separate from parents sometimes erupt, paradoxically, into frank rebellion by the adolescent. Similar basic problems may be expressed as a continuing dependence upon parents far into adulthood for all kinds of social and intellectual pursuits. Excesses of acting out expressed through fighting, destruction of property, and other antisocial activities may crystallize into an antisocial character struc-

ture and, through harmful involvement with a punitive society, into a delinquent career. Sexual experimentation under unfortunate guidance may result in short periods of homosexual activity or a true homosexual character, promiscuity, unwanted pregnancy, or a continuing sexual search that is never satisfied. If adolescent problems are not resolved by the period of late adolescence, one often sees clinical examples of the continuing uncertainty, groping, self-deception, and turning away from life decisions so well discussed by Peter Blos in "Prolonged Adolescence."[4] Extreme egocentricity and disregard for the needs of others may become a part of character structure and make the work of treatment difficult. Intransigent views held for defensive purposes may alienate adolescents from their peers and from life experiences. Inhibited characters, shading into schizoid adaptations, crystallize during this period of life.

The hallmark of all the characterological problems described here is a relative lack of anxiety on the part of the adolescent about his behaviors and symptoms, together with extremely limited reality-testing ability, poor judgment, and little concern for future results of his acts. He is driven to continue his compulsively destructive demands on himself, his parents, and society and cannot easily learn to modify his voracious wishes and fantasies.

The basis of transformation of transient disorders into characterological ones often is the unconscious reinforcement of such symptoms by parents or society. Adolescents have great difficulty in finding reliable people with whom to share their perplexity and from whom, through sharing, to gain some insight into the meaning of their distorted behavior. In addition, if the society offers a great deal of secondary gain for disturbed behavior in the form of support of unusual behavior or increasing tolerance for alloplastic solutions to conflicts, the adolescent is faced with a great struggle to internalize his problems and then, necessarily, live with considerable anxiety and guilt. The easier and more usual way is for symptoms to become ingrained into character structure.

Neuroses

Though neurotic reactions may manifest themselves from early childhood through adult life, and all adult neuroses have at their core a childhood neurosis, it is rare for a true, well-structured neurotic reaction to occur until relatively late in the teenage years. The very interplay of surging motor development and activity, increasing societal involvement of the adolescent, and his need to turn from parents and other adult figures works against the internalization of conflict into anxiety, hierarchically organized defenses, and the ability to develop a sustained, therapeutically useful transference relationship.[1]

Younger adolescents often express conflicts through neurotic mechanisms, particularly phobic and conversion symptoms, but the symptoms are short-lived, changeable, and unintegrated into character and defense structure. Such symptoms, like the transient disorders described above, are almost the rule rather than the exception in adolescence. They represent, for the most part, examples of partially integrated sexual thoughts and fears that are rampant during this age span. Highly dramatic symptoms, such as fainting, seizures, blindness, and paralyses, still occur with great frequency in young adolescents and are often mistaken for neurological disorders.

Similarly, adolescents may experience overwhelming anxiety or panic reactions in response to loss, sexual fears, or guilt feelings. Such reactions present the clinician a difficult problem in differential diagnosis, for they may border on schizophrenic disorganization. Adolescents experience an intensity and anguish in their anxiety reactions that leaves little room for reality testing and investigation of the bases of an act or concern they have experienced. In all these symptom reactions, separated from those of character problems by the presence of extraordinarily intense anxiety, a striking peculiarity is the unintegrated, almost catastrophic quality they project to the clinician. Like a summer lightning storm, their pathological significance can only be assessed by observing them over time. Fortunately, many such reactions are completed in a few days, and the adolescent is able to return to his previous level of healthy functioning, often with little recollection or concern about the depth of danger or pain he had experienced.

Many adolescent depressive reactions and suicidal attempts are examples of the results of overwhelming anxiety that cannot be endured. They develop in response to what seem to be small stresses, are almost totally unamenable to immediate therapeutic correction, and are totally alien to the adolescent's usual way of functioning. They tax the therapeutic ingenuity and strength of the clinician.

Only in middle and later adolescence do we see a crystallization of obsessive compulsive neuroses with their attendant rituals, highly organized ambivalent thought patterns, and barely controlled anxiety. Though such reactions have their roots deep in early childhood and, retrospectively, can be seen as developing earlier in life, it is only when they begin to cripple the patient that they are clinically visible. Many compulsive adolescents get a great deal of secondary gain from their compulsive activity because of a number of factors. They often are highly productive and effective in prescribed, organized school work. Their hobbies and recreational activities, involving intricate, demanding skills, as expressed in stamp collecting or model making, are highly prized by the adult society. It is only when the adolescent must make his own social and career decisions and become more independent that his compulsive way of life is threatened by anxiety and disorganization.

Adolescents with hysterical character structures combining a great deal of histrionic quality, a seemingly infectious quality of relationship to others, a wish to please at all costs, and a brightness of affect, traverse the early years of adolescence quite successfully and without anxiety because they do please their teachers, parents, and other adult figures. When an hysterical mode of adaptation is no longer effective in life, a great deal of anxiety, depression, acting out, and disorganization may supervene. This occurs when the support and reflected appreciation of his elders are no longer sufficient, and the adolescent must begin to function independently and gain a sense of his own autonomy and significance from within himself rather than from others. Such adolescents founder when the supports of the adult world are taken away and they are exposed to the competition, sexual realities, and societal demands of an increasingly independent existence. Their symptoms may take the form of histrionic suicide attempts, hysterical psychosis, and caricatures of family roles.[2] When a family has depended on a great deal of repression, superego control, and overly rigid unwritten rules in order to control its children, the confrontation with the larger world is both painful and disorganizing for the adolescent.

Schizophrenia

Schizophrenia is the characteristic major psychiatric disorder of adolescence. It increases in incidence dramatically from the age of fifteen and reaches a peak during late adolescence and early adulthood, leveling off toward the end of the third decade. The borderline, or schizoid, personality, which had been protected by the dependent world of childhood, finds life made more difficult by the greater freedom and demand of adolescent social, educational, and sexual experience. Such schizoid, or borderline, adolescents find their adjustment made more precarious during this time, become anxious, and often regress into overt schizophrenic reactions. At times these reactions are slow in development, and at others they may be catastrophically acute in onset.[19]

Though simple and hebephrenic schizophrenic reactions become visible during early and middle adolescence, the characteristic reaction is that of an acute catatonic episode. Catatonic reactions are by far the most frequent schizophrenic disorganizations seen during this period and, side by side with the acute conversion reactions, constitute the bulk of emergency psychiatric difficulties during adolescence. Catatonic episodes can develop in a matter of hours and express themselves in great motor inhibition or overactivity, highly overactive and paranoid thought and speech patterns, totally inhibiting panic or desperate grandiosity. Fears centering around homosexuality, sexual inadequacy, or sexual guilt, together with a remarkable concern with philosophic and religious issues of a grandiose nature, almost universally accompany such reactions. Characteristically, catatonic patients have the ambivalent wish to change themselves or feel that they have been transformed into another sex. They wish to change the world immediately, to purify it and bring news to everyone else that has been given them in a revelation. Quite often such wishes are put into action in totally inappropriate and aggressive ways that are disturbing to the people in the patients' environments.

Though not clearly schizophrenic reactions, we see a number of severely obsessional and panphobic syndromes in adolescence. These patients suffer from all manner of doubts, fears, inhibitions, distressing thoughts, and severe relationship problems. It is the very pervasiveness, changing quality, and life-inhibiting nature of these symptoms that characterize them.

Fortunately, most schizophrenic reactions in adolescence, if well treated, result in successful compensations, entire restitution, or cure. The clinician may be surprised to observe a severe catatonic reaction clear up within a matter of several days. However, such resolutions are dependent on prompt attention and accurate knowledge of a patient's preoccupations.[9]

Psychotic Depressions

True psychotic depressions and manic episodes begin to express themselves overtly toward late adolescence. It is rare to see a full-blown manic episode during middle adolescence, and totally hopeless, self-castigating, delusionally impoverished depressive syndromes accompanied by weight loss, lack of pleasure in life, and total inhibition of external activity occur infrequently during the early and middle adolescent periods. However, syndromes of extreme withdrawal and psychotic suicidal pressure may, on occasion, be seen during middle adolescence.

Finally, it is most rare to see a cyclical manic-depressive syndrome until late adolescence. It is of passing interest that mania appears to be the last major psychiatric disorder to express itself in the human life span, except for the systematized paranoid schizophrenia disorders that may occur occasionally during later life.

Psychosomatic Disorders

Psychosomatic or psychophysiological disorders are particularly prevalent in adolescence because of the easily disrupted balance between surging bodily growth and psychological and social development occurring during this period. The teenager, pushed by hormonal changes and asked to take over regulation of himself in many new aspects of his life, may well express the conflicts engendered by such challenges either in the creation or exaggeration of somatic symptoms. Beginning with growing pains and motor awkwardness and extending into well-defined psychosomatic disorders, the adolescent is subject, because of the immense developmental pressure he is undergoing, to a large variety of psychophysiological stresses. Stresses may affect the functioning of the autonomic nervous system, motor activity, or sensory function. They may result in emotional conflict complicating the problems of acne, control of diabetes and other endocrine diseases, and in prolonging invalidism and regression following major orthopedic procedures. During adolescence, the most studied psychosomatic disorders, such as asthma, peptic ulcer, ulcerative colitis, certain types of headaches, and vascular problems, become significant medical and psychiatric entities.

Anorexia nervosa is, perhaps, the most characteristic adolescent psychosomatic disorder and will be described in some detail. It is a relatively rare, exceedingly intriguing, and serious disturbance of metabolic and psychological functioning that can be considered either a disorder of regulation or a psychosomatic disorder. Its onset is primarily in early adolescence, and it is far more frequent in girls than

in boys. Symptoms include decreased ingestion of food, hyperactivity, and general bodily dysfunction. Patients with this disorder refuse food, maintain that they have eaten more than they do, and dispose of food or hide it so that it does not have to be ingested. They also induce vomiting in themselves and, being exceedingly concerned about food, eat foods with minimal caloric value. Additional symptoms are amenorrhea and the secondary symptoms of inanition including electrolyte imbalance and slowed metabolic functioning in general. It is because of the electrolyte imbalance and the results of starvation that the disorder is so serious a medical emergency.

Because of the exceeding perfectionism, unusual and profound fears of oral impregnation, and depression, anorexia nervosa patients often consider suicide and make suicide attempts. Character structure in the disorder varies, primarily on the continuum of the severity of anorexia. Anorexia nervosa can be seen in hysterical characters, schizophrenic reactions, compulsive reactions, and frank depressions. However, the primary qualities are a refusal of food together with a denial that intake has been diminished, a frantic attempt at activity to decrease weight, and an intense preoccupation with food and food preparation. Regardless of general reality functioning, the patient with anorexia nervosa is truly delusional in regard to the fear of ingesting food.[3]

The course of all these disorders, whether they are primarily psychological in origin or exaggerations of somatic disease, often is crucially determined by the conflicts and challenges experienced by the adolescent.

Historically and Culturally Linked Symptom Expressions

A new group of psychiatric disorders has descended on the clinician in the last decade. The symptoms, if they may be called clinical symptoms, present as antitheses to or caricatures of conventional values and life styles of adult society. They are more a reflection of world view than any variety of conventional psychopathology.[8,17,21,24] However, these problems do confront the psychiatrist because of medical-legal difficulties arising from them, appeals from frantic parents, and rare requests for help from adolescents themselves. Keniston[18] summarized the issue as a "continuous disengagement by youth from adult institutions, confrontation with alternative moral viewpoints, and the discovery of corruption in the world."

The symptoms of these disorders include drug use and abuse,[26,27] changes in living habits, and radical departures from previous modes of movement into the adult world.[29] They confront the psychiatrist as a turning away from conventional expectations about thrift, a future orientation, ambition, usual career patterns, the importance of higher education, concern for amassing property, and living within the legal system. Instead of settling down, the late adolescent wants to be nomadic and moving. Instead of a belief in doing and accomplishing, his thing is "being" and not thinking about consequences. Language and conceptual thought have given way to quietude, contemplation, and meditation. Instead of an interest in developing greater competence in rational technological procedures, he has turned to mystic, magical, irrational routes of seeking his fate. Adult standards of dress, life style, and decorum are jarred by the adolescent's hippie clothes, seemingly casual sexuality, politically revolutionary ideas, comfort with violence, concern with transcendental meditation, loud rock music, mystical need for being on the road, and belief in "good vibes" that make speech unimportant. The interest of adolescents in protest trips, communes, rock festivals, coffee houses, free pads, and new communities within decaying parts of cities pose crucial problems in adolescent development practices, the nature of psychopathology, and clinical care.

❨ Conclusion

The adolescent period is the first one in which symptoms and behavior can be grouped into well-defined psychiatric categories. Whereas the younger child is seen as a behavior problem, the adolescent, unable to keep his deviant behavior and thoughts under the protection of his family or to successfully continue to inflict such behavior on the society, has one of three roads to travel. He may crystallize nonadaptive behavior into characterological defects, such as acting out and ego restriction, in which case he is either punished or ignored by the society. He may also turn his developmental concerns and thoughts inward in the form of anxiety, expressed as various kinds of neurotic, psychosomatic, or motor symptoms. Finally, symptoms may be expressed through suicidal behavior, depression, and schizophrenic disorganization.

It is of the greatest importance that the clinician dissuade himself from the conventional view that adolescence is a disease in itself, or, at least, that it is only one disease. Too often, clinical writing about adolescence emphasizes the problems of inhibited or rebellious adolescents, with concomitant suggestions for ways of developing therapeutic relationships and strategies that will foster expression of impulse or offer control. However, there is no single therapeutic alliance, drug treatment, way of speaking with an adolescent, or method of working with parents that can encompass the great number of now well-defined syndromes of the period. It is the responsibility of the clinician working with adolescents to establish a differential diagnosis of the adolescent and his parental and social network and then to offer a specific treatment plan for the disorder uncovered.

This chapter has emphasized the great importance of assessing symptoms over time, seeing them in the context of the developmental periods and challenges of the adolescent and of understanding the social setting in which the behavior occurs. Ensuing chapters will expand greatly on each of the categories described here. They will emphasize the importance of understanding the adolescent as a constantly developing organism who needs support and medical and educational intervention in order to allow him to continue to grow effectively and adaptively. Most of the disorders of adolescence can be seen as the result of unavailability of supportive help during developmental crises. When such help is available, transient disorders can be understood and lived through so that they do not develop into the more serious psychiatric difficulties described throughout the rest of this volume.

(Bibliography

1. ADATTO, C. P. "On the Metamorphosis from Adolescence into Adulthood." *Journal of the American Psychoanalytic Association*, 14 (1966), 485–509.
2. BARTER, J. T., et al. "Adolescent Suicide Attempts." *Archives of General Psychiatry*, 19 (1968), 523–527.
3. BLISS, E. L., and BRANCH, C. H. H. *Anorexia Nervosa*. New York: Hoeber-Harper, 1960.
4. BLOS, P. "Prolonged Adolescence." *American Journal of Orthopsychiatry*, 24 (1954), 733–742.
5. ———. *On Adolescence: A Psychoanalytic Interpretation*. New York: The Free Press, 1962.
6. BRUCH, H. "Psychological Aspects of Obesity in Adolescence." *American Journal of Public Health*, 48 (1958), 1349–1353.
7. CONRAD, J. *Youth*. In *Three Short Novels*. New York: Bantam Books, 1960.
8. DOUGLAS, J. D. *Youth in Turmoil*. Chevy Chase, Md.: National Institute of Mental Health, 1970.
9. EASSON, W. M. *The Severely Disturbed Adolescent*. New York: International Universities Press, 1969.
10. ERIKSON, E. H. *Identity: Youth and Crisis*. New York: Norton, 1968.
11. FREUD, A. *The Ego and the Mechanisms of Defence*. New York: International Universities Press, 1946.
12. ———. "Adolescence." *Psychoanalytic Study of the Child*, 13 (1958), 255–278.
13. ———. *Normality and Pathology in Childhood*. New York: International Universities Press, 1965.
14. FREUD, S. "Three Essays on the Theory of Sexuality." Standard Edition, 7:125–248. London: Hogarth, 1953.
15. GROUP FOR THE ADVANCEMENT OF PSY-CHIATRY. "Psychopathological Disorders in Childhood: Theoretical Considerations and a Proposed Classification." VI, Report no. 62. New York, 1966.
16. HALL, J. W. "The Analysis of a Case of Night Terror." *Psychoanalytic Study of the Child*, 2 (1946), 189–227.
17. HUGHES, H. S. "Emotional Disturbance and American Social Change, 1944–1969." *American Journal of Psychiatry*, 126 (1973), 21–28.
18. KENISTON, K. "Student Activism, Moral Development, and Morality. *American Journal of Orthopsychiatry*, 40 (1970), 577–592.
19. KNIGHT, R. P. "Borderline States." *Bulletin of the Menninger Clinic*, 17 (1953), 1–12.
20. LOURIE, R. S., and WERKMAN, S. L. "Normal Psychologic Development and Psychiatric Problems." In R. Cook, ed., *The Biological Basis of Pediatric Practice*. New York: McGraw-Hill, 1968.
21. ROSZAK, T. *The Making of a Counterculture*. New York: Doubleday, 1969.
22. SPIEGAL, L. A. "A Review of Contributions to a Psychoanalytic Theory of Adolescence." *Psychoanalytic Study of the Child*, 6 (1951), 375–393.
23. TANNER, J. M. *Growth at Adolescence*. Springfield, Ill.: Charles C Thomas, 1962.
24. WERKMAN, S. L. "Adolescence: 20th Century Predicament." *American Association of University Women's Journal*, 59, no. 4 (1966), 185–187.
25. ———. "Identity and the Creative Surge in Adolescents." In J. H. Masserman, ed., *Science and Psychoanalysis*. New York: Grune & Stratton, 1966. Pp. 48–57.
26. ———. "What Next? Youth and Drugs." *Rocky Mountain Medical Journal*, 66 (1969), 32–36.
27. ———. "Adolescent Drug Addiction." In S. L. Copel, ed., *Behavior Pathology of Childhood and Adolescence*. New York: Basic Books, 1973.
28. ———, and GREENBERG, E. "Personality and Interest Patterns in Obese Adolescent Girls." *Psychosomatic Medicine*, 29, no. 1 (1967), 72–80.
29. WEST, L. J., and ALLEN, J. R. "Flight from Violence: Hippies and the Green Rebellion." *American Journal of Psychiatry*, 125 (1968), 364–370.

CHAPTER 15

PSYCHOTHERAPY
OF ADOLESCENCE

E. James Anthony

❪ Historical Introduction

FOR REASONS that would strike a responsive chord in the minds of most practitioners, Freud[19] included therapy among the three "impossible" professions, the other two being teaching and governing. The psychotherapy of adolescence may demand, at different times and for different adolescents, the exercise of all three, which might well make it the most impossible of the impossible professions and therefore the one most avoided in practice. Anthony[3] has this to say about such evasiveness:

Psychotherapists, confronted by the adolescent, have put forward as many reasons and rationalizations as parents and adults in general for treating the adolescent with special care and caution or not treating him at all. They have argued cogently in favor of treatment but by other therapists and in other institutions. Many have concluded, on the basis of sound reason, that it is better to leave adolescents psychotherapeutically alone during adolescence because of their well-known proclivity to act out and drop out [and because] the vivid metaphors they have coined possess a strong deterrent quality. "One cannot analyze an adolescent in the middle phase," says one prominent author; "it is like running next to an express train." Another likens adolescence to "an active volcanic process with continuous eruptions taking place, preventing the crust from solidifying." Once the psychotherapist gets it into his head that he has to deal with a bomb that might explode or a volcano that might erupt or an express train that will out pace him, he will approach the treatment situation with very mixed feelings. If one adds to this array of stereotypes the reputation that even the mildest adolescents have for resorting to slight delinquencies at the least provocation, then the psychotherapist's reason for bypassing adolescence is easier to understand if not to condone.

A major source for the difficulties arising in the treatment of this particular age group stems not only from fixed preconceptions of the adolescent as a patient but also from rigid insistences on treating him by a single method.

Flexibility is the hallmark of good treatment practice at this stage, and to discard this principle is to ask for trouble. As far back as 1904, Freud[20] provided a balanced statement on this point: "There are many ways and means of practicing psychotherapy. All that lead to recovery are good. . . . [W]e have developed the technique of hypnotic suggestion, and psychotherapy by diversion of attention, by exercise, and by eliciting suitable affects. *I despise none of these methods and would use them all under proper conditions.*"* If this is true for psychotherapy, it is even more so for adolescent psychotherapy. Later on, Freud did change to the exclusive practice of analytic psychotherapy because, he said, it penetrated more deeply, carried furthest, brought about the most marked transformations, and offered a more meaningful and interesting experience to the therapist. He also had, naturally, a considerable investment in the practice of psychoanalysis. Though Freud never treated children, he had some experience in treating adolescents in both early and late stages and had developed considerable understanding of their psychopathology way back at the end of the last century. What follows is a contrasting account of a case of night terror as envisioned by Freud and by a contemporary psychiatrist (Debacker[10]).

Case History

A thirteen-year-old boy in delicate health began to be apprehensive and dreamy. His sleep became disturbed and was interrupted almost once a week by severe attacks of anxiety accompanied by hallucinations. He always retained a very clear recollection of these dreams. He said that the Devil had shouted at him: "Now we've got you!" There was then a smell of pitch and brimstone and his skin was burnt by flames. He woke up from the dream in terror, and at first could not cry out. When he had found his voice he was clearly heard to say: "No, no, not me; I've not done anything!" Or "Please not! I won't do it again!" Or sometimes: "Albert never did that!" Later, he re-

fused to undress "because the flames only caught him when he was undressed." While he was still having one of these devil dreams, which were a threat to his health, he was sent into the country. There he recovered in the course of eighteen months, and once, when he was fifteen, he confessed: "I didn't dare admit it; but I was continually having prickly feelings and overexcitement in my parts; in the end it got on my nerves so much that I often thought of jumping out of the dormitory window."

Freud refers to Debacker's conclusions as "an amusing instance of the way in which the blinkers of medical mythology can cause an observer to misunderstand a case." The sad thing is that such medical mythologies still continue to flourish in the present day and age.

Some question has been raised as to whether Freud explored the period of childhood and adolescence with as much openness as he investigated the adult. Lack of investigation of the early periods of life prevented him from making further discoveries, and his work with the younger group bears all the characteristics of self-fulfilling prophesy. In the case of Little Hans,[18] for example, he remarked: "Strictly speaking, I learnt nothing new from this analysis, nothing that I had not already been able to discover (though often less distinctly and more indirectly) from other patients analysed at a more advanced age." In 1900, he wrote to Fliess as follows:[22] "The new case is an interesting one, a girl of thirteen whom I am supposed to cure at high speed and who for once displays on the surface the things I generally have to unearth from beneath superimposed layers. I do not need to tell you that it is the usual thing." There is a certain developmental logic in assuming that what occurs earlier is merely buried deeper and that the instinctual substratum is the same at all ages. Nevertheless, this point of view tended to overlook the fact that a thirteen-year-old girl is confronted with tasks specific to her phase of the life cycle and with which she deals in ways specific to her developmental status. For the same reasons, she needs to be regarded psychotherapeuti-

* Italics mine.—E.J.A.

Comparison of Interpretations by Freud and Debacker

INTERPRETATION (FREUD, 1899)	INTERPRETATION (DEBACKER, 1881)
1. One would infer that the boy masturbated when younger, that he probably denied it, and had been threatened with severe punishment for his bad habit.	1. The influence of puberty on a boy in delicate health can lead to a condition of great weakness and can result in a considerable degree of cerebral anemia.
2. The onset of puberty and the tickling feelings in his gentials had probably revived the temptation to masturbate.	2. Cerebral anemia produces character changes, demonomanic hallucinations, and very violent nocturnal and perhaps diurnal anxiety states.
3. There was a struggle to repress these emergent feelings and impulses as a result of which a suppression of libido took place and transformed it into anxiety; this anxiety had then taken over the role of punishment with which he had been threatened at an earlier age.	3. The demonomania and self-reproaches are attributable to his religious education.
	4. Recovery took place as a result of physical exercise and the regaining of strength at the passing of puberty.
	5. The predispositions to this brain condition are probably genetic and congenital (past syphilitic infection in the father).
	6. They have classified this case among the apyretic deliria of inanition arising from cerebral ischaemia.

cally differently than in childhood or adulthood and to be treated technically in a different way. One has, however, to remember that this was in 1900 and that Freud was almost singlehandedly creating the discipline of psychotherapy. If one remembers this, one can better understand why he frequently extrapolated from one age to another, trying out a variety of techniques that he was in the process of developing systematically. In the same year, he wrote again to Fliess:[22] "I have a new patient, a girl of eighteen; the case has opened smoothly to *my collection of picklocks.*" With Dora, he was to find his most generally applicable and powerful "picklock," the transference analysis. He continued to experiment boldly with the psychotherapy of adolescence, and some of his methods can still be usefully applied today. A fourteen-year-old boy came to him for psychoanalytic treatment suffering from multiple tics, hysterical vomiting, and headaches.[21] How to persuade an adolescent boy to communicate, much less associate, at the start of therapy is a difficult problem for any psychotherapist in any era, but Freud tackled it in his usual imaginative style.

I began the treatment by assuring him that if he shut his eyes, he would see pictures or have ideas, which he was then to communicate to me. He replied in pictures. His last impression before coming to me was revived visually in his memory. He had been playing at draughts with his uncle and saw the board in front of him. He thought of various positions, favorable or unfavorable, and of moves that one must not make. He then saw a dagger lying on the board—an object that belonged to his father but which his imagination placed on the board. Then there was a sickle lying on the board and next a scythe. And there now appeared a picture of an old peasant mowing the grass in front of the patient's distant home with a scythe.

With this set of visual associations available to him, Freud was able to uncover the psychopathology related to a most unhappy family situation, demonstrating that it was the boy's suppressed rage against his father that had stimulated the apparently meaningless set of pictures and that represented the masturbation and castration moves in the operation of a serious oedipal conflict.

The so-called false connection, or transference discovery, of Freud was adapted superbly by Aichhorn[1] in his treatment of wayward adolescents, which he carried out extensively during the 1920s and 1930s. The transference relationship was not analyzed in the systematic way of psychoanalysis, but the pressure of transference was used to force action into specific channels and maintain it there. Aichhorn, as Freud pointed out,[19] intuitively and sympathetically practiced his own brand of therapy with delinquent adolescents, and psychoanalysis did little more than provide him with a theoretical framework. Since Freud himself was then of the opinion that wayward youth could not be analyzed because the analytic situation could not be set up, he was appreciative of the value of this analytically oriented influencing technique. This, in fact, was what it was, and it was, therefore, understandable that Aichhorn should compare his approach to high-powered salesmanship. Salesmen, like psychotherapists, pursued a definite goal with their clients, and the client needed to be softened up before he could be persuaded. In order to do this, the salesman sets up a situation of dependency in which he plays the role of superior, knowledgeable adult, at the same time reducing the client to the position of a helpless child who has surrendered himself to someone's will. The salesman becomes cathected by libido and is transformed into a transference figure. For Aichhorn, a number of "shopping situations" existed in the treatment of adolescents, and his method of "planned influencing" including the parents, who also needed to be kept in a state of dependence.

In a very modern sense, Aichhorn was extremely conscious of the transference network surrounding the treatment of the patient, which helped to modulate the parental response to the child's antisocial acting out during therapy. The resilience of the parent to be criticized, to be critical of herself or himself, and to be influential in the treatment, is gradually strengthened. Toward termination, the transference relationship is resolved, the parent is made an equal partner in the situation, and the libido displaced onto the therapist is returned to the child.

The therapeutic work with the parent can parallel the therapy of the adolescent child, and the family crisis with which treatment frequently began is gradually replaced by ongoing psychotherapy. The alternation of passive and active phases can surprise the patient into making profound changes. An empathic understanding of the parental superego can help such changes to be made and consolidated. Aichhorn's "shock" techniques and active-passive alternations, if used skillfully, can undoubtedly bring about dramatic changes in the life style of the adolescent patient. To use it successfully, the incorruptibility of the therapist has to be above question. When Aichhorn counsels the therapist to agree with whatever the delinquent says, share his views, and side with him against other people in order to win him over, there is an appreciable danger in becoming, or seeming to become, an adult delinquent in the process. Where the "juvenile impostor" is concerned, the approach can be startling. The therapist could plan a criminal project in detail with the young delinquent, drawing his attention to various ways of improving his methods of stealing. The various disconcerting maneuvers—taking the loot from him, planning a robbery with him, and finally, giving him money for his needs—are designed to leave the young person in a state of tension until the next session. Aichhorn was very successful with this "timely use of the factor of surprise" that allows the therapist to keep a step ahead of his patient. The method aimed at creating a dependency relationship and overcoming the initial and inevitable feelings of mistrustfulness. Much of this can perhaps be best understood as a preparation for bringing apparently unreachable and untreatable adolescents into treatment.

The borderline and psychotic adolescent was for a long time excluded from the psychotherapeutic situation, until Sechehaye[34] described a method of "symbolic realization" whereby the therapist would enter into contact with his patient at the exact level of his regression, however archaic this might be. Thus, a patient at a preverbal stage could be reached better by physical care than by words. For instance, a gift of an apple could be made a symbol of gratification and could thereby ensure the continuity of communication and contact.

The Preconditions for Psychotherapy

The psychotherapeutic treatment of adolescence demands a working knowledge of normal adolescence as well as the characteristic psychopathology of the period.

Normal Adolescence

Many normal adolescents are recipients of psychotherapy because clinicians who deal with them are not altogether familiar with the wide range of healthy reactions that occur at this stage. What would be designated, in terms of intensity, as a clinical disturbance in other parts of the life cycle is no more than an expectable disequilibrium at adolescence. The line of demarcation between mental health and illness is never sharp at any age, but it tends to be especially fuzzy during this transitional period from childhood to adult life. Transitional phenomena are characterized by rapid change, and previous and subsequent balances and compromises between internal and external forces and circumstances give place to unpredictable oscillations of feelings and behavior. Adolescence constitutes the most revolutionary step in human development. The revolutions involve massive physical and psychological changes that affect appearance, the mode of thinking, and the phase of reacting and interreacting. The revolution may be so sweeping that, as Anna Freud[16] remarked: "The picture of the former child becomes wholly submerged in the newly emerging image of the adolescent." The pregenital reactivations of preadolescence are replaced by the genital impulses of early puberty, and the new urges carry new dangers with respect to incestuous wishes and feelings. The need to keep these under control requires a constant deployment of defenses, but the emerging drives are sometimes so strong that a breakthrough from time to time is almost inevitable.

The whole situation is in a constant state of flux, so that we rarely meet the same adolescent twice. He is always in a state of shifting defensiveness, changing defenses, or releasing drives. In the interpersonal sphere, he moves forward to the accompaniment of a constant rearguard action against his parents. He both wants to be rid of them and to keep them tied to his needs and gratifications. He fluctuates between independence and helplessness, between progression and regression, between idealization and disparagement of the parent, between love, hate, and studied indifference. In his efforts to break the tie, he turns to his peers, treating the group as a whole as a surrogate to which he transfers his drives and identifications, receiving in turn its support and solace in his adolescent predicament.

The pains of this period can be so intense that adults in general suppress their memories of it. Adolescence, according to Anna Freud,[17] is quintessentially an interruption of peaceful growth, and therefore a steady equilibrium during this phase is by definition abnormal. It is important for the diagnostician to bear in mind that abnormality is the major characteristic of normality at this time. A Group for the Advancement of Psychiatry report, dealing with the same issue, pointed to the recurrent alternation of episodes of disturbed behavior with periods of relative quiescence stemming from experiments in submission and rebellion, in control and free expression.[25] The report emphasized that an alternation of this nature is frequently nothing more than "a temporary and essentially normal outburst of a more primitive behavior." Under ordinary conditions, the drives are once again brought under control, and the ego gains additional strength through the mastery of the new experience.

If one can speak of the normal abnormality of adolescence, one can surely describe a normal psychopathology of adolescence. To some extent, Deutsch[11] did this with respect to the female, and Erikson[14] depicted, in his epigenetic chart, the stage of role confusion that forms the negative pole to an integrated ego identity. The normal adolescent girl remains, said Deutsch, "completely childish" in her deepest being for a long period during puberty. She is frightened of her new self-confidence and her new responsibilities and, at the same time, is becoming increasingly aware of some of her frailties.

The watchful adolescent psychotherapist is alert to the increase of narcissism and its importance in the process of maturation and in the strengthening of the ego. The adolescent becomes acutely aware of the "I am I," and though this narcissistic force works toward a unification of the personality and an increase in self-confidence, a little excess of it leads to the "arrogant megalomania" that can make interpersonal relationships (and these include those with the therapist) at times exasperating. This narcissistic ego of adolescence is extremely sensitive to frustration, especially love frustrations, to the breaking of promises, to disappointment in the expectation of admiration, and to criticism, especially on the part of parents.

The second trait typical of the adolescent girl is her masochism, which Deutsch[11] regarded as an "elemental power in feminine mental life." The association between pain and pleasure derives from the genital trauma aggravated by the onset of menstruation, both combining to produce the female castration complex. One type of masochism originates in an infantile tie to the mother and the other from an overattachment to the father, with a concomitant masculinity complex. The third central attribute of adolescent femininity is passivity, which is in part a further conse-

quence of the genital trauma but also has constitutional and evolutionary antecedents. It is as though the little girl is awaiting true development into adolescence, "for something to happen to her," and unless this occurs, she remains unawakened and predisposed to frigidity. Her greater passivity makes her more prone to identification, more inclined to fantasy, more governed by subjective impressions and inner perceptions, and more apt to intuitive judgments. All in all, she has a lesser "reality potential" than the adolescent boy.

The psychotherapist, therefore, must be prepared for all three elements to enter into the therapeutic relationship. He will be constantly confronted by the girl's expectation that something will happen to her, that something will be given to her, and that in due time, the deficiencies in her developmental experience and endowment will be made up to her. The nuclear fantasies associated with these trends are narcissistic-exhibitionistic ones, involving fame in some form, the adoration and admiration of many, and masturbatory dreams in which she is the cynosure of these fantasies. The passive-masochistic fantasies involve the idea of violent seduction and rape in which a female figure forces the girl to submit to painful sexual acts performed by men. In dreams, terrifying male persecutors with knives in hand are breaking in at the window for the purpose of stealing valuable objects.

Passivity and masochism are less prominent in male adolescents, but the bisexual conflicts, the guilty reactions to masturbation, the anxieties over the changing body image and worrying incestuous dreams occur as frequently.

On the cognitive side, psychotherapy is enhanced by a new capacity for abstract thinking, for dealing with thoughts instead of things, for chains of free associations, and for a capacity to integrate and systematize large collections of ideas.[33] The adolescent patient becomes able to look at himself, to examine the processes of his mind, and to construct theories about his feelings, particularly when he is defensively prone to intellectualization. In addition, his newly integrated identity furnishes him with a sense of continuity and a perspective of past, present, and future, making him free to roam in thought and fantasy over wide sections of time and space. He has transcended the period of latency in which the child is incarcerated within the confines of the present and the concrete. For the first time, the individual at this stage of his development can see himself in perspective, can examine his life both internally and externally, and can formulate plans and programs for the future.

Diagnosis and Treatment Planning

Having acquired a good working knowledge of the normal range of adolescent responses, the adolescent psychotherapist must further orient himself to clinical diagnosis within the context of adolescence. He will then come to realize that the disorders of this period fall roughly into four categories: (1) those that begin in childhood and terminate in adolescence (many cases of enuresis, asthma, and epilepsy); (2) those that begin in childhood and continue through adolescence into adult life (personality disorders of various types); (3) those that begin in adolescence and terminate in adolescence as phase-specific disorders (situational maladjustment, identity confusion, and some cases of obesity and anorexia nervosa); and (4) those that begin in adolescence and continue into adult life (schizophrenia and a few manic-depressive psychoses). The classical psychoneuroses may fall into any of the four categories, but a careful anamnesis will generally disclose antecedents in a forgotten infantile neurosis.

All syndromes, except the massive inhibitions and the schizoid character disorders, acquire an additional adolescent flavor of mood swings, episodic changes in behavior, acting out, identity problems, intellectual and ascetic defenses, masturbatory and bisexual conflicts, and a general coating of narcissism and egocentrism. These adolescent elements superimposed on the basic psychopathology generate a quality of crisis characterized by more available affects, more fluid defenses, and freer communications. It is not surprising that many therapists, in practice, begin their treatment of an adolescent disorder by the technique of crisis intervention and subsequently proceed with the usual psychotherapeutic procedure. Nevertheless, it is at this stage that the neuroses of later life take on their characteristic configuration. Jacobson[28] has drawn attention to patients suffering from protracted adolescent problems who may still, at age thirty or more, show a typical adolescent fluidity both in their moods and in their symptoms, so that their clinical manifestations may oscillate from neurotic to delinquent, perverse or borderline.

Adolescent depression is frequently phase specific and reminiscent of mourning and unhappy love affairs. Jacobson described adolescence as "life between a saddening farewell to childhood—i.e., to the self and the objects of the past" and the as yet unknown country of adulthood. There is a general feeling among those who care for adolescents that too much is asked of them within Western cultural life and that this is what provokes the violent crises of affect, the painful depressions and despair, the severe guilt and shame and self-consciousness, the hypochondriacal preoccupations, and the constant fluctuations between convictions and doubts, all enmeshed in feelings of isolation and loneliness. Within a short period of time, the adolescent has to make renunciations of the past, undergo mental and physical revolutions in the present, face painful initiations into the future, and, at the same time, make binding decisions about careers. During this clash between progressive and regressive forces, there would seem to be a pressing need for a moratorium, and psychotherapy may help to provide this.

The treatment planning must be done in conjunction with the adolescent and take into close account the realities of his external circumstances. In assessing his response to therapy, one has to evaluate the positive and negative, the therapeutic and antitherapeutic forces at work in the environment. What goes on in the other twenty-three hours may be crucial to the outcome of treatment. In assessing capacity for psychotherapy, one is concerned with basic attitudes of mind, such as introspectiveness, psychological mindedness, proneness to aggression, transference potential, ability to form a therapeutic alliance, tolerance for anxiety and frustration, and sufficient skills for conceptualization and communication. Negative indications for psychotherapy would be an adolescent with a weak ego and superego, suffering from a longstanding, severe disorder, with a basic difficulty in looking within, conceptualizing, and communicating, and whose symptoms offer a high degree of secondary gain. Unfortunately, because of disadvantageous upbringing, a large number of adolescents fall into this category of poor potential. In these cases, a long period of preparation for psychotherapy or psychotherapeutic "management," in Winnicott's term,[37] may help to increase the quota of treatable patients. Good treatment planning, as outlined by the Group for the Advancement of Psychiatry[26] entails consideration of intrapsychic modification, alteration of intrafamilial functioning, changes of peer-group interaction, modification of school or community setting, and possibly removal of the child to an altogether different environment for a period of time. The more internalized the syndrome, the more focused is the treatment on the psychotherapeutic situation; the more externalized the syndrome, the greater need to bring about concomitant shifts in the familial and extrafamilial environments.

The Adolescent as Patient

The adolescent is an unpredictable patient for whom it is difficult to plan a complete course of treatment. Since dropouts are so frequent as to be characteristic of adolescent psychotherapy, it is possible that wide fluctuations in resistance and accessibility exist and that it might be good practice to carry out psychotherapy intermittently. It would seem better to do this as part of the general plan than to have it occur at less desirable phases of the treatment. Experience has shown that the adolescent in the early phase has many of the characteristics of the child in late latency, such as heightened resistances, outerdirectedness,

increased activity and aggressiveness, decreased tolerance for one-to-one situations, and poor communicativeness. These factors tend to make psychotherapy short and difficult during these two phases. In the midphase of adolescence, the patient develops some of the typical fluidity of the era and talks a great deal without saying too much or making too many meaningful connections. Communication is used as abreaction, and insight and understanding are resisted. In the late phase, treatment already takes on qualities of adult therapy, and the patient can be treated as a young adult who is accepting of interpretations and is developing a taste for insightful communications. In general, therefore, the ease with which the adolescent assumes the patient role varies with the phase of adolescence.

The adolescent is not only a patient in the psychotherapeutic situation, but generally carries his role into his external environment, where he is likely to talk to his friends about his therapeutic experiences, dramatize the interchanges with his therapist, and act out when the transference resistances mount up. His friends may hear his dreams before his therapist, and he may come armed with their interpretations. He may also maintain a reserve therapist in the form of a good friend to whom he may go in times of crisis when his own therapist is not too easily available.

The adolescent is not the patient for routine psychotherapy. Fluctuations, reversals, sudden progressions and regressions generally mark the course of his treatment. The defenses are never quite the same from week to week, and the range is between early infantile types, such as projection, denial, and isolation, to repression, intellectualization, and asceticism.

With many adolescent girls, the affects are forever "bubbling," as though instinctual impulses were constantly threatening to break through. In such cases, and in contrast to adolescent boys, the wish is maintained on the safe side of activity, so that masturbatory fantasies and latent homosexual crushes are more likely to be activated by treatment than masturbation and homosexual activity. The incestuous impulse in blatant form is also much more likely to invade the consciousness in the therapeutic situation than would be the case with boys.

With both sexes, the treatment environment is regarded simultaneously or alternately as dangerous and safe, and the adolescent, after an episode of courageous revelation, is likely to take flight. For both sexes, also, seductiveness, both sexual and intellectual, is often a primary weapon to keep the therapist under control. The unwary therapist who allows himself to respond too positively to such a maneuver may find himself treated as a seducer, to the temporary detriment of his therapeutic function.

In addition to the kaleidoscope of bubbling affects, varied defenses, florid dreams and fantasies, the instinctual danger also tends to stimulate creativity, so that entrancing flights of fancy and rich chains of associations may occur. This fluid interplay between primary and secondary process tends to make the adolescent a most interesting patient. However, with the settling down of the instinctual upheaval characteristic of this period, there is also a recession in this creative and artistic elaboration brought into play in the therapeutic situation. Many therapists have experienced a sense of disappointment when the adolescent returns as an adult patient and, in contrast, appears dull and down to earth.

◖ Techniques of Individual Psychotherapy with Adolescents

As Geleerd pointed out,[23] the adolescent is biologically as well as psychologically a very different individual in the three phases of adolescence, reacting differently to treatment in each phase. She felt that the therapeutic approach had to vary accordingly. Although she was speaking of psychoanalysis, this is equally true of psychotherapy. Psychoanalysis with adolescents, like psychoanalysis in general, focuses on transference, the analysis of defenses, and the interpretation of unconscious, repressed material. Geleerd felt that the analysis of adolescents differs from that of the adult patient in several ways: A greater effort has to be made to increase the tolerance of the ego to pathogenic conflicts; more help is needed in learning to test reality; less consistent and systematic analysis of defense mechanisms is possible or even desirable; and working through is only feasible to a limited extent. She also thought that the analyst fulfills a parent role, but in a more neutral way than in child analysis, and that the management of transference is different.

The analysis of the first-phase adolescent is extremely hard, and the unconscious life of the child seems almost nonexistent. The analyst is rejected along with parents and other adult figures, and the sessions are mainly filled with battle accounts from the home front. The same long preparation is needed as with children in late latency.

In the midphase analysis, unconscious fantasies are more available, thus the treatment seems to move faster against a background of greater fluidity. Geleerd warned that the analyst may have to guard against creating chaotic conditions.[23] During this phase, the patient may develop a crush on his analyst, superimposed on the underlying transference relationship. The transference neurosis is now seen in intimate form, and the patient may from time to time prefer to lie on the couch.

The analysis of the late-phase adolescent is more similar to that of the adult. Geleerd suggested that the patient may require explanations and encouragement to accept sexuality or aggression, but such educational measures are generally self-defeating as well as undermining to the analytic process.[23] Contact with the family is generally avoided except in emergencies. It is generally agreed, however, that in contrast to adult analysis, the person of the analyst plays a greater role in adolescent analysis, and many adolescent analysts have adopted the intermediate posture of allowing the adolescent to lie on the couch but facing the analyst. By opening and closing the eyes, the adolescent can then control to some extent the impingement of the analysis on his reality and fantasy.

The adolescent also strives to keep the distance from his parents under control, but even when he reports them as remote figures, a simultaneous analysis of parent and adolescent soon discloses the considerable extent to which the child is influenced by the parent in his imitations, identifications, acting out, and unconscious wishes. The adolescent often seems to recapitulate the adolescent struggles of the parent. The confusion of personal identity with parental identity thus becomes a real menace to further development, especially as the adolescent is involved in the task of disengaging primary objects and the giving up of infantile ego states, referred to by Blos[8] as the second individuation.

Individual psychotherapy with the adolescent is essentially ego therapy, and the goal may be anything from symptomatic relief to the furnishing of insight into relative unconscious determinants of the manifest conflict. Generally speaking, however, the treatment deals only with conscious and preconscious material, and only occasionally does the therapist interpret unconscious content. The ego is strengthened through suggestion and support, which help to break down resistance and develop self-confidence, and through the abreaction of tensions. Confrontation and clarification are two important change-producing mechanisms.

The beginning of treatment with adolescents invariably requires special handling by the therapist both in analysis and in psychotherapy. An introductory phase has been recommended for both forms of treatment during which the initial negative reactions are gently resolved, the strangeness of the situation made more familiar, and the complex phenomenon of feeling at home gradually inculcated.

The so-called normal paranoia of adolescence is exacerbated by the peculiar conditions of therapy. The therapist is perceived as threatening, his technique as intrusive, the situation as dangerous, the confidentiality as suspect, and the complete circumstances as a trap. For the patient, the immediate implications are that he is crazy and that the differences he is experiencing in his mind and body are indications of brain degeneration. The compulsively disobedient adolescent will feel impelled to attack the authority figure of the therapist immediately, and the uncompromising adolescent will refuse to budge from his prepared position, which would preclude his becoming a patient.

Many have felt that Aichhorn's method[1] of taking a patient's part in order to win his confidence and bring him into a positive transference is essential at the beginning of psychotherapy with the adolescent. The patient must become convinced that he is not the focus of an adult conspiracy and that his therapist is not in league with his parents to bring him to heel. For this reason, many psychotherapists accord the adolescent full adult patient privileges, contracting with him regarding time and money, and refusing to see the parents at the beginning without the adolescent being present to hear the discussion. They continue with this principle during treatment when crises arise and parents are interviewed, but only in the presence of the patient. No phone calls are made or letters written without the concurrent knowledge of the adolescent. Whereas Aichhorn[1] felt that it is necessary to avoid becoming identified with the parents or seeming to side with them, Ella Sharpe[35] felt that these initial resistances are inevitable and respond to direct interpretation. The therapist should not fall over backwards in this sensitive situation but try and confront it head on. Treating the adolescent with velvet gloves may only increase his suspiciousness.

All therapists agree that the negativism of puberty is a formidable resistance to overcome and is a primitive defense against emotional surrender, or complete submission to the therapist and a sacrifice of identity. Even in the most rebellious cases, surrender is always around the corner.

The major elements that are potent in overcoming the initial negativism and mistrustfulness of the adolescent in treatment are the unruffled equanimity of the therapist, his steady regard for his patient, his concern for the patient's welfare, his intense preoccupation with the patient's productions, and his unconditional acceptance of all aspects of the patient. Erikson[14] pointed to the inferiority engendered in the adolescent patient when his negative identity is brought into contact and, therefore, comparison with the positive, well-integrated identity of the therapist. The patient is well aware of his poor identity and is equally anxious not to have it submerged or destroyed by the curative process. In cases of identity confusion, Erikson stated that it is sometimes necessary to reach rock bottom, "letting the ego die," before healthy reintegration can take place. In addition to being a conspiracy, a trap, and a means to enforce surrender, treatment may also be conceived as a punishment, especially when sadomasochistic tendencies are uppermost. If the negative feelings, however, are dealt with as soon as they arise in therapy, or are even anticipated by the therapist, confidence in the therapist and his treatment is established, allowing for the development of a working therapeutic alliance. A further measure of confidence is attained during the course of treatment when the therapist demonstrates his continued equanimity in the face of violent affective fluctuations and persistent negativism. In the case of girls, the therapist has not only to allow for the usual fluidity of the period but must also familiarize himself with the shifts in fantasy that occur during the menstrual cycle, as shown by Benedek.[6]

Some Specific Technical Considerations

The acting-out adolescent, as is apparent from Aichhorn's management of this problem,[1] can tax the patience and ingenuity of even dedicated psychotherapists, who may come to feel the same sense of helplessness and resentment generated in the parents of such patients. The therapist is torn between his ideal of therapeutic tolerance and acceptance and the pragmatic necessity for imposing restrictions; as a result, his treatment posture may become inconsistent and, at times, even incoherent.

Bergen[7] strongly advocated the use of limits. In her experience, the adolescent who acts out may look upon even severe restrictions as an indication of a basically friendly approach, and many therapists have experienced (with some alleviation of guilt) the diminution in anxiety when limits are firmly set. Bergen felt that the conflict with authority cannot be handed over to the administration; it needs to be treated and worked through in relation to the therapist's authority. The patient with a weak ego cannot be expected to handle his own controls and may respond with some relief to controls from the outside as a temporary measure. Permissiveness in this case could create feelings of omnipotence with terrifying consequences for the patient. Working patiently within limits may gradually bring about an internalization of controls in a regular sequence. Because of results ensuing from his wayward behavior, the patient is driven to seeking help; he is well received by the therapist who respects his wish to cooperate in the establishment of controls; the restrictions are found reassuring, and even attempts at rebelliousness carry elements of cooperation. The struggle follows the early developmental pattern of internalizing controls and needs to be taken step by step because, as Bergen[7] said, the patient "needs to feel his struggle."

Theory can sometimes help to support the therapist in the difficult management of such cases. Acting out can come to mean something much more than just obnoxious behavior indulged in by the adolescent in order to provoke his environment. The therapist may come to regard such behavior as a desperate attempt to draw attention to the patient's predicament, as a cry for help. The therapist may also think of acting out as the equivalent to remembering, and since the recovery of memories plays a considerable part in the intensive psychotherapies, such as psychoanalysis, a serious degree of acting out may render the patient untreatable by these methods.

Still other therapists view this form of behavior in the context of the transference relationship and the resistance to its analysis. Such therapists would tend to control acting out by means of interpretation rather than restriction, but they may also find that their interpretations are often not heard nor heeded.

Delinquent acting out raises additional problems for the psychotherapist who may find himself, to his dismay, involved in time-consuming administrative and legal situations. Eissler suggested[12] that the delinquent, unlike the neurotic, needs to be treated in two phases, the first of which is preparatory for the second. According to him, there are three indispensable steps in the treatment of delinquents. First, in keeping with Aichhorn's[1] approach, the therapist must work actively at establishing a positive transference relationship, something that happens automatically in the treatment of neurosis. Interpretation plays only a minor role during this initial phase and is given only if it serves the goal of preparing for the second phase. The abatement of delinquent symptoms occurs when a working relationship is established between the therapist and the patient, which itself is predicated on the patient's experience of the therapist as an omnipotent but benign being who will use his power for the patient's benefit but never to his detriment. In the next step, the therapist relinquishes this role and assumes his habitually more neutral position, and as a consequence the delinquent condition is neuroticized, with the aggression being gradually replaced by anxiety. Aichhorn[1] claimed that he could carry a delinquent patient through both treatment phases, but the technical skills required are so different that a relay of therapists is generally preferable. The method can backfire and lead to an increase in acting out or exploitation of the therapist. Cautious optimism is a prerequisite in the treatment of all adolescents[13] but particularly with the delinquent type.

Anthony discussed[4] the difficulties of treating the clinical depression of adolescents, which he regards as an extension of the normal and expectable sadness of young people caught up in the adolescent predicament, imprisoned, as it were, within a disturbing developmental phase with often a curious pessimism with regard to getting through it. He describes two different forms of the illness. (1) The type 1 depression tends to show a cyclical development related to variations in self-esteem brought about by approval or disapproval by an idealized parent figure. In one part of the cycle, self-esteem is high, the mood is elated, and the patient eats well; following a narcissistic injury, there is a swing into a second phase characterized by low self-esteem,

self-hate, and feelings of extreme helplessness. The psychopathology is mainly preoedipal and based on a marked symbiotic tie to the omnipotent mother. Shame, humiliation, inferiority, inadequacy, and weakness are the pervading affects, and narcissism and egocentrism are extreme. The mother is seen as sadistic, disparaging, and reproachful. (2) The type 2 depression is more oedipal in nature, with a great deal of guilt and moral masochism associated with a punitive superego. The feelings of self-disgust often begin in late latency, precipitated by disappointment at the breakdown of parental idealization, and this leads eventually to the aggression turned against the self in which both self and hated incorporate objects are annihilated. The management of the type 1 depression is a function of the therapist's sensitivity to the cycle of self-esteem and of his understanding that the two parts of the cycle reflect two parts of the total psychopathological picture. He therefore works carefully at the self-depreciating tendencies during the low phase and with the abundance of good feelings and their significance during the high phase. The acceptance of the patient throughout the cycle operates significantly to break up this phasic development and dispel the patient's magical conviction that good will inevitably follow bad and bad, good. The crises of self-esteem are tactfully and gently interpreted and any apparent reproachfulness on the part of the therapist brought into the open. In the type 2 depression, the ambivalent dependency on the therapist may be extreme, so that even routine separations at weekends may become castrophic in their impact. As times goes on and continuity in treatment is maintained, the therapist becomes a stable internal figure that eventually allows the patient to retain an equilibrium in his absence. With both types of depression termination may occasion a resuscitation of hopeless and helpless feelings and a demand for prolongation of therapy.

The schizoid adolescent may come to psychotherapy in adolescence with a long childhood history of distant and remote feelings with regard to people. The problem posed is not unlike that of the delinquent and, for the same reasons, requires a period of preparation during which a therapeutic alliance can be established. The technical difficulty of making contact with the inner life of the patient is considerable, since the more one presses forward, the more he retreats, and the pursuit itself becomes unreal.

Anthony described[2] an approach making use of primitive memories in the form of sensations that he termed "screen sensations," since they cover deep, nonverbal experiences of a sensory or kinesthetic type. The treatment of such patients is often punctuated by the emergence of peculiar and unusual sensations, vividly experienced and vividly described, that seem to haunt the patient for a while as if resonating with some distant remote past. The screen sensations lead back to other experiences in latency, the preschool years, and finally to infancy, when the reexperience in the therapeutic situation is an almost ecstatic Nirvana experience of timelessness and spacelessness, with the disappearance of the ever-constant fear of submersion and annihilation. In the preparatory phase, the therapist permits the development of an intense symbiotic relationship, and after the emergence of the screen sensations, he initiates the process of separation that generates a more treatable neurotic disturbance.

There are limits to the therapeutic development of such withdrawn individuals where even the establishment of the initial relationship is quite an achievement. In this context, Anna Freud[16] remarked: "There are many cases where the analyst would be wise to be content with this partial success without urging further treatment. A further, and deeper, involvement in the transference may well arouse all the anxieties described above and, again, lead to abrupt termination of the analysis due to the adolescent's flight reaction."

Bryt[9] discussed the perennial problem of dropout from psychotherapy of adolescent patients. In the lower socioeconomic stratum, the dropout rate has been exceeding 50 percent. The factors may include selecting patients with little "psychological literacy" (in Slavson's terms[36]), inflexibility of the treatment procedures, unrealistic therapeutic goals, lin-

guistic and semantic incompatibility between therapist and patient (as Hunt emphasized[27]), and finally pessimism on the part of the therapist. According to Bryt,[9] a meaningful semantic framework is a prerequisite to the talking treatment of psychotherapy.

❲ The Role of the Psychotherapist

More than at any other stage, the adolescent shows extreme awareness and sensitivity to the person of the therapist and, despite his characteristic self-absorption, may evince an avid curiosity about the therapist's background; age, sex, personality, and ethnic origins may assume vital positions in the progress of psychotherapy. Liking and being liked by the psychotherapist are also important prerequisites that may affect the dropout rate. The major factor is probably that of the sex of the therapist. For various reasons, some male psychotherapists are extremely uncomfortable with female adolescent patients, and some male adolescent patients are extremely disturbed and threatened by female psychotherapists. Geleerd[23] warned of the dangers of unconscious seductiveness on the part of the psychotherapist, and the situation can be made even more perilous when he misconstrues his approach as therapeutic. There is no doubt that countertransference is a major hazard in the psychotherapy of adolescents, and Anthony[3] discussed its various forms.

Psychotherapists, like parents, may develop stereotypic reactions to adolescent patients in addition to the classical countertransference. In a more interpersonal way, therapists may dislike their adolescent patients as individuals, as well as particular aspects of them. Stereotypes might take various forms. The psychotherapist may view the adolescent as dangerous and avoid him, or as endangered and overprotect him. In the course of treatment, the countertransference feelings may become erotic and disturbing, especially when the situation is a heterosexual one. Once again, the need to get close may be translated into physical closeness. The patient may further con-fuse the issue. When, for example, he treats the adolescent girl in a way that he reserves for his child patients, she may react disconcertingly like a mature woman, so that his innocent maneuvers take on the guise of seduction; when he treats her like an adult patient at an appropriate distance, she suddenly "melts away leaving behind a little girl who cannot understand why she may not be loved in the old way." The therapist may also find himself getting fully involved in the sexual life of his adolescent patients and probe for unnecessary details for "therapeutic" reasons. The blatant homosexuality of some adolescents under conditions of treatment may also evoke strong rejecting responses in the therapist and an increase in his severity and seriousness.

Again, the therapist, like the parent, may find it difficult to fit himself and the adolescent into the same therapeutic situation and may become disturbed at the marked fluctuations in the adolescent's moods and object relationships. He may react at finding himself treated as a transitional object to be taken up and put down at the whim of his patient. With the younger adolescent, he may become disgruntled at the patient's obvious boredom and restlessness, his open yawning, his lack of communicativeness, and his monotonous reporting of external events. Once, however, the psychotherapist has accepted the fluctuating and erratic reactions of his adolescent patients as part of the therapeutic situation, he may be able to settle down more easily and comfortably to incorporating such problems into his technical approach, even to the extent of regularizing breaks from treatment.

The therapist, like the parent, may also envy the youthfulness, the youthful activities, and the youthful loves of his patients and may find himself responding with resentment and reproachfulness to the "good things" happening to the young adolescent. At the close of therapy, he may find himself clinging unnecessarily to his patient and prolonging the termination phase. In the treatment of depression, Anthony described[4] the almost contagious development of depression in the psychotherapist, sometimes followed by a counterdepression of exaggerated professional good humor. The psychotherapist can also respond to the patient's narcissism; treatment then becomes an endless source of gratification and little more. The masochistic trends concomitant with the depression may provoke small exhibitions of sadism that may build up and assume monolithic proportions in the patient's mind so that the treatment situation becomes a torture chamber. Anthony also described[4] the type of countertransference generated in the male therapist when treating a female adolescent patient with a type 2 depression. In the up phase, the male therapist is likely to envisage the inner space actually furnished with good objects of all kinds to be both admired and envied. In the down phase, these good things are drained from the female patient, and the psychotherapist becomes suddenly conscious of her deficiencies, her ungivingness, and her castrated state. The inner space, as Erikson[14] put it, is "the center of despair in the woman," and its emptiness is apt to affect the man who is treating her.

⟮ Conclusion

The relative weakness of the adolescent ego has led to many doubts about treatability. There are some who feel that the adolescent is best left to treat himself and find his own solutions with some support from the therapist. There are others who feel that treatment itself is a sort of moratorium to the adolescent in which the habitual reviews of his life history, as well as the regular sequential development of a therapeutic session, can improve his time sense and give him the feeling of continuity that he needs. Gitelson[24] was against analysis and recommended what he called character synthesis, the putting together of the fragmentary experiences and feelings of the adolescent. Zachry[38] felt that adolescence was a good time to institute treatment because this was when the growing-up child became introspective and aware of internal conflict. Others have stressed the need to adapt psychotherapy to the adolescent rather than the other way around. Above all, it is important for the psychotherapist to recognize the normal abnormalities of adolescents and not to rush in to treating them. What is normal for an adolescent has never been better stated than by Anna Freud:[16]

I take it that it is normal for an adolescent to behave for a considerable length of time in an inconsistent and unpredictable manner; to fight his impulses and to accept them; to ward them off successfully and to be overrun by them; to love his parents and to hate them; to revolt against them and to be dependent on them; to be deeply ashamed to acknowledge his mother before others and, unexpectedly, to desire heart-to-heart talks with her; to thrive on imitation of and identification with others while searching unceasingly for his own identity; to be more idealistic, artistic, generous and unselfish than he will ever be again, but also the opposite: self-centered, egoistic, calculating. Such fluctuations between extreme opposites would be deemed highly abnormal at any other time of life. At this time they may signify no more than that an adult structure of personality takes a long time to emerge, that the ego of the individual in question does not cease to experiment and is in no hurry to close down on possibilities.

❪ Bibliography

1. AICHHORN, A. *Delinquency and Child Guidance.* New York: International Universities Press, 1964.
2. ANTHONY, E. J. "A Study of 'Screen Sensations.'" *Psychoanalytic Study of the Child,* 16 (1961), 211–250.
3. ———. "The Reaction of Adults to Adolescents and Their Behavior." In G. Caplan and S. Lebovici, eds., *Adolescence: Psychosocial Perspectives.* New York: Basic Books, 1969. Pp. 54–78.
4. ———. "Two Contrasting Types of Adolescent Depression and Their Treatment." *Journal of the American Psychoanalytic Association,* 18, no. 4 (1970), 841–859.
5. BALSER, B. H., ed. *Psychotherapy of the Adolescent.* New York: International Universities Press, 1959.
6. BENEDEK, T., and RUBINSTEIN, B. B. *The Sexual Cycle in Women.* Washington, D.C.: National Research Council, 1942.
7. BERGEN, M. E. "Some Observations in Maturational Factors in Young Children and Adolescents." *Psychoanalytic Study of the Child,* 19 (1964), 245–286.
8. BLOS, P. "The Second Individuation Process of Adolescence." *Psychoanalytic Study of the Child,* 22 (1967), 162–186.
9. BRYT, A. "Dropout of Adolescents from Psychotherapy." In G. Caplan and S. Lebovici, eds., *Adolescence: Psychosocial Perspectives.* New York: Basic Books, 1969. Pp. 293–303.
10. DEBACKER, F. *Nocturnal Hallucinations and Terrors in Childhood.* Thesis. Paris, 1881.
11. DEUTSCH, H. *The Psychology of Women: I. Girlhood.* New York: Grune & Stratton, 1944.
12. EISSLER, K. R. "Ego-Psychological Implications of the Psychoanalytic Treatment of Delinquents." *Psychoanalytic Study of the Child,* 5 (1950), 97–121.
13. ———. "Notes on Problems of Technique in the Psychoanalytic Treatment of Adolescents." *Psychoanalytic Study of the Child,* 13 (1958), 223–254.
14. ERIKSON, E. H. *Identity: Youth and Crisis.* New York: Norton, 1968.
15. Fraiberg, S. "Some Considerations in the Introduction to Therapy in Puberty." *Psychoanalytic Study of the Child,* 10 (1955), 264–286.
16. FREUD, A. "Adolescence." *Psychoanalytic Study of the Child,* 13 (1958), 255–278.
17. ———. "Adolescence as a Developmental Disturbance." In G. Caplan and S. Lebovici, eds., *Adolescence: Psychosocial Perspectives.* New York: Basic Books, 1969. Pp. 5–10.
18. FREUD, S. "Analysis of a Phobia in a Five-Year-Old Boy." In *Collected Papers.* Vol. 3. New York: Basic Books, 1949. Pp. 149–289.
19. ———. "Psychoanalysis and Delinquency." In *Collected Papers.* Vol. 5. New York: Basic Books, 1949. Pp. 98–100.
20. ———. "On Psychotherapy (1904)." In *Collected Papers.* Vol. 1. New York: Basic Books, 1949. Pp. 249–263.
21. ———. *The Interpretation of Dreams* (1900). In Standard Edition. Vol. 5. New York: Basic Books, 1949.
22. ———. *The Origins of Psychoanalysis.* New York: Doubleday, 1954.
23. GELEERD, E. "Some Aspects of Psychoanalytic Technique in Adolescence." *Psy-*

choanalytic Study of the Child, 12 (1957), 263–283.

24. GITELSON, M. "Character Synthesis: The Psychotherapeutic Problem of Adolescence." *American Journal of Orthopsychiatry*, 18 (1948), 422–431.

25. GROUP FOR THE ADVANCEMENT OF PSYCHIATRY. *Normal Adolescence*.

26. ———. *From Diagnosis to Treatment: Differential Treatment Planning*. In press.

27. HUNT, R. G. "Social Class and Mental Illness. *American Journal of Psychiatry*, 116 (1960), 1065.

28. JACOBSON, E. *The Self and the Object World*. New York: International Universities Press, 1964.

29. Kaplan, A. "Joint Parent-Adolescent Interviews in the Psychotherapy of the Younger Adolescent." In G. Caplan and S. Lebovici, eds., *Adolescence: Psychosocial Perspectives*. New York: Basic Books, 1969. Pp. 315–321.

30. KOLANSKY, H. "Some Comments on the Simultaneous Analysis of a Father and His Adolescent Son." *Psychoanalytic Study of the Child*, 21 (1966).

31. LEVY, K. "Simultaneous Analysis of a Mother and Her Adolescent Daughter: The Mother's Contribution to the Loosening of the Infantile Tie." *Psychoanalytic Study of the Child*, 15 (1960), 378–391.

32. LORAND, S., and Schneer, H., eds. *Adolescence*. New York: Basic Books, 1961.

33. PIAGET, J. *The Growth of Logical Thinking from Childhood to Adolescence*. New York: Basic Books, 1958.

34. SECHEHAYE, M. *Symbolic Realization*. New York: International Universities Press, 1951.

35. SHARPE, E. *Collected Papers on Psychoanalysis*. London: Hogarth, 1950.

36. SLAVSON, S. R. *A Textbook of Analytic Group Psychotherapy*. New York: International Universities Press, 1964.

37. WINNICOTT, D. W. *Collected Papers*. London: Tavistock, 1958.

38. ZACHRY, C. B. "A New Tool in Psychotherapy with Adolescents." In N. D. C. Lewis and B. L. Pacella, eds., *Modern Trends in Child Psychiatry*. New York: International Universities Press, 1939.

CHAPTER 16

INTENSIVE PSYCHOTHERAPY OF THE ADOLESCENT WITH A BORDERLINE SYNDROME

James F. Masterson

THE BORDERLINE SYNDROME emerged on the modern psychiatric scene during the early 1950s as a vague, ill-defined entity comprising symptoms that ranged from the neurotic, through the character disorder, to the psychotic.[36,48,69] Psychiatrists gave it little attention; for example, the sole article on this subject in any psychiatric textbook to this date was by Schmideberg in 1959.[58]

In the last ten years the concept of the borderline syndrome has been greatly refined by psychoanalytic study,* which found that the basic psychopathology existed not in the pre-

senting symptoms but in a specific and stable form of pathological ego structure, a developmental arrest. Rinsley[49-57] described the clinical manifestations, the psychodynamics, and the intensive treatment of this arrest in adolescents. Grinker, Werble, and Drye[24] classified the clinical manifestations of this pathological ego structure in adults. However, the cause of the developmental arrest remained unknown.

The more recent developmental studies of Mahler[37-44] on the contribution of the stage of separation-individuation to normal ego development and of Bowlby[6-8] on the psychopathology of separation at this time of life when applied to the borderline adolescent has led to

* See references 2–5, 11–13, 17–25, and 59–64.

the theory that the psychodynamic cause of the developmental arrest was a faulty separation-individuation.

This theory laid bare the underlying psychodynamic structure of the borderline syndrome and so enhanced the understanding of transference and resistance that intensive psychoanalytic psychotherapy became not only possible but the treatment of choice for many of these patients. Properly treated—with a combination of support and analysis—patients can and do work through much painful regressive affect that results in a dramatic attenuation of their disorder.

This chapter briefly outlines borderline syndrome theory and applies it to the diagnosis, psychodynamics, and treatment of the borderline adolescent. It supports the point of view of Rinsley[53] and takes issue with the point of view most recently expressed by Zetzel,[68] that the borderline patient is seldom capable of tolerating the painful affect integral to the emergence of regressive transference reactions. As illustrated in this essay, many, though not all, borderline patients—given the appropriate therapeutic support—can tolerate this painful affect. These issues are dealt with in more detail in other publications.[45-47]

❲ A Developmental Theory

Since the clinical picture of the borderline adolescent is not what it appears to be, appropriate diagnosis depends on an understanding of the underlying psychodynamics. The fact that the borderline syndrome is the root of the problem is concealed by the patient's defense mechanisms, which mask his feelings of abandonment, and by his chronological age, which belies the infantile state of his character.

To understand this syndrome it is first necessary to understand not only the theory of the contribution of the symbiotic and separation-individuation stages to normal ego development but more importantly, the developmental consequences that ensue when separation from the symbiotic partner is burdened by an abandonment depression. The theory of the former has been creatively worked out by Mahler and her coworkers in their developmental studies while that of the latter springs from application of the work of Mahler and Bowlby to the borderline adolescent.

❲ Role of Separation-Individuation in Normal Ego Development

The symbiotic relationship can be defined as one in which the functions of both partners are necessary to each. The child's image of himself and that of his mother is of one symbiotic unit. The mother acts as auxiliary ego for the child, performing many functions for him that his own ego will later perform. For example, she sets limits to both external and internal stimuli, and she helps him to perceive reality, tolerate frustration, and control impulses.

At approximately eighteen months, the child, under the impetus of the biologically predetermined maturation of ego apparatuses —that is, his own individuation—which includes the physical development of learning how to walk, the emotional growth task of separation from the symbiotic relationship begins. The child now undergoes an intrapsychic separation and begins to perceive his own image as being entirely separate and different from the mother's.

This achievement brings with it many dividends for the development and strengthening of the child's ego, as outlined by Rinsley.[52] The child introjects the functions the mother had performed, for example, reality perception, frustration tolerance, impulse control, thereby strengthening his ego structure. The capacity for object constancy, that is, the capacity to evoke the mental image of a person who is absent, develops, and the defense mechanism of object splitting comes to an end. These latter occurrences will enable the child later in life to repair object loss by mourning.

Three forces—(1) the child's individuation process, (2) the mother's encouragement and support (supplies), and (3) the mastery of new ego functions—press the child on his developmental pathway through the stages of separation-individuation to autonomy. A process of communicative matching occurs between mother and child in which the mother responds with approval to the child's individuation cues. The mother, as the catalyst of the individuation process, must be able to read and respond to these cues if the child is to pass through the stages of separation-individuation to autonomy.

❨ Role of Separation-Individuation in the Borderline Syndrome: A Developmental Arrest

This theory, developed by the author, is derived from the study of the borderline adolescent and his mother. The mother of the patient with a borderline syndrome suffers from a borderline syndrome herself. Her pathological needs impel her to withhold support and encouragement of the patient's separation and individuation; rather, she clings to the child to prevent separation, discouraging moves toward individuation by withdrawing her support.*

Abandonment Depression

Therefore, between the ages of one and one-half to three years a conflict develops in the child between the developmental push for individuation and autonomy and the withdrawal of the mother's emotional supplies that this growth would entail. The child needs the supplies to grow; if he grows the supplies are withdrawn.[1] Thus arise his feelings of abandonment (depression, rage, fear, passivity, helplessness, emptiness, and void). The depression contains feelings of starvation, of despair and death, of loss of vital supplies often expressed by patients as a loss of oxygen or blood or a body part.

These feelings are intolerable and are han-

* See references 1, 22, 57, 54, and 67.

dled by the defense mechanisms of ego splitting and denial.[14,15] Although separated from the mother, the child clings to her to defend himself against the return to awareness of these feelings. The splitting and denial are further reinforced by various defense mechanisms: acting out, clinging, reaction formation, obsessive-compulsive mechanisms, projection, denial, isolation, withdrawal of affect.

The abandonment feelings continue to exert their overwhelming but hidden force through the tenacity and strength of the defense mechanisms used to keep them in check. These defenses, however, block the patient from fully developing through the stage of separation-individuation to autonomy. He suffers from a developmental arrest. He is caught, so to speak, in midstream, en route between two stages of development: He has separated from the symbiotic stage but has not fully progressed through the separation-individuation stage to autonomy.

Narcissistic-Oral Fixation

In order to understand the disastrous consequences of these events for the development of the child's ego structure, we must shift to another framework, namely, Freud's psychosexual continuum, which has common meeting points with the one we have been discussing. Freud spoke[16] of two phases, the autoerotic and the narcissistic, that precede the oral phase of development. Symbiosis is a narcissistic phase, and separation-individuation is ushered in by orality. It is likely that the developmental arrest of the borderline occurs either in the narcissistic or early oral phase. The earlier this arrest occurs the more likely the patient's clinical picture will resemble the psychotic, and the later it occurs the more likely the clinical picture will resemble the neurotic. In either case the developmental arrest produces severe defects in ego functioning. The ego structure remains "narcissistic, orally fixated." Two key characteristics of this ego structure, so important to an understanding of the patient's reactions to separation, are the persistence of object splitting and the failure to develop object constancy.[32-35]

Prepuberty: A Second Separation-Individuation Phase

The child's defenses enable him to function until prepuberty—approximately ages ten to twelve—when a second marked developmental maturation of the ego occurs. This growth spurt, manifested by a thrust toward activity combined with a turn toward reality, is similar in scope to the maturation of the ego that occurred in the separation-individuation phase.[10] This maturation together with the need to further separate from the mother produces a recapitulation of the separation-individuation phase of development, that is, a second separation-individuation phase.

Precipitating Factors

All adolescents go through a second separation-individuation phase in prepuberty, owing to the maturational spurt of the ego. In some borderline patients this alone precipitates a clinical syndrome; in others this internal event combined with an actual external environmental separation exposes the patient to the experience he has been defending himself against since early childhood—separation from the symbiotic partner to whom he has been clinging. This, in turn, interrupts his defenses against his feelings of abandonment, and they return in full force. The environmental separation precipitates the intrapsychic feelings of abandonment.

These precipitating factors—either the second separation-individuation phase alone or in combination with an actual separation—reinforce the feelings of abandonment and produce a clinical syndrome via the need for an intensification of the defenses.

The clinical manifestations will depend on the patient's unique style of defenses against his feelings of abandonment. Regardless of the type of defense, however, the two diagnostic hallmarks of the borderline syndrome are the abandonment depression and the narcissistic oral fixation.

In order to illustrate how these patients experience and deal with these abandonment feelings, it is most useful to choose a clinical example and follow the lead of Rinsley,[50,53] who suggested that the adolescent's experience is similar to that of the infants studied by Bowlby. These infants had to undergo a physical separation from their mother by hospitalization at the very developmental period we are concerned with, namely, during the first two years of life.

Bowlby[5-8] described these infants as passing through three stages: (1) protest and wish for reunion, (2) despair, and (3) detachment if the mother was not restored. The adolescent is unable to contain the affect associated with the second stage, that of despair.

A physical or emotional separation so reinforces the abandonment feelings that the patient's defense mechanisms intensify to the point that the clinical condition results. These defenses against the depression, however, interfere with the work of mourning so essential to further ego development.

The clinical picture portrays the repetition in adolescence of an infantile drama—the abandonment depression engrafted to the separation-individuation process which effectively halts further ego development.

Diagnosis

There are as many clinical types as there are defenses. The acting-out adolescent is used in this chapter to illustrate the five clinical characteristics of the syndrome.

1. Presenting symptomatology: acting out. The function of the acting out is to defend the patient against feeling and remembering his abandonment depression. It may begin with mild boredom, or restlessness, or concentration difficulty in school, or hypochondriasis, or even excessive activity of all kinds (physical and sexual). Finally, more flagrant forms of acting out appear—antisocial behavior, stealing, drinking, marijuana, LSD, methedrine, heroin, glue sniffing, promiscuity, running away, car accidents, and hippie-like behavior, including long hair, sloppy dress, and unsavory companions.

2. Environmental separation experience. The separation experience itself, though sometimes blatant and obvious, is more often quite hidden. For example, actual separations such as in death or divorce are obvious, but the experience may often be precipitated by such subtle occurrences as an older sibling going away to college, or a grandparent, a governess, or maid becoming ill; or merely by some change in the focus of the symbiotic partner's behavior, such as a mother who becomes involved in an affair, or is herself too depressed to care properly for the child, or one who might have to give most of her attention to a sick sibling. It is important to keep in mind that neither the patient nor the parent has any awareness of the profound significance of the separation experience, so the therapist must ferret this out by himself.

3. Past history (narcissistic orally fixated character structure). The parents have borderline syndromes themselves and are most often quite unaware of the fact that the patient has failed to negotiate the usual developmental stages. The doctor must pursue the developmental history on his own, looking for signs of prolonged dependency and passivity, developmental defects in ego structure, such as poor frustration tolerance, poor impulse control, and reality perception, which give rise to a host of symptomatic expressions from very early in life. These may range from disciplinary problems at home and in school to difficulties in developing social skills with peers, and include such symptoms as enuresis and obesity. Once an accurate history has been obtained, the clinician must assess the developmental level of the patient's character structure, keeping in mind the enormous discrepancies that can exist between developmental level and chronological age.

4. Parental personalities.* The parents themselves have borderline syndromes and have suffered as much from a lack of parenting as do their adolescents. Consequently, the parents, never having been mothered cannot mother, and never having been fathered cannot father. They perceive their children as

* See references 1, 22, 54, 57, and 67.

parents, peers, or objects. They cling to the children to defend themselves against their own feelings of abandonment and cannot respond to the child's unfolding individuality.[22] Thus the child is subjected to scapegoating of the most extreme sort.

The fathers, passive, inadequate men, dominated by and dependent upon their wives, play very minor parental roles. The mothers are controlling women who need and vigorously battle to maintain the symbiotic tie with the child.

5. Pattern of family: communication. These families communicate mostly by acts, not words.[1,68] Consequently, the adolescent expresses his need for help by an act, a plea for help, that expresses as exactly and poignantly as any words the blind, hopeless, trapped crying out for succor and aid. The final act that brings the patient to treatment usually occurs as the end point of a long series of gradually escalated acts whose goal is somehow to break through the vacuum of unawareness and/or indifference of the parents—to make visible the adolescent's drowning in his own struggle with his feelings. Despite these acts, the intervention often is still not at the behest of the parents but rather some outside figure, such as a friend, a schoolteacher, or even the police or a wise judge.

Let us now turn to a characteristic clinical illustration.

(Patient Anne

Fate struck Anne, a sixteen-year-old adopted girl, a particularly cruel blow at the age of ten when the maid who had taken care of her died and her mother became chronically ill with porphyria. The mother and father had a very distant relationship, the father spending most of his time at work so that the patient was left alone to care for the mother.

Anne, always a behavior problem, was unable to tolerate the feelings of abandonment and responded with heightened acting out behavior both at home and at school. At home she was rebellious, stayed up most of the night, and slept during the day. In school she resented the teachers and dressed inappropriately.

As she entered her teens, she started to smoke marijuana. At age fourteen she was taken to see a psychiatrist who said she was hopeless and recommended that she be committed to a state hospital. Her parents refused to do this but took her out of the public school system after clashes with teachers and sent her to a private boarding school. After one year there, at age fifteen, she was suspended for violating a number of rules, including visiting a boy in his room. At this time she had sexual intercourse for the first time, soon feared she was pregnant, and had fantasies of running away, taking the baby with her, and working to support it. Fortunately for her this event did not come to pass. After being suspended she returned to the local high school, where she remained for only seven weeks before dropping out. She was taken to see another psychiatrist, started treatment, and again would not talk about herself. The psychiatrist sought more information by means of Amytal interviews, which were also unproductive. Several months before admission, her behavior got worse; she began leaving the house to take long walks during the middle of the night and dating boys who were taking heroin. Finally her doctor insisted that she be hospitalized. She was sedated and placed in the hospital against her will.

Anne began life with the handicap of having an unwed mother of whom little was known except that she was fifteen years old. Anne early suffered a second reverse when she was adopted at the age of six weeks, presumably because the couple was unable to have a child, owing to the father's sterility, but more probably in order to preserve an already shaky marriage. Surely, this was an ominous beginning for a new life.

According to her adopted mother, she was a difficult baby, crying constantly and banging her head during the first year of life. A Negro maid, Louise, was hired to care for her. The mother said, "The three of us took turns rocking her to sleep. She was a feeding problem. She didn't like anything, she spit everything out unless Louise cooked it for her."

She had difficulties in school beginning in the first grade and disobeyed teachers continually. At five she was told she was adopted and that she was the chosen one for her parents.

Her mother said she had so much difficulty in school that "I would be in school more than she would." The mother tried to discipline her by spanking her or taking things away, but "Anne would scream so that I couldn't stand it." During the first six years Louise was the only one who could handle her. Louise was overindulgent, did everything for her, and took sides with her against the parents. The mother frequently felt angry at the maid, yet acknowledged her inability to manage the patient without Louise's help. When Anne was eight and one-half the maid left. The patient looked forward to her infrequent visits. Then when Anne was ten, fate stepped in again; suddenly and unexplainably Louise stopped visiting. The die was now cast.

Anne's appearance on admission was striking—shoulder-length black hair, partially covering her eyes, pale white skin, her only makeup blue and white eyeliner, giving her an almost ghost-like appearance. She dressed either in bluejeans with a black turtleneck top and black boots or very short miniskirts. She wore one blouse cut out on the sides almost down to the waist without a brassiere. When visited by her parents (as we had not yet learned to prohibit visits), she would demand that they bring in all sorts of unnecessary items for her—five more shirts than she would need—and she was particularly hostile and contemptuous toward her father.

Phase 1: Testing[*]

This phase, which extends from the beginning of treatment to the control of acting out and the establishing of a therapeutic alliance, is obviously crucial. Why is this first phase so important and what is its significance to the patient?

The adolescent with a borderline syndrome is defending himself against an abandonment

[*] Rinsley[50,53-56] termed this phrase "the resistance phase of residential treatment."

depression. Driven by the wish for reunion, he clings to and spends his efforts to keep alive the pathologic symbiotic relationship with his mother. His façade of resistance, though tenaciously clung to, actually masks a feeling of utter hopelessness—his despair and dread of abandonment, which stems from the impasse that has evolved in his relationship with his mother.

Although aware, at some level, that he needs help, he is frightened that if he allows a relationship to develop with the therapist he will risk reexperiencing the abandonment of his earlier relationship. He wants reunion, not consolation of his loss. His first unspoken question then will be: "How do I know you, the therapist, are any different? Prove to me that you have the capacity to understand me. Nobody else ever has. Prove to me you will not abandon me." The aim of the testing process is to answer these questions.

There is no therapeutic alliance as we understand the term. Words at this point are not used to convey or express feeling but to manipulate and test. Behavior is the principal means by which the patient expresses his emotions.

He employs acting out not only as a defense against feeling and remembering but also as a vehicle for testing. Although basically ineffective and self-destructive, acting out is perhaps not so painful for him as risking trust and placing his all-embracing symbiotic needs in the hands of a person he, as yet, has no reason to trust.

The adolescent patient must then conceal his need for help and engage in an elaborate test that the doctor must successfully pass before the patient will feel enough trust to reveal his painful state. He makes a virtue out of a necessity by extolling the benefits of his acting out while hoping his doctor will have the ability and good sense to see through him.[26-29] After all, what else can he do? He is grappling with overwhelming primitive conflicts, that is, wishes for fusion and fears of engulfment, on the one hand, and abandonment, on the other.

Let us return to Anne to see how the therapist handled this testing phase of therapy. The principal drama takes place outside the usual psychotherapeutic arena of words in the world of action.

The content of Anne's initial interviews was more or less as follows. She did not want to be there. There was nothing really wrong. Why should she follow the stupid rules? People do not live by rules. She denied depression, but said, "No, it is just a feeling of vagueness, numbness, emptiness. I'm not really unhappy; it is just that I don't care. All I really want is out." She wondered why she did not feel more depressed in a horrible situation like this. She hoped something would happen so that she could get out of the hospital.

Anne's initial acting out consisted of her exhibitionistic appearance in wearing miniskirts, her negativistic, sarcastic, flip attitude toward the therapist, writing provocative letters to her friends about hospitalization, procrastination in school, phone calls to friends to make provocative statements, and failure to keep her room clean. Efforts to limit the acting out were begun by forbidding miniskirts, monitoring her letters, limiting the phone calls, and expecting her to be at school on time and to keep her room clean.

The anger that had previously been dissipated in this defiant behavior now began to come out more directly. For example, "I'm not picking up this room. You can tell the doctor that if I am in occupational therapy and she wants an interview, I'm going to refuse to come down. If she comes near me I'll throw something at her face." In short, she is saying the doctor is unreasonable, she does not understand her, and she is "square."

At this point the patient was totally unaware of the relationship between her acting-out behavior and her emotional state. For example, she did not realize that after an upsetting visit or phone call from her parents, she would resume acting out by staying up late and dressing inappropriately.

The first breakthrough in her awareness of the relationship of feeling to behavior occurred about ten weeks later, when the doctor forgot to leave an order giving the patient permission for a visitor. The patient was furious but rather than verbalize it she acted it out, refusing to go to bed on time, wearing eye makeup and perfume and a shirt borrowed from one of the male patients. She remained in the next interview only five minutes and said: "This interview is a waste of time. You forgot what was important. You demand things of me, but forgot what was important to me." And she stormed out.

In the next interview, it was pointed out to her that she expressed her anger at the doctor in the same destructive manner that she had with her parents. In addition, it was suggested that verbalization might be more constructive. Still angry, she denied any connection: "People are trying to change me. When I get out nothing will change, I will still be the same."

After many interviews dealing with the relationship of feelings to behavior, the patient began to control her behavior. She now dressed appropriately and participated well in school. Her acting-out defense thoroughly controlled, the feelings of depression and abandonment against which it had been a defense rose to the surface.

Phase 2: Working through the Abandonment Depression*

Passage of the patient from Phase 1: Testing, to Phase 2: Working through, is signaled clinically by control of the major part of the acting out, a consequent deepening of the depression, and spontaneous recall (this time with more appropriate affect and detailed memory) of the history of the separation and abandonment.

The patient has now fulfilled the conditions necessary for the working through of the mourning process and other emotional conflicts in the interviews, that is, (1) the patient is now aware of the relationship between feeling and behavior; (2) she has begun to check the impulses to act out, which allows feeling to rise into consciousness and which also impels her to remember her past.

At the same time that conflicts are brought to the interview for discussion rather than acted out, words are used to express feeling

* This phase corresponds with Rinsley's "definitive" or introject phase.[50,53-56]

rather than to manipulate the situation. Finally, with the conclusion of the testing process, the patient, assured of the therapist's competence and trustworthiness, allows a therapeutic alliance to develop, which makes the first dent in the patient's feeling of despair and hopelessness.

The patient enters into a transference, which later will have to be resolved. Nevertheless, this relationship breeds confidence and allows the patient to work through the rage and depression associated with separation from the mother.

This change in the patient's clinical condition warrants a parallel change in both the therapeutic focus and approach. The focus shifts from the environmental milieu and behavior to expression of the patient's feelings in the interview, with consequent recognition and working through of the conflicts. The goal of therapy in Phase 2 is to work through the rage and depression at the abandonment, which lays the groundwork for the repair of ego defects through new introjections and once again starts the patient on her development through the stages of separation-individuation.

Therapeutic technique shifts from controlling acting out to working through in the interview, that is, from limit setting to interpretation. With the deepening of her depression the patient institutes a secondary line of defense, such as withdrawal, evasion, and denial, which must be interpreted by the therapist, thus bringing the patient back to accepting and working through the depression. At the same time, the therapist supports and encourages verbalization as a superior alternative to acting out for relieving the depression and for eventual resolution of the conflict.

ABANDONMENT FEELINGS

"After Louise left I started getting really lonely." Doctor: "What did you think about her leaving?" Patient: "I don't know but I felt more acute loneliness. She used to stay with me. I didn't realize she was good for me until long after she had gone. Mother told me she didn't know where she was. I had the feeling that maybe something happened. I felt nostalgic, something that was part of me was taken away." Here Anne literally reports her feeling that the separation involved a loss of part of herself.

Doctor: "Was that about the time you began to have trouble in school?" Patient: "Yes, I started getting called down. I didn't do well in the first part of the seventh grade. In the summer I really got close to Jan and Bill. We used to stay over at one another's house. Jan and I were always freer, we had less of a front with each other than I had with other people. I really was terribly lonesome."

"Mother started getting sicker then. I'd come home to a different friend's house each night, and father stayed in New York City." Anne then reported her acting out as a defense against the depression. "I think I would have talked to anyone. I didn't know what I felt. I mainly acted. I did whatever I wanted to. I don't think I have ever talked to anyone really deeply. I wasn't aware of feeling lonely, but I thought I really needed somebody. I wasn't aware of feeling lonely until one or two years ago."

RAGE AT MOTHER

As the patient slid further into a trough of her depression she worked through her feelings of being abandoned by her mother-surrogate Louise and then confronted the basic conflict over separation-individuation with the mother. At this point she began to near the bottom of her depression where lay feelings of homicidal rage at the mother and suicidal depression. "I never remember a mother-daughter relationship, maybe just a bit when I was young. I ended up hating her. I wish I didn't. Talking to her makes me pissed off at the world. Sometimes I could pound her into the ground. Then she'd get sick, and I'd feel bad, and I'd take her to the hospital. A couple of times she would come up to slap me, and I'd push her away. I felt I could kill her a couple of times. I wound up feeling sorry for her."

RAGE AND ACTING-OUT BEHAVIOR

"I don't think she ever knew what it would be like to love without convenience." Anne then suddenly recognized the relationship between her behavior and her anger. "It is funny, I thought I was doing all those things because I wanted to do them.

"I spent a lot of time with Bill. I'd be upset and he would come to my house, and then when he left I would be upset again. We would watch television or go to a movie. I'd also go to Jan's house. But when I was thirteen or so, Bill and I broke up, and Jan moved away. Things were still groovy in a way, but we were more separated.

"Then I started to smoke pot and go out with Danny. When Jan and I got together we used to look back to when everything was okay—two years before when I wasn't smoking pot. My parents didn't hassle me as much about Bill, and I stayed away from them as much as I could. I had stuff to look forward to, such as being with Bill or going to Jan's.

"I think that there is a kind of loss that goes with smoking pot. I was kind of happy but I knew that it couldn't go on, but I didn't want things to change so radically. I had to have someone to hang on to. I figured I could focus all my attention on Bill and Jan. I was out of school, nothing to do, just waiting and waiting. My mother expected me to be rotten no matter what happened."

EXPRESSING DEPRESSION PATIENT IMPROVES

With the expression of the rage and hopelessness the patient began to improve. In an interview a few days later the patient said, "I don't know why, but I feel more comfortable now, calmer, waiting for something to happen. Up to now I have had no hope. I have thought things would go on just like before. But now things do seem to be getting better, perhaps not completely changing. In fact, I am coming back to when I was comfortable, and I kinda expect things to keep getting better."

JOINT INTERVIEWS

After the patient had passed the bottom of the depression, namely, homicidal rage and suicidal depression, and when the parents had become aware of their conflicts in the parental role and had to some extent begun to learn a more appropriate parental role, it was necessary for parents and patient to be brought together.

These joint interviews had a specific and limited purpose: They did not attempt to do family therapy as such but (1) to expose the family myth; (2) to restore more appropriate patterns of emotional communication in the family, the patient doing now what she was unable to do originally, namely, expressing her rage verbally and working it through with the psychotherapist, thereby relieving the pressure behind the acting out and discovering a new mechanism for dealing with family conflict; and (3) to find more constructive and newer ways of dealing with family conflicts on the part of both patient and parents. This initial confrontation always arouses great anxiety, which immediately leads to regression on the part of both patient and parents. However, after successful confrontation and catharsis of the underlying emotions, the family is freed to seek better patterns of adjustment. This crucial operation finally brings a strong ray of hope to the patient.

Phase 3: Separation*

As the adolescent enters the separation phase he develops great anxiety, since the impending separation from the therapist revives all the old feelings of being abandoned, which then come to dominate the issue of separation. The patient responds to this anxiety as of old by regressing and acting out to impel the therapist to keep him in the comfortable, dependent position and not require him to deal with the anxiety he feels about the move to autonomy, that is, to being on his own.

He is afraid he will be unable to cope with his own feelings, parents, and life situation. In addition, he fears that he will yield to the temptation to regress and be drawn back into the old bind of dependency with his parents.

Separation as an Abandonment

Anne talked about experiencing the impending separation from the therapist as

* Rinsley's phase of "resolution" (desymbiotization).[50,53-56]

abandonment, and at last perceived that she was handling this fear by acting out in an effort to get the therapist to hold her back as her mother always had.

The therapist reinterpreted her fears with a discussion of the difference between separation and abandonment and reassured the patient that she would not have to move away from the security of her relationship with her therapist any faster than she was able. Anne then began to work through her fears of being abandoned, in the setting of the impending separation from the therapist.

She recalled the day Louise left, at age ten, and her feeling that people could only get so close. Much as she loved and needed Louise, she could not hold on to her. She then remembered her loneliness and anger at her mother for not fulfilling her needs when Louise left. Patient: "When Louise left, mother was pretty cold to me. She would be sick and sleep a lot. I would get home from school and go to my room. There was nothing to come home to. My mother wasn't even around to say 'Hello.' She really wasn't a mother at all. As far as I was concerned she was a grownup living a world apart from me."

As the patient returned to her fear of doing things on her own, the therapist reassured her about her capacity to handle things herself, and of the therapist's support until she was on her own—pointing out that the patient's life had been characterized by either overindulgence or abandonment and that there was a middle course until she was able to be independent.

Final Improvement

She summarized her treatment: "I have gone through three stages here: First, it was really hard and everything was drag. Second, then I went back to being a little kid, running to you and mama. Third, now it is okay, I am growing up at last, I hope it will be more like a happy medium between the dependency I hated and the freedom I feared, like you have talked about for a long time now." After this interview, which was in the middle of June, the patient gave no evidence of any regressive tugs, nor any acting out, nor any depression.

❨ A Libidinal Refueling Station

Our early unsuccessful experiences in attempting to send these patients either home or to a boarding school after discharge have slowly led us to understand that the hospital treatment, effective as it is, is only a beginning for the following reason: The patient has not resolved his separation anxiety, which continues to frustrate any effort at a close heterosexual relationship because of fears of engulfment or abandonment.

The manifold problems associated with the oral fixation, particularly the demand for an exclusive dependent relationship, have not been fully worked through. Discharge from the hospital, that is, from the caretaking apparatus, over and above its abandonment significance, leaves the patient open to severe oral frustration with consequent rage and depression due to his continued emotional need for supplies in order to build ego structure.

In addition, although the patient is somewhat freed from the old environmental conflict with the mother, he now engages in an intensive intrapsychic battle between his push for individuation and the anxiety and guilt that spring from his introjected maternal image. Beyond this, the patient's discharge from the hospital again raises the mother's wish for reunion, which she implements to pressure the patient to regress and return to the old symbiotic union. The patient, for his part, suffering severe depression and guilt, is severely tempted to regress and rejoin the mother.

The issue which dominates all others, however, is the patient's continued need for emotional supplies and for relief from anxiety and guilt in order to continue on his developmental way to autonomy. To meet these issues we are now in the process of setting up another caretaking facility—a halfway house—which can be used as a libidinal refueling station until the patient is emotionally ready to go off on his own. Our patients will be able to put the halfway house to a use similar to that of the normal toddler who returns to the mother

for libidinal refueling as an aid in his journey. In addition, to minimize some of the separation anxiety, we have arranged to have the patient continue with his inpatient therapist for a second outpatient year.

In the meantime, we have been placing our patients with relatives or at boarding schools. Freed from the regressive pull of constant contact with their parents and supported by a continuing relationship with their therapists, the patients are far better able to cope with their intensive intrapsychic conflicts. The vicissitudes of this therapeutic struggle are described in other publications.[46,47]

Although the borderline adolescent's problem is severe, and therefore his therapeutic requirements high, there is no reason for discouragement. If we have understood and properly treated the patient's pathology, we will have made it possible for him once again to harness the enormous power of his own inherent growth potential to his own ego development.

❨ Bibliography

1. BATESON, C. F., MISHLER, E. G., and WAXLER, N. E. *Family Processes and Schizophrenia.* New York: Science House, 1968.
2. BENEDEK, T. "Adaptation of Reality in Early Infancy." *Psychoanalytic Quarterly,* 7 (1938), 200–215.
3. ———. "The Psychosomatic Implications of the Primary Unit: Mother-Child." *American Journal of Orthopsychiatry,* 19 (1949), 642–654.
4. ———. "Psychobiological Aspects of Mothering." *American Journal of Orthopsychiatry,* 26 (1956), 272–278.
5. ———. "Parenthood as a Developmental Phase." *Journal of the American Psychoanalytic Association,* 7 (1959), 389–417.
6. BOWLBY, J. "Grief and Mourning in Infancy and Early Childhood." *Psychoanalytic Study of the Child,* 15 (1960), 9–52.
7. ———. "Separation Anxiety." *International Journal of Psycho-Analysis,* 41 (1960), 89–113.
8. ———. *Attachment and Loss.* Vol. 1. New York: Basic Books, 1969.
9. DEUTSCH, H. "Some Forms of Emotional Disturbances and Their Relationship to Schiz-

ophrenia." *Psychoanalytic Quarterly*, 11 (1942), 301–321. (Also, rev., in H. Deutsch, *Neuroses and Character Types*. New York: International Universities Press, 1965. Pp. 262–281.)

10. ———. *The Psychology of Woman*. Vol. 1. New York: Grune & Stratton, 1944.

11. EKSTEIN, R., and WALLERSTEIN, J. "Observations on the Psychology of Borderline and Psychotic Children." *Psychoanalytic Study of the Child*, 9 (1954), 344–469.

12. FAIRBAIRN, W. R. D. "A Revised Psychopathology of the Psychoses and Psychoneuroses." In *An Object-Relations Theory of the Personality*. New York: Basic Books, 1954.

13. FRAIBERG, S. "Libidinal Object Constancy and Mental Representation." *Psychoanalytic Study of the Child*, 24 (1969), 9–47.

14. FREUD, S. "Fetishism" (1927). *Collected Papers*. Vol. 5. New York: Basic Books, 1959. Pp. 198–204.

15. ———. "Splitting of the Ego in the Defensive Process" (1938). *Collected Papers*. Vol. 5. New York: Basic Books, 1959. Pp. 372–375.

16. ———. "On Narcissism: An Introduction" (1914). *Collected Papers*. Vol. 4. New York: Basic Books, 1959. Pp. 30–59.

17. GIOVACCHINI, P. L. "The Submerged Ego." *Journal of the American Academy of Child Psychiatry*, 3, no. 3 (July 1964).

18. ———. "Maternal Introjection and Ego Defect." *Journal of the American Academy of Child Psychiatry*, 4, no. 2 (April 1965).

19. ———. "Transference, Incorporation and Synthesis." *International Journal of Psycho-Analysis*, 46, pt. 3 (1965).

20. ———. "The Frozen Introject." *International Journal of Psycho-Analysis*, 48, pt. 1 (1967).

21. ———. "Frustration and Externalization." *Psychoanalytic Quarterly*, 36 (1967), 571–583.

22. ———. "Effects of Adaptive and Disruptive Aspects of Early Object Relationships and Later Parental Functioning." In E. J. Anthony and T. Benedek, eds., *Parenthood*. Boston: Little, Brown, 1970.

23. ———, et al. "On Regression: A Workshop." John A. Lindon, ed., *Psychoanalytic Forum*, 2, no. 4 (Winter 1967).

24. GRINKER, R. R., WERBLE, B., and DRYE, R. *The Borderline Syndrome*. New York: Basic Books, 1968.

25. GUNTRIP, H. *Personality Structure and Human Interaction*. New York: International Universities Press, 1964.

26. HENDRICKSON, W. J., and HOLMES, D. J. "Control of Behavior as a Crucial Factor in Intensive Psychiatric Treatment in an All Adolescent Ward." *American Journal of Psychiatry*, 115 (1959), 11.

27. ———. *Institutional Psychotherapy of the Delinquent: Progress in Psychotherapy*. Vol. 5. New York: Grune & Stratton, 1960.

28. ———, and WAGGONER, R. W. "Psychotherapy of the Hospitalized Adolescent." *American Journal of Psychiatry*, 116 (1959), 6.

29. HOLMES, D. J. *The Adolescent in Psychotherapy*. Vol. 5. Boston: Little, Brown, 1964.

30. JACOBSON, E. *The Self and the Object World*. New York: International Universities Press, 1964.

31. KERNBERG, O. "Borderline Personality Organization." *Journal of the American Psychoanalytic Association*, 15 (1967), 641–685.

32. KLEIN, M. *The Psycho-Analysis of Children*, London: Hogarth, 1932.

33. ———. "Notes on Some Schizoid Mechanisms." In J. Riviere, ed., *Developments in Psycho-Analysis*. London: Hogarth, 1946.

34. ———. "Contribution to the Psychogenesis of Manic Depressive States." In *Contributions to Psycho-Analysis, 1921–1945*. London: Hogarth, 1948. Pp. 282–310.

35. ———. "Mourning and Its Relation to Manic Depressive States." In *Contributions to Psycho-Analysis, 1921–1945*. London: Hogarth, 1948. Pp. 311–338.

36. KNIGHT, R. P., ed. "Borderline States." In *Psychoanalytic Psychiatry and Psychology*. New York: International Universities Press, 1954. Pp. 97–109.

37. MAHLER, M. S. "Autism and Symbiosis: Two Extreme Disturbances of Identity." *International Journal of Psychoanalysis*, 39 (1958), 77–83.

38. ———. "Thoughts About Development and Individuation." *Psychoanalytic Study of the Child*, 18 (1963), 307–324.

39. ———. "On the Significance of the Normal Separation-Individuation Phase." In M. Schur, ed., *Drives, Affects and Behavior*, Vol. 2. New York: International Universities Press, 1965. Pp. 161–169.

40. ———. *On Human Symbiosis and the Vicis-*

situdes of Individuation. New York: International Universities Press, 1968.

41. ———, and FURER, M. "Certain Aspects of the Separation-Individuation Phase." *Psychoanalytic Quarterly,* 32 (1963), 1–14.

42. ———, and LAPERRIERE, R. "Mother-Child Interaction During Separation-Individuation." *Psychoanalytic Quarterly,* 34 (1965), 483–489.

43. ———, and McDEVITT, J. "Observations on Adaptation and Defense in Statu Nascendi." *Psychoanalytic Quarterly,* 37 (1968), 1–21.

44. ———, PINE, F., and BERGMAN, A. "The Mother's Reaction to Her Toddler's Drive for Individuation." In E. J. Anthony and T. Benedek, eds., *Parenthood.* Boston: Little, Brown, 1970.

45. MASTERSON, J. F. "Treatment of the Adolescent with Borderline Syndrome: A Problem in Separation-Individuation." *Bulletin of the Menninger Clinic,* 35 (1971), 5–18.

46. ———. "Intensive Psychotherapy of the Borderline Adolescent." *Annals of Adolescent Psychiatry,* 2 (1973), 240–268.

47. ———. *Treatment of the Borderline Adolescent—A Developmental Approach.* New York: Wiley, 1972.

48. RICKMAN, J. "The Development of the Psycho-Analytic Theory of the Psychoses, 1893–1926." London: Baillière, Tindall & Cox, 1928.

49. RINSLEY, D. B. "Psychiatric Hospital Treatment with Special Reference to Children." *Archives of General Psychiatry,* 9 (1963), 489–496.

50. ———. "Intensive Psychiatric Hospital Treatment of Adolescents: An Object-Relations View." *Psychiatric Quarterly,* 30 (July 1965), 405–429.

51. ———. "The Adolescent in Residential Treatment: Some Critical Reflections." *Adolescence,* 2, no. 5 (Spring 1967), 83–95.

52. ———. "Economic Aspects of the Object Relations." *International Journal of Psycho-Analysis,* 49, pt. 1 (1968), 44–45.

53. ———. "The Theory and Practice of Intensive Residential Treatment of Adolescents." *Psychiatric Quarterly,* 42 (1968), 611–638.

54. ———. "The Adolescent Inpatient: Patterns of Depersonification." *Psychiatric Quarterly,* 45 (1971), 3–22.

55. ———. "Residential Treatment of Adolescents." In G. Caplan, ed., *American Handbook of Psychiatry,* Second Edition, Vol. 2. New York: Basic Books, 1974.

56. ———. "Special Education for Adolescents in Residential Psychiatric Treatment: A Contribution to the Theory and Technique of Residential School." *Annals of the American Society of Adolescent Psychiatry.*

57. ———, and HALL, D. D. "Psychiatric Hospital Treatment of Adolescents: Parental Resistances as Expressed in Casework Metaphor." *Archives of General Psychiatry,* 7 (1962), 286–294.

58. SCHMIDEBERG, M. "The Borderline Patient." *American Handbook of Psychiatry.* Vol. 1. New York: Basic Books, 1959. Pp. 398–416.

59. SPITZ, R. A. *The First Year of Life: A Psychoanalytic Study of Normal and Deviant Development of Object Relations.* New York: International Universities Press, 1965.

60. WINNICOTT, D. W. "The Capacity To Be Alone" (1958). In *The Maturational Processes and the Facilitating Environment.* New York: International Universities Press, 1965. Pp. 29–36.

61. ———. "From Dependence Towards Independence in the Development of the Individual" (1963). In *The Maturational Processes and the Facilitating Environment.* New York: International Universities Press, 1965. Pp. 83–92.

62. ———. "The Development of the Capacity for Concern" (1963). In *The Maturational Processes and the Facilitating Environment.* New York: International Universities Press, 1965. Pp. 73–82.

63. ———. "Ego Integration in Child Development" (1962). In *The Maturational Processes and the Facilitating Environment.* New York: International Universities Press, 1965. Pp. 56–63.

64. ———. "Hospital Care Supplementing Intensive Psychotherapy in Adolescence" (1963). In *The Maturational Processes and the Facilitating Environment.* New York: International Universities Press, 1965. Pp. 242–248.

65. ———. "Psychotherapy of Character Disorders" (1963). In *The Maturational Processes and the Facilitating Environment.* New York: International Universities Press, 1965. Pp. 203–216.

66. ———. "The Theory of the Parent-Infant

Relationship" (1960). In *The Maturational Processes and the Facilitating Environment*. New York: International Universities Press, 1965. Pp. 37–55.

67. ZENTNER, E. B., and APONTE, H. J. "The Amorphous Family Nexus." *Psychiatric Quarterly*, 44 (1970), 91–113.

68. ZETZEL, E. R. "A Developmental Approach to the Borderline Patient." *American Journal of Psychiatry*, 7 (January 1971), 127.

69. ZILBOORG, G. "Ambulatory Schizophrenias." *Psychiatry*, 4 (1941), 149–155.

CHAPTER 17

PROBLEMS OF DELINQUENCY AND THEIR TREATMENT

John L. Schimel

⟦ A Definition and Diagnosis

DELINQUENCY is not a psychiatric concept but a legal one. It is, moreover,
a difficult term to define even legally.
In general it refers to "such behavior by a
young person as to bring him to the attention
of a court."[17] The upper age limit for juvenile
delinquency varies in different states from sixteen to twenty-one years. Eighteen is the usual
dividing line between misconduct and crime.
The courts in some states may, however,
transfer the child to a criminal court in case of
a serious offense, such as murder or rape.
Municipalities, counties, and states have their
own ordinances defining delinquency and prescribing legal remedies. These include not
only the fifty states but also Puerto Rico, the
District of Columbia, the federal government,
3,000 counties, and 16,000 municipalities.

The delinquent or juvenile offender is a
child or adolescent who has committed an act
that would be considered criminal if he were
older. There are, moreover, many acts that are
considered offenses only if committed by a
young person. These include truancy, disobedience, running away from home, staying
out late, consorting with unsatisfactory companions, getting married without parental
consent, and dropping out of school before the
legal age. There is also the factor of public
intolerance as a measure of delinquency.
Clearly one community will tolerate behavior
among the young that another community, or
even another neighborhood, will not.

The foregoing indicates some of the difficulties in defining delinquency. To overcome this
some states have rigorously defined those acts
to be considered delinquent. Others, and this
is the trend, have made the term purposefully

vague so as to allow the police and the courts the widest possible latitude in dealing with youthful offenders.[41]

The psychiatrist faces further ambiguities in his work in this branch of forensic medicine. He is expected to make a diagnosis, not only for his own guidance but for that of the court. The official nomenclature[15] offers a potpourri of possibilities related to delinquent behavior. There are several intriguing possibilities under behavior disorders of childhood and adolescence: unsocialized aggressive reaction of childhood (or adolescence); group delinquent reaction of childhood (or adolescence); and runaway reaction of childhood (or adolescence). There are also possibilities in conditions without manifest psychiatric disorder and nonspecific conditions, which include the entry of social maladjustment and dyssocial behavior. The latter is "for individuals who are not classifiable as antisocial personalities, but who are predatory and follow more or less criminal pursuits, such as racketeers, dishonest gamblers, prostitutes, and dope peddlers."

The foregoing are not idle concerns. The psychiatrist's diagnosis may have far-reaching consequences for his charge. Withal, both definition and diagnosis have to be made with a comprehensive knowledge of the setting and circumstances of both the community and the delinquent behavior. The actual clinical conditions seen in a court setting vary from the normal through the entire range of neurotic, sociopathic, and psychotic disorders.

(Scope of the Problem

During 1970 there were an estimated 1 million runaways in the United States, many of whom experimented with sex and drugs. There are no nationwide statistics on juvenile offenses. Estimates are made on figures reported by the Federal Bureau of Investigation and the Children's Bureau.[12,19] The involvement of young people in the total crime picture is high, 22.9 percent of all arrests reported by the FBI in 1966.[19] The incidence is actually higher in suburban areas than in urban areas, and the lowest incidence is found in rural areas. In 1967 an estimated 1.5 million arrests of people under eighteen were made, of whom half were referred to the juvenile courts. The children involved in court actions each year amount to 2.1 percent of all children aged ten to seventeen. It is estimated that one in every nine youths (one in six males) will appear in juvenile court before his eighteenth birthday. The percentage appears to be rising. The absolute number will rise with the anticipated increase of the 40 million youths age ten to eighteen in 1970 to 47 million in 1980. In addition to the number of children who appear before a court, an equal number are handled directly by the police or through a police juvenile bureau without reference to the court.

For every girl brought to court, there are four or five boys. The chief offenses of the boys fall into the categories of larceny, burglary, disorderly conduct, curfew violation, vandalism, auto theft, running away, and violation of the liquor and drug laws. The chief offenses of the girls are running away, larceny, and disorderly conduct. The problems of drug usage are dealt with in another section of this volume. The crimes begin early, with shoplifting starting at age six or seven. Girls, beginning at the younger end of the spectrum, range from incorrigibility to truancy to sex offenses. It appears that they exceed the boys in regard to shoplifting. Boys go from petty thievery to more serious stealing and then to assault. The acts fall into two general classes: (1) those injurious to others and (2) those injurious to the self, such as drug abuse and sexual activities. The cost is high, running into hundreds of millions of dollars for direct services to delinquents and their families as well as over a $100 million for property stolen by juveniles in addition to property destroyed through vandalism.[8]

Of all children whose cases reach the court approximately 14 percent are remanded to public training schools, an estimated 45,000 children each year. Three boys are committed for each girl. The boys stay an average of nine months, the girls one year. A small percentage stay two or more years. In 1967 these children were housed in 220 state and local training schools.[10,11]

The sheer scope of the problem of delinquency in the United States is staggering. United Nations reports indicate that juvenile delinquency is increasing in many other countries as well: England and Wales, the Union of South Africa, Australia, New Zealand, the Federal Republic of Germany, East Germany, Austria, Greece, Yugoslavia, France, Sweden, Finland, and the Philippines.

❲ Philosophy of Care

The problem of young people failing or being unable to live up to the standards set by adults is age-old, as are the legal remedies. Hammurabi's Code is the oldest known code of laws, dating back to 2270 B.C. in Babylon. The society was patriarchal, and deviant behavior by children was not tolerated. Punishment was severe. For example, the code states: "If a son strikes his father, one shall cut off his hands." In Biblical times, the punishment of death by stoning was prescribed for the "stubborn and rebellious son." Blackstone, writing in eighteenth-century England, reported the case of a boy of eight who was hanged for burning two barns. Harsh penalties for youthful transgressions continued throughout the nineteenth century. In New Jersey, a thirteen-year-old boy was hanged in 1828 for an offense committed when he was twelve. As late as 1965, among 331 prisoners under sentence of death in the United States, three were eighteen and three nineteen. Their offenses were either rape or murder.[8,9]

The legal concept of juvenile delinquency is a recent one. The first juvenile court in the world was established in Chicago, Cook County, Illinois in 1899. This was the culmination of a millennial process of softening attitudes toward transgressors, whether juvenile or adult. It may be well to keep in mind that the penalties meted out to adult offenders in the United States today are remarkably more severe than in other civilized countries. The talion law of the Bible of an "eye for eye, tooth for tooth" is still a dominant theme in American law and is reflected in the cry for "law and order." An offense that may merit a two-year sentence in France or Italy may call for ten or even twenty years to life in the United States.[38] (At the moment of this writing, a youth is facing the possibility of twenty years of incarceration based on possession of microscopic amounts of marijuana, which were found in the lining of his pocket.) Although the ostensible purpose of imprisonment for adults is alleged to be rehabilitation, the practice comes closer to savage repression.

Two assumptions underlie modern concepts of delinquency. One is that children under a certain age are not responsible or accountable for criminal acts. The second is that some children are in need of the protection of the courts.[10] The court in Cook County was delegated the responsibility for three categories of children: the dependent, the neglected, and the delinquent. All had become wards of the state. This trend eliminated most criminal trials for children, though it was not until 1945 that Wyoming enacted the necessary laws.

The early care of delinquents was largely custodial and disciplinary. Rigorous supervision and accountability were believed to result in the production of "good citizens," that is, reform. This is still the dominant trend. A recent review of the regulations of a training or reform school in New York State revealed few differences between it and a maximum security prison: one visit by one relative each six weeks, one letter a week, and so on. The other trend is the therapeutic, or psychiatric. The latter can be felt, rather than seen, throughout the entire system, from apprehension by the police, to detention, to court appearance, to training school. One might put it that the metaphor is slowly changing from that of the bad child in a good society to that of a sick or deprived child in a bad or neglectful society. The wherewithal to implement the latter metaphor is not only awesome but has not been forthcoming, except in sporadic instances.

There are a number of paradoxes involved in the more humane concepts of juvenile delinquency. A notable one lies in the protective function of the courts. The judge is seen as the wise patriarch[30] doing what is best for the child and the community, but in this role he is empowered to dispense with the protections of due process accorded all citizens by the Bill of Rights of the American Constitution. The juvenile courts may assume jurisdiction over children without proof of legal violation. Children have not had the right to legal counsel, to a jury trial, to refuse to answer questions, or to incriminate themselves.[41] In the 1967 Gault case the U.S. Supreme Court affirmed the need to apply the safeguards of the Bill of Rights to juveniles in the case of a boy sentenced to a long term in a correctional school without regard to due process. This decision is regarded by many workers in the field as a mixed blessing and is honored in the breech by many practitioners, since it would make the work more cumbersome in an already overburdened and undermanned system.

(Types of Delinquents

For a consideration of the types and kinds of delinquents, one may consult a plethora of sociological and psychiatric studies. One stumbling block is that the populations of courts, court clinics, and training schools are drawn primarily from the lower classes.[22,23,27] During the 1920s and 1930s it was actually believed that delinquency was extremely rare in the middle and upper classes. Dr. Sophia Robison[36] showed, in a 1936 study conducted in New York, that middle-class delinquents rarely reached the police or the courts. Many were referred to private agencies not primarily concerned with delinquency. A number were handled by the Bureau of Child Guidance. The upper-middle- and upper-class child is likely to be handled completely by the family and its circle of influential professionals. The child may be sent to a military school or private hospital rather than to a public correctional institution. The great leveler at the moment seems to be violations of the marijuana laws with the apprehension of children of governors and other high officials being announced regularly in the press. It would appear that very few children do not, at one

time or another, commit an act that could legally be termed delinquent.

There is a large group of delinquents who may be termed social delinquents.[42] These consist of individuals with relatively intact personalities. Their delinquent acts lie in an adherence to nonlegal values and norms which are shared with other members of various subcultural groups.[43,44] This is a crucial factor to consider in the troubled interface where middle-class psychiatrists meet lower-class individuals in the courts, the hospitals, the clinics, and in community psychiatry programs. The problem is an old one, which has manifested itself, for example, in attempts to design culture-free IQ tests. It may be difficult for the middle-class professional to construe different value systems as anything but pathological. Yet within groups of such social delinquents, some show leadership and a sense of responsibility within their own peer and/or subcultural group. Others may be incompetent within the deviant group. Alfred Kinsey has told of a campus policeman, holding lower-class sexual values, who would mind his own business if he saw a couple having sexual intercourse in a car. Heavy petting or fellatio, however, offended his sense of values, and he would arrest the couple.

Similar difficulties crop up more and more frequently in other social agencies such as the schools. The issue has recently been made very prominent by blacks. They protest that the middle-class white teaching cadres push their own values and regard the values of others as inferior or sick. The alienation between the teacher and the taught is clear and growing. Similar difficulties have been noted by psychiatrists attempting to comprehend and treat other social groups. In the 1970s no one can afford to mistake cultural differences for evidence of psychological defect.

Many delinquents are, nonetheless, suffering from the milder or more severe forms of psychological disability. They fall into various groups characterized as unable to internalize social norms or to restrain impulsivity.[18,24,25] The usual satisfactions that require conformity to group mores are not available to these children and adolescents. These youngsters may be, diagnostically, neurotics, sociopaths, or schizophrenics. Some who fall into the delinquent group are handicapped with a mental defect, often combined with another psychiatric disability.

❪ Role of the Professional

The role and function of the professional are determined by that point in the delinquent's career where their paths cross. Most delinquents do not get to the courts but are seen in clinics, public and private hospitals, the schools, and in private practice. In private practice, it is the rare adolescent who is not legally a delinquent if for no other reason than by violation of the marijuana laws. The problems are diverse, however. Some adolescents enter private therapy after being "busted" on a pot charge, and psychotherapy is a condition of their parole. For these relatively affluent youngsters the main form of therapy is individual, one-to-one psychoanalytically oriented psychotherapy. Interviews may be held with other family members, or a modified form of family therapy may be used.

In clinic and hospital practice, individual therapy is supplemented or replaced by group and milieu therapy. The latter methods are often heavily relied on because of the shortage of trained personnel. It should be noted, however, that group and milieu therapists are presenting rationales and statistics to indicate that their methods are and should be primary, particularly in view of the importance of group and peer relationships in the lives of adolescents.

The relation of the therapist to the delinquent varies with the circumstances. The white therapist with the black delinquent faces not only an age and culture gap but may also face militant antiwhite attitudes. The therapist dealing with the middle-class dropout, hippie, or radical youth may face a strong antiestablishment attitude in which he is an example of the establishment. The therapist dealing with the child in the court, in the training school, or with the youngster who must see a psychiatrist as a condition of his parole, must deal with an attitude (and a fact) that identifies him as an agent of the repressive forces of society. It takes a special skill and hardiness on the part of the therapist to endure and be useful in these situations.

Youngsters who are apprehended by the police generally follow a different track. In some urban centers there are specially trained and assigned youth police who may deal with minor problems on the spot. Some children are brought to the police station. Their parents are called, and the child is warned. Usually no record is made. The police may release the child to the parents with a referral to a social agency. Only one-half of the children taken into police custody are referred to the juvenile court. The screening of the child is done by a probation officer or social worker. The decision as to whether to place the youngster in detention until his court appearance is made by the intake worker, usually a probation officer. In 1965 it was estimated that 409,000 children had been placed in detention, although the number on any given day was about 13,000.[8]

In urban centers the psychiatrist may be attached to the court. His function may be primarily one of diagnosis and recommendation. Experimental clinics have been operated within the court system itself to provide therapeutic help to the offender and his family, such as the Treatment Clinic of the Family Court of New York City. Overall, however, the role of the psychiatrist in the juvenile courts has been limited. The difficulties lie not only in areas of finances and availability of personnel but also in the absence of well-established rationale of relevance of psychiatry to court procedures other than consultation.

❪ Rehabilitation

The goal of the training school is rehabilitation. The latter is a key concept in American penology. The basic notion is that enforced conformity to the rules of an institution (custodial care) will result in conforming behavior to the rules of the larger society, on release. A contradiction is involved here since the length of the period of confinement must also reflect the gravity of the offense and not necessarily the optimum period of confinement necessary for rehabilitation. The individual must pay his debt to society.

If the reader feels that the psychology of custodial rehabilitation is either mad or obscene,[29,38] he should, nevertheless, be reminded that this is the prevailing mode of dealing with juveniles in public institutions. Psychiatric literature on delinquency concentrates on experimental programs in which the psychiatrists play an important role and may give a misleading impression of the overall picture. Indeed, psychiatric programs fed sparingly into custodial units may be of dubious value for a number of reasons, not the least of which is the incompatibility of views of human nature and human possibilities between a custodial and a therapeutic approach.

Custodial care is still the rule rather than the exception in the training schools, although there has been a trend toward the therapeutic approach for the better part of a century. Even the regard for the individual expressed by custodial care of juveniles is of recent origin. Training schools were a development of the nineteenth century in both England and the United States. Prior to that time, dependent and delinquent children wandered the streets or were confined in a house of correction or workhouse along with vagrants, beggars, criminals, the senile, and the insane. The first program in the United States to separate juvenile from adult offenders was instituted in 1825 when the Society for the Reformation of Juvenile Delinquents opened the New York City House of Refuge. The state gradually took over this responsibility, and by 1850 the trend for state-supported training schools was well established.[8]

There have been numerous experimental units within the context of custodial care. With boys this has taken the form of schools specializing in vocational training, a combination of camp and school, and work camps, such as Illinois Youth Commission's forestry work camps. The amount of formal supervision and regimentation varies in these units, with the work camp being the most informal setting.

Does rehabilitation work? This is a knotty and controversial question.[21,39] Many boys and girls learn a trade while in training schools. Undoubtedly, many learn improved ways of stealing and the like. The majority do not return to the training school once they are discharged, nor are they apprehended as adult offenders later in life. Follow-up studies indicate, however, a high degree of neurotic suffering, sociopathy, alcoholism, and marital failures among those who have been residents in a training school.

❰ Toward the Therapeutic

The therapeutic approach has not made much of an impress on the total problem of juvenile and adult offenders. This has been true for a variety of reasons which I will touch on. In passing, one might mention the momentum gathering behind the therapeutic approach— well in advance of any proof of large-scale effectiveness of the therapeutic approach— and in spite of protests by black militants and others that mental health programs are a sop and not an answer to the social conditions that produce the enormous numbers of juvenile offenders, criminals, and the mentally ill.

Many of Freud's early followers were interested in applying his psychoanalytic theories to the problems of special groups in society. Otto Rank[3] was particularly interested in artists and writers; his views were also influential in the development of social work and social agencies in the United States. Alfred Adler's[3] concern with the influence of society on the individual and on the importance of social roles finally earned him the role of heretic among the early psychoanalysts. His interest led naturally enough to the effects of schools and teaching on children. He organized the first child guidance clinics in Vienna. Oskar Pfister[3] was the first from the field of education to receive analytic training and apply psychoanalytic concepts to his activities as teacher and pastor in Switzerland.

Franz Alexander, later to become the president of both the American Psychoanalytic Association and the American Academy of Psychoanalysis, developed an interest in the analytic study of the criminal while in Berlin. Together with a lawyer, Hugo Staub, he published, in 1929, *The Criminal, The Judge, and the Public*.[5] It was republished in 1956. In 1931, Alexander undertook a research project in criminal psychology sponsored by the Judge Baker Foundation in Boston with Dr. William Healy. The results of this study were published as *The Roots of Crime*.[4]

August Aichhorn[2,3] came to psychoanalysis from the field of juvenile delinquency. He had been a schoolmaster and an originator of day-care centers for working parents in Vienna before World War I. He became the director of a training school for children. Unable to accept the available explanations for delinquency, he undertook psychoanalytic training. His subsequent work laid the foundations for a therapeutic approach to delinquency. His classic work, *Wayward Youth*, was first published in 1925.

Aichhorn referred to his work, even before analysis, as a "psychology of reconciliation." His concept of "latent delinquency" pointed toward an inquiry into the causes of delinquency, such as an arrest in personality development resulting from a disturbance in early child-parent relationships. Aichhorn stressed the need for dealing with underlying determinants of latent delinquency rather than with the symptoms of manifest delinquency. He recognized the necessity of providing corrective emotional experiences with others in order to undo the effects of deficient past relationships. The transference was to be used as the critical leverage toward healthy change. Essentially an eclectic, and willing to experiment in almost any direction, Aichhorn was an innovator. The methods he used have been repeatedly discovered during the subsequent years. He utilized individual, group, family, and milieu techniques.

Aichhorn was a robust, jolly, and lively man. He knew the language of the gutter from his childhood and used it freely with his young charges. He knew the value of the joke and the wisecrack in easing the generation gap. He has, nevertheless, left evidence of a remarkably sensitive and intuitive grasp of clinical conditions. Although Aichhorn was unusual in his ability to deal with juveniles before his analytic training, the latter gave him the conceptual tools to formulate his insights and pass them on.

Aichhorn's work with seriously disturbed children and adolescents provided a model for much of the subsequent work done in the United States.[6,7,33–35] In a noted experiment he took twelve incorrigible boys and placed them in a group, with virtually no controls. When repressive measures were not used, it was interpreted by the boys as weakness on the part of staff. They practically demolished the premises and even threatened one another with knives, without staff interference. A period of quiet was followed by even wilder outbursts. After several months an emotional bond developed among the boys and with the workers and their behavior approximated the normal. A similar approach was used by Bruno Bettelheim[6,7] at the Sonia Shankman Orthogenic School in Chicago, a residential school for seriously disturbed children. Aichhorn's methods are also reflected in S. R. Slavson's activity group therapy for children, developed at the Jewish Board of Guardians in New York City.

Aichhorn also anticipated the ego-psychological and reality-orienting methods utilized with disturbed children. He suggested[2] that:

We must give the pupils experiences which fit them for life outside and not for the artificial life of the institution. The more the life of the institution conforms to an actual social community, the more certain is the social rehabilitation of the child. There is a great danger in an institution that the individuality of the child does not develop along lines best suited to his needs but that rules are laid down in accordance with administrative requirements which reduce the child to a mere inmate with a number.

There is probably no clearer statement of the therapeutic ethos for delinquents. The modern application of this aspect of Aichhorn's views is clearly expressed in *A Time to Heal: Cor-*

rective Socialization, by Goldfarb, Mintz, and Stroock.[25]

Experimental treatment methods abound, with behavior therapy, Eric Berne's version of group therapy, reality therapy, and other modalities being added as variations on themes laid down long ago, all reporting promising results. Long-range studies are necessary to validate their lasting effectiveness. A computer printout of the references on juvenile delinquency studies from 1965–1969 by the Department of Health, Education, and Welfare resulted in a single sheet of paper 430 feet long (about one-tenth of a mile). Each eleven-inch segment contained two or three abstracts, for an estimated 12,000 reported studies in a five-year period. The therapeutic approach requires heavy financial support, experimentation, and a built-in research design to validate its results.

Experimental therapeutic approaches tend to be added piecemeal to existing institutional structures. Strains develop between administration, existing staff, the community, and the therapeutic unit, all reflecting on the work with the juvenile population of the institution. It is suggested that the most important research, for the present, does not deal with treatment modalities as such but with their impact on the total structure into which they are introduced. The therapeutic approach in dealing with delinquents does not exist in a vacuum but within and as part of a complex societal matrix.[42]

❴ Retrospect and Prospect

On July 23, 1965, President Lyndon Johnson established a commission on Law Enforcement and Administration of Justice, through Executive Order 11236. The project was aided by hundreds of expert consultants and advisors, as well as by the FBI, the U.S. Bureau of Prisons, and the Department of Health, Education, and Welfare. The findings and recommendations of this commission were published in a number of large volumes.[31,32]

The recommendations of the commission make it clear that preventive measures are considered to be of primary importance. The therapeutic role can be seen to be a distinctly minor factor in the overall plan, in spite of evidence that psychiatric services for children are now woefully inadequate. Nevertheless, the following sampling of the commission's recommendations should be studied for the perspective they throw on the overall problem. The commission recommends:

Efforts, both private and public, should be intensified to: Reduce unemployment and devise methods of providing minimum family income. Reexamine and revise welfare regulations so that they contribute to keeping the family together. Improve housing and recreation facilities. Ensure availability of family planning assistance. Provide help in problems of domestic management and child care. Make counseling and therapy easily obtainable. Develop activities that involve the whole family together.

Efforts, both private and public, should be intensified to: Involve young people in community activities. Train and employ youth as subprofessional aides. Establish Youth Services Bureaus to provide and coordinate programs for young people. Increase involvement of religious institutions, private social agencies, fraternal groups, and other community organizations in youth programs. Provide community residential centers.

In order that slum children may receive the best rather than the worst education in the Nation, efforts, both private and public, should be intensified to: Secure financial support for necessary personnel, buildings, and equipment. Improve the quality and quantity of teachers and facilities in the slum school. Combat racial and economic school segregation.

In order that schools may better adapt to the particular educational problems of the slum child, efforts, both private and public, should be intensified to: Help slum children make up for inadequate preschool preparation. Deal better with behavior problems. Relate instructional material to conditions of life in the slums.

In order that schools may better prepare students for the future, efforts, both private and public, should be intensified to: Raise the aspirations and expectations of students capable of higher education. Review and revise present programs for students not going to college. Further develop job placement services in schools.

Efforts, both private and public, should be intensified to: Prepare youth for employment. Provide youth with information about employment opportunities. Reduce barriers to employment posed by discrimination, the misuse of criminal records, and maintenance of rigid job qualifications. Create new employment opportunities.

To the greatest feasible extent, police departments should formulate policy guidelines for dealing with juveniles. All officers should be acquainted with the special characteristics of adolescents, particularly those of the social, racial, and other specific groups with which they are likely to come in contact. Custody of a juvenile (both prolonged street stops and stationhouse visits) should be limited to instances where there is objective, specifiable ground for suspicion. Every stop that includes a frisk or an interrogation of more than a few preliminary identifying questions should be recorded in a strictly confidential report.

Communities should establish neighborhood youth-serving agencies—Youth Service Bureaus—located if possible in comprehensive neighborhood community centers and receiving juveniles (delinquent and nondelinquent) referred by the police, the juvenile court, parents, schools, and other sources.

In a review of *Crime, Law and Corrections*,[38] the author noted:

The practicing psychiatrist is committed to the notion that maturity and non-destructiveness are one. In his work he is daily reminded that the maturity of individuals directly correlates with the respect and compassion that have been accorded them. He observes repeatedly that recovery from mental illness depends on learning to recognize respect and compassion in others. These qualities must exist and be responded to for growth and recovery to occur. The psychiatrist knows that to grow a good man from a child, a patient or a delinquent adult requires the nurturing and fostering of a sense of self-esteem.

I regretfully surmise that large issues of justice tend to obscure the smaller ones that serve to dehumanize the many. The great mass of criminals (and the mentally ill) are from the societally demeaned by reason of race, color, creed, accident, fate and biological disadvantage, such as low intelligence. The society first neglects, then "protects" itself by demeaning through confinement and ostracism, thus thereby "deterring" other possible offenders and, mirabile dictu, "rehabilitating" the offender himself.

The psychiatrist (and his fellow social scientists) is by and large nonplussed by societal remedies for criminality. His theories force him to believe that such societal practices must lead to increased criminality and recidivism. Indeed statistics, and otherwise observable trends, do substantiate his theories. For the psychiatrist there is an Alice-in-Wonderland quality in the use of ever harsher penalties to remedy social situations brought about by harsh realities. He has seen this exacerbating process during Prohibition. He sees it in regard to abortion, gambling and the use of drugs.

It is evident that there will be increasing effort to comprehend the nature of the criminal (and the delinquent) and experimentation in his rehabilitation. There will be an expansion of supervised probation opportunities to an increasing number of offenders, an extension of minimum security units for prison and reformatory inmates, as well as a reduction of the average length of confinement in correctional institutions. It seems clear that the problem of criminals and correction must become part and parcel of the community mental health centers and programs, with heavy emphasis on early case finding and prevention.

⫽ Bibliography

1. ABBOTT, G. *The Child and the State*. Chicago: University of Chicago Press, 1938.
2. AICHHORN, A. *Wayward Youth*. New York: Viking Press, 1935.
3. ALEXANDER, F., EISENSTEIN, S., and GROTJAHN, M. *Psychoanalytic Pioneers*. New York: Basic Books, 1966.
4. ———, and HEALY, W. *The Roots of Crime*. New York: Knopf, 1935.
5. ———, and STAUB, H. *The Criminal, the Judge, and the Public: A Psychological Analysis* (1931). Rev. ed. New York: The Free Press, 1956.
6. BETTELHEIM, B. *Love Is Not Enough*. New York: The Free Press, 1950.
7. ———. *Truants from Life: The Rehabilitation of Emotionally Disturbed Children*. New York: The Free Press, 1955.

8. CAVAN, R. S. *Juvenile Delinquency*. 2d ed. Philadelphia: Lippincott, 1969.

9. ———, ed. *Readings in Juvenile Delinquency*. 2d ed. Philadelphia: Lippincott, 1969.

10. CHILDREN'S BUREAU. *Institutions Serving Delinquent Children, Guides and Goals*, no. 360. Rev. ed. Washington, D.C.: U.S. Government Printing Office, 1962.

11. ———. *Statistics on Public Institutions for Delinquent Children*. Washington, D.C.: U. S. Government Printing Office, 1964.

12. ———. *1966 Juvenile Court Statistics*, Statistical series, no. 90. Washington, D.C.: U.S. Government Printing Office, 1967.

13. CLINARD, M. B. *Sociology of Deviant Behavior*. New York: Holt, Rinehart & Winston, 1963.

14. COHEN, A. K. *Delinquent Boys: The Culture of the Gang*. New York: The Free Press, 1955.

15. COMMITTEE ON NOMENCLATURE AND STATISTICS OF THE AMERICAN PSYCHIATRIC ASSOCIATION. *Diagnostic and Statistical Manual of Mental Disorders*. 1968.

16. EISSLER, K. R., and FEDERN, P., eds. *Searchlights on Delinquency: New Psychoanalytic Studies*. New York: International Universities Press, 1949.

17. ENGLISH, H. B., and ENGLISH, A. C. *A Comprehensive Dictionary of Psychological and Psychoanalytical Terms*. New York: Longmans, Green, 1958.

18. ERIKSON, E. H. *Childhood and Society*. New York: Norton, 1950.

19. FEDERAL BUREAU OF INVESTIGATION, U.S. DEPARTMENT OF JUSTICE. *Uniform Crime Reports for the United States*. Washington, D.C.: U.S. Government Printing Office, 1966.

20. GLUECK, S., and GLUECK, E. *One Thousand Juvenile Delinquents*. Cambridge, Mass.: Harvard University Press, 1934.

21. ———. *Juvenile Delinquents Grown Up*. New York: The Commonwealth Fund, 1940.

22. ———. *Unravelling Juvenile Delinquency*. Cambridge, Mass.: Harvard University Press, 1950.

23. ———. *Family Environment and Delinquency*. Boston: Houghton, Mifflin, 1962.

24. ———. *Delinquents and Nondelinquents in Perspective*. Cambridge, Mass.: Harvard University Press, 1968.

25. GOLDFARB, W., MINTZ, I., and STROOCK, K. W. *A Time To Heal: Corrective Socialization*. New York: International Universities Press, 1969.

26. HEALY, W., and BRONNER, A. F. *New Light on Delinquency and Its Treatment*. New Haven, Conn.: Yale University Press, 1936.

27. HOLLINGSHEAD, A. B., and REDLICH, F. C. *Social Class and Mental Illness*. New York: Wiley, 1958.

28. McCORKLE, L. W., ELIAS, A., and BIXBY, F. L. *The Highfields Story: A Unique Experiment in the Treatment of Juvenile Delinquency*. New York: Holt, Rinehart & Winston, 1957.

29. MENNINGER, K. *The Crime of Punishment*. New York: Viking Press, 1968.

30. NATIONAL PROBATION AND PAROLE ASSOCIATION. *Guides for Juvenile Court Judges*. New York, 1957.

31. PRESIDENT'S COMMISSION ON LAW ENFORCEMENT AND ADMINISTRATION OF JUSTICE. *Corrections*, Task Force Report. Washington, D.C.: U.S. Government Printing Office, 1967.

32. ———. *Juvenile Delinquency and Youth Crime*, Task Force Report. Washington, D.C.: U.S. Government Printing Office, 1967.

33. REDL, F. *When We Deal with Children: Selected Writings*. New York: The Free Press, 1966.

34. ———, and WINEMAN, D. *Children Who Hate*. New York: The Free Press, 1951.

35. ———, and WINEMAN, D. *Controls from Within*. New York: The Free Press, 1952.

36. ROBISON, S. M. *Can Delinquency Be Measured?* New York: Columbia University Press, 1936.

37. SCHIMEL, J. L. "Franz Alexander, Father of Psychosomatic Medicine." *The Physician's Panorama*, 3, no. 2 (February 1965).

38. ———. "The Role of Rationality in Crime and Corrections: An Epilogue." In Ralph Slovenko, ed., *Crime, Law and Corrections*. Springfield, Ill.: Charles C Thomas, 1966.

39. SCHREIBER, P. *How Effective Are Services for the Treatment of Delinquents?* Children's Bureau Report, no. 9. Washington, D.C.: U.S. Government Printing Office.

40. SLAVSON, S. R. *Reclaiming the Delinquent*. New York: The Free Press, 1965.

41. STROUSE, J. *Up Against the Law: The Legal*

Rights of People under 21. New York: New American Library, 1970.

42. VINTER, R., and JANOWITZ, M. "Effective Institutions for Juvenile Delinquents: A Research Statement." In L. Hazebrigg, ed., *Prison Within Society.* New York: Doubleday, 1969.

43. WHYTE, W. F. *Street Corner Society: The Social Structure of an Italian Slum.* 2d ed. Chicago: University of Chicago Press, 1955.

44. YABLONSKY, L. *The Violent Gang.* Baltimore: Penguin Books, 1966.

CHAPTER 18

EATING DISTURBANCES IN ADOLESCENCE

Hilde Bruch

(Definition

THE TERM "EATING DISTURBANCES" is used here to refer to those conditions where body size and manipulation of food intake are used to solve or camouflage inner and outer adjustment problems. Clinically these disturbances are recognized as obesity, characterized by excessive accumulation of fat tissue, and psychologically by helpless ineffectiveness in the face of bodily urges and social demands, or as anorexia nervosa, extreme leanness and cachexia, representing an overrigid effort at establishing a sense of control and identity while suffering from an all-pervasive sense of ineffectiveness.[3] Severe psychiatric problems are also encountered in those who maintain what looks like a normal weight but who are continuously preoccupied with their appearance and dietary manipulations, a group referred to as "thin fat people."[2] Others alternate between phases of rigid reducing followed by rapid weight increase, seemingly unable to stabilize at any weight; they may lose and gain a total of as much as 500 pounds during the adolescent years.

There is probably no other group of people as concerned and preoccupied with their physique and appearance as adolescents, before and after pubescence. They are forever worried about their size, whether they are too tall or too short, about the adequacy of their sexual maturation, and about their attractiveness in general; but most of all they are preoccupied with their weight. The fear of being too fat, or rated as such, parallels the weight consciousness of our society, which condemns even mild degrees of overweight as ugly, undesirable, and a sign of self-indulgence. Formerly an exceedingly rare disorder, anorexia nervosa seems to be on the increase in Western countries, where slimness is experienced by adolescents as the only respected state.

(Growth in Adolescence

Adolescence, the period of active growth and maturation, is characterized by marked changes in eating habits and fluctuations in body weight. Growth during adolescence fol-

lows a specific human pattern, rigid in its sequence but varying considerably in intimate
details from one individual to another.
Growth in stature precedes gain in weight.
The filling-out process is greater in girls than
in boys and appears to be determined, more
than any other factor involved in this complex
process of growth, by external factors. It is not
uncommon during this period of active growth
for some individuals to become plump and for
others to become overslim. It is important to
differentiate these normal variations from
pathological disturbances of weight and size.
Once growth and weight have stabilized, these
normal deviations are relatively easy to correct,
as is exemplified by the numerous plump
adolescents who are successful with reducing
programs and remain slim, though often with
life-long attention to their eating habits. No
information is available on the relative frequency of normal as compared to pathological
weight excess. Plumpness or normal weight
excess probably represents the more common
form of obesity in adolescence, and such patients will not come to the attention of psychiatrists, at least not for problems related to
their weight. However, under unfavorable
conditions this temporary plumpness may become the starting point of progressive weight
increase resulting in severe obesity, or, with
excessive emphasis on dieting, it may lead to
anorexia nervosa.

(Biological Aspects

There has been in recent years growing
awareness that obesity is a rather complex, far
from uniform, condition with disturbances in
many areas.[14] There is evidence of hereditary
factors in some cases, of disturbances in depo-
sition and release of fatty acids,[8] of other
metabolic malfunctioning or endocrine imbalance, and of variations in the number of fat
cells in the adipose tissues.[12] Another line of
investigation has focused on disturbances in
the central mechanisms of weight regulation.
Extensive studies on animals with experimentally produced microscopic lesions of the hy-

pothalamus and other midbrain regions have
elucidated the importance of different cell
groups in influencing appetite and satiation.
Newer studies emphasize that not only the
eating function but also spontaneous activity
and motivation are affected by these lesions.
The most up-to-date studies on regulation of
food and water intake suggest that there are
no locations for any specific behavior in any
hypothalamic compartment but that the functioning of the nervous system must be approached in an integrated way.[18] An enormous amount of information has accumulated
through the study of experimental and genetic
obesity in animals. Interesting as these findings are, it is not known to what extent these
animal obesities are relevant for man. Their
importance lies in the fact that they illustrate
vividly that there are different disturbances
which have a final common pathway insofar
as they lead to abnormal accumulation of adipose tissue.

Clinical interest has gone through definite
cycles. During the 1930's concepts of endocrine malfunctioning dominated the field, but
these were conceived of in rather simplistic
terms. Early psychiatric studies were as much
preoccupied with proving the irrelevance of
the endocrine factors as with establishing definite psychodynamic profiles. At present there
is renewed emphasis on biological disturbances and a much more open-minded approach to psychiatric problems and their interaction with physiological factors. Patients
who come to the attention of a psychiatrist
have usually undergone exhaustive medical
studies in the expectation of finding a definite
organic cause. In none of the fat patients referred for psychiatric treatment had there
been evidence of endocrine or metabolic disorders, and very few had obese relatives; nor
have I seen a case of a thus far unrecognized
tumor of the brain associated with obesity,
although I have observed several young patients with postencephalitic obesity. In the
latter instance, the detailed psychiatric inquiry
revealed that the acute changes in weight and
eating pattern, and other behavior disturbances, had followed a febrile disease which had

not always been recognized as encephalitis. Such patients had developed suddenly, without relationship to an upsetting life event, an uncontrollable urge to eat; they would eat whenever food was available, unrelated to recognizable or definable emotional stress. The clinging and hostile interaction with the family, characteristic of obese patients with emotional disorders, as well as a possessive but mistrusting attitude on the part of the parents, were absent.

In anorexia nervosa, too, opinion has fluctuated widely concerning the role of organic factors.[3, pp. 211-226] Gull, in 1873, suggested, by naming the disorder "anorexia nervosa," that mental stress was the causative factor. Lasègue, who described the condition at the same time, ascribed it to the symptom complex of hysteria, which he conceived of as a constitutional disability. The whole discussion was thrown into new focus when Simmonds, in 1914, observed cachexia in cases of emboli in the pituitary gland; for the next two or three decades anorexia nervosa was attributed to hypopituitarism. An extensive literature developed to differentiate the psychiatric syndrome of anorexia nervosa from the effects of endocrine dysfunction. There is at present a tendency to consider all somatic manifestations as secondary to the starvation, a formulation that is not entirely satisfactory. Recent studies suggest that though most of the functions of the anterior pituitary gland are preserved, there is growing evidence that the release of gonadotropin is impaired and gonadal failure may persist even after the malnutrition has been corrected.[21]

⟪ Social Aspects

Western culture on the whole has been critical, even contemptuous, of obesity. In the United States, preoccupation with weight, with the demand to be slim, has reached such proportions that every fat person, adolescents in particular, faces some problems in his social relations. The attitude toward obesity and the frequency of its occurrence vary inversely with social class, occurring seven times more often in lower-class women than in those of upper-class status.[17] This suggests that an upper-class fat youngster will encounter more serious psychological and sociological problems than one growing up in a lower-class environment where the attitude toward obesity is less negative.

Though recognition of this attitude is long standing,[3, pp. 9-24] systematic studies are of recent origin. By comparing a group of obese girls in a reducing camp with girls in a typical summer camp, Monello and Mayer illustrated, through administration of projective tests, the damaging effect of this cultural pressure on obese adolescents.[16] The obese showed heightened sensitivity to and obsessive preoccupation with the state of being fat, combined with a tendency to be passive and to withdraw in the face of group isolation. In evaluating the body image of obese people, the positive or negative attitude toward their own appearance, Stunkard and Mendelson found that obese adults who had been of normal weight during adolescence felt much less derogatory toward their appearance than those who had been exposed to social rejection and blame for being fat during childhood and adolescence.[3, pp. 87-105; 25]

Cahnman conducted a sociological study focused on the stigma of obesity and concluded that the obese teenager is discriminated against and made to understand that he deserves it, and thus he comes to accept this treatment as just.[5] As a result, he is unable to escape his condition and settles down to live with it. He becomes timidly withdrawn, eager to please, and tolerant of abuse. Whatever avenues of escape he chooses, he interprets himself in the way that is indicated to him and responds to expectations by accepting the dominant negative attitudes regarding his obese condition.

In my experience, based on several quite distinct population groups, individual obese youngsters will react to this widespread social prejudice according to their sense of competence and independence. The first observations were made during the Depression years on fat children coming from lower-middle- and lower-class homes, often of immigrant background. Conspicuous was the bewilderment of the mothers who could not understand why anybody should object to a child being big and plump. Part of this group was followed into early adulthood; the figures are incomplete and give only approximate percentages of the outcome.[3, pp. 134–150] Less than one-third outgrew the condition during adolescence, with the encouragement of friends or by separation from their homes. A few made a good general adjustment, though they remained moderately overweight. Reevaluation of the early records showed that those who had done well in the long run had been accepted by their parents as being heavy, and had not been exposed to relentless pressure to reduce. Those who remained fat or became super-obese had been literally persecuted for being fat by their families and had shown evidence of serious emotional disturbances as children; quite a few became frankly psychotic.[3, pp. 175–193] They had arrived at adolescence with a low self-esteem and a sense of helplessness, and they reacted with guilt and depression to the critical cultural attitude. Observations in private practice, on middle- and upper-class obese adolescents, led to the same conclusion, that an individual's security and competence were the determining factors for the way he reacted to the damaging social pressure.

⟮ Psychiatric Aspects

Psychiatrically, too, obesity and anorexia nervosa are not uniform conditions. In anorexia nervosa two distinct syndrome groups can be recognized. The first is the typical or primary syndrome with relentless pursuit of thinness as a final step in a desperate struggle for control, for a sense of identity and effectiveness.[3, pp. 250–284] These patients are not primarily anorexic, though frantic preoccupation with food and the most bizarre eating habits may develop in the course of their illness. Many indulge in enormous eating binges with

subsequent vomiting, alternating with periods of starvation. Characteristically, they are hyperactive to an unusual degree and deny their cachexic appearance. Less frequent is the atypical or secondary form where weight loss is incidental to some other problem and is often complained of or valued only for its coercive effect.[3, pp. 227–249] The eating function itself is disturbed, and food is endowed with various symbolic dangerous meanings. The conflicts of conversion hysteria and other psychoneuroses prevail in some cases; in other cases these conflicts are manifest symptoms of schizophrenic reaction or severe depressive illness. These atypical cases vary considerably in the severity of illness and the accessibility to treatment. When these patients have been sick for a long time they look deceptively like cases of true anorexia nervosa and are often labeled with this diagnosis.

It is more difficult to subdivide the enormous number of obese patients. The psychiatrist will rarely see patients from probably the largest group, those who are overweight on a constitutional basis or exhibit temporary fluctuation in weight. If they suffer from a psychiatric illness, it is not related to the weight, except that in periods of stress such patients are apt to use the excess weight as a focus for self-belittling, or an alibi for difficulties. This is commonly observed in overweight adult patients. The pattern of reactive obesity is also more commonly seen in adults, with the onset of obesity directly related to a definite upsetting event, and the overeating and ensuing obesity serving as a defense against anxiety and depression. When reducing is enforced the depression will become manifest.[24]

The characteristic form of obesity for childhood and adolescence is developmental obesity, in which disturbances in the eating and activity pattern are intrinsically related to the whole process of growth and development.[3, pp. 151–174] There are many obese adults who are just older representatives of this type. Whether or not they have been heavy as children, concern with size and weight and inability to tolerate frustration or delay in gratification have been central issues in their total development. Many have been fat as far back as they can remember, and their size has always been an important factor in their self-concept and in the environment's reaction to them. Much as the large size is complained of, they cling to it because they fear that by losing body substance they will lose their special strength and power. These obese adolescents engage in megalomanic daydreams of some special and outstanding achievement. Nothing they ever achieve comes up to the exaggerated expectation of what they feel they could or are expected to do. They are quite unrealistic in their ambitions and want to be the first and best in everything. If not recognized as special, or if success does not come without effort, they will give up in sullen despair. Such dreams of glory are usually camouflaged by a façade of indifference and are revealed only in the course of therapy. In the anorexics the special achievement is the very control over the body through self-starvation, or their defying nature by staying thin though eating enormous amounts, followed by throwing up.

Not infrequently reality checks break down and a psychotic picture becomes manifest. A dramatic account of such a breakdown of a fat young girl has been told in *I Never Promised You a Rose Garden.*[9]

In spite of the glaring differences in the outer picture, obese and anorexic patients have certain basic disturbances in common. Underlying their manifest stubbornness and negativism is a devastating sense of ineffectiveness, a feeling of being unable to control their bodies and body functions and to direct their lives in general. They often complain about feeling empty and that they are controlled by somebody else; they act and behave as if their center of gravity were not within themselves and as if they were the misshapen and wrong product of somebody else's actions. They lack discriminating awareness of the signals of bodily needs; specifically, they are unable to recognize hunger and satiation or to discriminate between bodily discomfort and anxiety or other psychological tensions. They have failed to achieve the sense of ownership of their own bodies. They do not experience themselves as effective, separate, and self-directed beings with the ability to identify and to control their bodies. Their failure in weight regulation is not based on some organic defect, as has often been assumed in the past, but on this deficit in self-awareness.

It is this lacking sense of ownership that colors the way obese and anorexic adolescents face the problems of adolescence. Like other adolescents they must prepare themselves for self-sufficiency and independence and emancipate themselves from their families; in particular, they must overcome their dependency on their mothers. Adolescents who develop manifest eating disturbances are poorly equipped for these tasks. The more deficient an individual is in his sense of personal and bodily identity, the less equipped he is to deal successfully with these important new steps. Quite often the adolescent has been overprotected and overcontrolled as a child, with few experiences outside the home, so that the need to grow beyond the family's attitudes and values becomes a threatening experience. Frequently, he is also deprived of the support and recognition from his peer group that helps the normal adolescent in his struggle for liberation.

The inability to eat normally sets fat and anorexic adolescents apart. The question is raised as to how such a basic bodily function as eating develops so that it can be misused in such an inappropriate and distorted fashion. The abnormal eating patterns do not occur in isolation but are always associated with other difficulties in the area of active or passive self-awareness. Detailed reconstruction of the early life experiences, from patients' accounts and transference behavior, and from observations of the transactional patterns during family sessions, suggested that the individual expressions of their needs and discomforts had been disregarded. Characteristically, these patients had been given adequate, even excellent care, from a physical angle, but it had been superimposed according to the mother's concepts of what the child needed instead of being geared to child-initiated clues.[4]

❮ Conceptual Model of Early Development

In order to understand how this pattern of interaction would lead to inaccurate learning of hunger awareness and deficient sense of ownership and self-directiveness, a simplified conceptual model of human development was constructed, with emphasis on the underlying functional processes and transactional patterns. Two basic forms of behavior need to be differentiated from birth on, namely, behavior that is initiated within the infant and behavior in response to stimuli. This distinction applies to both the biological and the social-emotional field. Behavior in relation to the child can be classified as responsive and stimulating. The interaction between the environment and the infant can be rated as appropriate or inappropriate, depending on whether it serves the survival and development of the organism or interferes with it.

Appropriate responses to clues coming from the infant, initially in the biological field and subsequently in the social-emotional field, are essential for his diffuse urges to become organized into differentiated patterns of self-awareness, competence, and effectiveness. If confirmation and reinforcement of his initially rather undifferentiated needs and impulses have been absent, or were contradictory or inaccurate, then a child will grow up perplexed when trying to identify disturbances in his biological field or to differentiate them from emotional and interpersonal disturbances; thus an obese person will feel "I need to eat," instead of anger or another appropriate emotion. He will be apt to misinterpret deformities in his self-body concept as externally induced, and will be deficient in his sense of separateness, will experience his body image in a distorted way, and will feel passive and helpless under the influence of internal urges and external forces. These symptoms are also characteristic of schizophrenia; it seems that this developmental scheme offers a clue for the close association of severe eating disorders with schizophrenia.[3, pp. 175-193]

The reconstructed early feeding histories are often conspicuous by their blandness. This applies in particular to anorexia nervosa, where parents often stress that the patient had been unusually good, happy, and normal as a child. Such parents feel that there is nothing to report, that the child had never given any trouble, had eaten exactly what had been put before him, and did not fuss about food. If a mother's concepts are not out of line with the child's physiological needs, he may offer the façade of normality. Obesity in a child may be a measure of a mother's overestimation of his needs or of her indiscriminate use of food as a universal pacifier. The gross deficit in initiative, inner controls, and active self-awareness, including the inability to regulate one's food intake, becomes manifest when the child is confronted with new situations and demands for which the misleading routines of his early life have left him unprepared. Not having developed an integrated body concept, he will feel helpless when confronted with the biological, social, and psychological demands of adolescence. In some, progressive obesity or anorexia becomes manifest under the stress of puberty itself; in others, the illness becomes manifest only at the time of additional new demands, such as entering a new school, separation from home, or when a reducing regime is superimposed.

Though abnormal eating patterns and disturbed body size are the outstanding symptoms, developmental deficits are encountered in many other areas. Conspicuous in the obese are the poor muscular skills, the inability to derive pleasure from athletic activities, and in the anorexics, aimless hyperactivity, a symptom that usually precedes loss in weight. Though somatic pubescence may be observed as adequate, with onset at an average or even early age, one may find serious disturbances in the psychosexual maturation of the adolescent. Amenorrhea and lack of sexual desire are consistently associated with anorexia nervosa. Obese adolescents, too, suffer from confusion and concern about their sexual adequacy. According to popular prejudice, fatness in the male indicates lack of masculinity, and an obese youngster may be paralyzed by the fear of such a defect. Surprisingly few develop overt sexual deviations, such as transvestism or homosexuality; and in fact, these deviations probably occur no more frequently than among the nonobese. Though fatness in a woman looks like an exaggeration of the female form, many adolescent girls have as serious conflicts about their sexual identity as boys; in many it appears to be a more urgent problem. Some are quite outspoken about having wanted to be a boy, and the hope lingers on that they will be changed one day, or that they will be recognized as belonging to what the Greeks called the third sex, namely, being a man and a woman at the same time.[3, pp. 151–174]

(Corroborative Evidence

The clinical deduction of a deficit in the perceptual and conceptual awareness of hunger has found support from direct observations. Through a series of ingenious experiments in which external factors were manipulated, Schachter demonstrated that obese subjects are affected in their eating habits by external cues, such as the sight of food, its taste and availability, or apparent passage of time, whereas subjects of normal weight will eat according to enteroceptive determinants.[22] Stunkard observed that fasting obese women, during contractions of the empty stomach, failed to report awareness of hunger or desire to eat, whereas nonobese women would usually report such sensations.[24] Coddington and Bruch observed that obese and anorexic patients were significantly more inaccurate than healthy normal subjects in recognizing whether or not food had been introduced into the stomach.[6]

The observation of numerous functional deficits in animals reared in complete isolation supports the assumption that seemingly innate functions require learning experiences for their organization. Monkeys raised on wire mothers, when fully grown, were grossly abnormal, apathetic, stereotyped in their response, and incapable of grooming behavior or of mating, though having undergone physiologic puberty.[10] Such isolate monkeys were also deficient in regulating their food intake and exhibited hyperphagia of the same magnitude as monkeys with hypothalamic lesions.[15]

This model of development as circular, reciprocal transactions between parent and child is also in good agreement with other studies of infancy, though as far as I know, no one else has expressed this in quite as simple and general terms. Piaget spoke of these reciprocal processes as "accommodation," the transformations induced in the child's perceptual schemata and behavior patterns by the environment, and as "assimilation," the incorporation of objects and characteristics of the environment into the child's patterns of perception behavior.[19] Escalona spoke of the infant's experience as the matrix of his psychological growth, and gave many details of the reciprocal transactions between mother and child.[7] Mahler described in detail the individuation-separation processes as circular, when infants were observed in the actual presence of their mothers.[13] While living with families who had produced a hospitalized schizophrenic child, Henry recognized the highly inappropriate ways, duplicated with monotonous sameness day in and day out, with which such mothers would superimpose their own concepts in the feeding situations.[11] In a study aimed at defining factors involved in the development of a child's attachment to his mother, Ainsworth and Bell observed that the differentiating factors were not related to the technique of feeding but to the relevance of the mother's response to the infant's signals of his needs.[1] Mothers who tended to treat too broad a spectrum of clues as signals of hunger, or who wanted to produce a baby who would sleep and make little demand, would overfeed their babies, who were rated overweight at age three months and continued to be overweight at age one.

Modern neurophysiological thinking has moved in converging directions. Pribram spoke of the servomechanism type of neural organization and suggested that two reciprocally acting mechanisms of control exist and that feedback is ubiquitous in the organization of the nervous system.[20] He proposed a model of brain function that is memory-based rather than drive-based, which means the traces of past and ongoing experiences enter into the organization of patterns. Morgane, through his studies of the regulation of the food and water intake, pointed out that the old concepts of localization and hypothalamic centers are no longer tenable and that a general system approach to several interrelated brain stem areas is necessary for a more useful understanding of brain functioning.[18]

❰ Therapeutic Implications

These considerations are not only of theoretical interest but also of practical importance. Treatment results, medically as well as psychiatrically, have often been unsatisfactory. My experience has been gained chiefly through psychoanalysis and intensive psychotherapy of many obese adolescents and fewer anorexics, who, though intelligent and gifted, had failed in fulfilling the promise of their talents and in achieving interpersonal intimacy; many had experienced unsuccessful psychoanalytic therapy.

Examination of the therapeutic situation as a transactional process suggested that the classical psychoanalytic setting, with the patient expressing his secret thoughts and feelings and the therapist interpreting their unconscious meaning, contained elements that implied the painful reexperience of something that had characterized their whole development, namely of being told by someone else what they felt and how to think. The recognition that a profound sense of ineffectiveness, with deficits in awareness of and control over the body and its functions, was the key issue led to a reformulation of what is essential in the therapeutic process. [3, pp. 334–376] These patients need help in becoming alerted to any self-initiated feelings, thoughts, and behavior. Thus they may gradually develop awareness of their own participation in the treatment process and in the way they live their lives.

Discriminating awareness of sensations may be experienced in a bodily function other than eating. It may be as trivial as putting on a sweater because the patient, not mother, feels chilly, or in some small scene in which he recognizes that his own behavior has an effect on other people. Some may never achieve true awareness of physiological hunger. As they learn to discriminate other emotional states and body sensations, and feel more in control of their behavior, the frequency of their misinterpreting various psychological situations as urge to eat will gradually diminish. With increasing competence they may become capable of following a dietary regime.

❰ Case Illustrations

Case 1

This history will serve as an example of normal adjustment in an upper-class obese girl who at age eighteen, five feet one inch tall and weighing 175 pounds, was seen in consultation on request of her mother who complained that her daughter always regained the lost weight after she had put her on a diet. This was an attractive girl who wore clothes flattering to her figure and who felt that her mother tried to run everybody's life. She had always had a supportive friend in her grandmother, from whom she felt she had inherited her makeup, her quiet and considerate temperament, and her short stocky figure. The girl realized that being plump had not been the same social handicap fifty years ago as it is now. However, she had found out that she functioned better, did better in her studies, and was socially more responsive when she had what she felt was her natural weight. When she tried to reduce, and she has repeatedly lost ten or twenty pounds, she felt so tense and uneasy that she had decided that it was better for her to maintain her present stable weight.

She was grateful for the support of her view that her general functioning was more important than her weight. About a year later she became engaged to an attractive young man with whom she shared many interests. When she raised the question that her weight might be socially embarrassing, he replied that he was marrying a person not a figure. Their marriage turned out well. Ten years and two pregnancies later her weight was exactly what it had been at age eighteen, too plump by contemporary fashionable standards but not interfering with an active and meaningful life.

Case 2

In this case, obsessive concern with weight and figure was a camouflage for deep-seated self-doubt and confusion. This eighteen-year-old girl, a senior in high school, had become so depressed that she had to interrupt her studies. She had always felt she was destined to lead a lonely life because no man could love her because she was "too fat" and a brilliant student. She was tall, five feet eight inches. Her weight had never been above 135 pounds, but since age fifteen she had been obsessed with dieting. She had forced her weight down to 110 pounds but then was acutely unhappy and embarrassed by remarks about her being too skinny. She tried to be less conscientious about her school work in a effort to be like everybody else, but then was unhappy when her grades dropped. For a while she dated a young man and took part in social activities. She became alarmed and severely depressed when she gained some weight, to about 125 pounds, and now missed the remarks about how thin she looked.

Though extreme, concern like hers is akin to that of many modern adolescents who feel attractiveness is measured in pounds and inches, and who will use any degree of plumpness as alibi to avoid social, in particular sexual, contacts.

Case 3

In anorexia nervosa the picture is usually so complicated by the severe problems that self-starvation provoke in a family that it is often difficult to recognize the dynamic constellation at the time of its development. Situations with information before the illness are of particular interest. In the case of a socially prominent upper-class family, there had been a consultation about an older daughter, who was markedly obese at age eighteen, when the younger,

anorexic girl was only twelve years old. The mother asked for help because she resented her daughter's obesity and was aware that her own concern was excessive. She spoke in glowing terms about her younger daughter, who was the ideal child. Her teachers would refer to the latter as the best balanced girl in school, and relied on her warmth and friendliness when other students had social difficulties. After the anorexia developed it could be recognized how the anxious and often punitive concern with the older sister's obesity had influenced the younger girl's thinking and self-concept, convincing her that being fat was an almost shameful and deplorable fate. The rapid weight increase during puberty horrified her, and she felt she was deserving of respect only by being thin. This conviction precipitated a starvation regime, and her weight dropped from 125 pounds to 80 pounds. This coincided with her beginning to realize that life was not just filling the mold into which her parents had poured her, but that she was expected to be master of her fate. The frantic preoccupation with her weight and body was an effort to establish mastery, at least in one area.

Case 4

This sixteen-year-old fat boy, only 61 inches tall and weighing over 200 pounds, threatened to drop out of school because he felt he was not able to be as good as he should or wanted to be. He had been sickly as a child, and he had often heard it said that he owed his life to his mother's devoted efforts. She had been outraged when he grew fat as an adolescent, and it was a crowning insult when his school record went down. After he had made considerable progress in therapy he confessed one day, "What's the use of going to school and studying if you cannot be the best in everything?" This preoccupation interfered with his studying. When he sat down to do his homework, the question flashed through his mind, "Even if I tried hard, who guarantees that somebody else will not do it better?" In his frustration he would eat whatever he could find, though he hated being fat. He wished that he were six years old again, starting first grade; then he could make A's all through the school years, and he would not need to worry. Even if he tried now, it would not be good enough, because he had not been the best student throughout school, and his life was ruined.

Once this topic had been touched on he revealed the most amazing overambitious plans which would make his life worth living. He had seen a movie about the first ascent of the highest mountain. "That movie shows exactly how I feel. The only one who counts is the one who goes on a mountain for the first time. That is something special. The rest, all those mountain climbers, they just do exercise, they don't count."

From then on he spoke by the hour about his dreams of achievement. To be known, to have a famous name, and to be remembered, that was what counted. There were two main ambitions: one was to do something so great, something so helpful for mankind, that his name would be remembered even after 500 years. But he would not hesitate to commit a crime in order to get his name in the papers. In his dreams of doing something spectacular he compared himself to great people of the past. Galileo was his hero. "If you are not doing something great, if your name is not remembered, then I don't see why we should live at all. One day you will die, you will get buried; it would be much better not to have lived at all."

If he could not be remembered for having done something great, then he would not mind being remembered as the most vicious or the most conceited person, just as long as he were to become well known. "I would be glad to be remembered if it were only for being conceited," and he spoke of Wagner, the composer. His therapist agreed that Wagner had this reputation, but added, "But that is not why he is remembered. In addition he was a superb musician: he is remembered for his music; he delivered the goods." This comment touched on what troubled him the most: He was afraid that he could not deliver the goods; his deepest fear was not being good enough in anything, and he had tried to build himself up

with all these glorious daydreams. Nothing but the extraordinary and spectacular could protect him against this terror of being nothing, of not feeling really alive.

Mention was made of his great size making him outstanding and conspicuous. He hesitated and then admitted that his fatness was something special; it did set him apart. Though he said he hated it, there was a certain gratification in having his family continuously talk and worry about his enormous size; being so large was something extraordinary. Such pride in size is expressed by many fat people, all the embarrassment and humiliation notwithstanding.

Case 5

The discrepancy between unrealistic aspirations and inner conviction of incompetence may result in psychosis. A sixteen-year-old boy, who had been obese most of his life, suffered an acute psychotic episode shortly after entering a liberal boarding school of his own choosing. There had been continuous conflicts at home about his insolent behavior and his greedy and unmannered eating. He expected to make friends at this school where no one remembered him as fat and awkward, which he felt had made him lonely and friendless. He hoped to become a member of the football team. He had lost some weight during the preceding summer, and his muscles had developed. He was confident that his large size, which until then had been the source of his suffering, would now become an asset.

The first day of practice was a terrible disappointment. The workout was hard and demanding, and there was no glory in it at all. He stumbled on the staircase and sprained his ankle, and thus was dropped from the team. This was a great relief to him, but it also meant the end of his dreams of glory.

The many rules and regulations at the school were disturbing to him. He had built up a case against his father for insisting on punctuality, cleanliness, and courtesy, and now he discovered that the rules at home had been lax in comparison with the rules at school. This insight, however, did not give him any relief, for it left him without justification for his hostile feelings and hatred. He could not concentrate on his studies and became increasingly worried about failing. Then he began to worry about his mental state and became really panicky.

He made some efforts to participate in group activities, but he could not make real contact. He withdrew more and more into a fantasy life in which he was the leader of a group of boys who, as a kind of people's court, controlled the student body. He was the chief executioner and dealt out the punishments. He loved the position of power, but was afraid that he might abuse his power and that the others might take revenge. It frightened him that he would like to kill someone and get away with it, but it also delighted him that he had this feeling of power over life and death. He was unable to differentiate between fact and fantasy, and when recounting this would insist that he really had been head man, the most respected boy in school.

Actually he had spent most of the time in the infirmary with vague complaints, chiefly headaches and abdominal pain. He became furious when it was suggested that his stomach pains might be related to the enormous amounts he ate; his weight had risen to approximately 280 pounds. He became more and more involved in his aggressive notions, and one evening staggered to the house of the headmaster, telling a gruesome tale about a bloody fight between two other boys in which he had interfered to prevent them from killing each other. He was afraid that they would now turn against him, and he no longer felt safe. The delusional nature of this story was recognized, and he was sent home. He was admitted to a psychiatric hospital where he made a recovery after a lengthy treatment. His weight stabilized at 200 pounds, somewhat heavy for his height but not as conspicuously fat as he had been as a young adolescent.

Case 6

This history is given as an example of a schizophrenic reaction with extreme passivity and helplessness in a young girl who had been perfect in her parents' eyes until age fourteen, when she became plump. The father, a self-made man, was obsessively concerned with appearance and position and insisted that his wife and daughter should be slim. When fifteen years old she was persuaded to go on a diet with her mother, who subsequently maintained her weight loss. However, for the patient a period of weight fluctuation of between 105 and 170 pounds began. After entering college she soon returned to her parents' home, sleeping constantly and desiring to be left severely alone. After a course of electroconvulsive therapy (ETC) she became extremely antagonistic, suspicious, and threatening toward her parents. Less than a year after she moved out of her parents' home she was admitted to a psychiatric hospital, having progressively gained weight.

Outstanding in her behavior was her conformity, her complete inability to say no to any request, her complaining of emptiness when no one told her what to do, her mentioning that in the past, "Mother always knew what I was thinking." She was preoccupied with food, felt that it had human characteristics, only it was better. "It is always there. People are not comfortable, but with food you don't have to make excuses, you just take. With people you have to be polite all the time and you can't say No." She ate without awareness of hunger, experiencing only an undifferentiated, uncomfortable feeling. "I feel so empty, I do not know who I am." She would wake up from sleep intensely anxious. "I feel pulled down on my bed; all my muscles are pulled back. It is a horrible experience that I cannot move." Awake, too, she suffered anxiety attacks with the feeling of floating, of having no body. Often she felt befuddled, not knowing whether she was asleep or awake. At times she was confused about temperature sensations, not knowing whether she felt warm or chilly.

This girl who had been raised as an exhibit for her vain parents gave the façade of normalcy until she was separated from them, when, without autonomy or self-reliance, she felt unable to protect herself against demands by any one she met. Her inability to control her weight was only one aspect of this developmental deficit, with obesity as the leading complaint.

⟨ Bibliography

1. AINSWORTH, M. D. S., and BELL, S. M. "Some Contemporary Patterns of Mother-Infant Interaction in the Feeding Situation." In *Stimulation in Early Infancy*. New York: Academic Press, 1969. Pp. 133–170.
2. BRUCH, H. *The Importance of Overweight*. New York: Norton, 1957.
3. ———. *Eating Disorders: Obesity, Anorexia Nervosa, and the Person Within*. New York: Basic Books, 1973.
4. ———. "Hunger and Instinct." *Journal of Nervous and Mental Disease*, 149 (1969), 91–114.
5. CAHNMAN, W. J. "The Stigma of Obesity." *Sociological Quarterly*, (1968), 283–299.
6. CODDINGTON, R. D., and BRUCH, H. "Gastric Perceptivity in Normal, Obese and Schizophrenic Subjects." *Psychosomatics*, 11 (1970), 571–579.
7. ESCALONA, S. K. "Patterns of Infantile Experience and the Developmental Process." *Psychoanalytic Study of the Child*, 18 (1963), 197–244.
8. GORDON, E. S. "New Concepts of the Biochemistry and Physiology of Obesity." *Medical Clinics of North America*, 48 (1964), 1285–1305.
9. GREEN, H. *I Never Promised You a Rose Garden*. New York: Holt, Rinehart & Winston, 1964.
10. HARLOW, H. F., and HARLOW, M. "Learning To Love." *American Science*, 54 (1966), 244–272.
11. HENRY, J. "The Naturalistic Observation of the Families of Schizophrenic Children." In R. H. Ojemann, ed., *Recent Research Looking Toward Preventive Intervention*. Iowa City: State University of Iowa, 1961. Pp. 119–137.
12. HIRSCH, J., and GALLIAN, E. "Methods for the Determination of Adipose Cell Size in Man and Animals." *Journal of Lipid Research*, 9 (1968), 110–119.
13. MAHLER, M. S. "On the Significance of the Normal Separation Individuation Phase." In M. Schur, ed., *Drives, Affects, Behavior*. New York: International Universities Press, 1965. Pp. 161–169.
14. MAYER, J. "Some Aspects of the Problem of Regulating Food Intake and Obesity." In C. V. Rowland, Jr., ed., *Anorexia and Obesity*. Boston: Little, Brown, 1970. Pp. 255–334.
15. MIRSKY, I. A. "The Saul Albert Memorial Lecture: Some Comments on Psychosomatic Medicine." *Excerpta Medica of the International Congress*, 187 (1968), 107–125.
16. MONELLO, L. F., and MAYER, J. "Obese Adolescent Girls: Unrecognized Minority Group?" *American Journal of Clinical Nutrition*, 13 (1963), 35.
17. MOORE, M. E., STUNKARD, A., and SROLE, L. "Obesity, Social Class, and Mental Illness." *Journal of the American Medical Association*, 181 (1962), 962–966.
18. MORGANE, P. J., and JACOBS, H. L. "Hunger and Satiety." *World Review of Nutrition and Dietetics*, 10 (1969), 100–213.
19. PIAGET, J. *The Construction of Reality in the Child*. New York: Basic Books, 1954.
20. PRIBRAM, K. H. "Toward a Neuropsychological Theory of Person." In E. Norbeck, D. Price-Williams, and W. M. McCord, eds., *The Study of Personality*. New York: Holt, Rinehart & Winston, 1968. Pp. 150–160.
21. RUSSELL, G. F. M. "Anorexia Nervosa: Its Identity as an Illness and Its Treatment." In J. H. Price, ed., *Modern Trends in Psychological Medicine*. Great Britain: Butterworths, 1970. Pp. 131–164.
22. SCHACHTER, S. "Obesity and Eating." *Science*, 161 (1968), 751–756.
23. STUNKARD, A. "The 'Dieting Depression': Incidence and Clinical Characteristics of Untoward Responses to Weight Reduction Regimens." *American Journal of Medicine*, 23 (1957), 77–86.
24. ———. "Obesity and the Denial of Hunger." *Psychosomatic Medicine*, 21 (1959), 281–290.
25. ———, and MENDELSON, M. "Obesity and Body Image: Characteristics of Disturbances in the Body Image of Some Obese Persons." *American Journal of Psychiatry*, 123 (1967), 1296–1300.

CHAPTER 19

DRUG PROBLEMS
AND THEIR TREATMENT

Matthew P. Dumont

ADOLESCENT DRUG USE will compel a moment of truth in American psychiatry. No issue is more deeply felt by the public. No issue more urgently demands a comprehensive approach encompassing preventative as well as therapeutic and rehabilitative interventions. And no issue more unequivocably challenges our traditional techniques.

The manner in which the mental health professions respond to the widespread anxiety about youth and drugs will be a final common path to a host of other ambient problems. Questions about professionalism and nonprofessionalism, the sick versus the criminal role, our relationship to public policy and legislation, and mental health aspects of the generation gap and social revolution all become inescapable when one engages the issue of drug abuse. In short, it represents a crisis for us as well as society, and depending on whether we can develop new coping capacities, we may be overwhelmed and completely ineffectual or develop a reinvigorated professionalism.

It must be emphasized at the outset that traditional techniques are ineffective. Individual psychotherapy has shown itself to be incapable of interrupting a pattern of drug dependence in significant numbers of patients. The fact that as a treatment modality it is a precious and inequitably distributed commodity additionally militates against a heavy investment of public and professional resources in that direction. The traditional mental hospital approach with whatever combinations of individual and group psychotherapies, occupational and recreational activities, and milieu approaches has demonstrated no greater effectiveness.[5,7,9,11]

In some minds incarceration itself has been viewed as an appropriate response to drug use by a society whose capacity for terror and rage has never been sounded. There may be little to argue with against this position as long as it is unhesitantly justified as a measure to protect otherwise wholesome communities from the dangerous behavior of the addict. If, however, there is the slightest inclination to think in terms of modifying the behavior of the drug user himself, incarceration cannot be perceived as a rational measure. Not only does it not work, but it perpetuates an environmental press of criminality, alienation, and hopelessness that exacts an incalculable toll on individual welfare and ultimately on society itself. Even those institutions most preoccupied with security cannot maintain an environment free of illicit drugs.

The quarantine notion of community protection, which implies that innocent children will be saved from exposure to an infectious process of drug use by incarcerating a critical mass of users, ignores the pervasiveness of the problem. Even conservative estimates of illicit drug use among the young indicate a prevalence of 40.9 percent.[8]

Finally, to consign to prison a number of individuals who are selected arbitrarily or, worse, through a process of social, racial, or political bias as the bearers of a social problem is to close our minds to the sources of that problem outside the individual.

In the final analysis, the hasty imposition of either patienthood or criminality on a large population of drug-dependent youth evades the reality of illicit drug use as a collection of behavior behind which is as broad a panoply of individual, familial, and sociocultural forces as any behavior in the human condition.

There is no single psychological profile to the drug user. And while there are rough constellations of social variables that distinguish modal users of different types of drugs,[1] there is no sociogram of the drug user with any predictive value. It may have been true two decades ago that skin color, social class, and family disruption provided correlations with drug addiction,[3] but it is not true today.

There has been a rapid growth of heroin use among white adolescents of all social classes and family backgrounds. The most salient influence on a young person's proclivity to drug use is a contingent one, peer-group pressure.[1] Ball[2] concluded:

In the case of both marijuana smoking and heroin use, the adolescent peer group exercised a dominant influence. The incipient drug user asked his older addict friends to be included in the group's primary activity.

There was no evidence that the onset of drug use was a consequence of proselyting, coercion or seduction.

Onset was, nonetheless, a group process.

The implication of these observations is profound. We are not dealing with a population that is uniquely pathological or criminal.

A societal response to drug use premised on psychopathology or criminality is, then, worse than worthless. Not merely will it be ineffectual in interrupting drug use but it may, by its expectations, actually generate secondary behavior patterns of an ego-alien or dyssocial type.

Two states in this nation, New York and California, in their anxiety about widespread drug use within their borders, have, at great expense, developed large, locked, centralized, medically dominated institutions to treat addicts with the help of an involuntary civil commitment code. Without even the adversarial protections afforded a criminal, an addict may, on the opinion of a physician, be involuntarily committed to such an institution. Not surprisingly the evaluations of these programs[10] are attesting to their uselessness. But apart from their representing civil libertarian monstrosities, I would suggest that there is no more devastating thing that can be done to a human being who is not essentially pathological or antisocial than to be called sick and treated like a criminal.

One additional caveat must be alluded to before we discuss feasible alternatives. The practices of mental health have never existed in a political vacuum. The societal response to drug use in particular has throughout history been colored by an establishmentarian hostility to forces perceived as politically threatening. Blum et al.[1] noted that seventeenth-century Moslem rules provided for the death penalty for coffee drinking as "the coffee house had become a meeting place for leisured political malcontents who were thought to be secretly hatching plots against established political and religious authority." The pharaohs suppressed drinking in houses of beer and wine for the same reason. Blum et al. concluded that "the holders of power responded violently to new drug use, which was symbolic . . . of rebellion, separatism, or other dissatisfaction with the status quo."

We may not indulge the fantasy that contemporary America is immune from such irrationality. We seem to be entering a time in history when the young are looked on with fear. The polarization of generations, along with the growing fury of the color line, has created a political ambience in this country that many have likened to the onset of German fascism. It is the young and the black who are perceived as the users of illicit drugs. It should not be difficult for us to understand how such issues as preventive detention, "no-knock" entry, and involuntary civil commitment as applied to drug abuse may be perceived as having political significance.

These, then, are the issues against which a plan of public policy concerning the treatment of drug problems must be laid out: the ineffectiveness of traditional professional approaches, the inappropriateness of incarceration, the salience of peer-group pressure, and a sensitive political context.

With this background, a renewed and focused interest has been expressed toward the phenomenon of the ex-addict-run self-help program. A psychiatrist's initial exposure to such a program is likely to be intensely negative. One may observe that a man is wearing a dunce cap on which is written the words: "Ask me why I'm wearing this," as if his humiliation is to be compounded by having to be reiterated at every encounter. Another man is made to submit to his hair being shaved off. A woman is wearing a stocking on her head. A couple is told that they may not have a relationship. An adolescent girl is ordered to scrub a dozen toilet bowls. If there should be any complaints, even greater indignities may be imposed as well as a verbal whiplash, furious and obscene. These are frequent occurrences in ex-addict, self-help residential treatment centers such as Synanon, Daytop Lodge, and Marathon House. On a more constant basis, there is a distinct hierarchy of privileges and authority, with those at higher levels able to command obedience from those at lower levels. Such a system makes no pretentions to be democratic and egalitarian. Its constituents are junkies who are not, so the argument goes, responsible enough to make decisions about themselves, let alone other people. Until they "mature," they must be treated as though they were babies or crazy.

There are some interesting similarities and some even more interesting differences between such a setting and the more traditional psychiatric inpatient facility. Psychiatrists, as a group, tend toward liberal and egalitarian sentiments. They are, as a result, revolted by the paramilitary specter of controls and sanctions in the ex-addict centers. Controls and sanctions are, nonetheless, a conspicuous component of life on a psychiatric ward. They may be stated in terms of therapeutic decisions in case conferences, but patients tend to see punishments and rewards for what they are.

While psychiatrists like to think of the patient as the raison d'être of mental hospitals, studies by sociologists have demonstrated that the patient holds distinctly lower status as an actor in the social system. Even when this is recognized, it is not articulated by the hospital staff as it offends the official ideology of medical personnel who are supposed to minister to a patient's needs, to serve him and treat him without violating his dignity. In some progressive psychiatric wards, attempts are made to minimize the low-caste status of patienthood by a variety of patient-government techniques. Rarely is significant decision-making authority vested in the patient, however, and when it is, there are intermittent assumptions of control by the physicians.

Psychiatrists tend to be revolted by the denigration of new patients in the self-help centers, and adhere to a formal rhetoric of dignity and respect for patienthood. The informal, unstated, and perhaps unconscious role sets in psychiatric units may still relegate the patient to an undignified position however. It is also possible that the conflicted messages that the psychiatric environment communicates to the patient are perceived as an indication of deceitfulness and hypocrisy on the part of the staff or are not consciously perceived at all, in which case such messages may be pathogenic.

In the self-help center there is little or no difference between the formal and the informal hierarchy. In a sense, there is only a formalized, informal hierarchy with decision-making openly and unashamedly a peer-group phenomenon. Attitudes about each member are expressed freely so that everyone knows who is loved, who is hated, who is feared, and who is respected. One achieves both status and authority as a result of peer-group allocations of love and respect. For this reason there tends to be charismatic leadership at the top of a self-help program. It is a system that is predicated on personal skills being recognized and rewarded.

By contrast, there is a marked distinction between formal and informal hierarchies on a psychiatric ward. The special case syndrome has only lately been recognized, but it has always been part of the drama on inpatient units. While physicians are nominally in control of the ward, the informal authority structure frequently finds the nurses having most to say about day-to-day issues. There is, as a result, a certain amount of confusion about who is in charge, a confusion that is difficult to articulate and define and to which new patients are particularly vulnerable. Added to this confusion among the professional groups impacting on the patient is an ambiguity about authority structure within the professions. There may be therapist-administrator splits among the psychiatrists, specialist-generalist splits among the nurses, and group-work-casework splits among the social workers. Each distinction is another arena of subtle, unstated jockeying for position carrying an antitherapeutic potential. What seems to characterize the psychiatric ward is a kaleidoscopic array of diffuse authority structures, an inarticulate ecology of control mechanisms into which is thrust the patient, already burdened with the ambivalence about authority that characterizes drug dependence.

The ultimate sanctions imposed by self-help programs are distinctly different from those of psychiatric units. Recidivism or hustling in the self-help program, if perceived to be intractable, may result in exclusion. Participation in the program is deemed to be a privilege and an opportunity, perhaps the last one for attaining true independence and freedom. Being put out on the street is being condemned to the inherent slavery of continued addiction. There is no need for locked doors or restraints in such an environment; the peer-group ideology perceives escape and acting out as comprising inherent bondage.

In the psychiatric ward, peer-group pressures may be opposed to the institutional press. While the hospital expects obedience and conformity ("primary adjustment" in Goffman's terms), the peer group, particularly when adolescent, frequently demands rebellion, elopement, and illicit drug activity as a condition for acceptance and respect. The hospital responds to such behavior with more restraints, constantly reinforcing the challenge to rebel. Adolescent treatment units in psychiatric settings are, therefore, marked by a preoccupation with locked doors, chemical restraints, and all the other paraphernalia of external controls. The ultimate sanction in such an environment is further restriction and isolation, progressing to chronic hospitalization in a maximum security situation. It is difficult for controls to be internalized when they are so readily forthcoming from the institution.

The most important distinction between the authority structure of the self-help program and that of the psychiatric ward is that the former is open and the latter closed. No matter how oppressive or humiliating one feels at the bottom of the ladder in the self-help program, the possibility of reaching the top is always present. In fact, achieving the top is the purpose of the program. The only obstacles to achieving that purpose are self-imposed. The demonstration of self-control, honesty, and respect is the means to attain freedom from addiction as well as enhanced prestige and authority. Graduation from the program may mean a life of involvement and autonomy outside or the assumption of managerial responsibility within the program or a related one.

On a psychiatric ward, regardless of how

well one behaves, how much "health" one manifests, or how successfully one juggles the conflicting expectations and fealties, one can never attain the position of a nurse or a doctor. Authority, diffuse as it is, remains forever unattainable, and regardless of one's inherent or emergent capacities, the low status of patienthood remains an onus until the moment of discharge, when the stigma of ex-patienthood may continue to exact its toll.

If we look at the two environments as laboratories for experimenting with life styles, or as educational institutions rather than treatment facilities, their differences are brought into sharp relief. In the self-help program, the individual is trained to perceive himself as an agent who has a broad array of options, each of which will stimulate a different response. In the psychiatric environment, the patient must be trained to manipulate the conflict forces from the environment as well as his own behavior in order to achieve some autonomy and gratification. Freedom, there, is perceived as an accidental phenomenon or one that involves a capacity to play roles well, if inauthentically.

The psychiatric ward trains the patient to act more competently in the kind of world he is accustomed to, where the individual must carve out a life space within ambiguously but rigidly defined environmental constraints. It is a world where mastery is an arbitrary and capricious business, frequently lacking in equity and justice. The self-help program trains people for success in a different kind of world, one in which a man may order his affairs in concert with others and where mastery is a function of one's own competence as a human being. Such a program has implications far beyond a group of drug-free individuals. It seems to be directed toward a restructuring of society itself, utilizing its graduates as the agents of change.

The "concept" program of the ex-addict-run therapeutic community is one manifestation of a spectrum of drug programs oriented around the self-help principle. Some of these programs are beginning to depart from the exclusive reliance on ex-addict staffs. Professionals with a variety of credentials and nonaddict (straight) nonprofessionals are increasingly being found in positions of responsibility. The implication is that having broken through the artificiality and arbitrariness of the old professional hegemony over human services,[11] it would be foolish to be locked into an equally artificial but newer credentialism. Being an ex-addict is not a standard of competence. New standards are being forged in these programs and will, when they emerge, deal with such issues as communication skills, sensitivity, empathy, and self-mastery, regardless of the formal education or lack of it commanded by the trainee.

A broad array of nonresidential, community-based, self-help activities are developing throughout the nation: hot lines, drop-in centers, runaway houses, free clinics, and a host of other acute social and health service facilities, all relying on youthful, indigenous, and nonprofessional staffs with the backup, training and support of occasional professionals. Young people in trouble with drugs have been turning to facilities with such names as "The Open Door," "The Kool'Aid," "Bridge," "Help," "Concern," "Sanctuary," "Place," to be talked down from a bad trip, for a meal, for a place to sleep, or because of a feared overdose, as a way of getting back home or just for someone to talk to. These services are conspicuous for their informality, accessibility, and lack of concern for protocol, records, appointments, and other amenities of more established service systems. They generally convey an atmosphere of openness, dedication, and youth. These programs frequently survive on a week-to-week basis, with inordinate energies being expended to raise funds for rent, food, or an occasional salary. They are frequently harassed by local authorities, who provoke police surveillance or unduly rigorous enforcement of zoning, public health, or safety ordinances. Despite this, the morale is usually quite high in these centers, where a sense of common destiny, the accoutrements of a counterculture, and interminable encounter sessions sustain the cohesion and commitment of the staff.

The therapy that such programs provide differs from the traditional group psychotherapy administered by mental health professionals in two major ways. (1) It focuses more on the health and competence of the client than on his pathology. (2) The orientation is almost exclusively on the here and now. While the programs vary widely in the intensity, frequency, or formality of group experiences, there is rarely any preoccupation with the nomenclature of pathology or with the origins of current behavior in the distant past. An uncovering technique is premised not on exploring a repressed oedipal conflict but on identifying as vividly and urgently as possible the immediate behavior of an individual in a social system.

The emergence of such self-help programs has an importance greater than the provision of an array of services for young drug users. These programs represent models for other human-service systems, which will have to meet their manpower needs by developing pragmatically trained nonprofessionals rather than relying on a system of elitist guilds. They are models for helping relationships where the gap between the person giving the help and the person receiving the help is not so vast, so imperialistic, nor so exploitative as it has been in the past.

Perhaps even more importantly, the self-help program has an implication for the rest of society as a model for institutions for the young. The school has rarely shown itself to be a societal arrangement for meeting the current needs and recognizing the current capacities of youth. It not only has done a rather poor job of meeting society's own needs but it has emerged as a joyless, alien, stultifying environment imposed on that part of the population usually referred to as society's hope but treated as its refuse. These programs provide models for new ways to deal with the young, where they may learn important skills, such as how to communicate, how to get along with peers and authorities, how to organize, and, perhaps the most important skill of all, how to help a fellow human being. In many communities they are the only places where adolescents may congregate without being told to move on or buy something.

As examples of institutions for the young, self-help programs have implications for the primary prevention of drug abuse that may be more profound than any other effort, including the expenditure of millions of dollars on drug-education curricula in school systems which in other ways do violence to young minds.

I have not discussed the role of methadone maintenance as a treatment technique. It has shown promise as a method controlling illicit drug use and the associated criminal behavior in adult populations of hard-core, long-standing recidivist opiate addicts. It has not been demonstrated to be an appropriate treatment for youthful drug users. Federal guidelines, as well as clinical and ethical constraints, would indicate some caution in the widespread experimentation with a technique that consigns people to an indefinite opiate addiction.

A final word about the role of government vis-à-vis drug programs: It is clear that municipal and county agencies should facilitate rather than interfere with the development of community-based programs of the self-help variety. Given the political environment and the relative incompetence of civil-service dominated bureaucracies, state government should not itself be the provider of service to drug users. As an administrative unit, state government is appropriate for the establishment of standards, the evaluation of performance, and the allocation of resources. Local communities are too impoverished to support drug programs and federal and private sources are too capricious.

Finally, as the first rule of medicine, *primum non nocere* might serve as a first principle of public policy. It would appear that the imposition of criminal sanctions on the use of drugs has resulted in harm. A rational and compassionate society should not feel the need to further punish the victims of its own negligence.

❲ Bibliography

1. BLUM, R., et al. *Society and Drugs.* Vol. 1. San Francisco: Jossey-Bass, 1969.
2. BALL, J. C. "Marijuana Smoking and the Onset of Heroin Use." In J. O. Cole and J. R.

Wittenborn, eds., *Drug Abuse*. Springfield, Ill.: Charles C Thomas, 1969. Pp. 117–128.

3. CHEIN, I., et al. *The Road to H*. New York: Basic Books, 1964.

4. COLE, J. O., and WITTENBORN, J. R. *Drug Abuse*. Springfield, Ill.: Charles C Thomas, 1969.

5. DONNELL, J. A. *Narcotic Addicts in Kentucky*. Chevy Chase, Md.: National Institute of Mental Health, 1969. Pp. 32–42.

6. DUMONT, M. "The New Face of Professionalism." *Social Policy*, 1, no. 1 (June 1970), 26–31.

7. DUVALL, H. J., LOCKE, B. A., and BRILL, L. "Follow-Up Study of Narcotic Addicts Five Years after Hospitalization." *Public Health Reports*, 78 (March 1963), 185–193.

8. GELINEAU, V., JOHNSON, M., and PEARSALL, D. "A Survey of Adolescent Drug Use Patterns," *Massachusetts Journal of Mental Health*, 3, no. 2 (Winter 1973), 30–40.

9. HUNT, G. H., and ODOROFF, M. E. "Follow-Up Study of Narcotic Drug Addicts after Hospitalization." *Public Health Reports*, 77 (January 1962), 41–54.

10. KRAMER, J. C. "The State Versus the Addict: Uncivil Commitment." *Boston University Law Review*, 50, no. 1 (Winter 1970), 1–22.

11. VAILLANT, G. E. "A Twelve Year Follow-Up of New York Narcotic Addicts: The Relation of Treatment to Outcome." *American Journal of Psychiatry*, 122 (January 1966), 727–737.

CHAPTER 20

DEPRESSION AND SUICIDE

James M. Toolan

I N 1961 GRINKER et al.[23] stated, "It is a curious phenomenon, that, although depressions are so frequent, not only in hospital practice but also among ambulatory patients seeking clinical and private office care, very few investigations have been made on this syndrome as contrasted with the intensive work carried out on schizophrenic, psychosomatic and other psychiatric conditions." Over the past ten years this situation has been partially corrected. Numerous studies have been published, mainly on the possible biochemical basis of depression and even more frequently on the response of depression to various antidepressive medications. Almost all the work done has been concerned with the adult patient.

The question of depression in children and adolescents has continued to receive little attention. The indexes to Kanner's *Child Psychiatry*[27] and the first edition of the *American Handbook of Psychiatry*[5] do not include the term. Beck,[7] in a 370-page monograph on depression, failed to refer to depression in children and adolescents, while Klerman,[32] in a very recently published review of clinical research in depression, did not cite a single paper on this topic.

Why is there such a striking discrepancy in the attention paid to depressive reactions in adults as compared with children and adolescents? Several factors are responsible. Some authors, among them Rochlin, have concluded, on purely theoretical grounds, that "clinical depression, a superego phenomenon, as we psychoanalytically understand the disorder, does not occur in childhood."[39] Others have stressed the absence in children of the usual clinical signs and symptoms that characterize depression in adults. As Lehman[33] wrote,

There has always been agreement among clinicians about the phenomena that characterize the psychiatric condition which we call depression or sometimes melancholia. The characteristic symptoms are: a sad, despairing mood, decrease of mental productivity and reduction of drive; retardation or agitation in the field of expressive motor responses. These might be called the primary symptoms of depression. There are also secondary symptoms—feelings of helplessness; hypochondriacal preoccupations; feelings of depersonalization; obsessive-compulsive behavior; ideas of self-accusation and self-depreciation; nihilistic delusions; paranoid delusions; hallucinations; suicidal ruminations and tendencies.

We seldom encounter similar clinical pictures in children and preadolescents. This has led Rie,[38] following a review of the literature on depression in children, to conclude, "An examination of the implications for child psychopathology of the dynamics of adult depression, including the roles of aggression, orality, and self-esteem, generates serious doubt about the wisdom of applying the concept of depression to children." He then stated: "There may be room to believe that the fully differentiated and generalized primary affect characterizing depression, namely despair or hopelessness, is one of which children—perhaps prior to the end of the latency years—are incapable."

Recently, however, several authors concluded that depressions do occur in children and adolescents. I have indicated[47] that in order to recognize depressions in children and adolescents "we have to cease thinking in terms of adult psychiatry and instead become accustomed to recognizing the various manifestations by which depression may be represented in younger people." A few earlier papers also indicated that even the classical type of depression might occur in the very young. In 1946 Spitz and Wolf[44] described a group of institutionalized infants with symptoms of withdrawal, insomnia, weeping, loss of weight, and developmental retardation. Some of these symptoms progressed to stupor and death. The authors coined the term "anaclitic depression" to describe what would better be called an infantile depression. Separation from the mother between the sixth to eighth month, for at least a three-month period, was postulated as the cause of this reaction. The better the mother-child relationship had been, the more severe the reaction following separation. In the same year Goldfarb[22] described intellectual and social retardation in a group of institutionalized children as owing to emotional deprivation, but did not use the term "depression."

Engel and Reichsman[17] described an infant with a gastric fistula who spontaneously developed a depressive reaction and in whom they could induce a depression experimentally. After the infant recovered from depression and marasmus, she would react with a de-pressive-withdrawal reaction when confronted with a stranger, but would recover when united with a familiar person. The authors believed this reaction was due to loss of the mother and the infant's awareness of her helpless state. Sandler and Joffe[40] posited a similar explanation for childhood depression. Bowlby,[12] who exhaustively studied the effect of separating a child from its mother, described three stages that the child undergoes when separated from the mother: protest, despair, and detachment. All these can be considered as various stages of depression in youngsters, though Bowlby[12] preferred to use the term "mourning."

Earlier, Despert[16] stated that "depression in children is not so uncommon as a survey of the literature would indicate." Out of 400 children she treated, 26 were described as having "depressive moods and/or evidencing preoccupation with suicide or expressing realistic suicidal threats." Eleven children who reacted to the death of a parent with depression were described by Keeler.[00] He noted that children often mask such feelings and recommended the use of psychological testing to help the clinician recognize these emotions.

A six-year-old boy with acute poliomyelitis, who developed a severe depression, was noted by Bierman, Silverstein, and Finesinger[10] to resemble adult depressives. "He looked sad and depressed, so much so that the interviewer was prompted to record that he had at times what one would call in an adult a melancholic facies. He talked in a low, weak, sad voice." This depression lasted for two months after his departure from the hospital. The authors noted that the youngster "said very little directly about his disability, but in his doll play and psychological test performance a great deal was revealed which bears on the topic of body damage and hence on the narcissistic injury. The extent and severity of the perceived damage far surpassed those of the disability as objectively measured." Lowered self-esteem, similar to that seen in adult melancholics, was emphasized by the authors.

In an eight- to eleven-year-old age group seen in outpatient therapy, Harrington and Hassan[24] noted that seven girls out of a group of fourteen were depressed. They described "a common syndrome of weeping bouts, some flatness of affect, fears of death for self or parents, irritability, somatic complaints, loss of appetite and energy, and varying degrees of difficulty in school adjustments." They also noted the comparison to the clinical picture seen in adult neurotic depressives and related the depression to self-depreciation and ego weakness.

Agras[2] studied the relationship of school phobia to childhood depression in seven children between the ages of six and twelve. He suggested the term "depressive constellation" to describe a propensity toward depression in both mother and child. He described "a syndrome comprising depressive anxiety, mania, somatic complaints, phobic and paranoid ideation" which he believed to be "close phenomenologically to the depressive disorders of adults." Campbell[14] also related school phobias to depressive reactions in children, though he believed them to be a variety of manic-depressive disorders. Homesickness in children was described by Statten[45] as a "symptom complex, usually associated with separation from home, which reflects an underlying depressive state, to which a child is attempting to adjust."

Sperling[43] introduced the term "equivalents of depression" in children. She and I[47] emphasized that the clinical manifestations of depression in children differ from the picture as seen in adults. Both studies mentioned anorexia, gastrointestinal disorders such as ulcerative colitis, and sleeping difficulties as indications of depression, especially in infants and younger children. They also both noted that the mothers of such children are often depressed. Ling, Oftedal, and Weinberg[35] described headaches as a symptom of depression in ten out of twenty-five children with the presenting complaint of headache. He also noted a strong family history of depression in such cases.

In the latency-aged child I[47] described behavioral difficulties such as truancy, disobedience, temper tantrums, and running away from home as depressive equivalents. I added, "The youngster is convinced that he is bad, evil, unacceptable. Such feelings lead him into antisocial behavior, which in turn only further reinforces his belief that he is no good. The youngster will often feel inferior to other children, and that he is ugly and stupid." Preadolescents exhibit similar behavior. Denial is frequently utilized as a means of avoiding facing depressive feelings. Boys find it especially difficult to express depressive feelings, as they often regard them as evidence of weakness.

Younger adolescents may evidence depression by boredom, restlessness, an inability to be alone, a constant search for new activities. Many adolescents exhibit such symptoms occasionally, but the persistence of these traits should be suspect. Depression may also be manifested by feelings of alienation, isolation, and emptiness. The tendency of adolescents to group together in fraternities and communes is often an attempt to find support in each other and relief from such feelings. Many will resort to the frequent and excessive use of drugs and alcohol to escape their painful emotions. Sexual activity, often of a promiscuous nature, is frequently attempted to alleviate feelings of depression and loneliness. Such behavior, though temporarily successful, often leads only to guilt and further depression. Many a teenage girl has become pregnant out of wedlock in the vain attempt either consciously or unconsciously to escape feelings of boredom and depression.

Bodily complaints encountered in adolescents who are depressed are often similar to symptoms found in depressed adults. Fatigue is a frequent presenting complaint. It is especially significant when present upon awakening in the morning. Hypochondriacal complaints and bodily preoccupations should always make one suspicious of an underlying depression in any adolescent.

Difficulty in concentration is one of the most frequently encountered complaints presented by depressed adolescents. Teachers, guidance counselors, and physicians should always take this complaint seriously. Previously bright students will begin to fail academically, much to the amazement of parents and faculty alike. These students will become discouraged, convinced that they are not able to cope with their studies. Such a conclusion can only diminish their already weakened self-esteem and lead to further depression. Nicoli,[37] studying dropouts from Harvard University, concluded that "depression is by far the most frequent and the most significant causal factor in the decision to interrupt or terminate one's college experience." He related the depression to an

awareness of a disparity between the ideal self as a uniquely gifted intellectual achiever and the real self as one of thousands of outstanding students struggling in a threateningly competitive environment. This awareness, gradual or abrupt, results in the clinical picture frequently observed in the dropout; feelings of lassitude, inadequacy, hopelessness, low self-esteem, and inability to study.

We have very little information as to the effect that depression, occurring during the adolescent years, will have on future psychic functioning. Hill[25] wrote that "suicide is significantly more common in depressed women who lost their fathers at age ten to fourteen, and to a lesser extent at fifteen to nineteen. Men and women whose mothers died in the first ten years of their lives also attempted suicide more often." This suggests that these children may have become depressed following their parents' death and continued as depressed adults. I believe that though some may spontaneously overcome depressive feelings during adolescence, many do not. One can only speculate what influence depressive feelings during adolescence can have on the psychotic depressions of the involutional years.

Many depressed adolescents utilize denial and acting out as a means of avoiding depressive feelings. Such acting out may lead to serious delinquent behavior, as described by Kaufman and Heims:[29] "A crucial determinant (in delinquency) is an unresolved depression, which is the result of the trauma which these children have experienced." They noted further: "We consider the delinquent acts of taking and doing forbidden things or expressing resentment and hostility to the de-

priving world as the child's pathologic method of coping with the depressive nucleus." Burks and Harrison[13] came to a similar conclusion, viewing aggressive behavior on the part of many delinquents as a method of avoiding depression. Kaufman and Heims[29] theorized that delinquents suffer from a severely impoverished self-image and a profound emptiness of ego, comparable to the emptiness of the schizophrenic ego.

During midadolescence classical depressive reactions are frequently encountered. In addition to many of the classical signs and symptoms of depression, the adolescent often exhibits a confused self-identity. He may complain of being isolated, unworthy, and unlovable. Such a youngster may appear to resent his parents, yet in reality is overly dependent on them. Separation from home and parents, owing to leaving for service or college, will often lead to a profound homesickness and depression. The separation from the parents, though often eagerly desired, is experienced as a loss of love.

In reviewing the histories of depressed adolescents, one discovers that many exhibited behavioral difficulties prior to the onset of their depressive symptoms, difficulties which have previously been called "depressive equivalents."[47] Thus the thesis that such symptoms are manifestations of depression in younger persons would appear to be substantiated. It is of interest that the behavioral difficulties usually disappeared when the overt clinical picture of depression developed.

In a discussion of depression in children some mention must be made of the incidence of manic-depressive psychosis. There is almost unanimous agreement that manic-depressive reactions are extremely rare in children and young adolescents. Kasanin and Kaufman[28] were able to describe only four effective psychoses before sixteen years of age, and all four cases presented initial symptoms after fourteen years of age. Anthony and Scott,[4] after an extensive review of the literature on manic-depressive psychosis from 1884 to 1954, discovered only three cases in late childhood that they felt qualified for the diagnosis; they added one case of their own where the initial symptoms occurred at twelve years of age. Campbell[14] is one of the few authors to believe that manic-depressive psychosis is not unusual in children. His views have not received much recognition. Hyperactive, manic-like behavior is often observed in children and adolescents, but on careful clinical observation and study it is almost always diagnosed as the symptoms of a hyperactive, brain-damaged child or an excited schizophrenic.

Psychological testing can be most helpful in recognizing depression in children and adolescents. As already mentioned, many depressed youngsters find it difficult to openly face and discuss their painful feelings. In fact, many will utilize denial to a considerable degree and cover up their depressive feelings with aggressive behavior. One must always bear in mind that the psychodiagnostic picture is often different from that seen in adult depressives. Anger is usually openly expressed, while depressive feelings remain in the background, the reverse of the usual adult patterning. There may be a diminution of color responses on the Rorschach. The Rorschach also shows images of body emptiness, as well as angry, aggressive, sadistic ones. On the WISC or WAIS, one usually finds a higher performance than verbal score—once again the reverse of that seen in adult depression. This patterning is similar to that shown by sociopaths and may be related to the tendency toward acting out already described.

Dream and fantasy material can be of assistance in the study of depression in children and adolescents. They often dream of dead persons calling them to the other world. Not infrequently they dream of being attacked and injured. On other occasions their dreams will picture bodily emptiness or loss of various parts of the body. Kaufman and Heims[29] and I[47] interpreted such loss of bodily parts to a loss of a significant relationship rather than to castration anxiety. The fantasies of depressed youngsters constantly refer to the theme of being unloved and unwanted. They frequently fantasize that they belong to another family. Fantasies of running away from home and of being dead are also frequently encountered. Associated with both these is the recurrent thought that someone (usually the parents) will be sorry for having treated them so badly.

❨ Diagnosis

The new classification of the American Psychiatric Association[3] is very unsatisfactory concerning the classification of childhood disorders. Depression is not even mentioned. Faux and Rowley,[19] however, proposed the following categories of depression in children and adolescents:

Grief Response (Functional Depression)
　Overt depression manifested by feelings of futility, guilt, unworthiness, or self-destruction.
　Depression masked by manipulative expression.
　Depression masked by denial.
　Depression masked by hostility.
　Depression associated with withdrawal and fantasy.
Endogenous Depressive Diathesis (A term that implies an idiopathic constitutional tendency; possibly the early manic-depressive should be so categorized.)
Depression Associated with Cultural Deprivation (A circumstance in which there is insufficient stimulation, which results in listlessness and apathy.)
Depression Associated with Physical Incapacity (Medical disorders: diabetes, polio, muscular dystrophy, etc. Mutilation: amputations, burns, etc.)
Drug-Induced Pseudo-Depression (A type of reaction that occasionally occurs when hypnotics, anticonvulsants, or sedatives are used in the treatment of emotional or physical disorders.)

❨ Therapy

The management of depressive youngsters must of necessity be individualized. The approach will vary, depending on age, family composition, clinical picture, facilities available, and so on. The infant diagnosed as anaclitic, or with infantile depression, needs an immediate change in his living arrangements. Such an infant needs one significant person to care for him, ideally his mother. We must not forget Spitz's and Wolf's[44] warning that such children may not recover if the clinical condition continues beyond three months. While the therapy of such youngsters is important, the prevention of such reactions is even more so. Infants should be separated from their mothers only when absolutely necessary. If infants and children need hospitalization, mothers should be encouraged to visit daily, to care for and feed the child. If an infant must be placed in an institution (for example, prior to adoption), every effort should be made to assign one adult to care for him.

The management of children and early adolescents who mask a depression with behavioral difficulties must be similar to that suitable for acting-out youngsters in general. As a rule, such youngsters do not realize that they need help, and often their parents do not either. These youngsters are usually referred by school and court authorities. Psychotherapy as a general rule is often a difficult pursuit, since they not only do not recognize the need for help but use denial and projection to avoid facing their painful feelings of depression and emptiness. The therapist must help the youngster realize that he is unhappy and that his acting out is a symptom of his depression. Patience is required, as usually a considerable time will elapse before the patient is able to confront and talk about his depressive feelings. One must avoid premature interpretations lest the youngster be frightened and discontinue therapy. Such youngsters will often test the therapist to prove to themselves that he cares for them, no matter what they do or how they behave. One must also bear in mind the fact that they may appear to earnestly desire and need a close relationship with the therapist, but will often become anxious if they achieve such closeness, fearing that they will lose it as they have lost other significant persons in their lives. If therapy does succeed with these youngsters, the therapist must be alert to the appearance of frank depressive symptoms, which necessitates a different technical approach.

Working with the more overtly depressed adolescent patient presents different problems. Some therapists become frightened of the potential suicidal risk and unnecessarily urge hospitalization. Other therapists may become bored and impatient at the slow progress and find it difficult to listen to a continual recital of hurt, unhappy feelings. Still others may be unduly sympathetic, thus encouraging the patient to preserve his depressive feelings, since relinquishing them may mean loss of the therapist's interest and concern.

The depressed adolescent, even more than most patients, must depend on the therapist relationship as his main support. He must be able to trust the therapist and rely on him. Only then will he gain the strength and courage necessary to confront his depressive feelings. These depressed patients are often very demanding of the therapist's time, attention, and concern. They swing between trust and distrust for a considerable period of time before they can realize that the therapist will not desert them. Since most depressed patients feel unworthy and unlovable, it is understandable that they doubt that anyone can truly care for them. Therapy with the depressed adolescent in general is facilitated by the patient's recognition that he is unhappy. Unlike the acting-out, depressed child, these patients are usually desirous of help. Not infrequently, however, they have to convince their parents, teachers, physician, and so on that they require psychiatric care. All too often their complaints are tossed off lightly as growing pains or with "All adolescents are unhappy at times" or "Pull yourself together and stop feeling sorry for yourself." It is not unusual for such an adolescent to resort to a suicidal attempt in order to have his problems taken seriously.

In most instances, depressed adolescents require intensive therapy. Simple techniques, such as support, suggestion and reassurance, or environmental manipulation, appear to resolve the problems, but all too often the improvement will be short-lived. Placement away from home is seldom indicated unless the suicidal risk is high. In fact, it is extremely important to have the parents actively involved in the therapeutic program so they can be helped to understand the feelings of loss of love that affect their child. The parents also will often need help with their own feelings of responsibility and guilt. For these reasons many believe family therapy to be of great value in treating depressed adolescents. At this moment, however, it is too early to evaluate the effectiveness of this new technique, compared with individual therapy of child and parent.

Most clinicians appear convinced that antidepressant medication is of great assistance in the management of adult depressive reactions. Children and adolescents appear to respond less favorably. One might speculate that perhaps younger patients metabolize these compounds differently than older patients. Close clinical observation would appear to indicate, however, that whenever the child or adolescent originally presents a clear-cut depressive picture, the response to antidepressant medication is similar to that observed in adults.[15,21] A less favorable response is seen in the depressive reactions manifested by behavioral difficulties. Ling et al.[35] reported favorable responses to antidepressant medication in youngsters, aged four to sixteen, presenting headaches as a mask for their depression.

There appears to be very little use of electroconvulsive therapy (ECT) in treating the depressive reactions of children and adolescents. During the past ten years, many clinics have discontinued electroconvulsive therapy in adult depression, except following an unsuccessful trial of antidepressant medication or where the suicidal risk is evaluated as being very high, so that the therapeutic time lag that occurs with antidepressant medication is dangerous. At present, very few child psychiatrists use electroconvulsive therapy. I would recommend that it be used only as a last resort with adolescents who present a clinical picture of overt depression, when psychotherapy and medication have proven ineffective.

(Suicide

Suicide and suicidal attempts are not infrequent in childhood and adolescence, although even professional persons have been slow to recognize that fact. This has been due in large part to the belief that adolescents do not become depressed and hence are unlikely to commit suicide. As a matter of fact, the rate of suicide among adolescents has shown the greatest rise of any age group. The rate at ages fifteen to nineteen years rose nearly 50 percent, from 4.0 per 100,000 during 1950–1952 to 5.9 per 100,000 during 1960–1962. Jacobziner[26] stated that

Suicide in adolescence has increased and is assuming proportionally greater importance as deaths from other causes decline. Of the total number of reported suicides in the United States in 1962, 659 individuals were less than 20 years old. One was a white male seven years of age, 102 were between ten and fourteen years, and 556 were in the fifteen to nineteen age group. A total of 499 were male and 160 female, a sex ratio of over 3:1.

Suicide ranks as the fourth leading cause of death in the fifteen-to-nineteen age group. It is surpassed only by accidents, malignant neoplasm, and homicide, and it surpasses deaths from tuberculosis, leukemia, nephritis, rheumatic fever, appendicitis, and all contagious diseases. It should not be overlooked that all figures for reported suicide are underestimated, probably more so for children and adolescents than for adults. The Suicide Prevention Center of Los Angeles estimated that up to 50 percent of all suicides are disguised as accidents. Since we are increasingly aware that many accidents are attempts at self-destruction, and accidents currently lead all the causes of death in childhood and adolescence by a large margin, the inference to be drawn is apparent.

Males consistently outnumber females in deaths by suicide, in all age groups throughout the world. The incidence of suicidal attempts, however, shows a reverse sex ratio; females greatly outnumber males at every age. I[48] reported an incidence of seven to one in studying the Bellevue Hospital adolescent population[26]. If it is difficult to obtain accurate figures for suicides, it is almost impossible to do so for attempted suicides. Jacobziner[26] estimated the ratio of attempted suicide to actual suicide at 100 to 1.

There have been surprisingly few studies on suicidal attempts by children and adolescents. Bender and Schilder[8] reported on eighteen children under eighteen years of age who threatened or attempted suicide. They were described as reacting to an intolerable situation. They felt unloved, became angry, and then felt guilty for having such feelings. Balser and Masterson[6] reported thirty-seven attempted suicides out of a group of 500 adolescent patients. I[48] reviewed the statistics of Bellevue Hospital in New York City for 1960. Of approximately 900 admissions to the children's and adolescents' units, 102 were for suicidal attempts and threats. Of these, eighteen were under twelve years of age, and eighty-four were between twelve and seventeen years of age. The youngest child was a five-year-old boy who attempted suicide on several occasions by burning himself with a gas heater and pouring scalding water over himself.

Analysis of the patients reported shows many came from disorganized homes. Less than one-third resided with both parents. Fathers were conspicuously absent from the homes. First children were disproportionately represented. Diagnostically, behavior and character disorders composed the largest group. In general they were immature, impulsive youngsters who reacted excessively to stresses that were often of a minor nature. The patients were divided into five categories in terms of dynamics.[48]

1. Anger at another which is internalized in the form of guilt and depression. Usually the parents or parent substitutes were the original objects.
2. Attempts to manipulate another, to gain love and affection or to punish another. Such attempts were often directed against the parents, with the fantasy of "You will be sorry when I am dead. You will realize how badly you treated me."
3. A signal of distress. The youngster often feels impelled to make a dramatic gesture to call the parents' attention to his problems, which the parents have often overlooked or ignored.
4. Reaction to feelings of inner disintegration, for example, in response to hallucinatory commands.
5. A desire to join a dead relative.

Schrut[42] described nineteen adolescent patients who attempted suicide. His group was noteworthy for hostility and self-destructive behavior. He postulated a mechanism similar to mine,[48] namely, the child felt rejected and became angry with his parents. This caused the parents to become increasingly angry with the child, and thus a destructive cycle was established.

The proper evaluation of suicidal patients is never a simple matter, but it is especially challenging in the case of children and adolescents. It is not unusual to encounter an adolescent who has made a serious suicide attempt and yet appears angry, not depressed, as an adult would be in the same situation. All suicide attempts, no matter if the threat to life was minor, should have a thorough psychiatric evaluation. Whenever possible a period of observation in a hospital is indicated. This can usually be arranged in the pediatric service of a general hospital if an inpatient psychiatric service is not available. Hospitalization not only protects the child against harming himself, but enables one to evaluate the child in a neutral setting, as well as the parents and family situation, before making definitive therapeutic plans. In addition, it may interrupt the conflict often present between suicidal patients and their parents. It is not unusual for parents to minimize the suicidal potential of their child's actions, or even to be angry with him for causing them personal distress and for disgracing the family. If the child does return home, the parents must be actively involved in the treatment program, otherwise efforts to help the child will usually fail.

⟮ Discussion

We can now conclude that while young children do not show depressive reactions similar to those seen in adults, such symptoms are present in adolescents from approximately age fourteen. Is this because the child under fourteen does not become depressed, or does he manifest depression in a different fashion? Although there is no general agreement on this point, careful analysis of the evidence would indicate that the latter is the case. This should not surprise one, as for many years child psychiatrists and child analysts debated the existence of childhood schizophrenia. It was maintained by many analysts on clinical grounds that children could not become schizophrenic. It is now established that children can become schizophrenic, even though the clinical picture differs from that seen in adults. It is significant that the clinical picture in childhood schizophrenia begins to resemble that of the adult also at approximately fourteen years of age. We must be constantly aware that the child is a developing organism and therefore expect the clinical picture to vary with the maturational level of the child. We should not allow theoretical formulations to influence our clinical judgment. As Boulanger[11] wrote,

A psychoanalyst may very well be reluctant to perceive in a child the equivalent of an adult's melancholia, for he is besieged at once by all the points of theory which are unsettled and passionately disputed within the school: the organization and function of the ego, superego, and object relationships, the origin of the Oedipus complex and the complexities of the instinctual development, the purpose of masochism and the validity of the death instinct.

The classical papers of Abraham[1] and Freud[20] postulated that a harsh, punitive superego turned aggression and hostility against the self, leading to depression. The depressed person was considered to have identified with the ambivalently loved lost object. The oral component of depression was emphasized by both Abraham[1] and Freud.[20] Klein[31] described what she called the depressive position of childhood in oral terms. She considered this to be a normal developmental stage for all infants. Her theory has not, however, met with a very favorable reception. Most psychoanalysts since Abraham[1] and Freud[20] have theorized that depression follows the loss of a significant love object, whether the loss be fantasy or reality. Bibring[9] advanced the theory that self-esteem is the key to understanding depression. "Depression can be defined as the emotional expression of a state of helplessness and powerless-

ness of the ego, irrespective of what may have caused the breakdown of the mechanism which established . . . his self-esteem." He indicated that the basic mechanism is "the ego's shocking awareness of its helplessness in regard to its aspirations."

The concept of self-esteem has assumed such significance in the theory of depression that Rie[38] was led to ask "at what point in the child's life such an experience develops with sufficient intensity to constitute what has been called low self-esteem." Quoting Erikson[18] and Loevinger,[36] he went on to state, "It may be no accident that this level of ego identity, or ability to conceptualize oneself, and the typical adult manifestations of depression are both generally agreed to occur at the earliest during adolescence." Rie[38] believed that an affect of helplessness is an essential picture of depression. After quoting Schmale[41] and Lichtenberg[34] he concluded, "There may be reason to believe that the fully differentiated and generalized primary affect characterizing depression, namely despair or helplessness, is one of which children perhaps prior to the latency years, are incapable."

The modification of Bibring's[9] theory of the significance of self-esteem in depression by Sandler and Joffe[40] answers the objections of Rie.[38] They "stress rather the basic biological nature of the depressive reaction, related to pain (and its opposite, 'well-being'), rather than the psychologically more elaborate concept of self-esteem." They continued that depression "can best be viewed as a basic psychobiological affective reaction which like anxiety, becomes abnormal when it occurs in inappropriate circumstances, when it persists for an undue length of time, and when the child is unable to make a developmentally appropriate reaction to it." They also revised the theory of the loss of the desired love object:

While what is lost may be an object, it may equally well be the loss of a previous state of the self. Indeed we would place emphasis on the latter rather than on the fact of the object-loss per se. When a love-object is lost, what is really lost, we believe, is the state of well-being implicit, both psychologically and biologically, in the relationship with the object. The young infant who suffers physical and psychological deprivation in the phase before object-representations have been adequately structured may show a depressive response to the loss of psychophysical well-being. Even an older child, who can distinguish adequately between self and object-representation, may react with depression to the birth of a sibling; a reaction which is not in our view an object-loss but rather a feeling of having been deprived of an ideal state, the vehicle of which was the sole possession of the mother. . . . If his response is characterized by a feeling of helplessness, and shows a passive resignation in his behavior, we can consider him to be depressed.

Thinking in developmental terms, Sandler and Joffe[40] realized that, as the child grows older, the object loss becomes of greater significance than the loss of the state of well-being embodied in the relationship to the object. They summed up their definition of depression "as a state of helpless resignation in the face of pain, together with an inhibition both of drive discharge and ego function." They were aware that some children will make strenuous efforts to regain the former state of well being, that some may react with anger and aggression, while others will regress to more immature levels.

The thesis that depression is a reaction to loss, either of an object or a state of well-being, with a feeling of diminished self-esteem and helplessness, enables us to understand the various manifestations of depressive reactions at different ages. The result of any object loss will depend on the individual's ability to tolerate pain and discomfort, be it physical or mental, and the developmental stage when such loss occurs. The younger the child the more serious the consequences. The infant may remain fixated in his ego development or even regress. At times, the impairment of ego development will hinder intellectual growth. The ability to form adequate object relationships may be significantly impaired. This will interfere with the ability of the individual to identify with significant figures in his life. Such disturbances in the process of identification will adversely affect the development of the superego, ego ideal, and the whole personality structure.

When the loss takes place during latency and early adolescence, the youngster will often exhibit hostility and anger toward the person whom he feels has betrayed and deserted him. This often leads to serious acting out and delinquency, which may temporarily help ward off painful feelings of helplessness and impotence. These defensive operations unfortunately seldom if ever prove successful and only lead to further conflict with the parents, who become increasingly antagonistic toward the child, who desperately needs their love and support. Some children will inhibit the expression of anger toward their parents and turn it against themselves. Such a child will consider himself to be evil, and such a self-image will lead to the acting out so commonly seen in depressed children. This behavior will reinforce the child's poor self-image, further lower his self-esteem, and increase his feelings of helplessness and depression.

Numerous defensive operations are used by children and adolescents to guard against the painful feelings of depression. The most frequently encountered are regression, repression, denial, and projection. We often note displacement onto somatic symptoms during adolescence. A reversal of affect is seen in some youngsters. Toward midadolescence, significant maturational changes occur in ego functioning, especially in the area of reality testing. The youngster will use denial to a lesser extent; he will see his parents' role in his object loss. This will not only increase his anger toward his parents but will also increase his guilt for having such feelings. The hostile feelings toward the parents become directed in midadolescence toward their introjects within the youngster, since, as I described elsewhere,[46] the superego does not fully develop until midadolescence. These changes, plus the knowledge that reality will not change and that he will not regain his lost love object, reinforce the adolescent's feelings of lowered self-esteem and helplessness and produce the clinical picture of overt depression.

Another factor that contributes to the formation of depression in adolescence is the resolution of the Oedipus complex, with its sense of parent loss. This sense of loss is increased when the child leaves home for the first time for boarding school or college. Many youngsters at that period still need parent substitutes with whom they can relate in order to diminish their feeling of parent deprivation. Others meet this need by relating closely to their own peer group, as is clearly illustrated in the so-called family communes. Those who fail to obtain some close relationship at this period frequently succumb to serious depressive reactions.

Finally, no review of the factors associated with depression in children and adolescents should overlook a possible role of the endocrines. A therapist cannot ignore the fact that many depressions occur and/or are accentuated concurrently with periods of endocrine imbalance or stress, for example, puberty, menstruation, and the postpartum and menopausal periods. What such a role may be is as yet completely unknown, though it is hoped that current studies will help elucidate the role of the hormones, particularly those, including the hypophysial secretions, related to sexual function.

In sum, a comprehensive review of the literature reveals controversy as to whether children under twelve years of age become depressed. The evidence indicates that they do, but that the clinical picture varies considerably from that seen in adult depressives. From fourteen years on, adolescents often exhibit the usual adult depressive symptoms. A theoretical explanation for depressive reactions in children and adolescents is offered to explain the varying clinical picture in terms of maturational changes.

❴ Bibliography

1. ABRAHAM, K. "Notes on the Psychoanalytic Investigation and Treatment of Manic-Depressive Insanity and Allied Conditions." In *Selected Papers*. London: Hogarth, 1927.
2. AGRAS, S. "The Relationship of School Phobia to Childhood Depression." *American Journal of Psychiatry*, 116 (1959), 533–536.
3. AMERICAN PSYCHIATRIC ASSOCIATION *Diagnostic and Statistical Manual of Mental Disorders*. 2d ed. Washington, D.C., 1968.
4. ANTHONY, J., and SCOTT, P. "Manic-Depressive Psychosis in Childhood." *Journal of Child Psychology and Psychiatry*, 1 (1960), 53–72.
5. ARIETI, S., ed., *American Handbook of Psychiatry*. Vol. 2. New York: Basic Books, 1959.
6. BALSER, B., and MASTERSON, J. F. "Suicide in Adolescents." *American Journal of Psychiatry*, 115 (1959), 400–405.
7. BECK, A. T. *Depression*. New York: Hoeber, 1967.
8. BENDER, L., and SCHILDER, P. "Suicidal Occupations and Attempts in Children." *American Journal of Orthopsychiatry*, 7 (1937), 225–234.
9. BIBRING, E. "The Mechanism of Depression." In P. Greenacre, ed., *Affective Disorders*. New York: International Universities Press, 1953.
10. BIERMAN, J., SILVERSTEIN, A., and FINESINGER, J. "A Depression in a Six-Year-Old Boy with Acute Poliomyelitis." *Psychoanalytic Study of the Child*, 13 (1958), 430–450.
11. BOULANGER, J. B. "Depression in Childhood." *Canadian Psychiatric Association Journal*, 11 (1966), S309–S311.
12. BOWLBY, J. "Childhood Mourning and Its Implications for Psychiatry." *American Journal of Psychiatry*, 118 (1960), 481–498.
13. BURKS, H. L., and HARRISON, S. L. "Aggressive Behavior as a Means of Avoiding Depression." *American Journal of Orthopsychiatry*, 32 (1962), 416–422.
14. CAMPBELL, J. D. "Manic-Depressive Disease in Children." *Journal of the American Medical Association*, 158 (1955), 154–157.
15. CONNELL, P. "Suicidal Attempts in Childhood and Adolescence." In J. G. Howells, ed., *Modern Perspectives in Child Psychiatry*. Edinburgh: Oliver & Boyd, 1965.
16. DESPERT, J. L. "Suicide and Depression in Children." *Nervous Child*, 9 (1952), 378–389.
17. ENGEL, G. L., and REICHSMAN, F. "Spontaneous and Experimentally Induced Depressions in an Infant with a Gastric Fistula." *Journal of the American Psychoanalytic Association*, 4 (1956), 428–453.
18. ERIKSON, E. H. "Growth and Crisis of the

'Healthy Personality.' " In M. J. E. Senn, ed., *Symposium on the Healthy Personality*. New York: Josiah Macy Jr. Foundation, 1950.

19. FAUX, E. J., and ROWLEY, C. M. "Detecting Depressions in Childhood." *Hospital Community Psychiatry*, 18 (1967), 31–38.

20. FREUD, S. *Mourning and Melancholia* (1917). Standard Edition. Vol. 14. London: Hogarth Press, 1949.

21. FROMMER, E. A. "Treatment of Childhood Depression with Antidepressant Drugs." *British Medical Journal*, 1 (1967), 729–732.

22. GOLDFARB, W. "Effects of Psychological Deprivation in Infancy and Subsequent Stimulation." *American Journal of Psychiatry*, 102 (1946), 18–33.

23. GRINKER, R. R., et al. *The Phenomena of Depressions*. New York: Hoeber, 1961.

24. HARRINGTON, M., and HASSAN, J. "Depression in Girls During Latency." *British Journal of Medical Psychology*, 31 (1958), 43–50.

25. HILL, O. W. "The Association of Childhood Bereavement with Suicidal Attempts in Depressive Illness." *British Journal of Psychiatry*, 115 (1969), 301–304.

26. JACOBZINER, H. "Attempted Suicides in Adolescence." *Journal of the American Medical Association*, 191 (1965), 101–105.

27. KANNER, L. *Child Psychiatry*. Springfield, Ill.: Charles C Thomas, 1960.

28. KASANIN, J., and KAUFMAN, M. R. "A Study of the Functional Psychoses in Childhood." *American Journal of Psychiatry*, 9 (1929), 307–384.

29. KAUFMAN, I., and HEIMS, L. "The Body Image of the Juvenile Delinquent." *American Journal of Orthopsychiatry*, 28 (1958), 146–159.

30. KEELER, W. R. "Children's Reaction to the Death of a Parent." In P. Hoch and J. Zubin, eds., *Depression*. New York: Grune & Stratton, 1954.

31. KLEIN, M. "A Contribution to the Psychogenesis of Manic-Depressive States." In *Contributions to Psychoanalysis*. London: Hogarth, 1948.

32. KLERMAN, G. L. "Clinical Research in Depression." *Archives of General Psychiatry*, 24 (1971), 305–319.

33. LEHMANN, H. E. "Psychiatric Concepts of Depression: Nomenclature and Classification." *Canadian Psychiatric Association Journal*, 4 (1959), S1–S12.

34. LICHTENBERG, P. "A Definition and Analysis of Depression." *Archives of Neurology and Psychiatry*, 77 (1957), 519–527.

35. LING, W., OFTEDAL, G., and WEINBERG, W. "Depressive Illness in Childhood Presenting as a Severe Headache." *American Journal of Disabled Children*, 120 (1970), 122–124.

36. LOEVINGER, J. "A Theory of Test Response." In *Invitational Conference on Testing Problems*. Princeton, N.J.: Educational Testing Service, 1959.

37. NICOLI, A. M. "Harvard Dropouts: Some Psychiatric Findings." *American Journal of Psychiatry*, 124 (1967), 105–112.

38. RIE, H. E. "Depression in Childhood: A Survey of Some Pertinent Contributions." *Journal of the American Academy of Child Psychiatry*, 5 (1967), 653–685.

39. ROCHLIN, G. "The Loss Complex." *Journal of the American Psychoanalytic Association*, 7 (1959), 299–316.

40. SANDLER, J., and JOFFE, W. G. "Notes on Childhood Depression." *International Journal of Psychoanalysis*, 46 (1965), 88–96.

41. SCHMALE, A. "A Genetic View of Affects with Special Reference to the Genesis of Helplessness and Hopelessness." *Psychoanalytic Study of the Child*, 19 (1964), 287–310.

42. SCHRUT, A. "Suicidal Adolescents and Children." *Journal of the American Medical Association*, 188 (1964), 1103–1107.

43. SPERLING, M. "Equivalents of Depression in Children." *Journal of the Hillside Hospital*, 8 (1959), 138–148.

44. SPITZ, R., and WOLF, K. M. "Anaclitic Depression: An Inquiry into the Genesis of Psychiatric Conditions in Early Childhood." *Psychoanalytic Study of the Child*, 2 (1946), 313–341.

45. STATTEN, T. "Depressive Anxieties and Their Defences in Childhood." *Canadian Medical Association Journal*, 84 (1961), 824–827.

46. TOOLAN, J. M. "Changes in Personality Structure During Adolescence." In J. H. Masserman, ed., *Science and Psychoanalysis*. New York: Grune & Stratton, 1960.

47. ———. "Depression in Children and Adolescents." *American Journal of Orthopsychiatry*, 32 (1962), 404–415.

48. ———. "Suicide and Suicidal Attempts in Children and Adolescents." *American Journal of Psychiatry*, 118 (1962), 719–724.

CHAPTER 21

TRANSITION
FROM SCHOOL TO WORK

Irwin M. Marcus

THE ISSUE OF WORK appearing in a text on psychiatry implies that a relationship may exist between personality and work. "Transition" suggests that there are possible developmental lines that may be traced from early childhood through adolescence and into adulthood; these have significance for vocational behavior.

Even in Anna Freud's[9] systematic and unique studies of normality, the concept of developmental sequences is limited to particular, circumscribed parts of the child's evolving personality. The basic interactions between intrapsychic phenomena at various developmental levels and environmental influences appear to be far more complex than some behaviorists would admit. The variables are myriad on the long road from the young child's egocentric view of life and his auto-erotic play to his games, hobbies, school activities, and arrival at work.

Available evidence indicates that, prior to puberty, the child's concept of work is in terms of adult activities and that whatever

vocational interests he expresses are linked to his wishes to grow up. Ginzberg et al.[11] and others agreed that the young child's ideas of work are in the realm of fantasies and are unrelated to either actual interests or abilities. I have treated little girls who expressed wishes to do the kind of work their fathers do or to be a father's secretary as variations of the Oedipal wish for possession of the father. These children perceive their mothers' housework and daily chores as unhappy experiences and verbalize their rejection of a future in that direction. I wonder if I am witnessing the buds of future women's liberation advocates. Many young boys have expressed their wishes to work with their fathers. I have seen this both in those who had experienced closeness and pleasure in a mutually satisfying relationship and in others whose fathers paid only slight attention to them or were primarily involved through discipline and punishment. The boy's need for closeness and identifications with his father obviously influences these early expressions of occupation goals. In other instances, the children are merely expressing their admiration of seemingly omnipotent heroes such as the astronauts who now walk on the moon; their football, baseball, and basketball favorites; and movie stars. Yes, some little girls still want to be movie stars. Children who reach the stage of gratifying relationships with me while in therapy have on occasion expressed the wish to be a doctor or specifically a psychiatrist. My own daughter, at three years of age, was once invited to the stage in the presence of a large audience and, when questioned by the master of ceremonies regarding what she wanted to be, shouted into the microphone, "Superman!"

Following more than two decades of provocative and intensive study of personality factors in occupational choice, Roe[30] concluded that there is little evidence that both specific and general early life experiences can be related to the choice of adult work. She found that there are many choice points along the road to maturity. Thus, personality can be considered as only one significant factor in the decisions made at a given occupational choice point. Education, personal talents, interests, and experience, as well as external variables in the environment, such as the prevailing economic situation, the societal attitude toward one's race, culture, or religion, and the ever-changing industrial technology influence the ultimate field of employment. It is no secret that prejudicial attitudes still exist in certain industries against particular groups. If, due to government pressures and publicity, hiring does occur in these industries, the opportunities for advancement are still quite limited. When information of this sort sifts down to a college group, the students who feel that the situation will influence their future veer away from certain vocational areas. Males and females have characteristically different developmental lines in their life history, so that understanding factors in the transition from school to work necessarily involves concepts that are not equally relevant to both.

Tiedeman, O'Hara, and Baruch[39] have shown that sex role and family status are no less significant than the self-concept in influencing occupational choice. It should not come as a surprise that their studies indicate that interest and personality inventories are more effective as predictors of choice of work than are aptitude tests. They confirmed the impression of Ginzberg et al.[11] impression that the self-concept in boys is in the process of consolidation during the high school years. The interests stage during the sophomore year of high school is followed by the development of work values toward the senior year. Rather than attempting to predict vocational choice, many serious researchers in this field are turning their attention to studying the vicissitudes of personality-environment interaction that crystallize into vocational identity. Holland[16,17] developed a vocational preferences inventory based on six environmental types: realistic, intellectual, social, conventional, enterprising, and artistic. He engaged in longitudinal studies of National Merit Scholarship finalists to relate their choice of major study in college to their scores on his scale.

In the past decade, Flanagan and associates[8] began a massive study of 440,000 students from a representative sample of high schools in our country with the focus on such personality variables as interests, abilities, and aptitudes. Their goal is to follow the work patterns for a twenty-year period, but the fluctuating environmental factors and any understanding of individual development will obviously have to be absent. They do plan to include data concerning certain characteristics of the school and community environment. In this way, the social environment is not completely ignored. Super and his associates[33,88] spent more than thirty years striving toward an understanding of the transition from school to work to strengthen the frame of reference necessary for helpful vocational counseling. Super felt that the counselor's role should not be a static one based on the assumption that the occupational traits are already fixed and therefore predictable. The accumulating evidence about the transition phenomenon toward work indicates that a dynamic role for the counselor is more appropriate. The counselor must try to understand which factors are crucial for each individual during the developmental stages toward an occupational choice and promote this exploration process. Vocational psychologists can easily become entangled in the maze of phenomena associated with theories of personality that deal with the self-concept. If the transition to work is significantly influenced by the student's picture of himself, the researcher must struggle with techniques to be employed or developed to search out the components that constitute a self-concept. In fact, there is considerable variation in even conceptualizing self-concept (note Eissler,[2] Erikson,[4] Fenichel,[6] S. Freud,[10] Greenacre,[12] Hartmann, Kris, and Loewenstein,[14] Jacobson,[18] Josselyn,[19] Kohut,[20] Levin,[22] Spiegel,[31] Sullivan,[32] and Wheelis[40]). Thus, theories that link self-concept and work can be thorny and much too complex for practical counseling.

The foregoing survey of authorities serves as a background for a closer examination of the previously mentioned work of Ginzberg et al.[11] who conceptualized the transition to work as a very general form of behavior requiring viewpoints from a multidisciplinary team of psychologists, psychiatrists, and sociologists. They viewed the transition toward vocational choice as a process that evolves over eight or ten years, while passing through a series of stages. This process has a degree of irreversibility in that earlier decisions will, in turn, limit the options for later decisions. Finally, they considered compromise prominent in every decision. Therefore, to a large degree, personal attributes are in interaction with environmental circumstances, and the work direction in the transition during maturation is funneled by the total situation, not just the self-concept Ginzberg el al. viewed the transition from school to work as going through an initial fantasy phase between ten and twelve years of age, followed by a tentative period from puberty into middle adolescence to about seventeen years of age, and finalized by the realistic stage, which extends into early adulthood. The fantasy phase is self-explanatory. During the tentative period, the adolescent begins to consider his abilities and interests more seriously. Those who have done poorly in mathematics and science are less prone to speak of careers requiring facility in these areas; however, the subjective approach is still prominent. The adolescent's preoccupation gradually shifts from his interests to his impression of his capacities and to values as with job status. However, the realistic stage includes the necessary compromises with environmental opportunities and actual awareness of skills, ability, and so on, as mentioned above.

In late adolescence, the exploratory activity, with its associated inquiries, varies with the initiative, curiosity, and aggressiveness of the individual. I have had those in this age group call me to discuss the field of psychiatry specifically as well as medicine in general. Such calls have come from those who do not know me personally but have heard my name or been in an audience where I have been a speaker. Similarly, girls have asked me about social work as a career. Ginzberg et al.[11] believed that the realistic phase concludes with crystallization and specification of a work choice. The significant issue in their concept of sequential phases is the irreversibility feature; namely, the academic selections along the road continue to limit the available options for later decisions. Thus, the time factor during the transition period from school to work is such that the later the decision, the less freedom for a change in direction.

The identity crisis, as described by Erikson,[3] is complex in its dynamics from both the intrapsychic and multienvironmental factors. In New Orleans, as in other old communities, the "who" of identity is reinforced by emphasis on who are the adolescents' relatives and ancestors and who has membership in the private Carnival Krewes and social clubs. There is, however, a noticeable shift occurring in each new wave of the generations, and the old advantages of snobbery for maintaining fixed social status and stabilizing identity are giving way. The grandchildren of some of this community's more outspoken anti-Semites are close friends with Jewish children. Many girls now feel that debuts are a waste of time and money and are shunning the exclusive clubs their families have depended upon for "sucking up" status for their identity. (I refer to "sucking" because it is the easy way to obtain nourishment; all one needs is a mouth.) Real and meaningful identity comes from one's own performance and personal development, not from ancestors and exclusive clubs. (The ancestor worshipers remind me of the potato —the best part being underground.) Work as a significant factor in one's identity is gradually replacing the traditional value systems of the past. Many of the youth of today wish to become involved in work activities that foster the preservation of the natural environment and the improvement of human relationships on a worldwide basis. Such young people are more interested in *what* they can do in life, and they wish to be identified on the basis of their goals rather than on who their friends may be or how much money their work will generate. Thus, the progress throughout schooling becomes a key issue in the work goals and identity that can be achieved by an individual. Where work identity becomes a pillar in the self-esteem structure, positions of less gratification and status as well as positions that involve delayed retirement can and often do trigger a depressive reaction or other forms of mental disturbance. Therefore, the psychiatrist and physicians in general should understand these work-identity interactions and related problems when confronted with patients.

Neff[28] considered the work personality as having a semiautonomous function. This is consistent with my own psychoanalytic observations[25] that individuals with severe character problems can continue to function effectively in skilled and complex occupations. The transition from school to work occurs within the matrix of total personality development. This developmental process is well known to students of human behavior. It is academic and possibly philosophical to argue whether the sexual and aggressive needs and feelings are the primary drives, the vicissitudes of these instincts leading to interest and pleasure in mastery, or whether mastery is a separate basic drive (Hartmann,[13] Hendrick[15]). Motor patterns and their associated pleasure were seen by Mittelmann[27] as an independent urge intimately connected with almost all other functions of the individual. Lantos[21] identified the latency period as the time when the transition from pleasure in motor activity to pleasure in mastery occurs. Erikson[3] similarly placed the shift in stages at this period when the child wants to learn to do things and to enjoy accomplishment. He called this phase the sense of industry, when the child enjoys recognition and prestige from producing things. During this stage, the child may feel inadequate and inferior when confronted with his unresolved conflicts and when comparing himself unfavorably with the adult world of parents and teachers, or with more effective children. Neff[28] felt that the concept of the superego should include internalization of other social and cultural demands in addition to the earlier childhood precepts of parental prohibitions. Thus, he saw the compulsion to work as a superego demand, and I would suggest an additional related factor, namely, the influence of the ego ideal with its images of the level of achievement desired in one's strivings. In my psychoanalytic work, I have found the entire transition phase from school to work influenced by conflicts in certain individuals.

One man, who was in his late twenties, was having great difficulty maintaining a consistent work level. He was about to lose a crucial position in his employment because he acted out his rage toward a superior authority. He was at that time withdrawn from his coworker peers and usually behaved in an ingratiating manner to his superiors. His school record was erratic, very poor in his earlier years with an apparent learning disability and gradual improvement later, after his father died during the patient's midadolescence. The withdrawal from peer-group relations was a chronic pattern during his school years; however, in his early teens there was a brief episode of homosexual submission to a peer. The patient's father was a successful businessman with an excellent reputation, from whom the patient received a mixture of affection and criticism. The worst conflicts occurred around the issue of the patient's poor performance in school. The patient was frequently reminded of his ultimate destiny, that he would end up as a bum, garbage collector, or a street cleaner if he did not "shape up" and do his school work.

The patient not only had a learning problem in his earlier schooling but was also clumsy in sports and subjected to teasing by his peers for his timidity and ineptness. In his early teens he was sent to military school to "make a man of him." Unfortunately, he was "made" there, but not into a man. He felt humiliated by this homosexual experience in which he was in the passive role and felt used, nor did he gain the friendships he sought through his submission. When told of his father's death, he felt guilty and confused by an awareness of the impulse to laugh. His relationship with his mother was worse than with his father. He had been cared for during early childhood by a series of nursemaids and felt no warm ties to his mother. He both hated and feared his mother's powers because she could dismiss his caretakers.

The early phase of his psychoanalysis was very rough on me, the psychoanalyst. He depreciated and attacked me with every vicious phrase he could muster. This was a difficult period, as I thought the analysis would have a better chance of supporting the stress after a phase of building trust and rapport. However, he had been repressing and suppressing so much rage for so long in his life that he obviously welcomed the opportunity to unload on me. My ability to "take it" became the testing ground for the trust. It also became clear that he did not want to listen to me, just as he always struggled against listening to teachers, because that meant he would have to be passive and submit to my penetrating comments. He finally revealed that he suspected that if he dropped his attacking defense, he would be helpless, and I would then use him sexually. The paranoid mechanisms and homosexual conflicts will not be elaborated on here. I merely wish to extract a few vignettes to demonstrate the relationship between this man's developmental history, personality patterns, and transition to a work style. He revealed his association of knowledge with power. Thus, if he learned more than his father, other authorities, and his peers, he could then "clobber the shit out of them." His learning disturbance continued to bother him even after his father died, though it was not so paralyzing as in

earlier years. Increasing data indicated that this disability was related to his guilt-ridden defenses. He wished to avoid integrating knowledge and the approach to any degree of successful achievement in order to prevent the destructive revengeful fantasies he harbored and feared would erupt in the wake of success. He was in constant fear of being unable to answer pertinent questions by superiors regarding his work activities. He had a history of changing schools and an urge to continue to alter his place of living. If this pattern had continued, from school to work, his record of being an unreliable, transient, and unstable worker would have fulfilled his father's dreaded prophecy.

The foregoing example emphasizes the importance of personality factors that influence work achievements in an adverse manner. Obviously, to arrive at a successful level of work ability, individuals must be capable of cooperative relationships with their superiors and peers and not be blocked by intrapsychic conflicts in achieving their capacity for competence.

The following is a brief example of the complex interaction between personality factors and work attitudes. This example, in contrast with the inhibitions in work, is in the area of work compulsions as a style of living. I analyzed a man in his midthirties who worked from about 7:00 A.M. to about 10:00 or 10:30 P.M. with another five or six hours on Saturday and Sunday. His work style was similar to that of many physicians, attorneys, and businessmen I have treated. Some of these patients were single; others were married. The avoidance of a wife and/or children at home did not appear to be a determining feature of their pattern. With specific individual variations, each of the men in this category felt deprivations regarding his reaction to the type of mothering he experienced in his childhood. In one instance, the mother was depressed, withdrawn, and bedridden; in another, she died early in his childhood; in a third case, his mother remarried following his father's death, and the patient felt rejected by his mother's attention to her new husband, preceded by her depression and her working outside the home following her husband's death. The deprivations are experienced as oral needs and threats to survival. All the above patients had problems regarding overweight from overeating and/or difficulty controlling their alcoholic consumption. The patient in this example had learning problems all the way through his schooling and into his college education. He failed in one college and held on marginally in another. He was very superior intellectually and ingested considerable information, but refused to give it back when confronted with examinations. His toilet training had been traumatic: He was subjected to enemas and had to show his defecated products before he was allowed to flush the toilet. The analysis revealed the association in his mind of examinations with having his bowel irrigated and his product checked over. Furthermore, in his compulsive work pattern, he identified his work with his mother and the financial compensation with her feeding him. He felt close to his mother, happy and secure while working, but he felt depressed and anxious when away from his occupational activities. This patient was not an example of the Sunday neurosis phenomenon described by Ferenczi[7] or the sublimation of aggression and hostility through work suggested by Menninger.[26] Anxiety is aroused when the person is faced with inactivity, and defense mechanisms are utilized to contain the anxiety, with resulting symptom formation.

The transition from school to work involves much more than a mere change in environment. It is also a change from supportive, friendly relationships with parental and school authorities to impersonal work authorities— the institution, company, or corporation. There is a change in living style and often in community environment. The necessary reorganization of personality orientation to one's self and others may produce a postadolescent identity crisis or a self-image crisis, to use Wittenberg's[41] concept. The anxiety level may be of sufficient intensity to create a variety of symptoms, including a transient depersonalization. The latter may occur not only in borderline character pathology but also in the neurotic and even so-called normal or healthy

person. The feeling is one of confusion toward one's self-image, the familiar continuity regarding sameness of one's personality seems lost, and the ability to feel comfortable and oriented toward the environment is similarly changed. I have seen this phenomenon in people who changed from high school to college, in others who changed jobs in the same city or changed cities in the same corporation, and in a number of immigrants from a variety of countries such as Germany, England, France, South America, and Asia. I approached these disturbances without drugs or hospitalization. I drew the patients' attention back to their memories of their previous more secure environment and orientation and fostered the reintegration from that point forward. So far, the technique has been successful in my private practice (since 1948), an adequate period of experience.

The adolescent revolt against his own superego, which is identified with the parental and authority restrictions, allows him to feel more independent in the reorganization of his personality. However, in the transition to the work world, which in the young adult may be characterized as the postadolescent phase, the conflict is somewhat different. The task of establishing an equilibrium between ego ideals and superego is pushed by the necessity to make a number of significant, serious decisions for adult life. Space does not permit a theoretical discussion of whether superego and ego ideal concepts are to be viewed as a single functional unit or as separate concepts (Arlow and Brenner,[1] Erikson,[4] Jacobson[18]).

Conflicts between ego ideals and superego stir the self-image crisis. Wittenberg[41] distinguished the pseudoideal from the true ego ideal. The former is linked with the grandiose, omnipotent fantasies of childhood. Learning problems in the college years may be in certain instances a result of such impossible expectations and a rigid, cruel superego demand for fulfillment of the superman achievements. The ensuing feelings of discontent, failure, and severe self-hatred and projected or real perception of disappointment in the parents have led some students to drop out and run away. In others, these feelings have led to the sad situations of suicide or serious drug usage cop-outs.

I am now psychoanalyzing a twenty-three-year-old white woman who arrives with filthy feet, either with sandals or barefoot, wearing loose, baggy, shredded blue jeans and a sweatshirt. She smells from avoiding usual bathing activities, but is intensely idealistic about ecology and voices a devotion to cleaning up our polluted environment. She has suffered severe feelings of inferiority, inadequacy, and guilt over her rejection of parental and community values. Although she is a college graduate, she has avoided the discipline of a remunerative occupation and has felt that she must work toward saving mankind from its self-destructive course. She feared that treatment might force her into the social mold she abhors, because she saw the therapist as a representative of middle-class social values. As she has come to perceive the focus of therapy as an opportunity to understand her conflicts, an opportunity allowing her to choose from a range of options besides the single one she had felt compelled to adopt, she has learned to trust the therapist. Her dread, almost panic, of maturation and adulthood became clear and has helped her to understand her tendency to cling to men who wished to control and dominate her. She felt a sense of security in adopting their values, joining their causes, and identifying with the sense of excitement they engendered in her. Their apparent comfort in being rebels, criticizing society, and living a Bohemian life gave her the stimulation she felt was really living. Gradually, she has realized she had merely substituted one mother for another—regarding controls, dependency, and demands. The one advantage of the present "mother" over the original one is the many forms of pleasure she can experience in bed. In bed, she and her mentor can reverse roles: There he wants her to be the aggressor and dominate him. However, she has as much conflict regarding her sex role in bed as she has in her "baby" role in the rest of their relationship.

The above is another vignette illustrating the self-image dilemma between superego and pseudoego ideals during this transition phase of life. The maturational conflicts are complex during development and interfere with the choice of work and the choice of mates. Marriage to a man who has decided on a career within the established system could gratify her wish to be a mother and have a secure and stable family life, but such a choice is unacceptable as long as she pursues her pseudoego ideal. She could feel as if she has submitted to her superego mother, which she would consider a regression to childhood. Yet, she unconsciously acts out her wishes to be the everlasting child by enjoying the pleasures of every impulse and avoiding as much reality and self-discipline as possible. Behind her wish for equality of the sexes, her women's liberation activities, and her preference for the loose shirts concealing her breasts and the pants zipping in the front is her envy of the male. She resented a man reacting to her with "Oh, she's a girl" recently when she put on a dress for a special occasion. He had previously seen her only in her typical costume. Wishes for a baby would come to the surface in her fantasies during intercourse and, as in many instances of this constellation, the wishes are acted out unconsciously by laxity in the use of contraceptives. She became pregnant and panicked at the thought of having a baby or even marrying the father. Her escape fantasies first went to suicide, but, as she worked with the issues in treatment, she finally decided to go on living and had an abortion. Then she had to force the conflict between her ego ideal of being a good mother and the reality of seeing herself as a woman who would destroy her baby.

Understandably, psychoanalytic work with young men and women during their self-image dilemma is difficult and must be done with thoughtfulness, kindness, and as much understanding as one can muster from training and experience. A rigid, harsh superego that demands fulfillment of several ego ideals can be a constant source of conflict and symptom formation, particularly depression. To be a good parent and spend time at home with one's child and spouse may be opposed by the wish to be dedicated to one's work and achieve success according to whatever values are used in measuring that goal. The conscience can lash out at the self-image either way, producing a continuous state of discontent, irritability, and a sense of failure. One defensive maneuver intended as a solution to a superego-ego ideal or pseudoego ideal conflict is to attack the representatives of the superego. In the preceding case illustration, the young woman was intent on humiliating her parents and thus diminishing their values and influence on her. When the superego is projected to the society or government, the hostility is in that direction. The provocations are brought to a point where attacks from these sources are unconsciously welcomed to rationalize and justify the conclusion that authorities are indeed bad and the "system" must be destroyed. The newspapers and television coverage have given us ample evidence of these destructive counteracts by these young people who are having great difficulty in navigating the transition from school to work.

The transition may lay dormant for many years and break out after ten or twenty years of a seemingly happy marriage and work situation. I can offer two brief examples. One concerns a married woman in her early forties and the mother of six children who decided that her husband had prevented her from having her own identity. She felt that all through the marriage she was expected to do all the things necessary to foster his social aspirations and personal pleasure and to help him fulfill his self-image. She felt empty, drained, and exhausted from the rapid succession of births and subsequent child-care requirements as well as an overwhelming boredom with the friends he considered of value to him. When the children were older, she enrolled in postgraduate courses and began a series of affairs. She had married shortly after college and was a bright, gifted, attractive woman, but felt frustrated about her own self-image and ego-ideal system, which included much more than motherhood and being a wife. Her individual activities, outside of the home, gave her an exciting sense of autonomy and a freedom from the symbiotic and unconsciously incestuous attachments to her husband. She felt much more of a sexual identity and a clearer impression of her ego boundaries when with other men in her academic milieu. Her husband and their social life were seen by her as a single unit and a threat to her survival as an individual. Much to his surprise, she suddenly announced to him that she wanted a divorce. After these circumstances occurred, treatment was sought because she was uncertain of her decision and troubled by the conflict with her superego and with the various pressures her husband brought to bear on her.

The other example is a male in his forties who had married after high school and walked out on his wife after their silver anniversary. They, too, had several children and appeared to be inseparable during their married life. He sold his successful business and decided he wanted to have a fresh start in life. This fresh start included dating girls in their early twenties and a lack of decision regarding his work interests. His wife was so shocked she became suicidal and was hospitalized. Their marriage also had all the earmarks of the symbiotic and unresolved aspects of psychosexual and identity conflicts.

The various defense mechanisms utilized in the struggles accompanying transition from school to work include projection, regression, denial, identification, and acting out. When pathological degrees of narcissism, ambivalence, and defense mechanisms weaken reality testing, the symptoms will vary with the character structure. The desperate effort to cling to waning youth in the transition from school to work is revived when people have delayed this consolidation of their personality, as in the two preceding examples. They attempt to look, act, and think young. The reality of the adult world appears boring, and they seek their last chance to live an exciting life and recapture or develop their sense of individuality and identity. Both groups—the young people in transition and the older ones who try to return to a new transition—have in common an aggressive, firm, and anxious desire to return to living by the pleasure principle. There is an underlying depressive longing for freedom and happiness without the burden of responsibilities to anyone but themselves and a wish for fulfillment of their self-image.

The adolescents in transition are alert to the effect of their behavior, achievements, and goals on their parents' self-image. They have difficulty at times deciding whether they are gratifying themselves or their parents when they are progressing in an acceptable direction. Similarly, if hostility and parental conflict are high, they feel both cryptic pleasure and guilt when their parents are embarrassed or enraged at unacceptable directions. I reported a study of learning problems in adolescents where these conflicts entered into the school failures.[23] In another study of 110 student nurses, I found that the autonomy need—to handle their own problems and make their own decisions regarding the pursuit of nursing as a career or to drop out and explore other work goals—prevented many girls from consulting others with their problems. They avoided not only the available student advisors but also their own peer group. The fear of outside influence on their identity struggles and sensitivity regarding their self-images led to impulsive decisions to drop out of training. The student nurses would present false excuses to the director of their school to rationalize their action. As a result, the school did not know how to approach or to solve the real problem of their relatively high dropout rate. My study of this group in transition from school to work led to an approach that favorably influenced the problem.[24]

In conclusion, the transition from school to work does involve problems of personality interaction with academic, social, and economic factors. The personality factors can enhance or disturb the development of the work behavior. However, the crystallization of a work personality allows for semiautonomous function. Thus upheavals in nonwork areas of the personality may not necessarily influence work patterns. On the other hand, disorders in the development of a successful transition from school to work cannot be solved by simply placing the person in a training school. This chapter, hopefully, will contribute some understanding of the interaction and vicissitudes of the dynamics involved.

([Bibliography

1. ARLOW, J., and BRENNER, C. *Psychoanalytic Concepts and the Structural Theory.* New York: International Universities Press, 1964.
2. EISSLER, K. R. "Problems of Identity." In panel reported by D. L. Rubinfine, *Journal of the American Psychoanalytic Association,* 6 (1958), 131–142.
3. ERIKSON, E. H. "Growth and Crises of the Healthy Personality." In *Identity and the Life Cycle. Psychological Issues.* Monograph 1. New York: International Universities Press, 1959. Pp. 50–100.
4. ———. "The Problem of Ego Identity." In *Identity and the Life Cycle. Psychological Issues,* Monograph 1. New York: International Universities Press, 1959. Pp. 101–164.
5. ———. *Childhood and Society.* 2d ed. New York: Norton, 1963.
6. FENICHEL, O. "Identification." In *The Collected Papers of Otto Fenichel.* Vol. 1. New York: Norton, 1953. Pp. 97–112.
7. FERENCZI, S. "Sunday Neurosis" (1919). In *Further Contributions to Psychoanalysis.* 2d ed. London: Hogarth Press, 1950. Pp. 174–176.
8. FLANAGAN, J. C., et al. *Design for a Study of American Youth.* Boston: Houghton Mifflin, 1962.
9. FREUD, A. *Normality and Pathology in Childhood.* New York: International Universities Press, 1965.
10. FREUD, S. "On Narcissism: An Introduction" (1914). *Collected Papers.* Vol. 4. London: Hogarth Press, 1948. Pp. 30–59.
11. GINZBERG, E., et al. *Occupational Choice: An Approach to a General Theory.* New York: Columbia University Press, 1951.
12. GREENACRE, P. "Early Physical Determinants in the Development of the Sense of Identity." *Journal of the American Psychoanalytic Association,* 6 (1958), 612–627.
13. HARTMANN, H. *Ego Psychology and the Problem of Adaptation.* New York: International Universities Press, 1958.
14. ———, KRIS, E., and LOEWENSTEIN, R. M. "Comments on the Formation of Psychic Structure." *Psychoanalytic Study of the Child,* 2 (1946), 11–38.
15. HENDRICK, I. "Work and the Pleasure Prin-

ciple." *Psychoanalytic Quarterly*, 12 (1943), 311–329.

16. HOLLAND, J. L. "Some Explorations of a Theory of Vocational Choice." *Psychological Monographs*, 76 (1962).

17. ———. "Explorations of a Theory of Vocational Choice and Achievement." *Psychological Reports*, 12 (1963), 547–594.

18. JACOBSON, E. *The Self and the Object World.* New York: International Universities Press, 1964.

19. JOSSELYN, I. "Ego in Adolescence." *American Journal of Orthopsychiatry*, 24 (1954), 223–237.

20. KOHUT, H. "Forms and Transformations of Narcissism." *Journal of the American Psychoanalytic Association*, 14 (1966), 243–272.

21. LANTOS, B. "Work and the Instincts." *International Journal of Psycho-Analysis*, 24 (1943), 114–119.

22. LEVIN, D. C. "The Self: A Contribution to Its Place in Theory and Technique." *International Journal of Psycho-Analysis*, 50 (1969), 41–51.

23. MARCUS, I. M. "Learning Problems." In G. Usdin, ed., *Adolescence*. Philadelphia: Lippincott, 1967. Pp. 94–110.

24. ———. "From School to Work: Certain Aspects of Psychosocial Interaction." In G. Caplan and S. Lebovici, eds., *Adolescence: Psychosocial Perspectives*. New York: Basic Books, 1969. Pp. 157–164.

25. ———. "The Marriage-Separation Pendulum: A Character Disorder Associated with Early Object Loss." In I. M. Marcus, ed., *Currents in Psychoanalysis*. New York: International Universities Press, 1971. Pp. 361–383.

26. MENNINGER, K. "Work as Sublimation." *Bulletin of the Menninger Clinic*, 6 (1942), 170–182.

27. MITTELMANN, B. "Motility in Infants, Children, and Adults." *Psychoanalytic Study*

of the Child, 9 (1954), 142–177.

28. NEFF, W. S. *Work and Human Behavior.* New York: Atherton, 1968.

29. O'HARA, R. P. "Roots of Careers." *Elementary School Journal*, 62 (1962), 277–280.

30. ROE, A. "Personality Structure and Occupational Behavior." In H. Borow, ed., *Man in a World at Work*. Boston: Houghton Mifflin, 1964.

31. SPIEGEL, L. A. "The Self, the Sense of Self, and Perception." *Psychoanalytic Study of the Child*, 14 (1959), 81–109.

32. SULLIVAN, H. S. *Conceptions of Modern Psychiatry.* 2d ed. New York: Norton, 1953.

33. SUPER, D. E. *Appraising Vocational Fitness by Means of Psychological Tests.* New York: Harper & Row, 1949.

34. ———. "A Theory of Vocational Development." *American Psychologist*, 8 (1953), 185–190.

35. ———. *The Psychology of Careers: An Introduction to Vocational Development.* New York: Harper & Row, 1957.

36. ———. "The Critical Ninth-Grade: Vocational Choice or Vocational Exploration." *Personnel and Guidance Journal*, 39 (1960), 106–109.

37. ———, and OVERSTREET, P. L. *The Vocational Maturity of Ninth-Grade Boys.* New York: Teachers College Press, 1960.

38. ———, STARISHEVSKY, R., MATLIN, N., and JORDAN, J. P. *Career Development: Self-Concept Theory.* Princeton, N.J.: College Entrance Examination Board, 1963.

39. TIEDEMAN, D. V., O'HARA, R. P., and BARUCH, R. W. *Career Development: Choice and Adjustment.* Princeton, N.J.: College Entrance Examination Board, 1963.

40. WHEELIS, A. B. *The Quest for Identity.* New York: Norton, 1958.

41. WITTENBERG, R. *Postadolescence.* New York: Grune & Stratton, 1968.

CHAPTER 22

THINKING ABOUT THINKING ABOUT HEALTH AND MENTAL HEALTH

Edgar Auerswald

JESUS OTERO AND HIS WIFE, Maria, grew up on the same street of a small, rural Puerto Rican village. They saw each other at a distance for many years without speaking much. Jesus spent most of his time with the boys of the village, while Maria was with the girls. They admired each other at a distance.

Like most of the other families of the village, the families of Jesus and Maria were poor. Work in the fields paid poorly, and the families were barely able to scrape out an existence. Most of the villagers, especially the young, dreamed of getting away and finding a way to make money. While they liked the warm sun and the beauty of their land, they were tired of worrying each day about where food for tomorrow would come from or how to buy tarpaper to cover the latest leak in the roof of the ramshackle huts they lived in.

At the age of nineteen, Jesus finally summoned up enough courage to declare his admiration for her to Maria, who, at eighteen, responded with wild delight. Within the year they were married.

Maria took her place with the women of the village. Within six years she bore three children, first a girl, then a boy, then another girl. Maria was happy with her children and her place among the women. She saw her parents every day. She spent her days on the streets of the village with her two sisters and the other mothers and their children. She knew that her children were safe there, since if she lost track of them, the other women would be watching. There was much gossip to chatter about. True, she sometimes went hungry so her children would have enough to eat, but Jesus would come with food before she got too hungry.

Jesus, however, was not so happy. It was hard to feed five mouths, and he sometimes had to borrow from friends when money ran out. He spent his time, like the other young men of the village, either working or with his friends. He wished he had more money for beer, since he liked drinking with his cronies. Mostly he was unhappy at the thought that his life would always be like this. He could not see any way to change it. And since his children were born, he had little time with Maria. There was no way for them to be alone in the little two-room hut they lived in. Even when they made love late at night, Maria kept silent so as not to wake the children. Jesus's fondest dream was to find a way to get enough money to build a house, but there seemed no way in their village.

Jesus had an older brother, whom as a boy he had both admired and envied. Jesus considered his brother Juan to be smarter than he was, and there was no doubt he was more successful with the girls. Juan had many girls, and he had not married. Shortly before Jesus had married Maria, his brother had left their village and gone to Ponce where he had learned the trade of a bricklayer. Subsequently, he had gone to New York where, after a period of struggle, he had been able to get into the bricklayer's union. He had begun to make what to him and Jesus was a great deal of money, and, still unmarried, he wrote a couple of times a year to Jesus about the good life he was leading with money and girls in New York. Jesus envied him. He loved Maria and his children, and he did not want to lose them, but he wished he could do as Juan had done and keep his family too.

One day he wrote to his brother, swallowing his pride a bit, and asked Juan if he could lend him enough money to get him to New York and to buy enough food for his family for a month or two until he could find himself a job. His plan was to send money back to his family and at the same time to try to save enough to bring them to New York. Maybe there he could get better jobs if he worked well and hard. It seemed just possible to him that if he was lucky he might be able to then save enough to come back to his village some day

and build his house and maybe even to start a small business of his own. Maybe he could build houses for other people for a living.

Juan's answer to his letter was discouraging. Juan said that he was willing to save money for a loan to Jesus, but it would take a few months for him to do so. He wrote, however, that he did not approve of Jesus's plan because New York was a bad place for families. There was not much sun or fresh air for children, the streets were dangerous for them, and it was hard for the women to take care of them. Good housing, he also wrote, was very expensive, and cheap housing was bad. The apartments smelled, and there were rats in the buildings. He advised Jesus not to come.

Jesus argued with Juan by mail, using as his arguments that there was no way he could better himself in the village, and that in New York his children would be able to go to school all the way through high school, unlike their village where the school had only recently expanded from six grades to eight. After several letters, Juan finally wrote that, although he felt that Jesus would be making a mistake, if he still wanted a loan to come himself to see what it was like, he would save the money for him. Jesus excitedly wrote back that he did indeed still want to come.

When he told Maria that he was going to New York, she was, at first, dismayed. It frightened her to think of leaving the village, and she had heard that life for a woman was very hard in New York. But Jesus was so elated at the plan, and she understood how impatient he felt with the restrictions of their village. She could not find it in herself to destroy his joy. So she hid her dismay and tried to act excited herself. In a few days, she had convinced herself that the plan might be for the best. And it was true that her children could get more schooling. But she would miss her mother and father and her sisters and her friends.

Several months later, a money order arrived from Juan, and three weeks later, carrying his clothes in a paper box bound with string, Jesus set out for San Juan and the plane to New York. His excitement grew with his first experience of flying. The sight of New York City below him as his plane descended was overwhelming. His way of later describing how he felt was that it was like the clouds were his. Juan was waiting to meet him at the airport. Jesus cried as he embraced his brother.

It did not take long for Jesus to find a job despite his very limited English. Juan had tried to get him an apprenticeship as a bricklayer, but had not been able to do so. There were a great many men seeking such apprentice jobs, and Juan knew no one who could give preference to a newly arrived man who spoke virtually no English. But one of his friends who managed a diner had agreed to hire Jesus and train him to be a short-order cook. So within a few days Jesus was at work. He lived with Juan, who asked no rent. By living sparingly, Jesus was able to save money rapidly. He had arrived in New York in late spring, and by the end of the summer he had saved enough to pay for his family's fare to New York. He set out accordingly to find a place for them to live. For the first time, he hit a snag in his plan.

Jesus's take home pay was $89 a week and change. He had been living very meagerly on $20, sending $30 to Maria and saving the rest, which added up to about $160 each month. He wanted to begin paying off his loan from Juan, and he knew that it would be difficult to maintain his family in New York on the $50 he had been allotting them. He figured that he could spend $100 for rent.

Juan's room, in which he was living, was on the West Side of Manhattan, and Jesus began his search in that neighborhood. He found nothing that he could afford. As he branched out into other areas of the city, he fell more and more into despair. Tenement apartments, which he could afford, were universally filthy and in disrepair. Apartments he liked were all too expensive. It took him five months before he finally rented a place in a tenement building on the Lower East Side. The apartment had four small rooms that were, he felt, livable, and, unlike most of the tenements he saw, there seemed to be enough heat, and the toilet and the appliances worked. Jesus bought

mattresses, a table, and chairs and sent off a money order to Maria for fare for her and the children.

A few weeks before Maria made her trip to New York, an incident occurred in her village that was to play a part in her life at a later time. The incident involved an old woman who lived alone on the edge of the village who had been assigned a particular role in the community. Some of the elders of the village, who loved to tell stories of the early days of their lives when belief in witchcraft and the occult was widespread, had teased Maria and her friends when they were children by telling them that the old woman was a witch. Their teasing was only half in jest, since they half-believed that she might have some kind of dark powers. The old woman was hit on the head one day by a stone thrown by one of a group of boys at play, one of whom was Maria and Jesus's son. The old woman had fallen, stunned, although as it turned out she was not seriously hurt. But when back on her feet, enraged, she had turned on the women who had run to her aid, one of which was Maria, and screamed: "A curse on you! A curse on all of you!" The hate in her eyes momentarily terrified Maria, on whom the old woman's gaze had landed.

Jesus and Juan met Maria and the children when they arrived on their low-fare midnight flight. Unlike Juan, Maria had found the flight frightening, and the children, sensing her fear, had been restless. She was relieved and happy to see Jesus, but she was tired, and the bus ride to Manhattan seemed endless. She could barely get herself to believe that all that time they were in one city. She later said that she felt that she had been swallowed by the city. On the subway ride in Manhattan to the Lower East Side, she clung so tightly to Jesus that he complained that she was hurting him. She was not able to respond to the poorly lit apartment, and, with the children asleep, she fell exhaustedly on to the mattress she shared with Jesus. She was too tired to enjoy his love-making.

In the morning she felt better. The two windows in the apartment faced east, and there was sunlight until midmorning when the sun disappeared behind a building and was hidden for the rest of the day. She took stock of the apartment, found that there was more space than their hut in the village had provided, but it was filthy and there were many cockroaches. She set about cleaning the apartment after Jesus left for work. She ventured out of the apartment once, clutching the money Jesus had given her, to go the the store he had pointed out across the street to buy soap and food, but the store was huge, and she could not see what she wanted. She finally found soap and a can of beans. She tried to pay the man in the white apron, but he had said something in English she could not understand and had pointed down the aisle. She could not tell what he had pointed at, but she walked down the aisle in the direction in which he had pointed and found several lines of people paying for food. She joined one line, wondering if it was the right one, then realized her children had disappeared. She found them in one of the aisles pushing a cart with someone else's food in it. She scolded them, but then she began to feel as if she could not breathe. Gasping, she left the soap and beans on the nearest shelf and fled back across the street to the apartment.

When Jesus arrived home that evening, he found Maria sitting on the mattress on which they slept. It did not appear that she had done anything to the apartment. The children were dirty, and seemed unattended. There was no food. He was at first annoyed, but then realized something was wrong. When he asked Maria what it was, she told him of her experience in the supermarket. She emphasized that she had not been able to breathe. She said her breathing was all right now, but that she felt very frightened. She missed her sister, and she did not like it here in New York. Jesus said he thought the city was all too new and big for her, but that it would be all right soon. He took her with the children back to the supermarket, and they bought food and cleaning supplies. Later, Juan came to visit and they reminisced about their childhood days in their village. Maria relaxed and laughed at their reminiscences. She seemed better, and the next day she set about cleaning the apartment. She asked Jesus to do the shopping for her until she felt more sure of herself. He agreed.

For the next two weeks, Maria seemed all right. She went with Jesus to the school four blocks away to enter the two oldest children. They were told that, even though this school was closer for them, they lived in the district served by another school, nearly twice the distance. They registered their children at the other school. Maria asked Jesus if he would take the children to school the next morning. They argued a bit when he objected, telling her she would have to start doing more things outside the apartment if she were ever to feel comfortable in the city. But she insisted, and he agreed. Jesus was working when school let out, so Maria went to get the children. When she arrived at the school she could not, at first, find her children, and she again found it hard to breathe. Her children found her gasping for breath seated on the steps of the school. Nevertheless, for the next two weeks she went each day to collect her children. But, with the exception of an occasional trip to the supermarket, which she had learned to negotiate, she stayed in the apartment.

After two weeks, at Jesus's insistence, she also began to take her children to school in the morning. For one month she kept up this routine. She complained bitterly to Jesus about her loneliness. There were no other Spanish-speaking people in their tenement, only two elderly Jewish women and a number of black families, how many she did not know. None made any effort to be friendly. She had tried a couple of times to make friends with some of the other Spanish-American mothers who came to the school. They had been nice to her, but they seemed busy with their own families, and she had been unable to get any of them to carry on a sustained interchange. Juan brought girls with him twice when he visited, but they were very different from Maria, and she could not talk with them about the things they were interested in. They were not married and were interested in clothes, men, dancing, and having a good time. Both had been in New York for many years. They knew little about rural Puerto Rico. Jesus was not home much either. He had his men friends, and he behaved much as he had back in the village, spending time after work with his friends.

It was not until about four months after the arrival of Maria and the children that Jesus began to worry seriously about her. His concern began in earnest when she confided in him one evening that she was terrified of the men who stayed in the hallway each afternoon, because she was convinced that were there because they wanted to kill her. She begged him to stay home the next day to send them away. Jesus reassured her, telling her that she was imagining things. After a week of evenings during which she continued to plead with him, he did stay home one day. He discovered that Maria was indeed partially right. There were men in the hall for an hour or so about noontime. They seemed to be waiting for someone to arrive to open the door of an adjoining apartment. They were agitated and noisy for a while, but after getting into the apartment next door, they left by ones and twos within a few minutes. It was not Jesus, but Juan, who later surmised that the men were junkies and that someone was using the apartment next door to deal dope from. Juan cautioned Jesus to leave them alone lest they give him trouble, and suggested that Jesus install a second lock on his door. He also said that perhaps Jesus should look for another apartment.

What Jesus did not know was that, for two weeks before confiding in him, Maria had been so afraid to leave the apartment that she had stopped taking the children to school. He only found out about it two weeks later when the following events took place.

The absences of Maria's children had come to the attention of the school attendance officer, who made a routine visit to the Oteros' apartment to find out why the children had been absent. He found Maria in bed, unkempt, paying little attention to the children. The oldest child had answered his knock at the door and told him that Maria was not feeling well. He had asked if he could speak to her anyway for a moment.

The child took him to the mother's bed. The attendance officer explained who he was and asked why she was not sending her children to school. Maria, speaking rather vaguely in Spanish, which the attendance officer understood fairly well, although it was not his native language, said something about being afraid to go out when those men were in the hallway and about noises on the street that bothered her. The attendance officer asked her about her husband who she said was at work at the restaurant. She could not tell him the name of the restaurant or where to find it. She did have a telephone number, however. When the attendance officer asked her if she was sick, she answered: "I have asthma." The attendance officer observed that her breathing seemed all right at the moment. She answered: "Yes, but I am afraid."

The attendance officer then explained to her that she was required by law to send her children to school. Maria fell silent. When she did not speak for several minutes the attendance officer said goodbye and left, feeling uneasy.

Back at his office, he described what had happened during his visit to the Otero home to the supervisor of the district's guidance program, who said she thought that Mrs. Otero must be emotionally disturbed and that someone ought to get her husband to take her to see a doctor. The attendance officer then called the number Maria had given him. He told Jesus on the phone about his visit and that he would have to do something about getting his children to school. He added that he thought Jesus should know that he had found Maria's behavior strange and that he thought she might be sick. He suggested that Jesus should take her to see a doctor.

Accordingly, Jesus took Maria to see a doctor in a local public clinic the following day. A Spanish-speaking aide interviewed her for the purpose of filling out the fact sheet of her record and, at the end, asked her why she wanted to see the doctor. Maria told the aide that she had asthma attacks. Her statement was duly noted in the area of the record sheet marked "chief complaint." After a three-hour wait, Maria saw the doctor who asked her about her asthmatic attacks. Maria could not speak English and the doctor could not speak Spanish, so another Spanish-speaking aide was enlisted to act as interpreter. Maria described her episodes of shortness of breath, and the doctor told her that what she described did not sound like asthma. He listened to her chest with his stethoscope and said he could hear nothing abnormal. He scheduled her to have a chest X-ray and some routine blood and urine tests later in the week and gave her an appointment for two weeks hence to see him again. He told her if she had another attack to come back directly to his office so he could listen to her chest during the attack.

The very next evening, Maria and Jesus appeared back at the clinic. That morning Jesus had insisted Maria take the children to school. He had returned in the evening to find that she had not done so, and he had become angry. He was fed up with her fears and complaints, especially since the doctor had found nothing wrong with her. He had shouted at her and stomped out of the apartment to find his cronies. He had come home late, slightly drunk, and feeling somewhat remorseful over his outbreak of anger, to find Maria seated in the kitchen gasping for breath and seemingly unable or unwilling to talk to him. He had become alarmed and had awakened his oldest child to tell her that she would have to watch over the others while he took Maria to the emergency room.

The surgical resident in the emergency room, who spoke Spanish, questioned Maria and Jesus and learned why she was there and that she had been there at the clinic the day before. He read the note the previous doctor had written which concluded with: "Diagnosis deferred, possible anxiety reaction with hyperventilation syndrome. Rule out bronchial asthma." He listened to Maria's chest and heard no signs of asthma. He then asked her if she was afraid of something. Maria told him she was very much afraid of the men in the hall who wanted to kill her. He asked Jesus about this fear, and Jesus said it was nonsense. He then asked Maria why they would want to kill her. She answered "Perhaps because of the curse." The resident doctor asked what she meant, and she told him of the

old woman back in the village who had put a curse on her. The doctor then took Jesus aside and said that he thought Maria might be suffering from a mental illness, but that, since he was not a psychiatrist, he could not be sure. He told Jesus that about a mile away at a large medical center there was a twenty-four-hour walk-in psychiatric service. He said he would call there and tell them to expect Jesus and Maria. The clinic ambulance would take them there.

The psychiatrist at the walk-in clinic talked to both Jesus and Maria at some length. He then wrote out a report that listed Maria's symptoms as follows: frequent panic attacks, breakdown of social function, somatic delusions (asthma) and paranoid delusions, seclusiveness, breakdown of judgment, little or no insight. He described her affect as labile. He ended with a diagnosis of acute schizophrenic reaction, precipitated by stress (culture shock) or moving. He was inclined to give her tranquilizers and send her home with an appointment to come to the psychiatric outpatient clinic. Two things, however, changed his mind. First, he asked Maria if she had ever wanted to kill herself. Maria had answered that she had begun to think of it very recently. Second, when he told Jesus that his wife was mentally ill, Jesus had appeared reluctant to take her home, saying he feared what she might do to the children. Jesus, who was given no further explanation by the doctor, was responding to his concept of mental illness. Crazy people in his mind were people who got out of control and harmed others. While he could hardly believe that Maria could do such a thing, he had ceased to be certain the moment the doctor told him that Maria was mentally ill. The psychiatrist, in the end, decided that Maria should be hospitalized for a while, not long, he told Jesus. Maria protested at first, but when the doctor emphasized that she would be safer in the hospital, and when Jesus promised he would see her every day and see to it the children were all right, she agreed reluctantly.

Maria stayed in the hospital for four weeks. She was given rather large doses of tranquilizers at first, which made her lethargic, and

Jesus found her uncommunicative and strange. The doses were lowered over the last week of her stay, and she seemed to become her old self again. She no longer expressed the idea that the junkies in the hall wanted to kill her or that her trouble was due to the old woman's curse. She accepted the doctor's explanation that she had had a nervous breakdown and was now better. She made friends with some other Spanish-American women on the ward, and when she left she seemed much happier than at any time since her arrival in New York.

Beginning with the night of her hospitalization, however, things had gone from bad to worse for Jesus. Returning to the apartment, devastated by the discovery that his wife was mentally ill, he had tried to take stock. First of all, he was broke. He had not been able to save anything since his family had arrived. He still owed Juan the money for his original loan, and now he would have doctor and hospital bills. His job provided no insurance. Now he did not see how he could even keep up his job without help from somewhere. Someone had to care for the children. He called Juan to tell him what had happened. Juan suggested he try to get Maria's sister to come to New York to take care of the children. In the meantime, he would try to get one of his girlfriends to watch the children for a few days. Jesus said he had no money to bring Maria's sister to New York. Juan did not offer to lend him more, and Jesus did not want to ask him to do so.

Jesus stayed home from work for two days. The third morning one of Juan's girlfriends appeared, and he was able to go to work. He paid the girl a few dollars that night, and, for the next week, she spent her days at the apartment. Then she announced she was sorry, but she could not help any longer. Juan could find no one else to help, but one of the men Jesus had come to know on his job got his wife to agree to take care of the children at her own home while Jesus was working. She lived a half-hour by subway from the Lower East Side, however, and after a few days, she, too, said she had done all she could do. Jesus missed more work, and his boss

called and said he would have to get back to work or be replaced. Jesus spoke to the doctor about having Maria come home, but the doctor said it would be at least another week, since he did not want to send her home until the dosage of the drugs she was being treated with could be brought down to maintenance levels. He referred Jesus to the social worker on the service where Maria had been hospitalized. The social worker had called around to various homemaker services but unearthed no promise of immediate help. She stayed with the children the next day, getting the two oldest to school and keeping the youngest with her through the day. But she could not continue to help this way, and Jesus missed work the next two days. The result was that his employer called and told him not to bother coming back. He had been replaced on the job.

Two days later Maria came out of the hospital. She was still taking drugs, which sometimes made her sleepy, but to Jesus she seemed better. She was determined, however, to go back to Puerto Rico. Jesus was able to borrow a little money from Juan for food for the next week. He also found a part-time job washing dishes in another diner. But over the next two weeks it became clear that they could not make ends meet. Accordingly, when the social worker from the hospital came to visit, Jesus agreed to let her help them apply for welfare payments. Jesus got some coaching from some of his cronies on how to deal with the welfare department. He was told that any money he earned would be deducted from the check, but that, if the welfare department thought he had abandoned his wife and was not to be found, his wife could get the full check, and if he could then find a job he could save money and get himself out of debt. He was uneasy about this plan, since it was dishonest, but he saw no other way of getting out of the trouble he was in. He was afraid Maria would get sick again. If she were on welfare, she could also get Medicaid help. He talked with Maria about this plan. She agreed to tell the welfare worker that he had disappeared, as long as Jesus would agree to let her and the children go back to Puerto Rico as soon as they could save the money. Accordingly, Jesus moved back to Juan's apartment and Maria began collecting the welfare check.

Two weeks later Jesus was able to find another job as a short-order cook, and he began paying Juan back and saving money for his family's return to Puerto Rico. He spent weekends and some evenings with his family, but he and Maria lived in constant fear that their collusion would be discovered by the welfare department. They were especially afraid they would be discovered by the social worker from the hospital who would tell the welfare worker. As a result of this fear, Jesus's visits got less and less frequent.

In the meantime, Maria was again finding life very difficult. She was beginning again to have more anxiety attacks, including the sense of being unable to breathe. Some days she was afraid to go out to take her children to school, but she now allowed them to go by themselves. This frightened her more, however, and she lived in constant fear that something would happen to them on the street. She would not let them out to play after school hours. The children, who became bored and restless while cooped up in the apartment, fought frequently with each other, and she felt she could no longer control them, especially the boy, Julio. The social worker who came to visit, seeing the return of Maria's fears, raised the question of whether she might not benefit from another stay in the hospital. Maria objected. She did not want to go back to the hospital. Her self-esteem was at an all-time low, and she felt she would be all right again if she could just get back to her village. She could not see how the hospital could help her. The next time the social worker came to visit, she kept her children quiet and did not answer the door.

It took Jesus about four months to get out of debt and save enough money for the trip back to Puerto Rico. But, finally, the entire family boarded the plane for the trip back. When they arrived in their village they were greeted warmly, and a friend made room for them until they found a place to live. Maria's family and friends were shocked at her appearance on their arrival. But within a few weeks she seemed her old self. She was back on the streets of her village with her sisters and her friends. She was happy again. Before her supply of tranquilizers ran out, she stopped taking them.

Jesus, however, was far from happy. He was again scrambling to find money. There was no work in the fields for him, though finding such work was only a matter of time. He did odd jobs for the local storekeeper. He did enjoy seeing his friends, but he could not shake the feeling of failure. He had kept aside enough money to return to New York, and within a few weeks he had decided that was what he would do. Maria did not want him to go, but when he became adamant that he could see nothing for himself in the village but years of sameness ahead, she could not argue. Accordingly, Jesus went back to New York. He lived with Juan again, found a job and began saving money. Before long, lonely for a woman, he began to take out some of the girls he met through Juan. And, before long, Maria realized she was not missing Jesus very much. He was in New York, which was a place she wanted to forget.

Jesus and Maria's son, Julio, was eight years old when Jesus returned to New York. He missed his father desperately when the latter first left. Through habit, he kept looking for him to appear. Then he would suddenly realize Jesus was not going to appear, and it would make him feel very sad. Sometimes when this happened he would go off by himself and cry. Other times, he would feel very angry at his father for having left, and, as time went by, he got more and more angry at his mother, too, because she did not seem to care very much that his father was gone. There were other angry boys in the village like him, some of them angry for the same reasons.

Julio was a lithe and handsome boy who was well coordinated, and he was a good fighter. He fought readily when provoked, and with the pervasive feelings of anger he felt so often, he was easily provoked. He was a bright boy, but he did poorly in school because he could not keep his mind on the work. His teacher tried to help him, but her attention made him feel embarrassed in front of the others in the schoolroom, and then he felt angry again, and he had trouble paying attention to what she was trying to teach. He fell behind the rest of the class. His fights with other boys became more numerous. When they sometimes called him dumb he would strike back, and his reputation as a troublemaker began to grow. He began to stay away from school more and more often.

Maria despaired at her son's behavior. Julio was sometimes nasty to her, and often she did not know where he was. She tried to talk to him often, but he would listen sullenly and not answer. His behavior did not change. Finally, in desperation, she tried beating him. This only made him more sullen, and, when one day he exploded and fought her back, she stopped.

During the more than two years of Jesus's absence, his letters had become less and less frequent. Although the money he sent arrived like clockwork every month, the money order was often all that was in the envelope. Maria knew that Jesus must have other women or, perhaps, even another woman. She did not really expect a man like him to do without a woman. Sometimes, as she lay alone at night, she herself needed a man to the point of desperation. She sometimes felt she was wasting the best years of her life. She was an attractive woman, and since the men of the village knew she was without her husband, there was no lack of opportunity. But she had been taught very strictly that a good woman must remain faithful to her husband. And the village was small, so that even if she took a man secretly, her actions would not remain secret very long.

Maria thought about going back to New York with her family to live with Jesus, but she became frightened and her breath became short even thinking about it. So she began to write Jesus more and more often telling him how much she needed him, begging him to come back to the village.

It made her unhappy sometimes when she realized that her letters did not always fit her feelings. She vaguely knew that it was not Jesus especially she wanted. There were times when she had to make a special effort to remember his face. It was somebody she

wanted, somebody to be her man and to help her with Julio.

Jesus answered some of her letters. He said he could not come back to live in the village because there was nothing for a man to do there. He was working for a construction company now and was in the union. His bosses liked him, and there was a chance he could become a foreman. He could not leave. He encouraged her to come to New York. But his encouragement was not very forceful, and Maria could tell that his heart was not in it. But she kept on writing. After a few months of these letters, Jesus wrote that he was coming back to the village, not to stay, but to visit. He had two weeks vacation from his job and had saved enough money for the fare.

Jesus had been away for two and a half years. He seemed much older and more self-assured to Maria when he arrived. And she thought he looked handsome. He was different in many ways. He talked much more, and sometimes his talk was about things that she could not really get into place in her thoughts. It was not that she could not understand him, she told herself, but he seemed to be talking of things important to another world than her own. He made her feel vaguely stupid. She had been right when she had thought his heart was not in his letters when he asked her to come to New York. Although he was now asking her face to face, it was clear that he was hoping she would refuse. She did, and she sensed the relief he tried to hide. She told him that New York had made her sick and that even the thought of returning made her begin to feel that way again.

It was several days after he arrived before he made love to her. Lying in his arms, she realized that the two of them had, in many ways, become strangers. By the time the first week of Jesus's stay had passed, both he and Maria knew they would never live together as man and wife again. Their realization remained unspoken, but their talk turned to what to do about their children, especially Julio.

During these first days of his visit, knowing of Julio's troubles, Jesus had tried to get close to his son. His efforts had ended in frustration. Although Julio had stayed near Jesus almost everywhere he went, he had become sullen and silent whenever Jesus tried to talk to him. The only time he smiled and seemed more open was when Jesus would play catch with him in the village street. But when Jesus tried to turn their talk from baseball to school or to Julio himself, Julio's sullenness returned. Early in the second week of his stay Jesus realized that a five-dollar bill was missing from his pocket. When he asked Maria if she had seen it, Maria said she had not. When further search proved fruitless, Maria said she suspected that Julio had taken it. She broke down and cried then and poured out her despair and helplessness about Julio's behavior. She begged Jesus to do something. Jesus could not think of anything to do. He had not been confronted with Julio's behavior this way before. He was not at all certain Julio had taken his money, and he did not want to accuse him of it unless he was sure. He thought that if he did, and he was mistaken, that Julio would be so hurt he would never talk to him again.

Days passed, and Jesus felt more and more unhappy about Julio and himself. Several times he thought Maria was about to ask him to take Julio back to New York with him when he returned. But she never asked him, and he was not sure whether the idea was hers or purely his. He was torn in two directions by the thought. Having Julio in New York, he knew, would drastically change his life there, and he was not at all sure what would happen to Julio. There were so many ways for a boy to get into trouble on the streets there. Although he kept his thoughts about his idea to himself, he began to get an eerie feeling that somehow the decision had been made and that, even though no one had even spoken about this possibility, Julio would be going back with him. Finally, two days before he was due to leave, he blurted out a question to Julio. He asked his boy if he had ever wanted to come live in New York with his father. For a moment Julio looked like he was about to cry, but he did not. It seemed to Jesus that a long time passed before Julio nodded his

head. Two days later, using money Maria had saved from Jesus's checks, Jesus bought a ticket for Julio, and the two of them boarded the plane.

Here I must stop and say a word about my own involvement in the above story. At the time that Maria was hospitalized in New York City, I had recently begun to work in the neighborhood health center to which Jesus had taken her on the night of her "breakdown." I had become interested in the seemingly large number of recently arrived Puerto Rican women who were showing symptoms similar to Maria's. I had alerted the emergency room staff to notify me when such situations appeared there and, accordingly, had been told about Maria on the morning after Maria's hospitalization. Subsequently, while Maria was in the hospital, I visited her. I also paid a visit to Jesus and to the attendance officer. The purpose of my visits was to collect some data I hoped to use as part of my effort to understand why so many such women seemed to be so devastated by the transition from Puerto Rico to New York. I also followed what happened to Jesus, Maria, and their family until their return to Puerto Rico. I had written a rough version of their story, trying as much as I could to do so from their vantage point. I had put it away in a folder in my files where it had stayed for six years until I pulled it out again as a result of the following events.

Having been asked by Gerald Caplan, the editor of this book, to contribute a chapter having to do with the delivery of services for adolescents, I had written the conceptual presentation that appears later in this chapter and had been casting about in my head for a story about an adolescent which I could use to illustrate the points I had made. I had settled on another story, and, a bit frantically, since I was already late in submitting my chapter, I had begun to write it. Then I ran into Jesus.

I was hurrying through the lobby of a West Side Manhattan hospital heading for a committee meeting when I saw him. I was late for the meeting, and I think I would have blocked out my recognition of him had he not been so obviously in distress. My attention was caught first by the look of pain on his face, and it was a moment before I realized who he was. Even then, my impulse was to hurry on, but his eyes caught mine, and I could not. I went up to him and said hello. He seemed in a daze, and there were tears on his cheeks. I thought he did not remember me, so I told him who I was, and how and where we had touched before. His tears welled up, and he began to cry. Then he told me his son was dead. Julio had died sometime the night before in the hospital emergency room of an overdose of heroin. He had been fourteen years old.

We sat down in the lobby, Jesus and I, and talked. I talked to him twice more after that, and from these talks I was able to reconstruct the rest of the story above, and some of what happened after Jesus brought Julio back to New York. I will shorten this latter part of the story since it is a repetitious saga of hopelessness and despair well known to those who are trying to help people in our big cities.

When Jesus and Julio arrived in New York, Jesus once again enrolled his son in school. Julio was never able to make it there. Within two months he was suspended for fighting. Jesus, like Maria, tried to control him with physical punishment, to no avail. Julio was then brought to court two times in the next six months, the first time for injuring another boy's eye in a street fight, the second time for stealing a bicycle. At the second appearance the judge remanded him to a state training school.

According to Jesus, at the training school two things happened. Julio learned to read, and he began to experiment with drugs. He stayed there for nearly a year before returning home to stay with Jesus. Not long after he had returned, Jesus had come home one night and found him lying on the floor. He was fully conscious but strangely euphoric. When he announced to Jesus he was taking heroin, Jesus had again become angry and yelled at him. Julio had retorted that he did not care what Jesus thought and then had gone to bed. Later Jesus heard him call for his mother in his sleep. The next day Julio did not come

home, and Jesus did not see him alive again.

Throughout this time, Jesus and Julio had been involved with a veritable multitude of people who tried to help. Julio had been "treated" briefly during his disastrous New York stay by two psychiatrists and a school psychologist. Involved at other times had been a school guidance counselor and three social workers, one from the court clinic, one from the training school, and one from the psychiatric service in the hospital where I had met Jesus. The last of the psychiatrists he saw was also working in that hospital. He had seen Julio only once, right after Jesus had discovered his son's heroin addiction. The note of that visit in the boy's hospital chart, which I looked up, was sparse. It said only three things: (1) that the psychiatrist had not been able to get Julio to talk much about himself, (2) that the psychiatrist suspected Julio's behavioral problems were the result of an "underlying schizophrenic process," and (3) that Julio needed a "residential program for adolescent addicts" of which there was none quickly available.

A nagging and useless guilt has accompanied me as I have compiled the last segment of this story. At best, it is a story of massive failure of the helping systems. At worst, it is a story in which the helping systems contributed to the final tragic end. I keep thinking back to the first time Jesus and Maria asked for help, and telling myself that if I had known then what I know now I could have changed the story. I think I could have. To tell you how, I must present the conceptual issues about which I had written just before my last contacts with Jesus.

One of the difficulties in writing these days is that the nature of life, at least in urban America, is such that it seems increasingly impossible to address human problems within the framework and idiom of any single discipline. I find myself bouncing from one vantage point to another, speaking sometimes as a psychiatrist, sometimes as a public health worker, sometimes as a behavioral scientist, sometimes as an epistemologist, sometimes as an ecologist, sometimes as a father concerned about the future of his children, and sometimes as a man simultaneously concerned about himself and other human beings.

From some of these vantage points I am less than erudite, and often it is difficult to find language, since I cannot stick to the idiom of one discipline. So be it. We live in an era of rapid and accelerating social change which is becoming so rapid that there seems no other way to capture what is happening at a point in time than to pounce on it from many directions and to hope in this fashion to understand a little for a moment of where we are. In the end, of course, what one man captures in this way may have more to do with where he is than with where we are. But, in today's world, that is the best any one man can do, I think. At any rate, much of what follows is not really a psychiatric essay written by a psychiatrist. It is rather one man's perception while circling around some issues that seem important.

The incredible growth of human technology during the past quarter century is teaching us much. We are, for example, learning more and more about how the human brain processes information. Despite the continued elusiveness of a full understanding of precise mechanisms, we can be reasonably certain now that the biologically mature human brain, like its extension, the computer, requires prior organization, that is to say, programming, if it is to effectively carry out its data-processing function. Some programs are built into the species and are passed on to individuals through the process of genetic transfer. But cybernetic understanding has taught us that, as part of the process of growth and maturation, the brain is fully capable of programming and reprogramming itself in increasingly complex ways. The brain can accomplish this through learning, when and if it receives sufficient information input delivered in such a way as to allow such a process to occur, and providing that prior programming is such that it allows the information in question to enter the space in which the storing and processing take place.

Before continuing, I had better say a word about how I am using the word "program", lest

I sound as if I am robotizing human beings. Nothing could be further from my intention. (1) Obviously, human beings are living systems with all of the unique properties inherent therein. (2) They possess human capacities shared by no other living organism. (3) Human programs are of a complexity far beyond the capacity of even the most sophisticated of today's computers. (4) Human programs contain affective components that are not fully reproducible with current technology. The use of the word "program" however, becomes justifiable, in my opinion, when we recognize that human beings do, nevertheless, respond individually and collectively in repetitive ways, given fixed conditions and the same input. (We now have a reproducible model of what Freud tagged the "repetition compulsion.") In this sense, the computer analogy holds. Also, I would like to point out that it is the use of symbolism in thought, or, in other words, the way man processes information, that makes him unique, not his capacity to feel, as some contend. There is abundant evidence that all mammals, at least, have feeling responses. Feelings, furthermore, are a form of information in the cybernetic sense.

It is heuristically useful, in my opinion, to think of learned human programs according to the numbers of human beings who share them. Those programs shared by all people, or by very large segments of humanity, that determine the structural links between programs shared by smaller segments are probably what we refer to most often as epistemological. When we talk of "universal man," "Eastern man," or "Western man," we are referring to prototypes directed by this order of programming. Therefore, a rough subdivision of epistemologies would include Western, Eastern, and universal. I shall refer to these programs herein as first-order programs.*

We use a variety of adjectives to describe programs shared by large numbers of people, but less in number than those who share epis-

---

* As usual, I find myself in language trouble. "Epistemology" is the best non-neologistic word I can find to describe what I mean, but I am using it narrowly, in a sense, when I use it to describe only first-order programs.

temological programs. A list of such adjectives might include "cultural," "political-economic" (ideological), "scientific-disciplinary" (theoretical), and, perhaps, "theological." These are second-order programs.

Another group of programs, involving still fewer people, would be generally subprograms of the above and might be called "social systems programs" (third-order programs). These would consist of those programs shared by those who populate organized systems of many sizes, such as governmental systems, political parties, social welfare systems, and corporations. The programs shared by health workers in health systems would be included in this group.

Families, both nuclear and extended, and educational systems share additional programs, which should, I believe, be thought of separately from other social systems programs because of their special relevance to the growth, development, and socialization of children.

Finally, some programs occur as idiosyncratic outcomes of an individual's experience, programs that are unshared and unique to the individual. These fourth-order programs determine much of that which we call individuality and, perhaps, creativity.

I would like to emphasize that I am not attempting here to classify human programs. What I mean to suggest is simply some rough divisions that are heuristically useful. They also allow me to make a point. I believe that mankind is beginning to understand that members of our species must stop bickering and killing one another over cultural, ideological, theoretical, social, familial, and individual differences and turn at least a major portion of our attention to an even more basic issue, namely, those differences that create conflict between large groups, resulting from what I have called epistemological programs. In order to understand differences, of course, we must first understand the nature of these programs.

I submit that three basic epistemological programs are currently discernible on "spaceship earth." That program with which we have been most familiar here in the United States might be called the Western epistemological program. The precise historical origins of this program are, of course, buried in the darkness of unrecorded history, but teleologically, it seems likely that the events that shaped the program as it now exists, were, at least in part, the same events that formed the notion of monotheism. The image of the omniscient, omnipotent individual, coupled with the notion of a single truth, and the dichotomized polarities of good and evil, right and wrong, healthy and sick, and so on seems to have formed the basis of Western thought. To this day, Western man emphasizes the primacy of the individual and organizes his thinking in terms of such polarities. This epistemological program demands, for example, that the second-order ideological programs of communism and capitalism be considered one good and one evil. When such a program directs the thinking and actions of nations, conflict is inevitable and irreconcilable, since, to maintain its position, one must be read against the other.

Similar conflicts occur in the social organization directed by third- and fourth-order social programs, which, in turn, are directed by either ideology. In our country, organized under the capitalist ideology, people are programmed in competitive techniques. The "good" thing to do is to strive to win in a social environment that values socioeconomic and/or academic success. Thus, the individual within this society has assimilated a program that directs him to climb vertical socioeconomic and academic ladders. The rules and regulations of this social program state that such behavior is good, and lead our citizens to feel good about themselves when they succeed in ladder climbing. Such success is viewed as an individual achievement. The image created is that somewhere in the clouds at the top of the ladder is a position of ultimate wealth and power and omniscience (God in his heaven).

Our behavioral sciences have evolved their body of theory largely as a result of the focus on the primacy of the individual as directed by the Western epistemological program. People either make it or they do not, and if they do not, instead of being considered good and feeling good, they are tagged with a variety of labels having evil connotations. They are considered sick, criminal, lazy, or stupid. It is again necessary to have both elements of the usual dichotomy present. That is to say, if some people are to be considered as having made it, there must be some who do not make it. Without both there is no yardstick against which to measure what constitutes making it. Therefore, our society needs to perpetuate the presence of a group of people that are sick, criminal, lazy, or stupid. However, since the individual man is prized, it is not possible under this epistemological program for our society to fully ignore those individuals at the bottom of the ladder. Therefore, we have also evolved a number of institutions designed to care for them—social welfare systems, mental health systems, social rehabilitation programs, and the like. The dilemma of which we are becoming increasingly conscious is that these so-called systems must carry out their work in the context of the epistemological dichotomy described above. They must carry on their work in two ways: One way reflects their origins as helping organizations; the other reflects the requirement that they maintain the social structure that created them. Therefore, they cannot go too far in their helping functions lest they bite the hand that feeds them. They cannot hoist too many of those they help too high on the competitive level. They cannot be so successful that the balance between those at the top and those at the bottom of the ladder is seriously upset.

Stability is maintained in this arrangement through the use of blame systems,* which are, it would seem, the inevitable outcome of the good-evil dichotomy. Everyone can feel like a good guy despite the presence of clear injustice if he can identify the bad guys or the intractable set of bad conditions. For example, the tragedy at Kent State as the ultimate prototypical expression of campus violence set off

a welter of charges and countercharges as to who or what was to blame—the weak college presidents, communist influence, permissiveness, the fascist national guard, lack of presidential leadership, you name it.

In space-time terms, the Western epistemological program is essentially a linear program. Space is filled with vertical, spiritual, academic, and socioeconomic ladders, and time is thought of as clock time—horizontal, sequential, and ticking off at a steady rate. Progress is defined as that which creates higher rungs on the ladders, and knowledge is accumulated through a set of parallel linear efforts based on inductive or deductive exploration of linear cause and effect relationships. We call this "specialization," and we have evolved a variety of specialized disciplines, each with its own language, to deal with various pieces of the human condition. The specialized operations that knowledge accumulated in this fashion suggests are organized into programs to solve problems. The recognition that such specialization limits the range of variables that can be used to explore cause and effective relationships has led each discipline to join in so-called interdisciplinary efforts. Such efforts, however, are usually so caught in the vertical hierarchical aspects of our social disorganization and in language difficulties that they are barely able to use limited input from outside the dominant discipline of the organizational system that mounts the program. Thus, we have evolved hospitals whose physicians (those of the dominant discipline) are helped by ancillary staff. We have social welfare agencies and schools who hire psychiatrists as consultants and psychiatric clinics who use social workers to see collateral clients. Psychiatric clinics establish educational therapy programs, housing agencies hire social workers to deal with problem families, and so forth. Also, the notion that to solve a problem with a program staffed by those whose discipline gives them a claim to be experts in that problem leads to a proliferation of programs as problems arise. We require money (our funding organizations routinely fund programs), and each program is concerned with delving deeper into the causes of the problem

---

* Many will disagree with this language since it is usual to consider value systems as the providers of social stability. In my opinion, in the dichotomy of the Western program, blame systems, which are the other side of the value system coin, are much more useful stabilizers than values.

by narrowing the field in order to gain more detailed expertise. Each discipline gradually assumes a vantage point that diverges from those of other disciplines, and at the interfaces between disciplines there is overt or covert war. Complex problems seldom get solved. Instead, progress is made.

The second discernible epistemological program might be called the Eastern epistemology. I am on thin ice when I lump all Eastern thought into one program. But in the service of brevity in this chapter, I will comment on only one aspect shared by several Eastern programs in terms of some areas of similarity to and difference from the Western epistemological program.

The Eastern program, too, emphasizes the value of the individual man and the notion of attainment in a concept of space filled with a vertical hierarchy. The Eastern hierarchy, however, has not been classically primarily socioeconomic or formally academic. It has been spiritual. The ultimate attainment has been defined as a state of oneness with the forces of the universe.

The Eastern view of time, like the Western view, is linear, but, paralleling the emphasis on spiritual attainment, the view of life and death differs markedly. While the Western program focuses Western man on a single lifetime, during which he must qualify for a Godlike existence after death, the Eastern program gives each man more time; it is assumed that many lifetimes are needed to attain that final rung at the top of the spiritual ladder, lifetimes that are not even viewed as necessarily human since the hierarchical program includes all living things. Just where a given individual resides on the hierarchy of species, and on such ladders as the socioeconomic, is thought to be preordained by his performance during the last lifetime. Thus, socioeconomic competitiveness has been less, and the value of the preservation of life in a single lifetime has also received less weight. To the Westerner, life in the East has seemed cheap, and fatalism about one's status has seemed to be the rule. As in the Western program, a kind of universal blame system also maintains the sta-

bility of this arrangement. The blame is put on fate.

Currently, as a result of increases in East-West interchange, Western intrusion into the populations sharing the Eastern epistemology is leading gradually to change in the countries involved (that is, socioeconomic hierarchies have become ascendant), while, to a much lesser extent, the Eastern epistemology has influenced some of those programmed the Western way.

What I wish to emphasize here, however, before going on to the third epistemological program, is that, regardless of differences in space-time and life-death concepts, both Eastern and Western epistemological programs emphasize the ultimate attainment of the individual man within vertical hierarchies in linear time. There is little or no concern for the viability of the species in either program except, perhaps, for the implicit notion that the survival of the species will be automatically ensured by the creation and maintenance of conditions that promote the possibilities of individual attainment.

Despite the present state of the societies based on the Western epistemology, which I have depicted with somewhat pejorative language, the Western program, in evolutionary terms, has been extraordinarily productive. It spawned what we have called science, which in turn provided knowledge that was used for the development of technologies, which in turn produced extraordinary tools to be used for the acquisition and storage of more knowledge, ultimately useful for survival purposes. Whether or not our species would have been better off if this form of civilization had not evolved is a moot question. It is unanswerable, and, even if there were a ready answer, it would, at this time, be useless. The Western program, as a relatively recent part of the evolutionary process, is with us, together with its products which have become necessary for survival. Because there are so many of us, survival would not be possible if we threw out what we have learned. What the Western program has not and cannot produce is a way of thinking that allows us to collectively learn how to use the knowledge and technology we have accumulated during the era of its ascendancy. It is time for epistemological reprogramming, and thanks to what we have learned in the era of Western thought, we now know that this can be done. Reprogramming according to the Eastern epistemology, I believe, will not suffice, since fundamental space-time concepts in Eastern and Western programs are not all that different.

This brings me to the third epistemological program. I began by describing this program as the universal program, a description that fits in one sense, since like the Eastern program this program begins with a view of man in the time and space of his universe. The term "universal," however, is confusing when it is recognized that the program is not universally shared. Also, the nature of the program is such that the term "ecological,"* as originally defined, seems more appropriate. Therefore, I will henceforth refer to the third program as the ecological epistemological program.

It seems likely that at least the rudiments of the ecological program have been around on our planet for millennia, if one accepts the likelihood that primitive man could not have survived without developing means of acting collectively. Isolated tribes, who lived directly off the natural resources of the territory they occupied, would, one would expect, develop tribal structures that were designed to enhance the survival chances of the whole tribe. The prolongation of individual life was probably seen as dependent on programs designed for group survival by maintaining a balance with nature. This way of thinking is the keynote of the ecological epistemology. What information we have relevant to so-called primi-

---

* Again, the choice of the adjective "ecological" raises a language problem. In this instance I am using the word "ecology" in the sense of its original definition, which is the study of beginnings and endings in universal time and space. In popular usage, the meaning of the word has been constricted to the point that some use it almost euphemistically to denote environmental cleanliness or aesthetic quality or as a synonym for conservation.

tive tribal cultures that exist at present or have existed in the recent past show, rather clearly I believe, this basic tenet of the ecological program. In the absence of the knowledge accumulated by Western science, efforts to explain natural phenomena are, in these cultures, heavily mystical, but the concern for staying collectively in tune with nature for survival purposes is evident.

Most important, however, is the observation that the ecological epistemological program is now shared by a rapidly growing segment of people throughout the world. A large percentage of those who share this program presently is made up of those who are growing up in the incredible information environment provided by the evolution of a technology that has allowed millions to see and hear man's escape from the confines of his planet during the occurrence of these events, while at the same time observing the social chaos resulting from the inadequacies of the Western program. A large number of young human beings, together with a smaller number of those no longer so young, having been the continuous recipients of information from sources that span the globe, and, having viewed planet earth from the vantage point of its moon, have become clearly aware of the degree to which our species is hell bent on its own destruction. They begin their thinking with concern for the viability of species man as one living species striving with other living organisms to maintain its survival in its physical environment. Inherent in this program is the recognition that the exclusive focus on the attainment of the individual in hierarchically organized space, a view shared by Western and Eastern programs, is antithetical in the end to individual survival since, if the species disappears, so, of course, do the individuals who comprise it.

While the subprograms of the Eastern and Western epistemologies are well developed, widely shared subprograms have yet to form clearly among those who share the ecological epistemology. Only fragments are discernible, but some trends are apparent. For example, it would appear that most second-order programs (ideological, disciplinary, and theological) may not develop at all, with the exception of a kind of universal cultural program. Such terms as "postideological," "postdisciplinary," and "posttheological" have been appearing side by side with the phrase "universal culture" in the new civilization literature. Useful information acquired over the years as these second-order programs evolved in Eastern and Western epistemologies will be used, I believe, in the design of a universal cultural program and in third- and fourth-order programs.

Third-order social systems programs, though poorly formed, seem to be evolving in a direction based on the use of new technology to do more with less in the manner propounded by Buckminster Fuller. The thrust of these new programs would be toward the design of human support systems combining new special configurations of group living with media technology used locally and in networks. The aim would be to link people with people and to provide structural rigidity for groups of people and intergroup relations rather than complex value systems and concomitant blame systems.

And, from this trend, there seems to be emerging an emphasis on the idiosyncratic individual program. People are encouraged to experiment with novelty, to do their own thing, as long as they adhere to a single value system. This value system might be stated as follows: While doing your own thing, you cannot behave in ways counter to ecological necessity or to the maintenance of the integrity of other living beings.

Space in the ecological epistemology is conceived as filled with process in which hierarchical organization appears transiently but not permanently. Space is filled with the model of the universe. It is galactic and planetary. "Spaceship earth" is not a euphemism. It is a serious descriptive phrase. Space is filled with moving, changing, interacting systems. Time is seen as multidimensional. Clock time is conceived as linear and limited in concept. Rates of change, including acceleration and deceleration of rates, are assumed.

Those who share this epistemological program currently tend, in moments of anger, to construct blame systems, but they are short-lived and transient. They have no structural function, and the emphasis on continuous process in multidimensional space-time does not call for the fixing of linear cause-effect relationships.

It may perhaps be unfortunate that a good deal of the activity of those who share the ecological program has been directed at assessing what is wrong with second- and third-order programs (cultural, ideological, disciplinary, theoretical, theological, and social systems programs) developed out of the Western program. The criticism leveled at the ecological thinkers that they should stop carping at the old and come up with something new, or shut up, is probably well taken, if a bit unfair in timing. The problem, however, is that whenever one observes the currently programmed state of Western society through the template of the ecological perspective, one is seduced by despair into describing what one sees in a kind of desperate outcry that says, "My God, look what we're doing." Having said this, I must now confess that I cannot fight the impulse. Since this is an essay about health care, especially mental health care, I propose to describe what one sees, on the terrain of New York City at least, when one looks at our current system of providing help for people who need it, through the eyes provided by the ecological program.

If we momentarily screen out of our vision all but the service systems, what do we see? For the most part, we see vertically organized bureaucratic pyramids standing on the city terrain like windowless skyscrapers, with guards at their doors to assure that no one gets in except those who will accept help in a manner defined by the system inside. (In psychiatric clinics and social agencies we call the guards "intake policies.") Each intake policy, however, operates differently, and each is considered a separate program to deal with a specific piece of human need.

Inside each skyscraper are workers who operate according to a prescribed linear progression. Doctors, for example, follow a standardized linear procedure. Get the presenting symptoms. Take a history of the development of those symptoms. Do a physical exam for signs of illness. Get what laboratory tests are needed. Make a diagnosis. Treat the illness diagnosed. Follow up the treatment. If the illness is one with a biological etiology, and a way of treating it is known, the person, who in that setting is no longer a person but rather a patient who belongs to a particular doctor, will get help. The person whose symptoms are part of a set of conditions that include elements of complex life situations originating outside the skin, beyond the purview or competence of the specialist he consults, may not only get no help, he may even have to deal with input from the specialist, which complicates his situation adversely.

Individual people who are parts of families, which are parts of larger systems, and so on, move about on the terrain seeking help for complex problems of living. At the door of each skyscraper they either accept the definition as prescribed or they do not. If they do not, they get no help, so that most often they will accept it.

Thus, what we see are helping systems designed to deal with parts of problems being called on for help by people whose program leads them to believe that whole problems originate within themselves, but who are themselves only parts of problems. A kind of collusion between helper and helpee narrows the view of each. Together they attempt to get the lights back on by replacing the fuse. When it is the fuse that is defective, they succeed, but, too often, it is the whole power network that has broken down, and, unhappily, in the system that has evolved from the Western epistemological program, there is no one assigned to the task of dealing with the whole network.

Those agencies, especially those of government which one would hope could deal with these conditions, are themselves organized in the same piecemeal fashion. They are, furthermore, populated by people who share the Western epistemology, and while proclaiming the need for integration, continue attempts to solve problems defined in piecemeal fashion by more and more piecemeal programs, which progressively narrow their targets. In typical Western fashion, these agencies and their personnel cling to the notion that this is the right course to take.

Until very recently, failures have almost never been explained as the ultimate result of a basic epistemological program. As mentioned above, the usual way to explain failure is to find someone or some system to blame. Those whose thought is determined by the Western program usually blame some human system near the opposite pole of the socio-politico-economic hierarchy from where they perceive themselves or a system whose second-order programs are the dichotomous opposite of their own. Capitalists will blame communists, and vice versa. The poor blame the rich; the rich, the poor; liberals blame conservatives; and so on ad infinitum. Viewed ecologically, it seems inevitable that this progression of events can lead only to further fragmentation, further construction of blame systems, more conflict at more interfaces, and a continued rise in the outbreaks of violence, which is currently so frighteningly discernible on the terrain of our lives.

Having succumbed to my impulse to view the world governed by the Western epistemological program through ecological lenses, I fervently wish I could indulge another impulse. If it were possible to shout out of the printed page, I would do so, because I believe that MAN IS AN ENDANGERED SPECIES AS LONG AS THE MOST POWERFUL NATIONS ON EARTH CONTINUE TO CHART A COURSE DETERMINED BY THE WESTERN EPISTEMOLOGICAL PROGRAM. But I also believe that IT IS POSSIBLE TO INTERRUPT OUR HEADLONG RUSH TO OBLIVION BY CHANGING THE WAY WE THINK ABOUT OURSELVES IN OUR WORLD IN THE UNIVERSE, THAT IS TO SAY, BY CHANGING THE EPISTEMOLOGICAL PROGRAM THAT GOVERNS OUR THOUGHT.

By this time, some of you are likely to be asking: What has all this to do with health care, and, especially, mental health? Or, why write all this for this book? The answer, I think, is fairly simple: Because we, as health care professionals, have accepted the task of sustaining the lives of people. We have sold ourselves as those most expert at performing this task for the most part. It is we who have been replacing the fuses and wondering why the lights failed to go on. Ecology has been defined as the study of beginnings and endings of human beings in time and space, that is, with life and death. Is it not, therefore, our task to confront these issues? It is, of course, obvious from what I have said that I believe strongly that it is not only our task, but also that it is imperative that we get on with it without delay.

Now, let us narrow our sights a bit and zoom down on what is happening at this point in time in that arena we have labeled the field of mental health. Among the growing group of those who share the ecological epistemological program are health professionals of various disciplines who work in programs in this arena. As a result, a few organized systems of response to human need have been appearing here and there in communities under the aegis of mental health programs, which in design and operations flow from the ecological perspective. Since there are fundamental conceptual discontinuities between them and traditional mental health programs, the result is that two discontinuous operational styles now can be seen, each of which shows the characteristics of the epistemological program from which it flows. Let us look briefly at how each operates in space-time.

As we would expect, space in the traditional (Western epistemological) mental health program (a third-order social system program) is filled hierarchically. In the typical organization there is a dominant discipline, usually psychiatry, served by ancillary disciplines. The system responds to people in trouble as those at the bottom of the hierarchy by labeling them "sick" and calling them "patients." There are levels of patienthood determined by the functional capacity of the patient to successfully fit in and succeed in various arenas of social function. The system decides who is succeeding in school or job, in family roles, in other social contexts. Levels of nonsickness, or mental health, are assigned accordingly. Diagnostic labels describing the kind of sickness carry connotations that slot the patient at various levels. Within single diagnostic categories there are levels, for example, the ambulatory schizophrenic, who is president of the bank, versus the back-ward schizophrenic. The choice of treatment modality frequently depends on which rung the patient occupies on the socioeconomic ladder. The ambulatory schizophrenic bank president is more likely to be seeing a psychoanalyst privately three times a week because he can afford to buy the time, while the back-ward schizophrenic gets shock or chemotherapy and, eventually, nothing but custodial care. The banker may move down on this ladder if he loses his job and his money, but it is unlikely that the back-ward patient will move up in any appreciable way.

Available operating space is usually assigned according to organizational hierarchy. That is to say, the director has a large office, although he may seldom work directly with patients, while the social worker who sees families may have to cram them into a cubbyhole, and aides and students share an office. Time in this system is conceived of as linear clock time. Work going on in the fixed space of offices is also fixed in time in appointment schedules. This is considered efficient use of time even though the rhythm of appointments does not relate to the rhythm of the patient's life. The two rhythms get into synchrony by chance from time to time or in those instances where the adherence to regularly scheduled appointments is circumvented. The hierarchical nature of the program stands out once again when we recognize that patients are expected to wait till the time slot they are assigned to see their therapist (only when the wait is clearly intolerable can the assigned rhythm be broken), while therapists are not expected to wait for their patients.

Within this system, deviation is allowed under the banner of innovation. Some programs, for example, make home visits, others reach out, and still others even go so far as to abandon offices and move into storefronts or trailers. Most such innovative programs never abandon their fundamental epistemological program, but they do abandon some of the rules of their social system program, at the expense of becoming suspect in the eyes of others in their field. Papers are written on the need for innovation; these also contain warnings about the danger that innovation will not be integrated with sound practice; that is, change is fine as long as nothing fundamental changes or, in other words, as long as change can be rationalized within the basic epistemological program.

Blame systems are discernible throughout this system. Mothers, fathers, siblings, and families as units all come in for their share of blame in the determination of cause-effect factors, which are considered in explaining the distress of those served. Failures in helping efforts are explained through blame systems. Helpers will blame past and present family relationships, fixed pathology in patients, organizational restrictions in which government, politicians, or administrators are at fault, other helping systems or workers, or, occasionally, themselves for poor results. Sometimes, insufficient knowledge is admitted, but, even in these instances, a blame system seems apparent since there is an assumption that if the experts were closer to omniscience, all could be solved. The limiting aspects of the epistemological program are almost never considered.

To date, very few programs have evolved that are populated by those who share the ecological epistemological program. The differences in space-time concepts show up operationally in such programs only briefly, since they usually develop as offshoots of larger more traditional programs. Such efforts are usually treated as foreign bodies by the parent organizations sooner or later, organizations that, in the absence of an understanding of the epistemological issues, tend to assess these efforts in terms of second-order programs. These programs are, as a result, viewed within an ideological or theoretical dichotomy and are considered too radical. After a period of time, depending on how visible their operations become to the policymakers in the parent body, such programs are either phased out or converted to innovative programs again directed by the Western program. Usually, these programs are accused of having aban-

doned sound practice. Until this foreign-body reaction takes over, however, the differences can be momentarily observed.

In these programs, too, one sees what one would expect to see according to the basic epistemological program.

Space is viewed as filled with process (change), which provides its structure. In other words, structure and process are not considered separately. Change is assumed to be proceeding in time at a rate that may be constant or accelerating or decelerating. Processes assume shapes with discernible boundaries, which may be fleeting or may exist for long periods of time; that is, they are relatively stable or unstable. These identifiable shapes are thought of as systems. System stability, which is relative, is thought of as a function of the capacity of the system to control internal processes and to respond to external processes within a viable range. A constant exchange of energy and information between systems is assumed. In general, living systems are thought of as less stable than nonliving systems. These living systems, too, require constant energy and information input. The range of environments within which a living system can survive is thought to be determined by the capacity of the system to store energy and information (for example, a camel can survive in the desert because it can store the elements it needs to produce its own energy in an arid environment, while man can survive there if he has stored the information he needs to allow him to plan to have camels to carry the elements he needs to survive there). No living system can survive, therefore, without environmental supports. Some organisms, in addition to supports from the physical environment, require support from other organisms. Man, especially, requires information from other men. Our young must learn if they are to survive. People must know what is going on if they are to respond with appropriate action (behavior).

Thus, in the provision of help, the emphasis in such programs is on information collection and the sharing of information and also on the mobilization of needed support systems. Calls for help are viewed as ecological phenomena, as part of the never-ending change process, which emanates from a shape of events occurring at someone's expense. It is assumed that the shape of events can be redirected in a manner that will relieve the distress of the person thus affected. An attempt is made to eliminate factors that tend to fix the shape of the situation encountered, including those factors in the helping system that can contribute such fixatives. Thus, maximum mobility in time and space is sought.

Fixed appointment schedules and exclusive office practice are abandoned. Disciplinary boundaries and hierarchies are avoided. Emphasis is placed on the capacity of the helping system to move rapidly into the space-time of the system of shaped events out of which the call for help came and to effect change using whatever skills are needed in a manner designed to alleviate the distress therein.

For the sake of clarity, it should be emphasized that, at the time they form, such helping systems are not interested primarily in social systems change. The dichotomous separation between events inside a person's skin and those outside is not made in response to a call for help. It is assumed that the process producing the cry occurs in a shape of events that includes elements from inside the skin and outside over a span of time. Each shape is different, and relief of distress can be obtained only when key elements are affected regardless of where they originate. In my opinion, the argument so frequently encountered currently in the community mental health arena, as to whether social-systems change or intrapsychic change is more relevant to the lives of people, can only occur among those who share the Western epistemology. It is a theoretical (second-order program) conflict in which each position needs the other to survive.

One experience of those among us who have attempted to work in helping systems using the ecological way of thinking is that story after story begins to surface in day-to-day work, each illustrating in some manner how the Western program directs its service systems to simultaneously work for and against their goals. In the limited space available for this presentation, I have only been able to tell one, the story of Maria and Jesus and Julio.

Before sailing off into conceptual space, I wrote that I thought I knew how the Oteros' tragedy could have been averted. From what I have written it is clear, I hope, that I believe the key to that statement is that the problems of the Oteros be confronted by a group of people who order their data according to the ecological epistemology. Let me then present my fantasy of what I fervently wish had happened.

If we pick up the story at the point that the attendance officer has convinced Jesus that he and Maria need help, let us imagine that he knew of a mobile team made up of people with a mix of skills in biological, psychological, and social health care who had enlisted him as a listening post for trouble in his community. Having spotted the trouble, the attendance officer spoke to Jesus about this group that might be able to assist him and Maria with their difficulties and asked his permission to call them. Jesus consented. The attendance officer accordingly called the mobile unit and reported his experience with the Otero family.

Upon receipt of the attendance officer's call, a pair of workers from the mobile unit were dispatched to call on Maria. They had been working in their community for some time, and they were aware of a frequent shape of events that evolved when women from rural Puerto Rico arrived in New York. They knew that the size and complexity of city life were often completely beyond the capacity of these women to absorb. These women had lived in surroundings that had not prepared them for coping with the city in cognitive terms. They were unable to orient themselves to the complexities, and they rapidly became confused and anxious. These workers knew, too, that women such as Maria, in their efforts to cope without adequate cognitive tools, tended to construct explanations for their fears that were based on their past experience, since they could not explain their dilemma in a manner based on an understanding of their present state. Such explanations, of course, because they were not related to present realities, were, by definition, delusional.

In addition, these mobile workers knew that primary sociopsychological supports for women in Puerto Rico in villages such as Maria's came from other women, not from men (including husbands). The intimacy and chatter and mutual child rearing of the women on the streets of the village made up the major portion of their lives. From experience, the mobile workers also knew that women who arrived in New York and settled near relatives or other women they knew seldom had trouble acclimating themselves to their new environment because the women-to-women supports were immediately established and the newcomer was taught by previous arrivals how to negotiate the city.

Knowing all this in advance, the mobile workers knocked on Maria's door prepared to explore the circumstances of Maria's problem within this context. They found, of course, that these conditions were at issue in explaining Maria's state. Having verified this, the mobile workers knew how to proceed. They first asked Maria if there was any other woman Maria knew and liked in Puerto Rico who had preceded her to New York City. Maria came up with two names. The workers next arranged to have a telephone installed in the Oteros' apartment. They traced down the two women Maria had mentioned and arranged for a telephone for them. They also arranged for them to visit Maria, using the unit minibus for transportation the first few times. They encouraged Maria to call these friends on the telephone daily for awhile. They then assigned a Puerto Rican volunteer from the community, whom they had recruited for precisely this task, to oversee Maria's education in the geography of the city and the ways to negotiate it. The volunteer introduced her to supermarkets with Spanish-speaking employees. She introduced her to an organized group of Spanish-American mothers who did work for the school to which her children went. She visited Maria almost daily for a few months, babysat for her during the day and on the evenings when Maria and Jesus went to the English class the mobile workers had helped them enroll in. They explored job goals with Jesus and helped him construct a plan to get training for more skilled work with more pay. They helped the Oteros enroll in the neighborhood health center of which the mobile unit was a part. Biopsychosocial family health care was provided in this center by family health units, again made up of people with various skills. Having done these things, the mobile unit turned the job of monitoring the Oteros' life state over to the family health unit in which they had enrolled, but they remained available and encouraged Maria and Jesus to call them again at any hour of the night or day if they felt the need.

With this kind of help Maria's anxiety fell away. Her delusions never formed, or if they had formed before the mobile unit moved in, they melted rapidly into insignificance. Maria maintained her self-esteem. She was not labeled mentally ill. Instead she recognized that her difficulties were the same as those experienced by many women who had come to the city as she had.

What the rest of the Oteros' story to date might have turned out to be if the helping systems had responded this way, who can say? It is unlikely, of course, that they would have lived happily ever after. But I am reasonably certain that the story would not have progressed as it did. Maria's "schizophrenia" would have been prevented, at least. Jesus would have had a better chance to realize his dream. The Otero family would most likely have remained intact. And, I would like to think, Julio might very well be alive today.

I have ranged over a broad terrain in this chapter, from a story about a single family to a statement that man is an endangered species. Some of what I have tried to say is highly fragmentary or, conversely, highly generalized, especially the efforts to delineate the major tenets of the various epistemological programs. As a result, many questions can and should be raised that are not confronted here. A dialectic over these issues is badly needed. I have attempted, however, to make one major point, which I would like to reiterate in conclusion.

Western thought has been constructed in such a way so as to facilitate the assemblage of scientific data or information. As a result, man has learned an incredible amount about himself and his universe in a very short time. But most of us who have been programmed according to the Western epistemology find ourselves in a difficult dilemma. The Western program is not useful, and in fact is frequently harmful, when our effort to use our accumulated knowledge is directed by it. The Western program, in my opinion, is, in the end, destructive as the basis of a format for helping one another and for survival of our species. Though perhaps we should maintain the Western program for use in further scientific and technological endeavor, we must reprogram the epistemological program that governs our ways of dealing with one another and with the world and universe we inhabit. As an endangered species, human beings can afford to do no less. We can no longer afford to fail with the Marias and Julios of the world because, when we do so, we may very well be thinking and acting in ways destructive to ourselves and our children. The fact that the Oteros are poor and that they are Puerto Rican is nearly irrelevant. We are all sharing the same boat. We are all Maria, or Jesus, or, perhaps, even Julio.

CHAPTER 23

OUTPATIENT TREATMENT OF ADOLESCENTS AND THEIR FAMILIES

Jacob Christ

TREATMENT PROGRAMS for adolescents are of relatively recent origin, for until a decade or so ago few psychiatrists studied the specific problems of adolescents in any depth, and treatment of adolescents by psychotherapeutic methods was generally considered difficult at best and most likely unrewarding.[11] Changes have come about rather rapidly, both in regard to our knowledge about adolescents and in the relative pessimism with which treatment of adolescents had been considered. There is now a multiplicity of approaches to the troubled teenager, all practiced by an increasing number of interested professionals. A specialty of adolescent psychiatry as such does not exist as yet, but a number of psychiatrists have now a heavy load of adolescent patients.

It is possible to subdivide the knowledge and the corresponding treatment approaches into three major categories. (1) Knowledge primarily centered around the individual and his development during adolescence comes to a large extent from psychoanalytic sources. Erik Erikson's[10] contribution on the identity crisis of the adolescent and Peter Blos's[4] work on adolescence considerably illuminated the field of individual dynamics and outlined specific intrapsychic and psychosocial features of adolescence. (2) It was recognized that group formation and group behavior by peer identification are an intrinsic part of adolescence. Various psychotherapeutic approaches now utilize groups. Adolescent discussion groups, activity groups, and work with natural groups, as in streetcorner work, have been widely practiced and described in the treatment of disturbed youngsters (group treatment of adolescents will be discussed in another chapter). (3) Approaches to the family as a whole, either by separate interviews with the patient, the parents, or other relatives, or by therapy for the total family have greatly increased the available knowledge of family dynamics. The emphasis in family therapy is not so much on the one disturbed adolescent as on the disturbance in the family as a whole. For instance, unhealthy family structure, communication gaps, or splits in the family are identified and understood in their pathogenic significance.

❰ The Individual Adolescent and His Developmental Task

Erik Erikson[10] defined the adolescent's predicament as "finding an identity" and, indeed, the words "identity crisis" have become a common diagnostic term used, and sometimes misused, when one talks about disturbed adolescents or young adults. Having an identity connotes both an inner oneness with oneself and the assurance of possessing a recognizable posture in society. The opposite of having an identity is identity diffusion. The adolescent or young adult who has not "found himself" and is puzzled as to who he is and where he belongs is often said to suffer from identity diffusion. More specifically, Peter Blos[4] in his work on adolescence recognized several stages, which can perhaps best be summarized by dividing them into two major sections. Two distinct and separate psychological tasks are there for the adolescent to master. During the earlier part, roughly between eleven and fifteen years, he must come to terms in one way or another with the issues of biological maturation. There is early in adolescence a marked upsurge in instinctual drives, probably caused by the hormonal changes during early puberty. On the psychological level, the young man or woman must relive the crucial, emotionally loaded family constellations that his earlier development has imprinted on him. Most of this reliving remains unconscious under normal circumstances, the only visible symptom being the well-known restlessness, unpredictability, and moodiness of the early teenager. Separa-

tion from the parents and in particular the abandonment of the powerful parental images will lead into the second major phase, perhaps most commonly associated with the ages sixteen to eighteen. This is the stage of individuation, in which an adolescent becomes the person he is to be and gains a feeling of selfhood, an identity, and hopefully a place of his own in society.

As for the first stage of adolescence, prepuberty or early puberty, its arrival is marked by the breakdown of what has been described as childhood identity or a preliminary identity by Theodore Lidz.[15] This childhood identity emerges in the early grammar school years and the child's teacher in the second or third grade often describes rather well his various assets and liabilities and, circumstances permitting, places him into the kind of educational setting most appropriate to him. This identity of the child is incomplete and, in particular, is characterized by the existence of two relatively separated psychological worlds, the outer world of school, family, and life performance and the rather more chaotic inner or fantasy world, which is fed by stories told, by reading, or by television. This latter inner world is by and large repressed and only rarely directly accessible to adults. It is the destiny of this repressed inner world to resurface. Its energy is destined to shake up the relatively smooth performance that is expected from an elementary school child. The turbulent teenage behavior will reveal much of the repressed inner world if properly listened to. Later, in a new synthesis, an even performance will once again become the expected norm.

The awakening of the forces of this second world, the unconscious world of fantasy fueled by the instinctual drives, takes place in somewhat different form for boys than it does for girls. In boys one sees characteristically a degree of developmental regression, in particular in the area of cleanliness, appearance, and readiness to accept authority. Dirtiness in physical habits, dirty language, and increased defiance toward all rules become prevalent and either a provocative or a passive-aggressive stance is taken by the typical twelve-year-old. There is also little inclination to open up to adults. Parental authority, in analogy to early childhood experience, is perceived as inhumanly powerful, merciless, overwhelming, and very restrictive. In technical terms, the superego once again takes on the aspects of the archaic superpower that it was in early childhood. The defiant twelve-year-old takes the same stance vis-à-vis parental authority emanating from both the father and the mother that he once took toward his then much bigger parents when he was in the process of mastering his aggressive drives as a three- to five-year-old.

If by virtue of trauma or deprivation an adolescent remains in this preadolescent stance, we may expect something similar to the psychology of the delinquent. There is a defiant stance toward the world. The superego is harsh, punitive, and monumentally powerful. The delinquent tends to project these qualities on the outside world, and he then finds in them the characteristics of his future persecutors, be they the school authorities, the police, or whoever. The delinquent must continuously prove that he is really master of his own destiny by defying all these powers. He will ordinarily not show much evidence of the subsequent developmental phases of adolescence; in particular, he will remain friendless, he will be unable to experience loss or grief or depression, and the relations with the opposite sex will have a peculiarly possessive, almost impersonal, quality to them. Thus, delinquency may be understood as the result of a preadolescent fixation.

It may be understandable why an attempt at psychotherapy in this stage has grave handicaps. The young adolescent will rarely trust a therapist to the point of sharing his inner world with him. The therapist will in all likelihood have to intervene in the family situation and may be the most useful as a counselor to the parents, who may well be puzzled and disturbed by the developments in their offspring.

Matters are somewhat different with girls. As with boys, a degree of developmental regression comes about in early puberty, but rather than leading to rebelliousness and defiance, the early pubertal girl will experience a feeling of helplessness and inadequacy, which, however, has to be denied vigorously. Conflict with the mother is likely over privileges that normally are assigned to older girls or grown-up women, such as the purchase of articles of clothing, freedom to be out later at night, and the use of lipstick and other makeup. Inevitably, the young woman's demands for being in on whatever feminine fashions command appears premature to the worried mother. A feature of early adolescent years described by Helene Deutsch is the so-called adolescent triangle. It is observable that girls, much more than boys, develop best friends, also called "chum relationships," in the early teenage years. Sometimes some considerable affective freedom is permissible between two girls, and at any rate, it appears that the secure relationship with the girl friend is much more important than any heterosexual relationships, which may be tried as a great adventure but never carried too far. It is with the chum of the same sex that one exchanges confidences about what one does or does not dare do, and it is the support of the chum that is most needed in a crisis.

If this derivative of the dependent relationship on a person of the same sex is not acknowledged in one form or another or is not available to the young adolescent girl, as in boys, the result may be delinquency and in particular, repetitive promiscuity. The denial of dependency may lead to acting extra grown up, and premature sexual behavior, often called pseudosexuality, is the common feminine equivalent of adolescent delinquency. The manifest sexual behavior should not deceive one, for here again truly affectionate and personal ties to the partner in love are out of reach for the promiscuous adolescent, whose main aim is to hide defensively her as yet strong dependency.

Psychotherapy with disturbed girls of this age group is equally difficult as that with boys of the same age. By and large, a female professional will do better than a male, precisely because of the existence of this developmental problem of dependency.

The characteristics of the second major

phase of midadolescence and individuation are definitely less conspicuous for the onlooker but probably more painful for the adolescent himself. At the beginning, approximately age fifteen, phenomena referrable to depression can often be observed. The adolescent has moved further away from his family, perhaps not physically but certainly in his feelings, and he has, most importantly, relinquished some claims for fantasy satisfaction through the parents. The images of the parents as strong, powerful, and good people have vanished. Parents have been recognized as human and as failing. Adolescents will not fail to let their parents know how disappointed they are with them. Naturally, adolescents will seize on realistic weaknesses of their parents, but the great emotional push behind the sometimes violent criticism of the parents is not owing to real failures but to the great disappointment about the falling down of the once so powerful parental images. On the social scene, some of the same phenomena seem to occur: Young people are disappointed with what society, the university, the politicians should have been. Their request is for more contact with those who are older, with an order of things better than the present one and with recognition of the young as full persons. The middle adolescent, indeed, feels rather deprived. His parental images do not hold up, his own resources are not yet sufficient, his depressive moods are not easily understandable, often not to himself. Acknowledgement of this state of distress is particularly difficult since society expects the teenager to continue with the tasks he is involved in, be they in the direction of adaptation to a wage-earning position or further education.

Some typical defenses against this midadolescent depression are so general that they are often ascribed to adolescence per se. A common one has aspects of grandiosity to it, and as such denies the basic feeling of helplessness. Heightened attention to oneself, narcissism, often appears in the form of self-righteousness, arrogance, or petulant argumentativeness. Sometimes the same narcissism may be manifested in a more passive way by a heightened concern with body, body building, or appearance. The importance of clothing for boys and girls and the concern with appearance, often with long hours spent before the mirror, belong here. A degree of exhibitionism is often part of this. Openness to ideologies belongs in this phase as well, as do the cultural fads, anywhere from unconventional clothing to drug use. Another defense against the depressive situation of the adolescent is delinquency. To make something happen is often a way out of having to bear unbearable tension. A delinquent act will release tension and will create a new situation where the enemy will be external, identifiable, and possibly fallible. A very transparent case example follows.

A sixteen-year-old boy was caught stealing hubcaps in a shopping center. He was easily caught by a police officer and was sent by the court for treatment. His counselor heard in the first interview that he had lost a girlfriend and therefore had done what he did. The story of the lost girlfriend and the young man's concern about how to gain her back became very repetitive, and ultimately his terrible disappointment with his parents came to the fore. His father had not achieved the status of suburbanite that some of his friends' fathers had. His mother was impervious to him when he craved her attention. He saw his home situation and by implication himself, as mediocre or poor, and he had not as yet found comfort with a peer group nor was he comfortable with young girls. His depressed state had become unbearable to him, and by acquiring a Mustang hubcap, he had asked for help, unconsciously and yet fairly obviously.

The later phase of individuation is characterized by the adolescent's search for someone or something to get involved with. Since the retreat to the safety of an affectionate relationship with the parents becomes more definitely closed, the adolescent is looking for affectionate ties with contemporaries of the opposite sex. Inevitably, frustrations ensue, and a first disappointment of a significant love relationship often constitutes a major crisis in the life of an adolescent and will revive the earlier state of depression and helplessness. Vice versa, a steady boyfriend or girlfriend relationship can do a great deal for the maturation of a teenager. The formally unattached and seemingly drifting young person now has a focus and acts in general much more purposefully. While the relationship with the sexual partner may not progress and may eventually end, much else in the life of the adolescent may progress. A characteristic of adolescent choice of partners is that it is very strongly based on similarity. The prerequisites of understanding each other completely, feeling the same about everything, having all the same interests are telltale signs that identification is a stronger binding force at this stage than object choice. The two adolescents who are boyfriend and girlfriend frequently belong to the same group, have double dates with other group members, and in general will do everything to create the impression that they are alike. Such a relationship will often protect an adolescent from exploring further relationships and will provide a safe haven where he has temporary freedom from coming to terms with himself, with his future career, and with society at large. In a larger sense, the questions of choice of work or career and choice of education will usually be posed at this stage. An adolescent may here identify with the values of his family and embark on living a life very similar to that of the parents, or he may choose the avenue of conflict and identify with others or with other causes. Expectably, the great majority of adolescents between sixteen and eighteen will appear more or less in harmony with their parents. Often the identification of the young person with the parent of the same sex is a premature one, and undesirable traits of the parents are taken over along with the desirable ones, unreflected and unrevised. A delay in late adolescent identity formation may bring about the dangers of identity diffusion. But it may also provide what Erikson[10] has called a moratorium for the adolescent to find his own separate identity and may as such provide a more creative solution to the issue of finding an identity.

Perhaps it is apparent that, both in the phase of adolescent helplessness or depression and in the later individuation phase, a therapist can be extremely helpful. The later adolescent is usually much less reluctant to talk about matters with someone recognizable as genuinely concerned and able to understand.

❪ The Adolescent in His Peer Group

Group formation is not particular to adolescence. From at least age four onward, group formation takes place among children and is effective in influencing their behavior. Group phenomena are observable through childhood, and their presence is not only acknowledged but widely utilized by teachers, educators, recreational directors, and others. What makes adolescent group formation different is that it has escaped from the control of the adult world and is the first and principal vehicle for self-assertion of the adolescent against parental authority. The authority of the group in time takes precedence over the authority of the parents, and as all parental rules are challenged, they are in the early teenagers' mind superseded by the rules that the group demands. Group rules often are far more stringent than parental rules, but also are far more binding on the teenager. Early adolescent boys are particularly prone to rely on their group, often called a gang, for protection, recreation, and activity. Considerable cohesiveness is usually achieved, leadership is contested and eventually decided on, internal rules are enforced, and strangers are unwelcome. Manifestations of affect within the group are usually poorly tolerated; there is no overt display of feeling, the emphasis is on action and on impressing one's peers with one's achievements, be they aggressive or sexual in nature. By comparison, girls are relatively less groupy. They tend to form closer relationships on an individual basis and are less amenable to organized collective activity. In later adolescence, groups are often mixed, and while activities are less rigidly controlled and the group does not have the gang-like quality of the earlier boys' groups, the group of friends may be a great support in times of crisis. In particular, the somewhat narcissistic or grandiose midadolescents will tend toward group formation as a tool for finding a common goal or purpose, ultimately as a solution to the inner tension, which sometimes is unbearable. It is evident that the disturbed youngster who does not have a group of friends to fall back on will have fewer resources to deal with his problem than his contemporary who is a solid member of a group of friends.

Strategies for group psychotherapy with adolescents generally take into consideration the developmental needs of the adolescents in regard to group formation. Groups of younger teenagers are generally of one sex and led by a leader of the same sex, whereas groups of older adolescents, fifteen and over, are often sexually mixed. By and large, it is easier to bring a group of younger boys together than it is to collect a group of younger girls for therapeutic purposes. In the practice of community mental health centers, it is often opportune to form a group of adolescents, for instance, in an effort to deal with problems around drug abuse. The generally favorable response from such groups may be understood through the phenomenon of identification; it is often easier for a teenager to identify with a contemporary than with an adult and what the peer-group member misses in sophistication, he may gain in terms of intensity of emotional involvement. The newer programs of adolescent self-help for drug problems in particular—crisis intervention through hot lines, where help is given over the telephone, or home counseling—all bespeak the power of adolescent peer identification. A phenomenon as complex as the epidemic of drug use, however, also requires dealing with the parents of the teenagers involved, and quite often a parents' group will meet as well as a teenagers' group. There is a definite advantage in having the same group leader or group leaders for the parents as well as for the adolescents, as will be discussed later. The often used argument that confidentiality is jeopardized when the therapist also deals with parents presupposes a concept that therapy is done by revelation of confidential secrets. The relative power of peer-group identification and the advantage of having a fuller picture of family interaction more than make up for what lack of trust may result from the therapist's dealing with parents as well as with the teenagers.

❰ The Adolescent and His Family

As private practitioners or clinics tried to render service to young people and their families, it became apparent that the traditional medical model of treating an adolescent problem situation as a disease suffered by an individual member of the family, was totally unsatisfactory. To begin with, finding the so-called disease becomes an elusive task, as for instance in the rebellious youngster who tries to emancipate himself from his overbearing mother or father through an attempted runaway episode. Moreover, excessive focusing on one-to-one individual psychotherapy, if necessary with several family members, results in long waiting lists, which in turn create dissatisfaction. A clinic or practitioner then can serve only a small fraction of those in need of help. More specifically, a waiting list, or any delay in providing help, often results in a situation quite different from the one for which help was originally sought. If one allows an acute problem to wait for a number of weeks, and many adolescent problems are acute problems, then the problem is no longer an acute one but may have been resolved in an unsuitable fashion. In practice, it is often the case that if no help is given immediately, no help can ever be given to meet that particular situation. However, speedy evaluation by looking at the situation as a whole will provide clues for a possible conflict resolution.

Perhaps a change in focus must be specified: rather than treating disease in one person, one tries to define a problem in interpersonal terms. The solution then is not to cure the one person labeled as the patient, with no change in the others, but to change the entire system, which is, in this case, the family. In practice, one would try to understand any adolescent problem situation from at least two viewpoints: On the one side are the concerns of the adolescent in his development, and on the other side is the ongoing family interaction as described by the various participants or as observable in a family interview.

Any practice of adolescent psychiatry, whether by an individual or by a clinic team, should contain the following types of diagnostic interviews which should ideally be held within a relatively short time of one another: (1) an interview with the adolescent alone, which should cover his own view of himself, his complaints, and his view of his family; (2) an interview with the available parents, either separately or jointly, to review their point of view about the youngster's problem and their point of view of their respective spouses; (3) a family interview involving parents, the adolescent himself, and as many siblings as can be present. There need not be a set order in which these interviews are held. What is most important is that findings from all three settings be pooled or brought together to bring about a full understanding of the situation.

A fifteen-year-old girl, a high school student in a suburb, was referred after having taken several aspirin tablets. She reported disagreements, especially with her father, about discipline, in particular about privileges of going out and going with a boyfriend. She described her father as drinking too much and being irritable while recovering from coronary heart disease. She appeared mildly depressed in the interview and appeared somewhat fearful, particularly when describing her father's behavior. She also described some claustrophobia in elevators and recalled fears of the dark as a child. However, her side of the story was not the only one. The parents, in a joint interview, first confirmed the father's coronary heart attack, his drinking, and his irritability. However, as far as the patient's behavior was concerned, they had noted for some two years that she had become inconsiderate of others, in particular her younger siblings, that she had begun to skip school quite frequently in the last few weeks, and that she had started to lie to them about her whereabouts and to go out on the sneak during the night. Moreover, she had begun to tell her younger siblings stories about her supposed sexual exploits. In addition, the parents volunteered information that alcoholism had been a problem in

both their respective families. Both the father and the mother as teenagers, had been forced into deceiving their own peers about their parents' sad state. They had, in a sense, been lying out of shame. Their view, however, was that the present problems were all with their daughter. An interview with the full family finally revealed a marked split between the three older children and the parents over the issue of discipline and, in particular, the restrictiveness of the parents. Reassuringly, however, during the interview, some serious negotiations took place in which parents and children for the first time confronted one another with the intent of solving some problems. During subsequent interviews, the young patient realized in her individual interviews that she had indeed been fearful for her father's life, in particular, in view of his irrational behavior after his heart attack. She recognized that her suicide attempt had been in a sense an imitation of her father's own carelessness about himself. The family as a whole continued the negotiations started in the family session, and to the parents' surprise, the children's requests were much more reasonable than they had anticipated. Inasmuch as the parents had been deceiving others when teenagers themselves, they had assumed that their children would surely deceive them. When this did not turn out to be the case, common plans for the family could be made, and communications were reestablished.

If one proceeds with treatment on the basis of one single aspect of the information only, treatment may well be ineffective. An adolescent who reports at length about the irrational behavior of parents and the parents' restrictiveness often fails to reveal to the therapist his or her own destructive behavior. An exclusively individually oriented therapist may easily accept the thesis of the persecuted adolescent, and therewith he is no longer helpful. If the parents only are consulted, the teenager may emerge as the victimizer of the family and the cause of all the problems, and a therapist relying on parents only may overlook the tendency of the same parents to have the child stand in for their own negative qualities, for instance, the quality of deceitfulness.

James Anthony[1] outlined typical schematized attitudes that prevail about adolescence, including the adolescent as the victim as well as the adolescent as the tyrant or victimizer. Family therapy has introduced the new notions that pathology in adolescents may be owing to faulty family structure, to communication failure, or to existing rifts within the family. Family structure and, in particular, the nature of the marriage of the parents has been related to psychosis by Lidz, Fleck, and Cornelison,[16] while communication failures, such as the "double bind," have also been seen as closely related to psychosis.[3] While family therapy has gained much information from the study of schizophrenia, quite often total family problems become visible also in families with less disturbed adolescents. A persistent alliance between father and teenage daughter with sexual or seductive overtones may lead to the teenager's inability to be successful with boyfriends and eventually to leave home. An overbearing mother who constantly checks on her teenage daughter may force her into sexual exploits by constant provocation without being aware of it. A depressed father may force a son into major and dramatic acts to get him to pay attention. Each time, the family setting per se will be most revealing. Quite often such circumstances are not talked about, and the participants usually are not aware of them.

Family treatment has become a much practiced modality in the treatment of adolescent problems and has found wide acclaim, in particular for those problems that tend to be more refractory to individual approaches, such as delinquency, drug abuse, and psychosis. It presupposes that a family is present and available for therapeutic work. It is likely to be more successful where the family is more or less intact and where problems are clearly due to family circumstances rather than, for instance, to social problems. It is a particularly suitable vehicle for the treatment of adolescents in a crisis situation, such as a suicidal attempt or gesture, a runaway episode, or a sudden change in the adolescent's behavior. Flexibility should be maintained. In some sessions the adolescent himself, about whom the problem was in the first place, may not show up for the family sessions; yet the family may profit.

⟮ Diagnostic Considerations

From the preceding considerations, it should follow that diagnosis of an adolescent problem has several dimensions to it. The following will be considered in sequence: (1) the overt symptomatology; (2) the individual dynamics and, in particular, the issues of adolescent development; (3) peer-group and societal influences on adolescent behavior; and (4) the interaction and the dynamics of the adolescent's family.

1. The overt symptom has perhaps sometimes been underestimated in its importance, in particular, for the prognosis of the adolescent disorder under consideration. The manifest disorder can be presented as lying within the adolescent himself; that is the representing difficulty is in the areas of thought or feeling of the teenager. A teenager who presents his discomfort openly is able, for instance, to talk about his depression, display appropriate affect, or report his inner difficulties, and will, by and large, have a fairly good chance to overcome his problems with proper help. This is true even for pictures that at first appear rather menacing, such as expressed feelings of unreality, dissociation, or, even occasionally, hallucination. Such psychotic-like symptoms should not automatically lead to hospitalization of the young person but first to a detailed investigation of his own development and the pertinent family circumstances. The same is true with symptoms manifested primarily in the physical area, which are not uncommon in adolescence. Endless physical tests are usually of no avail, whereas recognition of, for instance, a depressive situation, will go a long way toward reversing the disability.

In contrast with symptoms that point inward, such as the ones described above, action symptoms that point outward are of different clinical significance. While indeed a runaway episode or an episode of drug taking may be due to the same depressive constellation that in another youngster will show as manifest depression, the fact that outward action has been taken will of necessity change the nature of the intervention. Dealing with outward action and its significance is often very painful for the teenager, and more likely than not, he will try to avoid confrontation with the therapist rather than translating his actions into words or feelings. The same is true where aggressive action or delinquency has been chosen as the way of dealing with unbearable tension. Confrontation is usually avoided and any one-to-one psychotherapy has an additional hurdle to overcome. The patient sees himself as having been caught and wants to deal only with the realities of the situation, while the therapist is seeking evidence for inner problems or inner feelings. Quite often the two will not meet on any common ground.

It is with these latter action symptoms that a socially oriented approach shows more promise. Exploration of family dynamics leading to the problematic action is often fruitful. Treatment will, more likely than not, proceed along the lines of group therapy, or if severe delinquency is the problem, treatment in a structured milieu is indicated. In summary, one would try to distinguish principally between two types of presenting symptoms, those directed toward the inside, such as feeling, thought disorder, and to an extent, physical symptoms based on emotional grounds and, on the other hand, action symptoms where pathological interaction with the environment is the main issue.

2. An individual developmental assessment of the youngster will often need to be made with the help of parents or others who may have information on the teenager's behavior. One may search for characteristics dating from childhood, such as relative activity or passivity of the child, energy spent at various activities, such as studying, sports, games, relative sociability with peers or grownups, openness of contact, or closed-mouthness. In particular, one would look for the main adolescent developmental landmarks. Was there an upsurge of aggression in early puberty? Were there good peer relationships at that time? Was there a renewed interest in the parent of the opposite sex? Were there episodes of depression or moodiness? Has there been a boyfriend or girlfriend? One might fi-

nally explore the topic of identification through the individual adolescent's development. Does he physically resemble his father or his mother? Has he acted like his father? Has his father fostered some closeness during the grammar school years and brought interests to life? Does he have at present hero figures or adored celebrities? Would he like to grow up like his father and choose work similar to his? The answers to questions such as these will often go a long way to reveal salient conflicts within the adolescent as, for instance, passivity in the face of an active achieving father and resulting conflicts or similar syndromes. It must be stated that quite often the adolescent alone will not be able to answer a good number of these salient questions. While the matter of confidentiality has been stressed in individual therapeutic work with adolescents, it must be said that quite often salient conflicts will not come to the fore without extraneous information being available to the therapist.

3. Peer-group and sociocultural influences are of definite importance in understanding adolescent problems. One is, however, ill advised to accept at face value statements frequently made both by the parents and the adolescent that the cause of all difficulty lies with the group of friends that the patient hangs around with. Peer-group influences are certainly one influence, but by no means the only one. Group codes are very binding on the adolescent, yet in most instances there is a way out from the particular group with which he has chosen to affiliate. It is the same with cultural influences. Assumptions about upbringing of children held by immigrant parents are frequently at variance with current norms in the United States. A degree of cultural conflict results, with the teenager caught in the middle. Reconciliation of the conflicting value systems is often not an easy task and may be accompanied by symptoms of stress. Exposure to racial discrimination may be another stress that will affect the teenager with particular severity. The solution lies often in a strengthening of the home base, which will make the teenager's origin acceptable in his own eyes and in the eyes of his parents. Parents who

are highly critical of themselves for being different from what they perceive as the dominant segment of society will tend to underrate their own authority and leave the youngster to establish his own values, often by destructive rather than constructive means. The therapeutic intervention may be then primarily along the lines of supporting the parents' authority or cultural or racial identity. The challenging teenager will then encounter a clearer message from his family as to his ethnic, cultural, or racial identity, which he then may choose to accept or reject.

4. A clear assessment of family interaction is of the utmost importance in adolescent problem situations. A look at the parents' marriage and at the parents' interactions with both the identified patient and other siblings will reveal a great deal of the origin of adolescent behavior. Typically, the advent of sexuality in the pubertal girl will have an effect on the father. He may either defend himself against the impact of a young mature woman in the family and pay no attention to the growing daughter, or he may by contrast accede altogether too much to her seductive attitudes and therewith put her under a burden of guilt, at least in her fantasy life. Where the father and mother are alienated from each other, quite often the children are expected to take sides with one or the other. Destructive splits and guilt-laden alliances result from such marital alienation. Where the father is often absent or ineffectual, an adolescent son will come under considerable pressure to be the man in the house. He can avoid this predicament by being absent as much as possible, or in turn he will suffer from unconscious guilt, which quite frequently can be acted out in aggressive or delinquent behavior. Delinquency will externalize the guilt and give it a quality of reality where the most immediate concern becomes dealing with the realistic adversary. Scapegoating behavior is not uncommon in families, and some adolescents make good scapegoats, who will by their problems, as it were, hide the conflicts between the spouses. A youngster who destroys household goods in order to reunite father and mother against himself may in fact preserve the marriage, which without his destructive behavior would fall apart. Knowledge of family dynamics quite naturally will lead to a different focus in treatment, and instead of dealing with a defiant youngster, one may choose to remedy the marital situation between the parents.

(Strategies and Tactics for the Treatment of Adolescents

It should be understood that for an area as complex as the one discussed, no single treatment will yield consistently satisfactory results. Just as diagnosis has to be multidimensional, treatment approaches must be of many sorts and adapted to what the situation requires. Each approach has its strong sides and its drawbacks, often several approaches have to be used simultaneously, such as individual, group, and family treatment. Imagination must be used to devise the proper method, and frequently the approach may have to be changed as necessities require. Flexibility and openness to change are perhaps the two most useful rules. In the end economics and available resources often dictate what type of treatment will be given, and a wise clinical decision for treatment planning will, of course, consider feasibility along with desirability of a given approach or technique.

Whenever possible the treatment of an adolescent problem situation should first be attempted on an outpatient basis and with active participation of the family. Even in cases where psychotic syndromes are present, much understanding can often be gained from an exploration on an individual and family basis. Institutionalization for acute situations should be reserved for life-threatening circumstances. For chronic situations, it will be important first and foremost to assess the strength of the youngster and the family's resources to deal with a given problem. Repetitive crises, which often occur in the matrix of a chronic unsatisfactory situation, can sometimes be dealt with by crisis intervention methods. However, where it has become clear that neither the teenager nor the family has means at their disposal to extricate themselves from a destructive situation, a change in milieu may be necessary. It is in those circumstances that school away from home or institutionalization may be necessary. A structured milieu has often beneficial effects in those cases where clearly no structure had been provided by the parents and where either physical or emotional deprivation had been a problem. It needs to be understood that institutionalization for chronic problems will usually require some considerable time, and the adolescent hospitalized or institutionalized will often fight hard battles with the caring personnel.

Individual psychotherapy with an adolescent has a better chance the more the adolescent is able to develop trust in the therapist and with this trust create a unique relationship with him. Several factors stand in the way of such a trusting relationship. A young adolescent sees a therapist as a mouthpiece for the parents, the school, or the established order, and will deny the therapist any personal identity of his own. The therapist will not be treated as a person, much less as someone with whom one would share intimate feelings. Sharing of such feelings is reserved for peer-group members. The therapist may be viewed as of little use when action has been in the foreground of the picture. A youngster who is hospitalized or treated for his actions in one way or another will usually find a therapist only important when he agrees to act as an advocate to secure freedoms, privileges, or supplies which the youngster feels he needs. Acceptance then is a conditional one and is predicated on the therapist's actions rather than on his skill or his willingness to deal with underlying feelings or problems. Choras and Stone[7] remarked that a therapist under those circumstances will only begin to make an inroad with a patient when he can in some ways become important to the patient for something that he, the patient, himself wants. The difficulty of playing along with the patient for the sake of a good relationship should, however, be mentioned. A therapist who compromises himself or his own ways for the sake of an adolescent will often get into considerable difficulty, inasmuch as sooner or later there will always be a point where a therapist will have to say no. His skill will be tested by the manner in which he will be able to refuse something to a young patient without losing the young patient's respect or affection. It deserves to be said that where individual therapy comes about, even if it is on a short-term basis, a beneficial openness and fluidity of the situation are created for the individual adolescent. Where an ongoing relationship is available on a personal basis, development may take place and a very personal and meaningful experience ensues. This is much in contrast to family confrontation or crisis intervention-oriented maneuvers with a number of people. In these situations, an actual pressure for quick resolution of the pathogenic issue is present, and obviously a practical advantage comes about because everyone tries to come to terms with the matter; yet no therapeutic relationship ensues, and the role of the therapist is limited and tied to the crisis only. In the individual setting, the process of progress may be slower but possibly more meaningful for the individual adolescent.

In establishing indications for individual psychotherapy with an adolescent, one should first take stock of the individual adolescent's ability to cooperate with a therapist. Much useless individual treatment might be done when this precondition is not met. However, the symptoms and complaints that the adolescent may present can be of great variety and number. Given the teenager's ability to make an investment in the therapeutic relationship, possibly even only a small one, symptoms of feeling disorder, thought disorder, and also, to an extent, action disorder are amenable to psychotherapy. Technical difficulties are considerable. The question of "How does the patient get to the doctor's office or to the clinic?" will always have to be settled. How much should the parents know of what is being said in the therapeutic hours? What are the limits to which the therapist can go in hiding potentially dangerous information from the responsible relatives? Questions such as these will usually have to be answered and by and large will have to be answered in each case differently. The younger the adolescent, the more necessary the communication of one sort or another with the family will have to be. One frequent issue that therapists of adolescents have to deal with is the "no show," that is, the patient who does not come for appointments, and once again, procedures will have to be worked out in a flexible manner rather than according to a rule set once and for all.

Group treatment with adolescents has a natural advantage inasmuch as the forces of identification with a potential peer group can be made to work. The emotional impact of observing one's own experience expressed by someone else in the same situation is quite usually a powerful one and one that facilitates personal involvement and emotional interchanges. It is possible to organize adolescents either in groups containing only one sex or in mixed groups. Younger adolescents between ages twelve and fifteen usually are seen in groups containing only one sex, with a leader of the same sex. Commensurate with one's developmental stage, the opportunity to come to terms with members of one's own sex, forming identifications and ego ideals, is the most urgent task. The therapist will proceed somewhat in the manner of a child therapist, and activities of one sort or another are usually required. Young adolescents in particular need movement for tension release, and they will mediate their difficulties through action more readily than through words. Moreover, activity groups will need to be more structured than the typical group psychotherapy of the adult, and the leader acts more as a role model than as an interpreter of feelings. Groups of delinquents, even if they should be older than fifteen, by and large fall into the same pattern of the leader-centered and well-structured group containing members of only one sex. This is once again in consonance with the developmental level, which is often preadolescent or early adolescent for the delinquent. Jacobs and I[13] have described the need for structuring and limit setting in such groups. Characteristically, regressive stances occur in an adolescent group. Flight, fight, and resorting to eating are common and need to be built into the group's climate. One may socialize

fighting tendencies by bringing in competitive games and the tendency to resort to eating by having some organized means for providing refreshments during the session. The management of the group per se can become a task for the participants, and in recognizing their feelings toward one another and ways of dealing with one another, they may learn the elements of democratic procedure.

Groups of adolescents past the age of fifteen can often be mixed and may follow the pattern of becoming a group of friends. While it becomes possible here for members to thwart the purpose of the group, for instance, by pairing off and taking oneself in this way out of the group, by and large the needs of even these older adolescents to have group support will permit these groups to be successful. A measure of structure is necessary even in groups of older adolescents, and adult leadership will still need to be rather more active. However, at this stage it becomes possible to institute groups on the discussion model that are not very different from adult psychotherapy groups. Such groups may be called "rap sessions," "club meetings," or by any other name; quite often the impact on the adolescents is strong and, if properly conducted, very therapeutic.

Indications for group treatment of adolescents are usually wider than those for individual treatment. Disorder manifested as action is apt to be the most common cause for referral to group treatment. A group by its nature provides a relatively protected social system in which the adolescent can test out his social skills or, vice versa, become aware of his social shortcomings. The problem one faces in the treatment of a disturbed youngster usually is not the one of deciding on the benefit of belonging to a group but on finding the right type of group and the proper setting in which he can work therapeutically. Many adolescent groups are sponsored by recreational organizations where the activity model by and large prevails. Mental health centers have been somewhat slow in providing appropriate settings for adolescents, which would mean several kinds of groups—younger adolescents, older adolescents, activity-related, or more discussion-like groups. Finally, closed institutions, such as hospitals or penal institutions, may utilize group approaches, usually of the variety containing only one sex, as a means toward better social adjustment in delinquent or very disturbed youngsters. In the main, groups are indicated when the goal is a change in social behavior. The technical difficulties of such groups usually have more to do with the operating assumptions of the particular social setting, such as hospital, clinic, or recreational organization, that is, where the group takes place, than with the individual adolescents themselves. It is important for the therapist of adolescent groups to have a clear view of where he and his group fit in with the sponsoring organization or what type of interaction he may bring into the adolescent group. Trying to fit oneself into a larger social system is in a sense the task of the adolescent, and a relatively protected therapeutic group provides one of the best introductions to this end.

Family treatment may follow a rigorous model, where the total family and only the total family is seen by the therapist, or, better, may follow a more flexible arrangement where the treatment may be family oriented and yet an opportunity may be provided for individual sessions and sessions with the parents alone, as well as total family sessions. It is this less rigid, family-oriented model that seems to yield in most instances fairly precise information on the nature of the adolescent problem and often permits relatively short treatment focused on the salient issue and concentrated on the place or people who are most capable of solving the problem. In other words, where rapid problem-solving is needed, one may not only try to identify a suitable focus for intervention but also try to find the important people who are most likely to respond to helpful intervention. It may be noted that a family of any size called together to deal with a crisis around an adolescent might be considered a group or, perhaps more specifically, a problem-solving group. The family perceives itself as having been called together to deal with an issue, the issue being the problem around the adolescent. Ordinar-

ily, such a family would not come together for problem-solving purposes, and in many cases, the experience of sitting together and trying to resolve the difficulty is a new experience itself. A family that is, as it were, forced together for the specific purpose of solving a crisis will usually do so in fairly short order, if only to relieve discomfort. The more important therapeutic issue is to arrive at a rational solution rather than a makeshift solution based perhaps on attaching blame or guilt to someone either inside or outside the family. Quite likely the identified patient will serve as scapegoat in a poor crisis solution, and his ejection from the family might be decided upon. If outsiders are to be blamed, quite often the school authorities, police, or peers of the adolescent will do, and occasionally the therapist receives the blame. One may find in family problem-solving sessions that crises will calm down rather quickly to a point where most family members are no longer anxious or helpless. However, crises, even if they are solved quickly, are not always solved adequately with family sessions alone. Long-term family therapy has been practiced and described and has resulted in profound attitude changes in parents as well as in the younger members of their families. It may be indicated in cases of psychosis or serious behavior disorder.

In summary, it may be said that treatment of adolescents by whichever method is a challenging and oftentimes difficult task. Unfortunately, experiences with medication are rarely positive, so that the psychological and social approaches remain the most important tools in the treatment of the adolescent. It is important to apply all approaches—individual, group, and family—in a flexible manner in order to arrive at the best understanding and the most expedient handling of adolescent problems.

❲ Bibliography

1. ANTHONY, J. "The Reactions of Adults to Adolescents and Their Behavior." In G. Caplan and S. Lebovici, eds., *Adolescence: Psychosocial Perspectives*. New York: Ba-

sic Books, 1969. Pp. 54–77.

2. BALSER, B. H., ed. *Psychotherapy of the Adolescent*. New York: International Universities Press, 1957.

3. BATESON, G., JACKSON, D. D., HALEY, J., and WEAKLAND, J. H. "A Note on the Double Bind." *Family Process*, 2 (1962), 154–161.

4. BLOS, P. *On Adolescence: A Psychoanalytic Interpretation*. Glencoe, Ill.: The Free Press, 1962.

5. BOSZORMENYI-NAGY, I., and FRAMO, J. L., eds. *Intensive Family Therapy: Theoretical and Practical Aspects*. New York: Harper & Row, 1965.

6. CAPLAN, G., and LEBOVICI, S., eds. *Adolescence: Psychosocial Perspectives*. New York: Basic Books, 1969.

7. CHORAS, P., and STONE, A. A. "A Strategy for the Initial State of Psychotherapy with Adolescents." *American Journal of Psychotherapy*, 24, no. 1 (January 1970), 65–77.

8. DEUTSCH, H. *Psychology of Women*. New York: Grune & Stratton, 1944. Vol. 1.

9. ———. *Selected Problems of Adolescence*. Monograph Series of the *Psychoanalytic Study of the Child*, Monograph No. 3 International Universities Press (1967).

10. ERIKSON, E. H. *Childhood and Society*. New York: Norton, 1950.

11. FREUD, A. "Adolescence." *Psychoanalytic Study of the Child*, 13 (1958), 255–278.

12. HOLMES, D. J. *The Adolescent in Psychotherapy*. Boston: Little, Brown, 1964.

13. JACOBS, M. A., and CHRIST, J. "Structuring and Limit Setting as Techniques in the Group Treatment of Adolescent Delinquents." *Community Mental Health Journal*, 3, no. 3 (Fall 1967), 237–244.

14. JOSSELYN, I. M. *The Adolescent and His World*. New York: Family Service Association of America, 1952.

15. LIDZ, T. *The Person: His Development Throughout the Life Cycle*. New York: Basic Books, 1968.

16. ———, FLECK, S., and CORNELISON, A. R. *Schizophrenia and the Family*. New York: International Universities Press, 1965.

17. LORAND, S. and SCHNEER, H. I., eds. *Adolescents: Psychoanalytic Approach to Problems and Therapy*. New York: Hoeber, 1961.

18. MASTERSON, J. F., Jr. *The Psychiatric Dilemma of Adolescence*. Boston: Little, Brown, 1967.

CHAPTER 24

RESIDENTIAL TREATMENT OF ADOLESCENTS

Donald B. Rinsley

R ESIDENTIAL, inpatient, or hospital treatment refers to a comprehensive therapeutic process addressed to the adolescent whose psychopathology is of a degree that warrants his removal from his usual familial and social environments, with subsequent admission into full-time institutional care. Such treatment is reserved for those adolescents who have been unable to harness or channel their instinctual energies and hence have failed at utilizing peer and adult relationships to sustain psychosocial growth.[7] For such adolescents, residential treatment must provide two basic therapeutic ingredients. (1) It must provide accurate diagnosis, sensitive understanding, and adequate psychiatric treatment of the adolescent's illness. (2) It must provide cognitive-intellectual and emotional growth experiences, including education, and occupational, recreational, and vocational modalities appropriate for the patient's age and cognitive development and for the nature, degree, and chronicity of his illness. These two ingredients are, as it were, so intimately interrelated as to preclude application of the term "residential treatment" to any purportedly therapeutic inpatient program essentially devoid of either. Thus, whereas the healthy adolescent pursues age-appropriate growth experiences per se and the adolescent in outpatient treatment pursues them along with his therapeutic process, the inpatient adolescent receives them as a carefully prescribed, integral part of his residential therapeutic experience, and the residential setting must be staffed to provide them.

As employed here, the term "residential treatment" has reference to a complex, full-time inpatient process provided within a service, setting, or unit specialized for and adapted to the needs of patients in the early and middle periods of adolescence (ages twelve through seventeen years), and not to services or wards that attempt concomitantly to provide treatment for a mixed population of adolescent and adult psychiatric patients. Although controversy continues regarding the advisability of treating adolescents on adult mental hospital wards,* there is growing awareness that optimal care, which implies intensive, reconstructive treatment conducive to lasting, healthy personality change, is best carried out amid the adolescent peer group by professional staff, specially trained in techniques most appropriate for the adolescent, who serve as healthy identificatory models for him.[15,35,40,42] Finally, granting that childhood psychopathology develops from, and in turn gives expression to, pathological familial relationships, adequate residential treatment must include the means conducive to therapeutic modification of such relationships, including intensive parallel or concomitant casework treatment, family therapy, and, in some cases, individual psychotherapy or psychoanalysis for parents.

⟨ Developmental and Diagnostic Considerations

Irrespective of presenting symptomatology, the adolescent who is a candidate for residential treatment is invariably found to have failed at the interrelated developmental tasks of separation-individuation and emancipation.[27,28] The more precise extent of that failure depends on whether his difficulties arose prior to or after the inception of the mother-infant symbiosis during the first postnatal year of life. Following the formulations of Kanner and of Mahler in the case of infants and younger children,[8,18,19,21-23] it is possible to divide the great majority of adolescent inpatients into two major etiologic-diagnostic groups.

Group 1.   Presymbiotic Adolescents

Adolescents diagnosed as presymbiotic (autistic-presymbiotic) are traditionally viewed as suffering from nuclear, or process, schizophrenia. Their pervasive psychopathology has been present since early infancy; they are severely disorganized, show perceptual-

sensory, cognitive, affective, and expressive-motoric dyssynchronies and often display the "soft" neurological signs found in schizophrenic children, whom Bender has termed "pseudodefective."[3-5] The term "presymbiotic" applies to them from recognition of their failure to have achieved a satisfying relationship with a mothering figure, hence to have received the protection of the maternal stimulus barrier during the period of maximal vulnerability of the infantile ego. As a consequence, there remain profound, chronic defects of the ego boundaries, with persistence of introjective-projective defenses and reliance upon magic-hallucination, scotomatization, and denial. The term "autistic" applies because these adolescents live amid an inner world replete with a welter of mixed ideal and horrific bad internal objects, which are fused with endopsychic sensations and images, and hence with their primitive perceptual notions of their bodily processes, organs, and products. As a result, meaningful relations with others are impossible, and the prospect of closeness or intimacy is likely to provoke inordinate clinging, withdrawal, or attack. These adolescents are admitted to the hospital with long histories of developmental lags and of psychosocial and educational failure; many are stigmatized as brain-injured or retarded. The overwhelming majority receive postadmission WISC full-scale IQs in the borderline retarded range or below.[35,40,42] A variety of diagnostic labels are regularly accorded the presymbiotic adolescent.[42] (See Table 24-1.)

Group 2.   Symbiotic (Borderline) Adolescents

Adolescent inpatients classifiable under this rubric have indeed experienced the elements of a need-satisfying mother-infant object tie; their psychopathology reflects their failure to have separated from it, and hence to have undergone any significant degree of individuation. Some of these adolescents are overtly, even floridly, psychotic, while others present their psychopathology in the form of hyperactive, impulsive, megalomanic, asocial, or

* See references 1, 2, 7, 11, 15, 29, 46, 48, and 49.

TABLE 24–1.

AUTHOR'S TERMINOLOGY	EQUIVALENT DIAGNOSES	OFTEN MISDIAGNOSED
Presymbiotic psychosis of adolescence	Nuclear schizophrenia Process schizophrenia Childhood schizophrenia pseudodefective type[5] Childhood schizophrenia, (organic group)[9] Schizophrenia, childhood type Schizophrenia, catatonic type (occasional) Schizophrenia, hebephrenic type (occasional) Kanner's syndrome: infantile autism (rare)[18,19] "Atypicality"[32]	Mental retardation, moderate to severe Psychosis with: Mental retardation Organic cerebral impairment Chronic brain syndrome, due to various causes Various syndromes of ego and developmental arrest[7]

antisocial (pseudopsychopathic) behavior, or else by means of a wide spectrum of anxiety-laden, obsessive-compulsive, phobic, and hysteriform symptomatology (pseudoneurosis).[5, 6,27,28] Irrespective of specific symptoms, careful study discloses heavy reliance upon an autistically organized inner world, the content of which centers upon mother-child fusion and reunion fantasies, which must at all costs be protected from the scrutiny of others.

Within this group are found some adolescents labeled as "brilliant but crazy," including the odd or strange "model student" and occasional examples of the "childhood genius," whose purported genius reflects massive pseudointellectual overcompensation rather than genuine originality or creativity. Just as the presymbiotic adolescent is often misdiagnosed as feebleminded, mentally retarded, or brain-damaged, so is the symbiotic adolescent frequently misdiagnosed as psychoneurotic, characterologically disordered, or else suffering from some sort of phase-specific adjustment reaction or turmoil state supposedly specific for adolescents.[24–26,50] The postadmission WISC full-scale IQs of symbiotic adolescent inpatients range from borderline through superior scores. Some are indeed intellectually gifted but have achieved below their educational potential as a consequence of the in-

roads of their illness, while others have achieved brilliantly in academic work at the expense of otherwise healthy peer-group and wider social and interpersonal relations. Sudden or insidious decompensation occurs in these adolescents, as it often does in younger symbiotic primary school children, when the requirements of the school and the wider social environment threaten to overwhelm the youngster's precarious, guarded autistic personality organization.[35,40,42] Table 24–2 records some of the numerous diagnostic labels regularly assigned to the symbiotic adolescent.[42]

Historical and examinational findings regularly demonstrate the following characteristics of the adolescent who is a candidate for intensive residential treatment.

1. Major signs of ego weakness, including substantial reliance on such primitive defenses as projection, introjection, regression, and denial; impairment of the synthetic function of the ego, with ensuing disruption of self-environment relations and decomposition of perceptual, cognitive, affective, and motor functions; predominance of anxiety of the instinctual type with associated failure of normal repression; impairment of object relations; serious impairment, or lack of, basic trust; persistence of primary-process (autistic; dereistic) thinking, with reliance on transitivism and

TABLE 24–2.

AUTHOR'S TERMINOLOGY	EQUIVALENT DIAGNOSES	OFTEN MISDIAGNOSED
Symbiotic psychosis of adolescence	Borderline syndrome of adolescence[27, 28]	Adjustment reaction of adolescence
	Reactive schizophrenia	Adolescent turmoil
	Childhood schizophrenia, pseudoneurotic type[5] pseudopsychopathic type[6]	Psychoneurosis (anxiety, phobic, hysterical, depressive, obsessive-compulsive, "mixed," and so on)
	Schizophrenia, childhood type	
	Schizophrenia, chronic undifferentiated type	Various schizophreniform conditions
	Schizophrenia, catatonic type (occasional)	Personality disorder, especially delinquent, antisocial, schizoid, and the like
	Schizophrenia, hebephrenic type (occasional)	School phobia (rare)
		Various syndromes of ego and developmental arrest[7]

gestural and word magic; persistent infantile grandiosity and serious difficulties with self- and sexual identities.[38]

2. Major problems with instinctual drives, including burgeoning or extreme failure of inner controls, leading to profuse if fluctuant acting out, confusion, and turmoil; and schizoid patterns indicative of massive ego constriction, leading to withdrawal and alienation.

3. Failure of interpersonal relations, including inability to utilize intrafamilial and wider social and peer relationships in the service of self-control and self-direction.[7]

4. Inability effectively to utilize proffered environmental supports for ego functioning, including those of the family and the wider cultural environment, particularly the school.[7]

5. Presence of latent or overt classical thought disorder, which conveys failure to have achieved a significant measure of abstract categorical (operational) thinking by early adolescence. (When viewed against a background of sudden, progressive, or chronic psychosocial distress, the presence of classical thought disorder may be considered pathognomonic for the adolescent who requires intensive residential treatment.)

(Diagnosis of the Family

Irrespective of social class, the family of the adolescent inpatient will almost invariably be discovered to have raised and dealt with him as if he were something or someone other than who he in fact is; that is, to have apersonated or depersonified him.[41] A consequence of parental psychopathology, such depersonification operates according to a general pattern, which Johnson and Szurek[16,17] first described in the case of the delinquent or antisocial child and adult, and severely inhibits and distorts identity formation.[41,45,47]

Detailed study of the families of adolescent inpatients discloses their similarity to the pervasively disturbed families described by Bateson, Lidz, and Wynne,[30] the relationships within which have been subsumed under the term "amorphous family nexus."[51] Such families are organized essentially along autistic lines, with such features as the pervasive use of double-bind communications; blurring of age, generational, and sexual roles; shifting and fluid individual identities; patterns of irrational thinking with distorted perception of the extrafamilial world; inadequately controlled or pathologically overcontrolled instinctual urges, and diffusion and obfuscation of leadership and authority. The adolescent's psychopathology thus represents, in sum, his prior internalization of these pathogenic patterns, his immense ambivalence toward them, his inability to communicate about them, the secondary gain of his efforts to comply with them, and his miscarried efforts to break free of them.

([The Residential Milieu: General Considerations

The genuinely therapeutic residential milieu is neither a school, foster care home, detention facility, recreational center, nor correctional institution, although at various times it functions in all these roles. Rather, it comprises a small psychiatric hospital, the staff of which represents a group of competent professionals, each with a well-defined role, whose main tasks include the detection, control, clarification, and interpretation of the patient's symptomatic behavior. The setting should be reasonably self-contained, with an ongoing inservice training program for its staff, in order to limit or eliminate the classical clinical-administrative dichotomies that seriously complicate and often vitiate the performance and goals of intensive treatment.[10]

The fundamental, general functions of the residential milieu for the seriously ill adolescent include:[31]

1. Removal of the patient from the pathogenic family nexus and from the extrafamilial environment, the demands and expectations of which have overwhelmed him.
2. Shelter and protection, including interpersonal, pharmacological, and physical devices to graduate and limit incident stimulation, hence to offer protection against ego trauma.[31,34,39,44]
3. Appropriate, consistent (hence predictable) external controls, the purpose of which is to transduce communications inherent in symtomatic verbal and nonverbal behavior into secondary-process language.
4. Opportunities for controlled therapeutic regression, with emergence of transference responses, which in turn reveal the spectrum of the adolescent's particular, overdetermined coping mechanisms, including those that represent his resistances to treatment.[35,40,42,43,44]
5. Recognition and diagnosis of the manifold of pathogenic, depersonifying communications and role and identity confusions characteristic of the patient's family nexus.
6. Appropriate, intensive use of the techniques of confrontation, clarification and interpretation vis-à-vis the patient and his parental surrogates, in order to expose and alter their apersonative patterns of communication.
7. Promotion of the adolescent's need to identify with the residential staff as good objects, with concomitant emergence of his endopsychic nucleus of bad (internal) objects.[35,40,42]
8. Provision of such ego-supportive modalities as ongoing education (residential school), recreational and occupational therapies, and, for some older adolescent inpatients, vocational training as part of their overall treatment.

([The Resistance Phase of Residential Treatment

Irrespective of the route by which the adolescent and his parents have entered the combined residential treatment process, and whether voluntary or otherwise, they quickly develop a variety of resistances to it.* These resistances, whether gross or subtle, intense or fleeting, serve to disguise and protect the pathogenic family nexus, the congeries of wishes, needs, fantasies, and role distortions

---

* See references 33, 35–37, 40, and 42–44.

which all parties to the nexus share in common, including the secondary gains subserved by the family members', especially the patient's, symptoms. In the case of the presymbiotic adolescent, the resistances, often herculean, serve to ward off staff members' access to the enormously primitive inner world of part-object representations, exposure or loss of which the adolescent perceives as a threat to his very existence. In the case of the symbiotic adolescent, the need is to draw attention from the welter of primitive refusal and reunion fantasies that comprise the matrix of his psychopathology. In the case of the parents, the resistances aim toward deflecting the family therapist's or the caseworker's attention from the various depersonifying themes characteristic of the parent-child relationship as well as to deny or assuage the guilt associated with them.

Resistance behavior conveys the adolescent's particular spectrum of archaic, overdetermined coping devices, particularly in relation to authority or surrogate figures from the past. Its recognition, clarification, and interpretation are best carried out in a closed ward or cottage, where comprehensive external controls and carefully titrated privileges serve to bring the adolescent into engagement with, and prevent his avoidance or evasion of, staff members.

The most important forms of resistance behavior that adolescent inpatients regularly demonstrate are the following:[40,42,44]

1. Identification with the aggressor, including some forms of early positive transference, and imitation or mimicry of adult staff members in a counterphobic effort to ward them off.
2. Leveling, which represents the adolescent's effort to depersonify staff members into peer or sibling figures.
3. Flirtatiousness and seductiveness, which convey efforts to sexualize relationships with staff figures, thereby to deflect their attention from other actions, fantasies, preoccupations, and sensory-perceptual experiences.

4. Oversubmissiveness, which has obvious counterphobic intent.
5. Scapegoatism, either active, by which the adolescent sets up a wardmate or motivates him toward proxy acting out, or passive, exemplified by the adolescent who masochistically collects injustices or actually sets himself up to be assaulted or punished by peers or staff members.
6. Outright rebelliousness, ambivalently aimed at warding off staff members through provocative or wildly disruptive behavior as well as provoking patient-staff contact through application of necessary physical restraints or controls.
7. Transference diffusion (also termed "transference splitting," a notable form of which is often called "manipulation"), including gossiping and talecarrying and various efforts to "split" staff members or even whole shifts of aides or child-care workers, thereby to conceal thoughts, feelings, and other subjective experiences behind the ensuing confusion.
8. Persistent avoidance, including classical negativism, apathy, somnolence, daydreaming, various seizure and dissociative phenomena, refusal to eat, and efforts to provoke restriction and isolation.
9. Somatization, by which physical complaints become the metaphorical vehicle for body language communications as well as a means of deflecting staff attention from thoughts, feelings, fantasies, and delusional preoccupations.
10. Peer-age caricaturing, also termed "out-typifying one's self," by which the adolescent attempts to deny or ward off attention to disturbing subjective experiences through actions that appear as slight exaggerations of behavior traditionally viewed as "typical of teenagers."
11. Clique formation, in which peer- or small-group interactions are used to

preclude engagement with staff members.

12. "Craziness" and "pseudostupidity," the aim of which is to arrest or paralyze staff attention to disturbing inner experiences, whence the message "I am too crazy (stupid) to bother about, so why don't you leave me alone (or let me out of here)."

13. "Intellectual" pursuits, including literary, graphic artistic, and scientific pursuits and projects, which have basically autistic significance, notably if indulged in without careful staff supervision.

14. Elopement or running away, a complex, overdetermined act in response to a variety of aggressive, erotic, reunion, and rescue fantasies. Although running away may and often does have positive therapeutic meaning, its occurrence during the resistance phase of treatment almost always betokens an anxious need to preclude therapeutic engagement.

Analysis of the adolescent inpatient's resistance behavior and metaphors requires the staff's sustained and comprehensive attention to every nuance of his daily actions and interpersonal relationships. Concomitantly, the parents (or, in some cases, other surrogate figures) bring to the caseworker or the family therapist resistance communications which in turn reflect their own anxiety, guilt, and patterns of depersonifying their child. These last comprise the following general categories:[41,44]

1. The child as "thing," inanimate object or externalized part of one's self, a narcissistic part object lacking an identity of its own apart from that of the parent. (This category of depersonification is found amongst seriously disorganized, i.e., psychotic, parents.)

2. The child as parent figure, which reflects the classical parent-child reversal of roles.[45]

3. The child as spouse, which reflects serious age and generational conflicts, with notably incestuous overtones and actions.

4. The child as sibling, in which the parent lives out with the child earlier sibling rivalries and conflicts derived from the inability to have separated from symbiotic ties with his or her own parents (i.e., the child's grandparents).[27,28]

5. The child as lifelong infant, reflective of the parent's own unresolved infantile needs and anxiety over assumption of genuinely adult goals and values.

In symbiotic cases, the adolescent's and the parents' resistances serve to protect, as it were, the parent-child tie, separation or emancipation from which evokes fresh charges of anxiety and guilt in both, which lead in turn to further regressive efforts at mutual clinging. Successful working through of the separation requires rigid control of parent-child contacts and correspondence; when accomplished, it signifies beginning resolution of the so-called loyalty problem, such that the parent in effect bids the child to trust and begin to identify with the staff members, and the child proceeds so to act. Even within an intensive, interpretive, carefully supervised residential milieu, such resolution ordinarily requires from twelve to eighteen months of concentrated work by all concerned.

In presymbiotic cases, the problem is more difficult and the outcome of the resistance work more problematic. Often, there are no available parents whom the adolescent can begin to objectify and from whom he might separate; hence the resistance work must center on the enormously difficult task of separating him, as it were, from the welter of magic-hallucinatory, mixed idealized, and terrifying internal objects amidst which he lives. Although no time limits can be assigned this process, some adolescents in this situation have managed to accomplish the resistance work within a five-year period of intensive residential treatment.

In both symbiotic and presymbiotic cases, successful completion of the work of the resistance phase of residential treatment betokens the inception of the adolescent's significant and enduring identifications with the staff members, and of the parents' identification with and acceptance of their child's treatment, personified in the family therapist or the caseworker. The stage is now set for the beginning of the next, or definitive, phase of residential treatment, the hallmarks of which are (1) accelerating emergence of the adolescent's heretofore suppressed autistic preoccupations and coping efforts and (2) progressive clarification and amelioration of the family's pathogenic nexus of mutual depersonifications.[42]

⟨ The Definitive Phase of Residential Treatment

Entrance into the definitive phase of residential treatment initiates what often proves to be a period of regressive storm and stress for the severely ill adolescent. It means giving up the core of bad introjects central to his psychopathology, the efflorescence of anxiety and guilt, which his symptoms have in part held from conscious awareness, emergence of the last vestiges of the powerful infantile-megalomania common to unseparated personalities devoid of basic trust, and the onset of various degrees of regression in all areas of psychological function.[35,40,42] The whole process signals the ultimate failure of the adolescent's traditional splitting defenses and confronts him with the anxiety and guilt that attend the inception of whole-object relations. Thus, the adolescent proceeds to grieve or mourn the loss of his introjects, however pathogenic they may have been, with emergence of the exceedingly painful "mixed," or "impure," depression of childhood.[27,28,35] During this period, he begins to speak of how "bad," "evil," and "destructive" he has been, and by his regressive experiences and actions mounts an eleventh-hour plea to the staff to remit the therapeutic pressure on him, to desist from further efforts to empty him of his objects, as it were. The staff understandably find it difficult to continue, as their powerful countertransference to the adolescent's experience of impending annihilation motivates them

to restore him to his former state. Of signal importance in sustaining this introject work are the identifications with the staff the adolescent has developed toward the end of the prior resistance phase of treatment.

Of particular impact on the adolescent during this phase of his treatment is the failure of the secondary gain of his illness, a result that ensues in part from his parents' ongoing work in the family therapy or concomitant casework process, such that they begin to signal to him that they no longer need to depersonify him. Thus, he becomes doubly bereft as he perceives the departure of his bad introjects as well as his parents' failure to continue reinforcing his symptomatology. If he traverses this period successfully, the adolescent will have begun to objectify himself and his parents, hence to have given up his infantile ties to them.

⟨ The Resolution Phase of Residential Treatment*

Completion of the definitive phase of residential treatment ordinarily requires another year of intensive therapeutic work. As it begins to draw to a close, the adolescent becomes prepared for increased and unsupervised visits and passes with his family, and for the assumption of ever-wider responsibility for his own actions. His earlier identifications with the staff have supplied him with the nucleus of "good" introjects, which he had long lacked, and his increasing capacity to objectify himself and his parents now serves to preclude reimmersion in whatever remnants of the family's original depersonifying nexus of communications may persist. By now he has successfully worked through the paradigmatic "loss"

* Masterson[27,28] independently described three analogous phases in the intensive psychiatric treatment of the adolescent with borderline syndrome: his phase 1, testing, corresponds with the resistance phase, his phase 2, working through, with the definitive phase, and his phase 3, separation, with the resolution phase above described. Lewis,[20] also working in a residential setting, confirmed the phasic nature of adolescent residential treatment, with particular emphasis on resistance and later introjection.

of his original, archaic, pathogenic internal objects, which will have strengthened him for the mourning he must now perform as he begins to separate from the residential staff and milieu that have become so important to him. The latter will require several months of combined interpretive and supportive therapeutic work, accompanied by concomitant working through by the family as they prepare to "reacquire" their child.

⟨ The Basic Goals of Residential Treatment

For the presymbiotic adolescent, the full residential setting provides a highly concrete, compulsively styled, maximally predictable environment, as free as possible from peer-competitive experiences, and organized to support the one-to-one, or individual, therapeutic process, which is essential for the treatment of the nuclear schizophrenic adolescent. The individual therapist may be a psychotherapist, psychoanalyst, specially skilled residential teacher, or occupational or recreational therapist whose work with the patient interdigitates closely with that of the other residential staff members and who receives intensive individual or group-process supervision to promote recognition and resolution of the enormously difficult countertransference problems that such work entails. The goal of the individual therapeutic process comprises catalysis for the crystallization of basic ego nuclei and points toward establishment of the patient-therapist symbiosis symbolic for the earlier mother-infant symbiosis, which the adolescent had never achieved. Once established,

the patient-therapist symbiosis requires extended efforts directed toward eventual desymbiotization, which signals the adolescent's first real efforts toward separation-individuation. The whole process may be diagrammed as in Figure 24–1.[42] In the case of the presymbiotic adolescent, establishment and beginning resolution of the patient-therapist symbiosis occur during the resistance phase of treatment. During that period, the patient comes to develop and work through the transference psychosis, symbolic of the enormously primitive and archaic experiences resulting from early object loss. Among the various factors contributory to the exceptional difficulty of this work, three emerge with particular clarity. (1) The patient's early resistances assume herculean proportions. (2) Staff countertransference of similar proportions emerges exceedingly rapidly. (3) Many such adolescents are products of thoroughly disorganized, fragmented pseudofamilies, or else have long since lost contact with parents and other family members; as a result, there is often little, if anything, in the way of family therapy or concomitant casework treatment, and the resistance phase of treatment becomes prolonged.

For the symbiotic adolescent, essentially locked within a prolonged, unresolved mother-infant fusion tie, the therapeutic goal comprises desymbiotization with attendant separation and individuation. To this end, the major focus of the work of the resistance phase of treatment becomes the recognition and interpretation of the adolescent's fantasies, which center on megalomanic control of and reunion with family members, particularly the mother. As these recognitions and interpretations proceed, the residential program increasingly emphasizes progressive socialization, gradu-

FIGURE 24–1.

Resistance Phase of Treatment	Definitive Phase of Treatment	Resolution Phase of Treatment
Establishment of Symbiosis ↓		
Beginning Resolution → of Symbiosis	Continued Resolution → of Symbiosis	Desymbiotization and Separation

ated expansion of privileges, peer-competitive participation (including residential school and occupational and recreational therapy classes), and increased personal responsibility. Although individual psychotherapy may be prescribed and is often helpful, it is not considered essential for the symbiotic adolescent, who often works best with a skilled residential psychiatrist directly in the ward or cottage area on a day-to-day basis. In particular, willy-nilly prescription of individual psychotherapy is contraindicated, especially during the resistance phase of treatment, lest the adolescent proceed to incorporate it into his splitting defenses, thereby vitiating its impact upon him. The process may be diagrammed as in Figure 24–2.[42]

(Clinical-Administrative Structure of the Residential Service

Effective intensive residential psychiatric treatment represents the opposite of the pathogenic familial-social nexus, within which the adolescent's psychopathology has developed and to which it gives expression. This treatment includes establishment and maintenance of stable staff roles, clear-cut and predictable lines of authority, firmly and equitably enforced rules of dress and conduct to which patients are expected to adhere, and rapid and effectual staff communication and consensus regarding every aspect of the patient's daily experience and behavior. Within such a setting, the residential psychiatrist assumes leadership of the ward or cottage therapeutic team, which is composed of the nurse and psychiatric aides or child-care workers.

The residential psychiatrist possesses final authority in determining and implementing the overall therapeutic plan for each patient, in collaboration with the other ward or cottage staff members, and prescribes indicated educational and adjunctive therapeutic activities and classes. The residential psychiatrist collaborates closely with the caseworker or family therapist, and with his patients' group and individual psychotherapists, none of whom carry administrative responsibility for the ward or cottage treatment areas.

Ideally, an intensive residential psychiatric service should be reasonably self-contained; if the adolescent service is a part of a larger general, teaching, or public or private mental hospital, its staff should be able to evolve and implement its clinical-administrative program devoid of coercion or pressure to conform to general institutional rules inapplicable to an adolescent residential program. Its ongoing diagnostic and therapeutic work should be carried on, with but rare exception, only by full-time staff members. By and large, part-time visiting or attending staff, lacking comprehensive daily knowledge of the patients, complicate the therapeutic work by falling easy prey to the adolescent's redoubtable tendency to manipulate them and to split and divide them from the full-time staff members.

If the residential setting also serves as an affiliated teaching service, it becomes essential for the various trainees, particularly the general and child psychiatric residents and fellows who serve as residential psychiatrists, to receive intensive supervision by experienced senior staff members who are themselves actively immersed in the therapeutic work of the service. Such supervision, which not rarely

FIGURE 24–2.

Resistance Phase of Treatment	Definitive Phase of Treatment	Resolution Phase of Treatment
Recognition and Exposure of Symbiosis ↓		
Beginning Resolution → of Symbiosis	Continued Resolution → of Symbiosis	Desymbiotization and Separation

assumes therapeutic qualities, serves to expose and minimize the serious transference-countertransference binds that trainees are prone to experience in their work with seriously ill adolescents.[12,13,15] The same is true as well for the various full-time staff members themselves, for whom individual and group-process in-service training and supervision are ongoing needs.

⟨ Group and Family Therapy

In a very real sense, the therapeutic ward or cottage program comprises a more extended form of group therapy. For the hospitalized adolescent, formal, dynamically oriented group psychotherapy has a definite place, subject to several qualifications:

1. Formal group psychotherapy is optimally conducted with a mixed- or same-gender group of adolescents numbering not more than six, with or without a recorder, in addition to the group psychotherapist.
2. Group psychotherapy is contraindicated for presymbiotic adolescents until they are well along in the definitive phase of treatment.
3. Group psychotherapy is of little therapeutic value and may indeed exert negative therapeutic effects in the case of symbiotic adolescents during the resistance phase of treatment; that is, before they have engaged with the ward or cottage staff. The exception is the psychotherapeutic group conducted directly in the ward or cottage treatment area, integrated into the mainstream of daily ward or cottage activities.
4. With hospitalized adolescents, the conduct of the group sessions should follow a carefully prescribed and enforced structure regarding time and place, promptness of arrival, and behavior during the sessions. Although the patients may in various degrees participate in setting and maintaining the structure,

a passive, or laissez-faire, approach to it by the therapist is contraindicated. The notion of participatory democracy in an adolescent residential service is often an illusion that disguises staff countertransference and scotomatizes the adolescent inpatient's very serious difficulties with ego functioning. The therapist must therefore unequivocally convey to the group that he is in full and complete control of it at all times.

Again, regularly scheduled meetings between the hospitalized adolescent and his parents, under the supervision and with the scrutiny of the caseworker, constitute a form of family therapy of particular diagnostic and therapeutic value to all concerned, especially as such meetings serve to promote exposure and resolution of the parents' and the adolescent's resistances. The parents should have their own meetings with the caseworker for discussion of problems not directly related to their difficulties with their child, as well as for consideration and analysis of the events that transpire during the patient-child meetings, as these may be correlated with the details of the child's ongoing work in the ward or cottage.

⟨ Residential School and Adjunctive Therapies

The therapeutic and specific values of residential school and of occupational and recreational therapies lie in their firm integration as parts of the overall therapeutic program of the residential treatment service, and not as ends in themselves.[14,42] Thus, the teachers and the occupational and recreational therapists have concomitant status as full therapeutic team members, and the specific skills they impart or catalyze subserve the adolescent's particular therapeutic needs.

In the case of the presymbiotic adolescent, the disorganizing effects of peer competition necessitate assignment to the one-to-one class. In school, the specific goal of imparting basic cognitive skills succeeds only if the student-teacher relationship flourishes. Often, the residential teacher becomes, in effect, the adolescent's psychotherapist, as she labors to catalyze the youngster's blighted capacity to learn. The same general considerations apply to occupational and recreational therapies, in which the therapist utilizes specific professional skills and modalities to generate and reinforce the nuclear object relationship so essential for the process schizophrenic adolescent.

In the case of the symbiotic adolescent, residential school and adjunctive therapies represent opportunities for desymbiotization. In them, the symbiotic adolescent is urged toward competition and socialization, with ensuing exposure of his infantile grandiosity and opportunities for relinquishing it through the consensual process.

In all cases, the therapist must set and maintain a firm structure in which the adolescent is expected to perform and must be skilled in therapeutic process in addition to the specifics of his or her particular professional expertise.

⟨ Some Pitfalls of Residential Treatment

The variety of pitfalls common to residential therapeutic services for adolescents amount, on careful analysis, to symbolic repetitions of the antecedent depersonifications to which the adolescent inpatient has previously been exposed. To them, the patient responds either directly or metaphorically with the message, "You don't understand me!" Under such circumstances, the patient has three alternatives. (1) He may dissimulate and appear to comply. (2) He may proceed to act out and "raise the roof." (3) He may run away.[36]

Some of the common pitfalls are:

1. Substantive and euphemistic mis- or underdiagnosis of the borderline or frankly psychotic adolescent with such labels as character disorder, psychoneurosis, adjustment reaction, or some form of deviant development.[24-27]

2. Countertransferential adultomorphization of the adolescent, reflected in laissez-faire, overpermissive, pseudoanalytic, and pseudodemocratic approaches, which profoundly overestimate the youngster's coping and adaptive capacities and scotomatize his difficulties with self- and sexual identities.

3. Open-ward treatment of the adolescent during the resistance phase of his work, prior to engagement with the ward or cottage staff.

4. Capitulation to the warding-off demands inherent in the adolescent's regressive actions and experiences during the early part of the definitive phase of treatment, thereby terminating his underlying need and efforts to desymbiotize.

5. Failure to regulate and control parent-child correspondence and visits, and consequent failure to effect parent-child separation, with resultant persistence of their mutually depersonifying communications.

6. Failure or unwillingness to utilize necessary legal controls to ensure the adolescent's continued residential treatment during those times when his and his parents' fear of exposure of their pathogenic nexus motivates efforts to remove the patient against medical advice.

7. Premature or willy-nilly use of individual psychotherapy for the symbiotic adolescent during the resistance phase of treatment.

8. Use of part-time, visiting, or attending staff members and of school classes and adjunctive therapies not intimately integrated with and subservient to the basic therapeutic purposes of the residential service.

⟨ Bibliography

1. BEAVERS, W. R., and BLUMBERG, S. "A Follow-Up Study of Adolescents Treated in an Inpatient Setting." *Diseases of the Nervous System*, 29 (1968), 606–612.

2. BECKETT, P. G. S. *Adolescents Out of Step: Their Treatment in a Psychiatric Hospital.* Detroit: Wayne State University Press, 1965.

3. BENDER, L. "Childhood Schizophrenia: Clinical Study of 100 Schizophrenic Children." *American Journal of Orthopsychiatry*, 17 (1947), 40–56.

4. ———. "Childhood Schizophrenia." *Psychiatric Quarterly*, 27 (1953), 663–681.

5. ———. "Schizophrenia in Childhood: Its Recognition, Description and Treatment." *American Journal of Orthopsychiatry*, 26 (1956), 499–506.

6. ———. "The Concept of Pseudopsychopathic Schizophrenia in Adolescents." *American Journal of Orthopsychiatry*, 29 (1959), 491–512.

7. EASSON, W. M. *The Severely Disturbed Adolescent: Inpatient, Residential and Hospital Treatment.* New York: International Universities Press, 1969.

8. FLIESS, R. *Ego and Body Ego: Contributions to Their Psychoanalytic Psychology.* New York: Schulte, 1961.

9. GOLDFARB, W. *Childhood Schizophrenia.* Cambridge: Harvard University Press, 1961.

10. GRALNICK, A. *The Psychiatric Hospital as a Therapeutic Instrument.* New York: Brunner/Mazel, 1969.

11. GREAVES, D. C., and REGAN, P. F. "Psychotherapy of Adolescents at Intensive Hospital Treatment Levels." In B. H. Balser, ed., *Psychotherapy of the Adolescent.* New York: International Universities Press, 1957. Pp. 130–143.

12. HENDRICKSON, W. J. "Training in Adolescent Psychiatry: The Role of Experience with Inpatients." In D. Offer and J. F. Masterson, eds., *Teaching and Learning Adolescent Psychiatry.* Springfield, Ill.: Charles C Thomas, 1971. Pp. 21–38.

13. ———, HOLMES, D. J., and WAGGONER, R. W. "Psychotherapy with Hospitalized Adolescents." *American Journal of Psychiatry*, 116 (1959), 527–532.

14. HIRSCHBERG, J. C. "The Role of Education in the Treatment of Emotionally Disturbed Children Through Planned Ego Development." *American Journal of Orthopsychiatry*, 23 (1953), 684–690.

15. HOLMES, D. J. *The Adolescent in Psychotherapy.* Boston: Little, Brown, 1964.

16. JOHNSON, A. M. "Sanctions for Superego Lacunae of Adolescents." In K. R. Eissler, ed., *Searchlights on Delinquency.* New York: International Universities Press, 1949. Pp. 225–245.

17. ———, and SZUREK, S. A. "The Genesis of Antisocial Acting Out in Children and Adults." *Psychoanalytic Quarterly*, 21 (1952), 323–343.

18. KANNER, L. "Autistic Disturbances of Affective Contact." *Nervous Child*, 2 (1943), 217–250.

19. ———. "Problems of Nosology and Psychodynamics of Early Infantile Autism." *American Journal of Orthopsychiatry*, 19 (1949), 416–426.

20. LEWIS, J .M. "The Development of an Inpatient Adolescent Service." *Adolescence*, 5 (1970), 303–312.

21. MAHLER, M. S. "On Child Psychosis and Schizophrenia: Autistic and Symbiotic Infantile Psychoses." *Psychoanalytic Study of the Child*, 7 (1952), 286–305.

22. ———. *On Human Symbiosis and the Vicissitudes of Individuation.* Vol 1. *Infantile Psychosis.* New York: International Universities Press, 1968.

23. ———, and GOSLINER, B. J. "On Symbiotic Child Psychosis: Genetic, Dynamic and Restitutive Aspects." *Psychoanalytic Study of the Child*, 10 (1955), 195–212.

24. MASTERSON, J. F. *The Psychiatric Dilemma of Adolescence.* Boston: Little, Brown, 1967.

25. ———. "The Psychiatric Significance of Adolescent Turmoil." *American Journal of Psychiatry*, 124 (1968), 1549–1554.

26. ———. "The Symptomatic Adolescent Five Years Later: He Didn't Grow Out of It." *American Journal of Psychiatry*, 123 (1967), 1338–1345.

27. ———. "Treatment of the Adolescent with Borderline Syndrome: A Problem in Separation-Individuation." *Bulletin of the Menninger Clinic*, 35 (1971), 5–18.

28. ———. *Treatment of the Borderline Adolescent: A Developmental Approach.* New York: Wiley, 1972.

29. MILLER, D. H. "The Treatment of Adolescents in an Adult Hospital." *Bulletin of the Menninger Clinic*, 21 (1957), 189–198.

30. MISHLER, E. G., and WAXLER, N. E. *Family Processes and Schizophrenia.* New York: Science House, 1968.

31. NOSHPITZ, J. D. "Notes on the Theory of Residential Treatment." *Journal of the*

American Academy of Child Psychiatry, 1 (1962), 284–296.

32. RANK, B. "Intensive Study and Treatment of Preschool Children Who Show Marked Personality Deviations, or 'Atypical Development,' and Their Parents." In G. Caplan, ed., *Emotional Problems of Early Childhood*. New York: Basic Books, 1955. Pp. 491–501.

33. RINSLEY, D. B. "Psychiatric Hospital Treatment with Special Reference to Children." *Archives of General Psychiatry*, 9 (1963), 489–496.

34. ———. "Thioridazine in the Treatment of Hospitalized Adolescents." *American Journal of Psychiatry*, 120 (1963), 73–74.

35. ———. "Intensive Psychiatric Hospital Treatment of Adolescents: An Object-Relations View." *Psychiatric Quarterly*, 39 (1965), 405–429.

36. ———. "The Adolescent in Residential Treatment: Some Critical Reflections." *Adolescence*, 2 (1967), 83–95.

37. ———. "Intensive Residential Treatment of the Adolescent." *Psychiatric Quarterly*, 41 (1967), 134–143.

38. ———. "Economic Aspects of Object Relations." *International Journal of Psycho-Analysis*, 49 (1968), 38–48.

39. ———. "Extended Experience with Thioridazine in the Treatment of Hospitalized Adolescents." *Diseases of the Nervous System*, 29 (1968), 36–37.

40. ———. "Theory and Practice of Intensive Residential Treatment of Adolescents." *Psychiatric Quarterly*, 42 (1968), 611–638.

41. ———. "The Adolescent Inpatient: Patterns of Depersonification." *Psychiatric Quarterly*, 45 (1971), 3–22.

42. ———. "Theory and Practice of Intensive Residential Treatment of Adolescents." Rev. ed. In S. C. Feinstein, P. Giovacchini, and A. A. Miller, eds., *Adolescent Psychiatry*. Vol. 1. *Developmental and Clinical Studies*. New York: Basic Books, 1971. Pp. 479–509.

43. ———, and HALL, D. D. "Psychiatric Hospital Treatment of Adolescents: Parental Resistances as Expressed in Casework Metaphor." *Archives of General Psychiatry*, 7 (1962), 286–294.

44. ———, and INGE, G. P., III. "Psychiatric Hospital Treatment of Adolescents: Verbal and Nonverbal Resistance to Treatment." *Bulletin of the Menninger Clinic*, 25 (1961), 249–263.

45. SCHMIDEBERG, M. "Parents as Children." *Psychiatric Quarterly*, Suppl., Part 2, 22 (1948), 207–218.

46. SCHMIEDECK, R. A. "A Treatment Program for Adolescents on an Adult Ward." *Bulletin of the Menninger Clinic*, 25 (1961), 241–248.

47. STRAGNELL, G. "Psychopathological Disturbances from the Avoidance of Parental Responsibility." *New York Medical Journal and Medical Records*, September 6, 1922.

48. TOOLAN, J. M., and NICKLIN, G. "Open Door Policy on an Adolescent Service in a Psychiatric Hospital." *American Journal of Psychiatry*, 115 (1959), 790–792.

49. WARREN, W. "Inpatient Treatment of Adolescents with Psychological Illness." *Lancet*, 262 (1952), 147–150.

50. WEINER, I. B. "The Generation Gap: Fact and Fancy." *Adolescence*, 6 (1971), 155–166.

51. ZENTNER, E. B., and APONTE, H. J. "The Amorphous Family Nexus." *Psychiatric Quarterly*, 44 (1970), 91–113.

CHAPTER 25

DROPOUTS AND WANDERERS OF THE HIP GENERATION

Toward a Gestalt-Ecological View

James R. Allen

O N OCTOBER 21, 1967, crews of antiwar demonstrators besieged the Pentagon. According to the *East Vilage Other*, their numbers included contingents of "witches, warlocks, holymen, seers, prophets, mystics, saints, shamans, troubadors, minstrels, bards, roadmen, and madmen." Eventually they performed a great exorcism, casting "mighty words of white light against the demon-controlled structure." That mighty ziggurat did not rise into the air, but the demonstrators had given expression to a new form of political action, an ever-changing pageant and crusade, a motley mixture of politics and put-on.

The greatest difficulty in the study of members of this hip generation is a lack of solid data. Its members need to protect themselves from enemies, whether outraged neighbors, tourists, or flocks of would-be pilgrims. Researchers are likely to find themselves accessories either before or after some fact, and to discover it difficult even to grasp the perspectives of members of several life styles, let alone discover some higher level of abstraction that makes sense of them all. Citizens of this country have prided themselves in making the United States a great melting pot. The obverse of this phenomenon is the very human tendency to treat difference not as difference, and therefore as an opportunity for growth, but rather as a battleground for self-esteem. "We differ" becomes "One of us must be right, and one wrong"; life is treated as a zero-sum game, where the gain of the winner is assumed equivalent to the loss of the loser. What is the division of people into "straights" and "hippies," "freaks" and "jocks," those over and those under thirty, but a new version of the categories of the elect and the damned?

Because of this paucity of solid data, descriptions of the hip generation are not unlike descriptions of Rorschach cards, more descriptive of the viewer than the viewed. Much depends on whether the phenomenon is perceived as a worldwide social movement, as the expression of geographically limited communities of deviants, as contemporary varieties of bohemian subculture, or some combination of these. Much depends on the degree of emotional disequilibrium the observer expects of adolescence and youth, and on the extent to which he accepts or rejects postindustrial Western society. The hip generation treats as unreal those very things the straights have taken seriously—security and power, status and position in hierarchies, and the "glories of our blood and state," in short, the attributes and manifestations of a society based on cadres of willing workers and willing consumers. Unlike deviant groups of the past, they reject many of the goals of the larger society and are ambivalent about the means: "The American way of life" one slogan reads, "may yet be the death of us all."

Much depends, too, on the viewer's historical perspective, the extent to which he sees the past and future as continuous. Aspects of discontinuity have been expressed in frameworks that are philosophical, as in Jasper's "second axial period,"[29] theological, as in the noosphere of Teilhard de Chardin,[14] historical, as in Toynbee's "etherealization,"[60] Reich's change from "Consciousness 2" (the New Deal and its concomitant attitudes of mind and way of life) to "Consciousness 3,"[41,47] and the revolt Roszak[48] described against the irrational rationality of "objective consciousness." Within a sociological framework, a similar view found expression in Sorokin's[55] concept of change from a sensate to an ideational or idealistic sociocultural order and in the Fromm-Bachofen hypothesis[1] of change from a patriarchal to a matriarchal culture. In the anthropological literature, Margaret Mead[37] described a change from cofigurative culture, where the prevailing mode of behavior is the behavior of contemporaries, to a prefigurative one, characterized by the young teaching the old. The framework for members of the hip generation, however, is more likely to be astrological; this is the "dawning of the age of Aquarius." Whether or not a new man really is aborning is probably less important than the vague uneasiness that he might be; the myth of Faustian man, which has sustained industrialized man since the Renaissance, seems to have run dry.

Dropping out, like running away or the taking of drugs, may be benign or malignant, and occurs in youth belonging to all categories of psychiatric classification, including variants of normal, a fact foreclosing generalizations except for those at such high levels of abstraction that their clinical usefulness is limited. These behaviors may be symptomatic of faulty development, or may be primarily defensive or adaptive, part of the separation and restorative processes of adolescence. Their roots may lie not in ideological movements, social disorganization, or in inner conflict alone but rather in their reciprocal complementarity at a time when the intellectual development elaborated by Piaget[45] makes it possible for youth to think ideologically.

Difficulties in classifying behaviors and assigning them to given classes of individuals with specific psychological profiles or similar background are confounded by such hybrids as the "Jesus freaks," "high" on their versions of Christianity, and the "Christ Patrols," motorcycle gangs of evangelic "missionaries," and the troublesome fact that the young individuals in the same groups seem to demonstrate markedly differing forms of behavior. The defensive aspects of such alternations are inherent in the defense mechanisms described by Anna Freud[19] in her characterization of adolescence; however, these aspects are probably also the outcomes of reciprocal interactions among inner needs, peer groupings, and social movements.

This chapter is a sketch of some of the more striking aspects of these systems—ideological movements, social change, and the personality of youth—and their interdependent interactions. It ends with a brief description of two strands in the networks of treatment. In the space available, it cannot be complete, and the author has been content to sketch not the moon but only a finger pointing to the moon. Implicit throughout is an assumption of the desirability of phase congruence or balance between subsystems within the individual and in the symbiotic interactions between the individual and those systems that form his environment.

◖ Ideological Movements

Dissent and Its Manifestations

Since there are as many forms of dissent as there are dissenters, any attempt to point out types runs the risk of oversimplification at lower levels of abstraction. Dissent is not synonymous with pathology, and normality is not necessarily conformity, an example of confusing statistical norms with health. Dissidence can be political, economic, cultural, religious, or any combination of these, but such terms as "hippie" are often used without regard to the actual goals or beliefs involved.

The width of the generation gap divides its observers. Most studies seeking to compare the political stance of parents and their offspring, whether Young Americans for Freedom or Students for a Democratic Society, suggest that the young are merely extending the values of their parents.[33] In their twenty-year longitudinal study of fifty-two children in Kansas, Toussieng, Morarity, and Murphy[59] found that one-third of these youth had quietly developed values differing very markedly from those of their parents, yet none openly rebelled, protested, or took drugs. Based on criteria of openness to their own senses and experiences and on the nature of their value systems, they delineated five psychosocial categories along a continuum: (1) obedient traditionalists, (2) ideological conservatives, (3) cautious modifiers, (4) passionate renewers, and (5) awareness seekers.

The findings of the Gallup, Harris, and Fortune polls prior to the 1968 presidential election suggested that there is more disagreement among the young themselves than between the generations.[33] The dissenters, however, are often highly talented and can succeed in making themselves and their goals highly visible. They arouse deep and ambivalent feelings—envy, guilt, nostalgia, repulsion, and admiration; they fall heir to what Anthony[5] called our stereotypes of adolescence, persons dangerous or endangered, whom parents wish to eject, yet whose loss they mourn. It is from the atom that swerves that change derives: The number of the early Christians, for example, has not proven the same as their impact. Although perhaps a minority compared with their peers, the total number of young dissenters is great and appears to grow, a phenomenon complicated by the growing proportion of young people in the general population. There are now in the United States as many people between ages fourteen and seventeen as between twenty and forty-three.

Although many young people remain largely uncritical of wider society, at least as manifested in conformity of behavior and outlook, the minority is highly visible. An obvious number break specific rules of society and are consequently perceived as deviant, but there are more who break the same rules but are not so perceived, and some who are obedient but perceived as deviant, the sheep in wolves' clothing. (At least one eight-year-old carries a "joint" in his wallet, not to smoke but to impress his siblings and his friends.)

The hip generation has inherited what Matza[36] described as three subterranean traditions of youth: bohemianism, committed to expressive authenticity, monasticism, and romanticism; radicalism, guided by apocalyptic vision, evangelism, and populism; and delinquency, manifested in aggressive celebrations of power, a spirit of adventure, and a disdain for work. Whether pursued with fiery passion or cold aloofness, bohemianism leads to unconventional art and unconventional personal experience; radicalism, to political activity; and delinquency, to victimization and status offenses, activities prohibited among juveniles but which, within limits, may be pursued by adults. The hip generation also embraces religious tradition, not in any narrow denominational sense but in the more general semantic sense of *re-ligare*, a "binding back" to basic aspects of the universe. This can underwrite a variety of expressions, including the mystical and the occult, but it can also underwrite black magic and an "escape from freedom."

About Two Axes: A Psychosocial Classification

It is useful to consider dissenters of the left as psychosocially oriented at any given point in time, according to the interaction of two axes. The ordinate defines preference for how power and wealth should be distributed, ranging from those who, like some black militants, want a piece of the pie of industrialized society, through those wanting to keep the piece they have, to those who renounce the entire pie. The abscissa represents a distribution between two extremes, with political and social activism at one pole and internal transformation at the other, a continuum from revolution to reformation ranging, as Roszak[49] suggested, from political activism arising from the New Left sociology of Mills,[33] through the "Freudo-Marxism"[48] of Brown[9] and Marcuse,[35] to the Gestalt-therapy "anarchism" of Goodman,[23,44] and the psychedelic aesthetics and eclectic mysticism of Watts[61] and Ginsberg.[22]

There is not necessarily harmony between these groups: Militant blacks, Chicanos, and blue-collar workers in many parts of the country, for example, have not been happy at all with the hippies and their fellow travelers. Here are white, middle-class youth turning their backs on the very things the less affluent are striving to attain, and who, like the black rebels' parental generation, make a patient, gentle adjustment to deprived circumstances.

In reality, these neat distinctions, however useful heuristically, bleed one into another. Many a communard has seen himself as beginning a new society: "If," some ask, "there is no one willing to be ruled, who can be the rulers?" The yippies and their followers at the Chicago convention, for all their put-ons, were classified, like the "provos" in the Netherlands, as the political arm of the hippies. Marcuse,[35] theoretician of the New Left, attacked the puritanical and methodological bases of industrialization on both sides of the Iron Curtain. In short, hip-bohemianism seems to be in the process of elaborating personalities and life styles that parallel, if not follow from, New Left criticism and that, in times of increased emphasis on law and order, may substitute for it.

(Social Changes

Antinomianism: Gnostic Heresies and Growth Centers

The normal task of adolescence and youth of integrating the discrepancies between a past to be left behind and a future to be found is especially marked during periods of rapid social change. The requirements of the old order offer a satisfying world image to many young people; however, in every individual and in every generation there seems potential for the reciprocal aggravation of individual conflict and social ill.

When external standards fail, the individual is forced to find some ordering principle within himself. In this light, many hip activities can be viewed as attempts to find a new orientation: astrology, magic, folk ballads, populism, and a glorification of childhood are all means of orienting oneself in a universe that is neither ordered nor absurd but just is.

We tend to overthrow the institution that represents the unbelievable or discredited and attempt to form new ones. It appears that many young people have lost faith in the ideals and political channels that have appealed to youth in the past; the best they can do to replace them is to grope toward some vague and usually unworkable form of participant democracy.

Rapid social change has a number of consequences. It makes traditional values less believable, perhaps less useful; past systems of power and meaning may seem no longer adequate, even in the absence of alternative systems. It also makes the future less predictable.

One means of adapting to these conditions is to concentrate on what is known, the present and the self, to turn attention to the "now," celebrate the moment, and search for some truth within, whether it be sought through direct revelation, intuition, or mysticism.

This particular mode of adaptation, the antinomian,[1] has become prominent during other periods of great social change. During the early centuries of the Christian era, for example, the gnostic heresies arose. These cults rejected the authority of the church, turned inward in their search for truth, founded utopian communities, and practiced spiritual exercises to achieve union with the Holy Ghost. Some of their members engaged in civil disobedience, refusing military service, and spent their time denouncing the establishment of the day. Similar changes occurred during the Anabaptist movements of the time of the Reformation, and in the periods following the French Revolution and Napoleonic wars, the failure of the Russian revolution in 1905, and the defeat of Germany in World War I.

Today, at the level of psychotherapeutic practice and institutions, a comparable phenomenon can perhaps be seen in the current interest in self-actualization, sensory awareness, inner rhythms and inner selves, the founding of the American Humanistic Psychology Association, and the 200 "growth centers" that have sprung up across the country during the past five years.[26]

Drug usage reflects and is reflected in antinomianism: Drug experience emphasizes the now and the self. In 1848, the drug was hashish; in 1870, absinthe; in 1967 it was a psychedelic, followed by epidemics of stimulants, depressants, and opiates. It is often difficult, if not impossible, to untangle the extent to which chemical agents produce their changes by direct chemical action on the brain, by giving permission for change, or by merely acting as an explanation for change, as good and as bad as all explanations. At one time, many young people seemed to use the psychedelics in the hope of change, as frogs into princes; however, as time has gone on, more have come to use these drugs less in the hopes of change than merely to make their swamps more colorful.

Mobility, Fragmentation, and "Schizoid Factors in the Personality"[17]

It has been reported[33] that the average American now moves five times across state lines and changes his occupation three times.[55] One of the concomitants of this mobility has been the breakdown of the primary community where a man was known as a total being. This has, in turn, contributed to our knowing others only in regard to one aspect of their personality and to their knowing us in only one role, that is, to the fragmentation of both the self and the other into roles and aspects that become more and more specialized. Such sociocultural factors reinforce the psychological characteristics Fairbairn[17] termed "schizoid" and hypothesized as typical of all human beings at the deepest level of their psyches. *The Divided Self*,[31] a related concept, has helped make Laing an underground psychiatric hero. Whether experienced within, or projected onto the environment, it can be difficult indeed "to get it all together."

Contemplatives, Futurists, and "Heads"

There are subtle ways in which each culture conditions its members to perceive and create their subjective worlds.[32] Proxemics, the study of man's personal and social use of space as a means of structuring relationships, suggests that people of different cultures selectively screen out different sensory data; hence they inhabit different worlds and develop different sets of ideas taken as "common sense." Perhaps, as Tart suggested,[57] the "normal state" of consciousness for any individual is the one most adaptive and appropriate to his particular time and place. Projecting our own psychology on all "normal" people, however, we tend to assume that our "normal state of consciousness" is exactly the same as that of all "normal" people.

As a baseline, there appear to be two subjective and functional modes of being-in-the-world: (1) an action mode characterized by clear boundaries between self and nonself, a lineal concept of time and consequent cause-and-effect sequence, and (2) a receptive mode, characterized by indistinct or nonexistent boundaries between self and nonself, timelessness and synchronicity.

Within Western culture, we have developed rather strong negative attitudes toward altered states of consciousness and have strongly favored the active mode of being-in-the-world. Our particular version of this mode is a spectator-spectacle world view, in which observer and observed can be separated and reality is structured into sequential arrangements of cause and effect. As an essential aspect of the development of a technologized world, this view has served us well; it has also brought the threat of imminent ecocatastrophe to the inhabitants of spaceship earth.

In common, contemplatives, futurists, and "heads" share a questioning or an indifference to some of the basic unspoken assumptions of this "normal" waking state. These assumptions, at least in the United States, of the white middle class have included: (1) the assumptions of inevitable competition and a winner and a loser in all transactions, rather than the possibility of "double wins"; (2) the assumption that man is a species separate from other species and is lord of the universe; (3) the assumption that the bigger the better; (4) the assumption of lineal time; and (5) the assumption of the inevitability of the nuclear family.

The drug-user and the contemplative may have experienced other states of consciousness and other modes of being, each associated with alternative paradigms.[52,57] While remaining in a "normal" state of consciousness, the futurist and ecologist may use a systems framework, while the militant rejects what he despairs he can never achieve or what he sees as inseparably bound to evil.[2]

Living successfully in the twenty-first century is likely to depend on different criteria than successful living in the Industrial Age, and so may our definitions of mental health.

Even a person's relationship to reality cannot be assessed without delineating whose description of what reality is being utilized as the norm.

(Youth

Members of the hip generation range in age from pubescents to adults. However, the majority fall within that period known as youth; Toussieng et al.,[59] for example, reported accelerated psychological development, a kind of telescoped and condensed adolescence. In the populations they studied, the *Sturm und Drang* had ended by the ninth grade. It seems characteristic of postindustrial societies that they have come to sanction this stage of development between adolescence and the beginning of adulthood, a stage defined sociologically by disengagement from society, developmentally by continuing opportunities for growth, and psychologically by a concern with the relationship of the self to society and the universe.

During this period, the young person may be subject to conflicts at a number of levels. Using the framework developed by Anna Freud[19] and the Hampstead group, these may be listed as follows:

1. Developmental interferences consist of whatever disturbs the typical unfolding of development. It is sometimes difficult to distinguish environmental demands and opportunities that do not fit for a youth from those that he experiences as unreasonable but to which his objections most likely represent his rationalization of oppositionalism, power conflicts, omnipotence, and moral absolutism. Our culture does not currently honor convincingly either its goals or the type of personality it creates. This, coupled with the disorganization of social structures, the gnawing unease that somehow systems have got out of control, and the corruption of professed ideals deprives young people of optimum conditions for the articulation of their potentialities. In the absence of a facilitating environment, youth must find its own raison d'être, and tends to celebrate what it can do.

Not infrequently, parents—and society—directly or indirectly encourage the young in the very things they later condemn; for years, one mother of a thirteen-year-old runaway had moaned, "Oh, you won't run away. If anyone does any running away around here, it will be me."

2. Developmental conflicts arise when environmental demands are made at an inappropriate developmental stage or when maturational levels are reached and are accompanied by psychological difficulties.

The period of adolescence and early youth is a period of destruction of the ties with parents and their internal representations, with subsequent periods of mourning or its psychic partners, denial and elation, and their replacement by suitable new representations.[28,51] Schechter[51] suggested that in the more severe deviations from normal either (1) the parents are not given up but are kept inviolate by idealization, (2) the attachment to the parents is so completely withdrawn, and without replacement, that it is necessary for the young person to regress to pathological self-investments, or (3) the energy is directed toward inappropriate, unrewarding and often sadistic objects. When the partially lost objects are not replaced by another suitable or valued one, the young person may experience himself as moorless, unattached, alone and apart, yet omnipotent.

Following the fate of omnipotentiality in youth, Mindlin[40] noted that its distortions can lead to unquestioned and excessive identification with parental objects at one extreme and to excessive change and lack of commitment at the other.

Identity formation and heterosexual intimacy are tasks of adolescence and early adulthood. Yet, during times of rapid social change there may be serious disadvantages to their solidification too early. In his recent reformulation, Erikson[16] suggested that the young person must pass through a phase of "ego diffusion," expanding the boundaries of his self to include a wider identity, cognitive certainty, and ideological conviction. If his efforts misfire and he is unable to work out a clear formulation of life and his role in it, he ends up

in "ego confusion," which is usually accompanied by retrogression to an earlier psychosexual state. Retrogression to the oral stage leads to a premoral position where morality is denied; retrogression to an anal stage leads to an amoral position of flaunting accepted standards; retrogression to an Oedipal stage leads to "anti-authoritarian hypermoralism", while retrogression to a latency stage leads to "pre-ethical pragmatism."

Erikson[16] suggested that an incapacity or refusal to conclude the stage of identity on the terms offered by the adult world can lead to group retrogression. In pathological states, mistrust may seem to submerge trust, shame and doubt to submerge autonomy, guilt to submerge initiative, and inferiority to submerge industry. However, because of their repression of a necessary minimum of distrust, members of the hip generation have frequently found themselves the victims of predators, pilgrims, and microbes. The negative revival of the second stage of infantile development becomes manifest in willful impulsivity, shamelessness, contempt, and defiance, characteristics not uncommon among members of motorcycle gangs. A negative revival of the phallic phase may result in hypermoralistic antiauthoritarianism, seizure of the seats of power, and expectation of amnesty because it's "all in the family." Revival of the latency stage is manifest in a dropping out for the sake of doing "one's own thing"; in time, such people may erect a commune of superiority masking the sense of inferiority that is the residue of the school age.

In extending Piaget's account of the changes in the structure of moral reasoning, Kohlberg[30] has defined three stages: (1) During the preconventional stage the concepts of right and wrong are defined in terms of what leads to personal gratification or that which one can do without getting caught. (2) During the conventional stage of development, good and evil are seen as absolute. (3) During the first phase of the postconventional stage, the concept of right and wrong is determined in the framework of a social contract. This, in turn, is supplanted by the highest postconventional phase, one in which the individual is devoted to personal principles that may transcend conventional morality. By age twenty-four, 10 percent of middle-class males have reached the highest postconventional phase, while another 26 percent are at the social-contract phase. The work of Smith[55] and Kohlberg[30] indicates that the same banners will be waved by people of several different levels of moral development.

3. Interstructural conflicts are conflicts between hypothesized personality structures, for example, between drive activity and internalized demands. At times, specific external factors may stir up conflicts latent within the personality which otherwise might have caused no distress. At times these conflicts may be initiated by regression of any of the hypothesized psychic structures; for example, superego regression may be precipitated by renouncing those who formed the internalized models. Between the ages of sixteen and twenty, Kohlberg reported,[30] a number of individuals moving toward postconventional morality regress briefly to the preconventional stage, the "Roskolnikoff syndrome."

4. Intrastructural conflicts are conflicts within hypothesized systems. Many a draft-eligible young man has been caught between two alternative moral frameworks: should he heed the demands of patriotism and duty or the call toward reverence for all human life?

5. Externalized conflicts are any of the above conflicts which may be projected onto the environment and fought there, perhaps intermingling with real developmental interferences. The sense of a generation gap, for example, can be a distancing device substituting ideological differences for inner conflict; on the other hand, as a sign in the London office of The Rolling Stone reads: "Don't adjust your mind, reality may be faulty."

6. Phase discrepancies between or within hypothesized psychic structures occur as a result of hypertrophy or underdevelopment of certain personality functions. Some young wanderers, for example, drift about because, however developed they may be intellectually or in other areas of functioning, they are not tied to family or friends by the usual emotional ties. Similarly, in some activists one may find a high degree of moral development, which leads to ruthlessness and destructive zealotry because it is not tempered by a concomitant development of empathy, compassion, or the capacity to love.

Mental health workers vary significantly in the degree of disturbance they expect to find in adolescence and young adulthood. A shift from the study of troubled youth in the consulting room to the study of nonclinic populations in their milieu brings with it a shift of interest from psychopathology to syndromes of mental health and a concomitant emphasis on the processes of coping and adaptation. Whatever the internal psychological state of a youth, his passage to adulthood is likely to be relatively smoother in a society where there is a consensus in the value systems, meaningful rewarded adult roles, and clearly defined transition points.

⟦ The Hip: A Brief History

The term "hippie" may be a derivative of the old English wrestling term "on the hip"; if you get your opponent there, you have him under control. It may derive from "hipster," an underworld term for a burglar who "cases the joint" and therefore is "in the know," or even from "on the hip," the reclining position once favored by smokers of opium. In any case, in varying forms of "hip" and "hep," it passed through jazz and underworld circles before emerging as the diminutive "hippie."

It would be convenient if the hip generation and its counterparts were card-carrying movements with elected representatives and clearly enunciated manifestoes. Moral, attitudinal, and behavioral criteria have been continuously drawn up and then changed. One of the characteristics of the true hippie of 1967, as described by West and I,[4] was the reply, when we asked a resident of Haight-Ashbury to define a "hippie": "What's a hippie? Those are your IBM cards, your blinders. I'm a free man, or as free as anyone can be in this society." In a like manner, when historians begin scrutinizing the minutiae of history, they may quibble whether the Dark Ages ever did exist.

Today, however, the cultural constellations known as the "hip generation" are variegated, similar to those of the medieval crusades that acquired and lost members along the road of march.

By autumn 1966, the Haight-Ashbury district of San Francisco had emerged as a watering place of West Coast hippiedom. On the basis of psychiatric interviews with 100 street hippies, West and I[4] delineated a picture of the hippies, or as they preferred to be called, members of the New Community, or in a more Teilhardian manner,[14] a Conscious Community. They were middle-class, white, well-educated youth in their early twenties. They espoused a world view based on brotherhood, altruism, tolerance, and nonviolence. They tended to meet one another from the position, "I'm OK, and you're OK (or potentially so)," a position that not infrequently they felt they had reached through the use of psychedelic chemicals. Though most had a gourmet taste for drugs, none were addicted, and some had gone to the nonchemical "turn-ons"—mantra chanting, meditation, and Yoga. They favored readings, music, and clothes that were exotic then by the standards of most of America; but these were not essential, and the beads, bare feet, and long hair were generally regarded as only the outward signs of inner grace. As one runaway phrased it, "You can have inner grace without the outward signs or all sorts of outward signs and no grace at all."

The latter were the so-called plastic hippies. While many flocked to Haight-Ashbury in search of part or all of the promise of the hippie myth—brotherhood, truth, love, sex, drugs, or a therapeutic community of sorts—moochers and entrepreneurs also arrived. Only a fraction of the pilgrims were hippie material. Similar findings were reported by Yablonsky,[63] who surveyed 700 hippies in locations as far ranging as Galahad's Pad in New York's East Village and the Gorda Commune in Big Sur, California.

Careers in Hippiedom

By 1967, the West Coast hippie way of life seemed to evolve through a series of stages:

1. The state of dissatisfaction. Our subjects were predominantly intelligent, college-educated twenty-year-olds of white middle-class background, from which they sought an exit, less in anger than with feelings of impotent disillusionment, the rather sad conviction that the world of their parents was unable to offer relevant models of competence. These were mostly thoughtful and sensitive young people with idealistic and liberal values, often articulated but less obviously practiced by their parents. A few could see themselves as having picked up the torch of humanism where their parents let it fall. Perhaps it was their parents' recognition of this that was sometimes responsible for their continued support. In many ways, they reflected a successful education: Given the freedom to think their own thoughts, to feel their own feelings, and to speak out, they now took a stand against the trappings of an affluence which they experienced as unfulfilling.

2. The search. The state of dissatisfaction was followed by a search for meaning in the light of a good educational background and from an initial posture of financial security. The mass media, hot and cool, underground and establishment, directed their search toward hippie enclaves; the media supplied the guidebooks and manufactured stereotypes for youth to live out.

3. The association. Association with other searchers who seem to have discovered a "way" is the next step. Specialized vocabularies reveal that they are acquired in interaction: The term "freak," for example, has a meaning for "freaks" that the bourgeois would never suspect, a linguistic celebration of the rejected, typical of expressive social movements. The terms "head" and "freak" take on a master status, constraining the recipient to structure more of his identity and activity in these terms. Associating with other heads, the head is publicly labeled and treated according to the popular diagnosis of the cause of his alternative life style.

Harassment arrests and calculated degradation are not uncommon; in many areas, official action has legitimatized nonofficial action; after neighborhood programs, local toughs and vigilantes have assumed the role of defenders of the faith and of the system. On his side, the hippie may use techniques of neutralization valid for him and his group but not for society as a whole—to see himself as a kind of billiard ball, more acted on than acting; to concentrate on the harm of unlawful acts ("Who gets hurt?"); to disguise injury as moral under the circumstances (for example, to take from the rich, i.e., liberate, and give to the poor, Robin Hood style); to condemn the condemners ("hypocrites" and "pigs"); or to sacrifice demands of the larger society to those of the smaller. Lack of interaction with surrounding groups leads to unbridled fantasy and self-fulfilling prophecies on both sides.

Society is so integrated that activities and social arrangements in one sphere of activity mesh with activities and social arrangements in other spheres. This leads to the dropout.

4. The dropout. From the viewpoint of the middle class, this is the end; for the hippie, it is the beginning. Once he has dropped out he is likely to participate in some loosely organized liaison with others, a primary group between himself and the rest of the world—a family, commune, tribe, or clan—which provides him with the set of perspectives and understanding about what the world is like and heightens a sense of common identity and destiny. A distrust of organization and structure make it difficult for any form of control or leadership to emerge; consequently, group memberships and allegiances tend to be ephemeral and shifting. In time, some find themselves trapped, maintaining a position and a set of beliefs that no longer fit, either because the would-be hippies equate change with recantation or because of drug effects, both psychological and legal. The integration of these people back into society, or society's integration into them (for their numbers grow) may be one of the great tasks of the future.

We have now witnessed a flowering of the life styles that are recognized by outsiders as hippie and whose participants experience a shared identity. The real threat of the hippie, in whatever is pushed under that label, is the attraction of his way of life rather than his immediate political potential. The message is carried by hundreds of underground papers, posters, rock music, collective gatherings, and above all, by word of mouth.

For the younger age groups today, there may be neither disillusionment nor search; the hip alternatives are part of their ambiance, and one of the few images of man toward which they can hope to grow without having to give up a sense of enchantment and play, an image of man as man as opposed to a machine, and into which they can escape from a world that would be as shocked by the official rejection of moral principles as by their practice. It is also a style beneath which the crazed, the criminal, and those bereft of competence in dealing with the world may find both an identity and a protective shield.

The politicization of the Western mind can be traced through three major stages: (1) Opposition to feudalism culminating with Rousseau and the *philosophes*. (2) Marx, Lenin, and the German Social Democrats culminating with the opposition to capitalism. (3) Today, the machine is the evil and all earlier inequities have somehow fused with it into pyramids of power. The solution for some is to make up a community of those whom they love and respect and who share common goals. Ours has been the heyday of the nuclear family, but according to latest United States census reports, 51 percent of the population today no longer lives in families.

Translated into life styles in 1971, there are a number of ways of living the hip way of life. It is possible to live in a commune and beat the system at its own games, a path often followed by successful rock groups and a growing number of committed people, often over twenty-five or even thirty, who seek to cope in a more successful manner in our current society. They pool resources for investment, purchasing, shelter, and education facilities for their children. It is possible to take a relatively low-paying job, such as in the post office, and follow the local version of the hippie life in one's spare time. It is possible to drop out and live on the border of things, participating in shadow campuses and free universities. It is possible to go underground in a more political sense. As the proponents of law and order make activism more dangerous, many have decided that political change must follow a reformation in life style. Yet, this too is political, for where else can we look for the beginnings of an honest revolution but in what Buber[11] called "prerevolutionary structure making"?

At a time of escalation in man's wants, the *Gemeinschaft* way of life of the commune reverses this process. It takes a great deal of improvisation, using whatever examples one can find: French communities of work, the Hopi and other Indian tribes, seventeenth-century Diggers, American religious communities of the turn of the century, and the Arcadian and Utopian traditions.[21,34] If they have truly dropped out, these people may see themselves as both sane and successful, having escaped the hangups of technology, and see those who remain as the tragic casualties of a doomed culture.

Communes are explicit social systems. Differing widely one from the other, they offer opportunities for experimentation in living. There are at least three major varieties of stable communes: religious, utopian, and those built around the desire to optimize coping capacity, a kind of cooperative model. As a social system, each commune can be analyzed along a number of continua: boundary maintenance, the complexity and nature of the interaction of subunits, relationship to other social systems both horizontal and vertical, methods of socialization and social control, and locally relevant functions, such as production, distribution, and consumption. A significant recent development is the emergence of collectives of communes sponsoring a number of joint projects, such as a food-purchasing cooperatives.

Some experimental communities are highly planned; some, following Skinner's *Walden Two*,[53] are even based on behaviorism. Others are more the outcome of a drifting together of lost souls, not infrequently recapitulating their families of origin.

In nonreligious experimental communities, celibacy is rare. Free-love groups are short-lived because the sexually uncommitted are usually uncommitted in general. The most general pattern seems to be nonpromiscuous "swinging" with other members of the commune, or group marriage, a form where each of three or more participants considers himself pair-bonded with at least two of the others. Same-sex bonds between females seem the most frequent; but same-sex bonds between males seem more important to the success of the marriage.[46]

For those who come to it with critical inadequacies, the tribe, commune, or clan may be merely an heir to their discarded family; for some, such groupings offer a truly facilitating environment that facilitates both their being and their becoming. It is perhaps for these people that the *Whole Earth Catalog*,[62] a listing of "how-to" books and designs for the communard, is dedicated: "You are as gods, and might as well get used to it."

The hippies have improvised rituals and rights that allow them to shout, to stamp, and to play; thereby, they may have created an approximation to Norman Brown's[9] "politics of no politics." Preoccupation with self-actualization, however, can lead to domination by others. Mystic being in the moment may slip into hedonistic living for the moment. Doing one's thing, respect for oneself and others as they are, can become an advertising slogan for hip capitalism and hip consumerism, a new version of the culture of leisure and a euphemism for being "out of gear."[60]

Persecutors, Rescuers, and Victims: From Byronism to Bonapartism

With the smoking of a marijuana pipe of peace at the great Human Be-In in January 1967, the peace-loving hippies of Haight-Ashbury and the notoriously violent "bikers" (motorcyclists) celebrated an uneasy alliance. Each group seemed intrigued to share vicariously in the life of the other, and each group more clearly defined itself by contrast with the other. Both were sensitive to violence, but in outwardly opposite ways. In common they shared a fluidity of identity, anti-intellectualism, ambivalence toward technology, and scorn for what they regarded as the hypocrisy of the straights. The motorcyclists in Haight-Ashbury were arranged along a Great Chain of Being, with the Hells Angels at the top. At the bottom were the street commandos, who could not afford motorcycles but only the exoskeleton of denim, leather, and dirt. For them, there was no righteous wrath and no target; the act or threat of violence seemed an end in itself, and to hurt or to be hurt bestowed some measure of meaningfulness.

It is interesting that members of the hip generation, with their talk of love and peace, somehow attract violence, thus increasing both their sensitivity to it and their defenses against it. As attacks have continued, some have traded their flowers for weapons; foreground becomes background, opposites merge, and Byronism shades into Bonapartism. The muddy pleasures of Woodstock brightened 1969; 1970 brought murder at Altamont.

Members of the hip generation seem to have become part of a great drama triangle of victims, persecutors, and rescuers. The roles may change, victims becoming persecutors and persecutors victims, but the system remains. This particular phenomenon is exacerbated by projection on both sides; thus, some commentators could once herald the hippies as comparable to the early Christians, possibly dirty but certainly innocent and pure, while others could see only diseased bands of useless, filthy, drug-taking gypsies, the quintessence of parasitic degeneracy. This phenomenon may be exacerbated by adolescent absolutism and a tendency to separate objects into the loved and the hated. It has certainly been exacerbated by the tendencies of both sides to use their group as a protective shield against guilt feelings and to sanctify aggression in the name of good.

Beneath the beads and behind the songs often lies a desperate sense of futility and of being wasted. Loving everyone and everything may disguise an inability to love anyone or anything. In loose aggregates of nongroups with their shifting populations, each person, in doing his own thing, can find the most comfortable distance for himself, but he may also lose contact with all but himself. In Yablon-sky's sample of almost 700 hippies,[63] 49.4 percent had been locked up: 270 in jail, 87 in mental hospitals, 33 in prison. Zaks' survey of 432 yippies in Lincoln Park in 1968 noted their clearly positive feelings toward their parents and toward educational goals, despite little confidence in society in general and school systems in particular, little racist feeling, and little interest in organized structure.[64] Although 42 percent had constructive suggestions, only 12 percent could see any positive future for the country. The younger they were, the higher they scored on tests of anomie, suicidal preoccupation, and manifest anxiety and the greater their feelings of hopelessness, isolation, purposelessness, and the nonvalue of existing in society. "Freedom," Janis Joplin was to wail, can be "just another word for nothing left to lose." Jerry Rubin, the yippie, put it: "The hippie-yippie-SDS movement is a white Nigger movement. The American economy no longer needs young whites and blacks. We are waste material. We fulfill our destiny in life by rejecting a system which rejects us." For many of these young people, drug usage offers a way to ease inner tension, a semblance of group belonging, and a means of social protest; it also provides a means for self-punishment and for self-destruction.[4]

The roots of the amotivational syndrome of aimless, ahedonic drifting, probably lie in a combination of psychological, social, and chemical factors, varying from person to person and for the same person at different times, a Gordian knot complicated by multiple drug usage and social reinforcements. Long-term use of stimulants may, for example, produce a kind of rebound depression. Many drugs interfere with the coordinates of space and time. Most of us in Western society construct our lives along a linear flow of time, the future before us and the past behind, a time span of limited duration, our three score and ten. If, as a result of psychedelic drug usage, an individual comes to feel tuned in to all of space and all of time, then this one life span—and with it the goals of the immediate future—becomes of little importance. Yet it is with the goals of the immediate future that most of us structure our lives; without them, there is danger of finding oneself caught in a morass of existential despair. The concomitant decrease in competitiveness, aggressiveness, and striving has usually been interpreted medically in terms of avoidance, passivity, or even brain damage. However, among members of the countercultures, these qualities may be viewed differently, sought after, and socially reinforced for a time as valuable both to the individual and to society.

Rap Centers, Psychedelic Gurus, and the Mental Health Worker

Solutions to the problems of the hip generation are numerous: Some are traditional, some nontraditional; some emphasize prevention, others treatment and rehabilitation; some emphasize the psychological level, others the social, the moral, or the medical. Two bright strands in these interlocking networks have been the development of nonestablishment health facilities and the opportunity for consultation to the communes.

During the past decade, three particular trends have emerged in the delivery of health services: (1) the growing demands of the consumer, (2) the popularity of like treating like, and (3) the spread of nonestablishment, if not downright antiestablishment, health facilities—calm centers, hot lines, rap centers, and free clinics. The latter serve a number of functions. They are centers for free medical care and counseling, havens for bad trippers, bridges to more traditional agencies, social-educational centers of the settlement-house type, and, as in the case of the free university, structures offering educational courses more traditional educational institutions could or would not offer.

In general, these centers eliminate formalism in the roles of patient and therapist. Appointments rarely are necessary. Discontinuity in care-givers is the norm, and little seems to trouble the clients, whose lives are dominated by brief contacts. Approaches differ from area to area and time to time, but the thrust of such services is usually to provide young people, who generally do not see themselves as ill, with immediate access to a caring and concerned human being. Record-keeping is generally suspect; personal identification often goes no further than pseudonyms.

The major long-term result of these alternative institutions may prove to be an enhanced understanding between people of varying life styles, the formation of cadres of informed middle-class volunteers trained in meeting the young and the poor, and perhaps the development of a new base of political power. Some of these centers have served as springs whence more adequate community services may flow; others have probably hindered recognition of the need of education for living and more adequate medical care for all.

In such facilities, professional helpers are not infrequently dismayed to find they are held in low esteem. This is the result of a number of factors, including the disappointing experiences of many street people at local general hospitals, the establishment images of organized medical and mental health workers, and competition from the self-help groups. In their roles as helpers, some local residents may find an identity, a position of prestige and value, perhaps for the first time in their life; as a stalwart of one free clinic put it, "Before I came here, I didn't know who I was, and could do nothing. Now I know I'm a helper and can help people." Unfortunately, to maintain an identity as a helper one needs people to help; the rolls may change, but the system remains. In some centers, psychedelic gurus have formed cliques that have become the real power of the center, sometimes without the knowledge of the nominal directors. Because of the meaningfulness of being a helper, and because of the shifting nature of the hip population and its lack of recognized spokesmen, those directing these nonestablishment institutions are forever in danger of maintaining an organization which no longer fits the needs of their constituents.

Tilting with persecutors, well-meaning rescuers from the mental health professions may waste their time and indeed feed community resistance to their efforts. Some come to help and are upset and angered to find their roles already performed by indigenous workers; some come to criticize and instruct in matters moral—and are soon ousted. Some find themselves caught up in a kind of forced choice based on the assumption that if two life styles differ, one must be good and one bad; the good is only as good as the other is bad; they find themselves pushed either into some caricature of the establishment position or into going native. Many professionals can work comfortably with disinfectant but not incense; with the sound of sirens but not of rock; under the gaze of Osler or Freud but not of Buddha. For some, not to denounce what they see as excess is to sanction it. They may indeed be met with threatened lawsuits on such charges as contributing to the delinquency of minors, assault, that is, treating minors without parental consent, frequenting a disorderly house, and creating a public health hazard. Finally, it is difficult to live in two worlds at once: I once found myself nonplussed when a member of a local motorcycle group offered what his group most valued, a willingness to mug the enemy of my choice!

Consultation in the Communes

Some communards seek mental health consultation to clear blocks to their growth and development, both as individuals and as a group. Consultation, as Caplan[12] described, can be of many types, and what is needed or requested varies from group to group. However, the initial invitation is frequently from a deviant member of the community.

At the program level, I have noted a frequent need for information and planning about hygiene, child care, and the less useful sequellae of improvisational programlessness. At this point, we may have conflicting findings regarding the rearing of children in groups; however, it is certainly clear that parenting by many may degenerate into good parenting by none in an unpredictable world of frequent movings, short-lived relationships, and shifting rules. Although idealized, children seem not infrequently treated more as toys than as human beings. A few parents, entranced by

the liberating effects of LSD, have even given it to their infants to "immunize" them against the hangups of the world.

Sometimes it seems useful to hold workshops for an entire commune, a combination of individual, group, and family therapy. While communards are heir to all the problems of mankind, I have been especially impressed with the frequency of problems arising from individual members not taking responsibility for their own feelings while taking responsibility for the feelings of everyone else, of resentments over unequal distribution of labor, of Oedipal furies despite manifestoes of sexual freedom or group marriage, of authoritarianism or political paralysis resulting from the majority being unwilling to impose their decisions on the minority, and of issues of closeness and intimacy, of being close yet free, the oscillations between anxiety attendant on isolation and the threat of engulfment.

"On the Street": Psychotherapeutic Interventions

In choosing his psychotherapeutic technique, each mental health worker will probably at least attempt to be in touch with himself, his patient, and the context, and not with technique alone. In addition to our usual psychotherapeutic armamentarium, less well-known approaches seem fruitful for work in rap centers, communes, and on the street. I have found two of these especially useful: Gestalt therapy and transactional analysis.

Gestalt therapy, as elaborated by Perls,[43, 44] is an existential approach emphasizing awareness in the here and now, contact, the completing of unfinished situations, and the integration of fragmented aspects of the personality. Its emphasis on what is as opposed to our fantasies of what should be and on self-support parallels antinomian emphasis on the now, with its consequent celebration of the senses; its rather Taoist[38] emphasis on experience and the trusting of inner rhythm fits with antinomian tendencies to distrust authority and intellectualization and to elaborate the truth within. Its emphasis on the integration of disowned parts of the personality counteracts tendencies toward "the divided self,"[31] a disembodied spirit in a disenchanted body. It is noteworthy that much of the social criticism of Paul Goodman,[44] one of the intellectual architects of the great dropout, seems to have its roots in his work as a Gestalt therapist. This treatment approach does, however, require an abstracting ability that may be temporarily impaired by drug usage.

Transactional analysis[3,7] is a deceptively simple framework utilizing the concepts of inner selves (parent, adult, child), basic existential positions, and a life career, or "script," to make sense of what goes on within and between individuals.[3,6] Because of this apparent simplicity, it is especially useful in helping people become aware quickly that their psychological interactions are understandable, and hence controllable, that they are not as corks tossed about helplessly by every ocean wave, but that they can make decisions and carry them out, mindful of what fits for them, others, and their environmental context. Unfortunately, transactional analysis can also be used not to promote growth and development but to refine control and manipulation, thereby confirming suspicions that mental health workers are less interested in growth and development than in coopting strays back into the system.

Permission and Protection

In working with members of the hip generation, I have found it useful to have the client consider his script, or life plan, how he sees his present in terms of his past and his future, in order to determine what permission he currently needs. The therapeutic encounter can be seen as making this permission explicit. Ultimately, the client will need to give this to himself. When he does and begins to restructure his life, he may need protection, for any significant life change is likely to require major changes in a person's relationships and activities, leaving him in a transitional period of uncertainty, unwilling to continue on as he

had, yet uncertain what to do in its place.

Within the context of his family each young child is enveloped in expectations, hopes, and fears of how life is to be for him. These messages, or "injunctions," arise from within the total family context, usually totally beyond the awareness and intentions of his parents, and are sometimes the very opposite of their later verbal messages.[3,7,24]

The child may not pick up these injunctions, or he may refuse to accept them, perhaps finding alternatives from the lady next door or the parents of some other child. Based on these injunctions, however, and on his limited life experience, he may decide how life will be for him, then selectively screen his world to support and reaffirm this decision. For example, a child who is unwanted or for whom there really is no place because his parents are fighting, divorcing, or otherwise troubled may pick up the injunction "Don't be." On this basis, as the Gouldings and I[24] have pointed out, he may make one of the following early decisions: (1) "When things are bad enough I'll kill myself." (2) "I'll hang on, no matter how bad things get." (3) "I'll get even even if it kills me." (4) "I'll show you, even if it kills me." (5) "I'll get you to kill me." He is then in a position to spend his life collecting and treasuring the appropriate feelings to support this decision, in this case probably feelings of depression, anger, and guilt.

I once spent an evening with a motorcycle gang that was preparing to battle the police and drinking in celebration of their expected deaths. For all their braggadocio, the message was clear. As one young man put it, "We will get them to kill us, and that will show just what kind of people they are." In short, this was the current reaffirmation of the early decision "I'll get you to kill me."

Other family contexts lead to different injunctions, different decisions, and a collection of different feeling states. For example, the injunction "Don't make it" (often with the later verbal message "Work hard"), is likely to be followed by the decision "I'll never make it" and feelings of helplessness, frustration, and anger.

Cutting across standard diagnostic categories, these permissions and the corresponding injunctions may be outlined as follows:[3,7,24]

1. Permission to exist. (Injunction: "Don't be.")
2. Permission to experience one's own sensations, to feel one's own feelings, to think one's own thoughts as opposed to what others may think one should think or feel. (Injunctions: "Don't be you, be me." "Don't think——." "Don't feel ——.")
3. Permission to be oneself as an individual of appropriate sex, and age, and with a potential for growth and development. (Injunctions: "Don't be you." "Don't grow up." "Don't leave me." "Don't be a child.")
4. Permission to become aware of one's basic existential position, that is, one's basic stance toward self, others, and the environmental context. (Injunction: "Don't become aware of where you're at.")
5. Permission to change this existential position, to experiment, to learn, and to practice in an atmosphere of feedback and support. (Injunction: "Don't be OK.") This is usually reinforced by expectations of calamity, should change occur.
6. Permission to find satisfaction in love and work, that is, to be a sexually mature human being able to validate one's own sexuality and the sexuality of others, and to "make it." (Injunctions: "Don't grow up." "Don't be sexually mature." "Don't leave me." "Don't make it.")
7. Permission to be emotionally close to others. (Injunction: "Don't be close.")
8. Permission to find some meaning in life. (Injunctions: "Don't be OK." "Don't be integrated." "Don't get it all together.")

This progression of permissions reflects the old adages—"Know thyself." "Be thyself." "Develop thyself." However, it also suggests specific levels of therapeutic intervention. Each of our currently popular modes of therapy covers a number of levels and may reso-

nate at still other levels. This is also modified by the personality and expertise of the therapist. At level 2, for example, we find much of the work of Hilde Bruch,[10] the sensory explorations of Elsa Gindler, Charlotte Selver, and their pupils,[52] and some aspects of yoga,[25] movement, and dance therapies.[26,42] In contrast, level 8 touches a new problem of identity: "Even if I know who I am, what difference does it make?" Long the province of religious and mystical traditions, this problem has particular impact today because we have increasing evidence that our politicians and scientists have set in motion systems that more and more control them. Ultimate meaning is an important element in some yoga traditions,[25] Jungian therapy, Frankl's logotherapy,[18] peak-experience therapy,[8] psychosynthesis,[6] meditation and its currently popular technological counterparts in the training of alpha and theta waves.[25,42,57]

Such an approach makes explicit the role of the mental health worker; he helps his client balance tendencies within his development and thereby get on with his total growth and development. This model of help is cast in the framework neither of sin nor of sickness but of growth, an important emphasis especially when working with people who regard themselves as neither criminal nor ill.

In summary, the heralded rebellion of the cultural constellations now known as the hip generation is largely one of lateral insurgency; these young people have gone off in directions other than the current mainstreams of industrialized society and are in the process of exploring their own values and alternative institutions. If their parents could personify pure evil, then they might represent pure good, but neither do, and the Aquarian Age seems a time when we more frequently must choose between two goods or two evils rather than between good and evil. Ultimately, whether we view this phenomenon as an escape, threat, or serious search for the most viable shape that human life may take depends, in part, on our own personal hopes for the future. It is also a manifestation of the period of transition from childhood to adulthood. In *Demian*,[27] Hermann Hesse described this transition for Emil Sinclair, a young man caught between two worlds, his middle-class well-ordered home where "straight lines and paths . . . led into the future" and a dark world of chaos into which a descent is not necessarily evil but an expression of boldness and intelligence, and perhaps even a necessary antecedent to real order: "Many people experience the dying and the rebirth—which is our fate—only this once during their entire life. Their childhood becomes hollow and gradually collapses. Everything they love abandons them and they suddenly feel surrounded by the loneliness and mortal cold of the universe. Very many are caught forever in this impasse—the dream of the lost paradise."

(Bibliography

1. ADLER, N. "The Antinomian Personality." *Psychiatry*, 31, no. 4 (November 1968).

2. ALLEN, J. R. "Contemplatives, Futurists and 'Heads': Paradigms and Altered States of Consciousness, 1971." *The Paseo Center Drug Book*, Pasco Center, Oklahoma City, December 1971. (Available as a reprint of the National Drug Abuse Education Center, University of Oklahoma Medical Center, Oklahoma City, 1971.)

3. ———, and ALLEN, B. A. "Introduction to Counseling: Part II. Transactional Analysis." Reprint of the National Drug Abuse Education Center, Oklahoma City, December 1970. Published in part as "Scripts: The Role of Permission." *Journal of Transactional Analysis* (April 1972).

4. ———, and WEST, L. J. "Flight from Violence: Hippies and the Green Rebellion." *American Journal of Psychiatry*, 125 (September 1968).

5. ANTHONY, E. J. "The Reactions of Adults to Adolescents and Their Behavior." In G. Caplan and S. Lebovici, eds., *Adolescence: Psychosocial Perspectives*. New York: Basic Books, 1969. Pp. 54–78.

6. ASSAGIOLI, R. *Psychosynthesis*. New York: Viking Press, 1965.

7. BERNE, E. *The Principles of Group Treatment*. New York: Grove Press, 1966.

8. BINDRIM, P. "Facilitating Peak Experiences." In H. Otto and J. Mann, eds., *Ways of Growth*. New York: Viking Press, 1968.

9. BROWN, N. O. *Love's Body*. New York: Knopf, 1968.

10. BRUCH, H. "Obesity." In G. Caplan and S. Lebovici, eds., *Adolescence: Psychosocial Perspectives*. New York: Basic Books, 1969. Pp. 213–227.

11. BUBER, M. *Paths in Utopia*. Boston: Beacon Press, 1968.

12. CAPLAN, G. *The Theory and Practice of Mental Health Consultation*. New York: Basic Books, 1970.

13. CASTANEDA, C. *A Separate Reality: Further Conversations with Don Juan*. New York: Simon & Schuster, 1971.

14. DE CHARDIN, T. *The Phenomenon of Man*. New York: Harper, 1959.

15. *East Village Other*, November 1–15, 1967.

16. ERIKSON, E. H. "Reflections on the Dissent of Contemporary Youth." *International Journal of Psycho-Analysis*, 51, pt. 1 (1970).

17. FAIRBAIRN, W. R. D. "Schizoid Factors in the Personality." In *The Object-Relations Theory of the Personality*. New York: Basic Books, 1954.

18. FRANKL, V. "Beyond Self-Actualization and Self-Expression." *Journal of Existential Psychiatry*, 1 (1960), 5–20.

19. FREUD, A. "Adolescence." *Psychoanalytic Study of the Child*, 13 (1958).

20. ———. *Normality and Pathology of Childhood*. New York: International Universities Press, 1966.

21. FRYE, N. "Varieties of Literary Utopias." *Daedalus*, Spring 1965.

22. GINSBERG, A. *Planet News: 1961–1967*. San Francisco: City Light Books, 1968.

23. GOODMAN, P. *Compulsory Miseducation*. New York: Horizon Press, 1964.

24. GOULDING, R. "New Directions in Transactional Analysis." In C. J. Sager and H. S. Kaplan, eds., *Progress in Group and Family Therapy*. New York: Brunner-Mazel, 1972.

25. GREEN, E., and GREEN, A. "On the Meaning of the Transpersonal." *Journal of Transpersonal Psychology*, 3 (1971).

26. GUSTATIS, R. *Turning On*. New York: Macmillan, 1968.

27. HESSE, H. *Demian*. New York: Holt, 1948.

28. JACOBSON, E. "Adolescent Moods and the Remodeling of Psychic Structures in Adolescence." *Psychoanalytic Study of the Child*, 16 (1961).

29. JASPERS, C. *The Perennial Scope of Philosophy.* R. Mannheim, transl. New York: Philosophical Library, 1949.

30. KOHLBERG, L. *Stages in the Development of Moral Thought and Action.* New York: Holt, Rinehart & Winston, 1970.

31. LAING, R. D. *The Divided Self.* Baltimore: Penguin, 1965.

32. LEE, D. *Freedom and Culture.* Englewood Cliffs, N.J.: Prentice-Hall, 1959.

33. LIPSET, S. M., and RAAB, E. "The Non-Generation Gap." *Commentary,* 50, no. 2 (August 1970).

34. LOCKWOOD, M. "The Experimental Utopia in America." *Daedalus,* Spring 1965.

35. MARCUSE, H. *An Essay on Liberation.* Boston: Beacon Press.

36. MATZA, D. "Subterranean Traditions of Youth." *Annals of the American Academy of Social Science,* 338 (November 1961).

37. MEAD, M. *Culture and Commitment.* Garden City, N.Y.: Doubleday, 1970.

38. MERTON, T. *The Way of Chuang Tzu.* New York: New Directions, 1969.

39. MILLS, C. W. *The Sociological Imagination.* New York: Grove Press, 1961.

40. MINDLIN, E. "Omnipotentiality, Youth and Commitment." *Journal of the American Academy of Child Psychiatry,* 4 (1965).

41. NOBILE, P., ed. *The Con III Controversy: The Critics Look at the Greening of America.* New York: Pocket Books, 1971.

42. ORNSTEIN, R., and NARANJO, C. *The Psychology of Meditation.* New York: Viking Press, 1971.

43. PERLS, F. *Gestalt Therapy Verbatim.* Lafayette, Cal.: Real People Press, 1969.

44. ——, HEFFERTINE, R., and GOODMAN, P. *Gestalt Therapy.* New York: Dell, 1951.

45. PIAGET, J. *Psychology of Intelligence.* New York: Harcourt, Brace & World, 1950.

46. RAMEY, J. W. Emerging Patterns of Behavior in Marriage. Paper presented at Groves Conference on Marriage and the Family, San Juan, May 5–7, 1971.

47. REICH, C. *The Greening of America.* New York: Random House, 1970.

48. ROBINSON, P. A. *The Freudian Left.* New York: Harper & Row, 1969.

49. ROSZAK, T. *The Making of a Counter-Culture.* Garden City, N.Y.: Doubleday, 1969.

50. RUDHYAR, D. *Directives for a New Life.* Palo Alto, Cal.: Ecology Center Press, 1971.

51. SCHECHTER, M. "A Psychological Field Theory of Adolescence." *Minnesota Medicine,* 51 (December 1968).

52. SELVER, C., and BROOKS, C. V.W. In H. Otto, ed., *Explorations in Human Potentialities.* Springfield, Ill.: Charles C Thomas, 1966.

53. SKINNER, B. F. *Walden Two.* New York: Macmillan, 1962.

54. SMITH, H. C. "The Triple Choice: Social, Political, Cultural." *American Journal of Orthopsychiatry,* 39, no. 1 (1969).

55. SMITH, M. B. "Morality and Student Protest." In *Social Psychology and Human Values.* Chicago: Aldine, 1970.

56. SOROKIN, P. A. *The Crisis of Our Age.* New York: Dutton, 1941.

57. TART, C. Seminar series, Esalen Program on "The Psychology of Human Consciousness." University of California, Santa Barbara, Summer, 1971.

58. ——, ed. *Altered States of Consciousness.* New York: Wiley, 1969.

59. TOUSSIENG, P., MORARITY, A., and MURPHY, L. Cool Voices: Midwestern Youth Face the Future. In preparation.

60. TOYNBEE, A. J., Jr. *A Study of History.* Oxford: Oxford University Press, 1935.

61. WATTS, A. *The Book on the Taboo Against Knowing Who You Are.* New York: Collier Books, 1967.

62. *Whole Earth Catalog.* Portola Institute, Menlo Park, California, 1971.

63. YABLONSKY, L. *The Hippie Trip.* New York: Pegasus, 1968.

64. ZAKS, M., HUGHES, P., JAFFE, J., and POLKART, M. B. Yippies at the Chicago Democratic Convention, 1968. Paper presented to the 46th annual meeting of the American Orthopsychiatric Association, New York, March 1969.

CHAPTER 26

COPING IN EARLY ADOLESCENCE

The Special Challenges of the Junior High School Period

Beatrix A. Hamburg

COMING OF AGE IN AMERICA is an increasingly lengthy, challenging, and fascinating process. It represents the most dramatic example of the complex processes involved in negotiating a critical period of normal development. It illustrates the shifting interplay between the biological, psychological, and cultural demands on the individual. At the present time much of the focus of attention has been on the failures of coping in this era, especially as indicated by higher suicide rates, prevalence of drug abuse, and increase in violent behaviors. I have viewed adolescents from the perspectives of developmental psychology, school consultation, and clinical psychiatry. This chapter represents an effort to delineate the phases of adolescence and to explore the significant variables operating within each phase. The major emphasis will be on early adolescence. The adaptive challenges posed by superimposed tasks have generally been underestimated, if perceived at all. It seems important to sharply define this early adolescent period. The implications for future research efforts and some clinical implications will also be discussed. Late adolescence is only briefly discussed here because there is more than ample discussion elsewhere.

In general, the adolescent receives enormous attention in both the popular media and in scientific writings. Even in the scientific literature, however, with rare exceptions, neither in title nor content is there any allusion to the vastly different populations that are lumped together under the generic term "adolescence." There is every reason to believe that the adolescent period can and should be divided into three distinct eras, which have their characteristic tasks, challenges, and coping possibilities. It is also likely that it may bring additional clarity to our thinking to make some further distinction within eras, in terms of sex, ethnic, and possibly class differences, particularly if one focuses on the "culture of poverty" as separate from the more affluent sectors of the population in terms of child-rearing practice and outcome.

One possible explanation for the lack of differentiation within the universe of adolescence is the relative recency of the construct. It is generally conceded that the cultural invention of adolescence is a byproduct of the Industrial Revolution.[2] Prior to that there had apparently been no need to provide for a hiatus category to deal with the individual who was biologically no longer a child but whom the society did not find it convenient to induct into adult roles, particularly occupational niches. Such a need does exist in today's highly technological and rapidly changing world.[7] Gertrude Stein is reported to have said that America is the "oldest modern country in the world." By this she meant that we have had the longest experience as a mechanized, highly industrial nation. As a corollary of this, we also have the longest experience with adolescence, or a teen culture.

A definition of adolescence is not easy. It can be stated that both the beginning and the end of adolescence share in common a change in status: at the beginning, a change in biological status and at the end, a change in psychosocial status. It is important to recognize that a significant shift in status represents a major disequilibrium, in that the prior tested solutions and habitual ways of functioning no longer can apply without modification or regrouping. Thus, the initiation of adolescence represents one crisis and the termination of adolescence represents another. It is clear that in former times, when the shift to adult social roles temporally overlapped with the biological change in status, there was but a single critical period in going from childhood to adulthood. With the insidious lengthening of the adolescent period, we have now arrived at a situation in which there are two largely nonoverlapping critical periods in the transition from childhood to adulthood. In fact, I should like to propose that our adolescence is now sufficiently lengthy to provide a demonstrable interval between these two periods which deserves consideration in its own right. Furthermore, the sex differences in the negotiation of the early, middle, and late phases of adolescence are noteworthy.

There has been a tendency for those interested in adolescence to focus their discussion of the subject in terms of either one or the other of the critical periods. By and large, the heaviest emphasis and the bulk of the literature have been on the male in late adolescence who is being socialized into adult roles, or to put it another way, the identity crisis[9] of the male. A great deal has been written about both the internal processes of these young men as well as the cultural factors that impinge on youth and the ways in which they influence socialization. Unfortunately, the inference has often been drawn that the conclusions thus reached pertain to all ages and stages of adolescents and speak equally validly for the female as for the male.

The smaller number of discussions that deal with the biological or hormonal changes tend to see these as almost exclusively libidinal in impact and as independently compelling and controlling a wide range of behaviors, "explaining" all or most of adolescence. The importance of each of these approaches is undeniable. But our adolescent transition is now too complex to be comprehended by any single approach.

It is difficult to set the boundaries of adolescence in a precise way. It is immeasurably easier at the lower or younger level when, by definition, one is dealing with pubertal change as the criterion. However, even here there are problems. There are difficulties in the appropriate categorization of the individual whose hormonal timetable is either notably advanced or retarded with respect to his age mates.

The boundary difficulties are enormously more complex at the upper or older end of adolescence. The age at which individuals are admitted to adult occupational roles is constantly being raised, and thus, in the most meaningful way, adolescence is being lengthened. While the occupational role is most salient, there are other adult roles that must be negotiated, namely, autonomy or living independently of parents; intimate or monogamous sexual relationship; the assumption of adult responsibilities of voting, age of conscription into the army, age for legal drinking, and legal responsibility for making valid contracts. These rights and responsibilities have no regular pattern. There are also some accommodations in terms of admission to adult sexual roles at an earlier age. Accompanying this, there is a trend toward earlier marriage, at times while individuals are still quite dependent on parental support. The recent move to grant the vote to eighteen-year-olds represents the admission of this group to a significant adult status in terms of societal responsibility. The very ambiguity about the termination of adolescence is variably experienced as stress in its own right.

❨ Early Adolescence

There is a dominant theme that gives focus to the issues of each era. The dominant theme of early adolescence is pubertal change. I have intentionally avoided the term "sexual change," despite the fact that pubertal changes are, of course, a response to changes in the sex hormones. Puberty is also a time of general growth spurt. There are striking increments in height, changes in facial contours, fat distribution, pelvic proportions, and muscular development. These are at least as important as the changes in the genitalia and secondary sex characteristics, and they function independently in shaping the course of adolescent development.

The current information about the biological changes involved in the onset of puberty reveals that the pubertal events result from an interaction between sex hormones and the cells of the hypothalamus. In childhood, until eight or nine years of age, there are trace levels of circulating gonadal hormone. Evidence in mammals[5] indicates that prior to puberty the cells of the hypothalamus are sensitive to these minute amounts of circulating hormone, and there is a resultant feedback system set up, in which the anterior lobe of the pituitary, via the hypothalamus, is inhibited from secreting gonadotropins which would otherwise evoke secretion of sex hormones in functional amounts. The significant change of puberty is the maturation of the cells of the hypothalamus and their escape from the restraining influence of minute qualities of gonadal hormone. The factors influencing this maturation of the brain in man are not yet elucidated.

It is the case, however, that the onset of puberty has shown a secular trend toward an increasingly earlier age. Tanner[23] estimated that a lowering of the age of menarche by four months per decade would represent the trend of the past 100 years. The average age in 1860 was 16.5 and is now 12.5 years. The onset of puberty in females can be sharply defined by menarche, which is a distinct event that can be precisely recorded. It is known that the comparable events of puberty in males show a lag of roughly two years.[3] However, it is assumed that the pubertal events in males reflect the same secular trend as females. This finding is generally attributed to better nutrition. It is acknowledged that other factors, as yet unelucidated, may well play a role. In any case, it is significant to note that the biological onset of puberty is at increasingly earlier ages. The generational change is noticeable, though not striking. However, the net effect over historical time has been to further extend the span of adolescence by causing a lowering of the age of onset at the same time as social factors are extending the upper limits.

Menarche, as was mentioned, is a notable event that serves as a convenient marker for pubertal events. It is not, however, the initial event of puberty. After ages eight or nine, there is a gradually increasing excretion of estrogens in girls which becomes accelerated at about age eleven. Initially, this excretion is not cyclic; it becomes cyclic about eighteen months prior to menarche. Menarche almost invariably occurs after the peak of the height spurt is passed. While menarche does not mark the initiation of pubertal changes, neither does it signify their completion. Its occurrence marks a definitive and mature stage of uterine growth, but not full reproductive function. There is usually a period of twelve to eighteen months of infertility postmenarche, and maximum fertility probably is not reached until the early or middle twenties. Significant development of secondary sex characteristics also precedes menarche. Beginning growth of the breast is usually the first sign of puberty. This is then followed successively by growth of pubic and axillary hair.

The first signs of impending puberty in boys occur typically at age thirteen (two years later than the girls).[3] The initial signs are some enlargement of the testes and penis followed shortly thereafter by height growth spurt. The changes occur roughly one year after testicular cell growth and the secretion of male sex hormone by the cells of the testis.[24] The enlargement of the larynx occurs a little after the spurt in height, and the voice deepens during the period when development of the penis is approaching completion. The growth of pubic, axillary, and facial hair occurs in sequential order.

Typical or average ages have been given in this brief summary of pubertal changes, but the range of ages for all of these changes is very large.

Mention must now be made of the social setting in which the biologically changing early adolescent finds himself. By and large, the institution of the junior high school will be his school experience. Theoretically, the junior high school was designed to ease the transition from the experience of self-contained classroom and single teacher throughout the day, existent in the elementary school, to the large population, large campus, rotating classes and multiple teacher situation of the high school. In fact, junior high schools, as they now exist, duplicate in all particulars the conditions of the high school, so that the transition is not

eased but, instead, the radical shift in school experience is displaced downward by two years. As generally followed, the system involves elementary school for six years and then junior high school for two or three years followed by high school for three or four years. As it works out, the entry into junior high school is timed with significant pubertal changes in most girls. There are, however, only a small number of early-maturing boys who have comparable pubertal changes at this time. The implications of this for the adolescent's development will be discussed later.

For all the students, however, entry into junior high school is interpreted as a drastic change in status. It is the true badge of entry into the teen culture. It is also the case that the academic demands, both in quantity and quality of performance expected, show a sharp increase. Achievement pressures begin to be applied from all directions. There is, as mentioned, the new experience of a very large institution with a succession of six or seven different teachers each day whose personal relationship with the student cannot have the same meaning or intensity of elementary school days. There are ultimate advantages as well as disadvantages to this system, but it is, nonetheless, a sharp discontinuity with the past.

Parents also view the junior high school student as entering a new world. They expect to treat their child differently and think of him now as an adolescent. As mentioned previously, the stereotype thus evoked refers to late adolescents, and so parental attitudes and behaviors tend to derive from this model. The applicability of the late adolescent model for providing useful prescriptions for dealing with early adolescents will be examined.

Finally, it is worth noting some of the continuities with the past that do exist. The early adolescent continues to live with his parents, and the issue of actual physical separation from them and living on his own, or autonomy, is remotely viewed, if perceived at all. There is a sharp increment in the school demands, but he is a student and continues to think of himself as continuing to exist in the student role for considerable years ahead.

There is no pressure for real commitment to an adult work responsibility. Though going steady may or may not be the custom in a particular community, there is rarely any question of a more than playful relationship to the opposite sex.

Coping Implications

PUBERTAL CHANGE

A primary task is coping with the impact of undeniable change in body configuration. The widespread concern of the early adolescent with his body has been generally sensed and has been documented in nationwide surveys of thousands of adolescents by the Purdue Opinion Polls. Their figures show that 52 percent of adolescents report a dissatisfaction with their weight. Generally boys tend to want to gain and girls to lose weight; 24 percent of girls want to improve their figures. Thirty-seven percent of boys would like to change their body builds. Twelve percent are deeply concerned about pimples. Thirty-seven percent are dissatisfied about their posture. Frazier and Lisonbee[10] studied 508 tenth-grade students and found that among tall girls, 49 percent were very concerned about their height and 39 percent of short boys expressed equally great concern. In their sample, 82 percent of the students expressed concern about pimples or other skin problems. Sixty-seven percent of the entire group expressed a desire for some type of physical change. It has been found[10,13] that when junior high school students were asked what they did not like about themselves, physical characteristics was the most predominant response. There was a very much lower percentage of high school students who responded in this way. In the stage of early adolescence, the individual feels himself faced with the problem of accepting his emerging shape and size as the physique that will characterize him throughout adult life. The psychological development of the individual is related to the course of his physical development.

It has not been so obvious that the timing of puberty would have significant and differential consequences for boys and girls.[1] In actuality, there is a great range of chronological ages over which pubertal changes occur. Children mature at different rates. Mary Cover Jones[14] and associates have done long-term investigations of the different impacts and varying outcomes of early versus late maturity in boys and girls. Skeletal age was used as a stable and reliable index of physical maturity. On the average, the physically accelerated and physically retarded adolescents of the same chronological age are separated by two years in skeletal age. In girls, as early as eleven years of age all of the late maturers are shorter than the mean for the early maturers. At the mean age of fourteen, the height distributions for early and late maturers show an extreme separation with no overlap. At the peak of growth, early-maturing girls are not only taller than their girl classmates but actually much taller than most of the boys in the class. From that age onward, the differences tend to decrease, and by eighteen or nineteen the mature heights of the early- and late-maturing girls are very similar.

Strength tests in boys show that late maturers are relatively weak and are low in tests of athletic ability. Early-maturing boys are more masculine (mesomorphic) in their builds, and late-maturing boys more childish (slender and long-legged) in their builds. Late maturers are likely to be perceived and treated as immature by both adults and peers.

These classic studies[14] revealed that systematic comparisons between the behavior and personality characteristics of early- and late-maturing adolescents have indicated that acceleration in growth tends to carry distinct advantages for boys but disadvantages for girls.

In early adolescence early-maturing boys are given more leadership roles, are more popular, excel in athletic ability, are perceived as more attractive by adults and peers, and enjoy considerably enhanced heterosexual status. When studied at seventeen years of age,[20] the early-maturing boys showed more self-confidence, less dependency, and were more capable of playing an adult role in interpersonal relations.

The findings on the late-maturing boys

showed more personal and social maladjustment at all stages of adolescence. When studied on follow-up at age seventeen, this group showed negative self-concepts, prolonged dependency needs, rebellious attitudes toward parents, strong affiliation needs, and profound feelings of rejection by the group. Interestingly, the two groups did not differ in needs for achievement and recognition.

The early reports of systematic comparisons among girls aged eleven to seventeen showed that early-maturing girls were seen as "submissive, listless, or indifferent in social situations and lacking in poise. Such girls have little influence upon the group and seldom attain a high degree of popularity, prestige or leadership."* Late-maturing girls in early adolescent years were seen as relatively more outgoing and assured. They were described as being confident and having leadership ability.

In early adolescence early-maturing boys and, to a somewhat lesser extent, late-maturing girls share a fortuitous adaptive advantage. Early-maturing girls stand in an intermediate position adaptively despite their extreme position developmentally. A possible explanation for this may be that while their body configuration and tallness are viewed by the girls themselves and by others as discordant, this occurs while in the elementary school setting. Essentially this means that the task of coping with physical change occurs as the single major challenge confronting the early-maturing girl. She does not have the superimposed academic and social pressures inherent in junior high school. Her status with her peer group is buffered by halo effects, which can continue to operate because she is remaining in a stable social setting and does not have to establish herself with new peers. Also, despite the fact that her appearance is different both to herself and others, the changes are recognized by all concerned as desirable steps toward maturity. Finally, within the continuity of the elementary school period, parents are less likely to alter their expectations of her or drastically change their accustomed ways of relating to her. She is usually perceived by them as a large child rather than an adolescent. Again, needed stability may thus be achieved. In instances where the parents collaborate in permitting an early shift to adolescent behaviors at ages of nine or ten, there is much more turmoil, as she strives to find a niche.

The late-maturing boy is at the most severe disadvantage. He is at least as highly discordant as the early-maturing girl, but under much less favorable circumstances. He continues to look like an elementary school boy at a time when it may be important to him to be as grown up as possible. He has a developmental lag of about four years as compared to the average girl of the same age and perhaps two years in relation to the age-matched boy. His inevitable discordance in size may put him at risk of a particularly slavish devotion to as much superficial conformity as is available to him. Despite these efforts at acceptance, he is likely to suffer considerable emotional distress.

There is every reason to further investigate the possibility that much of the unpredictable moodiness, hostility, depressions, and other signs of emotionality, which are so perplexing and troublesome to those dealing with early adolescents, may in fact, be substantially related to the significant changes in sex-hormone levels characteristic of pubertal development. In females it is well established that at the other times of major change in the levels of sex hormones, such as pregnancy and menopause, there is a notable corollary effect on mood. For some females, there is an even more fine-tuned sensitivity to the circulating levels of gonadal hormone such that there is a cyclicity of mood that is dependent on the hormone changes of the monthly menstrual cycle.

It has been established that in nonhuman mammalian males of several species there is a rise of aggressive behavior at the time of onset of puberty.[18] There are persuasive impressions that the same phenomenon exists in humans. Now that newer technology permits accurate measures of male gonadal hormone levels, an opportunity exists to explore this definitively in man in conjunction with a variety of behavioral indices and social indicators.

* See reference 14, pp. 455–456.

If these sex-hormone–mood correlations are established for puberty, they would offer an important new insight into one of the distressing aspects of early adolescent behavior. At present, the adolescent casts about to find exclusively psychosocial justifications for his moods. Often, the adults dealing with him are hurt and baffled by his moody behavior. Unfortunately, many adults tend to automatically react in a counterpunitive style, and thus a downward spiral of negative interaction may ensue, leading, at times, to explosive outbursts on both sides. Both parent and child would feel better knowing that the mood had, in part at least, a biological base.

PSYCHOSOCIAL CHANGE

The entry into junior high school catapults the early adolescent into the new world of the teen culture and imposes a drastic and demanding change in the format of school experience. It is a time of inevitable crisis and reorganization for all children who are a part of this system.

Prior to the invention of junior high school, a child typically continued in the self-contained classroom until the end of eighth grade. He then went to high school for the succeeding four years. As mentioned previously, the commonest plan at present is for the child to start junior high school after the completion of sixth grade. There is, therefore, a loss of two years of the elementary school setting, at present. In the prior arrangement, the child had the opportunity of dealing with the stiffer academic expectations of the seventh and eighth grade in the context of a teacher who knew him well and in a peer group where he had secure status and a network of support. He also had the cushion of knowledge of his prior competence in the same setting to bolster him in attacking the new challenges. Similarly, it was also possible to move toward heterosexual explorations in a safe structure. Dating behavior was initiated with partners who were well known. It was possible for dating couples to combine this new activity with retaining membership in the long-standing, same-sex cliques or groups. There was the likelihood of going back and forth between the new group of dating couples and the prior reference group, where there could be information exchange and a chance to validate impressions. There was a great richness of resource in forming one's opinions about members of the opposite sex. Currently, there is a far greater tendency to go steady without prior dating experience and for the couple to have a rather isolated existence with intense mutual dependence.

With the sudden entry into a new role status, the early adolescent may feel himself in need of a new set of behaviors, values, and reference persons. Although no child can escape the necessity for reorientation and reorganization at this time, there would appear to be class and cultural differences in the experiencing of this crisis.

It is noteworthy that it is a consistent finding of large survey studies of adolescents that there is far less turbulence than more theoretically oriented sources and case studies would lead one to expect. It now seems likely that the bulk of other types of professional literature may represent a sampling effect. It should also be noted that the surveys have typically been studies of public high school populations and not of junior high school populations per se. The relative calm of this high school era as a general phenomenon will be discussed later. However, there is retrospective material in these same studies which gives rise to inferences about junior high school students. (Incidentally, paucity of material and the great need for research directly on junior high school students should be mentioned.) The survey material has, by design, tended to include all strata of the population in representative numbers. This means that the middle classes, upper-lower through lower-middle, contribute by far the largest total number of students. There is reason to believe (and this will be elaborated on further) that the lower-lower, upper-middle, and upper classes have disproportionately influenced the usual literature on adolescence. In contrast, the bulk of students in the survey studies come from the nonprofessional white-collar and blue-collar families who are moderately affluent and traditional in their orientation. They and their children tend to expect a continuity of generations in terms of values and occupational niches. There is mutual expectation of conformity or very little early striving toward autonomy. By and large, these individuals live in stable communities, and the children respect and wish to emulate their parents. Religious values and affiliations tend to be stronger than in the surrounding classes.

Offer[21] extensively studied two large groups of adolescents in public high schools in Illinois. He called them "modal adolescents," and he found that among his modal adolescents only very few were members of deviant groups where parental values would be seriously challenged. "The relationship between the subjects and their parents was stable, consistent and empathic."[21, p. 223] The same findings are reported by Douvan and Adelson[6] in their survey of 3,500 adolescents in Michigan. They also concluded that the process of detachment from the parents seems less dramatic and full of conflict than tradition and theory hold.

The early adolescents in the traditional families are buffered in meeting the combination of crises of early adolescence. They continue to have and want to utilize the guidelines and resources of the parents in developing new strategies for dealing with the pubertal and school challenges. They are, therefore, less subject to peer pressure. The impact of the teen culture on them is less striking. It should be remembered that the early adolescent, the junior high school student, is typically between twelve and fourteen years of age. There is a four- to six-year period before the issue of actual separation from the home and parents will become real. A strong posture of independence at this early stage is not, therefore, linked with a valid developmental transition.

When the child had continued into eighth grade in an elementary school setting, there was further stability in the parent-child relationship. The mutual perception of change in social status and role was postponed until ninth grade and occurred after some mastery of the self-image problems related to pubertal changes had taken place. However, the modal adolescents of today, with their multiple superimposed developmental crises of early adolescence, show effects of the stress. In discussing his students, Offer[21, p. 70] noted that "in our subjects rebellion manifested itself most clearly in early adolescence, at ages twelve and fourteen." Even at worst, however, this defensive behavior on the part of the traditionally oriented early adolescent is within bounds.

Undeniably, the extreme disturbance of behavior described in much of the literature on adolescence does actually exist. It occurs in families where there is expectation by both parent and child of sharp discontinuity between the child and adolescent role, and also where there is repudiation of parental values. These families tend to cluster in two groups. One is the lower-class, disadvantaged population. The other is the upper-middle-class and intellectual group. The latter, the enlightened, high-status parents, have usually derived their prescriptions for dealing with their adolescents from professional sources. Unfortunately, as mentioned previously, virtually all the literature, although not explicitly stated, deals with the late adolescent phase. These parents find, therefore, an emphasis on the need for independent decision-making and the development of autonomy. In an effort to foster the perceived value of independence in the child, there may be a significant renunciation of parental prerogatives. This is not appropriate for the early adolescent. In fact, it is contraindicated. There is a heightened need for parental stability and guidance at the time of major biological, school, and social discontinuity. The early adolescent cannot possess the competence and mastery needed for independence. Instead, the early and midadolescent phases are the training grounds and preparation for the achievement of autonomy by the time of late adolescence. The success with which these earliest phases are negotiated will, of course, affect the final outcome of adolescent development.

In the poverty group, the adolescent finds a heightening of an already preexisting tendency to find his guidance and support among peers rather than adults—the street gang. There have frequently been weak or missing fathers. In response to this, the adolescent males often tend to adopt styles of exaggerated masculinity, including hyperindependence, high risk-taking, and aggressive behaviors. Of course, father absence occurs sporadically in all social groups. Wherever it occurs the negative impact on the development of the adolescent male is significant. Grinker, Grinker, and Timberlake[11] emphasized the history of strong identification with father and father figures as significant in the cluster of conditions found in his sample of emotionally healthy college freshman males.

Where there is a lack of firm parental guidance and availability of the parent as model and coping resource, there is a more urgent need for the individual to uncritically seek peer support and adopt the badges of conformity. While this uncritical allegiance to the peer group may be useful in allaying immediate anxieties, it has serious limitations. The peer group at this stage is usually too shallow and rigid to afford the necessary resources for growth and development. When the peer group is organized around drugs and/or acting-out behaviors, there is potential for considerable damage.

The pseudoindependence of this era is often characterized by a challenging and abrasive interpersonal style. In fact, the use of arguments and an adversary stance may represent a style of information-gathering. If the significant adults can react without rancor they are usually rewarded, after some delay, with finding that their ideas and values have been incorporated by the early adolescent. However, many parents are hurt by this new adversary behavior of their children and retire in a self-protective retreat when their overtures are rebuffed. These are the ingredients of the generation gap. With the distancing of parent and child, there is often a relaxation of the demands previously made on him, and a lessening rather than a more appropriate increase in the responsibilities expected of him. Parents may lose touch with the activities and friends of their child under the rubric of privacy for the child.

There are data on the relation between parental interest and involvement and the adolescent self-image.[22] Data from the same source[22] deal with the effects of level of self-esteem on behavior. Rosenberg has studied 5,077 juniors and seniors in public high schools throughout New York State. He studied parental interest as indicated by the parents' knowledge of and relationship to their child's friends, parents' reactions to academic performance, and their responsiveness to the child as judged by dinner table interactions. There is retrospective information pertaining to the early adolescent period. He concluded[22] that low parental involvement and interest are highly correlated with low self-esteem in the child. He said[22, p. 138] it is "not the punitive responses which are most closely related to low self-esteem but the indifferent ones." He pointed out that low self-esteem leads to characteristic responses. The individual is more vulnerable in interpersonal relations (deeply hurt by criticism); he is relatively awkward with others (finds it hard to make talk, does not initiate contacts); he assumes that others think poorly of him or do not particularly like him; he tends to put up a front to people; he feels relatively isolated and lonely. There is low faith in people. In some "this low faith in people takes the form of contempt for the great mass of humanity; among others, mistrust, and among still others, hostility."[22, p. 182] "Low self-esteem makes them relatively submissive or unassertive in their dealings with others. . . . It is, thus apparent that the individual's self-conception is not only associated with attitudes towards other people, it is also associated with his actions in social life and the position he comes to occupy in his high school peer groups."[22, p. 205]

CLINICAL IMPLICATIONS FOR EARLY ADOLESCENTS

An important aspect of the difficulties experienced by early adolescents lies in the fact that each of the three superimposed tasks involves drastic discontinuity with the past. Therefore, at a time of great stress, the individual is severely limited in his ability to draw on past learning and information in trying to cope with the new tasks. Many persons are also somewhat handicapped in ability to 'integrate new experiences because they have not yet reached the final stages of cognitive development in which their introspective and abstract thinking processes are well-developed. As a result, most early adolescents are quite dependent on environmental supports in attempting to anticipate and regulate responses to the challenging tasks at hand. This tendency applies to many individuals who differ in such important variables as rate of maturation, sex, ethnicity, or socioeconomic status.

It might enhance the coping ability of early adolescents to receive prior education about the forthcoming pubertal period. Sketchy information is now given by some schools to fifth- and sixth-grade children on menarche and secondary sex changes. In addition, it would probably be helpful for children in late elementary school to become aware of the implications of the wide range of normality and the timetables for various manifestations of pubertal change which affect the total body image. In this time of intense concern over body image, the early adolescent is particularly vulnerable to real or imagined assaults on his bodily integrity. It seems reasonable that elective surgical procedures should be avoided at this critical period. When medical or surgical interventions are required they should be discussed with the patient with an understanding of his heightened anxiety and need for clear information about the ultimate consequences for his bodily intactness and attractiveness.

Available evidence supports the concept that parental interest, guidelines, and support, particularly of the same-sex parent, offer the most effective help to the early adolescent in negotiating his tasks. There is a need for public understanding of a differentiated view of adolescence and specific information on early adolescence. Rather than accepting the notion of the generation gap as modal and even somehow growth promoting, parents need education about the underlying needs of early adolescents. They need to be supported in carrying out appropriate parental functions and in learning about effective communication with their children.

IMPLICATIONS FOR RESEARCH WITH EARLY ADOLESCENTS

Very little research has been directed primarily to the early adolescent period in terms of its specific coping challenges. At the same time, it has become clear that the junior high school period is a time of major stress and impaired coping ability. The roots of this high rate of distress in the junior high school population need to be further studied. It might be fruitful to study the transition from elementary school to junior high school in a fashion similar to the study of the transition from high school to college carried out by Coelho, Hamburg, and Murphey.[4] Some educators are experimenting with alternatives to the traditional sequence of elementary, junior high, and high school. These deserve study in terms of the psychosocial and coping outcomes, in addition to curricular and learning considerations. The shift from thinking in terms of concrete operations to mature abstract thinking has not been studied in detail in this era to learn about the variability, rate of change, or other attributes of cognition peculiar to the early adolescent period. It is a clinical impression that information processing in this era is significantly different from that in middle and late adolescent periods. There seems to be a general tendency to have difficulty in reasoning about things that are outside of direct, personal experience.

The desirability of further investigation into the relation of gonadal hormone to the moodiness of adolescence has already been mentioned. There is also a need to investigate the possible relation of gonadal hormones to aggressive behavior in males. It is, of course, important to study the problem of aggressive and antisocial behavior in the broader psychosocial aspects as well. Finally, there is a need to look at the ways in which the peer group can be more reliably used as a constructive coping adjunct. At Stanford, we have initiated a peer counseling program in which students are encouraged to assume a helping stance toward their fellow students and are given skills and information to bring to their role.

This is but one of many models for utilizing the potential of the peer group. We need to explore as many as possible.

In general, there is a need for interdisciplinary research on early adolescence, linking biological and psychosocial variables. This critical period of turbulence and potentiality deserves far more study than it has so far received.

(Midadolescence

The high school years, when students are roughly between the ages of fifteen through eighteen, constitute the midadolescent period. It comes to an end with the graduation from high school. New adaptations are necessary then because of the imminence of taking a job or going to college and the actuality of separation from home and nuclear family.

While in high school there are no distinctive new challenges or changes in status. The format of school and the intellectual demands are an extension of the junior high. There are bodily growth and developmental changes which are the continuum of the pubertal changes. Finally, there is the continued socialization into the adolescent roles. The midadolescent is given increasing social responsibility and privilege, for example, driving the automobile, though he still does not have the voting rights or legal responsibilities that come after age eighteen at the earliest. There is an opportunity in the midadolescent era to work at familiar problems with greater depth and differentiation. The caricature-like, exaggerated quality of the prior period yields to the greater experience and emerging individuality of the midadolescent. Also, there is a gradual shift from the here and now perspective to a future orientation.

In general, midadolescence is an interval of quiescence and consolidation. The survey studies cited earlier were typically done on this age group, and the investigators were uniformly impressed by the tranquility of the group as a whole.

The adaptations are smoother in high school not only because the tasks are less new and challenging but also because the coping assets within the individuals are greater at that time, owing to maturational effects. By the time of high school, full cognitive development has been achieved. This makes new dimensions possible in dealing with psychosocial as well as intellectual tasks. The midadolescents are capable of useful introspections.[12] They are interested in exploring the various facets of an issue, and they can learn a great deal by debates and intellectual discussions as a means of information gathering. Horizons are broader, and new connections of ideas can be made. The true relevance of a number of things can now begin to be appreciated. There is less response simply to the novel, exotic, or contradictory aspects of the environment but a more differentiated approach to their milieu. There is a real concern with values and ideals.

Likewise, interpersonal transactions are more differentiated and constructive. There is a more highly critical use of the peer group. There are planned experimentations and role rehearsals. Instead of previous stereotypy, peers are used in a variety of roles such as helpers, foils, critics, and models. The previous concern with exploratory learning about the opposite sex in general terms is giving way to the nurture of specific relationships in which there is mutuality and the beginning of tenderness. The midadolescent is making many refinements in his self-image and sense of identity.

There is a chance now to confirm some aspects of this new self in functional terms. There are added privileges and responsibilities that lead to new contracts with the parents and meaningful moves toward independence. The earning of the driver's license and use of the family car is an excellent example. In less affluent families it may be the obtaining of a work permit and opportunity to prove one's worth in the labor market in terms of responsibility and productivity.

In all these ways, the midadolescent, though somewhat more quiet, is making real progress and is laying the groundwork for definitively dealing with the salient issues that are to confront him in late adolescence.

⟨ Late Adolescence

Graduation from high school is the critical event that ushers in the stage of late adolescence for most young people. The long continuum of student life in secondary school while living under the protection and restraint of the nuclear family comes to an end. Some individuals may move directly into adult roles of marriage and full-time work responsibility. For most of the group, however, the post-high school era is the psychosocial moratorium of which Erikson[8] has written so persuasively. There is a more or less extended period of time in college or apprentice training when the search for identity can be pursued.

As has been mentioned previously, this is the era so amply represented in the literature. Therefore, only a brief synopsis of the major developmental tasks of this period need be set forth.

Autonomy is a key issue. Most other tasks are derivative from this.

The search for identity could be restated as "now that I am free to be the kind of person I choose, what is it that I care about." Away from the family, but under the protection of college and the general attitudes of tolerance that society affords members of this age group, there is a chance to try out modes of independent functioning.

Another task is the renegotiation of the relationship to the family. The separation usually does not mean estrangement. The goal is to achieve a more adult-adult relationship based on mutual respect and more equality. This generally involves a more realistic appraisal of the family with an acceptance of shortcomings and an appreciation of the assets.

The commitment to work is an important task. The late adolescent needs to define and pursue a goal in which his talents are used, interests are focused, and a sense of efficacy is established. The end point is reached when a particular adult work role is achieved. The choice of an alternative life style, where no such adult occupational niche is sought or occupied, represents a prolongation of adolescence despite the chronological age.

When the individual moves out of the family into the community, there is a heightened need to define himself in relation to his new situation and also more broadly in relation to the existing society. For different individuals this is a more or less difficult task. For different reasons both the disadvantaged minorities and the elite intellectual groups tend to find this an arena of great challenge and often turbulence.

Finally, there is the challenge of heterosexual adjustment and intimacy. Despite the new permissiveness, it is still the case that the majority of young people do not establish a mature, stable heterosexual relationship until late adolescence. This task is not derived from autonomy needs but stands in its own right as a major challenge. Mutuality and the ability to relate tenderly and with trust are the issues of importance in this task.

Kenneth Keniston[16] proposed a separate developmental era in his "Youth: A 'New' Stage of Life." On close reading, however, it seems more likely that he is describing a specific kind of resolution of the universal problems of the late adolescent period. The tasks he describes are not different from those set down by Erikson in his description of the search for identity. Keniston stated,[16, p. 649] "Youth, as a developmental stage is emergent; it is an 'optional' stage, not a universal one." The distinguishing criterion for the designation of "youth" that Keniston cites is the attainment of postconventional moral reasoning, as described by Kohlberg.[17] By this is meant a stage in which an individual comes to feel that his personal principles transcend not only conventional morality but even the social contract. This variant of adolescence has been adopted by a vocal and highly publicized minority and as such seems to be best included in the general category of late adolescence rather than viewed as a separate life stage. It is more aptly described as a different life style and seen as but one of the several alternative broad strategies available for coping with the psychosocial pressures of this age period.

(Bibliography

1. ADAMS, J. F. "Adolescent Personal Problems as a Function of Age and Sex." *Journal of Genetic Psychology*, 104 (1964), 207–214.
2. ARIES, P. *Centuries of Childhood*. New York: Knopf, 1962.
3. BLIZZARD, R., JOHANSON, A., GUYDA, H., RAITI, S., and MIGEON, C. "Recent Developments in the Study of Gonadotrophin Secretion in Adolescence." In F. Heald and W. Hung, eds., *Adolescent Endocrinology*. New York: Appleton-Century-Crofts, 1970.
4. COELHO, G., HAMBURG, D., and MURPHEY, E. "Coping Strategies in a New Learning Environment." *Archives of General Psychiatry*, 9 (1963), 433–443.
5. DONOVAN, B. T., and VAN DER WERFF TEN BOSCH, J. J. "The Hypothalamus and Sexual Maturation in the Rat." *Journal of Physiology*, 147 (1959), 78–92.
6. DOUVAN, E., and ADELSON, J. *The Adolescent Experience*. New York: Wiley, 1966.
7. EISENBERG, L. "Student Unrest: Sources and Consequences." *Science*, 167 (1970), 1688–1692.
8. ERIKSON, E. H. *Identity and the Life Cycle. Psychological Issues*. Monograph 1. New York: International Universities Press, 1959.
9. ———. *Identity: Youth and Crisis*. New York: Norton, 1968.
10. FRAZIER, A., and LISONBEE, L. K. "Adolescent Concerns with Physique." *School Review*, 58 (1950), 397–405.
11. GRINKER, R. R., SR., GRINKER, R. R., JR., and TIMBERLAKE, J. A. "A Study of 'Mentally Healthy' Young Males (Homoclites)." *Archives of General Psychiatry*, 6 (1962), 27–74.
12. INHELDER, B. *The Growth of Logical Think-ing from Childhood to Adolescence*. New York: Basic Books, 1958.
13. JERSILD, A. T. *In Search of Self*. New York: Columbia University Press, 1952.
14. JONES, M. C. "Self-Conceptions, Motivations and Interpersonal Attitudes of Early- and Late-Maturing Girls." In R. E. Grinder, ed., *Studies in Adolescence*. New York: Macmillan, 1963. Pp. 454–465.
15. ———. Psychological Correlates of Somatic Development. Presidential address, Division 7, American Psychological Association, September 1964.
16. KENISTON, K. "Youth: A 'New' Stage of Life." *The American Scholar*, Autumn 1970, pp. 631–654.
17. KOHLBERG, L. "Development of Moral Character and Moral Ideology." In M. L. Hoffman and L. W. Hoffman, eds., *Review of Child Development Research*. Vol. 2. New York: Russell Sage Foundation, 1964. Pp. 383–431.
18. LUNDE, D., and HAMBURG, D. "Techniques for Assessing the Effects of Sex Hormones on Affect, Arousal, and Aggression in Humans." In A. B. Astwood, ed., *Recent Progress in Hormone Research*. Vol. 28. New York: Academic Press, 1972. Pp. 627–663.
19. MARTINI, L., and PECILE, A. *Hormonal Steroids 2*. New York: Academic Press, 1965.
20. MUSSEN, P. H., and JONES, M. C. "Self-Conceptions, Motivations, and Interpersonal Attitudes of Late- and Early-Maturing Boys." *Child Development*, 28 (1957), 243–256.
21. OFFER, D. *The Psychological World of the Teen-Ager: A Study of Normal Adolescent Boys*. New York: Basic Books, 1969.
22. ROSENBERG, M. *Society and the Adolescent Self-Image*. Princeton, N.J.: Princeton University Press, 1965.
23. TANNER, J. M. *Growth at Adolescence*. 2d ed. Oxford: Blackwell, 1962.
24. WOLSTENHOLME, G. E. W., and O'CONNOR, M. *Endocrinology of the Testis*. Boston: Little, Brown, 1967.

PART THREE

Sociocultural Psychiatry

CHAPTER 27

PSYCHIATRIC
EPIDEMIOLOGY

John C. Cassel

IT IS NOT THE PURPOSE of this chapter to review the current state of knowledge in psychiatric epidemiology nor to present in any details the methods of epidemiology. For both these purposes there is a moderately extensive and reasonably adequate literature available.* Rather the intention is to present some of the critical issues in this field, issues that, unless resolved, severely limit the potentialities of epidemiological inquiry, and to indicate some approaches to their solution.

The contribution that epidemiology can make to furthering knowledge of any disease or disorder is directly dependent upon the adequacy with which three interrelated, but analytically separable, problems can be resolved. These three problems are:

1. The adequacy with which cases can be identified and separated from noncases.
2. The utility of the theories invoked to

explain the processes determining the condition being studied.
3. The skill with which the independent variables are selected as indicators of these determinant processes.

While these issues are central to any epidemiological inquiry, psychiatric epidemiology presents some unique problems, especially in the designation and ascertainment of cases. This topic, including the definition, classification, and measurement of psychiatric disorder or mental health status, has been the subject of numerous conferences, debates, and studies.[42,50,52] There is as yet, however, little consensus among experts and until comparatively recently, a lack of clarity in much of the thinking in this area. To a large extent this confusion can, in my opinion, be traced to the failure of earlier attempts to recognize that in any inquiry the classification scheme used and the phenomena to be measured will be determined in large part by the purposes of the study. That is, no single classification scheme is likely to be equally useful for all purposes.

---

* See references 15, 16, 22, 24, 26, 29, 31–33, 38, 39, and 43.

❪ Classification and Ascertainment of Mental Disorder

In the field of psychiatric epidemiology, one of the clearest statements of the relationship of the classificatory scheme to the purposes for which such a scheme is to be used is that made by Gruenberg.[17] He clearly differentiated some eight or nine such purposes which, without doing violence to his ideas, could be categorized into three major groups.

1. Studies concerned with aiding the planning of health services, including a determination of priorities, facilities, personnel, necessary finances, and so on.
2. Studies concerned with the processes of recovery from mental disorders.
3. Studies concerned with the determinants of genesis of mental disorders.

It is the failure to separate out the distinctive needs, in terms of both classificatory systems and underlying theories, of studies concerned with recovery from those concerned with genesis of disease that has perhaps been responsible for much of the confusion in the past. Implicit in this lack of distinction is the notion that the causes of any illness are the same as the causes of lack of recovery from that illness. Even though as early as 1943 Halliday[20] eloquently identified the advantages of making such a distinction, his advice has largely been overlooked in epidemiological studies, in which both the research strategy and the classificatory systems used are frequently based on the implicit assumption that these two sets of causes are identical. A few familiar examples may help make this point clear. Knowledge of abnormalities in carbohydrate and fat metabolism, including the role of insulin, has improved our ability to treat diabetics (that is, to understand something of the recovery process). This knowledge, however, is of very limited utility in explaining why diabetes occurs or why, for example, the rates in the United States have been increasing over the last half century. Further, some of those factors suspected as

being important in the genesis of diabetes (dietary factors and sedentary living, for example) may also be antecedents to diseases (such as coronary heart disease) usually classified separately from diabetes. By the same token, knowledge of the relationship of cigarette smoking to cancer of the lung has increased our knowledge of genesis but has been of no use in changing our approach to treatment. In the field of mental disorders the identification of the social breakdown syndrome by Gruenberg[18] is a good illustration of this point. According to this concept the factors responsible for much of the disability that accompanies mental disorder in many patients are independent of the factors responsible for the initial condition. Reduction of disability can thus be accomplished by changing these relevant factors even though we may be ignorant of the causes of the underlying mental disorder.

The implications for a classificatory scheme of making a distinction between studies concerned with recovery from those concerned with onset are clear. In psychiatric epidemiological studies concerned with the recovery process (including the effectiveness and efficiency of various modalities of medical care and health services), existing clinical classifications should be the basis for case definition. Further, ascertainment can, without too much loss, be restricted to those under some form of psychiatric care. What is required is an improvement of the reliability with which such cases are labeled (that is, improvement in the standardization of criteria to be used and the ability of the investigators and clinical personnel to apply these criteria). Such attempts are currently being undertaken by a number of investigations, one of the most notable of which is that being conducted by the mental health section of the World Health Organization. The complexities of this problem of standardization should not be underestimated. According to Wing[50] they include:

1. Determination of the dividing line between psychotic and nonpsychotic conditions.
2. Decisions to be made when there are

combinations of different forms of psychosis in the same person.

3. The influence of known or suspected etiological factors on diagnosis (for example, the effect of prior knowledge that the patient was taking amphetamines in the decision as to whether to label the condition "amphetamine psychosis" or "schizophrenia [drug induced]").

4. The effect of knowledge of previous diagnoses. (For example, in a patient presenting with a condition that under most conditions might not be called psychotic, the knowledge that there had been an earlier clearcut episode of schizophrenia might lead some clinicians to rediagnose schizophrenia.)

5. Social and cultural factors that influence diagnosis.

While it would appear that none of these problems is insuperable, requiring mainly the elaboration of a consistent set of rules (if necessary, arbitrary rules), the point to be made is that even the most satisfactory solution of all these difficulties will not provide a useful classificatory scheme for the other two major purposes, namely, administrative purposes and studies concerned with the determination of the factors responsible for the onset of disease.

For administrative purposes, particularly for the planning of health services, it is crucial not only that cases outside as well as within the current treatment network be counted but that such cases be classified as to whether their condition is regarded as susceptible to the current technology of treatment or rehabilitation and as to whether such conditions are preventable. A beginning of such a classification is included in the guide to the control of mental disorders published by the American Public Health Association.[3]

The greatest difficulty of all lies in the development of a suitable classificatory scheme for purposes of studying the genesis of mental disorders. Here, in addition to the problems posed by attempting to ascertain cases in the community as well as those under treatment (with all the attendant problems of variation in intensity of contact between the investigator and respondent and the problem of intra- and between-observer reliability), two rather special problems emerge.

The first of these relates to the various factors that can lead to a person becoming labeled as a psychiatric case. Gruenberg[17] identified five such factors, which alone, or in combination, are involved in this labeling.

1. The result of an appeal for help, that is, as a result of symptoms and complaints on the part of the respondent.
2. The result of concern or fears in others.
3. The result of trouble to others.
4. The result of breaking the law.
5. The result of a failure in functioning.

The importance of such a categorization is that it makes clear a well-known but often overlooked fact as far as epidemiological studies are concerned. The labeling of an individual as a psychiatric case is usually the result of the product of two sets of potentially independent factors, the intrapersonal disorders of mood, thought, and behavior (number 1 in the above scheme) and the existing social standards and level of tolerance for deviant behavior (numbers 2 through 5 in Gruenberg's scheme). The majority of patients under psychiatric care (particularly in psychiatric hospitals) will be under such care by virtue of both sets of factors, but the relative importance of each set may vary systematically in different sorts of people. Thus it is theoretically possible that the majority of lower-class patients in a psychiatric hospital are labeled as cases by virtue of their interpersonal difficulties (that is, violation of the existing social norms) whereas upper-class individuals with the same label may be patients largely by virtue of their intrapersonal difficulties (symptoms, complaints, and so on). The situation will be further confounded when individuals not under treatment are to be included in the study and labeled as cases. Almost by definition the majority of these will not have disturbed the social norms and expectations to the same degree as will those who are under treatment. This may mean that their intrapersonal disturbances are not so severe as in treated patients, or alternatively that the tolerance of deviance, and the expectations for performance, by significant others are different in the case of community cases compared with treated patients. In order then to ensure that like things are being measured, particularly when comparisons between communities are to be made (where both sets of factors may be expected to vary), it would seem desirable to develop two separate classificatory schemes. (1) The first of these would be concerned with measuring disturbances in mood, thought, and behavior as reported by the respondent, independently from degree of disability or those aspects of impaired function which are dependent upon the views or expectations of others. Such an approach forms the basis for one part of the classification used by Leighton[31] ("behavioral patterns or syndromes"); by the new instrument, the present state examination, being developed by Wing et al.;[51] and to some extent by the approaches being used by Dohrenwend[15]—the structural interview schedule and psychiatric status interview (although these latter two do not make this crucial distinction as clearly as might be desired). The central problem here is not only the development of reliable instruments but being able to determine the frequency and duration of the symptoms rather than just their presence or absence at the time of examination. The organization of these symptoms into clusters and the development of syndromes are an elaboration of this approach, which also requires that this classificatory system be kept distinct from that concerned with failure of interpersonal functions. (2) Classificatory systems having to do with the failure of interpersonal functions (called level of disability by Leighton[31] and, more broadly, level of functioning by Gruenberg[17]) would form the basis for a separate classificatory scheme. The relationship between these two sets of indices would be an important research topic in its own right and might yield a third set of classifications.

Even if this problem of separate classificatory systems can be resolved, however, it still leaves unanswered the problems of what signs and symptoms (or other measures of disturbed intrapersonal functioning) are to be measured. It is here that the crucial role of the underlying theory subscribed to becomes apparent. The preoccupation on the part of many investigators with distinguishing between physical and psychological symptoms or signs, for example, is in my opinion an indication of subscription to a theoretical model that in light of current knowledge has outlived its utility. As this problem cannot be reviewed out of context of the theories concerning the nature of disease and its causes, with particular reference to the role of environmental factors in etiology, these will be now discussed in some detail.

⟨ Theories Concerning the Nature of Disease and Its Causes

Throughout history there has been a conviction in medicine that certain environmental factors are important in the etiology of disease. The specific factors deemed worthy of study, however, have varied considerably over time from the "airs, waters, places" of Hippocratic times to the microchemicals and microorganisms of today. Quite clearly the factors selected for study (from an almost infinite number of possibilities) are heavily dependent on the existing theories of the nature of disease and its causes and the existing level of technology. Comparatively recent findings tend to suggest that we need to modify some of these existing theories to allow for the possibility that one of the more important aspects of the environment for man (from a disease etiology point of view) may be the presence of other members of the same species.

Paradoxically, some of the more convincing evidence supporting this point of view comes from animal studies. To a large extent, these have been concerned with variations in the size of the group in which the animals interact and in situations that lead to confusion over territorial control. A number of investigators have shown, for example, that as the number of animals housed together increases, with all other factors such as genetic stock, diet, temperature, and sanitation kept constant, maternal and infant mortality rates rise, the incidence of arteriosclerosis increases, resistance to a wide variety of insults, including drugs, microorganisms and X-rays, decreases, and there is an increased susceptibility to various types of neoplasia.[*] Lack of territorial control in mice has been shown to lead to the development of marked and persistent hypertension, to increased maternal and infant mortality rates, to reduced resistance to bacterial infections, and to decreased longevity.[23]

In addition to demonstrating the health effects of variations of the social milieu, further animal studies have provided clues as to the processes through which they may be produced. Changes in group membership and the quality of group relationships have been shown to be accompanied by neuroendocrine changes, particularly, but not exclusively, by changes in the pituitary and adrenocortical systems.[34,35] The changes in some of these hormones, such as the 17-hydroxycorticosteroids and the catecholamines, especially if prolonged, can, in turn, markedly affect the homeostatic mechanisms of the body and the responses to a wide variety of stimuli. The evidence, then, from a series of studies would seem to be both sound methodologically and reasonable from a biological point of view.

Convincing as this animal work would appear to be, the relevance of these findings to human health, however, is as yet unproved, and considerable doubt exists as to the appropriate analogues in the human social system. Attempts, for example, to demonstrate that increased population density and crowding are related to poorer health status have been unconvincing and have led to confusing and often conflicting results.[8] A careful review of some of these studies taken in conjunction with the animal work would suggest that for future research in this area to be profitable we should abandon a search for the direct human counterpart to animal crowding or territorial confusion and concentrate instead on some more general principles, or hypotheses, that

can be derived from these data. In my view, four such principles seem worth considering.

1. The social process linking high population density to enhanced susceptibility to disease is not the crowding per se but the disordered relationships that, in animals, are inevitable consequences of such crowding. These, while manifest by a wide variety of bizarre and unusual behaviors, often have in common a failure to elicit anticipated responses to what were previously appropriate cues and an increasing disregard of traditional obligations and rights. Thus, under crowded conditions, habitual acts of aggression (including ritualized aggression), subordination, or cooperation on the part of one animal fail to elicit appropriate reciprocal responses on the part of another. Characteristic obligations and responsibilities become blurred (for example, female rats cease caring for their young and male-female relationships become disturbed to a point where the equivalent of gang rapes have been reported in rats under conditions of high population density). The failure of behavior patterns to accomplish their intended results (that is, to lead to predictable responses on the part of others) leads frequently to repetition of these behaviors with, presumably, concomitant chronic alterations in the autonomic nervous system activity and hormonal secretions associated with such activity. These, in turn, alter the homeostatic mechanisms of the organism, leading to increased susceptibility to disease.

This hypothesis would suggest that in human populations the circumstances in which increased susceptibility to disease would occur would be those in which, for a variety of reasons, individuals are not receiving any evidence (feedback) that their actions are leading to desirable and/or anticipated consequences. In particular this would be true when these actions are designed to modify the individual's relationships to the important social groups with whom he interacts. Such circumstances might occur in a variety of situations.

It is highly probable that when individuals are unfamiliar with the cues and the expectations of the society (as in the case of migrants

[*] See references 1, 2, 4, 7, 12, 14, 28, 40, and 44.

to a new situation or of individuals involved in a rapid change of the social scene, such as the elderly in an ethnic enclave caught up in the process of urban renewal), their actions would be unlikely to lead to the consequences they anticipate and thus, owing to the chain of events suggested above, they should be more susceptible to disease than are those for whom the situation is familiar. Some circumstantial evidence supporting this point of view exists. Scotch[41] and his collaborators found that blood pressure levels among Zulu who had recently migrated to a large urban center were higher than both those who had remained in their rural tribal surroundings and those who had lived for more than ten years in the urban setting. In two independent studies, Syme[46,48] demonstrated that occupationally and residentially mobile people have a higher prevalence of coronary heart disease than have stable populations and that those individuals displaying the greatest discontinuity between childhood and adult situations, as measured by occupation and place of residence, have higher rates than those in which less discontinuity could be determined. Tyroler and Cassel[49] designed a study in which death rates from coronary heart disease, and from all heart disease, could be measured in groups who were themselves stable but around whom the social situation was changing in varying degree. For this purpose they selected forty-five- to fifty-four-year-old white male rural residents in the various counties of North Carolina and classified these counties by their degrees of urbanization. Death rates for coronary heart disease and all heart disease showed a stepped gradient with each increase in the index of urbanization of the county. In a further study Cassel and Tyroler[9] studied groups of rural mountaineers, one of which was composed of individuals who were the first of their family to engage in industrial work while the second comprised workers in the same factory drawn from the same mountain coves and doing the same work for the same pay as the first group, but who were the children of previous workers in this factory. The underlying hypothesis was that the second group, by virtue of their previous experi-

ence, would be better prepared for the expectations and demands of industrial living than the first and would thus exhibit fewer signs of ill health. Health status was measured by responses to the Cornell Medical Index and various indices of sick absenteeism. As predicted, the first group had higher Cornell Medical Index scores for both physical and emotional symptoms and higher rates of sick absenteeism, after the initial few years of service at each age, than had the second.

A second set of circumstances in which the individual would not be receiving any feedback that his actions were effectively modifying the situation might occur where there is some evidence of social disorganization. This, while still being far from a precise term that can be accurately measured, has proved to be a useful concept in a number of studies. In the hands of several investigators, for example, various indicators of social or familial disorganization have been related to increased rates of tuberculosis,[25] mental disorders,[31] deaths from stroke,[37] and prevalence of hypertension.[21]

Clearly, though none of these studies prove that this postulated psychosocial process is an important determinant of the higher disease rates, they are all at least consistent with such a notion.

2. Not all members of a population are equally susceptible to the effects of these social processes. Systematic and regular differences have been observed with the more dominant animals showing the least effects and the subordinate ones having the most extreme responses.[11] These differences are manifest both in the magnitude of the endocrine changes as well as in increased morbidity and mortality rates. Conceivably these findings may, in part, explain the high levels of blood pressure found in American blacks, who not only usually occupy a subordinate position in society but whose lives are frequently characterized by considerable evidence of social and familial disorganization. At the very least, such findings would suggest that studies aimed at identifying the health consequences of migration should distinguish those migrants who occupy subordinate positions in their host

countries from those who occupy positions of power or prestige.

3. The third principle is concerned with the available protective factors, those devices that buffer or cushion the individual from the physiological or psychological consequences of social disorganization. These would seem to be of two general categories, biological and social. Under biological factors would be included the adaptive capacities of all living organisms, the capacity, given time, to adjust physiologically and psychologically to a wide variety of environmental circumstances. In animals, this is illustrated by the higher responses of laboratory-naïve animals to given stimuli than of veteran animals[36] and to the much lower rate of pathology in animals born and reared in crowded conditions than in animals transferred to these conditions some time after birth.[27] In humans, the finding that death rates from lung cancer in the United States, when controlled for cigarette smoking, are considerably higher in the farm born who migrated to cities than in lifetime urban dwellers (despite the longer exposure of the latter to atmospheric pollution[19]) would seem to be evidence of the same phenomenon.

In addition to these biological adaptive processes, various social processes have also been shown to be protective. Chief among these are the nature and strength of the group supports provided to the individual. In rats, for example, the efficacy with which an unanticipated series of electric shocks (given to animals previously conditioned to avoid them) can produce peptic ulcers is determined, to a large extent, by whether the animals are shocked in isolation (high ulcer rates) or in the presence of litter mates (low ulcer rates).[13] The territorial conflict that led to elevated blood pressures[23] was produced by placing mice in intercommunicating boxes. Hypertension only occurred, however, when the mice were "strangers." Populating the system with litter mates produced none of these effects.[23] In humans, small group studies have shown that the degree of autonomic arousal that can be produced by requiring solutions to what in reality are insoluble tasks is more extreme if the group is made up of strangers than when it is made up of friends.[5] Modern studies on the epidemiology of tuberculosis in the United States and Britain have shown that the disease occurs more frequently in marginal people, that is, in those people who for a variety of reasons are deprived of meaningful social contacts.[6,25]

If these three hypotheses are correct, it would imply that the health consequences of disordered social relationships will not be universal, affecting all people in the same manner. A more adequate formulation would hold that such consequences will depend on (1) the importance or salience of the relationships that become disordered; (2) the position of the individuals experiencing such disordered relationships in the status hierarchy; (3) the degree to which the population under study has been unprepared by previous experience for this particular situation (that is, has had insufficient time to adapt); and (4) the nature and strength of the available group supports.

4. The final general principle that can be derived from the animal experiments relates to the manifestations of ill health that might be anticipated under conditions of social change and disorganization. The model of disease causation provided by the germ theory has accustomed us to think in monoetiological specific terms. Accordingly, much of the work concerned with social or psychological antecedents to disease has attempted to identify a particular situational set (usually labeled "stress" or "a stressor") that would have a specific causal relationship to some clinical entity, analogous, say, to the relationship between the typhoid bacillus and typhoid fever. Such a formulation would appear to be clearly at variance with the animal data, a striking feature of which is the wide variety of pathological conditions that emerge following changes in the social milieu. A conclusion more in accordance with the known evidence would be that such variations in group relationships, rather than having a specific etiological role, would enhance susceptibility to disease in general. The specific manifestations of disease would be a function of the genetic predisposition of the individuals, their metabolic states, and the nature of the physicochemical or mi-

crobiological insults they encounter. This concept of generalized susceptibility would be consistent with the situation in the United States, where it has recently been demonstrated that those regions of the country having the highest death rates from cardiovascular disease (age, race, sex specific) also have higher than expected death rates from all causes, including cancer and infectious diseases.[45] This illustration, of course, does not necessarily document that social processes are responsible for such an increased susceptibility, but does lend credence to the view that variations in generalized susceptibility may be a useful concept. Somewhat more direct evidence is provided by industrial studies in the United States, which have shown that managers in a company who, by virtue of their family background and educational experience, were least well prepared for the demands and expectations of executive industrial life had the highest rates of all diseases, physical illness as well as mental, major as well as minor, long-term as well as short-term.[10]

From this formulation it would appear that an initial aim in epidemiological studies (including psychiatric epidemiological studies) would be to identify these individuals at highest risk to disease or disorder in general. The manifestations of such increased susceptibility could be quite widespread and include many clinical entities that for therapeutic purposes are currently regarded as separate diseases. A second level question would then address itself to the determinants of the manifestations in the susceptible populations. Why are there disturbances in mood or thought on the part of some individuals and hypertension or tuberculosis in others? Here I suspect the answers are most likely to come from genetic studies, from studies of the combined effect of genetic and experiential factors on metabolic patterns, and from studies of physicochemical and microbiological insults.

The decision, then, as to the appropriate classificatory scheme to be used in studies concerned in the genesis of disease and, from such a decision, the instruments and techniques to be used to gather such information is, I submit, inextricably bound to the theories espoused by the investigator.

This chapter should not necessarily be read as a plea to accept this particular theoretical formulation, but rather that, in epidemiological studies in general and psychiatric epidemiological studies in particular, the onus is on the investigator to make his theoretical formulation explicit and the information to be obtained both for the classification of cases and characterization of the independent variables congruent with it.

(Bibliography

1. ADER, R., and HAHN, E. W. "Effects of Social Environment on Mortality to Whole Body X-Irradiation in the Rat." *Psychological Report*, 13 (1963), 24–215.

2. ———, KREUTNER, A., and JACOBS, H. L. "Social Environment, Emotionality and Alloxan Diabetes in the Rat." *Psychosomatic Medicine*, 25 (1963), 60–68.

3. AMERICAN PUBLIC HEALTH ASSOCIATION. *Mental Disorders: A Guide to Control Methods.* New York, 1962.

4. ANDERVONT, H. B. "Influence of Environment on Mammary Cancer in Mice." *Journal of the National Cancer Institute*, 4 (1944), 579–581.

5. BOGDANOFF, N. D., BACK, K., KLEIN, R., ESTES, E. H., and NICHOLS, C. "The Physiologic Response to Conformity Pressure in Man." *Annals of Internal Medicine*, 57 (1962).

6. BRETT, G. Z., and BENJAMIN, B. "Housing and Tuberculosis in a Mass Radiography Survey." *British Journal of Preventive and Social Medicine*, 11 (1957), 7.

7. CALHOUN, J. B. "Population Density and Social Pathology." *Scientific American*, 206 (1962), 139.

8. CASSEL, J. C. "Health Consequences of Population Density and Crowding." In press.

9. ———, and TYROLER, H. A. "Epidemiological Studies of Culture Change: I. Health Status and Recency of Industrialization." *Archives of Environmental Health*, 3 (1961), 25.

10. CHRISTENSON, W. N., and HINKLE, L. E., Jr. "Differences in Illness and Prognostic Signs

in Two Groups of Young Men." *Journal of the American Medical Association*, 177 (1961), 247–253.

11. CHRISTIAN, J. J. "The Potential Role of the Adrenal Cortex as Affected by Social Rank and Population Density on Experimental Epidemics." *American Journal of Epidemiology*, 87 (1968), 255–264.

12. ———, and WILLIAMSON, H. O. "Effect of Crowding on Experimental Granuloma Formation in Mice." *Proceedings of the Society for Experimental Biological Medicine*, 99 (1958), 385–387.

13. CONGER, J. J., et al. "The Role of Social Experience in the Production of Gastric Ulcers in Hooded Rats Placed in a Conflict Situation." *Journal of Abnormal and Social Psychology*, 57 (1958), 216.

14. DAVIS, D. E., and READ, C. P. "Effect of Behavior on Development of Resistance in Trichinosis." *Proceedings of the Society for Experimental Biological Medicine*, 99 (1958), 269–272.

15. DOHRENWEND, B. P., and DOHRENWEND, B. S. *Social Status and Psychological Disorder*. New York: Wiley, 1969.

16. DUNHAM, H. W. *Community and Schizophrenia*. Detroit: Wayne State University, 1965.

17. GRUENBERG, E. M. "Epidemiology and Medical Care Statistics." In *The Role and Methodology of Classification in Psychiatry and Psychopathology*. Washington, D.C.: U.S. Government Printing Office, 1965. Pp. 76–99.

18. ———. "The Social Breakdown Syndrome: Some Origins." *American Journal of Psychiatry*, 123 (1967), 1481–1489.

19. HAENZEL, W., LOVELAND, D. B., and SIRKEN, M. G. "Lung-Cancer Mortality as Related to Residence and Smoking Histories." *Journal of the National Cancer Institute*, 28 (1962), 947–1001.

20. HALLIDAY, J. L. "Principles of Aetiology." *British Journal of Medical Psychology*, 19 (1943), 367.

21. HARBURG, E., et al. Stress and Heredity in Negro White Blood Pressure Differences. Progress Report to National Heart Institute, 1969.

22. HARE, E. H., and WING, J. K., eds., *Psychiatric Epidemiology*. London: Oxford University Press, 1970.

23. HENRY, J. P., MEEHAN, J. P., and STEPHENS, P. M. "The Use of Psychosocial Stimuli To Induce Prolonged Hypertension in Mice." *Psychosomatic Medicine*, 29 (1967), 408–432.

24. HOCH, P. H., and ZUBIN, J., eds. *Comparative Epidemiology of the Mental Disorders*. New York: Grune & Stratton, 1961.

25. HOLMES, T. H. "Multidiscipline Studies of Tuberculosis." In P. J. Sparer, ed., *Personality Stress and Tuberculosis*. New York: International Universities Press, 1956.

26. JACO, E. G. *The Social Epidemiology of Mental Disorders*. New York: Russell Sage Foundation, 1960.

27. KESSLER, A. Interplay Between Social Ecology and Physiology, Genetics, and Population Dynamics of Mice. Doctoral Dissertation, Rockefeller University, 1966.

28. KING, J. T., LEE, Y. C. P., and VISSCHER, M. B. "Single Versus Multiple Cage Occupancy and Convulsion Frequency in C$_3$H Mice." *Proceedings of the Society for Experimental Biological Medicine*, 88 (1955), 661–663.

29. LANGNER, T. S., and MICHAEL, S. T. *Life Stress and Mental Health*. New York: The Free Press, 1963.

30. LEIGHTON, A. H., LEIGHTON, D. C., and DANLEY, R. A., "Validity in Mental Health Surveys." *Canadian Psychiatric Association Journal*, 11 (1966), 167–178.

31. LEIGHTON, D. C., HARDING, J. S., MACKLIN, D. B., MACMILLAN, A. M., and LEIGHTON, A. H. *The Character of Danger*. New York: Basic Books, 1963.

32. ———, and LEIGHTON, A. H. "Mental Health and Social Factors." In A. M. Freedman and H. I. Kaplan, eds., *Comprehensive Textbook of Psychiatry*. Baltimore: Williams & Wilkins, 1967. Pp. 1520–1533.

33. LIN, T. and STANDLEY, C. C. *The Scope of Epidemiology in Psychiatry*. Geneva: World Health Organization, 1962.

34. MASON, J. W. "Psychological Influences on the Pituitary-Adrenal-Cortical System." *Recent Progress in Hormone Research*, 15 (1959), 345–389.

35. ———, and BRADY, J. V. "The Sensitivity of the Psychoendocrine Systems to Social and Physical Environment." In D. Shapiro, ed., *Psychobiological Approaches to Social Behavior*. Stanford, Calif.: Stanford University Press, 1964.

36. ——, BRADY, J. V., POLISH, E., et al. "Concurrent Measurement of 17-Hydroxycorticosteroids and Pepsinogen Levels During Prolonged Emotional Stress in the Monkey." *Psychosomatic Medicine*, 21 (1959), 432.

37. NESER, W., CASSEL, J., and TYROLER, H. A. Stroke Mortality in the Black Population of North Carolina in Relation to Social Factors. Presented at the American Heart Association Meeting on Cardiovascular Epidemiology, New Orleans, 1970.

38. PASAMANICK, B., ed. *Epidemiology of Mental Disorder*. Washington, D.C.: American Association for the Advancement of Science, 1959.

39. PLUNKETT, R. J., and GORDON, J. E. *Epidemiology of Mental Illness*. New York: Basic Books, 1960.

40. RATCLIFFE, H. L., and CRONIN, M. T. I. "Changing Frequency of Arteriosclerosis in Mammals and Birds at the Philadelphia Zoological Garden." *Circulation*, 18 (1958), 41–52.

41. SCOTCH, N. A. "Sociocultural Factors in the Epidemiology of Zulu Hypertension." *American Journal of Public Health*, 52 (1963), 1205–1213.

42. SELLS, S. B., ed. *The Definition and Measurement of Mental Health*. Washington, D.C.: U.S. Government Printing Office, 1968.

43. SROLE, L., LANGNER, T. S., MICHAEL, S. T., OPLER, M. K., and RENNIE, T. A. C. *Mental Health in the Metropolis*. New York: McGraw-Hill, 1962.

44. SWINYARD, E. A., CLARK, L. D., MIYAHARA, J. T., and WOLF, H. H. "Studies on the Mechanism of Amphetamine Toxicity in Aggregated Mice." *Journal of Pharmacology and Experimental Therapy*, 132 (1961), 97–102.

45. SYME, S. L. Personal communication.

46. ——, BORHANI, N. C., and BUECHLEY, R. W. "Cultural Mobility and Coronary Heart Disease in an Urban Area." *American Journal of Epidemiology*, 82 (1965), 334–346.

47. ——, HYMAN, M. M., and ENTERLINE, P. E. "Cultural Mobility and the Occurrence of Coronary Heart Disease." *Health and Human Behavior*, 6 (1965), 173–189.

48. ——, HYMAN, M. M., and ENTERLINE, P. E. "Some Social and Cultural Factors Associated with the Occurrence of Coronary Heart Disease." *Journal of Chronic Diseases*, 17 (1964), 277–289.

49. TYROLER, H. A., and CASSEL, J. "Health Consequences of Culture Change: The Effect of Urbanization on Coronary Heart Mortality in Rural Residents of North Carolina." *Journal of Chronic Diseases*, 17 (1964), 167–177.

50. WING, J. K. "International Comparisons in the Study of Functional Psychoses." *British Medical Bulletin*, 27 (1971), 77–81.

51. ——, BIRLEY, J. L. T., COOPER, J. E., GRAHAM, P., and ISAACS, A. D. "Reliability of a Procedure for Measuring and Classifying 'Present Psychiatric State.'" *British Journal of Psychiatry*, 113 (1967), 499–515.

52. ZUBIN, J., ed. *Field Studies in the Mental Disorders*. New York: Grune & Stratton, 1961.

CHAPTER 28

SOCIAL DISINTEGRATION AND MENTAL DISORDER

Alexander H. Leighton[*]

I T IS WIDELY RECOGNIZED that when circumstances force isolation on an individual, he is apt to show psychophysiological disturbances and symptoms of psychiatric disorder, such as depression, anxiety, and delusions. The sources of isolation generally lie in some disruption of the communications the individual has with other people. Most influential, as a rule, are matters that affect ties with family members because of their strong emotional character, but ties with friends, neighbors, coworkers, bosses and employees are also significant, owing to the bearing they have on such matters as self-esteem and identity. If the disruptions are sudden, they may be regarded as crises; if they are continuing, they may be considered in terms of chronic stress.

Those circumstances that force isolation on individuals are usually imbedded in society and culture. It is this fact that provides the frame of reference for the present chapter, in which I consider social and cultural influences in relation to mental health and mental illness.

The total field is large and parallels those that focus on genetics and on organic factors.

⟨ A Concept of Psychiatric Disorders

The term "psychiatric disorder" is here employed to designate everything commonly found between the covers of a general textbook in psychiatry. It is thus a category such as surgical disorder or medical disorder. I do this as a means of outlining the territory of reference and to avoid the more restrictive connotations of such terms as "mental illness," which might imply psychosis, or "emotional

* The ideas expressed in this chapter are derived from research conducted over many years. I wish to express a strong sense of gratitude to the colleagues who have participated and to the foundations that have given support. Chief among the latter are the Milbank Memorial Fund, the Carnegie Corporation of New York, the Ford Foundation, and the National Institute of Mental Health.

disturbance," which might exclude the cognitive.

The mass of information in a psychiatric text has a number of components: descriptions of behavior, including verbal statements about subjective states; theoretical explanations of these behaviors; descriptions of entities in which behavior and explanations are combined so as to constitute diseases, or illnesses, reaction types, or so on; a nosological system for naming and ordering the entities; and recommendations for treatment according to entities.

The possibility of valid generalization about textbooks stops somewhere close to here. Beyond this point one encounters differences and controversy among clinicians regarding phenomena, theory, and the most suitable ways of organizing the subject matter. There are, for example, the psychoanalysts, the organicists and the eclectics, and there are of course many divisions and crossovers among these. From outside psychiatry and psychology comes theory about sick roles, social determinism, and challenges to a lot of things vaguely labeled "the medical model."

A situation of this sort makes scientific investigation difficult, but not impossible. One course is to adopt certain limited definitions, to hold them tentatively but use them systematically, and to see if they provide a basis for improved definitions and sharper issues for research. This procedure can be described as employing operational definitions in order to advance through successive approximations.

With this in mind, suppose we select that part of the field covered by psychiatric texts concerned with describing behaviors (including both physiological phenomena and expressions about subjective states). This restricted area is still of considerable size in that it contains all the behaviors of major interest to psychiatry, but it does exclude etiological implications and the conceptualization of entities. A tentative ordering can be achieved by accepting, for the time being, such traditional groupings as anxiety, depression, and schizophrenia. We may conceptualize these as patterns, commonly referred to as symptom patterns. Inasmuch, however, as the word "symptom" has connotations of some underlying entity (for example, a disease), it is probably better to say "behaviors of psychiatric interest" (BPI).[5]

The utility of this procedure is that it permits counting the frequency of BPIs in populations and enables one to do so independently of etiological assumptions or interpretations. This is a step toward setting up indicators of psychiatric disorder that can be treated epidemiologically. But more is needed. In addition to discovering something about types and frequencies of BPIs, it is also desirable to learn something about severity.

The notion of severity, as employed clinically, has as a rule two dimensions. One is degree of manifest disability or impairment; the other is the implied seriousness of the condition. This usually involves some expectation with regard to eventual outcome. For example, an anxiety symptom pattern and a schizophrenic symptom pattern could be equally impairing, but the schizophrenic pattern would be considered more serious.

Let us again take the phenomenal rather than the speculative meaning and, rejecting the concept of seriousness, limit ourselves to the disability or impairing aspect, and utilize criteria that bear on interference with work, family, and community roles. Impairment by reason of a BPI can thus be estimated along dimensions from none to severe. There is an advantage here in having a measure of independence between BPI and impairment. In population studies, for example, BPIs can be tabulated and analyzed with or without reference to degree of impairment.

The operational conception of psychiatric disorder presented thus far may be summarized as an array of behavior patterns each of which can vary along a dimension of impairment. Several questions immediately arise, of which two are: Why select this particular conception? What relationship does it have to clinically identifiable psychiatric disorders?

The selection arises from the kinds of questions we wish to ask of nature. Any research on the relationships of societal and cultural factors to psychiatric disorders has to be concerned with the untreated just as much as with the treated, and with the well just as much as with the people who have disorders. This means sampling surveys of total populations, and this in turn puts boundaries on the kind and amount of data that can be obtained from all subjects in a standard manner. Under these circumstances, data on behavior patterns of psychiatric interest are much more feasible than are data pertinent for psychiatric diagnosis (or what Oppenheimer calls "interpretanions").[11]

A second major reason (pertinent to the sociocultural questions we desire to ask) is the need to avoid building causal relationships into the ways the phenomena are defined. It is true, of course, that most of the etiological concepts in dynamic psychiatry are not directly social, but they are indirectly. Mother-child relationships, for example, are differentially affected by cultural variations and by differences in socioeconomic class levels. Further, the repertoire of symbols and their significance may vary markedly under the influence of such factors.

A third point is the fact that clinicians appear to agree among themselves much better regarding BPIs and ratings of impairment than they do on diagnostic formulations.

What is the relationship of BPI to clinically identifiable psychiatric disorders? The last word has not been said on this, but several studies indicate that if an individual has been found by survey methods to have marked BPIs and a significant degree of impairment, a psychiatrist conducting an independent assessment is highly likely to find that the individual is manifesting some kind of clinically identifiable type of disorder. Conversely, it is very rare for the person low in BPIs and who is not impaired to be adjudged as suffering from a psychiatric disorder.[7] There are exceptions in both directions, but it appears safe to say that there is strong association between BPI rating systems and any of several different diagnostic orientations.

This is perhaps enough to indicate the concepts (BPI) with which societal and cultural factors will be approached. There remain still, of course, numerous questions, but they would require more space than is available here.

One, however, may be touched upon in conclusion: What definition of pathology is being employed? I am using a functional definition. Borrowing from Virchow, I would like to suggest that pathology is not only a matter of lesion but of danger to the organism. BPIs are considered pathological when:

1. They constitute a behavior pattern that in some degree places in jeopardy the survival of the individual. Subjective suffering and social disability are both aspects of this.
2. The malfunctioning is self-perpetuating, that is, it tends to persist despite efforts of the individual and/or others to exert control.

(A Concept of Sociocultural Disintegration

Up to this point we have been discussing psychiatric disorders and, by implication, personality. The focus, in short, has been on the individual level of integration, not on biochemistry, cells, organs, or such psychological faculties as cognition and affect but on the functioning of a total system made up of these components.

In this section I should like to direct attention away from individuals to societal systems. This constitutes a major jump, something like moving from cells to a whole person. The meaning of "societal system" may be illustrated by a village or a town. Such a community is a system in that it has patterns of interpersonal behavior that are essential to the survival and welfare of the whole. These patterns enable the group to obtain what is needed for subsistence, protection against weather and disease, control of hostility and other forms of disruption, the creation of new members and their education, disposal of the dead, networks of communication, storage of information, ways for arriving at decisions and taking united action, and much else. Such collective, patterned activities have been called the "functional prerequisites of a society."[1]

A societal system is an integer distinct from the individual level by virtue of having properties that are more than the sum of the components. The components contribute, of course, but the net result is behavior of the whole, consisting in patterns that could not be produced by multiplying individual behaviors. It is rather the product of many, various, and reciprocal behaviors on the part of individuals.

I am putting emphasis on this matter of a "jump" because all of us who have been engrossed in the study of personality have considerable difficulty in thinking of human groups in other than additive terms. Although societal phenomena are dependent on the organic and psychological characteristics of individuals, they can be studied in their own right, and such of course is the business of the social psychologist, the sociologist, and the anthropologist.

To further develop the point, let us note that societal systems (communities) continue to exist while the individuals who compose them enter and leave. The analogy to cells in some parts of the body suggests itself. To a certain degree societal systems are independent of the individuals who compose them, for they can outlast many generations and even survive when large numbers of the constituent individuals are killed, as in an epidemic or war. Conversely, a societal system may flounder, fail in fulfilling its functional prerequisites, and eventually disappear without there being a commensurate mortality among the individuals who compose it. As ghost towns demonstrate, these people may survive through moving away and being absorbed in other systems.

Let us take a moment now to expand the notion of societal system beyond the example selected at the start, a town. What has been said about towns can also be said about larger clusters of people, such as cities. It can be said too of countries and tribes that are composed of many cities and towns. In such cases, the cities and towns are subsystems within the larger whole.

It is also evident that subsystems of another kind exist within the above types of groupings, namely, institutions such as government, in-dustry, and schools. These also exhibit behavior patterns that are more than the sum of individual components, and they generally have a life that extends beyond that of these components.

If a societal system has functional prerequisites, it is evident that it can function well or badly. Historians and statesmen have long had a somewhat organismic view of human groups even though they may not have developed it fully. In Western civilization, writing about functional and malfunctional societal systems appears to have begun in the Greek city states, in the setting of their fierce competition with each other, and their successes and failures. Plato's theories and his attempt to apply them to Syracuse are well known. Gibbon's *Decline and Fall of the Roman Empire* was an effort to look back and comprehend the widespread, catastrophic malfunction of Mediterranean societal systems that ushered in the Dark Ages.*

The notion of societal systems and the notion of good and bad functioning at the societal level are basic to understanding the concept of sociocultural disintegration. It was in relation to this background that my own studies of human groups in disarray[6] led to the ideas summarized in the remainder of this section.

As a beginning, let us imagine two contrasting human groups. One, at an ideal pole of sociocultural integration, we shall call the "model." This is a perfectly functioning community in which subsistence, protection, communications, and all the other functional prerequisites of a society are operating smoothly. In contrast to this, at the opposite pole of utter sociocultural disintegration, is the "collection." Here there is no system, but instead a collection of human beings whose procuring of food, shelter, defense against attacks, and so on are purely individual matters. A passive

* Our present-day understanding of societal functioning takes much of its origin from the sociologist Emile Durkheim and the anthropologists Bronislaw Malinowski and A. R. Radcliffe-Brown. To this should also be added the influence of general systems theory as illustrated in the writings of Ludwig von Bertalanffy and Kenneth Boulding.[12]

inert mass of human beings can be supposed, but it is easier to visualize the conflict of individual interest leading to Hobbes's war of all against all.

It is unlikely that either the collection or the model has ever existed in pure form, but postulating them helps to make two points. (1) A town or other similar type of societal system must be somewhere between these two extremes. Thus, though it may be far from perfect, it may still, in practical terms, be functioning pretty well; or it can be toward the disintegrated pole and gravely impaired with regard to its functional prerequisites and so have little margin separating it from extinction. Such a condition is manifest in such matters as failures of communication, lack of leadership and followership, broken homes, fragmentation and confusion of shared values, and increased intragroup hostility and violence. Degree and type of integration or disintegration thus constitute a frame of reference in terms of which communities can be compared with each other, or the same community with itself at different points in time.* (2) Both integration and disintegration are always going on in any given community at the same time, like anabolism and catabolism. The total process may be looked upon as a dynamic equilibrium that now swings toward greater integration and now toward less. I would suggest, however, that communities moving overall toward the pole of disintegration pass ultimately a threshold from beyond which the ordinary integrative processes are powerless to recall them. There is descent then into a state of chronic malfunction, or possibly extinction of the community.

This frame of reference highlights three questions: What causes communities to reach a state of irreversible disintegration? Can measures of prevention be developed? Once such disintegration has occurred, can it be cured?

At the present moment in history, the im-

portance of these matters hardly needs underlining. It is manifest that sociocultural disintegration is an exceedingly widespread phenomenon. The rise of crime; economic maldistributions; the inadequate coping of administrative bodies; strikes by police, sanitary engineers, transportation workers, hospital staffs, and others; and the melting away of shared values and recognized codes of ethics and conduct are all specific examples of impairment with regard to functional prerequisites such as subsistence, division of labor, communication, protection of various kinds, control of hostility, united action in problem-solving, and so on.

The questions of cause, prevention, and remedy are much in discussion. There is a certain amount of scientific information available for use, but this is overlaid by much else stemming from folklore, political and economic interests, and the blindness of aroused passions. While a behavioral science approach might be of service in solving the problems, the irony is that the scientific approach itself requires a base in a well-integrated societal system. So far as knowledge of cause goes, there appears to be evidence that poverty, migrations, population increase, and rapid social and cultural changes constitute factors that both initiate and then become an expression of sociocultural disintegration, making up many interwoven vicious circles.

Our problem in this chapter is the relationship between sociocultural disintegration and psychiatric disorders. We shall, therefore, deal with the causal factors in sociocultural disintegration only insofar as psychiatric disorders constitute one of them.

⟮ A Theory of the Relationships of Psychiatric Disorders and Sociocultural Disintegration

Sociocultural disintegration, as we have seen, involves societal malfunction. This is part of the definition. Our theory states that this societal malfunction increases the prevalence of psychiatric disorders in the population of the

---

* Discussion of the techniques for measuring integration and disintegration are beyond the scope of this chapter. Suffice it to say that they exist at a first approximation level and that refinement of instruments is a major area for investigation.

affected societal system.[4] This process occurs in multiple ways, some of which may be described as follows.

1. Through an increase in the frequency of organic diseases. This occurs because the functioning of medical institutions (for example, hospitals, outpatient care, and public health services) shares in the disintegration and also because economic difficulties and failures in the coordination and administrative aspects of the societal system result in an increase of unsanitary conditions and a reduction of food resources leading to widespread malnutrition. In short, the more a community is disintegrated, the less it is able to protect itself against organic disease.

As illnesses based on infection grow, and as accidents and malnutrition increase, there is a proportional increase in those psychiatric disorders in which the organic component plays a major role. These may include brain damage from syphilitic and viral diseases, damage to the central nervous system by lack of B-complex and other vitamins, and brain damage from poorly conducted parturition and from prenatal illnesses, such as rubella.

This is probably enough for illustration. The central idea is that even though some of the diseases of civilization, such as those based on a too rich diet, might be improved by disintegration, the net effect would be major increase in morbidity with a consequent increase in all psychiatric disorders in which organic factors play a key part in the etiological complex. In practical terms we would expect to see this in war-shattered populations and those torn up by uncontrolled migrations, such as the septic fringe and deteriorated core of many cities. We would expect it in populations whose societal systems had been disintegrated because of economic disasters and in communities where the process of social and cultural change had become accelerated to the point that the consequent failures in function were so marked and so widespread as to push these systems beyond the threshold of spontaneous recovery.

Furthermore, as the general level of morbidity rose, one could expect that this too would become progressively more and more

of a factor in the disintegration process, adding a new malfunctional cycle to the numbers already in progress. That is to say, the more people ill, the fewer to manage the roles in the societal system. The ill thus constitute a diminution in the system's resources for recovery and an increment toward disintegration. BPIs from intellectual deficiencies, emotional labilities, and other manifestations of brain damage would constitute a significant part of this morbidity.

2. Through failure of the child-nurturing and child-rearing patterns of the societal system. Due to economic breakdowns, the dissolution of codes of conduct, and the evaporation of shared sentiments, the growing child must experience many influences detrimental to the growth of a well-functioning personality. There would be a greater frequency of maternal deprivation, inadequate or absent father figures, and such incongruities and discontinuities in peer relationships as render the interpersonal medium in which personality formation occurs both noxious and distorting.[*]

Altogether, then, where social disintegration has lasted long enough to see generations grow up through its noxious influence, there would appear more and more individuals with impairing BPIs of the type associated with neurosis, psychosis, and personality disorders. As with the mainly organically based psychiatric disorders, these would add in turn to the forces making for sociocultural disintegration. Such would be particularly true of the personality disorders, with their asocial, dyssocial, and antisocial manifestations.

3. Through stress applied during youth, middle life, and old age. The notion here is that BPIs are in part manifestations of psychological strain derived from experiencing the world as a sea of frustrations, terrors, and disappointments. Very little works out according to hopes, and almost nothing has meaning. Such conditions are due to the lack of shared values, lack of standards and codes of behavior, and lack of opportunity for satisfaction of

---

* Beiser[2] analyzes this process in relation to Erikson's eight ages of man.

such basic needs as freedom from fear, access to love and respect, a sense of belonging to a worthwhile group, and opportunity for the expression of spontaneity.

The above theory of stress and strain requires some elucidation: Personalities are seen as dynamic systems, and certain conditions of the societal environment constitute stress to which the systems react. When the stress is prolonged and severe, the reactions have a tendency to become chronic, malfunctional, and to persist after the stress has been removed. In other words, manifest psychiatric disorders emerge.

In accepting societal stress as part of the etiological complex involved in the production of psychiatric disorders, it is not necessary to scrap psychodynamic theories. It may well be that many people have neurotic personalities as a result of experiences in early life. Social stress theory would assume that some of these could be so severe as to be evident in even the most benign environment. It would also assume that most people are able, under favorable conditions, to control or adapt their neurotic tendencies so that no very impairing BPIs result. Under stress from societal disintegration, however, the functional adaptations give way, and impairing BPIs emerge. The more severe and prolonged the disintegration, the greater the stress and the larger the proportion of people in the population who would manifest disorder. Finally, it can be assumed that when stress is sufficiently prolonged and severe, even persons without a neurotic predisposition will suffer damage to the personality and begin to show malfunctional, hard to reverse patterns of behavior characteristic of psychiatric disorders.

As indicated under points one and two, here also the psychiatric product of sociocultural disintegration becomes a contributor and adds to the network of interlinked deteriorating cycles, which, like chain mail, resist efforts to penetrate and modify. Anxiety, hostility, and delusional behaviors increase, short-term remedies such as drugs and the excitement of violence are sought, whereas long-range and cognitive efforts decline.

(Illustrative Findings and Interpretations

In the Stirling County study, covering ninety-seven communities, a number of settlements were identified as exemplifying disintegration, and others, integration, utilizing sociological and cultural criteria. Neither group was at the extreme of the continuum, nor was it static; what the labels indicate is that within the range offered by the county, some communities lay more toward disintegration and others more toward integration. To this may now be added what became an evident fact: Differences between these two categories of settlements were considerable, with most of the ninety-seven communities occupying a place between the settlements at the extremes.

When the prevalence of BPIs and their degree of impairment were assessed by means of samples, it was found that by and large the disintegrated groups had a much higher prevalence rate of impairing BPIs than did the well-integrated groups.

This statement sums up the findings in a very by and large fashion. The observations that underlie it are numerous and various, and the statistical treatment is intricate. It is necessary to incorporate qualifications and to consider alternatives at numerous points in the course of building logical inferences.[8,9]

A few selected major points may be noted as follows.

1. The settlements in question were small, ranging in size from 100 to 450. Generalization from these to other societal systems of different size and composition is not as yet justified on the basis of any well-controlled body of data. The theoretical frame of reference, however, does postulate a strong relationship between societal disintegration and high prevalence of psychiatric disorders and would expect it to be demonstrable in many different kinds of communities and without regard to size. From this point of view, the Stirling County study results constitute specific instances of general process relationships, dis-

sected out by the research and made visible. Parallel studies conducted in Nigeria have given similar findings.

2. The study dealt exclusively with adults. Hence it remains for future investigation to probe the theoretical expectations regarding the noxious effect of growing up in a disintegrated societal system. The expectation, however, remains highly plausible because the characteristics of child-parent and child-peer relationships in such situations fulfill criteria of noxiousness from the viewpoint of virtually any psychological theory of development from psychoanalysis to operant conditioning.

3. The sample of respondents used in Stirling County to estimate the prevalence of BPIs were the same individuals who contributed a major part (though not all) of the data pertaining to estimates of community integration and disintegration. This raises the possibility of one variable being contaminated by another. People suffering from anxiety and depression, for example, may see their communities in more negative terms than do others. Conversely, lack of social control may appear at the individual level as personality disorder of the sociopathic type.

The above is a serious problem, and it is highly desirable to develop techniques that employ different samples for the two main sets of variables and that base estimates of integration-disintegration on observed behaviors, excluding respondent opinions.

On the other hand, despite the need for such progressive refinement, the issue does not really call in question the correlation of high frequency of disorder with marked sociocultural disintegration. There are plenty of BPIs and indicators of disintegration that are not open to any reasonable suspicion of contamination. Psychophysiological manifestations and behaviors characteristic of anxiety are not individual expressions of such societal variables as lack of leaders, deficient communications, or broken families. It is more plausible to suppose they are either cause or consequence.

4. The correlations demonstrated in the Stirling study do not prove that the societal factors are the cause of the psychological. It

could be either way, or both together interacting, the joint result of some third influence. Our theoretical frame of reference suggests the high probability that in the present state of the world, there are many physical and sociocultural forces at work creating disintegrated societal systems, and that chronologically the beginning of the interacting, malfunctional cycle (or spiral) is most commonly a tear in the social fabric. If our theoretical orientation bears resemblance to what is going on in nature, then a prime issue for the welfare of mankind is to find where effective intervention can be applied. It appears virtually certain that the individual treatment level alone will not suffice. Discovering ways to prevent or reverse sociocultural disintegration is thus a central issue in the mental health field.

Figure 28–1 depicts the distribution of im-

FIGURE 28–1.   **Variation in ABCD Ridit with Age and Sex.**

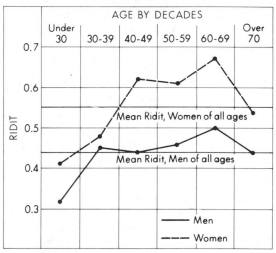

(Reprinted from D. C. Leighton et al., *The Character of Danger: Psychiatric Symptoms in Selected Communities*, Vol. III [New York: Basic Books, 1963], p. 255. Reprinted with permission.)

pairing BPIs according to age and sex. The statistic used here is the "ridit"[9] rather than percentage, and this is done in order to be congruent with previous publications. For the purposes of this chapter it is probably sufficient to note that 0.50 is the mean for the entire Stirling County sample. Ridits above this are indicative of more psychiatric disorder than the mean, and ridits below indicate less. The ridits are based on ratings which in turn are based on BPIs.

Table 28–1 shows the ridits according to disintegrated areas, well-integrated areas, and the county. The figures suggest not only the predicted relationship between psychiatric disorder and sociocultural disintegrative process but also a marked difference between men and women in this relationship. Attention may be drawn to the following:

1. Overall, women have a higher prevalence rate than men. This difference increases with age.
2. Both sexes have the highest rates in the middle years, and both have some dropping off of frequency with age.
3. In disintegrated areas, there is little difference between men and women; what difference there is appears to be toward greater frequency in men.
4. In well-integrated areas, the marked sex difference persists, but it may be in either direction. Thus in one integrated community the men have a higher rate than the women, albeit both are lower than the mean. In another integrated community, the women have a very much higher rating than the men: The women are ten ridits above the mean ("more ill"), while the men are ten units below. This suggests that what may be a benign environment for one sex may be noxious to the other. Disintegration, however, is apparently bad for both.

Further work conducted since 1952 suggests that differences of this sort may be associated with role stress. In other words, in sociocultural systems undergoing marked change, certain societal roles come under more stress than others, and sometimes the most stressful roles are those determined by sex, in some cases male, in other cases female. There is also some evidence to suggest that similar differences apply to roles determined by age, so that in one population certain younger roles may be more stressful, whereas in others the pressures are felt in roles characteristic of older persons. All these points are invitations for further research in areas that are of maximum significance at the present time.

❨ Some Implications

The BPI approach opens possibilities for re-examination and new understanding regarding the nature of psychiatric disorders. This is by means of opportunities for reliability and numerical treatment.

For example, BPIs can be derived from representative samples of community populations and analyzed through multivariant methods.[a] By these techniques it should be possible to find out which BPIs hang together in such a manner as to indicate dimensions. What is presently considered psychoneurotic anxiety, for example, may be resolved into several distinctive patterns. Further, since BPI surveys gather data from individuals along the entire range from those with none to those with highly impairing BPIs, it is possible for patterns to emerge that constitute syndromes not previously recognized by psychiatry. This could be the case if the syndromes are mild or if they are of such a nature as to lead the individuals so affected to avoid medical consultation.

TABLE 28–1.   **Mean ABCD Ridits for the Disintegrated Areas, Fairhaven and Lavallee, and the County by Sex**[*]

| | DISINTEGRATED AREAS | WELL INTEGRATED | | WHOLE COUNTY |
		Fairhaven	*Lavallee*	
Men	0.68	0.43	0.47	0.44
Women	0.65	0.60	0.40	0.55

[*] Modified from D. C. Leighton et al., *The Character of Danger: Psychiatric Symptoms in Selected Communities*, Vol. III (New York: Basic Books, 1963), p. 330.

A revised and refined descriptive psychiatry based on BPIs would facilitate the investigation of etiologies on both a wide and more intensive basis. Because of its nature, this procedure does not in itself foreclose on explanations, but rather opens questions for inquiry. It anticipates that a given BPI may be a final common path for more than one cause or for several causes in combination. The way is, therefore, prepared for systematic study and, where consistent relationships can be found between etiological factors and particular pattern characteristics, a diagnosis in the full sense of the word may become possible.

Conversely, there is the possibility of uncovering the range and variation of BPIs that may be associated with a given noxious factor.

The above comments refer to all kinds of possible causes, not just to those that are social and cultural. Further, within the sociocultural field, the comments have wider applicability than the elucidation of the relationship of mental health and mental illness to integration and disintegration. Disintegration can account for only a part (albeit an important part) of the disorder variance in populations. For example, there is much evidence to indicate that integrated communities can develop mass delusions and shared passions that are self-perpetuating and highly dangerous for survival. History is full of examples, many of which focus on religious and political ideologies. Without depending on such dramatic extremes as the crusades, witch hunts, or the dancing manias of the Middle Ages, it should still be possible to examine the process of social cohesiveness and its relationship to BPIs. The use of drugs and alcohol, antisocial behavior such as violence, and the spread of apprehension, despair, and suicide are contemporary examples in which both disintegration and integration play a part, with the latter taking the form of closely bound groups, somewhat detached from the larger society. They apparently arise, at least in part, as a reintegrative reaction to disintegration, but they can often serve to augment rather than stem the general trend toward disintegration.

Conceptualizing psychiatric disorders in terms of BPIs provides a way to avoid becoming polemically stuck on such issues as the appropriativeness of the medical model and whether, after all, mental illness is a myth, the product of role definitions. The real, underlying problems are rather those concerned with how the BPIs affect individuals and the community in which they live. Are the patterns disturbing to the person? Are they disturbing to others? Are they easily reversed, or do they require special methods? If so, what methods: drugs, psychotherapy, group therapy, development of coping abilities, or alteration of the societal environment? If several of these together, what is the best combination?

A further point about BPI surveys derives from the fact that they bring to the fore persons who are at the zero end of the range, that is, persons in the population who do not have BPIs and who by this definition are healthy. These constitute a type of individual little examined in psychiatry. Their comparative study with persons who are impaired owing to BPIs sets the stage for describing patterns of health and elucidating their etiologies, utilizing procedures parallel to those employed with regard to BPIs. This means an empirical approach, something very different from much previous work on positive mental health, in which the starting point was frequently a theoretical or ideal construct for defining a mentally healthy personality.

The assessment of sociocultural systems in terms of the integration-disintegration frame of reference leads to theory that has some explanatory power. It provides, for example, an answer to the question as to why so many studies have found a high frequency of psychiatric disorders in the lower socioeconomic class levels: The stress of life in these classes is essentially that of living in a socioculturally disintegrated environment. In the Stirling County study there are some incomplete data that suggest that when low socioeconomic status is not accompanied by sociocultural disintegration, the prevalence of BPIs is no greater than in the white-collar levels. A study in Sweden of a rural area has suggested that when the lowest socioeconomic class is well integrated it may have a low prevalence of disorders.[10]

The potential for explanation is not limited to matters of class difference. It can also be called upon to explain why rapid cultural change sometimes does and sometimes does not involve a high frequency of BPIs. The same applies to populations undergoing migration. In other words, one can say that low socioeconomic class, rapid cultural change, and migration have in common that they constitute a state of risk with respect to sociocultural disintegration. If the disintegration occurs, there is a rise in the frequency of impairing BPIs. If adaptation of the societal system occurs without disintegration, no rise in BPIs will take place. What is needed now is further work to define the limits of this explanatory power and to delineate the processes involved more specifically.

The usefulness of disintegration theory, however, depends in part on the further development and refinement of method so that the data will be at the same level of objectivity, reliability, and susceptibility to numerical treatment as the BPIs.

On the basis of such methodological advances, it should be possible to begin the investigation and definition of disintegration thresholds, that is, the point beyond which reversal of trend toward organizational breakdown becomes impossible without intervention from the outside. Related to this are a host of problems regarding the nature of the threshold. Chief among these, from a mental health point of view, is the impact on the societal system of increasing the frequency of impairing BPIs. Is the threshold in a large measure determined by a saturation point of BPIs in a population such that coping behavior is overwhelmed and a downward spiral established?

The causes of integration and their relationship to mental health and mental illness are a field of investigation comparable with that of studying the causes of disintegration, and largely open to the same kinds of method. Its importance attaches to the possibility of discovering how benign cycles may come into existence, that is, the counterpart of the vicious cycles and downward spirals. How do mutually reinforcing trends toward integration and low BPIs appear? Further, is the beneficial dimension of integration (so far as mental health is concerned) a curvilinear one? Is there an optimal point of integration beyond which the BPIs begin to rise again because the societal system is too rigid to accommodate human needs? As patterns of mental health become clearer, will it be possible to identify levels and types of integration that are stultifying with regard to these modes of adaptation? Do societal systems have a built-in tendency to oscillate about some optimal point of integration, due perhaps to overintegration leading through increased BPIs toward disintegration?

Turning now to the practical implications for service, the central issue is: How much of what has been said in previous pages can be accepted as a legitimate basis for action? From this point of view, I would like to suggest that the following assumptions are tenable.

1. There is considerably more psychiatric disorder in populations generally than is being reached by any existing system of delivering services. Much of this is low level in the sense that hospitalization is not indicated, but it represents a considerable amount of suffering and great hampering of interpersonal relations among millions and millions of people.
2. Certain kinds of societal conditions are strongly associated with high frequencies of disorder in populations. Many of these conditions are open to modification.

If one is willing to accept these two assumptions, it follows that the weight of evidence and the force of logic call for revision of service patterns and the development of action programs aimed at modifying noxious sociocultural factors. The theory of sociocultural disintegration can be of help in establishing priorities and in giving some idea of the processes with which change efforts will have to cope.

Arguments against attempts to improve the sociocultural environment (such as some clinicians have made) can no longer be justified by saying, "There is no proof that preventive measures work." To insist on such proof prior to action is to demand more than is demanded for psychotherapeutic effort. Instead of "Prove it before we do it," the emphasis can be placed on "Let us do it, but with controls so we can learn from the doing and evaluate the results."

If we consider first the matter of dealing with individuals who are burdened with impairing BPIs, it seems likely that there will continue to be a place for some long-term one-to-one psychotherapy with and without the aid of drugs. Aside from this, however, is the pressing need for psychiatry to set up the present trend toward redefining its roles and functions so that many of these can be conducted by paraprofessionals and by professionals who have shorter periods of training. The same applies to the other mental health professions, namely psychology, social work, nursing, and occupational therapy. In particular, one may note the importance of having these five professional groups continue to work together to redefine their respective roles in order to achieve a more efficient distribution of tasks. These activities would span treatment, the reduction of disability, counseling, and crisis intervention.

When we turn to the problem of change in noxious sociocultural factors, it appears very likely that there is need for the development of a new kind of professional whose competence might be in at least three fields: mental health, societal systems, and applied behavioral sciences. If we take the mental health center as an example, this professional could hold a position with some such title as "Director of Community Relations." The aim would be for him and his staff to work with the other human services in the community and in the planning phase of new developments with a view to environmental enrichment and the reduction of noxious influences. His methods would be catalytic and facilitative, with two main objectives: (1) to interject mental health considerations where needed in the present services and planned enterprises of the community, and (2) to stimulate the develop-

ment of planned change where this is not occurring but is needed from a mental health point of view. As part of these objectives he would be concerned with helping to bring the other members of the mental health center in contact with those parts of the community in which they are needed and where they would have opportunity of being influential. He could augment their knowledge of the community, aid in identifying high-risk groups, and assist in the development and adjustments of the center's own plans and policies.

There are many other implications of a practical nature, but since the notion of this new kind of mental health professional, the community catalyst, is the most outstanding, it is perhaps the appropriate place to stop.

⟪ Bibliography

1. ABERLE, D. F., et al. "The Functional Prerequisites of a Society." *Ethics*, 9 (1950), 100–111.

2. BEISER, M. "Poverty, Social Disintegration and Personality." In M. Palmer, ed., *The Human Factor in Political Development*. Waltham, Mass.: Ginn, 1970. Pp. 118–142.

3. BENFARI, R. C., and LEIGHTON, A. H. "Comparison of Factor Structures in Urban New York and Rural Nova Scotia Population Samples: A Study in Psychiatric Epidemiology." In I. Kessler and M. Levin, eds., *The Community as an Epidemiologic Laboratory: A Casebook of Community Studies*. Baltimore, Md.: Johns Hopkins Press, 1970. Pp. 235–251.

4. LEIGHTON, A. H. "Psychiatric Disorder and the Social Environment: An Outline for a Frame of Reference." In B. Bergen and C. Thomas, eds., *Issues and Problems in Social Psychiatry: A Book of Readings*. Springfield, Ill.: Charles C Thomas, 1966. Pp. 155–197.

5. ———. "Is Social Environment a Cause of Psychiatric Disorder?" In R. Monroe, G. Klee, and E. Brody, eds., *Psychiatric Epidemiology and Mental Health Planning*. Psychiatric Research Report, no. 22. Washington, D.C.: American Psychiatric Association, 1967. Pp. 337–345.

6. ———. "Cosmos in the Gallup City Dump."

In B. Kaplan, ed., *Psychiatric Disorder and the Urban Environment: Report of the Cornell Social Science Center.* New York: Behavioral Publications, 1971. Pp. 4–12.

7. ———, LEIGHTON, D. C., and DANLEY, R. A. "Validity in Mental Health Surveys." *Canadian Psychiatric Association Journal,* 11 (1966), 167–178.

8. ———, et al. *Psychiatric Disorder among the Yoruba.* Ithaca, N.Y.: Cornell University Press, 1963.

9. LEIGHTON, D. C., et al. *The Character of Danger: Psychiatric Symptoms in Selected Communities.* New York: Basic Books, 1963.

10. ———. "Psychiatric Disorder in a Swedish and a Canadian Community: An Exploratory Study." *Social Science and Medicine,* 5 (1971), 189–209.

11. OPPENHEIMER, H. *Clinical Psychiatry: Issues and Challenges.* New York: Harper & Row, 1971.

12. SHELDON, A., BAKER, F., and McLAUGHLIN, C. P. *Systems and Medical Care.* Cambridge: Massachusetts Institute of Technology Press, 1970.

CHAPTER 29

PSYCHIATRIC DISORDERS IN URBAN SETTINGS*

Bruce P. Dohrenwend and Barbara Snell Dohrenwend

T HE CITIES are bearing the brunt of technological and social dislocations in
modern society. They cannot house,
let alone educate, and in some cases they are
not even able to feed or provide adequate sanitation for their populations. They are crime
ridden and sometimes riot torn. So goes the
story from New York to Tokyo with stops
around the world. What are the consequences
for the people who live in these disturbed centers of modern societies?

One answer is suggested by psychiatric critics of the social order such as Lawrence K.
Frank,[29] who wrote in 1936:

Our so-called social problems . . . are to be
viewed as arising from the frantic efforts of individuals, lacking any sure direction and sanctions

or guiding conception of life, to find some way of
protecting themselves or of merely existing on any
terms they can manage in a society being remade
by technology. Having no strong loyalties and no
consistent values or realizable ideals to cherish,
the individual's conduct is naturally conflicting,
confused, neurotic and antisocial. . . . (pp.
339–340)

Our aim in this chapter is to examine the empirical evidence bearing on such speculations
with a view to analyzing the theoretical,
methodological, and practical issues posed.

◖ Some Incongruities between Speculation and Fact

Popular and influential speculations such as
Frank's[29] have led to a number of studies designed to put them to the test. One is the investigation by Goldhamer and Marshall[37] of

* This work was supported in part by Research
Grant MH 10328 and by Research Scientist Award
IK5-MH14663 from the National Institute of Mental
Health, U.S. Public Health Service.

hospital first admissions between 1840 and 1940 in the state of Massachusetts. As Glazer[34, p. 117] noted in an essay introducing their work,

It would appear a truism to assert that man, subjected to an increasingly inhuman (or at any rate nonhuman) environment, increasingly breaks down under the strain. And indeed, all around us are huge installations which we know house many thousands of the mentally disordered, and the budgets of state governments groan under the pressure of maintaining them and building more. Surely all this, if not new, is far more characteristic of our present-day lives than of life a hundred years ago. But *are* we sure?

The finding of Goldhamer and Marshall that the rates of functional psychoses of the early and middle years had not varied over a hundred-year period would seem to indicate that in fact we cannot be sure that a change has occurred. Their finding is restricted, however, to treated rates and does not include the full range of psychiatric disorders. Moreover, Goldhamer and Marshall raised the possibility that the conditions of urban life had been sufficiently established by 1840 so that they would have had to go back another hundred years to test the effects of the most important changes. Unfortunately, such data are not available.

Nevertheless, Goldhamer and Marshall's findings are surprising, in part because they are based on treated cases. It has long been known that rates of treated psychiatric disorder vary with the availability of treatment facilities, which surely must have increased from 1840 to 1940, and with public attitudes toward their use.[18, pp. 5–7] In fact, conclusions about the traumatic psychiatric effects of industrialization have been criticized for their reliance on treated rates of disorder, usually treatment in mental hospitals. Though such investigations typically show much higher rates of first admissions to mental institutions for persons residing in urban than for persons residing in rural areas,[87] Mott and Roemer[75] noted:

Not only are mental hospital beds considerably less available to rural people, but rural attitudes are such that even with mental institutions available, the rural family is more typically opposed to "committing" one of its members. The social milieu in rural areas, in fact, not only discourages institutionalization of mental cases but actually creates less urgent need for it. Even when conclusions are drawn from mental hospital admissions within one state, therefore (with the same facilities supposedly being available for both rural and urban residents), one cannot be impressed with findings of lower rural mental disease rates. (pp. 140–141)

Accordingly, Mott and Roemer suggested that World War II Selective Service statistics on psychiatric rejections based on actual examinations of potential inductees provide more suitable evidence. On the basis of their analysis of some of this evidence, they concluded[75, p. 141] that "Selective Service examinations in this country, in fact, have shown the highest rates for most mental disorders to occur in the most rural communities. Star[93] and Ginzberg, Anderson, Ginsberg, and Herma[33, pp. 189–192] showed, however, that such comparisons on the basis of national Selective Service statistics are extremely difficult to interpret, owing to the vastly different diagnostic procedures and administrative practices applied at the various induction stations as well as the strong influence of educational level on the rejection rate.

The problem of unreliability in diagnostic standards is less prominent in a study of one particular induction station than in comparisons across induction stations. Thus, by investigating men examined at the Boston Armed Forces Induction Station from both rural and urban communities during the winter, spring, and summer months of 1941 and 1942, Hyde and Kingsley[50] provided some useful data on the problem that suggest that rural and urban differences are vastly more complicated than was suggested by Mott and Roemer.[75] Hyde and Kingsley found that Boston, the largest city in the area, had the highest rejection rates for total psychiatric disorder and for the subtypes of chronic alcoholism and psychopathic personality. The most rural areas (described as semirural by the investigators), however, were a close second in total rates and highest in rates of mental deficiency, psychoneurosis, and psychosis. Intermediate on most rates were the moderate sized cities, small cities, and towns, which were categorized by the investigators as of generally higher socioeconomic level than either Boston or the semi-rural communities in these comparisons. As Hyde and Kingsley[50] emphasized, however, the population served by the Boston induction station was predominantly urban. The rural versus urban contrast may not, therefore, be as sharply drawn in this study as we would like.

A more clearly rural setting provided the basis for a study by Eaton and Weil,[25] who noted the views of a famous skeptic:[26, p. 47] "In some happy corners of the earth, they say, where nature brings forth abundantly whatever man desires, there flourish races whose lives go gently by, unknowing of aggression or constraint. This I can hardly credit; I would like further details of these happy folk." Their own review of the existing literature led Eaton and Weil to agree with Freud's skepticism and to suggest that speculations associating simple rural life with good mental health were based on anecdotal observations of primitive societies that might be psychiatrically incomplete. To provide more systematic data they set out to study the Hutterites, a group with a strong reputation for mental health based on just such anecdotal accounts.

The Hutterites are an ethnic enclave of about 8,500 persons who have lived for more than ninety years in the United States and Canada. They comprise a religiously oriented and self-sufficient communal society with a secure agrarian economy. This extraordinarily stable Hutterite society has been highly effective in providing cradle to grave support for its members. Has it also protected them from psychiatric disorder?

On the basis of direct interviews and key informant reports from members of the Hutterite population, Eaton and Weil arrived at a rate of psychosis that ranked the Hutterites as third highest of ten populations with which they were compared, higher, for example, than the urban and far from affluent eastern health district of Baltimore. Noting that population comparisons are difficult to make given the methodological problems involved in epidemiological studies, the investigators[25, p. 209] concluded cautiously that the "findings do not confirm the hypothesis that a simple and relatively uncomplicated way of life provides virtual immunity from mental disorders."

Inkeles and Smith[52] reached a far less conservative conclusion on the basis of their recent study of young male farmers, industrial workers, and urban nonindustrial workers in six countries: Argentina, Chile, East Pakistan, India, Israel, and Nigeria. Drawing from batteries used in a number of well-known previous studies conducted mainly in the United States,[39,61,65,92] these investigators[52, p. 85] obtained a "psychosomatic symptom test" to measure "mental health" or "adjustment." Their results led them[52, pp. 110–113] to conclude:

We believe . . . that . . . the theory which sees the transition from village to city and from farm to factory as inherently deleterious to mental health must be, if not wholly discarded, at least drastically reformulated. . . . Our investigation suggests that in developing countries . . . salubrious experiences are no less enjoyed by those who have moved to the city and have taken up industrial employment than by those who continue to pursue the bucolic life of cultivators in the bosom of their traditional villages.

The generalizations we can make from this study are limited, however, since the psychosomatic symptom test used to measure mental health is hardly adequate to measure the full range and variety of types of psychiatric disorder.[17] Moreover, the samples studied do not represent the populations of the rural and urban communities from which they were drawn. They are instead work-site samples of young men who, as the authors pointed out, were all adapted in the sense that they held steady jobs. Results from such selected samples, as the work of Indik, Seashore, and Slesinger[51] with a similar symptom inventory suggests, cannot be extrapolated to general populations. It seems possible, for example, that in focusing on work-site samples of employed persons, Inkeles and Smith missed the most pathogenic aspects of urban living.

As possible indication of the nature of these more pathogenic features, consider the picture portrayed by Calhoun's[9] experiments on the effects of crowding on rats. Calhoun[9, p. 144] observed closely a phenomenon that is "the outcome of any behavioral process that collects animals together in great number"; it is called a "behavioral sink." In his own experiments, this sink took the form of an especially high concentration of animals around a particular (but not the only) food source that was located in one of the central pens in which the experimental animals were placed and in which they bred.

As Calhoun[9, p. 144] noted, "The unhealthy connotations of the term are not accidental: a behavioral sink does act to aggravate all forms of pathology that can be found within a group." Thus, for example, "Females that lived in the densely populated middle pens became progressively less adept at building adequate nests and eventually stopped building nests at all."[9, p. 145] Some males were "completely passive and moved through the community like somnambulists. They ignored all the other rats of both sexes and all the other rats ignored them."[9, p. 146] And still another type of male developed who took no part in the general status struggle but functioned as a kind of oversexed rapist who also engaged in cannibalistic behavior. In general, the effects of crowding, most prominent in the behavioral sink, were to disrupt "vital modes of behavior such as courting of sex partners, building of nests and the nursing and care of the young."[9, p. 139]

How accurate, however, are these investigations of rats as experimental analogues of major conditions and consequences of modern urban living? Some results from a study of "the city that has probably the highest residential densities ever known in the world"[74, p. 18] suggest that the nightmare vision Calhoun's experiments call forth is more fantasy than fact when applied to human beings. The city is Hong Kong and the study, recently reported by Mitchell,[74] is based on three large-scale sample surveys of both adults and children. Mitchell's description[74, p. 21] will give you some idea of the meaning of the word "density" as applied to the inhabitants of dwelling units in Hong Kong:

The median size dwelling unit in the urbanized areas of the colony has 400 square feet, and the median square feet per person is 43. Thirty-nine percent of the Hong Kong respondents report that they share their dwelling unit with nonkinsmen; 28 percent sleep three or more to a bed; 13 percent sleep four or more to a bed. . . . High density dwelling units could be labeled "poor housing," for they are the most likely not to have tap water, flush toilets, and cross ventilation. They are also most likely to have only one room per unit, to have ten or more people in the unit, and to have two or more unrelated families sharing the same unit.

In striking contrast to what might be expected on the basis of sheer extrapolation from Calhoun's results, Mitchell found no relationship between density per se and measures of strain consisting of a battery of psychosomatic symptoms similar to those used by Inkeles and Smith[52] and items on impairment of functioning focusing on withdrawal from family roles and withdrawal from work roles. He concluded that after suitable controls are introduced on such factors as income, density within dwelling units shows only a limited range of effects. Moreover, these effects do not appear to extend to those symptom and impairment data he collected that were most directly relevant to measuring psychiatric disorders. Let us note, for future reference, however, that among the limited range of effects Mitchell reported is one bearing on parental supervision of their children. The higher the density in the dwelling unit, the less the tendency for the parents to discourage their children from leaving the house. The side effect of this is to reduce the parents knowledge of and control over their children.

Rates of Psychiatric Disorders in Rural and Urban Settings

Whatever their limitations, the investigations described above are quite sufficient to give us pause about the accuracy of popular speculations linking urbanized, technologically oriented social settings to psychiatric disorder.

Do we have, then, any other evidence with which to resolve the questions of fact these speculations pose? Fortunately, over the last half century there have accumulated forty epidemiological studies carried out in a variety of social settings in America, Europe, Asia, and Africa with the aim of counting not only treated cases but also untreated cases of a wide range of psychiatric disorders.

In an earlier analysis[18, pp. 11–12] we found that these rates, most of which represent prevalence for a limited time period, ranged from under 1 percent to 64 percent in the communities studied. Inquiry into what could account for variation of such magnitude produced a series of disconcerting answers. There were no consistent differences in total prevalence rates according to the geopolitical area of the world nor, within geopolitical areas, according to urban or rural study site. Rather, the variability was found to be related to differences in thoroughness of data collection procedures and, even more, to contrasting conceptions of what constitutes a case of psychiatric disorder.[18, pp. 95–99]

Given the major methodological differences that these variable rates reflect, direct comparison of the rates obtained by different investigators is frustrating and uninformative. It is possible, however, to compare different studies in terms of the relationships between disorder and various factors, such as age, sex, and social class. In this way, in previous analyses[18, p. 17] we found consistent relationships between rates of overall psychiatric disorder and social class; we also[18, pp. 24–31] found consistent relationships between various subtypes of disorder and sex as well as social class. We will see, then, whether further analyses of this type will enlighten us about rural versus urban differences.

Seven of the epidemiological investigators or teams of investigators reported data from both rural and urban segments of the populations they studied, with two reporting data for two settings each divided into rural and urban portions. Thus, we can look at nine comparisons of rural and urban rates. As Table 29–1 shows, in one comparison the total rate is higher in the rural setting; there is one tie; and in the remaining seven comparisons the urban rate is higher than the rural rate. Note, however, that most of the differences are not large.

Table 29–2 gives us some indication of why the rural-urban differences in total rates are generally small. While some types of psychiatric disorder tend to be more prevalent in urban settings, there are others that tend to appear more frequently in rural settings. That is, total rates for all psychoses combined tend to be higher in the rural than in the urban area in these comparisons, and this appears to

TABLE 29–1.   **Percentage of Psychiatric Disorder Reported for Investigations Including Both Urban and Rural Study Sites**

URBAN	RURAL	URBAN MINUS RURAL	AUTHOR(S)
0.8	1.7	− 0.9	Kato[55]
1.1	1.1[a]	0.0	Lin[66]
1.11	1.03	+ 0.08	Kaila[53] (study 2)
1.28	1.07	+ 0.21	Kaila[53] (study 1)
3.0[b]	2.7[b]	+ 0.3	Tsuwaga et al.,[98] Akimoto et al.[1c]
13.5	11.7	+ 1.8	Piotrowski et al.[83] (Ciechanow)
45.0	40.0	+ 5.0	A. H. Leighton et al.[64]
18.1	13.0	+ 5.1	Piotrowski et al.[83] (Plock)
34.1[b]	20.2[b]	+13.9	Helgason[44]

a Rate for more rural of two relatively rural areas studied.
b Calculated by B. S. Dohrenwend.
c Studies carried out by overlapping teams from the Neuropsychiatric Department of Tokyo University.

TABLE 29–2. **Percentage Rates According to Diagnostic Category from Studies Reporting Results for Both Urban and Rural Sites**

	URBAN	RURAL	URBAN MINUS RURAL	AUTHORS
Rates of Psychosis	0.00	2.00	−2.00	A. H. Leighton et al.[64a,b]
	5.29[c]	6.50[c]	−1.21	Helgason[44d]
	0.77	0.99	−0.22	Piotrowski et al.[83a] (Ciechanow)
	0.37[c]	0.49[c]	−0.12	Tsuwaga et al.,[98] Akimoto et al.[1e]
	0.27[c]	0.34[c,f]	−0.07	Lin[66]
	1.01	0.65	+0.36	Kaila[53] (study 1)
	0.80	0.31	+0.49	Piotrowski et al.[83a] (Plock)
Rates of Schizophrenia	0.00	1.00	−1.00	A. H. Leighton et al.[64a,b]
	0.36[c]	1.34[c]	−0.98	Helgason[44d]
	0.21	0.18[f]	+0.03	Lin[66]
	0.39	0.21	+0.18	Tsuwaga et al.,[98] Akimoto et al.[1e]
	0.64	0.38	+0.26	Kaila[53] (study 1)
Rates of Manic-Depressive Psychosis	0.07[c]	0.29[c]	−0.22	Tsuwaga et al.,[98] Akimoto et al.[1e]
	2.18[c]	2.34[g]	−0.16	Helgason[44d]
	0.05	0.07[f]	−0.02	Lin[66]
	0.27	0.25	+0.02	Kaila[53] (study 1)
Rates of Neurosis	0.19[c]	0.25[c]	−0.06	Tsuwaga,[98] Akimoto et al.[1e]
	0.18	0.07	+0.11	Lin[66]
	7.13	5.29	+1.84	Piotrowski et al.[83a] (Ciechanow)
	9.28	7.14	+2.14	Piotrowski et al.[83a] (Plock)
	77.00	71.00	+6.00	A. H. Leighton et al.[64a,b]
	14.18[c]	6.30	+7.88	Helgason[44d]
Rates of Personality Disorder	0.00	7.00	−7.00	A. H. Leighton et al.[64a,b]
	0.14[c]	0.07[c,f]	+0.07	Lin[66]
	0.85[c]	0.25[c]	+0.60	Tsuwaga et al.,[98] Akimoto et al.[1e]
	1.25	0.65	+0.60	Piotrowski et al.[83a] (Ciechanow)
	3.04	0.62	+2.42	Piotrowski et al.[83a] (Plock)
	13.61[c]	4.62[c]	+8.99	Helgason[44d]

[a] Age range limited.
[b] Figures for symptom patterns that may or may not be cases.
[c] Calculated by B. S. Dohrenwend.
[d] Life-time prevalence given urban or rural residence at end of observation period.
[e] Studies carried out by overlapping teams from the Neuropsychiatric Department of Tokyo University.
[f] Rate for more rural of two relatively rural areas studied.
[g] Not including alcoholism and drug addiction for which rates are calculated separately by Helgason;[44] the rate for alcoholism and drug addiction is also greater in urban than rural residents.

be so also for the manic-depressive subtype though not for schizophrenia, which may be equally frequent in rural and urban settings. By contrast, the rates for neurosis and personality disorder are higher in urban than in rural settings in all but one comparison for each type of disorder.

These results are obtained, of course, on the basis of only nine rural versus urban comparisons and can hardly be considered representative in any systematic sense of the term. Yet the studies date from 1942 to 1969; take place in Europe, Asia and Africa; involve cities as different as Tokyo, Reykjavik (in Iceland), and Abeokuta (in Nigeria); and report overall rates of disorder ranging from 0.8 percent to 45 percent. The consistency in direction of most of the urban-rural differences reported in these studies, despite the diversity of time, place, and method of assessing disorder they represent, suggests that the results be taken seriously. On the basis of this evidence—and it is the best we have available—there appears to be a tendency for total rates of psychiatric disorder to be higher in urban than in rural areas, owing at least in part to an excess of neurosis and personality disorder in the urban areas. If we accept these results at face value, our next question is why this should be so.

(The Issues of Explanation

Although the environment of the city dweller is often harsh and sometimes threatening, we cannot, without first inquiring into other possibilities, infer that the relatively high rates of psychiatric disorder in urban settings are a consequence of these unfavorable environmental conditions, as some social critics have suggested. Consider, for example, a line of argument that provides quite a different explanation. It starts by noting that cities also provide concentrations of industry and commerce, wealth and power, art and entertainment that make them magnets for rural people. Migrants seeking greater opportunity, challenge, or perhaps, anonymity than rural environments provide are drawn to the city in large numbers. Perhaps, then, they bring with them the psychiatric problems that we find to be relatively concentrated in urban areas rather than developing them in reaction to the urban environment.

Straightforward evidence to resolve this issue is not available. That is, no one has yet surveyed members of a rural population for evidence of psychiatric disorder, or perhaps a proneness to develop such disorder, at one point in time and then followed this population to determine which members migrated to urban areas and what the migrants' impact was on the rates of disorder in the areas to which they migrated. Attempts to solve this problem have largely relied, then, on two types of studies that provide less direct evidence.

1. The first are cross-sectional studies comparing rates of treatment for psychiatric disorder among migrants as against nonmigrants, with the latter group drawn either from the area from which the migrants emigrated or from the area into which the migrants immigrated. Most of these studies have not focused on rural migration to cities but deal rather with the issue of whether migration is in general a selective process with respect to treated psychiatric disorder. Murphy's[76] comprehensive review of these studies led him to conclude that the relatively high rates of hospitalization among migrant populations reported in early studies, for example, Ødegaard's[80] pioneering investigation of Norwegian migrants to Minnesota, were by no means universal. The findings of these studies taken together argue, therefore, against any generalization concerning the psychiatric characteristics of migrants as a group.

Furthermore, more recent work by Ødegaard dealing specifically with rural to urban migration within Norway failed to establish any clear conclusions because of problems involved in interpreting the meaning of hospital admissions. Ødegaard[81] noted that the excess of hospitalization among migrants to Oslo resulted at least in part from the tendency to hospitalize cases of senility, general paresis, and alcoholic psychoses that might have been kept in homes in a rural area. Similarly, Astrup and Ødegaard,[2, p. 122] finding a relative increase over time in rate of first admissions of migrants compared to nonmigrant residents of Oslo and Bergen, wrote

One might conclude that the immigration to the larger cities has changed in character, but there is nothing to lend positive support to this theory. Most likely the explanation is that since 1930 the hospitalization of senile psychoses has increased rapidly in Oslo and to some extent in Bergen, while in the (less urban) remainder of the country this increase has been much less marked.

Thus, these cross-sectional comparisons of migrants and nonmigrants have yielded no definite conclusions about the psychiatric differences or similarities of the two groups.

2. A study by Helgason[44] of untreated as well as treated psychiatric disorder in the life histories of an age cohort drawn from the population of Iceland overcomes some of the difficulties of the cross-sectional studies. In this investigation, Helgason utilized the excellent records available in Iceland to reconstruct migration histories. Thus, he was able to compare the life expectancy of morbidity in nonmigrants and in two migrant groups: those who had moved to Reykjavik, the capital and only city in Iceland, and those who had moved elsewhere within Iceland.

His results for psychoses indicate no difference in the life expectancies for this type of disorder in the two migrant groups. Since both migrant groups have lower rates than nonmigrants, moreover, these results do not suggest that psychotics selectively migrate from country to city. By contrast, the life-time expectancies for neuroses, for alcoholism and drug addiction, and for psychopathic personality are all higher in the group that migrated to Reykjavik than in the group that migrated elsewhere within Iceland, and in general the figures for the Reykjavik group are higher than those for the nonmigrant group as well. These results suggest then, the possibility of selective migration to the city among neurotics and those with personality disorders. It is, of course, also possible to infer that the city environment induced these conditions in the migrants.

Helgason's results, based on his classification of the subjects according to where they were living at about the age of fourteen, provide some additional information on this point. In every comparison those who were resident in urban communities at about fourteen had higher life expectancies for neurosis and personality disorders than those who lived in rural communities at this age, and these higher rates for early urban dwellers were generally of the same magnitude as the rates for migrants to Reykjavik. Since the residence of youngsters of age fourteen would not have been selected in terms of their own personalities or predispositions, these results suggest that the excess of neurosis and personality disorders in urban areas was not due solely to selective migration on the part of those who had become predisposed to the disorders in rural areas. On the contrary, the most parsimonious explanation of Helgason's results for neurosis and personality disorder is that they are primarily induced by stresses in the urban environment. At the same time, it remains possible to explain these results in terms of a genetic predisposition to neurosis or personality disorder that leads to migration to the city and is passed on to offspring who are raised there. Thus, while Helgason's results are suggestive, they do not entirely resolve the issue of the relative importance of the urban environment, on the one hand, and of genetic inheritance, on the other, in the etiology of these disorders. Moreover, there is some question as to whether the results of Helgason's study can be generalized to more populous and heterogeneous societies, even though they are consistent with our findings in Table 29–2, showing higher rates of neurosis and personality disorders in urban areas. Are there further clues from other epidemiological studies that will help unravel this puzzle?

(Social Class and Psychiatric Disorder in Urban Settings

In a previously published analysis of the epidemiological studies,[18] in which attempts have been made to count untreated as well as

TABLE 29-3. **Epidemiological Studies Classified According to Urban or Rural Study Site and Relation of Rates of Overall Psychiatric Disorder to Social Class[a]**

MAXIMUM IN LOWEST SOCIAL CLASS	MINIMUM IN HIGHEST SOCIAL CLASS	PERCENTAGE		d	AUTHORS	NUMBER OF STUDIES
		Minimum	Maximum			
			URBAN STUDY SITES			
Yes	Yes	2.7	4.0	1.3	Dube[21b]	10
		0.7	3.7	3.0 ⎱	Cohen et al.[12c]	
		1.1	6.6	5.5 ⎰		
		14.3[d]	20.5[d]	6.2	Hare and Shaw[43e]	
		30.0	37.8	7.8	Taylor and Chave[96f]	
		7.3	16.6	9.3	Hyde and Kingsley[49]	
		17.4[d]	29.4[d]	12.0	Bellin and Hardt[3g]	
		5.0	17.0	12.0	Gillis et al.[32]	
		1.6	15.1	13.5 ⎱	Gnat et al.[36h]	
		6.0	25.4	19.4 ⎰		
		12.5	47.3	34.8	Srole et al.[90]	
		—	—	—	Cole et al.[13i]	
Yes	No	2.3[d]	2.9[d]	0.6	Tsuwaga et al.[98j]	1
No	No	6.2	13.6	7.4	Pasamanick et al.[82]	1
			RURAL STUDY SITES			
Yes	Yes	0.8	0.9	0.1	Hagnell[41g,k]	4
		1.4[d]	3.2[d]	1.8	Akimoto et al.[1j]	
		19.5	27.0	7.5	Bremer[4g]	
		—	—	—	D. C. Leighton et al.[651]	
Yes	No	1.2[d]	2.5[d]	1.3	Brugger[6m]	2
		10.3	29.7	19.4	Primrose[84]	
No	No	3.4[d]	5.3[d]	1.9	Brugger[8m]	4
		45.0	54.1[d]	9.1	Llewellyn-Thomas[69n]	
		7.4[d]	25.7[d]	18.3	Brugger[7m]	
		0.0	22.7[d]	22.7	Strotzka et al.[94]	

a Excluding studies conducted in a mixture of urban and rural study sites.
b This study includes a small rural minority not reported separately. The figures given here are for adults at two educational levels. Dube[21] reported that family income was not related to rate of disorder, but this finding is confused by the fact that the study population included both single and extended family units, and the rate of psychological disorder was higher in the latter, implying that per person, income might be inversely related to rate of disorder.
c Data for whites only reported for two wards separately.
d Calculated by B. S. Dohrenwend.
e Males and married females only.
f Based on survey data without supplementary physicians' reports included in total rate.
g Subjects divided into only two strata.
h Rates for two cities reported separately.
i Cole et al.[13, p. 395] do not report rates but state: "Four-fifths of the families in the lower social strata contained at least one mentally ill member, while less than one-half of the upper-stratum families were thus affected."
j Distribution of population in socioeconomic strata was reported only by number of families; since Japanese census reports do not include information on family size by socioeconomic strata, rates were calculated on the basis of equal family size in all four strata.

treated rates of disorder, we reported that the most consistent finding was an inverse relationship between overall rates and social class. In twenty of the twenty-five investigations that included data on social class, the highest rate was in the lowest social stratum. Some of these studies were done in urban settings and some in rural. It is possible, therefore, to inquire whether there are differences in the nature of this relationship in rural and urban areas.

As Table 29–3 shows, the results are striking. The inverse relationship between class and overall rates of psychiatric disorder is mainly an urban phenomenon. Taken together with the findings shown in Table 29–1 of higher overall rates in urban settings, this suggests that whatever processes produce psychiatric disorders, they are more concentrated in cities and are strongly related to the class system in such settings.

([The Social Causation-Social Selection Issue

In 1939, Faris and Dunham[28] published their classic ecological study of psychiatric disorder in the city of Chicago. Their well-known finding was that the first admission rates for most psychoses, including schizophrenia, were highest in the central slum section of the city and decreased regularly as one moved out toward the well-to-do suburban areas. The explanation they favored at the time was that "the patterns of rates reveal that the nature of the social life and conditions in certain areas of the city is in some way a cause of the high rates of mental disorder."[28, p. 170] More specifically, it is the "terrifically harsh, intensely individualistic, highly competitive, extremely crude, and often violently brutal"

social life[22, p. 174] that predisposes to disorder in general, and related social isolation that contributes to schizophrenia in particular.[22, pp. 177-178]

Since this work, two extremely influential urban investigations stemming from social environmental orientations to etiology have been published in the United States: the New Haven Study,[47] and the Midtown Study.[90] The investigation of treated rates of disorder according to social class in New Haven was motivated by a view that "psychiatrists work with phenomena that are essentially social in origin."[47, p. 11] Similarly, the Midtown Study investigators of the prevalence of treated and untreated psychiatric disorder in a section of Manhattan in New York City took as their "most fundamental postulate" the proposition that "sociocultural conditions . . . have measurable consequences reflected in the mental health differences to be observed within a population."[90, pp. 12-13]

These theoretical orientations are examples of what can be grouped under the broad heading of social causation approaches. To varying degrees, they are quite compatible with the sick society analogy, with the addition that they locate the sources of the social organism's greatest pain in its slums and low-status groups. Note, however, that while the results of these studies were in the main consistent with their theoretical positions and hypotheses, both sets of researchers, like Faris and Dunham before them, were aware of a major problem: Their findings do not enable them to rule out plausible alternative explanations from opposing theoretical points of view.[47, p. 360; 72]

As early critics[71] of the research of Faris and Dunham pointed out, downward social drift of previously ill persons can plausibly explain the concentration of cases in the slums of Chicago. Nor does a finding in the New

---

k Annual incidence rates.

l Results reported in ridits rather than percentages.

m Occupations grouped by B. S. Dohrenwend into three strata: high (self-employed merchants, manufacturers, and farmers, and middle-level civil servants); middle (merchants, manufacturers, and farmers employed by others, and low-level civil servants); and low (workers and servants).

n Occupations grouped by B. S. Dohrenwend into three strata: high (independent business and salaried workers); middle (fishermen and farmers); and low (laborers). Two categories of persons grouped separately by Llewellyn-Thomas[69] were excluded: housewives and miscellaneous.

Haven Study that most lower-class cases of disorder had originated in that class rather than having drifted down to it resolve the problem. As Gruenberg[38] pointed out, in a society such as our own where upward social mobility is the norm, it is quite possible that the healthy members of the lower class have been selected upward, leaving behind a residue of ill. Both downward drift and the notion of residues are main varieties of what can be termed social selection hypotheses.[23] These alternatives to the social causation hypotheses, we should note, are compatible with genetic theories of etiology.

Consider in light of this social causation-social selection issue the two broad types of disorder that we found above to be more highly concentrated in urban than in rural settings: neurosis and personality disorder. By either the social causation or the social selection arguments as developed above with reference to urban settings, both types of disorder should be more consistently concentrated in the urban lower class than in the rural lower class. As Table 29–4 shows, this is not the cause with neurosis. In urban as well as in rural settings, the highest rate is as likely to be found in a social class other than the lowest as it is to be found in the lowest social class. This suggests that the social causation-social selection issue must be reformulated with reference to neurosis, and we will return to this problem later on.

By contrast with neurosis, Table 29–5 shows that rates of personality disorder are consistently highest in the lowest class. Note, however, this is true in rural as well as in urban settings. What this suggests is that the inverse relationship between personality disorder and social class is so strong that it holds

TABLE 29–4. **Epidemiological Studies Classified According to Urban or Rural Study Site and Finding of Highest Rate of Neurosis in Lowest or Other Than Lowest Social Class[a]**

MAXIMUM IN LOWEST SOCIAL CLASS	PERCENTAGE			AUTHORS
	Minimum	*Maximum*	*d*	
	URBAN STUDY SITES			
Yes	1.34	8.01	6.67	Pasamanick et al.[82]
	29.00	47.00	18.00	Gillis et al.[32b]
	—	—	—	Cole et al.[13c]
No	0.00	0.32[d]	0.32	Tsuwaga et al.[98]
	2.90	4.70	1.80	Hyde and Kingsley[49]
	30.00	49.30	19.30	Langner and Michael[63]
	RURAL STUDY SITES			
Yes	0.11[d]	0.28[d]	0.17	Brugger[6]
	0.00	0.33[d]	0.33	Akimoto et al.[1]
	50.00[e]	70.00[e]	20.00	D. C. Leighton et al.[65b]
No	0.00	0.46[d]	0.46	Brugger[7]
	4.40	6.74	2.34	Bremer[4]
	7.16	15.74	8.31	Primrose[84]

a Excluding studies conducted in a mixture of urban and rural sites.
b Figures are given for symptom patterns, which may or may not be cases.
c Without giving actual figures Cole et al.[13] reported that neuroses were found to be about twice as frequent in lower-level families as in upper-level families.
d Calculated by B. S. Dohrenwend.
e Approximations estimated from Figure 15 in D. C. Leighton et al.[65, p. 289]

across the differences in rural and urban class systems, even though, as we saw in Table 29–2, there is less personality disorder in rural than in urban areas.

We also saw, in Table 29-2, that total rates of psychosis contrasted with both personality disorder and neurosis in that the psychosis rates were not consistently found to be higher in urban than in rural settings. As Table 29–6 shows, they contrast with these two other types of disorder again in that they tend to be inversely related to social class in urban settings though not in rural settings. This suggests that the relationship between social class and psychosis is not strong enough to hold in rural settings.

It should be noted, however, that the broad category of psychosis masks some strong differences in subtypes of disorder such as manic-depressive psychosis and schizophrenia. Only seven of the epidemiological studies including untreated as well as treated cases reported data on schizophrenia and manic-depressive psychosis according to class. None showed the highest rate of manic-depressive psychosis in the lowest class. Manic-depressive psychosis thus appears more nearly to resemble neurosis than personality disorder in its relation to class.

For schizophrenia, five of the seven showed the highest rate in the lowest class. Of these five, three were rural[4,6,7] and two reported

TABLE 29–5. **Epidemiological Studies Classified According to Urban or Rural Study Site and Finding of Highest Rate of Personality Disorder in Lowest or Other Than Lowest Social Class[a]**

MAXIMUM IN LOWEST SOCIAL CLASS	PERCENTAGE			AUTHORS
	Minimum	*Maximum*	*d*	
	URBAN STUDY SITES			
Yes	3.4[b]	9.7[b]	6.3	Hyde and Kingsley[49]
	0.0	7.0	7.0	Gillis et al.[32c]
	4.5	14.9	10.4	Langner and Michael[63]
	—	—	—	Cole et al.[13d]
No	0.43[e]	0.96[e]	0.53	Tsuwaga et al.[98]
	RURAL STUDY SITES			
Yes	0.19[e]	0.46[e]	0.27	Brugger[6]
	0.00	0.59[e]	0.59	Akimoto et al.[1]
	7.49[e]	11.17[e]	3.68	Bremer[4]
	0.99	15.20	14.21	Primrose[84]
No	1.90[e]	3.31[e]	1.41	Brugger[7]
	13.23[f]	15.69[f]	2.46	D. C. Leighton et al.[65c]

[a] Excluding studies conducted in a mixture of urban and rural study sites.
[b] Calculated by B. S. Dohrenwend by addition of figures given by Hyde and Kingsley[49] to one decimal place.
[c] Figures are given for symptom patterns, which may or may not be cases.
[d] Cole et al. do not give actual figures but report[13, p. 395] that " 'acting out' types of aberrations [tend to be more frequent] in the [lower] levels."
[e] Calculated by B. S. Dohrenwend.
[f] Calculated by B. S. Dohrenwend from combination of estimates for personality disorders and sociopathic behavior made from Figure 16, in D. C. Leighton et al.[65, p. 290] These categories were combined despite not being mutually exclusive because, of 128 cases in the two categories, only 10 are in both.

rates according to class for combined rural and urban study sites.[44,66] The two exceptions were Japanese studies, one done in an urban[98] and the other in a rural community.[1] More recent results from Japan suggest, however, that these two studies may be exceptions in Japan also, since on the basis of nationwide investigation of untreated as well as treated disorder, schizophrenia was found to be inversely related to class.[56] For schizophrenia, moreover, studies based only on treated rates[24,28,40,47,73,99] have tended to show the same inverse relationship with class as the studies we reviewed. On the latter types of studies (there are about a dozen reported or reviewed in the references cited above) only one did not show the highest treated rates of

schizophrenia in the lowest social stratum.[11] It would seem, then, that schizophrenia is similar to personality disorder in that its inverse relationship to social class is so strong that it tends to hold in rural as well as in urban settings.

These findings on neurosis, personality disorder, total rates of psychoses, and rates for the manic-depressive and schizophrenic subtypes suggest, then, that different types of psychiatric disorder show markedly different relationships to social class and to urban versus rural settings. These differences suggest, in turn, that social causation and social selection processes in urban areas must be very different for the different types of disorder. How can we investigate these differences?

TABLE 29–6.   Epidemiological Studies Classified According to Urban or Rural Study Site and Finding of Highest Rate of Psychoses in Lowest or Other Than Lowest Social Class[a]

MAXIMUM IN LOWEST SOCIAL CLASS	PERCENTAGE			AUTHORS
	Minimum	Maximum	d	
URBAN STUDY SITES				
Yes	0.16	0.45	0.29	Hyde and Kingsley[49]
	0.00	4.00	4.00	Gillis et al.[32b]
	3.60	13.10	9.50	Langner and Michael[63]
No	0.21[c]	0.60[c]	0.39	Tsuwaga et al.[98d]
	0.08	0.87	0.79	Pasamanick et al.[82]
RURAL STUDY SITES				
Yes	0.56[c]	0.92[c]	0.36	Bremer[4d]
No	1.35[c]	1.48[c]	0.13	Brugger[7d,e]
	0.42[c]	0.72[c]	0.30	Brugger[6d,e]
	0.00	0.47	0.47	Primrose[84]
	0.25[c]	1.30[c]	1.05	Akimoto et al.[1d]
	—	—	—	D. C. Leighton et al.[65b,f]

a Excluding studies conducted in a mixture of urban and rural sites.
b Figures are for symptom patterns, which may or may not be cases.
c Calculated by B. S. Dohrenwend.
d Functional psychoses only.
e Rates for lifetime morbidity.
f It is estimated in D. C. Leighton et al.[65, p. 291] that the rate in the lowest employed occupational stratum is either equal to or slightly lower than the two middle strata; estimates are not presented here because, with rates in the range of 1 or 2 percent, error in estimation would be unduly large. Stratum 5 was not considered in this comparison because it is composed largely of retired people, thereby confounding age with social class.

❨ A Quasi-Experimental Strategy

It is possible to conceive in the abstract of straightforward approaches to the problem. There are, however, strong ethical and practical obstacles to the actual undertakings that would be involved.

Consider, for example, the possibility of initiating a massive prospective study of the relation between social mobility and disorder over several generations. This would supply the missing data on family histories of disorder, thereby overcoming some of the problems involved in interpreting the etiological implications of studies of social mobility and schizophrenia.[18, pp. 41-48] It would also extend the mobility studies to other types of psychiatric disorder. A major practical problem here, however, is the career aspirations of the initiators of such programs, who would have to leave them to succeeding generations of researchers to carry to completion. To date, researchers have not been able to tolerate such self-denial. Even Mednick and Schulsinger's remarkable plan for a twenty-year follow-up of high-risk subjects was designed "to maximize the probability that the investigators would still be alive at the conclusion."[70, p. 272]

Another straightforward approach would be to design experiments involving the manipulation of hypothesized genetic and environmental pathogenic factors to determine their effects. A fascinating model of how this might be done was provided recently by Thoday and Gibson.[97] The subjects were flies; the characteristic to be explained was the number of bristles they developed; and the environmental variable was temperature. The investigators' procedure was to divide the flies into two groups on the basis of the number of their bristles, raise them under different temperature conditions, retain offspring in each generation in their group or transfer them to the other group on the basis of number of their bristles, and assess the results of nine generations. The important point, of course, is that the subjects of the experiment were flies. They enable investigators to solve all or most of the design problems, including that of history, the very problems that constitute insurmountable practical and ethical difficulties when our subjects are human beings and the effect in which we are interested is psychiatric disorder.

More impressive research has been done on the etiology of schizophrenia than on any of the other types of psychiatric disorder with no known organic basis. The strongest of this research has been made possible by the identification of natural experiments. The prime examples are the control of heredity provided by the phenomenon of monozygotic twins[54,60] and the strategies centering on adoption.[45,57] In such strategies, however, the powerful experimental contrasts so far have been on the genetic rather than on the social environmental side of the nature-nurture issue.[18, pp. 39,40] Are there other natural contrasts that would make it possible to develop quasi-experimental strategies for investigating the etiological implications of the relations among urban environment, social class, and psychiatric disorder?

We have argued that at least one such set of conditions does exist and that it provides, potentially, a key to a crucial test of the social causation-social selection issue for any type or combination of types of psychiatric disorder that are inversely related to social class.[18] The conditions are provided by the processes whereby ethnic groups are assimilated in relatively open-class urban societies. Let us try to summarize this quasi-experimental strategy as it would apply in New York City.*

The history of New York City has been marked by successive waves of new immigrant groups: the Irish and Germans in the 1840s, the Jews and Italians starting in the 1880s, the blacks after World War I, and the Puerto Ricans after World War II. With the possible exception of non-Jewish Germans, the initial conditions of these new groups in the city have been those of poverty, slums, and working-class jobs. The Jews, the Irish, and, to a lesser extent, the Italians have moved up over succeeding generations into relatively affluent

---

* The following description of the quasi-experimental strategy is adapted from B. P. Dohrenwend and B. S. Dohrenwend.[18, pp. 49-55]

and largely middle-class circumstances. In this process of assimilation, these three ethnic groups have achieved a substantial share in the wealth and power of the city.

In sharp contrast to these now relatively advantaged ethnic groups are the blacks and Puerto Ricans, who are concentrated geographically in the city's slums and occupationally in its low-paying unskilled and semiskilled jobs. Glazer and Moynihan summarized[35, p. 5] the economic picture in the city, stating that

the economy of New York . . . is dominated at its peak (the banks, insurance companies, utilities, big corporation offices) by white Protestants, with Irish Catholics and Jews playing somewhat smaller roles. In wholesale and retail commerce, Jews predominate. White collar workers are largely Irish and Italian if they work for big organizations, and Jewish if they work for smaller ones. The city's working class is, on its upper levels, Irish, Italian and Jewish; on its lower levels, Negro and Puerto Rican.

Some Assumptions

With the above illustration of different stages of ethnic assimilation in mind, let us make some assumptions:

1. That there is an almost universally shared norm in open-class societies that upward social mobility is desirable.
2. That serious psychiatric disorder involves disability that decreases the probability of upward social mobility and increases the probability of downward social mobility.
3. That there is greater downward social pressure on members of disadvantaged ethnic groups, such as blacks and Puerto Ricans, than on their social-class counterparts in more advantaged ethnic groups, such as white Anglo-Saxon Protestants, Jews, and Irish.
4. That there are no genetic differences between ethnic groups that are more likely to predispose the members of one than the members of another to develop serious psychiatric disorder.

On the basis of these assumptions, it is possible to derive from opposing social environmental and genetic theoretical orientations alternative predictions about rates of disorder in different ethnic groups within the same social class.

The Social Environmental Prediction

If the rate of disorder in a particular social class is a function of the amount of environmentally induced stress experienced by members of this class, we should find higher rates of disorder among persons in disadvantaged ethnic groups than among persons from advantaged ethnic groups in the same social class. In other words, the greater social pressure exerted on these relatively disadvantaged ethnic groups (for example, blacks and Puerto Ricans in New York City) would be expected to produce an increment in psychopathology over and above that produced by the lesser social pressure, at any given class level, on members of more advantaged ethnic groups (for example, white Anglo-Saxon Protestants and Jews in New York City).

The Genetic Prediction

By contrast, from a genetic point of view we would expect just the opposite. For if disorder is mainly an outcome of genetic endowment, we would expect the rate in a given class to be a function of social selection processes whereby the able tend to rise or maintain high status and the disabled to drift down from high status or fail to rise out of low status. Since the downward social pressure is greater on disadvantaged ethnic groups, such as blacks and Puerto Ricans, we would expect many of their healthier members to be kept in low status, thereby diluting the rate of disorder. In contrast, with less pressure to block them, the tendency of healthy members of more advantaged ethnic groups to rise would leave a residue of disabled persons among the lower-class members of these advantaged ethnic groups, thereby inflating their rate of disorder. Thus, social selection should function to give a lower rate of disorder in disadvantaged than in advantaged ethnic groups if social class is held constant.

The Problem of Disorders Not Inversely Related to Social Class

We noted that these predictions can be tested for any types of disorder that pose the social causation-social selection issue by dint of their inverse relationship with social class in urban settings. This is the case for total rates of disorder, total rates of psychosis, and also for two more discrete subtypes, schizophrenia and personality disorder. Results for the various types of disorder thus investigated could differ, thereby providing detailed specification of more precise effects of social environmental stresses and genetic endowment.

It will be recalled, however, that two major subtypes of psychiatric disorder—neurosis and manic-depressive psychosis—did not show an inverse relationship with social class. What does this imply about social selection and social causation processes in relation to these types of disorder?

The lack of an inverse relationship with social class would imply that social selection processes play little or no part in the distribution of these disorders. From a genetic point of view, the most likely reason would be that neurosis and manic-depressive psychosis are less disabling than the types of disorders that are inversely related to class. From a social causation point of view, by contrast, various theorists[59,63] have suggested that there are class differences in the factors mediating social pressure that make middle-class individuals particularly vulnerable to neurotic breakdown. A major axis in this conception involves a distinction between lower-class conformity values and middle-class autonomy values.[59] Note that this conception does not contradict the implication of other observations supporting our basic assumption that the quantity of pressures is greatest on the lowest class. Rather, the distinction being drawn is a qualitative rather than a quantitative one; it centers on a difference in the type of pressure experienced by persons from the middle rather than the lower class.

On the basis of these considerations, tests of the genetic and social causation alternatives for neurosis and manic-depressive psychosis would differ somewhat from the tests set forth above for types of disorder that are inversely related to class. Since we still assume that there are no differences in inherited disposition to disorder between ethnic groups, and since there would be less opportunity for social selection to play a part in the distribution of these less disabling disorders, the prediction from a genetic orientation would be of no difference in rates of neurosis and manic-depressive psychosis for members of advantaged versus disadvantaged ethnic groups from the same social class. However, social pressure would still be greater on members of disadvantaged ethnic groups, so we would again predict, from a social causation point of view, that the disadvantaged ethnic groups would show higher rates of neurosis and manic-depressive psychosis if class is held constant.

The Importance of Replication

Replication of the quasi experiment in varied national and cultural settings could provide a cumulatively powerful test. Thus, results for blacks and Puerto Ricans by contrast with more advantaged ethnic groups in New York City would be strengthened if they could be replicated for sets of advantaged and disadvantaged ethnic groups including, for example, Indians and Pakistanis in London or migrants from southern Italy to the northern industrial city of Milan. Such replications, if successful, would tend to rule out alternative explanations of the results in any single urban setting as being due to idiosyncratic genetic factors or idiosyncratic stressful circumstances.

⟨ State of the Facts Bearing on the Quasi-Experimental Strategy: Problems and Prospects

If the preceding theoretical analysis is correct, we may have something quite rare—a major substantive issue that could turn on what deceptively appear to be simple questions of fact, for example, the question of whether the rates of various types of disorder are higher or lower or the same among blacks and Puerto Ricans in New York City relative to their class counterparts in more advantaged ethnic groups. Unfortunately, the epidemiological studies that we reviewed do not provide data on rates of various subtypes of psychiatric disorder for contrasting ethnic groups with class controlled.

Nevertheless, some ongoing research may soon provide highly relevant data: for example, Lee Robins' prospective study of antisocial behavior in samples of white and black males in St. Louis[86] and Langner's recently begun follow-up investigation of impairing symptoms in samples of children, some of them now adolescents and young adults, in a section of New York City.[62] Moreover, the existence of several psychiatric case registers, such as the one in Rochester, New York,[31] may, if cross-checked by community interviews, make possible relevant comparisons on rates of schizophrenia.

It is possible, in fact, to envision a series of investigations in which the quasi-experimental strategy would be replicated in large metropolitan regions. This would involve field studies focused on sets of advantaged and disadvantaged ethnic groups sampled in such a way as to permit control of social class across ethnic comparisons. The sampling problems are difficult but far from insurmountable. In New York City, for example, they would involve oversampling lower-class white Anglo-Saxon Protestant and Jewish respondents since these groups are mainly middle and upper in class composition. By contrast, black and Puerto Rican lower-class respondents would be undersampled since lower-class persons are in the majority in these ethnic groups. It might even be possible, in addition, to sample relatives of a number of the subjects in ways that would enable us to use the ingenious family set method recently developed by Harburg, Schull, and their associates;[42,89] this would permit a more direct assessment of the role of genetic factors in our results.

The most serious obstacles to further research are centered in the problem of how to conceptualize and measure different types of psychiatric disorder in the sets of contrasting class and ethnic groups in the urban areas to be studied. As was reported earlier, differences in the concepts and methods used in previous studies are the main reasons for the great differences in rates of disorder reported by different investigators. Moreover, since the evidence for the validity of the measures of psychiatric disorders used in these studies is sparse,[18, pp. 95–109] there is no way to choose on the basis of objective criteria the more valid among them for purposes of conducting further investigations. Our own earlier studies in the Washington Heights section of New York City, rather than supplying more of the necessary facts, have uncovered more methodological problems in how to conceptualize and measure psychiatric disorder in contrasting class and ethnic groups.[18, pp. 57–94]

There are, however, major clues from this work and from the previous epidemiological studies on the nature of the methodological problems and, by implication, how to formulate them—the necessary first step toward a solution. Look again at Table 29–3. Note the high rates of disorder reported in some of the investigations. The Midtown Study, for example, reported a rate of 47.3 per cent in the lowest social class.[90, p. 230]

Where else have there been reports of such high rates of distress in nonpatient groups? We turned for an answer to descriptions of reactions to stress situations, including accounts of the Nazi concentration camp experience,[27] combat,[91] bereavement,[67] and forced relocation from neighborhood homes as a result of urban renewal.[30]

From a review of this research,[10, pp. 110–130] it is evident that previously normal persons will show psychiatric symptoms in stressful circumstances. In some severely stressful conditions, moreover, the symptoms can seem serious indeed. Noyes and Kolb,[78, p. 455] for example, describe pseudopsychotic, or three-day, psychoses in reaction to combat. For the most part, however, such symptoms tend to be transient unless supported by secondary gain. Only in the most severe circumstances, such as those of maternal and stimulus deprivation in infancy[5] and the concentration camps for Jews under Hitler,[27] do we have strong evidence of persistent psychiatric disorder being produced by contemporary stress situations. It appears, therefore, that most situationally induced symptomatology, unless supported by secondary gain, tends to be transient and stands in sharp qualitative contrast to the persistent and intransigent symptomatology observed in psychiatric patients.[101]

Consider the possibility, then, that many or perhaps even all psychiatric symptoms are something like elevated temperature. The same set of symptoms seen at any given time may indicate vastly different underlying problems.[10, pp. 131–132] The overwhelming majority of the epidemiological studies of general populations were conducted at only one point in time. To date, they have provided little reliable information about the persistence of symptomatology over time in the context of changing situations.[100] In sum, there is no way to tell in most of these studies whether the symptoms observed were situationally specific or persistent manifestations of personality defect, including, perhaps especially, defects that are genetic in origin.

We[20] and others[48,68] have found that stressful events—events such as a death in the family, a serious physical illness or injury to the breadwinner, marriage, or birth of a first child —that disrupt an individual's usual pattern of activities are far from infrequent in general population. Moreover, there is strong evidence that the harsher stress situations induced by such events are more frequent in the environment of lower class than in the environment of higher-class groups.* These considerations have led us to conclude that while the epidemiological studies of general populations have demonstrated an inverse relationship between social class and symptomatology, the psychiatric implications of such symptomatology are very much in doubt.

We think, then, that the symptoms reported in these epidemiological studies have been of two main types:

* See references 18, pp. 131–150; 19; and 20.

1. Those mainly generated by stressful social situations and (a) transient in the absence of secondary gains or (b) persistent when supported by secondary gain.
2. Those mainly generated by personality defects and persistent or episodically recurrent even in the absence of secondary gain. Such personality defects would certainly include and may even, we have argued,[18] consist for the most part of problems that are genetic in origin.

We regard the distinction between situation-generated symptomatology and personality defect-generated symptomatology as being of central importance to the conceptualization and measurement of psychiatric disorder. If we can distinguish what is situationally specific symptomatology from what is not, we can further specify the alternative predictions of the quasi-experimental research strategy outlined above. That is, we can compare the rate of situation-generated symptomatology by contrast with the rate of defect-generated symptomatology across the sets of contrasting ethnic groups, with social class controlled. We would expect the rates for individuals who show mainly the situation-generated symptomatology to conform more nearly to the social causation prediction; by contrast, we would expect the rates for individuals who show mainly the defect-generated symptomatology to conform more nearly to the social selection or genetic prediction. What is needed to test these predictions is the development of adequate measurement procedures for the study of different types of symptomatology and related ability and disability in role functioning over time and in the context of changing social situations in contrasting class and ethnic groups.

(Implications

The U.S. Bureau of the Census defines as urban all central cities with populations of 50,000 or more, the remainder of the county in which they are located, and contiguous counties that are integrated with them socially and economically. Each of these central cities and its satellites is called a standard metropolitan statistical area, and in 1900 only two-fifths of the population of the coterminous United States lived in such settings. This fraction had increased to about half by 1920; to three-fifths by 1950; and to almost two-thirds by 1960.[95] Today (as of the 1970 census), almost three-quarters of our somewhat more than 200 million people live in one of these approximately 230 urban settings,[58] with fully one-third of the population in the 25 largest and still rapidly growing metropolitan regions of the country alone.[77] We have been transformed from a rural to an urban society since the turn of the century.

The great cities of an industrial society such as ours are collecting points for people of widely varying backgrounds, interests, and financial means to pursue them. This diversity and continuing change in population are matters of compelling importance. News of population shifts appear in *The New York Times* as soon as the Bureau of the Census releases 1970 data on black migration to the central city from the south, or on migration of white middle-income groups to the suburbs. We read, for example, that while about 12 percent of the United States population as a whole is black, blacks make up slightly more than one-fifth of the population in our central cities.[88] And of the approximately 6 million Mexican Americans in the country, about 80 percent live in urban barrios such as East Los Angeles.[85]

These shifts of population to urban areas are world wide. In an industrial city such as Milan in northern Italy, for example, only about 500,000 of its 1.7 million population were born there.[46] Almost half the remainder are estimated to be among the 6 million southerners who moved north following World War II. They share some basic characteristics with their counterparts, such as blacks in New York or Chicanos in Los Angeles: They are new to the city; their customs and manners are different; and they have little in the way of financial resources or occupational skills, the essential equipment for developing socially acceptable modes of mastering urban ways of life.

In this context, we suggest that the major research and service goals of community and social psychiatry might well be, first, to discover and understand more fully relations between the social phenomena of urbanization on the one hand and psychiatric disorders on the other, and second, on the basis of this understanding, to find ways of delivering effective services to individuals from groups with the most extensive and severe psychiatric problems.[15] In terms of these goals, and against a background of the increasing urbanization briefly but vividly illustrated by the figures given above, what are the actual and potential contributions of the work that we have been describing?

Despite important studies by Eaton and Weil,[25] Goldhamer and Marshall,[37] Inkeles and Smith,[52] and Mitchell[74] that have led us to question the popular stereotypes of urban living, we have shown that the best evidence suggests that overall rates of psychiatric disorder are indeed higher in urban than in rural areas; not all types (there is no evidence that total rates of psychosis are higher in urban than in rural areas) but important subtypes such as neurosis and personality disorder are responsible for this result. Moreover, within urban areas, not only the total overall rates but total psychoses, schizophrenia, and personality disorder are disproportionately concentrated in the lowest social class. One of these (schizophrenia) is psychiatrically the most severe and debilitating of the disorders with no known organic basis; the other (personality disorder), with its strong antisocial subtypes, is the most threatening to others and hence most socially disapproved.[14,16] These research results thus decisively nominate the low-status groups in urban settings as the primary target, from both a psychiatric and a public point of view, for programs in community and social psychiatry.

In settings where rates of such disorder are highly concentrated, there is a compelling immediacy in the need for action, for these are also, as Mitchell's[74] results showed, the areas where greatest crowding is likely to lead to lapses in parental supervision of their children. Let us underline this need with some comments by the novelist Joyce Carol Oates[79, p. 12] that suggest its urgency more vividly than the figures we have given:

It is a fact of slum life that children dominate in sheer numbers. The more impoverished the neighborhood, the more children to run wild in its streets and on its sidewalks, both powerful and helpless. The fear of anarchy, shared by all of us who have been children, materializes in the constant struggle of children to maintain their identities, striking and recoiling from one another: in miniature they live out tragic scenarios, the pressure upon the human soul in our age, the overcrowding of life, the suffocation of the personality under the weight of sheer numbers, noise, confusion.

Locating the primary target is one thing; there are many, after all, who have suspected that it was there right along. Specifying how to approach this target is quite another. If we have documented more amply that the highest rates of psychiatric disorder are to be found in the lowest-class groups residing in urban settings, we have also shown that the etiological implications of this finding are very much at issue. Thus, the facts about psychiatric disorder in urban settings that would be most relevant to the formulation of psychiatric programs of prevention and treatment are, in the main, still missing.

Yet, just as twin and adoption studies have made possible major advances in demonstrating that there is a significant genetic factor in the transmission of schizophrenia, so there is the possibility that new strategies for research on psychiatric disorder in general populations, such as the quasi-experimental design outlined above or others to be developed, will lead to breakthroughs in basic knowledge of the role of social environmental factors and their relative importance in etiology. To do so, we would argue, such designs should be no less concerned with social mobility, ethnic and class diversity, and the nature of assimilation processes than are the press, politicians, and government officials, for these are the salient social realities of modern urban life.

(Bibliography

1. AKIMOTO, H., SHIMAZAKI, T., OKADA, K., and HANASIRO, S. "Demographische und psychiatrische Untersuchung über abgegrenzte Kleinstadtgevolkerung." *Psychiatria et Neurologia Japonica*, 47 (1942), 351–374.

2. ASTRUP, C., and ØDEGAARD, Ø. "Internal Migration and Disease in Norway." *Psychiatric Quarterly*, 34, suppl. (1960), 116–130.

3. BELLIN, S., and HARDT, R. "Marital Status and Mental Disorders among the Aged." *American Sociological Review*, 23 (1958), 155–162.

4. BREMER, J. "A Social Psychiatric Investigation of a Small Community in Northern Norway." *Acta Psychiatrica et Neurologica Scandinavica*, 62, suppl. (1951).

5. BRONFENBRENNER, U. "Early Deprivation in Animals and Man." In G. Newton, ed., *Early Experience and Behavior*. Springfield, Ill.: Charles C Thomas, 1968. Pp. 627–724.

6. BRUGGER, C. "Versuch einer Geisteskrankanzahlung in Thüringen." *Zeitschrift für die gesamte Neurologie und Psychiatrie*, 133 (1931), 352–390.

7. ——. "Psychiatrische Ergebnisse einer Medizinischen, Anthropologischen, und Soziologischen Bevölkerunguntersuchung." *Zeitschrift für die gesamte Neurologie und Psychiatrie*, 146 (1933), 489–524.

8. ——. "Psychiatrische Bestandaufnahme im Gebeit eines medizinischanthropologischen Zensus in der Nahe von Rosenheim." *Zeitschrift für die gesamte Neurologie und Psychiatrie*, 160 (1937), 189–207.

9. CALHOUN, J. B. "Population Density and Social Pathology." *Scientific American*, 206 (1962), 139–148.

10. CLAUSEN, J. A. "Mental Disorders." In R. K. Merton and R. A. Nisbet, eds., *Contemporary Social Problems*. New York: Harcourt, Brace & World, 1961. Pp. 127–180.

11. ———, and KOHN, M. L. "Relation of Schizophrenia to the Social Structure of a Small City." In B. Pasamanick, ed., *Epidemiology of Mental Disorder*. Washington, D.C.: American Association for the Advancement of Science, 1959. Pp. 69–94.

12. COHEN, B. M., FAIRBANK, R., and GREENE, E. "Statistical Contributions from the Eastern Health District of Baltimore: III. Personality Disorder in the Eastern Health District in 1933." *Human Biology*, 11 (1939), 112–129.

13. COLE, N. J., BRANCH, C. H. H., and ORLA, M. "Mental Illness." *Archives of Neurology and Psychiatry*, 77 (1957), 393–398.

14. DOHRENWEND, B. P. "The Attitudes of Local Leaders Toward Behavioral Disorder." In L. C. Kolb, V. B. Bernard, and B. P. Dohrenwend, eds., *Urban Challenges to Psychiatry: A Case History of a Response*. Boston: Little, Brown, 1969. Pp. 63–90.

15. ———. "The Challenge in Retrospect and Prospect: A Research-Oriented View." In L. C. Kolb, V. B. Bernard and B. P. Dohrenwend, eds., *Urban Challenges to Psychiatry: A Case History of a Response*. Boston: Little, Brown, 1969. Pp. 461–474.

16. ———, and CHIN-SHONG, E. "Social Status and Attitudes Toward Behavioral Disorder: The Problem of Tolerance of Deviance." In L. C. Kolb, V. B. Bernard, and B. P. Dohrenwend, eds., *Urban Challenges to Psychiatry: A Case History of a Response*. Boston: Little, Brown, 1969. Pp. 91–118.

17. ———, and CRANDELL, D. L. "Psychiatric Symptoms in Community Clinic and Mental Hospital Groups." *American Journal of Psychiatry*, 126 (1970), 1611–1621.

18. ———, and DOHRENWEND, B. S. *Social Status and Psychological Disorder: A Causal Inquiry*. New York: Wiley, 1969.

19. DOHRENWEND, B. S. "Social Class and Stressful Events." In E. H. Hare and J. K. Wing, eds., *Psychiatric Epidemiology: An International Symposium*. London: Oxford University Press, 1970. Pp. 313–320.

20. ———, and DOHRENWEND, B. P. "Social Class and the Relation of Remote to Recent Stressors." In M. Pollack, L. Robins, and M. Roff, eds., *Life History Research in Psychopathology*. Vol. 2. Minneapolis: University of Minnesota Press, 1972, pp. 170–185.

21. DUBE, K. C. "Mental Disorder in Agra." *Social Psychiatry*, 3 (1968), 139–143.

22. DUNHAM, H. W. "Mental Disorder in the Community." In A. M. Rose, ed., *Mental Health and Mental Disorder: A Sociological Approach*. New York: Norton, 1955. Pp. 168–179.

23. ———. "Social Structures and Mental Disorders: Competing Hypotheses of Explanation." In *Causes of Mental Disorders: A Review of Epidemiological Knowledge, 1959*. New York: Milbank Memorial Fund, 1961. Pp. 227–265.

24. ———. *Community and Schizophrenia: An Epidemiological Analysis*. Detroit, Mich.: Wayne State University Press, 1965.

25. EATON, J. W., and WEIL, R. J. *Culture and Mental Disorders*. New York: The Free Press, 1955.

26. EINSTEIN, A., and FREUD, S. *Why War?* League of Nations, International Institute of Intellectual Cooperation, 1933.

27. EITINGER, L. *Concentration Camp Survivors in Norway and Israel*. London: Allen & Unwin, 1964.

28. FARIS, R. E. L., and DUNHAM, H. W. *Mental Disorders in Urban Areas: An Ecological Study of Schizophrenia and Other Psychoses*. Chicago: Chicago University Press, 1939.

29. FRANK, L. K. "Society as the Patient." *American Journal of Sociology*, 42 (1936), 335–344.

30. FRIED, M. "Grieving for a Lost Home." In L. J. Duhl, ed., *The Urban Condition*. New York: Basic Books, 1963. Pp. 151–171.

31. GARDNER, E. A. "The Use of a Psychiatric Case Register in the Planning and Evaluation of a Mental Health Program." In R. R. Monroe, G. D. Klee, and E. B. Brody, eds., *Psychiatric Epidemiology and Mental Health Planning*. Psychiatric research report, no. 22. Washington, D.C.: American Psychiatric Association, 1967. Pp. 259–281.

32. GILLIS, L. S., LEWIS, J. B., and SLABBERT, M. *Psychiatric Disturbance and Alcoholism in the Coloured People of the Cape Peninsula*. Cape Town: University of Cape Town Press, 1965.

33. GINZBERG, E., ANDERSON, J. K., GINSBERG, S. W., and HERMA, J. L. *The Lost Divisions*. New York: Columbia University Press, 1959.

34. GLAZER, N. "Trends in Mental Disorder." In A. M. Rose, ed., *Mental Health and Mental Disorders.* New York: Norton, 1955. Pp. 117–122.

35. ——, and MOYNIHAN, D. P. *Beyond the Melting Pot.* Cambridge, Mass.: Massachusetts Institute of Technology Press, 1963.

36. GNAT, T., HENISZ, J., and SARAPATA, A. A Psychiatric-Socio-Statistical Study of Two Polish Towns. Paper presented to the First International Congress of Social Psychiatry, London, August 1964.

37. GOLDHAMER, H., and MARSHALL, A. W. *Psychosis and Civilization: Two Studies in the Frequency of Mental Disease.* New York: The Free Press, 1953.

38. GRUENBERG, E. M. "Comments on 'Social Structures and Mental Disorders: Competing Hypotheses of Explanation' by H. W. Dunham." In *Causes of Mental Disorders: A Review of Epidemiological Knowledge, 1959.* New York: Milbank Memorial Fund, 1961. Pp. 265–270.

39. GURIN, G., VEROFF, J., and FELD, S. *Americans View Their Mental Helth.* New York: Basic Books, 1960.

40. HÄFNER, H. and REIMANN, H. "Spatial Distribution of Mental Disorders in Mannheim, 1965." In E. H. Hare and J. K. Wing, eds., *Psychiatric Epidemiology· An International Symposium.* London: Oxford University Press, 1970. Pp. 341–354.

41. HAGNELL, O. *A Prospective Study of the Incidence of Mental Disorder.* Stockholm: Svenska Bokforlaget Norstedts-Bonniers, 1966.

42. HARBURG, E., SCHULL, W. J., ERFURT, J. C., and SCHORK, M. A. "The Family Set Method for Estimating Heredity and Stress. I." *Journal of Chronic Disease,* 23 (1970), 69–81.

43. HARE, E. H., and SHAW, G. K. *Mental Health on a New Housing Estate.* New York: Oxford University Press, 1965.

44. HELGASON, T. "Epidemiology of Mental Disorders in Iceland." *Acta Psychiatrica Scandanavica,* 173, suppl. (1964).

45. HESTON, L. L. "Psychiatric Disorders in Foster Home Reared Children of Schizophrenic Mothers." *British Journal of Psychiatry,* 112 (1966), 819–825.

46. HOFFMAN, P. "Milan Being Inundated by New Migration from South." *The New York Times,* November 5, 1970. P. 2.

47. HOLLINGSHEAD, A. B., and REDLICH, F. C. *Social Class and Mental Illness.* New York: Wiley, 1958.

48. HOLMES, T. H., and RAHE, R. H. "The Social Readjustment Rating Scale." *Journal of Psychosomatic Research,* 11 (1967), 213–218.

49. HYDE, R. W., and KINGSLEY, L. V. "Studies in Medical Sociology: The Relation of Mental Disorder to the Community Socioeconomic Level." *New England Journal of Medicine,* 231 (1944), 543–548.

50. ——. "Studies in Medical Sociology: The Relation of Mental Disorders to Population Density." *New England Journal of Medicine,* 231 (1944), 571–577.

51. INDIK, B., SEASHORE, S. E., and SLESINGER, J. "Demographic Correlates of Psychological Strain." *Journal of Abnormal Psychology,* 69 (1964), 26–38.

52. INKELES, A., and SMITH, D. H. "The Fate of Personal Adjustment in the Process of Modernization." *International Journal of Comparative Sociology,* 11 (1970), 81–114.

53. KAILA, J. Über die Durchschnittshaufigkeit der Geisteskrankheiten und des Schwachsinns in Finnland." *Acta Psychiatrica et Neurologica,* 17 (1942), 47–67.

54. KALLMAN, F. J. "The Genetic Theory of Schizophrenia: An Analysis of 691 Schizophrenic Twin Index Families." *American Journal of Psychiatry,* 103 (1946), 309–322.

55. KATO, M. "Psychiatric Epidemiological Surveys in Japan: The Problem of Case Finding." In W. Caudill and T. Y. Lin, eds., *Mental Health Research in Asia and the Pacific.* Honolulu: East-West Center Press, 1969. Pp. 92–104.

56. ——. Personal communication, May 31, 1970.

57. KETY, S. S., ROSENTHAL, D., WENDER, P. H., and SCHULSINGER, F. "The Types and Prevalence of Mental Illness in the Biological and Adoptive Families of Adopted Schizophrenics." In D. Rosenthal and S. S. Kety, eds., *Transmission of Schizophrenia.* London: Pergamon Press, 1968. Pp. 345–362.

58. KNEELAND, D. "Thousands Flee the Towns of America's Lonely Plains." *The New York Times,* February 14, 1971. Pp. 1, 68.

59. KOHN, M. L. *Class and Conformity: A Study of Values.* Homewood, Ill.: Dorsey Press, 1969.

60. KRINGLEN, E. *Heredity and Environment in the Functional Psychoses: An Epidemiological-Clinical Study.* Oslo: Universities Forlaget, 1967.

61. LANGNER, T. S. "A Twenty-two Item Screening Score of Psychiatric Symptoms Indicating Impairment." *Journal of Health and Human Behavior,* 3 (1962), 269–276.

62. ———, HERSON, J. H., GREENE, E. L., JAMESON, J. D., and GOFF, J. A. "Children of the City: Affluence, Poverty and Mental Health." In V. L. Allen, ed., *Psychological Factors in Poverty.* Chicago, Ill.: Markham, 1970. Pp. 185–209.

63. ———, and MICHAEL, S. T. *Life Stress and Mental Health.* New York: The Free Press, 1963.

64. LEIGHTON, A. H., LAMBO, T. A., HUGHES, C. C., LEIGHTON, D. C., MURPHY, J. M., and MACKLIN, D. B. *Psychiatric Disorder among the Yoruba.* Ithaca, N.Y.: Cornell University Press, 1963.

65. LEIGHTON, D. C., HARDING, J. S., MACKLIN, D. B., MACMILLAN, A. M., and LEIGHTON, A. H. *The Character of Danger.* New York: Basic Books, 1963.

66. LIN, T. "A Study of the Incidence of Mental Disorder in Chinese and Other Cultures." *Psychiatry,* 16 (1953), 313–336.

67. LINDEMANN, E. "Symptomatology and Management of Acute Grief." *American Journal of Psychiatry,* 101 (1944), 141–148.

68. LINDENTHAL, J. A., MYERS, J. K., PEPPER, M. P., and STERN, M. S. "Mental Status and Religious Behavior." *Scientific Study of Religion,* 9 (1970), 143–149.

69. LLEWELLYN-THOMAS, E. "The Prevalence of Psychiatric Symptoms within an Island Fishing Village." *Canadian Medical Association Journal,* 83 (1960), 197–204.

70. MEDNICK, S. A., and SCHULSINGER, F. "Some Premorbid Characteristics Related to Breakdown in Children with Schizophrenic Mothers." In D. Rosenthal and S. S. Kety, eds., *Transmission of Schizophrenia.* London: Pergamon Press, 1968. Pp. 267–291.

71. MEYERSOHN, A. "Review of 'Mental Disorders in Urban Areas: An Ecological Study of Schizophrenia and Other Psychoses.'" *American Journal of Psychiatry,* 96 (1940), 995–997.

72. MICHAEL, S. T. "Psychiatrist's Commentary." In L. Srole, T. S. Langner, S. T. Michael, M. K. Opler, and T. A. C. Rennie, *Mental Health in the Metropolis: The Midtown Manhattan Study.* New York: McGraw-Hill, 1962. Pp. 327–335.

73. MISHLER, E. G., and SCOTCH, N. A. "Socio-Cultural Factors in the Epidemiology of Schizophenia: A Review." *International Journal of Psychiatry,* 1 (1965), 258–293.

74. MITCHELL, R. E. "Some Social Implications of High Density Housing." *American Sociological Review,* 36 (1971), 18–29.

75. MOTT, F. D., and ROEMER, M. I. *Rural Health and Medical Care.* New York: McGraw-Hill, 1948.

76. MURPHY, H. B. M. "Migration and the Major Mental Disorders." In M. B. Kantor ed., *Mobility and Mental Health.* Springfield, Ill.: Charles C Thomas, 1965. Pp. 5–29.

77. *The New York Times,* March 23, 1971.

78. NOYES, A. P., and KOLB, L. C. *Modern Clinical Psychiatry.* 6th ed. Philadelphia: W. B. Saunders, 1963.

79. OATES, J. C. "An American Tragedy." *The New York Times Book Review,* January 24, 1971.

80. ØDEGAARD, Ø. "Emigration and Insanity: A Study of Mental Disease Among the Norwegian-born Population of Minnesota." *Acta Psychiatrica et Neurologica,* 4 suppl. (1932).

81. ———. "Distribution of Mental Diseases in Norway: A Contribution to the Ecology of Mental Disorder." *Acta Psychiatrica et Neurologica,* 20 (1945), 247–284.

82. PASAMANICK, B., ROBERTS, D. W., LEMKAU, P. W., and KRUEGER, D. B. "A Survey of Mental Disease in an Urban Population: Prevalence by Race and Income." In B. Pasamanick, ed., *Epidemiology of Mental Disorder.* Washington, D.C.: American Association for the Advancement of Science, 1959. Pp. 183–191.

83. PIOTROWSKI, A., HENISZ, J., and GNAT, T. "Individual Interview and Clinical Examination to Determine Prevalence of Mental Disorders." In *Proceedings of the Fourth World Congress of Psychiatry, Madrid, September 5–11, 1966.* Excerpta Medica International Congress series no. 150. Amsterdam: Excerpta Medica, 1968. Pp. 2477–2478.

84. PRIMROSE, E. J. R. *Psychological Illness: A Community Study.* London: Tavistock, 1962.

85. ROBERTS, S. V. "Chicanos Stirring with New Ethnic Pride." *The New York Times,* September 20, 1970. Sec. 4.

86. ROBINS, L. N., MURPHY, G. E., WOODRUFF, R. A., JR., and KING, L. J. "The Adult Psychiatric Status of Negro School Boys." *Archives of General Psychiatry,* 24 (1971), 338–345.

87. ROSE, A. M., and STUBB, H. R. "Summary of Studies on the Incidence of Mental Disorders." In A. Rose, ed., *Mental Health and Mental Disorder: A Sociological Approach.* New York: Norton, 1955. Pp. 87–116.

88. ROSENTHAL, J. "Black Exodus to Suburbs Found Increasing Sharply." *The New York Times,* July 12, 1970. Pp. 1, 22.

89. SCHULL, W. J., HARBURG, E., ERFURT, J. C., SCHORK, M. A., and RICE, R. "A Family Set Method for Estimating Heredity and Stress: II." *Journal of Chronic Disease,* 3 (1970), 83–92.

90. SROLE, L., LANGNER, T. S., MICHAEL, S. T., OPLER, M. K., and RENNIE, T. A. C. *Mental Health in the Metropolis: The Midtown Study.* Vol. 1. New York: McGraw-Hill, 1962.

91. STAR, S. A. "Psychoneurotic Symptoms in the Army." In S. A. Stouffer, L. Guttman, E. A. Suchman, P. F. Lazarsfeld, S. A. Star, and J. A. Clausen, eds., *Studies in Social Psychology in World War II. The American Soldier: Combat and Its Aftermath.* Princeton, N.J.: Princeton University Press, 1949. Pp. 411–455.

92. ———. "The Screening of Psychoneurotics in the Army: Technical Development of Tests." In S. A. Stouffer, L. Guttman, E. A. Suchman, P. F. Lazarsfeld, S. A. Star, and J. A. Clausen, eds., *Measurement and Prediction.* Princeton, N.J.: Princeton University Press, 1950. Pp. 486–547.

93. ———. "The Screening of Psychoneurotics: Comparison of Psychiatric Diagnoses and Test Scores at All Induction Stations." In S. A. Stouffer, L. Guttman, E. A. Suchman, P. F. Lazarsfeld, S. A. Star, and J. A. Clausen, eds., *Measurement and Prediction.* Princeton, N. J.: Princeton University Press, 1950. Pp. 548–567.

94. STROTZKA, H., LEITNER, I., CZERWENKA-WENSTETTEN, G., and GRAUPE, S. R. "Socialpsychiatrische Feldstudie über eine landliche Allgemeinpraxis." *Social Psychiatry,* 1 (1966), 83–87.

95. TAEUBER, I. B. and TAEUBER, C. "People of the United States in the Twentieth Century: Continuity, Diversity, and Change." *Social Science Research Council Items,* 25 (1971), 13–18.

96. TAYLOR, L. and CHAVE, S. *Mental Health and Environment.* London: Longmans, Green, 1964.

97. THODAY, J. M., and GIBSON, J. B. "Environmental and Genetical Contributions to Class Difference: A Model Experiment." *Science,* 167 (1970), 990–992.

98. TSUWAGA, T., OKADA, K., HANASIRO, S., ASAI, T., TAKUMA, R., MORIMURA, S., and TSUBOI, F. "Über die psychiatrische Zensusuntersuchung in einem Stadtbezirk von Tokyo." *Psychiatria et Neurologia Japonica,* 46 (1942), 204–218.

99. TURNER, R. J., and WAGENFELD, M. O. "Occupational Mobility and Schizophrenia: An Assessment of the Social Causation and Social Selection Hypotheses." *American Sociological Review,* 32 (1967), 104–113.

100. TYHURST, J. S. "The Role of Transition States—Including Disasters—in Mental Illness." In *Symposium on Preventive and Social Psychiatry.* Washington, D.C.: U.S. Government Printing Office, 1957. Pp. 149–169.

101. WILSON, R. S. "On Behavior Pathology." *Psychological Bulletin,* 60 (1963), 130–146.

CHAPTER 30

THE EPIDEMIOLOGY
OF SCHIZOPHRENIA

Ernest M. Gruenberg

WE WANT TO UNDERSTAND the distribution of schizophrenic disorders in human populations and the factors that contribute to high and low rates, because without such understanding we cannot plan treatment programs or appraise our efforts at prevention. Behind every action program for any disorder there lies a picture of the condition's epidemiology; sometimes this picture is firmly based on established facts, but more often it is inferred from limited data mixed with general theoretical preconceptions. The uses of epidemiological knowledge are grouped under seven conventional headings:[32] (1) historical trends, (2) community diagnosis, (3) individual risk, (4) beyond the clinical horizon, (5) identification of syndromes, (6) working of the health services, and (7) the search for causes.

(Historical Trends

Are schizophrenic conditions becoming more common, less common, or is their rate of occurrence stationary? Is it a condition, such as intestinal ulcers and lung cancer; a growing health problem; or, like tuberculosis and rubella in the United States, a problem of declining importance?

There are no data suitable for providing a firm answer to this question. In thinking about the various possibilities, several general facts should be kept in mind. Ackerknecht pointed out that there is a tendency for progressive thinkers to believe that social progress leads to more mental disorder.[35, p. 23] The term "schizophrenia" itself was coined by E. Bleuler during 1911[5] to symbolize a shift in conception from the earlier picture of dementia praecox and the universally deteriorating course that the name implied. Hence nomenclature and diagnostic criteria took a big step. Since then E. Bleuler's move away from Kraepelin's view of a uniformly deteriorating condition has gone furthest in the United States, where the concept of schizophrenic conditions in the absence of psychotic disruption of mental functioning has developed.[1, p. 23] This concept is clearly symbolized in the term "pseudoneurotic schizophrenia,"[24] which, in effect, says that there are cases of schizophrenic disorder that masquerade as neurosis. The tendency to regard psychiatric patients with no gross overt psychotic manifestations as schizophrenic has gone further in the United States than in Europe and most other parts of the world.[12] In Denmark,[27] attention to psychogenic psychoses removes from the schizophrenic category many cases that even other Europeans would regard as schizophrenic. Hence, appraisal by clinical records over time is bound to be difficult, since the criteria for making the diagnosis have been shifting during the past century.

But these changes have not affected such investigators as Manfred Bleuler,[6] E. Bleuler's son, who said, "When I speak of schizophrenia, I mean real psychosis. I excluded from the study border-line cases, as for instance pseudoneurotic patients who had never been psychotic in the social sense. . . ." He followed 208 of 216 schizophrenic patients admitted to his hospital in Zurich in 1942 or 1943. He followed them until death or 1963, using a description of the various courses developed by E. Bleuler. Figure 30–1 tells his story. He emphasized that the 1965 percentages are based on familiarity with his own similar cohort published twenty-five years earlier and with the still earlier studies of his father and of Kraepelin: "catastrophic schizophrenia is dying out. . . . By 1941 the rate had gone down to 5–18 per cent [of an earlier cohort]. . . . This most terrible form of schizophrenia has become increasingly rare. . . . In my material not a single psychosis beginning after 1942 has developed in this way."

Despite some weaknesses in these studies,

FIGURE 30–1. **Long Courses of the Schizophrenias According to Catamneses of 316 Schizophrenics Completed in 1941.**

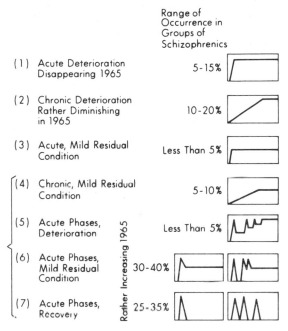

Reprinted from M. Bleuler, "A 23-Year Longitudinal Study of 208 Schizophrenics and Impressions in Regard to the Natures of Schizophrenia" in D. A. Rosenthal and S. S. Kety, eds., *The Transmission of Schizophrenia.* (Oxford: Pergamon Press, 1968, p. 5. Reprinted with permission.)

they deserve special attention because of the author's high qualifications for forming judgments on the matter. His impressions and data are not out of keeping with other evidence. The most malignant forms of schizophrenic psychoses are becoming rarer and the more benign forms more common than before, at least as percentages of cohorts newly admitted to a service. This method of appraising a change in the frequency of the most severe forms of a condition has a weakness: The proportion of newly admitted patients who pursue the malignant course in later cohorts as compared to former cohorts could drop because the number of milder cases being admitted has risen. But when M. Bleuler said that none of his cases starting after 1942 showed the most malignant course he saw earlier, the argument is strengthened.[14]

Data on schizophrenic patients in mental

hospitals and in outpatient clinics suggest a modified course resulting in a falling prevalence of schizophrenia since 1955, but these data can also be interpreted in other ways. The number of schizophrenic patients in United States mental hospitals was rising steadily from the earlier part of the century until about 1955, when it leveled off at about 150 per 100,000 population (age adjusted) and began to decline steadily.[38] The schizophrenic first admission rate to mental hospitals rose steadily from about 18 per 100,000 in 1950 to almost 20 in 1962. (The subsequent decline to about 17 per 100,000 in 1964 is due to a technical factor in the statistical reporting system. In 1962 the state mental hospital systems agreed to standardize their definition of "first admission" so as to refer to a patient's first psychiatric inpatient experience rather than, as had often been the practice, a first admission to a particular hospital or particular state hospital system.)

A rapid decrease in the length of hospitalization episodes explains this drop in the prevalence of hospitalization for schizophrenia while the first admission rate for the condition was rising. The shortened stay of all mental hospital admissions since 1955 is a well established phenomenon, and its impact has been felt by schizophrenics at least as much as by patients with other diagnoses. It is due to earlier releases in the face of falling death rates in mental hospitals.[38]

Do these shortened hospital stays since 1955 reflect a shortened schizophrenic episode and thus a lowered schizophrenic syndrome prevalence in the population? Or is it simply a matter of using outpatient treatment to replace inpatient treatment for the same disorder? Or have we, as some have suggested,[33] simply shifted the burden of chronic care from the hospitals to the community? The rapid dissemination of thorazine and other phenothiazines and medications for treating chronic mental disorders since 1955 has been held by some to account entirely for this large shift in the locus of the chronic mental patient. If the shift is attributable to new drugs, it must be assumed that the new drugs had an effect on the types and severity of symptoms associated with the mental disorders, including schizophrenic disorders. And if the types and severity of symptoms have been changed so as to reduce the need for mental hospital care, presumably some manifestations of the schizophrenic syndrome have indeed been prevented. But as Chapter 47 makes clear, the problem is, in fact, not that simple. When the new drugs were introduced, there was already in motion a trend toward reducing the length of hospital stay, partly in an effort to retain the patients' functional assets and community ties in order to prevent chronic deterioration.[17] In addition, beginning in the late 1960s, there was a policy shift by state governments to reduce mental hospital stays and to reduce the mental hospital census not only as a better way of caring for patients but also as an expression of anti–state-hospital sentiment, in particular, and a taxpayer's revolt against publicly supported personal services, such as hospitals and schools. It cannot be assumed, therefore, that the patients released in short order after mental hospital admission are indeed functioning at a higher level than admissions during earlier years; they may be functioning with the same types and severity of symptoms as their predecessors but only in a different location.

This is why the data on the level of functioning of cohorts of mental hospital admissions over time are important for appraising whether a lowering of the prevalence of severe manifestations of the schizophrenic syndrome has actually occurred. To help conceptualize this issue and to work out methods for researching it, the social breakdown syndrome was developed. The evidence indicates that severe disability in personal and social functioning associated with schizophrenic disorders has become rarer as unified clinical teams moved the services to a pattern of community care.[19] The annual incidence of new long-term episodes of chronic social breakdown syndrome was halved with the introduction of comprehensive services rendered by unified clinical teams in a community where the services for the severely ill patient are closely integrated with the entire network of community services.[20]

Direct evidence regarding the prevalence or incidence and average duration of schizophrenic episodes is lacking. Viewing the social breakdown syndrome as a secondary complication of schizophrenic conditions as well as of other severe mental disorders made it possible to study and report on whether that secondary complication became less common without answering the question as to whether similar changes had occurred in the schizophrenic syndrome or only in other severe mental disorders.

In discussing the possible reasons why the latest cohort of admissions to the Burghölzli Clinic in Zurich showed a benign course as compared to the earlier cohorts of admissions to the same clinic, M. Bleuler[6] was uncertain as to whether this could in part be attributed to the fact that failure to release patients "at the right moment" does not occur any longer. If his data are looked at only in the context of what happened over many decades in a single hospital's patients, it is difficult to find the appropriate information. But if those changes are seen as part of a widespread tendency to modify the way in which hospitals are used in caring for patients with serious mental disorders, additional light can be thrown on this interesting speculation.

In the overall picture of changing patterns of care some services run ahead of the general movement and to some extent act as trail blazers, while others lag behind, remaining unchanged over the same time period. If we look at the pioneering developments inaugurated by Rees, Macmillan, and Bell (see Chapter 47, "The Social Breakdown Syndrome and Its Prevention") as having been due to the characteristics of those hospital directors rather than to any special local characteristics of the mental disorders in the communities they served, we can contrast the way mental disorder syndromes evolved in their communities to the way the same syndromes evolved in other communities during the same period to get evidence about the way in which the shift in the pattern of psychiatric care, which we refer to here simply as "community care," ameliorates the course of the schizophrenic disorders. Their experience was in the decade before the tranquilizing drugs became available. More systematic data, gathered in Dutchess County since 1960, show that a similar effect was achieved beginning well after these new drugs had been incorporated into psychiatric practices.

Putting these two sets of observations together with M. Bleuler's observations[6] regarding the relatively low frequency of catastrophic courses in later cohorts of schizophrenics points to the conclusion that community care of the chronic schizophrenic patient reduces the risk of chronic deterioration in that condition. To some this conclusion will appear inevitable and without need for further corroboration, while to others the conclusion will appear repugnant and the evidence for the conclusion inadequate. I take a position that falls between these two reactions: I find the conclusion inevitable but recognize that the evidence for it is inadequate. From an abstract scientific point of view it may not appear to matter very much when we come to a conclusion on the issue. But from a practical point of view the way this evidence is evaluated makes an enormous difference. While the evidence is not absolutely conclusive that community-care patterns prevent chronic disability, it would be wrong today to say that anyone who wishes to reinstitute locked-door, isolated psychiatric services, physically and socially far removed from the world where the patients formerly lived and to which they will return if they recover sufficiently, is perfectly entitled to do so. On the contrary, the evidence is sufficiently strong to put a person who advocates such a view on the defensive; the burden of proof that this will not worsen the outcome for his patients has now become his. Those who advocate movement toward community-care patterns of delivering psychiatric services have a strong case that this leads to less chronic deterioration. The fact that some new, still unsolved problems in patient care have emerged out of community care does not weaken this case. The recurrently collapsing patient who escapes the after-care system and gets into deeper and deeper personal and social problems actually exists. Some released patients are living under indefensibly bad hygienic conditions and in situations of social isolation that cannot be regarded as beneficial. Present evidence suggests that if the solution to these problems is sought by a return to long-term state hospital care, damage will be done. Many other patients will be kept in long-term care because of a fear that they will pursue such a course. (Our present ability for predicting this outcome is not good.) Apparently, the recurrently collapsing patient is less damaged by his failures than by long-term institutionalization. The systems of after care need to be strengthened, and less intensive forms of supervision than total institutions will have to be expanded (unless some new, effective treatment or preventive measure for the schizophrenic condition itself is discovered).

If the decrease in the frequency of chronic deterioration is a consequence of changed patterns of patient care (rather than historical trends in the nature of the condition or new specific treatments), there are two possible views as to what kind of change in patient care has occurred and is occurring. Some see community care as undoing a noxious form of bad care that previously produced the formerly common chronic deterioration. Others see community care as representing an innovation in social psychological insights that helps protect the patients from deteriorating tendencies. This is an interesting theoretical controversy, which will continue for a period; the arguments and evidence amassed on each side will be beneficial to psychiatry because they will force a new perspective on the distinction between iatrogenic illness and the effect of the social environment on treatment and human functioning.

❰ Community Diagnosis

Knowledge of the size of the schizophrenic problem in a community, of which part of the population has the highest rates of occurrence, and of what part of the psychiatric load schizophrenic conditions represent, can help in planning.

One simple way to look at the frequency of schizophrenic conditions is to look at the people in psychiatric treatment on one day. Yolles and Kramer[38] showed that people aged forty-five to sixty have the highest rate of residence in state and county mental hospitals. In this age group, about 200 out of every 100,000 residents of the United States are patients in such a mental hospital with a diagnosis of schizophrenia on any given day. They are more than 60 per cent of all mental hospital patients in that age group. This fact accounts in part for psychiatry's preoccupation with the schizophrenic syndrome and provides a measure of its importance as a form of mental disorder. At every age between sixteen and sixty-five years, more than half the mental hospital patients are schizophrenic.

But these are only half the psychiatric patients with schizophrenic disorders; there are almost as many schizophrenic patients in the other psychiatric facilities. In Maryland in 1963, about 1.3 people per 1,000 were in state and county mental hospitals (age adjusted rate). If Veterans' Administration, general and private mental hospitals, outpatient clinics, and long-term leave from mental hospitals are added the rate is 2.3 per 1,000.[38, p. 83] In Dutchess County, New York (where the age group sixteen to sixty-five numbers about 100,000), in 1970 there were 140 schizophrenic patients in mental hospitals and at least as many in other facilities on one day. Two-thirds of the latter were in the mental hospitals' after-care clinics.[36] Schizophrenic cases do not dominate the caseloads of these other psychiatric facilities as much as they dominate those of government mental hospitals (state, county, and Veterans' Administration), where they make up half the caseload. In outpatient clinics, general hospitals, and private mental hospitals, schizophrenic cases are only about one-fourth of the adult caseload.

These summary figures give a picture of the impact of schizophrenic patients on clinical services in terms of the caseload at any one point in time. They also provide a glimpse of how large a problem schizophrenic disorders appear to be when viewed from the clinician's perspective.

This picture can be further enlarged by looking at the rate at which new schizophrenic cases come to the clinical services. In the mental hospitals, the number of first schizophrenic admissions per year was about 16 per 100,000 for all ages (adjusted). The age group with the highest first admission rate is twenty-five to thirty-four years, where it is twice the overall rate. This peak incidence rate is more than twenty-five years younger than the highest prevalence rate for schizophrenic patients in mental hospital residence. This twenty-five-year difference between the age group with the highest first admission rate for schizophrenic patients and the age group with the highest prevalence rate of patients in residence may well account for the commonly held clinical view that schizophrenic disorders tend to be long-lived and carry a poor prognosis.

The people who reside in the center of an urban area are admitted to mental hospitals with a diagnosis of schizophrenia much more often than the people who live on the outskirts of the city. This was first shown to be so by Faris and Dunham,[11] who used the Park and Burgess theory of urban social ecology to test a hypothesis about communication functions in different parts of the city and how defects in social communication can favor schizophrenic disorders. In the rooming house center, first admission rates for schizophrenia were more than 700 per 100,000 per year and dropped to 250 at the periphery. We can look on this finding in several different ways. The easiest is to interpret these findings as indicating that a person with a schizophrenic psychosis is much more likely to be admitted to mental hospitals if he lives in the city's center than if he lives in the periphery. Medical care facilities are well known to be used differentially by different parts of the community.

A second interpretation is to see the findings as indicating that living in the city's center somehow increases the probability of a schizophrenic disorder. This, in fact, was the hypothesis advanced by Faris and Dunham. Their argument is strengthened by the fact that admissions to mental hospitals for other diagnoses do not display the same patterns as the predicted rates for schizophrenic admissions. Thus they have produced evidence that the differential first admission rates to mental hospitals by different parts of the city have a definite pattern for schizophrenic admissions, but a different pattern for organic disorders and no particular pattern for manic-depressive psychoses. Hence they can argue that the pattern observed for schizophrenic admissions is not due to a simple difference in hospital utilization rates.

A third interpretation, the drift hypothesis, states that during the preclinical phases of schizophrenic disorders people will tend to drift into the anonymous central city and thereby artificially inflate the admission rates from that part of the city. This hypothesis is difficult to refute, or even test, because it poses great methodological research problems. Dunham[9,10] reviewed the studies bearing on this issue. The other side of the drift hypothesis is even more difficult to deal with. It has to do with the notion that a generation that starts life in the central city will, to the extent possible with successful job careers, migrate out of the central city to the periphery and that a family with a chronic schizophrenic member will have less successful job careers and, therefore, be less likely to succeed in moving to the more desirable city periphery. The preclinical state is associated with a failure to achieve the upward social mobility that other people in the same neighborhood have experienced. The concept of differential migration of those at high risk of later showing a particular disorder as compared to those at low risk of exhibiting this condition was first introduced into the general field of epidemiology by investigators concerned with the distribution of mental disorders. Ødegaard's investigation[34] of the relationship between migration from Norway to Minnesota and the probability of later mental disorders remains as the most thoroughly executed of such studies. It did show a slight association between migration and later mental hospital admission for schizophrenic psychoses. (The methods employed have since then turned out to be of great importance in the study of diseases associated with occupations; it has been found that the people in a given occupation may show a lower than expected prevalence of certain chronic disorders because those who leave the occupation are at higher risk of showing the condition later in their lives.)

These are the most important efforts to clarify variations in psychiatric treatment rates for schizophrenic disorders. More generally, in the absence of very detailed investigations, differences in treatment rates are most likely to be owing to differences in the way the psychiatric services are organized and the utilization rate of alternate forms of care. Certainly, the current statistics on changes in mental hospitals and community mental health centers are properly looked on as reflecting radical changes in policy regarding how to make psychiatric services available. At the present time it is reasonable to look on these medical care statistics as indicating changes in the way the services relate to a pool of schizophrenic people in the population and to recognize that this pool is of undetermined size and is undoubtedly larger than the population receiving psychiatric services.

(Individual Risk

By counting the frequency of new cases of schizophrenic disorder arising at each age, an accumulated risk over a span of years can be computed. Thus Yolles and Kramer estimated on the available data that about 3 percent of all U.S. males who reach their fifteenth birthday will experience an episode of schizophrenic disorder before they die.[38] European data based on more conservative criteria for hospitalization and for schizophrenic diagnoses lead to estimates of around 1 percent.

This risk is not the same for all groups of people. It is higher in the first-degree relatives of schizophrenic patients than in the first-degree relatives of other people. To study this difference a group of people are selected as control persons for some schizophrenic cases, matching for age, sex, and whatever else the investigator thinks relevant (from each patient's town's birth register, for example). Geneticists measure the extent to which sec-

ondary cases among the relatives of the "probands" (the schizophrenic cases) are greater than the risk among relatives of the controls. This is one way of measuring the familial aggregation of cases of a disorder; but sharing some pathological genes is not the only way by which characteristics become clustered in families. Socially inherited characteristics (such as poverty, wealth, nationality) also tend to aggregate in families.[29] Families tend to share a physical environment so that waterborne diseases also tend to aggregate in families. Members of the same household sometimes infect each other with viruses and bacteria, and households tend to be made up of related persons.

Insurance companies frequently use information about the risk of a condition to compute insurance premiums: A company using the 3 percent risk factor would try to get enough in premiums to average out the costs of benefits. Since first-degree relatives of schizophrenic cases are known to be at a much higher risk than other people, an insurance company might wish to use such a relationship to exclude relatives from their customers.

(Beyond the Clinical Horizon

In the section on community diagnosis we saw how the fact that patients in mental hospitals on any day are older than the new admissions, gives the impression that the schizophrenic condition tends to be long lasting and progressive. If patients who leave the hospital are followed over the next few years one gets a different impression. These data show a very variable outcome, some patients deteriorating steadily, some showing varying periods of remission with intermittent relapses, and others showing a nearly complete or complete remission after a first episode of severe symptom formation with a lifetime of successful functioning and no further relapses.

The very variable course schizophrenic disorders take, described by E. Bleuler in 1911, has been repeatedly confirmed by later investigators.[6,21]

E. Bleuler's main argument for reformulating the concept of dementia praecox into the group of schizophrenias was his recognition that the natural course was more variable than Morel and Kraepelin had believed. Morel's concept of *démence précoce* and Kraepelin's fondness for classifying disorders on the basis of outcome may be thought of as arising from experience when the mental hospital was mainly used as an institutional placement of last resort and most of its patients failed to adapt to life. By the end of the nineteenth century, outpatient work had become more extensive and when clinicians such as E. Bleuler[35] saw cases in this broader different clinical context their perception of the condition's course changed.[18]

In a similar fashion, when investigators began doing follow-up studies, they exposed themselves to people with this disorder who had recovered and found that these recoveries were more common than had been thought by clinicians who only remain aware of the patients who remain in care or who return to care. Hence our picture of the schizophrenic syndrome's course and of its distribution in the population changed as clinical services extended beyond the hospital's walls.

There is every reason to believe that as with many other conditions, such as tuberculosis, coronary heart disease, hypertension, and measles, pulling together the case records of the clinicians and clinical agencies serving a community will reveal a picture of the condition's frequency in the population, but that these clinical reports will only represent a portion of the total load of morbidity. There are several reasons for knowing this to be so. (1) Histories taken at the time of admission to clinical services reveal a period of time before seeking treatment when the new patient was clearly ill. During those months he was unknown to the clinicians and was not, in fact, anyone's patient. (2) Follow-up studies of people who have left treatment frequently reveal the existence of cases that a clinician would regard as examples of a schizophrenic condition, but at that point in time the person is no one's patient. (3) A limited number of morbidity surveys have been done, and each

has added some cases previously not known to the clinicians serving the population surveyed. They have produced prevalence rates up to 900 per 100,000 in surveys in which household interviews were carried out by the investigators (that is, four times as high as reported prevalence rates for schizophrenic hospitalizations, which range up to about 200 per 100,000[9,38]).

These figures give an approximate idea of the size of the schizophrenic population lying below the clinical horizon. The reason why so little reliance can be placed in the data lies in the overall state of our knowledge regarding the schizophrenic condition. Being defined as a descriptive entity without clear margins, there is inevitable controversy regarding the identification of cases. The existence of such controversy is not a sufficient reason for regarding the condition being studied as subjective; many things are obviously objective but do not have sharp edges: storms, the earth's atmosphere, cities, mountains, the oceans, for example. Nor does our difficulty in defining the condition in words provide a good enough argument to convince one that the whole idea is without substance: We find it hard to describe odors and colors but that does not convince us that each of us is having a purely private experience when a rotten egg is opened or the sky changes color. Efforts to find cases of schizophrenic disorder in community surveys will continue as long as the syndrome remains a puzzle and a challenge to psychiatry. But we cannot expect to obtain too clear a picture with the rather elementary cameras now available.

There are two main reasons to wish for a clearer picture regarding the size of the schizophrenic problem. One is its relevance in the planning of treatment facilities. The extent to which this is a pressing need for knowledge depends on our view of the effectiveness of existing treatment techniques. If we think we have a very effective treatment that will relieve distress or prevent the progress of a progressive condition, we will want to find the early and milder cases. The second motive for wishing to get a fuller picture of the size and distribution of the schizophrenic syndrome in human populations is the desire to discover causes. Morbidity surveys regarding schizophrenia have generally been motivated by this second need. For reasons that must be left to the social historian of psychiatry, these have mostly been efforts to measure the lifetime risk of developing the syndrome at some point in one's life as a consequence of an hereditary defect. The psychiatrists with a bias in favor of a genetic etiology have done the most to find hitherto unrecognized cases of schizophrenia in the community. Because they have tended to think of the condition as a result of an inherent characteristic of the individual, they have tended to see the variations in the clinical picture during the individual's lifetime as a methodological problem rather than as a topic for investigation. Hence, they have been content in their community surveys to ascertain people with schizophrenia either at the present or at any earlier time.

But we should recognize that household interviewing does not favor the location of people with schizophrenic syndromes if the individuals have not formerly been mental patients or had some other serious disruption of their social functioning. In fact, a rereading of Bleuler's monograph setting forth the clinical picture of the schizophrenias makes it clear that setting criteria for diagnosis in the absence of marked secondary signs and a current complaint would be extremely difficult. Studies have tended to count the number of people who have ever in their lifetimes manifested the schizophrenic syndrome. Such studies can only answer the question, "What proportion of people born will at some time in their lives be regarded as schizophrenic?" The most carefully gathered data on this question are heavily dominated by episodes of psychiatric treatment, even when the entire population at risk was contacted personally.[22,23] These figures are best thought of as an index of the frequency with which individuals are fated to exhibit a clinically recognized schizophrenic syndrome prior to their sixtieth birthday. If one thinks that the condition is due to some particular gene configuration as the key causal factor, one provides evidence that in the United States, where diagnostic criteria are broad, there is a 2 to 6 percent lifetime risk.[38]

Because morbidity surveys yield so little information regarding the distribution of schizophrenic conditions in human communities, they are not dealt with further here. They have been competently reviewed elsewhere.[38]

Because identification of the syndrome in the absence of treatment is not yet feasible, owing to the state of our concepts regarding its nature, some investigators have been tempted to postulate that all schizophrenic persons will ultimately turn up in the treatment statistics. While this is a convenient theory for those who have access to medical care statistics but cannot make the diagnosis in previously untreated people, it is not logically tenable as a scientific formulation of what the medical care statistics relate to.[16,37]

(Identification of Syndromes

The emergence of schizophrenia with a variable course from the concept of dementia praecox with a progressive dementing course was described above as a result of changing perspectives arising from an extension of clinical work and follow-up studies. The identification of a more heterogeneous, less stereotyped syndrome emerged out of this process. This is a good example of how epidemiology contributes to the identification of a syndrome.

This schizophrenic condition has been further modified in the course of time as the effects of institutionalism, later dubbed institutional neurosis by Russell Barton,[3] became visible as a characteristic of some people who spend long periods in overly structured long-term mental hospitals, whether the condition for which they were admitted was schizophrenia or some other serious mental disorder.[18] By recognizing some manifestations of withdrawal and deteriorated functioning as a consequence of a specially structured social environment, these complications were seen as less related to the schizophrenic disorder than previously.

Still later, a syndrome that generally starts outside of the hospital and often leads to hospitalization—extreme withdrawal or extreme aggressive behavior—became identified as common to many of the mental disorders, and its course was found to be fairly independent of the diagnostic type of mental disorder present. When it was observed that this syndrome's course was highly influenced by the ways in which the delivery of health services was organized, it took on a name, "social breakdown syndrome," and its manifestations were in a sense also removed from the concept of schizophrenia as such.[2,15] This process is described in Chapter 47, "The Social Breakdown Syndrome and Its Prevention."

⟨ Working of the Health Services

Health services are of value to the extent that they lower the prevalence of disease or disability or postpone death. Knowledge regarding whether health services succeed in lowering the prevalence of schizophrenia comes only from epidemiological information. At the present time, there is no technical basis for seeking to lower the prevalence of schizophrenia by lowering its incidence; no established techniques exist that, if applied, would lead to that expectation. Even if the number of new cases of schizophrenia that start each year (annual incidence) were to remain the same, if the average duration of the episodes could be reduced, the prevalence would also be reduced. There is some reason to think that the average duration of schizophrenic episodes is getting shorter. This was discussed earlier in the section on historical trends.

But even if the annual incidence and average duration of schizophrenia are not being changed by the health services, the amount of disability associated with schizophrenia apparently is being reduced. Much of the disability in personal and social functioning associated with schizophrenia is preventable by organizing the delivery of psychiatric services so as to give close attention to the maintenance of the patients' health functions, minimizing any possible loss of self-esteem, and by maintaining and strengthening family and community ties. (See Chapter 47, "The Social Breakdown Syndrome and Its Prevention.")

One means of accomplishing this goal is by providing more informally accessible treatment closer to the patient's home, by making inpatient care more accessible and more flexible, and by reducing the periods of hospital care, even if this means repeated hospitalizations for some people. The principle behind this approach is that patients released back to community care as early as possible in their recovery will suffer less disruption of personal and community relationships; maintenance of these relationships is important for the prevention of disability.

Experience in trying to implement policies favoring shortened hospital stays and maximum flexibility in the use of inpatient and outpatient resources suggests that greatest success is achieved when a unified clinical team has continuing responsibility for patient care at all stages of care, regardless of whether the patient is in inpatient or outpatient care at any time. This unified clinical team must be part of an inpatient service and be able to do its own after care and its own precare screening as well as have access to all the other related community services, such as day hospital, adult outpatient clinic, child guidance clinics, public health nursing services, and welfare agencies.[20] Under these conditions, the number of outpatient schizophrenic patients becomes as large as the number of inpatient schizophrenic patients on the average day. In Dutchess County, New York, where such a pattern was established in 1960,[25] this approximate equality had occurred by 1969. At that time, the median stay of all admissions to inpatient care from Dutchess County (age sixteen to sixty-four) had dropped to less than twenty-one days. At that time, for New York State as a whole the median stay was fifty-five days.

The unification of inpatient and outpatient responsibility in a single clinical team appears to affect the way in which staff members deal with specific patients. This is probably due to the fact that decision regarding patient placement is made by the same staff who will be responsible for dealing with the consequences of their decision. The indications for release of patients and for their readmission depend on judgment regarding the consequences of each decision. In many concrete situations, we cannot judge with certainty what will happen after a move is made or what will happen if no move is made. A unified clinical team is in a better position to make these decisions less binding on themselves and less binding on the patients. They are also in a better position to learn from their experience.[31]

❲ The Search for Causes

Knowledge of the distribution of schizophrenic disorders in human populations can presumably lead to new insights regarding causal mechanisms. In medicine, in general, the clues pursued by epidemiologists often arise from the observations of clinicians who observe a connection among their cases that strikes them as different from the patterns they have seen in other disorders. At other times, clues emerge from tabulations of routinely collected information, or the careful organization of information about the occurrence of an illness. It was the ophthalmologist Gregg who first called attention to an epidemic of congenital cataracts and linked this to an epidemic of rubella after a long-time interval between epidemics when people had been free of the condition. From this emerged our present knowledge of how fetal rubella affects the development of the eye, of the heart, and especially of the central nervous system. It was the anesthesiologist Snow who, after studying the history of records regarding epidemics of cholera, concluded that it must be a waterborne disease caused by a living organism and proceeded to a series of classic epidemiological studies of epidemics in progress that demonstrated this fact long before any bacilli had been visualized and been shown to be capable of causing disease. Epidemiological studies of schizophrenia have been dominated by the frequent clinical observation that the condition appears to cluster in families. Another series of studies[11] arise from a notion that the schizophrenic condition might be accountable to a specific set of distortions of interpersonal communication embedded in the structure of human communities. This series of investigations began in Chicago in the 1930s and have been pursued vigorously since. They were described briefly in the section on working of the health services. Dunham[9,10] summarized the state of these inquiries so well that it is unnecessary to recapitulate these investigations here.

The same line of reasoning has led to a large number of studies that are not specific for diagnosis but are related to mental disorder in general.[8] These investigations cannot throw light on the distribution of one disorder as contrasted to other disorders because such inquiries do not sort the population by type of disorder. Schizophrenia epidemiology cannot exploit those data. This assertion does not, however, dispose of the notion that mental disorders as a whole might have an understandable distribution in the population. If symptom formation is looked on as a matter of choice[30] rather than as an inherent product of the condition—the clinical diagnosis—it makes sense to sum up the causes of schizophrenic disorder with those of the other functional psychoses and neuroses. Some would exclude the organic psychoses and mental retardation from this summing process, but the evidence regarding symptom choices could be used to argue that mental disorder symptoms in the presence of brain disorder are not universal and that these are just as logical to include as not. These arguments that all mental disorders might have a common epidemiology are not refuted by the known facts about the differential distribution of schizophrenia and manic-depressive psychoses as brought out, for example, by Faris and Dunham.[11] These could simply reflect differential symptom formations in the presence of some fundamental disorder, as yet unidentified. Thus, we see that abstract arguments do not produce definite reasons for the pursuit of one course rather than the other. This is an example of situations where choices must be judged by their products. If an approach proves fruitful in elucidating a hitherto obscure issue, it will become the approach of choice until a still more fruitful one is found. Since none of these approaches has been outstandingly fruitful in giving us practical insights into the nature of schizophrenia, they will not be given further attention here.

The studies on gene theories of schizophrenia have been equally persistent and have repeatedly led to apparently conclusive results only to fall because of technical inadequacies of the studies or because the data do not conform to any defendable gene model. These two courses of inquiry, while not actually incompatible, take their starting point from two opposing clinical impressions regarding the nature of the condition. The social origin set of studies arises because it is so clear that schizophrenics continue to carry on normal mental functions in so many instances, even while grossly psychotic. In addition even after years of dilapidated, apparently totally destroyed personality functioning, schizophrenic patients, for no obvious reason, begin to display normal mental functioning.[6] Hence, it is tempting to think of schizophrenia as a response of the person to a current situation and as quite different from organic psychoses, which seem to take an entirely different course in that when functions are lost they stay lost.

In contrast, if attention is paid to the apparent unmodifiability and hopelessness of some schizophrenic patients, one is tempted to think that there must have been something wrong with them even before they became manifestly mentally ill. In many case histories, there are clues that point in this direction, suggesting the presence of a handicap even before any sign of disordered functioning was observed. Every large caseload contains many patients who are long-term problems for the care-taking staff. They may have intermittent short-term episodes of social breakdown syndrome and hospitalization, but between these episodes they exhibit serious, apparently uncorrectable handicaps in living and maintain only a marginal social adjustment with more or less severe symptoms of disordered mental

functioning. Some of these patients appear to be mentally retarded. Some are regarded as schizophrenic. Those sticky, incurable, either excessively inactive and dependent or intermittently misbehaving individuals who are seen as schizophrenic are so obvious to the working clinicians that it is tempting to regard their condition as due to an inborn defect of the organism.

Kety and his associates[28] conducted the most serious and important recent attempt to isolate genetic from environmental factors in the causation of schizophrenia. The record systems and social practices of Denmark provided them with a complete list of people who had been legally adopted by courts in the City or County of Copenhagen by biologically unrelated parents ($N = 5,483$). The country's psychiatric register and other medical, social, and police and military agency records were searched, and 507 were found to have had admissions to psychiatric facilities; of these, thirty-three were judged to be schizophrenic by a set of criteria carefully worked out among the investigators. A group of thirty-three matched controls was selected from the list of adoptees who had not been admitted to a psychiatric facility. They were matched for age at adoption, age, sex, socioeconomic status, time spent with biological parents, time spent in institutions, and time spent with foster parents prior to adoption.

The index cases (schizophrenics) had 150 biological relatives (parents, siblings and half-siblings), while the control group had 156. These were located in the population register, and then the psychiatric register and other records were screened for the same people. The records of all forty-seven relatives who had been in psychiatric facilities were reviewed carefully in a blind fashion, and sixteen were considered in a schizophrenic spectrum.

These sixteen cases among relatives called schizophrenic by the investigators in their blind diagnoses were unequally distributed between the two groups of biological relatives: 3 were found in the 156 relatives of the control adoptees and 13 in the 150 relatives of the index, that is, schizophrenic, adoptees. The percentage odds against this distribution occurring through sampling variation are very great, more than 99 percent probability.

Because of the way different types of schizophrenic syndromes and other mental disorders were distributed among the two sets of relatives, the authors concluded[28] that their data were "compatible with the thesis that the schizophrenia in the probands represents some polygenic inadequacy transmitted through heredity but receiving its ultimate expression and differentiation on the basis of a complex interaction among genetic factors or between them and the environment."

In this view, schizophrenia is not a simple Mendelian gene disorder, such as phenylketonuria or hemophilia. A single gene defect lays the ground for the whole schizophrenic spectrum syndrome. The available data force us to think of a dominant gene with a very low penetrance, that is, most people who have the defective gene never exhibit a schizophrenic syndrome.[17] Furthermore, because of the relatively low fertility of known schizophrenics as compared to the rest of the population, this gene would tend to disappear over several generations, which the available evidence contradicts. There are two ways of maintaining a single gene defect in the presence of these facts: (1) one can assume a fairly high mutation rate, leading to new, not inherited, cases; or (2) one can assume that the many carriers of the gene who do not exhibit the schizophrenic syndrome are more fertile than the rest of the population.[26] If one is attracted to the alternative explanations available to account for the data, hypotheses become more complex and inherently more difficult to test. The difficulty in testing them and their complexity is not an overwhelming argument against them; the only strong argument is the razor discovered by William of Occam, the fourteenth-century thinker to whom is attributed the law of parsimony: Do not multiply hypotheses unnecessarily.

Another variety of causal theory associated with an inborn condition looks toward an injury during the period of fetal development.

The argument for considering this type of hypothesis is weightier than is generally recognized in psychiatric circles because the advances in knowledge regarding prenatal injury are not widely known among psychiatrists interested in schizophrenic research; they are more widely known and more attended to by people concerned with the causes of mental retardation and the causes of congenital anomalies, such as anencephaly, harelip, and clubfoot. The types of insults seem to be less important than the stage of embryological development when they act. Infections, injuries, toxins, and malnutritions have all been implicated in congenital anomalies. In general, the risk of these events rises with undesirable physical and social environments, and this is presumably what the investigators using the Danish population controlled for when they selected their controls as coming from similar socioeconomic backgrounds. But if this possibility is considered, it may explain the higher frequency of deaths among the biological families of the index (schizophrenic) adoptees as compared to its frequency among the controls' biological families. The percentage odds against the possibility that the higher death rate among the biological mothers of the schizophrenic adoptees is owing to sampling variation are 94 percent. A larger proportion of the fathers died as did a larger proportion of the half-siblings. It is enough to make one uneasy about rejecting the possibility that the schizophrenia, in fact, being investigated was something emerging at least in part from unfavorable environments leading to central nervous system damage during fetal development. The fact that some of the excess deaths were suicides can be used to weaken this argument.

Neither the sociogenic theories nor the gene theories can be refuted by today's evidence. Nor can one reject the theory of a fixed defect arising after conception but early in life. On the contrary, each can be defended with some evidence. On review of the evidence, it seems fair to say that further progress will not be made by opposing these theories but will more likely emerge from a new kind of approach to the etiology of schizophrenia that either straddles these three notions or looks in an entirely new direction.

Since each of the three approaches assumes a long-standing difference in the organism, the obvious way of seeking to straddle these approaches is to seek a direct way to identify this difference through an examination of the organism at a level somewhere between the gene composition and psychopathological. The identification of such a difference between schizophrenic individuals and other people would immediately open a new door to further investigations with the hope of untangling the knot. If one could show that schizophrenic individuals have a difference (or defect) that is otherwise relatively rare in the population, one could then investigate the epidemiology of that difference. One would also be able to search for explanations as to why those people who have the difference and do not show schizophrenia are different from others with the difference. One could begin to search for cases of schizophrenic disorder that do not exhibit the difference and see if they have characteristics to distinguish them from other types of schizophrenic cases.

With so much promise, it is no wonder that biochemists have invested so much (as yet unsuccessfully) in trying to locate a metabolic difference common in schizophrenics but rare in other people. So have some psychologists. One promising line of approach is suggested by Belmont, Birch, and Belmont:[4] A defect in the cross-sensory recognition of sensory stimuli, in the presence of intact intrasensory mechanisms and of motor pathways and of intelligence, produces a set of defenses that can lead to schizophrenic syndromes. This possibility has been investigated among childhood schizophrenics with reported positive results. But, of course, we do not know whether childhood schizophrenia is the same disorder as adult schizophrenia. Nor does there exist at present an adequate test for intersensory integration of stimuli among adults.

It is almost certain, at any rate, that the next step forward in unraveling the causes of the schizophrenic syndromes will be through either some such intermediate mechanism that can be ascertained or in an entirely new direction.

(Conclusion

This review of current knowledge regarding schizophrenia's epidemiology deliberately started out with no attempt to define the condition being studied. In a stock-taking of our present state of knowledge it is a good approach, because it leaves us open to shifting views of its nature as we take account of the different evidence on the matter. In the conduct of a single piece of research this procedure would not be defendable. If others are to be able to interpret research data, the investigator needs to present the criteria used in that particular study as clearly as possible.[16] Serious attempts to incorporate into our understanding the results of investigations conducted by others require that we master the investigator's methods and research approaches to the maximum extent possible.

The nature of the group of schizophrenias cannot be settled by argument, but will in time become settled through careful, thoughtful investigations. On today's evidence, it is a good bet that this group of disorders will become broken into several subjects as our knowledge advances and that each subject will come to be seen as a manifestation of a condition that has other manifestations and that some cases of the condition will show no clinical pathology. Clinical investigations and laboratory investigations will play a part in this process. Epidemiological investigations may provide the key that unlocks the mystery (as they did with respect to pellagra, lung cancer, and fetal rubella) or laboratory investigations may provide the key (as they did in syphilis), or clinical investigations (as occurred in epidemic pleurodynia—Iceland disease).

Future epidemiological studies of schizophrenia will benefit from recognizing the fact that we now know that the epidemiology of inpatient care for this condition and the epidemiology of social breakdown syndrome associated with the condition are each distinct from the epidemiology of schizophrenia.

¶ Bibliography

1. AMERICAN PSYCHIATRIC ASSOCIATION. *Diagnostic and Statistical Manual of Mental Disorders.* 2d ed. Washington, D.C., 1968.

2. AREA COMMITTEE ON MENTAL HEALTH. *Mental Disorders: A Guide to Control Methods.* New York: American Public Health Association, 1962.

3. BARTON, R. *Institutional Neurosis.* Bristol: Wright, 1959.

4. BELMONT, L., BIRCH, H. G., and BELMONT, I. "Auditory-Visual Intersensory Processing and Verbal Mediation." *Journal of Nervous and Mental Diseases,* 147 (1968), 562–569.

5. BLEULER, E. *Dementia Praecox, or the Group of Schizophrenias.* New York: International Universities Press, 1950.

6. BLEULER, M. "A 23-Year Longitudinal Study of 208 Schizophrenics and Impressions in Regard to the Nature of Schizophrenia." In D. A. Rosenthal and S. S. Kety, eds., *The Transmission of Schizophrenia.* Oxford: Pergamon Press, 1968. Pp. 3–12.

7. BÖÖK, J. A. "Genetical Etiology in Mental Illness." In *Causes of Mental Disorders.* New York: Milbank Memorial Fund, 1961. Pp. 14–33.

8. DOHRENWEND, B. P., and DOHRENWEND, B. S. *Social Status and Psychological Disorder: A Causal Inquiry.* New York: Wiley, 1969.

9. DUNHAM, H. W. *Community and Schizophrenia: An Epidemiological Analysis.* Detroit, Mich.: Wayne State University Press, 1965.

10. ———. "Epidemiology of Psychiatric Disorders as a Contribution to Medical Ecology." *International Journal of Psychiatry,* 5, no. 2 (1968), 124–146.

11. FARIS, R. E. L., and DUNHAM, H. W. *Mental Disorders in Urban Areas: An Ecological Study of Schizophrenia and Other Psychoses.* Chicago: University of Chicago Press, 1939.

12. GENERAL REGISTER OFFICE. *A Glossary of Mental Disorders.* Studies on medical and population subjects, no. 22. London: Her Majesty's Stationery Office, 1968.

13. GOFFMAN, E. *Asylums.* New York: Doubleday, 1961.

14. GROUP FOR THE ADVANCEMENT OF PSYCHIATRY. *Problems of Estimating Changes in Frequency of Mental Disorders.* New York, 1961.

15. GRUENBERG, E. M. "Application of Control Methods to Mental Illness." *American Journal of Public Health,* 47 (1957), 944–952.

16. ———. "Epidemiology and Medical Care Statistics." In M. D. Katy, J. O. Cole, and W. E. Barton, eds., *The Role and Methodology of Classification in Psychiatry and Psychopathology.* Public Health Service publication, no. 1584. Washington, D.C.: U.S. Government Printing Office, 1968. Pp. 76–79.

17. ———. "From Practice to Theory: Community Mental Health Services and the Nature of Psychoses." *Lancet,* April 5, 1969. Pp. 721–724.

18. ———. "Hospital Treatment in Schizophrenia: The Indications for and the Value of Hospital Treatment." In R. Cancro, ed., *The Schizophrenic Reactions: A Critique of the Concept, Hospital Treatment and Current Research.* New York: Brunner/Mazel, 1970. Pp. 121–136.

19. ———, BENNETT, C. L., and SNOW, H. B. "Preventing the Social Breakdown Syndrome." In F. C. Redlich, ed., *Social Psychiatry.* Association for Research in Nervous and Mental Disease research publication, no. 47. Baltimore, Md.: Williams & Wilkins, 1969. Pp. 179–195.

20. ———, and HUXLEY, J. "Mental Health Services Can Be Organized to Prevent Chronic Disability." *Community Mental Health Journal,* 6, no. 6 (1970), 431–436.

21. ———, and KOLB, L. C. "The Washington Heights Continuous Care Project." In L. C. Kolb, V. Bernard, and B. S. Dohrenwend, *Urban Challenges to Psychiatry.* Boston: Little, Brown, 1969. Pp. 269–292.

22. HAGNELL, O. "The Incidence of Mental Disorders in an Entire Population: A Prospective Study." *Acta Socio-Medica Scandinavica,* suppl. (1969), 33–37.

23. ———. "A Prospective Study of Mental Disorders in a Total Population." In F. C. Redlich, ed., *Social Psychiatry.* A.R.N.M.D.

research publication, no. 47. Baltimore, Md.: Williams & Wilkins, 1969. Pp. 22–46.

24. HOCH, P. H., CATTELL, J. P., STRAHL, M. O., and PENNES, H. H. "Course and Outcome of Pseudoneurotic Schizophrenics." *American Journal of Psychiatry*, 119 (1962), 106–115.

25. HUNT, R. C., GRUENBERG, E. M., HACKEN, E., and HUXLEY, M. "A Comprehensive Hospital-Community Service in a State Hospital." *American Journal of Psychiatry*, 117 (1961), 817–821.

26. HUXLEY, J., MAYR, E., OSMOND, H., and HOFFER, A. "Schizophrenia as a Genetic Morphism." *Nature*, 204 (1964), 220–221.

27. JUEL-NIELSEN, N., and STROMGREN, E. "Five Years Later: A Comparison Between Census Studies of Patients in Psychiatric Institutions in Denmark in 1957 and 1962." *Acta Jutlandica*, medical series, 13 (1963).

28. KETY, S. S., ROSENTHAL, D., WENDER, P. H., and SCHULSINGER, F. "The Types and Prevalence of Mental Illness in the Biological and Adoptive Families of Adopted Schizophrenics." In D. Rosenthal and S. Kety, *Transmission of Schizophrenia*. Oxford: Pergamon Press, 1968. Pp. 345–362.

29. LILIENFELD, A. M. "A Methodological Problem in Testing a Recessive Gene Hypothesis in Human Disease." *American Journal of Public Health*, 49 (1959), 199–204.

30. MENNINGER, K. A., MAYMEN, M., and PRAYFER, P. *The Vital Balance: The Life Process in Mental Health and Illness*. New York: Viking Press, 1963.

31. MILBANK MEMORIAL FUND. "Mental Hospitals Join the Community." *Milbank Memorial Fund Quarterly*, 42, no. 3 (1964), pt. 2.

32. MORRIS, J. N. *Uses of Epidemiology*. 2d ed. London: Livingstone, 1970.

33. NUFFIELD PROVINCIAL HOSPITAL TRUST. *The Burden on the Community: The Epidemiology of Mental Illness*. London: Oxford University Press, 1962.

34. ØDEGAARD, Ø. "Emigration and Insanity." *Acta Psychiatrica et Neurologica*. 4, suppl. (1932).

35. ROSEN, G. "Social Stress and Mental Disease from the 18th Century to the Present." *Milbank Memorial Fund Quarterly*, 37 (1959), 5–32.

36. SOLOMON, M. Personal communication.

37. WORLD HEALTH ORGANIZATION STUDY GROUP ON SCHIZOPHRENIA. "Report of Meeting Held in Geneva, September 9–14, 1957." *American Journal of Psychiatry*, 115 (1959), 865–872.

38. YOLLES, S. F., and KRAMER, M. "Vital Statistics." In L. Bellak and L. Loeb, eds., *The Schizophrenic Syndrome*. New York: Grune & Stratton, 1969. Pp. 66–113.

CHAPTER 31

THE EPIDEMIOLOGY
OF MENTAL RETARDATION

Zena A. Stein
and Mervyn Susser

M ANY DIFFERENT and unrelated causes give rise to mental retardation.* Yet the single encompassing diagnosis of mental retardation has meaning in that it predicts, for the majority of affected children, limited development and a lifelong career of dependence. Epidemiology, which is the study of the determinants and distribution of health disorders in populations ("epi" meaning "upon," "demos" meaning "the people"), must recognize both the heterogeneous

causes and the common elements of mental retardation. In their concern with etiology and prevention, epidemiologists must recognize the heterogeneity of causes. In their concern with the planning and evaluation of care, they must recognize a condition of dependence that generates common needs. In the present chapter, weight will be given to both these concerns. Knowledge of causes and prevention depends mainly on studies of incidence; knowledge of planning and evaluation depends mainly on prevalence.

Incidence describes the frequency with which disorders arise in a population during a defined period of time. The search for causes of the trends and distributions of health disorders is best pursued by studies of incidence, because incidence relates disorders to circumstances that exist at or before the time of onset of a disorder, and time order is an essential criterion in establishing causal relations.

* A number of terminologies are available and in use in different classifications.[3,89] The use of the term "retardation,"[16,46,219] not entirely satisfactory, relates to attempts to evade the stigma that has come to attach to such other terms as mental deficiency or mental subnormality (the latter introduced, for the same reason, in the British legislation of 1959).[194] Unlike these terms, retardation does not necessarily imply a permanent state of dysfunction. It better describes that particular syndrome of mild mental retardation from which recovery does occur than all the conditions it has been made to designate.

Since prevalence describes the amount of disorder existing in a population at a particular time, regardless of time of onset, it affords a useful measure of the existing load of disorder to be provided for. But prevalence is less useful in the search for causes of the existing disturbance or disorder. It gives a cross-sectional view of a population's experience at one time and cannot establish with precision the circumstances in which disorders of long and variable duration arise.

Disorders of long duration have a good chance of appearing in a prevalence census. In severe mental retardation there is no recovery, and duration is synonymous with survival. Thus, the long-lived will swell and bias the numbers of the mentally retarded population who contribute to prevalence, while some who contribute to incidence will not live long enough to enter a count of prevalence. Hence, prevalence and incidence are not interchangeable terms for measuring frequencies. The divergence between incidence and prevalence is exaggerated where duration varies widely and where it changes through time. Both these circumstances hold for the duration of severe mental retardation. The relation between prevalence and incidence can be simply stated: The prevalence of a condition is a function of its incidence and its duration. When either incidence or duration is known, inferences about the other term can be drawn from prevalence studies.[128]

A special problem in the epidemiology of mental retardation is the definition of the case. Cases, to be counted, must be distinguished from noncases, but the lines of demarcation are blurred by confused definition. Recognized mental retardation is a social attribute. Recognition is a consequence of failures to perform the social roles demanded of individuals at each stage of life. The order of society determines how taxing these roles shall be. What is expected in particular social roles, therefore, varies with time and among societies, and among the classes of a single society.

The manifestation of mental retardation as a social attribute contains at least three components: organic, functional, and social. A primary organic component refers to a structural or physiological disorder; this we shall term "impairment." Impairment of the brain or its metabolism is diagnosed by the methods of clinical pathology and clinical medicine. A psychological or functional component, which we shall term "disability," arises from the individual's psychological reaction to the limitation imposed on function either by organic impairment or by psychic and social forces. In mental retardation, functional disability is expressed in intellectual deficit and is diagnosed by the methods of clinical psychology and psychological medicine. The social component of mental retardation is defined by the special social roles assigned to the retarded individual. This social limitation we shall term mental "handicap"; it describes a social role, the manner and degree in which primary impairment and functional disability alter expected performance. Handicap is diagnosed by the methods of sociology and social medicine.

These organic, psychological, and social criteria yield different frequencies of mental retardation and make quite different contributions to our understanding of the condition. The components of mental retardation measured by each criterion do not have a one-to-one relationship with each other and are made apparent by different circumstances. Impairments that can be recognized at birth, and for which a one-to-one relationship with functional disability and mental handicap can be predicted, as in Down's syndrome, are not common. Cerebral palsy is an impairment recognized by the signs of brain damage. Only about one-third of all cases of cerebral palsy suffer the functional disability of subnormal intellect or are assigned the special social role of the handicapped person.

Conversely, recognized functional disability cannot always be related to definitive organic lesions. In a large proportion of cases of mental retardation, even with severe intellectual deficits, a specific clinical diagnosis cannot be made. In these cases, the presence of organic impairment is merely assumed.* Severe mental retardation of unspecified diagnosis thus

* In severe mental retardation, brain lesions have been found in about 90 percent or more at autopsy.[56]

describes a residual class, a dump heap of cases that is heterogeneous in terms of origins and types of organic impairment. Yet it is a homogeneous class in that all members share a degree of functional disability and social handicap.

In mild mental retardation, on the other hand, the intellectual deficit and functional disability of the cultural familial syndrome is preceded by no detectable organic impairment at all, and is not always accompanied by the social role of mental handicap. If it is accompanied by handicap, the role may often be temporary, between the phases of pubescence and young adulthood. The social role of mental handicap is occasionally assigned to individuals who have neither impairment of the brain nor intellectual disability.[135] Their social roles are inadvertently acquired by their admission to "treatment" because of a combination of behavior disorders and lack of social support.[169,183] Thus, a proportion of the inmates of many institutions for mental retardation have neither detectable clinical lesions nor IQ scores below the normal range.[149]

In studies of incidence, the order of usefulness of each criterion ascends from social, through psychological, to organic. The practical reasons for this order emerge from the information each criterion yields when analyzed by age. To take first the social dimension of mental handicap in early life, incidence is a difficult measure to apply, or even to conceptualize. Failures in role performance emerge gradually without a sharp point of onset. In the dependent state of infancy, role failures may go unrecognized, or may even be denied by some parents, and they become apparent only at school ages, when social roles are better defined. The incidence of functional disability is also difficult to measure at young ages. Psychometric measures in infants do not predict adult intellectual function as well as measures in older children, and early in the life cycle they may fail to identify the functional disability of new cases.

By contrast, some impairing conditions, for instance, Down's syndrome, are from the moment of birth the clearcut entities that epidemiologists most desire for incidence studies. Yet even these conditions are not without measurement problems. The life of a unique individual begins with the formation of a zygote. Some aberrant chromosomal arrangements preclude zygote formation altogether; some permit the zygote to divide but are incompatible with fetal survival; other's permit a bare few days of extrauterine life; and the trisomy 21 of Down's syndrome is compatible with survival in spite of a high risk of death from fertilization onwards. Indeed, most of the impairments of severe mental retardation have their onset in intrauterine life. At best, therefore, incidence counts are based on the emergence of impairment at birth, and unknown numbers are aborted early in fetal life. It is an uncertain assumption that the impaired survivors fairly represent impairments among all conceptions. If the assumption is incorrect, the associations with impairment that are taken to point to causes may in fact be the misleading results of selective survival.

In studies of prevalence, the order of usefulness of the social, psychological, and organic criteria is reversed. We have noted that prevalence best establishes current needs for treatment and care. In mental retardation, these needs rest principally on the social component of the condition, which embraces all the other components. The prevalence of the social role of mental retardation is more easily established than is the prevalence of disability and impairment. The individuals among children and adults who are socially defined as mentally retarded, by their backwardness at school or by their failures in occupational roles, can often be identified from records and interviews. To determine levels of functional disability requires psychometric testing. For school children, test scores may be no more difficult to come by than their educational performance, but for adults, tests will usually have to be specially undertaken among a reluctant population. To determine organic impairment requires still more elaborate clinical examinations and more laborious surveys.

The distinctions among the organic, functional, and social dimensions of mental retardation have theoretical as well as descriptive significance. For instance, the observation that all organic impairments need not be expressed in functional disability leads to the hypothesis that learning can fully compensate for impairment. Thus, any demonstration that retarded brain growth in fetal or infant life need not be accompanied by measurable intellectual disability in later life has significance for hypotheses about the basis of functional intelligence. Again, the demonstration that functional deficits need not be directly translated into social handicap confirms that social roles can accommodate a wide range of performance around the average. The demonstration that functional deficits at pubescence need not persist leads to the hypothesis that assigned roles and achieved social status may themselves improve and maintain levels of role performance. These hypotheses have significance for preventive programs and methods of care.

Another important distinction to make in the epidemiology of mental retardation is between severe and mild degrees of mental retardation. Severe retardation comprises at most one-quarter of the total. Usually diagnosed at an early age, its many known and unknown causes,[16,129] rooted in persisting organic impairment of the developing brain, are distributed fairly evenly across the social classes. Mild retardation comprises at least three-quarters of cases, is diagnosed later during childhood or even during pubescence and adolescence, and no more than one-quarter of those affected are rooted in organic impairment. The remainder, with functional disability and social handicap but without definite organic impairment, are concentrated in the lower social classes and associated with poverty and its concomitants.* Thus, the origin and prevention of much severe retardation must be sought in impairing preconceptual and perinatal factors that affect all classes; the origin and prevention of much mild retardation must be sought in postnatal factors that influence the acquisition of functional disabilities and social roles.

In the section on incidence that follows, some proven and some possible causes of mental retardation will be discussed. Some are

rare, but we have concentrated on causes that could be prevented by a comprehensive program for mental retardation. The review is selective, and many causes have not been dealt with, for instance, those of genetic origin.[126,127,129] The causes we shall consider are (1) chemical and physical agents in the environment; (2) infections; and (3) sociomedical factors including poverty, prenatal and perinatal factors, nutrition, and demographic factors. In the section on prevalence, we discuss the prevalence of severe and mild retardation separately, and then consider the implications of the trends for treatment and care.

This discussion has so far elaborated the simple and emphasized the complex side of epidemiological measures. These complex issues must be respected, but they are intended to clarify, not to invalidate, the accumulated knowledge on which advance in the field must always be based. Our review will proceed with that object in mind.

(Causes and Incidence

Technological development has added to the possible causes and perhaps to the incidence of mental retardation. The side effects of medical treatments, industrial processes, and warfare expose people to pervasive chemical and physical agents. We therefore begin with a brief outline of some chemical and physical antecedents of mental retardation.

Chemical Factors

Such drugs as lysergic acid diethylamide (LSD) can affect the chromosomes.[47,98,193] Because chromosomal abnormalities underlie some types of mental retardation, notably Down's syndrome, drugs attract suspicion as possible causes of mental retardation. Such drugs as thalidomide,[117,124] and perhaps LSD,[224] affect later fetal development, and they also attract suspicion as causes of mental retardation. Proof is lacking, however, that drugs, taken during gestation for therapy or for psychedelic effects, cause mental retardation.

* See references 22, 119, 165, 170, and 185.

The heavy metals, mercury and lead, are proven causes of mental retardation, and people have been exposed to them by ingestion of drugs, and by pollution of food, water, air, and housing. In addition to the "hatters' shakes" and other forms of mercury poisoning,[94] there is little doubt that mercurials in teething powders still in use after World War II were responsible for the infantile neuropathy known as "pink disease" (acrodynia).[216] Mercury levels high enough to cause alarm have recently been found in fish in the United States and Europe. The well-documented Minamata Bay outbreak in Japan[197] in the 1950s justifies the alarm. Over a period of several years a number of women who during pregnancy habitually ate shellfish taken from the bay bore children afflicted by cerebral palsy and mental retardation. These shellfish concentrated mercury discharged from an industrial plant. Control of the mercury contamination promptly reduced the incidence of the condition. In the United States, during 1969, at least one family suffered severe mental effects from mercurial poisoning, and the mother of the family, pregnant at the time, gave birth to a child with neurologic defects and perhaps mental retardation. In this incident, the family had eaten the meat of pigs fed on mercury-treated grain, a treatment intended to protect the planted grain from pests.[179]

Lead poisoning has long been known to produce lead encephalopathy. Often fatal in young children treated tardily, a proportion of those who survive the encephalopathy are mentally retarded.[18] A history of pica is common, and usually the source of lead can be identified in peeling leaded paint in the home. Children from two to four years of age are most often affected, as might be expected from the association with pica.[8]

Acute lead encephalopathy is uncommon. A question of great concern, however, is whether more chronic and milder forms of lead intoxication give rise to mild degrees of mental retardation, neurological disorders, and behavior disturbances.* In Chicago,[24,163] Cleveland,[82] New York[99] and Baltimore,[41] lead encephalopathy occurs mainly in particular areas, the so-called lead belts. Numbers of children from the lead belts have high levels of lead in their blood, sometimes associated with lead deposits and radiological signs in bones and basophilic stippling of red cells. The peak age for these syndromes is the same as for lead encephalopathy, namely two to four years, and many have a history of pica. Some cities, in an effort to detect dangerous sources of lead and to treat those with high blood lead levels, have initiated mass blood testing programs for children in affected areas.[84,121]

The effect on mental function of lead intoxication without encephalopathy, as indicated by high blood levels, is not yet established, but there is good reason to assume that high levels are noxious. In areas where children are at risk, the only safe course for cities to follow is to enforce housing standards, educate parents to the danger, and systematically screen the infants at risk. Although the assumptions of screening programs are not proven and need testing, programs intelligently applied can test their own assumptions in the course of application.

Physical Factors

Among known physical agents that can cause mental retardation, by far the most serious is ionizing radiation. The sources studied have been, first, therapeutic and diagnostic irradiation and, second, the atomic bombs exploded over the populous cities of Hiroshima and Nagasaki, at the order of President Truman, as Japanese resistance was collapsing at the end of World War II.

Pelvic irradiation of mothers early in pregnancy can lead to cerebral damage in the child. Clinical observations date from 1929. Decisive epidemiological observations date from the Hiroshima bomb, August 6, 1945.† A twenty-year follow-up has established that the effects of the bomb included shortened stature, microcephaly, mental retardation, and leukemia. Microcephaly has a high correlation

---

* See references 131, 137, 143, 157, and 211.

† See references 140, 141, 158, 217, and 221.

with brain size, and it is tempting to use head circumference as an indicator to retarded brain growth and organic impairment. The main stimulus to the growth of the skull is thought to be the growth of the brain. As a manifestation of nuclear irradiation, microcephaly proved to be to some degree independent of the functional disability of mental retardation. This independence is reflected in the fact that three-quarters of the microcephalic subjects did not exhibit notable mental retardation. On the other hand, sixteen of eighteen cases of marked mental retardation, about 90 percent, had microcephaly. It seems not unlikely that microcephaly caused by nuclear irradiation reflected impaired brain growth and cell depletion, and that this organic impairment became apparent in dysfunction only in the one-quarter of subjects most severely affected.

The susceptibility of the fetus to irradiation varied with the dose and with fetal age, and there was some interaction between these two factors. Both microcephaly and mental retardation increased in frequency as the dose of radiation increased. Where fetal exposure occurred earlier than about twenty weeks after the last menstrual period, the incidence of both conditions was distinctly higher than with later exposure. Mental retardation was concentrated particularly in the period about ten weeks after conception. A review of twenty-six case reports of fetal injury after medical irradiation has also shown the fetus to be most vulnerable at seven to fifteen weeks.[58] With heavy doses of radiation, however, the difference in susceptibility between early and late gestation in both microcephaly and mental retardation was diminished although still present.

Effects of irradiation have been sought in children whose mothers or fathers were irradiated before the children were conceived. In the cohort of Japanese children who were born between 1948 and 1959, and whose parents had been exposed to the atomic explosions, effects of preconception exposure were not detected in the incidence either of congenital abnormalities or of mental retardation.[147] Indeed, the cases of Down's syndrome found among 5,582 exposed mothers proved to be only half the expected number.[171]

Because of the small numbers of cases that are found with cohort studies of rare conditions, the question of the relationship between irradiation of the gonads before conception and subsequent mental retardation is still a matter of debate. In a case-control study, Sigler, Lilienfeld, Cohen, and Westlake[176] compared the radiation experience of mothers and fathers of 216 cases of Down's syndrome and 216 controls matched for maternal age. Mothers exposed to fluoroscopy or to therapeutic radiation had a relative risk of seven to one. The information about irradiation was derived from family reports. The validation of these reports from clinical records was not extensive, and on this ground the result awaits confirmation.

The findings of Sigler et al. get support from a prospective Canadian enquiry by Uchida, Holunga, and Lawley.[203] On the other hand, in other studies besides that of the atom bomb cohort, a relationship between preconceptual irradiation and Down's syndrome has not been found.[34,190] If the findings of Sigler et al. are confirmed, the attributable risk (that is, the rate in the population attributed to maternal irradiation over and above the rate attributed to other causes) would not be large; however, the information could be used immediately to reduce incidence. Clarification should therefore be sought without delay.

Infections

The infections that influence the incidence of mental retardation are a mixed bag.[13,174,205] They include bacterial meningitis, congenital syphilis,[12,85] toxoplasmosis,[10,218] and viral encephalitis. On the one hand, changes in infectious diseases have led to a fall in the incidence of organic impairment and of mental retardation generally, or can be assumed to have done so. On the other hand, survival from attacks that would once have been fatal has led to a rise in the prevalence of impairments and to a consequent rise in the incidence of subsequent functional disability and mental handicap.

Known infections have probably never been responsible for more than a small minority of cases of mental retardation. Even rubella, so grave a hazard to the embryo,[50,138] is an uncommon cause of mental retardation unless the syndrome is complicated by lesions of the sense organs.[132] In an English epidemic, congenital rubella without complications of the sense organs did not lead to a reduction in mean IQ in affected children followed over ten years.[175] Influenza infection during pregnancy has appeared on occasion to increase the incidence of oesophageal atresia, of cleft palate, and anencephaly, but no association with intellectual deficit or mental handicap has been discovered.[111]

In general, viral encephalitides contribute a small and sporadic number of cases to the pool of mentally retarded persons.[139] In epidemics, among infants the rate of fatalities and of brain damage with subsequent mental retardation is high, but the condition is an uncommon one overall. Measles encephalitis, for instance, is a rare cause of mental retardation. In the United States, between 1960 and 1966, about 250 cases of measles encephalitis were reported each year.[204] Eighty percent survived, and an estimated one-third of these were under two years of age. An estimated one-third of these young survivors (about twenty-two per year) might have been left with severe mental retardation. These numbers depend on reporting and may underestimate by as much as a factor of ten.

The possibility exists that even uncomplicated measles may have mental sequelae.[77] The postulated effects of measles, like the fatalities it causes in malnourished populations,[145] may depend on the interaction of infectious agent and host characteristics.[152] In one series of studies in the United States,[23,76, 77,105] reading readiness at school entry was used as an index of intellectual disability. In poor communities, children with a history of measles were retarded in reading readiness compared with controls. In better-off communities, children with a history of measles were not retarded. Better-off children are perhaps

more resistant to damage from infection than those in poverty.[21] In addition, it is likely that the better-off children are better able to compensate, by learning and favorable experiences, for whatever temporary or permanent organic impairment measles may cause.

With successful and widespread immunization, any organic impairments and functional retardation caused by measles will disappear. In the United States, reported measles morbidity reached a nadir in 1968 following on a new national program; the rise in the subsequent two years probably relates to reduced effort rather than to reduced efficiency of vaccination.[205] The immunization that controls measles is itself a rare cause of encephalitis and mental retardation. Encephalitis with resulting mental retardation can also follow immunization against pertussis.[14] There is no doubt, however, that with regard to mental retardation, more is to be gained than lost by immunization against these diseases.[15,31]

The history of tuberculous meningitis illustrates that the effects of treatment on incidence have not always been in one direction. During the first decade after World War II, new treatments changed tuberculous meningitis from a uniformly fatal condition to one that permitted survival. Because a proportion of the early survivors had gross impairments of the brain, they added to the incidence of disability and handicap from mental retardation.[103] In the 1960s the incidence of primary tuberculosis and its complications continued to decline, and treatment also became more effective, so that fewer new cases of mental retardation due to tuberculous meningitis appeared.[123,201]

A somewhat comparable effect may be observed with other meningitides. There has been a sharp decline in the case-fatality rate of bacterial meningitis since modern treatments were introduced.[59,178] Although the proportion of survivors with mental sequelae may also have declined, the larger overall number of survivors could have generated a number of cases of mental retardation as large in the years subsequent to chemotherapy and antibiotics as in the years before.

Infections that occur at and around birth,

some caused by agents discovered only in recent years, have attracted suspicion as neurological pathogens.[175] Cytomegalovirus has been implicated as a cause of mental retardation.[87] It is also associated with infantile spasms and fits, and possibly with microcephaly, both common in mentally retarded populations. The pathogenesis is not clear; the virus seems to be harmless in the majority of the newborn from whom it is isolated.[182] Mycoplasma, virus-like agents, have also been suspect as a cause of mental retardation.[36] Firm evidence is lacking. Congenital toxoplasmosis is a rare but well-documented protozoal cause of mental retardation.[71,197] Antibodies to toxoplasma developed at the third and fourth months of gestation in 2 per 1,000 of a large series of pregnancies studied longitudinally in the cities of the eastern United States.[174] Congenital toxoplasmosis was observed in five offspring of mothers who developed antibodies, an incidence of 0.25 per 1,000. Since antibodies in mothers are detectable, prevention of this cause of mental retardation by aborting the fetus is technically within reach.

The incidence of mental retardation due to known infections has surely declined. Social change has improved host resistance and immunity, effected environmental control, and provided the techniques to prevent or to treat such infectious diseases as syphilis, bacterial meningitis, pertussis, measles, mumps, and rubella.[57] Further gains from the control of infectious diseases seem to be within reach. A reduction in incidence of small but uncertain magnitude should follow better understanding of the encephalitides, toxoplasmosis, and cytomegalovirus.

Social Class and Poverty

An association between mild mental retardation and social class has been recognized at least since the beginning of the century. Observers have been in doubt about which was the antecedent variable, that is, which was cause and which consequence. As the selective racial theories of social Darwinism lost force, so poverty of the environment has been given greater prominence as a causal antecedent rather than a consequence of mental retardation. The cultural-familial syndrome associated with poverty is a form of mild intellectual disability without detectable clinical lesions and is by far the most common type of mild mental retardation.[119]

In two industrial cities of Lancashire, England[183,184] the incidence of the condition (defined by an IQ between 50 and 80 and the absence of detectable clinical lesions) was not more than 0.26 per 1,000 among children in publicly financed schools of high social standing; the rate was 3.8 per 1,000 among the schools of lowest social standing, a relative risk at least fifteen times higher. In Aberdeen, Scotland, a similar distribution was also found to hold good.[22] A family study in Lancashire demonstrated that the syndrome was familial. It was virtually specific to demotic families. These were families of the lowest social strata, defined by occupation and education, that showed no signs of upward social mobility in the occupational and educational experience of three generations. Among aspirant working-class and higher-class families, which did show signs of upward social mobility, the typical syndrome was not found.

The specificity of the syndrome for families typed by cultural characteristics legitimizes the "cultural-familial" label.[195] Other features suggest that it is also cultural in origin. A degree of intellectual and social recovery tended to occur in young adulthood. Unlike those with neurological lesions, those with the syndrome were found to have made IQ gains in young adulthood. They made social gains as well. Provided they came from functioning nuclear families, most were adapted to normal social roles. Only those from nonfunctioning dysmorphic families broken in early childhood were institutionalized or otherwise handicapped.

Much other evidence[170,186,194] indicates that poor cultural environment can depress intelligence test scores. This environment effect best explains the fact that the tail end of the normal IQ distribution is substantially lower among the lowest social classes, which include demotic families, than among higher classes.

Seen in this context, IQ scores in the range 50–80 are the pathological outcome of adverse cultural environment.[184,185] The mental retardation attributed to the demotic culture presumably occurs in individuals endowed with relatively low innate intelligence or high sensitivity to the environment. Adverse environment depresses their performance below the threshold for normality in the society at large. The genetic component in mental performance probably explains a large proportion of individual variation but a much smaller proportion of the variation between groups.

Although the cultural-familial syndrome is a characteristic of certain types of family, this does not require that the causes of the condition reside within the environment of the families alone. Members of demotic families share, outside the family, the same harsh social and physical environment and impoverished educational experience. The external as well as the internal familial environment could contribute to the association of mild mental retardation and social class.

Compared with those better off, the children of the poor have experienced higher prematurity rates at birth, more infectious diseases with less treatment and more severe effects, more malnutrition; they have enjoyed less enduring family ties and been burdened with a greater frequency of all kinds of functional disabilities and physical handicaps. They have been poorly housed and poorly schooled, have suffered discrimination in social and public life, and have had a high liability to conviction for crime. These elements, too numerous to receive adequate treatment in this chapter, could each contribute to intellectual disability and to the assignment to members of the affected classes of the role of mental handicap. In the sections that follow, two attributes of the poor, the high risk of having prenatal and perinatal complications and inadequate nutrition, have been selected for discussion.

Prenatal and Perinatal Factors

Relationships between circumstances of birth and later intellectual function have been much studied, but the causal connections are still not clear. We exclude from discussion those chromosomal and genetic abnormalities, fetal malformations, and intrauterine infections that are in themselves both antecedents of mental retardation and of perinatal difficulties. The list that remains is long, since it includes factors related to the mother as well as the child, for instance, maternal factors like toxemia, short and long labor, malpresentations, unattended deliveries, antepartum hemorrhage, low birth weight, multiple births, neonatal anoxia, and bilirubinemia. The discussion will be limited to three factors for which there are substantial data: (1) low birth weight, (2) toxemia, and (3) multiple births. Even with regard to these three common and easily recognized conditions, the causal connections are difficult to disentangle.

1. Studies of perinatal mortality show that birth weight is either in itself a crucial factor in survival[25,30,196] or an indicator of other crucial factors that lead both to death and to retarded prenatal development. Low birth weight can account for the great part of perinatal mortality. Low birth weight also has associations with mental retardation,[*] and similar associations hold for short gestation and for retarded intrauterine growth measured by combining the two indices.[7]

Low birth weight cannot be assigned a causal or a direct mediating role in mental retardation without equivocation. Low birth weight itself has heterogeneous causes, known and unknown. Its association with mental retardation is reduced when those cases are excluded in which the causes of mental retardation antedate birth weight and retard development, as with Down's anomaly and phenylketonuria. With very low birth weights, preexisting congenital defects seem to account for much of the high risk of mental retardation.[69] Where congenital defect does not accompany low birth weight, brain damage appears to be a necessary intervening factor between low birth weight and mental retarda-

---

[*] See references 67, 104, 153, 209, 210, 212, and 213.

tion. In one series of infants of very low birth weight,[125] the risk of cerebral palsy was high among those with short gestation periods. The risk of mental retardation was raised only among those with cerebral palsy, but not in the remainder.

With moderate degrees of low birth weight, a consistent association with mental performance also is not found.[66] The interconnectedness of the postulated causal factors obfuscates the contribution of birth weight to measured intelligence. Thus, the social-class gradients of birth weight[30,104] and IQ[172] are sharp and parallel,[75] to the disadvantage of the lower classes. When the closest possible control of social class has been applied, by comparing sib pairs, only a small difference in IQ has been found between sibs of different birth weight (excepting the few pairs with gross weight differences between members).[161] This finding suggests that among the complex of variables associated with social class, a moderate difference in birth weight is not the likely intervening link between social environment and measured intelligence in school children. Similarly, within families with a mildly retarded child, the affected child is no more likely than his sibs to have been of low birth weight or small for the period of gestation.[7,22] These observations strengthen the view that certain forms of mild mental retardation, and particularly the cultural-familial syndrome, depend primarily on membership in families of distinctive character and milieu.

The distinction between organic impairment and dysfunction may be at the root of the apparent incoherence of the relationship of mental performance with low birth weight. Most factors causing functional disability act postnatally. If prenatal factors cause mild impairment, a plausible hypothesis is that this impairment can be compensated for by acquired functional abilities. Compensation may occur only in favorable circumstances. Some studies, but not all, point to interaction between the effects of low birth weight and social class on mental retardation. In these, moderately low birth weight was associated with mental retardation or lowered IQ only among the lower classes and not among the

higher. Moderately low birth weight seems to be neither a sufficient nor a necessary cause of mild mental retardation, but it may be a contributory cause in unfavorable circumstances.

2. Preeclamptic toxemia is often associated with other obstetric complications. It is difficult to isolate its role as a cause of mental retardation because other complications confound the results.[6] Another difficulty is that the epidemiology of toxemia is far from clear. Some studies indicate that toxemia is less frequent in times of starvation[177] and among the lower social classes. Studies of the relationship of toxemia with retardation must control for such factors, which may themselves produce the observed variations. Thus in Aberdeen, Scotland, children with preeclamptic toxemia scored above the normal in IQ, but when social class was controlled, the infants of toxemic mothers were at a slightly higher risk of mental retardation.[22] In that result, however, the toxemia was almost always associated with other obstetric complications. One Canadian study, which controlled for both social and obstetric factors, also concluded that a small amount of intellectual handicap could be attributed to toxemia.[26]

3. Multiple births are associated with a raised risk of mental retardation.[17,27] In some cases, as with low birth weight, retardation can be attributed to evident fetal abnormality. Twins and triplets experience many perinatal complications that relate to mental retardation more often than singletons: curtailed gestation, low birth weight, intrauterine growth retardation, long and short labor, toxemia, malposition, antepartum hemorrhage are all more common among them. Their intellectual retardation, however, is greater than can be accounted for by these factors alone.

Explanations of the mental retardation of twins must also weigh the contributions of prenatal organic impairment and postnatal experience. Among single survivors of twin births, mean IQ is approximately normal at eleven years of age, whereas among pairs of survivors, mean IQ is several points lower.[160] Single survivors differ from pairs of survivors in their postnatal experience, and their better intellectual performance can be attributed to postnatal causes rather than to chromosomal, intrauterine, or intranatal causes.*

In sum, low birth weight, toxemia, and multiple births are all closely associated with perinatal mortality and organic brain impairment. Where impairment is gross, mental retardation is often severe. Where impairment is not gross, its contribution to intellectual function in later life is overshadowed by postnatal experience. This is not to deny that these three natal circumstances have some predictive power in relation to mental retardation. This predictive power rests in the main on their association with other factors, such as congenital anomalies, neurological lesions, or socioeconomic status. In assessing causes in the individual case, these related factors always need evaluation.

Nutrition

In recent years, malnutrition has been strongly canvassed as a cause of mental retardation.[51] In animal experiments, diets sufficient only to keep the animals alive damage the central nervous system.[40,191] Effects include neuromotor and behavioral abnormalities[9,42,53] as well as reduced brain weight and changes in the histology and biochemistry of spinal cord and brain.[62]

The period of most active growth of a target organ (whether measured by cell numbers or by cell size and differentiation) is supposedly the time of its greatest vulnerability to insult. The theory of the critical period postulates that to interdict growth processes of an organ at the time of maximum growth and vulnerability will not only retard the processes but will prevent their taking place at later life stages.[63,215] In the human brain, two periods of maximum growth are thought to be early in gestation and in the months just before and after birth. The proliferation of neurone and glial cells takes place in the early phases of gestation, and growth in their size in the later phases.

In humans, nutritional deprivation can seldom be pinpointed in time, as a test of this hypothesis requires. No evidence bears on malnutrition during the postulated period of maximum vulnerability early in gestation, and that which bears on late prenatal and early postnatal life is scant. Starvation of the mother during the late prenatal period leads to low birth weight in the infant,[177] and other forms of malnutrition may possibly also cause low birth weight.[19] According to one investigator, study of a few infants who died of acute malnutrition during the first year of life showed a marked deficiency of cell number in the brain. The deficiency of cell number was more marked in infants of low birth weight, which pointed to a process initiated prenatally. Infants who died of acute malnutrition in the second year of life did not have a deficiency of cell number in the brain, which suggested that after early infancy malnutrition did not affect proliferation.[214]

In published reports of mental retardation supposedly induced by malnutrition, the earliest episodes of malnutrition have been in the postnatal months.[39,55,192,220] Thus, among sixteen marasmic infants admitted to hospital in Santiago, Chile, during the first six months of life, usually when a diet of flour and water had been substituted for breast feeding, several were found to be severely retarded later in childhood.[142] During the second and third years of life, an association of malnutrition and mental retardation has not been demonstrated as yet, and in adulthood severe malnutrition has not been associated with mental retardation, aside from pellagrinous dementia.

If mental retardation is caused by malnutrition, this cause is likely to be associated with forms of mental retardation that are commoner among the poor. In industrial societies food deficiencies, like mild mental retardation without organic impairment, are concentrated almost exclusively among the poor. The more severe degrees of mental retardation show no more than a slight predilection for the poor. In the United States, Sweden, and Great Britain, therefore, it would be safe to predict that any malnutrition-induced syndrome would be a form of mild mental retardation and would be

---

* It is possible but unlikely that both the survival of single twins and their better performance are the outcome of environments more favorable than those in which pairs survive.

reflected in indicators of function and role, rather than of impairments.[182] In the developing countries of Asia, Africa, and South America, little is known of the distribution of the different forms and degrees of mental retardation. In these harsher environments, malnutrition-induced cases of severe mental retardation may conceivably occur.

Demographic Factors

Maternal age is a major factor in the incidence of Down's syndrome.[120,136,156,162] The chances of bearing a child with Down's syndrome increase sharply with the age of the mother at the time she conceives. Parity and paternal age are closely linked with maternal age, but do not add to the risk of Down's syndrome.

The incidence rates at birth of Down's syndrome, for each maternal age, exhibit a high degree of stability at different times and places.* The proportionate contribution of older women, however, varies with the demographic trends affecting all births.[154,188] The frequency of all births depends on the age-specific fertility rates among women of different ages and on the proportion of women of different ages comprising the child-bearing population. Both are highly variable. The proportion of all births with Down's syndrome, therefore, is also variable.

The natural variation in child bearing points to the possibility of reducing the frequency of retardation by voluntary restriction of fertility. Knowledge and techniques are available with which to reduce significantly the incidence at birth of Down's syndrome.[122] Women in their later years of fertility are clearly a salient target group for a preventive program. So too are those few at risk of transmitting the condition genetically. Public attitudes and laws about contraception and abortion are changing, methods of prenatal diagnosis have been developed, and the problem is ripe for attack.[52,188] The hazard to older women needs to be made widely known and contraceptive advice and methods made fully available to older couples. For older women who fall pregnant, whether by accident or design, prenatal diagnosis could contribute an important part to a preventive program. The existence of a fetus with Down's syndrome can be diagnosed by amniocentesis, with reasonable accuracy and apparent safety, fourteen to sixteen weeks after conception.[146] Should a diagnosis of Down's syndrome be made by intrauterine aspiration, it should be mandatory to offer the mother the choice of a therapeutic abortion. Where the laws permit, there seems good reason to advise elective abortion.

The affected embryo can be identified in the amniotic fluid, just as in Down's syndrome, in a growing number of genetic diseases.[122,146] Several are causes of mental retardation. Theoretically, these forms of mental retardation can also be reduced in incidence by identifying women at high risk and monitoring their pregnancies by amniocentesis. Some of the inborn errors of metabolism, enzyme defects inherited through autosomal recessive genes, serve as examples. Some defects in lipid metabolism affecting the mucopolysaccharides (Hurler syndrome, Hunter syndrome)[127] and the sphingolipids (Tay-Sachs disease)[148] and some defects in sugar metabolism[98] are causes of mental retardation.[126] In these conditions, the birth of an affected child is often the first indication, too late for prevention, that a couple is at high risk because each member is heterozygous for the gene. In some cases, the prediction of high risk can be made before conception. Information on kin and biochemical methods of detecting heterozygosity sophisticate prediction and permit prenatal confirmation and action. In other cases, notably the enzyme defect in protein metabolism expressed in phenylketonuria, high risk can be predicted before conception, but prenatal diagnosis has not been achieved. The risk is recognized from family and obstetric history and from phenylalanine levels in the blood compatible with heterozygosity for the gene. Action must therefore be taken before conception or after birth. Mothers with still higher levels of phenylalanine blood levels compatible with homozygosity have a high risk of giving birth to a child already affected by the

* See references 48, 120, 130, 156, and 206.

TABLE 31–1.   Rates from Selected Prevalence Studies of Mental Retardation: By Period, Location, Age Group, and Case Source

SOURCE OF REPORT	PERIOD	CASE SOURCE	LOCATION	AGE SPECIFIC RATES PER 1,000			AGE GROUP
				Severe < 50IQ	*Mild* > 50IQ	*Total*	
Great Britain							
Royal Commission[202] (Tredgold)	1904	Key informants, schools, agencies	Manchester, Glasgow, and Belfast			12.0 7.4 5.0	Elementary school children
E. O. Lewis[118]	1925–1927	Key informants, and screening of schools; psychometric validation	3 urban areas 3 rural areas	3.76 6.14	17.14 33.56		7–14 7–14
Goodman and Tizard[80]	1960	Official register	Middlesex, England, and Wales	3.61			10–14
Kushlick,[109] Susser[194]	1961	Official register	Salford	3.25			10–19
Kushlick,[109] Susser[194]	1961	Official register	Salford		6.60		15–19
Kushlick[108]	1964	Special census of local agencies	Urban and rural Wessex	3.75			15–19
Innes and Kidd[97]	1968	Official register	Northeast Scotland	3.70	9.50		15–19
Birch et al.[22]	1970	Screening of schools, psychometric validation	Aberdeen	3.40	23.70		8–10

	Year	Method	Location			Age
United States						
Lemkau et al.[116]	1933–1936	Agency records; household sample census	Baltimore, eastern county	3.30	40.30	10–14
Oregon State Board of Health[151]	1962	Agency records	Oregon	3.30	19.30 30.30	under 20 12–14
Lemkau and Imre[115]	1966	Complete household survey, school screening, psychometric validation	Maryland rural	13.89	71.00	10–14
Netherlands						
Hartogh[88]	1954	Questionnaire to households	Gelderland, towns and villages	3.20	37.90	10–14
Sorel[180]	1968–1969	Administrative and psychometric screening	Amsterdam	7.34	9.50	13
Australia						
Krupinski et al.[106]	1963	Agency records	Victoria	1.91	4.56	12–14
Sweden						
Akesson[2]	1964	Agency records, key informants	Western Sweden, rural	5.50		10–20

raised maternal level;[86] in such cases the only successful prevention known is to prevent conception or induce abortion.

These various diagnostic advances point to the possibilities of screening programs. Large-scale screening has been practiced for some years in order to detect disease and prevent or treat it. For rare autosomal recessive genetic conditions, phenylketonuria programs serve as a prototype. In the course of the development of these large-scale screening programs, guiding principles for planning and evaluation have evolved. Screening tests must be sensitive enough to detect virtually all at risk and avoid false negatives. They must be specific enough to avoid false positives, each of which may entail extensive further diagnostic studies. Statistical tests are available to evaluate efficiency in terms of sensitivity and specificity.[128] The influence of frequency of the condition on the efficiency of screening should also be taken into account. Given efficient detection, its timing must be early enough to permit intervention while prevention or treatment is possible. Finally, intervention must be shown to be not only possible but effective, often a difficult challenge. Most screening programs proceed on these assumptions; all too few actually test them.

(Prevalence

Prevalence studies of mental retardation, like those chosen for illustration in Table 31–1, are difficult to interpret and compare. The difficulties reside in differences in the methods used to find cases and in the criteria used to define them. It can be seen from Table 31–1 that the disparity between surveys is much reduced provided comparisons are limited to specific age groups with the gross impairment of severe mental retardation. When there is little or no impairment, as with mild mental retardation, and ascertainment depends on functional and social criteria that differ from one survey to another, the disparities between rates remain marked. Apart from these methodological considerations, variation in rates is to be expected. The mentally retarded population, sensitive like other populations to the social environment, is both dynamic and unstable. It is dynamic in that there is continual recruitment of new individuals and loss of old ones.[187] It is unstable in that the balance between losses and recruitment is changing. The time trends for severe and mild mental retardation diverge sharply and will be considered separately.

The Prevalence of Severe Mental Retardation

Losses to the mentally retarded population are occurring at a slower rate than before because the death rate is declining and survival is improving. For evidence we turn to Down's syndrome, an excellent epidemiological index. The diagnosis is one of the least equivocal in medicine, and the population is one of the most complete and representative within the whole class of mental retardation. Life tables constructed for cases of Down's syndrome show an undoubted increase in longevity over the last generation.[33,49] Prevalence at the age of ten years appears to have risen from 1 in 4,000 in 1929 to 1 in 2,000 in 1949 and to a possibly still higher rate in 1960.

Improvements in medical and surgical treatments, in public health and the techniques of immunization against infectious diseases, and in the physical environment and accident control all reduce mortality in Down's syndrome. They prolong life without in any way modifying the accompanying mental retardation. The major cause of death in the past, respiratory infection, has been much reduced by antibiotic treatment. In most cases, death is now due to associated anomalies, such as those of the heart or gut.[74] Leukemia kills a fraction (about 1 in 95).[73] Half of the infants born with Down's syndrome die before their fifth birthday, but those who survive beyond it tend to continue in reasonably good health for several decades, so that in later life presenile symptoms and diabetes are coming to be recognized as common among them. In industrial societies, Down's syndrome now makes the largest single contribution to the prevalence of severe mental retardation both in the community and in residential institutions.

Down's syndrome serves as a paradigm for all forms of severe mental retardation. The total number of handicapped persons for whom families and communities must make provision has risen. Thus surgery prolongs the life of children with spina bifida and hydrocephalus,[164] conditions accompanied often by severe physical handicap and sometimes by mental handicap. During the decade 1950 to 1960, in the United States, the peak rate for deaths attributed to all congenital anomalies shifted from the under five age group to the five to fourteen age group.[144]

Survival is reflected in the prevalence of all forms of severe mental retardation. In Salford, England, data compiled from community registers pointed to a life span for severely retarded people that was longer in 1963[194, p. 289] than in 1948, and even longer in 1968.[78] In the interval 1948 to 1963, there was an average increase in the rate of the registered population of 4.75 per 100,000 per year. Table 31–2 shows that this increase in the population was accompanied by aging. The most notable increment was to the older age groups. Within the short period of fifteen years, a longer life span had evidently produced a notable increase in the prevalence of severe mental retardation.

In general, the available evidence from developed countries points to a changing trend in recruitment to the mentally retarded population.[80,187] The trends suggest a fall in incidence as well as a rise in longevity. New cases of Down's syndrome are probably occurring less frequently than before because older mothers have curtailed their child-bearing period. New cases of other types of severe mental retardation have probably declined even more dramatically. In England, the prevalence of Down's syndrome at ten years of age observed in 1960 by Goodman and Tizard[80] was higher than that observed by Lewis thirty-five years earlier; the prevalence of other kinds of severe mental retardation at the same age in 1960 was only two-thirds as high. In the face of prolonged survival for all kinds of severe subnormality, a decline in the prevalence of mental retardation other than Down's syndrome most likely came about through a considerable decline in incidence.*

To sum up, in severe mental retardation advances in public health, medicine, and surgery, and social change generally have reduced the incidence of impairment and intellectual disability at a slower rate than they have increased survival and prevalence.

Prevalence of Mild Mental Retardation

Longevity is not of major significance in the prevalence of mild mental retardation. The social handicap of mild mental retardation consistently has maximum prevalence in the second decade, building to a peak at adolescence, with a sharp decline into early adulthood and through the third decade.[45,83,118, 150,155] Death rates at these ages have been

* Another possibility is that cases of mental retardation that would once have been classified as severe are now classified as mild. If so, in order to accommodate such reassignment, the decline in the prevalence of mild mental retardation must be even more marked than we suggest.

TABLE 31–2.   **Registered Severely Subnormal Population in Salford[194] in 1948 and 1963 Compared: Age-Specific Rates per 100,000 by Ten-Year Age Groups[a]**

| | AGE GROUPS | | | | | | | |
	0–9	10–19	20–29	30–39	40–49	50–59	60–69	N
January 1, 1948	70	290	270	221	96	49	39	147
January 1, 1963	152	209	182	198	180	113	61	238

[a] The increased rate in the 0–9 year age group is the result of an active case-finding program instituted about five years before 1963.

low during recent times; the room for variation is too little to affect prevalence to the same degree as in severe retardation.

The age distribution of mild mental retardation is the result of the limited duration of the state of mental handicap in the majority of cases of this condition.[186] Diagnostic labels are assigned only after role failures are recognized,[133,134] usually at school,[61] and the child is referred for psychometric and medical review. In early adulthood, the labels tend to be removed once the affected individuals resume normal occupational or domestic roles.[5,37,150]

The duration and age distribution of mild mental retardation are not solely a matter of the assignment of the role of mental handicap to individuals with intellectual deficits. It is also a matter of the duration of intellectual dysfunction. The dysfunction that ordinarily underlies mild mental handicap seems to be, as noted above, of two broad types: One type is associated with organic impairments, usually prenatal in origin, and accounts for about one-quarter of cases; the other type is not associated with organic impairment and accounts for the remainder.

The intellectual deficit associated with organic impairment seems to be stable and permanent.[183] The undemanding roles of early childhood are within the capacities of these affected individuals. At pubescence, as educational demands in particular become more exacting, deficiencies in capacities for role performance become relatively greater. Social[135] recognition leads to the assignment of the diagnosis of mild mental retardation and the role of handicap.

The deficits associated with no detectable impairment, on the other hand, are not stable. A synthesis of the evidence suggests that the duration of these deficits runs concomitantly with the duration of handicap. Thus, the high frequency of mild mental handicap after pubescence can be linked with a decline in IQ. A number of studies suggest that the intellectual performance of groups at a marked social disadvantage grows progressively poorer up to adolescence, an outcome that can be attributed to a cumulative effect of exposure to an adverse environment.[81,114,208] Similarly, the

sharp fall in the frequency of mild mental handicap in early adulthood can be linked with IQ. As noted above,[186,187] persons with the cultural-familial syndrome have been shown to make gains in IQ in adolescence and young adulthood.[43,44]

More needs to be known about the distribution of IQ losses and gains and the size of the contribution of age changes to the frequency of mild retardation. We can conclude that for children at a marked social disadvantage pubescence is a highly vulnerable period. The handicap of such children appears greatest at just those ages when a competitive school system and specific socialization to the adult world begin to make their greatest demands. Although in cultural retardation a degree of intellectual and social recovery occurs without special treatment, it is uncertain how much permanent damage remains.

A decline in the prevalence of mild mental retardation should be expected. The social conditions that underlie the substantial fraction of cases without impairment are undeniably less harsh for the populations of industrial societies taken as a whole. In this instance, countervailing rises in longevity would affect only the prevalence of the smaller fraction of cases with impairment. Longevity would not affect the substantial social component that gives rise to disability and handicap of limited duration. Available evidence indeed points to a decline in prevalence.[185,186] This appears from cross-sectional surveys made in England over an interval of about four decades,[35,72] and from the Scottish surveys of national intelligence in 1932 and 1947.[172] In Sweden, too, after World War II, there was a decline in rejections for induction into the army because of poor mental performance.[159]

Since social change included improvements in nutrition, employment, social mobility, and education as well as reduction in mortality and morbidity rates, the decline in the prevalence of mild mental retardation cannot be related to any specific element of the social change. Improvement in the social environment of groups at a marked social disadvantage, however, can be expected to bring about a further decline in the prevalence of mild mental retardation. It seems likely that the greatest advantage will come from a serious attack on poverty and its cultural concomitants.

The Prevalence of Psychiatric Disability and Mental Retardation

The interrelationships between psychiatric disability, mental retardation, and organic impairment have been analyzed,[22,166,167,207] particularly in a recent study in the Isle of Wight, in the south of England.[166,167]

Among children with physical disorders, the proportion with psychiatric disability was about double the proportion in the general population. Among children with neuroepileptic symptoms and signs, the proportion was about five times as high. Among children with intellectual disability (measured by IQ), the proportion with psychiatric disability was still higher. The more severe the intellectual disability, the higher the rate of psychiatric disability. No single diagnosis among the mentally retarded population accounted for the high rate. Children had a high rate of psychiatric disability whether or not their intellectual disability was accompanied by signs of brain damage.

A prevalence study gives inadequate grounds for determining the time order of associations between manifestations, and therefore of the causal sequence among them. The bare facts do not permit a sure distinction to be made among conjunctions of physical, cerebral, intellectual, and psychiatric disorders that, on the one hand, have a common source in some antecedent underlying impairment and, on the other, arise successively in consequence of one another. In this study, a plausible interpretation seems to be that the high rate of psychiatric disability that occurred together with neurological disability (indicated by fits or spasticity) and severe intellectual disability had a common source in brain damage. In mild mental retardation in the absence of brain damage another explanation must be found for the raised rate of psychiatric disability. The excess of psychiatric disability that occurred both with mild mental handicap and physical handicap seems more likely to have been a consequence of the handicapped condition.

Implications for Care

The existence in the population of an increasing number of impaired individuals who will survive into later childhood and adulthood with severe mental retardation makes urgent the need to develop and apply new knowledge in its amelioration. The need focuses on three objectives: (1) to limit functional disability and social handicap in impaired persons; (2) to cultivate the maximum intellectual and social potential of those affected; and (3) to provide families and communities with appropriate supportive services to carry the burden of dependency.

The reduction of the prevalence of intellectual disability and mental handicap can be approached in two main ways. In some conditions, treatment of the underlying impairments can control their impact on intellectual function and role performance. In other conditions, the direct improvement of intellectual function and role performance can be attempted.

The effect on intellectual disability of controlling underlying impairment has been best elaborated, if still imprecisely, in phenylketonuria.[20,64] Here, dietary treatment in infancy and childhood has reduced the degree of intellectual disability, and perhaps its prevalence, in the cohorts of phenylketonuric infants identified at birth.

That the prevalence of functional disability can be reduced by means that develop intellectual function is indicated by several studies among the mildly retarded. First, longitudinal data on adolescents admitted to an institution for the mentally deficient showed that they continued to make IQ gains into their late twenties.[43,44] Second, in a cohort study of subjects labeled "educationally subnormal" at school, IQ gains were found in young adulthood among those with cultural-familial retardation.[183] Third, a special education program, begun in the preschool years and maintained for about three years, improved the performance of mildly retarded children.[102] Fourth, an experimental program of social and sensory stimulation, which started with pregnancy in retarded mothers and continued for four years, is reported to have shown remarkable benefits for stimulated children compared to controls.[90] Thus, improvement in the intellectual function of mildly retarded individuals is known to occur,[65] and the application of pedagogic and social techniques offers promise of accelerating the improvement. Widespread use of these methods would be necessary if there were to be any hope of inducing changes in the prevalence or in the distribution of the degree of disability.

The severity of mental handicap can be reduced by developing the full social potential of mentally retarded individuals. In adults, social adequacy can often be achieved by those with mental handicap. We have noted that the sharp decline in the age-specific prevalence of mild mental retardation from the mid-twenties coincides with the somewhat delayed adoption of adult roles by mildly retarded persons. The young man or woman who marries, or who acquires economic independence through working, no longer occupies the social role of a retarded person. According to follow-up studies of mildly retarded men and women, two-thirds to three-quarters have settled well in the extramural environment. To socialize individuals affected by mild mental retardation to adult roles can be expected to advance their recoveries, and thereby to reduce the prevalence of handicap.

The concept of socialization can equally well be applied to severely retarded individuals. Severely retarded children living in a large institution, when they were removed to a smaller home and given more individual attention, improved both their mental scores and their social skills compared with matched controls.[200] Among adults, when moderately retarded people were encouraged to achieve semi-independence by living in residential hostels and taking up supervised work, the level of dependency declined accordingly.[32] On the other hand, resettlement of residents from an institution into the outside world has

often proved difficult;[70] the difficulties point to the need for support and assistance beyond the immediate transition.[168]

Comprehensive and coordinated programs aimed at pedagogic, social, and residential improvements are needed to reduce the severity of mental handicap.[1,107,109,194,200] These programs, being recent, can be expected to do more in the future if they are properly planned and funded.

(Bibliography

1. ADAMS, M. *Mental Retardation and Its Social Dimensions.* New York: Columbia University Press, 1971.

2. AKESSON, H. O. *Epidemiology and Genetics of Mental Deficiency in a Southern Swedish Population.* Sweden: The Institute for Medical Genetics of the University of Uppsala, 1961.

3. AMERICAN PSYCHIATRIC ASSOCIATION. *Diagnostic and Statistical Manual of Mental Disorders.* 2d ed. Washington, D.C., 1968.

4. BACOLA, E., BEHRLE, F. C., and DE SCHWEINITZ, L. "Perinatal and Environmental Factors in Late Neurogenic Sequelae in Infants Having Birthweights from 1,500 to 2,500 Grams." *American Journal of Diseases of Children,* 112 (1966), 369–374.

5. BALLER, W. B. "A Study of the Present Social Status of a Group of Adults Who, When They Were in Elementary Schools, Were Classified as Mentally Deficient." *Genetic and Psychological Monographs,* (1936), 165–244.

6. BARKER, D. J. P. "Low Intelligence and Obstetrical Complications." *British Journal of Preventive and Social Medicine,* 20 (1966), 58–66.

7. ———. "Low Intelligence: Its Relation to Length of Gestation and Rate of Foetal Growth." *British Journal of Preventive and Social Medicine,* 20 (1966), 58–66.

8. BARLTROP, D. "The Prevalence of Pica." *American Journal of Diseases of Children,* 112 (1966), 116–123.

9. BARNES, R. H., MOORE, A. U., REID, I. M., and POND, W. G. "Learning Behavior Following Nutritional Deprivations in Early Life." *Journal of the American Dietary Association,* 51 (1967), 34–39.

10. BARON, J., YOUNGBLOOD, L., SIEWERS. C. M. F., and MEDEARIS, D. N. "The Incidence of Cytomegalovirus, Herpes Simplex, Rubella, and Toxoplasma Antibodies in the Microcephalic, Mentally Retarded." *Pediatrics*, 44 (1969), 932–939.

11. BAZSO, J., MALAN, M., SOOS, A., PIPAK, J., and ZSADANY, O. "The Later Effects of Prenatal Malnutrition on the Physical and Mental Development of Twins." In B. W. Richards, ed., *Proceedings of the First International Congress on Scientific Study of Mental Deficiency*. Reigate, Surrey: Michael Jackson, 1968.

12. BENDA, C. E. "Congenital Syphilis in Mental Deficiency." *American Journal of Mental Deficiency*, 47 (1942), 40–48.

13. BERENDES, H. W. "The Role of Infectious Diseases in the Causation of Mental Subnormality: A Brief Overview." In U.S. Department of Health, Education and Welfare, *The Prevention of Mental Retardation Through Control of Infectious Diseases*. Public Health Service publication, no. 1692. Washington, D.C.: U.S. Government Printing Office, 1968. Pp. 5–22.

14. BERG, I, M. "Neurological Complications of Pertussis Immunization." *British Medical Journal*, 2 (1958), 24–27.

15. ———. "Neurological Sequelae of Pertussis with Particular Reference to Mental Defect." *Archives of the Diseases of Childhood*, 34 (1959), 322–324.

16. ———, and KIRMAN, B. H. "Some Aetiological Problems in Mental Deficiency." *British Medical Journal*, 2 (1959), 848–852.

17. ———, and KIRMAN, B. H. "The Mentally Defective Twin." *British Medical Journal*, 1 (1960), 1911–1917.

18. ———, and ZAPELLA, M. "Lead Poisoning in Childhood with Particular Reference to Pica and Mental Sequelae." *Journal of Mental Deficiency Research*, 8 (1964), 44–53.

19. BERGNER, L., and SUSSER, M. W. "Low Birthweight and Prenatal Nutrition: An Interpretative Review." *Pediatrics*, 46 (1970), 946–966.

20. BERMAN, D. W., WAISMAN, H. A., and GRAHAM, F. K. "Intelligence in Treated Phenylketonuric Children: A Developmental Study." *Child Development*, 37 (1966), 731–747.

21. BIRCH, H. G., and GUSSOW, J. D. *Disadvantaged Children, Health, Nutrition and School Failure*. New York: Grune & Stratton, 1970.

22. ———, RICHARDSON, S. A., BAIRD, D., HOROBIN, G., and ILLSLEY, R. *Mental Subnormality: A Clinical and Epidemiologic Study in the Community*. New York: Williams & Wilkins, 1970.

23. BLACK, F. L., and DAVIS, D. E. M. "Measles and Readiness for Reading and Learning: II. New Haven Study." *American Journal of Epidemiology*, 88 (1968), 337–344.

24. BLANKSMA, L. A., SACHS, H. K., MURRAY, E. F., and O'CONNELL, M. J. "Incidence of High Blood Lead Levels in Chicago Children." *Pediatrics*, 44 (1969), 661–667.

25. BRIMBLECOMBE, F. S. W., and ASHFORD, J. R. "Significance of Low Birth Weight in Perinatal Mortality." *British Journal of Preventive and Social Medicine*, 22 (1968), 27–35.

26. BUCK, C., GREGG, R., STAVRAKY, K., SUBRAHMANIAM, K., and BROWN, J. "The Effect of Single Prenatal and Natal Complications Upon the Development of Children of Mature Birthweight." *Pediatrics*, 43 (1969), 942–955.

27. BULMER, M. G. *The Biology of Twinning in Man*. Oxford: Clarendon Press, 1970.

28. BURT, C. *The Backward Child*. London: University of London Press, 1937.

29. BUTLER, N. R., and ALBERMAN, E. D., eds. *Perinatal Problems: The Second Report of the 1958 British Perinatal Mortality Survey*. London: Livingston, 1969.

30. ———, and BONHAM, D. G. *Perinatal Mortality*. Edinburgh: Livingstone, 1963.

31. BYERS, R. K., and RIZZO, N. D. "A Follow-Up Study of Pertussis in Infancy," *New England Journal of Medicine*, 242 (1950), 887.

32. CAMPBELL, A. C. "Comparison of Family and Community Contacts of Mentally Subnormal Adults in Hospital and in Local Authority Hostels." *British Journal of Preventive and Social Medicine*, 22 (1968), 165–169.

33. CARTER, C. O. "A Life Table for Mongols with the Causes of Death." *Journal of Mental Deficiency Research*, 2 (1958), 64–74.

34. ———, EVANS, K. A., and STEWART, A. M. "Maternal Radiation and Down's Syndrome." *Lancet*, 1 (1961), 1042.

35. CATTELL, R. B. "The Fate of National Intelligence: Test of a Thirteen-Year Predic-

tion." *Eugenics Review,* 42 (1950), 136–148.

36. CHANOCK, R. M. "Mycoplasma Infections of Man." *New England Journal of Medicine,* 273 (1965), 1199–1206, 1257–1264.

37. CHARLES, D. C. "Ability and Accomplishment of Persons Earlier Judged Mentally Deficient." *Genetic and Psychological Monographs,* 47 (1953), 3–71.

38. CHASE, H. "Infant Mortality and Weight at Birth: 1960 United States Birth Cohort." *American Journal of Public Health,* 59 (1969), 1618–1628.

39. CHASE, P. H., and MARTIN, H. P. "Undernutrition and Child Development." *New England Journal of Medicine,* 282 (1970), 933–939.

40. CHEEK, D. B., GRAYSTONE, J. E., and READ, M. S. "Cellular Growth Nutrition and Development." *Pediatrics,* 45 (1970), 315–334.

41. CHISOLM, J. J. "Chronic Lead Intoxication in Children." *Developmental Medicine and Child Neurology,* 7 (1965), 529–536.

42. CHOW, B. F., BLACKWELL, R. Q., BLACKWELL, B., HOW, T. Y., ANILANE, J. K., and SHERWIN, R. W. "Maternal Nutrition and Metabolism of the Offspring; Studies in Rats and Man." *American Journal of Public Health,* 58 (1968), 668–677.

43. CLARKE, A. D. B., and CLARKE, A. M. "Recovery from the Effects of Deprivation." *Journal of Midland Mental Defective Society,* 4 (1957), 58–62.

44. ———, CLARKE, A. M., and REIMAN, S. "Cognitive and Social Changes in the Feebleminded: Three Further Studies." *British Journal of Psychology,* 49 (1958), 144–157.

45. CLARKE, A. M., and CLARKE, A. D. B. *Mental Deficiency: The Changing Outlook.* 2d ed. London: Methuen, 1966.

46. CLAUSEN, J. "Mental Deficiency: Development of a Concept." *American Journal of Mental Deficiency,* 71 (1967), 727–745.

47. COHEN, M. M., MARINELLO, M. J., and BACK, N. "Chromosomal Damage in Human Leukocytes Induced by Lysergic Acid Diethylamide." *Science,* 155 (1967), 1417–1419.

48. COLLMAN, R. D., and STOLLER, A. "A Survey of Mongoloid Births in Victoria, Australia, 1942–1957." *American Journal of Public Health,* 52 (1962), 813–829.

49. ———, and STOLLER, A. "Data on Mongolism in Victoria, Australia." *Journal of Mental Deficiency Research,* 7 (1963), 60–68.

50. COOPER, L. Z. "German Measles." *Scientific American,* 215 (1966), 30–37.

51. COURSIN, D. B. "Relationship of Nutrition to Central Nervous System Development and Function." *Federation Proceedings,* 26 (1967), 134–138.

52. COWIE, V. "Amniocentesis: A Means of Pre-Natal Diagnosis of Conditions Associated with Severe Mental Subnormality." *British Journal of Psychiatry,* 118 (1971), 83–86.

53. COWLEY, J. J., and GRIESEL, R. D. "Some Effects of a Low Protein Diet on a First Filial Generation of White Rats." *Journal of Genetic Psychology,* 95 (1959), 187–201.

54. CRAVIOTO, J., DE LICARDIE, M. S., and BIRCH, H. G. "Nutrition, Growth, and Neurointegrative Development: An Experimental and Ecologic Study." *Pediatrics,* 38, suppl. (1966), 319–372.

55. ———, and ROBLES, B. "Evolution of Adaptive and Motor Behavior During Rehabilitation from Kwashiorkor." *American Journal of Orthopsychiatry,* 35 (1965), 449–464.

56. CROME, L. "Pathological Aspects: General Sources of Information." In L. T. Hilliard and B. H. Kirman, eds., *Mental Deficiency.* London: Churchill, 1957. Pp. 86–87.

57. DAUER, C. C., KORMS, R. F., and SCHUMAN, L. M. *Infectious Diseases.* Cambridge, Mass.: Harvard University Press, 1968.

58. DEKABAN, A. S. "Abnormalities in Children Exposed to X-Radiation During Various Stages of Gestation: Tentative Timetable of Radiation Injury to the Human Fetus: Part 1." *Journal of Nuclear Medicine,* 9, suppl. 1 (1968), 471–478.

59. DESMIT, E. M. "A Follow-Up Study of 110 Patients Treated for Purulent Meningitis." *Archives of the Diseases of Childhood,* 38 (1963), 391–396.

60. DEXTER, L. A. "On the Politics and Sociology of Stupidity in Our Society." In H. S. Becker, ed., *The Other Side: Perspectives in Deviance.* New York: The Free Press, 1964. Pp. 37–49.

61. ———. *The Tyranny of Schooling: An Inquiry into the Problem of "Stupidity."* New York: Basic Books, 1964.

62. DICKERSON, J. W. T., DOBBING, J., and

McCance, R. A. "The Effects of Undernutrition in the Postnatal Development of the Brain and Cord in Pigs." *Proceedings of Royal Society of Medicine*, 166 (1967), 397–407.

63. Dobbing, J. "Vulnerable Periods in Developing Brain." In A. N. Davison and J. Dobbing, eds., *Applied Neurochemistry*. London: Blackwell, 1968. Pp. 287–316.

64. Dobson, J., Koch, R., Williamson, M., Spector, R., Frankenburg, W., O'Flynn, M., Warner, R., and Hudson, F. "Cognitive Development and Dietary Therapy in Phenylketonuric Children." *New England Journal of Medicine*, 278 (1968), 1142–1144.

65. Doll, E. A. "Is Mental Deficiency Curable?" *American Journal of Mental Deficiency*, 51 (1947), 420–428.

66. Douglas, J. W. B. "Premature Children at Primary Schools." *British Medical Journal*, 1 (1960), 1008–1013.

67. Drillien, C. M. "Studies in Mental Handicap: II. Some Obstetrical Factors of Possible Aetiological Significance." *Archives of the Diseases of Childhood*, 43 (1968), 283–294.

68. ———. "The Small-for-Date Infant: Etiology and Prognosis." *Pediatric Clinics of North America*, 17 (1970), 9–24.

69. ———, Jameson, S., and Wilkinson, E. M. "Studies in Mental Handicaps: Part I. Prevalence and Distribution by Clinical Type and Severity of Defect." *Archives of the Diseases of Childhood*, 41 (1966), 528–538.

70. Edgerton, R. B. *The Cloak of Competence, Stigma in the Lives of the Mentally Retarded*. Berkeley: University of California Press, 1967.

71. Eichenwald, H. F. "Congenital Toxoplasmosis: A Study of One Hundred Fifty Cases." *American Journal of Diseases of Children*, 94 (1957), 411–412.

72. Emmett, W. G. "The Trend of Intelligence in Certain Districts of England." *Population Studies*, 3 (1950), 324–337.

73. Fabia, J., and Drolette, M. "Malformations and Leukemia in Children with Down's Syndrome." *Pediatrics*, 45 (1970), 60–70.

74. ———, and Drolette, M. "Life Tables Up to Age 10 for Mongols with and without Congenital Heart Defect." *Journal of Mental Deficiency Research*, 14 (1970), 235–242.

75. Fairweather, D. V. L., and Illsley, R. "Obstetrical and Social Origins of Mentally Handicapped Children." *British Journal of Preventive and Social Medicine*, 14 (1960), 149–159.

76. Fox, J. P., Black, F. L., Elveback, L., Kogon, A., Hall, C. E., Turgeon, L., and Abruzzi, W. "Measles and Readiness for Reading and Learning: 3. Wappingers Central School District Study." *American Journal of Epidemiology*, 88 (1968), 345–350.

77. ———, Black, F. L., and Kogon, A. "Measles and Readiness for Reading and Learning: 5. Evaluative Comparison of the Studies and Overall Conclusions." *American Journal of Epidemiology*, 88 (1968), 359–367.

78. Fryers, T., Freeman, H. L., and Mountney, G. H. "A Census of Psychiatric Patients in an Urban Community." *Social Psychiatry*, 5 (1970), 187–194.

79. Gibbs, F. A., Gibbs, E. L., Carpenter, P. R., and Spies, H. W. "Electroencephalographic Abnormality in 'Uncomplicated' Childhood Disease." *Journal of the American Medical Association*, 171 (1959), 1050–1055.

80. Goodman, N., and Tizard, J. "Prevalence of Imbecility and Idiocy Among Children." *British Medical Journal*, 1 (1962), 216–222.

81. Gordon, H. *Mental and Scholastic Tests Among Retarded Children*. Educational pamphlet, no. 44. London: Board of Education, 1923.

82. Griggs, R. C., Sunshine, I., Newill, V. A., Newton, B. W., Buchanan, S., and Rasch, C. A. "Environmental Factors in Childhood Lead Poisoning." *Journal of the American Medical Association*, 187 (1964), 703–707.

83. Gruenberg, E. M. "Epidemiology of Mental Retardation." *International Journal of Psychiatry*, 2 (1966), 78–134.

84. Guinee, V. F. Statement on Lead Poisoning. Paper presented to Subcommittee on Housing of the House Committee on Banking and Currency, 1970.

85. Hallgren, B., and Hollstrom, E. "Congenital Syphilis: A Follow-Up Study with Reference to Mental Abnormalities." *Acta*

Psychiatrica et Neurologica, 93, suppl. (1954), 1–81.

86. HANSEN, H. "Epidemiological Considerations of Maternal Hyperphenylalaninemia." *American Journal of Mental Deficiency*, 75 (1970), 22–26.

87. HANSHAW, J. B. "Cytomegalovirus Complement-Fixing Antibody in Microcephaly." *New England Journal of Medicine*, 275 (1966), 476–479.

88. HARTOGH, P. H. *Social Aspects of Mental Retardation in Zutphen and Bommelerwaard.* Stichting Gelderland voor Maatschappelijk Werk, 1957.

89. HEBER, R. *A Manual on Terminology and Classification in Mental Retardation.* 2d ed. *American Journal of Mental Deficiency* monograph supplement, 1961.

90. ———. An Experiment in Prevention of "Cultural-Familial" Mental Retardation. Paper presented to the Second Congress of the International Association for the Scientific Study of Mental Deficiency, Warsaw, Poland, 1970.

91. HILLIARD, L. T., and KIRMAN, B. H. *Mental Deficiency.* Boston: Little, Brown, 1965.

92. HOCKEY, K. A., and HAWKS, D. V. "An Analysis of Birth Weight and Period of Gestation in Relation to Mental Deficiency with Particular Reference to Small for Dates Babies." *Journal of Mental Deficiency Research*, 11 (1967), 169–184.

93. HOLZEL, A., and KOMROWER, G. M. "A Study of the Genetics of Galactosaemia." *Archives of the Diseases of Childhood*, 30 (1955), 155–159.

94. HUNTER, D. *The Diseases of Occupations.* 4th ed. Boston: Little, Brown, 1969.

95. HUSEN, T. "The Influence of Schooling Upon IQ." In J. J. Jenkins and D. G. Paterson, eds., *Studies in Individual Differences.* New York: Appleton-Century-Crofts, 1961. Pp. 677–693.

96. IMRE, P. D. "The Epidemiology of Mental Retardation in a Southeastern Rural U.S.A. Community." In B. W. Richards, ed., *Proceedings of the First International Congress for the Scientific Study of Mental Deficiency*, Reigate, Surrey: Michael Jackson, 1968.

97. INNES, G., and KIDD, C. B. "The Operational Significance of Regional Morbidity Data on Mental Deficiency." *Health Bulletin*, 25 (1967), 1–5.

98. IRWIN, S., and EGOZCUE, J. "Chromosomal Abnormalities in Leukocytes from LSD-25 Users." *Science*, 157 (1967), 313–314.

99. JACOBZINER, H. "Lead Poisoning in Childhood Epidemiology; Manifestations and Prevention." *Clinical Pediatrics*, 5 (1966), 277–286.

100. KATZ, C. M., and TAYLOR, P. M. "The Incidence of Low Birthweight in Children with Severe Mental Retardation." *American Journal of Diseases of Children*, 114 (1967), 80–87.

101. KENNEDY, W. A. *A Follow-Up Normative Study of Negro Intelligence and Achievement.* Monographs of the Society for Research in Child Development, no. 34. Chicago: University of Chicago Press, 1969.

102. KIRK, S. A. *Early Education of the Mentally Retarded.* Chicago: University of Illinois Press, 1958.

103. KIRMAN, B. H. "Tuberculous Meningitis as a Cause of Mental Deficiency." *British Medical Journal*, 2 (1958), 1515.

104. KNOBLOCH, H., and PASAMANICK, B. "Mental Subnormality." *New England Journal of Medicine*, 266 (1962), 1045–1051, 1092–1097, 1155–1161.

105. KOGON, A., HALL, C. E., COONEY, M. K., and FOX, J. P. "Measles and Readiness for Reading and Learning: 4. Shoreline School District Study." *American Journal of Epidemiology*, 88 (1968), 351–358.

106. KRUPINSKI, J., STOLLER, A., MACMILLAN, C., and POLKE, P. "Survey of Mental Retardation Amongst Victorian Children." *Journal of Mental Deficiency Research*, 10 (1966), 33–46.

107. KUGEL, R., and WOLFENSBERGER, W., eds. *Changing Patterns in Residential Services for the Mentally Retarded.* Washington, D.C.: U.S. Government Printing Office, 1969.

108. KUSHLICK, A. "The Prevalence of Recognized Mental Subnormality of I.Q. Under 50 Among Children in the South of England with Reference to the Demand for Places for Residential Care." In D. Jakob, ed., *Proceedings of the International Copenhagen Conference on the Scientific Study of Mental Retardation.* Vol. 2. Det Berlingski Bogtrykkeri, 1964. Pp. 550–556.

109. ———. "Community Services for the Mentally Subnormal. A Plan for Experimental Evaluation." *Proceedings of the Royal Society of Medicine*, 58 (1965), 374–380.

110. LECK, I. "Examination of the Incidence of Malformations for Evidence of Drug Teratogenesis." *British Journal of Preventive and Social Medicine*, 18 (1964), 196–201.

111. ――――, HAY, S., WITTE, J. J., and GREENE, J. C. "Malformations Recorded in Birth Certificates Following A2 Influenza Epidemics." *Public Health Report*, 84 (1969), 971–979.

112. ――――, and MILLER, E. L. M. "Short Term Changes in the Incidence of Malformations." *British Journal of Preventive and Social Medicine*, 17 (1963), 1–12.

113. ――――, RECORD, R. G., McKEOWN, T., and EDWARDS, J. H. "The Incidence of Malformations in Birmingham, England, 1950–1959." *Teratology*, 1 (1968), 263–280.

114. LEE, E. S. "Negro Intelligence and Selective Migration: A Philadelphia Test of the Klineberg Hypothesis." *American Sociological Review*, 16 (1951), 227–233.

115. LEMKAU, P., and IMRE, P. D. "Results of a Field Epidemiologic Study." *American Journal of Mental Deficiency*, 73 (1969), 858–863.

116. ――――, TIETZE, G., and COOPER, M. "Mental-Hygiene Problems in an Urban District." *Mental Hygiene*, 25 (1941), 624–646; 26 (1942), 100–119, 275–288.

117. LENZ, W., and KNAPP, K. "Fetal Malformations Due to Thalidomide." *German Medical Monthly*, 7 (1962), 253–258.

118. LEWIS, E. O. *Report on an Investigation into the Incidence of Mental Deficiency in Six Areas, 1925–1927.* (Part IV of Report of the Mental Deficiency Committee, Being a Joint Committee of the Board of Education and Board of Control.) London: His Majesty's Stationery Office, 1929.

119. ――――. "Types of Mental Deficiency and Their Social Significance." *Journal of Mental Science*, 79 (1933), 298–304.

120. LILIENFELD, A. M. *Epidemiology of Mongolism.* Baltimore: Johns Hopkins Press, 1969.

121. LIN-FU, J. S. "Screening for Lead Poisoning." *Pediatrics*, 45 (1970), 720–721.

122. LITTLEFIELD, J. W. "The Pregnancy at Risk for a Genetic Disorder." *New England Journal of Medicine*, 282 (1970), 627–628.

123. LORBER, J. "Long-Term Follow-Up of 100 Children Who Recovered from Tuberculous Meningitis." *Pediatrics*, 28 (1961), 778–791.

124. McBRIDE, W. G. "Thalidomide and Congenital Abnormalities." *Lancet*, 2 (1961), 1358.

125. McDONALD, A. *Children of Very Low Birth Weight.* London: Heinemann, 1967.

126. McISAAC, W. M., CLAGHORN, J., and FARRELL, G., eds. *Advances in Mental Science: I. Congenital Mental Retardation.* Austin: University of Texas Press, 1969.

127. McKUSICK, V. A. *Heritable Disorders of Connective Tissue.* 3d ed. St. Louis: Mosby, 1966.

128. MacMAHON, B., and PUGH, T. F. *Epidemiology: Principles and Methods.* Boston: Little, Brown, 1970.

129. MASLAND, R. L. "The Prevention of Mental Retardation: A Survey of Research." *American Journal of Diseases of Children*, 95 (1958), 3–111.

130. MATSUNAGA, E. "Parental Age, Live-Birth Order and Pregnancy-Free Interval in Down's Syndrome in Japan." In G. E. W. Wolstenholme and R. Porter, eds., *Mongolism.* Ciba Foundation study group, no. 25. Boston: Little, Brown, 1967. Pp. 6–22.

131. MELLINS, R. B., and JENKINS, C. D. "Epidemiological and Psychological Study of Lead Poisoning in Children." *Journal of the American Medical Association*, 158 (1955), 15–20.

132. MENSER, M. A., SYDNEY, M. B., DODS, L., SYDNEY, M. D., and HARLEY, J. D. "A Twenty-Five Year Follow-Up of Congenital Rubella." *Lancet*, 2 (1967), 1347–1350.

133. MERCER, J. R. "Social System Perspective and Clinical Perspective: Frames of Reference for Understanding Career Patterns of Persons Labelled as Mentally Retarded." *Social Problems*, 13 (1965), 18–34.

134. ――――. "Who Is Normal? Two Perspectives in Mild Mental Retardation." In E. G. Jaco, ed., *Patients, Physicians and Illnesses.* 2d ed. New York: The Free Press, 1969. Pp. 66–85.

135. ――――, BUTLER, E. W., and DINGMAN, H. F. "The Relationship Between Social Developmental Performance and Mental Ability." *American Journal of Mental Deficiency*, 69 (1964), 195–205.

136. MILHAM, S., and GITTLESOHN, A. M. "Parental Age and Malformations." *Human Biology*, 37 (1965), 13–23.

137. MILLAR, J. A., BATTISHINI, V., CUMMING, R. L. C., CARSWELL, F., and GOLDBERG, A. "Lead and Aminolaevulinic Acid Dehydratase Levels in Mentally Retarded Chil-

dren and in Lead Poisoned Suckling Rats."
Lancet, 2 (1970), 695–698.

138. MILLER, H. C., CLIFFORD, S. H., SMITH,
C. A., WARKANY, J., WILSON, J. L., and
YANNET, H. "Special Report from the
Committee for the Study of Congenital
Malformations of the American Academy
of Pediatrics: A Study of the Relation of
Congenital Malformations to Maternal
Rubella and Other Infections—Preliminary
Report." *Pediatrics*, 3 (1949), 259–270.

139. MILLER, H. G., STANTON, J. B., and GIB-
BONS, J. L. "Para-Infectious Encephalo-
myelitis and Related Syndromes: A Critical
Review of the Neurological Complications
of Certain Specific Fevers." *Quarterly
Journal of Medicine*, 25 (1956), 427–505.

140. MILLER, R. W. "Delayed Radiation Effects
in Atomic-Bomb Survivors." *Science*, 166
(1969), 569–573.

141. ———, and BLOT, W. J. "Small Head Size
after In-Utero Exposure to Atomic Radiation." *Lancet*, 2 (1972), 784–787.

142. MONCKEBERG, F. "Effect of Early Marasmic
Malnutrition on Subsequent Physical and
Psychological Development." In N. S.
Scrimshaw and J. E. Gordon, eds., *Mal-
nutrition, Learning, and Behavior*. Cam-
bridge, Mass.: Massachusetts Institute of
Technology Press, 1968. Pp. 269–278.

143. MONCRIEFF, A. A., KOUMIDES, P. O., CLAY-
TON, B. E., PATRICK, A. D., RENWICK,
A. F. F., and ROBERTS, G. E. "Lead
Poisoning in Children." *Archives of the
Diseases of Childhood*, 39 (1964), 1–13.

144. MORIYAMA, I. M. *The Change in Mortality
Trend in the U.S.* National Center for
Health Statistics, series 3, no. 1. Washington, D.C.: U.S. Government Printing Office,
1964.

145. MORLEY, D. "Severe Measles in the Tropics." *British Medical Journal*, 1 (1969),
297–300, 363–365.

146. NADLER, H. L., and BERBIE, A. B. "Amniocentesis in the Intrauterine Detection of
Genetic Disorders." *New England Journal
of Medicine*, 282 (1970), 596–599.

147. NEEL, J. V., and SCHULL, W. J. "The
Effect of Exposure to the Atomic Bombs
on Pregnancy Termination in Hiroshima
and Nagasaki." *National Research Council
Publication*, 461 (1956), 151–163.

148. O'BRIEN, J. S., OKADA, S., FILLERUP, D. L.,
VEATH, M. L., ADORNATO, B., BRENNER,
P. H., and LEROY, J. G. "Tay-Sachs Disease:
Prenatal Diagnosis." *Science*, 172 (1971),
61–64.

149. O'CONNOR, N., and TIZARD, J. "A Survey
of Patients in Twelve Mental Deficiency
Institutions." *British Medical Journal*, 1
(1954), 16–18.

150. ———, and TIZARD, J. *The Social Problem
of Mental Deficiency*. London: Pergamon,
1956.

151. OREGON STATE BOARD OF HEALTH. *Mental
Retardation Prevalance in Oregon*. 1962.

152. PANUM, P. L. *Observations Made During
the Epidemic of Measles on the Faroe Islands in the Year 1846*. Cleveland: Delta
Omega Society, 1940.

153. PASAMANICK, B., and LILIENFELD, A. M.
"The Association of Maternal and Fetal
Factors with Development of Mental Deficiency: I. Abnormalities in the Prenatal
and Paranatal Periods." *Journal of the
American Medical Association*, 159
(1955), 155–160.

154. PENROSE, L. S. "The Incidence of Mongolism in the General Population." *Journal of
Mental Science*, 95 (1949), 685–688.

155. ———, BERG, J. M., and LANG-BROWN, H.
The Biology of Mental Defect. New York:
Grune & Stratton, 1963.

156. ———, and SMITH, G. F. *Down's Anomaly*.
Boston: Little, Brown, 1966.

157. PERLSTEIN, M. A., and ATTALA, R. "Neurologic Sequelae of Plumbism in Children."
Clinical Pediatrics, 5 (1966), 292–298.

158. PLUMMER, G. "Anomalies Occurring in
Children Exposed *In Utero* to the Atomic
Bomb in Hiroshima." *Pediatrics*, 10 (1952),
687–692.

159. RAYNER, S. "An Investigation of the Change
in Prevalence of Mental Deficiency in
Sweden." *Hereditas*, 51 (1964), 297–314.

160. RECORD, R. G., McKEOWN, T., and ED-
WARDS, I. H. "The Investigation of the
Difference in Measured Intelligence Between Twins and Single Births." *Annals
of Human Genetics*, 34 (1970), 11–20.

161. ———, McKEOWN, T., and EDWARDS, J. H.
"The Relation of Measured Intelligence to
Birth Weight and Duration of Gestation."
Annals of Human Genetics, 33 (1969),
71–79.

162. ———, and SMITH, A. "Incidence, Mortality
and Sex Distribution of Mongoloid De-
fectives." *British Journal of Preventive and
Social Medicine*, 9 (1955), 10–15.

163. RENNERT, O. M., WEINER, P., and MADDEN,

J. "Asymptomatic Lead Poisoning in 85 Chicago Children." *Clinical Pediatrics*, 9 (1970), 9–13.

164. RICKHAM, P. P., and MAWDSLEY, T. "The Effect of Early Operations on the Survival of Spina Bifida Cystica in Hydrocephalus and Spina Bifida." *Developmental Medicine and Child Neurology*, 11, suppl. 11 (1965), 20–26.

165. ROBERTS, J. A. F. "The Genetics of Mental Deficiency." *Eugenics Review*, 44 (1952), 71–83.

166. RUTTER, M., GRAHAM, P., and YULE, W. *A Neuropsychiatric Study in Childhood*. Philadelphia: Lippincott, 1970.

167. ———, TIZARD, J., and KINGSLEY, W., eds. *Education, Health, and Behavior*. London: Longmans, Green, 1970.

168. SAENGER, G. "The Adjustment of Severely Retarded Adults in the Community." *New York State Interdepartmental Health Resources Board*, 1957, p. 176.

169. ———. *Factors Influencing the Institutionalization of Mentally Retarded Individuals in New York City*. Albany: State Interdepartmental Health Resources Board, 1960.

170. SARASON, S. B., and GLADWIN, T. "Psychological and Cultural Problems in Mental Subnormality: A Review of Research." *Genetic and Psychological Monographs*, 57 (1958), 3–290.

171. SCHULL, W. J., and NEEL, J. V. "Maternal Radiation and Mongolism." *Lancet*, 1 (1962), 537–538.

172. SCOTTISH COUNCIL FOR RESEARCH IN EDUCATION. *The Trend of Scottish Intelligence: A Comparison of the 1947 and 1932 Surveys of the Intelligence of Eleven-Year-Old Pupils*. London: University of London Press, 1949.

173. SCRIMSHAW, N. S., TAYLOR, C. E., and GORDON, J. E. *Interactions of Nutrition and Infection*. Geneva: World Health Organization, Monograph no. 57, 1968.

174. SEVER, J. L. "Perinatal Infections Affecting the Developing Fetus and Newborn." In *The Prevention of Mental Retardation Through the Control of Infectious Diseases*. Public Health Service publication, no. 1692. Washington, D.C.: U.S. Government Printing Office, 1968. Pp. 37–68.

175. SHERIDAN, M. D. "Final Report of a Prospective Study of Children Whose Mothers Had Rubella in Early Pregnancy." *British Medical Journal*, 2 (1964), 536–539.

176. SIGLER, A. T., LILIENFELD, A. M., COHEN, B. H., and WESTLAKE, J. E. "Radiation Exposure in Parents of Children with Mongolism (Down's Syndrome)." *Bulletin of the Johns Hopkins Hospital*, 117 (1965), 374–399.

177. SMITH, C. A. "Effect of Wartime Starvation in Holland on Pregnancy and Its Products." *American Journal of Obstetrics and Gynecology* 53 (1947), 599–608.

178. SMITH, E. S. "Purulent Menningitis in Infants and Children: A Review of 409 Cases." *Journal of Pediatrics*, 45 (1954), 425–436.

179. SNYDER, R. D. "Congenital Mercury Poisoning." *New England Journal of Medicine*, 284 (1971), 1014–1016.

180. SOREL, F. M. *Prevalence of Mental Retardation*. Tilburg: Instituut voor Arbeidsvraagstukken van de Katholieke Hogeschool, 1970.

181. STARR, J. G., BART, R. D., and GOLD, E. "Inapparent Congenital Cytomegalovirus Infection." *New England Journal of Medicine*, 282 (1970), 1075–1078.

182. STEIN, Z. A., and KASSAB, H. "Nutrition." In J. Wortis, ed., *Mental Retardation*. Vol. 2. New York: Grune & Stratton, 1970. Pp. 92–116.

183. ———, and SUSSER, M. W. "Families of Dull Children:
I. "A Classification for Predicting Careers." *British Journal of Preventive Social Medicine*, 14 (1960), 83–88.
II. "Families of Dull Children: Identifying Family Types and Subcultures." *Journal of Mental Science*, 106 (1960), 1296–1303.
III. "Social Selection by Family Type." *Journal of Mental Science*, 106 (1960), 1304–1310.
IV. "Increments in Intelligence." *Journal of Mental Science*, 106 (1960), 1311–1319.

184. ———, and SUSSER, M. "The Social Distribution of Mental Retardation." *American Journal of Mental Deficiency*, 67 (1963), 811–821.

185. ———, and SUSSER, M. "Mild Mental Subnormality: Social and Epidemiological Studies." In F. Redlich, ed., *Social Psychiatry*. New York: Research publication no. 47. Association for Research in Nervous and Mental Disease, 1969. Pp. 62–85.

186. ———, and SUSSER, M. "Mutability of In-

telligence and Epidemiology of Mild Mental Retardation." *Review of Educational Research*, 40 (1970), 29–67.

187. ———, and SUSSER, M. "Change Over Time in the Incidence and Prevalence of Mental Retardation." In J. Hellmuth, ed., *The Exceptional Infant*. New York: Brunner/Mazel, 1971. Pp. 305–340.

188. ———, and SUSSER, M. "The Preventability of Down's Syndrome." *HSMHA Health Reports*, 86 (1972), 650–658.

189. STERN, H., BOOTH, J. C., ELEK, S. D., and FLECK, D. G. "Microbial Causes of Mental Retardation: The Role of Prenatal Infection with Cytomegalovirus, Rubella Virus, and Toxoplasma." *Lancet*, 2 (1969), 443–448.

190. STEVENSON, A. C., MASON, R., and EDWARDS, K. D. "Maternal Diagnostic X-Irradiation Before Conception and the Frequency of Mongolism in Children Subsequently Born." *Lancet*, 2 (1970), 1335–1337.

191. STEWART, R. J. C., and PLATT, B. S. "The Influence of Protein-Calorie Deficiency on the Central Nervous System." *Proceedings of Nutritional Society*, 27 (1968), 95–101.

192. STOCH, M. B., and SMYTHE, P. M. "Does Undernutrition During Infancy Inhibit Brain Growth and Subsequent Intellectual Development?" *Archives of the Diseases of Childhood*, 38 (1963), 546–552.

193. STUBBS, V., and JACOBSON, C. B. "LSD and Genetic Damage." *George Washington Magazine*, 26 (1968), 26–31.

194. SUSSER, M. W. *Community Psychiatry: Epidemiologic and Social Themes*. New York: Random House, 1968.

195. ———, and WATSON, W. *Sociology and Medicine*. 2d ed. London: Oxford University Press, 1971.

196. ———, MAROLLA, F. A., and FLEISS, J. "Birth Weight, Fetal Age and Perinatal Mortality." *American Journal of Epidemiology*, 96 (1972), 197–204.

197. TAKEUCHI, T., and MATSUMOTO, H. "Minamata Disease of Human Fetuses." In H. Nishimura, J. R. Miller, and M. Yasuda, eds., *Methods for Teratological Studies in Experimental Animals and Man: Proceedings of the Second International Workshop in Teratology, Kyoto, 1968*. Tokyo: Igaku Shoin, 1969. Pp. 280–282.

198. THALHAMMER, O. "Congenital Toxoplasmosis." *Lancet*, 1 (1962), 23–24.

199. THOMSON, A. M. "Prematurity: Socio-Eco-nomic and Nutritional Factors." *Bibliotheca Paediatrica*, 8 (1963), 197–206.

200. TIZARD, J. *Community Services for the Mentally Handicapped*. London: Oxford University Press, 1964.

201. TODD, R. M., and NEVILLE, J. G. "The Sequelae of Tuberculous Meningitis." *Archives of the Diseases of Childhood*, 39 (1964), 213–225.

202. TREDGOLD, A. F. *Mental Deficiency (Amentia)*. London: Ballière, Tindall & Cox, 1908.

203. UCHIDA, I. A., HOLUNGA, R., and LAWLEY, C. "Maternal Radiation and Chromosomal Aberrations." *Lancet*, 2 (1968), 1045–1048.

204. U.S. DEPARTMENT OF HEALTH, EDUCATION AND WELFARE. National Communicable Disease Center. *Annual Encephalitis Summary*, 1963, 1964, 1965, 1966, 1967, and 1968.

205. U.S. DEPARTMENT OF HEALTH, EDUCATION, AND WELFARE. *The Prevention of Mental Retardation Through the Control of Infectious Diseases*. Public Health Service publication, no. 1692. Washington, D.C.: 1968.

206. WAHRMAN, J., and FRIED, K. Paper Presented to the New York Academy of Sciences and National Foundation March of Dimes Conference on Down's Syndrome (Mongolism), 1969.

207. WEBSTER, T. G. "Problems of Emotional Development in Young Retarded Children." *American Journal of Psychiatry*, 120 (1963), 37–43.

208. WHEELER, L. R. "A Comparative Study of the Intelligence of East Tennessee Mountain Children." *Journal of Educational Psychology*, 33 (1942), 321–334.

209. WIENER, G. "Scholastic Achievement at Age 12–13 of Prematurely Born Infants." *Journal of Special Education*, 2 (1968), 237–250.

210. ———. "Relationship of Birth Weight and Length of Gestation to Intellectual Development at the Age of 8–10 Years." *Pediatrics*, 76 (1970), 694–697.

211. ———. "Varying Psychological Sequelae of Lead Ingestions in Children." *Public Health Report*, 85, no. 1 (1970), 19–24.

212. ———, RIDER, R. V., OPPEL, W. C., FISCHER, L. K., and HARPER, P. A. "Correlates of Low Birth Weight: Psychological Status at Six to Seven Years of Age." *Pediatrics*, 35 (1965), 434–444.

213. ——, RIDER, R. V., OPPEL, W. C., and HARPER, P. A. "Correlates of Low Birth Weight: Psychological Status at Eight to Ten Years of Age." *Pediatrics Research*, 2 (1968), 110–118.

214. WINICK, M. "Cellular Growth in Intrauterine Malnutrition." *Pediatric Clinics of North America*, 17 (1970), 69–78.

215. ——, and NOBLE, A. "Cellular Response in Rats During Malnutrition at Various Ages." *Journal of Nutrition*, 89 (1966), 300–306.

216. WINTERS, R. W. "Salicylate Intoxication." In H. L. Barnett, ed., *Pediatrics*. 15th ed. New York: Appleton-Century-Crofts, 1968.

217. WOOD, J. W., JOHNSON, K. G., YOSHIAKI, O., KAWAMOTO, S., and KEEHN, R. J. *Mental Retardation in Children Exposed In Utero to the Atomic Bomb: Hiroshima and Nagasaki*. Atomic Bomb Casualty Commission technical report no. 10–66. Washington, D.C.: U.S. Government Printing Office, 1966.

218. WORLD HEALTH ORGANIZATION. *Toxoplasmosis: Report of a WHO Meeting of Investigators*. Technical report no. 431. Geneva, 1969.

219. WORTIS, J., ed. "Introduction: What Is Mental Retardation?" *Mental Retardation*. Vol. 2. *An Annual Review*. New York: Grune & Stratton, 1970. Pp. 1–6.

220. YAKTIN, U. S., and McLAREN, D. S. "The Behavioural Development of Infants Recovering from Severe Malnutrition." *Journal of Mental Deficiency Research*, 14 (1970), 25–32.

221. YAMAZAKI, J. N., WRIGHT, S. W., and WRIGHT, P. M. "Outcome of Pregnancy in Women Exposed to the Atomic Bomb in Nagasaki." *American Journal of Diseases of Children*, 87 (1954), 448–463.

222. YERUSHALMY, J., and MILKOVICH, L. "Evaluation of the Teratogenic Effects of Mecizine in Man." *American Journal of Obstetrics and Gynecology*, 93 (1965), 553–562.

223. ZAVON, M. "Mercury Poisoning." In H. L. Barnett, ed., *Pediatrics*. 15th ed. New York: Appleton-Century-Crofts, 1968. Pp. 320–321.

224. ZELLWEGER, H., McDONALD, J. S., and ABBO, G. "Is Lysergic Acid Diethylamide a Teratogen?" *Lancet*, 2 (1967), 1066–1068.

CHAPTER 32

PSYCHOSOCIAL ASPECTS OF PREJUDICE

Eugene B. Brody

(A Definition of Prejudice

THE DEFINITION of negative ethnic prejudice offered by Allport[4] is useful for general discussion purposes: "Ethnic prejudice is an antipathy based upon a faulty and inflexible generalization. It may be felt or expressed. It may be directed toward a group as a whole or toward an individual because he is a member of that group." As Allport pointed out, "the net effect of prejudice, thus defined, is to place the object of prejudice at some disadvantage not merited by his own conduct."

This is a highly condensed definition encompassing a number of factors, many of which were discussed at individual length by Allport:

1. The prejudiced attitude and its associated beliefs are hostile, rejecting, and deprecatory.
2. The basis of the rejection is categorical and not related to the actual behavior of the target.
3. The prejudice is not usually modifiable through the ordinary learning, reward-and-punishment experiences. The negative attitude is even less modifiable than the specific beliefs associated with it. Information concerning the target individual or group is selectively received and may be so modified as to support the categorical judgment. This information is used to rationalize the persisting belief system and behavior based on it.
4. When the prejudice is threatened by information penetrating the defensive barriers the person holding it may become emotionally disturbed.
5. The prejudice may not always be reflected in immediately congruent behavior. There are many degrees of negative action that may be carried out against the target of prejudice.

The definition of prejudice as an unjustified antipathy expressed in attitudes, feelings, and beliefs is operationally useful. Its unjustified nature requires a series of psychological devices to protect its integrity: selective and modified perceptions, rationalizations, and resistance to change. Its basis in faulty generalization, however, suggests its link to prevailing value systems. These are statements of what is considered worthwhile by a society, and they are basic to its normative guidelines for living, whether contained in institutionalized (automatic and shared) patterns of behavior or embodied in a system of external restraints such as a legal code.[18] Values involve a shared recognition of what is considered proper, right, or desirable by a group. Such recognitions and normative guidelines are always evoked by prejudiced individuals; they are, of course, central to group behavior organized to destroy an individual scapegoat available because of his membership in a target category, or to fight another group designated as the upholder of heretical if not merely incompatible values.

⟨ The Significance of Prejudice

Prejudice, dogmatism, intolerance, and closed mindedness are major obstacles to collaboration for more satisfactory human living. They impair the native human capacity to relate effectively to others of differing appearance, background, beliefs, or behavior. Such impairment impoverishes and distorts individual life experience, both for the prejudiced person and his target. By treating a person as a member of a category rather than as a unique individual they dehumanize him and thus facilitate aggression against him. This process of dehumanization is involved in the preparation of troops to destroy an enemy (in contrast to other human beings), or of members of a dominant oppressor group to destroy a minority perceived as inferior or less than human. It can also reduce any potential discomfort suffered by dominant group members who profit from economic exploitation or cultural aggression. In this respect, prejudice may be regarded less as a psychological problem than as a social device, that is, one aspect of an ideology and value system necessary to maintain elitist economic and educational ar-

rangements. The systematic exclusion of less advantaged, immigrant, or culturally distinct groups from full participation in the cultural experience of the majority is one way of perpetuating social distance between the two groups and preserving the former's status as a minority vulnerable to exploitation.[14,16] Institutionalized prejudice (outside of individual awareness), and the virulent intergroup hatreds associated with ethnic, religious, and national identifications, can distort, impoverish, and ultimately destroy the lives of entire societies and cultures.

Intergroup hatreds sustained by shared perceptual rigidities are rationalized by shared ideologies. As Abraham Meyerson stated, man "uses his reason to justify his prejudices. . . ." When intergroup tensions reach the point of war, that is, organized attempts by one society to destroy another, they involve collective behavior based on a common ideology. A society at war, one dominated in its behavior by common prejudice, and one working toward the achievement of a constructive goal share certain common properties. Each constitutes what Talcott Parsons called a collectivity, that is, a group committed to action on the basis of a shared value system. Actions taken on the basis of prejudice, thus, may involve the same mechanisms as those motivated by nondestructive, nonprejudiced aims. Human construction and human war (intramural as well as international) both require collective or cooperative behavior. The balance in one direction or the other is determined by the values and prejudices of the society's leaders. The leaders' outlook in turn will have, inevitably, been influenced by the social context in which they developed and live as adults. Beyond this their decisions will be a function of the small groups with which they consult: The shifting explicit convictions of these group members will again vary with their implicit or unconscious values and prejudices. Fixed beliefs about the goals of a target group, inability to submit certain types of evidence to rational scrutiny, invarying fear of the stranger, and a persisting anxiety-based need to demonstrate one's own strength and that of one's own group can contribute to the mutual reinforcement of increasingly risky decisions within the executive body.

⟨ Prejudice as a Subject of Psychiatric Study

Prejudice is a particular concern of psychiatrists and other students of human behavior because of its obvious relation to problems of character structure, anxiety management, adaptation, and mental illness. It may reflect only an unthinking conformity with prevailing group values and practices. When, however, a hostile or deprecatory attitude cannot be modified by experiences that demonstrate its irrationality and when the possessor of the attitude avoids confrontation with facts that may threaten it, or with the beliefs associated with it, it seems likely that it serves some necessary psychological function for him. A tenaciously embraced antipathy toward a group, or toward a person because he is a member of that group, reflects a functional impairment in reality testing; it may also produce behavior in the prejudiced person that is maladaptive, destructive, or borders on the clinically paranoid. Thus, he becomes a legitimate object of psychiatric study.

The victims of prejudice are also objects of psychiatric concern. Prejudices held by members of a power-holding majority may be translated into action that limits the freedom of thought or achievement of members of a target group, usually defined as a minority whether in terms of numbers or of distance from the sources of societal power. In this instance, the prejudices of one group may influence the mental health of another. The most significant example in United States history concerns the black population. A special aspect of this is the influence of school segregation on the psychology of both black and white children. The psychiatric aspects of attempts to reverse the process, including the evoked resistances, have been explored in detail.[51]

The psychology of the victim may be complicated by the fact that he is often conscious of his difference from the power-holding majority by virtue of high social visibility. A person may be socially visible (that is, identifiable by others as belonging to a particular group) because of sex or age; skin color or physiognomy; characteristic behavior including speech, religious, or dietary habits; clothing; or nature and area of residence. A person with high social visibility due to fixed physical characteristics has the greatest difficulty in passing, should he desire to do so, as a member of the majority.

Social visibility may diminish rapidly and markedly in those migrants who physically resemble the majority as they become acculturated and resocialized into their new setting. For them true assimilation is an eventual possibility. However, adequate enculturation in their previous settings is important. Social histories contrasting with those of blacks whose culture was smashed in their slave period are seen in the United States Jewish and oriental minorities, although these last are, themselves, visible through skin color and physiognomy. A major difference lies in the fact of a strong, transplantable, complex culture capable of providing solutions to new problems and a sense of identity in a new milieu. Members of segregated groups with a strong cultural or religious heritage may reveal their insecurities and try to resolve their problems through overachievement. The main point is that they are able to do this and that their achievement gains consistent recognition within their own groups of origin because it fits their cultural heritage. Since all complex cultures have much in common, such achievement also has significance for and is rewarded by the dominant system as well. As Erikson[*] pointed out, "ego identity gains real strength only from the wholehearted and consistent recognition of real accomplishment, i.e., of achievement that has meaning in the culture." Minorities with strong cultural heritages and values may even strengthen their group identities when surrounded by a dominant society possessing enough values congruent with their own to permit them to survive and to play a

* See reference 37, pp. 426–442.

functional role within it. Minority group members with no intact history or culture of their own, however, who can acquire only distorted fragments of the values and achievement techniques of the majority, have little chance of reward for activities with real cultural meaning. Following Erikson again, they have diminished opportunity for developing the sense of reality that comes from a life way that is an individual variant of a stable group identity.[12, p. 4]

([Prejudice and Minority and Majority Social Worlds

Almost all studies of ethnic prejudice deal with the attitudes of majority groups toward minorities. The characteristics classically associated with minority group status have in the past been exemplified by black Americans: high social visibility, relative distance from sources of community power, incomplete access to social, educational, and economic opportunities, incomplete participation in the dominant culture, and certain other behavioral restrictions; these may include segregation imposed by the surrounding community, as well as a degree of self-segregation.[32] A final minority group characteristic is the subordinate group's accommodation to the surrounding community through the adoption of certain aspects of the dominant culture (enculturation) as it gives up aspects of its own culture (acculturation).

In recent years the minority group concept has been applied to a number of nonethnic groups. Adolescents, for example, are socially visible because of age-linked characteristics; they are remote from the sources of social power, deprived of full participation in economic and decision-making aspects of the culture, and often unjustly blamed for events in which they had no personal hand.[21] In the late 1960s and early 1970s, influenced in part by the successes of black militancy and widespread attacks on traditional organizations (often associated with United States military involvement in Indochina), other groups that

had passively endured discrimination began to assert their own rights. Women protested economic discrimination and lack of equal access to educational opportunities denied them because of sex. The Women's Liberation movement also became associated through some of its leaders with efforts to remove prejudice against female homosexuals and to improve their opportunities for satisfactory living in a heterosexual, male-dominated society. At the same time the Gay Liberation Front gathered strength, permitting many Americans who had hidden their homosexuality not only to admit but to assert it. In 1971 an event occurred that dramatizes the rapid changes in public climate about this issue: A leader of this movement ran for Congress from the District of Columbia with the Gay Liberation ideology as his major issues. This climaxed what he described as two decades of development of the homophile movement.[58] It has two basic precepts. (1) Homosexuals are fully the equal of heterosexuals and should have full equality in employment, civil rights, and the like. (2) Homosexuality is not pathological in any sense. In this last respect he accused[60, p. 22] psychiatry of prejudice, stating that it "has a pathologic psychological need for sexual hobgoblins."

Aside from blacks, a number of other American ethnic groups have been identified as targets of prejudice and discriminatory action at the hands of the majority. These include Puerto Ricans, Mexican-Americans (Chicanos), American Indians, and Eskimos. In each instance, individuals are the targets of antipathy and placed at a disadvantage, despite personal characteristics, because of membership in a particular ethnic category. Thus, prejudice has the effect of homogenization: The majority rob a minority group person of his unique individuality by perceiving and dealing with him as a member of a class.

Information Deficit and Stereotyped Perceptions

The continued existence of a power-holding majority elite and a powerless discriminated against minority has been based in part upon the maintenance of a degree of social distance between them. The social distance concept was made operational by a scale devised by Bogardus.[10] Another conceptualization of this situation is that of Rohrer and Edmundson[77] and others who think in terms of two social worlds: the social world of whites and that of blacks. Members of two different social worlds may have significant but incomplete contact with each other. Their relationships are not emotionally reciprocal. With this way of relating they have only partial and sometimes distorted information about each other. Such a relative information deficit promotes a tendency on the part of one group to think in stereotyped terms about the other. Perceiving members of other groups in terms of stereotypes permits, as indicated above, rationalization of their categorical rejection; it also serves an economic function by maintaining simplicity and by avoiding ambiguity of perception.[3,4,61,90] Lacking sufficient data, they continue to view each other on the basis of invalid generalizations. Although such generalizations need not always be hostile and may be modified with additional information, they provide one model of prejudice construction. Public opinion has often been influenced by leaders and information transmitters in such a way as to perpetuate the social distance between groups, and hence information deficit and stereotyped perceptions. This influence need not be explicit or consciously manipulative; it is commonly built into the culture. Thus, attitude and feelings acquired during socialization and reinforced by selective reporting in the mass media[39] and pronouncements of local leaders promote anger, fear, and defensive separation between groups. To the degree that one is a stranger he can be more easily perceived as an enemy.

At various points in history the separation between groups has been reinforced by law. In these instances the law can be understood as the codification of behavioral regulations that, while embodying historically evolved prejudices and stereotypes, are deliberately aimed at maintaining a status quo viewed by the power holders as politically, economically, or socially desirable. The twentieth century has seen the rise and fall of anti-Semitic laws in Germany and the accelerating elimination of legal barriers to full personhood and civil rights of untouchables in India and blacks in the United States.

An example of stereotyping not involving ethnic groups concerns the beliefs held about each other by members of the two social worlds of mental hospitals: the patient world and the staff world.[24] The effect of relative lack of information about the sources of interpersonal power is also seen in the development of paranoid ideas about the experimenters in subjects of sensory deprivation studies.

Evoked Behavior and Reference Group Theory

Two related factors tend to perpetuate the stereotyped ideas developed by members of one social group about another. One is associated with what has been called the "self-fulfilling prophecy." This pertains to the person who has a fixed idea about another, for example, that the other is aggressive; he, thus, tends to behave toward the other in a way that actually elicits responsive aggressive or hostile behavior. This elicited behavior, confirmatory of the original belief, tends to reinforce it.[71]

The other factor is the reference group, which provides a person with the social or interpersonal standards by which he judges himself.[62,72] A man's major normative or comparative reference group is usually the immediate community of peers in which he lives. His behavior may, however, be determined in important ways by standards held by members of some other group to which he attributes high value. If he has only fragmentary contact with this emulative reference group, his knowledge of its actual standards and valued behavior patterns may be both fragmented and distorted. This makes it likely that his behavior when dealing with emulative reference group members (generally the power-holding majority) will be a caricature of what these members regard as desirable and will tend to reinforce their prejudiced, stereotyped ways of perceiving the particular outgroup he represents.

To some degree the minority group member's use of the majority group for emulative reference purposes may be considered an aspect of the process of social accommodation and enculturation. Minority groups do not have complete access to the social institutions and cultural life of the larger societies of which they are a part. This is particularly true if, as in the case of American blacks, they have high social visibility and have been underprivileged and of low social class. In the course of accommodation to the larger power-holding society, the minority adopts fragments of the latter's values and goals. Among these can be stereotyped beliefs concerning people of varying religious, national, racial, or ethnic background, including themselves. This factor may contribute, for example, to the presence of anti-Semitic prejudice in black college students. Anti-black stereotypes, and particularly those regarding relative shades of skin color, while originating in the needs of the majority, also contribute to the frame of reference in which American blacks see themselves.[22] The elements of self-perception seem to become particularly important as the minority group member, of whatever category, becomes upwardly mobile and has increasing, and emotionally meaningful, contact with the majority social world. Such a person, with one foot in the majority world and the other in his own, but not feeling completely accepted by or comfortable in either, has been labeled as a "marginal man."[5,32] The marginal man's uncertainty of belongingness has been considered by Kurt Lewin[66,67] as productive of self-hatred and high sensitivity to anything in his group of origin that does not conform to the values of the dominant group. He may be especially prone to adopt deprecatory stereotypes regarding his own group of origin.

The era ushered in by the 1954 U.S. Supreme Court anti-school segregation decision has seen a progressive change in the normative and comparative reference groups for the American black community. The elements of this change have increasing relevance, as well, for the Mexican-American, American Indian, Puerto Rican, and to a lesser degree, the Eskimo communities. (Within the U.S. Oriental communities these changes are still minimal.[40,89]) The new reference group concept, assuming vigorous and visible form in the Black Power movement of the 1960s, embodies much of the ideology presented by Frantz Fanon in *The Wretched of the Earth* (1961).[38] Key aspects of Fanon's thinking include a perception of the world divided into colonies and colonialists, of the native black owing his oppressed and self-hating existence to the latter, and of the need for violence in the process of decolonization both as a means of reversing the social structure and of gaining dignity and self-esteem as a man for the formerly oppressed. This and other works helped provide the American black leader with a similar view of his own people and of a future to be gained not through integration but separation. In effect, it initiated a transformation of the normative-comparative reference group to one with emulative value as well. The gradual abandonment by blacks of an unattainable emulative goal, namely, to be white, must have incalculable benefits for personality development and liberation. A consequence of this is a recently published volume of essays by black authors entitled *The Black 70's*.[6]

The need for a new black identity was also involved in the concept of negritude used by Leopold Senghor, the poet president of Senegal, as a rallying cry for worldwide black culture building. The low self-esteem engendered by discrimination, by dominant group attitudes and restrictions, requires a sense of identity as an antidote. This sense is crucial to the transformation of a minority from an aggregate of individuals bound together only by an awareness of common misery into a collectivity committed to action on the basis of shared values.

It was as part of this process of individuation from the accommodated state of a subordinate formerly slave people, acquiring available fragments of the dominant culture, that a new search was initiated for values and practices from the African homeland. Although the uncritical phases of this effort have been succeeded by a more mature realization that the current Afro-American identity is something separate from black Africa as well as white America, cultural revitalization is recognized as a valid effort toward the promotion of self-esteem and renewed capability. Cultural revitalization is a prominent element in the mobilization of Mexican-Americans and American Indians as well as Alaskan Eskimos in their new efforts to gain political power.

Institutionalized Prejudice, Racism, and Individual Conflict

The preceding discussion has recognized the automatic, unconscious nature of much prejudiced behavior and the degree to which its psychological precursors are socialized into young Americans. The term "racism," to designate some aspects of this, became widely used in the late 1960s. A distinguished black actor and writer[30] defined "racism" as "a belief that human races have distinctive characteristics, usually involving the idea that one's own race is superior and has a right to rule others." This observer characterized the English language as an enemy, referring to "the enormous trap of racial prejudgment that works on any child who is born into the English language." If language is, indeed, recognized as a major source of the symbols involved in cultural experience, the degree to which color or ethnically linked words are deprecatory or anxiety inspiring becomes obvious as a determinant of unconscious racist attitudes.

Racism has been operationally defined by Wilkinson[86] as behavior of whites toward blacks based on a concept of white superiority. As the principles of white superiority are culturally learned, racism may be regarded as institutionalized. He traced the development of this concept in the United States to its early slavery of the dehumanizing Dutch-English type, with slaves considered as chattels. The myths and stereotypes arising from this pe-riod, many of which reflected the slaveholders' needs to rationalize their positions, became part of the American milieu, a "cultural blanket" with "effects on both blacks and whites alike."

Any practice imbedded in the culture may be considered contagious since it is socially transmitted from one generation to the next and since it is constantly reinforced during adult life. Pierce,[76] in fact, labeled United States racism as "a public health and mental health illness" made up in important part of "micro-aggressive episodes" perpetrated by whites against blacks on the basis of culturally learned "offensive mechanisms." Pierce[76, p. 268] also emphasized the role of social institutions in perpetuating racist perceptions and behavior by both blacks and whites:

the education system has succeeded in preparing generation after generation of Blacks to accept the docile, passive positions of abused, disenfranchised, second-class citizens. It is a summation of collective micro-offenses by the majority that permits police department after police department to tyrannize Black communities . . . which applies economic terrors to poor Blacks who have the temerity to demand what the law provides . . . to minimize the social importance of any Black or any Black achievement so that Blacks will see themselves as useless, unlovable, unable.

The underrepresentation of blacks in professional ranks has been attributed to racism both in its specific and general aspects. While various solutions have been proposed, the statement by Williams[88, p. 67] embodies a feeling expressed by many: "a Black nationalist orientation, coupled with the implementation of Black studies, will more effectively deal with the problem of Black professional underrepresentation than the integrationist ethic." Williams linked this conclusion with his awareness of the identity problem of the black professional who has "made it" in the white society. This problem was delineated by Beisser and Harris[7] in terms of the conflict between the black role and a particular professional role. As Williams[88, p. 68] summarized their point of view, "The dilemma . . . is often solved by compartmentalization and denial of Black identity. While performing as a professional, the individual denies the existence of his blackness. He is either a Black man or a professional, but finds it difficult to be both at the same time." Since the professional part of the person has been mainly white oriented and white educated, and survival in a white academic institution requires the virtual suspension of his black identity, total involvement in the black nationalistic (but not necessarily separatist) ethic, using one's professional skills, may solve the dilemma: "Black professionals should concentrate heavily on building organizations of Black people, for Black people, and by Black people."[88, p. 68]

As noted above, the discriminatory practices prevalent against one section of the population, the blacks, have until very recently been so widespread and so effectively rationalized that they have been openly espoused with no guilt by otherwise humane and sensitive individuals. Exclusionary anti-Semitic practices, on the other hand, have tended to be less open, hidden in part by the reluctance of the community and of even the victims themselves to acknowledge what is going on beneath the surface of a traditionally democratic and equalitarian society. This may be due to the diminishing social visibility of Jews over the years and their significant involvement in the cultural, business, and professional life of the nation. These exclusionary practices have been particularly pernicious to the degree that bystanders, living in communities where discrimination has existed long before their arrival, are in a sense coerced into becoming accomplices.[36] Institutionalized patterns of segregation influence a person whose psychodynamics might not result in his becoming an ardent holder of prejudice.[8,48] If he is going to live in a community, he must go along with prevailing patterns.[87] This involves not only conforming but learning how to discriminate and teaching one's children how to do the same. Sometimes the bystander is "too polite" to object and will not even acknowledge to himself that his freedom of choice regarding personal associations is being curtailed.[36,75] At some

level, however, he is aware that his behavior is not compatible with the American credo. If the resultant guilt or other tension is not handled by repression or by increasing congruence of behavior and ideals, it may become necessary to rationalize the discriminatory behavior by the adoption of the originally rejected prejudiced ideas. This is another way in which prejudice may be considered contagious.

The conflict between institutionalized social practices and traditional ideals with respect to the role of the black in the United States was discussed by the distinguished Swedish social scientist Gunnar Myrdal, in the early 1940s, under the title *The American Dilemma*.[73] The very existence of such a dilemma, of a conflict between values and actual behavior, differentiates the United States from the older stratified societies in which discrimination is not incompatible with the value systems. It also emphasizes that the prevention of prejudice cannot be viewed solely in terms of individual psychodynamics and psychopathology. Resolution of this conflict requires modification of general community customs and adoption of measures to keep patterns of prejudiced behavior from becoming imbedded in community custom, that is, from becoming institutionalized. Once institutionalization takes place, a behavior pattern is doubly difficult to eradicate. As Talcott Parsons[74] defined it, an institutionalized pattern of behavior represents an unthinking conformity to what is considered right, proper, legitimate, and expected in a society. We may add that it has a psychoeconomic function in that it reduces the number of decisions that any individual must make in his daily life and has a self-esteem building function to the degree that the person is supported and rewarded for conforming to the norms of his society. It is unlikely that under ordinary circumstances a person will be inclined to abandon a socially rewarded way of behaving that, in addition, saves him the energy expense and tension involved in making decisions about individuals who might more easily be automatically dealt with as members of a class.

The Psychodynamics of the Prejudiced Person

Problems of Reality Testing

The most general statement about people whose interpersonal attitudes and beliefs reflect categorical judgments that are based on faulty generalizations and are not modified by contrary evidence is that they suffer from impaired reality testing. In a volume prepared for UNESCO, Marie Jahoda[56] reviewed a body of empirical evidence pointing to this deficit as central in many who feel hostile to racial outgroups. One dramatic illustration is Hartley's[52] finding that a large proportion of those who disliked blacks and Jews also expressed dislike for three nonexistent groups to which he gave imaginary names and against which he advocated restrictive measures. This finding strongly suggests that prejudice is one behavioral manifestation of a particular type of character structure and that prejudiced attitudes and beliefs or dogmatism and intolerance can become apparent in a variety of social contexts, and with a variety of targets. The possible relation of prejudice to character is supported also by its fluctuations with severe personality disruptions. One example was the disappearance of strong anti-black prejudice and the emergence of presumably defended against problack feeling in a white Southern woman during an acute schizophrenic psychosis; these prejudices reappeared with resolution of the psychotic episode.[44]

The inadequate reality testing of the prejudiced may be considered an expression of the active selection, modification, or scotomization of incoming information that threatens a key belief or attitude. In other words, it has a prejudice-protecting function. The prejudice is also protected by the characteristic tendency of its possessor to regard incompatible realities that he cannot deny as exceptions to the rule. Thus, the modesty and straightforwardness of a Jewish acquaintance does not change one's views on the ambitiousness and deviousness of Jews in general; the acquaintance is consid-

ered an exception who proves the rule. On the other hand, a Jew who is aggressively ambitious is seen as living confirmation of the prejudiced point of view. Every datum is perceived as support for the fixed attitudes and beliefs.[9,28,36,84]

Unconscious Conflict and Prejudice

Prejudice sometimes becomes an obsession that dominates its possessor's psychological life. In this case, an active reminder of the target person may provoke an emotional storm. All these factors suggest that the tenaciously held, carefully protected prejudice is closely connected with unconscious irrational needs.[1,4,9,56,70] When behavior is so strongly rooted in unconscious factors and so dominated by what Freud called primary-process thinking, rational efforts to modify it are usually unsuccessful. Symptomatic behavior, in general, is not responsive to frontal, logical approaches. Its modification requires changes in unconscious conflicts, which underly the anxiety or guilt, motivating the employment of (only partially successful) defensive maneuvers, which are in turn reflected in the symptomatic behavior in question.

What are some of the psychological conflicts that underlie prejudice? Much early writing presents the basic hypothesis that members of a minority become targets of prejudice because they are convenient scapegoats who can be loaded with the sins of others and driven out of the community.[68,91] Another way of saying this is that the outgroup, or minority, is a readily available target for the displacement or projection of unacceptable wishes or feelings of the majority. Because it serves this social function, its existence becomes important for the reduction of the majority's anxiety and guilt and for the maintenance of the majority's self-esteem.

The nature of the unacceptable wish that is projected or displaced may vary, and the target appears to be selected in part on the basis of social circumstances. Thus, the deprived, lower-class American black, slowly rising from the status of a slave without an integrated family or a cultural heritage, is considered in terms of a particular set of accusatory preju- dices as lazy, dirty, untrustworthy, sexually amoral, and physically dangerous. According to some authors, in this sense he has symbol- ized for some white Americans their own unacceptable sexual, aggressive, and depen- dency wishes. For these individuals, the adop- tion of anti-black prejudice may offer some partial solution to their own problems involv- ing repressed, instinctual wishes.[4,56,61,69]

The Jew, with a culturally determined em- phasis on the importance of learning and with a supporting family background that fa- cilitates his upward mobility and business suc- cess, becomes the recipient of a different set of stereotypes. Anti-Jewish prejudices include fixed beliefs about a Jew's ambitiousness and his moneygrabbing and controlling propensi- ties. An anti-Jewish prejudice may provide a partial solution for problems involving wishes for power and control over others as well as those involving potentially explosive thoughts and feelings.[1,4,9,42,56]

The sensual and impulse-gratifying stereo- type of the black, or Jew, makes him a symbol that can also provide disguised gratification for those who are themselves inhibited and conflict ridden. Some accusatory tendencies of prejudiced people are illuminated by this for- mulation. Thus, a white woman with uncon- scious sexual desires for black males may come to believe that such men have aggressive sex- ual designs on her. Or white males who are insecure about their sexual capacities may perceive black males as threatening the white women who are their own legitimate sexual objects. There is some evidence that those with the greatest guilt about their own sexual desires have the greatest tendency to develop hostile prejudice involving sexual fears.[4,69,70]

Projection is facilitated when an available target, the outgroup class or individual, lacks a clearly defined, unambiguous structure of its own. According to Ackerman and Jahoda,[1] "for the anti-Semite the Jew is a living Ror- schach inkblot." In addition to being unknown for many and thus mysterious and possibly evil, because of historical circumstances he may be regarded as strange and alien, making him a particular object of interest for those

who, themselves, feel evil or self-alienated. This quality of strangeness and difference is attributed by many contemporary Argentine psychoanalysts to the practice of circumcision. Garma[45] believed that the specific term "anti- Judaism" should be used, noting that accord- ing to Freud the roots of this attitude are found in the fact that Jews: (1) practice cir- cumcision, which evokes the fear of castration in others, and (2) consider themselves to be God's chosen people. Both these factors may contribute to their perception by others as different, special, and potentially threatening.

Prejudice and Character

Much attention has been paid to charac- terological features that may predispose a person to acquiring and holding on to preju- diced ideas, that is, to incorporating them into the structure of his defensive and need-grati- fying system. Narcissistic[65] and sadomasochis- tic tendencies[43] have been noted as impor- tant, particularly for the person who might be prone to translate his prejudice into discrimi- natory or persecutory action. Adorno and his colleagues,[3] in one of the most significant studies in this area, summarized the charac- teristics of the prejudice prone in terms of the concept of authoritarian personality. This per- sonality type was described as one needing strong external supports, depending on con- ventional values, and sensitive to interpersonal status criteria and dominance, since these are important to the maintenance of his sense of inner security. Related features are uncritical submission to dominant group authorities, punitive reactions to violators of conventional norms, cognitive rigidity, cynicism, tendency to projection, and unusual interest in the sex- ual behavior of others. Many of these features are relevant to Rokeach's[78] definition of dog- matism, characteristic of individuals with a closed mind. The inflexibly organized belief system about reality, which is basic to the defi- nition of dogmatism, depends on a core of be- liefs about absolute authority. Perceptions of the world in general are strongly influenced by the perceiver's relation to authority figures. It has been demonstrated that open-mindedness (the flexibility and responsiveness to new evidence of one's belief systems) is partially related to one's ability to receive, evaluate, and act on relevant information received from the outside on its own intrinsic merits. Such open-minded individuals are more capable than others of discriminating between a message and its source and are less influenced by high status.

Prejudice and Identity Conflict

Jahoda[56] pointed to Jean-Paul Sartre's[80] "Portrait of the Anti-Semite" as an intuitively arrived at picture bearing much similarity to the empirical studies of the authoritarian personality. Jahoda's own review of the evidence[56] focuses on the importance of identity problems, stating that the authoritarian personality "bears the mark of an unresolved conflict, the conflict about one's identity, to an extraordinary extent." Such conflict requires a clearcut and sharp categorization of the world and a disinclination to examine motives that may result in a weakening of the perceptual structure necessary to maintain some sense of identity. For such a person, another who is easily definable on the basis of differences from himself may constitute both a threat and an attraction.[14,23,31]

Identity conflict may have its roots in disturbed patterns of parental identification. A father may be physically absent or personally remote, or he may be experienced as overwhelming and frightening. In neither instance is he available as a model or object of identification for his growing son. Why such developmental problems should result in prejudice vulnerability and dogmatism in one instance, in paranoid schizophrenia in another, and in homosexuality in yet another is unclear. However, there is evidence as noted above that problems in sexual identification similar to those present in clinically paranoid or homosexual individuals contribute to the identity conflict of the authoritarian personality. This is supported in part by the intense sensitivity to interracial sex relations found among members of dominant white groups and by the great energy expended on maintaining social

and legal barriers against miscegenation by the most prejudiced members of such groups.[3,42] Other psychodynamic factors that contribute to efforts to maintain these barriers (which are regularly crossed) include guilt over wishes to transgress or over earlier transgressions, projection of hostile or sexual wishes, and so on. Reflections of sexual identity conflict in the white Gentile's castration fears may be reflected in stereotyped ideas about the black's large genitals and potency or about the Jew's passionate nature. Destruction of the outgroup male, viewed in this sense, removes a possible sexual competitor and a basic threat to the ingroup male's psychosexual integrity.

Another approach to the issue of intrapsychic conflict among the prejudiced was suggested by Loewenstein, who found a valuable source of data in the development of transference feelings arising during the course of psychoanalysis.[68] He concluded that, with a Jewish analyst, the transference becomes organized on the basis of the patient's latent anti-Semitism. During the anti-Semitic stages of analysis, the Jew who is hated and feared by the patient in the person of his analyst usually represents to him a deformed image of his father or even of himself. The tendency to react in this way appeared to be most intense in those patients in whom it was possible to identify marked ambivalence toward father figures. Such a finding in the psychoanalytic situation is not completely surprising in view of the significance of the analyst as a paternal authoritative figure who cares for his patient but at the same time deprives him of the dependent closeness that he craves. There is, however, other evidence suggesting the importance of deep-seated ambivalence toward parental figures with this regard. For example, an early study of anti-Semitic college girls found them to have a sharper cleavage than more tolerant students between conscious feelings and ideas and those at an unconscious level.[23] One reflection of this cleavage lay in the difference between their declarations of affection for their parents and their thematic apperception test interpretations of parental figures as mean and cruel and daughters as jealous, suspicious, and hostile. Unprejudiced subjects who were more openly critical of their parents revealed less hostility in projective techniques and revealed fewer fantasies of their parents' deaths. Similarly, a positive correlation was found between indexes of prejudice and of ambivalence toward parents and other authority figures in a population of medical students.[82]

Allport,[4] reviewing the investigation of college girls and related studies, identified a series of personality elements as concomitants of prejudice. These were, in addition to ambivalence toward parents, moralistic tendencies, a need for definiteness, a tendency to dichotomize, externalization of conflict, excessive devotion to social institutions, and authoritarianism. He considered all of these characteristics "as devices to bolster a weak ego unable to face its conflicts squarely and unflinchingly. They are . . . the earmarks of a personality in whom prejudice is functionally important."

⟨ Psychosocial Consequences of Discrimination on the Victim

Symptomatic Responses

A deeply held, prejudiced attitude or belief must inevitably influence the social behavior of its possessor. No matter how well schooled he is in dissimulation, his behavior with members of the group toward whom he harbors antipathetic or deprecatory feelings will communicate the message: You are inferior, dangerous, hated, or otherwise obnoxious. As has already been noted, his discriminatory behavior and, indirectly, his attitudes will also influence the thoughts and feelings of peers, who, as they become aware of his position, must decide whether to lose his friendship and respect and adopt a different point of view or to undergo a series of conflict-engendering psychological maneuvers to enable them to conform comfortably with his beliefs. The situation becomes more generally pathogenic to the degree that prejudice is institutionalized

and requires both parents and children to learn how to think and feel in this way. This is a kind of learning that involves the selective submergence of incompatible tendencies in order to maintain their membership and status in the power-holding social group.[36]

Most of the early American work on discrimination was concerned with the static and relatively isolated social world occupied by the Negro.[41,57,85] Davis and Dollard[29] focused on the system of caste-like restrictions and the frustrations and aggressive feelings that these restrictions may produce. They concluded, however, that social class membership as it is translated into child-rearing practices is more important than caste (that is, than discrimination) in shaping the habits and goals of black children.

More recent studies, aside from those concerned with school segregation, have been based on studies of patients and have paid particular attention to family structure.[50] A frequently reiterated viewpoint is that of Kardiner and Ovesey,[59] who noted the central role of the mother in many black families and her lack of respect for her husband who cannot act according to white ideals or prototypes. Her dual significance as the provider both of economic and emotional stability for the family forces her to behave with her children in such a way that they often see her as frustrating rather than dependable. The father may be absent or, when present, passive and remote, though occasionally violent. In the broad sense of the word, a long history of discrimination has produced a family structure resulting in "continuous frustration in childhood [which creates] a personality devoid of confidence in human relations with an eternal vigilance and distrust of others."

Similar statements about the working black mother refer to her neglect of her children and of the father's tendency to compete with his children for dependency gratification from the mother.[81] Ambivalent dependency on the mother has been related also to a tendency to emphasize somatic complaints.[79] A more general recognition of the stressful quality of a continuing and pervasive discrimination and of the behavioral modifications necessary for survival under such conditions is contained in the formulation that a personality organization "which clinicians would ordinarily consider to be schizoid" is "an adjusted personality organization for Negroes in American society . . . since it serves to protect the core or ego aspects of personality. . . ."[72]

Discrimination as symbolic castration has received particular attention, and the black man, according to evidence presented by Kardiner and Ovesey, and also by Frazier,[41] has a significant problem in maintaining his masculine status not only because of the structure of his family, but also because of the emasculating pressure of the white society against which effective retaliation is impossible.[59] It is perhaps significant in this respect that a sample of young black male psychiatric patients displayed a marked lack of interest in using contraceptive techniques. This is interpreted as one way of gaining recognition of masculine status within the black social world and also within the complacent yet suppressive white world.[33]

The emasculation may assume specific developmental significance for the young black boy in his awareness that his father and father surrogates must behave as though they are weak, inferior, or vulnerable in relation to white males. It is immediately obvious that this situation may also apply to the sons of any discriminated-against, subjugated group. On the other hand, the minority group becomes stronger to the degree that it has a distinctive cultural heritage that can serve as a focus for identity formation for the young boy; this is a significant difference between, for example, the Jew and the black.

Conscious awareness of relative inadequacy and lack of real power associated with unconscious conflicts concerning potency are also suggested as possible determinants of psychopathology in mobility blocked socially and economically deprived members of the lower class, illiterate, poverty-stricken populations of certain underdeveloped countries.[20]

Another specific feature of the discriminated-against minority group member is his retaliative hostility against his oppressors. In some instances, this may take the form of anti-social gestures of defiance, including criminal behavior. The immediate target of the gesture, however, may be a member of his own group, particularly one who may symbolize some aspect of the power-holding segment.[31] The black man's refusal to use contraceptives may be an example of this. In other instances the hostility may be repressed and dealt with by reaction formations. Behavioral reflections of this would be characteristic docile, submissive, passive, and inappropriate cheerful and pleasant behavior. "Uncle-Tomism" among blacks, behaving in terms of a caricature of the cheerful servitor, may be an example of this. There are perhaps such other more subtle ways of discharging hostile tension, as through jokes using the dominant society as the disguised object. Any efforts at psychological and physical survival using any innate or culturally supported talent or socially available channel can certainly contribute to ambitious, hypervigilant, or even devious behavior in any individual member of a discriminated-against minority. Similarly, resignation in the face of overwhelming odds may result in apathy, indolence, and unwillingness to assume responsibility.

Most of the researcher's attention has perhaps been devoted to the issue of self-hatred in the discriminated-against person, particularly the black in America.[59,60] This self-hatred has been interpreted as a function of inability to express hostile wishes against the whites and of guilt derived from hating the whites and has also been related to identification with the powerful white group in that introjected white attitudes result in self-hatred: It is impossible to become white, and the black's reactive aim-inhibited hostility, using the introjected attitudes, is directed against himself.[35] This unattainable wish to be white, which is a response to the social context in which the person lives, is conceptualized by Kennedy[63] as a hostile ego ideal. The conflict-inducing value of having acquired the goals and standards of a hated group against which the expression, and even the full consciousness, of hostile feelings may not be possible is suggested by a study of schizophrenic black men. They showed more hostility against blacks and a greater tendency to identify with whites than did nonschizophrenic controls. The latter showed "a greater tendency to accept their own group membership, exhibited more fantasied retaliation against whites, more covert, deeply buried white identifications, and a closer approximation to a Negro ego-ideal."[48] In a similar vein Hendin[53] noted that suicide becomes a problem at an early age for the black urban male because of an early sense of despair that life can never be satisfying. In a psychoanalytic scrutiny of twenty-five suicidal patients, he was impressed by the prominence, in contrast to white subjects, of unconscious murderous rage reflecting "the frustration and anger of the Black ghetto." Other behaviors have been described as concomitants of the discriminated-against minority state. Milner[72] stated that "an undiscriminating, paranoia-like antipathy for 'all whites'" may be present that "does not allow a person to evaluate and react to white persons as individuals. Kardiner and Ovesey[59] described acting-out and essentially self-narcotizing techniques that permit the black to deal with feelings of difference, loneliness, and low self-esteem. Prominent elements of perplexity and confusion in young schizophrenic black men have been related to caste and class effects, which combine to widen the gulf between reality's threats and demands and the young men's actual capacities to perceive and act. It was also postulated[12] that the black man's constant need to deny the threatening or provocative aspects of the white world and to repress or displace wishes that might bring him into conflict with that world contributes to a semantic impoverishment or reduction in the connotative richness of the symbols that he uses.

Early Predispositions

The behavioral characteristics and inferred unconscious conflicts of minority group adults have their origins in early experiences as members of a segregated and otherwise discriminated-against group. There is increasing evidence that self-awareness in a member of a weak or vulnerable group occurs very early in life and that the black child's recognition that dark skin color is associated with lower power and prestige has been demonstrated at four to five years of age.[25–27,48,55] In more general terms, a black psychiatrist, Adams,[2] described the black child's identification with his parents as anxiety laden, particularly when parental insecurity and impotence in the face of social reality are obvious. He stated that the child might "turn to the white group for identification as a defense against this anxiety," but that at some point the child would inevitably encounter a final rejection. Erikson[37] touched on this problem of split identifications with the dominant whites and the inferior blacks when he postulated an early disruption of the continuity of the black child's identity as he becomes aware of his black identity. Recent studies have shown that young black boys in a border Southern city have significant psychological problems around the issue of low self-esteem, self-directed hostility, and identifications. An important determinant of parental identity conflict appears to be the mixed messages given them by their mothers concerning the importance of equal status and achievement, on the one hand, and the impossibility of attaining them, on the other.[13] Investigation of a comparable group of white boys from the same area indicated that even those with little personal contact with blacks tended to perceive them as symbolic of unacceptable or dangerous impulses in themselves. They too might be considered to suffer from identity problems related to color. They too were their mother's sons since, like their black counterparts, they constantly received from them mixed messages about the significance of skin color. In this case, one message stressed the importance of granting equal rights and privileges to blacks, while the other emphasized the blacks' dangerous aggressivity, potentially uncontrollable sexuality, laziness, and unreliability.[14]

Adaptation or Regression

Low self-esteem and hopelessness as a concomitant of distance from social power may perhaps be most easily studied in groups whose lack of self-determination is magnified by their lack of the verbal symbols necessary for the exchange of culturally important information. The migrants who accumulate on the rims and in isolated pockets of the great South American cities constitute such a group. As Willems pointed out,[16] in Brazil they do not as yet form a true urban proletariat, but rather a poorly assimilated agglomerate of individuals who have transplanted rural ways of living into the metropolitan area.

Andean Indian serfs studied by Klein[64] revealed through interviews and projective testing a self-concept dominated by despair and a perception of themselves as impotent and ineffectual in the face of a powerful and malevolent world. Their defensive preferences were those that might be characterized in an adult North American as indicating pathological regression or incipient behavioral disorganization. These included a defensive avoidance of sensation, defensive immobility, limited communication because of danger of exposure, and a pervasive perception of others as power oriented and hostile. Yet these people functioned as members of their oppressed village society, and the culture of their group, including the attitudes and values passed on from generation to generation, tended to perpetuate their reality situation by limiting their aspirations and conscious desires. In short, their perceptions and attitudes seem more logically interpreted as adaptive than as indicating vulnerability to disorganization.

Without question, deprivation, discrimination, contempt, and exclusion from full participation in the dominant culture all have an impact on character and behavior. But to what degree may these concomitants of minority group status be regarded as adaptive, and to what degree as regressive or disorganized? And to what degree is it justifiable to generalize from one minority group to another?[19] For example, the data of unsystematic observation and of mental hospital statistics suggest that both lower-class black men and women are prone to develop more dramatically psychotic states with interpersonal stress associated with alcoholic intoxication or with the stress of jail incarceration than are whites of similar age and sex. Derbyshire and Schleifer[34] demonstrated that lower-class blacks of both sexes show more florid symptomatology, and particularly, more temporal disorientation, on being identified as psychotic by virtue of public disturbance than is the case in comparable white disturbers of the peace. The phenomena are not seen, however, among the Jewish or Oriental minorities. In other words, minority status cannot be treated as a unitary concept any more than social class. The key may not be access to total societal power after all but rather the available quality and range of alternative solutions to problems associated with the lack of such access. This requires an adaptive or functional view of minority behavior, as well as scrutiny of what features of the life of a particular group have protective significance. The two interrelated protective and problem-solving assets of any individual or group are education and membership in a viable ongoing cultural process. These assist in the provision of a broad repertory of interpersonal and intrapsychic problem-solving techniques with a sufficient number of alternatives to meet a variety of circumstances. Without this, the institutionalization of passivity can constitute a protection against behavioral disorganization.[19, p. 239] This is quite different from the protective patterns used by European migrants to North America. For them the ultimate goals were involvement in the dominant culture, assimilation, at least on occupational terms, and the acquisition of economic power. In the absence of resources the only response to threat, the only alternative to disintegration, is passivity. This means group withdrawal into parallel personal cocoons that shut out the disturbing stimuli of the hostile environment and help avoid the potential flooding of their inner worlds with phantoms of their own making. I described[19, p. 240] this phenomenon in lowest-class illiterate South American peasants as cultural regression or hibernation. I contrasted this picture of adaptive or adjustive cultural regression with a type of cultural evolution that can be described as coping rather than adjusting, or as actively rather than passively adapting. A major example now in an early phase of evolutionary change is that of the black in America. The civil-rights movement and its offshoots, such as the Black Power idea, are beginning to unite blacks into a true collectivity with a commitment to common socially significant goals and values.

❡ Prejudice, Group Rigidity, and Flexibility: Other Areas of Concern

The psychological precursors and concomitants of prejudice are involved to varying degrees in most human and intergroup relations. Ethnocentrism, for example among Puerto Ricans in New York City is positively correlated with generally unfavorable attitudes toward prevention and cure of illness through medical and public health means.[83] Inability to free oneself from negative preconceptions concerning strangers, and persistent limiting of one's emotionally secure world to that populated by those of like kind, impairs the freedom to seek medical assistance from technically qualified though impersonal or unfamiliar sources.

Rigidity, closed-mindedness, and the tendency to view other nations in stereotypes have been documented as sources of persisting conflict in the international system. Closed-mindedness, like ethnic prejudice, can cause national leaders to make progressive revisions in their general image of the world until disappointment is reduced to a tolerable level. This process is reminiscent of mental illness, since it involves the inability to adequately test reality.[11] Part of the resistance to attitude change at the international level is the tendency to judge the actions of others as inherently hostile, behavior that at the interpersonal level would be considered as paranoid. The hypothesis that there exist cognitive dynamics that tend to sustain bad faith images of the enemy, and that such dynamics have identifiable consequences for international relations, has been to some degree substantiated by detailed study of the publicly available statements of former Secretary of State John

Foster Dulles and his attitude toward a single subject, the Soviet Union.[54]

Finally, the possible resolution of group tensions and of individual prejudice has attracted a great deal of attention. The range of proposed solutions is great because of the variety of factors that perpetuate prejudiced feelings, attitudes and beliefs, and discriminatory behavior. It has become clear that discriminatory behavior can be modified while prejudiced feelings remain, albeit in a dormant state. Economic factors seem particularly important in this respect. Whites, for example, who would never do so otherwise, have lived uncomplainingly next to blacks while working in government jobs. The converse is also true. White soldiers, emotionally close to black comrades in combat, have reverted to discriminatory patterns after discharge as part of unthinking conformity to the context in which they find themselves. This, despite profound and moving shared experiences with blacks, and despite their acknowledgment on questioning of changed basic attitudes. It is evident that inertia is one of the significant factors perpetuating prejudiced behavior and attitudes among large segments of the population; this contrasts with the tenaciously held antipathy described earlier. Even in this latter instance, however, social changes promise to modify the behavior in question. If the symptomatically prejudiced share the personality dynamics of the authoritarian personality, particularly his uncertainty of gender identity and associated need for approval from father surrogates, it follows that their attitudes and behavior will be strongly influenced by that of the most powerful social and governmental figures. In other words, the unofficial, covert messages of the president and of other community leaders, as well as their official pronouncements and legislated attitudes toward discrimination, will be powerful antidotes or reinforcers of prejudice.

Two other elements would seem important for a social context in which ethnic prejudice directed against familiar minorities is minimized. One is the available experience of emotionally reciprocal relationships between majority and minority children. This reciprocity is essential for one to see the world through the eyes of the other. The second element is the vitalization of the historically defined minority so that its own deprecatory self-image is not continued.

The social context is changing significantly in the 1970s so far as institutionalized and individual black-white prejudice is concerned. There is no evidence, however, that prejudice in general is being eliminated. Many authors are concerned, for example, with the impact of United States Indochina involvement, increasing Middle East tension, and the possibility of a need for new scapegoats on the future of anti-Semitism in this country. Some see significant similarities between the social climate of the United States of the early 1970s, especially in relation to its assimilated intellectual Jewish population, and that of immediately pre-Hitler Germany.[46] It appears unlikely, given man's hierarchical and territorial proclivities, his sensitivity to threats from the unknown, his need to reduce the range of his decisions, and his primitive tendency to manage his guilt and anxiety by externalizing, that he is ready to abandon totally the advantages of closed-mindedness, scapegoating, and prejudice.

❪ Bibliography

1. ACKERMAN, N. W., and JAHODA, M. *Anti-Semitism and Emotional Disorder.* New York: Harper, 1950.
2. ADAMS, W. A. "The Negro Patient in Psychiatric Treatment." *American Journal of Orthopsychiatry,* 20 (1950), 305–310.
3. ADORNO, T. W., FRENKEL-BRUNSWIK, E., LEVINSON, D. J., and SANFORD, R. N., eds. *The Authoritarian Personality.* New York: Harper, 1950.
4. ALLPORT, G. W. *The Nature of Prejudice.* Cambridge, Mass.: Addison-Wesley, 1954.
5. ANTONOVSKY, A. "Toward a Refinement of the 'Marginal Man' Concept." *Social Forces,* 35 (1956), 57–66.
6. BARBOUR, F. B., ed. *The Black 70's.* Boston: Porter Sargent, 1970.
7. BEISSER, A. R., and HARRIS, H. "Psychologi-

cal Aspects of the Civil Rights Movement and the Negro Professional Man." *American Journal of Psychiatry,* 123 (1966), 733–738.
8. BELTH, N. C. *Barriers: Patterns of Discrimination Against Jews.* New York: Friendly House, 1958.
9. BETTELHEIM, B., and JANOWITZ, M. *Dynamics of Prejudice: A Psychological and Sociological Study of Veterans.* New York: Harper, 1950.
10. BOGARDUS, E. S. "Measuring Social Distance." *Journal of Applied Sociology,* 9 (1925), 299–303.
11. BOULDING, K. E. "The Learning and Reality-Testing Process in the International System." *Journal of International Affairs,* 21 (1967), 1–15.
12. BRODY, E. B. "Social Conflict and Schizophrenic Behavior in Young Adult Negro Males." *Psychiatry,* 24 (1961), 337–346.
13. ———. "Color and Identity Conflict in Young Boys: Observations of Negro Mothers and Sons in Urban Baltimore." *Psychiatry,* 26 (1963), 188–201.
14. ———. "Color and Identity Conflict in Young Boys: II. Observations of White Mothers and Sons in Urban Baltimore." *Archives of General Psychiatry,* 10 (1964), 354–360.
15. ———. "Cultural Exclusion, Character and Illness." *American Journal of Psychiatry,* 123 (1966), 446–456.
16. ———. "The Psychiatry of Latin America." (Editorial.) *American Journal of Psychiatry,* 123 (1966), 475–477.
17. ———. "Transcultural Psychiatry, Human Similarities and Socioeconomic Evolution." *American Journal of Psychiatry,* 124 (1967), 616–622.
18. ———. "Culture Symbol and Value in the Social Etiology of Behavioral Deviance." In J. Zubin, ed., *Social Psychiatry.* New York: Grune & Stratton, 1968. Pp. 8–33.
19. ———. "Minority Group Status and Behavioral Disorganization." In E. B. Brody, ed., *Minority Group Adolescents in the United States.* Baltimore, Md.: Williams & Wilkins, 1968. Pp. 227–243.
20. ———. *The Lost Ones. Social Forces and Mental Illness in Rio de Janeiro.* New York: International Universities Press, 1973.
21. ———, ed. *Minority Group Adolescents in the United States.* Baltimore, Md.: Williams & Wilkins, 1968.

22. ———, and DERBYSHIRE, R. L. "Prejudice in American Negro College Students." *Archives of General Psychiatry*, 9 (1963), 619–628.

23. CAMPBELL, A. A. "Factors Associated with Attitudes Toward Jews." In T. M. Newcomb and E. L. Hartley, eds., *Readings in Social Psychology*. New York: Henry Holt, 1947.

24. CAUDILL, W., REDLICH, F. C., GILMORE, H. R., and BRODY, E. B. "Social Structure and Interaction Processes on a Psychiatric Ward." *American Journal of Orthopsychiatry*, 22 (1952), 314–334.

25. CLARK, K. B. "The Development of Consciousness of Self and the Emergence of Racial Identification in Negro Preschool Children." *Journal of Social Psychology*, 10 (1939), 591–599.

26. ———. "Skin Color as a Factor in Racial Identification of Negro Preschool Children." *Journal of Social Psychology*, 11 (1940), 159–169.

27. ———, and CLARK, M. K. "Emotional Factors in Racial Identification and Preference in Negro Children." *Journal of Negro Education*, 19 (1950), 341–350.

28. COOPER, E., and JAHODA, M. "The Evasion of Propaganda. How Prejudiced People Respond to Anti-prejudice Propaganda." *Journal of Psychology*, 23 (1947).

29. DAVIS, A., and DOLLARD, J. *Children of Bondage*. Washington, D.C.: American Council on Education, 1940.

30. DAVIS, O. "The English Language Is My Enemy." *IRCD Bulletin*, 5 (1969), 13–15.

31. DERBYSHIRE, R. L. "Personal Identity and Ethnocentrism in American Negro College Students." *Mental Hygiene*, 48 (1964), 65–69.

32. ———, and BRODY, E. B. "Marginality, Identity and Behavior in the American Negro: A Functional Analysis." *International Journal of Social Psychiatry*, 10 (1964), 7–13.

33. ———, BRODY, E. B., and SCHLEIFER, C. "Family Structure of Young Adult Negro Male Mental Patients: Preliminary Observations from Urban Baltimore." *Journal of Mental and Nervous Disease*, 136 (1963), 245–251.

34. ———, and SCHLEIFER, C. Clinical Change in Jail-Referred Mental Patients. Paper presented to the American Orthopsychiatric Association, San Francisco, April 16, 1966.

35. DOLLARD, J. *Caste and Class in a Southern Town*. New York: Harper, 1949.

36. EPSTEIN, B. R., and FORSTER, A. *Some of My Best Friends*. New York: Farrar, Straus, & Cudahy, 1962.

37. ERIKSON, E. H. *Childhood and Society*. New York: Norton, 1950.

38. FANON, F. *The Wretched of the Earth* (1961). New York: Grove Press, 1963.

39. FISHER, P. L., and LOWENSTEIN, R. L. *Race and the News Media*. New York: Praeger, 1967.

40. FONG, S. L. M. "Identity Conflicts of Chinese Adolescents in San Francisco." In E. B. Brody, ed., *Minority Group Adolescents in the United States*. Baltimore, Md.: Williams & Wilkins, 1968. Pp. 111–132.

41. FRAZIER, E. F. *Negro Youth at the Crossways*. Washington, D.C.: American Council on Education, 1940.

42. FRENKEL-BRUNSWIK, E., and SANFORD, R. N. "The Anti-Semitic Personality: A Research Report." In E. Simmel, ed., *Anti-Semitism: A Social Disease*. New York: International Universities Press, 1948. Pp. 96–124.

43. FROMM, E. *Escape from Freedom*. New York: Rinehart, 1941.

44. GALLAHORN, G., CUSHING, J., and BRODY, E. B. "Anti Negro Prejudice Before, During, and After a Schizophrenic Episode in a Southern White Woman." *American Journal of Psychotherapy*, 19 (1965), 650–652.

45. GARMA, A. Repetition of Ancestral Traumata and Destructive Identifications in Anti-Judaism. Mimeographed report presented in part at Workshop on Racial Prejudice, Pan-American Psychoanalytic Congress, Acapulco, Mexico, February 1964.

46. GLAZER, N. "Revolutionism and the Jews: The Role of the Intellectual." *Commentary*, 51 (1971), 55–61.

47. GOLDENBERG, H. The Role of Group Identification in the Personality Organization of Schizophrenic and Normal Negroes. Unpublished Ph.D. dissertation, University of California at Los Angeles, February 1953.

48. GOODMAN, M. E. *Race Awareness in Young Children*. Cambridge, Mass.: Addison-Wesley, 1952.

49. GORDON, A. *Jews in Suburbia*. New York: Doubleday, 1959.

50. GROSSACK, M. M., ed., *Mental Health and Segregation*. New York: Springer, 1963.

51. GROUP FOR THE ADVANCEMENT OF PSYCHIA-

TRY. *Emotional Aspects of School Deseg-regation.* 2d ed. Washington, D.C., 1970.

52. HARTLEY, E. L. *Problems in Prejudice.* New York: King's Crown Press, 1946.

53. HENDIN, H. *Black Suicide.* New York: Basic Books, 1969.

54. HOLSTI, O. R. "Cognitive Dynamics and Images of the Enemy." *Journal of International Affairs,* 21 (1967), 16–39.

55. HOROWITZ, R. E. "Racial Aspects of Self-Identification in Nursery School Children." *Journal of Psychology,* 7 (1939), 91–99.

56. JAHODA, M. *Race Relations and Mental Health.* Paris: UNESCO, 1960.

57. JOHNSON, C. S. *Growing Up in the Black Belt.* Washington, D.C.: American Council on Education, 1941.

58. KAMENY, F. E. "Gay Liberation and Psychiatry." *Psychiatric Opinion,* 8 (1971), 18–27.

59. KARDINER, A., and OVESEY, L. *The Mark of Oppression: A Psychosocial Study of the American Negro.* New York: Norton, 1951.

60. KARON, B. P. *The Negro Personality.* New York: Springer, 1958.

61. KATZ, D., and BRALY, K. W. "Racial Stereotypes of 100 College Students." *Journal of Abnormal and Social Psychology,* 28 (1933), 280–290.

62. KELLY, H. H. "Two Functions of Reference Groups." In G. Swanson, T. M. Newcomb, and E. L. Hartley, eds., *Readings in Social Psychology.* New York: Henry Holt, 1952. Pp. 410–415.

63. KENNEDY, J. A. "Problems Posed in the Analysis of Negro Patients." *Psychiatry,* 15 (1952), 313–327.

64. KLEIN, R. "The Self-Image of Adult Males in an Andean Culture: A Clinical Exploration of a Dynamic Personality Construct." Ann Arbor, Mich.: University Microfilms, 1963.

65. LASSWELL, H. D. *Psychopathology and Politics.* New York: Viking Press, 1960.

66. LEWIN, K. "Self-Hatred Among Jews." *Contemporary Jewish Record,* 4 (1941), 219–232.

67. ———. *Resolving Social Conflicts.* New York: Harper, 1948.

68. LOEWENSTEIN, R. *Christians and Jews.* New York: International Universities Press, 1951.

69. MCLEAN, H. V. "Psychodynamic Factors in Racial Relations." *Annals of the Academy of Political and Social Science,* 244 (1946), 159–166.

70. ———. "The Emotional Health of Negroes." *Journal of Negro Education,* 18 (1949), 283–290.

71. MERTON, R. K. "The Self-Fulfilling Prophecy." *Antioch Review,* 8 (1948), 193–210.

72. MILNER, E. "Some Hypotheses Concerning the Influence of Segregation on Negro Personality Development." *Psychiatry,* 16 (1953), 291–297.

73. MYRDAL, G. *The American Dilemma.* New York: Harper, 1944.

74. PARSONS, T. *The Social System.* New York: The Free Press, 1951.

75. PETERS, W. "Who Chooses the People You Know?" June 1959. (Referred to by B. R. Epstein and A. Forster, *Some of My Best Friends.* New York: Farrar, Straus, & Cudahy, 1962.)

76. PIERCE, C. In F. B. Barbour, ed., *The Black 70's.* Boston: Porter Sargent, 1970. Pp. 265–283.

77. ROHRER, J. H., and EDMONSON, M. S. eds., *The Eighth Generation.* New York: Harper, 1960.

78. ROKEACH, M. *The Open and Closed Mind.* New York: Basic Books, 1960.

79. ST. CLAIRE, H. R. "Psychiatric Interview Experience with Negroes." *American Journal of Psychiatry,* 108 (1951), 113–119.

80. SARTRE, J.-P. "Portrait of the Anti-Semite." *Partisan Review,* 13 (1946).

81. SCLARE, A. B. "Cultural Determinants in the Neurotic Negro." *British Journal of Medical Psychology,* 26 (1953), 278–288.

82. SIEGMAN, A., and BRODY, E. B. Unpublished data on University of Maryland medical students.

83. SUCHMAN, E. "Social Factors in Medical Deprivation." *American Journal of Public Health,* 55 (1965), 1725–1771.

84. TUMIN, M. D. *An Inventory and Appraisal of Research on American Anti-Semitism.* New York: Freedom Books, 1961.

85. WARNER, W. L., JUNKER, B. H., and ADAMS, W. A. *Color and Human Nature.* Washington, D.C.: American Council on Education, 1941.

86. WILKINSON, C. B. "Racism and the Acquisition of Prejudice." *Journal of Operational Psychiatry,* 1 (1970), 55–60.

87. WILLIAMS, R. M., JR. *Strangers Next Door: Ethnic Relations in American Communities.* Englewood Cliffs, N.J.: Prentice-Hall, 1964.

88. ———. "The Black Professional: Issues and

Tasks for the 70's." *Journal of Operational Psychiatry*, 1 (1970), 67–72.

89. YAMAMOTO, J. "Japanese American Identity Crisis." In E. B. Brody, ed., *Minority Group Adolescents in the United States.* Baltimore, Md.: Williams & Wilkins, 1968. Pp. 133–156.

90. YOUNG, K. *An Introductory Sociology.* New York: American Book, 1934.

91. ZAWADSTI, B. "Limitations of the Scapegoat Theory of Prejudice." *Journal of Abnormal and Social Psychology*, 43 (1948), 127–141.

CHAPTER 33

PSYCHIATRIC PROBLEMS
OF THE BLACK MINORITY

Chester M. Pierce

THE MAJOR AND OVERRIDING psychiatric problem of the black minority is the withering effect of racism. Hence the sociocultural and community aim must be to dilute, undercut, and eliminate racism wherever and however it is located. Objective accounts of the results of racism can be found in many places such as Dr. John Norman's[7] book on ghetto medicine. Racism's results can be quantified in terms of statistical comparison between blacks and whites in regard to such indicators as unemployment, mortality rates, longevity, substandard housing, and education level.

Although many problem areas might be selected, this chapter will discuss those problem areas thought to be both most critical and yet least often related to psychological and emotional health. The areas selected include problems concerning mass communication, formal educational channels, demographic patterns, and seeking alternative futures. As each of these areas is discussed a general solution will be suggested in terms of how the black population might move to increase its self-esteem, which is the most critical need in America's solving its most pressing domestic issue.

Before addressing these areas, however, a few introductory remarks will be necessary to orient the reader. The reader should know that black psychiatrists may view both the problem areas and their solutions much differently from white colleagues, who in general tend to define the boundaries of psychiatric concern as no larger than those illnesses brought to the attention of the hospital, clinic, or consultation room. Second, the reader should consider that perhaps all that is written about blacks might apply to other nonwhite minorities and maybe even to the white poor. Finally, the reader should realize that since the overall aim of medicine is to help more people live longer and live better, it should not be surprising that the ultimate goal must be for blacks and whites alike to become planetary citizens, who see their province as the entire earth and who function as enlightened cosmopolites. The articulation of this long-range goal is a problem that has to be kept uppermost in mind while considering the short-term and intermediate goals and the problems that jeopardize their actualization. After defining racism, it will be the latter problem to which we turn.

(The Definition of Racism

Racism in America is the behavior that results from mental attitudes about skin color. In this society all persons, black and white, are barraged by ceaseless efforts that insist that white skin color is superior to black skin color. As a result of this insistence, it is not unusual for any white to be permitted, in terms of unwritten law as well as written law, to exploit, degrade, abuse, humiliate, minimize, terrorize, and tyrannize any black. The mental attitude about skin color, not economic status or social attributes, is what justifies this behavior for the white. Since blacks have been victimized to sustain similar attitudes, all too often they too adopt proracist attitudes and behavior in regard to themselves and to whites. Due to proracist attitudes in the United States, both blacks and whites do things that permit, promote, encourage, sustain, and insist that whites are superior and blacks inferior.

The fact that this mental attitude cannot be changed even in the face of contrary evidence makes it by definition a delusion. The tragic results of this delusion, afflicting virtually the entire population of this country, has had unsettling effects not only for us in this day but for the entire world now and for some time in the projected future.

A mental illness in which millions have been smitten of course makes racism a public health illness. Similarly, like all public health illnesses, such as smallpox or plague, the medical model would predict that such an illness cannot be treated on a one to one basis, that it would leave in its wake serious sequelae (both in terms of sociocultural and pathophysiological indices), and that it would require large sums of money to eradicate. Naturally, the most effective therapy would be prophylactic or preventive measures taken before the illness could seize a population. In sum, the society would have to commit itself and its resources to get rid of the pestilence.

Racism so far has been viewed as a mental health and public health problem. Another view that should be glanced at prior to a consideration of the problems of the black minority is that racism is an infectious disease, a perceptual disease, and a lethal disease.

This mental health and public health illness is contagious in the sense that an almost invariable experience is that wherever white Americans gather in concentration, save for exploitation, measures to discriminate and ignore blacks are instituted immediately. On a more commonplace basis, a clinical instance could be cited, such as the relative freedom of racial conflict in a classroom until the arrival of a new child, who presents with vigor his parents' and the societies' actual view of blacks. In such an instance, prolonged and bitter racial conflict ensues. Here old black-white friendships are strained, realigned, and perhaps ruptured, as a class of children in a schoolroom begins to act like the general society, when the only variable presented was the emphatic statements of presumed white superiority over the minority members of the class, who had dark skin. In the private school where this incident occurred, it took literally hours for the black parents to deal with their fifth-grade child as they attempted to aid the child in coping with the vicious dehumanization brought about by this circumstance.

Some things about racism that defy men of good will in coming to grips with the issues are a reflection of perceptual distortion. In almost any instance of a black-white negotiation, the black sees things in one way while the white sees them differently. The white man thinks that to ask a black to consult about a film on blacks after it is made is a grand gesture, and he should be applauded and cheered by a grateful black community. It does not occur to him to utilize such consultation when the film is being written and produced. Nor does it occur to him that blacks should not always have to be grateful.

The most terrible and extreme consequence

of racism is that it kills people—black and white. Black babies starving or being chewed up by rats are an example of a direct and easily visible problem. Less visible but equally fatal are deaths secondary to society's failures, such as those that precipitate drug abuse, the most immediate and pressing biosocial problem of black people. But whites are being killed also by their racism. For instance, a heavy bodily toll must be taken on thousands of whites as they commute back and forth to their outer cities. Much of the motivation for such commuting is to escape living near blacks.

Therefore, as one selects problems of the black minority, one must be aware of the ubiquitous effects of racism, a contagious and lethal mental and public health disease, which is characterized by perceptual distortion and false beliefs about skin color.

(Problems of Mass Communication

The mass media more often than not see to it that blacks are portrayed in ways that continue to teach white superiority. The unsophisticated argue how marvelous it is that blacks are now seen regularly in nonmenial as well as menial roles in films and on television. Yet the way blacks are presented on these media, in general, has immeasurable importance in keeping blacks in a reduced status. For instance, a black is more often the server than the served, for example, on a commercial the black pumps the gas while the white drives the car or the black woman is the cab driver while the white man's uncivil remarks give her a headache. The black can be predicted to be less often depicted as a thinking being. For instance, although he is the district attorney in a program, the black solves a case with his fists; an underling, who is a white police lieutenant, uses his brains to solve the same problem. That is, while the district attorney is being beat up, the lieutenant is deploying squad cars, securing laboratory assistance, and reasoning out his next move. Gratuitously,

that is, unnecessarily, the show depicts the lieutenant speaking with a force and an arrogance that would not be tolerated in a real life situation between a district attorney and his subordinate. A public service advertisement tells white and black adults and youths the testimony of white children getting eyeglasses. This resulted in better school grades and increased ability to concentrate. Then one sees a black child testify that getting one's eyes tested is "fun." Thus, the black is seen over and over in such guises as a server and a nonthinking physical creature. Even his own health is attended to only because it is fun and immediate. On the other hand, both whites and blacks are told that whites are clever and far-seeing and attend to their interest because it is intelligent. Further, for all the millions who watch television, essentially it is only a white who controls, decides, and plans.

The black, even while solving his problems at a physical level, is usually shown to be contained, controlled, and inhibited by authority. Often this authority reinforces the true life condition of police control and surveillance of ghettos. At other times, the authority takes improbable forms. For instance, a very popular cartoon show for children, "The Globe-Trotter," shows a group of tractable, handsome black athletes. Yet what the children of the nation see week after week is that such a group of black men are controlled and directed by a small, feisty, white grandmother. Thus, hour after hour, emotional and psychological sets are being molded whereby blacks and whites will accept as usual and routine that even a senescent white woman can boss around, direct, and guide capable black men.

All these and countless other examples show blacks as accommodating, controlled, dependent, and, of course, not creative or original in their thought. However, other mass communications do more of the same. Television is cited first because it happens to use up more of a child's life than school hours. That is, by age sixteen, most children will have spent more hours before a television than in a classroom.

Let us look at other forms of mass media. Movies make similar claims of increased use of blacks in more dignified roles. As an aside, there can be no solution until blacks can have decision-making input into mass media, instead of merely having increased public exposure. Until this is done, proracist teachings will continue unabated.

As an example of what movies do in terms of the problem under discussion, one can mention a movie entitled *The Landlord*. In this comedy a white man buys a tenement building in a ghetto. Among other adventures he encounters three black women. One woman reaches out and nourishes and protects him, with all the devotion that whites love to recount when they talk about their black "mammies." Another black woman, a beauty, goes to bed with this man the first night she meets him. But it is the third black woman who exemplifies on the screen all the problems we have touched on. She is a black mother. The writers have her initiate an overture to the white hero. When her husband is jailed (significantly, because he was protesting racial ills), she goes to bed with the hero. As a result she is impregnated. When the cuckolded husband returns, he discovers his plight and in justifiable wrath pursues the white. However, even though armed with a weapon, chasing an unarmed man, the black is seen as ineffective. When he finally corners his prey, the mass media producers do not permit the black man to deliver a blow to the white. Instead, this comedy shows the black man paralyzed to act and then immobilized by a straitjacket so he can be carted away in an ambulance. The story does not stop by telling its audiences that blacks, no matter what the provocation, do not resist or cannot give effective resistance to whites. The plot goes on relentlessly, as comedy, to show the white hero living with the black mother while she awaits his child and while her black husband, the political militant, is in a mental institution. Almost all films in movies or on television can be analyzed from such perspectives by blacks. The emotional damage such mass communications do is limitless and unknown.

What the reader must bear in mind is that these assaults to black dignity and black hope are incessant and cumulative. Any single one may not be gross. In fact, the major vehicle for racism in this country is offenses done to blacks by whites in this sort of gratuitous, never-ending way. These offenses are microaggressions. Almost all black-white racial interactions are characterized by white putdowns, done in an automatic, preconscious, or unconscious fashion. These minidisasters accumulate. It is the sum total of multiple microaggressions by whites to blacks that has pervasive effect to the stability and peace of this world.

These offensive maneuvers by whites stem from the mental attitude of presumed superiority. Thus, whites feel they can initiate actions, direct unilateral operations, and control blacks, whom they are told over and over are unthinking, physical creatures dependent and available for entertainment, gratification, and exploitation. Unfortunately, blacks too accept such communications, and by their proracist attitude and behavior they all too often accept the white definition of a black or of a black problem.

Offensive maneuvers are so rampant in this society that one cannot help but witness them each day even in places where the racial component is essentially homogenous. That is, the newspapers, periodicals, radio, and so on all add their weight to the problems emanating from television, movies, films, plays, and musicals. But there are other vehicles that damage, even if no black is a witness.

Whites, for example, would not pause to consider racism in statuary. In liberal and genteel Boston there is a statue of "The Emancipator." An heroic-sized Lincoln wears a beneficent mien and holds a roll of Clio with one hand and extends another hand, as if in a blessing, over a black man on his knees dressed in diapers and wearing chains on his wrists. Since emancipators are common themes in art, one can contrast this statue with renditions of Simon Bolivar seen throughout South America or even in Central Park South in New York or off Canal Street in New Orleans. In these places there is no gratuitous degradation of another human being as homage is given to the subject of the statue. Yet there are on public display few statues or re-

liefs of blacks that do not go to special lengths
to assure a viewer that the black is in the inferior role. Even a rendition of a slave, if this
is to communicate an historical past, need not
show him on his knees in a diaper. Anyone
who has viewed the powerful and awesome
"Slave" in the square in front of the palace in
Port au Prince, Haiti, gets a totally different
emotional and psychological impact than from
viewing the slave in Boston or the black who
walks behind the Teddy Roosevelt equestrian
(along with an Indian) in front of the Museum of Natural History in New York.

Space permits only a brief consideration of
one more mode of mass communication violence to black people. Again one must not look
for the gross and obvious. The subtle, cumulative miniassault is the substance of today's
racism. Thus, one must do content analysis of
newspapers or periodicals in order to reckon
the violence done daily to blacks. Even on
sports pages white rookie athletes are hailed
as certainties in their professions because they
"understand the game" or "can think out a
problem." Black rookie athletes are applauded
for their vaunted "raw power and speed" or
"blinding fast ball." Presumably, white athletes think and black athletes rely only on bodily prowess.

Yet the corrosive influences of biased content are placed more effectively and more
constantly on news pages. Here, for instance,
an ambiguous caption under a picture of a
white woman may give the impression that a
black attacked her when in fact her assailant's
color is unknown. Or by clever placement, in
areas where most readership concentrates, an
episode sympathetic to blacks is markedly
counterbalanced by an outraged innuendo
about a black political figure.

The solution to the problems caused by
mass media lies in developing ways for
every black American to become expert in the
analysis of propaganda. Once this is done
blacks will relate at entirely different levels to
themselves and to the majority. Every community psychiatrist therefore should inform
himself of the fundamentals of propaganda so
that he can be in an advisory and educative
role in helping masses of blacks understand

and dilute, if not counteract, the ceaseless
brainwashing that goes on via mass communications with the conscious as well as unconscious design to keep blacks ineffective, passive, hopeless, and helpless. In addition, psychiatrists must find ways to help blacks eliminate microaggressions used by all mass media
and copied in white-black real life encounters.

But that effort only reaches one aspect of
the system. Blacks must be more than propaganda analysts and change agents for mass
media. They must also act to make the school
system fail.

⟨ Problems Due to Formal Education Channels

The formal education channels must stop
turning out defeated, demoralized, passive,
poorly skilled blacks. When this is done,
blacks will be able to operate in an effective,
cooperative manner that will make useless the
debate about whether blacks should integrate
or segregate.

Yet at this moment in history we must deal
with the reality that most blacks go to segregated, inferior schools that are phenomenally
successful in their mission. The mission of a
school is to prepare children for their sociocultural and political reality as adults. In this
democracy, the sociocultural and political reality is that every black is a disenfranchised,
second-class citizen. The schools must be con-
gratulated for meeting this mission with such
thorough success. If masses of blacks truly believed the mouthings about democracy that
American schools and mass media proclaim to
the world, one could not have generation after
generation of black masses accepting their
second-class disenfranchisement with complacency and accommodation and often even
with incredibly good cheer. If the schools had
not succeeded in preparing the great mass of
blacks to accept their situation and function
as passive aggregations, there would already
have been a gigantic counterviolence to white
violence. But instead, despite the impressions
one gains from the mass media, the problem is

not that too many blacks are psychologically militant but on the contrary that, thanks to the schools and the mass media, most blacks are docile and accepting. It is, therefore, of interest and importance to understand how the school system can conduct such a distinctly successful program that masses of blacks are psychologically prepared to accept all sorts of ruthless, antidemocratic practices in a land that has boasted about its democratic practices from its beginnings, when it became the world's leading slave state, to the present, when most of the people on the globe consider it the world's leading aggressor state. It is not without exaggeration to expect that if black Americans can make the school system fail in its mission to them, perhaps the entire world will feel less anxious about the aggressive proclivities of the most powerful nation that has ever existed. To understand this potential contribution to world peace and the vital role that community psychiatrists can play in its actualization, we must first determine what factors have allowed the educational system to work so effectively on the black masses. A case illustration from a Boston junior high school may be illuminating.

In all truth it is more difficult for a visitor to gain entrance to this Boston inner-city school than it is to gain entrance to the U.S. Navy Electronics Laboratory in San Diego, the presumptive repository of our fleets' secrets. The visitor or the school child approaches a formidable structure complete with bars on the windows. The large steel doors on this fortress-like structure are bereft of handles; hence one must pound hard to await someone to open the door from the inside. Once inside, the visitor is questioned gruffly as to his business in the school and as to whether or not the school authorities downtown know of the visit and its purpose. If one passes this inquisition by the white guard, he is free to observe the true method that has resulted in the success of the school system. The point here to remember is that quality education is not the issue so long as the child is subjected to the abuses about to be described in this very obvious prison structure.

Like all successful brainwashing endeavors,

the black student is never permitted to have even the dignity and independence of controlling his vegetative wants. Thus the school system locks the lavatory, and the child is told, explicitly and implicitly, that it is locked because he and his kind are so sick that if they had free access they would pop dope and fight and smoke pot. The locked handleless doors are an occasion to remind the budding black citizen, both explicitly and implicitly, that he and his kind are so sick that if the doors were open, his community would ransack the building, raping and beating teachers.

Still better and more subtle brainwashing is accomplished. One notes that all these prisoner-students are wearing coats despite the warmth of the building. The prisoner-students are told that if hangers were provided, he and his kind are so sick that they would steal one another's garments. Theorizing perfect quality of education, it is difficult to see how such a prisoner-student could grow up to be proud, independent, cooperative, or helpful. He is told over and over, at every occasion possible, that he and his are worthless and valueless and defeated. A good bulk of his conscious hours are spent in actual custody and confinement where he is subjected to sustained depreciation.

If an observer at this school had had any experience working in a true prison setting, it would be apparent immediately that the entire genre was identical to a prison. Here too the inmates test the limits of how much they can do without losing "good time." Here too the inmates are told step by step what to do ("Didn't I tell you to use these stairs . . . stop . . . go that way"), as if the exertion of any independent thought would be molding a youth who might dare to imagine. And as all have known since the days that it was proverbial in ancient Greece, imagination is the friend of terror. Thus, the junior high schooler in this school, which could be replicated all over our nation's ghettos, is made unimaginative, limited, and concrete in his thinking process. It would not do to have blacks dare to imagine, for then they might become friends of terror. At the same time, the black is the victim of a torrent of propagandistic ideation, which serves to make him accept a reduced status. The youth, even if he worked hard in the school and even if he had a quality education and pleasant surroundings to study in at home, would hardly have esteem and confidence in himself and his group. But then, as if such a school experience is not sufficient, after being in custody all day long the youth returns to the general community, where the television, newspapers, movies, and radio continue the same lesson to the black. He is taught that he is an inferior person toward whom whites can and will take prerogatives they would never consider taking with another white, since it would do violence to their sense of human rights. By syllogism, therefore, the black must be subhuman.

As if this was not enough of a problem to the black minority, there now appears on the horizon an even more pernicious route to disenfranchisement via an education channel. It is pernicious, even though, like the public education system and the mass media, it should and could be looked to as a principal route to banish racism. This particular route is the almost incontestable certainty that within a decade thousands of black (and white) children will be subjected to institutionalized child care in the prekindergarten years of life.

An alarm must be sounded. The large monies to be made available for such child care can be a deliverer or an executioner for the black masses. Since the public school education system has been so effective in pacifying the masses of black citizens, the exact operation and goals of the prekindergarten educational schemes must be very carefully evaluated. If they do more harm than good, black hopes will be almost nonexistent because the two formal education channels will have neutralized blacks between ages zero to fifteen.

The general solution for the problem of the black minority relative to formal education is twofold. On the one hand, while our people are becoming more aware of how to eliminate the negative propaganda heaped on them, they must become much more able to command a knowledge of total systems and how these systems integrate with one another.

Once this is done, the black, whether he is a schoolboy or a taxi driver, will know how to strengthen the formal channels to his own advantage (including constructing alternative channels of formal education) as well as to educate himself and his peers at multiple informal levels. Black cohesiveness, which is synonymous with black pride and black selfhood, depends on knowledge of where and how to exert maximum effort to modify or eliminate racist institutions.

Here too the task for the psychiatrist may seem untraditional. Some readers will be uneasy about whether or not such functions belong to psychiatry. Yet, what a present-day psychiatrist does on Park Avenue or Wilshire Boulevard would be scarcely recognizable to the man who practiced psychiatry in 1900. The society demanded and required, as all through history, that health services be given in a certain manner. Thus the role of the psychiatrist who is serious about these problems of the black inner city must be to assume an educative role so that he can help influence masses of people. Thus, he must bring to bear the knowledge of psychodynamics and psychological interactions as he teaches the value to the black psyche of understanding and neutralizing propaganda and understanding and utilizing systems theory. Yet, here too there are other cognitive inputs that blacks must have gratified in order to be maximally effective, efficient, and happy. One more such set of cognitive needs will be mentioned before we pass on to the equally important area of affective education in the promotion of black mental health.

❪ Problems from Demography

All black children and adults must learn demography. In order to be able to justify one's existence and determine suitably egosyntonic life goals, it is necessary to know where you stand in relation to the rest of the society. The cognitive and quantitative definition of such knowledge constitutes the field of demography.

In America today, blacks are a segregated, urban people. A goodly majority of all black children who are born today will spend a significant portion of their lives in urban, segregated situations. In fact, perhaps only one out of ten will live in multiracial circumstances during childhood. This demographic trend of increasing black clusters in cities makes such an analysis the crucial consideration in planning black-white strategy.

In order to make wise decisions and implement them, blacks must start from this base and consider the myriad advantages and disadvantages that result from the reality that we are essentially (both quantitatively and qualitatively) an urban, segregated people.

The intragroup conflicts that will stall blacks in the coming decade might be greatly reduced if black people would begin to incorporate and utilize a wealth of demographic data in the solutions of problems that require group coordination. For instance, a black response to the separate questions of birth control and population control would require more than sentiment. The decision to be best for the total society, including ourselves, has to be based on data. Further, what is required in one circumstance may not be suitable in another. Blacks, with the help of such experts as community psychiatrists, have to begin to construct desirable alternative plans, based on demographic probability and possibility. A local neighborhood will need to know such things as job markets, housing plans, population migrations, and consumer power in order to bring about positive sociopolitical action.

At a national level, blacks must develop a critical social pathway. That is, utilizing demographic data and the best available communication and systems analysis, a long-range plan should be developed that embraces a black response to all possible white interventions. For example, what steps, in fine detail, would have to be taken if tomorrow white America became truly democratic? Or what steps would be required if tomorrow the homes of blacks (about 90 per cent segregated) were cordoned off as one step toward concentration camp existence? The psychology of leadership and the psychology of life in extremely stressful, exotic environments is replete with verification that people do best who have anticipated possibilities and rehearsed the use of options and how to develop them. Such planning in itself is psychologically helpful for both the individual participant and the group. The task of community psychiatry must be to use its expertise in encouraging blacks to plan and to believe that they are able and capable of controlling their own lives and their own institutions in a pluralistic society. The task will be made simpler if black children, from the time they can remember, begin to deal with demographic facts about buying power, occupational skills, health services, and political blocs.

There is a regrettable tendency in American society not to permit blacks to be powerful in any manner. Blacks, as a whole, fail to realize strengths, since the system focuses always on black weaknesses. As an example, black mental illness is the focus of concern for psychiatrists rather than the investigation of the factors that permit blacks to endure. If black strengths, especially group strengths (as opposed to individual skills, talents, strengths), were emphasized more, black esteem would be heightened.

Therefore, in a demographic sense blacks must be more conscious of the strength of the nonwhite world, both in terms of numbers and skills. The American black has something precious that could be emphasized and used to help the whole world to peace. Compared to white America, we are bereft of skills. But compared to the rest of the world, white and nonwhite, we have abundant skills. For instance, tomorrow, without any jeopardy to the health services of the nation, black doctors and personnel for an entire first-class medical school could be exported to, say, an African country in temporary distress. In no way would such a school be inferior. In the move toward planetary citizenship in the ever smaller world, American blacks must think more in mass terms in regard to white-nonwhite alignments and contributions. For a psychiatrist in a ghetto to concentrate on a work program training upholsterers, while neglecting to get blacks, particularly black youth, to have a better cognitive map of who we are and how we can or could relate to the rest of the world, is to be helping to apply a Band-aid in an instance requiring radical surgery.

So far we have considered how blacks think. It follows that how one thinks determines much about how he functions. But mental illness comes about not only from how one thinks and functions but also how one feels and believes. A problem in the black community is to make people feel and believe that they have hope. To do this requires a consideration of providing something that is not now provided.

(The Problem of Constructing the Future

Futurologists take the view that we can no longer afford to plan *for* the future but must plan the future itself. A society of affluence and technology no longer should plan for the welfare of illiterates. It must take steps to plan that there should be no illiteracy. In terms of problems of minority blacks, steps must be taken to ensure help for each black citizen.

For the community psychiatrist, hope might be broken down into psychodynamic components which would include provisions for self-confidence; provisions for feelings of being needed, wanted, and useful; and provisions for feeling satisfied and satisfying. Yet the component parts that will occupy us at present are those that relate to feelings of being loved, feelings of controlling one's own destiny, and feelings that one is aware of multiple, positive options that he may exert.

The emphasis on feelings and motivations must result in blacks taking antiracist, instead of proracist, stances in interpersonal interactions. Black people must be ever more sensitive about how and when to take counteroffensive measures against whites. This means, in practice, being aware of our options and feeling we must exercise them in the service of reducing racist behavior. The black would thereby be constructing his future, since all actions must be devoted to planning not for the effects of racism but for its elimination.

Broadly speaking, there are two sets of options for blacks. On the one hand are those options that must be viewed and selected for action that relate to macroproblems. These are the large and broad issues that engage the race as a group and that demand concerted group action as the group labors to control its own direction. For instance, macroproblems would include such issues as how to combat anti-intellectualism in the inner city, or how to control the police forces in a community, or how to make a viable black economic subsystem that would function to our mutual benefit in the richest land the world has known.

However, it is the set of microproblems that will require our present consideration. These are problems that arise in individual interactions, almost always secondary to a white's offenses, which are initiated and spewed out as microaggressions. These problems are micro only in name, since their very number requires a total effort that is incalculable, even though each single effort might be only a microeffort. The black must be taught to recognize these microaggressions and construct his future by taking appropriate action at each instance of recognition. He must see options for his behavior.

Here is an example witnessed recently in a well-to-do neighborhood, where a black couple and a white man, probably all of similar economic and educational circumstances, stopped at a newspaper machine. Recall that blacks and whites in America take proracist positions. Thus, a black is expected to defer to a white, to seek white guidance and advice, to accept white instructions, to laugh at himself in the presence of whites, and to minimize any black in comparison to a white. The white man, operating from presumed superiority, gave instructions, directions, and advice to the black woman as she tried valiantly, but unsuccessfully, to get the machine to operate. While laughing at her ineptitude she dropped a coin. She elected to tell her black companion to pick it up, although all the verbal interaction had been between the white and herself. She accepted the coin without any response of gratitude for the kindness rendered as he gave her the coin. However, in the same natural and unwitting manner, she extended another coin to its white owner, while dignifying her effort by statements of thanks. The white walked off with more evidence, even if unconscious to him, that blacks extend themselves to please him and that they defer to his judgment, accept instructions, laugh at themselves, and treat their own as inferiors. In this interaction, none of these negative aspects had to be reinforced by the black woman. She could have elected, for instance, to tell the white to pick up the coin or she could have let him reach out and ask for the other coin.

But this brings up the matter of awareness of nonverbal cues as vehicles for racism. To accept such cues forecloses the future for blacks. These cues are kinetic racisms. In a real sense, how skillfully a black comes to recognize and deal with them may determine whether the white world wears him out, as is all too often the case.

A few examples will suffice. A black man stands exactly at the usual place where a bus stops and where the sign says it will stop. A white man, the only other waiting passenger, stands some fifteen feet away. When the bus arrives it stops right in front of the white man. Or a line of people are waiting to get into a movie. People leaving the movie must cut across this line. If a black happens to be in the line, almost surely outgoing patrons will decide to cross in front of him. In crowded hotel lobbies, whites who must find a route through the maze will usually walk as close as possible to a black person, expecting him to yield ground, in order to give them both more space. On a crowded street, such as Fifth Avenue in New York, whites do not waver as they approach a black. Their expectation is that, since their life space is more prized and valuable than the blacks', it should be the black who gives ground, who moves out of the way, who dips his left shoulder and pulls in his arm as they pass each other. In restaurants or stores if a waitress or salesman approaches a group of customers and one happens to be black, there is a case of "ease of selection."

The selection is easy because you know who does not have to be served first. Being black in these United States means that in such routine interactions there is an ease of selection based on ideas of presumed superiority. That blacks can and will be offended is the first law. The second law states that, whenever possible, offend the black, even by kinetic means, so that there will be reinforcement of the ideas of white superiority and black inferiority.

Once a black is aware of these mechanisms and how they determine his and his society's future, he can predict occurrences and take steps to despoil them or at least dilute them.

For instance, a black at a dinner where the table is round can assume, before the fact, that he will be the last served by the waiters as they come in and ladle out food. That is, the service will start with the person next to him.

But suppose, for instance, one was boarding an airplane with assigned seats, and one saw a white cripple at the bottom of the stairs to the plane waving everyone to go ahead of him. Doubtlessly, in these circumstances, most anyone would have let a man on crutches go up the stairs ahead of him. However, if one was the only black in the line and he witnessed this behavior, he would have to be alert for the fact that the cripple would decide to go up the stairs when the black arrived. In this true story, had the black allowed the cripple to go up first he would have reinforced racism and at the same time aggravated himself psychologically and possibly psychosomatically. Thus, when in fact the cripple made his move to cut in front of the black, the black had to use greater mobility and nimbleness to get up the stairs first.

Another true story of anticipating and despoiling racism rooted in kinetics involves an airline hostess serving coffee to three men. She began at the aisle seat, then served the man in the middle and then the man in the window seat. At the next set of seats she was in trouble, because here too were three men (had there been a woman the problem might have resolved differently). Yet, by chance, black men occupied both the aisle and window seats, while a white man was in the middle.

Her dilemma was where to start. If she started on either the aisle or window seat she could not serve the white man first. The black on the aisle was sensitive to her problem. The hostess solved it by saying, "Coffee anyone?" as she stuck her tray under the nose of the white man, so that he could put his cup on first. The aisle black answered politely, "Thank you," as he deftly put his cup on the tray before the white could react. Had the black not been calculating her behavior in this situation there could have been another reinforcement that blacks can and will and should be offended.

A community psychiatrist will see dozens of episodes of microaggressions and kinetic racisms toward blacks. If blacks recognize and react to these in a different fashion, then indeed they are constructing a different future. The psychiatrist with his knowledge of interpersonal dynamics must help blacks to construct such alternative futures.

⟨ Conclusions

Community psychiatrists are concerned, and properly so, about such questions as the number of first admissions of blacks to state hospitals or whether blacks have special forms of mental illness or whether treatment of a black will have to be different from methods used to treat whites. These are problems and solutions will be sought. For instance, many black psychiatrists feel that traditional, middle-class, white methods of psychotherapy may not suit the needs of many blacks.

Yet the community psychiatrist who is concerned with the whole society should address also other issues in regard to the current black-white problems. An important question, for example, is by what means upper-class (and to some extent also upper-middle-class) white females perpetuate racism. Perhaps studies on the attitude formation of young, white, upper-class females would do far more in understanding racism than all sorts of studies by whites in the ghettos, as they choose to call the inner-city communities. It is the young, upper-class, white female who will become

wife and mother, whose influence as a culture transmitter needs to be studied. It is instructive to think how the white majority has sent white men to study blacks in black communities, but how unsettling it would be to consider sending black men to study white females in white communities. The very uneasiness such a thought promotes indicates how large a problem the community psychiatrist faces. The barriers are tough but hopefully not unyielding.

In the next decade perhaps more community psychiatrists will involve themselves in neighborhoods, schools, homes, mass media offices, and so on in an effort to help make blacks flexible, hopeful, thinking, adventuresome, cooperative citizens who control their own destiny. Much work needs to be done in which psychiatrists work with other specialists in matters ranging from developing curricula and games to producing movies and television (for a global electronics educational system among other usages) to advising government and industrial leaders.

Like Euripides, the community psychiatrist should see the entire world as his province. In this analogy the cities of America constitute the backyard of the community psychiatrist. And before he can go out to engage this wonderful world, he must put out the fire that burns in his backyard and threatens to burn even more. This dangerous fire in his backyard is racism. It must be put out before the whole province is destroyed.

The day may be close at hand when community psychiatrists and other consultants are used by blacks in their effort to decrease group divisiveness and reduce their acceptance of patronizing or condescending behavior from whites. Such blacks may project futures and predict critical pathways by using forecasting techniques such as trend analysis or correlation plotting. Such blacks may understand complex interlocking systems and make group plans while exemplifying deliberate individual behavior, which is regarded as essential in eliminating microaggressions by whites. For instance, they might have been schooled in informal or formal school systems to practice such maneuvers as never arguing with each other in the presence of whites. These blacks will understand the value of levity control and publicity control. Hence, they will not resort automatically and casually to laughter, jocularity, and cheerfulness when confronting whites in serious negotiations. Nor will they be indiscriminate about revealing or discussing plans with whites before the appropriate occasions and circumstances. Many such blacks will shun and avoid most petitions by whites to publicize them or their ideas. Such blacks will be a force to aid the entire black community to enhance its esteem. And surely these blacks would find other titles more positive to group image and solidarity than "Psychiatic Problems of the Black Minority."

([Bibliography

1. Butts, H. "White Racism: Its Origins, Interpretation and the Implications for Professional Practice in Mental Health." *Inter national Journal of Psychiatry*, 6 (1969).
2. ———. "Psychoanalysis: The Black Community and Mental Health." *Contemporary Psychoanalysis*, 2 (1971).
3. Christmas, J. J. "Sociopsychiatric Rehabilitation in a Black Urban Ghetto." *American Journal of Orthopsychiatry*, 39 (1969), 651–661.
4. Comer, J. "The Social Power of the Negro." *Scientific American*, 4 (1967), 21–27.
5. ———. "White Racism: Its Root, Form and Function." *American Journal of Psychiatry*, 6 (1969).
6. Grier, W. H., and Cobbs, P. M. *Black Rage*. New York: Basic Books, 1968.
7. Norman, J., ed. *Medicine in the Ghetto*. New York: Appleton-Century-Crofts, 1969.
8. Pierce, C. M. "Problems of the Negro Adolescent in the Next Decade." In E. B. Brody, ed., *Minority Group Adolescents in the United States*. Baltimore, Md.: Williams & Wilkins, 1968. Pp. 17–47.
9. ———. "The Need for Children's Domestic Exchange." *American Journal of Orthopsychiatry*, 4 (1969).
10. ———. "Offensive Mechanisms: The Vehicle for Microaggression." In F. B. Barbour, ed., *The Black 70's*, Boston: Porter Sargent, 1970. Pp. 265–282.
11. Pinderhughes, C. A. "Understanding Black Power: Processes and Proposals." *American Journal of Psychiatry*, 11 (1969).
12. ———. "Universal Resolution of Ambivalence by Paranoia with an Example in Black and White." *American Journal of Psychotherapy*, 4 (1970), 597–610.
13. Poussaint, A. "A Negro Psychiatrist Explains the Negro Psyche." *The New York Times*, Sunday magazine, August 20, 1967.
14. ———, and Ladner, J. "Black Power: A Failure for Integration Within the Civil Rights Movement." *Archives of General Psychiatry*, 4 (1968), 385–391.

CHAPTER 34

PSYCHIATRIC APPROACHES TO THE IMPOVERISHED AND UNDERPRIVILEGED

Harris B. Peck

I T IS ESTIMATED that approximately 35 million persons in the United States exist in conditions of want or near want. Even if there were no greater prevalence of psychiatric disorders among the impoverished, the psychiatric issues affecting almost one-fifth of the nation would appear to have substantial claims to a significant portion of American psychiatry's attention and efforts.

The 1958 publication of Hollingshead and Redlich's[13] *Social Class and Mental Illness* confirmed the extent of psychiatry's involvement with the poor but sharply delineated a pattern of highly discriminating distribution of resources. Indeed, it appeared from these studies that the mode of treatment depended as much or more on a patient's socioeconomic status as on the medical or psychological considerations.

Although the specific forms of discrimination vary for different settings, and for differ-

ent diagnostic entities, the basic pattern is familiar to most practitioners. The psychiatric profession appears to favor patients in the upper social class with the form of treatment it values most highly, namely, psychotherapy. Patients from lower socioeconomic strata are more likely to be assigned to custodial care or some form of organic therapy. Even in the realm of psychotherapy, private practitioners engage in directive psychotherapy with 85 percent of their class 4 and 5 neurotic patients, whereas 45 percent of class 1 and 2 private patients receive psychoanalysis or analytic psychotherapy.

A report to the Chicago Board of Health on the availability of physicians' services to poverty area residents found that a relatively small number of doctors practiced in the poverty areas, which have 88 percent black residents, and that psychiatry was the specialty least available to black areas.[6] Bahn[1] and others pointed out the way in which such discriminating distribution of psychiatric facilities forces patients into the legal system and then to the state hospital, where they tend to become part of the untreatable chronic population. A similar pattern has been described by Markler[21] for emotionally disturbed poor minority group youngsters in the school system. Whereas white middle-class students are likely to be defined as troubled and placed in a treatment school, lower-class Negroes and Puerto Ricans are likely to be defined as troublesome and placed in custodial institutions.

Some psychiatrists when confronted with this kind of data argue that these contrasting patterns of treatment are not so much a reflection of discrimination against lower socioeconomic or minority-group patients but rather a recognition of the special qualities and limited receptivity to certain forms of treatment associated with the life style of patients from lower socioeconomic categories.

Hollingshead and Redlich[13] noted that psychiatrists are for the most part drawn from the upper and middle classes and may thus be less accepting and understanding in relation to patients from class 4 and class 5 backgrounds. They suggested that psychiatric training should better prepare psychiatrists to deal with patients from other classes, that new therapeutic approaches should be specifically designed to deal with this type of patient, and that more nonmedical therapists should be trained to work with patients from impoverished areas in those cases where there are no associated medical problems.

Viola Bernard,[4] in a comprehensive review of some of the principles of dynamic psychiatry in relation to poverty, called attention to the need to consider both direct and indirect forms of psychiatric intervention. She pointed out that in addition to modifications in direct clinical contact with patients, psychiatrists can make important contributions through the application of psychiatric principles not only to the administration of mental health agencies but also to all of the nonpsychiatric public programs that have an impact on the life and health of the impoverished population. The need for both direct and indirect approaches

in the psychiatrists' intervention with impoverished and disadvantaged populations derives from the complex nature of poverty itself.

Attention must be directed at the actual conditions under which the poor live, as well as the social and psychological attributes associated with those conditions. In 1962, more than 1 million children were being reared in large families with six or more children and incomes of less than $2,000 per year. Families living under such conditions are hard put to provide opportunities for better health or education that might lead to change in their status. Clark[7] pointed out that the poor, living in deteriorated housing, identify with their physical surroundings and incorporate this identification as a part of the view of themselves. Thus, Scherl and English[36] suggested that a strategy of mental health among the poor should address itself to the outer as well as the inner reality and accept the fact that mental health is less valued than money, food, housing, jobs, and general health services.

Leighton,[17] working with a rural population with levels of unemployment and poverty higher than that of neighboring communities, found corresponding higher levels of socioeconomic disintegration and psychiatric disorder. He attempted both to improve social functioning and human relations in the community and to increase economic and educational opportunities. He reported that over a ten-year period the prevalence of mental disorders was reduced in association with improvement in the community's psychological climate and the level of sociocultural integration.

A number of clinicians working within psychiatric settings have attempted to appraise the deficiencies in traditional approaches developed with reference to middle-class populations and to modify them or offer alternative therapeutic approaches to the poor and to working-class clientele. James McMahon, in a paper[20] on the working-class patient, employed the terms "working class," "lower socioeconomic," and "the poor" interchangeably. He pointed out that mere changes in administrative procedures, such as the elimination of waiting lists, do not lead to any significant improvements in results. He suggested that clinicians and agencies have fostered a number of stereotypes about the poor and erected a host of barriers between themselves and such clients, thus interfering with effective treatment. McMahon felt that clinics that cite the emphasis of the poor on the here and now as a reason for their inability to engage in extended psychotherapy may be ignoring the findings of workers who have found that personal attitudes of the therapist are more likely to be associated with success in treatment than the use of one or another sophisticated therapeutic technique.

Rosen and Frank[35] pointed out that, in addition to lower socioeconomic status, the poor patient may frequently be a member of a minority group and thus have an additional obstacle to face in the attitudes of the therapist, who is most likely to be both white and middle class. Thus, the black patient must also overcome the biases, cultural blind spots, reactive guilt, and unconscious prejudice of the person to whom he comes for help. The attempt to select working-class patients who are good treatment risks leads to the formulation of lists of criteria for acceptance, including capacity for introspection and psychological thinking, self-control, a desire to relate to people, strong ego, and high motivation. As McMahon[20] pointed out, if a patient met all these demanding qualifications, he might very well not require treatment at all. He suggested that it might be more realistic "to initiate and continue needed psychiatric care if, and only if, the therapist's participation in the treatment is congruent, at least temporarily, with the patient's request, attitude and expectation." The patient who expects active assistance is likely to be discouraged by a passive, detached approach, and McMahon felt this accounts for a number of working-class patients who do not persist after one or two initial psychiatric contacts.

The poor person who is in psychological distress but also in the midst of an overwhelming life situation, and thus looks for specific help and advice, may be able to address himself to his psychological problems only after several initial sessions have been devoted to determining his specific concerns and assisting him to deal with some of his immediate life difficulties. Mendel and Rapport,[22] in dealing with chronic schizophrenics from lower socioeconomic groups, found that immediate and active assistance and encouragement are crucial in overcoming the inertia that is often associated with chronicity.

It may be that because the psychotherapeutic approaches developed in the United States have been so heavily influenced by psychoanalysis, some of its postures have been automatically applied to situations and populations, such as the poor, where they are not necessarily appropriate. For example, it may be true that recurrent crisis may limit a patient's ability to carry through a successful traditional psychoanalysis. However, this does not mean that the impoverished patients must be eliminated from consideration for other forms of psychotherapy, even though their lives may be characterized by periodic major disruptions in their situations. It is precisely at such times that people from a disadvantaged community are likely to ask for help, and a number of psychiatric agencies serving the poor have incorporated mechanisms for engaging patients in treatment at the point of crisis. These include walk-in clinics, twenty-four-hour staffing of hospital emergency rooms with psychiatric personnel, and provision for emergency phone calls. As Lindemann pointed out,[19] entry into a patient's life at a time of crisis not only relieves suffering and helps avoid a catastrophic outcome but may also provide opportunity to engage the patient at a time in his life when he may be more amenable to establishing a therapeutic relationship which may be maintained after the immediate crisis has been resolved.

Although patients from lower socioeconomic populations may be more accessible at points of crisis, almost all studies indicate considerable difficulty in actually maintaining more extended contact. A review of 499 psychiatric clinics throughout the United States found that 60 percent had fewer than five sessions.[1] Overall and Aronson[24] reported a dropout rate of 57 percent after the initial interview. Hollingshead and Redlich,[13] in commenting on this pattern, said that "patients are disappointed in not getting sufficient practical advice about how to solve their problems and how to run their lives. They express in word and action their lack of confidence in a talking treatment. They expect pills and needles . . . and also a gratifying, sympathy and warmth."

A study by Overall and Aronson[24] demonstrated that for a lower socioeconomic population, for the most part, the therapist's behavior was less active, less medically oriented, and less supportive than the patient anticipated and that where such expectations did not correspond with the therapist's behavior, the patient was less likely to return for treatment. The authors suggested "one way of reducing cognitive inaccuracies is to attempt during the initial phase of treament to re-educate the patient as to both his own and the therapist's role in the treatment." They urged that the patient's expectations be explored during the first interview so that both patient and therapist can more easily view and modify their roles.

A technique that allows both therapist and patient to become more active than in the usual interview situation is that of role playing. Riessman and Guldfob[34] gave several reasons why this technique appears to be particularly viable in working with the disadvantaged.

1. It appears to be more congenial with the low income person's style which is physical—concrete, problem directed, externally directed rather than introspective. . . .
2. It allows the practitioner to reduce, in an honest fashion, the role distance between himself and the disadvantaged individual. . . .
3. It changes the setting and tone of what often appears to the low income patient as an office ridden bureaucratic, impersonal foreign world.
4. It appears to be an excellent technique for developing verbal power in the educationally deprived person.

Riessman and Guldfob point out that despite the preference of the poor for informality, they like to have content that is structured and definite, and that role playing lends itself to this need in that it can be used to teach specific types of behavior. In working with the disadvantaged, Riessman discourages use of the more theatrical features often used with the more formal types of psychodrama. Combining role playing with other forms of treatment, such as family therapy or group therapy, seems to work with the poor patient. It is important that the various functions for which role playing is being employed, such as catharsis, self-awareness, or insight, should be explained and made explicit. Of course, this recommendation, directed at the poor, might very well be followed in introducing a new procedure to any patient with whom a therapist wishes to establish some common understanding of what is hopefully to become a mutual endeavor.

For the most part, psychoanalysis and psychoanalytic therapy have been largely designed for and directed at middle- and upperclass patients. One of the few systematic attempts to explore the application of psychoanalytic therapeutic approaches to a lower socioeconomic population was conducted under the auspices of the William A. White Institute. In a report of this project, Gould[10] explained that though the population was drawn from members of a trade union, he referred to blue collar, the disadvantaged, and lower-class patients, interchangeably. Though some of twenty-three patients treated in the study may have been above the poverty line, many of the approaches suggested appear applicable to the more seriously disadvantaged. Gould believed that resistance to psychotherapy was reduced by several factors built into the study.

1. The service was offered in a simple, direct, open manner.
2. It was voluntary.
3. It was immediately available.
4. The overtures came from the psychiatrists, thus eliminating the fear of rejection.
5. Trade union leaders offered their active support.

Several of the modifications in the treatment approach itself that appeared most productive were:

1. A more directive approach as reflected in specific and concrete questions initiated by the therapist proved productive.
2. Informality was established through an easy give and take manner such as having the therapist open a session with a remark or comment about some subject of mutual interest. Gould found that such exchanges often lead into material of great relevance to the therapy.
3. Role playing proved to be exceedingly productive.
4. Educational and guidance materials proved to be entirely compatible with psychotherapy when the pathology was not too severe.

Gould emphasized that because the lower socioeconomic person has less of a tendency to use intellectualization as a defense, this may make him more accessible to therapy than some of his middle-class neighbors. He also asserted that the usefulness of symptom cure should not be minimized, since it frequently was followed by further changes on a deeper level.

Although it is generally acknowledged that the poor are more likely than others to be exposed to psychological and social stress and hazards to their mental well-being, the treatment of pathology manifested by poor people has seemed to attract more interest than programs directed at the maintenance of their health or competence. In part, this may be a product of the prevailing treatment. Although manifestations of mental health certainly may be discerned in the one-to-one situation, they are almost inescapable when the patient is studied within the context of some relevant aspect of his social environment. Some workers in the field of mental health have begun to address themselves to the study and intervention into large social institutions as such. However, most clinicians have pre-

ferred to deal with the smaller subsystems comprising the patient's more intimate social milieu.[26] In practice this has led to a considerable amount of experimentation with such natural small groups as families or classroom groups and groups comprised of people from some common vocational, religious, social, or agency setting.

Christmas and Richards[5] surveyed agencies employing group psychotherapy with socially disadvantaged adults and found that the group approaches employed tended to be strongly influenced by the overall philosophical orientation of the agency. Institutions with more traditional medical or psychoanalytic orientation tended to be less innovative, made less use of groups, and "the effect of social forces was not generally thought worthy of professional consideration." Agencies with a sociopsychiatric or socioeconomic orientation concerned themselves with the overall functioning of the patient and with such matters as finance and job. The staff reflected values and attitudes of the deprived community in their practice and tended to minimize intrapsychic and individual determinants of behavior in favor of considerations of social forces. The groups conducted by these agencies frequently focused on contemporary happenings and concentrated on therapeutic group efforts to alter what is, by action, in the present.

The approach of Heacock,[12] in working with groups of young adults, is along these lines. He focused on coping mechanisms to deal with life crises and feelings of powerlessness. A number of other workers have developed groups with comparable approaches to clients on welfare which stress activity, socialization, and social learning.[8]

As noted in a previous report by Peck and Scheidlinger,[32] many of the groups employed with socially disadvantaged populations in contemporary mental health programs are more akin to rehabilitation or socialization than to psychotherapy. Practitioners employed in these programs frequently include nurses, occupational therapists, teachers, and social workers as well as the usual orthopsychiatric team. Scheidlinger[22] categorized these therapeutically oriented group practice models as follows:

1. Activity catharsis and mastery: includes groups for patients with severe ego damage often with occupational therapy, orientation and provision for activity, use of materials and release of tension.
2. Cognitive information: emphasis on teaching new facts and attitudes as in family life education groups.
3. Interpersonal socialization: includes groups that meet needs for security, belonging and companionship such as leisure time character-building activities, patient government, and hospital activity groups.
4. Relationship experience: includes group programs in halfway houses, rehabilitation programs, and patient social clubs.

When working with disadvantaged populations, therapeutically oriented group programs of the types described above frequently include provisions for work with the patient's family as a unit. Inclusion of pertinent members of the family in therapeutic work lends concreteness to the situation and helps the lower socioeconomic patient specify his concerns. Family treatment is an almost essential element for the psychiatric hospital in maintaining the involvement of such patients in the program.[25]

A number of workers have reported on the advantages of seeing the family in their own home. Levine[18] developed a home family therapy method for the disadvantaged where role playing and manual activities are utilized as the stimulus for eliciting and clarifying family communication patterns.

Although it is generally assumed that there is some relationship between the mental health status of disadvantaged populations and the institutions that form the social context within which the poor live, these have received relatively little attention from psychiatric workers. S. M. Miller[23] stated that

services aimed at individual treatment are not enough. Professionals and their organizations

have to support and encourage action which will deal with the larger American scene where poverty is being produced and maintained. The professional role cannot end with the limited services that it can provide, but must extend to pressure for the social changes which will make individualized professional services more meaningful and effective. . . .

Although some psychiatric workers accept this position, a number of considerations appear to be responsible for the caution with which the professional approaches the course recommended by Miller.

1. The relationships between poverty, mental illness, and mental health are not well defined or understood.
2. Questions have been raised as to the compatibility of social action or institutional change with the psychiatrist's professional role.
3. Psychiatrists feel ill equipped and without adequate information, knowledge, or the technical skill required to engage in institutional change.

Leighton[17] referred to three major links between psychiatric disorders and poverty.

1. The blocking and frustration of basic needs that living under conditions of poverty engenders. These include stresses derived from insecurity regarding shelter, food, protection from violence, deprivations of love and recognition, as well as the reinforcement of the effects of debility from chronic organic disease associated with poverty.
2. The absence of remedial resources in the poor environment. Not only are psychiatric resources lacking or in short supply, but there is also a scarcity of those services that might be provided by such gatekeepers as physicians, ministers, and teachers.
3. The malformation of personality owing to the individual's growing up in a deprived environment.

A variety of personal characteristics have been attributed to those who suffer the deprivations associated with poverty.[14] These almost invariably include.

1. Fatalism, which involves a belief in uncontrollable and predetermined external forces.
2. Orientation to the present, with the feeling that it is both useless and wasting of energy to focus on the future.
3. Authoritarianism, which comprises an overrating of the strengths of existing social structures as sources of authority.

Numerous additions to these characteristics have been provided by a variety of workers. However, a unifying approach is suggested by Haggstrom[11] who pointed out that "over time, the dependency relationships of the poor become institutionalized and habits, traditions and organizations arise in both the affluent community and in the neighborhoods of poverty, maintaining the relationships between them." Furthermore, he argued that "when social scientists have reported on the psychological consequences of poverty it seems reasonable to believe that they have described the psychological consequences of powerlessness."

Power is a central component of several of the major criteria of mental health, particularly mastery of the environment and autonomy as delineated by Jahoda[15] in her review of the literature on positive mental health. Jahoda acknowledged that severe deprivations are among the conditions that may preclude the development of autonomy or environmental mastery. For her, adaptation to such environmental conditions means "that a workable arrangement between reality and the individual can be achieved by modifications of either or both through individual initiative."

However, modification of many of the realities that confront the impoverished individual cannot be achieved through individual initiative. It is for this reason that Haggstrom[11] stated that one way in which the poor can remedy the psychological consequences of their powerlessness, and of the image of the poor as worthless, is for them to undertake social action that redefines them as potentially worthwhile and individually more powerful. Among the criteria for effective social action cited by Haggstrom are that

1. The poor see themselves as the source of the action.
2. The action affects in major ways, the pre-conceptions, values or interests of institutions and persons defining the poor.
3. The action . . . becomes salient to major areas of the personalities of the poor.
4. The action ends in success.

Programs that fulfill even these minimal criteria are not common on the American scene. For one thing, those institutions that play a prominent part in defining the poor are generally not receptive to programs that would permit the poor to see themselves as the source of the action. However, with the impetus provided by the war on poverty and often with assistance from the Office of Economic Opportunity, a number of different kinds of institutions became the setting for community action-oriented types of mental health endeavors during the 1960s. Because these programs by their very nature were colored by the institutional settings in which they were conducted, their manifest content varied from those that were specifically psychiatric to those that emphasized such matters as education, health, or welfare.

Kellam and Schiff,[16] working in a community mental health center in Chicago's southside, looked to a community advisory board for the determination of the program's priorities. In response to the community's wishes, they decided to direct the initial thrust of the program around a major attempt to alter the educational environment for a substantial portion of the community's children. Attention to the environment and the institutional structure of the school was dictated by the large percentage (roughly 70 percent) of the first-grade children evaluated by their teachers as manifesting some degree of maladaptation. Because such maladaptation appeared to reflect a complex of social and institutional factors, intervention was directed at the school staff, classroom, and parent meetings in an attempt to influence such elements as (1) the child within the social field of the classroom; (2) the social system of the school; (3) the child's family; and (4) the particular community in which the child lives.

If a mental health program based in a public agency is engaged in social action, it must devise some effective and appropriate means of securing participation of the residents of the community it serves. Such participation requires mechanisms through which the community provides sanction for the agency's activities and through which it can engage in such functions as the determination of policy —the selection of key personnel, the soliciting and disbursement of funds, and the setting of priorities.

Kellam and Schiff preceded the development of their program by the formation of a community advisory board. Peck and his co-workers,[27] at Lincoln Hospital in the South Bronx of New York City, attempted to engage the community through the recruitment of mental health workers drawn from the area. They enlisted them in the development of small storefront neighborhood units with programs designed to be responsive to the particular service needs of the local area, in which the neighborhood center was located. The centers were receptive to any and all types of requests for service, including housing, employment, welfare, health, and family problems. An important contribution of the community health worker was in teaching residents to negotiate the maze of bureaucratic agency procedures. Where needed services could not be secured because of limitations of the agency, residents were encouraged to come together to devise solutions to their common problems. This sometimes gave rise to collaborative programs with school administrators, the local housing authorities, and so on. In other instances, committees of clients and workers from the neighborhood units became involved in organizing tenant councils that worked on code enforcements and participated with the local welfare rights organization in a campaign to improve conditions at Lincoln Hospital itself. These activities led to increasing awareness by the community of the need for a more direct role in hospital policy. Ultimately, these developments, which began in the mental health services, spread to the rest of the hospital and gradually assumed the form of demands by the community for control of such matters as funding, the selection of key personnel, and determination of hospital priorities.

Similar developments have been reported in quite diverse types of programs in the Woodlawn district of Chicago, Topeka, New Haven, and Washington Heights in New York City. The introduction of such elements into the program as the recruitment of staff from the local areas, the development of a strong community advisory board, decentralization, and participation in community activities provides opportunities for the residents of a community to engage in activities that can reduce the sense of helplessness and powerlessness and reinforce such mental health functions as autonomy and environmental mastery. In addition, it may lead to changes in institutional structures that can help bring about improvements in services. It may also lead to conflicts, crises, and at least temporary disruption in services. However, several developments on the current scene give promise of providing considerable assistance and support for such community action-oriented mental health programs.

One of the problems encountered by neighborhood-based mental health units relates to the difficulty of introducing innovative institutional policies or procedures that may run counter to traditional agency or governmental practices in the area. One approach to this problem is through the growing number of neighborhood health centers with which community mental health programs are beginning to establish neighborhood units capable of initiating change in a collaborative fashion. Detailed plans for the structural relationship between primary, secondary, and tertiary health and mental health services are outlined in a recent article by Spiro.[37] In a paper on the neighborhood health centers and their relationship to mental health programs, Scherl and English[36] emphasized the central role of community participation and the recruitment of local residents for the staff of the neighborhood center: "the services are made more appropriate, responsive and effective by virtue of their being designed around the needs of people and by virtue of the participation of persons in the neighborhood. This participation is insured through employment of residents as non-professionals and in policy making by neighborhood health councils."

Scherl and English saw the neighborhood health center as sharing the mental health program's orientation so as to "provide one responsive to a reality based sense of hopelessness and anger." They believed that through a neighborhood health center, "the poor can gain a measure of mobility of action and independence and add a measure of power to their voices. . . ."

Neighborhood health and mental health centers that share this type of orientation and consolidate their programs may contribute to their mutual effectiveness in the following ways:

1. Negotiation with mandating and funding institutions may be more easily accomplished for overall health services rather than for mental health services alone.

2. Relations and negotiation with the community can be more comprehensive and economical when these are centered around overall health and mental health issues.

3. Legal, financial, and organizational problems can best be approached with a comprehensive health program. For example, communities that wish to become the direct recipient of funds should not have to establish separate corporate structures for health and mental health services.

4. Manpower and career programs based on the recruitment of community residents can be more effective if they are designed as health careers programs for all health services rather than being developed for mental health services alone.

Both neighborhood health and mental health programs in disadvantaged areas are becoming increasingly interested in recruiting manpower from their local communities. The utilization of such indigenous personnel has a number of potential benefits that, from the mental health point of view, may be multiplied if the mental health program is incorporated into an overall health careers program.[31] A health careers program can train local community residents for functions that may assist the health professional, substitute for him, or add new functions and activities to the center's repertoire. Where mental health personnel participate in the development of a broad health careers program, they may have an opportunity to motivate and prepare personnel working in nonpsychiatric health services. If such personnel become better oriented to mental health principles and priorities, they can help extend the mental health network into the day-to-day operations of the health services. In those programs directed at preparing candidates for careers in health rather than job training for entry level positions, the educational experience may make a major contribution to the individual's growth and interpersonal competence. The participation of mental health personnel in planning and conducting these health career training programs helps focus attention on the psychosocial components involved in such training. This may assist in avoiding or at least reduce some of the inevitable personal strains experienced by the trainee and possibly help contribute to making the training into a meaningful personal growth experience. Thus, under the rubric of training mental health personnel, it is sometimes possible to make a more positive impact on the individual's adaptation than if he were referred for treatment in the role of a patient.

Most of the earlier training programs were primarily in-service training programs designed to prepare the trainee for a specific job in a mental health organization. Though many programs are still conducted at this level, several recent developments tend to greatly improve the quality of such training, and the newer programs embody the following elements.

1. Integration of mental health training with overall preparation for the health field.
2. A career rather than a job orientation, which means horizontal as well as vertical mobility with each step in the training lending itself to progressive escalation toward greater competence, specialization or responsibility.
3. Provision for accreditation through affiliation with the relevant educational institutions.
4. Assurance of job security through association of training programs with civil service certification and continuing promotion opportunities.

The development of career programs, which introduce residents of impoverished communities into the health and mental agencies as colleagues as well as in their role as patients, embodies several of the elements that characterize some of the newer approaches to the poor.[9]

Mental health professionals are beginning to engage themselves with members of the disadvantaged community rather than carrying out procedures on it. As community residents move up ladders of the health and mental health staff hierarchies, they are being increasingly knowledgeable participants not only in the delivery of services but also in the research, planning, and training activities on which such programs are based. Thus, members of a disadvantaged community can look to leadership from neighbors who, from their vantage point inside the system, can contribute to the development of better informed, more sophisticated community health and mental health boards. If this model becomes generally accepted and applied across the broad range of human services, substantial change may be anticipated in some of the institutions and agencies that have been so ineffective in their delivery of services. If the poor can help transform these institutions, they will not only directly benefit from the resulting improvements in care but will learn new adaptive skills that contribute to the maintenance and preservation of both their physical and psychological well-being.

❨ Bibliography

1. BAHN, A. K. "Admission and Prevalence Rates for Psychiatric Facilities in Four Register Areas." *American Journal of Public Health*, 56 (1966), 2033–2051.
2. ———, et al. "National Report on Mental Health Clinics." *Public Health Reports*, 1959.
3. BARNWELL, J. E. "Group Methods in Public Welfare." *International Journal of Group Psychiatry*, 15 (1965), 446.
4. BERNARD, V. W. "Some Principles of Dynamic Psychiatry in Relation to Poverty." *American Journal of Psychiatry*, 122, no. 3 (1965).
5. CHRISTMAS, J. J., and RICHARDS, J. An Overview of Group Psychotherapy with Socially Disadvantaged Adults. Paper presented to the American Group Psychotherapy Association, 1967.
6. CHICAGO BOARD OF HEALTH. *Preliminary Report on Patterns of Medical and Health Care in Poverty Areas of Chicago, and Proposed Health Program for the Medically Indigent.* Chicago, 1966.
7. CLARK, K. B. *Dark Ghetto.* New York: Harper & Row, 1965.
8. FENTON, N., and WILTS, K. *Group Methods in Public Welfare Programs.* Palo Alto, Cal.: Pacific Book, 1963.
9. FISHMAN, J., and McCORMICK, J. "Mental Health Without Wall: Community Health in the Ghetto." *American Journal of Psychiatry*, 126 (1970), 10.
10. GOULD, R. "Dr. Strongclass, or How I Stopped Worrying About the Theory and Began Treating the Blue Collar Worker." *American Journal of Orthopsychiatry*, 37, no. 1 (1967).
11. HAGGSTROM, W. "The Power of the Poor." In F. Riessman, J. Cohen, and A. Pearl, eds., *Mental Health of the Poor.* New York: The Free Press, 1964.
12. HEACOCK, D. P. "Modification of the Stanford Technique for Outpatient Group Psychotherapy with Delinquent Boys." *Journal of the National Medical Association*, 58 (1966), 41.

13. HOLLINGSHEAD, A. B., and REDLICH, F. C. *Social Class and Mental Illness.* New York: Wiley, 1958.

14. IRELAND, L. M., ed. "Low Income Life Styles." Washington, D.C.: U.S. Government Printing Office, 1966.

15. JAHODA, M. *Current Concepts of Positive Mental Health.* New York: Basic Books, 1958.

16. KELLAM, S. G., and SCHIFF, S. K. *Adaptation and Mental Illness in the First Grade Classrooms of an Urban Community.* Psychiatric research report, no. 21. Washington, D.C.: American Psychiatric Association, 1967.

17. LEIGHTON, A. H. "Poverty and Social Change." *Scientific American,* 212 (1965).

18. LEVINE, R. A. "Treatment in the Home." *Social Work,* 9 (1964), 19–28.

19. LINDEMANN, E., and KLEIN, D. "Preventive Intervention in Individual and Family Crisis Situations." In G. Caplan, ed., *Prevention of Mental Disorders in Children.* New York: Basic Books, 1961.

20. McMAHON, J. "The Working Class Patient: A Clinical View." In F. Riessman, J. Cohen, and A. Pearl, eds., *Mental Health of the Poor.* New York: The Free Press, 1964.

21. MARKLER, B. A. "A Report on the '60' Schools: Dilemmas, Problems and Solutions." In Denton, Markler, and Waishauer, eds., *The Urban "R's": Race Relations as the Problem in Urban Education.* New York: Praeger, 1967.

22. MENDEL, W. M., and RAPPORT, S. "Outpatient Treatment of Chronic Schizophrenic Patients." *Archives of General Psychiatry,* 8, no. 2 (1963).

23. MILLER, S. M. "Poverty and Inequality in America: Implications for the Social Service." *Child Welfare,* 42, no. 9 (1963).

24. OVERALL, B., and ARONSON, H. "Expectations of Psychotherapy in Patients of Lower Socio-Economic Class." *American Journal of Orthopsychiatry,* 33, no. 3 (1963).

25. PECK, H. B. "The Role of the Psychiatric Day Hospital in a Community Mental Health Program: A Group Process Approach." *American Journal of Orthopsychiatry,* 33, no. 3 (1963).

26. ———. "A Small Group Approach to Individual and Institutional Change." *International Journal of Group Psychotherapy,* 20 (1970).

27. ———, chairman. "Symposium on Group Approaches in Programs for Socially Disadvantaged Populations." *International Journal of Group Psychotherapy,* 15 (1965), 423–483.

28. ———, KAPLAN, S., and ROMAN, H. "Prevention, Treatment and Social Action: A Strategy of Intervention in a Disadvantaged Urban Area." *American Journal of Orthopsychiatry,* 36, no. 1 (1966).

29. ———, KAPLAN, S., and ROMAN, H. *Community Action Program and the Comprehensive Mental Health Center.* Psychiatric research report, no. 2. Washington, D.C.: American Psychiatric Association, 1967.

30. ———, KAPLAN, S., and ROMAN, H. *Community Action Programs and the Comprehensive Mental Health Center.* Poverty and mental health psychiatric research report, no. 21. Washington, D.C.: American Psychiatric Association, 1967.

31. ———, LEVIN, T., and ROMAN, H. "The Health Career Institute: A Mental Health Strategy for an Urban Community." *American Journal of Psychiatry,* 129 (1969), 9.

32. ———, and SCHEIDLINGER, S. "Group Therapy with the Socially Disadvantaged: Current Psychiatric Theories." 8 (1968).

33. ———, et al. "Some Relationships Between Group Process and Mental Health Phenomena in Theory and Practice." *International Journal of Psychotherapy,* 13, no. 3 (1963).

34. RIESSMAN, F., and GULDFOB, J. "Role Playing and the Poor." *Group Psychotherapy,* 17, no. 1 (1964).

35. ROSEN, H., and FRANK, J. D. "Negroes in Psychotherapy." *American Journal of Psychiatry,* 119 (1962), 456.

36. SCHERL, D. H., and ENGLISH, J. T. "Community Mental Health and Comprehensive Health Service Programs for the Poor." *American Journal of Psychiatry,* 125, no. 12 (1969).

37. SPIRO, H. "Beyond Mental Health Centers." *Archives of General Psychiatry,* 21 (1969).

CHAPTER 35

A REVIEW OF
TRANSCULTURAL
PSYCHIATRY

Eric D. Wittkower
and Raymond Prince

T RANSCULTURAL PSYCHIATRY is the study of the effects of culture on the pattern, frequency, and management of psychiatric disorders. The expression is roughly synonymous with comparative, or cross-cultural, psychiatry or with ethnopsychiatry. Related areas include the study of the effects of culture on personality and on normal psychological processes: The former has been largely the province of anthropologists with psychoanalytic interests;[50,53,109] the latter, which is of more recent vintage and includes the study of cultural effects on perception, cognition, intelligence, motivation, and the like, is being developed largely by psychologists.[88,101]

(Historical Development

Psychiatrists have always had at least a desultory interest in the possible effects of culture on the illnesses they treated. One of their early preoccupations was with the question of the relation between mental illness and civilization; most authors,[51] including Esquirol, Tuke, and Maudsley, held an unrealistically rosy view of primitive life and assumed that mental illness was the price of progress.

We seldom meet with insanity among the savage tribes of men; not one of our African travellers remark their having seen a single madman. Among the slaves of the West Indies it very rarely occurs; and, as we have elsewhere shown from actual returns, the contented peasantry of the Welsh mountains, the western Hebrides, and the wilds of Ireland are almost free from this complaint. It is by the over exertion of the mind, in overworking its instruments so as to weaken them . . . that insanity may be said to take place in a great number of instances.[42]

Before the effects of the cultural dimension could make a significant impact on psychiatric theory, psychiatrists had to be exposed to significant numbers of mentally ill from different cultures; and for the effect of culture to be most visible, a high degree of contrast between the cultural background of the patient and the physician was required.

It was perhaps because of the lack of contrast that American psychiatry's first exposure to cultural variety was not too enlightening.[14] Between 1839 and 1844 some 400,000 European immigrants flocked into the United States. Superintendents of already crowded mental hospitals noted with alarm the flood of "pauper insane," mainly Irish and German peasants. Most seemed to regard the immigrant as a kind of inferior American. The intellectual harvest of the contact was scant and did not extend beyond comments about filthy habits, refusal to work, and lower level of intelligence. There was also some speculation about the Irish peasants' greater susceptibility to mental disorder and resistance to treatment.

Other circumstances proved more productive. Toward the end of the nineteenth century, the colonizing European powers began to build and staff lunatic asylums in their holdings in Africa, the Caribbean, and Southeast Asia. There was much greater contrast between the culture of the physician and the patients, and a number of reports of varying quality began to appear in the psychiatric journals of the mother countries.[5,16,25,29,39,41]

In spite of their lack of anthropological and epidemiological sophistication and their often condescending attitudes toward the natives, these early physicians made observations and raised questions that continue to be the concern of transcultural psychiatry. They de-

scribed unusual symptom patterns, such as *latah* and *koro*, and questioned whether some disorders were peculiar to certain cultures; they noted that psychotic episodes were often shorter lived than was typical in Europe and that intense depressions and suicides were less frequent; they commented on the apparent importance of Westernization of indigenes as a factor in producing disorder; they speculated about the usefulness of the indigenous healer in the treatment of psychiatric illness.

A major stimulus occurred in the 1930s when Freud's ideas began to make themselves felt in this area. Apart from his own provocative excursions into anthropology in *Totem and Taboo* (1912) and *Civilization and Its Discontents* (1930),[34] many of his basic insights were highly relevant to transcultural psychiatry: his emphasis on parent-child relationships in shaping personality and causing disorder suggested that cultures with grossly different patterns of child rearing might generate different psychiatric phenomena; his demonstration that nonrational behavior and symptoms could have intelligible meanings and defensive functions opened up whole new areas for exploration not only of psychiatric disorders but also of cultural institutions, such as religions and ceremonial behavior. Freud's work inspired colonial psychiatrists to broaden their horizons;[24,63] even more important, his work was a major force in drawing anthropology into closer contact with problems of personality and psychopathology.[96,102] The result was a major shift in the kind of data collected in the field. Anthropologists began to record detailed descriptions of child-rearing practices,[26,73,112] to collect biographical studies of individuals from non-Western cultures,[40,56,93] and to investigate specific cases of psychoses and neuroses among the peoples they studied.[23,27,44,60,61] With or without psychiatric assistance, attempts were also made to relate child-rearing practices to adult personality and to articulate psychiatric disorders with the mythology, conflicts, and modes of life of the people among whom the disorders were found. Sapir was a major influence in promoting anthropological interest in psychiatry; not only did he recommend the works of

Freud, Abraham, Ferenczi, and Jung to his students, but he actively encouraged them to undergo psychoanalysis.[57]

A final important factor in the development of transcultural psychiatry has been the appearance of Western trained psychiatrists who are themselves members of non-Western societies. Because of their intimate knowledge of their own cultures they have been able to correct biased impressions of foreign observers and to provide cultural explanations for previously ill-understood syndromes. For example, many Western authors had been impressed by the similarity of the belief systems of many primitive groups to the delusions of schizophrenics: The notion that witches and sorcerers can damage individuals from afar seemed very like the ideas of influence of psychotics; the belief that incantations can produce rain or energize medicinal plants was equated with ideas of omnipotence in schizophrenic thinking. Lambo[59] and others, defending themselves against what they regard as a denigration of the African native population, vehemently attacked this view. Lambo contended that magical beliefs play an integrative function in his own traditional Yoruba culture and cannot be interpreted as in any significant way comparable to the alienating delusions of a schizophrenic. Lambo's position is consistent with that of many anthropologists.

Several comprehensive reviews of transcultural literature have appeared during the past thirty years.[28,71,97,115,117] Today, works on the subject appear with increasing frequency and two periodicals are specifically devoted to these studies: *Psychopathologie africaine*, published in Dakar, and *Transcultural Psychiatric Research Review*, published in Montreal.

(Culture and Personality

Certain drives are common to all men, although variations in degree and quality do occur. For a prolonged period all infants are in a state of complete dependence on their mothers. Gradually they move from their symbiotic relationship with her to a state of self-differentiation: I is separated from non-I. Gradually, too, with physical growth, shifts take place in zone predominance regarding mouth, anus, and genitals, though this zonal orientation is less rigidly delineated than is often supposed. Type and character of child rearing depend not only on individual variations of mothers but also reflect sociocultural climate. Variations in early mother-child relationships may produce a variety of effects in the adult. For example, in many primitive societies babies are breastfed for two years or more, close cutaneous contact is maintained between mother and child for a prolonged period, and toilet training by Western standards is lax. It has been suggested that the protracted child-mother intimacy (Collomb's[20] extrauterine gestation) may account for the Western primitive differences in demarcation of ego boundaries, instinct, and impulse control and a variety of cognitive operations; perhaps the lack of emphasis on toilet training has its reverberations in absence of sphincter morality, disregard for time, and want of restraint in the expression of aggressiveness.

Several psychoanalytically oriented studies[20,85,103] suggested that ego development, preferred ego defense mechanisms, superego functions, object relationships, and reality appraisal differ significantly between members of primitive cultures and members of technological cultures. As regards ego defense mechanisms, it has been found that members of primitive cultures are more apt to deny their objectionable impulses, project them onto witches and sorcerers, or to regress, under stress, to infantile modes of behavior than are members of technologically advanced cultures who unconsciously prefer such ego defense mechanisms as suppression, repression, reaction formation, and sublimation.

But as has already been noted, many of these relationships between child-rearing practices and personality have been challenged, especially by non-Western psychiatrists and anthropologists.[67] When a Yoruba mother attributes the illness of her son to bewitchment by her cowife, the questions may well be asked: Is the mother's mode of thinking related to her own experiences as a child,[39] to the fact that all Yoruba think that way, to the absence of effective police control[111] in the Yoruba culture, or could it be that this manner of thinking is functional for the culture in providing an answer to why the child is sick and offering clear methods for attempting to cure him?

Many attempts have been made to arrive at a suitable phrasing of the complex processes whereby a given culture arrives at its specific social institutions, belief systems, and modal personalities. Kardiner,[53] who has worked closely with several prominent anthropologists (Mead, Linton, DuBois, and others), provided the basis for the following generalizations:

1. Social evolution obviously occurs but does not follow a unilinear course. Hence each society must be studied as an entity in itself.

2. In order to understand the institutions and beliefs of a society, one must reconstruct the problems of adaptation the society has faced (for example, the adaptations to climatic, subsistence, and territorial problems as well as pressures from neighboring groups).

3. There are often many institutional methods for solving a given adaptational problem. For example, in some communities in danger of outstripping their food supply, the solution might be female infanticide (Marquesas island[53]) or institutionalized abortion (island of Yap[100]).

4. Social institutions are the patterned relationships that accommodate the individual to the human and natural environment.

5. Not all institutional patterns and belief systems are equally successful in adaptive power, and some may be disastrous in generating high rates of individual stress or psychopathology. Some patterns that were once functional may subsequently become dysfunctional. For ex-

ample, on the island of Yap, where there used to be population pressures, today, owing to institutionalized abortion, the population has decreased alarmingly.[100]

6. The interaction of individuals in society creates new institutions: Some promote cooperation; others stimulate anxiety and rage. The success of a society depends on a balance in favor of the former.

(Psychocultural Stress

No culture has succeeded in solving its adaptational problems without some kind and degree of coercion. Child-rearing practices, initiation rituals, some form of apprenticeship or schooling, laws, and taboos are common techniques to compel individuals to follow social norms and rules. These techniques vary from extreme permissiveness to harsh severity. Invariably, at one time or another during the individual's life, some of these constraints will cause frustration. The negative effect of tensions arising from these constraints is ameliorated by training to tolerate them, by cultural mechanisms that serve as safety valves, by institutionalized niches for deviants and marginal individuals, and by psychological compensations for culturally standardized behavior. A few examples may be given. Most Americans have learned to endure tension arising from competition and from a much greater degree of social isolation than exists in most other cultures. Conversely, among the Pueblo Indians, most individuals have acquired the capacity to tolerate tensions arising from constant immersion in the extended family and other groups that allow little scope for individuality. In other societies, ritual trances, bullfights, and drinking provide permissible outlets for cultural tensions while priesthood or shamanism may serve as a refuge for deviant individuals who find in these roles much gratification and even power over their fellow countrymen.

Nevertheless, such mechanisms can only mitigate cultural stress factors. They do not eliminate them. This very fact, added to numerous evidences that mental illness is found in all human societies, tends to indicate that culture per se (envisioned as a mold imposed on human drives and as a constellation of stimuli for human thought, sentiment, and behavior) universally generates significant psychological and even biological tensions. Everywhere some individuals become mentally ill, whereas others become deviants, delinquents, or reformers.[114]

Psychocultural stress factors may be divided into three broad categories: cultural content, social organization, and sociocultural change.[113,114]

Cultural Content

Basically, the relationship between cultural content and mental disease lies in the degree to which some cultural elements create tension between individuals, or generate anxiety within them.

TABOOS

Prominent among these elements is what may be called "cultural deprivation of basic gratifications." Such deprivation exists when the rules and taboos imposed by culture on a population or on some social groups within it become so excessive that they frustrate essential human needs. Such taboos may be related to food, aggression, sex, personal initiative, and political or religious authority. For instance, when a culture prescribes an excessive load of taboos to women without due compensations in terms of prestige, as is the case in some North African societies, it has been shown[68] that mental disorders in women increase in frequency. However, the pathogenic effect of taboos should not be overrated. Their amount and rigidity predispose to mental disease not by themselves but rather in interrelation with other cultural elements, such as values.

VALUE SATURATION

No two individuals adopt the values of their society in an identical manner. While most individuals are reasonably guided in their thoughts, attitudes, and behavior by cultural values, some individuals are unable to accept them, whereas others become imbued by them almost to the extent of intoxication. This phenomenon may be called "value saturation." A typical example is that of an American, who though lacking all the intellectual, emotional, and material qualities necessary to become a good businessman, will devote his whole life to the vain pursuit of success. In this case, psychological tension may assume such proportions that mental disease ensues. Probably some cultures and subcultures tend to produce more saturation than others. Germany's collective obsession with racial purity culminated in the tragedy of the extermination camps.

In most cases of value saturation, it is not easy to draw the line between normal and abnormal. For instance, A. F. C. Wallace[111] cited the case of Aharihon, an Onondaga war captive who was the idol of Iroquois youth because they could recognize in him the ego ideal of their culture. However, Aharihon had embodied the Iroquois model of manhood, especially the virtues of bravery and cruelty, to such an extreme that he could also have been considered a killer.

VALUE POLYMORPHISM

Value polymorphism refers to the coexistence, within the same cultural system or within the same individual, of values that are antagonistic. There are three major aspects of value polymorphism: (1) It may encompass a culture as a whole. This occurs generally in complex societies where an individual may be confronted with different ideologies, moral norms, and religious dogmas. (2) Another aspect of value polymorphism is related to cultural discontinuity[9] and to role replacement.[110] The passage from the status of son to the status of father entails a discontinuity in terms of values and roles, for example, from dependence on others to the responsibility for others. This, of course, is the natural order of things. However, when a culture does not provide proper and clear strategies, such as *rites de passage*, for these changes in the individual's life, or when the transitions and the roles themselves are ambiguously defined, the individual may find himself confronted with contradictory values, unable to choose those that could introduce him to his future statuses. The passage from adolescence to adulthood in Occidental cultures is a good example. (3) The third aspect of value polymorphism is the excessive exposure of individuals to simultaneous statuses. All human beings have simultaneous statuses: Most adult females must be good daughters, good mothers, good wives, good daughters-in-law, and so on. Generally such status pluralism does not create excessive tensions. However, it can happen, especially in societies dominated by value saturation, that some of these statuses become incompatible. For instance, the business executive may have so much responsibility as to interfere with gratifications derived from his other roles as father, husband, and friend. Some cultures have taken care of value polymorphism by strategies to reduce anxiety. For instance, the Masai of Africa forbid young men engaged in military training and activities to marry, but they permit them to have sexual relations with young unmarried girls.

ROLE DEPRIVATION

The opposite of value polymorphism is role deprivation, that is, the withdrawal of culturally and psychologically significant statuses and roles from some categories of individuals. The most extreme case of role deprivation is the ritual execution or exiling of individuals guilty of some taboo violation, such as incest or giving birth to twins. Other examples of role deprivation are the enforced retirement of the aged in Occidental societies and their relegation to uselessness culminating in killing in some primitive societies, such as the Eskimos and some Australian tribes, and the discrimination against some minority groups, such as Negroes in North America, and inferior castes in India and Japan.

Wallace[109] cited the case of the Seneca who, when they realized their socioeconomic situation and their white neighbor's contempt for their language and culture, became quasi-pathological: "Many became drunkards; the fear of witches increased; squabbling factions were unable to achieve a common policy." A very similar reaction occurred in New Guinea when the Aborigines realized that they had actually been conquered. Heavy drinking was also among the quasipathological reactions observed among them.[11] While the Seneca, after their first reactions, developed a revitalization movement where old and new virtues were emphasized, the New Guineans devised the famous cargo cult.[64,116] Examples of similar reactions are plentiful and well documented by Lanternari.[62]

SENTIMENTS

Another sociocultural factor linked to mental disease is the culture-bound system of sentiments that prevails in a particular society. Some cultures have been described, often too sweepingly, as being generally characterized by jealousy, megalomania, fear of spirits, and fear of people. For instance, in Ghana, according to Field,[32] fear of sorcery and of evil spirits is so common and so intense that everyone is suspicious of everyone else. Among the aborigines of New Guinea, "both fear and aggression are deliberately fostered."[10] There is good reason to believe that the more intense such culture-bound sentiments are in a society, the more widespread will be mental illness.

Social Organization

Two aspects of social organization deserve special attention regarding their relevance to mental illness: anomie and rigidity.

"Anomie" refers to the lack of integration of social organization and is sometimes used synonymously with social disorganization. A relationship between anomie and increased frequency of mental disorders has been established in Leighton's well-known Stirling County study.[80]

It has been demonstrated that unemployment and poverty in the slums of the big North American cities and migration to urban areas in Africa and South America[72] are associated with high rates of mental illness. However, the correlation between anomie and mental disease is not so simple as may appear because a variety of factors combine in determining anomie and frequency of mental disorders.[31] Recent discussions on possible correlations between the so-called culture of poverty and mental health have also revealed the complexity of factors involved.[33] Movement of mentally ill persons into slum areas is one such factor. Nonetheless, there is plenty of evidence that lack of education, poverty, ethnic diversity, and especially anomie and migration tend to create tensions because they deprive the individual of significant statuses and gratifying roles (role deprivation) and produce value polymorphism.

The reverse of social disorganization is social rigidity. This term means that the overall social structure of a society has become so inflexible that individuals have no choice but to conform to prescribed social norms. Typically, in small communities dominated by traditional values and by a social structure that imposes on individuals specific statuses and roles, those unable to knuckle down to passive conformance feel so constrained that great emotional tension ensues; they will become marginal, delinquent, or psychologically disturbed. Some of them will move to the cities in the hope of finding proper niches but more often than not they experience anomie and other types of tension.

Sociocultural Change

Much research has been done on the effect of sociocultural change on mental health. Sociocultural change occurs, of course, everywhere, but it varies in rate and nature according to a complex set of technological, economic, social, and cultural factors.

Sociocultural change does not always produce adverse emotional reactions. Some cultures seem to have a fairly high degree of cultural elasticity that makes them adaptable to new situations and new culture traits; such is the case with the Kamba, a Bantu tribe of East Africa, a society characterized by individualism and structural "looseness."[81] Nor need reactions to contact necessarily be pathogenic; reactions to acculturation seem to vary

in relation to the cultural patterns that had prevailed among North American Indian tribes before their contacts with white Americans.[70]

However, it has also been demonstrated that sociocultural change due to contacts between different social and cultural groups can be very harmful, although, of course, such psychological damage is not due entirely to cultural change. Other factors, such as low social status and poverty, are also at work. Hallowell's[45] study of the Ojibwa clearly indicates that those Ojibwa who were partly acculturated had regressive personalities. It is also well known that most primitive people living on the fringe of a complex society are subjected to stresses that increase the incidence of mental illness. The plight of colonized people has often been mentioned in that respect. Sociocultural change owing to migration seems to be particularly stressful; it has been observed on all continents. For instance, it would seem that the migration of Peruvians from small mountain communities to sea level regions engenders physiological stress as well as psychological insecurity.[33]

Factors involved in social change are so numerous and so intertwined that it is almost impossible to pinpoint the specific effect of each one.[77] In brief, it can be concluded that sociocultural change is noxious to mental health, especially if it occurs in combination with one or more of the previously named stress factors, such as anomie, role deprivation, and value polymorphism.

◖ Culture and Psychiatric Disorder

Turning now to the psychiatric implications of the cultural stress factors described above, it should be stated that most psychiatrists subscribe to a pluralistic etiological view of mental disorder. One often neglected dimension of psychiatry is the cultural dimension. This cultural dimension will be dealt with under three headings: symptomatology of mental disorders, the question of the culture-bound syndromes, and frequency of mental disorder.

Symptomatology of Mental Disorders

Much of our information about symptomatology of mental illness in developing countries comes from a highly selected sample, that is, patients admitted to mental hospitals because of grossly disturbed behavior. Moreover, in many developing countries the mental state of the patient may be influenced by vitamin deficiencies, parasitic infestation, infectious diseases, malnutrition, and other organic factors. To some observers,[17] the clinical manifestations of mental disorders owing to cultural and organic factors are so atypical that Western diagnostic categories hardly apply at all. But most observers stress similarities rather than differences, simply pointing out variations in intensity, duration, verbalized content, and affective coloring of disorders. Occasionally, the differences have seemed so marked as to suggest a different fundamental category of disorder, and these have been called culture-bound syndromes. As more data accumulates, however, the concept of the culture-bound syndrome becomes less acceptable or, at least, is reduced to a play on words.

There is now general agreement that schizophrenia is to be found in all cultures and that the clinical subforms (simple, hebephrenic, catatonic, paranoid) occur everywhere, though in varying frequencies.[114] The alleged rarity of simple schizophrenia in some societies may be owing to the acceptance of low work performance by some communities: Without the work ethic, to be indolent on pathological grounds is not exceptional. States of excitement are not necessarily related to schizophrenia in some cultures. They occur as brief psychogenic episodes and are related to the tendency in some primitive populations to regress massively in response to stress.[12,22] While chronic schizophrenic catatonic states have become rare in Europe and America, they are common in India and other Asian countries. The frequency of catatonic stupors in these countries may be due to the teaching both by Hinduism and Buddhism of social and emotional withdrawal as an acceptable mode of reacting to difficulties; the frequency

of catatonic rigidity and of negativism in Indian schizophrenics may be due to a traditional passive-aggressive response to a threatening world. By contrast, the maintenance of social contacts in southern Italian schizophrenics, even in advanced stages, has been attributed to their traditional sociability and to their great family solidarity.[86] Observers from both Africa and India agree that paranoid formations in schizophrenic patients under their care are less systematized than in Euro-Americans.[49,58] It is obvious that varying cultural beliefs mold the content of delusions and hallucinations: An Eskimo who has never heard of Jesus Christ or General de Gaulle can obviously not imagine that he is either of them in his grandiose psychotic ideas; in the African bush an indigenous paranoid patient will accuse a witch of damaging him and will feel persecuted by spirits and not by X-rays, radio, or television. An Austrian psychiatrist[66] studied changes in schizophrenic symptomatology during the last hundred years; comparing the first half century with the second he found that ideas of persecution by God or demons have become infrequent and ideas of being persecuted by material agents more common. According to Japanese investigators,[4,48] paranoid schizophrenia has increased in Japan since World War II. Since then, in place of delusions regarding the Emperor, paranoid delusions have concerned themselves increasingly with the United States, the Communist Party, radio, and television.

A global survey carried out at McGill University[79] revealed that symptoms of endogenous depression in its classical form are most commonly found among Europeans, irrespective of where they live. Atypical features have been noted in other cultures. Outstanding among these are the frequency of hypochondriacal ideas, the frequency of persecutory ideas (hallucinations and delusions) in developing countries, and the rarity of suicide and feelings of unworthiness and guilt in, for example, Sub-Saharan Africa.[91]

Feelings of unworthiness and guilt in depressives are most pronounced in Euro-Americans; they also occur in Japanese, Chinese, Indians, and Arabs. Self-accusatory ideas may be concerned with trespasses on morality, on society, or on worship of ancestors or deities. Guilt feelings in depressives are absent in societies in which superego pressures are externalized: Feelings of having sinned can be experienced only if the concept of sin is part of one's religious belief system. Projection of id impulses and of superego censures onto the outer world, so common in developing countries, counteracts feelings of guilt but results in paranoid formations that may mask the depressive picture. As regards hypochondriacal sensations, incapacity to verbalize feelings may account for their frequency in depressed preliterates. It is also possible, as Collomb[20] suggested for the Senegalese, that prolonged skin contact between mother and child reinforces libidinization of the body and therefore predisposes to pathological body sensations in depressives.

The gross forms of conversion hysteria, such as abasia-astasia, blindness, and deafness have almost vanished in Europe and America. This diminution may be due to "a wider dissemination of education with an increase in sophistication, a less authoritarian social structure, and a decrease in sexual prudery and inhibition."[18] A shift in clinical manifestations of conversion hysteria from gross forms to anxiety has certainly taken place in Europe and America since World War I, but no such reduction in frequency or in the clinical forms of conversion hysteria has been reported in developing countries. Other hysterical features (perhaps related to the reasons given above for the somatization in depressives) are vague aches and pains, functional visceral disorders, and the sensation of burning frequently complained of in primitive societies.[84]

Are There Culture-Bound Syndromes?

There are some mental disorders that in the past have been labeled "culture bound." Further study suggests that these are not really separate syndromes ranking with schizophrenia and hysteria. Although they may be graced with a local name and imbued with a distinctive and perhaps exotic-sounding symbolism rooted in that culture, they are basically the standard syndromes described in the *American Psychiatric Association Manual*. If some specific instances of a disorder in a non-Western culture are difficult to label within that system, they are no more difficult than some instances of disorder that occur within Western culture. As Hallowell[43] said of the well-known cannibalistic *windigo* symbolism, which is sometimes expressed in the depressions and schizophrenias of the Cree and Ojibwa: "If enough cases of *windigo* were collected, it might become apparent that they fall along a continuum of states comparable to those seen in other cultures, and that only the content of the delusion is specific to the Cree or Ojibwa."

Koro[21,119] is another example. The fantasy that the penis will withdraw into the abdomen and that the patient will die is sometimes expressed in the schizophrenias or hysterias of south China and Taiwan. Not infrequently, sufferers of this disease clamp the penis in a box to prevent retraction. Some authors have regarded *koro* as exclusive to Southeast Asia. But Baasher[6] reported from the Sudan that several of his patients expressed fears that their penises were shrinking, and, like the Asiatic patients, attributed the damage to excessive masturbation. Similarly a melancholic Jewish American patient[13] complained of "the peculiar feeling that his sexual organs were somewhat foreign to his body and that at times he could not even feel that they were there. This impression was so strong that the patient would frequently grab himself by the sex organs in order to be certain that they were still there." Perhaps the most that can be said is that if fantasies regarding the damaged penis, its causes, and consequences were collected from around the world, there would be a much greater clustering and intensity of *koro*-like imagery in Chinese culture. Rin[94] explained its prominence by linking it with the traditional Chinese world view. The world is divided into the *yang* (male, hot, dry, and related to the sun, life, and the right side) and *yin* (female, cold, wet, and symbolized by the earth, death, and the left side of the body) principles. The belief is held that in patients with *koro, yin* predominates over *yang*. The shrinking of the penis is believed to be the result of this predominance, and the cure lies in taking medicines and foods rich in *yang*. The superstition is widespread that a corpse has no penis, which explains the fear of death resulting from its retraction.

A variety of other culture-bound syndromes can be interpreted in a similar way: the magical fear syndrome, *susto*, described in Latin America;[37,98] the *zar* sickness of North East Africa and Iran;[74,75] the brain-fag syndrome of some African groups;[89] and the crazy-moth syndrome of the Navaho.[52]

Another group of culture-bound disorders, the *latah* group of imitation reactions, require a different interpretation. This syndrome is usually triggered by a fright (a loud noise, unexpected gesture, even a stimulus word, such as "snake" or "tiger") which results in some or all of the following behavior: an exaggerated startle reaction, echolalia, echopraxia, coprolalia, copropraxia, and automatic obedience. The episode is usually brief—a few minutes to an hour or two—and there is usually no alteration of consciousness. The syndrome is commonly regarded as an idiosyncrasy rather than a disease, and the sufferer often provides unwilling entertainment for his associates. It could be argued that this group of imitation syndromes warrants a separate diagnostic category in an international classification. It seems to have much more to do with a type of ego structure more commonly found in primitive peoples than with the kind of cultural symbolism observed in *windigo* or *koro*. Its distinction lies in its structure rather than its content. But once again it is not culture bound.

This syndrome first attracted widespread medical attention when it was reported among French Canadian peasants in Maine and Vermont by Beard[7] in 1880. His report was translated widely in French, Italian, and German journals.[104] The report particularly provoked the interest of Gilles de la Tourette,[2,36] who probably erroneously linked the syndrome with the syndrome of coprolalia and tics, which still bears his name. Almost immediately, Beard's "jumping Frenchmen" were identified with the highly similar *miryachit*

reaction found in Siberia[46] and with the *latah* of Malay.[30] Virtually identical patterns have been described in Japan among the Ainus,[104] and among several cultural groups in Mongolia,[1] South Africa,[38] Burma, Java, and elsewhere.[118]

Generally speaking, the syndrome is common among those of lowly status who are self-effacing and docile in character. Domestic servants are common among the afflicted. This observation has led to one interpretation of its cause an an expression of a conflict between submission and rebellion arising from "an unconscious connection between submission and a dreaded and desired passive sexual experience."[1] Others have seen it as a mocking behavior involving identification with the aggressor[15] or as a primitive anxiety-relieving mechanism still available to children and primitive people, but not to adult Western man.[3] Murphy[76] commented on the frequency of Malayan childhood games with strong elements of suggestion which might offer training for entrance into such hypersuggestive states as *latah*. This concept receives support from the observations of similar games in rural Quebec and their possible relation to a pattern of startle response.[92]

Finally the famous *amok* reaction should be mentioned.[116,121] It was first described in Malaya but has since been seen in many other parts of the world. *Amok*, a characteristically male reaction, is usually precipitated by frustrating circumstances, but physical stresses, such as acute infections, sleep deprivation, and intoxications, may act as precipitating or reinforcing factors. Several phases have been described: After an initial withdrawal, there is a period of meditation with loss of contact with the world, persecutory ideas, and a mood of anxiety and rage; this is followed by a stage of automatism, the *amok* proper; suddenly the subject will seize a weapon and attack anyone in his way. He may commit multiple homicides, may mutilate himself, and is frequently killed by frightened neighbors. With recovery of consciousness the subject may pass into a phase of depression. There is usually amnesia for the *amok* period. Like *latah*, *amok* can more properly be regarded as a reaction occurring in individuals of primitive ego organization wherever they may be found rather than as a state bound to any particular culture. Reports[120] that in Malaya and Java the incidence of *amok* fell after the authorities jailed *amok* runners indicates that social measures can curb frequency and specific forms of such reaction types.

Frequency of Mental Disorder

Sweeping statements have been made regarding differences in the total frequency of mental disorders between vast geographical and cultural areas, such as Asia and North America. However, nothing definite is known about such gross differences. On a manageable scale, cross-cultural comparisons of total and relative frequency of mental disorders have been made, using hospital records, key informants, and field surveys of selected population samples. Hospital records are obviously ill suited for epidemiological purposes because of the multiple cultural and local factors that determine hospitalization. The key informant technique is valuable in identifying gross disturbances in smaller communities, but less useful in urban settings and for less visible types of disorder. Field surveys are beset with difficulties because of differences in the resistance of the population to interview, language equivalence problems, cultural differences in doctor-patient relationships, and the lack of comparability of studies by different investigators owing to differences in survey techniques.

Several investigators, however, have succeeded in overcoming at least some of these difficulties and have provided some preliminary findings. The work of Lin and Rin, of Leighton and his group, and particularly of H. B. M. Murphy deserve special mention in this regard.

Between 1946 and 1953, Lin and Rin surveyed three Chinese communities and four aboriginal Malayo-Polynesian groups on the island of Taiwan.[69,95] The aboriginal groups were at varying levels of social development and acculturation. Using a key informant and home-visit survey technique, they covered some 11,000 Aborigines and 20,000 Chinese.

Their method was such that only the major types of psychiatric disturbances were counted, but the investigators and the method used were the same for the various cultural groups so that there is some degree of comparability of rates of disorder within this survey. The gross findings were that the lifetime prevalence rates of total mental disorders was practically the same among the Aborigines (9.5 per 1,000) as among the Chinese (9.4 per 1,000). The most significant differences were found between one of the aboriginal groups, the Atayal (who were the most primitive and least acculturated but the most poverty stricken), and the Chinese. The Atayal showed significantly higher total rates of psychoses. Organic and manic-depressive rates were considerably higher among the Atayal but schizophrenic rates were lower than for the Chinese. Rates of alcoholism were much higher ($p > 0.001$) among the aboriginal groups compared with the Chinese. The authors explain these differences as owing to differences in rates of acculturation, general health conditions, and genetic factors.

Leighton[65] and his group, which included anthropologists and Western-trained indigenous psychiatrists, compared the mental health of rural Nova Scotians (Canada) with rural and urbanized Yoruba (Nigeria). A standardized interview, field survey of a probability sample of the populations was the major technique, but key informant and hospital data were also utilized. The technique was such that reliable data were obtained only on the minor psychiatric disorders rather than the psychoses. The findings showed fewer differences between the groups than expected. Definite psychiatric disorders were found in 21 percent of the Yoruba villagers, 31 percent of the urbanized Yoruba, and 31 percent of the rural Nova Scotians. Rates of significantly impaired individuals showed more marked contrasts: 15 percent for Yoruba villagers, 19 percent for urbanized Yoruba, and 33 percent for rural Nova Scotians. There was also an unexpected similarity between the groups in symptom patterns.

H. B. M. Murphy[78] used a key informant technique to determine active prevalence rates of schizophrenia (whether hospitalized or not) in fourteen Quebec villages of contrasting cultures, including Anglo-Protestant, French Canadian, Irish Catholic, Polish, and German. Significant prevalence differences were found between the communities.

There were also differences in sex distribution, age of onset, duration, pattern of hospitalization, and other characteristics. Murphy[78] explained the differences in cultural terms. For example, he suggested that the very high rates of schizophrenia among women in traditional French Canadian communities may be owing to severe role conflicts. The ideal woman in these communities is one who marries early, has many children, works hard, and is submissive to her husband. About a generation ago, however, higher education became available to women and an independent career beyond the home or convent became a possibility. Study of individual cases showed this role conflict "reflected in the symptomatology of the female schizophrenics attempting to avoid, to escape from, or to destroy the type of marriage which their society sought to tie them to." Similar conflicts, which vary according to culture, were associated with schizophrenia in the other groups. Murphy suggested that the following circumstances in a culture are commonly linked with the precipitation of schizophrenia: a problem of choice that affects the individual deeply; pressure by the community to make a definite choice; contradictions or confusions in the guidance the culture provides; chronicity in the sense that the problem persists until a decison is taken.

use of altered states of consciousness (psychedelic states, trance states, and mystical states); the relation of rites of passage to mental health; and many other aspects that fall within the legitimate province of transcultural psychiatry.

Questions have been raised as to the value of transcultural studies; some have regarded it as a preoccupation with exotica. We see the field as having both theoretical and practical implications. As with other branches of science, the comparative method provides a powerful aid to understanding and conceptualizing. Transcultural psychiatric studies help to distinguish the essential and universal from the peripheral and parochial. These studies are indispensable in arriving at conclusions about the basic factors shaping personality, the core characteristics of psychiatric disorders, and the essentials of preventive and therapeutic activities.

But there are also practical applications. Insights gleaned from transcultural studies are vital for equipping mental health workers who cross cultural boundaries. These include psychiatrists from developing countries who come to the Western world for training; mental health workers located in multiethnic settings; and social workers, physicians, nurses, and perhaps even economists and engineers who are involved in foreign aid programs. The field is in its infancy, valid insights are difficult to achieve and call for laborious interdisciplinary alliances, yet transcultural psychiatric studies would seem to have a definite place in our attempts to come to terms with our conflict-laden, rapidly shrinking, global village.

◖ Conclusions

In this review, we have briefly considered the history and some of the major findings and theoretical constructs of the field of transcultural psychiatry. Space limitations have not permitted a comprehensive coverage. For example we have omitted the area of comparative healing practices; of attitudes to the mentally ill according to culture, as well as the entire field of mental defect; the patterns of

◖ Bibliography

1. ABERLE, D. F. "Arctic Hysteria and Latah in Mongolia." *Transactions of the New York Academy of Sciences*, 11, no. 14 (1952), 291–297.
2. ABSE, D. W. *Hysteria and Related Mental Disorders.* Bristol: John Wright, 1966.
3. ARIETI, S., and METH, M. J. "Rare, Unclassifiable, Collective, and Exotic Psychotic Syndromes." In S. Arieti, ed., *American*

Handbook of Psychiatry. Vol. 1. New York: Basic Books, 1959. Pp. 546–563.

4. ASAI, T. "The Contents of Delusions of Schizophrenic Patients in Japan: Comparison between Periods 1941–1961." *Transcultural Psychiatric Research Review,* 1 (1964), 27–28.

5. AUBIN, H. "Introduction à l'étude de la Psychiatrie chez les Noirs." *Annals Medico-Psychologiques,* 94 (1939), 1–29.

6. BAASHER, T. A. "The Influence of Culture on Psychiatric Manifestations." *Transcultural Psychiatric Research Review,* 15 (1963), 51–52.

7. BEARD, G. M. "Experiments with the 'Jumpers,' or 'Jumping Frenchmen,' of Maine." *Journal of Nervous and Mental Diseases,* 7 (1880), 487–490.

8. BENEDICT, P. K., and JACKS, I. "Mental Illness in Primitive Societies." *Psychiatry,* 17 (1954), 377–389.

9. BENEDICT, R. "Continuities and Discontinuities in Cultural Conditioning." In C. Kluckhohn and H. A. Murray, eds., *Personality in Nature, Society, and Culture.* New York: Knopf, 1949.

10. BERNDT, R. M. *Excess and Restraint: Social Control among a New Guinea Mountain People.* Chicago: University of Chicago Press, 1962.

11. BURTON-BRADLEY, B. *Mixed-Race Society in Port Moresby.* New Guinea research bulletin, no. 23. Canberra: The Australian National University, 1968.

12. BUSTAMANTE, J. A. "La Reaction Psychotique Aigue, la Transculturation, le Sous-Developpement, et les Changements Sociaux." *Psychopathologie africaine,* 5 (1969), 223–233.

13. BYCHOWSKI, G. "Disorders of the Body-Image in the Clinical Picture of Psychoses." *Journal of Nervous and Mental Diseases,* 97 (1943), 310–335.

14. CAPLAN, R. B. *Psychiatry and the Community in Nineteenth-Century America.* New York: Basic Books, 1969.

15. CARLUCCIO, C., SOURS, J. A., and KOLB, L. C. "Psychodynamics of Echo Reactions." *Archives of General Psychiatry,* 10 (1964), 623–629.

16. CAROTHERS, J. C. *The African Mind in Health and Disease.* Monograph series, no. 17. Geneva: World Health Organization, 1953.

17. CAWTE, J. E. "Ethnopsychiatry in Central Australia: I. 'Traditional' Illness in the Eastern Aranda People." *British Journal of Psychiatry,* 111 (1965), 1069–1077.

18. CHODOFF, P. "A Reexamination of Some Aspects of Conversion Hysteria." *Psychiatry,* 17 (1954), 75–81.

19. COHEN, Y. A. *Social Structures and Personality.* New York: Holt, Rinehart & Winston, 1961.

20. COLLOMB, H. "Assistance Psychiatrique en Afrique: Experience Sénégalaise." *Psychopathologie africaine,* 1 (1965), 11–84.

21. ———. "La Position du Conflit et les Structures Familiales en Voie de Transformation," *Canadian Psychiatric Association Journal,* 12 (1967), 451–465.

22. ———. "L'utilisation des Données Culturelles dans un Cas de Bouffée Délirante." *Psychopathologie africaine,* 1 (1967), 121–147.

23. COOPER, J. M. "Mental Disease Situations in Certain Cultures." *Journal of Abnormal and Social Psychology,* 29 (1934), 10–17.

24. DAVIDSON, S. "Psychiatric Work among the Bemba," *Rhodes-Livingstone Journal,* 7 (1949), 75–86.

25. DHUNJIBOY, J. "Brief Resumé of the Types of Insanity Commonly Met in India." *Journal of Mental Science,* 76 (1930), 254–264.

26. DuBois, C. *The People of Alor.* Minneapolis: University of Minnesota Press, 1944.

27. EATON, J. W., and WEIL, R. J. *Culture and Mental Disorders: A Comparative Study of the Hutterites and Other Populations.* Glencoe: The Free Press, 1955.

28. ELLENBERGER, H. F. "Ethno-psychiatrie." In *Encyclopedie Medico-Chirurgicale.* Psychiatrie 37725 A10, no. 5. Paris, 1965. Pp. 1–22.

29. ELLIS, W. G. "The Amok of the Malays." *Journal of Mental Science,* 39 (1893), 325–338.

30. ———. "Latah: A Mental Malady of the Malays." *Journal of Mental Science,* 43 (1897), 32–40.

31. FARRIS, R. E. L. "Ecological Factors in Human Behaviour." In J. McV. Hunt, ed., *Personality and Behaviour Disorders.* Vol. 1. New York: Ronald Press, 1944. Pp. 736–757.

32. FIELD, J. M. *Search for Security: An Ethnopsychiatric Study of Rural Ghana.* Evanston, Ill.: Northwestern University Press, 1960.

33. FINNEY, J. C., ed. *Culture Change, Mental Health and Poverty.* Lexington, Ky.: University of Kentucky Press, 1969.

34. FREUD, S. *Civilization and Its Discontents.* London: Hogarth Press, 1930.

35. FRIED, J. "Acculturation and Mental Health among the Indian Migrants in Peru." In M. K. Opler, ed., *Culture and Mental Health.* New York: Macmillan, 1959. Pp. 119–137.

36. GILLES DE LA TOURETTE, G. "Jumping, Latah, Myriachit." *Archives de Neurologie,* 8 (1884), 68–71.

37. GILLIN, J. P. "Magical Fright." *Psychiatry,* 11 (1948), 387–400.

38. GILMOUR, A. "Latah among South African Natives." *Scottish Medical and Surgical Journal,* 10 (1902), 18–24.

39. GORDON, H. L. "An Inquiry into the Correlation of Civilization and Mental Disorders in the Kenya Native." *East African Medical Journal,* 12 (1936), 327–335.

40. GRANT, W. "Megato and His Tribe." *Journal of the Royal Anthropological Institute,* 35 (1905), 266–270.

41. GREENLEES, T. D. "Insanity among the Natives of South Africa." *Journal of Mental Science,* 41 (1895), 71–82.

42. HALLIDAY, A. Quoted in G. Rosen, *Madness in Society.* New York: Harper & Row, 1968. P. 183.

43. HALLOWELL, A. L. "Culture and Mental Disorders." *Journal of Abnormal and Social Psychology,* 29 (1934), 1–9.

44. ———. "Fear and Anxiety as Cultural and Individual Variables in a Primitive Society." *Journal of Social Psychology,* 9 (1938), 25–47.

45. ———. *Culture and Experience.* New York: Schocken Books, 1967.

46. HAMMOND, W. A. "Miryachit, A Newly Described Disease of the Nervous System and Its Analogues." *New York Medical Journal,* 1 (1884), 191–192.

47. HARTMANN, H., KRIS, E., and LOEWENSTEIN, R. M. "Some Psychoanalytic Comments on 'Culture and Personality.' " In G. B. Wilbur and W. Muensterberger, eds., *Psychoanalysis and Culture.* New York: International Universities Press, 1951.

48. HASUZAWA, T. "Chronological Observations of Delusions in Schizophrenics." In H. Akimoto, ed., *Proceedings of the Joint Meeting of the Japanese Society of Psychiatry and Neurology and the American Psychiatric Association, Tokyo. Folia Psychiatria et Neurologia Japonica,* suppl. no. 7. Tokyo: Japanese Society of Psychiatry and Neurology, 1963. Pp. 180–183.

49. HOCH, E. M. "Psychiatrische Beobachtungen und Erfahrungen an Indischen Patienten." *Praxis,* 48 (1959), 1051–1057.

50. HONIGMANN, J. J. *Culture and Personality.* New York: Harper & Row, 1954.

51. JILEK, W. G. "Mental Health and Magic Beliefs in Changing Africa." In N. Petrilowitsch, ed., *Contributions to Comparative Psychiatry.* Basel: Karger, 1967.

52. KAPLAN, B., and JOHNSON, D. "The Social Meaning of Navaho Psychopathology and Psychotherapy." In A. Kiev, ed., *Magic, Faith and Healing.* Glencoe: The Free Press, 1964.

53. KARDINER, A. *The Individual and His Society.* New York: Columbia University Press, 1939.

54. ———, and PREBLE, E. *They Studied Man.* London: Secker & Warburg, 1961.

55. KIEV, A., ed. *Magic, Faith and Healing.* Glencoe: The Free Press, 1964.

56. KLUCKHOHN, C. "A Navaho Personal Document." *Southwestern Journal of Anthropology,* 1 (1945), 260–283.

57. LA BARRE, W. "The Influence of Freud on Anthropology." *American Imago,* 15 (1958), 275–328.

58. LAMBO, T. A. "The Role of Cultural Factors in Paranoid Psychoses among the Yoruba Tribe." *Journal of Mental Science,* 101 (1955), 239–266.

59. ———. "Traditional African Cultures and Western Medicine." In F. N. L. Poynter, ed., *Medicine and Culture.* London: Wellcome Institute of the History of Medicine, 1969.

60. LANDES, R. "The Abnormal among the Ojibway." *Journal of Abnormal and Social Psychology,* 33 (1938), 14–33.

61. LANGNESS, L. L. "Hysterical Psychosis in the New Guinea Highlands: A Bena Bena Example." *Psychiatry,* 28 (1965), 258–277.

62. LANTERNARI, V. *The Religions of the Oppressed.* New York: Knopf, 1963.

63. LAUBSCHER, B. J. F. *Sex Custom and Psychopathology: A Study of South African Pagan Natives.* London: Routledge, 1937.

64. LAWRENCE, P. *Road Belong Cargo.* Manchester University Press, 1964.

65. LEIGHTON, A. H., LAMBO, T. A., HUGHES,

C. C., Leighton, D. C., Murphy, J. M., and Macklin, D. B. *Psychiatric Disorder among the Yoruba.* Ithaca, N.Y.: Cornell University Press, 1963.

66. Lenz, H. *Vergleichende Psychiatrie: Eine Studie über die Beziehung von Kultur, Soziologie und Psychopathologie.* Vienna: Wilhelm Maudrich Verlag, 1964.

67 LeVine, R. A. "Africa." In F. L. K. Hsu, ed., *Psychological Anthropology.* Homewood, Ill.: Dorsey Press, 1961.

68. Lewin, B. "Die Konfliktneurose der Mohammedanerin in Ägypten." *Zeitschrift für Psychotherapie und Medizin,* 8 (1958), 98–112.

69. Lin, T. "A Study of the Incidence of Mental Disorder in Chinese and Other Cultures." *Psychiatry,* 16 (1953), 613–636.

70. Linton, R. *Acculturation in Seven American Indian Tribes.* New York: Appleton-Century, 1940.

71. ———. *Culture and Mental Disorders.* Springfield, Ill.: Charles C Thomas, 1956.

72. Mangin, W. "Mental Health and Migration to Cities: A Peruvian Case." In V. Rubin, ed., *Culture, Society and Health.* Annals of the New York Academy of Science, no. 84. New York, 1960. Pp. 911–917.

73. Mead, M., and Bateson, G. *Balinese Character.* New York Academy of Sciences special publications, no. 2. New York, 1942.

74. Messing, S. D. "Group Therapy and Social Status in the Zar Cult of Ethiopia." *American Anthropologist,* 60 (1958), 1120–1126.

75. Modarressi, T. "The Zar Cult in South Iran." In R. H. Prince, ed., *Trance and Possession States.* Montreal: R. M. Bucke Memorial Society, 1968. Pp. 149–155.

76. Murphy, H. B. M. "Mental Disorders among the Malaysians of Southeast Asia, with Notes on Latah and Amok." *Transcultural Research in Mental Health Problems,* 7 (1960), 24–27.

77. ———. "Social Change and Mental Health." *Milbank Memorial Fund Quarterly,* 39 (1961), 385–445.

78. ———. "Cultural Factors in the Genesis of Schizophrenia." In D. Rosenthal and S. S. Kety, eds., *The Transmission of Schizophrenia.* Oxford: Pergamon Press, 1968.

79. ———, Wittkower, E. D., and Chance, N. A. "Crosscultural Inquiry into the Symptomatology of Depression: A Preliminary Report." *International Journal of Psychiatry,* 3 (1967), 6–22.

80. Murphy, J. M., and Leighton, A. H., eds. *Approaches to Cross-Cultural Psychiatry.* Ithaca, N.Y.: Cornell University Press, 1965.

81. Oliver, S. C. "Individuality, Freedom of Choice and Cultural Flexibility of the Kamba." *American Anthropologist,* 67 (1965), 421–428.

82. Opler, M. K. *Culture, Psychiatry and Human Values.* Springfield, Ill.: Charles C Thomas, 1956.

83. Osterreicher, W. "Manisch-Depressive Psychose fijeen Soendanese." *Medisch Maandlblad Djakarta,* 3 (1950), 173–175.

84. Parhad, L. "The Cultural-Social Conditions in a Psychiatric Out-patient Department in Kuwait." *International Journal of Social Psychiatry,* 11 (1965), 14–19.

85. Parin, P., Morgenthaler, F., and Parin-Matthey, G. *Die Weissen Denken Zuviel.* Zurich: Atlantis Verlag, 1963.

86. Parsons, A. "Some Comparative Observations on Ward Social Structure: Southern Italy, England and the United States." *Transcultural Psychiatric Research Review,* 10 (1961), 116–119.

87. Pfeiffer, W. M. "Psychiatric Peculiarities in Indonesia." *Transcultural Psychiatric Research Review,* 3 (1966), 116–119.

88. Price-Williams, D. R., ed. *Penguin Modern Psychology Readings/Cross-Cultural Studies.* Harmondsworth: Penguin Books, 1969.

89. Prince, R. H. "The 'Brain-Fag' Syndrome in Nigerian Students." *Journal of Mental Science,* 106 (1960), 559–570.

90. ———. "The Yoruba Image of the Witch." *Journal of Mental Science,* 107 (1961), 795–805.

91. ———. "The Changing Picture of Depressive Syndromes in Africa: Is It Fact or Diagnostic Fashion?" *Canadian Journal of African Studies,* 1 (1968), 177–192.

92. Rabinovitch, R. "An Exaggerated Startle Reflex Resembling a Kicking Horse." *Canadian Medical Association Journal,* 93 (1965), 130–131.

93. Radin, P. *Crashing Thunder: The Autobiography of a Winnebago Indian.* University of California publications in American archaeology and ethnology. Berkeley, 1920.

94. Rin, H. "A Study of the Aetiology of Koro

in Respect to the Chinese Concept of Illness." *International Journal of Social Psychiatry*, 11 (1965), 7–13.

95. ———, and LIN, T. "Mental Illness Among Formosan Aborigenes as Compared with the Chinese in Taiwan." *Journal of Mental Science*, 108 (1962), 134–146.

96. ROHEIM, G. "The Psychoanalysis of Primitive Cultural Types." *International Journal of Psycho-Analysis*, 13 (1932), 1–224.

97. ———. "Racial Differences in the Neuroses and Psychoses." *Psychiatry*, 2 (1939), 375–390.

98. RUBEL, A. J. "The Epidemiology of a Folk Illness: Susto in Hispanic America." *Ethnology*, 3 (1964), 268–283.

99. SAPIR, E. *Culture, Language, and Personality.* Berkeley: University of California Press, 1949.

100. SCHNEIDER, D. M. "Abortion and Depopulation on a Pacific Island." In B. D. Paul, ed., *Health, Culture, and Community.* New York: Russell Sage Foundation, 1955. Pp. 211–235.

101. SEGALL, M. H., CAMPBELL, D. T., and HERSKOVITS, M. J. *The Influence of Culture on Visual Perception.* Indianapolis: Bobbs-Merrill, 1966.

102. SINGER, M. "A Survey of Culture and Personality Theory and Research." In B. Kaplan, ed., *Studying Personality Cross-Culturally.* New York: Harper & Row, 1961. Pp. 9–90.

103. STAEWEN, C., and SCHÖNBERG, F. *Kulturwandel und Angstentwicklung bei den Yoruba Westafricas.* München: Weltforum Verlag, 1970.

104. STEVENS, H. "Jumping Frenchmen of Maine." *Archives of Neurology*, 12 (1965), 311–314.

105. UCHIMURA, Y. "Imu, eine Psychoreaktive Erscheinung bei Ainu-Frauen." *Nervenarzt*, 27 (1956), 535–540.

106. VAN WULFFTEN PALTHE, P. M. "Koro. Eine Merkwürdige Angsthysterie." *International Journal of Psycho-Analysis*, 21 (1935), 249–257.

107. ———. "Psychiatry and Neurology in the Tropics." In A. Liechtenstein, ed., *A Clinical Textbook of Tropical Medicine.* Batavia: de Langen, 1936.

108. WALLACE, A. F. C. "The Institutionalization of Cathartic and Control Strategies in Iroquois Religious Psychotherapy." In

M. K. Opler, ed., *Culture and Mental Health.* New York: Macmillan, 1959. Pp. 63–96.

109. ———. *Culture and Personality.* New York: Random House, 1961.

110. ———. "Mental Illness, Biology and Culture." In F. L. K. Hsu, ed., *Psychological Anthropology.* Homewood, Ill.: Dorsey Press, 1961.

111. ———. "Anthropology and Psychiatry." In A. M. Freedman and H. I. Kaplan, eds., *Comprehensive Textbook of Psychiatry.* Baltimore, Md.: Williams & Wilkins, 1967. Pp. 195–201.

112. WHITING, J. M. W., and CHILD, I. E. *Child Training and Personality: A Cross-Cultural Study.* New Haven: Yale University Press, 1953.

113. WITTKOWER, E. D., and DUBREUIL, G. "Cultural Factors in Mental Illness." In E. Norbeck, D. Price-Williams, and W. M. McCord, eds., *The Study of Personality.* New York: Holt, Rinehart & Winston, 1968. Pp. 279–295.

114. ———, and DUBREUIL, G. "Some Reflections on the Interface between Psychiatry and Anthropology." In I. Galdston, ed., *The Interface between Psychiatry and Anthropology.* New York: Brunner/Mazel, 1971.

115. ———, and FRIED, J. "Some Problems of Transcultural Psychiatry." *International Journal of Social Psychiatry*, 3 (1958), 245–252.

116. WORSLEY, P. *The Trumpet Shall Sound.* London: MacGibbon & Kee, 1957.

117. YAP, P. M. "Mental Diseases Peculiar to Certain Cultures." *Journal of Mental Science*, 97 (1951), 313–327.

118. ———. "The Latah Reaction: Its Pathodynamics and Nosological Position." *Journal of Mental Science*, 98 (1952), 515–564.

119. ———. "Koro: A Culture-Bound Depersonalization Syndrome." *British Journal of Psychiatry*, 3 (1965), 43–50.

120. ———. "The Culture-Bound Reactive Syndrome." In W. Caudill and T. Lin, eds., *Mental Health Research in Asia and the Pacific.* Honolulu: East-West Center Press, 1969. Pp. 33–53.

121. ZAGUIRRE, J. C. "Amuck." *Journal of the Philippine Federation of Private Medical Practitioners*, 6 (1957), 1138–1149.

CHAPTER 36

CROSS-CULTURAL STUDIES OF MENTAL DISORDER

An Anthropological Perspective

George A. DeVos

⟪ Areas of Cross-Cultural Work Related to the Concept of Mental Illness

ONE OF THE CENTRAL TASKS of comparative studies in transcultural psychiatry is to examine the various manifestations of so-called mental ill health in various cultures and the provisions therein for dealing with them. The cross-cultural investigation of mental health, therefore, raises a number of questions that have been dealt with only imperfectly by the studies done to date in cross-cultural work.

1. Does the concept of mental health inescapably involve culturally biased value judgments, or are there possible valid generalizations that can be made about faulty physiology or socialization that tend to produce similar distress systems definable as mental illness, irrespective of culture? Are these cross-culturally identified forms of mental or emotional disturbance generally recognized as such by the members of the culture?

2. Are the syndromes generally recognizable by the psychiatric profession of an invariant nature? What is essential or universal, and what is culturally specific in diagnosis of symptoms?

3. Are there any truly culturally specific forms of mental and emotional aberration?

4. How do different cultures define and treat mental illness? What is the relative efficacy of the respective forms of treatment? How does cultural expectation

color or determine the behavior of the mentally ill?

5. Are there true differential incidences of internal maladjustment or social maladaptation related to cultural differences?

6. There are questions related to comparative epidemiological differences and mental disorder, problems in the modern age derived from the rapidity of social change and mobility between groups of various culture backgrounds. What are the effects of geographic and social mobility or acculturation or change of cultures on mental health and emotional well-being?

7. We have not completely resolved issues concerning the relationship of various less psychiatrically defined forms of social deviancy to mental health. How, for example, do such phenomena as the use of drugs, forms of crimes or delinquency, situations leading to murder and suicide vary within specific cultures? To what extent are they due to environmental situations and to what extent do they result from structural personality variables leading to selective vulnerability?

The limited scope of this chapter does not permit exhaustive reporting of pertinent literature. What can be done, however, is to illustrate these topics by example and cite some sources for more detailed reading in the subjects considered.

⟮ Cross-Cultural Recognizability of Psychiatric Problems

There has been considerable controversy about whether severe mental illness is recognizable cross-culturally and whether, for example, individuals who are schizophrenic in Western culture are classified as "crazy" in most cultures. This issue is compounded with the fact that there does indeed seem to be some culturally specific role-playing behavior expected of individuals with severe mental pathology. The structural defect, therefore,

may be disguised or distorted perceptually in terms of patterned behavior induced in given cultures. For example, Weinstein and Schulterbrandt,[66] on the basis of research in the French Antilles, concluded that delusions function not as an escape from reality but, to the contrary, as a faulty adaptive attempt at maintaining feelings of reality and identity. Thus, to the degree that such an attempt is made, the delusional symbol chosen will be related to the cultures' preferred channels of social relatedness.

In some cultures, the psychotic is expected to be dangerous and excitable. One may suppose that with such an expectation there will be a higher incidence of aggressive behavior in one culture as compared with another, induced by defensive aggressiveness in dealing with an emotionally or mentally aberrant individual. It is my own subjective impression that hospitalized Japanese psychotics observed in the early 1950s, at a time prior to the introduction of tranquilizing drugs, were less aggressive compared with American psychotics. Fewer restraints were used in Japan as compared with the United States. The care and nurturing extended by attendants was more intensive compared to custodial treatment afforded by United States hospitals. Similarly, Benedict and Jacks[7] and also Marinko[49] reported less aggressive behavior for African schizophrenia.

To date, the anthropological evidence points up great divergencies in the labeling process of deviant behavior, including psychosis. Even in such contiguous areas as the highlands of New Guinea, one finds contrasting reports of the recognizability of what would be to us obvious psychosis.[40] In Edgerton's empirical work in the four East African tribes he examined, he found the general capacity to give fairly accurate descriptions of behavior said to characterize a psychotic person. These definitions of psychotic behavior were widely known even by those who had never witnessed them. In effect, there was a known pattern of expectations of psychotic behavior in which individuals could be readily placed. The less severe the mental or emotional problems, the more varied the pattern of recognition cross-culturally and the more varied the explanations for them. Edgerton,[21] in his conclusions after a general examination of the literature related to this problem, suggested that the recognition of mental illness cross-culturally is a social process that involves moral and jural considerations. Considering an individual as a mental problem in every society studied involves placing the individual in a status that carries with it some alteration of rights and responsibilities. It follows from this that the recognition process for most cultures is not primarily a problem of a medical diagnosis. As he pointed out, defining someone as "crazy" takes the form of a social negotiation involving not only the person afflicted but in some instances his family and lineage. This is so without denying the real disturbances in thought, affect, and conduct that require some form of psychiatric management, however it is defined. In given cultures, the diagnosis of mental illness has the effect of lowering the marriageability of members of a given family. Therefore, the definition of aberrant behavior is more likely to be put in supernatural terms that do not carry the stigma of hereditary taints rather than being put in medical diagnostic terms, which, for this culture, imply a family lineage with defective genes. It goes without saying that for many cultures including Western culture into the nineteenth century, the concept of possession by an outside force is one of the most generally held explanations for psychotic behavior.

⟨ Cross-Cultural Comparisons of the Essential Constituents of Psychiatric Diagnosis

A related problem to the recognizability of psychiatric symptoms cross-culturally is the question whether manifest symptoms of a given broad clinical diagnosis such as depression or one or another of the designated behaviors considered collectively under the rubric of schizophrenia are indeed invariant syndromes. It may well be that some charac-

teristics considered essential relate more to the cultural setting than to the structure of the given disturbance itself. Murphy, Wittkower, and Chance[53] made a comparative study of the syndrome of depression. They examined reports submitted by sixty psychiatrists from thirty different Western and non-Western cultures. They found certain elements almost invariably associated with what is diagnosed as depression. However, some symptoms usually considered to be related to depression in Western Christian cultures, namely, thought retardation, guilt, and self-depreciation, prove to be absent in some other settings. Murphy suggested that the essential psychiatric essence of depression does take on particular local cultural features. Differences can even occur within Western settings. Note, for example, variation in the nature of depression reported by Grinker[26] for Midwestern United States and Hamilton[30] for England.

Similarly, Murphy, Wittkower, Fried, and Ellenberger[54] stressed the pervasive presence of social and emotional withdrawal, flatness of affect, auditory hallucinations, and general delusions suggesting that the essential diagnosis of schizophrenia involves some general libidinal withdrawal of a very severe and regressive nature and a concomitant rupturing of the ego's capacity to differentiate internal processes from external stimuli. But manifestations that are considered symptomatic of schizophrenia are also markedly different, depending on the culture. For example, Wittkower and Rin[69] found that so-called catatonic rigidity, negativism, and stereotypical behavior are reported more commonly in India than in the other countries surveyed. Bazzoui and Al-Issa[5] found that schizophrenia patients in Iraq and Italy appear to show more expressive and aggressive traits than such patients in the United States.

Such surveys today indicate universality in the structural defects in psychological organization, even though final definitive word as to the exact nature of schizophrenic withdrawal is not yet in. Cross-cultural examination, however, is helpful in moving toward the solution of this still puzzling psychiatric problem.

⟨ Are There Culturally Unique Psychiatric Symptoms?

The psychiatric use of anthropological material started at a time when members of the Western European cultural tradition had an implicit faith in the fact that they were the end product of an evolutionary sequence. The maturational potentials of Western man were considered superior to those of members of more primitive cultures. Hence, compared with Europeans, members of so-called primitive cultures were expected to exhibit biologically more primitive evolutionary capacities as far as mental functioning was concerned. It was presumed, therefore, that one could successfully find normative examples of thought in primitives that survived only as aberrations or as forms of psychopathology among modern humans.

More recently, among the anthropologists there is an assumption that culturally unique patterns are to be found in mental illness since medical diagnoses of Western psychiatry are totally culture bound. Therefore, one would expect that socialization elsewhere would produce unique patterns related to unique features in psychosexual developmental experience. Those starting from either the premise of racial inferiority or of cultural relativity have therefore scrutinized the anthropological literature to find examples of aberrations uniquely limited to particular non-Western cultures.

A totally different point of view starts from assumptions emphasizing the universality of the psychic apparatus and the universality of given developmental sequences in psychosexual development. From this point of view, seemingly unique forms of mental aberration are merely interpreted as variations in the cultural content of overt behavior, rather than as the manifestations of truly unique differences in underlying maladjustive psychological structures.

Of those in transcultural psychiatry attending to what has been termed culture-bound reactive syndromes, P. M. Yap[73] has done the most systematic and detailed examination of the literature.

Among the most noteworthy of the culture-specific forms appearing in the anthropological literature is the phenomenon known as *amok*. *Amok*, as it appears in the Malayan and Philippine groups, has been well described by Beaglehole.[6] It starts with a characteristic depression. The depression deepens, and the person withdraws, going into some type of disassociated trance-like condition wherein his energies are mobilized. He then rushes into some form of violent attack. It is reported that others cannot restrain him, and he very usually is put to death as a final resort. These happenings are reported over and over in surveys of culturally peculiar behavior, yet the actual evidence of reported incidence of such behavior is limited to two or three authors. A graduate student, James Russell, who spent two years in Southeast Asia, carefully reviewed the published reports and reported incidence of *amok* and concluded that almost no actual reports of killing individuals who go berserk are to be found in recent years. Also, publications on *amok* are a spiral of secondary references based on very little eyewitness material. It may well be that *amok* occurs but rarely, perhaps no more frequently than similar behaviors in distraught individuals in other cultures, yet in the Malayan culture area there is a mythology about *amok* that may make it seem to be a more frequent occurrence than it actually is.

More recently there have appeared descriptions of a related type of berserk behavior called "wildman behavior," occurring in the New Guinea highlands.[56] Newman was able to give us some indication of the cultural and personal stresses occurring prior to its outbreak. It seems to have instrumental as well as expressive purposes. From an expressive standpoint, the individuals who become afflicted are usually under some kind of internalized strain to achieve a status of which they are incapable. They also have need to act out certain aggressive urges or unconscious attitudes. Instrumentally, by manifesting wildman behavior one alters status in such a way that the social expectations change. One gains the distinct impression from Newman's description and interpretations that it is a kind of disassociated phenomenon permitting affective display similar to what one finds in various forms of spirit possession such as what occurs in voodoo.[49],[50]

Usually possession phenomena, such as in voodoo or in trance, are not defined as pathological but simply as a part of religious ceremony and expected social behavior without any connotation of deviancy attached. The comportment of individuals under possession is culturally expected and sanctioned. In other cultures, possession is culturally defined as pathological and hence an illness. This is true for such behavior as *latah*, described by Van Loon,[64] and *imu*, described for the Ainu of Hokkaido by Wielawski and Winiarz.[68] In these disturbances, one finds such symptoms as echopraxia and echolalia, where the afflicted person, usually a woman, helplessly imitates what another person says or does. The onset is often caused by some traumatic fright related to fear of spiders, snakes, or even the names of such animals. Individuals in this state very often use obscene words or frank sexual gestures. Aberle[2] saw *latah* as a dissociated state that, from the standpoint of its social functions, is produced in individuals who have disturbance of ambivalence with respect to submissive behavior. Submission symbolically implies passive sexual experience related symbolically to being attacked. The individual fears being overwhelmed but at the same time is sexually attracted. Almost invariably, it occurs in individuals of submerged or subservient social position. This type of behavior is found in Japan, related to what is described as "fox possession" in many rural areas, or sometimes possession by other animals such as dogs.

Though the content is different, Lee[42] described the type of dissociative behavior occurring among the Bantu of South Africa. Women suffer a type of malady called *ufufuyana*. They have nightmares about the *tokoloche*, who is described usually as a bearded dwarf with a large phallus who assaults women at night. There are pains in the lower abdomen, sometimes with accompanying paralysis, and seizures with the appearance of incoherent talk seemingly in a strange language. Ambivalence about sexual interest is very obvious from the stated symptoms. Another related illness reported in literature is that of so-called Arctic hysteria or *pibloktoq*.[27] There is loss of consciousness, the individual is amnesic after the occurrence, behavior is uninhibited, the individual tears off his clothes, he wanders off, some are reported to eat feces. Also the individual seems capable of feats of strength beyond his ordinary capacities. In all these reports one has to distinguish between the social functions and the cultural definitions of dissociated behavior. First, as Newman[56] indicated, there are functional resolutions of personal impasses in what is culturally perceived as aberrant behavior. The same resolutions may occur in another culture by means of possession states that are considered normal within the culture. The social functions, or cultural definitions as well as the specific cultural content of behavior, whether it be *amok*, wildman behavior, *latah*, or possession and trance, must not be used to forego psychiatric or psychological considerations of the actual similarity in the use of mental mechanisms related to dissociation that may well be common to all these seemingly disparate activities. Nevertheless, the social psychiatrist must become aware of cultural patterns to the extent of understanding how particular internal stress is derivative of given cultural expectations.

Other illnesses of a nondissociative nature are sporadically reported. There are, for example, what might be called malignant anxiety situations in the *susto* reported in the Andean highlands. One finds symptoms of depression and anxiety following severe fright or shock. Interpretation given is that somehow there has been a loss of the soul. Such malignant anxiety often is found in places where there is a strong belief in malevolent witchcraft. Such belief is reported widespread in the anthropological literature of Africa, for example. The most severe form of this belief in sorcery is that of the Australian aborigines where deaths have been reported of individuals who have learned that sorcery has been worked on them.[9,11] Specific to Chinese culture is the appearance of extreme forms of fear related to the delusion that the penis is shrinking and may disappear into the body. This state, known as *koro*, flared up most recently in Singapore after a rumor of radioactive fish spread through the Chinese community there.

Yap[70-72] attempted to classify these various forms under a general syndrome of reactive psychoses, psychogenic reaction. Various forms of disordered consciousness have subcategories, primary fear reactions, morbid rage reactions, culture-specific phobia. The various forms of possession states are considered dissociated reactions. Yap's terminology "reactive psychosis" has much to recommend it, but might be misleading if we think of psychosis as related only to disruptions of early ego formation. Two features stand out in these various diseases despite some of the similarities in content. (1) There are dissociated states in which the person is in an altered state of consciousness. The person is out of his mind literally but in a manner that suggests the repressive mechanism of hysteria rather than the breakdown of ego boundaries characteristic for more severe forms of energy withdrawal found in schizophrenia. The terminology "hysterical psychosis" is, along with Freud's original use of the term "psychosis," used to indicate a condition whereby the ego is overwhelmed by instinctual forces. However, the chief mechanism of defense is repression rather than severe forms of projection or introjection with partial rupturing of ego boundaries as found in what is usually classified as psychosis and schizophrenia. (2) Some cultural forms are related to extreme states of panic or anxiety owing to given belief within the culture, either that the person has been condemned to death by sorcery or that he has lost his soul or that his penis will shrink inside his body. These beliefs are specific to given cultures, but an afflicted individual who defines himself as having become a victim of a

given condition feels a degree of panic leading to physiological as well as mental disorganization. The relationship of the former cases to possession is evident because in each instance ego dissociation occurs. The person is literally not himself when in the afflicted state or in the trance state. This is equally true for the rage situation of *amok* or wildman behavior or the hysterical response reaction to the use of a forbidden or anxiety-provoking term, which sends the individual into the dissociated state.

As will be discussed briefly in the conclusions, one can distinguish between social adaptation and internal adjustment in viewing any given human behavior. On the one hand, one can see some seeming aberrant behavior or expressed experience functionally related to social adaptation in some instances. For example, trance dissociation can be seen as nonpathological and, in effect, a socially desirable state in some instances. In other instances, uncontrolled behavior cannot be adaptively harnessed to social purpose in such a way as to give it a positive meaning, but is defined by the group itself as maladaptive and pathological. Seen on the other hand from an internal adjustment standpoint of psychiatry, the fact that the individual characteristically uses mechanisms such as repression gives some underlying unity to these various behavioral maneuvers whether they are in the context of socially sanctioned possession behavior or are called into play by individuals of low status who are in need of some excuse of the expression of pent-up feelings related to sex or aggression. Similarly, mechanisms of repression can be used to ward off ungovernable anxieties produced by a cultural belief.

⟮ The Epidemiology of Mental Disorder

Surveys attest to the differential appearance of mental disorders cross-culturally. The best approach to why these differences appear is to assess the various ways that culture can influence mental health. Leighton and Hughes[45] produced one of the best all-around compendiums of the impact of culture on mental disorder. They used, as a basis for their concept of culture, Hallowell's idea of shared psychological realities of patterns and emotions to describe what it is they mean by culture when they are talking about culture as causative of mental disorder. They discussed a large number of culture-specific disorders, already mentioned. They then discussed a series of propositions about the effect of culture on mental health.

1. Culture may pattern disorders.
2. Culture may produce personality types especially vulnerable to certain kinds of disorders.
3. Some cultures may be thought to produce a higher incidence of given psychiatric disorders through certain child-rearing practices.
4. Cultures may be thought to effect psychiatric disorders through types of sanctions and strictures on acceptable behavior.
5. Culture may perpetuate malfunctioning by rewarding it in certain prestigeful roles. (They quote Devereux[16] and Kroeber and Kluckhohn[38] here.)
6. Culture may be thought to produce psychiatric disorders differentially in given segments of the population through certain stressful roles. (They quote Linton[47] here.)
7. Culture may be thought to produce psychiatric disorders through the indoctrination of its members with a particular kind of sentiment. (They quote Leighton.[44])
8. Complexity of culture may, per se, be thought to produce psychiatric disorders, as voiced by Sigmund Freud in *Civilization and Its Discontents*.[22]
9. Culture affects breeding patterns selectively. (Laubscher[41] discussed Bantu cross-cousin marriage and the incidence of schizophrenia.)
10. Culture, through patterns of faulty hygiene, can produce toxic and nutritive deficiencies influencing mental functioning.[65]

(Culture Change and Mental Health

One may illustrate questions of stress related to change and acculturation by examining some recent specific research on the influence of urbanization cross-culturally.[18]

Abstract conceptualizations in regard to the stress of migration need to be tested in concrete detail in given settings, in given cultures, ranging from ancient civilizations to small isolated, so-called primitive groups who in previous ages were relatively cut off from external contact. Social psychiatry can interest itself in the human response to change, the patterns of adjustment and adaptation that occur given the various forms the stimulus of change takes. A specific issue subsumed under macro issues involved in the effects of industrialization generally is the question: Does urbanization per se cause stress on immigrants to a city?

There is already in American sociological and psychological literature considerable reference to the assumed psychological stress occurring during migration into the city on the part of rural populations. In the United States, recent large-scale epidemiological studies have produced conflicting results. For example, Malzberg and Lee,[48] doing a study of the difference between New-York-born black and white populations in New York compared with rural or foreign-born populations found a much higher incidence of mental illness in recently arrived foreign or minority group immigrants compared with those of similar origin growing up within the city. Ødegaard,[57] on the contrary, in doing an extensive study of mental illness for the whole of Norway, has found a higher incidence of mental illness in Norwegians who do not move into the city. What does anthropological research reveal is the case in different societies where urbanization within given cultures can be separated out from acculturation compounded by urban migration? I shall quote from a series of papers appearing in a recent symposium dealing with this subject as well as others examining responses to change.[18] Alex Inkeles[33] did a direct examination of the fate of personal adjustment in six different cultures. He cited empirical material that suggests that rather than leading to problems of stress, urbanization seems to be correlated with better mental health as measured by the medical-psychiatric indices used in his research. Increased education, rather than leading to less social cohesiveness as has been claimed by some, has a fairly consistent significant positive effect on adjustment as far as test measurements of psychosomatic symptoms indicate. Even exposure to mass media seems to operate integratively rather than causing internal disruption of any sort.

Employment and such occupations as factory worker, according to Inkeles's results, are not conducive to psychosomatic complaints in any of the cultures sampled.

Inkeles summarized his cross-cultural report by saying that whatever may cause psychosomatic symptoms in young men in developing countries, it is something other than exposure to modernizing institutions, such as school, factory, city life, and mass media. The act of migration itself within his sample is not related to the greater symptomatic appearance of problems. One of the principal difficulties with theories of urban transition as stressful is not due so much to an incorrect view of city life as to a mistaken and romanticized image of what village, rural, or tribal life is typically like. Inkeles opposed the view that the daily life of traditional villages in most cultures was inherently healthier than almost anything village residents might encounter in urban industrial settings. There is too ready an idealization of the economic security enjoyed, or the cooperation and affiliative nature of village interaction and the availability of emotional support in times of personal need or crisis. Any objective evaluation of the internal structures of village life in any of a number of cultures would attest to the relative infrequency of such idealized situations.

Similarly, Ernestine Friedl,[24] on the basis of intensive research in Greece, found that much of the suppositions about stress in the

city are due to a priori assumptions about theoretical polarities placing the village and the city in opposition to each other. In summarizing the literature, she indicated such ideal typical constructions are a Procrustean bed and hence poorly suited as conceptual tools for dealing with real situations. The polarized traits supposedly operative are invalid because they simply do not appear in an actual living context, such as rural and urban Greece. Such classification is too vague and imprecise to be used for comparative empirical studies. In sum, Friedl raised serious questions as to the acceptability for actual anthropological research of the often cited folk-urban, Gemeinschaft-Gesellschaft, particularistic-universalistic, and traditional-modern dichotomies. Friedl's research method demonstrates a more observational anthropological approach, in contrast to the survey approach taken in six cultures by Inkeles. Nevertheless the conclusions are similar.

Edward Bruner,[8] studying modernization of the Batak of Sumatra, made a cogent critique of some of the assumptions in the psychiatric literature about the relationship of rapid social change to stress. Bruner's interpretation of the anthropological data forwarded both by psychiatrists and anthropologists found evidence both of examples of internal conflict being produced by rapid change and other situations where no such manifestation of symptomatology of stress is reported. A central issue, therefore, is to separate out the variables, differentiating out those situations of change that induce conflict from those situations that do not.

Any further resolution to the questions raised depends on intensive investigation rather than simple correlational analysis. One possibility in resolving differences of results would be to attempt some generalization to the effect that rates of mental disorder may be a function of how successful the host culture is in providing ways of handling the stress aroused. The research problem, then, according to Bruner, would be one of investigating intensively the culturally provided solutions to stress. Mental illness simply becomes one alternative response to an attempted resolution of aroused stress. Second, the concept of stress itself must be examined in cultural context through the actual perceptions of the individuals involved rather than on an a priori basis derived from a Western perspective.

Bruner[8] offered his case study of the Batak of Sumatra as an illustration of a quite successful resolution of the possible stresses inherent in modernization. In Bruner's explanation of why the Batak have adapted themselves with facility, he indicated that it is a flexibility in role making rather than simply role taking. The Batak headmen who regulate the *adat*, or law, do not perceive the outsider's categories of traditional and modern, for example. Seen through the subjective experience of the Batak themselves, one finds that a Batak headman is flexibly adapting his behavior to changing situations and that the actors in his culture are in this sense, creative agents interpreting the changing world in which they live and testing their interpretations by the feedback they gain from their behavior. If there is flexibility and adaptability in the agents, because of such capacities in their adjustive mechanisms, then adaptation to modernization may go on with considerable facility and a minimal experience of stress.

What Bruner pointed out for the Batak is a sense of implicit confidence in their law. Their family and kinship networks remain intact and their belief system is modified without any sense of disruption. On the basis of Rorschach and thematic apperception test protocols gathered from both urban and rural Batak, Bruner found no evidence of differences related to their urban adaptation and internal adjustment. This contrasts heavily with Bruner's previous experience among American Indians, where renunciation of Indian identity seems to be necessary in order to take on change. Bruner pointed out that there is a choice necessary in the case of American Indians and American Negroes. There is an inherent opposition between being Indian and being white. A person has to make a choice; he cannot be both at the same time. But a Batak, in contrast, does not have to renounce his own social group or personal identity in order to urbanize because there is no felt opposition between being Batak and becoming a modern Indonesian.

Bruner was well aware that he was challenging some of the favorite tenets of Western sociologists, including that of Marx, which regard, as Bruner put it, "Religion or ideology as the frosting on the cake of economic reality and political power." For Bruner, it is precisely the belief that the *adat*, the *nomia* of the group, is unchanged that allows for such successful relative modernization and urbanization without anomie on the part of the Toba-Batak of Sumatra.

Takao Sofue[63] examined some of the new stresses faced by those left behind in village life as rapid urbanization continues in Japan. With the considerable population movement into the industrial economy of modern Japan, those left in agriculture are facing serious readjustments, both internally and socially necessitated by a progressively devitalized rural life style. There are a number of dilemmas occurring specific to particular rural positions within the primary family.

In sum, three basic points are touched on in these studies.

1. Urbanization does not of itself imply disruptive modernization.
2. There is difference in the psychocultural effects of urbanization in situations where those moving to the city move into cities that are part of their own culture as opposed to situations of immigration into a different culture.
3. Mental health in migratory situations is undoubtedly related to the degree of discrimination or receptivity of the migrant within the new setting. The American migratory pattern differs greatly from other migratory situations and cannot be used to generalize about the stress nature of migration and its adverse effects on mental health.

H. B. Murphy[52] suggested that mental illness and physical illness are not clearly correlated with mobility, since in some places immigrants have lower hospitalization rates, but do seem to be related to the size and coherence of the immigrant group. He suggested that the degree to which the immigrant is encouraged to individuate himself may help and hinder him, its penalties being higher hospitalization rates.

Marc Fried[23] suggested that forced relocations, in urban areas, for example, disrupt working-class communities and that this disruption results in very real grief. The way that people adjust to this disruption is in a sense the way they adjust to forced mobility,[23, p. 139] "the higher the status the larger the proportion who have been able to cope successfully with the social changes implicit in relocation." Thus, in a sense, people who were already making it best in the terms of the mobile society are those people who have the highest amount of status to fall back on. These people adjust best to the changed situation.

Various other studies, including some epidemiological surveys, indicated that the number of social maladaptations (as well as what seem to be overt manifestations of internal maladjustment) is differentially related to ethnic group membership as well as to patterns of social and geographical mobility. Some forms of stress seem to be related to cultural change as well as to minority status. Particular cultural patterns tend to induce types of manifest breakdown in individuals, given situations of change, in spite of the fact that evidence could not be found that these tendencies toward social maladaptation are in any way related to particular stresses during the early formative periods in socialization. Such problems are not limited to situations of extreme change, such as those occurring when there is contact between nonliterate and technologically advanced cultures. They may occur with migratory shifts of people from rural to urban settings.

For example, in a Rorschach study of acculturated and nonacculturated Algerian Arabs, Miner and DeVos[51] reported increased signs of intrapsychic stress in the content symbolism of a sample living in a minority status position in the city of Algiers prior to the Algerian revolution. An increase in anatomical and sado-masochistic content was also evident in records of Chinese-Americans reported by Abel and Hsu[1] and in Goldfarb's sample of American Negroes.[25] DeVos[17] discussed the implications of these findings (true also for Japanese-Americans) for some concept of chronic stress in situations of minority status.

Abrahams[3] discussed the effect of the matrifocal family structure among American blacks. The matrifocal family structure had its roots in slavery and is reinforced by the present difficulty of black males in finding work. Such economic difficulties tend to lead to frequent acts of desertion by the father and to consequent continued reinforcement of woman-dominated family patterns, with growing boys facing psychological problems concerning male identity.

(Ethnopsychiatric Healing Practices

It has been noted that in curing aberrant mental states ethnopsychiatric techniques are often at least as successful as, if not more successful than, Western ones. Hughes[32] gave a fairly general cross-cultural survey of healing practices, both physical and mental, and pointed out that the problems presented by public health, including mental health, within particular cultures are intimately related to the functioning of the social system.

The techniques used in therapy in various cultures seem to bear some relation to child-rearing practices. Kiev[35] and Whiting and Child[67] noted that magical medical beliefs are more often accepted for their compatibility with personality variables than for their actual physiological utility. A variety of authors have discussed the importance of faith in primitive psychotherapy and the many similarities between the techniques of primitive societies and those of modern societies. Hallowell[28] discussed the wide range of mental illness treated by Apache shamans; A. H. and D. C. Leighton,[46] the Navaho use of cultural values to help integrate the ill back into the world of the well; and Devereux,[14,15] detailed and incisive studies on the Mohave.

The volume edited by Ari Kiev, *Magic, Faith and Healing*,[36] brought together a number of thoughtful papers covering the fact that therapy of functional disorders is most efficacious with the symbolic representations and beliefs of the individuals treated. All psychiatry of functional disorders, including modern Western psychiatry, is therefore to some degree at least folk psychiatry. Of particular interest in this volume is La Barre's[39] article on the therapeutic effect of confession as a social therapy in given American Indian tribes. It is, in effect, both internally adjustive and socially adaptive to the individual, reintegrating him into the society. Jane Murphy[55] cited the psychotherapeutic aspects of shamanism in Eskimos. Prince[58] gave a cogent description of the nature of indigenous Yoruba psychiatry in Nigeria. Bert Kaplan and Dale Johnson[34] related peculiar native Navaho symptoms to their social adaptive and maladaptive meaning. They reported that the most prevalent form of Navaho psychopathology is what is termed "crazy violence" or "crazy drunken violence." The Navaho simply have no specific term but call it going crazy or being drunk. It is seen more often as a natural consequence of drunkenness rather than something that would be classified as mental illness, and as such is often dismissed as typical Indian drunkenness. These symptoms are so regular and recurrent among the Navaho that there can be little doubt that it has special significance. The individual, however, seems to use drinking in order to get into an altered state of consciousness wherein he can express behavior that otherwise would be unconscionable to him. Some of this so-called drunken behavior results in the murdering of family members and suicide on the part of the individual. When he is going crazy he does not care what he is doing; he goes wild. Kaplan and Johnson pointed out that this behavior differs somewhat from the usual hysterical situation in that the person knows he is acting crazy but does not care and aligns himself, in effect, with his worst side. In hysteria, on the other hand, the victim refuses to acknowledge his illness as his own, attributing his behavior to whatever has invaded him. In the crazy violence of the Navaho there is seemingly a heroic element of being willing to take the consequences of one's behavior. The individual avoids no pain, suffering, or trouble but has a reckless willingness to die and to be hurt. Psychodynamic interpretation would see this as a direct discharge into action of warded off instinctual impulses and inner tensions absent of ego control. The point is ultimately, when one reads the description of the psychopathology by Kaplan and Johnson, that it is not unique to the Navaho but is simply culturally institutionalized and a relatively frequent occurrence. This is the issue, not that we are discovering some unique mechanisms that work for the Navaho and are not to be found elsewhere.

The effectiveness of Navaho curing ceremonies appears to be based on two points. There is the elaborate procedure of purification itself, which convinces the patient and the community that the bad stuff is vanquished and can no longer cause trouble. The second point is that the concern and goodwill of the group is focused on the individual in the sense that he receives the "good vibrations" of his group and receives a moral boost that makes him motivated to feel better inside. In other words, the individual, the total mobilization of the community, and the procedure itself have a powerful force on the individual, suggesting to him that he can be and in effect is being cured.

⟨ Relationship of Socially Deviant Behavior to the Concept of Mental Health

Despite the increasing availability of cross-cultural evidence, there are a number of issues on the borderline of what are legitimately considered psychiatric problems, such as crises of adolescence, forms and patterns of sexual deviation, delinquency and crime, suicide, and social problems as related to the use of drugs.

For example, the forms taken by crime or delinquency in cultures or situations leading to murder and suicide are variously defined in different cultures, but from a social psychiatric standpoint may have common etiological features. There are highly divergent viewpoints among social scientists as to how much the appearance of such phenomena is owing to environmental induction and problems of adaptation versus how much to structural personality variables leading to a selective vulnerability toward deviant behavior in given individuals.

American, and more recently, European societies are perhaps unique in the degree to which various forms of deviant behavior are identified as indicative of internal maladjustments rather than maladaptations. In a survey[20] of the uses of psychological tests and writings of psychologists concerning delinquency compared with sociologists, one gains a general impression that psychologists are more prone to deal with middle-class samples of the population[4] and sociologists are more apt to deal with lower-class youth.[59,61] Questions of social maladaptation are more prepotent as determinants operative in lower-class youth, although maladjustive defenses are also apparent in some cases. In contrast, middle-class delinquents show more evidence of possessing neurotic maladjustments about aggression than do lower-class youth.

There is no question that the social adaptations of homosexuals differ from society to society. For example, Japanese and American cultural attitudes are highly divergent.[19] A systematic cross-cultural study of similarity or differences in underlying adjustment patterns in homosexuals awaits to be done.

Chafetz[12] noted that, cross-culturally, drinking and alcoholism are not the same. Alcoholism is a function of the cultural attitude toward the use of alcohol and the degree of social stress to which the drinker is subject. The use of alcohol by Indians (introduced by white contact throughout the Americas) has, almost from the beginning, been described by white observers as culturally and individually destructive both in North and South America. In such countries as Mexico and Peru, drinking continues to be recognized as a major social problem. For example, Simmons[62] noted that drinking and drunkenness were, in the Peruvian village he studied, virtually universal. The suppression of aggression remains a key problem in this culture, and alcohol serves to reduce much of the anxiety and strain by releasing aggressive as well as friendly feelings in normally shy and inhibited persons.

Hallowell,[29] Helm, DeVos, and Carterette,[31] and Coult[13] placed more emphasis on the release of aggression than on the release of friendliness. These anthropologists, among others analyzing the adjustive and adaptive use made of alcohol among Indians, pointed out that it fulfills a release function in respect to aggression for many Indian groups who are overcontrolled in daily face-to-face relationships.

⟦ Conclusions: The Distinction between Inner Adjustment and Cultural or Social Adaptation

The various issues and problems related to an understanding of the interpretation of culture and mental disorder discussed above are far from being resolved. It is the major contention of this chapter that a clear self-conscious distinction between adaptation and adjustment would help greatly in orienting further research. Moreover, the anthropologist and the sociologist, both theoretically and methodologically, must give greater respect to the realities of inner adjustment patterns as continuing integrative structures of personality and, as such, as being highly determinant of motivated human behavior. Given such respect, there should result more adequate contributions from anthropology and sociology to answering questions of issues to transcultural or social psychiatry.

For the most part, in the literature of psychology as well as anthropology and sociology, the concepts of adjustment and adaptation are loosely used in a roughly equivalent manner. They indiscriminately refer both to the internal structures we subsume under the concept of personality and, in many instances, to mutually adaptive processes of human communication and interaction that occur in social role relationships. More generally, they are used indiscriminately as concepts referring to man's response to his environment. Converse concepts, maladjustment and maladaptation, can refer to some deficiency or structural lack in a capacity for response in an individual or simply to some form of response itself that is inadequate to the purposes or survival of the individual. The term "adjustment," as used in this chapter, is not culturally and situationally relative; it assumes an ideal progression of maturation that is potential for all human beings, but the realization of which may be culturally fostered or deformed. It is often said today that to be well adjusted in a bad environment itself could be pathological. This is not the proper use of the term "adjustment" in the psychodynamic sense intended here. Indeed a person can be deformed maturationally by his culture in such a way that he adapts well to situations of human brutality. One cannot assume, therefore, that he is internally well adjusted in the psychodynamic sense. While it is possible for an internally well-adjusted person to survive in a bad environment, one presumes, however, that he will attempt to effect external changes in the environment, whereas a person who is maladjusted will not be so well equipped to bring about desired ameliorative change. To put it the other way is to define adjustment only in terms of adaptation rather than maturational potential. It is most helpful, therefore, to theoretically maintain a clear distinction between internal structuring of personality related to the concept of adjustment and social behavioral responses that can be seen as adaptive or maladaptive for the individual within his culture.

This distinction has been elaborately elucidated by Clyde Kluckhohn in his publication on Navaho witchcraft.[37] Kluckhohn, in a detailed study of the social and psychological functions of witchcraft beliefs and practices, kept this essential distinction. Adaptation, for him, was defined as the relationships of individuals within society. For example, witchcraft was functionally adaptive in deflecting aggressive feelings out of the group onto more distant outsiders. Internally, for the individual, Kluckhohn considered witchcraft beliefs to be adjustive in that they acted as an outlet for affective states that otherwise would be disruptive to psychological functioning. Witchcraft functions could be seen in some other contexts as relatively maladaptive to the social group, or as evidence of relative maladjustment in one person compared with another who had less need to have recourse to witchcraft but could handle his relationships more directly. In this latter sense, adjustive functions are to be viewed in the context of personality organization or personality structure.

The relationship between adaptation and adjustment can be, indeed, complex, whether examining behavior of one individual from two points of view or similar behavior of different individuals in different contexts. Theodore Schwartz[60] has introduced the innovative concept of pathomimetic behavior to explain the seeming appearance of maladjustive behavior as part of religious ceremony in some cultures. There can be socially adaptive forms of behavior that, for purposes of strengthening religious belief for the individual as well as in the group, mimic, either consciously or unconsciously, forms of behavior that usually are indicative of maladjustment of organic pathology. For example, a shaman may indicate behaviorally that he is possessed by a deity by exhibiting seizure phenomena of a type observed to occur in epileptics. In native medicine, epileptic seizure, a frightening form of behavior to behold, is usually explained as the intrusion of an alien force, often a deity, into the body. To indicate that he is possessed, therefore, the person manifests a seizure. In the case of the epileptic, the behavior is maladjustive in the personality structure sense. In the shaman, whatever his state of consciousness or self-hypnosis, the behavior becomes socially adaptive as symbolic of religious ecstasy. In pathomimetic phenomena, the possessed individual has somehow learned to manifest convulsions as a sign that a spirit has entered his body so that communication becomes possible with the supernatural. His manifest behavior may therefore simply be adaptive rather than maladjustive either in structure or function.

If we relate these distinctions between adaptation and adjustment directly to the field of psychiatry, one notes that the traditional problems in psychiatry have been to distinguish between structure and function in respect to organic adjustment problems versus functional adjustment problems. In social psychiatry, or transcultural psychiatry, however, a new dichotomy appears. The distinction must now be made as to whether or not relatively debilitating or painful personal adjustments or maladjustments are socially adaptive or not within a given cultural context.

Psychiatrists and psychologists, when viewing mental health, are usually concerned specifically with psychological adjustive mechanisms viewed within Western culture, and to this extent they can without care slip into ethnocentric value judgments that govern the diagnosis and treatment of what they perceive to be psychiatric illness. Anthropologists in turn are focused on patterns of social adaptation, that is, whether the individual remains, or how he remains, or how he was brought into, or excluded from, social participation. Caudill[10] suggested that comprehension of the working relationship between anthropology and psychology requires today, for the psychiatrist as well as others, some understanding of the concept of culture as a key concept, just as it is necessary for anthropologists to better understand personality structure or personality functioning as keys to motivated human behavior. He suggested that we avoid tendencies to reductionism in either group in studying the interrelationship of these systems.

For modern psychiatry, operating both within Western culture and outside, there is the disturbing consideration that knowledge of the causes of malfunctioning by itself may not help in the treatment of problem behavior —unless there is a sharing of beliefs and symbol systems between therapist and patient concerning the efficacy of treatment—to the degree that a malfunctioning is not based on an organic problem. To that degree, treatment is irreducibly symbolic, in the literal sense of the word. What has already been apparent to some social or transcultural psychiatrists in ex-

tending or reinterpreting the causes of mental health or illness is the necessity to clarify or differentiate between those concepts or definitions of behavior prevailing within a given culture and those concepts being imposed externally on the meaning of behavior from a Western psychiatric framework. If no attention is paid to indigenous perceptions of mental illness or to the meaning of its particular forms within a culture, there can be no therapeutic process.[73] Western trained psychologists or psychiatrists, using only traditional descriptive psychiatry or psychoanalytic formulations, can easily alienate themselves from symbolic communication with members of the culture in which they are functioning.

⟮ Bibliography

1. ABEL, T. M., and HSU, F. L. K. "Some Aspects of Personality of Chinese as Revealed by the Rorschach Test." *Rorschach Research Exchange*, 13 (1949), 285–301.

2. ABERLE, D. F. " 'Arctic Hysteria' and Latah in Mongolia." *Transactions of the N.Y. Academy of Science*, 14 (1952), 291–297.

3. ABRAHAMS, R. D. *Deep Down in the Jungle: Negro Narrative Folklore From the Streets of Philadelphia.* Hatboro, Pa.: Folklore Associates, 1964.

4. BANDURA, A., and WALTERS, R. H. *Adolescent Aggression.* New York: Ronald Press, 1959.

5. BAZZOUI, W., and AL-ISSA, I. "Psychiatry in Iraq." *British Journal of Psychiatry*, 112 (1966), 827–832.

6. BEAGLEHOLE, E. "A Note on Cultural Compensation." *Journal of Abnormal Social Psychology*, 33 (1938), 121–123.

7. BENEDICT, P. K., and JACKS, I. "Mental Illness in Primitive Societies." *Psychiatry*, 17 (1954), 377–389.

8. BRUNER, E. "Some Observations on Cultural Change and Psychological Stress in Indonesia." In G. A. DeVos, ed., *Responses to Change: Adjustment and Adaptation in Personality and Culture.* N.d.

9. CANNON, W. B. " 'Voodoo' Death." *American Anthropologist*, 44 (1942), 169–181.

10. CAUDILL, W. "The Relationship of Anthropology to Psychiatry in the Study of Cul-

ture and Personality." *Japanese Journal of Psychoanalysis*, 6 (1959), 468–482.

11. CAWTE, J. E. "Ethnopsychiatry in Central Australia." *British Journal of Psychiatry*, 111 (1965), 1096.

12. CHAFETZ, M. E. "Consumption of Alcohol in the Far and Middle East." *New England Journal of Medicine*, 271 (1964), 297–301.

13. COULT, A. Conflict and Stability in a Hualapai Community. Unpublished doctoral dissertation, University of California.

14. DEVEREUX, G. "Cultural Thought Models in Primitive and Modern Psychiatric Theories." *Psychiatry*, 21 (1958), 359–374.

15. ———. "Mohave Ethnopsychiatry and Suicide: The Psychiatric Knowledge and Psychic Disturbances of an Indian Tribe." *Bureau of American Ethnology*, 175 (1961).

16. ———. "Normal and Abnormal: The Key Problem in Psychiatric Anthropology." In *Some Uses of Anthropology: Theoretical and Applied*. Washington, D.C.: Anthropological Society of Washington, 1956.

17. DEVOS, G. A. "Symbolic Analysis in the Cross-Cultural Studies of Personality." In B. Kaplan, ed., *Studying Personality Cross-Culturally*. Evanston, Ill.: Row, Peterson, 1961.

18. ———, ed. *Responses to Change: Adjustment and Adaptation in Personality and Culture* (Abstracts Symposia, VIIIth International Congress of Anthropological and Ethnological Sciences. Tokyo: Science Council of Japan, 1968.)

19. ———, and MIZUSHIMA, K. "Criminality and Deviancy in Premodern Japan." In G. A. DeVos, *Socialization for Achievement: Essays on the Cultural Psychology of the Japanese*. Berkeley: University of California Press, 1971.

20. ———, and WAGATSUMA, H. "Family Life and Delinquency: Some Perspectives on Japanese Research." In W. Lebra, ed., *Mental Health Research in Asia and the Pacific*. Vol. 2. Honolulu: East-West Center Press, 1971.

21. EDGERTON, R. P., and PLAG, S., eds. *Changing Perspective in Mental Illness*. 1969.

22. FREUD, S. *Civilization and Its Discontents*. New York: Jonathan Cape & Harrison Smith, 1930.

23. FRIED, M. "Transitional Functions of Working Class Communities: Implications for Forced Relocation." In M. B. Kantor, ed., *Mobility and Mental Health*. Springfield, Ill.: Charles C Thomas, 1965.

24. FRIEDL, E. "Migration and Decision Making: A Greek Case." In G. A. DeVos, ed., *Responses to Change: Adjustment and Adaptation in Personality and Culture*. N.d.

25. GOLDFARB, W. "The Rorschach Experiment." In A. Kardiner and L. Ovesey, eds., *The Mark of Oppression*. New York: Norton, 1951.

26. GRINKER, R. R. *The Phenomena of Depression*. New York: Hoeber, 1961.

27. GUSSOW, Z. "Pibloktoq (Hysteria) among the Polar Eskimo." In W. Muensterberger and S. Axelrad, eds., *The Psychoanalytic Study of Society*. New York: International Universities Press, 1960.

28. HALLOWELL, A. I. "Fear and Anxiety as Cultural and Individual Variables in a Primitive Society." *Journal of Social Psychology*, 9 (1938), 25–47.

29. ———. "Aggression in Saulteaux Society." In C. Kluckhohn, H. A. Murray, and D. M. Schneider, eds., *Personality in Nature, Society and Culture*. New York: Knopf, 1953.

30. HAMILTON, M. "A Rating Scale for Depression." *Journal of Neurological Psychiatry*, 23 (1960), 1082–1086.

31. HELM, J., DEVOS, G. A., and CARTERETTE, T. "Variations in Personality and Ego Identification Within a Slave Indian Kin-Community." *Contributions to Anthropology*, bulletin no. 190, pt. 2. National Museum of Canada, 1960.

32. HUGHES, C. C. "Reference Group Concepts in the Study of Changing Eskimo Culture." In V. F. Ray, ed., *Cultural Stability and Cultural Change*. Seattle: American Anthropological Society, 1957. Pp. 7–14.

33. INKELES, A. "The Fate of Personal Adjustment in the Process of Urbanization." In G. A. DeVos, ed., *Responses to Change: Adjustment and Adaptation in Personality and Culture*. N.d.

34. KAPLAN, B., and JOHNSON, D. "The Social Meaning of Navaho Psychopathology." In A. Kiev, ed., *Magic, Faith and Healing*. New York: The Free Press, 1964. Pp. 203–229.

35. KIEV, A. "Primitive Therapy: A Cross-cultural Study of the Relationship Between Child Training and Therapeutic Practices

Related to Illness." In W. Muensterberger and S. Axelrad, eds., *The Psychoanalytic Study of Society.* Vol. 1. New York: International Universities Press, 1960. Pp. 185–217.

36. ———, ed., *Magic, Faith and Healing.* New York: The Free Press, 1964.

37. KLUCKHOHN, C. *Navaho Witchcraft.* Boston: Beacon Press, 1944.

38. KROEBER, A. L., and KLUCKHOHN, C. "Culture: A Critical Review of Concepts and Definitions." *Papers of the Peabody Museum,* 47 (1952), 1.

39. LA BARRE, W. "Confession as Cathartic Therapy in American Indian Tribes." In A. Kiev, ed., *Magic, Faith and Healing.* New York: The Free Press, 1964.

40. LANGNESS, L. L. "Hysterical Psychosis in the New Guinea Highlands: A Bena Bena Example." *Psychiatry,* 28 (1965), 258–277.

41. LAUBSCHER, B. J. F. *Sex, Custom and Psychopathology: A Study of South African Pagan Natives.* London: Routledge, 1951.

42. LEE, S. G. "Some Zulu Concepts of Psychogenic Disorder." *South African Journal of Social Research,* 1 (1950), 9–19.

43. LEIGHTON, A. H. "Mental Illness and Acculturation." In I. Galdston, ed., *Medicine and Anthropology: Lectures to the Laity.* Bulletin no. 21. New York Academy of Medicine, 1959.

44. ———. *My Name Is Legion.* New York: Basic Books, 1959.

45. ———, and HUGHES, J. H. "Cultures as Causative of Mental Disorder." In *Causes of Mental Disorders: A Review of Epidemiological Knowledge.* New York: Milbank Memorial Fund, 1959.

46. ———, and LEIGHTON, D. C. "Elements of Psychotherapy in Navaho Religion." *Psychiatry,* 4 (1941), 513–523.

47. LINTON, R. In G. Devereux, ed., *Culture and Mental Disorders.* Springfield, Ill.: Charles C Thomas, 1956.

48. MALZBERG, B., and LEE, E. S. *Migration and Mental Disease.* New York: Social Science Research Council, 1956.

49. MARINKO, B. "Psychoses in Ethiopia." *Transcultural Psychiatric Research,* 111 (1966), 152–154.

50. METRAUX, A. *Voodoo in Haiti.* New York: Oxford University Press, 1959.

51. MINER, H., and DeVOS, G. A. *Oasis and Casbah: Algerian Culture and Personality in Change.* Anthropological papers, no. 15. Ann Arbor: University of Michigan, 1960.

52. MURPHY, H. B. "Migration in the Major Mental Disorders: A Reappraisal." In M. B. Kantor, ed., *Mobility and Mental Health.* Springfield, Ill.: Charles C Thomas, 1965.

53. ———, WITTKOWER, E. D., and CHANCE, N. A. "Cross-cultural Inquiry into the Symptomatology of Depression." *Transcultural Psychiatric Research,* 1 (1964), 5–8.

54. ———, WITTKOWER, E. D., FRIED, J., and ELLENBERGER, H. "A Cross-cultural Survey of Schizophrenic Symptomatology." *International Journal of Social Psychiatry,* 9 (1963), 237–249.

55. MURPHY, J. M. "Psychotherapeutic Aspects of Shamanism on St. Lawrence Island Alaska." In A. Kiev, ed., *Magic, Faith and Healing.* New York: The Free Press, 1964.

56. NEWMAN, P. L. "Wildman's Behavior in a New Guinea Highlands Community." *American Anthropologist,* 66 (1964), 1–19.

57. ØDEGAARD, Ø. "A Statistical Investigation of the Incidence of Mental Disorder in Norway." *Psychiatric Quarterly,* 20 (1946), 382 ff.

58. PRINCE, R. "Indigenous Yoruba Psychiatry." In A. Kiev, ed., *Magic, Faith and Healing.* New York: The Free Press, 1964.

59. RECKLESS, W. C., and SMITH, M. *Juvenile Delinquency.* New York: McGraw-Hill, 1932.

60. SCHWARTZ, T. "A Cargo Cult: A Melanesian Type Response to Change." In G. A. DeVos, ed., *Responses to Change: Adjustment and Adaptation in Personality and Culture.* (Abstracts Symposia,VIIIth International Congress of Anthropological and Ethnological Sciences.* Tokyo: Science Council of Japan, 1968.)

61. SHAW, C. N., and McKAY, H. D. *Social Factors in Juvenile Delinquency.* Washington, D.C.: National Commission on Law Observance and Enforcement, 1931. Vol. 2, no. 13.

62. SIMMONS, O. G. "Drinking Patterns and Interpersonal Performance in a Peruvian Mestizo Community." *Quarterly Journal for the Study of Alcohol,* 20 (1959), 103–111.

63. SOFUE, T. "Postwar Changes in Japanese Urbanization and Related Psychological

Problems." In G. A. DeVos, ed., *Responses to Change: Adjustment and Adaptation in Personality and Culture*. (Abstracts Symposia, *VIIIth International Congress of Anthropological and Ethnological Sciences*. Tokyo: Science Council of Japan, 1968.)

64. VAN LOON, F. G. "Amok and Latah." *Journal of Abnormal Social Psychology*, 21 (1927), 434–444.

65. WALLACE, A. F. C. *Culture and Personality*. New York: Random House, 1964.

66. WEINSTEIN, E. A., and SCHULTERBRANDT, J. G. Cultural Aspects of Delusional Systems: A Study in the United States Virgin Islands. Paper presented to the Washington Psychiatric Society, 1960.

67. WHITING, J. W. M., and CHILD, I. L. *Child Training and Personality*. New Haven: Yale University Press, 1953.

68. WIELAWSKI, J., and WINIARZ, W. "Imu: A Psychoneurosis Occurring Among Ainus."

Psychoanalytic Review, 23 (1936), 181–186.

69. WITTKOWER, E. D., and RIN, H. "Transcultural Psychiatry." *Archives of General Psychiatry*, 13 (1965), 387–394.

70. YAP, P. M. "Mental Diseases Peculiar to Certain Cultures." *Journal of Mental Science*, 9 (1951), 313.

71. ———. "The Possession Syndrome: A Comparison of Hong Kong and French Findings." *Journal of Mental Science*, 106 (1960), 114.

72. ———. "Words and Things in Comparative Psychiatry, with Special Reference to the Exotic Psychoses." *Acta Psychiatrica Scandinavia*, 38 (1962), 163.

73. ———. "The Culture-bound Reactive Syndromes." In W. Caudill and T. Y. Lin, eds., *Mental Health Research in Asia and the Pacific*. Honolulu: East-West Center Press, 1968.

PART FOUR

Community Psychiatry

U.S. GOVERNMENTAL ORGANIZATION FOR HUMAN SERVICES— IMPLICATIONS FOR MENTAL HEALTH PLANNING

Bertram S. Brown and James D. Isbister

([**Historical Perspective**

THE AMERICAN PEOPLE have never suffered government gladly. From colonial times to the present, suspicion of government has always existed, among the governors as well as among the governed. Even the authors of the U.S. Constitution, while creating the federal system, agreed with Thomas Paine's comment that "government, even in its best state, is but a necessary evil; in its worst state, an intolerable one."

The concept of comprehensive social planning as a responsibility of government simply did not exist in the America of farms and frontiers. The scope of federal intervention in the social field grew sporadically, in response to the pressures of industrialization and the growth of cities, until the great economic depression of the 1930s, when individuals and states were willing to accept a series of federal governmental programs designed to bring the nation out of its economic stagnation.

The New Deal, in responding to the demands for help, created new mechanisms to regulate the economy and supervise some of the operating practices of corporate enterprises, which had developed during the nineteenth century. In establishing governmental controls, the New Deal departed from the philosophical bases of laissez-faire, propounded by Adam Smith and the classical British economists as the foundation for industrial growth. Even more significantly, in terms of the delivery of human services, the New Deal attempted to promote the general welfare with a variety of programs to assist individuals suffering the consequences of the depression. These programs included such social innovations as the Work Progress Administration, the Civilian Conservation Corps, and the National Youth Administration. These experiments in governmental planning of social benefits for its citizens were dropped when the economic ills of the depression dissipated in the frenetic preparations for war.

Urban unemployment rapidly disappeared. The factories producing war material became strong magnets, stimulating some of the greatest internal migrations in American history— from dust bowl farms to big cities, from South to North, and from the interior to the Pacific and Gulf coasts. So great was the demand for workers that for the first time women were drawn into the labor force in significant numbers.

Thus, World War II was a strong catalytic agent, forcing movements and social changes throughout the population; these served to create new problems and highlight others that had been largely ignored. Poverty, unequal participation of minority groups in any facet of society, transportation, and housing needs of a growing population began to be considered as national problems as technology developed, industry advanced, and the increasing population became more mobile.

By the end of World War II, an increasing number of American people came to the conclusion that national problems required national solutions. This change in public attitude resulted in the increased development of many of the domestic programs that had been initiated during the New Deal or earlier periods. These programs included development of national parks and recreational areas, national forests, water resources, soil conservation, and interstate highways, all related to the general physical environment to be shared by the total population. Other governmental controls proliferated among regulatory agencies, created under statutes designed to protect the public's rights to services by public utilities, railroads, airlines, communications, and other facilities that were being required to operate in the public interest.

Simultaneously, government began to assume in peacetime a greater responsibility to assist in helping individuals to share in the wealth, resources, and services of this country. As a result, the greatest growth in domestic programs of the federal government during the past twenty-five years has occurred in support of the delivery of human services designed to improve the quality of life in the American society.

The Employment Act of 1946 committed the government, as a matter of public policy, to maintain full employment throughout the nation and to pursue economic policies and develop programs to achieve that goal.

Federal housing legislation changed the living patterns of millions of Americans who were able, for the first time, to become homeowners rather than tenants, as the government underwrote support of low-cost housing.

Adoption of the Social Security Act provided for a measure of old age security for the majority of the people, and succeeding amendments to that statute continue to add to these benefits. Second only to the original statute has been the effect of Medicare and Medicaid. Still controversial, this system of federal support for the delivery of health care to the aged and the medically indigent continues to change. The basic provisions, however, have become a part of the public's expectations of governmental responsibility and the statutory patterns developed in this area have been adapted in other fields.

The Higher Education Act and the Elementary and Secondary Education Act were adopted in the belief that, though the federal government should not assume responsibility for curricula, it should provide assistance through federal grants to colleges, universities, and schools to finance the improvement of educational facilities.

Legislation and judicial discussions have brought the federal government more forcefully into the quest for civil rights and equal opportunity for persons of all races and creeds.

Through federal legislation, assistance to law enforcement agencies in the states is now available through grants designed to improve the system of criminal justice and to explore means to rehabilitate juvenile offenders.

The scope of the federal government's involvement in human services has broadened considerably since World War II. So, too, has its investment, with federal expenditures for social welfare programs—including health, education, income maintenance, housing, and veterans' benefits—growing from less than $5 billion in 1945 to more than $90 billion in 1971.[1]

Seldom during this period of growth has the federal government set out to provide services directly. Federal support of human services comes from grants in aid and other funding help, technical assistance, and staff leadership; all these are made available to the states, regions, and municipalities and the private sector, which actually organize and operate those services made possible through federal support. (Exceptions to this basic pattern are, of course, to be found: health care and treatment facilities operated by the armed services, the Veterans' Administration, and the Public Health Service are limited to specific segments of the population and do not serve the general public.)

(Current Considerations

Throughout all these developments, however, the federal government has only recently begun to tackle the problem of distributing human services on the basis of comprehensive planning. Based on the pragmatism of the legislative process in the United States, most of the federal government's support of health, education, and welfare programs has been supplied on a categorical basis, with grants in aid earmarked for specific utilization within fairly limited program categories.

In order to make sure that federal money is disbursed and spent in accordance with the mandates of the Congress and that quality control is maintained, the federal agencies responsible for administration of support have set standards of performance and formulated regulations binding on applicants for federal funds.

Development of this process has resulted in the creation, within the federal government, of a huge, centralized control mechanism. At the same time, even though the federal control mechanism is centralized, federal agencies have proliferated to such an extent that support of human services programs has been fragmented, and, from the point of view of applicants for federal support, what is known as "grantsmanship" has become complicated, unwieldy, often competitive, and frustrating.

This latter circumstance is probably the single most compelling factor underlying current clamor for change in the system. However, there are other prevalent attitudes that will give direction to impending changes in governmental organization for delivery of human services in the immediate future. There is, for example, a very real belief that too many federally supported programs are designed to perpetuate the power of the administering agency or institution, rather than to provide real services for the individual. From the people to the Congress, there is an increasing demand for cohesive administration, planned in such a way that support mechanisms are integrated to achieve maximum results at the level of the persons or communities in need of help.

The demands for equity in federally supported programs—a share of the action—have clearly put an end to paternalism in government or the Lady Bountiful syndrome in the private sector. Minority groups are actively protesting programs designed to improve their lot, unless individuals within the minorities have a major role in planning, administering, and operating them. This attitude is shared and expressed by all disadvantaged groups. If the age of docility has ended and the age of dissent is to have constructive results, future planning for the delivery of human services must be achieved by the clients of those service programs as equal partners within the power structure.

In actuality, the demands for equity and for participation cannot and should not be separated in program planning; but it is helpful to recognize that these demands come from several quarters and are based on disparate points of view. Therefore, although a wide consensus on these attitudes is apparent, there is an equally wide divergence as to the means by which federal support will be made effective.

To analyze these differences is to realize that they will not be easily resolved and furthermore, that the resolution will respond to the traditions of the swinging pendulum or to the cyclical changes that have often characterized public attitudes toward governmental participation in the daily lives of the people.

For example, decisions on the content of human services programs, and the administration and the delivery of those services, have been made, since World War II, to a great extent by professional experts. Probably at no time in the history of this nation has the cult of the professional expert and the specialist been so much in the ascendancy as in the formulation and administration of governmental policies since the 1940s. But today, dissent against the status quo of the establishment has brought with it a general questioning of the professionals' right to an exclusive expertise in designing and delivering human services. And the professionals themselves are questioning their respective and combined roles in terms of the comprehensive planning of the programs within their areas of responsibility. It is, therefore, almost certain that governance by professional experts will continue to yield to citizen pressures in the next few years.

This, however, is only a part of the change in patterns of administration. Another of the major developments is the current effort to readjust the assignments of responsibility and

control within the various levels of government itself.*

Almost everyone concerned will give at least lip service to the statement that the authority of the federal government and the control mechanisms centralized in Washington must be reapportioned. Concerning the manner of reapportionment, however, there is no general agreement.

State and municipal governments are reasserting their demands for control of federal support mechanisms, in making funds available for local and regional programs. The debate on differing means of funding, for instance, encompasses methods of revenue sharing, distribution of bloc grants as opposed to categorical grants, health insurance, educational vouchers, and family assistance programs, to name a few components of the methodology debate.

From all this has come a trend toward decentralization of the distribution of federal funds and the administration of federal support. Operational authority for many grant programs administered by the U.S. Department of Health, Education and Welfare, for example, has now been assigned to the ten regional offices of the department. It is too early to begin to evaluate the effects of this change; but it is not too early to point out that decentralization will be effective in direct ratio to its ability to be responsive to the people who need service.

Advocates of central control have produced a great amount of rhetoric about quality control of programs, but often there is little concrete evidence that quality control, per se, results from centralized administration. In terms of the cost of central control, it can be demonstrated that it is wasteful of time (in

---

* President Nixon has proposed a comprehensive reorganization of the executive branch of the U.S. government and set forth far-reaching plans for decentralization of governmental decision-making as part of the "New American revolution."[3] The plan would consolidate the present subject-oriented federal departments into four purpose-oriented departments: community development, human resources, natural resources, economic affairs. The Departments of State, Treasury, Defense, and Justice would remain as they are. Ink and Dean[2] wrote a widely disseminated article outlining the purposes of the decentralization plan.

producing results following appropriation of funds) and that the overhead of administering programs centrally is expensive.

It would appear that there will continue to be a need for the centralization of decisions on means and on certain standards. Within over-all guidelines for federal programs, authority to decide how the pieces of human services systems receiving federal support are to be organized and how the pieces are to aggregate in terms of their relevance to the local population will have to be made to an increasing extent by states and localities.

Much has been said about the uneven quality and quantity of resources among the several states. Certainly, the quality of the product, in any locale, will be circumscribed in relation to difference in values, variations in the quality of governmental and professional expertise, and financial capabilities.

However, these problems are not new, and at least some of them have been successfully attacked by the mental health community in the United States. Therefore, it is imperative that those who are charged with the responsibility for mental health planning in the 1970s realize that the recent past developments in mental health are, and must be, considered as prologue and that recent experience within the national mental health program can serve as a nucleus for expansion into a national human services program.

([Mental Health and Human Services

From the standpoint of treatment modalities, psychiatric practice in the United States has developed from a public system of custodial care of mental patients, through a period of intense professional concern with psychoanalytic treatment, into various short-term intensive therapies designed to alleviate symptoms of pathology and maintain the patient at his most productive level. These modalities co-exist today, but by far the greatest emphasis will continue to focus on the development of community based preventive and treatment measures.

The initial application of the concepts of community psychiatry began from the pressure of necessity. The literature is rich in its accounts of the chronological progression of the treatment of the mentally ill, from the points of view of psychiatry, muckrakers, do-gooders, concerned individuals, and citizens' voluntary groups. Suffice it to say that mounting pressures over the past century resulted in governmental organization for mental health services.

Querido[4] put it this way,

Since psychiatry is being realized as a special field of human behavior and since the behavioral sciences are coming of age, psychiatric problems have become centered in society instead of remaining isolated in the ivory tower of clinical procedure. And, to become a patient is no longer to acquire a condition, but the expression of a social role.

In this way, the psychiatrist and the facilities in which he plays a leading or an advisory role become elements in a homeostatic system which creates the conditions for the equilibrium we call mental health.

The creation of such a balance between the behavior and the environments of people is the ultimate objective of the current effort to establish a national program of human services in the United States. This is what the development of comprehensive, integrated community human services programs means. The challenge, in terms of mental health planning, is to develop the ability of all the relevant professions to augment crisis intervention with crisis prevention. Since, in large part, the directions of future mental health planning will be closely related to the nature and size of governmental support of research, training, and services, a brief review of the government's role in the past illustrates the significant change from a concern with mental illness to a concern for the development of mental health in the entire population.

From the mid-nineteenth century until 1940, the role of the federal government in support of mental health services was of no effective consequence. A few psychiatrists attempted to establish a federal posture in the area, following their experiences in treating the psychiatric casualties of World War I; but attitudes toward federal involvement had not developed sufficiently to cause an acceptance of responsibility within either the Congress or the executive branch. State governments had assumed the responsibility to provide for custody of the mentally ill and for whatever treatment could be financed. Public mental hospital systems were supported by state funds; psychiatrists and other physicians practiced within the system, separate and apart from the rest of the medical profession. Officials became protective of their prerogatives under the system, and professionals became defensive about the quality of care provided within these overcrowded and underfinanced institutions.

In retrospect, it becomes obvious that one federal statute brought about both public and professional rejection of insitutional incarceration as the national treatment of choice to which mental patients were committed by the courts. Under provisions of the Selective Service Act of 1940, men eligible for the draft received psychiatric screening as part of their medical examination. The high proportion of men diagnosed as emotionally or psychiatrically unfit for service in the armed forces drew national attention. During World War II, psychiatrists developed and utilized a variety of short-term therapies for psychiatric patients. The need for federal support of these developments was first recognized by the Congress with the adoption of the Mental Health Act in 1946. Adoption of this statute made possible the initial organization of the National Institute of Mental Health, to develop mental health research, manpower, and state programs through incentive grants designed to increase state expenditures for treatment programs.

Improved treatment and the demonstrated effectiveness of psychoactive drugs brought about the next congressional response to public demand in 1955. The Health Amendments Act (Title V of the Public Health Services Act) was adopted to provide federal funds to states to support demonstration projects in mental health services. To a limited extent, Title V programs contributed to the develop-

ment of community based mental health services; but the federal intent was to provide short-term aid to states rather than to establish a permanent supportive partnership.

More important in 1955 was the congressional resolution establishing the Joint Commission on Mental Illness and Health to undertake the first nationwide survey and analysis of mental illness in the United States. The commission report, *Action for Mental Health*, was published in 1961. It took just two years for the commission's findings to cause the Congress to adopt the Comprehensive Community Mental Centers Act of 1963. The intent of this act permitted a wide interpretation within which the federal government, the states, local governments, and private resources within communities could evolve coordinated patterns in providing mental health services.

The development of support mechanisms under the Centers Act and its succeeding amendments is a matter of legislative history; but even today, mental health professionals do not always appear to realize the role they have developed in terms of their responsibilities and opportunities for leadership in the projected expansion of mental health services into a comprehensive program of human services.

Under provisions of the Centers Act, provision of preventive services became mandatory in a publicly supported mental health program.

In order to establish state eligibility for federal funds under the statute, literally thousands of citizens voluntarily surveyed and catalogued the mental health resources of their states and prepared comprehensive state plans for the development of mental health services.

The regulations under which the Centers Act is administered have, in only five years, established the bona fides of outpatient, emergency, and partial hospitalization services as valid substitutes for twenty-four-hour-a-day inpatient services in the great majority of cases.

In practicing experience, mental health personnel have learned to identify a wide spectrum of social as well as pathological causes for the psychological and psychiatric troubles of the population. Such conditions as poverty, racism, narcotic and drug abuse, bad housing, and inadequate public transportation have become identified by mental health workers as symptoms of a malaise that cannot be treated solely within a medical modality.

Mental health community-based service needs have brought about the initial development of expanded insurance benefits under third-party payment programs.

Community mental health centers have planned their programs to serve people rather than to serve institutional systems. The concept of continuity of care, in which treatment is provided and adapted to the patient's needs, has been accepted as an operational verity. And, the meaning of the word "comprehensive" has been expanded to include the recognition of many social conditions as root causes of psychological disruptions, dissents, and violence.

Governments at all levels now accept responsibility (albeit of varying degrees) for support of the provision of services to enable the citizenry to live productive lives in the midst of an increasingly complex society.

There are opportunities for many comprehensive health and human services delivery programs to be built in the next few years on the foundations established by the mental health community. In a national sense, a mental health services program exists. In developing a broader human services delivery system, the mental health experience can serve as a pattern.

(Implications for Mental Health Planning

The development of a national, community-based program of mental health services is unique within the health industry of the United States, but its patterns for the delivery of services are still exploratory. Therefore, at a time when the public and governments are seeking to achieve better integration of all human services, mental health planners have opportunities to lead from their strength of experience.

The potential for political and leadership roles of mental health professionals is still to be fully realized, but the opportunity for development of that potential is at hand. Of primary importance will be the ability of professionals to change some of their traditional attitudes of separatism. In many instances, mental health professionals may have to forego the tradition of command in favor of leadership and working together with professionals from other disciplines as well as nonprofessionals and citizens in the pursuit of human service goals. If such leadership is successful, it can result in a cooperative advocacy for the delivery of human services and initiate planning procedures in which educators, the judiciary, ecologists, economists, physical and behavioral scientists, new careerists, and others must and can share. Initial efforts of this sort of collaborative mode of procedure are already evident. The immediate task is to expand and refine the process.

Based on their experience to date, mental health planners can suggest as fundamental to the delivery of services the following characteristic requirements.

1. Service programs must be based in local communities and made easily accessible to all residents of a given community.
2. Staffs of service programs must include men and women trained in a variety of disciplines, who will work together as teams to ensure coordination and continuity of services, in the same way that community mental health staffs are organized to provide continuity of care for their patients and clients.
3. Human services programs must be responsive to consumer needs, and the programs must be organized to include consumer participation in their development and operation.

Just as the mental health community has recognized the need for preventive intervention prior to crisis, the entire medical profession is now wrestling with the demand for service programs to prevent, as well as to treat illness. The public demand, consciously or not, goes further, in a growing recognition that health means more than the negation of illness, in physical as well as in psychiatric terms. This point of view is already bringing about new service delivery patterns. Medical group practice is increasing, and governmental support will be forthcoming in the establishment of health maintenance organizations. Health maintenance organization planning is based on the notion that interdisciplinary health teams can maintain the health of population segments to a greater extent than have the traditional treatment facilities.

Financing of services from the standpoint of federal support will undoubtedly continue to move toward some forms of revenue sharing, bloc grants, and increased efforts to involve the private sector of the financial community. And, basic to financing patterns will be the tremendous expansion of health insurance, based on indirect or third-party payment.

The widespread, although diverse, pressures for establishment of a national health insurance program of an as yet undetermined type will have a tremendous effect on the kinds of services to be delivered and the means for delivery.

These decisions are as yet unresolved, but mental health planners already have enough experience to predict to their colleagues what some of the results of such financing will be. Mental health services have generally been excluded in one way or another, and for various reasons, in health insurance programs. However, current data and experience establish that it is economically feasible and programmatically sound to provide mental health benefits on an equitable basis with benefits for general health care. Even as mental health services receive greater coverage in insurance programs, the planners must recognize that only when the benefit is comprehensive, with adequate, appropriate, and equitable benefits for inpatient and ambulatory care, will the maximum role of the entire care system be realized.

(Conclusion

Governmental bodies at all levels in our U.S. system are moving toward greater integration of human service programs. Concurrently, the federal government, whose involvement in the human services arena has grown so considerably during the past twenty-five years, is moving increasingly toward noncategorical and indirect methods of financial support for human services. These two phenomena will pose difficulties for mental health planners, since traditionally mental health services have been organized in relative independence and have been financed, in the main, through direct public appropriations.

The challenge for mental health leaders and planners will be to see whether they can achieve their goals through aggressive and cooperative action in the new mode. As we have indicated in this brief chapter, the experience of the mental health professionals is rich, and they have much to contribute not only in the further development of mental health services but also in the coming evolution of better integrated, more responsive total human service delivery systems.

(Bibliography

1. EXECUTIVE OFFICE OF THE PRESIDENT, OFFICE OF MANAGEMENT AND BUDGET. *The U.S. Budget in Brief.* Washington, D.C.: U.S. Government Printing Office, 1971.

2. INK, D., and DEAN, A. "A Concept of Decentralization." *Public Administration Review*, 30, no. 1 (1970).

3. OFFICE OF MANAGEMENT AND BUDGET. *Papers Relating to the President's Departmental Reorganization Program.* Washington, D.C.: U.S. Government Printing Office, 1971.

4. QUERIDO, A. "The Shaping of Community Mental Health Care." *International Journal of Psychiatry*, 7, no. 5 (May 1969), 300–311.

CHAPTER 38

HUMAN SERVICES AT STATE AND LOCAL LEVELS

The Integration of Mental Health

Harold W. Demone, Jr.

⟨ Definition of Human Services

MANY RECENT DEVELOPMENTS indicate a trend toward comprehensiveness and coordination of the many services traditionally supplied by separate disciplines or agencies. One of these is the growth of such organizations as community mental health centers, multiservice centers, neighborhood service centers, youth opportunity centers, neighborhood health centers, and health maintenance organizations, all of which offer two or more services customarily given independently of one another. Comprehensiveness is the goal. Using this very basic definition, the secretary of the Department of Health, Education and Welfare could say in January 1971 that there were more than 2,000 such units in the United States.

* The assistance of Mrs. Janet Bouton in library research and editing is gratefully acknowledged.

There has also been a very clear but less formal trend on the part of various professions to become more comprehensive within their own disciplinary boundaries. Previously separate free-standing public health clinics are now being integrated into broader medical care networks. The solo practice of medicine is almost completely linked to hospital inpatient and outpatient services, emergency wards, laboratories, and third-party payers. General hospitals are increasingly associated with extended care facilities, skilled nursing homes, and home care programs. Rehabilitation facilities are being designed as integral components of general hospitals and at the same time are enlarging their scope of concern to include nonmedical rehabilitation programs linked to community-based workshops, vocational training, and job placement. And, of course, the expansion of the psychiatric system to include both a variety of nonmedical care-giving agents and indirect services is a further extension of the premise.

Michael March[21] supported the observation that many of the new programs, such as those cited above as well as manpower centers and employment offices, "strive individually to become more comprehensive as they try to meet the complex needs of their clientele."

The trend toward integration of services is also being fostered at the federal level. Among the recommendations of the Task Force on the Organization of Social Services is that new funds be concentrated on comprehensive services.[33] This task force defined social services as including, but not being limited to, the following: (1) information, advice, and referral services, (2) advocacy and legal services, (3) personal counseling, rehabilitative, and therapeutic services (including clinical psychotherapy, family casework, and vocational counseling), (4) personal and home aides, especially to serve the aged, handicapped, ill, and families that need help at home, (5) homemaker services, (6) meals on wheels to meet the temporary needs of aged and ill, or the continuous needs of the aged living alone, (7) day schools for young children that offer child development programs involving parents, (8) rural campus and urban community centers for young people, (9) education programs for basic education, cultural knowledge, or formal education, (10) community social and recreation centers, (11) family planning services, (12) job placement and training services, (13) volunteer placement and opportunity services, (14) protective and foster care services for children and the aged, (15) home care services for persons recently hospitalized or institutionalized or for ill or handicapped persons who can remain at home with comprehensive assistance from the community.

The trend toward comprehensiveness and coordination is also apparent in the efforts of many state governments to combine several separate health and social service programs within one new department. At the moment, approximately twenty states have combined several services, and many others are seriously considering similar reorganizations.[29] As most of these state-level modernizations occurred

during the last decade, it is likely that a structural trend of sorts is at work.

As is often the case, changes occur first followed by conceptual efforts. Public administrators and social scientists have only recently attempted to extract theoretical constructs from this reality, and even these are still primarily descriptive definitions. Further complicating the task of defining human services is the lack of clearcut direction in the trend.

In their discussion of intersystem relations in human service organizations, Baker and O'Brien implied that the latter may be defined by reference to "the complex array of physical health, mental health, and social organizations as an intersystem field."[3] Harshbarger made the most elaborate effort to define human services.

In terms of their systemic properties, human service organizations might generally be described as based upon public resources, relatively structured, normative based and morally involving, social or socio-technical service oriented, and aimed at clients, residents, or members as primary beneficiaries and staff members as secondary beneficiaries. Organizationally, the nature of their efforts is to deal with those bio-social problems which arise from the vagaries and complexities of being human.[13]

An analysis of the various state-level human service arrangements yields an operational definition. Each human service agency, whether already in existence or proposed, usually includes the public health, mental health, and social welfare programs of the state, and thus these programs might be seen as the three essential human services. Other services that appear to be an optional part of the definition include vocational rehabilitation, employment, corrections, parole, youth services, legal services, and industrial relations. It is interesting to note that formal education, which is certainly a human service, is consistently excluded from the new state organizational integration. This omission is usually justified on the basis that it has traditionally been administered separately. Since most of the merged services have also traditionally been independent entities and have used this same reason to argue for continued autonomy, it is clear that other factors must be at work. One factor of particular significance is the reluctance to place such a massive proportion of the state budget under the control of any one agency. In Massachusetts, for example, the new Executive Office of Human Services consumed approximately 70 percent of the state's proposed operating budget during fiscal year 1972, the first full fiscal year of its operation. Adding state-supported educational programs would mean that the new Secretary of Human Services would control more than 80 percent of the state's total expenditures. An equally important factor might be that state departments of education are related to extensive local counterpart systems whose policy-making bodies are usually locally elected and are often politically powerful. To enforce cooperation on the part of each of these local units would be an overwhelming, if not impossible, task.

In contradiction to this formal statewide tendency to exclude education, however, there are some signs of an opposite local trend. Adult education and continuing education have been traditional components of many human service agencies. Also, the community school concept has been greatly expanded since it was originally advanced by the Mott Foundation about forty years ago. Although it was first intended to promote the use of school property for year-round community recreation, many social, health, welfare, recreation, and adult education activities are now included in this arrangement, making some schools major community centers. These programs may be administered singly or under multiple auspices, but in any case community school directors working with citizen advisory groups are often producing their own versions of a human service center.

❮ Rationale for Human Services

Inefficiency, compartmentalization, specialization, bureaucracy, program barriers, and service gaps are among the many shorthand terms used to criticize the existing public, governmental service system and to justify the move toward alternative human service models. The thrust of many of the new proposals clearly appears to be a reaction to these deficiencies. This can be seen, for example, in Michael March's[21] summary of the direction of the current movement:

It is toward *comprehensiveness* of services, toward *decentralization* of services into the ghetto, toward *concerting* of resources from different programs, toward *co-location* of service components, and toward operational *integration* of services so that they can be geared together in a *continuum* ordered in proper sequence and effectively administered without the present duplication and time-wasting which goes on for clients and for employees.

Economic factors have been significant in fostering this new movement. In addition to the alleged inefficiency, time-wasting, and duplication that contribute to unnecessary expenditures in providing services, the costs of human services are rising. In economic terms, the health industry alone will soon be the major industry in this country, and as such it is becoming a target for those interested in controlling its expenditures and a source of income for those interested in exploiting its potential. A typical comment about the health industry is that of Becker:[5]

Economic factors, quality of care concepts, and automation are just a few of the forces creating new pressures for a coordinated community-wide organizational pattern for the provision of health care. The inevitable result is to bring into a functional relationship all the segments of community health care without regard to whether the unit is public or private.

President Nixon, in his 1971 health message, after briefly noting much progress, went on to describe a lengthy service of organizational ills, stating that "60 percent of the growth in medical expenditures in the last ten years has gone not for additional services but merely to meet price inflation." He also noted[24] that "even those who can afford most care may find themselves impoverished by a catastrophic medical expenditure." In many areas of the nation, especially rural and inner city, "care is simply not available." "The quality of medicine varies unduly with geography and income. . . . most of our people have trouble obtaining medical attention on short notice." The President also criticized the focus on treatment to the detriment of prevention and early case finding.

Although economic factors in the sense of profit-making motives may help to account for increasing interest in a given subsystem, it is the concern with cost benefits that presses the individual fields, organizations, and disciplines to examine their interorganizational boundaries and concerns, thus fostering the move toward cooperation.

The current trend to reject specialization, combined with a long-standing antagonism toward complex organizations and their bureaucracies, makes it almost faddish to criticize the existing service delivery systems, and the effects of these criticisms are being felt. Agency boards are broadening their composition, community control is advocated, consumer participation is required, and job descriptions are being rewritten to admit nonprofessionals.

Not of significant influence in bringing about the growth of the human services concept, but important nevertheless for the rationalists among us, research findings generally support the major criticisms of existing service delivery systems. The quality and quantity of service delivery is not adequate, and comparative morbidity and mortality statistics indicate that the United States is behind many other Western nations in health care delivery. It is also clear that we are not doing as well as many European countries in providing such services as nursing home care, home care, financial assistance to the aged, and day care for young children.

The defender of the status quo need only follow a few clients through the present system in order for him to realize clearly that the care-giving network is poorly designed to meet the needs of those it purports to serve. A complex inter- and intraorganizational and policy arrangement surfaces, with boundaries that are often artificial and hamper the delivery of needed assistance. Such terms as "fragmentation," "overlapping," "duplication,"

"gaps in services," and "lack of coordination" take on concrete meaning for individuals who need services. For example, a working mother may enroll her four-year-old in Head Start but have no place for her two-year-old; a pregnant woman may receive health care at one clinic and take her children to another clinic, while there are no facilities for the father; screening and eligibility requirements may exclude those who most need rehabilitative services because they are poor risks; an individual or family with several problems may receive help for only one of them because the first agency to which it goes does not diagnose the other problems or does not refer the client on to other appropriate agencies; lack of aggressive and imaginative outreach may prevent certain people (for example, non-English speaking people, the aged) from being aware of the services available.

This situation was tolerated by the poor (out of necessity) and by others (out of lack of knowledge or indifference) so long as it was widely viewed as a problem only for the poor. But now the middle class is also finding that the costs of health care can destroy a family financially, that finding adequate and reasonably priced nursing home care for the elderly may be impossible, and that creative, professional day care for the children of many middle-class working mothers is not available. As the middle class begins to add its voice to that of the lower class, the pressure for change will become overwhelming. Subsidies, coverage for catastrophies, charges based on ability to pay, and free care are widely discussed alternatives.

⟨ Models

Just as the definitions are deduced from many and varying experiences so are the models. In two cases of neighborhood centers (service and health) they bear the imprint of the national organization which stimulated them, the Office of Economic Opportunity. Similarly, the many proposals reviewed by the Department of Health, Education and Welfare resemble the sponsors or disciplines that initiated them. Most will have a core service, but it in turn will share the common traits of the proposal writers (whether from public health, mental health, law, rehabilitation, or social welfare).

Focusing exclusively on the neighborhood or community level there are a number of alternatives that will be described and analyzed: (1) the advice and referral center; (2) the diagnostic center; (3) the one-stop multipurpose center; and (4) a linked comprehensive network.[1,21,25,29]

Information and Referral

The advice (or information and referral) service is a simple concept based on more than forty years of experience. A small group of generalists, knowledgeable about available services, make appropriate referrals and follow up.[8]

A typical big city health and welfare council would expect its noncategorical information and referral service to make between 5,000 to 10,000 referrals each year, itself coping with those problems lending themselves to immediate generic intervention. The added component in the contemporary model would be small information and referral centers distributed throughout the various neighborhoods. Whatever the final shape, the capacity to advise, refer, and follow up is integral to each model.

Advantages of the information and referral model, and of the diagnostic center discussed in the next subsection, are: (1) both programs are relatively inexpensive; (2) if the agencies cooperate referral is likely to be enhanced and simplified; and (3) since minimal organizational change is required, cooperation is enhanced.

Problems inherent in or precipitated by expansion of the information and referral model are: (1) by itself it can be counterproductive if adequate services are not available; (2) the service gaps, eligibility requirements, and other defects in the existing system are not necessarily affected; and (3) it requires a level of sophistication at both the interpersonal and interorganization level seldom appreciated by even its most vigorous advocates.

The Diagnostic Center

In this more medically oriented model the information and referral apparatus would be supplemented by skilled diagnostic staff. Thus referrals could be more specific, comprehensive service plans individually devised, and more extensive follow-up undertaken.

Although it suffers from many of the same disadvantages as the information and referral service, some of its advocates are urging that all clients be required to enter all organized care-giving mechanisms via the diagnostic center. As with some other proposals this suffers in its inapplicability to the real world. If the problem is identified and services are available, most patients prefer to go directly to the treatment program. Each time additional layers are introduced into the clinical system some slippage occurs. If all patients are required to go through a central service, the end result could be fewer services delivered to those in need.

One-Stop Multiservice Centers

This arrangement of services contains all of the program elements found in the preceding models and in addition has the internal capacity to follow through on selected problems. There are now approximately 200 health and service centers posited on this premise.

For most, the specific program stimulus is clearly identifiable. Federal funds were made available to develop a new center along the lines of a nationally designed model or against a set of guidelines. As long as funds are available, the development of comprehensive centers occurred at a rapid rate. With the drying up of federal funds, the reverse has occurred. It is unlikely that a nationwide spread of such centers will be further encouraged by the federal government, for not only did cost analyses fail to justify their repetition on a large scale, but their continued promotion in the poorer neighborhoods of urban areas would simply further the development of improved, but still segregated, ghetto programs.

In spite of these limitations, the comprehensive service center model may have substantial long-range effects. Some professions formally cooperated for the first time. Quality services were offered in the inner city. Community control was given a substantial opportunity. The potential integration of direct services and client advocacy was tested.

Even a so-called one-stop multipurpose center could not contain all needed services and be truly comprehensive, and would therefore still encounter some of the problems of the information and referral center or diagnostic center in having to relate to other service agencies to assure clients the full range of services.

Network

The Organization for Social and Technical Innovation (OSTI) and March[21] suggested the possibility of forming an urban network of centers that could control one or more major one-stop centers and several intake diagnostic and information referral components.

The network principle includes other options as well. Neither dependent on nor exclusive of large comprehensive programs this model would focus on building linkages between organizations to facilitate services to the client. Generic information and referral organizations and specialized services agencies would continue to coexist. The federal funds formerly used to stimulate the development of new nonreplicable organizations would instead be used to facilitate availability, access, continuity of care, and organizations more responsive to client needs. The organization first receiving the client would either assume the follow-up responsibility or refer to the information and referral service, would be compensated for this responsibility, and would have the capacity to purchase services as needed.

As an alternative to the comprehensive service procedure, Perlman and Jones[30] suggested three alternatives depending on the nature of the community's service arrangement. Where services are generally adequate, they suggested a primary focus on information and referral. Where gaps exist one organization could take the leadership by developing necessary gap-filling services, possibly bartering with other organizations to take them over eventually. Finally they suggested that where services are totally inadequate a comprehensive center might be developed to offer a range of services.

The multiple models of Perlman and Jones permit pluralism and marketplace decisions. A model that fails to acknowledge these realities can survive only as long as some outside ministering organization pumps funds into its veins.

Whatever the model, the services have to be available and the client has to be able to secure them.

Where gaps and barriers are individual in nature, the referring agent should be supported in his efforts to modify the individual constraining behavior. Where the problems are systemic, the aggregation of many individual experiences will give guidance to administrators and planners as they attempt to modify the structure.

(Organizational Issues

A series of other issues integrally related to the effort to develop more comprehensive services should also be identified: (1) auspice, (2) control, (3) center or program, and (4) core services.

Program Auspice

The long-standing public versus private role dilemma seems to be taking a new form. The government has clearly assumed the ultimate responsibility for providing a human service floor. Public welfare, Medicaid and Medicare, and many governmentally sponsored categorical services illustrate the stability of this development. The issue now is how the services can best be delivered. The alternatives are not very complex: The government can (1) own and operate its own service system (for example, mental hospitals, city hospitals, public welfare social services); (2) provide for a series of client advocates, counselors, and referral agents who can purchase for the client those needed services (for example, vocational rehabilitation); (3) give the client the capacity to purchase what he needs within certain guidelines (for example, Medicare); (4) contract with organizations to provide services to eligible clients (for example, some chronic disease, mental health and day care); or (5) employ some combination of the four.

It seems clear that the multiple roles required of the public administrator are extraordinarily demanding and often quite unrewarding. Thus, we are beginning to see a countermove in public administration designed to give the public administrator more flexibility in responding to policy changes. Grants in aid, contracts, and purchasing-power type arrangements are being used experimentally. Private nonprofit and private profit organizations may both see a health and welfare renaissance. Competition may be encouraged, and the effort to develop service oligopolies (for example, community mental health centers) may be reduced.[23]

Illustrative of this changing public administration principle* are the recommendations of the Services for People Task Force of the social and rehabilitation services of the Department of Health, Education and Welfare.[33] One of the recommendations is to "strengthen government and non-profit providers of social services by additional funds and by placing them in competition with providers that will operate social services for profit." Certain unspecified social services would be operated only by the government.[33] Another recommendation is that

The Federal Government should encourage agencies receiving Federal grants to develop, for major use, systems by which prescribed recipients may purchase social services from private agencies

when appropriate. Such types of social services as day care for children and vocational training and retraining, including counselling, should be considered particularly appropriate for use in such systems.[33]

It should be noted that not only does this type of recommendation violate certain cherished beliefs about the appropriate roles of governmental and nongovernmental organizations but it ignores the drive toward coordination, also a firmly held principle. Its effort to coordinate is, at best, indirect. By encouraging competition it permits marketplace decisions about coordination and duplication.

Program Control

Underlying many debates is the issue of control of the program. At present four identifiable but overlapping groupings are contestants in the struggle: (1) human service professions and their affiliated categorical program supporters; (2) active upper-middle-class volunteers, long invested in the voluntary health and welfare system; (3) community control and; (4) consumer control. Although used interchangeably, community and consumer control are not necessarily identical. For a small neighborhood-based organization the community and consumers could overlap substantially, but for organizations serving a metropolitan or larger area or a highly specialized purpose, consumers and community could differ substantially. Community control is territorially based. Consumer control is designed to assign ultimate authority to the users of the product or service.

Since each of the four alternatives suffers from its own unique limitations it is likely that mixed control mechanisms will become increasingly common. Modal types influencing the appropriate compromises will be neighborhood based, community wide and metropolitan or larger, all in turn influenced by the generic specialized nature of the organization.

In any case it is clear that both the community and consumer control movements, merely on the basis of their newness, have upset the always tenuous balance between the many existing forces.

---

* The traditional practice has been to purchase goods and nonrecurring services. If the service was a continuing governmental responsibility, the procedure was for the government to develop its own capacity.

Center or Program Emphasis

Particularly highlighted by the community mental health center movement but integrally related to most recent human service developments is the latent conflict between the center (or facility) and program advocates. In mental health the unfortunate congressional timing, which made construction funds available a year before state plans were completed, tended to give the community mental health movement a building (center) focus. Associated with this facility orientation was the pressure toward single ownership and management of all the mental health resources in a given catchment area. The goal was unrealizable, of course, but the investment of new financial resources in this center tended to reinforce already existing organizational strains. Furthermore, interorganizational difficulties were enhanced since neither the additional funds nor sanctions were adequate either to buy or to coerce the rest of the system out of existence. The pragmatic network approach, also permitted by the law and the guidelines, focused instead on the use and coordination of a variety of existing resources and the assigning of certain functions, such as linkage and client advocacy, to the center but not necessarily requiring a superordinate role for a center as such.

Core Service

The core service, in one form or another, is an essential part of most proposed models. The ABT consulting firm[1] described it thus: "Core services are so called because they consist of a nucleus of supportive activities which can be applied to any kind or number of programs."[1] The core service's functions can be described differently depending on the organization's focus: intake, outreach, diagnosis, referral, follow up, client advocacy, and case coordination are all used, sometimes interchangeably.

Demone and Long[8] listed a series of considerations that need to be included in the development of any type of core service: (1) well-trained core staff are indispensable; (2) properly selected, trained, and supervised volunteers can play a significant role in association with the trained professional staff; (3) storefront programs, despite their emotional appeal, lack staying power and are too small to be economically feasible; (4) the processes of receiving, counseling, diagnosing and referring, separately or collectively, are highly complex and must be done well and at considerable cost in some cases; (5) evaluation and monitoring are critical; (6) for effective referral an up-to-date resource file is necessary; start up time for a metropolitan area will be from three to six months; (7) the service experiences should be reported at least annually; facts, criticisms, opinions, and suggestions should be documented and made available to the public and appropriate organizations; (8) the information and referral component should be able to serve as a barometer of the incidence and distribution of community problems as well as the community's readiness and capacity to cope with them; (9) since an objective should be to place as few intermediaries as possible between caregiver and client the service should train the staff of individual agencies to serve as their own core staff; (10) directories of community services should be compiled and distributed; and (11) as a central source for suggestions and complaints about community services and agencies the service should be an aggressive advocate for its clients.[8]

The core service, information and referral center, and information, referral, and diagnostic center obviously build on one another, overlapping in certain of the basic services but clearly the core service is the most complex of the mechanisms.

⟨ Alternatives to Direct Services

Rather than require services for the disabled, handicapped, aged, and the poor, an alternative solution is gaining popularity. It is suggested that everyone should be guaranteed an adequate income. The assumption is that

many of the felt needs and service requirements will disappear if income is adequate.
Then "we will not have to plan for two kinds
of Americans, the average American and the
deprived American, as we do now."[31]

Social Action

A variety of social change procedures can
be subsumed under social action; from conflict
to compromise, from a focus on process and
democratic skills to the development of self-
help competencies. In common is a goal,
vague or specific. For direct service organizations increasing interest in social change is apparent. Mental health centers might include
this role under consultation; others might
speak of community organization or advocacy.

Although aggressive advocacy for the individual client is increasingly sanctioned for
service organizations, the larger systems-
oriented change role often creates counterproductive reactions. In his study of six social
action programs Grosser[11] found that "it is
not easy to negotiate with an agency for a
client on a *quid pro quo* basis and at the same
time attempt to change its policies or personnel." Furthermore, "The experience of the
projects illustrates that dispensers of public
agency services are congenitally and organizationally unable to distinguish between the
protest and service function when practiced
by the same organization. Thus the public
agency sees social action against itself as a
breach of faith. . . ."[11] Essentially, Grosser
suggested that organizations respond as people; they are unlikely to work harmoniously
with other organizations when under attack
by those same organizations.

Despite the naturalness of this defensive
organizational posture, the literature is ambivalent on this matter. The consultation firm
OSTI, for example, although acknowledging
that the dual roles of service and social action
can be incompatible, still suggested that the
neighborhood service center must take a real
leadership role in community action. OSTI
suggested that if they fail to act they will lose
credibility with their consumers and will be
seen as agreeing with the establishment. They

concluded:[28] "Sometimes a center has to risk
antagonizing its funding sources, and gamble
that it will find support elsewhere. Sometimes
this may be a wise gamble, for after all a center is designed to serve people and without
their trust and support, it cannot long survive." However, the trust and support of the
center's clients is a complex and volatile entity
which must be carefully handled. The disastrous experiences of the New York Lincoln
Hospital's mental health services in coping
with local citizens exemplifies the lingering
dilemmas confronting the human services administrator who seeks to combine social action
and clinical care.

Here again human service organizations are
faced with existential choices. The customary
solution is for direct service organizations to
limit social action activities to those that will
not impair securing services for their clients.
Major social action programs are mobilized by
nondirect service organizations, but even for
the latter the degree to which an agency follows a major conflict model may influence the
life span of the organization. Short-term ad
hoc organizations are better prepared to do
battle "to the end."

Perlman and Jones,[30] in their excellent
analysis of twenty neighborhood service centers in five different cities, found that "Social
action has shown a disconcerting tendency to
direct its strongest fire at the allies and benevolent neutrals close at hand, rather than at the
more distant enemy."

⟪ Service Areas

The Federal Community Services Act of 1966,
in referring to efforts designed to overcome
duplication and fragmentation, described the
new experiments in community-based programs as offering a wider variety of services
than previously. Community mental health
centers, neighborhood service programs for
the aged and poor, and welfare community
centers were cited as examples. Each moved
in its own direction, in essentially comparable
catchment areas, and focused on roughly the

same client population. The conclusion: Comprehensive centers, coordinated programs, and planning focused on the whole man are needed.[30]

Clearly two trends are at work simultaneously. (1) Each field is enlarging the definition of its role and function and necessarily conflicting with others similarly engaged in expansion. Comprehensiveness is perceived by competitors as empire building. (2) The other trend is regionalization. Although definitions of catchment areas, responsibilities, and extent of coverage may vary, the thrust toward a geographic coverage principle is essential to all models.

Experiments at regionalization are not new. In 1889 the Metropolitan District Commission was established in Massachusetts to deal with water, sewerage, and transportation problems in metropolitan Boston. Since that time countless other overlapping efforts have occurred. Recent federal guidelines from the Department of Health, Education and Welfare, Housing and Urban Development, and the Bureau of Management and Budget have all provided impetus for relating services on a territorial basis (the mental health catchment area concept is typical).

What is needed is a common philosophical base. A geographic building block solution offers the most flexibility, neighborhoods serving as the basic unit. A community of solution will vary according to needs and resources. If kidney transplant centers or air pollution control programs are desired, their territorial base can be constructed by combining several smaller areas into a larger region. Several mental health catchment areas could be combined as a watershed region. Whatever the human service, certain essential characteristics must be considered (geography, population density, political jurisdictions, economic and marketing areas, population trends and composition, transportation, existing and predicted service needs, and utilization and financial considerations).[9]

Given these concurrent trends toward regionalization and coordination of services and continuity of care, a logical conclusion is that the existing linkages by function (settlement house to settlement house, general hospital to general hospital, or mental health center to mental health center) may compete with catchment area relationships, especially if the latter are reinforced by special federal funding encouraging formal linkages at the delivery level.

A caution should be inserted here: For all its advantages, the service area model has a tendency to lock organizations into territory and constituents and reduce competition. Parochialism and ethnocentrism are dysfunctional, whether based on category or geography.

(**Mental Health and Psychiatry as a Human Service**

As each new comprehensive model is developed, tested, and modified, questions are raised about how various professions and fields will be integrated into or linked to it. Naturally enough, these concerns are expressed by the various disciplines, less so by the program designers.

A careful review of the literature suggests that the issue of discipline integration is not considered a significant problem by the program managers. Extensive manuals developed for the Bureau of the Budget and the Office of Economic Opportunity speak only briefly to personnel matters, not at all to the integration of disciplines. They focus on task analysis as a way to factor jobs into their component parts in order to facilitate the assumption of many responsibilities by paraprofessionals. Professionals are described as tending toward bureaucratization, inflexibility, and predetermined standards. Some tasks, it is recognized, will require certain technical skills, although it is also noted that the major societal problems are not responsive to an individual approach. Some professionals, it is suggested, may be able to learn how to relate to larger community problems. The one to one relation is encouraged only as it enhances community change and development.[1,28] It can only be assumed that the means by which the professional can effectively be integrated into the new developments is not significant.

Ignoring these issues may have serious consequences, however, for these groups have established identities and statuses. Some may be dysfunctional, but unless careful thought is given to the modified role and status of professionals, programs may be blocked or seriously delayed.

Mental health could contribute to this role analysis in two ways, one focusing on how each discipline (psychiatry, nursing, social work, and so on) would be related to the human service network and the other on how the field of mental health itself would be integrated. Not that introspection is new to mental health. The 1960s saw endless prose directed to both issues as mental health made its latest effort to escape from its institutional base. All the arguments and concerns about community mental health are potentially extrapolatable to the larger, more complex field of human services.

Organizational Problems in Mental Health

Intraorganizational problems have evolved around a series of issues; a sampling includes concern about the dominant role of the clinical medical model, the struggle by the non-medical professions for more status and influence, the conflict between the institutional and community oriented, the strain between treatment and consultation, and the competition resulting from sharply delineated catchment areas. Interorganizationally, the struggle to separate retardation from the mental health umbrella is perhaps the most vivid illustration of conflict.

The special linkage problem of state mental health, retardation, correctional, delinquency, and chronic disease systems is that approximately 90 percent of their annual operating budgets are institutionally based. Locked into physical sites, buildings, and civil service, their ability to transform themselves into community-based programs, categorically or comprehensively, is seriously handicapped.

To move mental health into a formal rela-

tion with the other direct personal services may either escalate such organizational problems at an exponential rate or allow the more open-minded leaders of the professions and fields a new opportunity to serve consumers more efficiently. It may permit a confrontation with or an alternative to the heavy institutional investment.

The Mental Health Profession and Human Services

Except for its identification as an integral component of organized medicine, psychiatry should have neither more nor fewer problems in working within the larger human service network than any other discipline. The essentially autonomous and omnipotent antiorganizational stance of organized medicine and its assorted specialities has always handicapped cooperative efforts. Nevertheless, the fundamental problems are the same for all disciplines and organizations. They soon find themselves structured for the convenience of the providers rather than the users. The differences between professions are principally a matter of degree.

The integration of mental health services in general will suffer the same problems as the efforts to link other services together: The specialization and domain fixation will continue to reinforce fragmentation even if the various specialists report to a single administrator.

The Goal of Mental Health Integration

Two goals, not necessarily compatible, should be distinguished. Either the mental health disciplines can be integrated with other care-giving disciplines so that they relate to each other maximally or the mental health disciplines can be integrated to modify the delivery system to the benefit of the consumer. Since we do not need smooth running organizations for their own sake, the latter goal must become superordinate. Necessary components of effective service delivery of particular relevance to mental health, and which it can stimulate, include: (1) the humanization of services; (2) insight into factors that enhance various forms of discrimination (age, sex, race, social class, income, and diagnosis); and (3) considerations of consumer input in decision-making. Thus, the specialized knowledge in the field of mental health could contribute to system improvement and not merely to system maintenance. There are also significant structural-functional (social and physical) issues with mental health components.

The Individual or Systems Approach

Since by definition the human services model is designed to deliver services to individuals, it contains the latent assumption that people have problems that can be treated. In part at least the assumption is that the individual is at least partly at fault. If the client could only be adequately motivated to correct these faults, his situation would improve.

Among the problems in the present health and welfare system that Thomas Walz[35] saw as contributing to the growth of new service models is the fact that the system has generally been based on a "social theory regarding the causation of social problems which has produced strategies incapable of dealing with the nature of the problems experienced by the majority of the poor in this country."

Several problematic issues concerning the role a mental health program should play have yet to be resolved within the profession, to say nothing of whether they are resolved in the minds of the larger community with which the program is required to cope. Typical is how broadly mental health (and mental illness) is to be defined. Should a comprehensive mental health center be concerned also with those who are "well," but who need help through especially difficult situations which could conceivably precipitate mental illness?[6]

It is possible, however, that these definitional problems might not engage the mental health field in continuous intensive dialogue if it were more closely allied with other services. Under these circumstances, for example, the man who was unemployed would ideally be given not only assistance in finding a job and/or receive job training but would also

have any additional personal problems diagnosed and would be referred to the proper place(s) to help him cope with these.

Walz[35] said that traditionally

The preferred methods for dealing with social ills have largely been those based on the psychological sciences in which the focus has been on curing or rehabilitating the individual within the context of his family. As long as individual deficiencies rather than the deficiencies of the social system were the principal target, large-scale measures of social reform were not emphasized. The resistance of the hard-core poor to traditional methods of service intervention appears to be sufficient proof of the invalidity of the social theory upon which the social welfare system has been based.

Many of the new comprehensive centers that have arisen in the past decade were in fact a direct and conscious attempt to apply a new theory about the causes of social ills, such as juvenile delinquency. The emphasis, according to the guidelines of the Juvenile Delinquency and Control Act of 1961, was on community organization and experimentation with new service delivery arrangements.

Despite these conscious public policy decisions about the nature of society, the etiology of social problems, and the validity of various intervention procedures, the various comprehensive service organizations eventually found themselves dealing primarily with individuals and their families rather than system and organization change. Perhaps in reaction to these larger unachievable claims the current human service movement appears to be viewed primarily as a better clinical instrument and not as a complex, multiorganization capable of solving all problems for all people.

From this perspective the mental health model has actually been substantially integrated into the larger social welfare network for some time. Schools of social work and graduate programs in vocational rehabilitation have long been psychoanalytically oriented. Inservice training programs for public welfare workers have been based on the verbal insight method.[34] Middle-class theories of motivation, treatability, socialization, and future orientation dominate.

The human service movement offers an important alternative to the mental health community. Most recently mental health has opted for organizational separatism with sanctioned links to the medical care and social welfare systems. The comprehensive human service program allows for a joining of all three, and other subsystems as well, without forcing choices among incompatible alternatives.

The community mental health center could serve as an integral or initial component of a larger linked system. Mental health specialists, in addition to their treatment and remedial responsibilities, can serve as consultants, collaborators, and educators. Most important is the leadership role they can play in reinforcing the concepts of the whole man from a whole family living in a whole community. This is an important vantage point for the press toward primary and secondary prevention aimed at the host, agent, and community.

❲ Bibliography

1. ABT ASSOCIATES. *A Study of the Neighborhood Center Pilot Program.* 4 vols. Washington, D.C.: U.S. Government Printing Office, 1969

2. AIKEN, M., and GAGE, J. "Organizational Interdependence and Intra-Organizational Structure." *American Sociological Review,* 33 (1968), 912–930.

3. BAKER, F., and O'BRIEN, G. "Inter-systems Relations and Coordination of Human Service Organizations." *American Journal of Public Health,* 61 (1971), 130–137.

4. BAUMGARTNER, L., and DUMPSON, J. "Health in Welfare: A Joint or Divided Responsibility." *American Journal of Public Health,* 52 (1962), 1067–1076.

5. BECKER, H. "New Problems in Public-Private Relationships." *Bulletin of the New York Academy of Medicine,* 42 (1966), 1099–1108.

6. BLACK, B. "Comprehensive Community Mental Health Services: Setting Social Policy." *Social Work,* 12 (1967), 51–58.

7. ———. *Community Planning for Health Education and Welfare: An Annotated Bibliography.* Washington, D.C.: U.S. Government Printing Office, 1967.

8. DEMONE, H., and LONG, D. "Information-Referral: The Nucleus of a Human-Needs Program." *Community,* 44, no. 6 (1969), 9–11.

9. ———, and SCHULBERG, H. "Regionalization of Health and Welfare Services." In R. Morris, ed., *Encyclopedia of Social Work.* Vol. 2. New York: National Association of Social Workers, 1971. Pp. 1083–1088.

10. DENNIS, M. "Improving Coordination of Welfare and Medical Services." *Children,* 12 (1965), 97–101.

11. GROSSER, C. *Helping Youth: A Study of Six Community Organization Programs.* Washington, D.C.: U.S. Government Printing Office, 1968.

12. GROSSMAN, H., and COX, R. "Coordination: Teamwork in a Small Community." *Public Administration Review,* 23 (1963), 35–39.

13. HARSHBARGER, D. *The Human Service Organization.* Mimeographed, December 1970.

14. KAHN, A. *Neighborhood Information Centers: A Study and Some Proposals.* New York: Columbia University School of Social Work, 1966.

15. KIRCHNER ASSOCIATES. *A Description and Evaluation of Neighborhood Centers.* Washington, D.C.: U.S. Government Printing Office, 1966.

16. LEVINE, S., and WHITE, P. "Exchange as a Conceptual Framework for the Study of Interorganizational Relationships." *Administrative Science Quarterly,* 5 (1961), 583–601.

17. ———, WHITE, P., and PAUL, B. "Community Interorganizational Problems in Providing Medical Care and Social Services." *American Journal of Public Health,* 53 (1963), 1183–1195.

18. LITTWAK, E., and HYLTON, L. "Interorganizational Analysis: A Hypothesis on Coordinating Agencies." *Administrative Science Quarterly,* 6 (1962), 395–420.

19. LOURIE, N. "Community Public Welfare Services." *Public Welfare,* 24 (1966), 65–72.

20. McENTIRE, D., and HAWORTH, J. "The Two Functions of Public Welfare: Income Maintenance and Social Services." *Social Work,* 12 (1967), 22–31.

21. MARCH, M. "The Neighborhood Center Concept." *Public Welfare,* 26 (1968), 97–111.

22. MOYNIHAN, D. "The Urban Negro *Is* the

Urban Problem." *Transaction*, 4 (1967), 36–37.

23. NEWMAN, E., and DEMONE, H. W., Jr. "Policy Paper: A New Look at Public Planning for Human Services." *Journal of Health and Social Behavior*, 10 (1969), 142–149.

24. NIXON, R. M. President's Health Message to the Congress of the United States. Mimeographed, February 18, 1971.

25. O'DONNELL, E. "An Organizational Twiggy: A Review of Neighborhood Service Centers." *Welfare in Review*, 5 (1967), 6–10.

26. ———. "The Neighborhood Service Center: Trends and Developments." *Welfare in Review*, 6 (1968), 11–21.

27. ———, and SULLIVAN, M. "Service Delivery and Social Action Through the Neighborhood Center: A Review of the Research." *Welfare in Review*, 7 (1969), 1–12.

28. ———, and SULLIVAN, M. "Organization for Social and Technological Innovation." In Office of Economic Opportunity, *Neighborhood Centers Draft Manual*. Washington, D.C.: U.S. Government Printing Office, 1969. P. 495.

29. ———, and SULLIVAN, M. Organization for

State Administered Human Resource Programs in Rhode Island. Report to the General Assembly by the Special Legislative Commission to Study Social Services, June 1969.

30. PERLMAN, R., and JONES, D. *Neighborhood Service Centers*. Washington, D.C.: U.S. Government Printing Office, 1967.

31. RAINWATER, L. "The Services Strategy vs. the Income Strategy." *Transaction*, 4 (1967), 40–41.

32. REID, W. "Interagency Coordination in Delinquency Prevention and Control." *Social Service Review*, 38 (1964), 418–423.

33. ———. "Services for People: The Preliminary Recommendations of the Task Force on the Organization of Social Services." *Welfare in Review*, 7 (1969), 9–13.

34. TANNER, V. *Selected Social Work Concepts for Public Welfare Workers*. Washington, D.C.: U.S. Government Printing Office, n.d.

35. WALZ, T. "The Emergence of the Neighborhood Service Center." *Public Welfare*, 27 (1969), 147–156.

CHAPTER 39

A REVIEW OF THE FEDERAL COMMUNITY MENTAL HEALTH CENTERS PROGRAM

Alan I. Levenson

MUCH OF THE HISTORY of the federal community mental health centers program can be traced to events that occurred during and just after World War II. During the war, there developed a great emphasis on acute treatment in the setting of the war zone itself. After the war, there arose a great public concern about the problem of mental illness and our national efforts to deal with the problem. Together, these two sets of circumstances paved the way for the efforts of the federal government to reshape the delivery of mental health services throughout the nation.

Statistics collected during World War II made it abundantly clear that mental illness was indeed a significant problem for this na-tion. Selective Service records showed that mental illness was present to a considerable degree even among young males, those who were considered for possible military service. Of all the men who were examined for the draft, approximately 5 million were rejected as medically unfit. Of those rejected, approximately 40 percent were excluded because of some neuropsychiatric defect. What is more, neuropsychiatric disabilities accounted for the largest single group of medical discharges from the military service.

The military and draft records were clear. Equally clear was the growing number of patients who were hospitalized in large state-run institutions for the mentally ill. At the time that World War II ended, there were approximately 450,000 patients hospitalized in these institutions. Most of them could be expected to remain in these institutions for long periods of time, and many of them had already been there for many years by the time the war ended.

Much of the public concern can be attributed to these and similar statistics. To a perhaps even greater extent, however, the general public was aroused by a series of state hospital exposés published in magazines and books. The general public was made painfully aware of the fact that those patients hospitalized in state institutions were receiving little, if any, active treatment, and their living conditions were close to intolerable. The writers of the exposés were still further stimulated in their work by the fact that the state hospital populations continued to rise for many years after the end of the war. Indeed, by 1955, the nation's mental hospitals housed some 550,000 patients.

Authors, legislators, and the general public all decried the deplorable state of mental hospital services. In addition, they called for a new approach to the problems of mental illness, one that in their view would be more humane and more effective. In part at least, the potential for a new approach seemed to lie in the experiences of World War II military psychiatrists. During the war, these psychiatrists substituted short-term treatment for the traditional long-term practices of prewar civilian psychiatry. A mental disorder developing on the battlefield was seen as an acute problem and not as the beginning of a chronic one. What is more, military psychiatrists quickly learned that their treatment efforts were more successful when the patients were provided with care close to the front lines. Traditional methods had called for the return of neuropsychiatric casualties to hospitals in the United States where they were scheduled to receive long-term care. Now, however, these practices were abandoned, and the neuropsychiatric patient was taken only a few miles from the front; he was treated on a short-term basis and was returned to duty as quickly as possible. The results of this method clearly demonstrated its effectiveness. Mental patients could indeed be treated quickly and returned to their premorbid routines.

Psychiatrists returning to civilian life after the war looked for opportunities to apply their new short-term methods. They were helped in this regard by two other postwar developments. One was the growth of available services for the mentally ill in community general hospitals. Prior to World War II there had been few general hospitals that offered psychiatric services. After the war, however, more and more general hospitals began to accept psychiatric patients. This made it possible for the mentally ill patient to receive needed hospital care locally and conveniently. The new general hospital psychiatric units thus provided the psychiatrist with a setting in which to practice his newly developed treatment methods. Both the establishment of the general hospital psychiatric units and the development of short-term methods of care were aided in turn by the second postwar development, namely, the introduction of tranquilizers and related psychotropics. The drugs made it possible for periods of treatment to be shortened; they also made it possible for general hospital staff and board members to become increasingly accepting of the mentally ill as regular patients.

Despite the use of new methods, the availability of new drugs, and the development of general hospital psychiatric units, however, the first ten years after World War II brought little in the way of change in patterns of treatment of mental illness. Most mentally ill patients were still confined to state hospitals, and their care typically continued to be a matter of many years' duration. Some psychiatrists applied the methods and the lessons of war time, but most maintained the traditional practices. Public demands seemed clear and professional expertise seemed equally clear, but little was done to implement change on a broad scale.

❰ Federal Efforts

The first step in the direction of federal involvement in the development of new types of mental health programs was the enactment of the Mental Health Study Act of 1955. As passed by the Congress, the Act provided for a thorough study of the nation's mental health problems and needs. Moreover, the study was to identify present and potential resources for dealing with the problems of mental illness.

The study was undertaken by the Joint Commission on Mental Illness and Mental Health, and the report of the commission, *Action for Mental Health*,[12] is regarded by many people as having provided the origins of the federal community mental health centers program. The report did indeed emphasize the provision of services for the mentally ill on a local basis. Moreover, it called for the increased use of local general hospitals and local psychiatric clinics as principal resources for this care, and it proposed that the long-standing reliance on state hospitals be abandoned. In fact, the report recommended that existing state hospitals be reduced in size and that no new large institutions be constructed.

Action for Mental Health[12] appeared in 1961, and it served as a statement of mental health needs and goals at the national level. During the years that followed, Congress sought to support similar efforts at assessment at the state level. Between 1962 and 1964, several million dollars were made available for state surveys and the development of state comprehensive mental health plans. Each state was to develop a plan consistent with its own situation, but it was expected that each plan would provide the basis for developing mental health services on a local level.

While the state planning efforts were underway, federal officials were planning for a large-scale national program to support the development of local mental health resources. The planning for this national program began even before the final report of the Joint Commission on Mental Illness and Mental Health had been filed, and the work culminated in the delivery of President Kennedy's[13] mental health message to Congress and the passage of the Community Mental Health Centers Act.[16]

The President's message referred to a "bold new approach" to the care of the mentally ill. Specifically, this new approach referred to the emphasis on community-based services offering local care. Whereas the mentally ill had previously been cared for in isolated state-supported institutions, now they were to be treated in local community-based facilities.

Clearly, this emphasis on local care was the major thrust of the new federal program, but for many observers there was a second, equally important, new approach introduced by the program: the concept of providing federal assistance for the provision of services for the mentally ill. State governments had assumed almost total responsibility for the care of the mentally ill since the middle of the nineteenth century; prior to that time, it had been local governments that had provided such services as were available. The federal government was involved in providing mental health services only for certain specified populations, for example, American Indians, military personnel, merchant seamen, drug addicts, and residents of the District of Columbia. Otherwise, the federal role had been restricted to the support of research and training. Now, however, in 1963, the President and Congress were proposing that the federal government begin to play a major role in the provision of mental health services for all Americans.

The federal government, of course, was not seen as being about to assume full responsibility for the care of the mentally ill. Instead, the federal Community Mental Health Centers Act called for the joint participation of federal, state, and local governments in this work. In addition, the legislative history of the act clearly shows the expectation that the new local programs would utilize both public and private funds for their support.

Still another element of basic strategy in the federal program was that the federal dollars were to be used as "seed money." Federal grants were to be made in a manner that would help local communities in establishing their own mental health programs, but once established it was anticipated that the federal support would quickly be phased out. In its place, the local program was expected to rely on financial resources in its own state and community.

⟪ The Federal Legislation

As originally conceived, the federal support for local mental health programs was to be provided in two forms: (1) grants for the construction of new mental health facilities and (2) grants to assist in meeting the costs of staffing the new facility. In effect, the construction and staffing grants were originally intended to complement each other, for the initial proposal provided that staffing grants would be available only to those local mental health programs that had received support for construction.

When Congress considered the proposed legislation, there was already a long history of federal support for the construction of health facilities. Indeed, the Hill-Burton hospital construction program had provided funds to assist in the cost of building local hospitals since 1946. Moreover, hospital groups throughout the country actively supported the idea of another health facility construction program, particularly one that might give further support to building programs in general hospitals. While federal construction support was well established, however, the concept of direct federal support for the provision of services was essentially unknown. There were very few federal programs providing funds to help nonfederal agencies to meet the costs of staffing a health care program. Moreover, there was active opposition to the idea of providing such federal support. Much of this opposition came from medical groups throughout the country. At the time, these groups were concerned about the development of any new federal program that supported services as opposed to facilities.

Given the history of federal involvement in health and mental health programs, the active support that was available for a new federal construction assistance program, and the active opposition to federal financial support for services themselves, it is hardly surprising that the legislation that was enacted in 1963 pro-

vided authorization only for a construction program. The Community Mental Health Centers Act of 1963[16] made no provision for staffing support. Nevertheless, the Act did depart significantly from previous federal health facilities construction legislation. Specifically, the Community Mental Health Centers Act established eligibility for federal support in terms of a carefully defined program of services. Earlier federal health facilities programs had defined eligibility simply in terms of construction requirements, but the new community mental centers program set forth rigid guidelines in regard to the services to be provided within the new facilities.

The 1963 legislation authorized federal construction support on a formula or grant-in-aid basis. This meant that, of the total amount to be appropriated by the Congress in any given year, a specified proportion would be allocated for each state. The state allocations were based on a formula that had been well established during the history of the Hill-Burton program. It provided for the distribution of funds on the basis of such factors as population and per capita income. Requests for federal assistance had to be initiated by the sponsors of individual community mental health centers, but it was required that each application be consistent with a previously approved plan for the development of community mental health services throughout each state. The development of this plan was the responsibility of a designated state agency, and this agency was also to be responsible for the administration of the federal grant program within the state. It was required that the state agency's plan identify the various geographic regions of the state and, furthermore, indicate the relative priority of need for additional mental health services within each region. Having done this, it was then the responsibility of the state agency, acting through a public advisory committee, to pass on each application for federal construction funds.

The federal construction program was thus heavily dependent on administration at the state level. To be sure, each request for a federal construction grant had to be reviewed by a national committee. Before reaching this committee at the federal level, however, each applicant agency had to receive the support of the public advisory group (or state construction council as it was often known) within its own state.

Because of the emphasis on administration at the state level, the operation of the program could not help but vary somewhat from state to state. In some states there was emphasis on the development of services in urban areas, while in others the emphasis was on the development of services in rural communities. In some instances the state mental health authority provided a considerable amount of assistance to local agencies involved in the development of construction grant applications, while in others the state agency played a much more passive role. What is more, the program was so structured that there was variation among the states in regard to the level of federal support. This variation was another feature derived from the existing federal program for the construction of hospitals. The level of federal support for each construction project varied from one-third of the costs of the construction to two-thirds of the cost. This proportion, the federal share, was predetermined for each state, and the same percentage was applied to all projects within that state. Each state's federal percentage, like its proportion of the total federal appropriation, was determined on the basis of the state's socioeconomic level.

This concept of a fixed federal share for construction grants in each state was reaffirmed by the Community Mental Health Centers Act Amendments of 1967.[18] These amendments renewed the construction program authorization in its original form. In 1970, however, the program was somewhat modified. Amendments adopted in that year[19] provided for a higher level of federal construction support for community mental health centers in poverty areas. More specifically, the amendments authorized a uniform 90 percent federal share for centers serving poverty areas in all states.

([Federal Support for Staffing

Although the original Community Mental Health Centers Act of 1963 failed to provide for staffing grants, the amendments of 1965[17] provided for this staffing support. During the two years following passage of the original Act, much had happened to clear the way for this additional form of federal support. For example, as the comprehensive mental health planning projects continued in each state, the concept of the community mental health center became more widely known and more readily accepted. This growing acceptance led citizens' groups, legislators, and professionals to become increasingly concerned about the availability of financial resources that could support the new centers. As a result, there was a steady increase in the extent of public support, and indeed public demand, for federal staffing assistance.

The federal staffing grants were authorized in such a way that they were to be administered quite differently from the construction grants. Rather than being a formula or grant-in-aid type of program, the staffing support was to be administered through project grants. This meant that each application was to be considered in nationwide competition, and each grant was to be awarded from the total pool of appropriated funds. There were to be no state allocations, and as a result, the state mental health agencies were to play a somewhat less significant role in regard to staffing grant applications than they had become accustomed to playing in regard to construction grant applications. The state agencies were asked to review each request for staffing support, but these agencies were denied the veto power that they were able to exercise in the case of individual construction applications.

The 1965 amendments also specified a standardized federal share for staffing support. Whereas states differed in the level of federal construction support to which they were entitled, every state was to receive the same level of federal staffing support. Each eligible community mental health center could receive federal support at the level of 75 percent of staffing support during the first fifteen months of operation. During the next twelve months, the center was eligible for federal support at a level of 60 percent of staffing costs. The federal percentage was then to drop to 45 percent for twelve months, and finally it was to drop to 30 percent for the final three months of the grant. This meant that each center could expect federal support for staffing during a total period of fifty-one months.

Another significant feature of the original staffing grant authorization was its rather narrow definition of eligible staffing costs. Under the terms of Public Law 89-105,[17] community mental health centers could receive federal staffing support only for the costs of professional and technical personnel. These personnel were defined as staff members with responsibility for direct patient care. Clearly, the legislation provided no federal support for costs of operation other than those relating to personnel, for example, rent, utilities, and supplies. Moreover, because of the definition of eligible staff, the federal support could not be used to help pay the salaries of purely administrative personnel, clerical staff, maintenance and housekeeping staff, or kitchen help.

The more recent history of the federal staffing legislation is similar to that of the construction legislation. The 1967 amendments to the Community Mental Health Centers Act renewed the program of staffing support with little change in its format. In 1970, however, the additional amendments[19] broadened the staffing program in several respects.

One major element of change was a lengthening of the period of time during which a community mental health center might receive federal staffing support. Whereas the initial legislation had provided for a maximum of fifty-one months of support, the 1970 amendments[19] increased the length of support to a total of eight years. Moreover, the 1970 amendments specified that a center could receive federal assistance at a level of 75 percent of eligible staffing costs during the first two years of this grant period, at a level of 60 percent during the third year, at a level of 45 percent during the fourth year, and at a level of 40 percent during the final four years. By increasing the level of the federal share and the length of time of federal support, these amendments substantially increased the federal government's financial commitment to each new community mental health center.

In addition, the 1970 amendments provided for preferential support for community mental health centers in poverty areas. Just as these centers were to be eligible for construction support at a level of 90 percent, so too they were to be eligible for staffing support at a much increased level. The length of federal support for staffing was again set at eight years, just as for centers serving nonpoverty areas. During the first two years of the grant period, however, a community mental health center serving a poverty area became eligible for federal staffing support at a level of 90 percent of eligible costs. The amendments further provided that the federal share was to be 80 percent during the third year of the grant, 75 percent for years four and five, and 70 percent for the final three years.

Also of great significance was the 1970 change in the definition of eligible staff costs. This change also provided for a substantial increase in the extent of federal support for each community mental health center. Prior to the passage of the 1970 amendments, centers could receive federal support only for those technical and professional personnel who met the rather narrowly defined criteria outlined above. Under the terms of the 1970 amendments, the federal staffing funds could be applied to the salaries of almost all center personnel. The only personnel excepted were to be those considered to be minor clerical staff, maintenance staff, and housekeeping personnel. Otherwise, all staff—clinical, administrative, and clerical—might be included in the federal grant.

❰ Concepts and Services

As originally conceived for the federal program, a basic purpose of the community mental health center was the provision of local services. The goal was the care of the mentally ill patient within his own community. In this way he was to have the advantage of having the support of family, friends, and job available to him. In order for local care to be provided, however, it is necessary that the community mental health center make its services maximally accessible. The accessibility must be achieved not only through the physical placement of the center within the community that it serves but also through the development of center services that are available on a twenty-four hour per day, seven day per week basis.

Clearly, for the community mental health center to serve a local population, it was necessary that there be created a mechanism for specifically identifying the community to be served by each center. In the course of developing the federal community mental health centers program, considerable thought and attention were paid to the issue of defining the community to be served. The mechanism chosen was to define the community in terms of a specified geographic area having a predetermined number of residents. This geographic area was designated the catchment area, and according to the federal regulations each center must serve a specific catchment area having a population of 75,000 to 200,000 residents.

These population limitations were based on an awareness of the center's need to develop economically feasible programs, on the one hand, and its need to relate to many other community agencies, on the other. Accordingly, the 75,000 minimum population was chosen because it appeared that a center serving fewer than 75,000 persons would not be able to mount an economically efficient program. On the other hand, the 200,000 maximum figure was chosen because it appeared that a center serving more than that number of people would be unable to develop strong program ties with other human service agencies. In actual fact, as community mental health center grant applications were processed, it soon became clear that these figures could not be applied to all communities. In some cases it was more reasonable for a center

to serve fewer than 75,000 persons, and in other cases it was more reasonable for the center to serve more than 200,000 persons. Accordingly, many mental health centers were awarded federal grants and at the same time granted an exception to the basic population requirements.

The concept of offering local and accessible services has constituted one of the basic principles of the federal community mental health centers program since its inception. Another basic principle has been that of offering comprehensive services to the population served. In regard to the community mental health center, the word "comprehensive" was defined as having several meanings. In order to be comprehensive, it was anticipated that a community mental health center would have to provide a variety of types of care, and it would have to provide this care for a variety of types of illness. Thus, each community mental health center must provide services for all residents in the community—the young as well as the old, the psychotic as well as the neurotic, the alcoholic as well as the school dropout. Moreover, the center must offer services that are appropriate for each individual patient's specific problem.

In an effort to provide the necessary variety of services, the federal community mental health centers program requires that each center offer a minimum five essential services: (1) inpatient care; (2) outpatient care; (3) emergency services on a round-the-clock basis; (4) partial hospitalization (at least day hospital care and, optionally, night hospital care); and (5) community consultation and education. In addition, it is recommended that each center offer an additional five services: (1) precare and aftercare for patients hospitalized in long-term care facilities; (2) diagnostic services; (3) rehabilitation services; (4) research and evaluation programs; and (5) training and education programs. A center that offers the five essential services is eligible for federal support, but according to the definitions of the federal program, a center is not comprehensive unless it offers all ten services.

It is easily noted that both the list of essential services and the list of comprehensive services emphasize the care of the patient who presents himself at the center with a mental disorder. In public health terminology, these services are oriented to secondary prevention (the reduction of prevalence of disease through early and active treatment) and tertiary prevention (the reduction of residual disabilities through rehabilitation and follow-up programs). In addition, it is a clear intent of the federal community mental health centers program that each center develop an active program of primary prevention. Such a program is one designed to reduce the incidence of mental disorders, that is, to reduce the number of new cases of mental illness that develop within the catchment area. In terms of the original concept of the federal program, the service to be principally involved in a center's efforts at primary prevention is its program of consultation and education. Consultation and education are seen as the mechanism through which the professional staff of the community mental health center can help other local caregivers to maximize their own ability to identify and help the person who is potentially mentally ill. Consultation and education efforts are directed largely at those professionals outside the mental health field who work with people in times of personal crisis. Thus, most community mental health centers have focused their consultation and education programs on schoolteachers, clergymen, probation officers, welfare workers, and others in similar positions.

Although a consultation and education program constitutes one of the required elements of service in a community mental health center, it is clear that consultation and education activities have received only limited emphasis in many of the early centers. The major emphasis has been placed upon the development of direct patient care services, while preventive programs of consultation and education have been given a much lower priority. Indeed, the typical early center has devoted only about 10 percent or less of its program efforts to consultation and education.

This limited development of consultation and education programs has been attributed to several factors. One of these is the relative newness of these activities as part of the mental health professional's work. Most mental health professionals have been trained in the provision of direct patient care services, both diagnostic and therapeutic. The practice of preventive psychiatry is a rather new development, and as a result it has not been included in the traditional training program curricula. A second reason for the limited emphasis on consultation and education services can be found in the fiscal circumstances of many centers. Even when a community mental health center receives a large federal staffing grant, the center must still find funds not only to match the grant but also to pay for those aspects of its operation that are not covered by the grant at all. Accordingly, most centers have emphasized the provision of services for which they could receive direct reimbursement or some other kind of financial support. Unfortunately, financial support for consultation and education programs is not readily available. Indeed, in many instances, the centers themselves have been expected to pay for the consultation services they have provided to other agencies. This has been particularly true during the early phases of the development of consultation programs.

Those responsible for the administration of the federal community mental health centers program have been well aware of and much concerned about the limited development of consultation programs. As a result, it is not surprising that the 1970 amendments to the federal Community Mental Health Centers Act[19] included a special provision to increase the amount of federal support available for these consultation and education services. Specifically, the amendments authorized supplemental grants to community mental health centers to assist them in meeting the costs of staffing their consultation units. These supplemental awards are to be provided in addition to any support for consultation and education services that is included in a basic staffing grant.

It must be noted that consultation and education services are not alone in having suffered from limited emphasis in the typical new community mental health center. As the first centers began operation, it quickly became evident that even their direct diagnostic and treatment services were restricted in respect to some patient groups. In particular, services were typically available on only a very limited basis for alcoholic patients, drug-abuse patients, and, to a lesser extent, children and adolescents. Accordingly, in an effort to strengthen the direct services for these patient groups, the Community Mental Health Centers Act amendments of 1970[19] included special provisions for supporting services for these groups. Specifically, the measure authorized special staffing grants to support these highly specialized services.

Many of the early centers found it difficult to establish specific services for children and other groups, and many centers found it difficult to establish specific consultation and education programs. In addition, many centers faced a more general developmental problem. The federal program guidelines required that a community mental health center offer all five essential services in order to be eligible for a federal grant. The regulations further required that all five services be operational within approximately ninety days of the starting date of the grant. For many centers, it was indeed difficult to establish all the services within the required time period. In many instances the problem was one of getting all the services going at the same time. Other communities faced a problem in organizing a planning effort that was adequate to lay the necessary groundwork for the creation and opening of a community mental health center. Both problems were particularly severe in communities that had previously had extremely limited mental health resources, and these problems were perhaps most severe of all in those poverty areas that lacked human service resources of almost every kind.

The existence and persistence of these problems made it clear that the federal community mental health centers program as originally conceived was deficient in regard to its support for local planning. Although state level planning had been emphasized by the comprehensive mental health planning support and by the construction plan requirements of the community mental health centers program itself, the original Act paid little attention to the need for local planning.

In an effort to correct this deficiency, the Act was amended in 1970 to provide assistance for local planning and also to give individual centers a longer period of time in which to implement their services. Specifically, these new provisions of the federal program were aimed at centers being established in poverty areas, and they were also aimed at centers in the process of establishing services for children and adolescents, alcoholics, and narcotic addicts. The 1970 amendments[19] authorized grants to assist in the "initiation and development" of those centers that are to serve poverty areas and those that are establishing services for one or more of the special population groups. These initiation and development grants can be made for a term of one year and can provide the recipient with up to $50,000. In addition, the amendments of 1970 allowed those centers that serve poverty areas to begin operation of their five essential services over a period of eighteen months. As a result, it is possible for centers to receive special federal support during the planning stage and also to receive staffing support while phasing in their programs.

Amendments to the original Community Mental Health Centers Act of 1963 have thus introduced continual modifications into the original program. One aspect of the program, however, has not been changed. This is the requirement that federal staffing funds be used only for the support of new services. The intent of Congress was originally and has continued to be that federal money be made available to help in the development of services that have not previously been available.

For operational purposes, however, it should be noted that a "new service" can be defined in any one of several ways for purposes of determining eligibility of federal support. Clearly a service is new and thus eligible for federal support if it has not been previously provided by the applicant agency or any predecessor of the applicant agency. Alternatively, a community mental health center can receive support for a new service if this particular service is to be provided through the use of a treatment method or delivery mechanism that has not been previously available. Finally, the federal law and regulations make it possible for a community mental health center to be funded for the operation of a service that has been in operation on a pilot or trial basis for a period of not more than nine months prior to the time of application for a federal staffing grant.

lished in each of the ten regional offices, and the recommendations of these committees now go directly to the National Advisory Mental Health Council for final review. It is the council, which has been established by federal statute to advise the surgeon general of the Public Health Service in regard to matters pertaining to mental health, that now makes the final recommendation regarding the approval or disapproval of each staffing grant application.

❬ Administration of the Federal Program

Responsibility for the operation and administration of the federal community mental health centers program has been vested in the National Institute of Mental Health (NIMH). Staff members of the NIMH have been assigned the task of reviewing and passing on each application for center funds. When considering a staffing grant application, the NIMH staff has exercised final and full authority. Each staffing grant applicant essentially makes his request directly to the NIMH, and it is the NIMH that acts directly on the application. As noted above, however, the mechanism of operation of the construction grant program is somewhat different. Essentially, the NIMH shares its authority for the review of construction grant applications with a governmental agency designated for each state. The federal reviewers have the final but not full authority. A construction grant application can be reviewed at the federal level only if it has been approved and forwarded by the state agency.

Originally the administration of the community mental health centers program was assigned primarily to the staff of the NIMH central office in Washington. As the program was first structured, the work of the several NIMH field officers was to provide consulta- to those applicants who sought federal funds. More recently, however, the review and approval role of the regional offices has been considerably strengthened. Construction grants are still reviewed by committees estab-

❬ Resources for Community Mental Health Centers

The operation of a community mental health center is dependent on three basic resources: money, staff, and physical facilities. The purpose of the federal community mental health centers program has been to provide assistance for centers in obtaining needed resources in all three areas. The federal approach has been to provide direct assistance in regard to financial resources, and thus indirectly the federal program has provided assistance to centers in obtaining the needed physical plant and personnel resources.

Unfortunately, the federal program has never provided funds at the rate originally intended. During the first four years of the operation of the construction program, Congress authorized a federal expenditure of $200 million. In actual fact, however congressional appropriations provided only $180 million during this time, and, moreover, because of administrative decisions made by the executive branch of the federal government, the amount of money actually available for expenditure by the NIMH during this time was only $135 million. In addition, it must be noted that in subsequent years the amount of money available for construction grants has been substantially less than the level anticipated by the original planners of the program.

The same unfortunate fiscal history can also be seen in regard to the staffing grant program. During the first three years of the program's existence, the congressional authorization amounted to a total of $73.5 million. Of this amount, less than $60 million was actually available for distribution to applicants. As in the case of the construction grants, the amount of federal money available for staffing grants has been less than the amount originally anticipated.

Clearly, it was never intended that federal money alone be used to bring about the creation of community mental health centers. It was anticipated that state and local governments would provide some of the needed financial support and that private resources would also be used in the development of local centers. Unfortunately, however, it has turned out that the availability of funds from all these sources has been quite limited. As a result, at a time when centers have been faced with limitations in availability of federal funds, they have often been unable to find alternative sources of financial support in their local communities or state governments.

Federal, state, and local governmental bodies have all been attempting to deal with expanding resources necessary to meet the total needs of the community mental health centers program. In a like manner, private resources have not been able to expand with sufficient rapidity. Originally it was expected, for example, that the growth of private health insurance would significantly aid in the funding of community mental health centers. In actual fact, however, the growth of health insurance benefits for mental illness has not fulfilled expectations. A case in point is the insurance coverage of day hospital care. Many health insurance policies still do not cover such care, and as a result centers are frequently denied this potential resource for the development of their partial hospitalization programs.

Conclusion

As of early 1971, the federal community mental health centers program had funded approximately 400 local programs, and approximately half of these had begun operation.

Some of the funded centers had received both construction and staffing grants, but the majority had received only one type of federal support. The typical center was established to serve a catchment area of about 150,000 persons, and the usual organizational structure included a general hospital and one or more affiliated mental health service agencies.

The original intent of the federal program was the establishment of 2,000 centers to serve the nation's entire population. This total number of centers is still the goal, but as the program has functioned for the past several years, the target date for achieving the goal has been pushed further and further ahead. At this point it appears that a nationwide system of centers could not be achieved prior to the 1980s. The gradually increasing delay is a function of limitations in the availability of both federal dollars and local and state matching dollars. Ultimately, however, it continues to be the intention of the NIMH that local mental health programs be established throughout the nation and that these programs take the form of community mental health centers. As such they will be able to offer comprehensive mental health services, and in addition they will be designed to function as one component in a still more comprehensive system of total human services.

Bibliography

1. BOLMAN, W. M., and WESTMAN, J. C. "Prevention of Mental Disorder: An Overview of Current Programs." *American Journal of Psychiatry*, 123 (1967), 1058–1068.
2. BROWN, B. S., and CAIN, H. P. "The Many Meanings of Comprehensive." *American Journal of Orthopsychiatry*, 34 (1964), 834–839.
3. CAPLAN, G. *Principles of Preventive Psychiatry*. New York: Basic Books, 1964.
4. DEUTSCH, A. *The Shame of the States*. New York: Harcourt, Brace, 1948.
5. FELIX, R. H. *Mental Illness: Progress and Prospects*. New York: Columbia University Press, 1967.
6. GINZBURG, E. "Army Hospitalization: Retrospect and Prospect." *Bulletin of the U.S.*

Army Medical Department, 8 (1948), 38–47.

7. GLASS, A. J. "Principles of Combat Psychiatry." Military Medicine, 117 (1955), 27–33.

8. GLASSCOTE, R., et al. The Community Mental Health Center: An Analysis of Existing Models. Washington, D.C.: Joint Information Service, 1963.

9. ——, et al. The Community Mental Health Center: An Interim Appraisal. Washington, D.C.: Joint Information Service, 1969.

10. GORMAN, M. Every Other Bed. Cleveland: World, 1956.

11. GROUP FOR THE ADVANCEMENT OF PSYCHIATRY. Public Psychiatric Hospitals. Report no. 5. Topeka, 1948.

12. JOINT COMMISSION ON MENTAL ILLNESS AND MENTAL HEALTH. Action for Mental Health. New York: Basic Books, 1961.

13. KENNEDY, J. F. Message from the President of the United States Relative to Mental Illness and Mental Retardation. House of Representatives document no. 58, 88th Congress, 1st Session, February 5, 1963.

Washington, D.C.: U.S. Government Printing Office, 1963.

14. OZARIN, L. "The Community Mental Health Center: Concept and Commitment." Mental Hygiene, 52 (1968), 76–80.

15. ——, and BROWN, B. S. "New Directions in Community Mental Health Programs." American Journal of Orthopsychiatry, 35 (1965), 10–17.

16. U.S. CONGRESS. Community Mental Health Centers Act of 1963. Public Law 88-164, Title II. Washington, D.C.: U.S. Government Printing Office, 1963.

17. ——. Mental Retardation Facilities and Community Mental Health Centers Construction Act Amendments of 1965. Public Law 89-105. Washington, D.C.: U.S. Government Printing Office, 1965.

18. ——. Mental Health Amendments of 1967. Public Law 90-31. Washington, D.C.: U.S. Government Printing Office, 1967.

19. ——. Community Mental Health Centers Amendments of 1970. Public Law 91-211. Washington, D.C.: U.S. Government Printing Office, 1970.

CHAPTER 40

THE CONTROL OF
EPIDEMIC DRUG ABUSE

Organizing a National Program

Stanley F. Yolles

TRADITIONALLY, in the United States social programs designed and operated to meet the health and welfare needs of the American people have developed through evolution rather than revolution. Typical of the national reluctance to change its laissez-faire attitudes is the fact that today, even though there is a growing acceptance of the need to establish a national health program to provide for the equitable delivery of health services throughout the population, the form and scope of such a program are matters of professional and political controversy.

In this frame of reference, therefore, it is understandable that the government and the people are experiencing extreme difficulty in evolving a national drug-abuse program. Drug abuse has been variously defined as a legal, moral, medical, health, or social problem. For many years, the federal government's effort to control the use of narcotics was predicated on the notion that the use of narcotics was a crime, per se, and that drug addicts should be punished as criminals. Whether from cause or effect, this federal attitude was reflected in public attitudes. The few professionals who advocated treatment rather than punishment were largely ignored.

As recently as 1966, federal concern over the abuse of illicit drugs continued to be limited almost entirely to narcotic addiction. Treatment of addicts was provided for by the federal government in the barred, prison-like environment of the federal narcotic hospitals at Lexington, Kentucky, and Fort Worth, Texas. With very few exceptions, states and local communities limited their concern with narcotic addiction to the enforcement of punitive statutes. The inadequacy of token treatment programs brought pressures to bear through the national legislative process, and in 1966 the Narcotic Addict Rehabilitation Act was adopted by the Congress.

Under terms of this statute, the federal government accepted a mandate to provide community-based treatment and rehabilitation for those narcotic addicts who elected to accept civil commitment in lieu of standing trial for federal offenses, as well as volunteers for civil commitment. Thus, the federal government took its first significant step toward the establishment of a national program designed to provide treatment and rehabilitation, rather than punishment, for narcotic addicts. Under the administration of the National Institute of Mental Health (NIMH), the bars came down at Lexington and Fort Worth, treatment replaced custodial care, and addiction research centers were established. However, in 1966 public concern over dangerous drugs other than narcotics was still moderate, and the Narcotic Addict Rehabilitation Act made no provision for treatment of other drugs of abuse.

The Narcotic Addict Rehabilitation program, with federal funding support, established community-based addiction treatment units through contracts with existing state and local agencies. In so doing, it paved the way for further developments throughout the comprehensive community mental health services program.

When the Community Mental Health Centers Act was adopted in 1963, no specific provisions were made for support of alcohol and narcotic addiction programs within the new community mental health centers. But, since such programs were not specifically excluded, a number of mental health centers organized treatment programs for alcoholics, while remaining ambivalent about narcotic addiction. Following the initiation of the Narcotic Addict Rehabilitation program, amendments to the Community Mental Health Centers Act were proposed, providing special incentives to initiate alcohol and narcotic programs. Numbers of congressmen and senators sponsored a variety of proposals for special alcoholism pro-

grams; but the sense of immediacy was lacking and for a variety of reasons, the programs were not funded. The NARA program continued its exploratory and deliberate expansion; proponents of amendments to the Community Mental Health Centers Act marshaled their forces in order to try again.

Then, in rapid succession, a chain of events occurred that affected the social and cultural life of the entire population: Lysergic acid (LSD) tripped out of the laboratory on to the campus; marijuana suddenly became a symbol of youthful defiance and "everybody's child" who smoked a "joint" became a criminal by definition under federal statutes; and then heroin jumped out of the ghetto and the gutter into the affluent suburbs and the armed forces. Public apathy changed to panic; the administration certainly began to doubt; and the great drug debate took center stage in the American consciousness.

In 1967 and 1968 various agencies within the federal government were moving on a collision course in their efforts to control drug abuse. The Department of Justice proposed legislation during 1969 providing for increased mandatory minimum penalties for everyone convicted of possession and/or use of illicit drugs. The proposed legislation would have forced the courts to deal with a youngster caught smoking his first marijuana cigarette in the same fashion as with a professional peddler of narcotics. Under federal law, marijuana was still legally classified as a narcotic, and in the proposed legislation, the scheduling of drugs in risk classifications attributed a higher risk to marijuana than to LSD, the amphetamines, and other chemical compounds classified as dangerous drugs. Proponents of these legislative proposals continued to believe that increased penalties for drug abusers would prevent drug abuse.

Some members of Congress, however, took another course. They requested information from the NIMH and the Food and Drug Administration on progress of research on LSD, marijuana, and other dangerous drugs and heard testimony on research needs as well as on means to support public information and education programs in drug abuse.

In 1968, the scope of research, either funded by the NIMH or utilizing LSD from NIMH supplies, covered a wide range of activity from surveys and epidemiological studies through basic biochemical and experimental psychopharmacological research. The NIMH during fiscal 1968 was supporting fifty-eight studies, at a cost of $3.4 million for research in the area of LSD and other hallucinogenic agents, including studies designed to measure the extent and trends of LSD and other hallucinogenic use. A number of studies produced findings that suggested that LSD can cause severe psychotic reactions and may cause chromosomal damage. When this information was disseminated among young people, use of LSD began to decline, indicating that factual information concerning risk of adverse effects had some effect on the rate at which a specific drug was abused. As a result, Congress appropriated funds with which the NIMH initiated the first drug information program using the mass media; other funds were provided the NIMH and the Office of Education for pilot programs designed to educate schoolteachers about drugs, so that they, in turn, could present the available facts about drug abuse to their students. The White House collaborated in this program by establishing a drug-abuse education program focus, through which television and radio executives, the clergy, and others were provided with drug-abuse information at a series of White House meetings. During subsequent months, research findings on the risks of abuse of amphetamines and other dangerous drugs provided additional data on the effects of these drugs. Even though abuse of the drugs continues, there is evidence that drug abusers accept the validity of current research findings. Methamphetamine is a case in point. Throughout the drug culture, the knowledge that "Speed kills" has been demonstrated, and the rate of its use has declined.

The situation surrounding the use of cannabis, however, is more complex. When the hippies, the flower children, and the college students overwhelmed the traditional American society, marijuana use became a symbol of dissent throughout the "square," or traditional,

adult population. The controversy over marijuana, therefore, was in actuality only one part of a much larger and deeper phenomenon, variously called "alienation of the young," the "generation gap," or "the flight from reality."

While, in actuality, parents and their children were in conflict over the rejection of an entire life style, what they talked about was marijuana, and most of the arguments were based on myth and fable rather than fact. At the time when marijuana became the catalyst for controversy within the entire phenomenon of drug abuse, information about cannabis was in short supply.

As early as 1964, the NIMH was supporting research to effect a synthesis of the tetrahydrocannabinols, since the only source of the natural plant came from confiscated supplies of varying potency, and efforts to extract tetrahydrocannabinol were inefficient. Early efforts were unsuccessful, but during 1966, Raphael Mechoulam in Israel synthesized tetrahydrocannabinol; during 1967 Petrzilka published a method for synthesizing it; and during 1968 the NIMH contracted for the production of research quantities of both delta-8 and delta-9 tetrahydrocannabinol for distribution to the research community.

By the time research into the effects of the drug itself began to be effective, however, the entire marijuana question had gotten out of hand, and any relationship between argument and rational thought was coincidental. Eventually, faced with legislation that would continue to equate drug-abuse control with law enforcement under the system of criminal justice, the medical and scientific communities began to add their testimony before Congress to that of law enforcement officials.

(Legislative Authorities

The immediate result as far as legislation was concerned was the 1970 adoption of the Comprehensive Drug Abuse Prevention and Control Act. Mandatory minimum penalties were abolished; marijuana was taken out of the classification as a narcotic; provisions for parole for first offenders were provided; and the Secretary of the U.S. Department of Health, Education, and Welfare was given the authority to establish the comparative risk of each drug included in the schedule of dangerous substances, on which penalties under the law are based.

Of major significance in the adoption of this statute is the fact that the federal government accepted the notion that a federal responsibility exists in the establishment of a program of treatment, rehabilitation, and prevention of narcotic and drug abuse as a national policy. The statute authorized support of a more comprehensive treatment program; grants for development of materials and curricula dealing with drug education; training of professionals in treatment methods, rehabilitation programs and health education; and a special project grants program for detoxification and other special services. Given adequate funding, this statute, with other existing authorities, makes it possible for the federal government to assume the leadership in developing a comprehensive national program.

Illustrative of the trend that brought about the passage of the Drug Abuse Prevention and Control Act was the adoption, earlier during 1970, of the Community Mental Health Centers Act amendments, which had been under consideration for months. The 1970 amendments reflected a new awareness within the Administration of the need to develop special programs for dealing with the problems of alcoholism and drug abuse and that federal support should be provided as an integral part of the network of community mental health services.

Testifying before Congress, Administration spokesmen said,

Preventive and curative services for drug abusers and for alcoholics must be a part of a comprehensive mental health system and should not lead to separate facilities and services. The mental health centers model is an ideal one in which to integrate facilities for services for alcoholism and drug abuse.

For a number of reasons, services for alcoholics and narcotic addicts at the community level will require very special efforts and incentives. There-fore, preferential matching of funds and a longer period of Federal support are necessary.[1]

The 1970 amendments signaled a renewed interest within the Administration in the community mental health services program and a realization that the 452 community mental health centers already receiving federal support could and should provide drug-abuse programs in areas where the need was greatest. The statute therefore provided for preferential support in poverty areas.

The President's budget for fiscal year 1972 had originally included $105 million for support of the mental health centers program. However, most of the money was committed to the funding of grants already made. Additionally, therefore, the Congress approved a $67 million supplementary request for treatment of narcotic and drug abuses and a $7 million supplemental for the alcoholism program. All this related to widened government perceptions of the potential role of the community mental health center in meeting social problems underlying the manifest illness or disturbance of an individual, which certainly is inclusive of the causes of narcotic addiction and drug abuse.

Meanwhile, under the Narcotic Addict Rehabilitation program, by fiscal year 1971, the federal government had funded a total of twenty-three narcotic addict community treatment units in twenty-one cities. Furthermore, in addition to support of continuing and new staffing grants, this program in fiscal year 1971 was projecting further support through contracts; funds for special projects; program evaluation; and initiation and development grants providing seed money for local programs.

The estimates of federal funds for drug abuse programs by category, shown in Table 40–1, are indicative of the shift in emphasis from law enforcement to treatment, rehabilitation, education, training and research. These estimates include funding in the federal agencies involved in drug abuse with the exception of the Department of Defense. In essence, events in the calendar years 1968 through 1970 had brought about increased federal support in all facets of the narcotic addiction program and had established the foundation for support of a comprehensive program to cope with the problem of abuse of other dangerous drugs as well.

TABLE 40–1. **Federal Funds for Drug-Abuse Programs: Estimated Budget Obligations**

CATEGORY	1969[a]	1970[a]	1971[a]
Law enforcement	$22.3[b]	$ 39.3[b]	$ 48.7[b]
Treatment and rehabilitation	$28.5	$ 38.5	$ 73.5
Education and training	$ 2.0	$ 10.0	$ 10.6
Research and other support	$15.1	$ 17.3	$ 21.9
Total	$67.9	$105.1	$154.7

[a] Fiscal years.
[b] Millions of dollars.

Throughout 1971, as federal agencies sought to reach agreement on the means to administer a comprehensive national drug-abuse program, the evident increase in the use of heroin among the population within the continental United States was compounded by the spread of heroin use among the armed forces throughout Southeast Asia.

Estimates of narcotic addiction in the United States are reported annually by the Bureau of Narcotics and Dangerous Drugs. Estimates of the size of the actual addict population in the United States can be approached by comparing these figures with those from the New York City Health Department's addiction register, as well as through extrapolations of the number of heroin-related deaths in New York. These data indicated that in 1969 there were approximately 104,000 heroin addicts in New York City alone. Thus, the number of addicts throughout the United States may have been as high as 250,000.

In the spring of 1971, a poll purported to show a 16.15 percent drug-use rate among servicemen in Vietnam; and by mid-1971, evidence of heroin addiction among servicemen returning from Vietnam brought about Presidential action.

On June 17, the President of the United States, in a special message to Congress, termed the drug problem "a national emergency." By executive order, President Nixon assigned central and overriding authority for federal efforts in solving the narcotic and drug-abuse problem to the White House; created the Special Action Office for Drug Abuse Prevention to direct and coordinate all federal programs relating to drug abuse; submitted legislation to establish the office; and increased his fiscal year 1972 budget request by asking Congress for a government-wide total of $371 million for drug-abuse programs, including the further testing of anti-addiction compounds.

The fact that the Congress had not acted on the President's request when it adjourned for Christmas 1971 is a measure of the political complexities inherent in establishing a national drug-abuse program. The Congress, for example, has the prerogative to review programs administered by agencies within the executive branch of the government. It also has the responsibility to hold these agencies accountable for the manner in which funds are used. The President's request to establish a central office for drug-abuse programs within the executive office of the President affects congressional prerogatives, because the proposal requests permission to transfer funds from one agency to another at the discretion of the White House.

Although concern over the spread of heroin use in the armed forces undoubtedly triggered the President's request to the Congress for centralized authority within his executive office, other data indicated that the drug scene at home was also undergoing significant change. It is difficult to secure information on the patterns of use of illicit drugs, because of the possibility of criminal action; it is also difficult to secure information about the careers of drug users and the factors influencing their drug use and other behavior. However, as interest in drug research increases and additional funds become available, it has been possible to analyze trends in drug abuse, estimate the extent of abuse, and project possible avenues for the development of a program of prevention, treatment, and rehabilitation.

For 1969, the number of users, categorized by the drug used, has been estimated as follows: heroin, 250,000; LSD, 1 million; amphetamines, taken orally, 4 million; marijuana, anywhere from 10 to 20 million; barbiturates, 2 million. The number of persons who inject amphetamines, mix barbiturates with other drugs, or use inhalants cannot be estimated, except to assume from available evidence that their numbers are small in comparison with the above estimates.

The extent of use is only one measure of the problem; but increasing use is an indicator of other factors in the quality of American life which must be considered to be drug related. During 1971, for example, using any of the measures available, drug use and abuse continued to increase within an ever-widening age group. The "recreational" use of marijuana is currently so widespread that it is no longer considered to be a symbol of dissent and rebellion by young people.

(Drug Research

Recent trends in narcotic addiction, outside the armed forces, indicate that typical patterns include increasing experimentation with heroin among middle-class suburban youth; intravenous use of methamphetamine as an adjunct to heroin; and more frequent overdoses. Addiction still tends, however, to be concentrated in the ghettos of large cities, where 80 percent of the addicts are male and about half the arrested addicts are in the twenty-one to thirty age group.

Preliminary results of an NIMH study of high school and junior high school students during 1971[3] indicated that present concern over heroin must not blot out other drug-abuse problems. One county that has had relatively high rates of drug use among its high school population has now conducted the same type of student survey for four consecutive years. Results for the 1970–1971 school year now show a marked increase in the use of

all drugs with the exception of tobacco. Alcohol use, which some have suggested might be replaced by marijuana use, showed the largest apparent increase over 1970 in this group of junior high and high school students.

During 1971, the NIMH was supporting some sixty-six projects in marijuana research at a total cost of nearly $3 million a year, a little more than three years since it mounted an intensive research program in this field. This federal program has achieved several major objectives:

1. It has made cannabis research respectable, so that highly competent researchers are entering the field without fear of adverse publicity, professional disapproval, or disapproval of law enforcement officials.

2. It has made available, in standard dosage forms of known potency, a wide variety of natural and synthetic materials basic to continued research.

3. Investigations have shown that delta-9-tetrahydrocannabinol not only is broken down in the body, but that some metabolites can be found up to six to eight days after a single administration. This suggests a long duration of action and possible interference with other drugs.

4. Toxicity studies performed during the past year have clearly shown a large safety index between the behaviorally active and the toxic doses.

5. Subjective and objective effects of single-dose, acute administration of cannabis and its active components have been greatly elucidated.

6. Present overseas studies of chronic effects of cannabis will be expanded, as will studies of the complex motivations of users, in an effort to determine the implications of cannabis use as they relate to human conditions that may trigger its abuse.

7. Research on other psychoactive drugs has also been accelerated. Current findings relating to the effects of amphetamines, for example, indicate that these drugs have potential for serious depen-

dency, addiction, and even death. The emergence over the past year or so of the youthful polydrug user heightens the need for additional research on the interrelationship of the effects of all drugs.

Within this new drug research climate, it will be possible within a very few years to make a determination of the comprehensive effects of these drugs, if funds and other resources are assembled to mount a research program actually responsive to the need for it. This objective must be considered to be a vital component of any effective national drug-abuse program.

The situation surrounding the use of methadone to control heroin addiction illustrates the current, fragmented, underresearched procedures now in vogue in adapting research findings to treatment. As a chemical blocking agent, methadone supposedly blocks the euphoric effects of heroin, but is itself an addicting drug. It is a short-acting drug; the drug substitutes one addiction for another, and as methadone becomes more readily available, it too has entered the illicit market. Because of the proliferation of small methadone programs, regulations to control its use were evolved in 1971 within the federal government. However, the subject is still highly controversial, and, while experts in the field agree that the search for better ways to block the effects of heroin must have the highest priority, methadone maintenance continues to expand as a hoped-for easy way out in treating heroin addicts. At best, methadone treatment can only be termed experimental, for the long-term effects of widespread usage of an addicting drug to block another addiction have yet to be experienced.

More work needs to be done not only in research on methadone but on other blocking agents, such as cyclazocine and noloxone, which are now in use. Research is already under way in developing longer acting cyclazocine and noloxone. L-alpha acetylmethadol, a longer acting derivative of methadone, which is currently effective up to seventy-two hours, is still in experimental use.

Obviously, research on the drugs themselves is not sufficient. Studies of the heroin user are being conducted simultaneously with treatment of the known addict. But psychosocial studies of heroin users who have escaped detection by law enforcement officers and the courts are limited to clandestine surveys within the heroin culture. Not until the user is assured of anonymity can this research provide anything approaching definitive data.

(Prevention, Treatment, and Rehabilitation

Given the current research climate and the increased knowledge provided through research findings, coupled with the new statutory authorities through which the federal government, states, and local communities can establish treatment and rehabilitation programs, physicians and other health professionals no longer have valid excuses to minimize medical and scientific interest and participation in the drug-abuse field.

The medical profession's role in narcotic and drug abuse has never been a completely pretty one, even though there have been periodic attempts to reform. The profession's responsibility has been intimately linked with addiction and drug abuse for many years, and not solely through treatment. The inexpert prescription of narcotics before, during, and after World War I is a matter of general knowledge.

More recently, medicine would find it difficult to defend prescription practices that provide patients with an almost unlimited supply of pain killers, barbiturates, amphetamines, and other drugs whose properties are now known to be addictive in certain dosages under certain conditions. In general, the medical profession as a whole has rejected its responsibility in the problem of drug-abuse control, as well as in accepting drug addicts as patients.

The profession has known for a long time that the drug habit is a way of life that takes the user out of real life and occupies all his time and thought. Some free themselves; others do not. Therefore, addicts for the most part need sustained help over a long period of time, and the post-addict needs definite support in the community.

For the user of "soft drugs" as well as for the narcotic addict, there are broader considerations which go beyond the acute effects of the use of any drugs of abuse. These considerations are of special relevance to psychiatrists. Among the subtle changes observed in chronic marijuana users, for example, are decreased drive, apathy, distractibility, poor judgment, introversion, depersonalization, diminished capacity to carry out complex plans or prepare realistically for the future, a peculiar fragmentation of thought, magical thinking, and progressive loss of insight.

Psychiatry needs also to be particularly concerned about the potential effect of any reality-distorting agent on the future psychological development of the adolescent user. Since adolescence is a time of great psychological turmoil, patterns of coping with reality developed during this period are most significant in determining adult behavior. Persistent use of an agent that serves to ward off reality during this critical period is likely to compromise seriously the future ability of the individual to make an adequate adjustment to a complex and demanding society. To date, awareness of these conditions has not been equated, to any significant extent, with the profession's acceptance of responsibility in the treatment of drug abuse.

A possible reason for disenchantment on the part of the entire medical profession with treatment in this field may be that physicians, like most other citizens, have tended to look at drug abuse as a single, homogeneous phenomenon and have been slow to realize that a national treatment program, assuming the current public acceptance of the need for it, can be effective if operated in a realistic climate of expectations and results.

Drug abuse ranges from minor experimentation up to and through serious involvement, dependency and death. Therefore differentiation should be made among at least four groups of drug abusers: (1) the uninitiated

and the abstainers; (2) the experimenters; (3) the moderate users; and (4) those for whom drugs have assumed a central role in life.

Simultaneously, in categorizing drug users, it is also necessary to arrive at a working definition of drug abuse, on which to base development of a drug program. Such a definition would be use of a drug or other substance with central nervous system activity in excessive amounts, or in a manner to produce any of the following: marked physical or psychological dependency; psychosis or serious personality disturbances; serious impairment of personal and social functioning, including significant behavioral toxicity; death or danger to life of the drug abuser or others; serious interference with personality and social development; biochemical, neurological, genetic, or other physical damage.

A program based on such a characterization would bring about the development of treatment modalities appropriate to the presenting situation and related to the risk and severity of the consequences, both to the patient and to society.

In recent months, professionals already involved in the drug field have been discussing the objectives and goals of a national drug-abuse program. Of importance in achieving any success has been the tentative beginning of a search for methods by which organized, traditional medicine and the free clinic movement can collaborate to minimize the adverse effects of drug abuse.

In 1971, approximately 150 free clinics existed throughout the United States, and in seeking help from them, drug abusers sense the safety of confidentiality and an empathetic concern for their problems. Without doubt, the element of trust between those who need help and those who seek to provide it is one of the necessary components of an effective service program.

A great deal of the polarization around drug abuse results from lack of communication. Schools, universities, neighborhoods, and community groups of all kinds have become involved in the effort to develop means of communication where drug abuse and other issues relevant to everyone who participates are included in the discussions.

Without doubt, the single most important part of a national drug-abuse program will be to establish veracity through educational programs aimed at substituting intelligent concern for panic and replacing propaganda with facts. As sensible education programs and community success in providing young people with interesting alternatives to drug highs begin to have an effect, it should be less difficult for the physician and other health professionals to become interested in and accepted by those in need of help.

Various types of motivational therapies are currently being used in the treatment of drug abuse, but their acceptance to date has been minimal and is sought, for the most part, only when the experimental drug abuser has become further identified with some part of the drug culture and rejects his experience.

Programs aimed at the prevention of drug abuse will of necessity continue to be experimental. For those already involved in drug abuse two kinds of programs must be provided: emergency (first aid) services for acute crisis situations and continuing care to minimize the effects of dysfunctional behavior which accompanies chronic drug abuse. Within the customary medical care system, any properly trained emergency service can prevent death or disability. The free clinic system, however, provides public health services, such as contraception and suicide prevention, as well as crisis intervention for the acute drug episode itself and may include treatment of such related conditions as venereal disease.

Beyond the response to a crisis, continuing care is required in one way or another by all drug abusers during the period of time when the individual attempts to learn new patterns of living, separated from drug highs. Such programs now in existence are usually fragmented, but each of them has shown enough promise to warrant expansion and refinement. They include the therapeutic community, methadone maintenance, narcotic antagonists, civil commitment programs, psychiatric care, theologically and ideologically based programs, and financial aid.

None of these alone, however, can be successful without the organization of long-term, easily accessible rehabilitation programs that are a part of continuing care and must be able to provide supportive aid in the community as a long-term service. Basically, all these program components imply a continuity of care for the drug abuser comparable to the continuity of care provided for emotionally disturbed individuals in comprehensive community mental health centers.

Community psychiatry has not, to any significant degree, made its skills and knowledge available to the drug abuser as yet; this is, no doubt, the immediate task to be confronted during the 1970s. Community psychiatry has already learned that many disturbed individuals can be maintained in the community if follow-up care is provided without time limitations. Pasamanick's[2] follow-up study of acutely psychotic schizophrenics demonstrated that for a thirty-month period, more than three-quarters of the experimental group could be successfully maintained at home. Five years after termination of the demonstration, however, Pasamanick and his associates undertook a subsequent study of the same patients. They found that gradual erosion of the original significant differences occurred on the usual clinic and aftercare services, so that eventually no differences in social or psychological functioning could be found. "This indicates," Pasamanick commented, "a need for the structuring of community mental health services on an intensive, aggressive basis, or we do nothing more than transfer custodial care to the community." The analogy in establishing a national prevention, treatment and rehabilitation program for drug abuse is self-evident.

(**Bibliography**

1. ASSISTANT SECRETARY FOR LEGISLATION, U.S. Department of Health, Education, and Welfare. Statement before the Subcommittee on Public Health and Welfare of the House Committee on Interstate and

Foreign Commerce, U.S. House of Representatives, 1969.

2. PASAMANICK, B., DAVIS, A. E., and DINITZ, S. "Five Years After an Experimental Demonstration: The Prevention of Hospitalization and Schizophrenia." *American Journal of Orthopsychiatry*, April 1972.

3. SAN MATEO DEPT. OF PUBLIC HEALTH AND WELFARE, RESEARCH AND STATISTICS SECTION. *The Use of Alcoholic Beverages, Amphetamines, LSD, Marijuana, and Tobacco Reported by High School Students and Junior High School Students.* San Mateo, Cal., 94403, 1968–1969, and preliminary release of 1970–1971.

CHAPTER 41

PRINCIPLES
OF COMMUNITY
MENTAL HEALTH PRACTICE

Portia Bell Hume

ESPITE WIDELY DIFFERENT opinions with respect to the nature of community mental health practice, there is a growing consensus among the more experienced practitioners that an arrangement of concepts and principles may be attempted as a step to encourage others to make their own synthesis out of their own experiences. There remain so many unknowns and questions to be investigated that it would be premature to present in a dogmatic way the principles of community mental health practice that are just beginning to emerge. However, more knowledge may already exist than some practitioners now care to apply in the face of economic considerations, manpower shortages, or professional pressures. Therefore, even provisional or incomplete principles may offer better guides than personal opinions, outmoded notions, the preferences of vested interests, or arguments based on expediency.

Experiences in community mental health practice that have been described in a rapidly growing literature exhibit considerable diversity. This may be due less to basically different viewpoints than to the necessity of accommodating administrative guidelines dictated by major sources of funds or to the obvious shortage of trained manpower available to community-based programs. A related, widespread phenomenon is the resistance of communities and consumers of mental health services to being stereotyped. On the other hand, there are reports of programs that replicate those essential elements without which an endeavor may not be said to exemplify community mental health practice. Such practice may be broadly defined, then, as an organized effort for the dual purpose of meeting a particular community's mental health needs while attempting to reduce mental breakdown in that community to a minimum. In other words, community mental health practice is oriented to mental health and not solely to mental illness; the approach to mental disorders is a preventive one based on a public health rather than on a medical model; each community's concerns and sanctions, along with the community's ability to organize its resources, shape the characteristics of practice in each example.

While comprehensive community psychiatry plays a major role in community mental health practice, it is not the whole of it. For example, the indirect services provided by community psychiatry are so called because they are extended beyond direct, clinical contacts with patients to a sector of the population likely to break down, that is, to people in trouble, who seek help from those who may become the consultees of the mental health consultants. It is those consultees, working in nonpsychiatric, care-giving agencies, professions, and organizations, who represent the community's most significant resources for the maintenance of mental health at the level of primary prevention.

The purposes that give direction to community mental health practice provide both long-range and short-term objectives that distinguish community mental health practice from more conventional approaches. Some of the latter may focus, for example, on the elimination of individual psychopathology, that is, on the visible, mentally disordered members of the population who seek diagnostic evaluation and treatment. Other approaches, emphasizing the link between noxious, societal factors and dangerous or deviant behavior that is equated with mental illness, may emphasize social and political action for either of two reasons: to protect society from the "insane" or to change the societal conditions held responsible for "the myth of mental illness." Whatever the merits may be of such partial or partisan approaches, the position, which amounts to a given in community mental health practice, relies on a sound body of scientific evidence for the multifactorial nature of mental disorders, a theory that is as basic to preventive psychiatry as to clinical psychiatry.

Traditionally, psychiatry has provided all kinds of services for identified, psychiatric patients, from special housing in hospitals, nursing, or foster homes to medical, surgical, dental, educational, and social services in intramural or extramural settings. By contrast, in community mental health practice, psychiatric patients are not segregated unnecessarily from the rest of the population; their eligibility for the basic community services available to other citizens is promoted in every possible way. An institutional approach to the mentally disordered and retarded is replaced in community psychiatry by a conviction that most psychiatric patients are best treated as close to home as possible, with a minimum of interference with their coping and working capacities and a maximum of protection against interventions likely to increase psychopathology and dependence.

"Mental health" is a term that, like "public health," cannot be abstractly defined; in practice, it refers to the application of public health approaches to the reduction of mental disability within the population identified with a geographically or functionally defined community. Community mental health practice may thus be further described within the conceptual framework of preventive psychiatry as a community's system for the delivery of services. At all three levels of prevention (primary, secondary, and tertiary) such a delivery system involves both the nonpsychiatric and the psychiatric resources of the community, that is, a complex network of care-giving agencies and professions; of both incorporated and publicly elected governing bodies; of both public and voluntary tax-supported services; of social institutions and human resources, both professional and nonprofessional. Most of the organizations and individuals participating in such a network do not have community mental health as their primary responsibility or basic reason for existence. For example, the detection, apprehension, prosecution, and defense of criminals are primary functions of police, courts, and correctional facilities. The professionals engaged in such public programs, as well as lawyers in private practice, have for ages been formally involved with forensic psychiatrists once known as alienists, but they are scarcely aware of their own mental health functions. Yet, community mental health practice relies on the acquired recognition and acceptance of their special mental health functions not only by nonpsychiatric professionals but also by the community's policy-makers, public officials, directors, and staffs of agencies affording services not generally identified with public mental health.

Within the network comprising a community mental health system, the component subsystems have varying degrees of responsibility for, and make different kinds of contributions to, all three levels of prevention of mental disability. In the process of identifying the mental health function that is specific to, or uniquely provided by, a particular profession or resource involved in community mental health practice, it is essential to preserve the integrity and independence of the individual or agency whose basic purposes are obviously more related to the general health and welfare of the community than to mental health in particular. Working relationships are coordinate, as between mental health professionals and agencies, whose primary responsibility is community mental health, on the one hand, and those other individuals or organizations secondarily contributing to the mental health delivery system, on the other hand; the former do not supersede or attempt to transform the latter into their own image and likeness. On the contrary, the optimal utilization of community resources in meeting the mental health needs of a community is achieved to the extent that differences of degree and kind with respect to mental health functions are preserved and clarified, rather than blurred or nullified. The coordinating principle that guides relationships between coequals is circumvented when coordination is attempted by merely placing previously independent entities under a single authority. This maneuver will not of itself produce coordination; at best, it may mandate a process of developing and maintaining the working relationship between equal but different contributors to the mental health system.

(The Community

The elements of community mental health practice are often described in stereotyped terms and classified like the bits and pieces of a mosaic. Here they are presented not so much as structural elements but as a community's ranked order of purposes, each of which is achieved through certain processes, methods, and components of practice. The functional elements of practice aimed at the achievement of each major purpose are thus seen as occurring in clusters, and each cluster demonstrates a principle that maximizes the chances of successful outcomes while minimizing the restrictions of more rigidly structured, goal-limited, and predetermined forms of practice.

Mental health practice is here viewed as more than a blueprint for the application of preventive psychiatry to any or all communities. However useful a conceptual framework and its related guidelines may be, principles derived from the adaptation of mental health practice to a community are precisely those that make it possible for potentialities to be realized within a given community matrix, that is, the parenchyma of mental health work. The community setting in and for which the work is done provides the driving force that vitalizes and shapes the organization of practice. Any organization needs some structure, but the point to be made is that the functional elements of a community mental health program take precedence over its structure. In other words, the structural elements are too frequently dictated by power struggles, professional boundaries and resistances, or institutional investments with resultant limitation or loss of important functions.

In the absence of indications by a community of its concern about mental health matters, the resultant practice may represent a conglomeration of the different schools of thought favored by individual practitioners or by consumers of mental health services. Unless a community's purposes are known, the direction taken by mental health practice may be haphazard and suffer from lack of planning for stated objectives, either short term or long range. Without a community's identification of its own priorities, it is difficult to initiate, let alone to evaluate, any element of community mental health practice. Each community varies in awareness of its mental health needs, degree of concern, and ability to take the initiative. Leadership and timing are essential to genuine, active community involvement in mental health.

In the systematic application to community mental health practice of a public health approach at three levels of prevention (primary, secondary, and tertiary), the population at risk refers to the whole, as well as to special sectors, of the populace inhabiting a particular community. Just as an individual in relation-ship to his environment is the focal point of clinical interventions, the population at risk in relationship to its community is the center of attention in the practice of preventive interventions, including those that are remedial and rehabilitative in nature. The ecological, socioeconomic, sociocultural, and political features that identify a community's profile constitute the environment that is as significant for community mental health practice as the familial and psychosocial milieu of an individual patient in clinical practice.

In epidemiological studies of a specific mental disorder, the community may be conceptualized as a population in which there are carriers of the host factors responsible for mental breakdown. At the same time, a community may be identified as the source of pathogenic, environmental factors (physical, psychosocial or interpersonal, socioeconomic, and sociocultural), which, in varying degrees, contribute to a particular form of organic, psychosomatic, or psychogenic mental disorder. The host factors of general significance for mental health are an individual's potentialities for adaptation, both inborn and epigenetic. Of paramount and comparable importance is the community's capacity to respond through its resources by forestalling or relieving individual likelihood of mental breakdown due to environmental deficits and hazards in conjunction with individual vulnerabilities. In short, community mental health practice need not be limited to belated, clinical, psychiatric interventions on the grounds of epidemiological ignorance about the cause of every mental disease. There are known, general, epidemiological factors contributing to the most commonly encountered forms of mental breakdown which provide the guidelines for preventive measures.

It is not useful to define too narrowly the community in community mental health practice. In specific aspects of program development the community means different things, such as a geographically or jurisdictionally defined area (for example, a neighborhood, city, county, state, region, nation); a population of a limited size in relationship to location ("catchment area"); or a community of interest making common cause in behalf of mental health, that is, a social system. Each of these definitions is useful for particular elements of practice. A generally useful and functional definition is one that conceives of a community as a system of systems. Here, intergovernmental, interagency, interprofessional, interpersonal, and administrator-consumer relationships, among others, are viewed as essential to the initiation, development, and effective utilization of all available resources for both remedial and rehabilitative measures as well as for interventions and provisions that safeguard mental health.

Every example of community mental health practice can be identified by its community setting and the nature of the population it serves. However hidden the community's involvement in the undertaking, or however indifferent a community may appear to be, the community is nevertheless a dynamic element of practice. The more openly the community mental health system is linked with other community systems, the more it can avoid fragmentation and dissolution. Community mental health practice should reflect the processes that can be, but are not always, generated and shaped by the community in which it is based, whether the endeavor be broad or narrow in actual scope, ambitious or modest in its objectives. These processes reflect more or less persistent efforts to keep open two-way channels of communication between systems, to replace a community's fear or complacency with constructive concern, to promote public airing of differing viewpoints, and to mobilize leadership. For a community to determine what actions for mental health will best meet its needs, a process of community organization is required, following the principles of appropriateness and community determination of policy.

The drawing of a community's boundaries through clarification of its component subsystems in terms of their potential, if not actual, mental health functions serves the purpose of identifying both the environment and the population to which community mental health practice must be related. The process involved is the systematic adaptation of a public health model to community needs. One of the methods employed is the uncovering of the latent interdependencies of health, education, and welfare subsystems, social and governmental institutions, the various professions, and labor-management organizations, to name the more obvious examples. Other methods involve applications of the principles of human ecology and demography to the population at risk of mental breakdown. The more stable and cohesive the community turns out to be, the more its population can be fitted into the concept of the catchment area designated in the guidelines of the National Mental Health Act of 1963. The more mobile, displaced, and dense the population at risk, the more it needs to be related to a system of systems (that is, a community) that has the capability of serving much larger and more heterogeneous populations that can be fitted into the federal guidelines. Whereas community mental health practice should be suitable and adapted to a community's mental health needs, it is equally true that the needs of certain kinds of populations can be met only by broadening the boundaries of the community.

([Community Organization for Mental Health

The ways in which a community becomes purposefully and willingly, as opposed to accidentally or coercively, involved in mental health practice are manifold. Persistent demands from minorities, who must be heeded, may or may not be representative of objectively evaluated, community needs; yet the most deafening clamor may express both a genuine concern and a valid need couched in terms that do not have to be taken so literally that they can be conveniently ignored. Demands from professionals also have to be evaluated and interpreted since they, too, may suffer from lack of objectivity with respect to the community's priorities and mental health needs.

The most frequently effective, initial spokesmen for mental health are neither consumers nor providers of services but rather veterans of organizations with a history of volunteered, successful leadership in other fields related to the welfare of the community. Such leaders are apt to qualify as experienced listeners, respondents, and catalysts who have earned a necessary degree of trust and who are, consequently, in the best position to form the nucleus of a group more broadly representative of the community's opponents, as well as proponents, of mental health. Every such nuclear group needs a base of operation. If there exists in the community some form of health and welfare planning council, it could be the most suitable vehicle for constituting a mental health committee. The alternatives for a voluntary group of citizens are numerous, since even the smallest communities are surprisingly rich in organizations, to which the potential mental health spokesmen already belong and within which an initial mental health effort can be mounted, leading perhaps to the eventual formation of a citizens' mental health association. In any case, those who undertake to advocate mental health in their community should be volunteers, although they may soon need to acquire the professional consultants and staffing assistance needed by any voluntary group with demanding work to do.

Community organization for mental health goes beyond the formulation of public policy in terms of goals to be implemented or actions to be taken in rapid response to expressions of needs that have not been examined or validated. The implementation and development of community mental health resources is the last, rather than the first, step in the process of community organization. The advocates for mental health enter into the community organization process (1) by investigating as objectively as possible the ways in which the community customarily behaves in responding to its mental health needs; (2) by surveying the professional or agency providers of clinical services to the mentally ill or retarded, as well as nonclinical services contributing to the maintenance of mental health; (3) by studying the utilization actually made of the resources in relationship to the utilization-patterns of the people who need such resources the most (that is, realities as opposed to unfulfilled potentialities); and (4) by identifying the major problems and gaps in the existing delivery of services. In short, the first step in the community organization process is fact-finding, from which a valid estimate of the community's unmet mental health needs begins to emerge while continuing to provoke questions that demand still further investigation. The data gathering could become an end in itself unless this process is accompanied by review and interpretation of the data from all sources for consistency and meaning. This aspect of the investigative process can be accomplished, as a rule, only through interviewing the providers of the data, instead of relying solely on written questionnaires.

Once the meanings of the assembled facts have become clear, recommendations for action begin to take shape. As they accumulate and are reviewed, some may be eliminated as duplications, while others may be combined. The next step in the community organization process is, therefore, a classification of groups of related recommendations under major headings, which in turn leads to giving a different kind of order to the recommendations, namely, the assignment of priorities. The whole question of which community mental health needs take precedence over which others is undoubtedly the most difficult part of the planning process, whose rationale depends, however on the setting of priorities. The community's broad policy on mental health is molded when a report of the survey is made public and the priorities are questioned, clarified, or debated in an open forum.

The eventual and never-ending phase of the community organization process, after all the planning, is the implementation of the priorities that have won community acceptance. The whole process of community organization represents the best possible method of public education in mental health. The reason is that, when education leads to action, as well as to increased information and knowledge, a learning process associated with active participation and personal commitments has been set in motion, continues, and finds expression in the smaller or larger preliminaries to, and engagements in, implementation of the priorities over however long a span of time is appropriate.

The initiators of the community organization process and all who participated in it acquire some new functions as mobilizers of implementation through the recommendations they have formulated. They also may continue to function indefinitely, on a voluntary basis, as investigators, interpreters, or evaluators of changing community mental health needs. That is to say, their advisory capability in relationship to the community mental health system, whatever form it takes, should not be lost to those who are given the authority and responsibility for implementing and developing a community mental health system.

A voluntary organization that has engaged in the surveying and interpretation of the data, as well as in the formulation of recommendations and priorities, has a choice between incorporating itself as an administrative board or commission or of looking beyond itself to the community's governing body or to an already incorporated, nonprofit, private agency to implement the planning group's recommendations. In such states as California, where enabling legislation provides state funds to reimburse 90 percent of city or county net costs for mental health services, the choice is likely to favor the local governing body as the most desirable locus of authority and responsibility. In other places, for example, in the State of New York, enabling legislation specifies a particular kind of administrative board for city or county programs supported by the state. Under the federal legislation for community mental health centers, the board may be constituted either as a public agency or as a privately incorporated board of directors such as a general hospital's board of trustees. But the possibility remains that the volunteers who engaged in the community organization process may find none of the above alternatives available or suitable to their purposes, and, consequently, they may incorporate themselves for the purposes of implementing and organizing the kind of community mental health system they recommend.

⟮ Implementation and Organization of a Community Mental Health System

It cannot be assumed that actual implementation and organization of community mental health practice will follow, even though a mental health survey of any community is bound to uncover some existing mental health resources as well as recommending new ones. Existing resources may range from isolated, individual, or agency efforts to meet the mental health needs of selected members or sections of the community all the way to well-endorsed and established programs of clinical, social, or community psychiatry. Whether to create *de novo* a community mental health system or to enable an existing program to better adapt to the ever-changing circumstances and priorities of the whole community, organization or reorganization is necessary to provide for the unmet or new community

needs identified by means of the community organization process. Whereas some organizational structure is essential, the functional aspects of organization can scarcely be over-emphasized. The structural elements should be strong enough to provide some stability and continuity without sacrificing the flexibility essential for coordinating the multiple functions subsumed under the heading of community mental health practice.

There needs to be a governing board, either privately incorporated or publicly elected, that accepts both the authority and responsibility for carrying out the general purposes developed through the community organization process. In order to do its job with respect to the given purposes, the board needs staffing and funding, along with continuing support and guidance from the community's advocates for a mental health program meeting community needs. For example, the financing of an organized program requires consideration of the various sources of funds, both public and private, and assessment of the alternatives or possible combinations of funds to be used. Whether the governing board be publicly elected or privately incorporated, public taxes are apt to be one source of financing, if not the major one; an informed electorate supporting the use of public funds for mental health services in private or public agencies needs to be heard from by any governing body before it makes decisions.

The options of a governing board with respect to funding go hand in hand with its options in regard to the locus of authority and responsibility for professionally directed mental health services. Before exercising either type of option, the board needs advice from the community, that is, a mental health advisory committee with three kinds of membership: as many community advocates as necessary to constitute a majority, one or more mental health professionals, and one or more representatives of the existing resources for mental health. Because of the possibility of conflicts of interests, the advisory committee, whose main function is to keep the community's mental health needs before the governing body, should not be dominated by either professional or competing, vested interests. When advice on professional matters or questions about augmenting or coordinating resources are sought by the governing body, ad hoc subcommittees, chaired by an appropriate member of the advisory committee, can be added at any time to fulfill such special advisory functions. Another example of the usefulness of ad hoc subcommittees would be a selection committee for the guidance of the board in appointing (or replacing, as the case might be) a director of community mental health services; the selection committee would spell out the qualifications to be included in the description of the position in terms of functions, authority, and responsibilities delegated by the governing board. To the extent that the director's responsibilities include most of the administrative decision making within the broad policies laid down by the board or embodied in enabling legislation, the mental health advisory committee may eventually serve the program director as well as the board; however, care should be taken lest the advisory committee lose sight of its primary responsibility to the governing board, become subservient to the program director, and permit the director to speak for the advisory committee to the governing body designated as the community's mental health authority for the organization of the community mental health system.

The role of the community mental health director is, organizationally speaking, a dual one. There is direct, line responsibility only for the mental health services under his or her direction. But there is another, quite different kind of responsibility for the development of coordinate relationships with the directors of nonpsychiatric public or private agencies, with professional and nonprofessional organizations, and with psychiatric agencies and professions, all of which may be engaged in some aspect of mental health practice of their own. An example would be the working relationship between the community's health officer and the mental health director. The latter's dual role exists no matter how comprehensive the program of community psychiatry may be for which a director has direct responsibility.

However, amongst the ingredients of comprehensive community psychiatry there are included the provision of the so-called indirect, consultative services and direct collaborative (sometimes called "liaison") services to joint cases, which afford coordinate working relationships at both directors' levels and below.

The responsibility for community mental health practice at the level of primary prevention is rarely authorized as such. It is, however, sanctioned, with or without informed consent or intent, as a secondary function or effect of such basic services as education, health, welfare, rehabilitation, social planning, and various types of counseling. The better such services are in accomplishing their primary purposes, the stronger their effect in supplying basic human needs and in reducing the deficits that increase the risk of mental breakdown by adding to individual vulnerability. Primary prevention is also furthered by immediate and supportive response to individuals experiencing a life crisis of either a predictable, developmental type or an accidental, traumatic, and unpredictable character. People in such trouble, to which no one is immune, have as greatly enhanced risk of mental breakdown as the deprived and underprivileged sector of a population. The latter are, however, in double jeopardy, and they require the utmost collaboration between the caregivers in community mental health practice. The first priority in the organization of community mental health practice by a mental health professional may well be to provide mental health education and consultation to nonpsychiatric agencies and professionals in order to enhance their potentials for primary prevention of mental breakdown. But, since authority for the latter is rarely made explicit within the only agencies and professions in a position to practice mental health at the level of primary prevention, the negotiation of working agreements is a responsibility of the mental health director. He is authorized to undertake such engagements as a major step in organization that cannot be neglected, although it may have to be preceded by a great deal of mental health education, that is, program-centered administrative consultation by the mental health director in behalf of the administrator of a health, welfare, or educational system.

There are a number of alternative patterns of organization from which to select the most suitable to the mental health needs of a particular community. Three of the most important are (1) a program representing comprehensive community psychiatry with inherent (potential if not actual) capability and responsibility to coordinate community mental health practice, (2) a program that is less than comprehensive while filling one or more important gaps in existing resources and assuming partial responsibility, at best, for coordination, and (3) a consortium (incorporated) of cooperating but independent mental health agencies, each of which gives up some of its autonomy by submitting to the consortium's board of directors for purposes of cooperation, coordination, and planning. Each pattern has its own advantages and disadvantages.

In favor of comprehensive community psychiatry is its potentiality for responsible planning with the community, program and staff development, plus program review and evaluation. The kind of manpower required for this organizational model is, however, exceedingly rare. Not only are clinicians with special kinds of expertise in clinical evaluation, consultation, and collaboration demanded, but also mental health consultants and administrators who (1) are capable of coordinating their mental health functions, both within and outside their own program, (2) are capable of functioning as change agents, (3) are competent to recruit, deploy, supervise, and develop the staff, (4) are sophisticated in community organization, program planning, and evaluation, and (5) above all, possess convictions about accountability and responsibility to the community.*

A somewhat less than comprehensive program is much easier and may represent a step toward an eventually comprehensive program.

It readily provides for demonstrably needed but hitherto missing services of particular and often familiar kinds, in which the mental health professionals feel most comfortable and competent and which demand less planning either within the program or in relationship to other agencies in the community. Such a program may be greatly needed and occupy a comfortable niche. But its role in the total community mental health system is precarious to the extent that it very easily may remain isolated from the community's other mental health resources with equal claims to mutual support.

The disadvantages mentioned above are considerably alleviated by a consortium, which provides a vehicle for separate mental health agencies to get together, a structural basis at least for cooperation without undue duplication of services. There are hazards, however, in a consortium of member organizations inevitably possessing unequal powers in their own right and optimistically assuming that coordination is guaranteed by the consortium structure alone. Unless the board of directors of the consortium is truly independent and stronger than that of its strongest member, it cannot provide to the member organizations equal opportunity for either growth or coordinate relationships. By and large, the consortium structure tends to invite struggles for power, competitiveness, and substitution of the easy appearance of cooperation for the far more demanding involvement in continuous processes of coordination and collaboration.

The kinds of services constituting the content of a community mental health system are determined by the priorities issuing from the planning process. In general, they fall into three categories of preventive services when a system is fundamentally focused on the mental health of the population: primary, secondary, and tertiary prevention. The amount of any service that is provided depends on a given service's position in the priority listing, as well as on the kind of manpower and total funds available to the community from all sources, that is, fees for clinical services, third-party payments, special and time-limited

---

* For a listing of the ingredients of a program representative of comprehensive community psychiatry, see my "General Principles of Community Psychiatry."[14]

grants, voluntary contributions, and money from federal, state, and local taxes. All but the first listed source of funds impose some restrictions or requirements on their uses, but a community mental health system cannot depend solely on fees for clinical services without making most of the population ineligible. Furthermore, clinical services are the most expensive unless they are limited to diagnostic evaluations and brief preventive-therapeutic interventions. On the other hand, the most economical use of mental health funds is made by the indirect services provided to the population at risk via the nonpsychiatric agencies and professions already reaching most of the population one way or another. Indeed, mental health consultation and education (if they are provided by sufficiently experienced and competent mental health consultants from any of the major psychiatric professions), when coupled with clinical, psychiatric consultation, and collaboration in the treatment of joint cases, may provide with the greatest economy of money and manpower most of the essentials of primary, secondary, and tertiary prevention. The economies thus effected with respect to the psychiatric elements in the community mental health system are beneficial not only to the population at risk but also to the nonpsychiatric collaborators who are able to be more effective with many of their clients or patients, when they are backed up by mental health professionals. The reason is that a variety of impending or actual mental health problems harass the providers as well as the recipients of health, education, and welfare services. The providers most frequently suffer either from insufficient knowledge and awareness of their mental health service potentials at any level of prevention or from the hampering theme interferences that represent agency or professional stereotypes with respect to mental illness or mental retardation.

Collaboration and consultative services, together with conjoint planning for the development of the community mental health system, constitute the essential, functional elements of practice to which psychiatric and nonpsychiatric personnel from every level within their respective organizations may con-tribute. The corresponding structural elements go by various names in community psychiatry, such as screening, emergency, detention, liaison, precare, after care, mental health consultation and education, public information and education, to name the common labels. The important administrative functions of community organization, planning, staff development, program development, and program evaluation are usually dismissed as administrative overhead, which is figured as a percentage of the total budget or inadequately itemized as training and research.

The clinical, psychiatric services mentioned above may be provided on either an inpatient or outpatient basis. Extended twenty-four-hour or partial hospitalization, as well as all-purpose or specialized outpatient clinics and residential treatment facilities represent desirable, but expensive, options, which must enjoy a very high priority rating in order to be justifiably included in a community mental health system. In any case, such inroads on the community's total budget for mental health services should not be used as an excuse for their displacing the more essential, psychiatric components of a community mental health system.

(Conclusion

Community mental health practice is too often characterized by good intentions and beliefs in the power of community or social psychiatry to provide solutions to major social problems with overriding, political, economic, or cultural complications. It is all too easy to ascribe a mental health component to group-determined, social behavior of the human species, and to be diverted from the demanding tasks of a public mental health program befitting the needs of a community where every member of the population is a potential consumer of mental health services. The popular techniques of group intake, group evaluation, and group treatment are justified by specious arguments implying a belief that social stereotyping is preferable to psychiatric labeling. Neither, of course, is desirable, and fortunately there are other alternatives. A belief in the personal value and uniqueness of the individual is a basic tenet of community mental health practice, and it applies to both the providers and consumers of services in a given community. The evaluation of an individual's mental health problems or needs has its counterpart in the evaluation of the mental health responsibilities of professional or paraprofessional providers of services, whose mental health functions become effective to the extent that the administrative interferences and professional inadequacies they experience in coping with their work are correctly diagnosed and removed. Furthermore, the life crises that affect the population at risk also affect the providers and administrators in a community mental health system, where both professional and administrative crises and deficits are not at all uncommon. A purely structural organization of community mental health practice is too easily fractured by the developmental and accidental crises that beset it. Organization along functional lines with reliance on processes, methods, and principles related to purposes is more adaptable to the vicissitudes of community mental health practice.

(Bibliography

1. BELLAK, L., ed. *Handbook of Community Psychiatry and Community Mental Health.* New York: Grune & Stratton, 1964.

2. BINDMAN, A. J., and SPIEGEL, A. D., eds. *Perspectives in Community Mental Health.* Chicago: Aldine, 1969.

3. BRICKMAN, H. R. "Community Mental Health: Means or End?" *Psychiatry Digest*, 28 (1967), 43–50.

4. CAPLAN, G. *An Approach to Community Mental Health.* New York: Grune & Stratton, 1961.

5. ———. *Principles of Preventive Psychiatry.* New York: Basic Books, 1964.

6. ———. *The Theory and Practice of Mental Health Consultation.* New York: Basic Books, 1968.

7. CARSTAIRS, G. M., et al. *The Burden on the Community: The Epidemiology of Mental*

Illness, A Symposium. London: Oxford University Press, 1962.

8. FREEMAN, H., and FARNDALE, J., eds. *New Aspects of the Mental Health Services.* Oxford: Pergamon Press, 1967.

9. GRUENBERG, E. M., and HUXLEY, J. "Mental Health Services Can Be Organized To Prevent Chronic Disability." *Community Mental Health Journal*, 6 (1970), 431–436.

10. ———, SNOW, H. B., and BENNETT, C. L. "Preventing the Social Breakdown Syndrome." *Social Psychiatry*, 47 (1969), 179–195.

11. GRUNEBAUM, H., ed. *The Practice of Community Mental Health.* Boston: Little, Brown, 1970.

12. HALLOCK, A. C. K., and VAUGHAN, W. T., Jr. "Community Organization: A Dynamic Component of Community Mental Health Practice." *American Journal of Orthopsychiatry*, 26 (1956), 691–706.

13. HUME, P. B. "Community Psychiatry, Social Psychiatry and Community Mental Health Work: Some Interprofessional Relationships in Psychiatry and Social Work." *American Journal of Psychiatry*, 121 (1964), 340–343.

14.* ———. "General Principles of Community Psychiatry." In S. Arieti, ed., *American Handbook of Psychiatry.* Vol. 3. New York: Basic Books, 1966. Pp. 515–541.

15. JOINT COMMISSION ON MENTAL HEALTH OF CHILDREN. *Crisis in Child Mental Health: Challenge for the 1970's.* New York: Harper & Row, 1970.

16. LAMB, H. R., HEATH, D., and DOWNING, J. J., eds. *Handbook of Community Mental Health Practice.* San Francisco: Jossey-Bass, 1969.

17. LEVINSON, H., PRICE, C. R., MUNDEN, K. J., MANDL, H. J., and SOLLEY, C. M. *Men, Management, and Mental Health.* Cambridge, Mass.: Harvard University Press, 1966.

18. PARKER, B. *Mental Health In-Service Training: Some Practical Guidelines for the Psychiatric Consultant.* New York: International Universities Press, 1968.

19. REID, K. E. "Community Mental Health on the College Campus." *Hospital and Community Psychiatry*, 21 (1970), 387–389.

20. RYAN, W., ed. *Distress in the City: Essays on the Design and Administration of Urban*

* Contains a bibliography of 250 references on the subject of community psychiatry.

Mental Health Services. Cleveland: Case Western Reserve University Press, 1969.

21. SELLS, S. B., ed. *The Definition and Measurement of Mental Health.* Washington, D.C.: U.S. Government Printing Office, 1968.

22. SHORE, M. F., and MANNINO, F. V., eds. *Mental Health and the Community: Problems, Programs, and Strategies.* New York: Behavioral Publications, 1969.

23. ZUBIN, J., and FREHAN, F. A., eds. *Social Psychiatry.* New York: Grune & Stratton, 1968.

CHAPTER 42

THE ELEMENTS OF A LOCAL SERVICE PROGRAM

Norris Hansell

⟨ Design Axioms for Local Services

DISCOVERIES emerging in the context of expansions of local service activity comprise one of the most active areas in contemporary psychiatry. The hardy rate of such discoveries suggests the time may yet be too early to expect the theory of local service design to become stable. Surprises and reformulations may lie ahead. Several axioms have reached general acceptance with the workers in the field and offer useful pathmarkers for individuals seeking to apply this experience.

1. The characteristic behavior of persons in distress[*] offers a useful basis for planning effective clinical services and supports for such services. Individuals in the midst of crisis cannot easily negotiate complex entrance arrangements. Once admitted to services, they often show an exquisite capacity to be drawn into new conceptions of identity and role. These newly acquired views may yield either helpful expansions of adaptive capacity or undesirable contractions of capacity. Some of the least desirable concomitants of service are movement into prolonged patienthood and recruitment into unnecessary dependence on continuing service. Much of this experience has been drawn together by Caplan[23,24] and Scheff.[169-171]

2. The expectable behavior of social networks around persons in distress[†] exerts an impact of substantial significance on clinical and supporting activities of local services. This impact can be drawn into constructive outcomes. At the time they present for clinical services, individuals in distress often are being actively extruded from their prior social contacts and relationships. In the context of declining social role performance, frightening behavior, and undependable or unexpected behavior, the surrounding network may demonstrate powerful efforts to extrude the individual from his remaining vital social attach-

---

[*] See references 81, 126, 177, 185, 191, and 195–198.

[†] See references 33, 38, 59, 60, 82, 106, 108, 140, 149, 159, 166–171, 191, and 206.

ments. Additionally, if an individual is removed for the purpose of contact with services, his attachment opportunities may "close over" without him, a factor that increases with duration of absence. Particularly helpful in achieving increased prospects for life opportunity are services that do not remove an individual from his usual location and that are focused on expanding his competence to manage current life problems in ordinary settings.* Reception service practices of a type that usefully involve the social network in the assessment of problems, and the design of a response, seem to soften the extrusive impact of the network. Such practices also may enhance the adaptive capacity of the individual as he operates in conjunction with his usual associates.†

3. The clinical linkage of previously separated local program elements, for example, inpatient care, outpatient counseling, and sheltered workshops, frequently has a surprisingly large impact on the effectiveness of such services. In fact, the service capacity of local programs appears as much related to linkages between elements as to excellent internal design of elements. A noteworthy fraction of persons with psychiatric distress present with a cluster of difficulties. An effective response therefore often requires a cluster of corresponding categories of service. The ability to sum several services, and to arrange them into a meaningful clinical sequence, is an important category of local capacity. The establishment of reliable arrangements for multiagency service activity is a characteristic early objective within local program construction. The bringing together of several existing program elements, for instance, employment counseling, job skill training, and a halfway house (a social setting intermediate between inpatient care and full independence from treatment), frequently has more impact and lower additional cost than originating a new service. The interactive arrangements provided any service element are therefore a critical feature of its design. Persisting practices that routinize op-

tions for multiagency service often develop as a side effect of approaching other problems, for instance, plans to receive patients into the correct category of service.

The establishment of a reliable capacity for multiagency activity emerges as a criterion aspect of service design. One path toward achieving such an objective uses formal contracting between two or more agencies each of whom agrees to receive and service all referrals, or all referrals of a particular risk group, sent by the parties to the contract. Such "symmetrical, non-decline referral agreements"[76] allow an agency to assume client-assessment or service-delivery responsibilities in behalf of all the services assembled by contract rather than in behalf of a narrower, one-agency capacity.

4. As categories and auspices of service become increasingly linked into cooperative clinical and planning activity, a series of basic changes seems to occur in the design of the coalescing services. Procedures to qualify persons for access to service tend to simplify and accelerate. Staffs often decide to work for the establishment of an increased range of types of clinical service. Such increased service variety allows increased design specificity to the types of risk and disability expressed in the local population. Staffs work to provide at least a beginning service approach to each significant type of clinical problem in the settlement, for example, young, old, retarded, addicted, migrant, and delinquent. Agency staffs often work toward the early establishment of a reception service, especially one using a design addressed to the reception of persons presenting with varying grades of distress and a variety of kinds of trouble. A reception service can originate in several ways. Sometimes it begins in an attempt to provide a single front door to the several agencies in a developing network. Sometimes it arises to make possible the arrangement of multiagency staff participation in assessments of individuals presenting for service. In other settings, reception services begin as emergency services, often attached to a general hospital. However they originate, reception services seem to mature into a more general and con-

---

* See references 72, 73, 75, 118, 150, and 195.

† See references 18, 20, 26, 46, 68, 72, 76, 81–82, 83, 99, 140, and 181.

tinuing role in receiving, assessing, routing, and monitoring patients as they move through a variety of contacts with elements of the local psychiatric service program.[12,13,31,73,113] Reception services often become a focal point for expanded mental health consultation services and for work to establish other new services. Wide citizen interest often grows from the abundant new service information that accompanies the process of adding a reception service to existing local services.

5. Professionals working within service operations undergoing substantial changes in clinical design are able to acquire new clinical skills with surprising speed if their leadership engages them with relevant information and resources for retooling. Skills often critical in local service programming are ones associated with the convening of groups, with the facilitation of normal human adaptive work, and with the rapid assessment of clinical status and social attachments. Convening skills are useful in assisting groups of citizens, or professionals, conduct productive meetings,[72,73] [76,149] and for bringing families and members of a social network into the treatment process.[73,76,79] Skills in convening also allow a treatment staff to take advantage of the fact that an assembled social network offers a greater capacity for adaptive change than does a distributed network. Skills for enhancing adaptive capacity of persons who are passing through stressful intervals of life are a central ingredient in many inpatient and outpatient programs.[75,76,99] Services that increase the likelihood of adaptive success are desirable because they approach the objective of reducing the need for extended intervals of treatment. Skills in the rapid assessment of symptoms, role performance, social attachments, and adaptive capacity* are important in making precise use of scarce service resources. Such skills are also necessary when using service settings that do not involve removal from the ordinary circumstances of life. Rapid clinical assessment practices also assist in providing prompt access to services during the flexibility of crisis[24] and in avoiding wait-

ing lists and other complex qualifying routines prior to service.

6. The leadership tasks for constructing local service programs seem to center around gaining an easy familiarity with the current state of affairs and combining it with personal confidence in a service strategy that provides increasing evidence of its value as time proceeds. Citizen, agency, and professional endorsements are necessary components of effective local service systems. Such support can be expected to derive not from strong professional pronouncements but from visibly successful services. The communal patterns of established medical practice and of social casualty management practice† form a background for citizen expectations for service and professional behavior. Evolution of some practices away from existing expectations is often required to approach the design of an improved service network. When such evolution appears as a series of small, cumulative steps it seems to have the best chance of enabling a persisting network.[61,151] The cluster and flow properties of a human settlement, its fields of dwelling, work, recreation, and assembly,§ offer place and occasion to a service program.[208] Desirable patterns of administrative mechanics for local service programs seem to strike a balance between necessary program precision and protection of the clinical creativity of personnel.** Another group of administrative design requirements grows out of the special folk customs and professional attitudes that cluster about an enterprise addressed to the management of a group of human conditions regarded as important but of disputed cause. Local service programs can be buffeted by changing waves of public and professional sentiment. Such waves of sentiment include peculiar mixtures of concern and neglect. Local programs also can become encumbered by ideological fixity, careless thrusts of innovation, and inattention to the simple and obvious.‡ A reasonable posture seems to be a con-

---

* See references 75, 76, 81, 118, 126, 165, and 186.

† See references 1, 36, 61, 85, 97, 101, 151, and 200.
§ See references 29, 42, 89, 130, 139, and 208.
** See references 5, 27, 44, 48, 58, 73, 187, and 190.
‡ See references 10, 15, 19, 34, 35, 64, 105, 152, and 174.

tinuing vigilance for the hazards of ideology and haste.

❲ Clinical Services to Individual Persons

Features That Describe a Service

A useful definition of the term "service" is an experience or event, purposefully provided by others, that occupies a brief portion of a lifetime and results in continuing enhancement of the adaptive capacity of an individual after its completion. Within the context of this definition, the term "service design" is understood to encompass those features of any service that are thought essential to accomplishing its desired effect. Because there are many kinds of psychiatric distress and disability, there are many categories of service and service designs. For most services the essential design features turn out to be the timing,[191] setting,[55,71] participants,[38,76,129,171] objectives,[127,128] type of adaptive enhancement,[11,23,24,55,74,75,94,124,181,199] duration of service,[55,73] and criteria of exit. Though local services show considerable variation and experimentation, most workers appear to be approaching the following trends in service design:

1. The timing of entrance to service is moving closer to the onset of symptoms or of social network collapse.
2. The sites of reception into service and of main service activities are moving closer to the individual's usual space of life.
3. The persons engaged in the service activities, in assessing the trouble, and in evaluating the treatment plan are growing in number. An attempt is increasingly made to include as many network persons and service personnel as can make an efficient, productive contribution. Much human adaptive work seems to require a corporate participation or component, provision for which emerges as an element of service design.
4. The objectives of service are becoming more explicit. There is earnest endeavor to specify the nature of the pending adaptive work or disability undertaken for service. Changes in these same specifics are increasingly regarded as the product of service and as the standard within which effectiveness of service is most precisely reckoned.
5. The behavior and operations of the service personnel, which comprise their service activities, are being more explicitly described. Special effort is given to determining which activities are necessary or essential for the intended service design. What do the service agents do to enhance the client's adaptive work? As such "active principles" become known, the service agents can refine their service designs.
6. The duration of service encounters is shortening as service designs become more precise. Local service personnel show a keen interest in unencumbering their service activity from unnecessary amounts of continuing contact and from other recruitatory practices.
7. Criteria defining the proper occasion of exit from service are growing more prominent in definitions of service design. Frequently, behaviors or events signaling that the objectives of service have been attained are defined early in service so their appearance can be promptly recognized.

Highly productive work toward the improvement of local psychiatric services can derive from a more explicit specification of the risk groups in need of service. Also useful are clearer allocations of responsibility, among the several agencies in a settlement, for delivery of the desired elements of service. Precise understanding of the interagency allocation of responsibility also can allow for reliable sequencing of several kinds of service contact as well as for simultaneous, complex service contacts.[72,75,76,79,158] Several questions recur at each effort to attain such understandings. What risk group is the service intended to benefit? What profile of disability is expressed by the risk group? What are the active ingredients in a service intending to reduce such a profile of disability? What is the value of the effect or desired outcome? How will an observer detect that the desired effect has occurred? What special problems can be expected in making links for this service with other elements of the local service program?

Ordinarily the local service elements needed within any settlement will include the following kinds of service to individual persons: Reception service, which provides access; inpatient service, which provides controlled environment for residence; day care and night care service, which provides a treatment-oriented social system for a part of each day but expects the patient to spend another part of each day in an independent social system; outpatient service, which provides intermittent services to enhance adaptive capacity; home care service, which provides service set in a person's place of residence and usually involves his family; shelter care service, such as a halfway house or sheltered workshop, in which the individual moves freely about the community some portions of the day or week, perhaps holding employment, but in which the setting of his work or residence is specifically modified so as to reduce a disability state; and after care and communal reentry service, which provides packages of service for persons who have been institutionalized for a long time, or repeatedly, and are now preparing to resume movement about the general community. Table 42–1 reviews several differences among these service types. Note for instance that the duration of service, or transit time, is characteristic for each category of service. Note also that the assets and liabilities of the several services are complementary, a fact that suggests why a large increment in productivity regularly occurs when a set of previously unlinked services become linked.

Reception Service

Tasks accomplished in a reception service are reception of persons for entry into appropriate elements of the treatment system, assessment of the disability and resources of the individual, and arrangement of commencement of clinical services. A large amount of planning and several complex decisions occur during the relatively short period encompassed by reception service. It is therefore useful to design the service in such a manner as to acquire adequate information from brief clinical contacts. The establishment of capacities for multiagency participation in reception work, for convening the family unit or other members of the social network, and for ombudsman activity[6] are useful steps toward making maximum use of the reception phase.*

Some assessments made during reception service and at passage from ordinary social networks into contacts with special, treatment networks seem to carry a capacity to label, forecast, and recruit persons into continuing casualty status.† It is therefore advantageous to develop a strategy of assessment that is maximally informative to service planning and minimally recruitatory. A series of assessments that explore a person, network, and situation is helpful. What is the current disability in role performance? What is the degree of clarity of identity and life objectives? What is the general health status, with special attention to aspects that interfere with usual roles or with the adaptive work, including schizophrenia,[118] brain damage, or drug use? What is the status of the affectional attachments and network relatedness? From such information reception workers can develop a treatment plan. The report of such information also originates the clinical service record and establishes baseline descriptions and formal objectives later used to assess the impact of the service delivered. Other important issues in the design of reception services are linkage with a general hospital facility,§ telephone service,[123,203] walk in (or unscheduled) reception capacity,[30,31,156,203] and mobile capacity for reception and assessment.[150,203] Assessments at entry to service are often made in the setting where an individual is lodged when psychiatric intervention is being considered, particularly when persons are in hospital emergency rooms, prisons, old persons' homes,

---

* See references 31, 75, 76, 79, 156, and 203.
† See references 24, 26, 55, 76, and 207.
§ See references 12–14, 47, 173, and 175.

TABLE 42-1. Differences among Principle Categories of Service within a Nonexporting Local Program of Services

COMPARISON FEATURE	RECEPTION	OUTPATIENT	INPATIENT	SHELTER CARE Day Care	Halfway House	Sheltered Workshop	TRANSITIONAL GROUPS
Usual reason individual presents for service in such setting	Nonresponsive to adaptive challenge	Role decline (Network intact)	Fixed, non-adaptive behavior / Addiction / Physiologic decline / Lethal behavior	Precarious network attachments	Plus atrophy of role or job skills	Plus expansion of role skills	No network / Heavy prior use of service / Need for recurring service or assessment
Objective within service	Entry	Start adaptive work	Alter behavior or physiology	Enhance attachments, roles, skills			Provide ready network for use in building own network
Asset of setting	Precise linkage to service(s)	Nonrecruitatory service	Control	Built-in network and resources for skill enhancement; setting modified to reduce impact of disability			Enhances performance of isolate
Liability of setting	Awkward with repeating users	Awkward with addicts, isolates	Recruitatory, Expensive	Risk of encounter becoming prolonged into life location rather than service			Technology is primitive
Usual transit time	Hours	Weeks	Days		Months		Years

and nursing homes. Assessment designs that do not require removal to a cloistered setting seem to preserve more opportunity for a plan of management that minimizes the use of institutionalization. Assessments in situ can provide opportunity to assess and involve the network and may offer pertinent skill-enhancing experiences for staff.[76,156,203]

Inpatient and Day Care Service

An inpatient psychiatric service is a key service element of a local program. It may also provide a home base for professionals who work in reception, outpatient, and consulting settings. The special characteristic of inpatient service, when conducted as an aspect of a larger local service program, is rich linkage with other types of local service. Such links allow movement of the objectives of inpatient service away from shelter and asylum[97,98] toward operations that enhance adaptive capacity for life in ordinary locations.[11,72,73,77] As inpatient service is more fully linked with other categories of service, average inpatient stays are shortening, now averaging fewer than twenty days.[144] Inpatient service can be conducted using practices that productively involve the family and network.[68,70,184] An inpatient setting can be a constructive place for commencement of coping work and for testing new life skills.[75,76,88,134] When hospital care is conducted in a manner that does not separate an individual from his usual life pattern and from his social network, it can provide an advantageous setting for the titration of psychotherapeutic drugs, for withdrawal from an addicting material, for assembling clinical planning information, and for drawing together the patient's fragmenting social network. Key professional activities in inpatient care, when conducted as an element of a network of services, are provision of a temporary social system* that can help a person return to usual function and arrangement of circumstances for the work of reconstructing a more permanent social network. If an inpatient service is distant from other local services, or included within a larger, regional hospital facility, for example, a state mental hospital, it seems important that the service be reaching toward increasing linkage with a network of extramural services rather than operating primarily as a component of the regional hospital plant. Administrative movement to accomplish these objectives is sometimes called "unitizing" a mental hospital.†

Inpatient service can offer hazards to a local service program. It is usually the most expensive element of local service. Unless used precisely, inpatient service can encumber so large a fraction of the program resources as to constrain their overall productivity. If offices, administrative activities, and clinical records for many parts of the local program are located at the inpatient service space, inpatient operations can divert attention from important events in the more distributed program elements. Also, inpatient service appears to carry more recruitatory effect than nonresidential services: It tends to separate an individual more completely from his network and from ordinary environments and draw him into a life pattern embracing extended contact with service networks and environments.[11,66,80,110] In some locations, the courts and the legal code governing movement to and through some forms of treatment status join in viewing the service network as if it were constituted principally of inpatient activity. Such a view can jeopardize development toward a network of more varied service elements. When the interested court is brought into service planning work, particularly around efforts for the court and service agents to relate as collaborators in planning an effective reception service, the court can be a force of consequence in developing a varied service network.[72]

Day care and night care, perhaps because they do not separate a person from the ordinary setting of his life throughout the whole of a twenty-four-hour period, appear to convey distinctly less recruitatory effect. They are relatively inexpensive and offer efficient extensions of the staff and other resources that comprise an inpatient psychiatric service

---

* See references 55, 93, 116, 129, 134, 163, 164, and 201–203.

† See references 11, 73, 107, 120, 183, and 208.

unit.[56,66,96] Hertz et al.[80] demonstrated that day hospitalization frequently offers a shorter, less expensive, and more valuable clinical product than inpatient care, in studies that seem to control for severity of illness and other important variables. In order to use day care, a patient must be able to travel back and forth between the service point and a residence or job and must not be addicted to a narcotic material. The productivity of day care service seems to be related to its special capacity to provide intense, precise service during one portion of a day, while allowing the individual to operate in ordinary locations for the balance of the day.

Outpatient Service

The volume and variety of outpatient service is in a phase of rapid expansion in the United States[101-103] and is likely to be the major element of local services in most areas. In this discussion we use the term "outpatient service" to designate service in which the patient moves with free social excursion about the community, is not located in a specially designed, residential facility, and comes intermittently to a place of service for contacts lasting minutes to several hours. The principal components of service provided in a psychiatric outpatient facility are psychotherapy, decision counseling,[75] application and monitoring of psychopharmacological agents, services that monitor the behavior of individuals who have experienced a significant episode of disability, and services that enlarge an individual's operating social network. The demonstration that expanded outpatient care tends to prevent, shorten, or reduce the frequency of return to inpatient care has been made for many risk groups and for many parts of the United States.[*] It has also been demonstrated for many communities that risk groups underrepresented in outpatient care, for instance, children, retarded persons, old persons, and delinquents, will tend to be overrepresented in inpatient care.[101-103] From these findings emerges the precept that outpatient services

for any territory can have the greatest impact on reducing the use of institutional modes of care if such outpatient services are designed for, and focused onto, persons and groups known to be likely to be institutionalized from that community.[†]

Within the overall group of persons at risk of institutionalization, those who often can use outpatient care most effectively are persons whose role performance and network linkages are substantially intact. Persons whose adaptive efforts and skills for maintaining their social attachments are discovered to be even partially operative usually can be serviced in outpatient settings.[75,76]

Several design features of outpatient care seem to expand its potential contribution to the overall service capacity for a settlement. If closely linked with a reception service, it can interrupt and control the routes to and from institutional care.[110,131] If linked with other categories of service, especially job training and general health services, it can provide the setting for groupings of service that benefit particular individuals.[81,82] The arrangements for groupings of interlocking services, often provided under several agencies' auspices, are most expeditious if they include service exchange agreements of the reciprocal, nondecline type.[76] Other important characteristics of effective local outpatient services are staff competence in the provision of temporary, task-directed relationships,[73] provision for convening the family unit or other portions of a patient's network,[21,73,75,203] funding arrangements to provide service access for migrant persons and poor persons,[73] and apparatus for participation by the service consumers in the design and assessment of services.[95,158,172]

Home Care Service

Judging from the best results reported,[11,45,83,150] home care may be advantageous and currently underutilized in local service programs. Perhaps it is not more prominent because of the cultural and organizational sup-

---

* See references 78, 101–103, 107, 110, and 120.

† See references 72, 73, 107, 156, and 203.

ports it requires. When the necessary professional skill, administrative support, and family interest are present, the use of the home as the setting for all, or a portion of, a program of care appears to offer advantages in cost and social outcome. The use of the home as a principal location, and the family as central providers of care activity, can result in prevention of hospital admissions,[11,150] significant expansions of staff skill,[20,76,155,203] expansion of the management options available to reception service workers,[11,76,137] reduction in extrusive activity by the social network[11,76,150,153] and a lower likelihood of future hospitalization.[137,150] Used with children, it bypasses a very difficult design requirement of residential services for children, the need to provide a special school and a substitute family unit during treatment. With elderly persons it bypasses the hazards attendant separating an individual from a nurturing family unit and familiar environments. With schizophrenic persons it can result in increased effectiveness of the family unit as a problem-solving entity during crisis periods.[150]

In order to deliver effective assessment and treatment work within the home, it is necessary for the family unit to have a suitable dwelling place and willingness to participate.[76,150] The home care staff group needs appropriate experience,[11] mobility, and rapid response capacity.[76] The capacity of the family to attempt care of a member in the home can be assessed in ordinary reception service settings or in the home. Professional ideological beliefs suggesting that home care cannot be expected to be successful may contribute to the existence of styles of practice that omit home assessments or treatment arrangements.[20,138] Home care is seldom useful as the setting for withdrawal from drug addiction or abuse or when the family cannot be diverted from a fixed pattern of extrusive sentiment, as assessed during reception service or during an exploratory home care visit.

Shelter Care Service

Included under the term "shelter care" are halfway houses, sheltered workshops, and expatient clubs. They are grouped together because of an identifying similarity: They couple the provision of a specially altered local environment, or group, with an absence of limitations on free movement about the community. Such programs attempt to enhance individual adaptive capacity by offering a special environment or group for a part of the time only. They envision competent engagement with ordinary life settings as the primary objective of service. Halfway house service usually follows inpatient service, a response to the fact that much of the adaptive work formerly done in inpatient settings can be accomplished more easily in other settings. Halfway houses embody a small social unit and a sharp focus on skill-enhancing objectives. Other features of shelter care environments may include an organized schedule of daily social activity,[50,91] an associated work setting for wages or for the acquisition of job skills,[32,50] sleeping and domiciliary provisions, often somewhat like a boarding house,[50,91,109] participation in a regularly convened social network comprised of persons with similarly precarious attachments,* decision counseling,[32,75,209] behavior monitoring and direct critique by professionals and by members,[50,91,209] and other outpatient services, including phenothiazine monitoring.[50,05] In all the variations of shelter care, the central objectives remain the expansion of role and job skills and the expansion of skills for maintaining a social network. The risk groups effectively serviced in shelter care settings cover the full range of diagnostic and symptom groups but have in common the atrophy of social attachments and job skills, sometimes derived from experiencing prolonged, or repeated, institutionalization.

Shelter care services have a capacity to flourish under a variety of auspices and organizational arrangements, including families[119] and expatient groups, whether local or affiliated with a larger grouping, such as Recovery, Incorporated or Alcoholics Anonymous,† and with or without continuing professional par-

---

* See references 50, 67, 91, 111, 124, and 199.
† See references 67, 109, 111, 124, 157, 199, and 205.

ticipation. Most shelter care organizations work toward autonomous financing and policy development and to involve all their members in the tasks and governing of the group.[65,91,109,205] Most tend to emphasize an intense, but transitional, membership in the group,[50] leading toward a goal of movement beyond the group into a social network comprised largely of persons without residential institutional experience. Shelter care organizations usually have a pipeline view of themselves and maintain ordinary expectations for conventional conduct. They tend to dissociate themselves from attitudes linked with careers of permanent residence in a sanctuary, or asylum, and from special expectations not compatible with general social excursion throughout the settlement.[33,50,97,205] Sometimes a few permanent figures maintain the philosophy and structure of the group,[109] while most members pass through with an average residence or active membership time of several months. Changes often destructive to the rehabilitative capacity of shelter care occur when it is conceived as a continuing method of care or when the average time in residence goes beyond about a year.[32,50] Key features of an environment organized to maintain a continuing flow of intense but transitional opportunities are a psychological set that emphasizes performance achievement as a personal identity element,[50,58,71] a daily organization around accomplishable tasks or role elements,[50,58] and a local culture that can detect competent, attractive performance by a person who presented to the service with an offensive reputation.* Linkage and ombudsman services of a character similar to those that are part of ordinary reception services can make a substantial impact on the productivity of shelter care service.[32]

Services for Repeating and Prolonged Users

Services termed "after care" are composed of elements not unlike other outpatient services but drawn into a focus on experiences

* See references 50, 127, 128, 164, 167, 171, and 196.

benefiting persons who have been in inpatient care, especially prolonged inpatient care. Such persons often need service after the inpatient phase. Services termed "re-entry" or "rehabilitative" use inpatient, outpatient, home care, and shelter care elements organized to achieve noninstitutional life for individuals who have been institutionalized repeatedly or for prolonged periods. Services designed to lower the likelihood of rehospitalization are often termed "after care." Services designed to assist a person to be able to move from a period of prolonged or repeated institutional care to continuing noninstitutional life are termed "re-entry" services. Although only a small percentage of a territorial population becomes hospitalized even once during a lifetime[101-103] for mental or social disability, a fraction of the group who do become institutionalized become multiple occasion and multiple type service users. Previously institutionalized persons are therefore a population of more than usual risk justifying a category of services of special focus in design and administration. The aftercare and re-entry categories of service can be expected to comprise major sectors of the steady service activity in most territories, approximating, perhaps, 20 percent of the reception work, 30 percent of the outpatient and linking work, and 40 percent of the inpatient work.[77,101-103,207] Whereas services for other risk groups may be omitted or ineffective and the service network will not be resultingly incapacitated, services for the group at high risk of continuing, or repeating, institutionalization must be effective or the troubles of this risk group will encumber the major part of the capacity of the service network.[100] The characteristic persons who present for multiple or prolonged service include social isolates,[69,101-103] migrants,[132,133] and persons with clearly defined, familial schizophrenia.[101-103,160] In addition to expanding the service capacity of the treatment system, effective aftercare and re-entry services can be expected to free significant amounts of resources previously committed to prolong institutional care for other use.[77,102] The successful introduction of such services to a local area can cause expansions in public understanding of the assets and liabilities of institutions as components of a strategy of casualty management.*

Phenothiazine medication can be expected to be helpful in many but not all situations in which a diagnosis of schizophrenia is made.[92, 145, 150, 179] This fact is sufficiently important to suggest the value of precise service design for this group. The appropriate clinical contacts used to be reliable over a period of years. Prolonged phenothiazine administration and monitoring can be done in group settings. Patients can make effective use of telephone and postcard methods for keeping in touch without unnecessary inconvenience and disruption to their employment and pattern of life.

Aftercare and re-entry services use substantial components of decision counseling,[75] employment training, linkage and ombudsman service,[79] and services to enhance group skills and affiliative capacity.[100, 179] Many persons at risk of prolonged, or repeating, hospitalization have no social network available for the daily maintenance of life patterns and personality.† Successful services to this group often provide direct assistance in identifying, linking, and maintaining a social network. An example of a method for providing service, which apparently enhances affiliative capacity, is the spin-off group.[72, 74, 76] The spin-off group method employs a highly structured routine for several months. There are meetings and a set of roles, conventions, and group exercises. The therapist group assistant works to spin off a competent, autonomous, continuing group after eight to ten get-ready meetings. The method is conserving of professional time and appears to be a precise response to the predicament of isolated persons. It appears that isolated persons, given assistance in formation of new, small groups, show significant improvements in general social performance and surprising release from psychiatric distress.[73, 74, 76]

Many service areas contain a substantial number of hospitalized persons who have ex-perienced years, even decades, of hospitalization. About half of those in state and county mental hospitals have been there more than a year, and one quarter for more than ten years.[53, 77, 100] Perhaps half of the persistingly resident group have a physiological status compatible with life outside an institution. But the atrophy of social and employment skills is often profound. Many local service programs are attempting service for this group. Several investigators have reported surprising results if the service program is suited to the presenting difficulties.§ Re-entry service programs for this group have been carried out in inpatient, outpatient, and shelter care settings. Common elements in several designs to service this group include a social system that expresses vigorous expectations for competent performance, combined with a finely structured daily routine and a focus on a closely organized, small cohort of persons in a similar performance status.** Movement toward full, independent excursion in the community proceeds in a series of graded steps, often augmented with ombudsman and linking services. Services for this group often last a year or more. The longer a service is expected to extend, the greater is the indication to define an observable feature of behavior that will signal an end point to service and the proper occasion of exit from service. Such a provision operates to reduce the risk of recurring recruitment into the social system of treatment on the part of individuals with precarious social networks.[76]

⟨ Services to Agencies and Groups

Consultation and Prevention

Services to agencies, collectivities, and, indirectly, to classes of persons at special risk are a characteristic feature of local service programs. Such services are required in federally funded programs[143, 154] and comprise an area of rapid technical development, often under

---

* See references 50, 68, 73, 77, and 150.
† See references 71, 75, 76, and 101–103.

§ See references 4, 11, 32, 46, 50, 52, 63, 77, 127, 128, and 179.
** See references 4, 52, 63, 77, 105, 127, and 128.

the terms "consultation" and "prevention."[24–26] As is the case with services to individuals, each example of such services is intended to benefit a particular risk group, focused on characteristic disabilities in the target group and organized around design features of setting, timing, participants, objectives, and end point. Activities in which the action responsibility remains with another professional, and in which the recipient has the option to decline the use of the information or observations comprising the service, are usually termed "consultation."[25] Services altering an environment or social aggregate, intended to reduce the occurrence or severity of disability in a group, and often provided in a manner not requiring individuals to enter formally into patienthood status, are termed "preventive."[24] Most local services to agencies and collectivities involve elements of both consultation and prevention. Services to groups derive their main design characteristics from relevant properties of the persons for which benefit is intended and from the specifics of an environment or experience thought beneficial.

The action ingredients in service endeavors to agencies and collectivities seem to be similar to those in services to individuals. They include components such as counseling, convening, facilitating adaptive work, teaching role skills, and advising regarding assessments for service and routing of persons in distress. These components appear to comprise the delivered service even though a wide range of rhetoric is used to describe such endeavor, employing such concepts as "facilitating normal growth and development" and "developing new institutions to enhance communal adaptation of migrants."* In such a rapidly developing field, efforts to provide service are generally enhanced if the desired change is simply identified. Frequently discussed categories of preventive endeavor include the increased use of personal crisis as a period of flexible growth rather than as an occasion for labeling an individual for removal,† the alteration of hazardous social roles in structured

organizations,[3,55,81,82,94] and the development of closer linkages between individual aspirations and group allocations of status, sometimes termed "the Hawthorne effect."[5,37,55]

The process of selecting groups likely to benefit from indirect services is often aided by using epidemiological data, particularly data from reception service settings. Data originating in reception services can give information on risk groups that are not successfully managed in their current setting or services and, therefore, are presenting for transfer to the mental health system. Data from inpatient and residential services can provide information on risk groups that have been presented to the mental health system but currently are not managed within its noninstitutional settings.[102,115,131,161,183] Other considerations can suggest the value of an indirect route in approaching the problems of a particular risk group. A concern to avoid risks accompanying psychiatric labels, such as patienthood roles and reputations,[33,76,166,167,171] combined with anticipation of higher leverage in approaches to larger numbers of persons with imminent but unexpressed trouble[2,17,112,204] frequently suggest indirect service designs. Indirect approaches sometimes excel in avoiding or reducing disability status but can present complex problems in program design, administration, and evaluation.§

Services to agencies and collectivities in many local programs are designed to benefit school-age children,[94,95,188] persons in nursing and old persons' homes,[189] aged isolates,[182] unwed mothers,[194] persons abusing drugs and chemicals, widows,[180,181] unemployed persons, and persons in welfare programs. Promising experience has accrued with respect to the design characteristics of programs associated with prepartal care, battered children, lead poisoning, children separated from families during hospitalization, and operations in institutions that operate as family and home to dependent children.[16,17,112] Because poor persons are overrepresented in many categories of institutional and disability status,[142] local service programs sometimes attempt to

---

* See references 24, 28, 81, 82, 84, 94, and 112.
† See references 16, 17, 24, 26, 126, 177, 185, and 191.

§ See references 16, 57, 78, 94, 141, 146, 183, and 207.

enhance by service the capacity of individuals or groups to extricate themselves from continuing poverty status. For example, some local programs attempt to facilitate capacity for decision and action within organizations of relatively powerless persons.[192] Some risk groups are included indirectly in service efforts through service to an agency or category of professionals with whom they are in direct relationships. The variety of such indirect services is large, and includes efforts through schools,[94,146,188] courts, police, and juvenile officers,[122,146] home visiting nurses,[11,137] clergy, undertakers,[180] physicians,[23,49,117] and welfare workers. Throughout many indirect services is the common element of influence on a critical turning point in life or on an event of role passage.[24,191] For example, indirect services to recent widows can be designed around direct services to groups that convene widows to help one another,[180,181] or by consulting with clergy[180] or undertakers[180] or physicians.[23,118] Efforts to increase the likelihood of successful accomplishment of the tasks of studenthood can be focused around consulting with teachers,[94,95] counselors, truant officers,[188] or school administrators,[94,95,188] or by convening groups of parents or groups of parents and school personnel.[94,95]

Children's Services

The volume and precision of children's services seem to lag in development in many territories, perhaps because additional design features beyond those usual for adult services are often necessary. The recent report of the Joint Commission on Mental Health of Children[90] reviewed the situation and termed it a "dire crisis." It recommended, even so, that expanded services for children are not likely to be effective in nurturing healthy growth, and preventing disability, unless such new capacity embodies a service model that emphasizes the maintenance of the child within a family unit, within a school, and within an ordinary communal environment. Therefore, they recommended enhancing local services for children via expanded reception, home care, and school consultation services, including psychi-

atric participation in interdisciplinary assessments of a child's performance in the studenthood role. They also recommended a heavy emphasis, in local services for children, on counseling and convening services.[76,90] For children who are institutionalized for service, they stressed the importance of smaller institutions, with a family-like social unit, and with opportunity for full participation in the standard program of the local school district.[90] Because of the catastrophic risks attending separation of a child from a family unit, school, and community,[16,26,81,135] most children's services in local service programs stress designs based around a noninstitutional location for the child, and on types of service to a social network that are supplemental rather than eclipsing to the existing family unit.[16,17,26,147] The school is the dominant setting for children's services whether or not such services are conducted under strictly educational auspices.[16,26,83,94,95,147] Apparently promising are designs that aim to increase the capacity of the school to help more children achieve a successful studenthood experience.[83,94,147] Designs that appear effective include services that convene parents for an exchange of experience, especially parents who have children in distress, in trouble in school, or before a court. Whatever the active ingredient in a service is thought to be—educative, task learning, role learning, counseling, or social attachment or relationship—the trend in children's services emphasizes offering such service to children's established social networks rather than through special systems that label children for unique handling or removal from the settlement.[26,90,147] Few see much productivity in extended inpatient care, of any design, because of its powerful capacity to recruit children into permanent casualty status and to separate them from families.[83,90] In spite of these facts, perhaps because reception service as well as outpatient and consulting services are in short supply in many territories, children are currently entering inpatient facilities in larger numbers and beyond their increased representation in the population.[101-103,176] Consulting programs to juvenile courts, to police officers with juvenile surveillance responsibilities, and to foster homes, foster parents, and well-baby clinics are usually productive.[16,26] The underlying strategic decision in many developing designs for children's services is one to offer intense, continuing service to the parents, schools, and institutions that provide environments for children. The focus on inputs to the environments of children is made in order to make effective interventions in the lives of troubled children without recruiting such children into special institutions and constrictive roles.

Services for Old Persons

Between 10 and 15 percent of the populations of most settlements can be expected to be persons sixty-five years of age or older. Perhaps 10 to 20 percent of this group can be expected to appear in reception, outpatient, or institutional service during an average year. Older persons are highly overrepresented in inpatient care admission rates and, once admitted, tend to remain until death. For most territories, between two-thirds and three-quarters of the institutionalized older persons are in nursing homes rather than public mental hospitals, a trend that is increasing.[51,53,93,102,104] Older persons are underrepresented in reception, outpatient, and shelter care service[101-104] as compared with their representation in residential service. Yet when such services are developed within a settlement, the use of institutional care declines substantially.[42,102,104] Of those older persons who become institutionalized in a mental hospital, more than two-thirds are social isolates, having either lost a spouse or never having been married.[102-104,125] A major fraction experienced a physical health crisis in the interval just prior to admission. The health decline was followed by a decline in role and network performance, culminating in a performance crisis leading to institutionalization.[125,182] Services for the elderly attempt to engage with declines and crises in physical health, deficits in adaptational and psychological capacity, poverty and its restriction of options, and general social isolation. Service efforts can focus on efforts to enhance adaptive work to manage events of loss by death, illness, and dignity disruptions coming in the later years, years that often seem oriented to the special experiences of the young-adult portion of the life cycle. Local service designs for elderly persons can be based on the premises that relatively small inputs of health service, and of convening, linking, and counseling service, will make significant improvements in the quality of life and that institutional service, when required, should work to maintain or renew an older person's social roles and network attachments. The setting for much of this service is in residences and in nursing and old persons' institutional homes. Reception services are helpful to older persons if they offer precise assessment, service planning, and service linkages. Reception service of a type that can develop access to a variety of local services, within the context of a presentation for institutionalization, can often avoid or postpone entrance to institutional life.[46,54,76,79] Home visiting and home care services, together with brief day care and shelter care services, can help many older persons avoid institutionalization in the context of a health or loss crisis.[136,182] Counseling and brief outpatient services can help many older persons handle the loss of a spouse without moving to restricted life styles, depression, or suicide.[22,53,75,125,182] It is well known that brain changes in older persons can lead to a wide range of troublesome behavior and positive findings on the mental status exam. But apparently it is not so well known that losses in the richness of a person's social attachments can produce similar findings. Services that facilitate development of new networks, of friends and task groupings, are a promising category of service for older persons. Such service is useful before, during, or instead of movement into institutional care.*

Services for Persons Abusing or Addicted to Drugs and Chemicals

From the standpoint of local services, persons who are addicted to or abusing chemicals offer special planning programs. Such persons

---

* See references 46, 72, 74, 76, 125, 136, 182, and 189.

often present with a biological (tissue) dependence on a chemical, a situation best managed in a controlled, hospital setting. The withdrawal phase of the care of addicts is strictly institutional, whereas much of the rest of local programming aims for noninstitutional designs. Addicts frequently present for service as a result of illegal behavior, for example, the possession or marketing of a chemical. Their service, under such circumstances, is framed within legal boundaries. In addition, the principal social network of many addicts, and alcoholics, is comprised of persons who are also addicts or who collaborate in the destructive use of the chemical.[86,87,193] Management in ordinary social networks and settings is, therefore, neither legal nor usually effective. Local programming for persons abusing alcohol or addicted to a narcotic chemical is based around health service and chemical withdrawal, or methadone maintenance,[39,40,41] followed by extensive, intensive efforts to develop a new life style within a new social network. Often a group of exalcoholic or exaddict persons combine efforts in a corporate attempt at revamping their whole life patterns.[193]

⟮ Bibliography

1. American Psychiatric Association. *Diagnostic and Statistical Manual of Mental Disorders*, 2d ed. Washington, D.C., 1968.
2. American Public Health Association, Program Area Committee on Mental Health. *Mental Disorders: A Guide to Control Methods.* New York: American Public Health Association, 1962.
3. Appel, J. W., and Beebe, G. W. "Preventive Psychiatry: An Epidemiologic Approach." *Journal of the American Medical Association*, 131 (1946), 1469–1475.
4. Appleby, L. "Evaluation of Treatment Methods for Chronic Schizophrenia," *Archives of General Psychiatry*, 8 (1963), 24–37.
5. Argyris, C. "Some Propositions About Human Behavior in Organizations." In *Symposium on Preventive and Social Psychiatry.* Washington, D.C.: Walter Reed Army Institute of Research, 1957. Pp. 209–230.
6. Assembly of the State of Hawaii.

"Hawaii Ombudsman Act of 1967." *Civil Code of Hawaii*, 1967. Ch. 96, pp. 441–444.
7. Bahn, A. K., et al. "Admission and Prevalence Rates for Psychiatric Facilities in Four Register Areas." *American Journal of Public Health*, 56 (1966), 2033–2051.
8. ——, et al. "Diagnostic Characteristics Related to Services in Psychiatric Clinics for Children." *Milbank Memorial Fund Quarterly*, 40 (1962), 289–318.
9. Baker, F. "An Open-Systems Approach to the Study of Mental Hospitals in Transition." *Community Mental Health Journal*, 5 (1969), 403–412.
10. ——, and Schulberg, H. C. "The Development of a Community Mental Health Ideology Scale." *Community Mental Health Journal*, 3 (1967), 216–225.
11. Becker, A., Murphy, N. N., and Greenblatt, M. "Recent Advances in Community Psychiatry." *New England Journal of Medicine*, 272 (1965), 621–626, 674–679.
12. Bellak, L. "A General Hospital as a Focus of Community Psychiatry." *Journal of the American Medical Association*, 174 (1960), 2214–2217.
13. ——, et al. "Psychiatry in the Medical-Surgical Emergency Clinic." *Archives of General Psychiatry*, 10 (1964), 267–269.
14. Blane, H. T., et al. "Acute Psychiatric Services in the General Hospital: Current Status of Emergency Psychiatric Services." *American Journal of Psychiatry*, 124, suppl. (1967), 37–45.
15. Bockhoven, J. S. "The Moral Mandate of Community Psychiatry in America." *Psychiatric Opinion*, 3 (1966), 24–39.
16. Bolman, W. M. "Preventive Psychiatry for the Family: Theory, Approaches, and Programs." *American Journal of Psychiatry*, 125 (1968), 458–472.
17. ——, and Westman, J. C. "Prevention of Mental Disorder: An Overview of Current Programs." *American Journal of Psychiatry*, 123 (1967), 1058–1068.
18. Brickman, H. R. "Some Basic Assumptions in Community Mental Health." *American Journal of Public Health*, 54 (1964), 890–899.
19. ——. "Mental Health and Social Change: An Ecological Perspective." *American Journal of Psychiatry*, 127 (1970), 413–419.

20. BROWN, B. S. "Home Visiting by Psychiatrists." *Archives of General Psychiatry*, 7 (1962), 98–107.

21. BURKS, H., and SERRANO, A. "The Use of Family Therapy and Brief Hospitalization." *Diseases of the Nervous System*, 26 (1965), 804–806.

22. BUTLER, R. N. "The Life Review: An Interpretation of Reminiscence in the Aged." *Psychiatry*, 26 (1963), 65–76.

23. CAPLAN, G. "Practical Steps for the Family Physician in the Prevention of Emotional Disorder." *Journal of the American Medical Association*, 170 (1959), 1497–1506.

24. ———. *Principles of Preventive Psychiatry.* New York: Basic Books, 1964.

25. ———. *The Theory and Practice of Mental Health Consultation.* New York: Basic Books, 1970.

26. ———, and GRUNEBAUM, H. "Perspectives on Primary Prevention." *Archives of General Psychiatry*, 17 (1967), 331–346.

27. CAPLAN, R. B. *Psychiatry and the Community in Nineteenth-Century America.* New York: Basic Books, 1969.

28. CHAPMAN, L. F., et al. "Human Ecology, Disease, and Schizophrenia." *American Journal of Psychiatry*, 117 (1960), 193–204.

29. CHINITZ, B. "New York: A Metropolitan Region." *Scientific American*, 214 (September 1965), 134–148.

30. COLEMAN, M. D., and ROSENBAUM, M. "The Psychiatric Walk-In Clinic." *Israel Annals of Psychiatry and Related Disciplines*, 1 (1963), 99–106.

31. ———, and ZWERLING, I. "The Psychiatric Emergency Clinic: A Flexible Way of Meeting Community Mental Health Needs." *American Journal of Psychiatry*, 115 (1959), 980–984.

32. CRISWELL, J. H. "Community Roles in Psychiatric Rehabilitation." *Welfare Review*, 8 (1970), 8–15.

33. CUMMING, J., and CUMMING, E. "On the Stigma of Mental Illness." *Community Mental Health Journal*, 1 (1965), 135–143.

34. DANIELS, R. S. "Community Psychiatry: A New Profession, A Developing Subspecialty, or Effective Clinical Psychiatry." *Community Mental Health Journal*, 2 (1966), 47–54.

35. DAVIS, K. "Mental Hygiene and the Class Structure." *Psychiatry*, 1 (1938), 55–65.

36. DEUTSCH, A. *The Mentally Ill in America.* 2d ed. New York: Columbia University Press, 1937.

37. DICKSON, W. J., and ROETHLISBERGER, F. J. *Counseling in an Organization: A Sequel to the Hawthorne Researches.* Boston: Harvard Graduate School of Business Administration, 1966.

38. DOHRENWEND, B. P., and DOHRENWEND, B. S. *Social Status and Psychological Disorder: A Causal Inquiry.* New York: Wiley, 1969.

39. DOBBS, W. H. "Methadone Treatment of Heroin Addicts." *Journal of the American Medical Association*, 218 (1971), 1536–1541.

40. DOLE, M. E., et al. "Successful Treatment of 750 Criminal Addicts." *Journal of the American Medical Association*, 206 (1968), 2708–2714.

41. ———, et al. "Methadone Treatment of Randomly Selected Criminal Addicts." *New England Journal of Medicine*, 280 (1969), 1372–1375.

42. DOXIADES, C. A. "Man's Movement and His City." *Science*, 162 (1968), 326–334.

43. ———. "Ekistics, the Science of Human Settlements." *Science*, 170 (1970), 393–404.

44. DRUCKER, P. F. "Management and the Professional Employee." *Harvard Business Review*, 30 (1952), 84–90.

45. DUMONT, M. P., and ALDRICH, C. K. "Family Care After a Thousand Years: A Crisis in the Tradition of St. Dymphna." *American Journal of Psychiatry*, 119 (1962), 116–121.

46. EPSTEIN, L. J., and SIMON, A. "Alternatives to State Hospitalization for the Geriatric Mentally Ill." *American Journal of Psychiatry*, 24 (1968), 955–961.

47. ERRERA, P., et al. "Psychiatric Care in a General Hospital Emergency Room." *Archives of General Psychiatry*, 9 (1963), 105–112.

48. ETZIONI, A. *A Comparative Analysis of Complex Organizations.* New York: The Free Press, 1961.

49. EWALT, J. R., et al. "How Non-Psychiatric Physicians Can Deal with Psychiatric Emergencies." *Mental Hospitals*, 15 (1964), 194–196.

50. FAIRWEATHER, G. W., et al. *Community Life for the Mentally Ill.* Chicago: Aldine, 1969.

51. FORD, A. B. "Casualties of Our Time." *Science,* 167 (1970), 256–263.

52. GALLIONI, E. F., et al. "Intensive Treatment of Back-Ward Patients: A Controlled Pilot Study." *American Journal of Psychiatry,* 109 (1953), 576–583.

53. GARDNER, E. A., et al. "All Psychiatric Experience in a Community." *Archives of General Psychiatry,* 9 (1963), 369–378.

54. ———, et al. "Suicide and Psychiatric Care in the Aging." *Archives of General Psychiatry,* 10 (1964), 547–553.

55. GLASS, A. J. "Principles of Combat Psychiatry." *Military Medicine,* 117 (1955), 27–33.

56. GLASSCOTE, R. M., et al. *Partial Hospitalization for the Mentally Ill: A Study of Programs and Problems.* Washington, D.C.: American Psychiatric Association, 1969.

57. GLIDEWELL, J. C. "Some Methodological Problems in the Evaluation of School Mental Health Programs." In L. M. Roberts et al., eds., *Comprehensive Mental Health: The Challenge of Evaluation.* Madison: University of Wisconsin Press, 1968. Pp. 195–220.

58. GOFFMAN, E. *Asylums.* New York: Doubleday, 1961.

59. ———. *Behavior in Public Places.* New York: The Free Press, 1963.

60. ———. "The Insanity of Place." *Psychiatry,* 32 (1969), 357–388.

61. GOODENOUGH, W. H. *Cooperation in Change.* New York: Russell Sage, 1963.

62. GORWITZ, K., et al. "Release and Return Rates for Patients in State Mental Hospitals of Maryland." *Public Health Reports,* 81 (1966), 1095–1108.

63. GOVE, W., and LUBACK, L. E. "An Intensive Treatment Program for Psychiatric Inpatients: A Description and Evaluation." *Journal of Health and Social Behavior,* 10 (1969), 225–236.

64. GREENBAUM, M. "Resignations Among Professional Mental Health Leaders." *Archives of General Psychiatry,* 19 (1968), 266–280.

65. GREENBLATT, M., et al., eds. *Mental Patients in Transition.* Springfield, Ill.: Charles C Thomas, 1961.

66. GRINSPOON, L., and COHEN, R. E. "Introduction of a Part-Time Hospitalization Program into an Acute Psychiatric Treatment Service." *New England Journal of Medicine,* 267 (1962), 752–756.

67. GROSS, H. J. "Self-help Through Recovery, Inc." In J. H. Masserman, ed., *Current Psychiatric Therapies.* Vol. 11. New York: Grune & Stratton, 1971. Pp. 156–160.

68. GROUP FOR THE ADVANCEMENT OF PSYCHIATRY. *Crisis in Psychiatric Hospitalization.* Report no. 72. New York, 1969.

69. GRUENBERG, E. M. "The Social Breakdown Syndrome: Some Origins." *American Journal of Psychiatry,* 123 (1967), 1481–1489.

70. ——— and WEISS, J. L. "Psychotic Mothers and Their Children: Joint Admission to an Adult Psychiatric Hospital. *American Journal of Psychiatry,* 119 (1963), 927–933.

71. ———, and ZUSMAN, J. "The Natural History of Schizophrenia." *International Psychiatry Clinics,* 1 (1964), 699–710.

72. HANSELL, N. "Patient Predicament and Clinical Service: A System." *Archives of General Psychiatry,* 17 (1967), 204–210.

73. ———. "Casualty Management Method." *Archives of General Psychiatry,* 19 (1968), 281–289.

74. ———. Expanding Affiliative Capacity in Isolated Persons: Technical Handling of the Spin-off Group Method. Unpublished manuscript, 1969.

75. ———. "Decision Counseling Method: Expanding Coping at Crisis-In-Transit." *Archives of General Psychiatry,* 22 (1970), 462–467.

76. ———. *Introduction to the Screening-Linking-Planning Conference Method: Excerpts from Discussions of Triage Problems.* Rockford, Ill.: H. Douglas Singer Zone Center, 1970.

77. ———, and BENSON, M. L. "Interrupting Prolonged Patienthood: A Cohort Study." *Archives of General Psychiatry,* 24 (1971), 238–243.

78. ———, and HART, D. W. "Local Service Growth: The Illinois Zone Plan." *American Journal of Psychiatry,* 127 (1970), 686–690.

79. ———, et al. "The Mental Health Expediter." *Archives of General Psychiatry,* 18 (1968), 392–399.

80. HERTZ, M., et al. "Day Versus Inpatient Hospitalization: A Controlled Study." *Archives of General Psychiatry,* 127 (1971), 1371–1382.

81. HINKLE, L. E., and WOLFF, H. G. "Ecologic Investigations of the Relationship Between Illness, Life Experiences and the Social

Environment." *Annals of Internal Medicine*, 49 (1958), 1373–1388.

82. ———, and WOLFF, H. G. "Ecological Observations of the Relation of Physical Illness, Mental Illness, and the Social Environment." *Psychosomatic Medicine*, 23 (1961), 289–297.

83. HOBBS, N. "Helping Disturbed Children: Psychological and Ecological Strategies." *American Psychologist*, 21 (1966), 1105–1115.

84. HOLDER, H. D. "Mental Health and the Search for New Organizational Strategies." *Archives of General Psychiatry*, 20 (1969), 709–717.

85. HOLLINGSHEAD, A. B., and REDLICH, F. *Social Class and Mental Illness*. New York: Wiley, 1958.

86. HUGHES, P. H., and JAFFE, J. H. "The Heroin Copping Area." *Archives of General Psychiatry*, 24 (1971), 394–400.

87. ———, et al. "The Social Structure of a Heroin Copping Area." *American Journal of Psychiatry*, 128 (1971), 551–558.

88. JACKSON, J. "Factors of the Treatment Environment." *Archives of General Psychiatry*, 21 (1969), 39–45.

89. JACOBS, J. *The Economy of Cities*. New York: Random House, 1969.

90. JOINT COMMISSION ON MENTAL HEALTH OF CHILDREN. *Crisis in Child Mental Health: Challenge of the 1970's*. New York: Harper & Row, 1969.

91. KANTOR, D., and GREENBLATT, M. "Wellmet: Halfway to Community Rehabilitation." *Mental Hospital*, 13 (1962), 146–152.

92. KATZ, M. M., and COLE, J. O. "Research on Drugs and Community Care." *Archives of General Psychiatry*, 7 (1962), 345–359.

93. KELLAM, S. G., and CHASSAN, J. B. "Social Context and Symptom Fluctuation." *Psychiatry*, 25 (1962), 370–381.

94. ———, and SCHIFF, S. K. "Adaptation and Mental Illness in the First Grade Classrooms of an Urban Community." *Psychiatric Research Report*, 21 (1967), 79–91.

95. ———, and SCHIFF, S. K. "An Urban Community Mental Health Center." In L. J. Duhl and R. L. Leopold, eds., *Mental Health and Urban Social Policy*. San Francisco: Jossey-Bass, 1968. Pp. 112–138.

96. KINDER, E., and DANIELS, R. S. "Day and Night Psychiatric Treatment Centers: Description, Organization, and Function."

American Journal of Psychiatry, 119 (1962), 415–420.

97. KIRKBRIDE, T. S. *Construction, Organization and General Arrangements of Hospitals for the Insane*. Philadelphia: Lippincott, 1856. (Portions reprinted in *Mental Hospitals*, 6 [1955], 14–20.)

98. ———. "Description of the Pleasure Grounds and Farm of the Pennsylvania Hospital for the Insane." *American Journal of Insanity*, 4 (1848), 347–354.

99. KLEIN, D. C., and LINDEMANN, E. "Preventive Intervention in Individual and Family Crisis Situations." In G. Caplan, ed., *Prevention of Mental Disorders in Children: Initial Explorations*. New York: Basic Books, 1961. Pp. 283–307.

100. KRAFT, A. M., et al. "The Community Mental Health Program and the Longer Stay Patient." *Archives of General Psychiatry*, 16 (1967), 64–70.

101. KRAMER, M. "Epidemiology, Biostatistics and Mental Health Planning." In R. R. Monroe, et al., eds. *Psychiatric Epidemiology and Mental Health Planning*. Psychiatric research report, no. 22. Washington, D.C.: American Psychiatric Association, 1967. Pp. 1–63.

102. ———. *Some Implications of Trends in the Usage of Psychiatric Facilities for Community Mental Health Programs and Related Research*. Public Health Service Publication, no. 1434. Washington, D.C.: U.S. Government Printing Office, 1967.

103. ———. *Applications of Mental Health Statistics*. Geneva: World Health Organization, 1969.

104. ———, et al. "Patterns of Use of Psychiatric Facilities by the Aged: Current Status, Trends, and Implications." In A. Simon and L. J. Epstein, eds., *Aging in Modern Society*. Psychiatric research report, no. 23. Washington, D.C.: American Psychiatric Association, 1968. Pp. 89–150.

105. KUBIE, L. S. "Pitfalls of Community Psychiatry." *Archives of General Psychiatry*, 18 (1968), 257–266.

106. KUTNER, L. "The Illusion of Due Process in Commitment Proceedings." *Northwestern Law Review*, 57 (1962), 383–399.

107. LaFAVE, H. G., et al. "The Weyburn Experience: Reducing Intake as a Factor in Phasing Out a Large Mental Hospital." *Comprehensive Psychiatry*, 8 (1967), 239–248.

108. LAING, R. D., and ESTERSON, A. *Sanity, Madness and the Family.* Vol. 1. *Families of Schizophrenics.* New York: Basic Books, 1964.

109. LANDY, D., and GREENBLATT, M. *Halfway House: A Sociocultural and Clinical Study of Rutland Corner House, a Transitional Aftercare Residence for Female Psychiatric Patients.* Washington, D.C.: U.S. Government Printing Office, 1965.

110. LANGSLEY, D. C., et al. "Avoiding Mental Hospital Admission: A Follow-Up Study." *American Journal of Psychiatry,* 127 (1971), 1391–1394.

111. LEE, D. T. "Recovery, Inc.: Aid in the Transition from Hospital to Community." *Mental Hygiene,* 55 (1971), 194–198.

112. LEMKAU, P. V. "Prevention in Psychiatry." *American Journal of Public Health,* 55 (1965), 554–560.

113. ———, and CROCETTI, G. "The Amsterdam Municipal Psychiatric Service." *American Journal of Psychiatry,* 117 (1961), 779–783.

114. LEOPOLD, R. L., and KISSICK, W. L. "A Community Mental Health Center, Regional Medical Program, and Joint Planning." *American Journal of Psychiatry,* 126 (1970), 1718–1726.

115. LEVY, L., and ROWITZ, L. "The Spatial Distribution of Treated Mental Disorders in Chicago." *Social Psychiatry,* 5 (1970), 1–11.

116. LEWIS, A. B. "Effective Utilization of the Psychiatric Hospital." *Journal of the American Medical Association,* 197 (1966), 871–877.

117. LIBERMAN, R. "The Part Played by Physicians in the Patient's Path to the Mental Hospital." *Community Mental Health Journal,* 3 (1967), 325–330.

118. LINDEMANN, E. "Symptomatology and Management of Acute Grief." *American Journal of Psychiatry,* 101 (1944), 141–148.

119. LINN, M. W., et al. "Family Care: A Therapeutic Tool for the Chronic Mental Patient." *Archives of General Psychiatry,* 15 (1966), 276–278.

120. LIPSCOMB, C. F. "The Yorktown Psychiatric Centre: A Five-Year Review." *American Journal of Psychiatry,* 127 (1970), 232–237.

121. LIPSITT, P. D. "Due Process as a Gateway to Rehabilitation in the Juvenile Justice System." *Boston University Law Review,* 49 (1969), 62–78.

122. ———, and STEINBRUNER, M. "An Experiment in Police-Community Relations: A Small-Group Approach." *Community Mental Health Journal,* 5 (1969), 172–179.

123. LITMAN, R. E., et al. "Suicide Prevention Telephone Service." *Journal of the American Medical Association,* 192 (1965), 21–25.

124. LOW, A. A. *Mental Health Through Will Training,* (1937). Boston: Christopher, 1950.

125. LOWENTHAL, M. F. "Social Isolation and Mental Illness in Old Age." *American Sociologic Review,* 29 (1964), 54–70.

126. LUDWIG, A. M. "Altered States of Consciousness." *Archives of General Psychiatry,* 15 (1966), 225–234.

127. ———, and FARRELLY, F. "The Code of Chronicity." *Archives of General Psychiatry,* 15 (1966), 562–568.

128. ———, and FARRELLY, F. "The Weapons of Insanity." *American Journal of Psychotherapy,* 21 (1967), 737–749.

129. ———, and MARX, A. J. "The Buddy Treatment Model for Chronic Schizophrenics." *Journal of Nervous and Mental Disease,* 148 (1969), 528–541.

130. LYNCH, K. "The City as Environment." *Scientific American,* 214 (September 1965), 209–219.

131. McINNES, R. S., et al. *An Analysis of the Service Relationships Between State Mental Hospitals and One Local Mental Health Program.* California Department of Mental Hygiene Biostatistics Bulletin, no. 23. Sacramento: State of California, 1962.

132. MALZBERG, B. "Mental Disease Among the Native and Foreign-Born White Population of New York State, 1939–1941." *Mental Hygiene,* 39 (1955), 545–559.

133. ———. "Rates of Mental Disease Among Certain Population Groups in New York State." *Journal of the American Statistical Association,* 31 (1936), 545–548.

134. MAROHN, R. C. "The Therapeutic Milieu as an Open System." *Archives of General Psychiatry,* 22 (1970), 360–364.

135. MASON, E. A. "The Hospitalized Child: His Emotional Needs." *New England Journal of Medicine,* 272 (1965), 406–414.

136. MESMER, R. "European Psychiatry: Observations Concerning the Care of the Aged,

Mentally Ill and Retarded." *Pennsylvania Psychiatric Quarterly*, 7 (1967), 1–16.

137. MEYER, R. E., SCHIFF, L. F., and BECKER, A. "The Home Treatment of Psychotic Patients: An Analysis of 154 Cases." *American Journal of Psychiatry*, 123 (1967), 1430–1438.

138. MICKLE, J. C. "Psychiatric Home Visits." *Archives of General Psychiatry*, 9 (1963), 379–383.

139. MILGRAM, S. "The Experience of Living in Cities." *Science*, 167 (1970), 1461–1468.

140. MISHLER, E. G., and WEXLER, N. E. "Decision Processes in Psychiatric Hospitalization." *American Sociological Review*, 28 (1963), 576–587.

141. MUMFORD, E., et al. "Ambiguities in a Secondary School Mental Health Project." *American Journal of Psychiatry*, 126 (1970), 1711–1717.

142. NATIONAL CENTER FOR HEALTH STATISTICS. *Medical Care, Health Status, and Family Income*. Washington, D.C.: U.S. Government Printing Office, 1964.

143. NATIONAL INSTITUTE OF MENTAL HEALTH. "Regulations for Community Mental Health Centers Act of 1963, Title II." *Federal Register*, May 6, 1964, pp. 5951–5956.

144. ———. *General Hospital Inpatient Psychiatric Services, 1967*. Public Health Service Publication, no. 1977. Washington, D.C.: U.S. Government Printing Office, 1969.

145. NATIONAL INSTITUTE OF MENTAL HEALTH PSYCHOPHARMACOLOGY SERVICE CENTER COLLABORATIVE STUDY GROUP. "Phenothiazine Treatment in Acute Schizophrenia." *Archives of General Psychiatry*, 10 (1964), 246–261.

146. NEWMAN, L. E., and STEINBERG, J. L. "Consultation with Police on Human Relations Training." *American Journal of Psychiatry*, 126 (1970), 1421–1429.

147. OJEMANN, R., ed. *The School and Community Treatment Facility in Preventive Psychiatry*. Iowa City: University of Iowa, 1966.

148. OZARIN, L. D., and LEVINSON, A. I. "The Future of the Public Mental Hospital." *American Journal of Psychiatry*, 125 (1969), 1647–1652.

149. PARSONS, T. "Illness and the Role of the Physician: A Sociological Perspective." *American Journal of Orthopsychiatry*, 21 (1951), 452–460.

150. PASAMANICK, B., et al. "Home vs Hospital

Care for Schizophrenics." *Journal of the American Medical Association*, 187 (1964), 177–181.

151. PAUL, B. D., ed. *Health, Culture and Community*. New York: Russell Sage, 1955.

152. PHILIPS, D. L. "Public Identification and Acceptance of the Mentally Ill." *American Journal of Public Health*, 56 (1966), 755–763.

153. POLLOCK, H. M. "Practical Considerations Relating to Family Care of Mental Patients." *American Journal of Psychiatry*, 92 (1935), 559–564.

154. *Public Law 88-164, The Community Mental Health Centers Construction Act*. Washington, 88th Congress, S 1576, October 31, 1963.

155. QUERIDO, A. "Early Diagnosis and Treatment Services." *World Mental Health*, 8 (1956), 180–189.

156. ———. "The Shaping of Community Mental Health Care." *British Journal of Psychiatry*, 114 (1968), 293–302.

157. RECOVERY INC. *A Directory and Manual*. Chicago, Ill.: Recovery Inc. (116 South Michigan Avenue, Chicago 60603), 1970.

158. REISSMAN, F. "Strategies and Suggestions for Training Nonprofessionals." *Community Mental Health Journal*, 2 (1967), 103–110.

159. ROSEN, G. "Mental Disorder, Social Deviance and Culture Pattern: Some Methodological Issues in the Historical Study of Mental Illness." In G. Mora, ed., *Psychiatry and Its History*. Springfield, Ill.: Charles C Thomas, 1970.

160. ROSENTHAL, D., and KETY, S. S., eds. "The Transmission of Schizophrenia." *Journal of Psychiatric Research*, 6, suppl. no. 1 (1968).

161. ROWITZ, L., and LEVY, L. "Ecological Analysis of Treated Mental Disorders in Chicago." *Archives of General Psychiatry*, 19 (1968), 571–579.

162. RUBIN, B. "Community Psychiatry: An Evolutionary Change in Medical Psychology in the United States." *Archives of General Psychiatry*, 20 (1969), 497–507.

163. ———, and EISEN, S. B. "The Old Timers' Club." *Archives of Neurology and Psychiatry*, 79 (1958), 113–121.

164. ———, and GOLDBERG, A. "An Investigation of Openness in the Psychiatric Hospital." *Archives of General Psychiatry*, 8 (1963), 269–276.

165. RUESCH, J. "The Assessment of Social Disability." *Archives of General Psychiatry*, 21 (1969), 655–664.

166. SARBIN, T. R. "The Dangerous Individual: An Outcome of Social Identity Transformations." *British Journal of Criminology*, 7 (1967), 285–295.

167. ———. "Notes on the Transformation of Social Identity." In L. M. Roberts et al., eds. *Comprehensive Mental Health: The Challenge of Evaluation*. Madison: University of Wisconsin Press, 1968. Pp. 97–115.

168. ———. "Schizophrenic Thinking: A Role-Theoretical Analysis." *Journal of Personality*, 37 (1969), 190–206.

169. SCHEFF, T. J. "Role of the Mentally Ill and the Dynamics of Mental Disorder." *Sociometry*, 26 (1963), 436–453.

170. ———. "The Societal Reactions of Deviance: Ascriptive Elements in the Psychiatric Screening of Mental Patients in a Midwestern State." *Social Problems*, 11 (1964), 401–413.

171. ———. *Being Mentally Ill*. Chicago: Aldine, 1966.

172. SCHIFF, S. K. "Community Accountability and Mental Health Services." *Mental Hygiene*, 54 (1970), 205–214.

173. SCHULBERG, H. C. "Psychiatric Units in General Hospitals: Boon or Bane?" *American Journal of Psychiatry*, 120 (1963), 30–36.

174. ———, and BAKER, F. "Varied Attitudes to Community Mental Health." *Archives of General Psychiatry*, 17 (1967), 658–663.

175. SCHWARTZ, M. D., and ERRERA, P. "Psychiatric Care in a General Hospital Emergency Room." *Archives of General Psychiatry*, 9 (1963), 113–121.

176. SEGAL, J., et al. *Mental Health of Children*. Public Health Service Publication, no. 1396. Washington, D.C.: U.S. Government Printing Office, 1965.

177. SELYE, H., and FORTIER, C. "Adaptive Reactions to Stress." *Psychosomatic Medicine*, 12 (1950), 149–157.

178. SHAKOW, D. "Psychological Deficit in Schizophrenia." *Behavioral Science*, 8 (1963), 275–305.

179. SHELDON, A., and JONES, K. J. "Maintenance in the Community: A Study of Psychiatric Aftercare and Rehospitalization." *British Journal of Psychiatry*, 113 (1967), 1009–1012.

180. SILVERMAN, P. R. "Services to the Widowed: First Steps in a Program of Preventive Intervention." *Community Mental Health Journal*, 3 (1967), 37–44.

181. ———. "The Widow-to-Widow Program: An Experiment in Preventive Intervention." *Mental Hygiene*, 53 (1969), 333–337.

182. SIMON, A. "Physical and Socio-Psychological Stress in the Geriatric Mentally Ill." *Comprehensive Psychiatry*, 11 (1970), 242–247.

183. SMITH, W. G., and HANSELL, N. "Territorial Evaluation of Mental Health Services." *Community Mental Health Journal*, 3 (1967), 119–124.

184. SPEAR, P. S., and DORAN, L. L. "Variables Related to Visiting Rate of Hospitalized Mental Patients." *Journal of the Fort Logan Mental Health Center*, 5 (1970), 77–83.

185. SPEIGEL, J. P. "Psychological Transactions in Situations of Acute Stress." In *Symposium on Stress*. Washington, D.C.: Walter Reed Army Medical Center, 1953. Pp. 103–112.

186. SPITZER, R. L., et al. "The Psychiatric Status Schedule: A Technique for Evaluating Psychopathology and Impairment in Role Functioning." *Archives of General Psychiatry*, 23 (1970), 41–55.

187. STANTON, A. H., and SCHWARTZ, M. S. *The Mental Hospital*. New York: Basic Books, 1954.

188. STICKNEY, S. B. "Schools Are Our Community Mental Health Centers." *American Journal of Psychiatry*, 124 (1968), 1407–1414.

189. STOTSKY, B. A. "A Controlled Study of Factors in the Successful Adjustment of Mental Patients to Nursing Homes." *American Journal of Psychiatry*, 123 (1967), 1243–1251.

190. STRAUSS, A., et al. *Psychiatric Ideologies and Institutions*. New York: The Free Press, 1964.

191. TYHURST, J. S. "The Role of Transition States, Including Disasters, In Mental Illness." In *Symposium on Social and Preventive Psychiatry*. Washington, D.C.: Walter Reed Army Institute of Research, 1957. Pp. 149–172.

192. ULLMAN, M. "Power: A Unifying Concept Linking Therapeutic and Community Process." In W. Gray et al., eds. *General*

Systems Theory and Psychiatry. Boston: Little-Brown, 1969. Pp. 253–265.

193. VAILLANT, G. E. "The Natural History of Drug Addiction." *Seminars in Psychiatry,* 2 (1970), 486–498.

194. VISOTSKY, H. M. "Project for Unwed Pregnant Adolescents." *Clinical Pediatrics,* 5 (1966), 322–324.

195. ——, et al. "Coping Behavior Under Extreme Stress." *Archives of General Psychiatry,* 5 (1961), 423–448.

196. WALLACE, A. F. C. "Mazeway Resynthesis: A Biocultural Theory of Religious Inspiration." *Transactions of the New York Academy of Science,* 18, series 2 (1956), 626–638.

197. ——. "Stress and Rapid Personality Changes." *International Record of Medicine,* 169 (1956), 761–774.

198. ——. "Mazeway Disintegration: The Individual's Perception of Socio-cultural Disorganization." *Human Organization,* 16 (1957), 23–27.

199. WECHSLER, H. "The Self-Help Organization in the Mental Health Field: Recovery, Inc.: A Case Study." In H. Wechsler, L. Solomon, and B. M. Kramer, eds., *Social Psychology and Mental Health,* New York: Holt, Rinehart & Winston, 1970. Pp. 456–473.

200. WEINBERG, S. K., ed. *The Sociology of Mental Disorders.* Chicago: Aldine, 1967.

201. WOODBURY, M. A. "Milieux, Symptoms and Schizophrenia: The Seven-Year History of a Psychiatric Ward." *Psychiatric Research Report,* 19 (1964), 20–36.

202. ——. "Object Relations in the Psychiatric Hospital." *International Journal of Psycho-Analysis,* 48 (1967), 83–87.

203. ——, and WOODBURY, M. M. "Community-Centered Psychiatric Intervention: A Pilot Project for the 13th Arrondissement, Paris." *American Journal of Psychiatry,* 126 (1969), 619–625.

204. WORLD HEALTH ORGANIZATION, EXPERT COMMITTEE ON MENTAL HEALTH. *Programme Development in the Mental Health Field.* Technical report series, no. 223. Geneva, 1961.

205. ZURCHER, L. A., and GREEN, A. E. *From Dependency to Dignity: Individual and Social Consequences of a Neighborhood House.* New York: Behavioral Publications, 1969.

206. ZUSMAN, J. "Sociology and Mental Illness." *Archives of General Psychiatry,* 15 (1966), 635–648.

207. ——. "Some Explanations of the Changing Appearance of Psychotic Patients." In E. M. Gruenberg, ed., *Evaluating the Effectiveness of Community Mental Health Services.* New York: Milbank, 1966. Pp. 363–394.

208. ——. "Design of Catchment Areas for Community Mental Health Services." *Archives of General Psychiatry,* 21 (1969), 568–573.

209. ——. " 'No-Therapy': A Method of Helping Persons with Problems." *Community Mental Health Journal,* 5 (1969), 482–486.

CHAPTER 43

COMMUNITY*
ORGANIZATIONAL ASPECTS
OF ESTABLISHING
AND MAINTAINING
A LOCAL PROGRAM

Raquel E. Cohen

To ESTABLISH A FOUNDATION on which a broad comprehensive mental health program can be established, the professional must leave the walls of the clinic and enter the community "turf."[31] Here he will be confronted with a complex situation, consisting of many dynamic components with which he is unfamiliar and for which his prior train-

ing and modes of thinking have not prepared him.[5,7,12,14,46] This chapter will address itself to the issues with which he will need to deal. Although there are no scientifically specified modes of proceeding, sets of phenomena that occur on a regular basis offer an opportunity to abstract conceptual principles, which provide guidelines for procedures in organizing a mental health program.[15,30,33,41]

Participation on a proactive basis in community organization and action to effect health-promoting changes requires joint planning and operation with individuals affected by these efforts in ways that would have been

* The word "community" in this chapter is used to denote the conglomerate of groups living and interacting within the boundaries of the geographical limits of the catchment areas. Mental health professionals are becoming increasingly aware of the variety of uses and meanings of the term, as noted in numerous reports and publications.[2,6,39,43,65]

unheard of and unacceptable a few years ago to most classically trained mental health professionals.[4,10,19,38,48] The psychiatrist will need to critically reexamine assumptions, experiences, traditions, and models that guided him in the past and to explore new pathways and develop innovative solutions to long-standing, long-neglected problems, aided by the findings of other disciplines, ranging from the political and managerial to the biological sciences, which are now just beginning to be integrated into the field of community psychiatry.[17,32,42,44,51]

([Primary Aspects of Organizing the Community Mental Health Program

As the mental health professional exercises leadership in organizing a local program he should attempt to accomplish the following:[11,12,28,29,55]

1. Investigate as many aspects of the community as possible, including the type of community he is entering and the group that may participate with him in his endeavors.[23]

2. Determine the degree of accord between his program interests and the interests of the community so that a basic equilibrium between his professional concerns and the expressed needs of the community—the consumer of his future services—is established.[22,58]

3. Determine the actual and potential sources of conflict between different groups, which is often marked by issues involving personal ambitions, hidden agendas, and external needs and demands. While assessing these factors it is important to remember that any assessment will not remain static; people change, individuals come and go, political parties shift. Dynamic changes over time will therefore occur and should be considered when making decisions.[54]

4. Organize elements perceived as salient into a gestalt, realizing that each element will modify the other, that is, what people think is important to them will be influenced by broader and possibly more powerful forces emanating from different levels of government and community leadership, which, in turn, may reflect national trends.[1,9,25] The mental health professional should give continuous attention to the interaction and influence of each component with and on the other to minimize the possibilities of error and the statistical probabilities of failure.

5. Find ways and develop techniques of helping different groups to compromise around community issues as the program starts. It is therefore important for the mental health professional to know about and assess the relevant factors comprising the human dynamics operating on local as well as broader levels in relation to his place and possibilities as a mental health leader in the community and, at the same time, to help groups relate to each other.[56,62] This needs apportionment of time which must become a refined technique. While remaining quite close to the grass roots of the community, the mental health professional should also be able to spend some time in informal meetings at national, state, and city governmental levels. There he will acquire information from policy decision-makers, who are in the position to radically influence programs in which a great amount of energy has been invested. This activity becomes crucial when we note that such programs can be truncated with the flourish of a signature which could very easily occur in the case of model cities and antipoverty programs.[52]

6. Acquaint and attempt to involve community members with his own aims through program planning and development. Here the priorities of citizens and representatives of other human services should be respected at the same time that the mental health professional seeks to incorporate his own interests and approaches.[24,31,57,61]

As the mental health professional participates in the community he will relate to members of area boards, executives, and consumers who serve as advisors, representatives, and "samplers" in their own districts and who can be a source of alliance about community activities; they are able to collect information because of their broad contact and can be extremely helpful to a program that is interested in permeating and participating in community affairs. Coordinating committees often bring together large numbers of directors of agencies, who in turn will be closely allied in the delivery of services.[57,69,70]

7. Attempt to find ways of developing a proactive mechanism, a modus operandi whereby the mental health professional avoids, on the one hand, being manipulated or becoming a passive acceptor of community wishes or, on the other, exerting rigid authoritative approaches. He therefore strives to anticipate certain problem areas, but always reacts to the felt needs of the consumer by recognizing sources of potential conflict, to achieve a balance between the expressed basic needs of community members and his own ideas and perceived options and to make decisions on what he feels will both benefit the community and be feasible for him to accomplish.[63]

8. Set realistic limits to what he can accomplish and find ways of dealing with the sense of frustration experienced by community members when they are not able to obtain everything they want.[59]

(Developing and Maintaining Sanction with All Operating Levels

Once the mental health professional has accepted the leadership to organize the local mental health program, successive approximations and explorations of and with the community are needed to establish priority of approaches and types of intervention. It is at this point that the professional must continue to review and clarify for himself the salient issues within the population for which he now is responsible. He must decide what approaches he has at his disposal to intervene at either primary, secondary, or tertiary preventive and rehabilitative levels and what manpower is available to implement any chosen intervention.[11,68]

When he ascertains what the felt needs of the significant groups in the community are, he must analyze their priority possibilities, the reality issues of community climate, and his own approaches and plans, which he attempts to keep flexible. He must enter into negotiations with representative groups to firm up these priorities and begin implementing the primary aspects of his program. As he negotiates with the different groups, who will be asking for disparate programs relating to vested interest in children, retardation, or drugs, he must realize that no group per se is homogeneous; ascertaining the different subgroups with respect to their ethnic, religious, and socioeconomic characteristics is therefore important.[45] Each subgroup will need and want different things and many times will not have the type of verbal spokesman who will bring this to the attention of the professional. Kellam[40] has delineated the various representative groups that are emerging as negotiators within mental health community programs. It is essential to pay particular attention to the silent subgroups, children, immigrants, and the sick and try to develop spokesmen or ombudsmen to give voice to their unexpressed needs and put them on a par with the powerful voices.

Once he has obtained enough knowledge on these issues, the mental health specialist should set up a priority order and weigh the items in relation to the size of the group affected and how an established priority will benefit the community as a whole. He should also try to ascertain what the needs of the middle class silent majority— the traditional community—are as compared to those of the lower socioeconomic groups, heretofore the silent community, which has emerged in the past decade as more voluble and often in conflict with traditional establishment sectors.[73]

With the data obtained he should be able to answer some of the following questions:

1. What are the crucial, emergent topical issues?
2. What are the felt needs of the population?
3. What are the crucial unmet problems as professionally defined?

4. Which and where are the populations at high risk? These are the vulnerable subpopulations susceptible to fall prey to trouble, due to the fact that they live under undesirable living conditions.
5. Where are the most noxious and violent areas in the community where deprivation, poor housing, cramped surroundings, and pollution exist in their most acute states?

Even though the mental health professional realizes that he cannot deal with all levels of psychopathology, he should be aware of the fact that for every patient treated in the community there also exist a considerable percentage of untreated and unknown cases, in addition to individuals who have a high potential for developing manifest psychopathology. Continuous feedback material from such caregivers in the community as policemen, welfare workers, nurses, and general practitioners should be accumulated in order to eventually develop a community epidemiological profile, which would include the factors that cause stress as documented by research findings, as well as the psychopathological symptoms and disturbances of that stress.[47,66]

(Finding Community Allies

The mental health professional in the community must find out who the salient caregivers are, in order to identify potential allies, who by their daily responsibilities and activities might be able to help in revealing and caring for high risk populations in the community.[67,68] The mental health professional should find out who is actually doing something about which problems, what approaches they are using, and the degree to which they are accomplishing the task of reducing some of the counterproductivity engendered by the social system, with special attention to rigidified bureaucracies that are unable to adapt to the multifaceted needs of multiproblem families.[60] As the professional becomes better acquainted with the ways in which some of these agencies or institutions perform their tasks, he should be tempered in his criticisms and ways in which he confronts them with their apparent insensitivity to the needs of the individual. The gap between adequate services and mobilization of resources within bureaucracies has a tradition and history that cannot be geared rapidly to meet individual needs. Needed change requires continuous efforts and inputs from many professionals, including the mental health worker, within a realistic, evolutionary climate. This challenge is also being met by a large number of multidisciplinary professionals especially interested in the quality of life for populations at high risk, who are intervening with a variety of techniques developed by their own disciplines.[26,27]

How does the mental health worker decide where to put his energies when working with caregivers and other social change agents? What helpful guidelines can he use in working with agencies having a direct impact on citizen well-being?

The criteria on which he will base his choice for collaborating with a care-giving system involves estimating two characteristics: (1) salience and (2) feasibility.[13] A system that would have high salience for the mental health professional would have among other characteristics (1) a high rank order relative to other systems in regard to its potential in satisfying current feelings of need in the community; and (2) a prognosis of serious consequences to the general mental health picture of the community if these needs are not satisfied. It must be recognized that a judgment on the salience of the system is relatively arbitrary, involving a complicated array of factors. It is particularly susceptible to influence by the spirit and value system of the times, in our time by the movement toward increasingly comprehensive human service systems.[3]

A system that offers the feasibility of collaboration with the mental health professional has the following characteristics:

1. Openness to the entry of the mental health professional so that he can accomplish

his task. There are various levels of openness, lack of defensiveness, flexibility, and degree of acceptability within our institutions. The mental health professional has to gauge within what institution it is feasible to promote change, what the inherent capacities are that lend themselves to effect change necessary for continually dealing with the problems in a sensitive and flexible manner. The following items must be looked at to ascertain the potential for gradual change: the structure of the agency; the type of leadership; the quality of the staff and staff relationships to administrative units within the government structure; the type of resources; and the source and steadiness of funding.

2. The climate of the times in terms of national priorities and the feelings of the community about the particular agency.

3. The permeating attitude within the agency toward the whole range of mental health issues.

Investigation of these items will elicit the data necessary to choose the target systems, agencies and institutions to organize and establish a local program.

By what methods can the mental health professional garner the data to accomplish his objectives?

1. The mental health professional can gather information by reading, talking, walking in the community, visiting with citizens from all walks of life, making lists of people who know and are active in different areas and systematically meeting with them to exchange information.

2. He can collect statistics gathered by others (U.S. census, antipoverty groups, health insurance programs) and monitor his own statistics so that he can find out who is using his facilities and for what purposes. This will give him data to develop many evaluations to feed back to his own program within short time periods in order to narrow the gap between relevant services and community needs.

3. He can use students and volunteers in spot surveys to gather data that provide the mental health professional with information about what people are thinking and feeling about specific problems in order to stimulate

citizens to study their own problems; citizen involvement and expressed needs might then be fed back to community leaders to help obtain their support for future mental health programs. They can also ascertain how people are using the mental health facilities and what changes or additions citizens could suggest about ongoing programs.

4. As data are accumulated, priority planning on the use of resources to achieve goals is determined. For example, collaborative planning with the general practitioners who will be affected by the specific program should be instituted. Subcommittees of these physicians will then develop their own ideas and present them to the director of the mental health program with suggestions and formulations concerning scope, directions, and goals.

It is obvious to any professional who has tried to develop a program that there will never be enough manpower to meet the needs indicated both by professional knowledge and by the expressed wishes of community leaders.[8,51,53] The task then becomes one of designing a program to produce the most effective, durable, and economical intervention. Community organization work by sociologists has delineated modes of stimulating changes by linking the community representatives in such a way that the effect of a particular program on one institution or one group of individuals will start a ripple effect through the community. That is, successful intervention in a highly visible or prestigious organization or institution will facilitate intervention in other community institutions. The converse is also possible: Unsuccessful intervention is followed by disastrous effects in the community.

(Implementation of Methods and Procedures to Organize the Program

1. The mental professional must be physically located in or near enough to the community to talk with citizens, caregivers, agency executives, and so on. Innumerable opportunities are available for participation in

meetings, task forces, councils, and representative citizens' groups. Whenever possible the mental health professional should, therefore, express his wish to offer his expertise in order to afford members of a community the opportunity to find out what he does and how he may be helpful. Whenever the opportunity arises, the mental health professional should capitalize on the multiple items on the agenda offered by almost any problem situation and use these as vehicles to make himself better known and to learn of and investigate the institutional components of the specific problem case. Information should be gathered about the agency and personnel involved and efforts made to meet as many people in the agency as possible to learn of their needs, problems, goals, and interests.

2. Establishing a reputation. When participating in and collaborating with community groups, a reputation of reliability is necessary. The community's fear that a newcomer will be a disruptive factor in the system is seen and felt in the reception given to mental health professionals. Suspicions and fears can arise when the mental health professional is insensitive to areas of conflict in any particular agency, and, for example, gives his attention and prestige to marginal or unpopular groups within an agency, or aligns himself with only one faction of the groups in conflict. To effect change within agencies or institutions which will be conducive to better community mental health programs, participation within some broad parameters of an agency's structure is imperative. Institutions need their own defenses in order to perform efficiently just as individuals do. A reputation for usefulness as opposed to meddling is very rapidly established and will influence the degree of help that the mental health worker will be able to offer within a particular community.

3. Usefulness. During the mental health professional's initiation period, his ability to demonstrate that he can be useful is the crucial test of his *rites de passage*, and is therefore of primary importance. It is obvious that his particular expertise is needed and wanted in the community. But this must be demonstrated in such a way that other professionals do not feel either inferior by their lack of knowledge or threatened by having to deal with mysteries they feel are known only to professionals in the mental health field. The mental health professional's task of earning a reputation of usefulness before he is known and asked to participate in community affairs is one of the delicate techniques that must be developed. Here an attitude demonstrating concern for the history of the problem at hand and a desire and ability to open options for community representatives when trying to understand the dimensions of their problems is helpful. It is imperative that the mental health professional's attitude and mode of communication impart to community members that "I" and "you" face the problems together and that collaboration can increase the possibility of solving them through the presentation and examination of views of dimensions of the problems as well as alternatives for their solution. The mental health professional must be cognizant of and sensitive to the differing, and often contradictory, expectations and fantasies regarding his capacities and abilities.[20] On the one hand he will be viewed as a total healer capable of solving all dilemmas; on the other, he will be viewed with caution, perhaps suspicion, as an interloper. He must therefore help community members become aware of his actual limitations and capacities and act with regard to them. That is, if they want help that does not fall within the mental health professional's scope he should be prepared to help them plan and get the type of resources that will meet the needs of the problem. In addition, whenever the mental health professional actively collaborates with the community, he should be aware that he is exposed to critical appraisal and be able to accept this in a comfortable and nondefensive manner, the same way he has learned to deal with his feelings in the one-to-one clinical relationship. It is at this point that the mental health professional has an opportunity to change the classical stereotypes and anxieties based on irrational expectations that both lay persons and professionals have about psychiatry and mental health professionals. At this juncture the relationship between the

community and the mental health worker becomes meaningful, enlarging the possibilities for enlisting the support of diversely oriented groups indigenous to or involved with the community; this is a crucial factor among the many that are conducive for successful community mental health programs.

❪ Maintenance of the Program

Once the mental health professional has acquired knowledge about his community and its salient needs, gained entry, developed ways of obtaining and maintaining sanction with all operating levels of the system, overcome negative stereotyped expectations, oriented himself to the social system of the community, investigated the administrative structure and functioning of the agency, started to plan and implement programs for change, developed and negotiated successive roles in conformity with the unfolding needs of the program, and learned to time interventions in relation to situational conflicts, how does he proceed to promote and maintain ongoing aspects of his program? How does the professional move from intelligence, reconnaissance activities, program planning and design, and program implementation to program maintenance, evaluation, and further development?

During this stage of his activities he must continue to relate usefully to those groups and forces in the community that sanctioned his program, but also to the differing and often conflicting groups essential to the development of the particular program in which he is involved.[34] Even though he may have earned a welcome from citizen leaders and individuals who collaborated with him, who guided and supported him to ascertain what the needed activities were, he must continually monitor the quality of his endeavors in the community. Obtaining appropriate sanction from influential power structure representatives—both lay and professional—leads to continuation and growth of a program and also calls for additional knowledge and techniques from the mental health professional.[50]

He should continue with an open approach, flexible and sensitive to the continuous messages obtained from helpful resource groups, and, at the same time, he must be able to organize them within an operational framework that allows for the gradual implementation of parts of the program rather than presenting or suggesting implementation worked out in advance of reactions and unforeseeable contingencies. With the passage of time he will develop clearer and more concrete plans to implement with and for the community, with established objectives that could be developed, set, and evaluated by both professionals and community representatives.

During this second phase of establishing the program and maintaining it at a level at which it has a good chance of being accepted by community leaders, flexibility and careful deployment of resources to aspects of the specific program are necessary.[64] The broad outlines may be set by what are considered by professionals to be sound principles, capable of being adapted to the specific needs of the community; the more concrete and binding principles or program outlines should be still left for a future date.[71] This is the time when the mental health program can start trying to define its own parameters along lines that will be harmonious with services in the community, with the aim of eventual participation without too much strain and stress, with ongoing community plans for the coming decade.[27,49] As the program advances, this type of open-ended organization can be extremely helpful for linking other systems and institutions and for emerging as the model for collaboration and implementation of comprehensive health or human services advocated by national leaders.[55] Federal forces have been able to influence mental health programs in the last ten years, and it is evident that they are pointing toward integration of services in the foreseeable future.

At the same time that the professional leader of the program develops the type of relationships that will allow him to plan with comprehensive health, welfare, and education agencies in the community, there should be a proliferation of small demonstration services within the community to begin implementing useful and responsive approaches to community needs. Within this small and concentrated effort the new staff that may be assembled, or the staff that has been already working in the community, but within the walls of the clinics, can begin learning the new techniques necessary to work in the community, as, for example, consultation to schools, development of storefront centers, collaboration within drug- or alcohol-abuse control programs.[69] In this way the staff has the opportunity to move out into community activities gradually, progressively, with continuous feedback into their own operations. To choose where and how to establish a specific service, the issues of feasibility and salience should be considered. Setting up small demonstration programs within the areas of primary, secondary, or tertiary prevention, according to the opportunities, will allow mental health professionals to be guided within a smaller limited setting by the same principles that they used in a macroscopic manner when learning about the community and considering broad approaches spanning the breadth and depth of community problems.

As more areas for activities related to mental health problems emerge in the community, the mental health professional will have increasing opportunities to reinforce their importance with community leaders and community representatives.[37] In one community where the psychiatric director was in the stage of maintaining the already established mental health programs, he divided his time between a group of activities that indicated the range necessary for the maintenance of the program. He participated whenever possible in any public and civic activities in which he could be a resource member or an interested participant. This included membership in a community council on drugs, the governor's task force on Spanish-speaking affairs, and a model city subcommittee on education and acting as a consultant to public agencies in the community, including schools. His activities paralleled the process of growth and the range of interaction necessary to achieve this purpose. The growth of the program appears to be based on the successful engagement of relationships between meaningful members of the mental health program with the appropriate individuals in the community, who could collaborate to implement formally or informally programs for the well-being of the community.[36]

As the community has started to organize self-help groups, grass roots organizations, and volunteer boards, more opportunities are emerging for the mental health professional to come into close contact with these large numbers of community leaders.[72] Functioning as a participant and interactive catalyst in an attempt to link groups with differing points of view on specific issues, distinct vocabularies, or propensities for taking stands that polarize large groups when making decisions on crucial issues makes for a tightrope approach for the mental health professional in trying to aid communication between sparring groups.[21,35] This is emerging as the antipodal steerage dilemma of mental health program activities.

This type of linking relationship has occurred more easily and frequently in the past because many of these individuals have been professional allies of the mental health worker. But an area of extreme importance and sensitivity, and the locus of community mental health problems today, is the mental health leader's attempts to relate to the various neglected groups in the community, specifically the minority groups that have emerged during the last few years who are alien, antagonistic, have different concerns, and give very little credence to what mental health represents. Some dramatic examples of difficulties encountered by mental health professionals as they try to relate to these groups emerge from the overlap or simultaneity of roles, for example, when community members participate in board activities and then move on to become paraprofessionals. As the indigenous representative progresses from an interested citizen to an enlightened one, who sees an opportunity to begin climbing the paraprofessional career ladder with hopes of upward movement to employment within the health system, the mental health professional finds it very difficult to negotiate and compromise with some of the demands established by these informed, knowledgeable and often militant individuals. Some demands may be novel and creative, while others, which often come to light in hidden agendas, serve the purpose of ambition of the participating community member inconsonant with specific program aims. Many a community meeting has been a shattering experience for mental health professionals if they are confronted with and accused of racism and discrimination, ascribed to them because they belong to the system or establishment. This may have nothing to do with either their individual predispositions or their activities, but they become the *causes célèbres* for pent-up expression of hostility and frustration engendered by the stressful living conditions of the very population that mental health workers want to reach. Going through the process of mitigating and neutralizing some of these feelings in order to develop cooperative working relations was one of the most painful learning experiences encountered by the mental health profession during the 1960s.

The issue that cuts across role and function is racism. Any white mental health practitioner working in a system staffed both by whites and blacks should always be aware of concerns about manifest and latent racism. When a member of such a system receives unusually high demands on his productivity and is under considerable tension, the always latent concerns and fantasies about racism (on both sides) can become manifest, with both sides projecting their frustrations and hostilities in a rhetorical barrage of racist epithets and accusations. This can be lessened if the mental health professional is able to participate in informal as well as formal activities within the community so that his knowledge and feeling for dimensions of problems is actualized directly, through interaction, rather than remaining expertise, which is often abstract and can create alienation.

Another area of difficulty occurs when the mental health professional works as a collaborator, consultant, or participant in areas in which increasing involvement with different value systems and aims within the human services agencies in the community is necessary and desirable. Here the professional is faced with the conflicts that arise when the problem-solving approaches of other agencies appear inappropriate to mental health values.[15,74] However, he must continually remember that there are many valid approaches to the same problems and must continue to have a genuine respect for opinions and approaches that, because of differences in professional background or experience, are foreign to him.[18] Mental health professionals trained in homogeneous, traditional clinical settings in which a given viewpoint and set of professional values tend to prevail, may find heterogeneity of backgrounds, opinions, and approaches which provide much of the substance as well as the form of interaction in working with a variety of professionals and lay groups quite difficult to handle. His impulse to be critical, to want to take over the job because he feels more competent, his wish for efficiency and rapid resolution of problems, will handicap him in allowing for a more evolutionary process of continuous development which will ultimately solidify his program. As the number of professional groups working in the community increases, the need for supportive backups, whether among peers or with consultants who have already resolved dilemmas and learned techniques for successfully negotiating within the community arena, is ever more welcome.

As the mental health professional becomes better known, trusted, and respected, he will very often be assigned the role of linking agency programs to promote comprehensive approaches to human problems. In most communities, agencies tend to work in isolation and to know relatively little about each other's programs. As the mental health professional moves laterally across agencies and upward across governmental levels, he will be able to identify gaps in the existent agency network and thus has an opportunity to link these agencies or systems, thereby utilizing the total program in order to provide different portions of the population who present problems, such as families, the elderly, or addicts, for example, with optimum care. Here the professional will encounter the divisive forces of power prerogatives, traditions, inertia, political pressures, and turf preservation, which impinge in such a way as to foster compartmentalization of professional efforts in the alleviation of human ills. He will tentatively try to define his own role in the linking activities, approach key agency leaders with the main focus on understanding their general needs and the problems which they are interested in participating. It is important to avoid arousing feelings of defensiveness by first handling in a careful way acute or sensitive areas of conflict and by introducing minimal material that might increase the suspiciousness that agencies manifest toward mental health workers.

As this broad activity of organizing the various components of his program into a comprehensive human services framework continues, many community groups are going to ask the professionals for services that, in most cases, cannot be met, owing to manpower and budget limitations. This means that many times the mental health worker will have to set realistic limits as to what clinical services can be provided. A clear statement of what type of services are possible at this stage of the program, as well as those that cannot be provided, should be presented. Many times the lack of services engenders disappointment in the community, but this can be partially mitigated by the offer to be helpful in providing alternative means of obtaining some aspects of the needed service and by linking and alerting a community to other agencies that might fulfill other aspects of the service. Here again, whatever help is offered should be accompanied by follow through to see that eventual successful completion of services is accomplished by the other units.

❲ Developing Formal Structures of Functioning with Community Units

As the mental health professional continues to move slowly, step by step, and to be sensitive to the interest and appropriateness of the community's needs, the process of growth of his program continues. The program will progress through several developmental stages, each indicating successful accomplishment of necessary tasks and successful resolution of conflictual and divergent needs.[17] How to ascertain what the needs are, how to find ways of balancing issues of knowledge, manpower, deep and acute problems within differing community groups, comprise the basis of practicing community psychiatry on a local level. Some indications that may be helpful in evaluating how the community organization aspects of the program are advancing include:

1. Sanction from most of the members of power and influence groups and from agency networks can be obtained in the majority of instances for specific programs.
2. Whether the program continues to unfold and seems to be accepted by a large number of community members.
3. Feedback that indicates a relatively good reputation of being useful.
4. Meaningful relationships with representative groups both in and out of the establishment continue.
5. Participation in the work of the local community agencies, in consultant, collaborator, or educator capacity, increases.
6. Participation as resource members to community boards, governmental agencies boards, and self-help grass roots organizations.
7. Increased demand of educational activities, such as speaking at PTA groups, in panel discussions of such clubs as Rotary or Lions, being invited as members for discussion groups with the clergy or public health nurses; in "rapping" sessions with minority groups, students, or self-help groups.

Much time and effort in interaction and negotiation must be spent in order to ensure an adequate accommodation between what the mental health professional is able and willing to do and what others want of him. These activities are in continuous evolution, part of a continuing process that will lead him to the clarification and conceptualization of his new roles and modes of functioning in the community as he tries to establish and maintain a mental health program. His relationship with the community will evolve as different facets of the program develop, influenced also by patterns inherent in institutional relationships and spontaneously arising conditions, which will offer him, in turn, new challenges and opportunities to chart the course and outline approaches for the professional of the 1980s.

⟮ Bibliography

1. ALLEN, A. "The Urban Setting: IV. The Black City Dweller—Mental Health Needs and Services." *Rhode Island Medical Journal,* 53 (1970), 267–270.

2. BACK, E. B. "The Community in Community Mental Health." *Mental Hygiene,* 54 (1970), 316–320.

3. BAKER, F. "Review of General Systems Concepts and Their Relevance for Medical Care." *Systematics,* 7 (1969), 209–229.

4. BANDLER, B. Current Trends in Psychiatry from the Academic Point of View. Paper presented to the American College of Psychiatrists, Third Annual Seminar for Continuing Education for Psychiatrists, Atlanta, Georgia, February 12–15, 1970.

5. ——. The Reciprocal Roles of the University and the Community in the Development of Community Mental Health Centers. Paper presented to the American College of Psychiatrists, Third Annual Seminar for Continuing Education for Psychiatrists, Atlanta, Georgia, February 12–15, 1970.

6. BELLAK, L., and BARTEN, H. H., eds. *Progress in Community Mental Health.* New York: Grune & Stratton, 1969.

7. BERNARD, V. W. "Education for Community Psychiatry." In L. C. Kolb, V. W. Bernard, and B. P. Dohrenwend, eds., *Urban Challenges to Psychiatry.* Boston: Little, Brown, 1969. Pp. 319–360.

8. BOWER, W. H. "Can 'Subprofessionals' Solve Psychiatric Manpower Problems?" *Roche Report,* 7 (1970), 1–2.

9. BROWN, B. S., and LONG, S. E. "Psychosocial Politics of the Community Mental Health Movement." *Research Publication of the Association for Research of Nervous and Mental Disorders,* 47 (1969), 289–306.

10. BUTLER, H. J. "Comprehensive Community Mental Health Centers, A Progress Report, 1969." *Journal of Psychiatric Nursing,* 7 (1969), 245–250.

11. CAPLAN, G. *An Approach to Community Mental Health.* New York: Grune & Stratton, 1961.

12. ——. *Principles of Preventive Psychiatry.* New York: Basic Books, 1964.

13. ——. *The Theory and Practice of Mental Health Consultation.* New York: Basic Books, 1970.

14. ——, and GRUNEBAUM, H. "Perspectives on Primary Prevention: A Review." *Archives of General Psychiatry,* 17 (1967), 331–346.

15. COHEN, R. E. "The Gradual Growth of a Mental Health Center." *Hospital and Community Psychiatry,* 19, no. 4 (1968), 103–106.

16. ——. "The Collaborative Co-Professional: Developing a New Mental Health Role." *Hospital and Community Psychiatry,* 24 (1973), 242–246.

17. ——. "Anatomy of a Local Mental Health Program: A Case History." *American Journal of Orthopsychiatry,* 42 (1972), 490–498.

18. ——. "Two for One: Collaboration Model." *Mental Hygiene,* 57 (1973), 23–25.

19. ——. "Principles of Preventive Mental Health Programs for Ethnic Minority Populations: The Acculturation of Puerto Ricans to the United States." *American Journal of Psychiatry,* 128 (1972), 1529–1533.

20. ——. "Working with Schools." In G. Caplan, ed., *American Handbook of Psychiatry* Vol. II. New York: Basic Books, 1974.

21. COLLINS, J., and GRANT, C. Mental Health Consultant at the Interface of Complex Social Systems. Working Paper for Training at the Laboratory of Community Psychiatry, 1970.

22. COOK, P. E. *Community Psychology and Community Mental Health.* San Francisco: Holden-Day, 1970.

23. COTTRELL, L. S. "Social Planning, the Competent Community and Mental Health." In *Urban America and the Planning of Mental Health Services.* New York: Group for the Advancement of Psychiatry, 1964. Pp. 391–402.

24. CRONKHITE, L. W., ALPERT, J., and WEINER, D. S. "A Health-Care System for Massa-

chusetts." *New England Journal of Medicine*, 284 (1971), 240–243.

25. DEMONE, H. W., and NEWMAN, E. "Mental Health Planning and Coordination." In H. Grunebaum, ed., *Practice of Community Mental Health*. Boston: Little, Brown, 1970. Pp. 687–701.

26. ELWELL, R. N. "Hospitals and Centers Move Toward a Single System of Comprehensive Services." *Hospital and Community Psychiatry*, 20 (1969), 175–179.

27. ENGLISH, J. Experiences in Administering a Comprehensive Health Service and Moving It Towards a Human Services Philosophy. Paper presented to the Inter-University Forum for Educators in Community Psychiatry, Parker House, Boston, Mass., March 30, 1971.

28. FREEDMAN, A. M. "Decussational Psychiatry: The First Phase in Community Mental Health Center Development." *Social Psychiatry*, 1968.

29. GLASSCOTE, R. M. "The Mental Health Center: Portents and Prospects." *American Journal of Psychiatry*, 127 (1971), 940–941.

30. ———, SUSSEX, J. N., CUMMING, E., and SMITH, L. H. *The Community Mental Health Center: An Interim Appraisal.* Washington, D.C.: American Psychiatric Association and National Association for Mental Health, 1969.

31. GRUNEBAUM, H., ed. *Practice of Community Mental Health*. Boston: Little, Brown, 1970.

32. GUERNEY, B. G., ed. *Nonprofessionals as Psychotherapeutic Agents*. New York: Holt, Rinehart & Winston, 1969.

33. HALLOCK, A. C. K., and VAUGHN, W. T. "Community Organization—A Dynamic Component of Community Mental Health Practice." *American Journal of Orthopsychiatry*, 26 (1956), 691–706.

34. HALPERT, H. P., and SILVERMAN, C. Problem-oriented Approaches to Interagency Cooperation for Mental Health Services. Paper presented to the American Public Health Association, Chicago, October 1965.

35. HERSCH, C. "Mental Health Services and the Poor." *Psychiatry*, 29 (1966), 236–245.

36. HIRSCHOWITZ, R. "Dilemmas of Leadership in Community Mental Health." *Psychiatric Quarterly*, Spring 1971.

37. HOLDER, H. D. "Mental Health and the Search for New Organizational Strategies." *Archives of General Psychiatry*, 20 (1969), 709–717.

38. HUME, P. B. "Principles and Practice of Community Psychiatry: The Role and Training of a Specialist in Community Psychiatry." In L. Bellak, ed., *Progress in Community Mental Health*. New York: Grune & Stratton, 1969.

39. KANE, T. J. "The Concept of Community Mental Health." *Journal of the Maine Medical Association*, 59 (1968), 256–258.

40. KELLAM, S. G., and BRANCH, J. D. An Analysis of Basic Problems and an Approach to Community Mental Health. Woodlawn Mental Health Center Working Paper, 1970.

41. ———, and SCHIFF, S. K. "An Urban Community Mental Health Center." In L. J. Duhl and R. L. Leopold, eds., *Mental Health and Urban Social Policy*. San Francisco: Jossey Bass, 1968. Pp. 112–138.

42. KISSICK, W. L. "Health Policy Directions for the 1970's." *New England Journal of Medicine*, 282 (1970), 1343–1354.

43. KLEIN, D. C. "Community and Mental Health—An Attempt at a Conceptual Framework." *Community Mental Health Journal*, 1 (1965), 301–308.

44. KOLB, L. C., BERNARD, V. W., and DOHRENWEND, B. P. *Urban Challenges to Psychiatry*. Boston: Little, Brown, 1969.

45. KOLMER, M. B., and KERN, H. M., Jr. "The Resident in Community Psychiatry: An Assessment of Changes in Knowledge and Attitudes." *American Journal of Psychiatry*, 125 (1968), 698–702.

46. LAUE, J. "Power, Conflict, and Social Change." In L. H. Masotti and D. R. Brown, eds., *Riots and Rebellion: Civil Violence in the Urban Community*. Beverly Hills, Cal.: Sage Publications, 1968. Pp. 85–96.

47. LEIGHTON, A. H. "The Stirling County Study." In *The Interrelations Between Social Environment and Psychiatric Disorders*. New York: Milbank Memorial Fund, 1952.

48. LEOPOLD, R. L. "The West Philadelphia Mental Health Consortium: Administrative Planning in a Multi-hospital Catchment Area." *American Journal of Psychiatry*, 124 (1967), 69–76.

49. ———, and KISSICK, W. L. "A Community

Mental Health Center, Regional Medical Program and Joint Planning." *American Journal of Psychiatry*, 126 (1970), 1718–1726.

50. ———. "Newer Approaches to Community Health." *Medical Clinics of North America*, 54 (1970), 671–682.

51. LEVENSON, A. I. "Organizational Patterns of Community Mental Health Centers." In L. Bellak, ed., *Progress in Community Mental Health*. New York: Grune & Stratton, 1969. Pp. 88–89.

52. MARMOR, J. "Social Action and the Mental Health Professional." *American Journal of Orthopsychiatry*, 40 (1970), 370–374.

53. MESNIKOFF, A. M., SPITZER, R. L., and ENDICOTT, J. "Program Evaluation and Planning in a Community Mental Health Service." *Psychiatric Quarterly*, 41 (1967), 405–421.

54. OSTERWEIL, J. "Mental Health Planning: Prelude to Comprehensive Health Planning." *Bulletin of the New York Academy of Medicine*, 44 (1968), 194–198.

55. OZARIN, L. D., and FELDMAN, S. Implications for Health Service Delivery: The Community Mental Health Centers Amendments of 1970. Paper presented to the American Public Health Association, Houston, Texas, October 27, 1970.

56. PECK, H. B. "A Candid Appraisal of the Community Mental Health Center as a Public Health Agency: A Case History." *American Journal of Public Health*, 59 (1969), 459–469.

57. ———, KAPLAN, S. R., and ROMAN, M. "Prevention, Treatment, and Social Action: A Strategy of Intervention in a Disadvantaged Urban Area." *American Journal of Orthopsychiatry*, 36 (1966), 57–69.

58. ———, ROMAN, M., and KAPLAN, S. R. "Community Action Programs and the Comprehensive Mental Health Center." *Psychiatric Research Reports of the American Psychiatric Association*, 21 (1967), 103–121.

59. RIESSMAN, F. "The New Approach to the Poor." *Psychiatric Research Reports of the American Psychiatric Association*, 21 (1967), 35–49.

60. ROGAWSKI, A., and EDMUNDSON, B. "Factors Affecting Outcome of Psychiatry Interagency Referral." *American Journal of Psychiatry*, 127 (1971), 925–934.

61. ROSENFIELD, L. S. "Planning Comprehensive Health Services." *Hospital and Community Psychiatry*, 19 (1968), 376–379.

62. ROSS, M. *Community Organization: Theory and Principles*. New York: Harper, 1955.

63. RYAN, W. "Urban Mental Health Services and Responsibilities of Mental Health Professionals." *Mental Hygiene*, 47 (1963), 365–371.

64. SALBER, E. J. "Community Participation in Neighborhood Health Centers." *New England Journal of Medicine*, 283 (1970), 515–518.

65. SANDERS, I. T. *The Community*. New York: Ronald, 1966.

66. SAPER, B. "Forecasting and Planning for Mental Health in Situations of Rapid Change." *Psychiatric Quarterly*, 43 (1969), 72–84.

67. SCHERL, D. J., and ENGLISH, J. T. "Community Mental Health and Comprehensive Health Service Programs for the Poor." *American Journal of Psychiatry*, 125 (1969), 1666–1674.

68. SHEELEY, W. F. "The General Practitioners Contribution to Community Psychiatry." In L. Bellak, ed., *Handbook of Community Psychiatry and Community Mental Health*. New York: Grune & Stratton, 1964. Pp. 268–270.

69. SHORE, M., et al. "Tufts Mental Health Area —Annual Plan." Prepared for the Dept. of Mental Health in the Commonwealth of Mass. Boston, 1972.

70. SPIEGEL, H., ed. *Citizen Participation in Urban Development: Cases and Programs*. Vol. 2. Washington, D.C.: NTL Institute for Applied Behavioral Science, 1969.

71. SPIRO, H. R. "On Beyond Mental Health Centers: A Planning Model for Psychiatric Care." *Archives of General Psychiatry*, 21 (1969), 646–654.

72. TURNER, J. B., ed. *Neighborhood Organization for Community Action*. New York: National Association of Social Workers, 1968.

73. ULLMAN, M. "Power: A Unifying Concept Linking Therapeutic and Community Process." In W. Gray et al., eds., *General Systems Theory and Psychiatry*. Boston: Little, Brown, 1969. Pp. 253–265.

74. WOLOSHIN, A. A., and WOLOSHIN, H. C. "Implementation Barriers to Community Mental Health Programs." *Psychotherapeutic Psychosomatics*, 16 (1968), 6–15.

CHAPTER 44

ORGANIZATION OF A COMMUNITY MENTAL HEALTH PROGRAM IN A METROPOLIS

Harry R. Brickman

INCREASING URBANIZATION is bringing greater attention to the supercommunity, or metropolis, as a locale for the delivery of mental health services. Social scientists[7,8] have for some time been describing the unique alienating and dehumanizing aspects of life in the metropolis, so that it is becoming increasingly evident that large urban areas of high population density differ qualitatively as well as quantitatively from smaller communities. With an increased awareness of the ecological aspects of community living, the stress-producing effects of the community itself are becoming more evident.[20,23]

The choice that seems to be available in the organization of metropolitan mental health services must inevitably reflect a basic choice in program philosophy: Is the metropolitan mental health program to be organized solely for the purpose of treating large numbers of patients, or is it intended to affect adverse living conditions in the metropolis? A public psychiatry program can be developed to develop and organize a proliferation of local treatment facilities for the mentally ill, or a community mental health program can be designed to make an impact on the psychiatric casualty-producing stresses of the community, as well as to treat and rehabilitate the casualties that do occur. The latter approach implies that the human living condition in the metropolis requires sufficient study and description so that both its casualty-producing and health-supporting potentials cannot only be identified but usefully employed in the mental health program.

❨ Alternatives for an Organizational Framework

If a program in a metropolis (or any other community for that matter) that limits itself to treatment of the poor alone is desired, its organizational framework is basically uncomplicated. Its characteristics will be those of a line health service delivery organization consisting of a collection of treatment and supervisory personnel, whose number and distribution will vary with the direct versus indirect responsibilities of the mental health program itself for the clinical treatment of identified patients. Its role in the community is essentially as a patient-processing system, dependent on public funding and community support. Its success can be measured in terms of numbers of patients treated, compared with those treated in state hospitals. A developmental end point of such a system is never contemplated in its design: Its role is to recruit psychiatric patients and to restore them to acceptable social functioning. Its sources of referrals can be almost limitless, since distress and emotional symptomatology are experienced by virtually all the social casualties of a community. Indeed, treating emotionally troubled deviant people as patients may be the most humane management available to them if their experiences as welfare cases, probationers, school deviants, and members of other community care-giving client groups are essentially dehumanizing.

Some metropolitan mental health programs have developed storefront and other similar service outposts in poverty neighborhoods, which attempt to venture beyond psychiatric services. Assistance in securing employment, welfare benefits, and other humane services is rendered directly and indirectly via indigenous aides to local residents, based on the mental health agency's conviction that other public agencies are unresponsive to the needs of their disadvantaged clients.

On the other hand, the organization of metropolitan mental health services that contemplate an impact on the community itself as well as on its casualties is much more complex, as it is necessarily closely articulated with the social framework of the community itself. In order to be effective, it must be intertwined with the network of stress-relieving social institutions in such a way as to nurture their effectiveness while standing ready to drain off the casualties that they are unable to effectively manage. Rather than serving as a connecting link between other social, health, and welfare agencies and their clients, assistance is rendered to personnel of these agencies to help them respond more effectively to their clients' needs.

Assuming that the choice of a broad community-oriented program is made, there are several key considerations in the organization of public mental health services in a metropolis. These include program ideology, community analysis and planning, program goals and policies, and organizational patterns.

❨ Program Ideology

The ideological orientation of a community mental health system is seldom specified, yet it is always implicit in any program. Sociological perspective informs us that, humanitarian motives aside, mental health programs are sanctioned in the community because they are fundamentally agencies of social control. Their role in the community is supported with the implicit assumption that they will identify those individuals who are peculiarly disruptive to smooth societal functioning and will assign these individuals the role of psychiatric illness. This officially sanctioned social role certification allows them to be relieved of many normative social expectations, either temporarily or permanently, dependent on diagnostic assessments relating to chronicity. As social control agents, mental health agencies are also expected to resocialize deviant people in such a way as to return them to nondisruptive social functioning whenever possible.

Imbedded in the social control function of a mental health program is the expectation that it will reflect and support the prevailing mores and social and cultural values of the community itself. Yet it is characteristic of large urban communities that efforts at social change, often violently confrontative of the status quo, are rampant. Epidemiological studies[8,12,23] have indicated that admission rates to psychiatric inpatient services are highest in areas of socioeconomic distress. If those working for social change wish to ameliorate socioeconomic distress, the socially sensitive mental health organization must obviously articulate itself with these groups as well as with those that certify and support its primary social control function.

An ideological principle of rehumanization can underlie an urban community mental health service that wishes to retain its vital effectiveness in a changing social ecology.[4] Organizational survival can probably be achieved by striking the necessarily fine balance between social control and social change. A humanistically oriented community mental health system can attempt to combat dehumanization by supporting the health-sustaining systems of the community. This may be accomplished by reducing through mental health education, consultation, and immediate clinical response in crises, the adverse effects of those casualty-producing systems that often paradoxically increase rather than reduce the bemused urbanite's experience of alienation and dehumanization. The Los Angeles County metropolitan mental health program is designed with this emphasis, but little formal research has been accomplished to prove the effectiveness of this approach. A relatively minor but possibly significant finding in Los Angeles County has been that lessened personnel turnover of social caseworkers occurs in neighborhood welfare offices that have received regular community mental health consultation. If a higher level of job satisfaction is experienced by welfare caseworkers, it is probably safe to conclude that their impact on clients may be less dehumanizing.

(Community Analysis and Planning

It is difficult to visualize a socially oriented mental health program that is not built on a foundation of basic socioeconomic and cultural data about the urban area to be served. Community analysis requires study and description of the sociopolitical and cultural attitudes of a community toward mental illness and mental health, as well as attitudes toward other public programs serving the less fortunate. Awareness of these aspects of the community's sociocultural climate will allow mental health planners to introduce their programs with the appropriate mixture of traditional public psychiatry and innovative, less conservative community-oriented activity. Geographical factors, such as natural neighborhood and community clustering and patterns of traffic flow, especially between home and work or home and shopping, along with other similar data, are obviously essential to the geographical placement of service delivery facilities. Socioeconomic residential patterns must be understood if a metropolitan mental health planner is to pinpoint areas of de facto segregation and other aspects of ghettoization. Patterns of mobility must also be understood: Recipients of public services in New York City utilize public transportation, primarily, while in Los Angeles County, the automobile prevails as the major transportation modality, even for the poor. These demographic data must be utilized in the development of geographic service areas, and decisions that determine populations to be served by facilities must reflect natural community groupings. Unfortunately, the federal community mental health centers program has enforced an arbitrary range of population to be served by federally funded comprehensive mental health centers, which, in Los Angeles County, as in several other large urban communities, has forced local mental health planners either to fit their understanding of natural community groupings into a Procrustean catchment area bed, or to decide against optimum use of the federal program in their communities.[2]

Community analysis must also include data on customary methods of dealing with mental and emotional illness not only in traditional local and state facilities but in public social systems, such as the schools, public health and welfare agencies, and law enforcement and correctional systems. These data are essential if the urban mental health program is to relate itself supportively to community caregiver services. Finally, community analysis must include a complete assessment of existing mental health and nonmental health resources, potential as well as actual.

The possiblities for further development and deployment of mental health resources can only be realized through a basically political analysis of the community's mental health constituencies. Among the questions to be explored are: Which groups are pressing for mental health programs and which are opposed? What are the patterns of demand for services? Are community demands primarily outpatient in nature? Which groups are interested in supporting living-working arrangements in the community for chronically mentally ill patients, and can they be mobilized to counteract the inevitable resistances to such a program? What are the attitudes of organized medical and other professional groups? What can be expected of local government executive and legislative officials in terms of willingness to fund mental health services? This type of community analysis must not stop after the initial phases of program planning. In order to guarantee the continued relevance of the mental health program to changing community pressures and needs, it can be maintained in the form of community liaison or advisory groups. These groups can serve as two-way communication channels between the program and appropriate elements of the community including consumers, providers, and other beneficiaries of the program. Such an activity, of course, not only gathers information from the community regarding problems and needs but also serves as a channel for general mental health education, as well as for generation and maintenance of a political constituency for the mental health program itself.

When a community organization and plan-ning function has been established, planning for actual mental health services has already seriously begun. Planning must be collaborative to be effective, with each major constituency of the mental health system—professional, provider, and consumer—actively contributing its perspectives to the total mental health plan. The nature of the interest in mental health services will, of course, vary with the constituency. For example, private sector providers will often seek the fullest possible flow of tax funds into their own programs and may strongly oppose new programs utilizing public agency personnel that they may regard as competitive. Particularly large and influential public agencies, such as public health departments or courts, may wish to divert a maximum of mental health program funding to specialized services that relate to their own primary functions. The task of evolving a program that balances perceived needs with often strident demands while still reflecting a definite program philosophy is often the most difficult one in the organizing of mental health services in a large metropolitan area.

❰ Program Goals

Following the initial stages of community analysis and organization, organization of services can best be built on a statement of program goals. The goals set for the program can be useful in the establishment of program budgeting, particularly as this form of fiscal planning continues to supplant the older type of line-item budgeting. Also a statement of expressed goals can serve as an acknowledged point of reference for the evaluation of the entire program. Organizational goals can be developed in relation to prevention, indirect services, and direct services in a metropolitan mental health program.[16] They should be a product of considerable discussion between professional staff people and the major mental health constituencies of the community and should reflect an amalgam of staff philosophy and professional concepts with the input of community constituencies. These in turn are to be juxtaposed with legislative and executive policy mandates within which all public programs must function.

An overall goal for the metropolitan mental health program is difficult to express in terms of mental health or mental illness alone. Given the universality of personal psychopathology, an individual's state of mental health is a relative rather than absolute phenomenon. Experienced clinicians recognize that absolute cure of mental illness is an ideal seldom actually attained. Similarly, absolute and complete mental health as the total absence of psychopathological symptomatology can never be completely attained. Realistically, the goal of any mental health effort, including the activities of individual clinical practitioners, is the reduction of social handicap resulting from psychopathology. Ultimately, the relative state of the individual's mental health or illness is the resultant of a number of factors: Basic personality, including such factors as ego strength and character differences, biological life strengths and stresses, and supports and stresses arising from the individual's experiences with his social milieu, including family, friends, work associates and other social factors. Since mental health services are sanctioned and supported as social control functions, it is ultimately the phenomenon of social handicap resulting from psychopathology to which they are addressed. Social handicap resulting from psychopathology obviously includes relative freedom from symptomatology. It also includes what is generally understood as successful coping behavior, signifying the individual's ability to live in reasonable equilibrium with his physical and social environment. Freud's definition of mental health— "*lieben und arbieten*" ("to be able to love and to be able to work")—broadly understood, might be a useful criterion for absence of social handicap. Translating this perspective into the identification of goals for a mental health program, it is convenient to utilize the concept of social handicap as a phenomenon to which the entire mental health program is remedially addressed. Reduction of social

handicap, therefore, can be a realistic overall goal for a metropolitan mental health program.

The overall goal of social handicap reduction can then be subdivided into a series of subgoals relating to primary prevention, indirect (community) services, and direct (clinical) services. The array of primary prevention services of a metropolitan mental health program can be designed to meet an overall goal of prevention of social handicap by two types of activities: those with a goal of development of a healthy society and those with a goal of helping make individuals symptom free. The development of a healthy society requires activities aiming at the elimination of disease, social alienation, crime, and discrimination from the community. Such activities can be carried on by mental health personnel by collaborative and consultative work with other life-supporting agencies and programs, such as health, human relations, probation, schools, and churches.

The subgoal of individual symptom reduction can be the aim of activities designed to increase knowledge among the general population concerning ways to anticipate and prevent personal crisis. This subgoal can also be the motive for promoting acceptance in the community of social and behavioral differences, including acceptance of persons who have had mental treatment and those who differ in life styles and ethnic status. Much of this activity can be carried out through the development of public information and education programs designed to reach the total population.

The reduction of social handicap is an overall goal for indirect or community services as well. A keystone of a metropolitan mental health program's preventive services that can be related to such a goal is the principle of preventing clients in other care-giving agencies, such as schools and health and welfare agencies, from becoming mental patients. Indirect services, chiefly mental health consultation, can be developed as a means of increasing the competence of other community care-givers to deal with the emotional problems of their clients, problems which produce, or at least aggravate, social handicap. Other related indirect services, such as mental health education, professional graduate and post-graduate training, program stimulation, and community organization can all be planned and evaluated in terms of meeting the goal of reduction of social handicap.

Assuming an optimum development of primarily preventive and indirect services, clinical services in a mental health program can also be related to reduction of the level of social handicap in the community. A focus on the living unit as the prime supportive (or noxious) social matrix for the patient suggests subgoals of clinical programs that displace individuals as little as possible from the living unit, and that indeed view the living unit as the basic unit of clinical intervention. Certain distinct principles of clinical program development logically follow such basic goals. These principles include the early establishment of practical service areas for clinical units equipped to carry full treatment responsibilities for their areas, with emphasis on broad coverage by utilization, wherever possible, of crisis intervention and brief treatment approaches. Immediate professional attention to, and disposition of, all treatment requests, as well as serious responsibility for continuity of care will assure minimal displacement of the individual from his immediate social matrix. This implies attention to a patient referral tracking system to coordinate and plan patient movement between service elements within an area, including the provision of humane transportation, where necessary, for patients who must be transferred within the complex of service units.

An important program implication of the overall goal of reduction of social handicap is the avoidance of chronicity. This would imply a narrowing of indicators for hospitalization, an emphasis on alternatives to inpatient treatment, and a minimization of holding functions of inpatient services, including the regrettable practice by some teaching centers of conducting psychiatric museums by holding patients on wards based on their suitability as teaching material for a succession of psychiatric residents and other trainees.

(Program Policies

Following agreement on goals, a further definition and basic statement of program-wide policies should be developed to guide the organization of services and to serve as a formal statement of organizational principles that can be discussed, supported, challenged, or modified as needed. Key organizational questions that need to be resolved in such a policy statement include (1) the role of constituency input in the development of programs, (2) the relative role of preventive services, (3) the relationship of the public mental health system to other mental health and generic services, (4) the outlines of a plan for planning, (5) delineation of the role of central office services versus those carried out in decentralized offices, (6) the principle of districting of services to be followed, (7) the principles to be applied in the assignment of professional staff to various duties, (8) the nature of the working relationship between private and public mental health resources as they develop in the metropolis, and (9) policies on special community problems such as drug abuse, alcoholism, and mental retardation.

In the development of the public mental health program of the Los Angeles County metropolis, a series of policy statements have evolved which are designed to govern mental health department activities related to overall program, planning, the organization and delivery of services, and interagency relationships. All these policy statements are related to the overall goals described earlier.

Policy statements governing new program development begin with the requirement that new programs must derive from identified community needs, resources, and citizen input, that they must provide for the maximum use of existing mental health and other services supportive of healthy social functioning, as well as maximum use of all existing sources of private and federal funds as well as state and county funds. In addition, new programs must maintain a balance among prevention, direct treatment efforts, and innovative approaches, in order to continue to develop a mental health service delivery pattern that regards community organization, mental health education, and mental health consultation as the foundations on which clinical services are to be provided. New programs are to be so structured as to allow for the use of the original referral of a potential patient as an opportunity for mental health education and consultation activity, wherever appropriate, as a desirable alternative to acceptance of the referred person into the clienthood ranks of the mental health system. Further statements emphasizing flexibility in hours and service response, ready availability of service, such as the absence of waiting lists, and the acknowledgment of responsibility of continuity of care are essential elements of a program development policy.

The matter of continuity of care deserves additional emphasis in the development and administration of community mental health programs in a metropolis. Agency professionals, faced with a multiplicity of demands for direct service, as well as other demands, will often make referrals of patients to other components of the mental health system, or to other care-giving resources, with little or no attempt to confirm the successful completion of their referrals. As a result, many patients fall between the planks of the system and experience exacerbation of their illness, which a responsible completion of the referral might have prevented. In order to obviate such discontinuity, the program must articulate a basic philosophy of responsibility for continuity of care. In Los Angeles County, this philosophy is only now being adequately developed and expressed. What is evolving is the concept of a human contract with a potential consumer as soon as he becomes a patient. An individual making a clinical contact at any point in the system is regarded as entering into a contract with all of the system, and such a contract binds the system to an agreement of responsibility for his clinical care until such

time as he is officially discharged as a patient or formally terminates his contract with the system. In order to implement such a philosophy, a patient tracking system is being designed that will provide up-to-date information on patient careers from the time of entry into the system until the time of discharge.

Policies governing planning activities call for participation by the widest possible range of citizens and special interest groups, utilization of all appropriate existing mental health and allied planning resources, sensitivity to local needs, and application of a variety of sources of knowledge about the community, its needs, and potential remedial programs. A continued planning dialogue between the mental health agency and the citizens of the community is mandated, including the widest feasible dissemination of the evolving annual plan in each major stage of its development. This reflects a legal requirement in California that each local mental health program prepare an annual plan for mental health services, as well as an annually updated five-year plan, which must receive endorsement by the official citizens advisory group as well as approval by the elected local government officials. An important feature of an official plan is the clearest possible statement of departmental and local government policies that has been evolved, or is being proposed, to achieve clearly stated departmental goals. Furthermore, specific activities and programs designed to implement policies and goals must be included in the plan.

A series of policy statements relating to the organization and delivery of services is also an essential feature of the development of a metropolitan mental health system. In the Los Angeles County program, policies emphasizing the decentralization of mental health services on the basis of mental health service regions have been established. The boundaries of these regions are based on generally recognized communities and neighborhoods. The exact placement of these borders conforms to the requirement that they follow census tract boundaries, so that up-to-date demographic information can be used in both the planning and evaluation of mental health services. In other communities, it may be preferable to use other demographic building blocks, such as postal zones, as basic units for the establishment of service areas. Departmental policies also include a provision that the quantity and type of each service delivered will depend on the characteristics of the patients served and the resources of each region, but that each region shall provide for a basic combination of services, which include community organization, mental health education, other preventive services, and treatment services. Furthermore, the delivery of services is required to be prompt, definitive, and comprehensive, minimizing impairment of function and displacement from the normal social milieu as well as ensuring continuity of clinical care. A further policy requirement is that all regional service professional staff shall, if possible, become competent to deliver all the services rendered. This provides for the widest exposure of clinicians to the entire spectrum of community mental health activity and tends to encourage the development of a unique community mental health professional identity.

A final series of policy statements concern the matter of interagency relationships. This is essential in view of the fact that the Los Angeles County mental health system attempts as much as possible to avoid the role of primary care-giving system in favor of riding on the shoulders of an enriched generic care-giving network. For this reason, the department is encouraged to take the necessary actions to support and encourage the development of the entire spectrum of personal services outside the mental health system, while integrating mental health services with the other systems. An essential part of such function is the identification of obstacles to the delivery of personal health, welfare, and educational services, the formulation of suggestions for the removal of obstacles, and the adoption of measures aimed at other public and private agencies that would contribute to the overall betterment of personal services of which mental health services are an integral part.

(Organizational Pattern

The actual organizational pattern of services must, of course, vary with the community and its possibilities for organizational expression of program goals and policies. In some communities, mental health services may be provided as part of a total public health services system. The advantage of such an approach is that the mental health system can be integrated with a hopefully well-established health services system, complete with community roots and a viable organizational structure. The major disadvantage of developing mental health as part of a health services system is the possibility that mental health services will tend to be too narrowly regarded as a branch of public medicine without sufficient flexibility to attempt innovative programs that, for example, may relate themselves more closely to public welfare, educational, or law enforcement agencies in the community. Also, mental health as a department of general health services may be forced to compete as if it were just another medical specialty, rather than a system for prevention or care of that most widespread form of personal disability which we define as emotional.

A separate public mental health agency can be established, with the advantage of greater visibility, greater potential flexibility, and greater opportunity to compete independently for public support. A separate mental health program is also better able to establish a network of working relationships with public programs outside of the traditional health system. An often-voiced disadvantage of the separate mental health system is an alleged tendency to divorce itself from other health services. Such a point would be considered debatable by those who consider the medical model in mental health programs more of a useful metaphor than an actual reflection of the existence of disease entities known as mental illness.

Perhaps one of the most important decisions to be made in the organization of mental health services in a metropolis relates to the problem of districting. It is widely acknowledged that workers in public agencies spend most of their hours in the care of multiproblem families. In the average urban community, the alienating and dehumanizing effects of public agency contacts with their clients are most often worsened by the fact that there is little or no communication among caseworkers and other caregivers working with the multiproblem family. Typically, such a family may have a spouse in the caseload of a probation department, another spouse in the caseload of the welfare department, and children in the caseloads of mental health, public health, employment, adoption, and a variety of other agencies. Typically, each of these agencies follows its own form of districting, rendering impossible the cooperative discussion of common caseloads. It would be well for the new mental health system to avoid adding to the existing confusion by setting up its own idiosyncratic districting grid. A better approach would be to examine all existing districting schemes already operative in the community and to attempt to gear itself to that districting scheme best related to its own mission. In the Los Angeles County metropolis, for example, the public mental health department chose to adopt the districting scheme of the public health department, among more than 100 separate existing districting patterns. Two reasons appeared paramount in this decision: (1) the anticipated close working relationship with public health services (although this is equally true of public welfare services, for example); (2) epidemiological research being facilitated by the fact that health department districting was based on census tracts as basic building blocks.

After deciding such matters as program goals and districting, organization of services is best set up in a metropolitan area with a maximum of decentralization possibilities. This assures flexibility in the program at the local neighborhood level, especially if relative autonomy is given to professional program people and if opportunities are provided for effective constituency input into the planning and development of services.

The actual mix of preventive and clinical services to be developed in each district will reflect perceived needs expressed through community liaison groups, and hopefully monitored by a well-staffed research and evaluation team, and the convictions of professional planners and administrators as to how new services should develop. One alternative in the design of programs is to assume the necessity for a complete range of services for each population group of a certain number or area and, depending on resources available, to go about establishing services on that basis. This is essentially the organizational principle embodied in the federal comprehensive mental health centers program.

Another approach is to start in a neighborhood with a basic core group of mental health professionals who carry out their services by beginning with community analysis and community organization. This is followed by the establishment of a significant amount of mental health education and consultation to community caregivers backed up by limited crisis-oriented outpatient services. Following these beginnings, and dependent on a continued monitoring of community needs, additional service components can be added so that eventually a comprehensive mental health service network is achieved. One of the advantages of this more gradual approach[3] is that it allows for the maximum reinforcement of community potential to manage emotional problems short of referral to the mental health system itself. It also makes it possible to fully develop alternatives to inpatient care, such as outpatient and partial hospitalization services, when psychiatric beds are in very short supply in the immediate neighborhood.

In view of limited resources, the organization of mental health services in a metropolis must make the fullest possible use of private mental health facilities and personnel, as well as those in the public sector. The relationship of the public to the private sector, however, must be carefully planned and developed. In some urban communities it has been characteristic of the combined private and public system for certain private facilities with large hospital services to tend to keep their beds filled by the active recruitment of patients in their districts. This may actually reflect a fundamental economic necessity rather than limitations of program philosophy on the part of professional staff in those institutions. Nevertheless, the public agency, for reasons not only of fiscal economy (bed services are the most expensive) but also of humanitarianism (chronicity must be prevented where possible), must bend its efforts to enforce some sort of hierarchical system of services in which inpatient services are utilized only if alternatives to hospitalization are not applicable to a patient's needs. One of the ways in which this can be accomplished is to retain for the public agency the function of gatekeeper for the total system. This implies that the public agency either actually serves as the sole referral resource for patients to be served by contract facilities in the private sector or develops a thorough, but practical means of monitoring and supervising actual clinical services being delivered to public patients in private facilities. This task is extremely difficult to perform since it is often characteristic of private agencies in some metropolitan areas to exert political pressure on the public mental health agency whenever the latter attempts to limit, for whatever reason, the freest possible flow of public funds into the contracting facilities.

Informing Qualities of the System

Last of all, some attention must be paid to what has been referred to as the "informing" qualities of the mental health system.[22] These are the sometimes hazily defined flavoring qualities of the program that distinguish it from other public programs in the community. The community philosophy that "informs" a mental health program may be an important factor in attracting young and idealistic mental health professionals for whose services many other agencies and situations may be competing. Some of these informing ingredients include the reputation of the program for interest in problems of youth, racial tensions, social change experimentation, innovation, and

serious evaluation and research. A specific informing ingredient would be the nature and extent of citizen and consumer, as well as provider, participation in critical program decisions. On the other hand, informing qualities of conservatism, limited program goals, and social control emphasis may prevail, in which the mental health program stolidly assumes a community role reinforcing the status quo by implicitly reacculturating its clients into sociopolitical conformity. A program can also be enriched or deprived by the presence or absence of political sophistication, creativity, and last, but not least, its role as a humanizing or dehumanizing force in the metropolis.

Bibliography

1. BRICKMAN, H. R. "Some Basic Assumptions in Community Mental Health." *American Journal of Public Health*, 54 (1964), 908–917.

2. ———. "Community Mental Health—Means or End?" *Psychiatry Digest*, 28 (June 1967), 43–50.

3. ———. "Community Mental Health: The Metropolitan View." *American Journal of Public Health*, 57 (1967), 641–650.

4. ———. "Mental Health and Social Change: An Ecological Perspective." *American Journal of Psychiatry*, 127 (1970), 4.

5. CAPLAN, G. *Principles of Preventive Psychiatry.* New York: Basic Books, 1964.

6. DUHL, L. J., ed. *The Urban Condition.* New York: Basic Books, 1963.

7. DURKHEIM, E. *Suicide.* Trans. by J. A. Spaulding and G. Simpson. Glencoe, Ill.: The Free Press, 1951.

8. FARIS, R. E. L., and DUNBAR, H. W. *Mental Disorders in Urban Areas.* New York: Hafner, 1960.

9. GLASS, A. J. "Psychotherapy in the Combat Zone." *American Journal of Psychiatry*, 110 (1954), 725–731.

10. GOFFMAN, E. *The Presentation of Self in Everyday Life.* Garden City, N.Y.: Doubleday, 1959.

11. GROUP FOR THE ADVANCEMENT OF PSYCHIATRY. *Preventive Psychiatry in Armed Forces.* Report no. 47. New York, 1960.

12. HOLLINGSHEAD, A. B., and REDLICH, F. C. *Social Class and Mental Illness: A Com-*

munity Study. New York: Wiley, 1958.

13. JOINT COMMISSION FOR MENTAL ILLNESS AND HEALTH. *Action for Mental Health.* New York: Basic Books, 1961.

14. KLEIN, R. J., and PARKER, S. "Goal Striving, Social Status and Mental Disorder: A Research Review." In S. K. Weinberg, ed., *The Sociology of Mental Disorder.* Chicago: Aldine, 1967.

15. LEIGHTON, A. H., CLAUSEN, J., and WILSON, R. N., eds. *Explorations in Social Psychiatry.* New York: Basic Books, 1957.

16. LOS ANGELES COUNTY DEPARTMENT OF MENTAL HEALTH. *Mental Health Plan for 1971–72.*

17. MERTON, R. K. *Social Theory and Social Structure.* Glencoe, Ill.: The Free Press, 1957.

18. MOED, G., and BRICKMAN, H. R. "Integration of Research into a Metropolitan Mental Health Program." In R. H. Williams and L. D. Ozarin, eds., *Community Mental Health: An International Perspective.* San Francisco: Jossey-Bass, 1968.

19. PARSONS, T. *The Social System.* Glencoe, Ill.: The Free Press, 1951.

20. RENNIE, T. A. C., SROLE, L., et al. "Urban Life and Mental Health." *American Journal of Psychiatry,* 113 (1957), 831–837.

21. RYAN, W. *Distress in the City: A Summary Report of the Boston Mental Health Survey 1960–62.* Massachusetts Department of Mental Hygiene, 1964.

22. SCHWARTZ, D. A. Personal communication, 1969.

23. SROLE, L., LANGER, T. S., MICHAEL, S. T., OPLER, M. K., and RENNIE, T. A. C. *Mental Health in the Metropolis.* New York: McGraw-Hill, 1962.

24. WHITTINGTON, H. G. *Psychiatry in the American Community.* New York: International Universities Press, 1966.

CHAPTER 45

COMMUNITY
MENTAL HEALTH
IN A RURAL REGION

Jackson Dillon

GUIDELINES for the development of mental health services in sparsely populated rural regions have not yet emerged. A search of the literature reveals the paucity of research on the subject. Such articles as exist are largely confined to foreign journals: Russia and China, in particular, have made serious efforts to provide adequate health services, including mental health programs, to rural peasant populations. Increased interest in the planning of rural health programs is apparent in recent U.S. publications.[2,18] However, authoritative studies describing models for delivery of rural mental health services are rare; exceptions include those of Kiessler,[9] who was able to supply both definitive and preventive services through consultation to caregivers, and Libo[11] (1966), who developed a community consultation program in rural New Mexico. The lack of mental health services in rural regions is paralleled by a lack of health services in general. A recent evaluation of neighborhood health centers[14] compared urban and rural centers on demographic and socioeconomic variables, health use characteristics, and health indicators. The most significant differences seemingly involved the availability of health services and the distances from such services in rural, as compared to urban, areas.

In both health and mental health rural populations are disadvantaged by (1) a lack of services, since health facilities tend to be located at population centers; (2) a lack of professionals, most of whom cluster around metropolitan training centers; (3) a lack of transportation, since travel by automobile up to 100 miles or more may be required to reach some specialty health services; (4) a lack of integration of services, which tend to be overlapping and fragmented in rural areas; and (5) a lack of involvement of professionals, who rarely understand or participate in rural affairs. However, rural areas provide certain advantages for the health worker. (1) He is welcome wherever he goes and his services are highly valued. (2) He finds more cohesive networks for communication and service to assist him, and informal caregivers who may become staunch allies. (3) His pioneer role in penetrating the community may facilitate innovative program development.

Each small rural community, like a neighborhood in a city, presents unique characteristics and needs. The physical and emotional isolation so characteristic of the rural region renders a public health approach essential if community mental health is to reach the people, merge scarce resources, surmount barriers of poverty, overcome ethnic bias, distance, and culture, and eventually provide effective service for the entire population.

❲ Delivery of Services in a Rural Region

Need for Decentralization

The community mental health center model is dedicated to narrowing the gap between services and consumer. As the effectiveness of reaching out into the community to provide necessary services was recognized, programs were developed at the local level in both urban and rural areas. Changes from centralized to broader community service have proceeded slowly, however. Predictably, the recipient favors neighborhood delivery of health service far more than the provider, although the opposite trend is apparent when professionals follow clients to the suburbs of large cities to provide local service. To leave the security of a successful office or clinic practice and provide service in the community is a risky step for the professional who fantasies reduced status, job insecurity, social stress, and other anxiety-provoking problems. Leaving the city to live and work in a rural region is even more threatening; yet, rural programs cannot develop unless professionals are willing

to relocate. Despite the need, professionals in the health areas continue to be in short supply in rural areas; thus far, efforts to relocate physicians through training subsidies have been disappointing.[1]

In the People's Republic of China extensive rural services were developed,[5] involving the rotation of urban planners, teachers, and clinicians to the rural areas for periods of nine months or more. American observers seem to interpret the rural assignments as punitive in nature; however, no criticism from those involved could be detected, and the success of the program was attributed to patriotic fervor. Effective use of indigenous workers was illustrated by the wide variety of tasks performed by the "barefoot doctor," and by other local organizational features of the Chinese program. The direct field experience of living and working in a rural area enabled policy makers and trainers to become familiar with class and cultural differences, and to mobilize relevant community resources.

In the United States, a reverse trend is noted: Planners rarely visit the rural community in person and health resources are largely found in urban areas. In rural regions an inverse relationship exists between quantity and quality of service and physical distance from providing agencies: Patients are expected to travel to population centers for all their health care needs. Rural upper and middle classes adjust to such financial and distance barriers, but for rural low-income families, the required travel may be an almost insurmountable burden: Problems of unreliable automobiles, expense, loss of work time, babysitting, long waits at the clinic, and so on. The rural poor are thus effectively prevented from seeking help, except for their most serious and urgent needs.

To provide quality health services in rural areas, the delivery of human services must be combined; it is unthinkable, for instance, to deliver quality mental health care to one family member and to ignore a tuberculosis victim, or a child with a toothache, in the same family. Schools, as centrally located care-giving agencies, could provide space for comprehensive services. Professionals, planners, and politicians must be convinced of the necessity for the relocation of services from traditional centralized settings to the rural community. The bias against providing such services is evident when officials disclaim the problem, blaming the individual "who could get to the [distant] facility if he were truly motivated or sick enough." Such prejudice must be overcome and strategies must be developed for reaching and treating all sectors in each community.

Design for a Rural Mental Health System

The following ideal goals were abstracted from the Tulare County (California) Five Year Plan for Mental Health (1970):

1. Provision of immediately available mental health service to each community grouping of 500 to 1,000 population.
2. Delivery of services to include a maximum of participation by indigenous community persons.
3. Integration of all human services into a unified delivery system.
4. Development of an informed and understanding community.

To provide immediate, appropriate mental health services in a rural area requires a network of small units, each offering a wide range of services, including diagnosis, therapy (group, family, music, activity), creative arts, mental health consultation, medication, and other modalities. Rapid evaluation and triage allows for an individually prescribed regimen, subject to change as the patient progresses toward recovery. With a variety of available services and prompt feedback of information from initial interventions, flexible short- and long-term therapeutic goals are possible. Central backup services should include business administration; intensive care on a small ward; coordinated, mobile, emergency services; and a close alliance with other medical and social services.

Program units should be small, staffed by a few skilled professionals, and semiautonomous in function. Trained nonprofessionals and citizen participants are essential elements. The commitment to serve all patients encourages creativity and innovation, leading to a therapeutic, self-fulfilling prophecy which virtually ensures success. Such activities as planning, research, training, and recruiting require collaboration between local staff, central administration, and outside consultants. Since the unit functions at the local level, mental health-related information concerning the population served is monitored continually, allowing for frequent program modification. A systems type analysis with regular study of selected indicators offers the most precision; however, a human analysis, with intuitive feel for the community, is also required.

Outreach Programs

HOME THERAPY

The time-honored approach of the visiting nurse and social worker is seldom employed by the psychotherapist; however, even a brief glimpse of the home scene may reorient the therapist as he becomes aware of factors not revealed in hospital or clinic visits. Significant other persons in the patient's social system are immediately available and frequently participate in the interview. Scheduling difficulties are simplified, particularly in family therapy, which is most effective when conducted in the home.

NEIGHBORHOOD THERAPY

Neighborhood therapy, a variation of home therapy, is effective in some communities. The customary need for privileged communication would seem to preclude neighborhood intervention, especially in the small rural community. However, in most instances the suggestion is warmly received by both the patients and their families. Acceptance is explored with each family until a neighborhood group is established. Meetings are held in a home or some other convenient place. Group members assume responsibility for planning and arrangements, and the therapeutic session frequently includes social and recreational activities. A loose therapeutic community is thus created, extending beyond the therapist and the session. Significant others, previously unknown to the therapist, join the group informally, and a supportive network is developed to assist rehabilitation of group members. Special features of neighborhood therapy are that the neighborhood group has (1) long-standing relationships, (2) common interests and goals, (3) continuing therapeutic alliances, (4) its own emotional resource system, (5) the opportunity to study therapeutic successes and failures at first hand, (6) the power to accept or reject the patient, and (7) the capability to reduce the stigma attached to the mentally ill.

The Satellite Clinic

With community cooperation a small, local, clinic facility may be established. The satellite approach is sometimes needed to develop meaningful services for a disadvantaged group that is unable or unwilling to use services offered at the mental health center. The clinic may initially operate only part-time while it bids for acceptance by the community. Services are patient and family centered, and carefully chosen indigenous workers form the core staff. Informal training experiences should be provided for community workers in the parent facility and in other community agencies. Cultural and sometimes language barriers must be bridged to accomplish the first goal of developing a meaningful communication system, a process that cannot be hurried or controlled. Once trust is established, clinical experiences customarily prove much the same as those encountered in conventional settings: Patients somehow seem more human and emotional problems less unusual.

The Community Team

An alternate method, the community team, functions much as the satellite clinic, but without a fixed base. Team members travel to isolated communities bringing components of the mental health program that seem most acceptable and appropriate for local needs. As in the satellite clinic, the team should include nonprofessionals and volunteers from the community who assist in linking the con-

sumers to the professionals. Crisis intervention techniques and the "anywhere" consultation, when used creatively, enable most clients to be managed as outpatients. For those who initially require hospitalization, the team can play a key role in follow up and rehabilitation.

The Community Representative

A carefully selected community representative is a valuable addition to any outreach program. In the small, rural community a volunteer or resident employee in the community can provide a variety of services otherwise seldom obtainable. Acting primarily in a liaison role between community and mental health center, the worker communicates with each. Emergency and crisis intervention services are enhanced by the ready availability of a staff member in the community; many aspects of both activity therapy and rehabilitation can be delegated to the indigenous helper. The community representative is both a spokesman and an informant, helping to build favorable relations between the mental health center and the public. Professional staff members may, at first, find it difficult to accord the local worker equal status and respect. Experience soon demonstrates the lack of role conflict, however, and much creativity can evolve from the shared program development that results.

In areas characterized by great distance between population centers, strategically located community representatives, working part-time with professional staff from the treatment facility, can form a network of services. The presence of a visible, reliable resource in the community reassures both patient and professional, adding stability to the total program. The community representative provides invaluable assistance in prevention programs, disseminating mental health information and education on a formal and informal basis by showing movies, distributing literature, and talking to groups. In reaching ethnic minorities where cultural and language barriers are difficult for an outsider to breach, a community representative can be an indispensable ally.

An Example: Kings View Rural Mental Health Services

Kings View Community Mental Health Center at Reedley, California, a private, non-profit corporation, has established contracts to provide decentralized programs with five San Joaquin Valley counties under California's Lanterman-Petris-Short Act.[10] Since 1969, services have been extended to a rural area of about 12,000 square miles, with a population of approximately 400,000. Mental health units, consisting of two inpatient facilities (twenty-six and sixteen beds, respectively), seven day treatment centers, and ten outpatient clinics, were installed in rural population centers. Instead of construction, leased or donated facilities were used. Immediate, appropriate services were provided, including crisis intervention, medication, individual therapy, group therapy, family therapy, activity therapy, rehabilitation, and outreach service. An individualized plan was established for each patient, with emphasis on continuity of care. The day treatment center provided definitive care for more seriously disturbed patients; when necessary, patients were hospitalized briefly (average seven to ten days) for stabilization, then transferred to the day treatment unit nearest to their homes. The system has provided quality inpatient and outpatient care for all identified patients: 7,000 cases were treated annually, as compared to the approximately 400 committed annually to California State Department of Mental Hygiene Hospitals in a previous year. The need for more outreach services became evident when statistics revealed that proportionate numbers of lower-class patients were seen by the hospital and emergency services, but relatively few obtained outpatient or indirect services. Scores of smaller settlements were receiving no local services; a search was initiated for more appropriate, community-based interventions, which soon led to a greater appreciation for, and understanding of, rural needs.

The Kings View experience has dispelled a number of myths about the chronic or long-term patient. Early evaluations demonstrated that acutely ill psychotics responded promptly to the intensive treatment program, but anxiety developed about management of the hard-core patient. Could the new system cope with the problem or would a new back ward finally be required? Eventually, the hard-core patient emerged as a repeater at the inpatient unit, who had somehow slipped past the network of outpatient services. A criterion was established, and special follow-up techniques were devised to cope with this target group: Home visiting, informal group meetings, social network therapy, injectable medication for those unable to follow instructions, hot pursuit for the excessively mobile, and so on. Patients' families, who at first were uncooperative, became allies when assured of the therapist's sincerity and of the reliability of the emergency services. As a consequence, disability was reduced and hospitalization was rarely required.

Encouraged by success, more interest and concern were generated for the chronic patient, and other subcategories, released from institutional care without follow up, were discovered: Veterans' Administration patients, parolees from the California State Correctional System, criminally insane and sex offenders released by the California State Department of Mental Hygiene, and board-and-care patients under supervision of the community services branch of the California State Department of Social Welfare. Supportive and rehabilitative efforts for all such patients were coordinated into the mental health system, with emphasis on the patient's adjustment to the community rather than to the institution.

❲ Community Approaches

Traditional Prevention Services

In rural communities, consultation to schools, pre- and postnatal clinics, visiting nurses, family planning services, and other agencies is readily accepted. Priority should be given to consultation with Head Start and child-care centers: Joint programming for early identification of children with emotional and learning handicaps has an immediate payoff to both mental health and the schools. Mental health information and education through films, mass media, tours, adult education programs, special workshops, and other means should be planned systematically to involve both the public and the care-giving agencies.

Integration with Other Agencies

A close working relationship with other human service agencies is essential in rural regions. Because of the paucity of services, lack of cooperation is more visible and destructive than in the city, where a variety of programs are available. Since rural resources are meager, interagency contacts are easily established. Following a favorable consultation period, joint programs may be developed that will provide service that is superior to that produced by either agency working alone. Domain boundaries become blurred, and new opportunities are discovered. The mental health center may at first furnish leadership in the venture because of the skills of its staff in group and interpersonal relations; later, the program will be truly a joint enterprise. In Tulare County a successful probational mental health crisis team, based at the mental health center, was formed using staff members from both agencies. Referrals to the probation department were diverted to the team, which intervened promptly in the home and in the school.

Serving the Entire Population

An essential feature of a successful, rural, mental health program is the commitment to serve the whole population and to supply immediate, appropriate treatment to all those in need. Any lesser commitment encourages defensive restriction of services at every level. To accomplish the program's objective, understanding of the small rural community as a social system is essential. A participant observer survey combined with anthropological consultation facilitates the understanding of the many cultural differences encountered. The classic studies of Goodenough[6] and Paul[13] provide useful clues to exploring the community. Unless cultural factors are considered, planning and administrative errors are predictable and will be repeated by each new program. Reports explaining the Mexican-American culture[4,15] have contributed to the understanding of communities in California; however, each community must be studied as a separate entity, and programs developed must be acceptable in terms of each community's folkways and mores.

Establishing Meaningful Contact

Valid assessment of the community is possible only through human interaction. Building trust is a prerequisite to success, and the mental health worker's attitude may be a critical variable.[8] Early impressions are often misleading; significant information is released only after the intervener has proven himself trustworthy in the ways the community has tested him. Culturally biased views, if any, may be immediately apparent to community members, and months of regular contact may be required before the mental health practitioner and the community resolve mutual prejudices and misconceptions.

Customarily, mental health professionals avoid political activity, but in the rural community, political involvement may be necessary. The mental health intervener will exercise political influence either knowingly or unknowingly; if the political aspect is defined as a constructive intervention, rather than as dangerous or unethical, the program's development may be facilitated. A responsive and responsible mental health worker may be invaluable to the community in obtaining its objectives and in avoiding political pitfalls.

Community Participation in Planning

Typically, health planning is initiated from above and proceeds downward: Federal and

state planners determine health needs and resources in rank order; cost effectiveness, available manpower, political considerations, and
budgetary restrictions are predicted; funding
is secured; and, finally, a rational plan is developed for presentation to community leaders. The consumer's right to be involved is
acknowledged; however, he is rarely present
or represented during deliberations. Unfortunately, many well-designed, well-intentioned
programs are unsuccessful because prior experience in the rural region has been neglected
and potential sources of difficulty have not
been identified. Service programs designed
under government or university auspices may
contain a hidden agenda (career building, research, political manipulation) that automatically precludes an egalitarian, creative relationship between intervener and community.[8]
New models are needed, both to involve the
community and to encourage participation in
planning by all concerned.

One alternative to the traditional model depends on consumer participation, effectively
reversing the traditional approach. Axioms of
this method are: (1) Act now, plan later. (2)
People come before program. (3) Deempha-
size money and construction. (4) Prepare for
predators. (5) Proceed aggressively.

Act Now, Plan Later

Community members, bored with unfulfilled promises and program failures, nevertheless remain willing to become involved in action programs that are considered appropriate
to felt needs. Such programs can be initiated
immediately and planning continued as development proceeds under the direct supervision
of the community. Prompt feedback concerning problems and failures allows for correction
of undesirable trends as they arise. Goals and
design of the program are changed as needed
until a functional fit that is acceptable to both
community and professional is achieved.

People Come Before Program

The first goal in planning a program should
be to engage all concerned in a working partnership and to secure full community sanction.
Professionals should advise sparingly, allowing

the community to share in designing and developing its own program. Communication
between consumer and planner and a creative
climate for community development are the
ultimate goals.

Deemphasize Money and Construction

Funding is an essential element, but should
never dominate planning. Guidelines of a
grant proposal may impose an artificial bureaucratic burden on the planning process and
stifle creativity in program development. An
all-voluntary effort, on the other hand, is easily initiated, is flexible, and allows more degrees of freedom. When money needs are
deferred, unexpected benefits sometimes appear. Resources may be mobilized from within
the community so that funding proves less
important than anticipated; as a result political power is retained by the community. The
interest and energy customarily devoted to
grant-writing procedures become available for
community dynamics and human interaction.
Community leaders who identify themselves
with the voluntary program frequently have
different goals and values as compared to
those who identify with the publicly funded
programs; later when the program matures so
that funding is introduced, the voluntary
leader usually proves more reliable and effective. Confrontations and power struggles, so
often identified with outside funding, may be
avoided.

Initiating construction to house programs
should likewise be undertaken with caution.
Once completed, a structure may fixate the
program. The trend in mental health toward
local treatment and phasing out of institutional services is apparent in California, where
several state hospitals have already been eliminated. Increased emphasis on community-
based programs can be anticipated in the
future: Existing structures within the community can frequently be modified and adapted
to the needs of mental health programs. Construction planning, delays, and costs are
avoided when facilities are leased rather than
purchased. The community should assist in
the selection of appropriate existing structures,
thereby ensuring community acceptance and

increasing the probability of success for the program.

PREPARE FOR PREDATORS

When a community-developed program shows signs of success, a variety of outside professionals and politicians may attempt to get some of the credit or perhaps to undermine the fledgling operation. From a systems theory viewpoint, violation of a domain boundary is seldom involved; rather, the outsiders seem motivated by fear of change and seek to restore a presumed equilibrium in the delivery of service. Forewarned, the community planners may be able to involve the invaders constructively in program development, since services are so welcome in the rural area.

PROCEED AGGRESSIVELY

Once initiated, the community program develops an identity and dynamic force of its own. As participants are recruited, a movement is generated which requires the coordinated expertise of both mental health workers and community leaders for its successful management. Good timing and a feel for community sentiment are important variables. Effective use of expert consultation and outside support to implement planning and program development enhances movement toward the goal.

Community Participation in Program Development

The core component in rural community mental health program development is the citizen participant. Volunteers from the community play a vital role in program planning and development, disseminating meaningful mental health information and education to the public, and arousing community support. Innovative programs invariably require citizen participation, as well as the extracurricular voluntary efforts of staff members. Creative solutions to rural mental health problems cannot be purchased; exciting components arise from the cooperative efforts of all concerned.

The emergent role of the citizen participant

in health and other human services has not been clearly defined. The modern volunteer is motivated primarily for self-actualization and career development. He is effective in his own life and seeks meaningful use of his talents. The chief barriers against using volunteers in ongoing service programs arise from the covert resistance of professionals, who fear a loss of prestige, and from the failure of administrators to consider the volunteer's personal needs, which might be quite different from those of the regular employee. Too often, the volunteer is given a useful but nonthreatening and perhaps meaningless role that effectively stifles creativity and extinguishes interest.

Rural mental health programs require a volunteer director who functions at the policy-making level in the organization. Duties include (1) recruitment and training of volunteers, (2) design of volunteer components for each project, (3) mediation between volunteers and professionals, (4) development of meaningful careers for citizen participants, and (5) promotion of additional volunteer human service programs in the community. Potential for prevention exists in the volunteer coordinator's ability to facilitate new volunteer programs. The newly established and rapidly expanding volunteer court movement[12,16] is an outstanding example.

Informed citizen participants can interpret the program's goals, needs, failures, and successes to the rural public far more effectively than professionals. Volunteers sometimes provide services not otherwise obtainable (for example, volunteer foster homes or evaluation of programs) and can assist the mental health center in the management of difficult cases, the development of prevention programs, and the resolution of political problems. Operationally, a constant interaction between the mental health center and citizen participants should be the rule in rural regions.

Volunteer bureaus are easily established in small rural communities, providing a pool of volunteer talent to be matched with service opportunities. With many volunteer positions available, the citizen participant can select an appropriate and stimulating role. As citizen participants develop an understanding of mental health principles and community problems, a growing constituency is formed to advocate for social change and furnish leadership in new community ventures.

A Community Alcoholism Program

The evolution of the Tulare County Alcoholism Council illustrates vividly the role of volunteers in community program development. Comprehensive programs for prevention and treatment of alcoholism are notoriously difficult to organize because of vested interests of service agencies and public denial of the problem. The planning process in Tulare County was initiated by the Mental Health Advisory Board; public meetings were sponsored to deal with the joint topics of alcoholism and drug abuse. Representatives of involved agencies, as well as interested citizens, attended the initial meetings. A decision to divide into interest groups led to the formation of a planning committee for alcoholism charged with investigating the current status of the problem in Tulare County. A talented housewife, formerly a teacher, volunteered as chairman, and others agreed to share leadership responsibilities. Members of the committee included one or more representatives from each local agency, representatives from Alcoholics Anonymous, volunteers from the general public, and individuals who were motivated by family or personal experience with alcoholism.

A survey of needs and resources was conducted by a social work graduate student who worked with members of the committee and with participating agencies. A comprehensive plan was developed which included both short- and long-term goals. Immediate steps were taken to raise funds for an alcoholism halfway house, to improve an alcoholism education program in local schools, and to establish detoxification facilities. The chairman and other volunteers made brief presentations throughout the county to service clubs, churches, and other civic organizations in an effort to reduce the stigma associated with alcoholism and to secure public endorsement. The political effectiveness of the committee's approach was demonstrated when the Tulare County Board of Supervisors voted unanimously to sponsor the program. Other alcoholism programs in the state were visited and funding agencies contacted by the chairman and members of the committee.

As support from the public and board of supervisors increased, the organization was incorporated, and the alcoholism council was able to obtain development funds. When legislation was enacted recently authorizing the diversion of public alcoholics to detoxification centers rather than to county jails, the council was ready with a master plan for a comprehensive alcoholism program. Mental health continues to play an active advisory role, but major credit for planning and development of the program must be given to the talented and dedicated volunteers.

Community Development Programs

In rural areas, mental health-related programs require broad community support in coping with prejudice and other barriers to social change. Comprehensive programs for children, senior citizens, alcoholics, drug abusers, the mentally retarded, and those with learning handicaps require the combined action of all available agencies and the dedicated support of concerned citizens. Acting alone, the mental health center cannot supply adequate services. However, leadership and organizational skills may be provided for the development of new projects, and mental health workers can advocate for the elderly, for children, and for disadvantaged groups who lack political power.

To provide leadership for rural projects, especially to those disadvantaged by poverty and/or ethnicity, is a difficult task. A total community approach is most effective, one in which the professional consultant temporarily sets aside his personal goals to work with the community on a program of its own choosing.[7,8] Success of the program increases the self-respect and self-confidence of community participants (in itself a significant mental health achievement) and leads to other self-help projects. Using Caplan's[3] model, the small rural community may be considered a consultee, much the same as an institution; similar techniques may be employed for entering the community, building positive relations, and developing a consultative role. Mental health projects may be introduced after the consultant has gained credibility and acceptance in the community.

Examples of Creative Partnership for Community Development

THE TULE RIVER INDIAN RESERVATION

My first contact with the Tule Indians was made on an informal visit to the reservation. Asking directions of a resident, I introduced myself and was directed to the tribal council headquarters, where I met two resident health aides who had been trained in an earlier health program. An invitation to a tribal council meeting resulted. In this, and subsequent meetings, I learned about current problems and had the opportunity to review the various proposals of public officials, businessmen, researchers, and others who had come to the reservation. A long series of projects had been attempted on the reservation, but nearly all had failed after a short time. One exception was the water system, which the public health engineers had been constructing over a period of fifteen years. Personnel and other bureaucratic changes had repeatedly delayed completion of the project; consequently many families were still carrying water from the river for household use. At the council meeting I was given the opportunity to explain my role in mental health and to offer assistance to the tribe in a project of its own choosing.

In subsequent discussions, priority was given to establishment of a dental clinic on the reservation. Although the furnishing of dental services would seem to bear little relationship to mental health, in order to honor my commitment, I explored possibilities for a dental clinic both with tribal leaders and with resources in the larger community over a period of several months. As a result of these efforts, plans for a voluntary dental clinic gradually evolved. A dental group from nearby Visalia, California, offered voluntary service on a regular basis; one of the dentists assumed the role of project coordinator. Other community resources became available; an architectural firm offered to draw plans for remodeling a tribal building to house a medical-dental facility; a dental supply firm furnished necessary equipment; the regional building trades council arranged for a volunteer labor force; and the U.S. Public Health Service supplied plumbing materials. Problems were encountered in obtaining donations of building supplies from dealers and wholesalers, but eventually a few cooperating firms were located.

The preparatory process required considerably more time than anticipated, but continued contacts with tribal members created opportunities for consultation on other matters. A volunteer medical student spent the summer on the reservation and assisted in expediting the project. The need for a dental assistant was paramount; however, unsuccessful academic experiences at nearby colleges in the past had resulted in a reluctance on the part of Indian youths to seek the necessary training for participation in tribal projects. Consequently, training on an informal basis was arranged for three female aides: (1) a medical aide was trained for six months in a general practitioner's office, with three additional weeks at a general hospital emergency room; (2) a dental aide was trained by the participating dental group in its main offices; and (3) a mental health aide was trained in the nearest Tulare County outpatient and day treatment center, with brief experience in an inpatient unit.

Consultation was requested by the tribe on a variety of matters. The health aides requested assistance in the following areas: preparation of a revised budget for the health project, development of an efficient medical record system, writing proposals for a health insurance program, and development of an evaluation program. Volunteer specialists were recruited to fill each request. As tribal leaders gained experience and confidence, other projects were successfully completed at the reservation, including a children's playground, a general store and service station, and the remodeling of a tribal building for a child-care program. A noticeable improvement of skills in dealing with the larger society emerged over a period of time. Negotiations with representatives of supply companies and unions concerning the clinic construction furnished valuable learning opportunities. Contacts with the statewide Indian organizations increased; tribe members were chosen for state Indian offices. The tribe sponsored a large fund-raising program in a nearby city, "An Indian Happening," the first of its kind in the area.

The favorable change in attitude and outlook of individuals in the tribe as a result of the successful projects was noticeable. Consultation requests became more sophisticated, telephone contacts increased, and meetings were occasionally held off the reservation. Even though construction of the medical-dental facility was delayed, the dental program was established in temporary quarters and became an immediate success. The dental aide worked with the dentists at the reservation and continued her training at their offices on a part-time basis. Federal Indian health funds became available and were used to hire a dentist to supplement the volunteer program. The physician who trained the medical aide encouraged her to undertake a medical prevention program that involved the collection of health histories and the administration of screening tests for diabetes and hypertension. A family planning clinic was introduced through the child-care program. An eye clinic was sponsored by the health department, and other specialty clinics were planned for the newly remodeled facility as it neared completion. The development of mental health services on the reservation was never discussed. Subsequent to her training, the mental health aide confessed that her assignment was the most frightening of all and that she was terrified during her first visits to the day treatment center. Her inner turmoil was not suspected by the mental health staff, who were impressed by her ability.

The need for mental health service has remained low in priority, but tribal members are now serving on the Tulare County Mental Health Advisory Board and the Tulare County Alcoholism Council, both policy-making boards, thus providing a direct link between the reservation and the mental health system. Although traditional mental health consultation was not the focus of the consultation relationship, the intervention is an example of primary prevention: Successful health programs have been developed on the reservation, the Tule River Indian health project has many trusted advisors, and some of the barriers to provision of health and mental health care have been lowered.

EARLIMART, CALIFORNIA

An intervention, similar to that of the Tule reservation, was attempted in a low-income area of southern Tulare County (approximately thirty square miles, population 14,-000). Farm labor, which is seasonal, provides the chief source of income. Human services of all types are virtually nonexistent. Ninety percent of the population is medically indigent, and approximately one-half receive some form of public assistance. Earlimart (population 2,900) is the largest community and is central to the service area.

The community was explored through several unrelated interventions. In the first, consultation was furnished to a young pediatrician who established a poverty clinic, Salud Earlimart.[17] The clinic was the only medical resource in the area, and bilingual health aides were employed to facilitate treatment of the largely Spanish-speaking population. The consultant psychiatrist visited the clinic weekly, developing a consultation relationship and providing direct service to clinic patients. The informal partnership led eventually to formation of a satellite mental health center. Services were gradually extended outside the clinic into the community, and to other population centers in the area, by a mental health team.

The second intervention involved Catholic Sisters, assigned as poverty workers to establish social and educational services in Earlimart. Regular consultation with the Sisters afforded additional opportunities to learn about the community. A third community contact was established through consultation with a psychologist serving the Head Start child-care program. A fourth intervention was initiated by the Tulare County Mental Health Advisory Board when a public forum was conducted to discuss mental health service needs with area residents.

Eventually the consultant was invited to meetings with all ethnic groups (black, Mexican-American, Anglo, Filipino, and so on) to explore community concerns; again the offer was made to assist the community with a project of its choosing. The highest priority, in this instance, was the need for a drug store (none being available in the area); the need for dental services ranked a close second. Developing a drug store proved to be an insurmountable problem; however, a community development was undertaken with the goal of establishing a free dental clinic. Free equipment was supplied by a dental supply firm, and dentists from several cities volunteered to serve twice monthly after the program was developed; one volunteered as coordinator, devoting two days per week of his time during the developmental phase. A board, representative of all communities in the area, was selected at public meetings to consult with the involved professionals and to determine clinic policies. The organization recruited community volunteers for fund raising, staffing of the clinic, and other aspects of the program. The Catholic Sisters of Charity furnished a house trailer for the clinic operation and worked with the volunteers in developing clinic procedure. Although inexperienced, the board made surprisingly effective decisions, each time reviewing the issues carefully with the professional advisors. Community sanction was evidenced by massive voluntary efforts and large attendance at fund-raising dinners, rummage sales, and the like. Gradual progress led to formation of a nonprofit corporation and plans for a building program.

Mental health services were expanded slowly in the community, with recognition that such services are threatening and difficult to introduce in a low-income, ethnic minority rural area. A favorable public image gained by assisting the successful dental project dispelled to some extent the mystique ordinarily associated with psychiatric treatment. Initially, group therapy sessions were conducted at the clinic, and outpatient services offered on a weekly basis. As the program developed, patients were seen in homes, in restaurants, in automobiles, in churches, or in any mutually convenient location. Neighborhood groups were started in nearby communities. The initial participants were chronic patients, who were enthusiastic about the opportunity for local treatment; soon new patients and their families joined the groups.

Two local residents, one Spanish-speaking, were employed for part-time service and were trained informally at other therapy centers in the county. One served as a volunteer coordinator in addition to other duties. Both were available for crisis intervention, expediting of individual treatment plans for patients, community work, and so on. A staff social worker began consultation with local school districts. Later a small house, near the Clinic, was rented to provide space for day treatment services. Services that formerly required a round trip of fifty miles or more became available at the local level, but the planning and development process was continued to ensure acceptable delivery of mental health service. Innovation and program change were encouraged with patients, aides, volunteers, and professionals collaborating in the planning. Opportunities for development of new projects continued to emerge, and models for delivery of rural mental health services have been improved as experience has been gained in the field.

(Trends

Rural delivery of mental health services has received an impetus from several sources. The federal community mental health centers program, which stresses delivery of services at a local level, has demonstrated the feasibility of alternate models to the traditional centralized system. In California, Lanterman-Petris-Short legislation has encouraged innovation and decentralization in pursuit of its goal of developing a single system of local mental health service. Rural regions have benefited along with urban and suburban areas. Finally, the current interest in health maintenance organizations, which would provide comprehensive health care through a system of national health insurance, may prove to be an additional stimulus to development of rural mental health programs.

⟮ Bibliography

1. AMERICAN MEDICAL NEWS. "Nearly Half of M.D.s 'Buy Out' of Rural Service." 15 (January 24, 1972) 7–8.

2. BLOOM, J. D. "Population Trends of Alaska Natives and the Need for Planning." *American Journal of Psychiatry*, 128 (1972), 112–116.

3. CAPLAN, G. *The Theory and Practice of Mental Health Consultation.* New York: Basic Books, 1970.

4. CLARK, M. *Health in the Mexican-American Culture: A Community Study.* Berkeley: University of California Press, 1970.

5. DIMOND, E. G. "Medical Education and Care in People's Republic of China." *Journal of the American Medical Association*, 218 (1971), 1552–1557.

6. GOODENOUGH, W. H. *Cooperation in Change.* New York: Russell Sage Foundation, 1966.

7. HATCH, J. "Community Shares in Policy Decisions for Rural Health Center." *Hospitals*, 43 (1969), 109–112.

8. ILFELD, F. W., Jr., and LINDEMANN, E. "Professional and Community: Pathway Toward Trust." *American Journal of Psychiatry*, 128, suppl. (1971), 75–81.

9. KIESLER, F. "Programming for Prevention." *North Carolina Journal of Mental Health*, 1 (1965), 3–17.

10. KINGS VIEW COMMUNITY MENTAL HEALTH CENTER. "Mental Health Services for Rural Counties." *Hospital and Community Psychiatry*, 22 (1971), 299–301.

11. LIBO, L., and GRIFFITH, C. "Developing Mental Health Programs in Areas Lacking Professional Facilities." *Community Mental Health Journal*, 2 (1966), 163–169.

12. MORRIS, J. A. *First Offender: A Volunteer Program for Youth in Trouble with the Law.* New York: Norton, 1970.

13. PAUL, B. D., ed. *Health, Culture and Community.* New York: Russell Sage Foundation, 1959.

14. ROMM, J. *Initial Analyses of Baseline Surveys for Neighborhood Health Centers.* Bethesda, Md.: System Sciences, 1971.

15. SAUNDERS, L. "Healing Ways in the Spanish Southwest." In E. G. Jaco, ed., *Patients, Physicians and Illness.* Glencoe, Ill.: The Free Press, 1960. Pp. 189–206.

16. SCHEIER, I. H. *Using Volunteers in Court Settings: A Manual for Volunteer Probation Programs.* Washington, D.C.: U.S. Government Printing Office, 1970.

17. STRESHINSKY, S. "The Doctor Who Practices What He Preaches." *Redbook Magazine*, 138 (1971), 78–80.

18. WILSON, V. E. "Rural Health Care Systems." *Journal of the American Medical Association*, 216 (1971), 1623–1626.

CHAPTER 46

THE MENTAL HOSPITAL AS A BASIS FOR COMMUNITY PSYCHIATRY

Israel Zwerling

IN HIS 1925 PRESIDENTIAL address to the American Psychiatric Association, William A. White stated "The State Hospital as it stands today is the very foundation of psychiatry."[30] Harry C. Solomon, in his 1958 presidential address,[27] stated:

The large mental hospital is antiquated, outmoded, and rapidly becoming obsolete. We can still build them but we cannot staff them; and therefore we cannot make true hospitals of them. After 114 years of effort, in this year 1958, rarely has a state hospital an adequate staff as measured against the minimum standards set by our Association . . . and these standards represent a compromise between what was thought to be adequate and what it was thought had some possibility of being realized. . . . I do not see how any reasonably objective view of our mental hospitals today can fail to conclude that they are bankrupt beyond remedy. I believe therefore that our large mental hospitals should be liquidated as rapidly as can be done in an orderly and progressive fashion.

It was not, of course, the mental hospitals that had changed in the thirty-three intervening years but rather the foundations of psychiatry and indeed the broader determinants of man's relationship to man, from which the most crucial elements of the foundations of psychiatry at any period derive. The historic processes that, starting during the latter half of the nineteenth century, had rendered the large mental hospitals into underfinanced, understaffed, geographically isolated custodial warehouses have been described,[5,22] and there is little doubt that a reaction to the shame of these hospitals was a significant component in the confluence of forces that led to the explosive development of community psychiatry programs during the late 1950s. The civil rights movement, the war on poverty, the Peace Corps, the Durham rule, the campus revolts were slogans current in the United States *pari passu* with community psychiatry, each in their own arena reflecting the same worldwide revolutionary shift in the fundamental relations of man and society. Bartlett[3] outlined the role the designation of mental hospital patients as "indigent" played in creating the "institutional amalgam of administrative, medical, legal, economic, welfare and political activities" which maintained the isolation of the mental hospital from the community it served; similar considerations may be extended to the fact that patients have been, in disproportionate numbers, black and foreign born. It is important to recognize that the changes in institutional structure and function that have made possible the current role of the mental hospital in community mental health programs derived from broader changes in the social structure rather than from revolutionary developments in pharmacotherapy; the open-door policy, day hospitals, the therapeutic community, and family therapy were all in clear development prior to the discovery of the antipsychotic properties of the phenothiazines. E. Linn's study[18] of St. Elizabeth's Hospital from 1953 to 1956, for example, reveals that a higher proportion of patients admitted in the later years than in the earlier years were discharged, though the use of tranquilizers had not as yet been introduced. A parallel may be drawn to the decline in morbidity and mortality from tuberculosis, which preceded the introduction of acid-fast specific antibiotic drugs, but reflected the introduction of improved social, hygienic, and housing conditions in the care of tuberculosis patients.

In order to participate significantly in the network of community mental health resources, mental hospitals must, to begin with, replace custodial practices with active treatment programs. The range of therapeutic approaches increasingly evident in contemporary mental hospitals is indeed extensive and includes organic therapies (pharmacotherapy and ECT), psychotherapies (individual, family, multiple family, and group), and sociotherapies (milieu therapy, occupational and recreational therapies, art therapies,

therapeutic community). The impact of these treatment approaches on the career of patients has been extensively described; duration of hospitalization has been dramatically decreased, and concurrently the incidence of the noxious symptoms of hospitalism, which Gruenberg[8] aptly called the "Social Breakdown Syndrome," has declined. L. Linn[19] demonstrated, in a study of twelve state mental hospitals scattered around the country, that higher discharge rates were not significantly related to the age, mental status, or physical disability of patients, nor to the aesthetics of the wards or the personal facilities available to patients; they were, however, related to the frequency of patients receiving visitors and the frequency of organized patient-doctor, patient-staff, and patient-patient interactions. Consistent with this report is the finding by Schulberg and Baker[26] that concurrently with the general improvement in services attending the shift of the Boston State Hospital toward a greater community orientation, the number of patients not receiving any form of treatment was reduced from 37 to 18 percent. The capability to provide appropriate treatment may not in actuality exist in all psychiatric institutions, but this is no longer the sole frontier of the mental hospital; equally challenging is the formidable problem of breaking down the barriers between hospitals and communities and of establishing integrated and coordinated programs with community-based facilities, to the end of providing continuity of treatment for patients.

The forces impinging on the evolution of community-oriented programs in mental hospitals are extremely uncertain and undefined.[33] The modalities of psychiatric treatment, the practices of mental hospitals, and the development of community psychiatry approaches are both independently and interdependently undergoing dramatic and rapid change. The unevenness of the rates of change inherent in the science and art of psychiatry is magnified by the immediate impact on each of fiscal support available from public funds at city, county, state, and federal levels for teaching, research, and service programs. The many other variables of place and circumstance—

rural versus urban location of hospital and community mental health center, presence or absence of a medical school affiliation by either or both, presence of an unusually large concentration of old persons, of children, of ghetto residents, or of addicts in the populations served by either or both—in addition to the unpredictable nature of fiscal support, psychiatric technical developments, and changes in the social matrix in which families and communities are imbedded, make it difficult to predict the nature of community programs mental hospitals are likely to develop in the future. What can here be described are the patterns that have characterized the significant number of mental hospitals that pioneered in developing community programs, in the expectation that these patterns are likely to continue to be applicable to those traditional mental hospitals that will be changing in the next decade.

❰ Unitization

The single most revolutionary change in mental health services that has characterized community psychiatry programs is the shift from professional responsibility for patients— self-identified or brought to the hospital, clinic, or office by some interested other person—to responsibility for population groups. Preventive programs, early case-findings efforts, community education and consultation services, storefront and satellite clinic units, and the use of indigenous nonprofessionals all existed as components of traditional psychiatric services, but were all qualitatively increased and were newly combined in a coordinated pattern of work only after the acceptance of responsibility for the mental health of all residents in a defined geographic area made it no longer feasible for mental health professionals to wait in their accustomed places for accustomed (hopefully "good") patients on whom to exercise their accustomed skills. Inherently, the potential adaptations available to a mental hospital for change toward a community orientation

would appear to be extremely limited by the traditional role of the hospital as the most classic institution in the medical model, and this limitation becomes virtually insuperable when the hospital is responsible for a huge geographic area. Historically, the sorting out of patients in such circumstances has rested on individual patient characteristics (acute versus chronic; male versus female; specific diagnostic entities, for example, alcoholics, geriatric patients, depressed patients who are candidates for ECT); the tragic consequences of this sort of triage, for example, the inevitable process of creating chronicity by the sheer device of establishing "chronic" wards, are too familiar.

A strikingly different perspective is afforded a mental hospital when it divides its wards into units or services on a geographic basis (ideally, in our experience, from 100 to 250 beds to serve a population of from 100,000 to 200,000), with the unit chief responsible for patients from a defined catchment area and for effecting appropriate liaison with all mental health-related agencies and institutions serving that area.[15,16] In those instances where receiving or screening centers—hospitals or clinics—serve the target community, a range of administrative forms for providing continuity of patient care and for the sharing of patient records rapidly develops. Some of the units find themselves serving areas that are relatively well supplied with clinical resources, while others serve barren areas. The advantages to the hospital of relating to community-based centers quickly become apparent, with reference to reduced admissions through both appropriate local treatment alternatives and more stable adjustments by patients to community life after discharge because of improved follow-up care. The most frequent sequence that follows is that hospital units serving "have-not" localities first establish their own community-based aftercare clinics; the clinics soon begin to intercept patients on their way to the hospital by offering outpatient short-term crisis therapy, in addition to treating discharged patients; crisis intervention in turn leads to consultation services, most frequently to schools, police, and family agencies; the hospital units begin to use ward space more flexibly, to accommodate to the needs of the outpatient clinics for day and night hospitalization; and by this time the hospital is generally seeking to formalize the network of services established by such units as community mental health centers. The literature is liberally sprinkled with references describing such a sequence.[4,12,20,24] In at least as many instances, centers are developed out of the associations between hospital units and their community-based partners. Rural hospitals, with some appropriate devices (satellite clinics, for example) to provide for the logistical problems of ensuring continuity of treatment, have undergone similar development.[6,13]

Although unitization of mental hospitals is the crucial and necessary cornerstone of a community orientation, it is not without its penalties. It is expensive; it requires considerably more staff members, with better training, to replicate admission processes and treatment programs for several units, and to cover the requisite liaison and outpatient positions, than to maintain a large custodial triage and storage center. The initial period after unitization is invariably a difficult one. Patients must be moved from hospital loci determined by age, sex, or duration of stay to geographic units. Staff relationships change profoundly from a vertical to a horizontal organization in which each service or unit determines the assignments of its staff members, rather than having department heads decide independently on hospital-wide programs for psychologists, social workers, nurses, activities therapists, and nonprofessionals. With this shift, there is inevitably a blurring of professional disciplines; a chief psychologist is more likely to maintain the unique disciplinary identity of the roles of his staff than is a unit chief who will need to get his job done by extracting from each staff member whatever skills he possesses regardless of professional title. Even more vexing is the almost immediate creation of totally new roles, particularly boundary-spanning roles between the hospital unit and its own mini-community. It is not at all infrequent for mental hospital stationery to bear the inscription

"Address all correspondence to the superintendent"; this obviously cannot be continued in a unitized hospital, but powerful traditions must be overcome before unit chiefs or their community liaison staff officers develop free mobility across the hospital boundary into the community. Finally, there is almost certain to develop a competitive relationship between units; while this may have a salutary effect, it may sometimes generate disruptive bitterness between competing units.

For all these risks, large mental hospitals must unitize their services as an essential first step if the hospitals are to break the shackles that have isolated them from the community they serve.

(Patient Flow and Staff Sharing

In a considerable number of instances, free-standing community mental health centers have focused principal attention on patients with acute psychoses, neuroses, and personality disorders and have given low priority to the chronically mentally ill, the addicts, the alcoholics, the elderly, patients with poor impulse control or prone to assaultive behavior, and patients with medical and neurological as well as mental illness. The flow of patients between such centers and the area mental hospitals has tended to be unidirectional, with virtually no referrals from the hospital to the center.

In the competition with hospitals for patients most likely to respond to currently available treatment regimens, the mental health centers enjoy many advantages. University and teaching hospital departments of psychiatry are increasingly responsive to the pressures for developing community psychiatry programs, but except when they happen to be located in the vicinity of a mental hospital, the trainee and teaching staffs of these departments are unlikely to follow patients into the public mental hospital. The community mental health centers then, given first contact with patients, with substantial teaching obligations and generally with better financial support than mental hospitals, may tend to treat selectively the acutely ill patients, that is, precisely the patients we already are best able to treat. The state hospital, conversely, ringed by mental health centers, can then expect only those patients who are least likely to respond to current treatment approaches to sift through the community-based screening units. Hospital staff members interested in active treatment will then tend to be attracted to the mental health centers, and this process, once begun, can develop its own momentum, so that a rapid sorting out of professional staff may be expected. It is thus likely in some instances that community mental health centers, designed in large part to reverse the tendency of large mental hospitals to promote chronicity in mentally ill patients, will become significant forces for promoting chronicity. Two contributions already published report precisely such a development.[29,33]

There are a number of advantages to mental health centers in this pattern of patient flow. The flexibility of the newborn centers in selectively addressing community needs is maximized by having the mental hospitals as a captive backstop. The hospitals at the same time serve as reservoirs of professional manpower for the centers. Geographic distances between centers and hospitals, which may present serious logistical difficulties to the development of close liaison arrangements between a hospital and a community-based center, pose no problem to this pattern; indeed, the extrusion of undesired patients from community mental health centers is promoted by greater distances between the centers and the state hospitals. However, the promotion of chronicity and the building in of discontinuity between community and hospital phases of treatment are too great a price to pay for these advantages.

An alternative model is one in which the mental hospital serves as the regional hub of a wide network of community-based mental health centers, with each geographic unit of the hospital fully integrated into the network of services designed for a defined catchment area or serving itself as the principal locus of a community mental health center. The essence of this model is a regionalization of mental health services around the mental hospital, in close parallel to the catchment area subregions served by community mental health centers; in the present instance, liaison patterns involve the flow of patients between a hospital and a center, rather than between a center and the agencies and institutions in the community served by the center.

A variety of patterns of patient flow have emerged from liaison arrangements of this latter sort. Most simple is a separation of functions between hospital and center based on duration of hospitalization, in which decisions concerning admission and discharge remain the prerogative of each institution. Records are completely shared. The decision to refer a patient from a center program for admission to the hospital is made by the center staff, but an independent decision to admit the referred patient is the responsibility of the hospital. Conversely, a discharge recommendation is made by the hospital staff, but must be independently accepted and implemented by the center staff. Differences in professional judgment as to admissibility or readiness for discharge are an expectable occurrence in such an arrangement and frequently lead to such shared efforts at resolution as joint hospital-center clinical conferences or service liaison committees. Generally, the centers assign liaison staff members to the hospital unit to which their patients are assigned to facilitate social service and after care treatment arrangements for patients being discharged from the hospital.

In a number of instances,[31] administrative structures have been established in which patient flow is regulated entirely by a joint center-hospital staff unit, although the hospital employees remain responsible to the hospital director for specific administrative requirements. In these instances, complete continuity of care can be approximated, with patients followed into and out of the mental hospital by the staff member or team most involved with their treatment programs. Such arrangements are fraught with administrative difficulties. Unless the pay scales, fringe benefits, and union affiliations of hospital and center staff members are identical, employees doing substantially the same tasks but under different conditions of employment will be working side by side, a circumstance that could not be maintained for very long. The mixed chains of command—functionally to the center and structurally to the hospital—represent a further administrative complication: Neither the center nor the hospital director can act freely in pursuit of his own goals without concern for the other. Where there is a single unifying authority (for example, the chairman of a medical school department of psychiatry with which both the center and hospital are affiliated or the commissioner of a state department of mental hygiene with authority over both hospital and local services), these difficulties are readily resolved. In the absence of a central authority, they represent formidable obstacles to the complete unification of decisions concerning patient flow between mental hospitals and community mental health centers.

Invariably, the other side of the coin of patient flow is staff deployment; provision for continuity of patient care must remain limited if staff assignments are rigidly maintained as either to the center or to the hospital. A number of staff-sharing procedures have been described,[34] all of which fundamentally rest on some measure of mutual trust between hospital and center administrations and some measure of joint responsibility for patient care and treatment.

(Central Specialized Treatment Services

One of the problems that plagues all attempts at the decentralization of health services is the replication versus the regionalization of expensive, infrequently utilized programs. Appropriate care and treatment of small numbers of patients within any community mental health center catchment area may require a facility beyond the means reasonably available to any single center, and yet readily supportable on a broader regional basis. In such instances, the mental hospital that serves a ring of community psychiatry programs may lend itself uniquely well to service as a special treatment center for these programs. Responsibility for patients while in these programs generally rests with the hospital, but in most instances the patients are at the same time in community-based treatment programs organized by the center, so that some liaison between hospital and center is forced on the cooperating institutions. Such specialized treatment programs include both facilities for special categories of patients, and specialized facilities for broad patient categories.

Examples of the former include facilities for treating mentally ill criminals, addicts, alcoholics, and patients requiring extensive physiotherapeutic as well as psychotherapeutic efforts. Some of the problems attending the establishment of a prison ward are discussed below; except for a large urban community, the number of mentally ill offenders is likely to be too small to justify the cost of a separate security unit for the population of a mental health center catchment area. Again with addicts and alcoholics, while the number of outpatients from one area may be substantial, the number requiring inpatient treatment especially adapted for their care and treatment is likely to be too small for a community-based inpatient service.

Examples of specialized facilities for broad patient categories likely to prove too costly to be supported on a local basis include sheltered workshops, halfway houses, and nursery school programs for preschool children of mentally ill mothers. Although many, if not most, community mental health centers provide vocational rehabilitation services for their patients, the close replication of the conditions of work in a large factory is prohibitive, and the range of on-the-job vocational training supportable by any single center is limited; a regional vocational rehabilitation center operated by a large mental hospital can provide such facilities for a number of mental health centers. Similarly, individual centers frequently have a number of apartments and/or foster home placements available for patients judged capable of the degree of competence for independent living required for such residence but who cannot afford the intermediary living experience between a hospital and community apartments represented by a halfway house. At the Bronx State Hospital, a program designed to provide rehabilitative training in family life and mothering behavior for patients with preschool children found it necessary to extend the nursery school experience for the children and the rehabilitative effects with the mothers long after the mothers had been discharged to outpatient treatment in community-based clinics.

Mention must be made of the specialized role of private mental hospitals. Klerman[11] indicated the large numbers of patients, other than those requiring long-term institutionalization, treated in the private sector, and Ozarin, Herman, and Osterwell[23] described the many instances in which private hospitals have participated in the development of full or partial community mental health centers. Kubie[14] suggested that the private hospital is uniquely suited for demonstration research seeking models for the hospital and community liaison. The increase in the number of private hospitals, and their widened geographic distribution, has made it possible for many private patients to be hospitalized near their homes and has stimulated the development of partial hospitalization and halfway houses in conjunction with these hospitals. With increasing pressure for the inclusion of reimbursement for psychiatric treatment by public and private health insurance programs, and with the growing tendency of medical schools and voluntary hospitals to extend patient care to low-income groups, it is likely that private mental hospitals will follow the route of the public hospitals in a shift toward greater integration of hospital programs with the communities served.

❪ Conceptual Issues

It was noted above that the crisis of mental hospitals, in transition from geographically isolated custodial institutions to community-oriented treatment centers, can only be understood in the light of simultaneous crises in health care delivery systems and in medical education, and these in turn must be viewed against the background of the broader matrix of social change in which they are imbedded. We have accepted as national policy that health is a fundamental human right, rather than a privilege for those who can purchase medical services, and we have thereby altered in a radical way the basis from which we view such issues as the numbers, kinds, and distribution of doctors needed to implement the evolving health policy. We have at the same time begun to alter the doctor-patient relationship so that the patient sees himself less as the fortunate recipient of the favors of his doctor and more as a consumer who insists on holding his doctor to account as firmly as he does all purveyors of services. Under the pressure of the vast, hitherto poorly attended, mental health needs of large segments of our population, we have trained a range of nonprofessional mental health workers and have inevitably been forced by the mounting urgency of the need to redress centuries-old racial inequities to open channels for the more talented of these nonprofessional workers, overwhelmingly from minority groups, to paraprofessional and professional status. The demands of patient-consumers for a new measure of accountability, coupled with the extraordinary skill and ability of many minimally trained mental health workers, have led to a major reevaluation of the role of the professional in the planning and administration of health care delivery systems and a challenge to the hitherto unquestioned primacy of the doctor, and of the medical board of the hospital, in decisions concerning the organization of health services to communities. As Zborowski[32] eloquently noted:

There are only two possible alternatives for coping with this array of problems: one dictated by fear and conservatism, and the other by the understanding of social processes and by progressiveness. The hospitals may move out of the ghetto to follow the migration of the white middle class and their physicians to the security of suburbia. Or they may remain in the old location. . . .

Many hospitals have selected the second alternative, although that course is far more difficult than the first. Hospitals have to be ready to become part of the community. . . . They must accept responsibilities in the community, not only as the hospitals see them, but as they are defined in conjunction with the community.

A number of unresolved problems attend the acceptance by a mental hospital of responsibilities in the community, one of the most immediate being the redefinition of the role of the community in determining hospital policy. It has become an accepted feature in the operation of community mental health centers that community boards enter into the formulation of center policy and philosophy. In some instances the boards have incorporated, have secured staffing grants, and have contracted with professional staffs to provide the mandated services; in other instances, boards have been serving in an advisory capacity, sometimes with carefully restricted areas in which their advice is solicited or offered. There is as yet no consensus as to the optimal relationship between community representatives and the administrative or executive staff of a center, and community boards have barely begun to emerge in relation to the operation of mental hospitals. However, it is abundantly clear that medical boards and administrators cannot long continue to exclude the outsiders (that is, the communities they serve) from the decision-making processes of their hospitals. The impact of the active participation of community boards in establishing hospital policies and practices can be expected to profoundly affect every phase of hospital life, including priorities for admission of patients, hiring and firing procedures, the use of patients for teaching and research, and even the selection of treatment programs.

A second set of issues relates to the role of inpatient treatment in the network of mental health services provided by and for a population group. Community attitudes toward mental illness and psychiatric treatment are inevitably altered away from awe and fear toward a greater acceptance of hospitalization without stigma by the transition of hospitals to a community orientation and by the provision of mental health services in general hospitals and community clinics and centers. At the same time, the development of such treatment centers in the community broadens the available options to hospital admitting officers from hospital or home to a range of intermediary alternatives, and this in turn demands that a meaningful set of criteria for hospitalization be formulated.

It is apparent that former President John F. Kennedy,[10] in the message to Congress that heralded the shift in national policy toward support of community psychiatry programs, anticipated the demise of the large mental hospital; it seems equally apparent that facilities for inpatient care and treatment will continue to be required. Further, with reference to the use of hospitals, the consequences of the creation of community alternatives to mental hospitalization are inextricably intertwined with the development of a wide range of alternative conceptual models to the traditional medical model for understanding and helping persons seeking mental health services. At one extreme, Szasz,[28] Liefer,[17] and others suggested that mental illness is a myth and expressed the concern that hospitalization is merely a device designed by a social system to coerce deviants into conformity with its norms. At another extreme, Kubie,[14] quite content with the illness model, expressed concern that the long-term benefits of community treatment and of psychoactive drugs are unproven and uncertain, and he urged that "years of observation of the delayed aftereffects of physiologic, chemical and psychological devices are essential for both the progress of our scientific knowledge and the immediate care of patients. It is extremely difficult if not impossible to carry on such a period of critical and sustained observation without hospital control and protection."

A recent contribution to this set of issues presented in the monograph, *Crisis in Psychiatric Hospitalization,*[7] reflected the lack of resolution that prevails; after listing three indications for hospitalization for diagnostic purposes, and five indications for hospital treatment, it offered the uncertain conclusion that "An individual's need for hospitalization

. . . involves an examination of his personal problems and an assessment of his personal and the community resources. If the totality of resources, including alternative management procedures, is inadequate, hospitalization may be clearly indicated." A complementary contribution, suggested by Schulberg and Baker,[26] is that an evaluation research program for outcome studies of mental hospital treatment must derive from an open-systems model and examine not only the hospital but the entire network of community mental health facilities.

Still another special set of conceptual issues confronted by the transitional hospital relates to the definition of the boundary between psychiatry and the law. The geographically isolated, long-stay custodial hospital with locked wards was functionally more similar to than different from jail, and the differentiation between madness and badness in deviant behavior was not of crucial moment. This is clearly not the case in an open ward community-oriented active treatment hospital, despite the parallel transition in penal institutions from a punitive to a rehabilitation focus; it is not unusual, among other gross differences, for the median duration of stay in a mental hospital to be less than three months.

The potential role of a mental hospital in providing a locked ward unit on a regional basis for patients who require such a unit is dictated by the demands of the judiciary rather than by treatment needs; it is, therefore, difficult to avoid the establishment of a custodial prison ward atmosphere. Many states provide for civil hospitalization of criminal offenders accused of misdemeanors, whose behavior in the course of their arrest and arraignment raises questions concerning their sanity or competence. If the judiciary demands the return of such patients after examination and/or treatment, a security unit is mandatory, and there is the risk of the locked ward atmosphere spreading through the hospital. On the other hand, if the patients are released by the judiciary to the hospital, as Lowenkopf and Yessne[21] showed, they constitute a very significantly different population

from the other patients: They are more frequently involved in sex offenses, in bringing alcohol or drugs to the wards, in assaultive episodes, and in more than one-third of the cases their treatment is terminated by elopement from the hospital. Referral to outpatient treatment clinics is rejected by the patients, and the clinics in turn are prone to refer these patients back to the hospital on the slightest indication. The community-oriented hospital will find the mentally ill criminal offender a serious problem, and it may be that some totally new and more suitable modality for treating these patients will emerge out of current efforts to resolve the dilemmas they create.

Perhaps the most difficult problem in the transition of a mental hospital to a community orientation is the change demanded in the philosophy of the hospital staff. Baker and Schulberg[2] demonstrated that mental health professionals working in mental hospitals fall in the lowest scoring category on their community mental health ideology scale. This is not surprising. The mental hospital is a highly centripetal institution: The hospital groups, the hospital milieu, the hospital activities and programs, and above all the hospital staff are the stuff of which remedy is fashioned. The patients "belong" to the staff, and the prevalent perspective among staff members holds that it is precisely "those people" in the family and community who have generated the forces that led to illness in their patients; to develop active alliances with "those people" is not congenial to the staff. Equally inimical to expectable hospital staff attitudes is the introduction of primary prevention as a major emphasis; there is a qualitative conceptual leap from the accustomed concern of staff members with secondary and tertiary prevention, involving people already identified as patients, to programs designed to forestall patienthood, a leap that staff members often find difficult and baffling. A not infrequent chart note will read, "Mary has been upset each time her mother has come to visit; I have therefore restricted the mother from visiting until further notice." For a hospital staff to develop a true dedication to community treatment requires a major change in the staff self-image, away from that of caretakers and more toward that of change agents.

❲ Conclusions

Kraft[12] pointed out that community psychiatry involves rather little up to this point in the way of new treatment techniques, but rather offers traditional treatment approaches in a new delivery system designed to bring more of the therapeutic effort to patients in the community. For a traditional mental hospital to serve as a base for a community psychiatry program, it must then first offer a wide range of active treatment programs aimed at the most expeditious return of the patient to his family and community. Large mental hospitals must be unitized, so that clusters of wards with a total of from 100 to 250 beds are organized to serve a population area of from 100,000 to 200,000 persons. Liaison arrangements between a hospital unit and the community-based mental health facilities in the geographic area served by the unit should aim for the free flow of patients and records and for the full sharing of staff. Of particular concern where a community mental health center and a large mental hospital fail to develop such liaison arrangements is the likelihood that the center will retain for treatment only those patients likely to respond rapidly to currently available treatment modalities and will concentrate patients likely to become chronic in the hospital. A mental hospital serving as the hub of a regional network of community facilities can offer a variety of specialized services, or services for special categories of patients, likely not to be supportable economically by the resources of community mental health centers for smaller patient populations. Finally, a number of conceptual issues are introduced by the transition of a mental hospital from a geographically isolated to a community-oriented center, among which are community participation and control, the problem of the priority in public mental health

programs of providing for the need for hospitalization, the nature of the relationship between the health system and the law system for dealing with deviant behavior, and the attitudes of hospital staff members.

Mesnikoff[22] made the observation that we are coming full circle in the history of our country regarding the treatment of mental illness—from family to county to state and now back to county and family—though at a significantly more sophisticated level and with a great deal of expertise available to support treatment in the community. Viewed in this light, the mental hospital must serve as one resource in a network of mental health services designed to support programs for the community-based treatment of the mentally ill.

❲ Bibliography

1. BAKER, F. "An Open-Systems Approach to the Study of Mental Hospitals in Transition." *Community Mental Health Journal,* 5 (1969), 403.

2. ———, and SCHULBERG, H. "The Development of a Community Mental Health Ideology Scale." *Community Mental Health Journal,* 3 (1967), 216.

3. BARTLETT, F. L. "Present-Day Requirements for State Hospitals Joining the Community." *New England Journal of Medicine,* 276 (1967), 90.

4. BOYLES, P., and WALDROP, G. "Development of a Community-Oriented Program in a Large State Hospital of Limited Resources." *American Journal of Psychiatry,* 124 (1967), 29.

5. CAPLAN, R. B. *Psychiatry and the Community in Nineteenth-Century America.* New York: Basic Books, 1969.

6. ELWELL, R. N. "Hospitals and Centers Move Towards a Single System of Comprehensive Services." *Hospital and Community Psychiatry,* 20 (1969), 175.

7. GROUP FOR THE ADVANCEMENT OF PSYCHIATRY. *Crisis in Psychiatric Hospitalization.* Report no. 72. New York, 1969.

8. GRUENBERG, E. "On the Pathogenesis of the Social Breakdown Syndrome." In B. Stone, ed., *A Critical Review of Treatment Progress in a State Hospital Reorganized Towards the Communities Served.* Pueblo, Colo.: Pueblo Association for Mental Health, 1963.

9. HECKER, A. "The Demise of Large State Hospitals." *Hospital and Community Psychiatry,* 21 (1970), 261.

10. KENNEDY, J. F. *Message from the President of the United States Relative to Mental Illness and Mental Retardation.* House Document 58, 88th Congress, 1st session. Washington, D.C.: U.S. Government Printing Office, 1963.

11. KLERMAN, G. "The Private Psychiatric Hospital in the Community Mental Health Era." *International Journal of Psychiatry,* 6 (1968), 437.

12. KRAFT, A. M. "The State Hospital: Cornerstone of Community Service." *Hospital and Community Psychiatry,* 18 (1967), 243.

13. KREYES, W. "Development of a Rural Community Psychiatry Service Based in a Hospital for Mental Diseases." *Canadian Medical Association Journal,* 98 (1969), 154.

14. KUBIE, L. "The Future of the Private Psychiatric Hospital." *International Journal of Psychiatry,* 6 (1968), 419.

15. LABURT, H., WALLACE, M., IMPASTATO, A., and SKLAR, J. "The State Hospital and Community Psychiatry." *Diseases of the Nervous System,* 29 (1968), 556.

16. LEVY, L. "The State Mental Hospital in Transition: A Review of Principles." *Community Mental Health Journal,* 1 (1965), 353.

17. LIEFER, R. *In the Name of Mental Health.* New York: Science House, 1969.

18. LINN, E. "The Community, the Mental Hospital and Psychotic Patients' Unusual Behavior." *Journal of Nervous and Mental Disease,* 145 (1967), 492.

19. LINN, L. "State Hospital Environment and Rates of Patient Discharge." *Archives of General Psychiatry,* 23 (1970), 346.

20. LITIN, E., TYCE, F., and RYNEARSON, R. "State Hospital to Comprehensive Area Mental Health Center." *Hospital and Community Psychiatry,* 17 (1966), 33.

21. LOWENKOPF, E., and YESSNE, D. The Mentally Ill Offender in a Civil Hospital. Paper presented to the American Psychiatric Association, 1971.

22. MESNIKOFF, A. M. The State Hospital as a Community Mental Health Center. Paper presented to the American Psychiatric Association District Branches, New York, November 21, 1969.

23. OZARIN, L., HERMAN, M., and OSTERWELL, J. "Private Hospitals in Community Planning." *Mental Hygiene,* 50 (1966), 24

24. PHILLIPS, G. "A State Hospital Moves Toward Community Psychiatry." *Journal of the National Medical Association,* 61 (1969), 140.

25. RABINER, C., and NICHTERN, S. "Psychiatric Service to Community." *New York State Journal of Medicine,* 69 (1969), 713.

26. SCHULBERG, H. C., and BAKER, F. "The Changing Mental Hospital: A Progress Report." *Hospital and Community Psychiatry,* 20 (1969), 159.

27. SOLOMON, H. "The American Psychiatric Association in Relation to American Psychiatry." *American Journal of Psychiatry,* 115 (1958), 1.

28. SZASZ, T. *The Myth of Mental Illness.* New York: Hoeber-Harper, 1961.

29. VON BRAUCHITSCH, H. "Community Psychiatry and the Future State Hospital." *Michigan Medicine,* 66 (1967), 308.

30. WHITE, W. A. "Presidential Address Delivered at 81st Annual Meeting of the American Psychiatric Association, May 12–15, 1925." *American Journal of Psychiatry,* 5 (1925), 1.

31. WILDER, J., KARASU, B., and KLIGLER, D. The Hospital "Dumping Syndrome": Causes and Treatment. Paper presented to the American Psychiatric Association, Washington, D.C., May 4, 1971.

32. ZBOROWSKI, M. "The Changing Urban Scene." *Hospitals,* 44 (1970), 33.

33. ZWERLING, I. "Some Implications of Community Psychiatry for State Mental Hospitals." *Cincinnati Journal of Medicine,* 50 (1969), 189.

34. ————. "Part-time and Shared Staff." *Hospital and Community Psychiatry,* 21 (1970), 59.

CHAPTER 47

THE SOCIAL BREAKDOWN SYNDROME AND ITS PREVENTION

Ernest M. Gruenberg

THE SOCIAL BREAKDOWN SYNDROME (SBS) is the name given to certain features of psychiatric patients' deterioration. It is a useful concept because it specifies those features of patient functioning, especially extreme withdrawal and aggressive behavior, that become less common when new systems of delivering psychiatric services are introduced.

The social breakdown concept emerged from experiments with new psychiatric service delivery systems.[15] Evaluation research of a later demonstration of this new psychiatric service delivery system in Dutchess County, New York, developed it further.[6]

This chapter traces the concept's evolution, beginning with the early open hospital systems, started in some communities during the late 1940s, and shows its evolution and elaboration up to the present. As our experience and knowledge grow, our thinking about the social breakdown syndrome changes. Less than half the social breakdown syndrome episodes occur in people with schizophrenic disorders, the others being scattered among a wide variety of diagnostic groups. (See Table 47–1.) Social breakdown syndrome's distribution in the population differs markedly from that of schizophrenia. (See Chapter 30, "The Epidemiology of Schizophrenia.")

⟮ The Open Hospitals

In August 1954, Dr. T. P. Rees (Warlingham Park Hospital, Croyden) and Dr. W. S. Maclay (British Board of Control) reported* on

---

* At the time of the Toronto Conference of the World Federation for Mental Health, in August 1954, an international symposium on problems of

how three open hospitals functioned in Britain, impressing many American psychiatrists who were present. The practical experience of these three programs in the community care of the severely mentally ill was accompanied by a remarkable lessening of the severe chronic troublesome behavior and extreme chronic withdrawal of mental patients. Psychiatrists previously had assumed that these phenomena were owing to certain severe mental disorders rather than secondary complications, which could be avoided by reorganizing the delivery of psychiatric services.

These three experiments started by trying to give patients with severe mental illness more humane care. Locked doors and physical or chemical restraints were used less, and short voluntary hospitalizations for short-term indications, more, and the emphasis was on the long-term availability of services while chronic patients lived in the community. The three mental hospitals, serving well-defined populations, carried the direction of change so far that their medical staffs were devoting half their time to patients who were out of the hospital, all the mental hospital wards were unlocked, and very few admissions used legal constraints. Patients rarely stayed more than two to three months following admission, and the hospital census was falling despite a greatly increased admission rate. (During the same period, mental hospital censuses were rising elsewhere.)

Patients' behavior as a whole had, to the surprise of the directors, taken on a different

appearance by the time the programs had reached that point. The chronically disturbed (suicidal, assaultive, destructive, or soiling) and the chronic severely withdrawn patients (mute, self-neglectful, staring, regressed) became extremely rare.

Notions regarding what causes symptoms in severe mental disorders required reexamination. Since treatment reorganization led to large-scale disappearance of severely disturbed or withdrawn behavior, some of the disturbed behavior appeared to change when staff-patient relations were modified. Hence, a secondary, sociogenic syndrome of severely disturbed behavior was postulated and became known as the "social breakdown syndrome." Earlier thoughts along the same line had not carried the idea so far.[22]

Only when three pioneer services had transformed the psychiatric care for entire communities into the new pattern of community care, interrupted by short-term hospital treatment in open hospitals with minimal legal restraints, did the large-scale change in patient functioning become obvious. This occurred during the early 1950s. The three pioneer services were those of G. Bell (Dingleton Hospital, Melrose, Scotland), T. P. Rees (Warlingham Park Hospital, Croyden, England) and Duncan Macmillan (Mapperley Hospital, Nottingham, England).

⟨ The New Delivery System

Macmillan, writing in 1957,[14] described how the integration of locally operated services and mental hospital services in Nottingham, England, began to become unified in 1945. Through "a policy of continuity of care" the

partnership in mental health and public health was held with the assistance of a grant from the new Hope Foundation of New York. During the following year, the surgeon general of the U.S. Public Health Service requested that the World Health Organization give Dr. Robert C. Hunt a traveling fellowship to study these newer developments in Europe. Partly as a result of his reports, Commissioner Paul Hoch (New York State Department of Mental Hygiene), in 1957, appointed a committee of six New York State mental hospital directors to study these open hospitals under the guidance of Dr. T. P. Rees, who had retired that year. (The Milbank Memorial Fund provided the grant that made this possible.) The committee's 1957 report to Commissioner Hoch was also presented in part at the Milbank Memorial Fund's thirty-sixth annual conference[16] and at the ninth mental hospital institute.[11]

social worker who first saw the patient in the community continued to see the patient in the hospital, took part in the arrangements for employment and return to the home, and then paid the aftercare visits upon the patient's discharge. The medical member of the hospital staff who first saw the patient either at the outpatient clinic or on a domiciliary visit to the home usually carried out the inpatient treatment and then arranged to see the patient at his aftercare clinic.

By 1952 this integrated system was operating in a city where the only mental hospital (Mapperley) had given up all locked doors and all forms of physical restraint.

We make every effort to treat the patient as a personality and to maintain and restore his self-confidence. We go to great lengths to obtain his cooperation . . . admission has to be repeated . . . but the end result with this repeated form of treatment is very much better, and the patient then adjusts to life in the community.[14]

Many symptoms that made unlocking wards difficult disappeared. They had been regarded as due to the psychosis but terminated with the removal of restrictions. "No proper staff-patient relationship is possible," until legal certification is removed.

It causes the community to regard patients as people apart, different from other human beings.

The resentment and the feeling of injustice which certification causes in the mind of the patient is intense and it lasts for many years. When patients are in a state of emotional upset, when their self-confidence is already seriously undermined and disturbed, to deprive them of civil rights, depletes that stock of self-confidence even more at this critical phase of their life. One can hardly imagine anything more likely to upset them. The depressed patient becomes more depressed. The delusional patients become more fixed in their reactions and consider that they

TABLE 47–1. **Clinical Diagnoses[a] of the 139 Prevailing Social Breakdown Syndrome Cases,[b] Ages 16–64, in the Dutchess County Study Population[c] and Their Status as Inpatients or Outpatients at the Time of a 1963 Point Prevalence Survey**

N	DIAGNOSIS	IN HOSPITAL	OUT[d]
72	Schizophrenia	57	15
11	Psychoneurosis	3	8
8	Psychosis due to circulatory disturbances	6	2
7	Psychosis with mental deficiency	6	1
5	Psychosis associated with organicity	4	1
4	Involutional psychosis	1	3
4	Alcoholic psychosis	3	1
4	Other nonpsychotic disorders	1	3
4	Psychosis due to epilepsy	4	—
4	Alzheimer's	3	1
3	General paresis	3	—
3	Psychosis with psychopathic personality	1	2
2	Manic-depressed psychosis	—	2
2	Psychosis or personality disturbance due to trauma	2	—
1	Conduct disturbance	1	—
1	Presbyophrenia	1	—
1	Psychosis with epidemic encephalitis	1	—
1	Psychosis due to intracranial neoplasm	1	—
1	Paranoid condition	1	—
1	Undiagnosed psychosis	—	1
139	Total	99	40

[a] Diagnosis categories are listed in the New York State Condensed Form of New Classification as approved by the American Psychiatric Association council and used in the New York State hospitals during 1963. Diagnoses were obtained from clinical records.
[b] Data-gathering methodology is described elsewhere.[3]
[c] The population ages sixteen to sixty-four was approximately 100,000 people.
[d] "Out" means in the community, including family care.

have justification for them. Withdrawal symptoms become more pronounced.[14]

This system had become fully operative before the phenothiazines and the new group of psychotropic drugs had been discovered. Like some other important advances in medicine and public health, the realization that more could be done to help psychotic patients control their disturbing symptoms through new methods of psychiatric service organization came to this country from the other side of the Atlantic, a process that was facilitated by the World Health Organization and other international health organizations.[15,16]

The Social Breakdown Syndrome Is Named

As Alfred Stanton stated,[21] perhaps the fact that it was named by a committee reflects the social mechanisms by which this preventable complication of mental disorders became recognized. The American Public Health Association's Program Area Committee on Mental Health stated[1] in 1962:

There is one type of mental malfunctioning which occurs in many different chronic mental disorders, particularly schizophrenia, mental retardation, and various organic psychoses. It is responsible for a very large part of the institutionalized mentally disordered; it is responsible for much of the other forms of extreme social disability seen in these illnesses. This form of mental reaction in the presence of mental disorders is largely a socially determined reaction pattern which the committee believes can be identified as a major target for community mental health programs today . . . this particular reaction . . . came into sharp prominence because of its great commonness and its sensitivity to improved organization of services. It has not had a name in psychiatric literature in the past. In the absence of a better term, it is called "The Social Breakdown Syndrome." . . . It is necessary to have a term to describe what one is talking about when one has found something so worth describing. It is largely because of current successes in dealing with this syndrome, it is believed, that for the first time in two generations the census of patients occupying beds in mental hospitals has started to decline in the English-speaking countries.

Many mental disorders, particularly the psychoses (both "functional" and "organic"), are frequently accompanied by distortions of personality function which are associated with more or less severe destruction of the affected person's social relationships. These reactions can be viewed as following one of three patterns: (a) withdrawal, (b) anger and hostility, (c) combinations of these two.

Withdrawal is manifested by loss of interest in the surrounding world, sometimes accompanied by intense preoccupation with an inner phantasy life. As patients withdraw in this way they lose interest in social functions such as work responsibilities, housekeeping functions, and ordinary social obligations. Interest in personal appearance, dress, bodily cleanliness and toilet also decline. In the end comes the standard picture of the deteriorated, dilapidated, unresponsive, soiling, helpless, vegetative creature who in former times inhabited our mental hospitals' back wards.

The pattern of anger and hostility is manifested by expressions of resentfulness, quarrelsomeness, and hostility. When more advanced along this path the patient may accuse others of intent to harm him and become physically aggressive and assaultive. He may turn his wrath upon physical objects and become destructive of windows, furniture, or household fixtures; or his wrath may become directed at himself and this may lead to self-mutilating activities or outright suicide.

In those instances where the pattern pursued mixes tendencies to withdraw and tendencies toward hostility and anger, combinations of the features of both paths may appear. In addition, there is a way of withdrawing aggressively by distortions of the usual responsiveness to other people, for example, by stubbornly echoing whatever anyone else says, by assuming bizarre poses of body position or speech patterns, by odd gesticulations, and so forth. These modes of response avoid the "nonresponsiveness" of pure withdrawal and the overt expressions of resentment such as cursing and striking out, while effectively preventing real personal contact and indirectly expressing resentment or enmity.

The Dutchess County Experiment

Experience had shown that the chronic social breakdown syndrome's frequency depends upon the social setting and the way other people and social institutions and medical facilities respond to the underlying disorders.[11] The first U.S. program to implement these ideas in the postdrug era was launched in Dutchess County, New York, in 1959.

Dr. Robert C. Hunt, then director of the Hudson River State Hospital, stated during 1959 that "our present methods are not very effective in preventing or curing the psychotic illnesses, but we do now have the tools to attack the associated disability. We can relieve much of the disability which has already occurred; we can prevent its future occurrence and minimize its extent."[12] He pointed to

a tradition in our society of almost automatically hospitalizing persons with psychoses; also a tradition and current practice of not using community psychiatric facilities for the seriously ill. It sometimes appears that the richer a community is in its health, welfare and psychiatric facilities—as in large metropolitan centers—the more difficult it is to bring them to bear to help the seriously ill person.

These factors were considered first even though "Hospitalization as such is among the causes of disability. This is especially true of the traditional, highly security conscious hospital." What was needed was "flexible continuity of care for the individual patients" by undoing "specialistic compartmentation," which fragments patient care.

The major hypothesis to be tested in this pilot program is that chronic hospitalization and disability can be reduced by supplying the population with a comprehensive psychiatric service based upon a small community-oriented, open public mental hospital so organized that there is maximum continuity of care over both inpatient and outpatient phases of treatment.[12]

It was implemented by organizing what is now the oldest geographically decentralized county unit in a state hospital. "This is simply a new method of organizing and administering present services with nothing particularly new in the services themselves."[12] The one new function, which is precare, is an emergency psychiatric consultation service to the community.

Those who commonly initiate moves toward hospital admission, such as physicians and police, are encouraged to first give us a call when they have a patient for whom admission is contemplated. A consultant can often give better service to the patient without hospitalization, by recommending certain treatment measures to the family physician, by referral to a psychiatrist or clinic, by placement in a nursing home, or by admission for day or night hospital treatment . . . patients who are admitted for full-time hospital care will, through this advance medical contact, have a healthier relationship with the staff and make greater use of voluntary admission procedures.[12]

It was hoped that this reorganization of services would result in less long-term hospitalization and less chronic deterioration.

⟨ The Research

The prevention of long-term hospitalization was to be achieved through encouraging the reorganized system of psychiatric service delivery to release patients before full recovery and to maintain these patients in the community unless need for rehospitalization would initially become less common through the shift in policy. If long-term hospitalization was not reduced in frequency, it would be postponed. In any case, its measurement presented no problem, and in fact it did become less common.[19]

The measurement of long-term deterioration presented much more difficult problems. First, since the mechanism for preventing long-term deterioration included encouragement of early releases, it was necessary to plan studies not only on patients currently in hospital but also on all former patients. Second, deterioration, though a dramatic enough phenomenon when observed in the mental hospital, was not clearly and objectively defined.

In order to execute that aspect of the research, lengthy discussions were held with those who had faith that the new system would make a difference in deterioration.[4] Their ideas regarding deterioration could be broken down into two general areas: disturbance and function loss. In order to test this hypothesis research techniques were developed with a questionnaire for ascertaining cases of deterioration covering sixteen areas. (See Table 47–2.) To conduct systematic research it was necessary to specify what bad functioning was in terms that could be recognized both in the mental hospital and in a patient living at home.[8,10] Because the researchable, hopefully preventable, condition was more precisely conceptualized than the older, broader term "deterioration," the newly specified condition was called "social breakdown syndrome" after the American Public Health Association 1962 publication.

In order to conduct the research, exact criteria were needed to specify whether or not a particular person was deteriorated in functioning at a particular time. It was necessary to define the behavior that would be regarded as illustrating each of the sixteen actions itemized in Table 47–2 in a repeatable, reliable way, not relying on the varying judgment of each data gatherer regarding each phrase's meaning. Selecting the ascertainable items and specific manifestations of severity required much pilot work. Making such rules is a time-consuming operation; training people to follow the rules takes a week or two; supervising their work and keeping the standards consistent require time and skill.[2] The criteria used were objective and left little room for variation due to observer differences. These detailed criteria can only be mastered through demonstration of the rules in concrete instances.

The data showed that symptom formation and symptom continuation were highly dependent on the social organization of treatment services and on staff and community attitudes. Several findings contribute greatly to understanding the social breakdown syndrome's characteristics.

It occurs in many different psychiatric conditions. Many cases occur outside the hospital. The 1963 prevalence of social breakdown syndrome (see Table 47–1) associated with a psychosis was 1.5 per 1,000, ages sixteen to sixty-four, in the whole population. The number of new chronic (over one year) episodes beginning each year dropped about 50 percent between 1960 and 1963.[6] This was the first demonstration that service reorganization can lower any disorder's frequency in the population for whom the delivery of services was reorganized.

This practical demonstration confirmed by evaluation research calls for a new theory about symptom pathogenesis to explain why reorganization prevents chronic social breakdown syndrome. This theory must explain why this way of organizing psychiatric services is associated with less chronic social breakdown syndrome than another.

◖ Social Breakdown Syndrome Manifestations

People working in these new community-care programs are often not aware that they are applying new and better ways of organizing

TABLE 47–2.

DISTURBED BEHAVIOR	SOCIALLY INTEGRATED BEHAVIOR
1. Danger of self-damage	1. Being away from the ward
2. Self-destructive acts	2. Making money
3. Control of physical movement	3. Work assignment
4. Disturbing noisiness	4. Occupational therapy
5. Resisting meals	5. Reading or writing
6. Soiling	6. Recreation
7. Not speaking	7. Having money
8. Help arising and dressing	
9. Help going to bed	

treatment, but think they are implementing changes brought about since 1955 by the tranquilizing drugs. These new drugs do make it easier to care for psychotic patients, both because they directly affect the patient's behavior and because they have a placebo effect on the staffs administering them. Both the pre-drug pilot programs of community care and the postdrug experiences at Graylingwell, Plymouth, Fort Logan, and Dutchess County showed very similar results. Reorganization without drugs showed major improvements. Drugs without reorganization sometimes show little improvement.[20] We can infer two types of symptoms from these findings: the direct consequences of mental disorder and the secondary complications whose appearance and continuation depend on circumstances and are apparently preventable. Those secondary manifestations that are mainly prevented by using the best systems of care we call the "social breakdown syndrome."[5]

Manifestations and Course

The social breakdown syndrome can be manifested by a wide range of overt disturbed behavior. Withdrawal, self-neglect, dangerous behavior, shouting, self-harm, failure to work, and failure to enjoy recreation are the main manifestations. Either troublesome behavior or functional performance deficit may predominate. Each type occurs separately or in conjunction with the other. Severity ranges widely. (Hallucinations, confusion, phobias, and other subjective experience were not included in the studies because, first, many patients in improved programs describe these symptoms and, second, the field study techniques developed could not systematically investigate subjective experiences. Their exclusion did not prejudge the possibility that these too may often be secondary manifestations in the same sense, readily modified by the social environment and therefore properly regarded as manifestations of the social breakdown syndrome.)

At present, under the best conditions, almost all SBS episodes end within a few weeks, and episodes lasting for months are very rare.

The onset is sometimes insidious, the course indolent, and the end the vegetative state described in textbooks. More commonly, onset occurs in a single, explosive leap, beginning with violent behavior or the sudden termination of all ordinary social roles, often accompanied by a confused or clouded state. About two-thirds of the episodes start outside the hospital. Spontaneous remission often occurs in days or weeks without admission or any treatment. Other cases progress for a while and then arrest for a long period at a particular stage, which is sometimes followed by recovery. Some other cases pursue a remitting course. First episodes and relapses show similar patterns. It is instinctive to compare these course patterns with those described for schizophrenia by Bleuler. (See Chapter 30, "The Epidemiology of Schizophrenia.")

SBS occurs among psychiatric inpatients and in people in need of hospital admission. The syndrome usually begins outside the hospital, its components being the common justifications for admission "incapable of caring for himself," "dangerous to self or others." Thus, the social breakdown syndrome describes the severe burdens the community experiences in dealing with these individuals, and these burdens account for the decision to extrude them from the community. SBS also describes common reasons for keeping a patient in the hospital, an indication that hospital admission does not always terminate SBS.

Social Breakdown Syndrome Pathogenesis

A pathogenesis of chronic SBS can be postulated. Seven steps lead to the chronically deteriorated picture formerly seen in the back wards of mental hospitals. The social breakdown syndrome describes the way in which the relationship between a person and his social environment breaks down. The syndrome seems to emerge as a result of a spiraling crescendo of interactions between the patient and the people in his immediate social environment.

1. The push, common in ordinary life, consists in a discrepancy between what a person

can do and what he is expected to do. Such discrepancies are ordinarily transient: They are eliminated by a change in performance, by escaping from the demanding environment, by a change in environmental demands, or by an explanation that relieves the individual of the responsibility for the discrepancy.

2. Heightened suggestibility. When the discrepancy persists, the failing individual on whom the demand is being placed is held responsible for his failure to perform as demanded. The individual and those making the demand agree about his responsibility. He wonders what is wrong with him. A diffuse uncertainty regarding his own nature and value system develops and produces hesitancy or impulsiveness (or both). He has become more dependent on current cues from the environment regarding right and wrong. This increased sense of uncertainty about himself, his values, and his customary ways of dealing with life produce a readiness to consider new ways of doing things, new ways of looking at things, new ways of looking at himself. This is the precondition for constructive changes in attitude and behavior that, when the environment is suitable, leads to corrective modifications of functioning. Every psychotherapist, every army sergeant, and every job supervisor has seen this process; such behavioral modifications are part of normal life. But inability to modify his behavior in the expected way creates a special danger when the individual accepts the environment's expectations.

A common way to deny that the expectations are appropriate is to conclude that those making the demands on the individual have misunderstood his true nature: They are asking something appropriate, but they are asking it of the wrong kind of person. He decides that for this task he is too young, too old, too short, too tall, too blind, too crippled, or too ignorant to be expected to do what was asked. The failing individual's sense of responsibility for his failure to comply with the demands is relieved, and since he no longer holds himself responsible for the discrepancy these explanations can be called "exculpating." (As will emerge below, the discovery of suitable exculpating explanations can play a large role in

preventing chronic SBS.) When the discrepancy between environmental demand and individual performance is not terminated that way, the individual takes an unsatisfactory step to rectify the situation. But this only arouses fears or resentment, further putting him out of gear with the people around him. This produces an increased need to satisfy increasingly urgent demands. But his response to this still more tense situation has the opposite effect, resulting in still more misunderstanding and hostility. This process of action reaction, reaction to the reaction, and reaction to that goes on either toward an explosion and social extrusion of the individual or toward his progressive withdrawal from interaction, and hence from his usual roles and functions. This is when the social breakdown syndrome begins.

3. Labeling. He is then labeled as "crazy" or otherwise not right in the head, leading to a vague or rejecting diagnosis, such as schizophrenic or psychotic or just plain mentally ill, and to the recommendation that he be sent to the hospital.

4. Extrusion. Admission to the hospital can itself contribute to the further development of the social breakdown syndrome. Formal legal commitment is most damaging with its petitioning mechanism by which those closest to the prospective patient join with the community establishment to engage in the labeling and rejection process.

5. Institutionalization. An overly sheltering hospital environment can further exacerbate the social breakdown syndrome. In his community, he may have been expected to do things he could not do, but in the old-fashioned hospital he is expected to do nothing except what he was told to do (or, of course, to try to run away). Whatever the patient's behavior, no one expresses surprise. He is called sick and is told that he must be cared for. Thus he is morally relieved of responsibility for his failures at the price of being identified as having a condition that makes his own impulses, thoughts, and speech largely irrelevant to any practical activities of daily life.

6. Compliance and isolation. The social

breakdown syndrome progresses another step when the patient, though still viewing himself as different from the other patients, complies with the older type of hospital's rules of accepted behavior to stay out of trouble. He becomes isolated from his former ties. The family is told that everything necessary will be done by the staff; visiting is restricted to a few hours; staff members familiar with the patient's case are often unavailable to the family.

7. Identification. Next the patient comes to identify with fellow patients, anticipate staff demands, "fit in," and become a "good patient." Sometimes he fits into one of the available rebellious roles for which the hospital is equally prepared. In time, whatever his former capacities were, his ability to carry out ordinary social exchanges and work tasks decreases and becomes awkward from disuse. The end of this process is most readily seen in the mental hospital's chronic wards.

(Prevention of Chronic Social Breakdown Syndrome

Even the best psychiatric service cannot today prevent all onsets of social breakdown syndrome because often it arises before the individual becomes a patient. Prevention of onsets may, in fact, be occurring among chronic patients, but no research data on this phenomenon are available at present.

Chronic SBS is prevented today by encouraging early recovery from episodes after they start (secondary prevention). The reform in practices regarding encouragement of early voluntary admissions to inpatient services is probably having such an effect. The fashion for early release, facilitated by the tranquilizing and antidepressant drugs, is also probably having this effect. Even the early releases produced by hard-nosed budget-cutting may have this effect in general in spite of inadequate aftercare; but if it is benefiting some patients by preventing chronic SBS it is seriously endangering others who are grossly neglected.

In addition to these preventive activities, which are going on for various reasons, the unified clinical team staff member is in a position to do many things to facilitate early recovery from a SBS episode.

When a patient presents the early manifestations of the social breakdown syndrome, or appears tense and fearful that he will lose control and either withdraw or become violent, the psychiatrist, or other professional, might do well to try to locate the nature of the demands the patient is unable to meet.

The internalized demand for a performance that the patient cannot carry out is rarely conspicuous. The patient does not see the conflict consciously. Clinicians do not usually focus on it, so they rarely enter the relevant facts in the medical record. Occasionally, however, the relevant facts are recorded, and then a reader of the record can identify this demand-performance conflict. The following brief summary of one such case throws light on three issues: (1) how the demand-performance conflict develops and is responded to; (2) how the patient's struggles in this conflict tend to bring his attempts at solution to the surface and how the consequent symptom formation attracts the clinician's attention; and (3) how the orderly response by a clinical team operating in a unified service helps lead to the social breakdown syndrome's early termination.[*]

A laboratory scientist was admitted to the mental hospital from a general hospital emergency room where he had been brought in a distraught state following an altercation with his children, the oldest of whom he threatened to throw out of the window. The argument began immediately after the patient had come home after he was discharged from a commercial salesmen's training program he had been attending. It was the first day of the training program. He had verbally abused the instructor in front of the class, passionately lecturing him on his dishonest attempt to brainwash the students into misrepresenting the firm's product when selling it. "Liar, thief, reprobate" were the burden of his accusation, but the wording and tone were much more

---

* The assistance of my associate, Danielle Turns, in locating such a psychiatric record and in developing the necessary camouflage is gratefully acknowledged.

abusive. Forcibly removed from the class-room, he was sent home, an unemployed trainee salesman.

This episode ended six months of trying to find work after having been included in a mass layoff. A rigid person with high stan-dards for his own performance at work and as a husband, he could not accept the much lower-status salesman role. But neither could he reject it as it represented his first work op-portunity in half a year.

This demand performance conflict's impor-tance was intensified by the fact that, after the mass layoff and during the period on welfare, his wife had lost interest in him and devel-oped interest in someone else. In addition, one of his relatives near his own age had long been a competitor for the position of family success. Although the competitor made more money, our man was in an adequate position so long as he was a professional in contrast to the nonprofessional supersalesman.

Our man took steps to rectify his situation: He tried to define those making the demands on him as not entitled to respect (the instruc-tor), but this maneuver only served to arouse fears putting him further out of gear with the people around him. This produced an in-creased urgency regarding his unsuccessful role as breadwinner and household head. His response to this tense situation was apparently to define his oldest son as unsuitable for mem-bership in the family. This led to increased hostility and also fear, which brought him to the general hospital admitting room following the explosion with his son. He was extruded from the household.

On arrival the complaint was not a demand performance contradiction but his bellicose behavior. The staff's diagnostic formulation referred to a schizophrenic psychosis and their treatment recommendation was tranquilizing medication and open-ward care. The bellicose behavior disappeared almost immediately on arrival at the hospital, and within a few weeks the patient was home again.

Since the episode of SBS behavior stopped abruptly we may ask how the demand per-formance conflict was resolved. Performance was clearly unimproved. But the troublesome

behavior was explained by the presence of a sickness, and this sick role also removed our man from the demand that he perform as had previously been expected, at least for the present. This cannot be done without paying some price, and this man had to pay in several ways. Being defined as mentally ill does not enhance self-respect or the respect of others, but the fact that the disorder was described as responsive to known treatments minimized this effect. Though frightened by the events, he and his family were sufficiently reassured regarding the prognosis so that the latter could supply some encouragement after he left the hospital and all could recognize that his unemployment in a bad market was not entirely his doing. The assurance that the clin-ical staff's interest would not end with release from the hospital further helped the patient and family to bring out whatever healthy functioning he could muster.

The initiation into the sick role was done in a way that aborted his severely disturbed be-havior and extreme subjective distress. Not only were the old mistakes—encouraging community rejection and impersonal admis-sion procedures—avoided, but there was an active constructive use of medical authority (to borrow a phrase T. P. Rees often used). Such constructive use of medical authority is the opposite of permissiveness because it iden-tifies the complained about behavior as unac-ceptable, insists that the patient can stop it (with help), defines his problem as a sickness requiring medical care, and takes on responsi-bility for terminating his condition (with the patient's cooperation). This was done in a manner to strengthen the family ties, not weaken them.

To understand how the staff's actions helped abort this episode, the actions must be viewed as forms of communication that alter the patient's view of himself and his relation-ships and alter the family's view of him. The relevant communications were implicit in the actions taken, not explicitly worded. Concern about the patient's behavior was taken seri-ously; questions to ensure understanding of the complaints reinforced the serious attitude. The inner distress and the belligerence were not denied or ignored but explicitly accepted as grounds for concern and as justifying special help. They did not indicate his worthlessness or undesirability but his need for help in dealing with a condition that he did not bring on himself and that the clinical staff would work on (but only with his cooperation). He needed treatment; he accepted treatment; and he accepted the transfer to the nearby mental hospital. (The legal compulsion of a health officer's certificate was used but could probably have been avoided, particularly if the mental hospital doctor had gone to the emergency room for a precare consultation. This would have lessened the damage to self-respect caused by the use of compulsion.) As soon as he arrived at the mental hospital, he saw his psychiatrist who spent time with him and with the family before going to the open ward. The psychiatrist told the family, in the patient's presence, that they could visit at any time and that he would likely be home in a short time. These steps rapidly redefined his situation in a hopeful way. By prescribing drugs to reduce tension and assure sleep the first night, the doctor further asserted his medical authority and responsibility, defined the complaints as due to something the doctor could be expected to know about and could help, and relieved any notions that the patient was responsible for his condition and therefore for his failures. The drugs' efficacy as predicted enhanced the validity of all these messages. Guilt and fears about his behavior were quickly reduced; he began to feel responsible at once; and his family was able to acknowledge their affection for him and to look forward to his hoped for early recovery.

This man will, of course, continue to be in trouble after he leaves the hospital. The wife apparently thought that "for better or for worse" did not oblige her to remain loyal when the labor market turned worse; she was not likely to become more loyal when "in sickness and in health" came to mean in sickness. He left her. A man so preoccupied with the outward symbols of success is not going to find it easy to adapt to a world in which the supersalesman is outrunning the competent professional in earning these symbols. He may

well need another period of inpatient care (he did).

But the quick resolution of the crisis must be recognized as an accomplishment, freeing him to struggle with these more longstanding problems. The method used was to modify expectations as indicated above, and the means used to modify these expectations were adherence to some old valuable clinical rituals in the needed way and under organizational conditions that gave them maximum effect. Careful attention to eliciting and recording the complaint and a complete and thorough present illness history are this ritual's main features. Attention to the complaint reinforces the notion that those making the complaint know what they are talking about and that the clinician regards it as a legitimate basis for going further. Taking the history implicitly questions any theories regarding cause expressed while stating the complaint and further asserts the medical authority to question and expect answers so as to relate this person's story to the doctor's prior experience with other patients. Such a history always involves asking about symptoms not present, and this suggests that things could have been worse.

This initial examination itself involves so many crucial transactions that the process can redefine the problem and the clinician's relationship to it to such an extent that the crisis atmosphere dissipates and a treatment plan begins. Precare consultations have been done in Dutchess County, New York, since 1960 by Dr. C. L. Bennett and his associates for patients referred as possible mental hospital admissions. In about two-thirds of the precare consultations a skillful clinician can define the patient's problem in such a way that alternative treatment forms can be arranged: outpatient treatment, day hospital treatment, social work family counseling, or advice to a general practitioner. In almost all of the other third, the patient has voluntarily entered the hospital phase of treatment before the consultation is over.[7]

At present, these are the mechanisms apparently being used to terminate incipient or new social breakdown syndrome cases. Whether a more conscious attention to the nature of the contradiction between the demands being put on the patient and his capacity to perform would lead to a more efficient and effective termination of these episodes cannot be said with certainty until some clinical groups try it. In reviewing a recent group of consecutive cases, the social breakdown syndrome stopped within two weeks of entering treatment in more than half the cases, yet only a few could tell what the contradiction between performance and demand was, and even in those, these contradictions did not enter into any clinician's recorded formulation of the case.

These preventive measures may be contrasted with what would have happened to a man with a similar episode when the 1930 depression began. After shouting at the teacher perhaps, but certainly after trying to eject his child from the window, the police would have brought him before a magistrate for an involuntary commitment. His wife and perhaps other relatives would have been urgently pressed to sign a petition begging relief from responsibility for his care and for the court to arrange care and treatment in a mental hospital. His admission would have started with a brief perfunctory contact with an admitting psychiatrist whose main preoccupation would have been with the state of the papers ordering the admission, and this would have passed through half a dozen people's hands in as many hours in order to process him into the hospital. During this whole period he would encounter no one with a substantive interest in his complaint or his view of it: fingerprinting, searching for scars and recording them, a rectal temperature, a compulsory X-ray, routine blood tests, inventory of property, a shower, and a switch to institutional clothing would all take priority. It might be several days before a psychiatrist sat down to take a history. It would usually be weeks before this initial clinical evaluation was reviewed through two echelons and finally reached the clinical director who would have to decide the diagnosis and treatment plan. All prior judgments would have been temporary. How would our patient have reacted to all this? We do not know enough to say, and we would not know

enough even if we were thoroughly acquainted with him and his mental status. But it is reasonable to suspect that the people whom M. Bleuler describes as pursuing the catastrophic course in a proportion of schizophrenic admissions prior to 1942 were not very different from him. (See Chapter 30, "The Epidemiology of Schizophrenia".)

Unified Clinical Teams

The preventive measures described are most easily executed when a single professional team takes comprehensive responsibility for the whole course of treatment: precare, inpatient care in an open hospital that minimizes restraint and legal coercion, and aftercare. This unified clinical team needs close ties with the whole complex of community services and access to a full psychiatric service (inpatient, outpatient, and transitional forms of treatment). Even today such a unified clinical team operation is rare.

Many communities in the United States currently offer services that include the five elements making up the comprehensive services required for federal funding of community mental health centers: inpatient services, outpatient services, emergency services, partial hospitalization, and consultation and education. But these elements are usually run by separate clinical teams.

Despite proliferation of such comprehensive mental health services, many people with severe mental disorders needlessly become chronically deteriorated in their social functioning because no single team is able to follow them throughout the entire course of their illnesses. Besides being concerned with treating the patients' mental disorders, the team must focus on the mission of preventing the chronic social breakdown syndrome.

No amount of coordination or working integration of fragmented clinical teams, each working in its own service, can be expected to overcome the fact that clinicians working in these fragmented teams will have to make decisions on insufficient information. It is obvious that they will not know enough about what the other clinical team would wish to do. It is obvious that the new clinical team will take time to learn about what was going on during the earlier period, even though some administrators are cleverly using office reproduction equipment so that records can get to them quickly. What is not obvious is that in our present state of ignorance no clinical team can have confidence regarding how the patient will make out in the next service; this arises from the unpredictability of the course of the chronic mental disorders. "Unpredictability" means we do not know enough to make predictions with any degree of confidence. Our state of knowledge in this matter is not any better than the weather predictor's ability to tell us about tomorrow's rain or sunshine. While pursuing efforts to learn more we can protect our patients optimally by making decisions tentatively and letting those familiar with the patient and his prior responses continue to care for him. And why not? Because of some mistaken ideas that it is inefficient to have clinicians working in more than one location. This arbitrary concept of efficiency will cost many man years of serious deterioration in our mental patients.[9,17]

Stanton correctly said, "I believe that statements like patients should be outside if they can be, or they should be kept out, or they should be gotten out, are stated uncritically." We can agree that the generalization that "It's better to be out of the hospital than in the hospital whenever possible, under all conditions," is nonsensical. Two contrasting models are current in the literature. In one, the mental hospital is seen as incorrigibly bad, nothing but damaging, and therefore every possible means should be used to keep people out and, once in, to get them out rapidly. The other model is that the mental hospital has never been static at any point in its history, has always been changing, has developed some patterns of excessive retention but can be transformed into an acute service with specific goals for each admission and can work in close conjunction and as an intimate part of comprehensive community service (when its physical location is appropriate). In the first model, a return to the hospital is seen as a failure of the release. If the patient is released from the hospital and comes back again within a year it is seen as a failure to set up an adequate community treatment program for him. In the second model, where the hospital is seen as an active and integral part of the community program, readmissions are expected and are part of the release plans. In fact, you can only release patients properly into the community in certain mental states when the hospital really is highly accessible for unpredictable as well as some predictable needs to return. The therapeutic community inpatient service and the revolving-door inpatient service, run as part of a unified clinical team's resources, relate the hospital's resources to the patients in entirely different ways. To make the whole life of the hospital part of a therapeutic experience for the patient, as developed by Max Jones, extends the milieu treatment concept into something much more dynamic and structured, creating an intensively planned set of relationships for each patient to work through. However, if the hospital is used for acute, intermittent care of psychotic patients with specific indications at certain stages of the disorder as part of a community-care treatment program, admission should not integrate the patients into hospital life. A therapeutic community in a hospital cannot provide quick rotation, revolving-door service. The two types of service interfere with each other. The therapeutic community involves patients in many aspects of hospital life—ward activities, patient government, and so on. It has unique advantages in changing attitudes and behavior.[13,18] But the revolving-door pattern deals with the patient's problems much in the way that a general hospital deals with such episodes as cardiac decompensation or appendicitis: The hospital is a special place to go to for a short period, for specific purposes. These patients interact with the rest of the hospital and the other patients only to the extent that it is necessary to get through the few days, or week or two, that they are there. An acute service should not be operated as a therapeutic community, nor should a therapeutic community be used to deal with the problems of acute decompensations in long-term community-care patients.

Hospitalization in a good community-care program has five main uses.

1. To provide a treatment that cannot safely be given on an outpatient basis, for example, to give a dangerous drug requiring continuous observation for safe administration, to adjust drug dosages where outpatient treatment would be unduly hazardous, or for electroshock treatments.

2. To protect the patient from his own uncontrolled dangerous impulses or the consequences of self-neglect, namely, the old legal justification for involuntary certification, that the patient is a danger to himself or others.

3. To remove a person temporarily from an environmental stress during a period when he cannot cope with the stress or cannot be helped to cope with it successfully.

4. To temporarily relieve the patient's associates who are managing to live with him but at significant costs to themselves, which include the loss of the caretakers' free time and the emotional energy mortgaged from other potential forms of emotional investment.

5. To communicate two ideas: (1) that the patient's difficulties are because of sickness and (2) that the hospital is available to the patient and to his family for assistance while living with a chronic incurable disorder (but not as an unloading clinic).

❨ Conclusions

A practical finding—that certain deteriorated behavior patterns of people with psychoses are prevented by altered systems of delivering psychiatric services with consequent changes in staff attitudes and practices—drew attention to the fact that this syndrome occurs in people with many different mental disorders. Hence, this syndrome is not inherent to the mental disorders, but is a secondary, modifiable syndrome. What was once looked on as the strongest evidence of the presence of certain psychoses became evidence of sociogenic secondary complications. (See Chapter 30, "The Epidemiology of Schizophrenia.") Much of this syndrome's pathogenesis and progress can be understood in terms of interactions between a patient and those around him.

❨ Bibliography

1. AMERICAN PUBLIC HEALTH ASSOCIATION PROGRAM AREA COMMITTEE ON MENTAL HEALTH. *Mental Disorders: A Guide to Control Methods.* New York: American Public Health Association, 1962.

2. GRUENBERG, E. M. "A Population Study of Disability from Mental Disorders." *Annals of the New York Academy of Sciences,* 107, no. 2 (1963), 587–595.

3. ———. "Evaluating the Effectiveness of Community Mental Health Services." *Milbank Memorial Fund Quarterly,* 44, no. 1 (1966), pt. 2.

4. ———. "Can the Reorganization of Psychiatric Services Prevent Some Cases of Social Breakdown?" In A. B. Stokes, ed., *Psychiatry in Transition, 1966–67.* Toronto: University of Toronto Press, 1967. Pp. 95–109.

5. ———. "From Practice to Theory: Community Mental Health Services and the Nature of Psychoses." *Lancet,* 1969, pp. 721–724.

6. ———, ed. *Evaluating the Effectiveness of Community Mental Health Services.* New York: Mental Health Materials Center, 1968. P. 402.

7. ———, BENNETT, C. L., and SNOW, H. B. "Preventing the Social Breakdown Syndrome." In *Social Psychiatry.* A.R.N.M.D. research publication, no. 47. 1969. Pp. 179–195.

8. ———, BRANDON, S., and KASIUS, R. V. "Identifying Cases of Social Breakdown Syndrome." In E. M. Gruenberg, ed., *Evaluating the Effectiveness of Community Mental Health Services.* New York: Mental

Health Materials Center, 1968. Pp. 150–155.

9. ———, and HUXLEY, J. "Mental Health Services Can Be Organized to Prevent Chronic Disability." *Community Mental Health Journal*, 6 (1970), 431–436.

10. ———, KASIUS, R. V., and HUXLEY, M. "Objective Appraisal of Deterioration in a Group of Long-Stay Hospital Patients." *Milbank Memorial Fund Quarterly*, 40 (1962), 90–100.

11. HOCH, P. H., HUNT, R. C., SNOW, H. B., PLEASURE, H., O'NEILL, F. J., TERRENCE, C. F., and BECKENSTEIN, N. "Observations on the British 'Open' Hospitals." *Mental Hospitals*, 8 (1957), 5–15.

12. HUNT, R. C., GRUENBERG, E. M., HACKEN, E., and HUXLEY, M. "A Comprehensive Hospital-Community Service in a State Hospital." *American Journal of Psychiatry*, 117 (1961), 817–821.

13. LAMBERT, R., and MILLHAM, S. *The Hothouse Society: An Exploration of Boarding School Life Through the Boys' and Girls' Own Writings*. London: Weidenfeld & Nicolson, 1968.

14. MACMILLAN, D. "Hospital-Community Relationships." *Mental Hospitals*, 8, no. 1 (1957), 29–50.

15. MILBANK MEMORIAL FUND. *An Approach to the Prevention of Disability from Chronic Psychoses: Part I. The Open Mental Hospital within the Community*. New York, 1958.

16. ———. *Steps in the Development of Integrated Psychiatric Services*. New York, 1960.

17. ———. "Mental Hospitals Join the Community: Proceedings of a Round Table and of a Work Shop at the 39th Conference of the Milbank Memorial Fund." *Milbank Memorial Fund Quarterly*, 42 (1964).

18. MODLIN, H. C., GIBSON, R. W., GRUENBERG, E. M., STANTON, A. H., and WILL, O. A., Jr. "Panel Discussion on Hospital Treatment." In R. Cancro, ed., *The Schizophrenic Reactions: A Critique of the Concept, Hospital Treatment, and Current Research*. New York: Bruner/Mazel, 1970. Pp. 168–185.

19. PATTON, R. E. "Record of Mental Hospitalization of Dutchess County Residents." In E. M. Gruenberg, ed., *Evaluating the Effectiveness of Community Mental Health Services*. New York: Mental Health Materials Center, 1968. Pp. 124–128.

20. SMITH, T. C., BOWER, W. H., and WIGNALL, C. M. "Influence of Policy and Drugs on Colorado State Hospital Population." *Archives of General Psychiatry*, 12 (1965), 352–362.

21. STANTON, A. H. "Indications for Hospital Admission of Schizophrenia Patients: Some Sociopsychiatric Considerations." In R. Cancro, ed., *The Schizophrenic Reactions: A Critique of the Concept, Hospital Treatment, and Current Research*. New York: Brunner/Mazel, 1970. Pp. 137–152.

22. ZUSMAN, J. "Some Explanations of the Changing Appearance of Psychotic Patients: Antecedents of the Social Breakdown Syndrome Concept." *Mental Hospitals*, 8, no. 4 (1957), 363–364.

CHAPTER 48

PROGRAMS TO CONTROL ALCOHOLISM

Morris E. Chafetz and Harold W. Demone, Jr.

BEFORE DISCUSSING the programs necessary to control alcoholism, a definition of the problem will be provided. As is the case in so many behavioral-social-psychological areas, definitions are primarily descriptive rather than causal. Nowhere is this more true than in the field of alcoholism.

The literature is replete with alternative definitions. In 1955, the World Health Organization[25] suggested that alcoholism "is a collective term for a 'family of problems' related to alcohol," with symptoms described as " 'craving' . . . ; 'withdrawal' . . . ; 'loss of control.' " Jellinek,[8] in 1960, defined alcoholism as "any use of alcoholic beverages that causes any damage to the individual or society or both." Keller,[11] in 1962, in meeting the criteria for public health purposes (that is, identification of alcoholic populations for epidemi-

ological study and control) defined alcoholism as "a chronic disease manifested by repeated implicative drinking so as to cause injury to the drinker's health or to his social or economic functioning." Chafetz and Demone,[5] in 1962, offered both a descriptive and etiological definition:

We define alcoholism as a chronic behavioral disorder which is manifested by undue preoccupation with alcohol to the detriment of physical and mental health, by a loss of control when drinking has begun (although it may not be carried to the point of intoxication) and by a self-destructive attitude in dealing with personal relationships and life situations. Alcoholism, we believe, is the result of disturbance and deprivation in early infantile experience and the related alterations in basic physiochemical responsiveness; the identification by the alcoholic with significant figures who deal with life problems through the excessive use of alcohol; and a sociocultural milieu which causes ambivalence, conflict, and guilt in the use of alcohol.

With the uncertainty of definition, it logically follows that epidemiological data will have wide variance. Based on the Jellinek formula, for many years the estimated alcoholic population of the United States was considered to be 4.5 million. More recently, estimates based on a national interview sample[3] suggest an "alcoholic population" in excess of 9 million. Of this population only 5 percent fall into the highly visible skid-row derelict model; the remainder are employed or employable, mostly family-centered individuals.

Whatever the number and definition, it is clear that the population directly involved is substantial, and as a nation, we are ill prepared to cope with the problem. Collectively, the effects are staggering.

([Extent and Distribution of Alcoholism and Alcohol Problems

It has been estimated[24] that more than 40 percent of all arrests, either in a public place or while driving, are for drunkenness. Out of 5 million arrests made in our nation during 1964, it is reported that more than 1,535,000 were for public drunkenness, 250,000 were for driving while intoxicated, and 500,000 involved alcohol-related offenses.

The 1968 *Alcohol and Highway Safety Report*[16] concluded that "alcohol contributes to about 25,000 of the approximately 53,000 fatal highway injuries in the United States annually (1966 and 1967)." The National Safety Council[15] estimated that alcohol plays a role in 6 percent of the 14 million run of the mill crashes that occur in the country each year and that cause disabling injuries.

Alcoholism as a cause of death (including cirrhosis of liver with alcoholism, alcoholic psychosis, and so on) annually appears on more than 13,000 death certificates.[14]

For 1968, out of 140,000 total male admis-

sions diagnosed as alcoholic to psychiatric inpatient services, 59,000 were admitted to state and county mental hospitals, 40,000 to general hospitals and 29,000 to Veterans Administration hospitals, and 6,000 to private mental hospitals and federally funded community mental health centers.[22]

The cost to the nation may be as high as $15 billion each year: $10 billion in lost work time, considering only the employed alcoholics; $2 billion in health and welfare costs, incurred by alcoholics and their families; and $3 billion in property damage, wage losses, and the like associated with traffic accidents. In addition, based on a conservative national estimate, [19] there are such costs as $100 million plus for police, court, and penal costs for the drunkenness arrests; health and welfare expenditures on behalf of alcohol abuse come to $300 million plus, of which only $85.5 million is directly programmed for rehabilitative care for the alcoholic population.

To these must be added the human cost of broken homes, deserted families, and the countless psychological problems common in children of alcoholic parents. It has been estimated that the life expectancy of alcoholics is about ten to twelve years less than the average.[7] And, through the alcoholic's impact on his family, the tragedy of death and disability related to alcohol abuse affects, at a minimum, one of every six Americans.

([Self-Help Movements

In any examination of programs aimed at controlling alcoholism, Alcoholics Anonymous must head the list. The Alcoholics Anonymous movement was created in a cauldron of despair, neglect, and desperation manifested in the persons of an alcoholic physician and an alcoholic stockbroker during a chance meeting in Akron, Ohio, in 1935. The prevailing influence of the Oxford and Washingtonian group movements is acknowledged and documented in all the historical descriptions of Alcoholics Anonymous. But Alcoholics Anonymous's determination to succeed was evidenced by the founders' determination to focus only on alcoholism rather than the broader social goals espoused by the two older organizations. The movement's drive for anonymity, to preclude the development of personality cults, and its single-minded focus on alcoholic persons, have made it a powerful and effective program. It does not allow for diffusion of energy into political or social causes. A.A. is almost a nonorganization; the program is the organization. In a sense, therefore, the banding together of alcoholics under the A.A. banner is a living example of a participant democratic procedure. It is the model for all self-help groups. There exists a general service board, consisting mainly of nonalcoholics, plus members. The board functions to sustain integrity and services of the general service headquarters. The headquarters is the common linkage to Alcoholics Anonymous groups all over the world. Although there is a general service conference charter, the conference is unincorporated; the charter is not a legal instrument.

If Alcoholics Anonymous has a single voice, it is through its publications, especially the monthly *Grapevine*, that the tone is set.

Since Alcoholics Anonymous is a loosely knit body, the exact number attending group meetings is unknown. In 1938, there were only three A.A. groups with approximately 100 members in all. In 1944, it is estimated that the figure rose to 10,000 members in approximately 300 groups in North America. By 1965, this figure was about 300,000 members in approximately 10,000 groups in the United States. Today, in the Washington, D.C. metropolitan area alone, it is estimated that there are about 125 groups. There are perhaps 450,000 to 500,000 alcoholics participating in A.A. all over the world: Africa, Asia, Australia, central and southern Europe, Canada, and areas not covered in the world directory.

Structurally independent of Alcoholics Anonymous but direct outgrowths of that organization are Al-Ateen, and Al-Anon. Al-Ateen is an organization of teenage children of alcoholics, and Al-Anon an organization of spouses and relatives of alcoholics. There are now more than 4,000 groups comprising Al-Anon in the United States, Canada, and thirty-five foreign countries. The Al-Anon Family Groups, as the organization is called today, has published a number of books, such as *A Guide for the Families of Problem Drinkers, Living with An Alcoholic with the Help of Al-Anon, The Dilemma of the Alcoholic Marriage,* and *One Day at a Time in Al-Anon.* About 50 percent or more of Al-Anon members are relatives of still drinking alcoholics who have not yet joined Alcoholics Anonymous.

(Voluntary and Other Alcoholism Organizations

The National Council on Alcoholism (NCA) is one of the nineteen member agencies of the National Health Council. It is a national voluntary health organization with fifty-five affiliates throughout the United States. It was organized in 1944 to "combat alcoholism through a national program of education, research and community services," and unlike Alcoholics Anonymous, has often engaged in public policy activities in support of enlarged governmental efforts. Similarly, it has provided important leadership in programs of public information and consultation to the many interested groups. Of particular emphasis during recent years has been an extensive industrial consultation program. Expenditures in 1970 of the NCA and its affiliates amounted to $2.7 million.

On the local level, the number of affiliated members of NCA has remained relatively stable over the last decade, the principal growth having occurred between 1950–1960. When contrasted to the substantial growth of voluntary associations in mental retardation and mental health, public ambivalence about alcoholism is underlined.

The North American Association of Alcoholism Programs (NAAAP), developed by administrators of government-supported programs for treatment, education, and research in alcoholism, was organized in 1949 and has served as a forum for the exchange of ideas and information among publicly and privately sponsored treatment, research, and education organizations.

The Center of Alcohol Studies at Rutgers (formerly at Yale), in addition to its continuing research, documentation, and publication activities, developed the Summer School of Alcohol Studies, which has served as a model for the development of many other schools and summer institutes throughout the United States and Canada. The center has been instrumental in the organization of many state alcoholism programs and publishes the *Quarterly Journal of Studies on Alcohol*, the world's leading journal in its field.

Counselors on Alcoholism and Related Disorders (CARD), a nonprofit organization incorporated in California in 1968, offers a three-unit training course in alcoholism, in cooperation with the University of California extension division, to "train those interested in working with the alcoholic as their vocation." In addition, CARD regional summer schools have become quite popular.

The Licensed Beverage Industries, Inc., and foundations such as the Christopher D. Smithers Foundation carry on research and education activities in the field of alcoholism.

❮ Industrial Programs

The following definition of "alcoholism" was included in the National Industrial Conference Board's report published in March 1970:[12] "Alcoholism: 'A highly complex illness.' It is a chronic disease characterized by repeated excessive drinking which interferes with the individual's health, interpersonal relations or economic functioning."

Business and industry in the United States have, during the past decade, become much more responsive to their employees who have alcohol problems. Since some 3 to 8 percent of the employees of a typical company are likely to be alcoholics, estimates of the annual dollar cost can be substantial as noted earlier. Nor is the executive immune; it has been estimated that perhaps 10 percent of the American executives are alcohol dependent.[9]

In 1947, recognizing the problem of the alcoholic employees, Consolidated Edison of New York began a company rehabilitation program. Gradually, programs by such major companies as Allis-Chalmers, Equitable Life, Kemper Insurance, Du Pont, and Raytheon, to name only a few, were initiated.

An industrial consultant of the NCA reported an increase of 357 percent in the number of companies developing new alcoholism programs from 1959 to 1965 (counting fifty companies with "formal programs in full operation" in the base year of 1959).[20] In a government report (1967),[13] it is stated that "more than 200 American firms maintain their own company programs."

From a 1968 National Industrial Conference Board survey,[12] it appears that there has been a shift from a disciplinary approach toward more positive programs of rehabilitation. The majority of companies in the study also feel that control programs more than pay for themselves.

The NCA estimated that, as of January 1968, there were about 3.1 million alcoholics in the nation's work force of 58.3 million (in business, industry, and civilian government), or 5.3 percent of that work force.

From the "Report to the Special Subcommittee on Alcoholism and Narcotics Committee on Labor and Public Welfare"[23] it is estimated that the prevalence of alcoholism among federal civilian employees ranges from 4 to 8 percent of the work force and costs the federal government from $275 to $550 million annually.

In the military, one of the earliest attempts to treat alcoholics in the armed forces was at the Fitzsimmons Army Hospital in 1950. In 1966, the air force initiated its Wright-Patterson Program for alcoholics. In a paper by A. N. Papas,[18] alcoholism is deemed "a threat to the well-being of the individual and the Air Force in peacetime as well as in wartime." In this treatment program it was reported that seventeen men out of thirty-four eligible for a six-month follow up remained sober, an abstinence rate somewhat higher than the results of most treatment programs, which usually give one year follow-up figures of one-third abstinent, but lower than that reported by industry, which reports success rates of up to 70 percent.

Today, many companies have effective alcoholism control programs. In a study of fifty companies, the number willing to rehire a recovered alcoholic (in 1968 as compared to 1958) rose from fourteen to eighteen, and the number that "probably would rehire" rose from eighteen to twenty-four.[12]

⟨ Government-Sponsored Alcoholism Programs

The federal program under the division of alcohol abuse and alcoholism within the National Institute of Mental Health (NIMH) had a total fiscal 1971 budget of $14 million: $6 million in grant support for research; $330,000 in intramural research; $1 million in grant support for training; $6 million in federal matching grants for construction and staffing of community-based services for the treatment of alcoholics, and $330,000 for a national information and education program.

On December 31, 1970, President Nixon signed into law the "Comprehensive Alcohol Abuse and Alcoholism Prevention, Treatment, and Rehabilitation Act of 1970," which established a National Institute on Alcohol Abuse and Alcoholism within NIMH and authorized $300 million for alcoholism programs over the period of fiscal years 1971–1973. If any substantial portion of these authorized moneys is appropriated for use, the programs of the NIMH in support of alcoholism activities at the state and local level, and through the awarding of grants and contracts, will be dramatically increased.

An additional federal program under the Department of Health, Education and Welfare's social and rehabilitation service made $25 million in rehabilitation grants, which could include services to alcoholics, available during fiscal year 1971. The Department of Transportation had an alcohol-related program of approximately $18 million and the Office of Economic Opportunity's program was approximately $10 million for fiscal year 1971.

The Veterans Administration has the largest alcoholism research program in the country,[10] since it also has the world's largest sample of alcoholic patients accessible for long-term study, treatment, and follow up. During 1965, 55,581 patients with principal or associated alcoholic diagnosis were treated in Veterans Administration hospitals. During 1968, this figure rose to 92,231. During fiscal 1969, Veterans Administration hospitals operated twenty-seven pilot alcoholism treatment units in participating hospitals, without special funding. During 1970, alcoholism research was funded at approximately $2.5 million.

As of July 1, 1970, only two states (Idaho and Illinois) lacked state alcoholism authorities as designated by their governors. Of course, the quality and quantity of state programs vary considerably. In fact, the province of Ontario, in Canada, has clearly developed North America's outstanding government-sponsored program. Referring only to actual medical, psychiatric, social, and rehabilitation services for alcoholics, the state alcoholism agencies expended more than $40 million during fiscal year 1970.

⟨ Generic, Noncategorical Service Systems

Many alcoholics, though they do not acknowledge their alcoholism, are already in contact with one or more major helping agencies, such as general hospitals; mental hospitals; community mental health centers; and welfare, rehabilitation, and family service agencies. Estimates indicated that alcoholism is involved in 10 to 25 percent of welfare cases.[21,26] Studies of patients admitted to hospitals after attempted suicide indicated 11 to 23 percent were alcoholics; in a study of completed suicides, 31 percent were found to be alcoholics.[17] A study in Maryland found that 25.4 percent of males admitted to psychiatric outpatient facilities were excessive drinkers, though more than half of these persons received diagnoses of other than alcoholism.[1]

In addition, state mental hospitals during fiscal 1970 received $174 million for treatment of alcoholism; state support for psychiatric wards of tax-supported general hospitals, community mental health clinics, psychiatric clinics, and vocational rehabilitation agencies was between $14 and $20 million.

The general hospital has had a mixed record in alcoholism. Early in 1958, recognizing the alcohol problem, the Morristown Memorial Hospital (in a New Jersey community of 18,000) established an alcoholic service, among the first of such specialized hospital services in North America. The service included a follow-up care unit in the alcoholic clinic. Since then, an increasing number of hospitals have opened their facilities to alcoholics, following the leadership of the American Hospital Association, but only a few other communities have established services similar to those of the Morristown Memorial Hospital.[12]

Since hospitals are not always ready or willing to admit alcoholics, or are overcrowded, the jail still remains the major single source of immediate care for the individual who is drunk in the streets. During recent years, a major movement has been under way to remove the offense of public intoxication from the criminal statutes. Both through state legislatures and the courts, this "crime" is under attack. Some success has occurred. The underlying issue is the ability of the health and social welfare system to accommodate this substantial influx of patients ordinarily described as unreachable.

The alcoholic has often also found refuge with the Salvation Army when few other social agencies were willing to work with him.

Recognizing the need for the care and study of alcoholism, in 1953 Massachusetts established an alcohol clinic at the Massachusetts General Hospital in Boston, a university-affiliated hospital. A pilot study to engage the alcoholic to enter into treatment was initiated. It was known that many alcoholics who make their first contact with a hospital through the emergency service do not follow through on treatment by seeking outpatient care. In a study of 200 male alcoholics admitted to the emergency service of the hospital, 100 were assigned to an experimental group for treatment, and 100 to a control group receiving no special treatment. Follow up of the 200 cases at the end of the one-year experimental period attested to the fact that the alcoholic can form a therapeutic attachment. Prior to the study no alcoholic came to the alcohol clinic as a consequence of emergency service admission; the study showed that 65 percent of experimental cases made initial visits in contrast to 5 percent of the control cases; that 42 percent of the experimental cases made five or more visits in contrast to 1 percent of the controls. Additional findings showed that the usual clinical approaches to difficult treatment groups must be reexamined and revised, that, in fact, the establishment of treatment relations can be highly effective.

At Memorial Hospital in North Conway, N.H., "a federally supported demonstration project designed to offer comprehensive services to persons with alcohol problems in a rural area" was begun in an effort to provide emergency psychiatric services in a nonteaching general hospital loosely linked for consultative and teaching purposes to members of the psychiatric and social service departments of Massachusetts General Hospital.[2]

In fifteen years, from 1944 to 1958, the incidence of alcoholism in New Hampshire more than doubled, and the estimated number rose from 17,000 in 1953 to 30,000 a few years later. The Alcohol Rehabilitation Unit was conceived for a rural village of 12,500 where there were no professionally trained mental health personnel; where the one hospital with university affiliation is 100 miles away; where a state-operated two day a month clinic for diagnostic evaluation problems in young persons is seventy miles in a different direction; where the few private practicing psychiatrists were some sixty to eighty-five miles away; where the state hospital is ninety miles away; and where not a single inpatient facility for persons with emotional problems exists within the county.[4]

Therefore, custodial care for alcoholism (in addition to that provided by general hospitals to patients admitted for delirium tremens, gastritis, and other acute medical manifestations of the illness) had to come from nursing homes, jails, houses of correction, and country infirmaries.

A case in point, which suggests the therapeutic potential of the unit, concerned an alcoholic of long standing (twenty years). Treatment attempts such as several admissions to the state hospital, commitment to the county farm, a live-in occupational arrangement in a neighboring state with attendance at A.A. seven nights a week, disulfiram therapy as an outpatient without other treatment, and confinement in the local "drunk tank" had all proved fruitless. After sixteen months of treatment, which included "direct involvement in the community and . . . consequent ability to be very active on behalf of the client, to be able to respond immediately and flexibly to any crisis with hospitalization, medication, or a quick home visit, to shore up wavering motivation and hope, and to enlist the aid of many people in the person's life," the patient's drinking was reduced to only one-tenth of what it had been during the past several years, and the patient's absenteeism at work decreased correspondingly. The patient was reunited with his wife, and his functioning, both as head of the household and as employee, improved substantially.[4]

Because of the effectiveness of the facility, we feel this approach to providing alcoholism services in rural areas is worthy of development for the future.

One of the more successful efforts at establishing an effective alcoholism program at a state hospital was at Mendocino State Hospital.[6] Here, 100 miles north of San Francisco, in the state having the second highest rate of alcoholism in the United States, Mendocino State Hospital serves San Francisco County, which has the highest alcoholism rate within California. In the first half of 1966, nearly 1,000 patients, men and women, were admitted to the alcoholism service. Patients are accepted by the alcohol service either by court commitment (about 17 percent) or by voluntary admission (83 percent). Mendocino is the only California state hospital that routinely accepts alcoholics on a voluntary basis.

A greatly enlarged staff, needed to cope with the high ratio of patients and to coordinate the new unified program that came into effect in 1965, was filled mostly by employees who had volunteered for the alcoholism program. Use was made of a variety of staff members, not assigned to the alcohol service, as group leaders for the alcoholic patients.

Between the end of 1965 and the middle of June 1967 admissions to the alcohol program rose to more than 2,600 each year, more than 96 percent voluntary, and comprised more than two-thirds of all of the hospital's admissions. Some of the reasons for the success of the program can be attributed to the exceptional leadership, the well-trained, well-qualified, and highly motivated staff, and the treatment of the alcoholic patient, allowing and encouraging him to take on responsibilities. Some senior patients' involvement in the program were in counseling all new admissions, acting as group leaders, presenting panel discussions on alcoholism in communities, and managing a nonstaffed residence. The program's effort toward the control and prevention of alcoholism by integrating many and varied resources resulted in its being designated as the California Department of Mental Hygiene's demonstration alcoholism service.

(A Future View

A look at potential positive results if programs are accelerated suggests that aggressive, carefully planned programmed efforts could produce impressive cost benefits.

It is estimated that the cost to the average industry would be $5 a year for each employee, or $300 million a year for the entire work force, to cover the costs of an educational campaign, training program, and the identification and referral of the alcoholic employee.* (The actual treatment would occur in community settings.) The benefits of such a program could mean a substantial reduction of the $10 billion annual loss of productivity (25 percent of the

---

* Based on estimates available in 1970.

salary of each alcoholic). Three and one-third million employed rehabilitated alcoholics (based on 50 percent rehabilitation success) × 25 percent of their average annual salaries equals $5 billion, minus the $300 million program cost, or an annual saving of about $4.7 billion a year, or roughly $15 saved for each $1 spent.

There are approximately 200,000 federal civilian employees who suffer from alcoholism. Based on a minimum of 50 percent of the employed alcoholics who can be rehabilitated, and a cost of approximately $15 million annually for such a program (without paying for treatment services), the benefit figures for the federal program are higher than the private sector (due to higher average salary) and would result in a savings of $250 million, or $17 saved for $1 spent.

To the governmental and industrial programs for education, identification, and referral must be added treatment costs, of course. It is impossible to estimate the precise treatment cost to industry and government since cost to a large degree is dependent on health services that are locally available. Where local health services are adequate, industry need only refer alcoholics and may not have to assume any financial burden. However, where there are inadequate health services, the question of who will pay costs varies with the health insurance benefits available, the industry's contribution, and the public's participation through governmental programs.

Based on a 50 percent chance of rehabilitating alcoholics who come into contact with health and care-giving agencies, 2.5 million alcoholics would be rehabilitated at a savings of approximately $4 billion at a cost of $400 million, or a cost benefit ratio of 1 to 10.

More than $100 million per year is currently spent in arrest and incarceration of public drunkenness offenders, and a large amount also is spent in health and welfare services for this population. Treatment of these individuals in the health system has a 20–25 percent chance of success while "treatment" in the criminal system has proven largely unsuccessful. In addition, a saving in police and court time would be achieved.

The reduction of automobile accidents and the annual death toll of 28,000 and 500,000 disability injuries (and several hundred thousand traffic arrests) and more than $1 billion in property damage, insurance costs, and medical services through treatment by identification, education, and environmental manipulations and instrumentation might roughly be set at 40 percent.

Federal programs for alcohol abuse among Indians would cost $7.5 million with cost benefits unestimable at this time but commensurate with cost benefits for the general alcoholic population of the nation.

Because of the long-term neglect and unique inherent stigma associated with alcoholism and drinking problems and the more than 9 million problem drinkers in the United States (as compared with 250,000 heroin users), the need for broad-based comprehensive programs is paramount.

A Note on Prevention

No examination of alcoholism programs can be complete without consideration of prevention. In alcoholism, the parameters for possible action are considerably enlarged when the traditional public health model of primary, secondary, and tertiary targets for prevention is used and the host, agent and environment continuum is visualized.

Typical of most alcoholism endeavors to date, which focus on the late stages of the alcoholic process, the bulk of this discussion focuses on tertiary prevention, that is, on programs developed to treat the severe casualties of the alcoholic illness. In some quarters, the identification in industrial programs of the alcoholic employee is labeled early intervention and does possess some features consistent with secondary prevention. There are other possible opportunities in secondary prevention outside of industrial programs. A focus on early case finding in youth-oriented settings, such as schools, colleges, YMCAs, religious organizations, and so forth could be productive. Once the stigma of alcohol-related problems is removed from the moralistic and punitive arena, these formal organizations are in a unique position to identify those whose dependence on and behavior with alcohol is beyond the social norm. As in early case findings, secondary prevention is highlighted.

Primary prevention, most desirable of all, remains challenging and nonspecific. Without the single fact or etiological agent of the infectious model, specific "vaccination" as a primary preventative is inhibited. The amorphous inputs to better health and living, such as resilient coping mechanisms, improved mental health, less poverty, and a lessening of a myriad of social health problems could of course contribute to changing the milieu of alcohol problems and thereby lower the incidence of alcoholic conditions.

Some specific alcoholic preventive methods, to date unproven, are possible. These include measures designed to make available and desirable alcoholic beverages of lower, rather than higher, alcoholic content; measures designed to promote a style of integrative drinking (alcohol with meals, sporting activity, religious and family feasts), instead of alcohol use in, by, and for itself. Certainly no preventive approach could hope to succeed without some public campaign to identify drunken behavior as unacceptable.

Whenever educational thrusts are introduced, school programs are suggested. The use of school systems in alcoholism education is not a new phenomenon, since the fervor of the prohibition experiment resulted in all mainland state legislatures enacting legislation requiring the schools to educate the young to the dangers of drink (most were written about the turn of the century). Although the "fear teaching" exemplified by the old alcohol laws is not much of an example, it illustrates the continuing dilemma and debate about whether or not the school system ought to have the goal of social problem prevention. On one hand, some contend that the degree of support for school programs of prevention merely reflects the state of knowledge: When specific preventive measures are unclear or unavailable (when we do not know what to do), we turn to the school system and ask it to assume the task. Those persons of such persuasion contend that we attempt to prevent sexual problems by sex education, mental illness by mental health education, and drug and alcohol abuse by drug and alcohol education. Others, who make a strong distinction between information and education, contend that the educational system reneges on its highest calling when it abdicates its implicit mandate to awaken and develop mechanisms of social responsibility among its young charges. The pros and cons of this important debate are beyond the scope of this chapter, but bear noting in any discussion of prevention.

(Conclusion

The examination of alcoholism programs illustrates that the significant function of a specialized alcoholism network is to demonstrate, stimulate, and train. The needs, implications, and extent of alcohol problems are such that it is unrealistic to expect a specialized system to cope with the immensity of the total alcoholic population and their families. They will and must become part of the total health care system. But the alcohol programs must demonstrate and, hopefully, thereby change the negative attitudes and improve the healing competence of the generic system. The advent of the new alcoholism legislation of the federal government is a major thrust in this direction. By its broad mandate of increased federal support to states with its formula grant provisions, by the removal of civil service barriers to employment of persons with prior alcoholism histories, by the strength of its confidentiality provisions, by the demand that all state health programs include planning for alcoholism, and by the creation of a National Institute on Alcohol Abuse and Alcoholism, the potential and initiative are at hand. What psychiatry and the other allied helping professions do with this significant achievement is up to them.

❲ Bibliography

1. BAHN, A. K., and CHANDLER, C. A. "Alcoholism in Psychiatric Clinic Patients." *Quarterly Journal of Studies on Alcohol*, 22, no. 3 (1961), 411–417.
2. BLAINE, H. T., MULLER, J. J., and CHAFETZ, M. E. "Acute Psychiatric Services in the General Hospital: II. Current Status of Emergency Psychiatric Services." *American Journal of Psychiatry*, 124, suppl. (1967), 37–45.
3. CAHALAN, D., CISIN, I. H., and CROSSLEY, H. M. *American Drinking Practices: A National Study of Drinking Behavior and Attitudes*. New Brunswick, N.J.: Publications Division, Rutgers Center of Alcohol Studies, 1962.
4. CHAFETZ, M. E., BLAINE, H. T., and HILL, M. J. *Frontiers of Alcoholism*. New York: Science House, 1970.
5. ————, and DEMONE, H. W., Jr. *Alcoholism and Society*. New York: Oxford University Press, 1962.
6. GLASCOTE, R. M., PLAUT, T. F. A., HAMMERSLEY, D. W., O'NEILL, F. J., CHAFETZ, M. E., and CUMMING, E. *The Treatment of Alcoholism: A Study of Programs and Problems*. Washington, D.C.: Joint Information Service of the American Psychiatric Association and the National Association for Mental Health, 1967.
7. HENDERSON, R. M., and BACON, S. D. "Problem Drinking: The Yale Plan for Business and Industry." *Quarterly Journal of Studies on Alcohol*, 14 (1953), 247.
8. JELLINEK, E. M. *The Disease Concept of Alcoholism*. New Haven: Yale University Press, 1960.
9. JOHNSON, H. J. News report. *U.S. News and World Report*, April 29, 1968.
10. KAIM, S. C. Prepared statement before the Special Subcommittee on Alcoholism and Narcotics of the Committee on Labor and Public Welfare, U.S. Senate 91st Congress, July 1969.
11. KELLER, M. "The Definition of Alcoholism and the Estimation of Its Prevalence." In D. J. Pittman and C. R. Snyder, eds., *Society, Culture, and Drinking Patterns*. New York: Wiley, 1962. Pp. 310–329.
12. NATIONAL INDUSTRIAL CONFERENCE BOARD. *Company Controls for Drinking Problems*. Personnel policy study, no. 218. New York: National Industrial Conference Board, 1970.
13. NATIONAL INSTITUTE OF MENTAL HEALTH. *Alcohol and Alcoholism*. Public health service publication, no. 1640. Washington, D.C.: U.S. Government Printing Office, 1967.
14. NATIONAL OFFICE OF VITAL STATISTICS. *Report on General Mortality*. Washington, D.C.: U.S. Public Health Service.
15. NATIONAL SAFETY COUNCIL. *Accident Facts*. Chicago: National Safety Council, 1966.
16. *1968 Alcohol and Highway Safety Report*. Washington, D.C.: U.S. Government Printing Office, 1968.
17. PALOLA, E. G., DORPAT, T. L., and LARSEN, W. R. "Alcoholism and Suicidal Behavior." In D. J. Pittman and C. R. Snyder, eds., *Society, Culture, and Drinking Patterns*. New York: Wiley, 1962. Pp. 511–534.
18. PAPAS, A. N. An Approach to Alcoholism in the Military. Paper presented to the first USAF Alcoholic Detoxification Symposium, Wright Patterson Air Force Base, Ohio, December 1968.
19. PITTMAN, D. J. "Public Intoxication and the Alcoholic Offender in American Society." In President's Commission on Law Enforcement and Administration of Justice, *Task Force Report: Drunkenness*. Washington, D.C.: U.S. Government Printing Office, 1967. Pp. 7–28.
20. PRESNALL, L. F. "Folklore and Facts about Employees with Alcoholism." *Journal of Occupational Medicine*, April 1967, pp. 187–188.
21. TASK FORCE ON ALCOHOLISM. *Massachusetts Mental Health Planning Project Report*. Department of Mental Health, 1965.
22. TAUBE, C. A. *Alcoholism Among Male Admissions to Psychiatric Inpatient Services —1968*. Statistical note 31, Survey and reports sect., Biometry Branch, Office of Program Planning and Evaluation, Washington, D.C.: National Institute of Mental Health, 1970.
23. U.S. COMPTROLLER GENERAL. "Report to the Special Subcommittee on Alcoholism and Narcotics Committee on Labor and Public Welfare, United States Senate." In *Substantial Cost Savings From Establishment of Alcoholism Program for Federal*

Civilian Employees. B-164031(2). U.S. General Accounting Office, 1970.

24. U.S. FEDERAL BUREAU OF INVESTIGATION. *Crime in the United States: Uniform Crime Reports, 1965.* Washington, D.C.: U.S. Government Printing Office, 1966.

25. WORLD HEALTH ORGANIZATION. *Alcohol and Alcoholism: Report of an Expert Committee.* Technical report series, no. 94. Geneva, 1955.

26. WYOMING STATE DEPARTMENT OF PUBLIC WELFARE. *Public Assistance Cases Where Alcohol Is a Factor Contributing to Need.* 1965.

CHAPTER 49

COMMUNITY PROGRAMS
IN SUICIDOLOGY

Edwin S. Shneidman

I MAGINE AN INEXORABLY straight line stretching across this page representing time. Imagine further your dividing this line into three unequal parts: the past (sinistor), the present (represented by a dot that can move, but only to the right), and the future (dexter). You would then see the three temporal units in relation to which each suicidologist—and every other practitioner in the world, for that matter—must work. Beneficent or therapeutic action can focus only on what may happen in the future, what is happening in the present, or what has happened in the past. That is to say, one can come or do (the Latin word "venire") only before (prevention), during (intervention or parivention), or after (postvention). The materials in this chapter on suicide vention are organized around these three key temporal concepts.*

---

* The same is true for "saying" ("diction"): one can predict (He *will* commit suicide); paridict (He *is* schizophrenic), or postdict (He *was* a rejected child). All diagnoses are paridiction; prognoses are predictions; and statements about case history materials are postdictions. In general, they have different epistemological status and different degrees of veridicality. The distinctions among them are often disregarded, a fact that leads to much obfuscation.

As will be easily recognized, these three terms run parallel in many ways to the traditional public health concepts of primary, secondary, and tertiary prevention. I believe that the proposed terminology is more accurate; further it avoids the necessity of such phrases as "preventive intervention,"[5] when what is really meant is postvention.

It is, of course, possible to achieve a useful understanding of suicide as related to community and mental health issues in terms of any one of a number of models or paradigms. At the outset, however, it can be argued that among the models from which one can choose, the medical model (with its notions of disease, cause, cure, and a specially anointed curer) seems especially limited and, at best, only marginally appropriate. In this connection, Drs. Bertram Brown and Eugene Long appraised the situation realistically.

The conceptualization of community response to self-destructive crises along a temporal dimension has the merit of avoiding much of contemporary underbrush. The three temporal points logically exhaust the possible times at which action—individual, dyadic, community, or otherwise—can be effected.

They focus on when (before, during, or after) rather than the less appropriate who (M.D., Ph.D., or D.D.) or where (inpatient, outpatient, at home, or on the telephone) or what (manic-depressive, paranoid schizophrenic, benighted citizen, perturbed housewife). This way of seeing the action has the additional advantage of opening the field to anyone who can help at any crucial point in time: a trained volunteer, a significant (or even insignificant) other, a psychiatrist, an epidemiologist, a demographer, a psychoanalyst, a vital statistician, a clergyman, a sociologist, a policeman, a health educator, a clinical psychologist—a whole panoply of individuals who can practice prevention, intervention, or postvention, whether as clinicians, research scientists, or empathic human beings seeking to help someone in duress.

⟨ Prevention

The etymological meaning of prevention is straightforward: It means to come before. Its implication is that it forestalls, wards off, precludes, averts, or makes unnecessary the dire or inimical events that otherwise would occur. In suicidology there are two main avenues to prevention:

1. To increase the acumen for recognition of potential suicide among all possible rescuers. The key to the reduction of suicide lies in recognition and diagnosis, the perception of the premonitory signs and clues. Most individuals who are deeply suicidal cast some verbal or behavioral shadows before them. Prevention lies in recognition. The task of early casefinding must be shared by both professionals and lay people. The early signs of suicide must be made known to each physician, clergyman, policeman, and educator in the land and to each spouse, parent, neighbor, and friend.

2. To facilitate the ease with which each citizen can utter a cry for help. The tabooed nature of suicide must be recognized. Part of a successful program of suicide prevention lies in reducing the taboos and giving a greater permissiveness for citizens in distress to seek help and to make their plight a legitimate reason for treatment and assistance.

In a much broader sense—in terms of long-range policy planning, for example—planning for prevention would have to include two major contradictory (but not mutually exclusive) goals: (1) reducing the number of suicidal deaths; and (2) reducing the stigma or taboo on suicide, so that even when it does occur, the mental health sequelae on the survivors would be less severe and less crippling. These two major goals would, of course, also be applicable in other mental health areas, such as schizophrenia or homosexuality.

With these notions in mind, the following are suggested as parts of a comprehensive program in suicide, especially relating to the preventive aspects of such a program.

A Redefinition and Refinement of Concepts and Statistics on Suicide

It would seem to be part of the elementary logic of a clinical science to believe that remediation optimally follows from one's understanding of the nature of the phenomena. Good conceptualizations (including definition and taxonomy) must precede any effective action (prevention, intervention, or postvention).

It is generally agreed that current statistics on suicide are grossly inadequate and that comparisons of suicidal incidents between cities, between states, and between countries, based on available figures, are at best sometimes inaccurate and often obfuscatory and misleading. The current inaccuracies are due to many reasons, including the following:

1. Confusion as to how to certify equivocal deaths, for example, those that lie between suicide and accident.
2. Dissembling on the part of police and physicians who wish to protect the family and public officials who wish to protect the reputation of their community.
3. Inaccurate record keeping, where what

could be known and ascertained simply is not accurately tabulated.

4. The irremediable inadequacies of the present concepts.

Two additional points should be made in relation to statistics. (1) An opportunity now exists to introduce improved classifications and to conduct pilot studies to determine (for the first time) the veridical suicide rates in some selected communities. (2) The specter exists that unless there is a refinement of the concepts related to self-destruction, there will never be accuracy of reporting, because the present concepts are simply not conceptually strong enough to accurately reflect the events they are purported to represent.

At all levels, special thought should be given to the redefinition and refinement of statistics and to the problem of record keeping to the end of suggesting new concepts and a comprehensive program for uniform national record keeping in relation to self-destruction. I have elsewhere suggested that the greatest difficulty in accurate reporting of self-destructive deaths is that it is currently tied to an archaic classification of deaths.[8] The greatest shortcoming of this present classification is that it completely omits the role of the individual in his own demise.

We would do well to abandon completely the NASH (natural, accident, suicide, homicide) classification of deaths, for it is Cartesian and apsychological in that it entirely omits the role of the individual in his own death and totally disregards the teachings of twentieth-century psychodynamic psychology. Instead, we should attempt to conceptualize all human deaths in terms of a motivational dimension of intention toward death. As a beginning, three large subcategories are suggested: intentioned, subintentioned, and unintentioned. These subcategories might briefly be defined as follows. An *intentioned* death is any death, from whatever cause(s) or of whatever apparent mode, in which the decedent played a direct, conscious role in effecting his own demise. A *subintentioned* death is one in which the decedent played an indirect, covert, partial, conscious, or unconscious role in hastening his own demise by such behaviors as imprudence, excessive risk taking, abuse of alcohol, misuse of drugs, disregard of life-extending medical regimen, death-risking life style, or the like. An *unintentioned* death is one in which the decedent played no effective role in effecting his own demise, in that the death is due entirely to assault or trauma from without or nonpsychologically tinged failure from within. The reader is referred elsewhere for a further explication of these notions.[8,9,11]

The traditional NASH classification of death robs us of the possibility of generating meaningful statistics. An approach that focuses on the intention of the individual, if used in conjunction with the traditional approach, might well provide an important step in the psychological understanding of a broad spectrum of deaths and lead to more effective assessment and prevention.

Special Programs for the Gatekeepers of Suicide Prevention

An important key to suicide prevention lies in detection and diagnosis. One of the most important findings from the last decade's experience in suicide prevention is that practically every person who kills himself gives some verbal or behavioral clue of his intention to do so. These prodromal clues are often in code, that is, are cryptic or disguised, but nonetheless they are clues, and one can learn to recognize them. These are the handles to prevention.

In practice, a variety of people hear the presuicidal clues—spouse, friend, neighbor, clergyman, policeman, bartender, physician, employer, and so on. However, it is a most important fact that more than 65 percent of all individuals who commit suicide have seen a physician (usually a general practitioner) within three months of the event. It is therefore crucial to have a program of education relating to detection and diagnosis that focuses on physicians and, secondarily, on clergy, police, and other gatekeepers.

There are a number of ways in which a program for educating general practitioners about the diagnostic indices of suicide can be done. These include the following:

1. Preparation of special educational materials for physicians focused on the premonitory signs of suicide. These materials can be in the form of brochures, pamphlets, long-playing training records, film strips, films, or the like.
2. Preparation of a similar program directed toward physicians in hospitals and clinics.
3. Instruction on suicide prevention in the medical school curriculum.
4. Courses on suicide prevention in postgraduate medical education in medical schools throughout the country.
5. The use of resources of the American Academy of General Practitioners (AAGP).
6. Special national and regional conferences on suicide prevention sponsored by the AMA and the AAGP, perhaps with co-sponsorship by the American Psychological Association and the National Association of Social Workers.
7. Suggestions that the drug companies train their drug detail men in suicidal prevention. Although every doctor in the United States does not read every journal or attend conventions, every doctor does see drug detail men. The major drug companies ought to be most willing to train these drug detail men in the principles and content of suicide prevention and to have them distribute appropriate literature to the physicians on whom they call. This could be done not only through the drug companies but with the additional coordination of the AMA, state medical societies, and so on.

Clinical experience over the past several years indicates that it is not only possible but advisable for physicians to ask direct questions about a patient's suicidal intent without any harmful effects. In interviews with 10,000 suicidal patients and reviews of 3,000 suicidal deaths, the staff at the Los Angeles Suicide Prevention Center found no evidence that such questions had ever harmed patients; indeed, the questions often relieved the patients and permitted them to discuss their problems with the physicians.[13]

Additional special programs, tailor made for clergy, police, educators, and others, should, without question, also be considered.

Carefully Prepared Programs in Massive Public Education

Massive public education is probably the most important single item for effective suicide prevention and at the same time one of the most difficult to put into practice in ways that would be both acceptable and effective. The basic notion is that one major avenue to reduction of suicidal deaths is through the use of the lay citizen for first-line detection and diagnosis. The rough model may be found in cancer detection, wherein more and more citizens know the prodromal clues for cancer (for example, bleeding from an aperture, a lump in the breast, a wart or sore that does not heal or that grows). The same model, with appropriate changes, might well be adopted in suicide prevention.

A study of massive public education might be done initially in a few carefully preselected communities. This study would need to involve experts in epidemiology, biostatistics, and the use of communication media. This type of study would need to be preceded by a long-term comprehensive study of the actual state of suicidal (and suicidal equivalent) incidents in those areas. The public education activities might include planned and careful use of all the public media: schools, television, newspapers, radio, advertisements, placards. These activities might be done in both usual and unusual places (where appropriate), such as doctors' offices, pool halls, or public lavatories.

One or two cities might be selected as large-scale pilot projects (or one or two sections of cities might be selected with equal catchment areas). There is the need for control scientific data in order to ascertain the effects and effectiveness of such a program of public education. In part, this can be done by selecting other cities (or sections of cities) comparable to the experimental cities in terms of the major variables thought to be relevant.

The use of certain carefully selected target cities as a pilot attempt in suicide prevention is in line with current scientific practice. There currently exist many concepts in suicide prevention that have been found useful; there is already a base of knowledge from which to predict a hope of success.

Although a program of massive public education would seem to be very important in any full-scale assault on the problem of suicide, it would need to be done with the reservations concerning the unanticipated consequences of public information and of popularizing the topic of suicide prevention. We do not know enough about the short-term effects of such a program. However, it needs to be further stated that this in itself is a legitimate subject for serious study and one in which sociology consultants would play an important role.

The Development of a Cadre of Trained, Dedicated Professionals

There do not exist at present trained professionals in sufficient number to man the proposed and planned projects in suicide prevention. There is an acute need for the creation of a core group of individuals who might then direct and staff the suicide prevention programs in the communities throughout the country. It should be pointed out that what is being proposed here is not the training of individuals to be specialists in suicide in the sense of only being therapists for suicidal people, but rather that individuals be given sufficient training in the basic ideas and facts about suicide and suicide prevention so that they can then act more meaningfully in their administrative and technical capacities.

The establishment of fellowships in suicidology at main centers of learning at several strategic places throughout the country would be most important. Already, it appears that there may be fellowships in suicidology programs soon on the West Coast, the Midwest,

and the Southwest. The concept seems viable, and the future seems to be one of expansion of such training sites. The main point to be made is that the establishment of these multiprofessional fellowships in suicidology will, within a relatively few years, create a corps of trained professionals specifically concerned with suicide prevention and able effectively to staff a variety of suicide prevention activities throughout the country.

❰ Intervention

Intervention has two meanings, either to come during or to come between. The first meaning of intervention is to come during the acute crisis. Its avowed purpose is to modify or reduce the intensity of deleterious effects of the crisis itself, in a word, to reduce the crisis to a noncrisis. The second meaning of intervention refers to activities that come between the present crisis and a potential subsequent crisis. Its avowed goal is to reduce the probability of another crisis. In this case, specifically of a future suicide attempt. In practice, some of the elements of effective intervention are as follows:

1. Attending to the perturbation and lethality elements in suicidal behavior.
2. Recognizing that self-destruction can be subintentioned and is not always overtly suicide.
3. Recognizing that suicidal behavior usually occurs in a dyadic context and taking account of the life-saving role of the significant other.

In general, effective intervention is accomplished by providing resources adequate to evaluate and respond to suicidal crises. Both facilities and personnel are needed. Personnel need to acquire relative skills and appropriate attitudes. Response to the suicidal individual and his significant other within their own cultural setting is the *sine qua non* for the reduction of the suicide rate.

Most suicide prevention activities are interventive in nature. In part, this is so because that is where the action is, but this fact does not gainsay another fact that great needs, especially for more fundamental research, lie in the areas of prevention and postvention. Intervention has the apparent attractions of immediacy, drama, and relatively quick response. The issue has been identified—he is suicidal—and the need is real. Intervention is a kind of secondary prevention, having to do with the effective treatment of an existing, identifiable (suicidal) crisis. The increase in the number of suicide prevention centers in this country from 3 to more than 130 in the past fifteen years is only one of several evidences of the legitimate appeal and humane worthwhileness of intervention. It is largely, but not entirely, the clinician's domain—his and the effective volunteer's.

Service and Treatment

Although there is great need for systematic research on intervention, the heart of intervention is the service itself. The challenge is a logistic and tactical one: that the services that can be rendered be made available to those who need them when they are required. This routinely means some kind of twenty-four-hour-a-day operation, usually involving the use of the telephone as the life-saving instrument. The use of the telephone willy-nilly changes the clinical interviewing task, presenting fresh challenges and offering new opportunities. Suicide prevention personnel need to become expert in quickly rating each caller's lethality,[10] his probability of committing suicide in the immediate future, as opposed to his perturbation or degree of upset or distress. Admittedly, workers at a suicide prevention center will probably handle more nonsuicidal calls (of individuals lonely, perturbed, intoxicated, psychotic, fundless but not lethal) than suicidal ones, yet they do well constantly to remember that their clinical goal is to keep people out of the coroner's office, to prevent their killing themselves, and that everything else takes its place subsumed under that primary aim.

The improvement of treatment procedures involves the search for new and improved methods. Within the last decade, a number of changes have already taken place. Among these can be listed a more active approach to treatment in general, the dyadic form of most treatment of suicidal persons actively involving the significant other, and a great movement out of the office into the community, using the resources within the community, the organized and unorganized helping hands of the community. In this special sense, it can be said that the best suicide prevention worker is the one who is able to get others to do most of the life-saving.

Studies of Special Groups

For any one of a number of reasons, the closer scrutiny of certain groups seems to merit special interest and attention. These groups, in the suicide domain, should include such readily identifiable high-risk groups as college students; military personnel; certain professional groups, such as physicians, particularly psychiatrists; the aged; and less readily identifiable high-risk groups, whatever their composition. On the topic of college students and suicide, there is currently a number of studies throughout the country. The identification of high-risk groups is a way of redefining individuals who manifest the prodromata or premonitory signs associated with suicidal behaviors. The key issue is whether groups of such high-risk persons can be found or whether this kind of search is not always a quest for specific individuals.

Selection and Training of Volunteer Groups

The manpower problem in suicide efforts is especially important. One way of addressing it is through fellowship programs, giving focused training to individuals who already possess graduate or professional degrees. Another way is to turn to the much larger resource pool of mature and willing individuals, carefully to select them and then rigorously to train them. This has been the route of many of the suicide prevention centers throughout the country, and there are some excellent reports of these experiences.[4] In general, selection has focused on such traits as flexibility and trainability, absence of overinvestment, or previous emotional difficulties, considerable maturity, and some experience with life's problems—the avoidance of "psychological virgins"—and the ability to quickly master the difference between a conversation (which is social and coequal) and an interview (which is clinical and betokens the helper and the helped). In the training of volunteers, many usual and innovative techniques have been employed (including the use of taped telephone calls, psychodrama, role playing, and the preceptor method) most of which cost very little but yet have the potential of enormous yield in dedicated and high-morale and low-cost personnel, usually the womanpower of the community.

⟮ Postvention

Postvention means to come after; either after a suicide attempt or after a completed suicidal act. There is much to be done for a person who has attempted suicide. We all know that suturing a wrist or gastric lavage does not treat the suicide attempt. That trauma is intrapsychic and interpersonal. Effective ways of reducing the suicide rate—always the primary goal—must include a heavy emphasis on postvention efforts for individuals who have attempted suicide.

As important as postvention for suicide attempt is, the other aspect of postvention may be even more important. It relates to helping the survivor victims of a completed suicide. When a suicide occurs, the story is not over; another narrative for the survivor victims has just begun. They have to live with their own guilt, shame, anger, perplexity, obsessions, in a word, with their own increased perturbation. Good mental health practice in a benign community ought unquestionably to provide for some postvention care of survivor victims of suicidal acts. It is not that these individuals then go on to commit suicide; rather it is that these individuals are more apt to become general mental health casualties in the clinics and in the hospitals.

The largest mental health problem in relation to suicide relates to the survivor victims, who outnumber the deceased in the order of five to one. Appropriate care or treatment of a surviving widow or, especially, surviving young children is obvious good mental health practice.[15] We know a good deal about the nefarious sequelae of a parent's suicidal death, and much is known relating to remedial and prophylactic psychological treatment of these unfortunates. Obviously, follow-up programs that study and help individuals who have attempted suicide are needed in order, at least, to learn more of the natural history of suicidal behaviors. Apropos of prophylaxis: Postvention of individuals in the present becomes prevention for the next decade, or even for the next generation. Postvention relates to the reduction in the amount of disability in the survivor caused by the irreversible suicidal event or in the individual who has attempted suicide subsequent to his first attempt.

Follow up of Suicide Attempts

We know that about eight out of ten people who commit suicide have previously attempted or threatened it, but the data relating to the percentage of people who have attempted or threatened suicide, who subsequently commit suicide, are contradictory and equivocal. The primary purpose of follow up of suicide attempts would be to prevent the commission of suicide. Some people who commit suicide do so the first time they attempt it, but the more common pattern is that of a series of attempts, with increasing lethality, and there are too many reports of individuals who have been sewn up or pumped out and released, only to complete the task within hours. Like the suggested programs for the gatekeepers and the program in public education, this also is meant to nibble at the suicide problem and to help effect a reduction in the suicide rate.

A program of follow up of suicide attempters could be done in sites where the conditions are propitious for success, and with especially cooperating hospitals, police departments, and public health officials. The actual follow up could be done by a variety of types of personnel, including public health nurses, social workers, psychologists. The data already available, particularly from the work of Stengel,[16] would serve as a beginning for further and better understanding.

There is great confusion about the relationship between attempted suicide and committed suicide. (Again, this confusion exists largely because clinicians and investigators fail to think in terms of lethality, as opposed to perturbation. A suicidal event, whether a threat, or an attempt, or a commission, is best understood in terms of its lethal intention, rather than its method or how much general upset accompanies it.) We need to know the characteristics of those with low lethality. Obviously, prevention of suicidal deaths lies in dealing with the former.

It might be well to pattern the follow-up procedures for suicide attempts roughly after that of health educators working with venereal disease or tuberculosis follow up and look forward to the time when suicide attempt follow up can be built into routine health services. The follow up could be seen as post-crisis follow up and would be a legitimate aspect of a comprehensive approach to suicide prevention. It is known that the most dangerous period with relation to suicide is within three months after a suicidal crisis. A follow-up procedure might be one effective way in saving some lives and would furnish excellent data for significant study and research.

Follow–up of Survivor Victims

It is not inaccurate to state that from the point of view of the survivor, there are two kinds of deaths: all the deaths from cancer, heart, accident, and so on, on the one hand, and suicidal deaths, on the other. If one stops to consider the kind of grief work and mourning that one has to do on the occasion of a death of a loved one who dies of a natural or accidental cause on the one hand, and then what he has to do for the rest of his life if his parent or spouse has committed suicide, the contrast is then clear. The individual who commits suicide often sentences the survivor

to obsess for the rest of his life about the suicidal death. The suicide puts his skeleton in the survivor's psychological closet. No other kind of death in our society creates such lasting emotional scars as a suicidal death. A comprehensive suicide prevention program should attend to the psychological needs of the stigmatized survivors, especially the children who survive a parent who has committed suicide.

Although this aspect of the program is not directed especially toward reducing suicide (dealing as it does with an individual who has already killed himself), because it relates to the survivors of the suicidal death, it is directly in the center of mental health concern. Today each citizen enjoys many rights in this country; we would hope that he might be granted the right to lead an unstigmatized life, especially a life unstigmatized by the suicidal death of a parent or a spouse.

The Los Angeles Suicide Prevention Center has pioneered in developing a procedure called the "psychological autopsy." This process is used in cases of equivocal suicidal-accidental deaths and consists of interviewing a number of individuals who knew the deceased, to obtain pertinent psychological data about the nature of the death. The relevance of this is that it has demonstrated that it is easily possible, and always therapeutic, to work with survivors of a suicidal death, especially immediately after the death and even for some interval thereafter.[6,10,17]

Studies of the effects of suicides on survivors need to be done. Two kinds of studies immediately suggest themselves: retrospective studies of individuals whose parent committed suicide one, five, ten, twenty years ago and prospective studies, where the suicide has occurred in the very recent past and the effects on the survivor are followed through time.

We do not at present know the cost of each suicide in terms of the deleterious mental effects on the survivors (how many survivors of a father's or a mother's suicide subsequently need mental hospitalization or other mental health care) and in ascertaining what these facts are, we need to develop special ways for effectively helping individuals who have suffered this kind of traumatic loss. Just as there are better and worse ways of responding to, for example, the loss of a limb or to blindness, so we must develop better ways to help survivors respond to the grim fact of suicide in their family, and thus to reduce the overall mental health toll.

Evaluation of the Effectiveness of Suicide Prevention Activities

Evaluation is a necessary part of effective follow up. The goal of effecting a reduction in suicidal deaths carries with it the simultaneous charge of doing so in such a way as to be able to demonstrate unequivocally that those lives have been saved.

Although, in the individual case, suicide can best be seen as reflecting "a damp, dismal November in the soul," it also seems to be that, in the large, suicide rates vary with such items as the nation's position in relation to peace and war; changes in the economic state of the nation (prosperity or depression); changes, in any one place, in the percentage and the role of blacks; and so on. All this is to say that it is an extremely thorny methodological problem in epidemiology to make a single test or to prove the effectiveness of a suicide prevention program in terms of a single measure, especially suicidal deaths. Nevertheless, efforts to establish the effectiveness of suicide prevention activities must, from both a scientific and moral point of view, be a part of a comprehensive suicide prevention program from its very beginning. Without this feature of rigorous evaluation there can be no accounting by any clinician or investigator, either to himself or to the scientific community.

This aspect of the total program, perhaps more than some of the others, requires close consultation with people in biometry, epidemiology, sociological methodology, research design, and statistics. Perhaps special committees might be formed specifically to deal with the issue of evaluation.

The basic issues in a suicide prevention program are: What can a local suicide prevention program do to lower the suicide rate of the people of that community, and how can we find out whether this is being accomplished?

In general, three levels of prevention have been envisaged: (1) primary prevention, in which the goal is to make it unnecessary for the suicidal crisis ever to occur; (2) secondary prevention (intervention), which has to do with the effective treatment of an existing suicidal crisis; and (3) tertiary prevention (postvention), which relates to the reduction in the amount of disability in the survivor caused by the irreversible (already occurred) suicidal event.

And if there are three levels of prevention, there are at least three criteria for the effectiveness of any suicide prevention program. The first, most obvious, and by far the most important is the reduction of suicidal deaths. The second is the evaluation of the effectiveness of various types of approaches to and treatments of suicidal phenomena. The third should not be entirely ignored: It is the reduction of the overall lethality in the individuals who make up a community. Just as one might ask what a random study of blood samples of individuals entering a business or government building would reveal in terms of barbiturate and ethanol levels, so in the same spirit one might ask what a random study would reveal in relation to individuals' lethality indices, that is, their general ties to life. A successful suicide prevention program should, in addition to overtly saving lives, also serve to lower the lethality level and suicidal index of a community. We need much baseline data in this area.

The very establishment of a suicide prevention program has a salutary effect on the mental health within its own community. It can provide a model for the effective approach to a variety of other sociopsychological blights, as well as provide useful information to help reduce the inimical effects of these blights. It would be hard to conceive that information generated in the area of suicide prevention would not have implications (both methodological and substantive) for accident fatalities, addiction, alcoholism, delinquency, homicide, schizophrenia, and other maladaptive and self-destructive patterns.

Suicide is, by definition, a certain kind of death and, as such, obviously relates to other kinds of death. Suicide has been defined as "the human act of self-inflicted, self-intentioned cessation."[9] Suicide relates to motivation and is intentioned (as opposed to unintentioned or even subintentioned); it is self-imposed (as opposed to death due to trauma from without, a psychological failure from within, or assault from others); it is total cessation (as opposed to partial deaths or temporary interruption of consciousness); it is individual (as opposed to the decimation or disappearance of a group); it is technically suicide (as opposed to the NASH [natural, accident, suicide, homicide] classification of modes of death used for reporting purposes in the death certificates [and statistics] in the Western world); and, in practically every ordinary case, it appears, from the point of view of the surviving relatives, to be stigmatizing (as opposed to honorific, uplifting, ennobling, comforting).

The extent of the community and mental health problems created by or associated with suicidal deaths is difficult, perhaps impossible to enumerate. The National Center for Health Statistics[7] estimated over 20,000 suicidal deaths in the United States each year. Some other experts on this topic, notably Dublin,[2] stated that this is a minimum figure, representing a significant underreporting. My own belief is that the veridical data are half again as high, a lot more than 30,000 self-inflicted deaths per year, and, if subintentioned deaths were added, the number would be ten times as high. Further, there are about eight suicide attempts for each reported suicidal death,[3] so that conservatively we are dealing with more than 180,000 suicidal episodes each year. The number of people alive in the United States who have attempted suicide at some time in their lives is estimated to be in the millions.[2] Although it seems obvious to say that the primary goal of any suicidal prevention effort is to save lives (that is, to effect a reduction in the suicide rate), it is no contradiction to state that, given the suicide figure at any given time, by far the more important mental health problems relate to the fate and well-being of the survivor victims of the suicidal deaths. If we can assert that the typical suicide directly affects four people (a surviving parent, a spouse, and two children), not to count the larger number the deceased less directly touches, then we are talking about the dire and inimical mental health sequelae imposed (usually for the lifetime of that person) on approximately 100,000 additional persons each year, burdens of guilt, shame, puzzlement, taint, fear, and mystery, which are never satisfactorily resolved and often reach through the generations, benighting many lives.

In the last few years, the special feasibilities of the suicide prevention centers have been explicated.[12] Specifically, the following feasibilities have been demonstrated: (1) of preventing suicide; (2) of discovering prodromal clues to suicide; (3) of doing meaningful research on this topic; (4) of using active therapeutic techniques, often involving the significant other; (5) of acting as a consultation service for established mental health agencies; (6) of working with a chief medical examiner-coroner, especially by use of the psychological autopsy procedure; (7) of having an around-the-clock service; (8) of employing a truly multiprofessional approach; (9) of conceptualizing some time-worn (and inadequate) concepts of suicide and death; (10) of "unbooing" some unnecessary taboos; (11) of showing the desirability of establishing regional training centers; and (12) of operating a specifically focused suicide prevention center.

In the past decade, there has been a spirited growth of suicide prevention centers throughout this country. The figures detailing this trend are themselves interesting. As recently as 1958 there were three more-or-less comprehensive suicide prevention centers in this country; in 1959, four; in 1960, five; in 1964, nine; in 1965, fifteen; in 1966, thirty; in 1967, forty; in 1968, sixty; in 1970, more than 130; the trend is up. Not all the centers of the future will be autonomous and have separate identification; indeed, most of them will be, as they ought, integral aspects of hospitals, universities, and especially of comprehensive mental health centers, but, nonetheless, they will exist. In terms of geographic distribution, suicide prevention centers now exist in more than half the states and in every major section of the nation. But, obviously, there is much to be done.

A suicide prevention center provides an example par excellence of a kind of service that, literally in order to stay alive (much less to function with any degree of effectiveness), needs to coordinate closely and well with a large number of agencies and key persons within the community. Perhaps more than most, the vention of suicide is a community mental health operation. Experience teaches us that the establishment of suicide prevention facilities within a community is an experience in liaison and coordination. The interest (or, at the least, the passive approval) of several pivotal groups should, in most cases, be secured: the local medical group, the police, local government, hospitals, resource therapists in private practice, some civic groups, a number of social agencies, and the press. A recent Public Affairs pamphlet[13] contained the following advice:

A suicide prevention center cannot open shop all at once like a supermarket. Rather, the entire process, if it would be successful, must be gradually and tactfully woven into the community. From the beginning, the organizers must solicit help—at the very least, cooperation—from the city or county medical authorities. The hospitals, the coroner's office, and the police chief should know about the beginning of any suicide prevention service. In fact, suicide prevention needs their help. This is reasonable, since the new service ultimately will ease police and hospital emergency-room workloads. But, on occasion, the suicide prevention service will have to call on them for help. The local press, radio, and television should be informed about what's afoot and asked to cooperate. If a story breaks before the budding suicide prevention service is ready, this premature news could be disastrous. Of course, the city government must know what plans are being made. If city officials are not the initial sponsors of such a community service, certainly their endorsement should be heartily pursued. Without local cooperation, successful suicide prevention is practically impossible.

The recent establishment of a new multi-professional discipline, suicidology, serves as the intellectual catchment area for a wide variety of scientists (epidemiologists, demographers, statisticians, sociologists, social psychologists, and so on), clinicians (psychiatrists, clinical psychologists, psychiatric social workers, trained volunteers, clergy, police, and so on), and educators (school and university personnel, health educators, and so on). Suicidology is the study of, and concern with, suicidal phenomena and their prevention. This term was chosen advertently in order to give the special visibility and identity such a new discipline required. As part of the activities of the new Center for Studies of Suicide Prevention at the National Institute of Mental Health, we had sought to create some sense of special excitement in the burgeoning fields of suicide and suicide prevention and to unite the interests of a number of kinds of people concerned either with suicidal phenomena or with suicide prevention. Suicidology seems to provide a reasonable solution. Already, in the recent past, the new profession seems to have taken hold. In 1968, the American Association of Suicidology was established.

Consistent with all this is the view expounded in this chapter of suicidal phenomena as sociopsychological blights (rather than an illness, disease, or set of statistics). Social and behavioral scientists would do well to focus, even to specialize, in the substantive areas of specific major sociopsychological blights, such as suicide, homosexuality, violence, urban perturbation, to name a few. Our stake—indeed, our responsibility—in suicide is a vital one. The suicidologist has the challenge to do exciting things in research, training and life-saving; his opportunities in community service would seem to be limited only by the limits of his own imagination and energy.

⟨ Bibliography

1. BROWN, B., and LONG, S. E. "Psychology and Community Mental Health: The Medical Muddle." *American Psychologist*, 23 (1968), 335–341.
2. DUBLIN, L. *Suicide: A Sociological and Sta-*

tistical Study. New York: Ronald Press, 1963.

3. FARBEROW, N., and SHNEIDMAN, E., eds. *The Cry for Help.* New York: McGraw-Hill, 1961.

4. HEILIG, S. M., FARBEROW, N., and LITMAN, R. E. "The Role of Nonprofessional Volunteers in a Suicide Prevention Center." *Community Mental Health Journal,* 4 (1968), 287–295.

5. LINDEMANN, E., et al., "Preventive Intervention in a Four-Year-Old Child Whose Father Committed Suicide." In G. Caplan, ed., *Emotional Problems of Early Childhood.* New York: Basic Books, 1955.

6. LITMAN, R. E., CURPHEY, T., SHNEIDMAN, E., FARBEROW, N., and TABACHNICK, N. "Investigations of Equivocal Suicides." *Journal of the American Medical Association,* 184 (1963), 924–929.

7. NATIONAL CENTER OF HEALTH STATISTICS. *Suicide in the United States.* Publication no. 1000, series 20, no. 5. Washington, D.C.: U.S. Government Printing Office, 1967.

8. SHNEIDMAN, E. "Orientations Toward Death: A Vital Aspect of the Study of Lives." In R. W. White, ed., *The Study of Lives.* New York: Atherton Press, 1963.

9. ———. "Suicide: Psychological Aspects: I." In *International Encyclopedia of the Social Sciences.* Vol. 15. New York: Macmillan, 1968. Pp. 385–389.

10. ———. "Suicide, Lethality, and the Psychological Autopsy." In E. Shneidman and M. Ortega, eds., *Aspects of Depression.* Boston: Little, Brown, 1969.

11. ———, ed. *Essays in Self-Destruction.* New York: Science House, 1967.

12. ———, and FARBEROW, N. "The Los Angeles Suicide Prevention Center: A Demonstration of Public Health Feasibilities." *American Journal of Public Health,* 55 (1965), 21–26.

13. ———, FARBEROW, N., and LITMAN, R. E. *The Psychology of Suicide.* New York: Science House, 1970.

14. ———, and MANDELKORN, P. "How to Prevent Suicide." *Public Affairs Pamphlet.* New York: Public Affairs Committee, 1967.

15. SILVERMAN, P. R. "The Widow-to-Widow Program: An Experiment in Preventive Intervention." *Mental Hygiene,* 53 (1969), 333–337.

16. STENGEL, E. *Suicide and Attempted Suicide.* Baltimore: Penguin Books, 1964.

17. WEISMAN, A., and KASTENBAUM, R. "The Psychological Autopsy: A Study of the Terminal Phase of Life." *Community Mental Health Journal,* monogr. no. 4 (1967), 1–59.

CHAPTER 50

MENTAL HEALTH PROGRAMS IN THE SCHOOLS

Irving N. Berlin

(Origins of Mental Health Programs

MENTAL HEALTH PROGRAMS in schools began as unorganized efforts by administrators and teachers to meet the need as public schools became widespread and mandatory in the 1930s.[3] Sensitive teachers and administrators with knowledge and understanding of their students learned and helped others learn the signs that alerted them to emotional problems and crises in a child's life. Their prompt concern was usually expressed by efforts to talk with the child, to gather information about the difficulties, and to talk with the parents. Innovative educators found ways of utilizing the school's resources, community physicians, settlement house workers, and so on on behalf of problems at home.

Increased attention and concern seemed to help the student.[66,99]

When public health nurses, school nurses, and health support services became a functional part of schools in the mid-1930s, they very quickly found themselves involved with mental health problems depending on their own sensitivity and capacity for empathy with children and educators. They became the resources for teaching hygiene, a short step to being consulted by girls and boys with worries that manifested themselves as psychosomatic problems. The work of Gildea, Glidewell,[41,42] and Kontar[42,43] and of Klein and Lindemann[56,58] and collaborators in Wellesley schools were efforts at helping parents, nurses, counselors, and teachers to understand children and to find ways to help them. They provided consultation, education, and referral resources to the schools and were able to demonstrate, by epidemiological research, some reduction of problems and greater ability of students to learn and cope with problems as a result of early case findings and intervention.[89]

(The Role of Child Guidance Clinics and Development of Pupil Personnel Services

World War I highlighted the fact that mental illness and emotional problems of crippling severity were widespread. The Rockefeller Foundation and Commonwealth Fund spearheaded the development of child guidance clinics and training programs for child psychiatrists.[70] Social workers and psychologists soon became part of the functional team, each with unique contributions. Influenced by Adolf Meyer's concepts of the need to understand the whole personality by understanding every facet of the child's life, that is, an evaluation of the total situation, especially the interaction of parents with their child, the clinics became resources for the few communities in which they were organized. Several school child guidance clinics were formed with foundation help in the late 1920s to permit more direct access of teachers to services and also help with classroom management.[65,70]

During this same period large urban school systems, faced with increased numbers of children with emotional problems, delinquent and aggressive behavior, began to pick sensitive teachers and train them through in-service work as counselors. Simultaneously, some schools of social work and a few departments of psychology began to interest their trainees in children's problems. At the University of Pennsylvania as early as 1908, Witmer, a psychologist, gave leadership to a guidance clinic which began in connection with the university. This program aroused widespread interest in work with children. Witmer involved his students in working with children, both in the clinic and in schools.[65]

Hitler's rise to power in the early 1930s brought a mass migration of psychoanalysts to the United States. Among them were child analysts. The Depression made teaching, training, and treatment in the burgeoning child guidance clinics rather than private practice necessary for many psychoanalysts from Germany and Vienna. Thus, Freudian concepts and methodology were taught and adapted for use in clinics. A few psychoanalysts worked as school consultants. Since Anna Freud, Aichhorn, Bernfeld, Erikson, and many others were interested in or trained in pedagogy and work with teachers, their ideas were disseminated.[10,101] With rare exceptions school mental health programs were conceived piecemeal to meet pressing needs, and little effort was made to assess how schools might become centers for early identification of problems—made possible when for the first time, most children would be observed by trained personnel. Certainly early identification of problems by teachers can be effective, as demonstrated by Bower,[19,20,21,22] but it was rarely taught or emphasized. The use of learning as a mental health tool was emphasized from the days of Witmer and Dewey.[1,61,88] However, planned school mental health programs using all school and community facilities were a rarity. Even today, despite the enormous increase in school problems, disruptions, and nonlearning behavior, such comprehensive programs are still rare.

(Mental Health Consultation in Schools

World War II brought an increased awareness of the mental health problems of the draft-age soldier. The great number of the rejections of draftees as mentally unfit for service and the vast numbers of servicemen, in and out of combat, who were treated for mental and emotional problems brought to sharp awareness the national need for training specialists to work with children and with schools.

Thus, in the late 1940s and early 1950s the first efforts at mental health consultation to schools were described in the literature.[11,18,27] Each author, working in his own way, began to describe his experiences and to account for results using a variety of theoretical approaches. At the nursery school level, Parker[79,80] described an educative consultation model to enhance the functioning of teachers with children. Other workers at the elementary and secondary levels described their work with teachers and administrators. The common theme that began to emerge was one of helping school personnel, educators, administrators, and other school workers to enhance their capacities to use educational methods more effectively in reducing children's difficulties in school. Caplan, from the Laboratory of Community Psychiatry at Harvard, began to describe a theory of mental health consultation that contributed to the awareness of many and enabled them to examine their work in the light of a theoretical model.[28,30,31,95] Thus mental health consultation in schools was written about, and various aspects were more consciously taught and applied. Caplan's framework was congruent with Berlin's early descriptions of the consultation process in schools.[9,11,12]

Sarvis and Pennekamp and Newman also began to describe their practice and formulate their theoretical base, borrowing in each case from their basic training and experience in intensive psychotherapy with children and adolescents.[78,96] Many other workers in the mental health professions became involved in a variety of consultation efforts with schools. Some chose individual work with teachers around problem children; others worked mostly with administrators when they could. Still others experimented with and delineated group consultation methods with teachers, counselors, and school health and mental health professionals.[40]

Inherent in all these efforts was the fact that problem children were so numerous that mental health clinics and workers as treatment resources could never catch up. Further, individual psychotherapy with children alone or including their parents did not produce rapid or miraculous results. Those on the firing line in the schools would have to become more effective in using themselves and the potentially therapeutic aspect of education more

productively on behalf of disturbed and disturbing children.

The simultaneous work in ego psychology by Anna Freud,[37] Hartmann, Kris, and Loewenstein,[46] Erikson,[36] and others and work on competence theory by White[100] began to clarify how the healthy aspects of the personality of a disturbed person or child can be used to aid in the reduction of the disturbance.

In recent books and papers, Sarvis and Pennekamp,[96] Newman,[77] and Berlin[13–15] have more clearly delineated their theoretical framework for school consultation. Sarvis and Pennekamp described vividly their experience in obtaining the close collaboration of teachers, administrators, counselors, school psychologists, and social workers in evolving a school team approach to the problem student. Newman described her methods, which were influenced by her collaboration with Fritz Redl. This approach is based on the life space interview concept, a very dynamic awareness, and understanding of both the teachers' and the students' problems in the context of the school environment and utilizes analytic and dynamic psychiatric theory via on the spot demonstrations of intervention using interpretations and sensitive behavioral confrontations to illustrate how, when, and where a disturbed child can be helped within the school context.[24]

❲ Example of a Methodology of Mental Health Consultation in the School

My paper on methodology of mental health consultation in the schools focuses on a five-stage process.[15] There are four or five steps involved in this method of mental health consultation, some of which tend to merge; but all are essential to effective mental health consultation.

The first step centers around developing a good working relationship so that the consultee does not feel suspicious or fearful that the worker will try to uncover unconscious motivations or pry into personal problems.

This is one obstacle all mental health professionals must overcome in consultation. The establishment of the collaborative relationship depends on the worker's task-oriented approach, in which only the work problems brought up for discussion are considered, but never in terms of possible underlying psychopathology. Perhaps the most successful way such a collaborative relationship is established is through the mutual consideration and evaluation of the origins of the troubles of the client. Consultant and consultee together consider the factors in the home environment, the living experiences, and the previous relationships of the client that may be etiological to the present troubles. Thus together they gather and evaluate the data that delineate the child's emotional troubles and personal and sociocultural deprivations. In this way the consultee does not feel personally responsible for the client's problems or burdened with the personal need to make up for the client's lack of nurturant and integrative experiences with important persons in the past. As a result of such exploration, the consultee can more realistically assess how much he can expect of himself in helping the client. He also comes to expect a collaboration with an expert colleague, who places no blame but instead focuses on enhancing the understanding of the client's learning problems.

The second step is an effort to reduce the consultee's anxieties and self-blame, his feelings of failure, frustration, anger, and hopelessness. These tensions are usually an admixture of reality problems and circumstances, the role problems common to the teaching profession, and the character problems that may interfere with the consultee's effectiveness. Mutual exploration of the genesis of the client's troubles may help reduce anxieties and usually lays the groundwork for a relationship in which the consultant's comments may be understood and considered, especially those comments that indicate his empathic understanding of the consultee's distress. The consultant most effectively conveys his understanding of these feelings, dilemmas, and anxieties by reporting experiences of a related nature that have engendered similar feelings in him. When the consultee talks of his hostile and anxious feelings as he is confronted by angry parents, the consultant can be helpful by relating how long it took him to learn that such anger was indicative of parents' hopeless and helpless feelings in dealing with the child. The teacher, counselor, or administrator thus learns that such anger is not directed primarily against the worker as a person. In this process the consultee's anxiety is externalized and reduced by the consultant's comments, which illustrate that these feelings and experiences are human and comprehensible and within his own experiences as a professional person and as a human being. Thus, the consultee's feelings of blame and guilt may be reduced, and he may feel less defensive. Because he feels understood he will be able to engage himself in the consultative effort.

The third step in consultation is designed to keep the collaboration task-oriented and to prevent the helpless dependency that may follow relief of anxiety. The consideration of etiological factors in the client's troubles and the consultant's diagnostic appraisal of the consultee's ego strengths are used to focus on the first step to be taken by the consultee to help the client. Thus, the teacher is engaged in consideration of how he can engage the student in the learning process. This needs to be a mutual consideration and agreement to work with the child in a particular way that the teacher considers consonant with his own capabilities. In this phase, the consultant needs to be wary of making unilateral recommendations or being seduced into prescriptions about the educative process in which the educator is the expert. Such recommendations will inevitably fail if the consultee is not involved in delineating and examining the educational aspect of the plan. The worker adds his expertise about the probable emotional impact of the method, consideration of how specific approaches may fit the child's particular psychological needs, and what emotional reactions might be anticipated and utilized in each plan. It is also very important that consultee and consultant agree on realistic and achievable goals. Goals need to be tentative ones, which can be tested and evaluated. Since each effort is experimental, neither participant need feel blame for any failure. Each is a collaborator in the discovery and refinement of techniques of educational approaches to the reduction of the difficulties. Recriminations endanger the consultative relationship.

The fourth step, a vital one, consists of follow-up meetings to evaluate, reconsider, modify, and try new approaches in the light of the teacher's experiences and the changes in the child. This enables the consultee to recognize that he can build on every tiny increment of learning, that each minute step is important and meaningful to the child's interpersonal experience and beginning sense of mastery. Thus, the consultee is encouraged to be content with tiny shifts, to recognize these, and to reward the child for his learning. He is helped to take satisfaction in his sustained and consistent efforts. Encouraged in continued consultations, the consultee begins to be more spontaneous and inventive in his approaches. At this stage one hears from the consultee how he has used his insights gained in consultation to work with other children.

The fifth step is the consolidation and disengagement from consultation. As the consultee works more effectively and feels more secure in his capacity to work and help a wider variety of disturbed children, he needs the consultant less. His increasing competence as a teacher, counselor, or administrator leaves him free to call the consultant when and if he needs help. In this process, then, the consultee is helped with his own situational or character problems by an understanding of the client's problems and by helping to deal more effectively with them. He also simultaneously unlearns his idiosyncratic and previously less effective attitudes and methods. Thus he learns to integrate attitudes and methods in the use of educative techniques that are more effective and can be used with many clients.

Since this is not a casework, patient, or client relationship, certain gratifications and rewards inherent in direct work may be missing and may initially make consultation less satisfying. Consultees who are helped to work more effectively usually do not express gratitude. Because they are engaged as collabora-

tors, they often may not recognize that they have been helped. Frequently the most successful consultation is indicated only by the evidence that the consultee does not require further consultation. As in all interpersonal processes, it is a slow one. An indirect process, it is once removed from the consultee's personality or character problems, and indications of success may not be seen for some time.

Consultation may be very anxiety provoking if the consultee feels overwhelmed. He may demand from the consultant answers that are not available. In these circumstances it may be very difficult to recognize that the consultee may be identifying with the attitudes and methods of the consultant as he helps evaluate the situation and begins to look for "bite-sized" approaches. The consultee may often not reduce his demands, but the consultant's persistence may help in finding an avenue of approach to tackle the problems a bit at a time. The identification of consultee with consultant has been found to be an important dynamic of the process. One often indirectly hears that a teacher reacts to the pressures from a difficult child or the overwhelming burdens of a difficult classroom situation with the same general approach and style that the consultant has used with the consultee.

Employing consultation methods with individual consultees seems to help both the consultee and the client function more effectively.

Only very recently did Caplan[32] complete his long awaited text on mental health consultation, which has very direct application theoretically and by detailed case examples for mental health consultation in the schools. Caplan clearly delineated the variety of consultation opportunities possible in the school setting from work with clients to consultee and program-centered efforts. Some of Caplan's students have also focused on the schools and have described their experiences and contributed to the theory of mental health consultation in the schools. Rappaport[87] focused on the social worker's role, and Bindman[18] and others on the psychologist's role as consultant in schools.

Rowitch,[94] in a seminal paper, describes the shift from case-oriented to program-oriented consultation in a day-care center. Here the basic procedures of the school are eventually altered to provide a more effective interpersonal and learning environment. Altrocchi, Spielberger, and Eisdorfer,[2] Kevin,[54] Berkowitz,[6] and others described variations of group consultation, each seeing the process as effective but as different in focus and emphasis. Altrocchi et al. and Kevin saw it as an enlargement of individual consultation with opportunities for the consultant's modeling of behavior helpful to each consultee in his problem solving. Berkowitz[6] viewed the process with any group of educators as moving from case to program consultation.

(Mental Health Programs and the Community

Despite many and varied school consultation models and efforts, integrated and effective school mental health programs are rare.[41] Rafferty's program in Baltimore[84,86] comes close to such a program, that is, close liaison with schools and work at various levels not only to enhance the school personnel's capacities to work with disturbed children but to work with educators to evaluate kindergarten and first-grade children. The free flow of children, educators, and mental health staff is fostered from inpatient and day-care services to outpatient service and return to school with close liaison at all times. The integrated activities, in every setting, of school and mental health center personnel in the service of a child are a unique and effective combination of talents, which enhances every professional's competence. It creates enthusiastic learning about children's functioning and dedication to the early recognition and prevention of psychological disorder. Parents are closely involved in each setting as partners in the work and as interested participants in learning how to help their children.

Blom and his associates, together with other mental health professionals,[7,75] work primarily with teachers' groups on an in-service basis to help sensitize them to the signs of early disorder and to help them evolve effective educational methods for helping alter the behavior and learning set of disturbed and nonlearning children.

The close working together of mental health professionals, community advocates, and parents to alter a ghetto child's chances for survival in the school is delineated by Kellam and Schiff in their work.[53,97] Such a program was not designed as a mental health program in schools but became one as the efforts to help teachers and children work together to help the child learn more effectively through group process in the classroom enhanced the total integrative functioning of both. Equally important, the program involved parents and community workers in an ever more effective collaboration with the school.

(Potential of School Mental Health Programs

Designed and utilized as secondary prevention, mental health programs that emphasize the early identification and remediation of learning and emotional problems have proven effective. School programs as they move into the preschool may have primary prevention opportunities. In the preschool and day-care settings, the identifications of developmental crises of children, nutritional and other indications of health, mental health, and learning problems may lead to their prevention. This requires the involvement of the family and the community in a joint enterprise with the school. The school must develop those relations with community agencies and especially with parents and the community they serve so that they can obtain collaborative mental health interventions supported by all concerned. The child and family advocate system proposed by the Joint Commission on Child Mental Health and currently being sponsored by the Office of Child Development, the Office of Education, and the National Institute of Mental Health may help to intervene early and to ensure more relevant and stimulating education.[20,22,26,35,39,51,102,103]

⟨[Community-School Mental Health Programs

On a large scale community-school mental health programs are new, although they reflect the learning from Lindemann and Klein in such projects as at Wellesley, and Gildea and Glidewell in projects at St. Louis.

A few such programs are in existence, and the rare ones are becoming very effective and are composed of known ingredients, but none specifically are directed to school mental health and effective learning. Historically they came about because of mass migration from rural to urban areas by minorities, the creation of enormous ghettos, and children who were not well prepared for learning. Families' reactions to the stresses of mass poverty in urban ghettos have resulted in many children with a myriad of problems which have overwhelmed school health and mental health resources.*

Schools have not changed in the last several decades to meet the growing urban problems. Teachers have been poorly prepared in newer, more relevant educational methods necessary for their jobs.† The rewards for learning need to be more tangible and the methods of teaching more innovative. As mental health personnel found that individual work with children was not feasible and evolved group techniques and consultation methodology, educators evolved creative, high-impact, high-interest classes.[52,55,68,71]

Most relevant to new modes of helping children has been the impact of parents, who as paid aides and volunteers have proven their worth, first to the education of preschool children and currently to elementary school children.

New programs are beginning to rely on professionally trained teachers as coordinators of volunteers. They spend their time helping volunteer parents and community persons learn how to help individual children and small groups. They have evolved highly attractive and effective learning games that volunteers can use with children who are failing in reading, math, history, and the like. Usually, volunteers can find time for work with individual children; most teachers are so involved in overall programming and total classroom monitoring that they have little time for individual work. The most emotionally disturbed children, those with severe ego defects due to early lack of nurturance and object constancy, can often, through working with a parent or interested community volunteer, begin to learn and to identify with the volunteer who is able to give the necessary time to the disturbed child.[73,91]

Consultation by mental health personnel to volunteers around some of the very disturbed children they serve has been quite effective. In one system such group consultation has not only provided a regular way of problem solving with the volunteers but has also permitted a healthy exchange of ideas. New learning for all, the integration of several community health and mental health services and school educational services on behalf of the child, and enhanced respect of each group toward the others have also occurred to the child's benefit.[57]

In some day-care, preschool, and Head Start programs the very young and very disturbed children require an enormous amount of individual attention that only a large number of community volunteers can provide. The attentive concern, for example, of a trained elderly volunteer has tremendous impact on disturbed nonlearning young children. In these same systems parent groups are involved in learning to help their children via games at home. They learn to provide prompt tokens as rewards that can be cashed in at school for toys and foods. These parents, rather than being alienated by their difficult nonlearning child who usually evokes a threat of retaliatory administrative action, learn to enjoy working with their child, often for the first time successfully.

The use of older children to teach younger children with learning and mental health problems has repeatedly proven effective. The older children prove to be effective objects for identification. Their interest and competence

---

* See references 25, 38, 60, 63, 81, 82, and 92.
† See references 44, 50, 59, 60, 72, 74, and 76.

in teaching younger children enhances their feelings of self-worth, and they are eager for mental health consultation. As consultees they learn quickly, raise relevant questions without hesitation, gather data effectively, and carry out mutually agreed on plans with energy and enthusiasm helpful to the disturbed child. They can also translate the objectives of their work to teachers and parents with clarity and vividness. Notably, student tutors also become better students and relate the mental health knowledge acquired to other situations, such as in their own class work. Some students look to entering the mental health fields themselves as important occupational objectives.[34,90]

(The Community Mental Health Center and School Mental Health

New school mental health programs for students of all ages have come from the consultation and education components of some community mental health centers. The heavy involvement of mental health aides and paraprofessionals in the centers means that the neighborhood problems as well as the school problems that contribute to mental health problems are potentially well understood by community members. The previous lack of collaboration of agencies with the school on behalf of a student and parent is reduced as the center begins to facilitate interagency collaboration using its facilities as part of the total system of services to be coordinated on behalf of its citizens. In some community mental health centers, mental health aides, teachers' aides, and health aides may be trained to be interchangeable, that is, to develop similar skills so that any of them can work with students and parents at home, at the day-care center, in the school project, and within the center's therapeutic day-care, inpatient, and halfway house services. Thus, one of the major road blocks may be overcome if a community mental health center begins to function to coordinate health, education, mental health, and even welfare services in its catchment area. To date such collaboration

and integration of services is still rare, but where they have occurred, they appear to be effective examples of how children can be served.[90]

(The Role of New Mental Health Workers in the Schools

To provide for needed personnel to help with mental health problems in schools, several new kinds of trained educators have evolved. The elementary school counselor in many areas is a consultant to several elementary schools and uses primarily an educational approach to mental health problems with some personal counseling for children and parents. Primarily the elementary school counselor tries to help teachers find ways to work with disturbed children via educational means. He is often trained to demonstrate such methods to teachers. In the main these are behavior modification methods, using token and social reinforcement.[46,47]

School counselors, social workers, and psychologists are developing new skills to add to the problem-solving techniques of their profession. They have developed group work techniques to help children and young adolescents. The counselors learn group counseling and special techniques of consulting with teachers. School psychologists have begun to abandon mass testing for involvement with teachers and troubled children using behavior modification techniques to help them learn to use clear rewards for successful learning and especially how to develop social reward systems. It has become clear that nurses, skilled counselors, social workers, and psychologists can in many of their functions work in the same ways.[21,23,49,69,93]

Added to these workers are the teachers' aides, volunteers, and older children as tutors. Importantly, parents can be helped to learn to work with their own and other children. Mental health professionals can collaborate with teachers to evolve models of helping others work with children. Incremental learning of teaching methods, as well as the use of observation and mental health consultation to help each worker overcome common problems in working with children, can also help reduce problems of working with severely disturbed children.

Very recently, school social workers and school psychologists have begun to learn mental health consultation methods in their course of training so that they can more effectively utilize their understanding of human behavior to help teachers work with disturbed children. Such in-house consultation is sometimes more effective than outside consultation because the consultant, as part of the school, knows the system, the administrators, the children, the teachers, the community, and all the various needs. Such efforts are often effective in working on system problems because they are common problems to all those concerned with children. Alliances within the system can be effected to solve the problems such as innovative teaching methods, more open community access to schools, more help to teachers with the teaching job to be done, as well as working out more effective methods of team teaching, helping schools to be more responsive to minority childrens' needs, and helping schools to develop more relevant courses. Such alliances, which utilize the mental health worker's skills to reduce expected and usual anxieties about change through mental health consultation and which focus on how needed change may reduce tensions in the schools, also promote better health and mental health programs for solving system problems.

Thus, what began as very sporadic and individual efforts to solve school mental health programs have now occasionally become system-wide programs in several large urban and rural areas.[45,64,67,83]

The role of the mental health worker has evolved into several roles. The generic role will always be relevant since some children will always require help for severe troubles via individual and group therapeutic methods.[84] Referrals of health and mental health problems and diagnosis of developmentally oriented psychological and learning problems, which lead to collaboration with educators, counselors, and remedial specialists to effect meaningful remediation, are clearly essential for some children. Many workers will also learn to use mental health consultation with individuals and groups to enhance the capacities of teachers, counselors, administrators, and sub-professionals to work more effectively with a wider spectrum of students with behavior problems. Mental health workers will also learn how to use group consultation to focus on system changes required to better educate a child population very poorly served by the schools for many years. One of their newest roles is that of school-community liaison. Here professionals with a particular feel for community problems, often minority mental health workers who have not moved too far from their communities, can help effect interaction between community and school around the needs of children, which are of concern to all.[5,17,95] Such interaction often leads to innovative changes in teaching and curriculum and parent participation in the program.

Recently mental health professionals have been able to help school personnel deal with confrontation in an integrative way. Thus, rather than wounded, angry, and authoritarian responses to various confrontations, they may help their colleagues in education to a more rational collaboration with students.[10,98] In some instances the mental health professionals' modeling of confrontation situations and illustrating the various kinds of common reactions and those that have led to integrative solutions may be helpful. Other workers' efforts to sensitize their colleagues to their students' feelings have helped. That is, increased awareness by educators of the kinds of anger that long-standing feelings of impotence, indifference of the educational system to needs of the poor, and racist attitudes have induced in students may increase collaboration with students to meet their specific needs. Effective collaboration helps students use their potency constructively to effect more and better learning. Hopefully, mental health professionals can also help their colleagues in education to increased awareness of how the schools from the early grades on can enhance the sense of effectiveness and ego mastery of students through participatory democracy first in the classroom, then in the community around the school, and then in the larger community.[17]

Mental health programs in the schools need now to focus on the use of recent research and knowledge to utilize the students' inherent ego strengths. Thus, the curiosity and investigativeness at every developmental level must be facilitated. Through both in-service exposure and mental health consultation, educators who were previously discouraged and weary have often rediscovered their skills and pleasure in involving each child in the excitement of learning. Simultaneously, as students acquire knowledge, they need help to use it for their own growth and to learn how to collaborate with others to solve the problems of their community and their society.[33]

Only a school program that uses its mental health workers inside and outside the system to help the teachers and administrators recognize and utilize the therapeutic effects of education will effectively deal with the many mental health problems in the school. It will utilize mental health consultation as one aid in the process of enhancing the competence of the faculty and students and their rapport with the community they serve.

In several of the most advanced school mental health programs, the mental health workers, both in the school system and outside, have begun to see their roles as catalysts to develop the capabilities of the administrators and educators in a school to anticipate problems and to recognize the very early signs of difficulties. Reexamination of previous experiences, where missed cues have resulted in exacerbation of difficulties, provides clues for primary prevention and early intervention or secondary prevention. School mental health programs in crises find it difficult to use their mental health personnel to focus on prevention as a major means of reducing crises. They tend to focus on treatment and administrative actions to deal with each crisis, which usually means the continuation of a crisis state. Efforts at gathering data about the nature and etiological factors of crises so that they can be anticipated and worked through are still rare. However, when carried out, they have led to effective preventive efforts.

School mental health programs still usually emphasize individual therapy of disturbed and disturbing children. The size of the problem without surcease has led to the use of mental health consultation as a means of dealing more effectively with problems in the classrooms. Massive school problems in both ghetto and suburban schools have led to widespread use of paraprofessionals and community resources. Only recently has there been a serious concern with the study of epidemiology and prevention of mental health disorders in the schools.

(Conclusions

Mental health programs in the schools have come a long way from the pioneering work of Witmer,[101] in the early 1900s, and didactic group mental hygiene efforts with parents, to recognition of individual children's problems and efforts at individual psychotherapy in the 1940s and 1950s. The 1960s saw consideration of efforts to meet growing needs with more effective methods of group work with children and mental health consultation with teachers and administrators to enhance their competence to help disturbed children within the school setting. Only recently, with the evolution of community mental health centers, has there been any effort to provide services close to the neighborhood. The massive problems resulting from in-migration of minorities into the ghettos—without responsive social and educational changes to alter the impact of poverty and discrimination—have required new patterns of mental health response to needs. These patterns of response tend to be community based and have utilized responsive mental health professionals as consultants to paraprofessionals and volunteers to provide greater manpower and impact on the ever-mounting problems.

In the schools, mental health programs depend on trained and responsive mental health professionals able to work effectively with parents, teachers' aides, and other paraprofessionals and students as teachers and consultees as well as with professional educators and administrators. Often their role is one of catalyst, to be alert to and anticipate the problems in such a system with its many diverse helpers and enormous needs in both educational and mental health spheres. As mental health workers learn to anticipate problems and honestly and openly raise them with all concerned, the needed changes within the systems and their relation to the community occur, and effective methods of helping children to learn and to grow are enhanced. As a result, others in the system begin to work toward anticipatory solutions of beginning problems, and prevention becomes possible.

❲ Bibliography

1. ALMY, M. "Intellectual Mastery and Mental Health." In H. F. Clarizio, ed., *Mental Health and the Educative Process*. New York: Rand-McNally, 1969. Pp. 107–119.

2. ALTROCCHI, J., SPIELBERGER, C., and EISDORFER, C. "Mental Health Consultation with Groups." *Community Mental Health Journal*, 1 (1965), 127–134.

3. ARIES, P. *Centuries of Childhood*. New York: Vintage Books, 1965.

4. BALSER, B. H. "Further Report on Experimental Evaluation of Mental Hygiene Techniques in School and Community." *American Journal of Psychiatry*, 113 (1957), 733–739.

5. BENNETT, E., and KAPLAN, F. "A Way of Thinking: Mental Health Professionals in Community Programs." *Community Mental Health Journal*, 3 (1967), 318–324.

6. BERKOWITZ, H. "Varieties of Mental Health Consultation for School Personnel." *Journal of Secondary Education*, 45, no. 3 (1970).

7. ——, ed. *A Report on School Consultation Activities*. Denver: University of Colorado Medical Center, 1969.

8. BERLIN, I. N. "Some Learning Experiences as Psychiatric Consultant in the Schools." *Mental Hygiene*, 40 (1956), 215–236.

9. ——. "Mental Health Consultation in Schools as a Means of Communicating Mental Health Principles." *Journal of the American Academy of Child Psychiatry*, 1 (1962), 671–679.

10. ——. "A History of Challenges in Child Psychiatry Training." *Mental Hygiene*, 48 (1964), 558–565.

11. ——. "Learning Mental Health Consultation: History and Problems." *Mental Hygiene*, 48 (1964), 257–266.

12. ——. "Mental Health Consultation in Schools: Who Does It and Why?" *Community Mental Health Journal*, 1 (1965), 19–22.

13. ——. "Consultation and Special Education." In I. Phillips, ed., *Prevention and Treatment of Mental Retardation*. New York: Basic Books, 1966. Pp. 270–293.

14. ——. "Preventive Aspects of Mental Health Consultation to Schools." *Mental Hygiene*, 51 (1967), 34–40.

15. ——. "Mental Health Consultation for School Social Workers: A Conceptual Model." *Community Mental Health Journal*, 5, no. 4 (1969), 280–288.

16. ——. "From Confrontation to Collaboration." *American Journal of Orthopsychiatry*, 40, no. 3 (1970), 473–480.

17. ——. "Professionals' Participation in Community Activities: Is It Part of the Job?" *American Journal of Orthopsychiatry*, 41 (1971), 494–500.

18. BINDMAN, A. J. "The School Psychologist and Mental Health." *Boston University Journal of Education*, 146 (1964), 5–10.

19. BOWER, E. M. *Early Identification of Emotionally Handicapped Children*. Springfield, Ill.: Charles C Thomas, 1960.

20. ——. "Mental Health in Education." In H. F. Clarizio, ed., *Mental Health and the Educative Process*. New York: Rand-McNally, 1969. Pp. 13–26.

21. ——. "The Modification, Mediation, and Utilization of Stress During the School Years." In H. F. Clarizio, ed., *Mental Health and the Educative Process*. New York: Rand-McNally, 1969. Pp. 344–352.

22. ——. "Primary Prevention of Mental and Emotional Disorders: A Frame of Reference." In H. F. Clarizio, ed., *Mental Health and the Educative Process*. New York: Rand-McNally, 1969. Pp. 294–303.

23. BRAUN, S. L., and LASHER, M. G. *Preparing Teachers to Work with Disturbed Preschoolers*. Medford, Mass.: Nimrod Press, 1970.

24. BRENNER, M. "Life Space Interview in the School Setting." In H. F. Clarizio, ed., *Mental Health and the Educative Process*. New York: Rand-McNally, 1969.

25. BROWN, B. S. "Definition of Mental Health and Disease." In A. M. Freedman and H. I. Kaplan, eds., *Comprehensive Textbook of Psychiatry*. Baltimore: Williams & Wilkins, 1967. Pp. 1519–1520.

26. CAPLAN, G. "Recent Trends in Preventive Child Psychiatry." In G. Caplan, ed., *Emotional Problems of Early Childhood*. New York: Basic Books, 1955. Pp. 153–163.

27. ———. "Mental Health Consultation in Schools." In *The Elements of a Community Mental Health Program*. New York: Milbank Memorial Fund, 1956. Pp. 72–85.

28. ———. *Concepts of Mental Health and Consultation*. Washington, D.C.: U.S. Children's Bureau, 1959.

29. ———. "Types of Mental Health Consultation." *American Journal of Orthopsychiatry*, 33 (1963), 470–481.

30. ———. *Principles of Preventive Psychiatry*. New York: Basic Books, 1964.

31. ———. "Problems of Training in Mental Health Consultation." In S. Goldston, ed., *Concepts of Community Psychiatry, A Framework for Training*. Bethesda, Md.: National Institute of Mental Health, 1965. Pp. 91–108.

32. ———. *The Theory and Practice of Mental Health Consultation*. New York: Basic Books, 1970.

33. CENTRAL ADVISORY COUNCIL FOR EDUCATION (ENGLAND). *Children and Their Primary Schools*. Vol. 1. London: Her Majesty's Stationery Office, 1966.

34. COWEN, E. L. "Emergent Approaches to Mental Health Problems: An Overview and Directions for Future Work." In E. L. Cowen, Gardner, and M. Zax, eds., *Emergent Approaches to Mental Health Problems*. New York: Appleton-Century-Crofts, 1967. Pp. 389–345.

35. EISENBERG, L., and GRUENBERG, E. M. "The Current Status of Secondary Prevention in Child Psychiatry." *American Journal of Orthopsychiatry*, 31, no. 2 (1961), 355–367.

36. ERIKSON, E. H. *Childhood and Society*. New York: Norton, 1930.

37. FREUD, A. *The Ego and Mechanisms of Defense*. New York: International Universities Press, 1955.

38. FRIEDENBERG, E. Z. *The Vanishing Adolescent*. New York: Dell, 1969.

39. GALLAGHER, J. J. *Teaching the Gifted Child*. Boston: Allyn & Bacon, 1964.

40. GIBB, J. R., and LIPPITT, R., eds. "Consulting with Groups and Organizations." *Journal of Social Issues*, 15 (1959), 1–74.

41. GILBERT, R. "Functions of the Consultant." *Teachers' College Record*, 61 (1960), 177–187.

42. GILDEA, M. C. *Community Mental Health: A School Centered Program*. Springfield, Ill.: Charles C Thomas, 1959.

43. ———, GLIDEWELL, J. C., and KONTAR, M. D. "The St. Louis School Mental Health Project: History and Evaluation." In E. L. Cowen, Gardner, and M. Zax, eds., *Emergent Approaches to Mental Health Problems*. New York: Appleton-Century-Crofts, 1967. Pp. 290–306.

44. GRAUBARD, P. S., ed. *Children Against Schools: Education of the Delinquent, Disturbed, and Disruptive*. Chicago: Follett, 1969.

45. GRIFFITH, C. R., and LIBO, L. M. *Mental Health Consultants: Agents of Community Change*. San Francisco: Jossey-Bass, 1968.

46. HARTMANN, H., KRIS, E., and LOEWENSTEIN, R. M. "Comments on the Formation of Psychic Structure." *Psychoanalytic Study of the Child*, 12 (1946), 11–38.

47. HEWETT, F. M. "Educational Engineering with Emotionally Disturbed Children." In H. F. Clarizio, ed., *Mental Health and the Educative Process*. New York: Rand-McNally, 1969. Pp. 386–397.

48. ———. *The Emotionally Disturbed Child in the Classroom*. Boston: Allyn & Bacon, 1970.

49. HOBBS, N. "Helping Disturbed Children: Psychological and Ecological Strategies." In H. F. Clarizio, ed., *Mental Health and the Educative Process*. New York: Rand-McNally, 1969.

50. HOLT, J. *How Children Fail*. New York: Delta Books, 1965.

51. JOINT COMMISSION ON MENTAL HEALTH OF CHILDREN. *Crisis in Child Mental Health: Challenge for the 1970s*. New York: Harper & Row, 1970.

52. JONES, R. M. *Fantasy and Feeling in Education*. New York: New York University Press, 1968.

53. KELLAM, S. G., and SCHIFF, S. K. "Adaptation and Mental Illness in the First Grade Classrooms of an Urban Community." In Greenblatt, Emery, and Glueck, eds., *Poverty and Mental Health*. Psychiatric research report, no. 21. Washington, D.C.:

American Psychiatric Association, 1967.

54. KEVIN, D. "Use of the Group Method in Consultation." In L. Rapoport, ed., *Consultation in Social Work Practice*. New York: National Association of Social Workers, 1963. Pp. 69–84.

55. KLEBANOFF, L. B., and BINDMAN, A. J. "The Organization and Development of a Community Mental Health Program for Children: A Case Study." *American Journal of Orthopsychiatry*, 32 (1962), 119–132.

56. KLEIN, D. C. *Consultation Processes as a Method of Improving Teaching*. Report no. 69. Boston: Boston University Human Relations Center, 1964.

57. ———. "An Example of Primary Prevention Activities in Schools: Working with Parents in Preschools and Early School Year Children." In N. M. Lambert, ed., *The Protection and Promotion of Mental Health in the Schools*. Public Health Service publication, no. 1226. Bethesda, Md.: U.S. Government Printing Office, 1965.

58. ———, and LINDEMANN, E. "Preventive Intervention in Individual and Family Crisis Situations." In G. Caplan, ed., *Prevention of Mental Disorders in Children*. New York: Basic Books, 1961. Pp. 283–306.

59. KOHL, H. *36 Children*. New York: New American Library, 1967.

60. KOZOL, J. *Death at an Early Age*. New York: Bantam Books, 1967.

61. KRUGMAN, M., ed. *Orthopsychiatry and the School*. New York: American Orthopsychiatric Association, 1958.

62. LAPOUSE, R. "The Epidemiology of Behavior Disorders in Children." In H. F. Clarizio, ed., *Mental Health and the Educative Process*. New York: Rand-McNally, 1969. Pp. 37–44.

63. LEIGHTON, D. C., et al. *The Character of Danger: Psychiatric Symptoms in Selected Communities*. New York: Basic Books, 1963.

64. LEOPOLD, R. L., and KISSICK, W. L. "A Community Mental Health Center Regional Medical Program and Joint Planning." *American Journal of Psychiatry*, 126 (1970), 1718–1726.

65. LEVINE, M., and LEVINE, A. "The First Psychological Clinic: Lightner Witmer, 1896." In M. Levine and A. Levine, eds., *A Social History of Helping Services*. New York: Appleton-Century-Crofts, 1970.

66. ———, and LEVINE, A. "The Visiting Teacher." In M. Levine and A. Levine, eds., *A Social History of Helping Services*. New York: Appelton-Century-Crofts, 1970.

67. LIBO, L. N., and GRIFFITH, C. R. "Developing Mental Health Programs in Areas Lacking Professional Facilities: The Community Consultant Approach in New Mexico." *Community Mental Health Journal*, 2 (1966), 163–169.

68. LIPPITT, R. "The Youth Culture, the School System, and the Socialization Community." In A. J. Reiss, Jr., ed., *Schools in a Changing Society*. New York: The Free Press, 1963.

69. LONG, N. J., and NEWMAN, R. G. "The Straws That Break the Teacher's Back." In H. F. Clarizio, ed., *Mental Health and the Educative Process*. New York: Rand-McNally, 1969. Pp. 282–288.

70. LOWERY, L. G. "Orthopsychiatry Treatment." In L. G. Lowery and V. Sloane, eds., *Orthopsychiatry, 1923–1948: Retrospect and Prospect*. New York: American Orthopsychiatric Association, 1948.

71. MacIVER, R. *The Prevention and Control of Delinquency*. New York: Atherton Press, 1966.

72. MINUCHIN, P., BIBER, B., SHAPIRO, E., and ZIMILES, H. *The Psychological Impact of the School Experience*. New York: Basic Books, 1969.

73. MINUCHIN, S. "The Use of an Ecological Framework in the Treatment of the Child." In E. J. Anthony and C. Koupernik, eds., *The Child in His Family*. New York: Wiley, 1970. Pp. 41–57.

74. MOORE, W., Jr. *The Vertical Ghetto*. New York: Random House, 1969.

75. MORSE, W. C. "Enhancing the Teacher's Mental Health Function." In E. L. Cowen, Gardener, and M. Zax, eds., *Emergent Approaches to Mental Health Problems*. New York: Appleton-Century-Crofts, 1967. Pp. 271–289.

76. NELSON, E. K., Jr. "Organizational Disparity in Definition of Deviance and Uses of Authority: Police, Probation, and Schools." In A. J. Reiss, Jr., ed., *Schools in a Changing Society*. New York: The Free Press, 1965.

77. NEWMAN, R. G. *Psychological Consultation in the Schools: A Catalyst for Learning*. New York: Basic Books, 1967.

78. ———, REDL, F., and KITCHENER, H. L. *Technical Assistance in a Public School*

System. Washington, D.C. Washington School of Psychiatry, 1962.

79. PARKER, B. "Psychiatric Consultation for Nonpsychiatric Professional Workers." *Public Health Monograph,* no. 53, 1958.

80. ———. "Some Observations on Psychiatric Consultation with Nursery School Teachers." *Mental Hygiene,* 45 (1962), 559–566.

81. PASAMANICK, B., and KNOBLOCK, H. "Epidemiological Studies on the Complications of Pregnancy and the Birth Process." In G. Caplan, ed., *Prevention of Mental Disorders in Children.* New York: Basic Books, 1961. Pp. 74–94.

82. ———, KNOBLOCK, H., and LILIENFELD, A. M. "Socioeconomic Status and Some Precursors of Neuropsychiatric Disorder." *American Journal of Orthopsychiatry,* 26, no. 3 (1956), 594–601.

83. PECK, H., and KAPLAN, S. "A Mental Health Program for the Urban Multiservice Center." In M. Shore and F. Mennino, eds., *Mental Health and the Community.* New York: Behavioral Publications, 1969.

84. RAFFERTY, F. T. "The Community Is Becoming." *American Journal of Orthopsychiatry,* 36 (1966), 102–110.

85. ———. "Child Population Service for a Total Population." *Journal of the American Academy of Child Psychiatry,* 6 (1967), 295–308.

86. ———, MACKIE, J., MAXWELL, A. D., and SILA, B. The Diagnostic Check Point for Community Child Psychiatry. Unpublished manuscript. School 95, Franklin Square School, Baltimore, Md., City School System.

87. RAPPAPORT, L. *Consultation in Social Work Practice.* New York: National Association of Social Work, 1963.

88. RATNER, J., ed. *Intelligence in the Modern World: John Dewey's Philosophy.* New York: Random House, 1937.

89. REID, D. *Epidemiological Methods in the Study of Mental Disorders.* World Health Organization public health papers, no. 2. Geneva, 1960.

90. REIFF, R., and REISSMAN, F. "The Indigenous Nonprofessional: A Strategy of Change in Community Action and Community Mental Health Programs." *Community Mental Health Journal,* Monograph no. 1, 1963.

91. REISSMAN, F. "A Neighborhood Based Mental Health Approach." In E. L.

Cowen, Gardener, and M. Zax, eds., *Emergent Approaches to Mental Health Problems.* New York: Appleton-Century-Crofts, 1967. Pp. 162–184.

92. ———, COHEN, J., and PEARL, A. *Mental Health of the Poor.* New York: The Free Press, 1964.

93. RIOCH, M. J., et al. "National Institute of Mental Health Pilot Study in Training Mental Health Counselors." In H. F. Clarizio, ed., *Mental Health and the Educative Process.* New York: Rand-McNally, 1969. Pp. 430–441.

94. ROWITCH, J. "Group Consultation with School Personnel." *Hospital and Community Psychiatry,* 19, no. 8 (1968), 45–50.

95. SARASON, S. *Psychology in Community Settings.* New York: Wiley, 1966.

96. SARVIS, M. A., and PENNEKAMP, M. *Collaboration in School Guidance.* New York: Brunner/Mazel, 1970.

97. SCHIFF, S. K., and KELLAM, S. G. "A Community Wide Mental Health and Health Program of Prevention and Early Treatment in First Grade." In Greenblatt, Emery, and Glueck, eds., *Poverty and Mental Health.* Psychiatric research report, no. 21. Washington, D.C.: American Psychiatric Association, 1967. Pp. 92–102.

98. SHAPIRO, T., and FROSCH, W. A. "Faculty Responses to Student Confrontation." *American Journal of Psychiatry,* 127 (1970), 599–605.

99. THOMPSON, M. H. *The History of Education.* New York: Barnes & Noble, 1963.

100. WHITE, R. W. "Competence and the Psychosexual Stages of Development." In M. Jones, ed., *Nebraska Symposium on Motivation.* Omaha: University of Nebraska Press, 1960.

101. WITMER, H. L. *Psychiatric Clinics for Children.* New York: Commonwealth Fund, 1940.

102. ZAX, M., et al. "A Teacher-Aide Program for Preventing Emotional Disturbances in Young School Children." In H. F. Clarizio, ed., *Mental Health and the Educative Process.* New York: Rand-McNally, 1969. Pp. 313–323.

103. ZIMILIES, H. "Preventive Aspects of School Experience." In E. L. Cowen, Gardener, and M. Zax, eds., *Emergent Approaches to Mental Health Problems.* New York: Appleton-Century-Crofts, 1967. Pp. 239–251.

CHAPTER 51

MENTAL HEALTH PROGRAMS IN WELFARE SYSTEMS

Alexander S. Rogawski

(Poverty and Psychiatry

THE DISPROPORTIONATE PREVALENCE of mental health problems and emotional disabilities in the lower socioeconomic segments of society has long been recognized and repeatedly documented.[3,24,40,49,77] Critical comments by Miller and Mishler[58] notwithstanding, Hollingshead and Redlich's[40] classic study on the relations between social class and mental illness demonstrated clearly that the lowest class almost invariably contributes many more psychiatric patients than its proportion of the population warrants.

By and large, mental health services for the poor have remained grossly inadequate in spite of many well-intended efforts. During recent years some improvements have been achieved as a result of the interest and involvement in community psychiatry. Many professionals lack the knowledge, the skills, and often the interest and the willingness to engage the poor in treatment.[7,33,68,73,74]

The psychological problems of the disadvantaged are often complicated by difficulties that threaten these people's very survival. It has been justly questioned whether some approaches, helpful to people from the middle and upper income groups, are relevant to the life styles or suited to the needs of the poor.[43]

Responsible psychiatrists must search for effective remedial approaches to psychological distress wherever it is found.[32,81,83,84] Even though "poverty is *not* primarily a mental health problem,"[31] psychiatrists must collaborate in efforts aimed at preventing and treating the psychological misery of the poor. The required expansion of psychiatric knowledge and expertise can be achieved only by thorough study of the problems and by personal exposure to the special conditions of poverty and its complex relation to mental health and illness.[28,38,57] The experience with the poor has motivated psychiatrists to reevaluate and restructure their professional roles and to modify concepts, methods, and techniques correspondingly.[2,7,25,33,68]

*

❲ Some Aspects of Public Welfare

Between 20 and 25 percent of the total United States population live on submarginal incomes below the level of the poverty income index by which the U.S. Department of Labor and the Office of Economic Opportunity define the poor. According to this index, in December 1969 a nonfarm family of four needed an annual income of $3,600 to meet the expenses of a minimum adequate standard of living. This amounted to about $70 per week.

A little more than one-fourth of the poor, as defined by the index, receive income from public assistance. The rate varies greatly among the states, depending on differences in eligibility requirements, levels of grants, the community's moral standards, and availability of other resources that keep many poor from applying for public relief. Currently, the number of recipients of public assistance exceeds 13 million people. Their number increases rapidly in periods of economic recession and growing unemployment, but it keeps mounting even during times of economic expansion and relatively full employment. The great majority of welfare recipients are too old, too young, too sick, or too disabled to be self-supporting.[61] Only a small percentage are able bodied and capable of being trained or retrained to be potentially self-supporting.

Families with children comprise the largest group of recipients today. In September 1970, 2,332,000 families with 6,498,000 children, comprising a total of 8,873,000, received public assistance nationwide. Most of these families were eligible for aid owing to the disability or absence of one parent because of death, divorce, or desertion. In twenty-six states a family could not obtain financial assistance as long as the father was living in the home, even if he was unemployed or unemployable. This rule has been blamed for the actual or alleged desertion of many fathers who wanted to render their families eligible for support by leaving the house.

More than 2 million aged over sixty-five years of age, one-half of them seventy-five or older, comprise the second largest group of recipients. Many of this group are also beneficiaries of old age insurance, but continued inflation has rendered their Social Security payments insufficient.

Almost 1 million recipients are either blind or disabled as certified by medical authorities. About 900,000 persons in urgent need of support fit none of the federal categories. These people, single adults or childless couples, must be aided under a county or a state-county general assistance program, which is usually so low that it barely keeps the recipient from starving.[18]

Public welfare is not limited to the provision of income maintenance and assistance payments. It is an organizing term, which for purposes of administration brings together a variety of supportive services—financial, medical, and social. These services include child welfare and child placement programs, preschool compensatory education, help with the education of children by providing aids for the development of children such as books or camping opportunities, medical assistance programs (Title XIX of the Social Security Act, often referred to as Medicaid), assistance with the procurement of appropriate medical care, rehabilitation services such as work incentive and concentrated employment programs, assistance with the securing of employment; homemaker services, volunteer services, food stamp programs; counseling with family problems and obtaining help for marital problems, family planning, legal services including assistance with a divorce, help with the obtaining of furniture or other household items, arranging for phone services and repairs, and assistance in the preparing of a budget. While the target population of these services is the very poor, public welfare offers in some areas other community services such as help with adoption and protective services for children as well as for adults. The boundaries and the focus of public welfare are constantly shifting to reflect legislative changes and reorganizations of service programs.[13] These changes add to the heavy burden of the job of the welfare worker.

When President Lyndon Johnson appointed the Commission on Income Maintenance Programs, in 1968, he described the attitudes toward welfare in his introductory remarks, "The welfare system today pleases no one. It is criticized by liberals and conservatives, by the poor and the wealthy, by social workers and politicians, by whites and by Negroes in every area of the nation."[49] There are many reasons for this general dissatisfaction. Public assistance programs as they are operated today were originally established by the Social Security Act of 1935 in reaction to the Depression. Federal and state governments assumed responsibilities for the poor that had previously been borne mostly by local voluntary and governmental bodies. The initial intention was for public assistance to be a supplementary and residual program of income security,[80] a temporary measure that would be phased out as soon as a comprehensive network of social insurance programs could take over. This expectation never came true. Because of complex social, economic and technological developments public assistance programs have grown and expanded, and their steeply rising costs have aroused the apprehension and the resentment of the taxpayers. They have in fact become a significant factor upsetting the fiscal stability of state and county budgets.

The basic objectives of welfare are quite ambiguous because of the widely differing values of various segments of the population. Some people would like to restrict public assistance to the doling out of just enough money to protect the smallest possible number of deserving poor from the consequences of extreme indigence so that the more fortunate citizens can preserve their peace of mind. These people feel that everyone is responsible for his own success or misfortune. Failure to achieve self-support is in most cases ascribed to a lack of initiative and diligence and, therefore, should not be rewarded or encouraged

by support. Other people, especially professionals, see public welfare as an instrument of social betterment, which could raise the general quality of life in the community by providing needy recipients with the means for a decent living and with appropriate social services to improve family and social functioning. Some welfare departments clearly state that they see their functions as including "advocacy for the consumer."[23] A considerable number of people expect welfare to aim especially at the reduction of dependency by encouraging any potentially capable recipient to develop toward the greatest possible degree of self-support. In the case of single parents, this position creates all kinds of complications.

The conflicts in values and objectives lead to passionate political controversies, which interfere with all truly constructive major welfare reforms. They also make it very difficult to conduct evaluative research and to assess the effectiveness and the impact of a program or of program components.[13] Furthermore, reflecting the ambivalent attitudes of the public at large, the staff of welfare departments are also confused about their goals. They experience tremendous frustrations in their work, which deprive them of the sense of direction essential for commitment to their difficult tasks.

The present welfare system has many obvious deficiencies and inequities. During the thirty-five years that have passed since the welfare system's creation, the world has changed dramatically, but public assistance and social insurance titles of the Social Security Act have not been altered correspondingly. The existing welfare mechanisms have been accused of being merely palliatives that institutionalize dependency.[44] As a rule the system provides substandard incomes that keep most recipients in abject poverty. Geiger[31] claimed: "One reason for the continuation of most people on public assistance is simply that the level of public assistance keeps them there struggling for the very essentials of existence." Hagstrom,[36] describing the "psychology of the powerlessness of the poor," asserted that the enforced dependency of the recipients "gives them little scope for action under their control" and therefore "dependency relationships become institutionalized and perpetuated."

There is no part of the welfare system that is not in need of basic overhaul.[34a] The brunt of criticism is usually directed at the Aid to Families with Dependent Children (AFDC) program because (1) participation rate and costs are increasing at a particularly fast pace; (2) the program seems to promote family break up; (3) there are unjustifiable discrepancies among the various states and regions of the country; and (4) the current legislation has built-in incentives to quit working.

The Family Assistance Plan (FAP), proposed by President Nixon, is attempting to remedy these deficiences. The most fundamental departure from present policy is the federalization of AFDC and its extension to the working poor.[41,49,66] The proposal is currently under consideration in Congress. Much discussion and delay can be expected before basic reforms of our current welfare legislation are passed, but such changes are inevitable. Anyone involved and interested in the fate of the poor must keep himself constantly informed of the developments and their implications.

After this very condensed introduction to some basic aspects of public welfare, the question could be raised as to why psychiatrists and other mental health professionals should get involved at all with a system that has such glaring shortcomings and that, in addition, is in a state of great flux. Notwithstanding the general lack of satisfaction with public welfare, it would be staggering to contemplate what would happen if this institution would not exist to reduce widespread human want and suffering until such time that a better approach and solutions have been found for the tremendous problems of contemporary poverty. A sizable proportion of all poor people in America, in fact most of the very poor, are greatly dependent on and affected by the welfare system. In addition to the recipients, the welfare workers represent a sizable army of providers of care in the community. They too are influenced by the structure and the limitations, as well as the opportunities of the system to furnish human services. The immense complexity of the problems will require for their solution lay people as well as a host of various professionals, economists, social planners, research experts, politicians, to name but a few. The victims of the system cannot wait until stabilizing legislation has been passed or until the present institution has been replaced by a better approach. People are suffering now, and the need for appropriate psychiatric expertise is urgent. The welfare system is one of the avenues by which psychiatrists and other mental health professionals can meet the poor and can learn from them about poverty and its problems. They can acquire new expertise, which can be used to humanize the system and assist in the development of a better design to replace it. Even as cautious an endorser as Gruenberg[35] stated in a reply to a paper by Riessman: "We all hope that current efforts to eliminate low living standards and personal indignities associated with extreme poverty will succeed rapidly. I suspect that psychiatrists have a significant, but minor, role to play in this process."

(History and Review of Literature of Mental Health Efforts in Welfare

Adolf Meyer advocated as early as 1909 that coordinated community mental health programs be established in which all care-providing agencies and resources, including the welfare establishment, would cooperate with psychiatric facilities.[12] It took many years before the first steps were taken to translate these suggestions into action.

There are relatively few reports that describe the development of collaborative relations between the staffs of welfare agencies and mental health professionals.[34b] Psychiatrists began to associate with social workers when they first noted that "Social work has needed the contributions of the psychiatrist because of the wide prevalence of emotional disturbance among its clients, and psychiatry has needed the assistance of social work in finding and meeting its community responsibilities."[15] The multidisciplinary team consisting of a psychiatrist, a psychologist, and a social worker was introduced during the early 1920s by the child guidance movement, but for a long time each profession maintained a distinct and separate role identity within the collaborative arrangement.[16]

Social Workers Assume Limited Treatment Responsibilities

About the middle 1930s the first reports appeared in which social workers in clinical or social agency settings were described as increasingly assuming treatment responsibilities with the support of a consultant psychiatrist.[75]

During the Depression private family agencies expanded rapidly by temporarily becoming the disbursing agents for the federal or state government. Eventually public relief departments were set up. Private agencies reverted to their previous smaller case loads and focused their attention on casework in the modern psychotherapeutic sense.[63] They invited psychiatrists to serve in staff positions or as consultants to diagnose, interpret, and evaluate the behavior of clients and treat them if so indicated. Later psychiatrists participated in agency in-service programs.[16]

The collaboration of the two professions taught psychiatrists to respect their social work colleagues. Even though the workers had less formal instruction, they were able to obtain a great deal of meaningful psychological information and insight, and they managed even cases with psychopathological symptoms surprisingly well. On the other hand, social workers discovered that psychiatric consultants were able to fortify them with "some quality of reassurance"[16] and that their effectiveness with clients increased as their anxiety abated. This kind of help was even more significant than whatever understanding was gained concerning the clients' psychodynamics. These observations are cited independently and repeatedly in many reports of this period.[14–16,63,75]

In 1946 Drake,[26] a welfare agency administrator, discussed the needs for consultants to local welfare departments and the pitfalls in their use. He defined as consultant, "One who gives advice or service the results of which are carried into action by the more responsible line officers of the agency." Psychologists and psychiatrists are listed last among the six groups of potentially helpful specialists. They should be employed "for mental testing and child guidance clinical service in connection with problem children, family adjustment cases, and children being studied for adoption or foster home placement." Drake called for a clear definition of the role and the responsibilities of the consultant as distinguished from the functions of a supervisor or administrator. "Consultants should always be consulted by agency executives before taking action involving the particular specialty in question."[26, p. 90] The specialist must be acquainted with the structure and the functions of the consultee agency so that he can address his interventions in the right form to the right person. Only in this way can confusion, mutual resentment, and injury to the morale of the agency staff be avoided. Drake made a strong plea for the use of consultants to supplement knowledge and skills of the regular welfare staff and recommended that consultants be taken into conferences on administrative matters to give them a sense of participation. Like in the army, "you can do almost anything to a man in the service except ignore him."

From the psychiatric consultant's side, Coleman[14] described in 1947, in a classic paper, a new method of psychiatric consultation which was "basically worker oriented rather than client oriented." Since social agencies help to carry a significant share of the neurotic burden of the economically less privileged segment of the population, Coleman felt that psychiatrists had to find a way to enhance the effectiveness of caseworkers. Even though the method of support and influence should be based on psychiatric knowledge and insight, no attempt should be made to change workers into psychiatrists. Social workers are invaluable to many clients in their specific professional role. Coleman stated that "the indication for psychiatric treatment is determined as much by the patient's ability to make use of it as by his neurotic suffering. Direct treatment is not the only way of relieving such suffering." He felt that most psychiatrists were quite unfamiliar with the functioning and the goals of social agencies, since during their training period they had been given little or no opportunity to work cooperatively with social workers. Thus they could not develop recognition and acceptance of the professionalism of social workers. Any psychiatrist wishing to function as a consultant must first acquaint himself with the social system of the agency, with the specific needs of the workers and their clients, and with the best way to respond to these needs. The psychiatrist appeared to be most helpful when he accepted the worker's presentation of the problem in an uncritical stance and when he was able to determine and to reduce the worker's emotional distress. Coleman admonished psychiatrists to limit their comments strictly to the professional problems and not to transgress into the workers' personal problems. This new method of consultation was a procedure *sui generis*, which had to be studied and mastered with special care. Coleman's paper has stood the test of time. Most of his recommendations apply to currently practiced forms of consultee-centered consultation without major modifications.

Coleman deplored that many psychiatrists felt their services could be utilized only by sophisticated workers with considerable education and skills. This limited psychiatric consultations mostly to the wealthier private agencies, whereas "public agencies, discharging a social responsibility which may be no less important, often have too few workers, trained or untrained, and rarely have enough psychiatric consultation." This description applied to public welfare agencies. Most welfare workers lacked then, as they still do, graduate education in social work. They had enormous case files, which made it difficult if not impossible to provide individualized case work. Prior to 1962, services were confined primarily to the determination of eligibility and to the provision of money payments, and psychia-

trists showed little interest in consulting with psychiatrically unsophisticated low status welfare workers. If consultants worked with public agencies it was usually with organizations that offered service for children, such as child welfare, foster home placement, and adoption.

In 1950, in an early report on consultation to a public welfare agency, Maddux[56] emphasized that even workers with limited training could effectively utilize the Coleman model of worker-oriented consultation. A psychiatrist delegated by a mental hygiene clinic to a local welfare agency for one and one-half days a week conducted conferences with individual workers and their supervisors whenever they requested it. He also interviewed selected clients for diagnostic purposes. Maddux described the enormous stress under which welfare workers must function. They are squeezed in the conflict between the needs of their clients and the demands of the taxpayers. As they respond to dependency needs of their clients, their own conscious and unconscious yearnings for dependency are aroused. Low salary ranges limit the hiring of graduates of social work schools, and most welfare workers have little or no relevant training even though they have usually graduated from college. The resulting rapid staff turnover prevents the building of ongoing relations between a client and the same caseworker. Large caseloads, enormous quantities of paper work, and complex regulations determining eligibility and availability of services restrict the time for constructive casework even further. But Maddux was not deterred from offering consultation by the lack of sophistication of the workers. He, too, confirmed the overriding need of the workers to be put at ease and reassured so that they could do their best under difficult circumstances: "The central aim of the consultant then becomes relief of worker anxiety."[56, p. 753] Theory and didactic instructions were of minor importance. At times the psychiatrist acted as a role model, for example, when demonstrating how he as a professional could remain acceptant of the worker in the face of a hostile assault, a situation that workers often had to face with their clients. Workers requested consultations much more frequently than diagnostic evaluations of their clients, which indicated that they found the consultations more helpful. Sometimes, diagnostic interviews with clients were combined with consultations with the workers. In spite of heavy time commitments to paper work, more than half of the workers in the agency asked for consultations. Those who kept returning for consultations showed "a progressive diminution in anxiousness with emergence of deepening interest in understanding their clients and increased ease in their contacts with clients."[56, p. 757] This demonstrated the usefulness of this method for staff development. Workers ranged widely in the degree of their sophistication and in their reactions to the procedure. Whenever a worker could bring himself to an initial interview, he returned one or more times, proving the reassuring effect of the experience with the psychiatrist. Maddux's paper contains some interesting case illustrations, which reveal that the aim of the consultation was not so much assistance in the specific case that had been presented but improvement of the worker's overall ability of helping future clients with similar problems. Some staff reacted with indifference, ambivalence, or outright hostility, but on supervisory and higher administrative levels the psychiatric consultant was enthusiastically accepted. The psychiatrist's position outside the channels of administrative responsibility added to his acceptability by the workers. He was seen by them as a friendly and potentially helpful visitor. An effort to involve some disinterested and even hostile workers was only partially successful. At no time were consultations foisted on unwilling staff.

Although psychiatrists worked in ever-increasing numbers in social agency settings, there were few generally accepted guidelines for their functions and the interprofessional working arrangements varied tremendously in different programs. Bernard[4] made an attempt to abstract more precise and realistic concepts from her own experience in an adoption agency. She considered consultation by individual case conference a core function, although psychiatrists could make many other contributions, such as the interviewing of selected clients for purposes of diagnosis or referral, participating in staff development projects, and involving themselves in discussions of treatment policies and program orientation. Bernard's model of consultation is primarily client centered and relies heavily on the application of psychodynamic interpretations. In all the cases she cited, the client was subsequently referred for psychiatric treatment. The consultant's intervention was not related to the worker's individuality. The support was an unspecified by-product of the consultant's knowledge and availability, "in addition to the dynamic and clinical explanations," which "significantly helped to reduce the worker's own anxieties and thereby enhanced the capacity for skillfully aiding the precariously maladjusted client."[4, p. 8] The involvement of several psychiatrists in the management of a single case makes this model uneconomical in terms of professional time and costs and would preclude its large-scale application within the framework of a community program.

The Mid-1950s: A Climate of Exploration

The middle 1950s were a time of stock taking in the mental health field. The Congress of the United States, in the Mental Health Study Act of 1955, directed the Joint Commission on Mental Illness and Health, as chosen by the National Institute of Mental Health (NIMH), to analyze and to evaluate the needs and resources of the mentally ill throughout the nation and to make recommendations for a national mental health program.[45]

In this climate of exploration, Lamson,[48] of the community services branch of NIMH, surveying the state of integration of mental health services in health and welfare community agencies, found two levels of action. (1) On the level of state government, in nearly all states at least one full-time professional person was responsible for the development of statewide community mental health services. This was frequently a psychiatrically sophisticated social worker who established liaison with the administrators and the staff of other human services, including welfare departments. Matters of common concern would be discussed in formal and informal administrative meetings defining needed resources and planning programs to remedy deficiencies. (2) On the local level, community mental health clinics had become aware that direct services to patients and their families alone could not meet the existing needs. They realized that consulting services and education offered to referring agencies could reduce case loads and number of referrals by upgrading the mental health skills of agency staffs. The new communication also improved coordination of services between participating agencies and counteracted attempts of some clients to play one agency against another.[40]

About the same time, attention was refocused from individuals on the importance of the family for the mental health of all its members. The concern for the family received new impetus through the 1956 amendments to the Social Service Act which emphasized services, "to strengthen family life and helping needy families and individuals attain the maximum personal independence of which they are capable."[80, p. 183] The legislation stimulated increased interest in staff development. Within a few years a number of relevant papers appeared which expressed the greater readiness of welfare agencies to utilize the help of psychiatrically sophisticated professionals.[20,21, 27,52,78] Social work schools progressively incorporated knowledge from dynamic psychiatry into their regular curriculum, and since psychiatrists were scarce, social workers were invited to act as mental health consultants.

In fact, social workers had been consultants in public assistance administration as early as 1939.[5] But while they were aware that agencies were made up of "human beings both wanting and resisting controls"[4] and while they employed social work principles based on mental health principles, such as respect for the person, confidentiality, self-determination, and individualization, their main attention was directed toward program implementations, personnel policies, and intergovernmental agency cooperation.[64] This kind of consul-

tation differed considerably from the types discussed here. They were defined as staff functions with responsibilities of the consultant "clearly defined and placed within the administrative structure of the organization."[19] Now social workers began to serve as extraorganizational mental health consultants.

Two faculty members of a graduate school of social work, Decker and Itzin,[21] visited at monthly intervals, essentially untrained staff of several county welfare agencies under the sponsorship of a state agency. They hoped to improve the workers' ability to render more intensive casework to their "most needful" families in the AFDC program. Cases were selected by the workers themselves. The consultations were primarily client centered. The consultants helped the workers to arrive at a diagnosis of the family and to develop a case plan. The results were quite spectacular, especially in cases that had not shown any improvement for a long time prior to the consultation. The effect was ascribed to the increased self-esteem and interest of the workers. As they gained self-assurance, due to the consultations, they were able to show more interest in their clients who in turn responded to the increase in attention with a gain of self-respect. Where the consultants noted deficiencies in individual line workers, they recommended supervision by the state social work staff.

The discrepancy in the perception of consultations by consultant and consultee respectively was illustrated by two companion papers published in 1957. Both the psychiatric consultant[78] and the administrator[20] of the corresponding consultee social agency described the consultation process and their expectations from their respective vantage points. The psychiatrist listed among the "requirements for consultants" such items as, "he should be well trained in dynamic psychoanalytic therapy," "should have had special training and experience in work with children," "should be paid an adequate fee," and, surprisingly, that "previous experience as a consultant is not essential." The low value assigned to prior consultation experience may account for his numerous references to "agency-consultant friction," "undercover motives" of the workers who select cases to "test" the consultant "to demonstrate the futility of expecting any good to come of casework or of consultation," who "maneuver the consultant into supporting an opinion with which the supervisor disagrees," and who finally cause the consultation to end "only in frustrating disintegration and more or less open antagonism." One gains the impression that this consultant had many unpleasant experiences, so that his paper, contrary to his expressed opinion, demonstrates how great the need is for a careful preparation of the consultant for his very special role. In the companion paper the administrator of the consulted social agency conceded that "consultations can be gratifying and productive of growth in both consultee and consultant" but only if the relationship is based on mutual respect, if the agency is clear what it wishes to gain from the procedure, if it is stable in its administration, in its staff and in its programs, and if the role of the psychiatrist consultant is precisely defined in advance. The author stressed that much thought must be given to the careful selection of the consultant. Attention must be paid not only to his professional background but equally to his personal fitness and ability to look at the process as a mutual learning experience, especially in its early stages. The psychiatrist must not be permitted to usurp administrative prerogatives, supervisory functions or believe that he is qualified to teach basic social work skills and techniques. Before the psychiatrist is asked to function fully as a consultant, he must be oriented about the agency and about the world of the clients. If several consultants serve an agency, one should be designated as the senior consultant, and he should be invited to help with the orientation of incoming consultants. The author's agency is never specified, but it was most likely a child welfare agency with a trained staff primarily interested in enhancing their skills in casework therapy and their knowledge in psychodynamics. Among the five listed indications for the use of consultation the first three refer to lack of knowledge, the fourth to psychiatric emergencies, and

only the last relates to "problems in the worker-client relationship."

An air of authoritarianism pervades the contributions of both the administrator and the psychiatric consultant. It is most clearly expressed in the stated policy of the agency that all workers had to present cases for consultation whether they liked it or not. As a rule, requests for consultation are left up to the individual worker and his supervisor.

It is evident from these two papers that this consultation relationship was fraught with tensions and painful complications. They were most likely caused by two major factors: (1) the consultant's lack of preparation for his task, and (2) the discrepancy between his conception and the agency's expectations concerning the consultation procedure and its functions. The administrator remarked that "Social agency staff sometimes complain that the psychiatrist doesn't listen enough,"[20, p. 8] a complaint that ought to have been heeded. Both authors agreed that the association of a psychiatrist with a social agency lent authority to the agency's decisions and facilitated some actions on behalf of their clients with professionals as well as with lay people in the community. The administrator added, however, that employing a consultant in order to borrow his authority was a "debatable" position.

Lifschutz, Stewart, and Harrison,[52] a psychoanalyst, a field social work supervisor, and a public welfare worker, respectively, pointed out in a paper published in 1958 that the psychiatric consultant "an increasingly familiar figure in the social agency" was now beginning to collaborate with public assistance agencies. They saw the consultant chiefly in a didactic and interpretative role. They concurred with Ormsby[64] that "Effective consultation educates and influences rather than takes over and directs." Two illustrative consultation examples were client centered and dealt with by psychoanalytic interpretations. The outcome of the first case was a referral to a psychiatrist. In the second case, the worker was assisted to help the client to make the decision to relinquish her child born out of wedlock. The consultant acted mainly as interpreter of the probable unconscious meaning of the client's social breakdown or of the contemplated interventions of the agency. No special attention was paid to the caseworker's individuality and her contribution to the problem, though the authors seemed aware of the feeling tone in the interplay between caseworker and client. One gains the impression that the consultees benefitted from the consultation mainly by sharing in the experience of looking at human events through the fascinating lens of psychoanalytic interpretation.

Nitzberg and Kahn,[62] a senior social worker and a clinical psychologist, staff members of a rural mental hygiene clinic, compared the method described in the preceding paper with their own consultation model, in which the aid given by the consultant's dynamic understanding of a given case[62, p. 85] was emphasized in contrast. They tried to develop the skills and background of workers "as well as to provide more immediate help on some specific problems." Over a period of four years, they met separately though concurrently with a group of welfare workers. The psychologist started earlier and discussed cultural values and attitudes, causes of emotional problems and attitudes toward people with disturbing behavior. The workers themselves changed the format by bringing up some of their own cases. As they became increasingly free to air their anxieties, the sessions seemed more effective. Then the social worker initiated monthly group case conferences. The psychologist now returned to semididactic sessions covering a wide range of psychological topics. This form of consultations was essentially a prolonged form of in-service training. In a statewide training program, the participants of the consultation program stood out by their ability to learn. The authors felt their greatest contribution consisted in the support they gave to the workers for service activities in which they were already involved. They were amazed at how well these untrained workers functioned in spite of heavy caseloads and extremely difficult working conditions. They were impressed with how much time and effort some workers devoted to individual cases. This is an experience reported by everybody who consults with welfare personnel.

Also in 1958, Eisenberg,[27] concerned with the uneconomic utilization of scarce psychiatrist manpower, suggested that child psychiatrists could make their greatest contribution to the mental health of the community by functioning as diagnostic consultants to a public agency, leaving the actual treatment to the agency staff. He felt that preoccupation with the individual psychotherapy model, reflecting the social matrix of contemporary psychiatric practice, often resulted in disrespect for the effectiveness of planned social conditioning as a therapeutic instrumentality. To make the best possible use of limited psychiatric time and manpower, he spent half a day each week at the foster-care division of the welfare department. He interviewed children who presented special problems and then met with case workers and supervisors to discuss the diagnoses, to formulate treatment plans, and to lay the foundations for effective casework by helping the workers to gain more insight into the psychodynamics of the case. The case worker was responsible for the development of a sustaining relationship with the children; for the interpretation of the clinic findings to foster parents, school, and court; and for the involvement of children into constructive group relations and activities. The case workers were thus the most important people in the life of these children, who were often severely traumatized by prior abandonment and rejection. Eisenberg reasoned that efforts invested in the case workers helping them to understand the problems they had to deal with would pay off in the long run by saving scarce and expensive psychiatric time. He likened his method of "manipulation of social space" to the use of the "therapeutic milieu" in inpatient facilities. He felt this approach was neglected by professionals because of the prevailing fashion to expect results only from "inner changes." With these children, who were in the custody of the welfare department by authority of the juvenile court, the method resulted in substantial and significant improvement. A somewhat superficial follow up revealed that where the consultant's recommendations had been followed the outcome was just as good as one could have expected if the child had undergone conventional psychotherapy. Furthermore, many of these children would have made very poor candidates for psychotherapy because of their tendency toward antisocial behavior.

In the same year, 1958, Bush and Llewellyn[8] described for the first time a statewide experiment with psychiatric consultation as part of an in-service training program. Several years later a follow up of the same program was published by Llewellyn and Shepherd.[53] The North Carolina State Board of Public Welfare initiated a psychiatric consultation service to foster deeper understanding of human behavior and to strengthen casework skills and agency services in a casework staff, many of whom had only limited training. Any county could request monthly two-hour consultations for three consecutive months with a team consisting of a consulting psychiatrist, the state supervisor of staff development, the area public welfare psychologist, and occasionally other invited consultants. The local agency prepared a summary of the case in advance, listing the chief problems and concerns and distributing it together with copies of all pertinent reports to all participants of the joint conference. Most of the time, the authors found that the true, more or less hidden, problem was not an "impossible" case but attitudes, expectations, and motivations that interfered with the agency staff's effective utilization of casework methods.

A planning session of the consulting team preceded each consultation. The written material was reviewed, and specific problems and needs of the particular area, community, or of the agency itself were discussed. In addition to the case worker who presented the case, as many members of the agency as could be spared attended the consultation. At the onset of the consultation the staff development supervisor from the state agency instructed the consultees what to expect from the consultation. The purpose was not to solve a specific problem or to evaluate a specific client psychiatrically but to serve as a springboard for a general discussion, which would hopefully improve the knowledge and skills of all participants. For a good part of the consultation the psychiatrist listened in silence until he gradually joined in the discussion. This gave him an opportunity to observe the group and to define for himself the nature and the probable causes of the workers' apprehension. Then he would attempt to reduce their tension by providing information, explanations, and interpretations of the client's behavior. This approach was based on the assumption that "agency-client relations can be enhanced through better understanding of the meaning of the behavior of the client and of the effect of environmental stress upon the client and his family."[53, p. 41]

All participants of the consulting team contributed according to their respective areas of expertise. An atmosphere of support was maintained throughout the session. The final period of the consultation was devoted to a discussion of a management plan based on the newly won insight into various aspects of the case. According to the authors, the procedure rallied the workers toward constructive thinking and realistic goals. The warm acceptance of the staff by the conference leaders seemed to contribute greatly toward an improvement in intra-agency relationships.

This particular consultation model was also an integral part of a statewide staff development program with the manifest intent to stimulate desire for more information about human behavior, to increase the self-awareness of the workers, and to stimulate their thinking of the role of casework and of the functions of the agency. A single session appeared to be much less effective than a brief series of three consecutive meetings. Characteristically, the first session was usually about a hard-core case, with the client clearly in the focus. By the time the third session had come around, the presentation frequently involved a relationship problem between a worker and his client. This was quite a contrast to the first meeting. A written summary prepared by the staff development supervisor and distributed to the agency personnel and the consulting team aimed at reinforcing the impact of the consultation. The local agencies were strongly urged to review the summary of their own staff developmental meetings. The consulting team often inquired about previously presented cases. This demonstrated to the workers their continued interest, but it also gave them a chance to get some feedback on the effectiveness of their efforts. An indirect evidence of the usefulness of this program is the fact that it has been continued now over a period of more than fifteen years with only minor modifications and most of the time under the guidance of the same psychiatric consultant.

The 1960s: Expansion of Mental Health Efforts

Several major developments occurred simultaneously in the 1960s, bringing about a rapid and extensive expansion of mental health efforts in public welfare systems throughout the nation.

1. Community oriented mental health services, established with funds provided by the Health Amendment Act of 1955 for demonstration projects, were beginning to get into operation and offered consultation services to public agencies.

2. Publication of the final report of the Joint Commission on Mental Illness and Health[45] in 1961 stipulated national interest and discussions and prepared the public climate for new mental health legislation and programs.

3. The Community Mental Health Centers Act of 1963 sparked the development of federally funded comprehensive community mental health services, which in several enterprising states had preceded the new federal legislation. One of the obligatory basic services of these new centers was consultation and education for other community agencies and resources.

4. Progressive changes in welfare legislation paralleled the legislative developments in the field of mental health. Amendments to the Social Service Act of 1962 introduced the principle that social services and money payments were companion parts of public agency responsibilities. Many public assistance departments changed their names to departments of public social services to emphasize the new philosophy. These program alterations were

not entirely humanitarian. Many legislators hoped that services would motivate recipients toward self-support, which would in turn reduce welfare costs. In order to make better social services possible, federal financial participation was linked to a progressive reduction of caseload per worker and a smaller number of workers per supervisor. In many programs, caseload coverage was restricted to sixty cases per worker. In the guidelines to the 1962 amendments, the welfare workers were presented as providers of services and as agents of change along the lines of traditional casework models.

The amendments failed to fulfill the expectations that welfare costs could be eventually reduced. Their immediate effect was a need and a demand for many more workers. The numbers of staff of welfare departments rose sharply and with them the welfare budgets. Because workers had fewer clients and because the focus was now clearly on more and better services, agencies intensified their staff development efforts to upgrade the capabilities of the staff. Consultation with sophisticated mental health professionals appeared a promising approach to staff development. The greater availability of mental health services by clinics, mental health centers, and even by contractually employed private practitioners coincided happily with the increased interests of welfare departments.

Simultaneously with these developments, the "other America" was once again rediscovered. Interest in all aspects of poverty increased sharply and culminated in the so-called war on poverty. At the same time, psychiatric professionals developed increasing interests in the community and in its relations to mental illness and health. Psychiatrists began to reexamine their roles and responsibilities. They searched for new concepts and methods that could be helpful to them in their new functions in nonclinical community settings.

Among the many significant contributions to the field of community psychiatry the comprehensive and concise conceptualizations of Gerald Caplan[9] have proved especially helpful to practitioner as well as programmer.

Over a period of twenty years, Caplan[11] refined the basic theory and practice of mental health consultation. He differentiated them from other specialized professional transactions, such as supervision, education, psychotherapy, casework, counseling, and collaboration. In this way, he made a major contribution to rendering consultation a basic clinical modality in community mental health services. His classification of the various types of consultation provided a taxonomy that permitted comparison and evaluation of the many different models of consultation presented in this survey.

Leaning heavily on Caplan's work, Rogawski[71] established a consultee-centered consultation program for the Los Angeles Department of Public Social Services (the former Bureau of Public Assistance), a mammoth agency employing several thousand social service workers. Rogawski did not begin to consult until he had spent several months in thorough orientation. During this time, he familiarized himself with the complex issues of welfare, studied the history and current practices and legislation of welfare, became acquainted with a large number of people working at different levels of the huge agency, sat in with social service workers while they were interviewing clients or accompanied them when they made home visits, learned how to compute a grant within the different aid categories, and finally began to experiment with several models of consultation. Because of the tremendous demands for professional support for the largely minimally trained welfare workers, he decided that group consultations with work units consisting of a supervisor and his or her five line workers promised to reach the largest number of staff. He referred to the work unit as a "work family," because relations in the unit resembled relations characteristic of families. At first he consulted alone, under the sponsorship of the local mental health department, but soon he was able to recruit additional psychiatrists from private practice as part-time consultants. They were available to specific districts for a few hours each week. Each new consultant had to go through an orientation phase during which he was familiarized with basic concepts of consultation. Then he became an observer in consultations with an experienced consultant. Finally, he would conduct consultations on his own, at first monitored and supervised by his preceptor, with whom he discussed the dynamics of the procedure following the consultation. The careful preparation paid off. The program enjoyed a favorable acceptance through all levels of the agency, and it has continued for a decade without a single major negative incident. Rogawski also integrated his consultations into a course on mental health consultation techniques for third-year psychiatric residents, many of whom joined the program after their graduation.

An even more ambitious program was described by Liben,[51] who combined psychiatric consultation and mental health education for a local welfare center with the training of psychiatric residents in community psychiatry. Two departments of the School of Public Health and Administrative Medicine and of the College of Physicians and Surgeons of Columbia University, a teaching hospital, the New York State Psychiatric Institute, the New York City Community Mental Health Board, and the Department of Welfare pooled their resources in the collaborative venture, which at once ran into hostile conflicts and resistance. While the psychiatric faculties wished to restrict the number of workers in contact with consultants in order to provide the most intensive service and the best learning experience for its residents, the agency staff insisted that all workers share equally in all aspects of the program and demanded the traditional models of instruction. A compromise was finally reached by arranging monthly seminars for the staff, with the attendance to be determined by the welfare agency, while the content was selected by the division of social and community psychiatry, and by providing weekly consultations with a limited number of welfare units. The monthly institutes included combined case conferences, videotapes demonstrating interviewing techniques, movie presentations with subsequent discussions, and lectures. As anticipated, these efforts had a limited impact on the welfare staff. But the contacts had a very welcome side effect in reducing the hostility between welfare and mental health personnel, and improving communication and relationships between them. They came to respect each other as they became aware of their respective problems. The consultee-centered case consultations were attended simultaneously by two to three units and their supervisors. The worker who presented a selected case prepared a psychosocial summary in advance, and after the meeting the respective supervisor summarized the discussion and the recommendations. Progress was reviewed in follow-up consultations.

The consultation approach seemed to be much more effective with regard to staff development. Success might be partly owing to the fact that each consultant prepared himself for the program in advance by reviewing the relevant literature and material that had issued from the experience of his predecessors. The first consultant always spent a "daily block of time for some weeks to develop the necessary data, as well as to make himself 'visible' in a nonthreatening way by interacting informally with various levels of staff."[51] This resembles closely the path pursued by Rogawski.

Common problems of the consultees were difficulties in perceiving both their limitations and their strength. Inexperienced workers tended to overidentify with clients and become overprotective or antagonistic. They reacted with guilt whenever they could not fulfill unrealistically high aspirations on behalf of their clients. Themes interfering with their professional functioning often included conflicts with their supervisors, with their colleagues, or with agency policies. At first, they seemed reluctant to refer clients to psychiatric resources. As they became aware that the psychiatrist consultants were human beings without dangerous and magical powers, they became more inclined to refer clients for psychiatric treatment. Group discussions often revealed misinformation or lack of information about appropriate referral agencies. The format of meeting in groups had the advantage that fellow workers who in the past had coped with a problem similar to the one presented in the consultation could offer help to the consultee. As a rule a worker was able to follow guidelines proposed by a fellow worker easier than what was introduced by the consultant.

The consultations resulted in a rise of self-esteem in the workers, greater objectivity toward the clients, fewer conflicts with supervisors, and even better understanding of the agency policies.

For the psychiatric residents, the experience was highly educational. They were able to see that they could help staff in their dealings with clients, and they learned to apply their psychiatric insights in the service of the ego functions of the consultees. They reviewed, used, and modified various models of consultation to develop their own conceptual framework for the consultation process.[9,10,82] Though the consultations were at first perceived as an opportunity of solving the problems in an individual case, the focus quickly shifted to common problems of the workers and to the improvement of their expertise. A measure of the success of the program could be demonstrated by the agency's request to continue, enlarge, and expand it.

⟨ Mental Health Programs in Welfare Systems: Current State

In preparation for this chapter, a search was made by the American Public Welfare Association through an assortment of materials received from state departments of welfare, which described a variety of divisional and specialized programs. The Association serves as a clearing house for the exchange of information and experience in the field of public welfare administration. Nothing pertaining to the administrative and professional arrangements between mental health programs and welfare systems could be located. Also, the Interstate Clearing House on Mental Health of the Council of State Governments could not provide any description of coordination of efforts in welfare and mental health.[17,79]

In 1961 Llewellyn and Shepherd[53] received

replies from the state welfare departments of all fifty states plus the Virgin Islands, Puerto Rico, and the District of Columbia to an inquiry about the utilization of psychiatrists in staff development programs, either locally or on a statewide basis. Three out of four states (73.6 percent) used psychiatrists, half of them only on the state level, one-fourth only on the local level, and one-fourth both on the state and on the local level. The authors suspected that the informality of their survey letter caused some ambiguity among their respondents. Even in states that denied the utilization of psychiatrists, some clients were probably referred at times for diagnostic evaluation. But two states insisted that they never made use of psychiatrists in any form. In 49 percent of the state agencies replying, psychiatrists were actively engaged in the education of welfare personnel by means of case conferences or other means of teaching. In an additional 24 percent of the sample, psychiatrists were involved in staff development without actively planning for it. In four states, psychiatrists functioned only as lecturers or seminar leaders. Only in two states were psychiatrists involved in a statewide staff development program: In North Carolina, Llewelyn, himself, employed psychiatric consultations as a training device to develop basic interpersonal skills, self-awareness, and mental health knowledge in workers of all programs at both state and county level; in Mississippi, statewide consultation services were used, but only for the education of child welfare workers.

Ten years have passed since this study, and I[72] decided to explore the current state of mental health programs in welfare systems by means of a questionnaire mailed to representatives, most often staff development specialists of welfare departments in all fifty states, the District of Columbia, and U. S. territories. The questionnaire could be completed partly by checks and partly by brief narrative. It inquired into the following areas: cooperation between mental health agencies and welfare staff; use of consultation programs; conditions of employment and types of mental health professionals; methods used by welfare staff to identify, evaluate, and serve emotionally and mentally disturbed clients; in-service training about mental health and illness issues; use of volunteer workers; employment of "new Careerists"; and compensation for services under the provision of Medicaid (Title XIX). Completed replies were received from forty-three states, the District of Columbia, and Puerto Rico. One state sent alternative information but refused to complete the form.

There were many obstacles interfering with the obtaining of the data. States differ widely in the administration of welfare and mental health programs. More than half of the states have completely separate departments for the two areas. A number of states have omnibus agencies combining under a single administrative official of cabinet rank the departments of health and welfare and other allied bureaus or divisions. While this may sometimes facilitate interprofessional communication, it is not always the case. For economic reasons the inquiry had to be limited primarily to state agencies. Some state officials were well informed about conditions on the local levels. In larger and more populous states staff development specialists were often incompletely acquainted about activities and arrangements by the county agency staff. This was revealed when in some instances replies from state officials were compared with information from local sources. A similar discrepancy became evident when the information from welfare staff was compared with the impressions of the mental health professionals in the same program. Psychiatric staff were always much more optimistic about the effect of their contributions.

Some informants from welfare departments expressed concern that the questionnaire method would evoke a rosier picture than the actual state of interprofessional cooperation warranted. One state official[72] wrote: "While the above questionnaire would indicate that there is mental health consultation and service available to the Division of Family Services in . . . , it is, in reality, woefully inadequate. The services provided are at best erratic and at worst non-existent. The services are confined to two or three metropolitan counties and practically non-existent in the rural areas." Expressions of similar sentiments recur throughout the replies from many states. Frustration with the inadequate supply and quality of mental health services may have been one of the reasons why seven states refused to participate in the survey, in spite of repeated correspondence urging them to return the completed questionnaire.

The following data are excerpted from the survey,[72] which will be reported in greater detail at a later date:

Cooperation between mental health agencies and welfare departments varied widely among the respondents. On the state level the focus was primarily on planning, development, and implementation of mental health programs involving welfare clients and staff. The contact was either formalized or on an informal basis, ranging from regularly scheduled weekly or monthly joint conferences to meetings set up for a specific purpose. Some respondents complained that there was no communication whatsoever. In New York City an office of psychiatry is an integral part of the Department of Social Services, budgeted by the agency, and functions on the basis of a joint agreement with the mental health commissioner, who appoints the director. This office provides evaluation and consultation services to the Bureaus of Child Welfare, Public Assistance, and Special Services, all operating divisions of the Department of Social Services. It also furnishes psychological evaluation and consulting services to the Bureau of Child Welfare, participates in centrally and locally initiated staff development programs, promotes liaison with state, city, and voluntary mental health systems, administers the psychiatric Medicaid program, consults with the executive staff of the welfare agency, and participates in policy decisions, research, and evaluation activities. Such intensive integration of the services seems unique, but movement toward greater communication and collaboration between welfare departments and community mental health agencies was reported from several states. In one state, the continuing education committee of the local branch of the American Public Health Association served as a common platform for welfare and mental health professionals to meet and to air common problems. In other states, communications and agreements were restricted primarily to certain specific issues, such as arrangements concerning persons who were both welfare clients and patients in mental hospitals. Arrangements between local agencies often seem quite independent from relations at the state government level. On the county level the focus is usually on service-related issues and on ways to upgrade and support the staff.

Five states claimed that they had no mental health consultations whatsoever. This reply may be due to a misunderstanding of the term. A sixth state, which also denied using consultations in general, reported in another section of the form that "consultation is obtained from mental health agencies in disability determination applications when there are symptoms of mental or emotional illnesses."[72] Obviously, recipients considered to be actual or potential mental patients are referred to psychiatric resources for diagnostic evaluation, although this procedure does not seem to be considered by some an act of professional collaboration.

About three-fourths of the responding state agencies indicated that they had individual or group consultation programs for their staff. Most frequently the consultations seemed client-centered, less often consultee-centered case consultations, and in only one-third of the states psychiatrists were invited to participate in administrative consultations. Five states reported that sensitivity groups were employed to improve staff relations. As indicated before, use of consultation was limited by the availability and accessibility of psychiatric resources. It varied considerably from region to region, even in the same state. Only sixteen state agencies reported the use of consultations as part of a regularly scheduled in-service training program in certain districts. Programs varied in frequency from once-weekly conferences to occasional meetings once or twice a year or special events scheduled in connection with perceived needs.

The following problems were cited as common indications for the requesting of a mental health consultation: adult or child behavior disorders indicating the presence of a mental illness; acting out behavior; marital conflicts and family disruptions; special problems, such as drug addiction; teenage abortions; illegitimacy; alcoholism; disturbed mothers neglecting or abusing their children; planning for placement of children, mentally disturbed adults, and, especially, aged and helpless persons; determination of eligibility for special programs of financial assistance or vocational rehabilitation; management of families with serious problems, such as a mentally retarded or psychotic youngster; obtaining help in the finding of mental health professionals or other psychiatric resources for the agency's children; learning problems; child-parent problems; emergency problems; precare and after care planning; clients in conflict with the community; changes in mental health legislation; and implementation of new treatment modalities.

The mental health consultants (psychiatrists, psychologists, and psychiatric social workers, and very rarely nurses and vocational guidance counselors) were usually furnished by a public health or a mental health agency, funded by the government or by private funds, federally or locally supported community mental health centers, outpatient clinics, family services and guidance clinics, state hospitals, psychiatric departments of general hospitals, and psychiatric training programs affiliated with a medical school or university. In some instances, welfare agencies employed private psychiatrists either on a part-time basis, on a contractual fee for service, or on a per diem basis. Only in rare instances were consultants directly employed by the welfare department. One funding resource for psychiatric manpower has been the Medicaid program (Title XIX).

The questionnaire permitted us also to gain an impression of the methods used by the welfare staff to identify emotionally and mentally disturbed clients and to serve them after proper evaluation.

Although almost all states seem to have some orientation program preparing the workers to recognize disturbed behavior, to deter-

mine the severity of the problem, and to initiate appropriate measures to deal with the problem, the level of orientation and continued in-service training seems to vary widely from state to state. All workers are taught some basic casework methods and learn how to elicit and evaluate historical information, how to review medical reports and recommendations, and how to use interpersonal relationships to stabilize disturbed clients and their families. In some departments much time is spent on teaching service workers how to provide emotional support by counseling as well as by concrete assistance, by group casework, and by appropriate referral and placement if so indicated. Herrick's[39] study of mental health problems in public assistance clients is an illustration of a high-quality in-service training effort and ought to be read by anyone who plans to consult with welfare workers.

The scarcity of mental health professionals, in general, and some reluctance to work with welfare clients and staff often force welfare workers to rely on their resourcefulness beyond their technical training. One respondent wrote: "Mental Health Professionals are limited in Idaho and consultation is limited both in quality and quantity. Because of the tremendous need, professionals tend to limit their time to the motivated client."[72] One respondent from another state wrote that the staff members tried not to engage themselves in continuous treatment of the seriously disturbed client but time and again found they had to remain available and work with psychotic and even potentially dangerous patients until such time as a psychiatric resource could become involved in the management of the case.

The replies to the survey reflect the great need for support by the psychiatric professions and the frustrations of the welfare staff when relevant collaboration with mental health professionals is lacking. One agency reported that in its state the emphasis in mental health seemed to be on the psychoanalytic model, and "this does not meet the needs of our client population." The director of staff development from another state stated: "It has been our observation of the approach of psychiatrists and social workers who have been involved in some in-service training that their approach is academically oriented and is not the job-related training that the local welfare department finds helpful, which subsequently leads to a breaking off of this kind of relationship." Several informants reported on discontinued interprofessional programs even though they politely claimed that the service was "discontinued following the reorganization of our service program."

⟮ Psychiatrists in Public Welfare

In view of the demonstrated need for psychiatric participation and the destructive consequences of disillusionment and discontinuation of interprofessional collaboration, the final section of this chapter will be devoted to a description of the various roles psychiatrists can assume within welfare systems.

The material presented in the foregoing sections of this chapter should make it obvious that any mental health professional wishing to function effectively within any part of a welfare system should prepare himself by expanding his traditional psychiatric expertise in several directions.

1. He must acquaint himself with the issues and conditions of poverty as they affect the life and the mental health of the poor, individually, in families, in communities, and in our society as a whole. He must learn about the legislative background and the current practices of welfare, and he would benefit from acquaintance with the history[47] and the values, means, and ends of public welfare.

2. He ought to be thoroughly familiar with the theory and practice of mental health consultation.[11] This should preferably include the rationale and the techniques of conducting the various types of consultation, the strategy of building a relationship with a consultee institution, and the ways of developing a program suited to the specific needs of the agency. Langsley and Harris[50] advocated, more than a decade ago, as most valuable preparation for such work, a supervised field experience in doing consultation with some agency during or after the psychiatric residency.

3. The mental health professional should refrain from plunging at once into activities even though he may be pressed for immediate intervention by some urgent problem of the agency. He should allocate some time for orientation in the agency in which he plans to function as clinician, consultant, or educator to become acquainted with specific conditions in the agency and to build rapport with his future consultees and colleagues. The reports of the experience of predecessors in the field cited in this chapter will prove invaluable as guides through the preparatory period.

Success or failure of a consultation program may ultimately be determined by the care given to the preparation of the consultant.

4. Finally, after learning about the needs of his agency, the psychiatrist should select from the range of possible functions those most fitting to the agency and to his own qualifications. Broad psychiatric knowledge, competence gained in basic psychiatric skills in the intensive one to one relationship, sensitivity for psychodynamic processes, the ability to listen with the "third ear,"[67] acuity of observation, and tact in interpersonal relations remain invaluable and essential prerequisites of any psychiatrist in a public agency.

There are several options available to a psychiatrist who wishes to work within a welfare program. He may serve as a (1) clinician, (2) mental health consultant, (3) participant in staff development, (4) mental health educator, (5) clinical researcher and program evaluator, or (6) participant in a new careers program.

Clinicians

A psychiatrist may provide diagnostic services for a welfare agency to assist in the planning of a therapeutic program, in decisions on placement of clients to board and care homes or referral to psychiatric facilities, and in the determination of eligibility for certain financial assistance programs (for example, Aid to

Totally Disabled) or for special medical services. Some psychiatrists are directly employed, on a part-time or full-time basis, to evaluate and to decide on requests for authorization of psychiatric treatment or special supportive services. Diagnosticians are especially important in programs concerned with child welfare to determine the suitability of children and their prospective substitute parents for adoption or placement in foster homes, to evaluate degrees of mental fitness or retardation, and to diagnose possible psychotic conditions.

Under the provisions of Medicaid (Title XIX) a psychiatrist in private practice may be reimbursed for treatment of medically indigent persons with or without special authorization, dependent on local regulations. Legal interpretations of federal regulations depend on state and local conditions and are unfortunately subject to changes in political climate.

Therapists treating welfare recipients ought to be informed about the various medical, social, and supportive services to which their patient is entitled. To gain this knowledge and to obtain services for the patient, the welfare worker should be included in the total management. The problems of the poor can rarely be resolved by psychotherapy alone even if combined with drug therapy. These patients usually need concrete assistance, which a worker acting as a supplemental ego may provide. Many psychiatrists are, unfortunately, not aware how much more can be done for their patient and his family if time is spent on communicating with the worker in a language free from technical terms and helpful to the worker to understand the client and his needs. In this communication, a psychiatrist's knowledge and experience with consultee-centered consultation are invaluable.

Mental Health Consultants

The various forms of consultations previously described represent the most important contribution a mental health consultant can make to the staff of a welfare agency. As a rule, he will be urged at first to conduct client-centered case consultations to help a case-

worker and his supervisor with an immediate problem. If he is sensitive and knowledgeable, the focus will soon shift to the consultees, to the determination of the interference with the workers' objectivity to the clients, and to attempts to remedy this interference with workers' optimal work efficiency. If the consultant follows the recommendations of experts,[11] defines his role carefully in advance, maintains good relations with the executives and administrators who must sanction his presence and with the line workers, supervisors, and middle management who must learn to trust and to accept him, he will most likely be retained by the agency for a long time. The more he is able to learn from and about the welfare personnel, the more helpful he will become, and the more likely that he will be invited to participate in administrative conferences, in program planning, and in discussions of policies. In this way psychiatrists may be able to contribute toward the humanization of human services.

Participants in Staff Development

The better acquainted the psychiatrist becomes with the welfare system, the more valuable he will be as teacher in orientation and in in-service programs. He may begin as a lecturer or seminar leader and progress to course consultant or training program consultant. If he has previously established good working relations with the agency staff as their mental health consultant, he may be given special credit by his audience, and he may overcome resistances in their mind which the uninitiated stranger may not be able to overcome.

In 1964 an intensive staff development effort was mounted, reported,[55] and, subsequently, carefully researched and evaluated[37] by the Los Angeles County Bureau of Public Assistance, which had to recruit large numbers of new social service staff to respond to the 1962 amendments of the Social Service Act. The program consisted of several parts. A nationally known sociologist, a psychoanalyst who was in fact the agency's own mental health consultant, and a highly experienced social work educator addressed almost 600 caseworkers and supervisors of all degrees of experience and sophistication in general sessions on the nature of the "normal family," on the "unique opportunity of workers to help people in crisis," and on the "social needs of the welfare family, respectively." These lectures were followed by intensive orientation workshops for workshop leaders and resource personnel, and, subsequently, all participants met in weekly intervals in four two-hour small discussion groups. The project was evaluated by a carefully designed research effort that revealed that workers with longer experience at the agency, even if they were formally untrained, were the most receptive to the learning of mental health concepts. They were able to attend to the needs of their clients for service because they were not so distracted by the handling of routine aspects of their assignment as less experienced workers. The presentation of the psychiatrist was the most popular. It was substantially more often designated as "pitched just right" because the workers appreciated "that the psychiatrist recognized the difficulty and the importance of the public assistance jobs and articulated their mental health components." Most likely, the psychiatrist was so well accepted because he had established the image of a supportive helper in his role as a mental health consultant.

Every teacher of welfare workers experiences the tremendous eagerness of the staff to learn. Partly this zeal is based on guilt and on the almost unrealistic hope that more education will enable the workers to help their clients with their enormous and overwhelming problems. Even though it is most questionable that seminars and lectures have a lasting and improving effect on the workers' skills and knowledge, traditional educational methods are highly popular with agency staff. It seems, however, that well-conducted consultations with small groups, because of their personal immediacy and relevance, are a far more effective means of education.

Mental Health Educators

The psychiatrist who works in a public welfare agency has excellent opportunities to broaden his experience and knowledge on human problems, especially as they concern the disadvantaged. As he absorbs this knowledge and thinks through his experience, he becomes uniquely qualified to bring his understanding to the attention of his colleagues. He can contribute to an improvement in the communication between the psychiatric and the welfare professionals and build respect for the dedicated efforts of the often misunderstood and much maligned agency staff. He may even reduce some of the widespread misinformation and the simplistic thinking concerning welfare policies and welfare practices in the population at large. Even though the physician's public image may be somewhat tarnished, he commands the respect of the public, and he may do a great deal toward the correction of erroneous impressions by presenting, in fairness, the serious and involved problems of poverty and the efforts toward its relief.

Clinical Researchers and Program Evaluators

Even though large sums of money are spent on public welfare, only insignificant amounts are allotted to research, in spite of its potentially great importance for public policies and programs. The opportunities of studying relations between impoverishment, powerlessness, and mental impairment, the psychodynamics of the helping process and its potentially destructive influence on recipients and their families are endless. Much clinical and social research is necessary to determine the importance of work and activities for the mental health of individuals. Also, we have no answers as to which approaches are best for the stimulation of motivation and independence in a society in which individual fate and life style are increasingly determined by supersystems beyond the control of single persons. New conceptualizations, perhaps supplied by the recent interest in systems theory, are required to permit evaluation of schemes proposed to alleviate poverty and their implications on the quality of life in communities and on the total fabric of our social institutions. In these endeavors, the interests of man ought to be also represented by the psychiatric expert.

Participants in New Career Programs

One of the most promising and innovative developments that has emerged from the war on poverty and that aims at the improvement of mental health services for the disadvantaged is the so-called new careers movement.[29,65,69] Essentially, this is the recruitment, training, and employment of people of disadvantaged background to provide human services for their neighbors or others with similar problems and life experience. The innovative core of the new careers effort is the challenge to traditional mental health professionals to learn from this new source of human service manpower how services can be rendered more relevant and effective by changes in techniques and strategies of service delivery. In this endeavor, help can also be expected from newly formed recipient organizations, such as the Welfare Rights Organization. It would transgress the frame of this chapter to elucidate the many and complex aspects of new careers. One of the exciting realizations issuing from the program was the discovery that the helper is the first to benefit from his being given the opportunity to help others.[67] The new careers program may thus serve simultaneously a number of problems: improvement of human services, rehabilitation of a large number of people of disadvantaged background, employment of unemployed or underemployed people in occupations from which they are unlikely to be phased out by technological progress, opening the door for large segments of population hitherto excluded from education and upward mobility, and initiating new thinking on social and mental health services.

An increasing number of welfare systems are beginning to integrate new careers into their organizations. Progress is slow because it arouses much resistance from administrative and professional quarters by challenging the status quo of service delivery and professional prerogatives. But the development seems inevitable, and fortunately so. Mental health professionals have been among pioneers and ardent advocates of new careers programs as participants in program planning, educators, collaborators, and providers of back-up services. While psychiatrists have experienced that involvement in innovative and still controversial areas can at times bring them pain and frustration, it is completely in the tradition of the profession to espouse causes in conflict with the established order on behalf of suffering man.

❲ Bibliography

1. ADLER, L. M., GOIN, M., and YAMAMOTO, J. "Failed Psychiatric Clinic Appointments: Relationship to Social Class." *California Medicine*, 99 (1963), 388–392.
2. BANDLER, B. "The American Psychoanalytic Association and Community Psychiatry." *American Journal of Psychiatry*, 124, no. 8 (1968), 1037–1042.
3. BEMMELS, V. G. "Survey of Mental Health Problems in Social Agency Caseloads." *American Journal of Psychiatry*, 121, no. 2 (1964), 136–146.
4. BERNARD, V. W. "Psychiatric Consultation in the Social Agency." *Child Welfare*, 33 (1954), 3–8.
5. BLAKESLEE, R. O. The Use of Consultants in Public Assistance Administration. Social Security Board, Washington, D.C., August 11, 1939. Mimeographed.
6. BRILL, N. O., and STORROW, H. A. "Social Class and Psychiatric Treatment." *Archives of General Psychiatry*, 3 (1960), 340–344.
7. BROSIN, H. W. "Federal Legislation, Local Psychiatric Societies, and Changing Patterns of Practice." *Mental Hygiene*, 51, no. 4 (1967), 479–485.
8. BUSH, E. D., and LLEWELLYN, C. E. "A Statewide Experiment with Psychiatric Consultation." *Journal of the American Public Welfare Association*, 16 (1958), 127–130.
9. CAPLAN, G. *Principles of Preventive Psychiatry*. New York: Basic Books, 1964.
10. ———. "Problems of Training in Mental Health Consultation." In S. Goldston, ed., *Concepts of Community Psychiatry*. Public Health Service publication, no. 1319.

Washington, D.C.: U.S. Government Printing Office, 1965. Pp. 91–108.

11. ———. *The Theory and Practice of Mental Health Consultation*. New York: Basic Books, 1970.

12. ———, and CAPLAN, R. B. "Development of Community Psychiatry Concepts." In A. Freedman and H. Kaplan, eds., *Comprehensive Textbook of Psychiatry*. Baltimore, Md.: Williams & Wilkins, 1967. Pp. 1499–1516.

13. CARTER, G. W. "Review of Research Findings in Public Welfare (a Five Year Analysis) March 1970." In H. Mass, ed., *Research in the Social Services: A Five Year Review*. National Association of Social Workers, 1971.

14. COLEMAN, J. V. "Psychiatric Consultation in Case Work Agencies." *American Journal of Orthopsychiatry*, 17 (1947), 533–539.

15. ———. "The Contribution of the Psychiatrist to the Social Worker and to the Client." *Mental Hygiene*, 37 (1953), 249–258.

16. ———, and APTEKER, H. H. "Division of Responsibility Between Psychiatrist and Social Worker in a Foster Home Agency." *American Journal of Orthopsychiatry*, 14, no. 3 (1944), 511–520.

17. COUNCIL OF STATE GOVERNMENTS. "State Mental Health Programs and Personnel Administration." Lexington, Ky.: Iron Works Pike, 1969.

18. COUNTY SUPERVISORS ASSOCIATION OF CALIFORNIA. *Public Welfare-Time for Change*. A county government study and platform for public welfare, final report. Sacramento, April 1970.

19. DAVIS, A. T. "Consultation: A Function in Public Welfare Administration." *Social Casework*, 37 (1956), 113–119.

20. DAVIS, W. E. "Psychiatric Consultation: The Agency Viewpoint." *Child Welfare*, 36, no. 9 (1957), 4–9.

21. DECKER, J. H., and ITZIN, F. H. "An Experience in Consultation in Public Assistance." *Social Casework*, 37, no. 7 (1956), 327–334.

22. DEPARTMENT OF HEALTH, EDUCATION AND WELFARE. Background Paper, June 1970: Amendments to the Family Assistance Act. Washington, D.C., June 10, 1970.

23. DEPARTMENT OF PUBLIC WELFARE, COMMONWEALTH OF PENNSYLVANIA. Regionalization of the Department of Welfare. Harrisburg, February 1969.

24. DOHRENWEND, B. P., and DOHRENWEND, B. S. "The Problem of Validity in Field Studies of Psychological Disorder." *Journal of Abnormal Psychology*, 70 (1965), 52.

25. DONADELLO, G. "Some Applications of Ego Psychology Theory to Practice and Programs in Child Welfare." *Child Welfare*, 46, no. 9 (1967), 493–497, 527.

26. DRAKE, R. "The Use of Consultants in a State Agency." *Public Welfare*, 4 (1946), 88–90.

27. EISENBERG, L. "An Evaluation of Psychiatric Consultation Service for a Public Agency." *American Journal of Public Health*, 48 (1958), 742–749.

28. FERMAN, L. A., KORNBLUH, J. L., and HABER, A., eds., *Poverty in America: A Book of Readings*. Rev. ed. Ann Arbor: University of Michigan Press, 1968.

29. FISHMAN, J. R., and MITCHELL, L. E. New Careers and Mental Health for the Disadvantaged. Paper presented to the American Psychiatric Association, San Francisco, Cal., May 13, 1970.

30. FROST, D., and ANDERSON, G. "A Health Department Stimulates Community Thinking for Mental Health." *American Journal of Public Health*, 40 (1950), 978–983.

31. GEIGER, H. J. "Of the Poor, by the Poor, or for the Poor: The Mental Health Implications of Social Control of Poverty Programs." In M. Greenblatt, P. E. Emery, and B. C. Glueck, eds., *Poverty and Mental Health*. Psychiatric research report, no. 21. Washington, D.C.: American Psychiatric Association, 1967. Pp. 55–65.

32. GOIN, M. K., YAMAMOTO, J., and SILVERMAN, J. "Therapy Congruent with Class Linked Expectations." *Archives of General Psychiatry*, 13 (1965), 133–137.

33. GREENBLATT, M., EMERY, P. E., and GLUECK, B. C., eds. *Poverty and Mental Health*. Psychiatric research report, no. 21. Washington, D.C.: American Psychiatric Association, 1967.

34. GROUP FOR THE ADVANCEMENT OF PSYCHIATRY. *The Consultant in a Family Service Agency*. Report no. 34. New York, 1956.

34a. ———. *The Welfare System and Mental Health*. Report no. 85. New York, 1973.

34b. ———. *Roles of the Psychiatrist in Welfare Agencies*. In preparation.

35. GRUENBERG, E. Discussion of Dr. Frank Riessman's paper in *Poverty and Mental*

Health. In M. Greenblatt, P. E. Emery, and B. C. Glueck, eds., *Poverty and Mental Health*. Washington, D.C.: American Psychiatric Association, 1967. P. 53.

36. HAGSTROM, W. C. "The Power of the Poor." In F. Riessman, J. Cohen, and A. Pearl, eds., *Mental Health of the Poor*. New York: The Free Press, 1964. Pp. 205–223.

37. HAMOVITCH, M. B., and NOVICK, M. B. "Research Evaluation of a Training Course for Staff of a County Public Assistance Agency." *Family Mental Health*, January 1966.

38. HARRINGTON, M. *The Other America*. New York: Penguin Books, 1964.

39. HERRICK, H. *Mental Health Problems of Public Assistance Clients*. Sacramento: Office of Planning, California Department of Mental Hygiene, June 1967.

40. HOLLINGSHEAD, A. B., and REDLICH, F. C. *Social Class and Mental Illness*. New York: Wiley, 1958.

41. HOSHINO, G. "A Conceptual Analysis of the Nixon Welfare Proposal." *Social Casework*, 51 no. 3 (1970), 157–166.

42. HOWARD, D. D. *Values, Means, and Ends*. New York: Random House, 1969.

43. IRELAN, L. M. *Low-Income Life Styles*. U.S. Department of Health, Education and Welfare, Welfare Administration publication, no. 14. Washington D.C.: U.S. Government Printing Office, 1968.

44. JACOBS, G. "The Reification of the Notion of Subculture in Public Welfare." *Social Casework*, 49, no. 9 (1968), 527–536.

45. JOINT COMMISSION OF MENTAL ILLNESS AND HEALTH. *Action for Mental Health*. New York: Basic Books, 1961.

46. JUSTIS, G. R. American public welfare association. Personal communication, August 11, 1970.

47. KLEIN, P. *From Philanthropy to Social Welfare*. San Francisco: Jossey-Bass, 1968.

48. LAMSON, W. C. "Integrating Mental Health Services into the Community Health and Welfare Program." *Journal of Psychiatric Social Work*, September 1955, pp. 243–249.

49. LANGER, T. S., and MICHAEL, S. T. *Life Stress and Mental Health*. New York: Macmillan, 1963.

50. LANGSLEY, D. G., and HARRIS, M. R. "Community Mental Health Activities of Psychiatrists." *Psychiatric Quarterly*, 34, no. 2, suppl. (1960), 314–325.

51. LIBEN, F. "Psychiatric Consultation for a Local Welfare Center." *American Journal of Public Health*, 59, no 11 (1969), 2013–2021.

52. LIFSCHUTZ, J. E., STEWART, T. B., and HARRISON, A. "Psychiatric Consultation in the Public Assistance Agency." *Social Casework*, 39, no. 1 (1958), 3–9.

53. LLEWELLYN, C. E., and SHEPHERD, K. B. Report of Survey of Use of Psychiatrists by Welfare Departments. North Carolina State Board of Public Welfare, 1961.

54. ———, and SHEPHERD, K. B. The Psychiatric Consultation Service: An Integral Part of Staff Development in a State Public Welfare Agency (mimeo-undated).

55. LOS ANGELES COUNTY BUREAU OF PUBLIC ASSISTANCE AND MENTAL HEALTH DEVELOPMENT COMMITTEE. *Family Mental Health Papers*. Los Angeles, January 1964.

56. MADDUX, J. F. "Psychiatric Consultation in a Public Welfare Agency." *American Journal of Orthopsychiatry*, 20 (1950), 754–764.

57. MAY, E. *The Wasted Americans*. New York: Harper & Row, 1964.

58. MILLER, S. M., and MISHLER, E. G. "Social Class, Mental Illness, and American Psychiatry: An Expository Review." *Milbank Memorial Fund Quarterly*, 37, no. 2 (1959), 174–199.

59. MOORE, R. A., BENEDEK, E. P., and WALLACE, J. G. "Social Class, Schizophrenia and the Psychiatrist." *American Journal of Psychiatry*, 120 (1963), 149–154.

60. MORTON, M., ed. *Public Welfare Directory*. Chicago: American Public Welfare Association, 1969.

61. NEW YORK STATE BOARD OF SOCIAL WELFARE. *Report from the Steering Committee of the Arden House Conference on Public Welfare*. Albany, March 1967.

62. NITZBERG, H., and KAHN, M. W. "Consultation with Welfare Workers in a Mental Health Clinic." *Social Work*, 7, no. 3 (1962), 84–93.

63. OLSON, E. "Psychiatric Developments in a Family Welfare Agency." *American Journal of Orthopsychiatry*, 7, no. 1 (1937), 96–102.

64. ORMSBY, R. "Group Psychiatric Consultation in a Family Casework Agency." *Social Casework*, 31, no. 9 (1950), 361–662.

65. PEARL, A., and RIESSMAN, F. *New Careers for the Poor*. New York: The Free Press, 1965.

66. RICHARDSON, E. Statement of the Secretary of Health, Education and Welfare before the Committee on Finance, U.S. Senate, July 21, 1970.

67. RIESSMAN, F. "The 'Helper' Therapy Principle." *Social Work*, 10 (1965), 27–32.

68. ——, COHEN, J., and PEARL, A., eds. *Mental Health of the Poor: New Treatment Approaches for Low Income People*. New York: The Free Press, 1964.

69. ——, and POPPER, H. *Up from Poverty: New Career Ladders for Nonprofessionals*. New York: Harper & Row, 1968.

70. ROGAWSKI, A. S. "The Unique Opportunities of Public Assistance Workers to Help Families in Crisis." In Los Angeles County Bureau of Public Assistance, *Family Mental Health Papers*. Los Angeles, 1964. Pp. 29–51.

71. ——. "Teaching Consultation Techniques in a Community Agency." In W. Mendel and P. Solomon, eds., *The Psychiatric Consultation*. New York: Grune & Stratton, 1968. Pp. 65–85.

72. ——. Mental Health Programs in Welfare Systems. Research project in progress.

73. ROSENTHAL, D., and FRANK, J. D. "The Fate of Psychiatric Clinic Out-patients Assigned to Psychotherapy." *Journal of Nervous and Mental Diseases*, 127 (1958), 330–343.

74. SCHAFFER, L., and MYERS, J. "Psychotherapy and Social Stratification." *Psychiatry*, 17 (1954), 83–93.

75. SLOANE, P. "The Use of a Consultation Method in Casework Therapy." *American Journal of Orthopsychiatry*, 6, no. 3 (1963), 355–361.

76. SOBEY, F. *The Nonprofessional Revolution in Mental Health*. New York: Columbia University Press, 1970.

77. SROLE, L., LANGER, T. S., MICHAEL, S. T., OPLER, M. K., and RENNIE, T. A. C. *Mental Health in the Metropolis*. New York: McGraw-Hill, 1962.

78. THOMPSON, W. "Psychiatric Consultation in Social Agencies." *Child Welfare*, 36, no. 9 (1957), 1–3.

79. TURK, R. L. Personal written communication from the secretary, Interstate Clearing House on Mental Health, The Council of State Governments, Chicago. July 27, 1970.

80. VASEY, W. *Government and Social Welfare*. New York: Holt, Rinehart, & Winston, 1958.

81. WELFARE PLANNING COUNCIL, LOS ANGELES REGION. *Mental Health Services for the Disadvantaged*. A position statement on the mental health development program. Los Angeles, October 1967.

82. WHITTINGTON, H. G. *Psychiatry in the American Community*. New York: International Universities Press, 1966.

83. YAMAMOTO, J. "Social Class in Psychiatric Therapy." In *Current Psychiatric Therapies*. New York: Grune & Stratton, 1965. Vol. 5, pp. 87–90.

84. ——, and GOIN, M. K. "On the Treatment of the Poor." *American Journal of Psychiatry*, 122 no. 3 (1965), 267–271.

CHAPTER 52

MENTAL HEALTH
PROGRAMS IN COLLEGES

Dana L. Farnsworth

THE MENTAL HEALTH of college students began to be a subject of particular interest in the second and third decades of this century. Stewart Paton at Princeton (1910), Smiley Blanton at the University of Wisconsin (1914), Karl Menninger at Washburne College (1920), Arthur Ruggles at Dartmouth and Yale (1921, 1925), Austen Fox Riggs at Vassar (1923), and especially, Clements C. Fry at Yale (1926) were among the first psychiatrists who saw the need for mental health services in American colleges and universities. They also introduced the idea that crippling emotional illness among students might be forestalled by working on the causes of distress before they led to the classic syndromes of illness, the same basic principle as is now being furthered by those in community and social psychiatry.[1,17]

Psychiatric services in colleges grew slowly after 1926, but since World War II and especially during the last fifteen years, there has been a more rapid rate of increase and a greater interest in the problems posed by college psychiatry. Clements Fry[25] polled all members of the American Psychiatric Association in 1947 and found that about 550 psychiatrists did at least occasional counseling in colleges, but only twenty-five were on a full-time basis. Gundle and Kraft's[34] national survey in 1953 found 101 colleges with special facilities set up within their health services to deal with emotional problems. Thirty-five full-time and 131 part-time psychiatrists were employed in these institutions. The most recent study[6] (1969) of college mental health programs in thirteen Western states indicated that some form of professional mental health assistance was available in three-fourths of the 102 colleges responding. Counseling centers predominated over medical-psychiatric services about two to one. Students used the service far more than did employees and faculty members in those services where they were eligible. These findings are probably representative of the entire country.

Reifler[46,47] recently reviewed the epidemiological aspects of college mental health and concluded that about 12 percent of college students are estimated to need mental health services each year and that such estimates, crude as they undoubtedly are, are remarkably constant over the past few decades. The incidence of psychoses appears to be constant also, and it is reasonable to anticipate that about two students in every thousand will become psychotic each year. Women use mental health facilities more than men, members of religious minorities more than others, while athletes and members of social fraternities use them less than the average. All superficial studies and observations reported have considerable consistency, but well-organized longitudinal studies of a cohort of students over a considerable period of time should give much more reliable information.

Few colleges and universities have a comprehensive mental health service, however, and this uneven distribution of services and disparity among different institutions as to what constitutes a serious problem makes statistical comparisons potentially misleading. The widely accepted estimate that 10 to 12 percent of all college students have emotional conflicts of sufficient severity to warrant professional help may be too conservative for institutions whose populations are relatively sophisticated about the nature of emotional conflict.

A large Midwestern university, for example, reported approximately one incidence of psychosis for every 1,000 students registered;[53] at Harvard, with an enrollment of 15,000, from twenty-two to fifty-four psychotic reactions per year occurred over a fifteen-year period. The average was about thirty.[8,18] We do not know the extent to which this indicates that Harvard has two to three times as many psychotic reactions as does the other institution. Harvard's more extensive mental health services and the sophistication of its students regarding emotional problems undoubtedly contribute to the higher figure by more accurate diagnosis and more complete reporting of data.[21]

The work of college psychiatrists constitutes one form of community psychiatry, and their experiences should be significant to other psychiatrists who are interested in preventive medicine and in applying psychiatric principles by methods other than the one-to-one relationship of psychotherapy. The goals of college psychiatry are broader than merely treating sick students and faculty members. Yet a college psychiatric service cannot approach realization of its most important goals if it is not solidly based on the information about the college and the psychosocial world of late adolescence and young adulthood which it obtains by treating some students, particularly in brief psychotherapy.

The maturational tasks of the late adolescent during his college years are comparatively simple if during his earlier life he has been fortunate enough to have good role models for emulation, parents who understood and loved him sufficiently to support him by firm, friendly, and consistent discipline and has acquired basically optimistic views of other people and his own relations with them. If he has had these favorable associations and influences, it becomes vital to his further development that the college attempt to construct an environment in which he can learn to become independent, deal with authority, cope with uncertainty and ambiguity, attain appropriate feelings of adequacy and competence, and develop standards and values with which he can live with comfort and self-esteem. All these qualities are complex and can seldom be taught directly, but the young person can acquire them if he has significant relationships with people who possess them. In brief, he needs warm, friendly, personal but critical interchange with a wide variety of faculty members as well as with his own peer-group members.

In addition to helping those in acute conflicts, the goals of a college psychiatric service include:

1. Changing attitudes of students, faculty, and employers toward emotional problems from aversion, fear or denial to understanding, tolerance, and cooperation in their management.

2. Improving relations between students and college staff in order to increase educational effectiveness.
3. Freeing the intellectual capacity of students to do creative and satisfying work.
4. Identifying and counteracting anti-intellectual forces that impede or prevent learning.
5. Creating a complex network of communication among all departments in the institution to facilitate early discovery of disabling conflicts. This must be done without creating the impression that there is a spy system, even one established for benevolent purposes.
6. Coordinating and integrating all counseling services in the institution, not in order to dominate or control but to see that all available resources are available to anyone needing them.[18]

College psychiatric services do not offer long-term or intensive psychotherapy, except in occasional cases when a student needing treatment but able to carry on academic work successfully is unable to afford private care and cannot gain entrance to a clinic in the community. To attempt to supply the full range of psychiatric services needed by all its students is beyond the present financial capacity of most colleges. Even if those responsible for administration and financial support were to alter their policies and assume the responsibility of providing psychiatric care for all those who need it, there would not be enough psychiatrists to meet the demands.

Various organizations and services exist in colleges for aiding those in emotional conflict, many of them antedating psychiatric services. In some colleges they still assume the functions that are seen, in other institutions, as more properly the responsibility of a psychiatric service operating within the health services. Academic, personal, vocational, and religious counselors cooperate in varying degrees with college mental health services. Limited psychiatric time is probably more effectively utilized in working with those who counsel college students than by treatment alone, though some psychotherapy is funda-

mental to an effective psychiatric service.

Ideally, within an institution all individuals and agencies that counsel students should cooperate with one another to ensure that any particular student needing help receives attention from the source best qualified to aid in the solution of his particular problem. A prime duty of a psychiatric consultant is to develop good relations with all such groups and thereby facilitate referral to him of those students specifically in need of psychiatric help. Above all, competition for student patronage between different advisory or counseling agencies should be avoided. There is more work to be done in aiding students with their academic and maturational problems than all personnel workers together can accomplish; the central issue is to learn how available resources can best be applied.

Some college psychiatric services practice group therapy, with satisfying results. So-called sensitivity training or encounter groups, which are nonmedical in nature, often appear on campuses under a variety of auspices. They are viewed by most college psychiatrists with considerable reservation, because of the propensity of these groups to attract persons already under emotional stress, with consequent precipitation of serious psychological reactions.

Emotional Illness among College Students

The clinical problems seen most frequently in college psychiatry are those in which emotional conflicts result in varying degrees of depression, anxiety, and psychosomatic symptoms. Schizophrenic reactions occur with little change in frequency from year to year. Manic reactions are appearing with decreasing frequency, although the evidence for this decrease is a clinical impression rather than comprehensive statistical data. Hysterical symptoms are more common in women than in men and are apt to be quite sophisticated, rather than manifesting the gross stigmata frequently encountered in those with the same complaint who have little education.

The prognosis for most college students with psychiatric disorders is excellent. Most of the patients are persons of superior intelligence who are in an early stage of illness, are highly motivated, and are still developing their adaptive and coping mechanisms. Results that might require months or years of effort in other patients are often obtained within days or weeks. Symptoms of psychopathology, which in other settings would be quite grave, are in this special population more likely to represent a transient reaction to stress.[16] It is rare, however, that the pressures of college life are the basic source of severe emotional decompensation, though they may precipitate the illness. Most students with severe emotional illness have a history of persistent family disharmony or difficulties with other interpersonal relationships.

Suicide

Suicide and suicide attempts are of acute concern to college administrators and psychiatrists. Whether the suicide rate among students is increasing is not definitely known, but indications are that it probably is not.[21] At Harvard University there were thirty-five suicides from 1946 to 1965, but the last seven years of this period had a 50 percent lower rate than did the first twelve. This coincides with the establishment of a comprehensive psychiatric service in 1958. The overall rate of suicide among college students is about 50 percent above that for noncollege students in the same age group.[51]

Although the suicidal act itself is frequently impulsive, nearly all students who commit suicide have been socially isolated or estranged, frequently for long periods of time, and in retrospect can be seen as having given prior indications of their distress.[44] College stresses or broken homes are not in themselves significant as causes of suicide; an unstable home life, death of a significant person in the individual's life, or loss of an important relationship are involved more often. Most, though not all, persons who commit suicide have been depressed. Use of hallucinogenic drugs has been known to bring about suicide, but this occurrence is not statistically significant.

Carmen and Blaine[9] made a study of sixty-nine suicide attempts at Harvard University from 1962 through 1967. Their figures are consistent with the general pattern that several suicide attempts occur for every completed suicide (the ratio is about four to one) and though men complete the act more often, women make more attempts. From the standpoint of management it is encouraging that twenty of the sixty-nine were treated in the college infirmary and were able to return to their studies without leaving college. Of the twenty-five who were hospitalized, three were able to complete their school work without taking a leave of absence. Some colleges require students who attempt suicide to withdraw at least temporarily from the institution, but the Harvard experience would indicate that this policy is not necessary and can work a needless hardship on students, who will respond quickly to therapy.

Early recognition of behavior that suggests strong depression or possible suicidal preoccupation, together with prompt medical intervention after attempts, has been instrumental in saving many lives. The most important element in preventing the suicide of any disturbed patient is a warm, friendly, supportive attitude on the part of his therapist.

(Emotional Problems of College Students

Many problems not ordinarily considered to be serious psychiatric disorders come to the attention of the college psychiatrist because there is no other person or group in the institution qualified to take primary responsibility for them. Among these are the nonmedicinal use of drugs, dropping out of college, apathy, psychosexual problems, and student unrest and violence. Most of these problems involve several people. Their presence does not presume psychiatric illness, yet failure to deal with them adequately may serve as a precipitant of serious emotional stress. In such situations opportunity for the students involved to discuss their quandaries with mental health workers, without thinking of themselves as patients, may be very helpful; in fact, many students will seek needed help only under such conditions.

Nonmedicinal Use of Drugs

Drug abuse has become widespread throughout all segments of society and is a particularly acute problem in schools and colleges. The capability of drugs to produce physical and mental changes has been exploited not only to escape from what the individual perceives as undue stress but as a way of expressing rebellion, identifying with peers, engaging in a quest for danger and excitement, and discovering more about oneself. The problem thus becomes an extremely complex one.

Drug use has become so ubiquitous that it is unwise for the psychiatrist to generalize concerning the role of drug abuse in emotional illness. The mature individual does not need to use these drugs in order to achieve satisfaction in his life, and their use is often a symptom of emotional problems. On the other hand, limited experimentation with drugs may simply be a part of growing up. Such use is not without danger, but it may be an expression of adolescence rather than disturbed maturity. And for certain individuals and in some cultural groups, occasional use of marijuana may represent conformity to a social norm rather than personality conflict. The psychiatrist should be careful to find out what an individual's drug use means to him, and not assume that particular emotional difficulties are present just because the individual has engaged in nonmedicinal use of drugs.

Work with persons who abuse drugs must deal not only with the role drug ingestion plays in the person's methods of coping with conflict but also with the actual disturbances of reasoning and perception that drugs can cause. Barbiturates and narcotics cloud the sensorium; amphetamines can cause paranoid thinking, thought fragmentation, and alternating mania and depression. The hallucinogens are known to precipitate psychotic reactions, sometimes long lasting. While these are more often seen in unstable persons with a history of hallucinogen use, they have also occurred in first-time users and apparently well-functioning individuals.

The amotivational syndrome[39] was first seen in persons who had used lysergic acid and related hallucinogenic drugs and has now been identified in persons who have used marijuana over a period of time. The individual becomes uninterested in productivity and customary social and intellectual striving; he becomes less able to organize his thoughts and actions, handle new material, formulate and carry through plans, or communicate in the ordinary manner with other persons. Often he feels that his reasoning, even as it becomes progressively more diffuse and in some cases chaotic, is clearer and more insightful. The syndrome resembles apathy (and in any particular individual, elements of both conditions may be present), but while the apathetic person usually desires to return to more productive functioning and is distressed about his physical and mental lethargy, persons whose drug use has led to an amotivational syndrome are likely to be pleased with their condition and feel little desire to change.

It was thought at first that this syndrome appeared in conjunction with drug abuse because the individuals involved tended from the beginning toward thought disorganization and low personal motivation, and that these qualities were likely to encourage the use of drugs and involvement in a noncompetitive culture. From 1965 on, however, marijuana use became more widespread, and psychiatrists had a chance to study regular, long-term use of this drug by persons seeking a social relaxant rather than a means of escape. They have seen a number of individuals who, they feel, are creative, intelligent, and highly motivated and yet have begun to show amotivational symptoms after a period of regular drug use. The evidence is still inconclusive, but a number of researchers do feel that marijuana use has a causative role in the development of this condition. Organic changes in the brain are feared by some observers.[7]

College psychiatrists are often asked to help

in managing patients who appear on an emergency basis with acute reactions to drugs. Overdoses of amphetamines, barbiturates, or narcotics are primarily medical emergencies rather than psychiatric ones. Patients suffering from panic or delusional behavior due to use of hallucinogenic drugs, however, usually recover spontaneously within a few hours. Tranquilizing medication will calm the patient, but his body then has to cope with two drugs rather than one. We have found that the great majority of these patients can be handled quite satisfactorily by having them rest in a quiet, well-lighted room, with someone whom they know and trust present for reassurance and as an orientation to reality. Physical or chemical restraints should not be used unless necessary. If the delusional state has not cleared within a day or two, it is possible that the drug has precipitated a psychotic reaction for which more definitive psychiatric care may be necessary.

We will be fighting a losing battle until we can win the confidence of students regarding the accuracy of our judgments concerning drug abuse. The facts are clear; what we now have to do is devise methods that will make it possible for them to make effective use of this knowledge.

Dropouts

So much publicity has been given to the dropout problem during the last few years that many persons think the phenomenon is something new. Actually, colleges have always suffered from a fairly high rate of attrition. For several decades the percentage of those who fail to graduate from the colleges they enter has held remarkably steady. About 40 percent of all college students graduate with the classes in which they entered; 20 percent drop out and then return or reenroll elsewhere and finish their studies; and 40 percent drop out and do not graduate.[18,49]

Large institutions, which accept a large proportion of those who apply, experience a higher rate of dropping out because they have more students whose academic ability is limited and whose motivation to stay in college is low. In colleges where entrance requirements are high, the screening process sorts out persons with low motivation and inability to do advanced academic work. When students drop out of these institutions, emotional factors are seen as more apparent. Institutional and administrative difficulties were formerly the main reasons given for leaving college, but the recent trend is toward uncovering the psychological and sociological causes.

Levenson[38] and his colleagues studied a series of eighty-nine students who had withdrawn for psychiatric reasons from colleges in the northeastern part of the United States and found that they had a high frequency of academic underachievement over a considerable period; low study ability; low social competence; inability to develop and maintain good relations with peers; and overestimation of their ability, followed by discouragement at early lack of success. Many of them had character disorders, with a strong tendency to act out their feelings. Family pathology was frequent; gross emotional disturbances were common. One-third came from broken homes, and another third had been subject to intermittent separation of parents. Out of forty-six who were treated, twenty-eight returned to college after being under treatment for two to eighteen months. Two of them subsequently dropped out of college. Several of the others made satisfactory adjustments in nonacademic pursuits.

The statistics concerning dropouts do not reflect the true situation, because students who leave one school and enroll at another are listed as dropouts, whereas they have not relinquished the academic enterprise but merely moved themselves into what is hopefully a more advantageous position. Most colleges realize this now and are not placing primary emphasis on lowering the dropout rate but are working toward getting each student into the kind of institution that is best suited to him and where he can work with satisfaction and a sense of confidence.

A student who leaves school may be abandoning his academic career more or less permanently, or he may intend to finish college but desires to take a semester or a year off in order to get a fresh perspective on himself and his life, experiment with a new life style, or effect certain steps in emotional and social growth. This moratorium[14] can be extremely helpful for the student who cannot or does not wish to go straight through with no pause or recapitulation. Unfortunately, the emotional stigma attached to dropping out has made it difficult for many students to take this step, even when it would be clearly to their advantage.

The rate of attrition depends partly on how much secondary gain the student achieves from staying in college. During the years from 1967 to 1970, when nearly everyone eligible for the draft might be called into active service, the dropout rate went down as students sought to maintain their draft-exempt status by staying in school. In 1970 and 1971, when draft calls became less frequent, the dropout rate rose again because young men who were not enrolled in college had a reasonably good chance of not being called up. The whole situation has so many variables that only approximations of what the incidence and causes of dropping out are can be determined; definitive studies will probably have to wait until the rate and intensity of social change diminish.

The fact that great numbers of those who drop out do return later would indicate that we need to redefine our own notion of the natural rhythm of education. Some students may go through in three years; others are simply not ready to complete their college work in the four years after finishing secondary school. Even those who leave college permanently do not necessarily represent a loss of potential talent to our society. Students who are not academically oriented, who do not learn well in a formal system of abstract instruction, or whose career aspirations call for a quite different kind of background may be moving toward a more effective use of their talents when they drop out.[18] Those who counsel students concerning the decision to remain where they are, change colleges, or leave entirely should have as their goal what is best for the individual.

The Apathy Syndrome

Walters[54] recently described a constellation of symptoms very common among college students which he refers to as "apathy." Every student, during the course of his college career, will feel apathetic occasionally when the stresses of work and his own aspirations become too great and his focus on his goals blurs temporarily. This phenomenon is sometimes called the "sophomore slump," for it often occurs during the reevaluation of goals associated with the second year of college, though it may occur at any grade level.

But some students develop a prolonged apathy, with prominent symptoms of indifference, indolence, lethargy, and dullness. As one student expressed his plight, "I can't make myself want to study." They suffer from reduced emotional stability, preoccupation with current work difficulties to the exclusion of past experiences and future expectations, and inability to study or engage in other activities which they see as valuable. They describe themselves as feeling only emptiness, physical lethargy, and intellectual impotence.

Frequently students with this syndrome feel compelled to present themselves as weak and inadequate. In the case histories studied, all the subjects had had a successful parent who had suffered actual injury or failure, and to them success and competition represented potential personal disaster similar to that experienced by the parent. Therefore, the student felt it necessary to avoid success and used apathy as a defense against the potential damage.

By living out his fantasies of being deficient, the patient also avoids facing the effects of his own aggressiveness. His strong feelings of hostility and rage toward particular people are partly diverted into anger at other persons and partly inward onto himself, producing feelings of guilt and failure. It is often frustrating for the therapist to work with a student suffering from apathy, because the patient is so prone to turning some of his strong feelings outward, promising success, and then turning near success into failure. The people who are trying to help him can be reduced to a feeling of impotence as great as that exhibited by the patient.

In a sense, apathy is a continuation and exaggeration of the defenses and solutions commonly used by the adolescent. Patients with this syndrome are experiencing a prolonged adolescence in that they have not yet been able to formulate clear goals, commit themselves to a realistic path of achievement, or form a mature adult identity.

Apathy may be self-limited, but it may also be a precursor of depression or various neurotic symptoms. It can also have a seriously detrimental effect on a student's academic performance and social adjustment. In many cases it is a clear indication that the student needs the opportunity to explore his own capabilities under different circumstances than those presented by the college. It is important that both student and administrators realize the problem is a maturational one, not laziness or irresponsibility, and that a leave of absence be arranged without fear of stigma. A moratorium can do a great deal toward developing that knowledge of self that permits utilization of the content of education.

Sexual Problems

The basic sexual problems of college students have not changed abruptly in the past few years, but attitudes toward them have done so. In many college communities the old rules about the times and regulations for men and women to visit in each other's rooms have been completely abolished. Use of contraceptives has become widespread, and treatments for venereal disease have become quite effective and nonpunitive. The result has been that any restraints that are exercised in sexual relationships arise from the minds of the individuals concerned rather than from the outer deterrents of fear of detection, disease, and pregnancy.

Whether this resultant freedom in attitudes has caused marked changes in sexual behavior remains unclear, but there is little doubt among college psychiatrists that the amount of premarital activity has increased. The focus of

their involvement has generally changed from dealing with the consequences of unwanted pregnancy to counseling with students on the psychological aspects of their relations and working in collaboration with internists and gynecologists who are familiar with contraceptive practices, particularly those involving antiovulation substances.

In some colleges there is a growing tendency to deal with the issues involved in relations between young men and women in educational and counseling terms rather than in the traditional one-to-one physician-patient relationship. By helping students to understand their interpersonal relationships, psychiatrists and other professionals can help students to deal realistically with various social situations and anticipate potential difficulties before they become actual problems. This is probably a desirable development, in fact the only one that gives promise of being a major help to all students, but it is still fraught with dilemmas. Some of these are analyzed in a recent series of publications.[22,23,33]

Homosexuality—both actual homosexual experience and worry about developing this orientation—is often an intense concern of young people who are still in the process of forming their sexual identity. The overly emotional reaction to this problem on the part of some persons connected with colleges has decreased, and psychiatrists can now handle it as a medical matter, with full confidentiality between physician and patient concerning the individual's interpersonal relationships. The privacy of the individual is scrupulously respected so long as his behavior does not offend others. Problems reflected in undesired homosexual encounters are handled in the same way as problems involving undesired heterosexual attentions. Numerous persons with problems concerning homosexuality do receive benefit, especially when the difficulties they perceive have not been of long standing.[18]

Student Unrest and Violence

The role of psychiatrists and mental health services in regard to the problems of student unrest and violence is an unsolved dilemma.[19]

Many of the protesting students do have emotional conflicts, and much protest activity takes forms that are at best immature and can be intensely destructive.[37] But labeling all protestors as emotionally disturbed is not justified. In fact, it might be argued convincingly that their dissatisfaction over social conditions connotes a higher than usual level of mental health. The individual emotional conflicts should, therefore, not be confused with political issues.

A fruitful sphere for discussion is the reason for the extreme behavior of some of the protestors, why they feel the necessity of abandoning reason and civility, and how all persons involved can learn to respect the feelings of one another in order that communication can continue. The interplay between disturbed interpersonal relations, personal problems such as career choice and fear of failure, and conflicts due to social conditions needs to be analyzed. The proper and feasible role of college mental health services in dealing with these problems needs continual reexamination, particularly with reference to how active a role mental health workers should take in attempting to effect social change, and how definitive they should be in labeling particular situations and behaviors as indicative of emotional illness or health.

Psychiatry has traditionally been apolitical, just as the colleges and universities have been, and though concern for the state of the college society is necessary, this does not mean that mental health services should become politicized and expected to take sides on every issue of public concern. This merely increases polarization of the issues. Certainly the health services must become increasingly sensitive to the feelings, opinions, and needs of students, without abandoning high standards of expected behavior and accomplishments. More resources are needed to allow the identification and removal of clear hazards to mental health and to impove those aspects of college life that foster independence, self-confidence, and a sense of meaning and accomplishment. Those with special interest in these preventive aspects should, however, balance their concern with the realization that what is a health hazard for one person may be a good growth medium for another.

⟨ Administrative Issues

Psychotherapy is the most important of the college psychiatrist's duties, but others that logically fall to him constitute a major opportunity to develop constructive attitudes and practice preventive psychiatry. He may be consulted by the administration about student behavior that suggests undue emotional stress, or concerning the suitability of some corrective measure rather than a punitive one. Admissions committees may seek his help in evaluating a student's potential; an applicant with prior emotional problems may ask him for diagnostic or prognostic information; student and faculty leaders may seek assistance in organizing social service programs or educational programs concerning such social problems as drug dependence or violence.

A college psychiatrist must not be, or even appear to be, the agent of the administration against the students or of the students against the administration. His appropriate place is within the health service, and his overriding responsibility is to his clients and to the medical code of ethics. He should be vigilant against being maneuvered, inadvertently or otherwise, into making administrative decisions that lie outside the field of medicine.

Confidentiality

The psychiatrist in a college or university, like his colleagues in other medical services for specific groups, has a dual responsibility—to his patients and to the organization.[4,17,18,45] He must work with students, administrators, faculty, counselors, police, and security officials, yet not use his influence or knowledge unfairly. Some critics of college psychiatry doubt that a psychiatrist can work with all these persons and not violate confidence (usually that of the students, they insist); but dozens of good health services are showing that it can be done. Indeed, it must be done if the health service is to be trusted and utilized at all.

The practices at Harvard University do not differ greatly from those of similar institutions and have been found effective in protecting the patient-physician relationship within a responsible social framework:

1. No information about the patient, gained in confidence, is divulged without his specific permission.
2. Psychiatric records are kept separate from other medical records, and extreme care is taken to protect them.
3. Psychiatric records are not used for screening purposes or made available to admissions committees, security investigators, or others, even with the patient's consent.
4. Stress is placed on the principle that records should include only sufficient detail to understand the illness, omitting details and names that are not necessary for accurate comprehension.
5. Parents or next of kin are not informed that a student is receiving treatment, unless hospitalization is necessary or the illness is very serious. (This includes students who are still minors.) In such cases the patient is informed of what is to be done, and why.

In rare instances, when a student's illness is so serious that his own life or the lives of others are endangered, it is sometimes necessary for the psychiatrist to take action against the patient's will or to inform the authorities of the situation. This serious step must never be taken except in genuine emergencies, and as a response to a real threat to life and safety. Likewise, psychiatrists do not inform administrators or authorities of any possible infraction of laws (either those of the institution or of the community) unless serious damage to the community or danger to others' lives is involved, as in bomb threats, homicidal intentions, and so on.

Curran[11] recently made a study of policies and practices concerning confidentiality in college mental health services. He found intense concern about maintaining confidentiality in all colleges. Though there were some variations, nearly all of them followed the standards formulated by the American College Health Association.

Involvement with Other Persons in the University

Some of the work of college psychiatrists consists of consultations in which there is no individual person who is specifically assigned the role of patient. Any time a teacher, administrator, or student is deeply troubled about the emotional reactions of someone for whom he has particular responsibility or concern, he should be able to discuss this with the college psychiatrist. The director of admissions may seek help in evaluating evidence of an emotional handicap in an applicant. The president and his associates may ask advice regarding the significance of bizarre or threatening communications to his office. The librarian may request an opinion about antisocial or destructive behavior of some who use the library (a more and more frequent occurrence). Individual faculty members may want to consult the psychiatrist when they receive a bizarre or irrational term paper or examination from a student.

Needless to say, the usual rules of confidentiality apply in all these situations just as they do in contacts with patients. The goal in such consultations is to attain a clear idea of the issues involved and some leads as to how they may be resolved. All these contacts with a wide range of people throughout the institution serve as opportunities for furthering everyone's understanding of the nature and diversity of emotional stress and the means of recognizing it.

Many of the consultations with individuals center on maturational issues and reality problems; a traditional psychiatric diagnosis from the official nomenclature may very well be unnecessary and inappropriate. Students who seek help for relatively transient problems should be urged not to type themselves as expatients just because they have consulted a psychiatrist. In an educational institution the psychiatrist, though his work is solidly grounded in the area of medicine, also functions as a special tutor in problems of emotional maturation. A student who sees the psychiatrist for assistance in this area should think of the interaction as a particular kind of educational assistance, not the manifestation of illness. Many colleges may find that the role of guiding emotional maturation is a new one for them, and they may have difficulty in understanding the psychiatrist's role in this work. This then becomes a new arena for the development of mutual understandings.

Training centers for college psychiatry are very few; the University of California and Yale and Harvard universities have the largest. Several universities with medical schools utilize the services of second- or third-year psychiatric residents, who spend a few hours each week or a few months at one time working under supervision in the psychiatric division of a student health service. This arrangement is usually very satisfactory to both the residents and the health services.

College psychiatry is a rapidly growing field, and new and better methods of working in a college setting are being developed as more institutions realize what a good mental health service can mean to them. Small colleges are at a particular disadvantage in organizing such services because of geographical and financial limitations. Patch[42] described the organization of a group mental health program for several colleges and showed that the idea is feasible.

(Conclusions

The mental health of college students does not seem to have become significantly worse or better during the six decades that some attention has been directed toward it. When effective services have been developed they have nearly always been continued, and those institutions that do not have them usually desire them. A good psychiatric service, with psychological and social service components, enables the college to deal with mental and emotional disorders as what they are, rather than in terms of punishment, academic failure, unsuitability for college life, or some other rationalization. Furthermore, the experience of living in a college community where a good mental health program is available (whether an individual uses it or not) seems to improve students' capacity to judge what good practice is, as well as their willingness to work for good programs in the communities in which they subsequently live.

(Bibliography

1. ANGELL, J. R. "Mental Hygiene in Colleges and Universities." *Mental Hygiene*, 17 (1933), 543–547.
2. BALSER, B. H. *Psychotherapy of the Adolescent.* New York: International Universities Press, 1957.
3. BLAINE, G. B., Jr. *Patience and Fortitude.* Boston: Little, Brown, 1962.
4. ———. "Divided Loyalties: The College Therapist's Responsibility to the Student, the University and the Parents." *American Journal of Orthopsychiatry*, 34 (1964), 481–485.
5. ———, and McARTHUR, C. C., eds. *Emotional Problems of the Student.* Rev. ed. New York: Appleton-Century-Crofts, 1961.
6. BLOOM, B. L. "Characteristics of Campus Community Mental Health Programs in Western United States—1969." *Journal of the American College Health Association*, 18 (1970), 196–200.
7. BRILL, N. Q., et al. "The Marijuana Problem." *Annals of Internal Medicine*, 73 (1970), 449–465.
8. CARMEN, L. "A Three-to-Five Year Study of Thirty-five Psychotic Hospitalized Students." *Journal of the American College Health Association*, 13 (1965), 541–550.
9. ———, and BLAINE, G. B., Jr. "A Study of Suicidal Attempts by Male and Female University Students." In D. L. Farnsworth and G. B. Blaine, Jr., eds., *Counseling and the College Student.* Boston: Little, Brown, 1970. Pp. 181–199.
10. COX COMMISSION. *Crisis at Columbia: The Cox Commission Report.* New York: Random House, 1968.
11. CURRAN, W. J. "Policies and Practices Concerning Confidentiality in College Mental

Health Services in the United States and Canada." In D. L. Farnsworth and G. B. Blaine, Jr., eds., *Counseling and the College Student*. Boston: Little, Brown, 1970. Pp. 293–314.

12. DESMIT, B. N. W. *From Person into Patient*. The Hague: Mouton, 1963.

13. ERIKSON, E. H. "Identity and the Life Cycle: Selected Papers." *Psychological Issues*, 1 (1959), monogr. 1.

14. ——. *Childhood and Society*. 2d. ed. New York: Norton, 1964.

15. ——, ed. *Youth: Change and Challenge*. New York: Basic Books, 1963.

16. FARNSWORTH, D. L. *Mental Health in College and University*. Cambridge, Mass.: Harvard University Press, 1957.

17. ——. *College Health Administration*. New York: Appleton-Century-Crofts, 1964.

18. ——. *Psychiatry, Education, and the Young Adult*. Springfield, Ill.: Charles C Thomas, 1966.

19. ——. "A Psychiatrist Looks at Campus Protest." *Psychiatric Opinion*, 6 (1969), 6.

20. ——. "Psychiatric Services in Colleges." In P. C. Talkington and C. L. Bloss, eds., *Evolving Concepts in Psychiatry*. New York: Grune & Stratton, 1969. Pp. 65–79.

21. ——. "College Mental Health and Social Change." *Annals of Internal Medicine*, 73 (1970), 467–473.

22. ——. "Sexual Morality: Campus Dilemma." In D. L. Farnsworth and G. B. Blaine, Jr., eds., *Counseling and the College Student*. Boston: Little, Brown, 1970. Pp. 133–151.

23. ——. "Sexual Morality and the Dilemmas of the Colleges." *Medical Aspects of Human Sexuality*, 4 (1970), 64–94.

24. ——, and BLAINE, G. B., Jr., eds. *Counseling and the College Student*. Boston: Little, Brown, 1970.

25. FRY, C. C. *Mental Health in College*. New York: Commonwealth Fund, 1942.

26. FUNKENSTEIN, D. H., ed. *Student Mental Health, an International View*. New York: World Federation for Mental Health, 1959.

27. ——, and FARNSWORTH, D. L. "The Future Contributions of Psychiatry to Education." In P. H. Hoch and J. Zubin, eds., *The Future of Psychiatry*. New York: Grune & Stratton, 1962. Pp. 70–82.

28. GALLAGHER, J. R., and HARRIS, H. I. *Emotional Problems of Adolescents*. Oxford: Oxford University Press, 1958.

29. GERSHON, S. "On the Pharmacology of Mari-

juana." *Behavioral Neuropsychiatry*, 1 (1970), 13–18.

30. GOLDSEN, R. K., et al. *What College Students Think*. Princeton, N.J.: Van Nostrand, 1960.

31. GROUP FOR THE ADVANCEMENT OF PSYCHIATRY. *Considerations on Personality Development in College Students*. Report no. 32. New York, 1955.

32. ——. *The Role of Psychiatrists in Colleges and Universities*. Report no. 17. Rev. ed. New York, 1957.

33. ——. *Sex and the College Student*. Report no. 60. New York, 1965.

34. GUNDLE, S., and KRAFT, A. "Mental Health Programs in American Colleges and Universities." *Bulletin of the Menninger Clinic*, 20 (1956), 57–69.

35. JOINT COMMISSION ON MENTAL HEALTH OF CHILDREN. *Crisis in Child Mental Health*. New York: Harper & Row, 1970.

36. KEELER, M. H. "Adverse Reaction to Marijuana." *American Journal of Psychiatry*, 124 (1967), 674–677.

37. KENISTON, K. *Young Radicals*. New York: Harcourt, Brace & World, 1968.

38. LEVENSON, E. A. "A Demonstration Clinic for College Dropouts." *Journal of the American College Health Association*, 12 (1964), 382–391.

39. McGLOTHLIN, W. H., and WEST, L. J. "The Marijuana Problem: An Overview." *American Journal of Psychiatry*, 125 (1968), 370–378.

40. MENNINGER, K., et al. *The Vital Balance*. New York: The Viking Press, 1963.

41. NIXON, R. E. *The Art of Growing*. New York: Random House, 1962.

42. PATCH, V. D. "Organizational Problems of a Multiple College Mental Health Center." In D. L. Farnsworth and G. B. Blaine, Jr., eds., *Counseling and the College Student*. Boston: Little, Brown, 1970. Pp. 249–261.

43. PEARSON, G. H. J. *Adolescence and the Conflict of Generations*. New York: Norton, 1958.

44. PECK, L., and SHRUT, A. Quoted by M. A. Farber in "College Suicide Study Discounts Impact of Drugs and Pressures." *The New York Times*, March 23, 1970, pp. 1, 29.

45. "Position Statement on Confidentiality and Privilege with Special Reference to Psychiatric Patients." *American Journal of Psychiatry*, 124 (1968), 175.

46. REIFLER, C. B. "Epidemiologic Aspects of College Mental Health." *Journal of the American College Health Association,* 19 (1971), 159–163.

47. ——, and LIPTZIN, M. B. "Epidemiological Studies of College Mental Health." *Archives of General Psychiatry,* 20 (1969), 528–540.

48. SANFORD, N., ed. *The American College.* New York: Wiley, 1962.

49. SUMMERSKILL, J. "Dropouts from College." In N. Sanford, ed., *The American College.* New York: Wiley, 1962. Pp. 627–657.

50. SUTHERLAND, R. L., et al., eds. *Personality Factors on the College Campus.* Austin, Tex.: Hogg Foundation for Mental Health, 1962.

51. TEMBY, W. D. "Suicide." In G. B. Blaine, Jr., and C. C. McArthur, eds., *Emotional Problems of the Student.* Rev. ed. New York: Appleton-Century-Crofts, 1961. Pp. 133–152.

52. UNGERLEIDER, J. T., et al. "A Statistical Study of Adverse Reactions to LSD in Los Angeles County." *American Journal of Psychiatry,* 125 (1968), 108–113.

53. WALTER, O. S. "Prevalance of Diagnosed Emotional Disorders in University Students." *Journal of the American College Health Association,* 18 (1970), 204–209.

54. WALTERS, P. W., Jr. "Student Apathy." In G. B. Blaine, Jr., and C. C. McArthur, eds., *Emotional Problems of the Student.* Rev. ed. New York: Appleton-Century-Crofts, 1961. Pp. 129–147.

55. WEDGE, B. M., ed. *Psychosocial Problems of College Men.* New Haven: Yale University Press, 1958.

56. WESTLEY, W. A., and EPSTEIN, N. B. *Silent Majority.* San Francisco: Jossey-Bass, 1969.

57. YOLLES, S. F. "Drugs and Behavior: National Concerns." *Medical Counterpoint,* 1 (1969), 6.

CHAPTER 53

MENTAL HEALTH
PROGRAMS IN INDUSTRY

Alan A. McLean

The communal life of human beings has . . . a two-fold foundation: a compulsion to work, which was created by external necessity, and the power to love. . . . *Eros* and *Ananke* have become the parents of human civilization.

SIGMUND FREUD[11]

THE PURPOSE OF THIS CHAPTER is to explore the application of psychiatric concepts in work organizations. The term "work organizations" is used to encompass mental health programs to be found both inside and outside private industry. Indeed there are probably fewer than 500 psychiatrists who serve the private sector of American business; many more are concerned with public institutions and agencies, military organizations, government, and universities. All are concerned with the individual adapting to an occupational setting.

❨ The Occupational Milieu

To intelligently view the role of the psychiatrist in the world of work it is important to review (1) the changing meaning of work in today's society, (2) the reasons employers seek psychiatric consultation, and (3) a brief history of earlier programs of occupational psychiatry.

The Changing Meaning of Work

"Over the years the changing nature of work has been the cause of the greatest continuing restructuring of American lives of any major force in our history." In making this statement to a 1967 meeting of state labor commissioners, then Labor Secretary Willard Wirtz went on to say that work satisfaction is as great a problem in our time as unemployment was during the 1930s and that the pace of change in work organizations is rapidly increasing. Not only has technology brought a restructuring of jobs, but change in society outside the world of work affects the job. It is within this context that mental health programs operate in the occupational setting. Before reviewing mental health practices, it would seem appropriate to examine both the work setting and current changing patterns of motivation for work.

Basic statistics suggest part of the picture. Fuchs[12] provided graphic demonstration of recent trends. He asserted that, if one considers the shift in the labor force in the field of education between 1950 and 1960, one finds that just the net increase in that period of time is greater than the total number of people engaged in the automobile and associated industries in 1960. Former Secretary of Health, Education, and Welfare Wilbur Cohen said that 70 million will be involved in all phases of education by the mid-1970s, more people than in the active noneducational labor force.[27] Further, comparing the services to industry from 1945 to 1965, the service sector increased by 13 million and the industry sector by 4 million; of the 4 million swelling the industry sector the vast increase was in white collar jobs, many in service-related industries.

Manufacturing techniques utilizing more automated processes and some frighteningly complex technologies present, in many industries, the need for frequent adjustment to job change. Skills are made rapidly obsolete; technical education is often outdated within five years of graduation. In fact, "The obsolescence of education in rapidly developing fields of knowledge has become about equal in rate to the obsolescence of an automobile."[15]

Gooding's sound journalistic study of the automobile industry cited recent dramatic attitude changes.[17] Younger workers are bringing new perspectives into the factory. They are restless, changeable, mobile, demanding, and therefore, have great difficulty adjusting to routine assembly-line operations. One-third of the hourly workers at Chrysler, General Motors, and Ford are under age thirty. One-half of Chrysler's hourly workers have been employed fewer than five years. Absenteeism has doubled in the last ten years at General Motors and Ford, with the sharpest climb in 1969. Midweek, 5 percent of General Motors hourly workers are absent each day; on Mondays and Fridays, 10 percent. Gooding concluded that younger workers have never experienced economic want or insecurity. They

realize that public policy will not allow them to starve, and this fact contributes to what management considers as a lack of sense of responsibility and a challenge to authority.

Job behavior is partly a result of the interaction between the industrial environment and demands of the individual for the satisfaction of what he considers legitimate aspirations. The age-old conflict of worker versus management is taking a different form. The overt and covert demands of the employee are increasingly for involvement, participation, and meaning in his work rather than for economic security.

Walter Reuther, late president of the United Auto Workers, discussed industry's problems with youth a few weeks before his death. Young workers, he said, are interested in a sense of fulfillment as human beings. In the auto industry, the young worker feels he is not master of his own destiny, and he is going to escape from it whenever he has an opportunity. This lack of involvement, Reuther felt, is a major factor contributing to absenteeism and poor worker performance. Observers from the behavioral sciences suggest that practices within the automobile industry are inconsistent with developments in society at large. They cite inflexible management practices, say that motivators are not built into jobs, and attribute younger workers' anger to a feeling that they are not a meaningful part of the work process. Some believe that workers who want a sense of self-development and who want to contribute are made to feel unimportant. While they want more control and more autonomy, they feel acted on rather than the acting agent.

The conclusions of the 1967–1969 Cornell Occupational Mental Health Conferences suggested that it is not only the automobile industry that fails to meet the needs of its workers. The result of an intensive study and interaction of 100 distinguished participants from many disciplines was published in 1970 under the title, *Mental Health and Work Organizations*.[23] The principal conclusion of the group was that old ideas about work and its meaning are no longer valid but that relatively few work organizations acknowledge this fact in their policies and practices. DeCarlo[9] gave perspective to this issue saying,

It is not unreasonable to consider the large organization, spawned and developed through the agencies of science and technology, as an entity with its own demands for survival, with its own personality and nature, and with its own peculiar demands upon its individual members. These demands may at times be at cross purposes with the individual existence of its members, often causing severe emotional reactions. Most psychiatrists would consider that the individual who is unable to adapt is indeed ill.

But could it be that madness lies the other way? If this is even partially true, and if we assume a kind of parity between the individual and the large organization, then we might do well to examine the relationships and the differences between the collective organization that is the personality and the collective personality that is the organization. It may well be that the organization is the one which must adapt the most to meet the characteristics, motivations, needs, and demands of the specific individual—at least more fully than has been the case in the past or present.

Perhaps one of the best ways of looking at probable future changes in the world of work is to explore the expectations of those about to join work organizations. The young automobile workers have their counterparts on college campuses who are also asking to "do their own thing" and will probably continue to do so when they enter the labor market. Three themes appear that relate to the probable work adaptation of these youths. (1) Many young people have completely rejected the idea of education as something one goes through in a packaged way to get a set of credentials. On campuses everywhere you hear the demand that education be meaningful. Many anticipate that they will make the same demands of their occupational experience, that they will be inclined to reject work that does not have what they consider to be real meaning. (2) The young are conditioned in our culture to the idea of instant success. To go to the moon, one simply spends enough money, and in ten years the astronauts are there. As a result it appears to have been relatively easy for young people to make the

transition in their own minds from the instant success of science to the demand for instant solutions to social problems. Many seem to feel that if we can get to the moon in ten years we ought to be able to change Columbia University or the telephone company in two years. (3) Youth is committed to the primacy of feelings rather than to logic. Logic, many of them have concluded, is something technicians can engineer in a black box; what is really important is what one feels. These are some of the attitudes now being carried into the work environment.

Motivation for Mental Health Programs

The changing expectations of workers both young and old is one of the more subtle reasons employers seek psychiatric assistance. There are more compelling, largely economic, reasons as well. Most large employers provide benefits that cover at least some of the treatment costs of psychiatric disorders for employees and dependents. The plans vary considerably: Some provide very little reimbursement; others do not discriminate between organic and psychiatric disorder under either major medical or hospitalization insurance plans and are very inclusive. Programs in the automobile and associated industries provide first dollar coverage for outpatient treatment, and other work organizations include psychiatric care in the clinics and hospitals they operate for employees. Such insurance is costly, and occupational mental health programs that can reduce the number of disorders requiring treatment are often viewed favorably by management.

A utilization rate for treatment of psychiatric disorder frequently is reported as 1 percent of covered populations in any given year. That is, an employer can anticipate that 1 percent of his employees will seek treatment for psychiatric disorder each year under a health insurance program that provides such coverage. Increasingly, psychotherapy and psychiatric hospitalization are both covered without discrimination.[1,30] General Electric reported that during 1968 psychiatric illness accounted for 3.1 percent of health insurance claims and

6.7 percent of benefits. The Health Insurance Plan of Greater New York reported 1 percent of members were referred for psychiatric treatment during 1966. Two percent of eligible workers covered at the Sidney Hillman Health Center were treated during a two-year period for "mental health problems related to work."

An in-company mental health program contributes to the early detection and referral of employees for treatment, and one might postulate that overall treatment costs would be less than without such an activity. If the mental health effort goes further and helps identify work situations that mobilize unnecessarily high anxiety levels, one might see even greater justification in economic terms alone.

WORKMEN'S COMPENSATION

One motivating force for occupational mental health programs is workmen's compensation insurance. Increasingly, workmen's compensation benefits are provided not only to victims of industrial accidents but to individuals with psychiatric disabilities that are in some way related to work. Held as compensable have been emotional disability caused by physical trauma, physical disability resulting from emotional stress, and disabling psychiatric disorder resulting from emotional stress.[19]

The case that focused attention on this matter was decided by the Supreme Court of the State of Michigan on December 1, 1960. By a five to three decision the court sustained an order of the Workmen's Compensation Appeal Board awarding compensation to Mr. James Carter for psychotic illness resulting "from emotional pressure encountered in his daily work as a machine operator." Mr. Carter's job was to remove burrs from a hub assembly, grinding out holes in the assembly with his drill and placing the assembly on a conveyor belt. Unless he took two assemblies at a time to his workbench, he was unable to maintain the pace of the job; in taking two assemblies he upset the production line. He was repeatedly instructed by his foreman not to take two assemblies, but when he only took one, he fell behind. In both instances he was criticized. On October 24, 1956 he developed an acute paranoid schizophrenic illness, and the referee awarded compensation for the disability that resulted from this. In the Carter case, the ruling was to the effect that it was not necessary to attribute the condition of the plaintiff to a single injury but that the series of events, the pressures of the job, and the pressures of his foreman "caused" an injury or disability under the law. One legal interpretation of this case was that "No single incident is essential to provoke or to sustain the claimant's right to recovery, but the cumulative efforts resulting in his concern about his job and his violation of the instructions of his foreman caused the condition of which he complained."*

During the past few years the courts have begun to construe workmen's compensation laws in such a manner as to relieve the employee of the burden of proving causal connection between his employment and his disability when the disability developed on the job. The courts in some instances will now presume that the disability is employment related unless substantial evidence is provided by the employer to the contrary. An example is the recent case of *Butler* v. *District Parking Management Company*, decided on June 8, 1966, by the U.S. Court of Appeals in the District of Columbia, which directed that compensation benefits be awarded to an employee. The court stated the facts and the law as follows:

After twenty years of employment as a parking lot attendant . . . appellant became ill during his working hours and did not report for work the following day and ensuing days. His claim is that the employment caused a mental breakdown, and it is not disputed that he was found to suffer a schizophrenic reaction. Section 20 of the . . . Compensation Act . . . provides: "In any proceeding for the enforcement of a claim for compensation under this act it shall be presumed, in the absence of substantial evidence to the contrary . . . that the claim comes within the provisions of this Act. . . ."

This provision places the burden on the employer to go forward with evidence to meet the presumption that injury or illness occurring dur-

---

* *Carter* v. *General Motors* 106 NW.2d 105 (Michigan Supreme Court, 1960).

ing employment was caused by that employment. . . . The employer offered no substantial evidence that appellant's injury was not work-related and hence has not met the burden imposed by the statute. . . .

Most workmen's compensation statutes contain provisions similar to Section 20 of the District of Columbia Workmen's Compensation Act, and it is not unreasonable to assume that in the future the universal practice will be to require the employer to disprove causal connection between employment and disability in cases of mental disorders rather than for the employee to prove that such causal connection exists. Since the proof of the negative of any issue is frequently impossible, the magnitude of the employer's potential liability looms even greater than in the past.

In addition to the interpretation of workmen's compensation statutes by the courts, separate legislation in 1970 stimulated major interests in occupational health. The Occupational Safety and Health Act now requires all employers to meet certain federal standards. These include detailed safety requirements, an elaborate reporting system for occupational injuries and illnesses, and a system of penalties to aid the enforcement of the act. Responsibility for administration of this legislation rests largely with the U.S. Department of Labor. The act, however, also created the National Institute for Occupational Safety and Health in the Department of Health, Education and Welfare. The latter organization is actively supporting research in occupational safety and health and developing standards to be administered by the Department of Labor. One of the early NIOSH projects involves support for a massive study of occupational stress. The stimulus for occupational health programs, physical and mental, will probably increase dramatically as a result of this congressional action.

Drug Abuse

Specific clinical and social problems have also stimulated the implementation of mental health programs in work organizations. A contemporary example is the increasing focus on drug abuse both as a national problem and as one involving employers. During the late 1960s significant concern developed about the misuse of drugs in industry. Particularly in the northeast and in the large urban centers, employees using heroin have created serious administrative problems in addition to the well-known personal and social disruption attendant addiction.

While no epidemiological studies have yet been completed, a survey in one metropolitan area showed that 60 percent of the larger companies screen job applicants for drug use. With the development of simplified thin-layer chromatography, many work organizations are screening the urines of applicants and, in some instances, employees on a routine basis. Informal reports suggest that in the New York City area, approximately 10 percent of applicants show some urine metabolite of a drug of abuse. Only 34 percent of organizations are said to have formal policies on drug abuse among employees.[13]

Among the reports are the following:

1. The Metropolitan Life Insurance Company reported that it first became concerned about misuse of drugs in its employee population during 1967, when increasing numbers of the younger employees developed patterns of absenteeism or lateness and frequently left their jobs for long periods of time, spent a lot of time in the washroom, had unauthorized visitors, and showed erratic and below par work performance. Occasionally they were seen in the medical department because of an altered state of consciousness. Most frequently, employees denied drug use and refused referral to rehabilitation agencies even though urine tests were positive for heroin.[8]

2. Bisgeier, the medical director of New Jersey Bell Telephone Company, reported a 1969 rate of heroin abuse among applicants of 4 per 1,000 and a 1970 rate of 8 per 1,000.[4]

3. The Manhattan–Brooklyn–Queens section of the New York Telephone Company found, that, between March and May of 1970, 9.8 percent of applicants had a positive chromatography for a suspicious drug. Of these, 58 percent were for quinine (used for cutting

heroin in the northeast), 4 percent amphetamines, 20 percent barbiturates, 3 percent morphine, 5 percent morphine plus quinine, 4 percent one of the phenothiazines, and the balance mixed drugs without morphine.[10]

Medical directors recognize that the problems related to the use of alcohol remain far more important to the work organization than those concerning the abuse of other drugs. And most firms with adequate employee health services have long-established programs to cope with the "problem drinker," a term preferred to "alcoholic" by most occupational physicians who feel they may become legitimately concerned about behavior stemming from the use of alcohol when it interferes with productivity or social relationships at work even though they recognize many of these cases may not properly be diagnosed as alcoholics.[33]

Thus we have disruptive and expensive overt psychopathology, specific subtypes of that pathology such as addiction, and legal requirements that stimulate employer interest in the development of mental health programs. These are in addition to the enlightened self-interest of some more sophisticated employers who seek greater understanding of work-related behavior for whatever reason.

The experience of several such programs suggests that one should make no attempt to "sell" such mental health programs on economic terms alone. During the first years of psychiatrists' consultation, the rate of referral for therapy by the organization's medical department is likely to soar and the utilization rate to increase considerably. Nor is it possible to cost out mental health services to justify the budget under which they operate. One cannot easily put an exact dollar value on somewhat better selection and placement of employees, or the training and enhanced sophistication of medical staff, members of management, and personnel departments. As a result of the work of the consultant, the communications among members of a work group are often greatly improved, problems being seen in a different light, but it may be difficult to see the results on a balance sheet.

Historical Considerations

"Industrial medicine exists; industrial psychiatry ought to exist. It is important for a modern psychiatrist not to hide his light under a bushel; he must step forth to new community duties. . . . [His] function [should] be preventative rather than curative. . . ."[32] This observation by Southard in 1920 predated by two years the first clearly documented industrial mental health program. To be sure, a variety of relevant research was completed or underway both in this country and Europe, and there were several generalized commentaries in the literature suggesting occupational roles for psychiatrists as well as nosologies relating psychopathology to work adjustment,[31] but 1922 saw the first full-time psychiatrist begin work in an American business organization when Giberson was employed by the Metropolitan Life Insurance Company. She remained with Metropolitan until her retirement in 1962. Her initial role was as a consultant in the employee medical department, her time being largely spent seeing individual patients referred by other physicians. In 1949 she left the medical unit to become personal advisor to employees and a consultant in the office of the president of the company.[14,15]

In 1924 another pioneer, V. V. Anderson, established a mental health service at the R. H. Macy's Department Store in New York. The first book on industrial psychiatry, which summarized this program in 1929, remains a classic.[2] Initially, Anderson was concerned with interviewing techniques in the personnel office and with the introduction of psychological tests during placement procedures. He also studied workers involved in accidents and effected a remarkable reduction in the accident rate of delivery truckdrivers for the store. In his clinical work he used the team approach, drawing on earlier experience in child psychiatry and enlisting the aid of a psychologist and social workers who worked on a broad array of employee mental health problems. The depressed economy of the early 1930s ended this activity, and it was a decade later before Macy's engaged the services of another psychiatrist, this time Temple Burling, who was particularly concerned with problems of morale and interpersonal relationships within various divisions of the company.[5]

Giberson's work was largely with individual employees and with the education of management personnel. Anderson, while also concerned with individual psychopathology, conducted the first applied mental health research in industry, and Burling was principally interested in interpersonal relationships. Thus, prior to the end of the 1930s the principal activities of occupational mental health consultants had been established. The core activity continues to be individual clinical case consultation directly with the employee or with an occupational physician. The psychiatrist works with personnel or administrative managers as well. The teaching of management and medical department staff, both formally and informally, is an important adjunct. Applied research concerned both with the incidence and prevalence of psychopathology and with factors in the work organization that unnecessarily mobilize anxiety is of increasing importance. Finally, the psychiatrist is seen as a facilitator of interpersonal communication and understanding. Giberson, Anderson, Burling, and the many who followed brought the following comment from Menninger,[25]

Their's was an unexciting day by day task of demonstrating not only to business men but also to their colleagues the contributions to the maintenance of mental health which psychiatrists could make in industry. Often they met apathy in both quarters. Sometimes they faced open hostility. And always skepticism. Perhaps not the least of their contributions is that they remained in the field.

Perhaps the greatest early stimulus to the study of industry as a social system came from Elton Mayo. In the 1920s he became interested in studies of fatigue and monotony at the Harvard physiology laboratory. In 1923 he investigated the high rate of turnover in a textile mill and noted that with the introduction of rest periods for workers in monotonous jobs, morale rose and turnover decreased. In 1927, Mayo and his associates undertook the now classic study of working conditions at the Hawthorne plant of the Western Electric Company in Chicago. These studies concluded that industrial enterprise has both economic and social functions. Production was demonstrated as a form of social behavior, and all the activity of the plant was viewed as an interaction of structure, culture, and the individual personality of workers. The alteration of any variable produced change in the other two. Reactions to stress on the part of individual employees arose when there were resistance to change, faulty control and communication systems, and poor adjustment of the individual worker to his structure at work.[24]

Early clinical studies of industrial accidents, fatigue, and psychiatric illness in the work setting began during World War I at the Industrial Fatigue Research Board in England. They were, however, given little currency in this country, even though our basic concepts of accident proneness and our first indications of the prevalence of psychiatric disorder in an industrial population derived from this work.[7,18]

⟮ Role of the Psychiatrist*

Several considerations are important for the psychiatrist who functions as a consultant in a work organization. Most psychiatrists have had little training for or experience in industry. In the community, hospital, and university, they are seen as authorities in dealing with mental disorder. The psychiatrist is not however an expert in the management of an organization, and there are many executives better able to resolve interpersonal conflicts in a corporation than psychiatrists to resolve intrapersonal conflicts in patients.

In commencing a consulting relationship, the psychiatrist must both give up many pre-

* Specific examples of qualifications of the psychiatrist for work in industry, other types of clinical experience, and case examples are cited elsewhere by Powles and Ross.[28] Patterns of occupational mental health programs also are well documented by Warshaw and Phillips.[33]

conceived, stereotyped ideas about work organizations and at the same time recognize that he is adding his skills to many that already exist. In large organizations with well-established medical departments there are occupational physicians and other medical specialists on the staff. Occupational nursing is a recognized specialty. Many organizations employ psychologists—clinical, industrial, and social—and there are experts in various facets of personnel administration. Members of the union hierarchy represent the employees' point of view to management, and there are those in management and executive positions with long years of experience in organizing men and materials around a common task. Each of these individuals correctly considers himself an expert in human behavior in his organization. Each is knowledgeable in some detail about one or another facet of the organization, and it behooves the psychiatrist at the outset to become acquainted with key figures in the other disciplines who concern themselves with its people.

In seeking the identity of the work organization he serves, the psychiatrist who is able to put aside industrial stereotypes will obviously be more successful than the one who does not. No two organizations, of course, are the same in any real sense. The individuality of an organization is made up of a vast array of variables. We might think of this in terms of the "personality" of the organization. This organizational personality or subculture represents the major purpose, policies, practices, affiliations, and values that define and symbolize the identity of the company. It is composed of those features usually put forth by members of the company management to represent its unique character. Much of the social environment is oriented to this concept. It can be identified by appropriate slogans, traditions, folklore, rituals, documents, and written statements. "But its home is in the minds of the members of the organization, and an imperfect reflection is in the minds of those who view the organization from outside."[3] This characteristic personality of each organization represents a strong social pressure for each

employee. Most of these factors of organization personality can be studied. We further recognize that some organizations are authoritarian in character and others are permissive. Certainly he who needs an authoritarian setting would be at sea in a permissive one. While not always true, a worker tends to gravitate to the job and to the industry and to the company or institution that suits his personality. His own personality in turn contributes to the overall personality of the organization.

The psychiatrist must study the actual situation in which he is to function, applying the classical natural history method of medicine to the study of a system of interpersonal relationships. As elsewhere, he is concerned with an initial set of observations, the development of various tentative diagnoses, and the formulation of hypotheses. He must test his hypotheses in many ways in his attempt to understand the size and the shape of the units and the events he observes—all this before he offers suggestions that might be thought of as treatment for the corporate personality. His identity is that of an expert in deviant human behavior. Both he and members of the work organization recognize this role from the beginning of a consulting relationship. Yet each may harbor a different interpretation of the role. Some psychiatrists feel they are properly concerned with the promotion of executives, evaluating and nominating candidates on the basis of freedom from psychopathology to be officers in an industrial organization. Others believe their background suits them for even more direct involvement in the economic affairs of the company, such as assisting with the marketing of a product, for evaluating the potential for default of creditors of the organization. Many believe it is unethical for a psychiatrist to function in industry at all, presuming that he would be asked to help management manipulate and exploit workers. None of these are real or proper views or activities.

Members of management also require guidance as to their expectations of the psychiatrist. They may be all too willing to abdicate responsibility for the administrative aspects of cases of psychiatric illness, in cases of applicants for employment with a history of such illness and in situations involving the establishment of corporate policy. The psychiatrist can evaluate and advise, but the responsibility for decision making lies with line authority.

The consultant has many valid concerns and activities. He is principally interested in the successful adaptation of the individual to his work organization. He is also concerned with facilitating organizational survival when it is threatened by individual deviant behavior or interpersonal and group strife. The legitimate satisfaction of appropriate psychological needs within an individual employee also becomes his valid concern. The provision by the organization for the security needs of its employees—both material and psychological—should be important to him. He is interested in how one deals with various personality characteristics. How does one cope with the aggressive or the passive dependent individual, the self-centered narcissistic person, or the paranoid? Job placement in keeping with these and many other personality characteristics frequently becomes his concern.

The traditional and obvious role of consultant to other physicians in an occupational medical unit differs in some respects from consultation in a clinic or a hospital. With his ongoing relationship to other professionals in such a department, he is able to play an active supporting role to the professional staff who have primary responsibility for working with the employee patient. In addition, the work organization allows a variety of techniques for early referral of the disturbed individual. For this reason the consultant is apt to see people as patients who are less ill than in other settings and therefore more amenable to therapeutic intervention. Such intervention often includes alterations in the work environment, and this too is frequently possible on his advice. Further, he is in a position to meet with the patient's supervisor and with those in personnel departments who are able to alter the job scene or make special arrangements for the employee–patient.

Most large companies have well-established management development programs designed to keep supervisory personnel abreast of contemporary administrative issues. Here is a ready-made setting for the psychiatric consultant to enter into formal dialogue with the power structure in the organization. Formal seminars and lectures can usefully orient such a group to concepts of unconscious determinism, specific ways of coping with unusual behavior, dealing with stressful interpersonal relationships and the emotional problems stemming from the role of manager or executive. The teaching role of the psychiatric consultant is of critical importance. In it, he establishes contact with key individuals and can be seen as a nonthreatening, helpful agent to whom members of the group can turn for assistance. He can also symbolize the corporation's concern for the individual with a disabling emotional problem.

In the clinical role, there is a continuing responsibility for ensuring appropriate placement of employees and potential employees. Can the individual applicant with a history of severe psychotic disorder be appropriately placed in the job he desires? Is the prognosis such that the organization is willing to assume responsibility for him as an employee? Would the job be stressful enough to trigger the development of further incapacitating symptoms? In such a capacity the psychiatrist is obviously principally the agent of the organization. While he is concerned with not allowing assignment that would jeopardize the health of the potential employee, his role is, to some extent, a protector of the interests of the company.

Patient Referral

The majority of the patients seen by the consulting psychiatrist are referred to him by another physician in the work setting. The physician, who is often a full-time employee, plays a pivotal role in detecting psychopathology in assisting managers who have observed disturbed or changed behavior in an employee to obtain a medical and, when indicated, psychiatric evaluation. Occasionally, a patient is referred directly by his supervisor when an obvious psychological problem exists or when it is known that the patient has been in psychiatric treatment or is returning to work following psychiatric hospitalization. Self-referrals are also frequent in most programs.

The psychiatrist may be asked to assess job applicants who appear to have emotional difficulties or who give a history of previous psychiatric treatment. Can the applicant tolerate the demands of the industrial setting? Does he have the ego strength and interpersonal skills to allow him to find satisfaction in his work, or will he be unable to be productive and experience additional disappointment and further loss of self-esteem and confidence? Are the organization and department willing to manage the possible psychological difficulties that might develop? Similarly, the psychiatrist is asked in certain cases to help determine the degree of an employee's disability and make recommendations as to whether he should return to work and under what circumstances.

Consultation and Evaluation

In evaluating a patient in the setting of an organization's medical department, the psychiatrist approaches the patient with very specific questions in mind: Is he presenting with mild to moderate neurotic traits, or is there a more serious process occurring that is on the verge of a disorganization? Is there a suicidal potential? What are the environmental structures that the patient can rely on for emotional and physical support during this period of distress—family, friends, church, and so on? Is the present situation an acute crisis, or is it an exacerbation of a chronic illness? What changes have recently occurred that may be related to the present emotional state? If the patient has experienced similar symptoms in the past, what did he find helpful or harmful in relieving his distress?

In addition to information from the patient, the consultant is in the fortunate position of being able to obtain the opinions and reactions of the medical department staff who have often seen the patient over the years for various physical and emotional complaints. His supervisor can add significant and helpful information as can members of the personnel staff. For example, is the employee particu-

larly productive, and has his productivity changed recently? How well does he customarily get along with his colleagues and supervisors in the work setting? Similarly, the medical staff can speak of the frequency of their contact with the patient and of their reactions to him.

Once a working diagnosis is formulated, the psychiatrist usually reviews his conclusions and recommendations both with the patient and the referring physician. It is at this juncture that he must be particularly tactful, nonthreatening, and positive. Often there is a suggestion for additional psychiatric attention. However, an occasional patient denies the seriousness of his problems and refuses appropriate or adequate treatment. Here, tactfulness, persuasiveness, and persistence are called for and often lead to a satisfying result. Occasionally, with some resistant patients, more serious emotional difficulties develop before the individual is willing to accept help. The alcoholic, for example, frequently denies the extent and consequences of his alcohol abuse and often does not accept help until he needs hospitalization.

Regardless of the recommendations made, another appointment is usually scheduled. In this way the consultant has the opportunity to reevaluate his initial impression, reinforce his previous recommendations, and determine the extent to which the patient has begun implementing the suggestions given at the previous meeting. If the patient refuses treatment and his condition is serious and is adversely affecting his work performance, he can often be motivated to obtain treatment by using job jeopardy as a leverage point.

The psychiatrist has a unique opportunity to influence the many interacting forces in the patient's life. Improving channels of communication with a clear, insightful understanding of the patient's difficulties with management, family, private physician, and medical staff can have a decisive effect on the patient's emotional state.

The corporate employer will tend to look to the psychiatrist who has gained initial acceptance in the company for a broad consultative role in relation to company policy, procedure, and practice. This may be one of the most significant roles he can play if one of his primary functions is with the stimulation of an environment conducive to the fostering of healthy patterns of behavior. To influence an organization away from a policy that fosters dependency upon it beyond reasonable work determinants, to help minimize the overreaction to a key authority figure's impulsively autocratic behavior—such a role has greater impact upon a company than the resolution of a single employee's disabling anxiety reaction, even though the latter remains the major clinical role of most consultants.

Frustrations

Some specific pitfalls that the consultant may anticipate seem worthy of mention: There is, in the members of the management of most work organizations, a residue of many of the common misperceptions of mental disorder. Thus, even the admission that there exists a psychiatrist on the payroll may be an anathema for some, perceived as an admission of corporate weakness. The presence of a psychiatrist can be interpreted by the more naïve as part of a coddling, overprotective, and permissive attitude toward employees. This is hardly surprising, since the values of the community, not of the mental health professional, are dominant at the helm of most companies. If one couples this view of a psychiatrist with the common personality characteristics of many who rise to the top, it is possible to identify some key frustrations for the consultant. The successful executive is often an individual who is aggressive, verbal, and extroverted and who prefers to consider objective facts rather than analyzing more subtle issues. He is not inclined to acknowledge the role of feelings and the importance of unconscious determinism. Those who tend to perceive the world in terms of black and white and who are accustomed to making daily decisions involving millions of dollars and thousands of people and whose principal goal is economic gain cannot be concerned principally with the mental health of employees.

This attitude suggests a number of problems for the psychiatrist who is interested in work adaptation of individuals and whose orientation is supportive of the employee. The psychiatrist may urge an expansion of health insurance to provide outpatient psychotherapy; top management may prefer a dental care plan. An employee with an acute schizophrenic illness may, after several months of disability, be urged by management to resign; the psychiatrist may strongly recommend his retention and efforts toward rehabilitation. The consultant may feel that a research group could benefit from improved communication; the research division's manager may question the application of psychiatric concepts in coming to grips with interpersonal issues even though they may be recognized as problems by members of the group.

Another frustration and an intriguing facet of mental health programs in some organizations is the way in which applied psychiatric research is handled. Some companies feel the results of such studies are internal and proprietary. They frown on publication. Of course, many do encourage publication of research on their employee populations, but others are highly selective of data to be released. Details of activities on behalf of the employees are common in today's literature. Data concerning utilization rates of various benefits covering treatment for employees and their families are generally available, but the corporations vary considerably in their willingness to release internal studies of the incidence and prevalence of mental disorder. The reasons vary and are seen by organizational management as legitimate, but it is unfortunate for occupational psychiatry that such work is not universally available. In the private sector of our economy, the mission of a company is to survive and grow profitably. Such organizations are not in the business of employee health care nor is employee health the principal concern of management. Most recognize an enlightened self-interest in maintaining a healthy population of workers, but published data that suggest high levels of psychopathology in their population are occasionally seen by management as an admission to competitors and to the general public that they are less than successful in maintaining a bright corporate image. While some sophisticated companies utilize carefully developed data for making changes that will relieve various job stresses and further the psychological health of employees, they are reluctant to see exposure of this material to the outside world. Because of this secrecy, there is no way of clearly identifying the extent of such research.

◖ The Job Corps

Perhaps the most extensive program of psychiatric consultation to components of a single work organization is that of the Job Corps. Part of the Manpower Administration of the Department of Labor (formerly in the Office of Economic Opportunity Job Corps), it provides a program of basic education and vocational training in a residential setting for young men and women aged sixteen through twenty-one from poverty backgrounds. There are 20,000 young men and women in active training in a wide range of occupations at fifty-seven Job Corps centers now in existence.

The program at each center consists of vocational training and work experience, basic education, counseling, and residential group living. Comprehensive health care is provided for all enrollees while they are at the centers. Recreational and leisure time activity programs, sometimes involving local communities, are also provided for corps members. In 1968, 84 percent of the centers had established some working contact with a psychiatric consultant, and some ninety-seven psychiatrists were so involved.[21] The pattern of participation is well described by Caplan, Macht, and Wolfe.[6] The rather unique concept of the psychiatrist's role is described as follows in a 1968 pamphlet, *Job Corps as a Community Mental Health Challenge*.[20]

Job Corps recognized that it needed clinicians to take responsibility for the care of those individuals who become ill while in the Corps. We offered to accept that responsibility within the broader context of assuming executive responsibility for all aspects of health and mental affairs.

This combined clinical and program responsibility provided our entree into the agency, and has supplied us with on-going sanction and a base from which to work. The blending of clinical and programmatic responsibilities was made possible by virtue of our role as physicians and as mental health specialists forming a part of a comprehensive health team. To implement the mandate provided us by the Director, we have had to repeatedly negotiate at all levels of the system, demonstrating our capacity to deliver on our promises and commitments.

Although we had carefully established our office in such a way that we had the opportunity to assist in all aspects of the agency's functioning related to mental health, we found that initially we were perceived only as experts in mental illness. The problem of reconciling our objectives and skills with the Job Corps' initial perception of what we could contribute, required two years' work. Our basic technique has been to make a diagnosis of the needs, resistances, and assets of the system and to gear our intervention to the system as we saw it.

The problem of altering our new associates' role perceptions of us has required an on-going educational process. At times we have had to return to our written mandate to enforce our involvement in issues having broad mental health implications. Gradually, the perception of our role has altered, allowing us readier access to all parts of the system. The delivery of services of high quality in the clinical areas has continued to form the base on which the remainder of the program is built. Were we to lose sight of this basic function, all else would soon topple.

Our work in the Headquarters, however, would be fruitless without the field Mental Health Programs, difficult as they have been to implement. They are the payoff, of course, for any programs centrally conceived. Thus, the Mental Health Program in the Job Corps is designed to be flexible regarding the changing needs of centers, but responsive to our overall objectives. Mental Health Consultation, Crisis Intervention, and Anticipatory Guidance techniques have been adapted to the particular needs of the Job Corps and its population. The actual implementation of the program can be conceptualized as a major "system-intervention." An intervention of this type cannot be achieved by fiat or by central office policy and program direction alone. It requires the effective coordination of individuals and program components not themselves subject to direct central authority.

At the Job Corps centers themselves, the consultants have worked with individual cases in problem areas in the center program and with general program issues. Behind-the-scenes consultation regarding case management is not unlike that pattern of consultation common in other work organizations. Psychiatrists work with center physicians, counseling staff, resident workers, and teachers on problems of individual corpsmen, sometimes seeing the individual, sometimes not. Less than half the consultants, however, are engaged in formal teaching for the members of the staff. The bulk of the consultants' work remains that of direct clinical psychiatric services including evaluation and diagnosis of enrollees, short- and long-term psychotherapy, and emergency psychiatric care. From this important clinical base, a substantial number of consultants have become actively engaged in mental health efforts that seem to have great potential to influence many of the programs in the centers.

⟨ Bibliography

1. AMERICAN PSYCHIATRIC ASSOCIATION. *Guidelines for Psychiatric Services Covered under Health Insurance Plans.* 2d ed. Washington, D.C., 1969.
2. ANDERSON, V. V. *Psychiatry in Industry.* New York: Harper, 1929.
3. BAKKE, E. W. *The Fusion Process.* New Haven, Conn.: Yale University Press, 1953.
4. BISGEIER, G. B. "How Many New Employees Are Drug Abusers." In W. W. Steward, ed., *Drug Abuse in Industry.* Miami, Fla.: Halos, 1970. Pp. 89–92.
5. BURLING, T. "The Role of the Professionally Trained Mental Hygienist in Business." *American Journal of Orthopsychiatry,* 11 (1942), 48.
6. CAPLAN, G., MACHT, L. B., and WOLFE, A. B. *Manual for Mental Health Professionals Participating in the Job Corps Program.* Washington, D.C.: Office of Economic Opportunity, 1969.
7. CULPIN, M., and SMITH, M. *The Nervous Temperament.* Medical Research Council Industrial Health Research Board report, no. 61. London: His Majesty's Stationery Office, 1930.
8. CUNNICK, W. "Drug Abuse in a Large Corporation." In W. W. Steward, ed., *Drug Abuse in Industry.* Miami, Fla.: Halos, 1970. Pp. 21–24.
9. DeCARLO, C. R. "Technological Change and Mental Health." In A. A. McLean, ed., *Mental Health and Work Organizations.* Chicago: Rand McNally, 1970. Ch. 10.
10. DuPONG, W. G. "A Statistical Analysis of Early Experience with Urine Chromatography for Drug Identification." In W. W. Steward, ed., *Drug Abuse in Industry.* Miami, Fla.: Halos, 1970. Pp. 157–158.
11. FREUD, S. "Civilization and Its Discontents." *Standard Edition.* Vol. 21. London: Hogarth Press.
12. FUCHS, V. *The Service Economy.* New York: Columbia University Press, 1968.
13. GARFIELD, F. M. "The Drug Problem in Industry." In W. W. Steward, ed., *Drug Abuse in Industry.* Miami, Fla.: Halos, 1970. Pp. 43–48.
14. GIBERSON, L. G. "Psychiatry in Industry." *Personnel Journal,* 15 (1936), 91–95.
15. ———. "Pitfalls in Industry for the Psychiatrist." *Medical Women's Journal,* 47 (1940), 144–146.
16. GLASS, B. *Science,* 170, no. 3962 (1970).
17. GOODING, J. "Blue Collar Blues on the Assembly Line." *Fortune,* 82, no. 3 (1970), 132–135, 158, 162, 167, 168.
18. GREENWOOD, M. *A Report on the Cause of Wastage of Labor in Munition Factories.* Medical Research Council report. London: His Majesty's Stationery Office, 1918.
19. LESSER, P. J. "The Legal Viewpoint." In A. A. McLean, ed., *To Work Is Human: Mental Health and the Business Community.* New York: Macmillan, 1967. Ch. 8.
20. MACHT, L. B., SCHERL, D. J., BICKNELL, W. J., and ENGLISH, J. T. *Job Corps as a Community Mental Health Challenge.* Washington, D.C.: The Office of Economic Opportunity, 1968.
21. ———, SCHERL, D. J., and ENGLISH, J. T. "Psychiatric Consultation: The Job Corps Experience." *American Journal of Psychiatry,* 124, no. 8 (1968), 110–118.
22. McLEAN, A. A. "Occupational Mental Health: Review of an Emerging Art." *American Journal of Psychiatry,* 122, no. 9 (1966), 961–976.

23. ———, ed. *Mental Health and Work Organizations.* Chicago: Rand McNally, 1970.

24. MAYO, E. *The Human Problems of an Industrial Civilization.* New York: Macmillan, 1934.

25. MENNINGER, W. C. "Preface." In A. A. McLean and G. C. Taylor, *Mental Health in Industry.* New York: McGraw-Hill, 1958.

26. MINDUS, E. *Industrial Psychiatry in Great Britain, The United States and Canada.* Report to the World Health Organization. Geneva, 1952.

27. NATIONAL CLEARINGHOUSE FOR MENTAL HEALTH INFORMATION. *Occupational Mental Notes.* Bethesda, Md.: National Institute of Mental Health, 1966.

28. POWLES, W. E., and ROSS, W. D. "Industrial and Occupational Psychiatry." In S. Arieti, ed., *American Handbook of Psychiatry,* Vol. III. New York: Basic Books, 1966. Pp. 588–601.

29. RENNIE, T. A. C., SWACKHAMMER, G., and WOODWARD, L. E. "Toward Industrial Mental Health: An Historical Review." *Mental Hygiene,* 31 (1947), 66–68.

30. SCHEIDMANDEL, P., CANNO, C. K., and GLASSCOTE, R. M. *Health Insurance for Mental Illness.* Washington, D.C.: Joint Information Service of the American Psychiatric Association and the National Association for Mental Health, 1968.

31. SHERMAN, M. "A Review of Industrial Psychiatry." *American Journal of Psychiatry,* 83 (1927), 701–710.

32. SOUTHARD, E. E. "The Modern Specialist in Unrest: A Place for the Psychiatrist in Industry." *Mental Hygiene,* 4, no. 550 (1920).

33. WARSHAW, L. J., and PHILLIPS, B.-J. A. "Mental Health Programs in Occupational Settings." In A. A. McLean, ed., *Mental Health and Work Organizations.* Chicago: Rand McNally, 1970. Pp. 196–236.

CHAPTER 54

MENTAL HEALTH PROGRAMS IN THE ARMED FORCES

Albert J. Glass

To APPRECIATE the unique contributions of military psychiatry, it is necessary to recognize its origin and development as a logical extension of military medicine. Military medicine was born of a necessity to conserve personnel, particularly in combat operations. Experiences of past warfare had repeatedly demonstrated a marked attrition of military manpower, of far greater magnitude than battle losses from infectious diseases, climate extremes, and other nonbattle injury and disease. Minimizing losses from combat causes was also important, for even relatively minor battle injuries could and did result in a large loss of trained manpower. Clearly, wars could be won or lost dependent on the ability "to conserve the fighting strength."*

Not until the latter half of the last century

* Motto of U.S. Army Medical Service

did advances in medicine make available an increasing technical capability of safeguarding military personnel from externally induced disease and injury. Thus, military medicine was fated to pioneer in the development of preventive and treatment techniques for disease and injury of environmental origin. It was therefore inevitable for military psychiatry to be created as a branch of military medicine in order to curtail manpower losses from mental disorders, when it became evident that such casualties were of situational or environmental origin.

(Military Psychiatry Before World War I

Prior to World War I, mental disorders in military personnel, as in civil life, were restricted to severe or bizarre conditions of psychotic proportions.[6, p. 5] Because of the low incidence of mental illness as then defined, which was ascribed to internal pathology rather than environmental causes, there was little interest or concern for these problems by the expanding activities of military medicine. Such cases were either discharged from the service or transferred to the Government Hospital for the Insane in Washington, D.C. (now St. Elizabeth's Hospital).

Situational causation of mental illness in military personnel was clearly demonstrated during the Civil War by the prevalent syndrome of nostalgia, which was characterized as a "mild type of insanity caused by disappointment and a continuous longing for home."[8, p. 639] However, psychiatric sophistication at that time was insufficient to grasp the concept of a situationally induced mental disorder. Instead, emphasis was placed on the innate vulnerability of youthful personnel as the cause for nostalgia. In the Russo-Japanese War (1904–1906), when mental disorders of combat troops were first treated by psychiatric specialists, their somewhat increased frequency was attributed to exposure to high explosives.[6, p. 4] However, these observations excited little comment.

⟦ World War I

From reports of the early fighting on the Western front in 1914, a new psychiatric disorder appeared that was of such frequency as to constitute a major loss of military manpower. Warfare had reached new heights of destruction and terror, and these new mental disorders seemed clearly to be of environmental origin. However, it was necessary that failure in the combat role be manifested by symptoms or behavior acceptable to the reference group and its leaders as constituting an inability rather than an unwillingness to function in battle. Similar but less frequent adaptive failure in previous wars was usually regarded as evidence of weakness and characterized as cowardice or other expressions of moral condemnation. Thus, initially, psychiatric casualties of World War I seemed to be a direct result of enemy shelling, hence the terminology of shell shock. By 1915–1916 the Allied medical services clearly recognized shell shock to be a psychological disorder, and terminology of the "war neuroses" came into common usage. But by this time, psychiatric casualties had achieved legitimacy as a disease and thus an inability to function in battle.

The 1914 shell shock cases from Allied combat troops were evacuated to the remote rear where they quickly overtaxed existing civil and military medical facilities. Later, special neuropsychiatric hospitals were established; but in rear facilities almost all shell shock casualties remained unimproved and refractory to treatment.[1,12] After many months, neuropsychiatric hospitals for the war neuroses were established in the zone of active military operations. The better results obtained in advanced positions prompted a further extension of treatment nearer the front in British casualty clearing stations and similar forward posts of the French medical services. In 1916 Allied psychiatrists and neurologists reported that a majority of the war neuroses could be returned to combat duty by forward treatment. With further experiences, the British and French medical services showed conclusively that the war neuroses improved more rapidly when treated in permanent hospitals near the front than at the base, better in clearing stations than even at advanced base hospitals, and better still when encouragement, rest, persuasion, and suggestion could be given in the combat organization itself.

Upon entry of the United States in World War I (April 1917), Major Thomas Salmon, the chief psychiatrist of the American expeditionary forces, and his associates, fully aware of the British and French experiences, gradually established a network of services for the war neuroses. The three-echeloned system that became fully operational during the last several months of the war[1,12] included:

1. Divisional psychiatric facilities, which held shell shock disorders for three to five days of rest, suggestions, and other

psychotherapeutic measures under supervision of the division psychiatrist.

2. Neurological hospitals, which received refractory cases from nearby divisional facilities and had a treatment capability of several weeks.

3. A special psychiatric base hospital located in the advanced communication zone, which provided prolonged treatment for the most resistant of the war neuroses in order to prevent chronicity and evacuation to the United States.

An important aspect of treatment at all levels was noted by Salmon and Fenton[12] as "an intangible and mysterious influence termed 'atmosphere.'" Perhaps this observation was the first direct reference to the environment of treatment, which included those feelings and attitudes of all medical personnel who came in contact with the war neuroses and sought to provide an urge or incentive for return to duty.

In retrospect, military psychiatry in World War I provided much of the conceptual framework on which has been based the current community mental health movement. Major contributions in this regard can be subsumed as follows:

1. Repeated demonstrations showed that situational stress and strain can produce mental disorder in so-called normal personnel as well as in those of neurotic predisposition. Previously, mental illness had been regarded as originating almost exclusively from physical and/or psychological abnormalities within the individual.

2. The development of treatment at the site of origin was a logical consequence of recognition that the war neuroses were caused by situational circumstances. It made possible a therapeutic rationale of prompt intervention measures with the objective of adjustment to the combat situation rather than evacuation to remote hospitalization with fixation of failure and symptoms of chronic disability. In time, the importance of location in the treatment of mental disorders has become a basic principle of the community delivery of services.

3. A network of supportive treatment facilities for the war neuroses from forward to rear areas was established by the American expeditionary forces. Only recently has the value of such a comprehensive network of services for mild to severe mental disorders become appreciated; it is in various stages of implementation as a linkage of community services with supportive state facilities.

4. Probably for the first time, the environment of treatment including its location, physical facilities, and the attitudes and behavior of treatment personnel was utilized as a therapeutic instrument. Later, this concept formed the basis for various types of milieu therapy and in military psychiatry became the principle of expectancy for return to duty.

⟨ Post-World War I

With the end of hostilities, the contributions of military psychiatry were largely disregarded. Psychiatry at this time was not prepared to grasp the significance of social or situational determinants of mental disorder or the importance of location and therapeutic atmosphere in its treatment. Moreover, extensive clinical experience with the persistent residual syndromes of the war neuroses in the postwar years created a widespread belief that these problems originated mainly from persons who were vulnerable to situational stress by reason of neurotic predisposition. The limited ability to cope with combat was deemed the result of faulty personality development and thus conformed to the psychoanalytic model of the psychoneuroses and was so generally diagnosed.

Military psychiatry after World War I became a permanent component of U.S. military medicine. Psychiatric units of open and closed wards with outpatient services were provided as sections under the medical services at all U.S. Army general hospitals. The practice of military psychiatry at these large Army hospitals was similar to that of civil mental facilities. But neither locally based treatment nor other concepts of social psychiatry as elaborated by the American expeditionary forces survived after World War I.

Curiously, during the period it was generally believed that the major lesson learned by military psychiatry in World War I was the importance of psychiatric screening at induction to remove vulnerable candidates for service and thus prevent the emotional breakdown of troops in peace or war. Yet none of the experiences of World War I indicated that studies were conducted or observations made on the validity of psychiatric screening.[1,12]

World War II

Because of the above-stated circumstances and other problems of need and expediency during the early phases of World War II, the contributions of military psychiatry of World War I were completely ignored. Instead, reliance was placed on psychiatric screening. The subsequent failure of the psychiatric screening program has been well documented.[*] As a result, there was little preparation for the management of psychiatric disorders, combat or otherwise. With expanding mobilization and the onset of hostilities, a high incidence of mental disorders soon overwhelmed existing medical facilities. The major available diagnostic category for these mainly situationally induced mental disorders was psychoneurosis with its implication of unresolved internal conflict from which symptoms were unconsciously derived. The newly built cantonment hospitals of World War II were soon filled with refractory symptomatic disorders in which psychological problems were a major component. The only resolution to this mounting caseload was medical discharge for psychoneurosis. Thus, mental illness became the major cause of manpower loss in the U.S. Army. As in World War I, combat psychiatric casualties were evacuated hundreds of miles to distant medical facilities where few could be restored to combat duty. Again, terminology for these cases was "psychoneurosis." With such labeling and its connotation of individual weakness, it was difficult for psychi-

atric casualties to be accepted by the combat group and its leaders as being the result of battle conditions; rather, they were considered the result of failure in induction screening.

Because of the above-stated events, efforts were made by individual psychiatrists and later by coordinated programs to establish locally based or forward treatment services. However, more than two years elapsed in World War II before sufficient organizational and operational capability was developed to deal adequately with the large incidence of wartime mental disorders. These changes occurred during 1943 and 1944, first in training bases in the United States and later in overseas combat theaters.

Extramural psychiatric units termed "consultation services" were gradually established at each of the training camps to provide outpatient treatment for symptom disorders and participate in the orientation of trainees. Later, psychiatric personnel included the function of consultation to trainer personnel in influencing decisions relative to facilitating the adjustment of trainees. By firsthand observation, psychiatrists of the consultation services became aware of the problems of trainees in dealing with separation from families and loved ones, lack of privacy, regimentation, unaccustomed physical activity, and other deprivations and changes incidental to the transition from civil to military life.[*] This function of consultation is perhaps the earliest demonstration of the utilization of indirect psychiatric services, which has now become an essential component of the community mental health approach to prevention.

During the later phases of the Tunisia campaign (March 1943), successful attempts were made to reestablish the World War I forward treatment for psychiatric casualties. Soon thereafter, a new terminology for psychiatric casualties was adopted. By directive, all psychiatric disorders in the combat zone were ordered to be designated as exhaustion regardless of manifestations. Other and more definitive diagnoses were permitted in rear medical facilities.[7] With the acceptance of exhaustion,

---

* See reference 6, pp. 375 and 740.

* See reference 6, pp. 349–371.

manifestations of combat psychiatric breakdown became less florid or dramatic. Psychiatric casualties did not need to portray "psycho" to communicate inability to function in battle. Beginning in March 1944, a three-echeloned system of services similar to that of World War I was implemented. The prolonged and diversified experiences of military psychiatry in World War II refined and elaborated on the accomplishments of World War I psychiatry as follows.

1. Causation. Perhaps the most significant contribution of World War II psychiatry was recognition of the sustaining influence of the small combat group or particular members thereof, termed "group identification," "the buddy system," or "leadership," which was also operative in noncombat situations. World War II clearly showed that interpersonal relationships and other situational circumstances were at least as important as personality configuration or individual assets and liabilities in the effectiveness of coping behavior. The frequency of psychiatric disorders seemed to be more related to the characteristics of the group than the character traits of the individual.

2. Treatment. During World War I and World War II, it was apparent that forward and early treatment afforded the opportunity of providing prompt relief for fatigue, loss of sleep, hunger, and other temporary physiological deficits. However, it was not until recognition of the sustaining influences of group and interpersonal relationships that the significance of treatment near or at the site of situational origin of psychiatric disorders was fully appreciated. Proximity of treatment maintained relationships and emotional investment in the core group. There existed in psychiatric casualties under conditions of forward treatment varying degrees of motivation to rejoin the combat group, which was heightened by improvement in physical well-being from recuperative measures of sleep, food, and the like. Also treatment in the combat zone provided an atmosphere of expectancy for improvement and return to duty. Forward location and brief simplified treatment clearly communicated to both patients and treatment personnel that psychiatric casualties constituted only a temporary inability to function. Conversely, removal of psychiatric disorders to distant medical facilities weakened emotional ties with the combat group with implications of failure, for which continuation of the sick role was the only honorable explanation.

3. Diagnosis. An important but as yet only a potential contribution of military psychiatry concerns the influence of diagnosis. World War I and World War II demonstrated that a definitive diagnosis in an early and fluid phase of a mental disorder can adversely affect the individuals so involved as well as exert a negative expectancy by treatment personnel toward improvement or recovery. Practically all available psychiatric diagnoses indicate the existence of organic or intrapsychic pathology, such as character and personality disorder, neurosis, psychosis, and brain damage. As yet, there is little usage of diagnostic designation for failure of adaptation, which would include both external and internal determinants of behavior. Even the addition of reaction to the usual diagnostic categories in World War II has been recently abandoned. For the above reasons, it is suggested that civil psychiatry would be as equally benefited as has been military psychiatry in avoiding the early use of definitive diagnoses, which place emphasis mainly on the liabilities of individuals and negate the setting in which failure of adjustment occurred. In the initial stages of patient contact, it would seem reasonable to utilize a general descriptive label and permit later events to determine the need for a more definitive diagnostic categorization.

(Post-World War II

Following cessation of hostilities, military psychiatry maintained a coequal status with medicine and surgery achieved in World War II. With other branches of military medicine, specialty medical training in psychiatry was instituted. Curiously, during the early postwar years, as following World War I, military psychiatry, like civil psychiatry, ignored the lessons of wartime experiences. Instead, attention was focused on the then prevalent psychoanalytic concepts and practice. At this time, there was a major need to explain symptoms and behavior on a dynamic rather than descriptive basis. The emerging field of social or community psychiatry had no conceptual frame of reference or special language. In contrast, psychoanalysis had a unified theory, considerable historical background, much literature, and a special vocabulary for expression and communication. At this time, military psychiatry in its training and practice emulated the expanding departments of psychiatry of the various medical schools. The wartime consultative services were largely discarded.

Korean War

After the abrupt onset of the Korean War on June 25, 1950, U.S. Army psychiatry moved rapidly to establish the World War II system of mental health services both at home and overseas. A three-echeloned network of services for psychiatric casualties was in operation during the early fall of 1950. The ineffective psychiatric screening of World War II was abandoned. A rotation policy of nine to twelve months in the combat zone, which had been unsuccessfully urged in World War II, was instituted after the first year of the Korean War. Mental hygiene consultation services were established at all major army bases in the United States. These units, utilizing psychiatrists, psychologists, social workers, and enlisted technicians, provided an expanded and flexible capability in furnishing direct care for referred problems and indirect consultation services for supervisory personnel.

As a result of the prompt implementation of the psychiatric lessons learned in World War II, during the initial year of severe combat in the Korean War the frequency of psychiatric disorders was less than one-half of the high incidence in World War II. Thereafter, a steady decline of the psychiatric rate occurred,

which during the last year of the Korean War reached almost to previous peacetime levels.[4]

Developments since the Korean War

During and following the Korean War, there has evolved an increasing application of social psychiatry principles in the practices of military psychiatry. This trend and its momentum were considerably influenced by the training and research activities of the neuropsychiatry division, which was established in 1951 and headed by David McK. Rioch. In this regard, symposia held at the Walter Reed Institute of Research in 1953 and 1957 brought together emerging civil and military concepts and experiences in social psychiatry and provided a needed body of theory and operational framework of reference for expansion in this area.

From the beginning of this era, emphasis in military psychiatry has been placed upon the activities of locally based mental health facilities, both in the field, at the division level, and on posts and bases, by Mental Hygiene Consultation Services (MIICS). These forward-level psychiatric units explored new approaches and developed innovative techniques in providing direct and indirect mental health services. Thus, over time, there have been incorporated into the regular operations of military psychiatry changes in the direction of social or community psychiatry as follows: (1) organizational flexibility and (2) field service program.

1. Organizational flexibility. An early basic change discarded traditional clinic procedure in which each referral was subjected to multiple examinations, including social history, psychological testing, and psychiatric evaluation, from which diagnoses and decisions for treatment or disposition were derived. Inevitably, such a time-consuming ritualistic arrangement produced long waiting lists and little flexibility in the utilization of personnel. In its place, a screening or triage function was assigned to an experienced social worker, who in the initial interview evaluated presenting problems with prompt referral to the appropriate staff

member. Waiting lists were abolished and routine psychological testing eliminated in favor of specific requests for such services, and psychiatrists were utilized mainly in consultation and supervision. All professional staff members were made available for evaluation and treatment with a free interchange of consultation. With achievement of organizational flexibility, the role of enlisted personnel changed from reception and clerical duties to active involvement and interaction with patients. Enlisted personnel became utilized in intake evaluation, the obtaining of collateral information, and counseling, dependent on training and experience. It was soon noted that enlisted specialists could readily obtain realistic accounts of situational problems and render effective counseling services. Enlisted staff members proved to be enthusiastic workers with considerable understanding of and empathy with the difficulties of fellow enlisted men. This more flexible organization and availability of staff permitted local military mental health services to make further advances.

2. Field service program. With time, it became apparent that more satisfactory results could be obtained when the location of evaluation and treatment was displaced from clinic facilities to the unit from which referral was made. In the field service program, an enlisted specialist responded to requests for mental health services by proceeding to the referring organization. Interviews were conducted with the subject and significant other persons in barracks, dayrooms, or offices. Experience demonstrated that more valid data could be obtained within the unit, from both the individual concerned and collateral information. Referring units came to appreciate that the objective of mental health services was adjustment rather than removal. The field service program was conducted almost entirely by enlisted specialists with back-up supervision usually by social work officers. In this program, the enlisted specialist always had the option of promptly bringing subjects to the clinic. His instructions were to deal with problems unless unable to communicate with the referred soldier or understand his situation. In time, 50 percent of referrals to the psychiatric unit for services were handled by the field service program.[5]

It is pertinent to review the development of the enlisted specialist in mental health services. During World War II, enlisted personnel with usually little or no previous training were made available through on-the-job experience to assist psychiatrists and nurses (also to some extent, social workers and psychologists) in order to expand the services of these scarce professionals. After the war, formal training programs were instituted to train enlisted specialists as neuropsychiatric technicians to work in psychiatric inpatient services and as social work and psychology technicians for clinic or divisional mental health services.[11] In addition, even larger numbers of enlisted specialists were made available through on-the-job training by the various mental health facilities. More recently, social work and psychology training have been combined to produce enlisted mental health specialists for function with field and post psychiatric services.[9] Such enlisted specialists may also be directly obtained from military personnel having bachelor of arts degrees, with graduate work or experience in a related field.

Command Consultation

During this period, there was increasing awareness that the majority of mental disorders in military personnel represented casualties or failures of adjustment in part at least due to circumstances or problems within the referring organization. As indicated previously, experiences in World War II and the Korean War had already demonstrated that the frequency of combat psychiatric casualties was, in addition to the intensity of battle, related to the characteristics of the group and/or its leadership. In this era, similar relationships were observed in the origin of psychiatric disorders from peacetime military activities.

Consistent with the above trend, the more flexible organization of local military mental health facilities following the Korean War made possible a wider utilization of professional and nonprofessional consultants to unit commanders at various levels; thus the term "command consultation." In this program, consultation services are usually initiated with commanders on the basis of a mutual effort to resolve the particular adjustment difficulties of an individual who was referred to the local mental health facility. After repeated instances of successful collaboration for specific individuals, a positive consultant-consultee relationship is established, which serves as a channel for more general issues of the command management of personnel. In this area, the consultant often has much to contribute, including epidemiological data, relative to the incidence of various categories of noneffective behavior, such as mental disorder, delinquency, and alcoholism. Soon specific problems are raised, such as screening for certain special schools, alteration of training procedures, and the identification of organizational problems. In essence, psychiatric personnel learn to serve as consultants in personnel management as restricted to conditions under which military personnel live, work, train, and fight. To perform this function, psychiatric personnel must have firsthand knowledge of unit activities as well as direct and collateral information concerning the maladjustment of referred individuals.[5]

Consultation was extended to such post special services as the judge advocate for offenders and the provost marshal in the problems of confinement. Out of these consultation activities, there arose a mutual concern with the problems of the military offender and the correctional process in post stockades and military prisons which led to the development of the stockade screening program.

With study of the correctional program, it became apparent that offenders in the five Army prisons who received sentences and a dishonorable discharge by general court martial had served one or more previous sentences in local post stockades for lesser offenses. Also the large majority of convictions both in stockades and prisons were for military type offenses, such as AWOL, desertion, and insubordination. Thus, the natural history of most military prisoners was clearly portrayed

as nonconformist behavior relative to military rules and discipline which was repetitive and often led to a prison sentence with dishonorable discharge. Intervention at the stockade level appeared to be a logical procedure to prevent extended noneffective behavior.

Accordingly, a program was gradually established on major posts in the United States and overseas that evaluated each admission to the stockade as to assets, liabilities, situational problems, and potential for adjustment in the military service. Local psychiatric personnel from divisions or post mental hygiene consultation services, mainly enlisted specialists and social work officers, accomplished such evaluations within the stockade and thereby became aware of correctional procedures at firsthand. Then followed mutual efforts with judge advocate, provost marshal personnel, and unit commanders to consider the potential of each stockade inmate. By this procedure, changes could be made in assignment, training, or other conditions for the individual offender to aid in adjustment on release with follow-up counseling usually by enlisted specialists. When it became apparent that attitudes and motivation of the stockade prisoner were such as to preclude effective adjustment in military service, administrative discharge was accomplished by agreement with the unit commander. Under these circumstances, before a record of repeated violations could be accumulated, a discharge under honorable conditions for unsuitability was usually given, which provided a more favorable opportunity for later adjustment in civil life. Within three to four years of the operation of this program, reduction of general prisoners was such that four of five Army prisons were closed, with a marked decline of dishonorable discharges.[5] This utilization of intervention has been extended to correctional programs of all branches of the armed forces.

(**Vietnam**

According to authoritative reports, military psychiatry in the Vietnam conflict achieved its most impressive record in conserving the fighting strength.[10,13] In its operations, enlisted mental health specialists were utilized for intervention, treatment, and consultation to a greater extent than previously practiced or even envisioned. The dispersed and intermittent nature of combat in Vietnam, with episodic search and destroy missions and perimeter fighting, made necessary a corresponding dispersal of divisional psychiatric services. The eight enlisted specialists in each combat division were assigned in pairs to each of four medical companies, which were distributed to provide medical services over the large area of division operations.

In a combat division of 15,000 to 18,000 men, psychiatric referrals averaged from 100 to 200 per month. Intake evaluations and counseling were performed by enlisted specialists, who conducted follow-up services. Enlisted specialists worked in close association with battalion and company medical officers who prescribed psychotropic and other medication as appropriate and provided for brief hospitalization as indicated. The division psychiatrist and division social worker visited the medical companies regularly for supervision. In addition, radio and landline communication enabled the enlisted specialist to contact these supervisors at any time. The more severe psychiatric problems were transferred to the division psychiatric treatment unit. Consistent with increased responsibility for direct services, enlisted specialists assumed an active role in providing consultation services, particularly for sergeants and junior officers.[2]

As a result of forward divisional mental health services, so few psychiatric disorders had been evacuated to rear medical facilities as to create the impression that psychiatric casualties were rarely produced by the unique nature of combat in Vietnam.[3]

(Conclusion

This chapter presents the historical development of military psychiatry in the U.S. Army. Particular emphasis is placed on its evolution into programs of social psychiatry, utilizing the principles of immediacy, proximity, and expectancy.

(Bibliography

1. BAILEY, P., WILLIAMS, F. E., and KOMORA, P. O. "In the United States." In *The Medical Department of the United States Army in the World War*. Vol. 10. *Neuropsychiatry*. Washington, D.C.: U.S. Government Printing Office, 1929.
2. BEY, D. R., and SMITH, W. E. "Mental Health Technicians in Vietnam." *Bulletin of the Menninger Clinic*, 34, no. 6 (1970), 363–371.
3. BOURNE, P. A. "Psychiatric Casualties in Vietnam, Lowest Ever for Combat Zone Troops." *U.S. Medicine*, May 15, 1969.
4. GLASS, A. J. "Observations Upon the Epidemiology of Mental Illness in Troops During Warfare." In Walter Reed Army Medical Center, *Symposium on Preventive and Social Psychiatry*. Washington, D.C.: U.S. Government Printing Office, 1958.
5. ———, ARTISS, K., GIBBS, J. J., and SWEENEY, V. C. "The Current Status of Army Psychiatry." *American Journal of Psychiatry*, 117 (1962), 675.
6. ———, and BERNUCCI, R. J. *Neuropsychiatry in World War II*. Vol. 1. *Zone of the Interior*. Washington, D.C.: U.S. Government Printing Office, 1966.
7. MEDICAL DEPARTMENT, U.S. ARMY. *Neuropsychiatry in World War II*. Vol. 11. In preparation.
8. *Medical and Surgical History of the War of the Rebellion*. Vol. 1. Washington, D.C.: U.S. Government Printing Office, 1870.
9. NOLAN, K. J., and COOKE, E. T. "The Training and Utilization of the Mental Health Paraprofessional Within the Military: The Social Work/Psychology Specialist." *American Journal of Psychiatry*, 127 (1970), 74–79.
10. OFFICE OF THE SURGEON GENERAL, DEPARTMENT OF THE ARMY. *The Mental Health of U.S. Troops in Vietnam Remains Outstanding*. Washington, D.C.: U.S. Government Printing Office, 1968.
11. RODEMAN, C. R. "The Technicians." In A. J. Glass and R. J. Bernucci, eds., *Neuropsychiatry in World War II*. Vol. 1. *Zone of*

the Interior. Washington, D.C.: U.S. Government Printing Office, 1966. Pp. 701–707.

12. SALMON, T. W., and FENTON, N. "In the American Expeditionary Forces." In *The Medical Department of the United States Army in the World War*. Vol. 10. *Neuropsychiatry*. Washington, D.C.: U.S. Government Printing Office, 1929.

13. TIFFANY, W. J., Jr. "Mental Health of Army Troops in Vietnam." *American Journal of Psychiatry*, 123 (1967), 1585–1586.

CHAPTER 55

PROGRAMS AND TECHNIQUES OF CRISIS INTERVENTION

Gerald F. Jacobson

THE DICTIONARY DEFINITION of "crisis"[4] is "a decisive or vitally important stage in the course of anything; a turning point." As such, its great importance in human existence has been known since the beginning of recorded time. Yet, though man has long known that crucial periods do affect his destiny, psychiatrists and other mental health professionals have shown little recognition of the significance of crisis until very recently.

The present state of the field is one of rapid growth; as often occurs when progress is rapid, different areas of the field are not fully integrated with one another. In order to organize the material for purposes of this presentation, three major areas will now be defined and briefly described: (1) crisis intervention programs, (2) crisis theory, and (3) crisis intervention techniques.

1. For purposes of this chapter, crisis intervention programs will be defined as organized facilities* (such as clinics) or components of organized facilities (such as crisis units of community mental health centers), staffed by mental health professionals and offering early-access, brief treatment to nonhospitalized persons.†[33] Early access means no or minimal delay; brief treatment means limits on total length of treatment or on number of visits. A frequent limit is six visits. For purposes of this essay, crisis intervention programs may or may not use crisis theory as their major theoretical base.

2. Crisis theory is defined as an important

---

* Strictly speaking, "program" refers to function; "facility" refers to the organization rendering the function. Both terms are used here interchangeably.

† For reasons discussed below, the term "patient" will not be used in relation to persons using crisis services. In spite of a recognized inconsistency, the term "treatment" will be used for lack of another readily available one in describing services rendered to a person in crisis.

and recently developed theoretical framework, originally based on the work of Lindemann[40,48] and Caplan[11-13] and subsequently further developed by others, including Bloom,[9] Harris et al.[26] Jacobson,[29,30,34] Kalis,[36] Kaplan and Mason,[38,39] Klein and Ross,[41] Langsley and Kaplan,[42] Morley and Brown,[50,51] Parad and Parad,[54] L. Rapoport,[57] R. and R. N. Rapoport,[58] Strickler,[63,64] and others.

3. Crisis intervention techniques are defined here as treatment techniques based on crisis theory and used by mental health professionals. Thus, while crisis intervention programs will be discussed regardless of their theoretical base, techniques will only be considered when they relate to crisis theory.* I will discuss crisis intervention programs, crisis theory, and crisis intervention techniques, concluding with a consideration of other subjects and current frontiers.

The experience at the Benjamin Rush centers in Los Angeles† is the source of significant parts of this chapter. The Rush centers offer treatment on the day of application if possible, and always within one week. Treatment is offered to anyone who desires it without regard to financial or diagnostic status, unless the applicant is already in treatment with a mental health professional elsewhere. Treatment is limited to six visits, and the average number of visits is four. Crisis intervention is carried out by a multidisciplinary staff, including psychiatrists, psychologists, social workers, and nurses, as well as trainees in all these disciplines. The methodology will be described in the section on crisis intervention techniques. At the conclusion of crisis intervention, referral is made to other facilities if necessary. The Rush centers are administratively independent divisions of the Los Angeles Psychiatric Service, a nonhospital community facility supported by private and public funds, which also operates ongoing outpatient treatment clinics and specialized programs for black and Spanish-speaking minorities. The Rush centers serve both middle- to lower-middle-class whites and a significant number of members of minority (black and Spanish-speaking) groups and of the poor of all races. One of the Rush centers is located in the Venice district of Los Angeles, sometimes described as "Appalachia-by-the-Sea." To date, approximately 12,000 different persons have been seen since the Rush centers began in 1962; the current rate is 2,400 different persons seen per year. The Rush centers have been described in a number of publications.§

([Crisis Intervention Programs

Crisis intervention programs are a recent and rapidly growing addition to the psychiatric scene. Only a limited number of reports have yet appeared in the literature. Table 55–1 summarizes eleven programs. This list undoubtedly contains omissions of program, either because they were overlooked or because they are too recent. A few reports have been omitted because the authors state that their program was in large part based on some of the programs that are listed. The table intentionally omits programs offering evaluation and referral services only. This omission does not reflect on the contribution of these programs, some of which provide comprehensive assessment followed by referral.[7,14,15] They do not offer treatment. Emergency services that also offer treatment are included.

---

* This omission is due to the necessity to keep this chapter brief and cohesive and with full recognition that some important contributions have come from clinics using other theoretical frameworks, such as the "Trouble-Shooting Clinic" at Elmhurst Municipal Hospital.[6] For a full discussion of brief psychotherapy in general, including some material on early-access, brief treatment centers using a different theoretical framework, the reader is directed to Small's *The Briefer Psychotherapies*.[61]

† The development of theory and practice at the Rush centers has been a team effort. I wish to acknowledge the important contributions that have been made by all of my coworkers, and most particularly by Dr. Wilbur Morley, Deputy Director, Los Angeles Psychiatric Service and Director, Venice/Oakwood Divisions, and Martin Strickler, A.C.S.W., Deputy Director, Los Angeles Psychiatric Service and Director, Whitworth and Robertson Divisions.

§ See references 2, 31–34, 49–51, 62, 63, and 65.

TABLE 55-1.   Crisis Intervention Programs in the United States

PROGRAM	LOCATION	YEAR STARTED
Wellesley Human Relations Service[10,40]	Wellesley, Mass.	1948
Walk-In Clinic of the Bronx Municipal Hospital[17,18]	Bronx, N.Y.	1956
Precipitating Stress Project, Langley Porter Neuropsychiatric Institute[26,37]	San Francisco, Cal.	1958
Trouble-Shooting Clinic at Elmhurst City Hospital[5,6]	New York, N.Y.	1958
Greater Lawrence Guidance Center[3]	Lawrence, Mass.	1960
Emergency Psychiatric Treatment Service, Kings County Psychiatric Hospital[25,67]	New York, N.Y.	1961
Benjamin Rush Center for Problems of Living[2,31-34,49-51,62,63,65]	Los Angeles, Cal.	1962
Walk-In Clinic at Metropolitan Hospital[52,66]	New York, N.Y. (East Harlem)	1962
Family Treatment Unit, Colorado Psychiatric Hospital[43-45]	Denver, Colo.	1964
Mental Health Clinic, Maine Medical Center[46,47]	Portland, Me.	1964
Intake Reception Clinic, Maimonides Hospital of Brooklyn[24]	Brooklyn, N.Y.	1964

Goals and Rationale

Goals and rationale of crisis intervention programs relate to two characteristics of these programs: ready access and brief treatment. They also relate to the kinds of persons who are served.

Ready access—immediately if possible, and always within a few days and with no waiting list—is offered in the expectation that the earlier a disturbance is treated, the less likely it is to result in more chronic and more severe malfunction. This is the same principle involved in prevention and early treatment of medical illness. To the extent that crisis intervention can prevent later and more serious disability, it helps to reduce human suffering and also results in more economic use of money and manpower. This preventive function is an important aspect of crisis intervention programs. Also, a crisis lasts up to six weeks, so that crisis intervention programs based on crisis theory can only be used if treatment is offered without delay.

Brief treatment usually consists of up to six visits. The rationale for brief treatment is that

many people do not want and/or do not need longer term treatment, but do want and need help in resolving immediate issues. Also, intervention at what Small[61] called "crisis—the propitious moment" can provide maximum impact per unit of mental health manpower because there is greater responsiveness to intervention and because rapid changes for better or worse occur in the course of a short period of time. Brief treatment, to be most effective, should not be an abbreviated or second-rate version of what some feel is the only real treatment, namely, longer-term therapy. Rather it should be of such a nature that it not only can be carried out within a brief time period but that it cannot possibly be extended without changing it qualitatively.[31] Crisis intervention techniques that meet this requirement are discussed later.

The third goal is that of offering treatment to all types of persons who need help and are not receiving it, with few if any exclusions. The rationale is the view that there are many persons who in subtle or obvious ways are excluded from mental health settings, except those of last resort, such as state hospitals. Hollingshead and Redlich[28] pointed out that those psychiatric services considered most prestigious, such as dynamically oriented outpatient treatment, are more readily available the higher the person's social class status. The poor are more likely to receive somatic treatment or drugs and, we may add, a round robin of referrals from one facility to the other without any treatment. The same type of overt or covert selection tends to apply to other groups, such as the aged, the less well educated, and, regardless of demographic characteristics, to persons severely disturbed and to those wishing help with immediate problems rather than character change. Crisis intervention programs can and do serve all population groups. If any discrimination is legitimate in crisis intervention programs, it will favor those less likely to get treatment, such as the poor or the psychologically most severely disturbed.

Organization

A number of organizational models for crisis intervention programs exist. In some cases they are administratively part of a hospital emergency room or of either the inpatient or outpatient services. Elsewhere, crisis intervention programs may be independent units. In my opinion, the optimum organization may be the last mentioned: a crisis intervention service independent of, and on a par with, inpatient, outpatient, partial hospitalization and other services. The need for a new component in the spectrum of mental health services has been reflected by the requirement that emergency services be one of the five required components of federally funded community mental health centers. (The other services are inpatient, outpatient, partial hospitalization, and consultation and education.)

Some advantages of autonomous status are as follows: When crisis intervention or emergency services are part of inpatient services, a conflict of interest is possible when staff are required to work actively for alternatives to hospitalization, particularly in instances where there is no shortage of beds. If there is a shortage of beds and an overworked staff, on the other hand, emergency services that are part of the inpatient service may not have the staff or time to provide more than evaluation for admission and more or less thorough referral to other units in the facility or community. When crisis intervention services are administratively part of the outpatient service, it is possible that ongoing treatment may be considered the preferred modality by many professionals and that crisis intervention may not receive the professional investment it requires to be successful.

It is desirable for crisis intervention programs to have as their primary function the provision of ready access, brief treatment. While they must, of course, be able to refer to other services, they should if possible be more than an entry control point that turns some people back and directs others to various services.

The physical location should follow from the above considerations. If the internal administrative arrangements and the attitude of the community make it feasible, all new cases coming to a facility (such as a community mental health center) may first be seen in the crisis intervention program. In that case, the crisis intervention program is also the emergency service, and it is available twenty-four hours a day. If this is done, it is desirable that the program have the authority to determine whether the person should be treated by crisis intervention techniques and whether and when he should be referred elsewhere in the facility or community.

In many cases it will not be feasible for the crisis intervention program to receive all admissions. When that is the situation, other ways must be found to decide who is seen in the crisis intervention program and who is seen elsewhere. At the Benjamin Rush centers we have solved our problem by placing the Rush center around the corner from the psychiatric clinic, which has a different name, street address, and application procedure. Admission to one clinic does not mean admission to the other. The names and functions of the different clinics are widely known in the community. With this arrangement the applicant decides whether to apply for crisis intervention or ongoing treatment.

In other settings there might, in addition, be

need of a central intake office, which directs applicants to any service, including the crisis intervention program. In such a case it is important not to lose the walk-in feature, which allows direct access to the crisis intervention program. If the crisis intervention service does not itself function as the twenty-four-hour emergency service, it must have a close working relation with a twenty-four-hour service in the facility or the community.

The question of what the maximum number of visits should be touches on many of the same issues. Some clinics have no firm maximum; some use the early-access, brief treatment clinic to see long-term cases who come regularly but infrequently. There is a definite case to be made for a firm time limit. The reason is similar to that for recommending an autonomous status for the clinic. We have already said that longer treatment is both easier and conforms more to the values of many psychiatrists and other professionals than crisis intervention services. Therefore, placing a firm limit on the number of visits assures that crisis intervention alone remains the focus of professional activity. At the same time, a firm limit is also helpful to the person in crisis, since he knows he must address himself to the current issues in his life without procrastination.

Any form of longer treatment, including low-frequency treatment, is in our experience more effectively carried out within the framework of a more conventional outpatient clinic. On the other hand, we have found, as did Raphling and Lion,[56] that some people use crisis intervention programs when they need them, and function on their own the rest of the time. We feel that this use of crisis intervention may sometimes be preferable to long-term treatment, especially for people with borderline states and severe character disorder. At the other end of the spectrum, intermittent use of crisis intervention may be helpful to people who function well except for occasional crises. The difference between ongoing treatment and repeated admissions is not so difficult to define as we thought it would be; rarely does one person have more than two admissions per year, and then they are usually around quite distinct issues. If

someone applies more often, an attempt is made to refer to longer-term treatment.

Problems

Crisis intervention programs must deal with a number of difficulties. Compared to more traditional outpatient facilities, they require new skills from professionals. In addition, work in crisis intervention programs is demanding, because the turnover means that the professional must deal with a succession of different people and problems rather than with a few familiar ones, as is the case in ongoing treatment. Also, it is hard to be continuously involved with acute problems. Further, crisis intervention programs challenge some of the value systems of psychiatrists and other mental health professionals, which include the belief that their goal should be to cure patients, rather than to help resolve circumscribed problems, however urgent. Coleman[16] and Gelb and Ullman[24] addressed themselves to some of these issues. For the above described reasons, there is a constant tendency on the part of many mental health professionals to revert to other models. This tendency must be counteracted if the crisis intervention program is to remain viable.

To deal with these problems, the crisis intervention program should provide a high degree of professional satisfaction to the staff and trainees involved. There should be adequate financial compensation; and there should be a recognition of the difficulty of the work. In addition, professionals in crisis intervention programs should have considerable supervision, both to deal with their inevitable anxieties about their clinical work and to assure that a change to ongoing treatment models does not occur.

(Crisis Theory

Origins

Crisis theory has evolved from a number of sources, the two most important of which are psychoanalysis and social work/sociology. The contributions of psychoanalysis are usually traced back to Freud's[23] use of brief treatment and his prediction, in 1919,[22] that new techniques modifying psychoanalysis would be available when the poor man, as well as the rich, would receive help for his mental suffering. The psychoanalytic contribution was further enhanced by Erikson's[20] concept of developmental crisis, with the crisis of adolescence as its prototype. Psychoanalytic concepts have made a major contribution to crisis theory as it exists today. Among components of crisis theory either derived from or significantly influenced by psychoanalytic theory is that of an equilibrium involving various forces and maintained by homeostatic processes. This concept is derived from that of the dynamic point of view in psychoanalysis, which is one of its four major viewpoints.* Also derived from psychoanalytic theory is the concept of coping, at least insofar as it reflects defense mechanisms. A comprehensive discussion of the relation of crisis theory to psychoanalysis is beyond the scope of this chapter.

Social work and sociology contributed some of the concepts relating to crisis as an important response to changes in the social orbit, that is, family, friends, work, religion, and so on. The concept of social role,[35] which is sometimes used in crisis theory, also comes from sociology. Social role relates to society's expectation that an individual carries out roles in relation to a social group, such as the family, work, or religion. When there is a sudden or major change involving one of these roles, a crisis may ensue. For example, the death of a spouse, in addition to its psychological meaning, also means the loss of the social role of spouse and a need to learn a new social role, that of widow or widower.

Some of the contributions of social work include the setting of limited goals related to enhancing adaptive abilities in dealing with specific life problems. The worker elicits the cooperation of the conscious ego in focusing on certain circumscribed issues, including those of role dysfunction. The importance of precipitating events is recognized. Character

change, though it may occur, is not the caseworker's main goal. Support is offered for those defenses that are used adaptively.

Some contributions have also come from psychology. The focus on individual strengths and growth potential in Rogerian counseling psychology[60] is similar to the emphasis on the opportunity for growth afforded by crisis. There are some similarities but also significant differences between the brief treatment approach of crisis intervention and the brief treatment approach of behavior therapy.[68]

One of the major original contributions to crisis theory is the work done by Lindemann[48] on grief reactions, first published in 1944. Lindemann found that there were distinguishable patterns of normal grief different from maladaptive responses to bereavement and that the latter could lead to long-term disturbances and in some cases to psychiatric illness. He noted that the first six weeks after the bereavement were crucial in determining whether normal grief or a more maladaptive resolution was likely to occur. Crisis theory was subsequently greatly advanced by the work of Lindemann and Caplan at the Wellesley Human Relations Service, established during 1948, and by their work at Harvard University. Many of the formulations in this discussion derive from the writings of Gerald Caplan.[11-13]

Major Principles

In the following, crisis theory will be defined as relating to individuals mainly; some concepts of crisis theory also apply to families and small and large groups.

The special contributions of crisis theory can be summarized by three major principles. (1) Crisis theory involves a high degree of attention to the phenomenon of psychological crisis, including its etiology, course, and outcome, and it involves a correspondingly intentional relative neglect of other psychological processes. Conventional psychiatric theory, on the other hand, emphasizes life-long psychological phenomena and may further selectively emphasize the phenomena of early childhood. Using the analogy of a microscopic examina-

---

* The others are genetic, economic, and structural.

tion of a given slide, most psychiatric theories use high magnification of the childhood period; crisis intervention uses high magnification of the phenomena of the current crisis. So conceptualized, crisis theory has no conflict with other approaches; rather it constitutes a selective emphasis on phenomena heretofore neglected. (2) Crisis theory emphasizes the potential of crisis not only for pathology but also for growth and development. This concept, early proposed by Erikson,[20] looks at crisis as both a danger and an opportunity. It is a danger because existing coping mechanisms are inadequate to deal with the current problem; it is an opportunity because new coping mechanisms may develop that can be used in both the present and future crises.* (3) Crisis theory, to a greater extent than most psychiatric theories, views men in the ecological perspective of himself in his human and natural environment. It is concerned with what goes on in the world around us, as well as within ourselves, and it conceptualizes the effects, for better or worse, of the interaction between these inner and outer worlds.

Crisis Phenomena

Crisis is described by Caplan as "an upset in a steady state."[57] When an individual is not in crisis, an equilibrium exists that is maintained with minimal awareness by the use of habitual problem-solving (or coping) mechanisms. Certain events may pose an actual or potential threat to fundamental need satisfactions and thus upset the equilibrium.† Events that threaten these needed satisfactions are defined as emotional hazards or, simply, hazards. They may relate to changes in the physical surroundings, social sphere, or biological function of an individual.

Whether or not a given event constitutes a

hazard depends both on the event and on its meaning to the individual. Some events are uniformly hazardous, such as bereavement. Others, such as marriage or promotion, are hazardous to persons whose previously learned coping mechanisms are not adequate to meet the tasks involved in the new situation. Strickler and LaSor[64] distinguished between the precipitating event, its emotional meaning, and the specific loss it threatens or implies.

A significant emotional hazard can trigger a crisis that, as Caplan defined it,[11] "Is provoked when a person faces an obstacle to important life goals that is for a time insurmountable through the utilization of customary methods of problem-solving. A period of disorganization ensues, a period of upset, during which many different abortive attempts at solution are made. Eventually some kind of adaptation is achieved, which may or may not be in the best interests of that person or his fellows."

Caplan[12] described four stages of crisis: (1) an initial rise in tension calling forth habitual problem-solving responses; (2) a further rise in tension and a condition of ineffectiveness; (3) a still further rise in tension accompanied by mobilization of external and internal resources; and (4) if all fails, a last stage of a major breaking point with disorganization of the personality. The latter stages are characterized by mounting anxiety and depression and by a sense of helplessness (being trapped) and hopelessness. They also involve varying degrees of regression of ego functions to more primitive levels than existed during more stable periods. This regression is reversible once the crisis is resolved. At any stage, the crisis can end if the hazard disappears or if a solution is found involving different ways to obtain the need satisfactions whose loss is threatened or, if this is not possible, if the loss is recognized and accepted. Most authors agree that the acute stage of crisis lasts no longer than four to six weeks after onset.

As already noted, one of the key points in crisis theory is that there is a range of possible outcomes in relation to adaptiveness. A diagram adapted from Hill[27] (see Figure 55–1)

---

* As Nietzsche said, "What does not kill you will make you stronger," or in Benjamin Franklin's words, "Crosses and losses make us stronger and wiser."

† Caplan[12, p. 32] stated that lists of needs are usually somewhat arbitrary. He proposed as "a useful working list" of needs one that would take into account three main areas: needs for exchange of love and affection, needs for limitation and control, and needs for participation in joint activity.

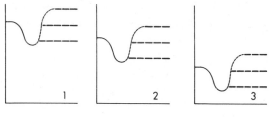

FIGURE 55–1.

helps illustrate this point. The vertical axes illustrate degree of adaptiveness of outcome; the horizontal axes represent time. Regardless of the level of adaptiveness of initial functioning, considerable variation in the end position of the adaptiveness scale exists.

Factors affecting crisis outcome include social and cultural prescriptions of behavior; influence of family and friends; influence of community caretakers, such as physicians and clergymen; and, of course, the effect of crisis intervention programs.

General criteria for adaptive outcomes of crisis have rarely been reported, though they have been described for particular crises, such as that of premature birth.[38] One important aspect of maladaptive outcome has received deserved attention: the role of crisis in psychiatric illness. Caplan[12, p. 35] pointed out that while crisis is not pathological in itself, it may constitute a turning point in the history of psychiatric patients. Confirming this view, Harris,[26] Kalis,[37] and Freeman[21] found that precipitating events were important factors in bringing people to seek outpatient treatment and Adamson and Schmale[1] found recent important losses in forty-five out of fifty admissions to an acute psychiatric service. The events precipitating the losses or threats of losses ranged from doctor's departure to broken romance to hysterectomy to sister's marriage.

In addition to psychiatric illness, maladaptive outcome of crisis at least as often, I believe, results in the deterioration of interpersonal relations. The ego regression characteristics of crisis result in increased use of the primitive mechanisms of projection, introjection, and denial. Hostility in the self is projected onto others and expressed in suspicious and hostile behavior. This behavior provokes at least partly realistic hostility from others. These others, perceived as hostile, both realistically and due to projection, are then introjected, resulting in further lowering of already low self-esteem. The low self-esteem is intolerable and leads to further projection. This vicious cycle may continue to suicide, psychosis, or the deterioration or dissolution of relationship. On the other hand, adaptive resolution results in a corresponding benign cycle, consisting of projection of one's own positive feelings of mastery and self-esteem, resulting in positive feedback and introjection of the positively viewed others. In practice, the outcome of any given crisis may include both positive and negative aspects. Deterioration or growth of long-term relationships may be characterized by repeated crises with varying outcomes, determined by whether positive or negative outcomes predominated the various crises that occurred during the course of that relationship.

Before leaving the subject of crisis theory, reference should be made to a volume edited by Parad,[53] containing many contributions to the subject, and to a summary article by Darbonne.[19]

(Crisis Intervention Techniques

We have discussed in the above section how crisis may, on the one hand, precipitate new or exacerbated psychiatric illness and deterioration of relationships, and how, on the other hand, it may result in increased effectiveness of functioning. These considerations make it clear that crisis intervention techniques have an important role to play. This section will describe crisis intervention techniques used by mental health professionals and based in significant part on crisis theory. This definition does not include two important areas: the first relates to techniques based on other theoretical frameworks; the second deals with techniques that in whole or significant part are used by non-mental health professionals. I have elsewhere[34] referred to and discussed some techniques in this last group.

Who is the person in crisis who should be treated? Considerable difficulty can be avoided by assuming that the person in crisis is the person who phones or comes for help, regardless of who is designated by that person as having the problem. Thus the person who calls or comes should be involved whenever possible; a tactful approach that does not imply that anyone is sick is necessary to involve someone who does not overtly seek help. A related recommendation is to see all people who come together, at least initially, since they are often involved in a common crisis.

Some activities carried out in crisis intervention programs and not specifically related to crisis intervention include the assessment of indications for hospitalization. These are usually limited to life-threatening behavior, since avoidance of hospitalization is an important goal.* Psychiatric diagnosis is necessary to the extent of ruling out organic factors and noting the nature and intensity of symptoms and of determining the general diagnostic category. Adjunctive drug treatment is used for the management of psychotic symptoms, severe depression, and overwhelming anxiety, with the clear understanding that it is not the main modality.

The remainder of this section deals with the specifics of crisis intervention techniques.

Principles

The principles and goals of crisis intervention parallel the three principles of crisis theory discussed above. The first principle of crisis theory is that which involves a high degree of attention to the phenomena of the current crisis, with a relatively intentional neglect of life-long psychological phenomena. Crisis intervention correspondingly selectively emphasizes the goal of achieving optimal crisis resolution. Chronic problems are deliberately disregarded during crisis intervention, sometimes a difficult task for the mental health professional, who feels he must cure everyone.

* Suicide prevention is an important part of crisis intervention. It will not be discussed in this chapter, except to say that the methods of crisis intervention described here may be very effective with suicidal persons.

The second principle is that crisis represents a danger as well as an opportunity. Crisis intervention aims at arresting and reversing ego regression and thus averting the danger of new or exacerbated psychiatric illness and/or deterioration of relationships. It seeks to return the individual to at least the precrisis level of functioning, and hopefully to a better one.

The third principle relates to the ecological perspective of man in his world. Crisis intervention aims at improving the relationship of the individual with the world in which he lives by helping him take appropriate action in solving specific problems.

The above conceptualization and the description of individual crisis intervention that follows is based on the application of crisis theory to the treatment program developed at the Benjamin Rush centers.

Individual Crisis Intervention

Some of the features of individual crisis intervention also apply to family and group crisis intervention methods, which are discussed below. The first step of the intervention is to identify the event that has disturbed the previously existing equilibrium. Sometimes the event is obvious, such as a separation or bereavement. Somewhat more often the person presents with the feelings of upset, helplessness, and hopelessness characteristic of crisis, but without identifying any important change in his life. In that case, the first task of the intervenor is to identify the event that has upset the equilibrium. With a diligent search it is almost always possible to find such an event within two weeks prior to the application for help. We find that unless a person's level of tension has risen to the point where he seeks help within two weeks after a given event, it is not likely that he will do so. Once this event is found it becomes the central point of the formulation of the crisis. Events before and after the key events are investigated and integrated into the overall formulation insofar as they are relevant to the key, or precipitating, event.

The search for the precipitating event is

veritable detective work. The intervenor is guided by a knowledge of the events that are generally hazardous for anyone. The most serious hazard overall is probably the loss of a spouse by death, separation, or divorce. Other generally hazardous events include death of a family member other than the spouse; jail terms for family members; serious physical illness; lengthy unemployment or retirement.* In addition to knowing which hazards are important regardless of age and sex, the intervenor should also know which areas are most important in producing hazards at different ages and for either sex. For example, emancipation of young adults from parents is an important source of hazard for all concerned; dating, engagement, marriage, and child-bearing are sources of hazards for young adults; successes and failures in work life may be sources of hazards at any age for men, and increasingly for women; hazards involving illness, bereavement, and aging occur in later life.

In addition to identifying the actual event, the intervenor must understand its emotional meaning in order to determine whether it constitutes a hazard. A bereavement, for example, may have a number of meanings, including the loss of emotional support, financial support, sexual satisfaction, or social role of spouse. The birth of a child may constitute a hazard for a man because he fears loss of dependent gratification from his wife and/or because he fears to compete with his own father and/or because he wanted a child of a different sex. In determining the meaning of a precipitating event, the intervenor looks for real or symbolic relationships with significant events in the past. For example, the loss of children by marriage may be especially difficult for persons who have never reconciled themselves to the loss of their parents.

Next, the intervenor formulates the dynamics of the current crisis. In doing so he will use the theoretical framework with which he is familiar. If he is psychoanalytically trained or oriented,[30] the formulation will include reference to unconscious instinctual and superego

forces, as well as to ego functions and to reality.† If the intervenor is primarily oriented to reality considerations, as in the case of some (though not all) social workers, most of the emphasis will be on reality factors and on ego functions, including changes in social roles. Keep in mind that we are discussing the conceptualization in the intervenor's mind, and not necessarily what will be shared with the person in crisis. Whatever his theoretical framework, the intervenor will arrive at as clear as possible an understanding of the nature of the psychological disturbance resulting from the hazard and of the possible new equilibrium that may result. For example, a man may respond to his wife's taking a job with a crisis involving feelings of pathological jealousy. The intervenor may recognize an upsurge of homosexual impulses. He will also recognize, on the ego level, a felt threat to the masculine role of provider. He may decide that the outcome may range from development of a psychosis to the taking of action that enhances the masculine self-image, such as an increase in heterosexual activity or achievement in competitive sports, or a redefinition of the relationship with the wife that results in renewed reassurance about his masculinity.

Treatment can be divided into cognitive, affective, and behavioral aspects. The cognitive aspects consist of communicating the intervenor's understanding to the person in crisis in language the latter can understand. He stays relatively close to the surface, so that the formulations can be assimilated within the available time.[33] Interpretations relating to ego functions and to reality are usually preferred; only rarely (especially with persons who have had previous treatment) can so-called deeper material be fruitfully integrated into crisis intervention. The intervenor must keep in mind that the goal of his comments is not to resolve long-standing conflicts but to help the person to understand better what his

---

* The above list is drawn from a list of hazards by Holmes and Rahe, used by Langsley et al.[44]

† The ability to understand unconscious material may be a two-edged sword in crisis intervention. It can be helpful if the intervenor can use it to improve the clarity of his perception of the crisis. It can be a hindrance if he feels impelled to use too much of what he knows as part of the intervention.

choices are now. It goes without saying that sensitivity, warmth, and empathy are necessary in crisis intervention, as in all psychotherapy.

It is not unusual for a person in crisis to react with an audible sigh of relief to the identification of the precipitating event and to a clear formulation of hazard and crisis. Dynamically, I believe this is due to an interruption of the regressive process which occurs as soon as the person in crisis recognizes a specific and therefore manageable problem in the present.

If the situation does involve a real loss, the next step consists of helping the person express appropriate affect, including grief. Other crisis-related affects, particularly anger, should also be ventilated, but care should be taken that the person deal with guilt over anger before expressing it and also that he be helped to direct his anger into appropriate, reality-oriented channels. Regressive, infantile affect should not be mobilized or encouraged.

Finally, work is done on finding new ways of coping with the changed reality situation. The intervenor rarely needs to give advice; with better cognitive understanding and with affective release, the person in crisis can mobilize his resources to find the solution best for him. Character change cannot usually be expected in crisis resolution, but some new coping can be learned, and existing coping can be modified and combined in new ways.

Coping mechanisms as usually defined include but are not limited to defense mechanisms. The classification of coping mechanisms is one of the areas in crisis intervention where much progress can still be made.* This limitation is not a grave one as far as practice is concerned, however. The intervenor conceptualizes usual coping behavior in everyday language, and in so doing makes reference to the thinking, feeling, and behavior of the person in crisis in relation to the person(s) and/or life areas involved in the crisis. A few examples derived from actual case material include coping with a difficult boss alternately

* An attempt to classify coping is currently under way as part of a research study at the Rush centers.

by submission and by rebellion; coping with the need to get enough heroin to satisfy an addiction by stealing in the company of a friend; coping with overwhelming rage by excessive drinking; coping with feelings of inadequacy by belonging to a motorcycle gang.

Having defined the significant coping mechanism, the reason why it is no longer available is determined. In the above examples, rebellion against the supervisor may have resulted in loss of a job; the friend who made the heroin addict's stealing possible was arrested; excessive drinking has led to serious physical illness; an accident made motorcycle riding impossible. The last step is the exploration of which of the available coping patterns is the most adaptive. The rebellious person may shift his rebellion to social issues and get his job back; the motorcycle rider may get recognition for artistic accomplishment, and so on. Adaptive coping also includes an acceptance of what is inevitable. Naturally, the development of new ways of coping does not occur overnight; but the outcome of the crisis will determine the direction that will be pursued.

The closing phase of crisis intervention consists of a review of gains made and of anticipatory planning in regard to the handling of future hazards. The question is then asked whether there are indications for referral to ongoing treatment. This question has intentionally been ignored until crisis resolution was complete. Now, for the first time, chronic disturbances are considered, with reference to the question whether there is need and motivation for longer-term treatment and whether appropriate treatment facilities are available. If so, referral for further treatment is made. As already mentioned, we found that some very disturbed persons either do not want further treatment or the very long-term treatment they need is not available. In such cases, the use of a crisis intervention facility when needed may be the best disposition.

The following case example illustrates individual crisis intervention; this was a case in which it took considerable work to understand the hazard. A wife complained of increased drinking by her husband. Nothing had apparently changed in the marital relationship. However, there was a shift in the wife's work situation, which had resulted in decreasing satisfactions for her there. This had caused her to put increased pressure on her husband, which in turn had increased his drinking. Intervention consisted of eliciting and then pointing out this chain of events and also of helping her recognize and express the disappointment of her job, while understanding that she was inappropriately displacing that disappointment onto her husband. The marital situation and the husband's drinking both improved after the wife—the only person seen —received crisis intervention.

Family Crisis Intervention

Emphasis on the family has been an important part of crisis intervention from its inception.[27,38,39] The most extensive report on family crisis intervention comes from the Colorado Psychiatric Hospital, as reported by Langsley and Kaplan.[42] Family treatment was used there as a successful alternative to psychiatric hospitalization. The principles of intervention included immediate aid, defining the crisis as a family problem, and focusing on the current crisis. The intervention included the identification of psychotic symptoms as an attempt to communicate and specific prescriptions for the family designed to bring about such changes of role assignments within the family as are required to restore the homeostasis disturbed by a particular event, such as the birth of a child. Tasks are assigned to the family, such as working out of dating rules for adolescents, if the adolescent's dating is part of the crisis. Home visits are frequently used, as are drugs. Occasionally, overnight hospitalization in a general hospital emergency room is employed.

Crisis intervention for this selected population of families of immediate candidates for hospitalization differs somewhat from other forms of crisis intervention. At the Rush centers, family members are automatically involved only when they present themselves on their own initiative, if the intervenor feels that the crisis involves more than one person, or because the resolution of the crisis for one person requires the cooperation of family members or may precipitate a crisis in other family members. As the above cited case shows, family problems may sometimes be treated by individual crisis intervention. When family crisis intervention is used, it is technically harder than individual crisis intervention. The hazards and coping pattern must be elicited for each family member separately and their interaction traced. The tendency to take sides in family disputes is one of the risks of family crisis intervention. Another is the tendency to become involved with chronic problems. This is a risk in individual treatment also, but it is more difficult to manage with families who wish to bring up conflicts and grievances accumulated over the years. The intervenor must sometimes forcefully bring them back to current issues.

Group Crisis Intervention

There are very few reports on the use of non-family crisis groups. Rosenberg conducted crisis groups with nursing students, as reported by Klein and Lindemann.[40] Peck and Kaplan[55] discussed crises in existing therapy groups, and Bloch[8] described an open-ended crisis group for patients in the lower socio-economic classes.

Crisis groups make up an important part of the crisis intervention at the Rush centers. Strickler and Allgeyer[63] formulated the methodology used in most cases: The hazard and crisis are assessed in an initial individual interview, and the person in crisis is then referred to a crisis group whose members explore ways in which each of them can cope with his specific problem. Crisis group attendance is limited to the same six sessions used in individual crisis intervention. Therefore, any group session has members who have progressed to varying stages of crisis resolution. The progress of older members is often very encouraging to those joining the group.

Morley and Brown[51] reviewed advantages and disadvantages of the use of crisis groups and concluded that it is highly effective with certain population groups, problems, and individuals. They described the manner in which members of a specific group help each other with such diverse problems as the arrest of one woman's children for theft, cessation of financial support of a psychotic patient by her mother, the breaking off of a relationship with a boyfriend, a bad lysergic acid "trip," and the loss of a job. Allgeyer[2] recently emphasized the unique usefulness of the crisis group for the disadvantaged.

(Social Class and Crisis Intervention

One of the goals of crisis intervention facilities is to reach population subgroups not served in traditional psychiatric outpatient clinics.[29,65] Dynamically oriented outpatient clinics particularly have not historically been responsive to the needs of the seriously disturbed, the aged, or the poor. As has been pointed out elsewhere,[29] crisis and crisis intervention represent a meeting ground on which patients and therapists from divergent cultural and social classes can and do meet. Crisis is rooted in those universally shared childhood experiences that precede the differentiation of individuals into cultural and social subgroups.

Experience has borne out the expectation that persons not characteristically referred to psychiatric clinics are indeed seen in crisis intervention facilities. Bellak and Small[6] noted that the Trouble-Shooting Clinic served a larger proportion of nonwhites than the proportion residing in the community. One of the key aspects of the walk-in clinic at the Metropolitan Hospital is their service to a deprived community.[52,66] Bloch[8] used his crisis group selectively for people from the lower socioeconomic classes. Persons from social classes 4 and 5, according to the Hollingshead and Redlich classification, represent between one-half and two-thirds of the population of the Rush centers.[32] Further,[65] the less educated as well as those over forty-five came as a result of newspaper publicity in significantly greater numbers than they did as a result of professional referral.

(Outcome Studies

There have been only a very few research studies related to outcome of crisis intervention. Langsley and Kaplan[42] reported on 150 cases treated by family crisis intervention at the family treatment unit, compared with an equal number of controls. The cases were compared in regard to whether psychiatric hospitalization occurred. Cases were randomly assigned, and there was no difference between test and control groups on fifteen population characteristics, including diagnosis and history of previous hospitalization. The results showed that none of the family treatment unit group was hospitalized for the presenting crisis. At six-months' follow up 83 percent of the experimental group still had not been admitted to a mental hospital. When subsequent hospitalization occurred it was briefer for the family treatment unit group than for controls, and there was no evidence that patients treated outside the hospital were more likely to become suicidal or homicidal or were more chronically disabled than patients treated in a hospital.

Bellak and Small[6] reported on 1,414 patients seen during a twelve-month period, of which 472 were followed up by both interview and rating scales. Seventy percent received brief psychotherapy and 8.8 percent required hospitalization. A symptom checklist showed a decrease in the mean score between just before and at the end of treatment, which was significant at the 0.001 level. The score remained unchanged at six-months' follow up.

At present a study of crisis intervention outcome is in progress at the Benjamin Rush centers.* This study will include experimental and control groups. Ratings will be made retrospectively, pretreatment, immediate posttreatment, and six-months posttreatment. Rat-

* This study is supported by a grant from the National Institute of Mental Health, No. MH 18846–01. Dr. Wilbur E. Morley is principal investigator.

ings will be done along dimensions of symptoms, affective disturbances, response to treatment, level of functioning, and coping behavior.

(Current Frontiers

Crisis intervention is now early in its second decade as a major component of the armamentarium of mental health programs. Some new areas of importance are beginning to emerge. One of these is the use of crisis intervention for alcoholics and drug abusers. Crisis intervention is not helpful in cases of the long-term drug user or alcoholic who has no acute conflicts about the use of drugs or alcohol. It appears to be highly effective if there has been a recent change in the person's life which resulted in difficulties in connection with their use. Such events include arrest and being placed on probation, "bad trips" with lysergic acid, and negative feedback from important others such as occurs when a wife or close friend seriously threatens to separate if the drinking or drug-abuse pattern continues. Crisis groups have been particularly helpful for drug abusers.

Lastly, the issue of identification of large populations at risk is important for the purpose both of preventing hazards and of implementing early intervention when such hazards do occur. Kalis[36] recently addressed herself to some of these issues. Thus crisis theory and crisis intervention are approaching the time when they must address themselves to the individual, his family, and the community and society in which he lives.

(Bibliography

1. ADAMSON, J. D., and SCHMALE, A. H. "Object Loss, Giving Up, and the Onset of Psychiatric Disease." *Psychosomatic Medicine*, 27, no. 6 (1965).

2. ALLGEYER, J. M. "The Crisis Group: Its Unique Usefulness to Divergent Racial, Cultural and Socio-Economic Groups." *International Journal of Group Psychotherapy*, 20 (1970), 2.

3. BAIN, M. D., et al. Crisis-Focused Treatment in a Child Guidance Clinic: A Preliminary Report. Paper presented to the American Orthopsychiatric Association, March 17–20, 1965. (Abstract in *American Journal of Orthopsychiatry*, 35 [1965], 2.)

4. BARNHART, C. L., ed. *The American College Dictionary*. New York: Random House, 1967.

5. BELLAK, L. "A General Hospital as a Focus of Community Psychiatry." *Journal of the American Medical Association*, 174 (1960), 2214–2217.

6. ———, and SMALL, L. *Emergency Psychotherapy and Brief Psychotherapy*. New York: Grune & Stratton, 1965.

7. BLANE, H. T., et al. "Acute Psychiatric Services in the Current Hospital: II. Current Status of Emergency Services." *American Journal of Psychiatry*, 124 (1967), 4.

8. BLOCH, H. S. "An Open-Ended Crisis-Oriented Group for the Poor Who Are Sick." *Archives of General Psychiatry*, 18 (1968).

9. BLOOM, B. L. "Definitional Aspects of the Crisis Concept." *Journal of Consulting Psychology*, 27, no. 6 (1963), 498–502.

10. BRAGG, R. L., et al. Tenth Anniversary Report of the Wellesley Human Relations Service, Inc., 1948–1958. Unpublished manuscript, 1958.

11. CAPLAN, G. *An Approach to Community Mental Health*. New York: Grune & Stratton, 1961.

12. ———. *Principles of Preventive Psychiatry*. New York: Basic Books, 1964.

13. ———, ed. *Prevention of Mental Disorders in Children*. New York: Basic Books, 1961.

14. CHAFETZ, M. E. "The Effect of an Emergency Service on Motivation for Psychiatric Treatment." *Journal of Nervous and Mental Diseases*, 140 (1965), 6.

15. COLEMAN, J. B., and ERRARA, P. "The General Hospital Emergency Room and Its Psychiatric Problems." *American Journal of Public Health*, 53 (1963), 1294–1301.

16. COLEMAN, M. D. "Problems in an Emergency Psychiatric Clinic." *Mental Hospitals*, May 1960, pp. 26–27.

17. ———, and ROSENBAUM, M. "The Psychiatric Walk-in Clinic." *Israel Annals of Psychiatry and Related Disciplines*, 1 (1963), 1.

18. ———, and ZWERLING, I. "The Psychiatric Emergency Clinic: A Flexible Way of Meeting Community Mental Health

Needs." *American Journal of Psychiatry*, 115, no. 11 (1959), 980–984.

19. DARBONNE, A. "Crisis: A Review of Theory, Practice, and Research." *Psychotherapy: Theory, Research and Practice*, 4, no. 2 (1967), 49–56.

20. ERIKSON, E. H. "Identity and the Life Cycle." *Psychological Issues*, 1 (1959), 1.

21. FREEMAN, E. H., et al. "Assessing Patient Characteristics from Psychotherapy Interviews." *Journal of Projective Techniques*, 28, no. 4 (1964), 413–424.

22. FREUD, S. "An Infantile Neurosis and Other Works." *Standard Edition*. Vol. 17. London: Hogarth, 1955.

23. ———, and BREUER, J. "Studies on Hysteria." *Standard Edition*. Vol. 2. London: Hogarth, 1955.

24. GELB, L., and ULLMAN, M. "Instant Psychotherapy" in an Outpatient Psychiatric Clinic: Philosophy and Practice. Paper presented to the American Psychiatric Association, Atlantic City, N.J., May 13, 1966.

25. HANKOFF, L. D., and WALTZER, M. D. An Evaluation of Emergency Psychiatric Treatment. Paper presented to the American Psychiatric Association, New York, N.Y., May 6, 1965.

26. HARRIS, M. R., et al. "Precipitating Stress: An Approach to Brief Therapy." *American Journal of Psychotherapy*, 17, no. 3 (1963), 465–471.

27. HILL, R. "Generic Features of Families Under Stress." *Social Casework*, 39, nos. 2 & 3 (1958).

28. HOLLINGSHEAD, A. B., and REDLICH, F. C. *Social Class and Mental Illness: A Community Study*. New York: Wiley, 1958.

29. JACOBSON, G. F. "Crisis Theory and Treatment Strategy: Some Sociocultural and Psychodynamic Considerations." *Journal of Nervous and Mental Disease*, 141 (1965), 2.

30. ———. "Some Psychoanalytic Considerations Regarding Crisis Therapy." *Psychoanalytic Review*, 54 (1967), 4.

31. ———. "Crisis Intervention from the Viewpoint of the Mental Health Professional." *Pastoral Psychology*, April 1970.

32. ———, et al. Operating Statistics and Characteristics of Patients, January 1, 1962–June 30, 1964. Benjamin Rush Center for Problems of Living, 1964.

33. ———, et al. "The Scope and Practice of an Early-Access Brief Treatment Psychiatric Center." *American Journal of Psychiatry*, 121 (1965), 12.

34. ———, et al. "Generic and Individual Approaches to Crisis Intervention." *American Journal of Public Health*, 58 (1968), 2.

35. JOHNSON, H. M. *Sociology: A Systematic Introduction*. New York: Harcourt, Brace, 1960.

36. KALIS, B. L. "Crisis Theory: Its Relevance for Community Psychology and Directions for Development." In D. Adelson and B. L. Kalis, eds. *Community Psychology and Mental Health: Perspectives and Challenges*. Scranton, Pa.: Chandler, 1970.

37. ———, et al. "Precipitating Stress as a Focus in Psychotherapy." *Archives of General Psychiatry*, 5 (1961), 219–226.

38. KAPLAN, D. "Study and Treatment of an Acute Emotional Disorder." *American Journal of Orthopsychiatry*, 35, no. 1 (1965), 69–77.

39. ———, and MASON, E. A. "Maternal Reactions to Premature Birth Viewed as an Acute Emotional Disorder." In H. J. Parad, ed., *Crisis Intervention: Selected Readings*. New York: Family Service Association of America, 1965. Pp. 118–128.

40. KLEIN, D. C., and LINDEMANN, E. "Preventive Intervention in Individual and Family Crisis Situations." In G. Caplan, ed., *Prevention of Mental Disorders in Children*. New York: Basic Books, 1961. Pp. 283–306.

41. ———, and ROSS, A. "Kindergarten Entry: A Study of Role Transition." In H. J. Parad, ed., *Crisis Intervention: Selected Readings*. New York: Family Service Association of America, 1965.

42. LANGSLEY, D. G., and KAPLAN, D. *The Treatment of Families in Crisis*. New York: Grune & Stratton, 1968.

43. ———, et al. "Family Crisis Therapy—Results and Implications." *Family Process*, 7 (1968), 2.

44. ———, et al. "Family Crises in Schizophrenics and Other Mental Patients." *Journal of Nervous and Mental Disease*, 149 (1969), 3.

45. ———, et al. "Followup Evaluation of Family Crisis Therapy." *American Journal of Orthopsychiatry*, 39 (1969), 5.

46. LEVY, R. A. "A Crisis-Oriented Community Clinic." *Mental Hospitals*, December 1965.

47. ———. A Practical Approach to Community

Psychiatry in a Remote City. N.d. (Described in L. Small, *The Briefer Psychotherapies*. New York: Brunner/Mazel, 1971.)

48. LINDEMANN, E. "Symptomatology and Management of Acute Grief." *American Journal of Psychiatry*, 101 (1944).

49. MORLEY, W. E. "Treatment of the Patient in Crisis." *Western Medicine*, 77, no. 3 (1965), 77–86.

50. ———. "Theory of Crisis Intervention." *Pastoral Psychology*, April 1970.

51. ———, and BROWN, V. B. "The Crisis-Intervention Group: A Natural Mating or a Marriage of Convenience?" *Psychotherapy: Theory, Research and Practice*, 6 (1969), 1.

52. NORMAND, W., et al. "Acceptance of a Psychiatric Walk-In Clinic in a Deprived Community." *American Journal of Psychiatry*, 120 (1963), 533.

53. PARAD, H. J., ed. *Crisis Intervention: Selected Readings*. New York: Family Service Association of America, 1965.

54. ———, and PARAD, L. "A Study of Crisis-Oriented Planned Short-Term Treatment: Parts I and II." *Social Casework*, 49 (1968).

55. PECK, H., and KAPLAN, S. "Crisis Theory and Therapeutic Change in Small Groups: Some Implications for Community Mental Health Programs." *International Journal of Group Psychotherapy*, 16 (1966), 2.

56. RAPHLING, D. L., and LION, J. "Patients with Repeated Admissions to a Psychiatric Emergency Service." *Community Mental Health Journal*, 6, no. 4 (1970), 313–318.

57. RAPOPORT, L. "The State of Crisis: Some Theoretical Considerations." *Social Science Review*, 36 (1962), 2.

58. RAPOPORT, R., and RAPOPORT, R. N. "New Light on the Honeymoon." *Human Relations*, 17, no. 1 (1964), 33–56.

59. RAPOPORT, R. N. "Transition from Engagement to Marriage." *Acta Sociologica*, 8, nos. 1 & 2 (1964).

60. ROGERS, C. R. *Client-Centered Therapy*. Boston: Houghton Mifflin, 1951.

61. SMALL, L. *The Briefer Psychotherapies*. New York: Brunner/Mazel, 1971.

62. STRICKLER, M. "Applying Crisis Theory in a Community Clinic." *Social Casework*, March 1965.

63. ———, and ALLGEYER, J. "The Crisis Group: A New Application of Crisis Theory." *Social Work*, 12 (1967), 3.

64. ———, and LaSOR, B. "The Concept of Loss in Crisis Intervention." *Mental Hygiene*, 54, no. 2 (1970), 301–305.

65. ———, et al. "The Community-Based Walk-In Center: A New Resource for Groups Underrepresented in Outpatient Treatment Facilities." *American Journal of Public Health*, 55 (1965), 3.

66. TANNENBAUM, G. "The Walk-in Clinic." In S. Arieti, ed., *American Handbook of Psychiatry*. Vol. III. New York: Basic Books, 1966.

67. WALTZER, H., et al. "Emergency Psychiatric Treatment in a Receiving Hospital." *Mental Hospitals* (1963), 595–597.

68. WOLPE, J., and LAZARUS, A. A. *Behavior Therapy Techniques*. Oxford: Pergamon Press, 1966.

CHAPTER 56

THE PERFORMANCE OF PARAPROFESSIONALS IN MENTAL HEALTH FIELDS

Alan Gartner and Frank Riessman

OUR MAJOR CONCERN in this chapter is to document the role of paraprofessionals* in promoting service for clients in the mental health and psychiatric fields; that is, we are mainly interested in the practice of the paraprofessional as it relates to the functioning of the patient or consumer.† Although he plays other roles (for example,

* Many terms have been used for the noncredentialed worker: "nonprofessional," "subprofessional," "new professional," "paraprofessional," "auxiliary," "aide," "allied worker," "community professional," "community worker," "new careerist," and so on. Recently, the term "paraprofessional" seems to be most widely accepted and is the one we shall use, although many of the workers themselves are beginning to prefer "new professional."[2]

† There is a huge and rapidly growing literature concerning paraprofessional programs in general, as well as mental health programs in particular. Illustrative is the recent publication of a bibliography on paraprofessional programs, which contains well over a thousand items.[26]

social change agent), our focus is on his input to service delivery. As we shall see, a number of major studies provide considerable evidence that the paraprofessional does indeed play a role in contributing to improved mental health of clients and patients both in hospitals and community settings.

Unlike public schools, where paraprofessionals are relatively new (although a significant minority of the staff), in the mental health programs they are of long standing and comprise a large majority of the employees.

Consideration of the role of paraprofessionals in mental health must begin first with an identification of just who it is one is discussing. If one defines as professionals those holding postbaccalaureate professional degrees and excludes those engaged in only maintenance and housekeeping activities, one can suggest three types of paraprofessionals.

1. The "old" hospital-based worker is typified by the psychiatric aide working in
a hospital setting, engaged in supportive
therapeutic work. He usually does not
have a college degree and is not indigenous to the community in which he is
working, though he generally comes
from a low-income background and is
frequently black or Puerto Rican.

2. The new middle-class paraprofessional
is typically a woman with a degree who
has received special training in mental
health skills and is generally engaged in
substantive therapeutic work. Margaret
Rioch's[31] program is perhaps best known
in this area. The women she trained were
middle class, mainly white, and held previous college degrees.

3. The indigenous paraprofessional is recruited from the community where he
works. He is usually employed, although
not exclusively, in mental health centers,
does not hold a college degree, and
is engaged in therapeutically relevant
work.

The first type, the old paraprofessional, is,
of course, the most common and the heart of
the staff of mental health hospital facilities.
The new paraprofessional is seen in the various efforts of the late 1950s and 1960s to meet
professional manpower shortages, while the
indigenous paraprofessional is largely the
child of the antipoverty and community mental health efforts. It is the last two to which we
will give special attention.

([The Old Paraprofessional

A highly significant well-controlled experiment conducted by Ellsworth[8] indicates that
the old type of paraprofessional could play a
powerful role in the improved treatment outcome for hospitalized male schizophrenics. "A
demonstration project in which the focus on
treatment was the development of the psychiatric aide as the rehabilitation agent" was
conducted at the Fort Meade, South Dakota,

Veterans Administration Hospital. Fort
Meade has a 600-bed hospital; for the purposes of the demonstration, patients of one
building were used as an experimental group
(N=122) and patients of two other buildings
were used as a control group (N=214). For
patients in both groups, the program was similar in use of medication, use of activity group
therapy, the process of reaching decisions regarding discharge, assignment of new admissions, and patient characteristics.[8, p. 87]

The demonstration program was designed
to raise the level of aide-patient interaction.
To do this effectively, the aide's role in the
hospital had to be altered, particularly as it
related to participation in decision-making. It
was found[8, p. 162] that a higher percentage of
experimental group patients were released to
the community during the thirty-month demonstration period, and a lower percentage of
them had to return to the hospital.

Postdischarge outcomes were based on six
indices: (1) level of behavioral adjustment;
(2) median days subsequently hospitalized;
(3) released versus not released; (4) percentage achieving twelve consecutive months in
the community; (5) good social adjustment;
and (6) discharge status six years later.

Both experimental and control groups were
divided into three subgroups, each based on
degree of schizophrenia. There were twenty-
one pairs of comparisons, and the experimental group did better on all twenty-one, in
thirteen of them at a substantial level of significance.[8, p. 161] "Although the chronically hospitalized patients group profited most by the
approach used in the experimental program,
the acute group of patients also responded
significantly.[8, p. 164]

Key factors in the aides' role seemed to be
the increased interaction with patients and
their new active participation in decisions regarding patients. The two factors were inter-
connected "as the active involvement of the
aide in the decision-making process was found
to be a necessary condition in sustaining aide-
patient interaction.[8, p. 165]

Ellsworth[8, p. 165] concluded: "Our project
has shown clearly that the role of a non-
professionally trained person can be

modified extensively in a psychiatric rehabilitation setting. When this modification takes the form of actively involving the nonprofessional in all phases of patient rehabilitation the treatment outcome for hospitalized male schizophrenics is highly significant."

⟪ The New Paraprofessional

Perhaps best known in this area is the early work of Margaret Rioch[31] and the studies of Robert R. Carkhuff[3] and Charles B. Truax.[33] These investigators, as well as a number of others reported in this section, provide evidence regarding the effectiveness of paraprofessionals as treatment agents.

In 1960, the adult psychiatry branch of the National Institute of Mental Health funded Rioch's Mental Health Counselors program.[31, pp. 683–684] It was designed to fill the need for staff to provide low-cost psychotherapy and at the same time to provide useful work for women with grown children. The value of these women was seen in their successful child-rearing experience and maturity. There were eight women chosen from eighty applications. Their median age was forty-two; seven were married, and one was widowed; they had an average of 2.4 children. All were college graduates, and three had postbaccalaureate degrees; six had held professional jobs; four had been psychoanalyzed. All their husbands held executive or professional positions. Their upper-class status is further shown by their ability to participate in a two-year training program without pay and with no guarantee of a job at the end of the program. All eight women completed the four semesters of training, which emphasized professional breadth, not technician specificity. It was limited to psychotherapy and emphasized on-the-job training. Most of the patients of the trainees were adolescents.

Blind evaluations were made by outside experts of trainees' taped interviews with clients, and trainees were not identified as such. On a scale from 1 (poor) to 5 (excellent), the rating of the interviews on eight factors ranged from 2.7 (beginning of interview) to 4.2 (professional attitude), with an overall global impression mean score of 3.4.[31] Evaluation of patient progress (N=49) showed that none changed for the worse, 19 percent showed no change; and 61 percent showed some change. Of these, 35 percent showed slight improvement, 20 percent showed moderate improvement, and 6 percent showed marked improvement.[31, p. 368] As to the counselors' faults, the director reported "they pleasantly reassure, protect and sympathize when it would be better to question more deeply and seriously. A second fault is a tendency to try to deal on a surface, common sense level with problems that are soluble only by eliciting unconscious conflicts."[32]

Similar to the Mental Health Counselors program, in terms of the background of the women trained as counselors, the Child Development Counselors program at the Washington, D.C. Children's Hospital differed from Rioch's program in that the counselors worked with patients of a different class background.[7] A similar cross-class effort was involved in the Albert Einstein College of Medicine mental health rehabilitation workers project, which also used mature women,[6] as did a Rochester, N.Y., program where housewives worked with emotionally disturbed young school children.[39] The many programs using college students as therapeutic agents crossed both class and age lines.[5,18,19,24,30] Still other programs used peers as therapeutic agents.[14]

In Australia, paraprofessional part-time volunteers (mature adults, successfully married) provided marriage counseling service. Some 270 persons served approximately 15,000 persons per year. The volunteers received weekly training for about a year and a half, primarily in a nondirective client-centered Rogerian approach. In about 15 percent of the cases, the problem was solved, and in another 35 percent of the cases marital relations were noticeably improved, according to Harvey.[17]

Aides trained in Rogerian play therapy worked with six Head Start children diagnosed by a psychologist as in need of psychotherapy, owing to uncontrollable, withdrawn, and inhibited behavior. "All six children treated by the aide showed signs of improvement during the treatment period," as reported by Androvic and Guerney.[1]

Similar to these efforts was the work of the Arkansas Rehabilitation Research and Training Center led by Charles Truax.[33] Here the effort has been to identify those characteristics that make for more effective counseling and for the use of lay counselors. Two major experiments are of interest. The first compared the work of lay therapists, clinical psychology graduate students, and experienced therapists.[33, p. 10] It involved 150 chronic hospitalized patients. "The variety of current diagnoses included manic depressive reactions, psychotic depressive reactions, and schizophrenic. . . ."[33, p. 9] Patients were randomly assigned to lay persons who had 100 hours of training, clinical psychology graduate students, and experienced counselors. "The lay mental health counselors were able to provide a level of therapeutic conditions only slightly below that of the experienced therapists and considerably above that of graduate student trainees."[33, p. 12]

Earlier work of the Arkansas group isolated three factors as critical to therapist's effect on patient: his communicating a high level of (1) accurate empathy, (2) nonpossessive warmth, and (3) genuineness to the patients. There were no significant differences between the three groups of counselors as related to communicating accurate empathy or nonpossessive warmth. On the third factor, communicating genuineness to the patient, the experienced therapists showed significantly higher performance.

Summarizing the effect on patients of the work of the lay therapists, Truax, the project director, wrote,[34] "Research evaluation indicated highly significant patient outcomes in *overall improvement, improvement in interpersonal relations, improvement in self-care, and self-concern, and improvement in emotional disturbance.*"[69]

The second study conducted at the Arkansas center addressed more closely the effect of paraprofessional counselors. Some 400 patients at the Hot Springs Rehabilitation Center, a large residential center, were randomly assigned in three different groups: (1) to experienced professional (masters degree) counselors; (2) to experienced counselors assisted by an aide under maximum supervision; and (3) to aides (former secretaries with little if any college but 100 hours of training) working alone under supervision. Within each of the three patterns, caseload was varied at either thirty or sixty; thus, there was a 3×2 experimental design. Two-thirds of the patients were male; two-thirds, white; all had personality or behavioral problems, and a sizable number had speech and hearing defects or were mentally retarded.[35, p. 333]

Performance under the three patterns of staffing was based on client work quantity, cooperativeness, work attitude, quality of work, dependability, ability to learn, and overall progress. On all measures, "The best results were obtained by the aides working alone under the daily supervision of professional counselors. The professional counselors working alone had the second best results, while the counselor plus the aide had the poorest effects upon clients."[35, p. 334]

The greater positive effects on client rehabilitation by the aides with their own caseload appeared to be "due both to the somewhat higher levels of warmth and empathy communicated to the clients by the aides and the greater motivation and enthusiasm of the aides."*[35] Carrying their conclusions beyond this project, the authors stated[36, p. 1014] that "The findings presented here are consistent with a growing body of research which indicates that the effectiveness of counseling and psychotherapy, as measured by constructive changes in client functioning, is largely independent of the counselor's level of training and theoretical orientation."

---

* The aides spent more time with clients, especially when they had high caseloads. The professionals, when they had high caseloads, spent less time with clients. The aides, in effect, appeared to feel that it was necessary to work hard to get to all the cases, while the professionals seemed to feel that with so many clients to see, it was impossible to get to all. However, "Overall, neither the total number of minutes spent in contact with individual clients nor the frequency of client contacts was related to the client's vocational progress."[34, p. 28]

Summarizing his review of many of the programs described above, Garfield[12] concluded, "The implication of all the programs . . . is that counselors can be trained in a clinical setting, in a reasonably short time, to perform a variety of functions."

The broadest examination of the work of paraprofessionals in mental health was Sobey's[32] study of over 10,000 paraprofessionals in 185 National Institute of Mental Health (NIMH) sponsored programs. As the data were presented in gross categories, one cannot, for the most part, distinguish the particular type of paraprofessional being employed, although it would seem that the category includes persons from all three of the groups we have delineated above—the old paraprofessional, the new middle-class paraprofessional, and the indigenous paraprofessional.

The major finding[32, pp. 155-156] related to the reason for the use of paraprofessionals is that

Nonprofessionals are utilized not simply because professional manpower is unavailable but rather to provide new services in innovative ways. Nonprofessionals are providing such therapeutic functions as individual counseling, activity group therapy, milieu therapy; they are doing case finding; they are playing screening roles of nonclerical nature; they are helping people to adjust to community life; they are providing special skills such as tutoring; they are promoting client self-help through involving clients in helping others having similar problems.

The basis for the use of paraprofessionals[32, p. 154] is illustrated in Table 56–1 by the responses of project directors to the question of whether, given a choice of hiring pro-

fessionals, project directors would prefer to utilize paraprofessionals for those functions that professionals had previously performed. In short, 53 percent preferred to use paraprofessionals over professionals for tasks previously performed by professionals, or to put it another way, only 32 percent preferred to use professionals.

As could be anticipated from the above, "overwhelmingly the project directors felt that the service performed by nonprofessionals justified the expense of training, supervision and general agency overhead."[32, p. 159] The directors saw paraprofessionals contributing across a broad spectrum of program activities including servicing more people, offering new services, and providing the project staff with new viewpoints in regard to the project population.[32, p. 161] Table 56–2 displays the directors' sense of these contributions.

The response to the last item in Table 56–2, relating to new viewpoints, suggests that a significant number of the paraprofessionals were indigenous workers. Also, in sixty-nine projects, the directors reported expanding the professional's understanding of the client group through association with the paraprofessionals.[62] The same thrust is to be seen in the comment that "the introduction of nonprofessionals was perceived as infusing the projects with a new vitality, and forcing a self-evaluation which although painful, led to beneficial changes for the field of mental health."[32, p. 175] The work style and personal attributes of the paraprofessionals were important, as they brought,

a change in atmosphere within the agency, and more lively and vital relationships among staff and

TABLE 56–1.   Utilization Preference in NIMH-Funded Projects: Professionals or Nonprofessionals

UTILIZATION PREFERENCE	NUMBER OF PROJECTS RESPONDING
Would clearly utilize professional staff	17
Would probably utilize professional staff	38
Uncertain	29
Would probably not utilize professional staff	36
Would clearly not utilize professional staff	55

TABLE 56–2. **Contributions by Nonprofessionals to Improvements in Service**

| IMPROVEMENTS IN SERVICE | Projects Reporting Degree of Nonprofessional Contribution (percentages) | | | |
	SUBSTANTIAL	MODERATE	SLIGHT OR NOT AT ALL	TOTAL NUMBER OF PROJECT RESPONSES
Service initiated/ completed faster	54	31	15	80
Able to serve more people	59	32	9	127
New services provided	57	27	16	141
More professional time made available for treatment	45	31	24	106
New viewpoints gained by project staff regarding population served	53	31	16	135

between patients and staff. . . . Improved morale, better attitudes toward patients, definite improvement in over-all quality of service were other improvements reported. The addition of youthful, untrained personnel within several hospitals makes the older trained personnel re-examine their own roles and the role, structure and function of the entire hospital.[32,p.174]

In summary, "Nonprofessionals were viewed as contributing to mental health in two unique ways: (1) *filling new roles based on patient needs* which were previously unfilled by any staff; and (2) performing parts of tasks previously performed by professionals, but *tailoring the task to the nonprofessionals' unique and special abilities.*"[33]*

The value of the use of new paraprofessionals is summarized by Carkhuff,[3,p.119] a former staff member of the Arkansas center: "In directly comparable studies, selected lay persons with or without training and/or supervision have patients who demonstrate changes as great or greater than the patients of professional practitioners."

* Editors' italics.

⟨ The Indigenous Paraprofessional

The characteristics of the lay counselor, as described by Carkhuff,[3, pp. 101-109] appear to apply as well to the indigenous worker.

1. The increased ability to enter the milieu of the distressed.
2. The ability to establish peer-like relationships with the needy.
3. The ability to take an active part in the client's total life situation.
4. The ability to empathize more fully with the client's style of life.
5. The ability to teach the client, from within the client's frame of reference, more successful actions.
6. The ability to provide clients with a more effective transition to more effective levels of functioning within the social system.

One of the earliest uses of indigenous paraprofessionals was at Howard University in the Baker's Dozen project of Jacob Fishman,

Lonnie Mitchell, and colleagues.[10,11,22,23] The Howard team's work has continued both there and at the University Research Corporation, whose many reports include consideration of mental health programs, primarily as part of new careers efforts.[25,27]

A 1969 survey of eighty community mental health centers found that 42 percent of all full-time positions were filled by indigenous workers. The figures were higher in drug-abuse treatment (60 percent) and geriatric services (70 percent).[27, pp. 14–15] A study in the same year, of paraprofessionals in ten community mental health centers in New York City, reported[13, p. 286] their "actual work as described by administrators varied from unskilled to highly skilled but more often is of the highly skilled variety." The work included interviewing, escort service, home visits, manning storefront offices, receiving complaints, collecting information, acting as translators, performing individual and group counseling, organizing community meetings, leading therapy groups, assisting patients in self-care, acting as patients' advocates with other agencies, casefinding, screening applicants, making case conference presentations, doing casework, giving speeches, planning after care services, and giving supportive psychotherapy to expatients.

Reiff and Riessman[28, p. 6] made the point that the use of the indigenous paraprofessional was part of the new concern for service to the poor. If the concern was only to meet professional manpower shortages, indigenity is unnecessary. However, if there was a concern to reach and serve those unreached and unserved, in short, if the propelling motive grew out of a critique of service performance, then the indigenous worker may be needed. The ability of the indigenous paraprofessionals is "rooted in their background. It is not based on things they have been taught, but on what they *are*."[28, p. 8] They are poor, from the neighborhood, minority group members, their family is poor, they are a peer of the client with common language, background, ethnic origin, style, and interests.* They can establish spe-

cial relations with clients: The paraprofessional belongs; he is a significant other; he is one of us. His life style is similar to that of the client, especially "the tendency to externalize causes rather than look for internal ones."[28, pp. 9–10]

Hallowitz, the codirector of the pioneering Lincoln Hospital Mental Health Services Neighborhood Service Center program, described a range of activities for the indigenous worker in such a setting.[15] These included expediting, being a friend in need, sociotherapy, supervised work, services to posthospital patients, services to the disturbed in the community, and self-help. The Lincoln Hospital Mental Health Services Neighborhood Service Center program began with an Office of Economic Opportunity grant, January 1, 1965. Three centers were established, each staffed with five to ten aides. They were seen as bridges between the professionals and the community. They are expediters, advocates, and counselors. Something of the power of their impact and the need for services in a community such as the South Bronx is shown by the service figure of 6,500 persons seen at two of the centers during the first nine months. The program offered services to the client's whole family, and it was estimated[30] that more than 25,000 persons were affected during that period.

Harlem Hospital employed indigenous workers in a variety of roles. Harlem residents interested in working with the aged provided outpatient geriatric psychiatric services. They made home visits, provided escort services, observed and reported on patient behavior, provided social services. About half of the study group of sixty cases were successfully managed.

Especially innovative was June Christmas's Harlem Hospital group therapy program, which uses indigenous aides.[4] The aides worked in a half-day treatment program for a small group of chronic psychotic posthospital patients. The aides participated as cotherapists in weekly group psychotherapy sessions,

---

* Perhaps the ultimate in the use of the indigenous worker is an NIMH-funded project to train twelve Navajo males as medicine men. They are to learn the fifty ceremonies of tribal traditions for treating illness and to work with the Public Health Service doctors regarding referrals and assistance.

acted as participants and expediters in the monthly medication group meetings, were members of the weekly therapeutic community meetings, and led the weekly client discussion groups. In addition, they performed case services, family services, and home interviews; surveyed patient needs; and provided community mental health education. The program was expected to hold one-third of the patients; it has held two-thirds.[37] A four-step career ladder—trainee, worker, technician, specialist—is in effect, gained, in part, through the efforts of union Local 1199 of the Drug and Hospital Workers Union.[26]

The Temple University Community Mental Health Center has trained indigenous workers as mental health assistants, workers whom they describe as "helpers first, then therapists."[20] Over time a work pattern developed where the mental health assistants "function as a 'primary therapist' providing on-going treatment and continuity of care which would include the procurement of ancillary (professional) services whenever appropriate."[20, p. 429] The assistant, a title the workers themselves preferred to "aide," worked with 96 percent of the patients in the clinic's first year. Two key factors in their work involved holding patients and by their availability preventing hospitalization.

While the percentage of patients' attrition between initial contact and first appointment is still high, it is a lower rate than that presented for comparable patient aggregates in usual clinic settings. The need to hospitalize patients contacting the crisis center and clinic has decreased by 50% due to the Assistants' availability for immediate outpatient care.[20, p. 430]

The Central City Community Mental Health Center in Los Angeles used community workers in a program designed to develop additional mental health manpower, train new workers, improve understanding between the disadvantaged and mental health personnel, increase the available services, and create new services appropriate to the disadvantaged. The community workers are used in the mental health facility itself, at a family service center, in various social welfare agencies, in a

public health project, in a public housing program, and to provide crisis intervention therapy in a suicide prevention program.[27, p. 12]

Among the other uses of indigenous paraprofessionals in mental health programs was as alcoholism counselors in a program of the Baltimore County health department; as paramedic technicians at a state residential school for the mentally retarded in Hawaii; as part of a home treatment team at the Veterans Administration Hospital in Tuscaloosa, Alabama; in a child guidance clinic component of a comprehensive mental health center in Rochester, N.Y.

(Formal Education and Performance

In a far-reaching study of seventeen state rehabilitation agencies, involving 209 counselors, 50 supervisors and 1,502 patients, the ratings of supervisors and patients were correlated with four levels of worker education: post M.A., M.A., B.A., less than B.A.

[H]igher levels of academic training of rehabilitation counselors do not result in higher supervisor ratings on the dimension of overall effectiveness of the counselor. . . .

[H]igher levels of academic training for rehabilitation counselors do not result in higher client reports of satisfaction with his counselor.[9, 524]

The lack of correlation between formal education and work performance has been cited in many of the reports described above. It may be that the type of formal education presently offered does not lead to improved paraprofessional performance because, as we have seen, training of untrained people has led to improved performance. New training approaches are beginning to develop at the college level.

Something of a new approach was developed in the new mental health college programs. A 1965 NIMH grant inaugurated at Purdue University the first two-year training program for mental health workers.[38] This was followed in 1966 by a Southern Regional

Education Board conference on the role of community colleges in mental health training. In 1967, two Maryland community colleges began such programs,[36] and by September 1968, twenty-six community colleges were offering similar programs, and fifty-seven by 1970. The programs[38, pp. 166–167] emphasized practicum, interviewing skills, counseling, use of community resources, and techniques of behavior modification.

In evaluating the Purdue program, various effects have been noted as regards changes in patient care—"humanizing" the hospital, opening closed wards, establishment of patient government, more use of recreation and work facilities, use of new treatment modalities such as milieu therapy and sociotherapy.[15]

These developments offer some countervailing tendencies to the finding of the survey of New York City community mental health centers, described above, that despite the fact that 70 percent of the center administrators rated the paraprofessional contribution as essential and another 22 percent rated him highly desirable, there is "little thought given toward developing the paraprofessional job into a worthwhile one."

And, perhaps encouraging is the fact that the graduates of the new Purdue program while working in mental health programs have chosen not to do so in traditional mental health facilities. It may be, as the authors suggest, that these new workers are disillusioned with the traditional medical model of mental health services.[13, p. 286]

The tensions involved between new personnel, new training, and traditional mental health practices have been well captured in a far-reaching article by Minuchin. He pointed out[21] that initially the use of paraprofessionals in mental health grew out of the manpower shortage.

For many professionals, a very important major assumption was implicit in this strategy, that we could maintain intact the traditional conceptualizations of mental illness and treatment, simply fitting the nonprofessional into the already existing structure of delivery of service. But the inclusion of paraprofessionals in the existing structure of delivery of service brought to a head a bipolarity of approaches to mental illness which was already incipient in the field.

At the one pole, where sociological thinking dominated, where pathology is seen as coming from the outside in, paraprofessionals have had less difficulty in fitting in. At the other pole, where the individual is very much a separate human being, the problem of fitting in has been very much greater. The paraprofessionals are seen[21, p. 724] as doing little more than "implementing the professional's recommendations and their supervision."

Minuchin's answer[21, p. 725] is that the field itself must be changed, indeed the very relationship of individual and society reconceptualized. As we have seen, the paraprofessional, initially introduced in a narrow framework, has in one way or another become a force for and focus around changes of a basic nature in the field. It is these changes, rather than minor tinkering within the present structure, that may be the shapers of the paraprofessionals' future role in mental health.

◖ Bibliography

1. ANDROVIC, M. P., and GUERNEY, B., Jr. "A Psychotherapeutic Aide in a Head Start Program: Part I. Theory and Practice." *Children*, 16 (1969).

2. BOYETTE, R., et al. "The Plight of the New Careerist." *American Journal of Orthopsychiatry*, 41 (1971), 237–238.

3. CARKHUFF, R. R. "Differential Training of Lay and Professional Helpers." *Journal of Counseling Psychology*, 15 (1968).

4. CHRISTMAS, J. J. "Group Methods in Teaching and Action: Non-Professional Mental Health Personnel in a Deprived Community." *American Journal of Orthopsychiatry*, 36 (1966), 410–419.

5. COWEN, E. L., et al. "A College Student Volunteer Program in the Elementary School Setting." *Community Mental Health Journal*, 2 (1966).

6. DAVIDOFF, I. F. et al. "The Mental Health Rehabilitation Worker: A Member of the Psychiatric Team." *Community Mental Health Journal*, 5 (1969), 46–54.

7. EISDORFER, C., and JOLANN, S. E. "Principles for the Training of 'New Professionals' in Mental Health." *Community Mental Health Journal*, 5 (1969).

8. ELLSWORTH, R. *Nonprofessionals in Psychiatric Rehabilitation*. New York: Appleton-Century-Crofts, 1968.

9. ENGELKES, J. R., and ROBERTS, R. R. "Rehabilitation Counselor's Level of Training and Job Performance." *Journal of Counseling Psychology*, 17 (1970).

10. FISHMAN, J. R., and McCORMACK, J. "Mental Health Without Walls: Community Mental Health in the Ghetto." *New Careers Perspectives*, 4 (1969).

11. ————, and MITCHELL, L. E. New Careers for the Disadvantaged. Paper presented to the American Psychiatric Association, San Francisco, Cal., May 13, 1970.

12. GARFIELD, S. I. "New Developments in the Preparation of Counselors." *Community Mental Health Journal*, 5 (1969).

13. GOTTESFELD, H., et al. "A Study of the Role of Paraprofessionals in Community Mental Health." *Community Mental Health Journal*, 6 (1970).

14. GUERNEY, B., Jr., ed. *Psychotherapeutic Agents: New Roles for Nonprofessionals, Parents, and Teachers*. New York: Holt, Rinehart & Winston, 1969.

15. HADLEY, J., et al. "An Experiment in the Education of the Paraprofessional Mental Health Worker: The Purdue Program." *Community Mental Health Journal*, 5 (1970).

16. HALLOWITZ, E. "The Expanding Role of the Neighborhood Service Center." In F. Riessman and H. S. Popper, *Up From Poverty: New Career Ladders for Nonprofessionals*. New York: Harper & Row, 1968. Pp. 94–101.

17. HARVEY, L. V. "The Use of Non-Professional Auxiliary Counselors in Staffing a Counseling Service." *Journal of Counseling Psychology*, 11 (1964), 348–351.

18. HOLZBERG, J. D., et al. "Chronic Patients and a College Companion Program." *Mental Hospitals*, 15 (1964), 152–158.

19. KREITZER, S. F. "The Therapeutic Use of Student Volunteers." In B. F. Guerney, Jr., ed., *Psychotherapeutic Agents: New Roles for Nonprofessionals, Parents, and Teachers*. New York: Holt, Rinehart & Winston, 1969.

20. LYNCH, M., et al. "The Role of Indigenous Personnel as Clinical Therapists." *Archives of General Psychiatry*, 19 (1968).

21. MINUCHIN, S. "The Paraprofessional and the Use of Confrontation in the Mental Health Field." *American Journal of Orthopsychiatry*, 39 (1969), 722–729.

22. MITCHELL, L. E., et al. *Training for Community Mental Health Aides: Leaders for Child and Adolescent Therapeutic Activity Groups; Report of a Program*. Washington, D.C.: Institute for Youth Studies, Howard University, 1966.

23. ————, et al. "Baker's Dozen: A Program for Training Young People as Mental Health Aides." *Mental Health Program Reports*, 2 (1968), 11–24.

24. MITCHELL, W. E. "Amicatherapy: Theoretical Perspectives and an Example of Practice." *Community Mental Health Journal*, 2 (1966), 307–314.

25. NATIONAL INSTITUTE FOR NEW CAREERS. *An Assessment of Technical Assistance and Training Needs in New Careers Projects Being Sponsored by the United States Training and Employment Service, Manpower Administration, U.S. Department of Labor*. Washington, D.C.: University Research Corporation, 1969.

26. ————. *New Careers Bibliography: Paraprofessionals in the Human Services*. Washington, D.C.: University Research Corporation, 1970.

27. ————. *New Careers in Mental Health: A Status Report*. Washington, D.C.: University Research Corporation, 1970.

28. REIFF, R., and RIESSMAN, F. *The Indigenous Nonprofessional: A Strategy of Change in Community Action and Community Mental Health Programs*. New York: National Institute of Labor Education, 1964.

29. REINHERZ, H. "The Therapeutic Use of Student Volunteers." *Children*, 2 (1964), 137–142.

30. RIESSMAN, F. and HALLOWITZ, E. Neighborhood Service Center Program. Report to the U.S. Office of Economic Opportunity on the South Bronx Neighborhood Service Center, December 1965.

31. RIOCH, M., et al. "National Institute of Mental Health Pilot Study in Training Mental Health Counselors." *American Journal of Orthopsychiatry*, 33 (1963), 678–698.

32. SOBEY, F. *The Nonprofessional Revolution in Mental Health*. New York: Columbia University Press, 1970.

33. TRUAX, C. B. *An Approach Toward Training for the Aide-Therapist: Research and Implications.* Fayetteville: Arkansas Rehabilitation Research and Training Center, 1965.

34. ———. *The Use of Supportive Personnel in Rehabilitation Counselling.* Fayetteville: Arkansas Rehabilitation Research and Training Center, n.d.

35. ———, and LISTER, J. L. "Effectiveness of Counselors and Counselor Aides." *Journal of Counseling Psychology,* 17 (1970), 331–334.

36. VIDAVER, R. M. "The Mental Health Technician: Maryland's Design for a New Health Career." *American Journal of Orthopsychiatry,* 34 (1969).

37. WADE, R., et al. "The View of the Professional." *American Journal of Orthopsychiatry,* 34 (1969).

38. WELLNER, A., and SIMON, R. "A Survey of Associate Degree Programs for Mental Health Technicians." *Hospital and Community Psychiatry,* 20 (1969).

39. ZAX, M., et al. "A Teacher-Aide Program for Preventing Emotional Disturbances in Young Schoolchildren." *Mental Hygiene,* 50 (1966), 406–415.

NAME INDEX

Note: Bold face figures indicate chapter pages.

SUBJECT INDEX